The First

American Frontier

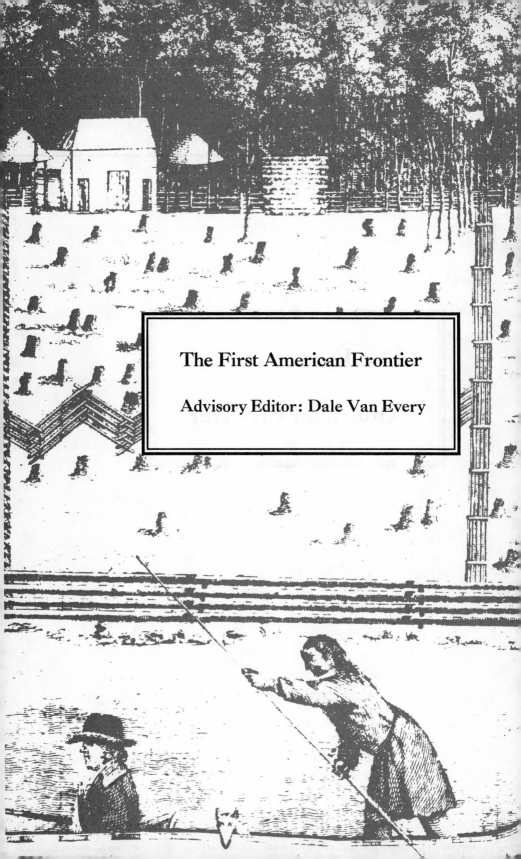

The First American Frontier

Advisory Editor: Dale Van Every

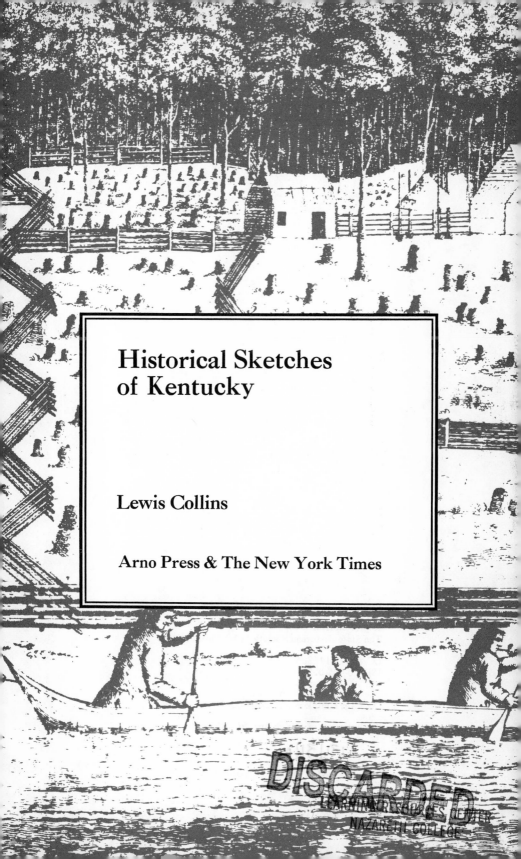

Historical Sketches of Kentucky

Lewis Collins

Arno Press & The New York Times

Reprint Edition 1971 by Arno Press Inc.

Reprinted from a copy in
The State Historical Society of Wisconsin Library

LC #   77-146385
ISBN 0-405-02836-9

The First American Frontier
ISBN for complete set: 0-405-02820-2

See last pages of this volume for titles.

134316

Manufactured in the United States of America

HISTORICAL SKETCHES

OF

KENTUCKY

CRITTENDEN

JOHNSON

CLARKE

SHELBY

KENTON

BOONE

DESIGNS BY EASTMAN

CHILDS SC NY

HISTORICAL SKETCHES

OF

KENTUCKY:

EMBRACING

ITS HISTORY, ANTIQUITIES, AND NATURAL CURIOSITIES, GEOGRAPHICAL,
STATISTICAL, AND GEOLOGICAL DESCRIPTIONS;

WITH

ANECDOTES OF PIONEER LIFE,

AND

MORE THAN ONE HUNDRED BIOGRAPHICAL SKETCHES OF DISTINGUISHED
PIONEERS, SOLDIERS, STATESMEN, JURISTS, LAWYERS, DIVINES, ETC

ILLUSTRATED BY FORTY ENGRAVINGS.

BY LEWIS COLLINS.

PUBLISHED BY
LEWIS COLLINS, MAYSVILLE, KY.;
AND J. A. & U. P. JAMES,
CINCINNATI.
1848.

JAMES & CO., Stereotypers, Cincinnati.

J A. & U. P. JAMES' Steam Press.

PREFACE.

THE late H. P. Peers, of the city of Maysville, laid the foundation for the work which is now presented to the reading community. Mr. Peers designed it to be simply a small *Gazetteer* of the State; and had collected, and partially arranged for publication, the major part of the materials, comprising a description of the towns and counties. Upon his decease, the materials passed into the hands of the Author, who determined to remodel them, and make such additions as would give permanency and increased value to the work. He has devoted much labor to this object; but circumstances having rendered its publication necessary at an earlier day than was contemplated, some errors may have escaped, which more time, and a fuller investigation would have enabled him to detect.

Serious obstacles have been encountered, in the preparation of the Biographical Sketches. Many of those which appear in the work, were prepared from the personal recollections of the Author; while others have been omitted, because he did not know to whom he could apply for them, or having applied, and in some instances repeatedly, failed in procuring them. This is his apology, for the non-appearance of many names in that department, which are entitled to a distinguished place in the annals of Kentucky.

In the preparation of the work, one design of the Author has been to preserve, in a durable form, those rich fragments of local and personal history, many of which exist, at present, only in the ephemeral form of oral tradition, or are treasured up among the recollections of the aged actors in the stirring scenes, the memory of which is thus perpetuated. These venerable witnesses from a former age, are rapidly passing away from our midst, and with them will be buried the knowledge of much that is most interesting in the primitive history of the commonwealth. It is from sources such as we have mentioned, that the materials for the future historian are to be drawn; and, like the scattered leaves of the Sybil, these frail mementos of the past should be gathered up and preserved with religious veneration. If the Author shall have succeeded, in thus redeeming from oblivion any considerable or important portion of the early history of the State, his design will be fully accomplished, and his labor amply rewarded.

Of all the members of this great republican confederacy, there is none whose history is more rich in the variety, quality, and interest of its materials. The poet, the warrior, and the statesman can each find subjects, the contemplation of which will instruct him in his art; and to the general reader, it would, perhaps, be impossible to present a field of more varied and attractive interest.

It is proper that the Author should state that he has received the assistance of many able pens, in the preparation of the work. The "Outline History," embracing about eighty pages, was written by John A. M'Clung, Esq., of Washington. William P. Conwell, Esq., of Maysville, has rendered important aid, particularly in the biographical department. He is the writer of the Sketches, among others, of the Hon. Henry Clay, Gen. George Rogers Clark, Col. Daniel Boone, and Gen. Z. Taylor. The author is also greatly indebted to Col. Charles S. Todd, of Shelby county; Henry Waller, R. H. Stanton, and William H. Wadsworth, Esqrs., of the city of Maysville; Noble Butler, Esqr. (author of a late and excellent

(3)

work on English Grammar), of the city of Louisville; Bruce Porter, Esq., of the town of Flemingsburg; Thomas W. Riley, Esq., of Bardstown; and Professor O. Beatty, of Centre College, Danville, for valuable contributions. Col. Todd furnished some seven or eight biographical sketches; among them, those of Gov. Shelby and Judge Innes. Mr. Waller prepared the whole of the county of Mason, Mr. Butler a large portion of the county of Jefferson, Mr. Porter a portion of the county of Fleming, Mr. Riley a portion of the county of Bullitt, and Mr. Beatty the article on the Geology of Kentucky. A distinguished citizen of the State contributed the interesting Sketch of the Court of Appeals.

The Historical Sketches of the several religious denominations, were prepared by the following gentlemen: Rev. John L. Waller, editor of the Western Baptist Review, Frankfort, of the Baptist church; Rev. W. W. Hill, editor of the Presbyterian Herald, Louisville, of the Presbyterian church; Rev. George W. Smiley,* of the Northern Kentucky Conference, of the Methodist Episcopal church; Rev. James Shannon, president of Bacon College, Harrodsburg, of the Christian Church; Rt. Rev. B. B. Smith, D.D., bishop of the Diocese of Kentucky, of the Episcopal church; Rev. Rich. Beard, D.D., president of Cumberland College, Princeton, of the Cumberland Presbyterian church; and Rev. M. J. Spalding, D.D., Vicar-General of Kentucky, Louisville, of the Roman Catholic church.

He also acknowledges his indebtedness to the following gentlemen, for information concerning their counties, for incidents connected with the early settlement of the State, or for biographical sketches, &c., viz:

James W. Carter, Esqr., of Adair county; W. F. Evans, Esqr., of Allen; J. W. Crockett, and J. H. Stovall, Esqrs., of Ballard; B. N. Crump, Esqr., of Barren; James M. Preston, Esqr., of Boone; Hon. Garrett Davis, Dr. Joseph H. Holt, Dr. William M. Garrard, and William C. Lyle, John G. Scrogin, and W. G. Talbot, Esqrs., of Bourbon; Rev. J. C. Young, D.D., president of Centre College, of Boyle; General John Payne, of Bracken; John Hargis, Esq., of Breathitt; Hon. John Calhoun, Joseph Smith, Joseph Allen, and Francis Peyton, Esqrs., of Breckinridge; W. T. Samuels, and Michael O. Wade, Esqrs., of Bullitt; B. J. Burke, and L. W. Moore, Esqrs., of Butler; Charles B. Dallam, and Marcus M. Tyler, Esqrs., of Caldwell; E. H. Curd, Esqr., of Calloway; Gen. James Taylor, and S. D. Smalley, Esqr., of Campbell; David Owen, Esq., of Carroll; G. W. Crawford, Esqr., of Carter; Daniel H. Harrison, A. G. Stites, and R. R. Lansden, Esqrs., of Christian; W. Flanagan, and Willis Collins, Esqrs., of Clarke; Dougherty White, and William Woodcock, Esqrs., of Clay; R. Maxcy, and E. Long, Esqrs., of Clinton; R. L. Bigham, and H. R. D. Coleman, Esqrs., of Crittenden; E. B. Gaither, and Th. T. Alexander, Esqrs., and Dr. David R. Haggard, of Cumberland; John P. Devereaux, Esqr., of Daveiss; A. M. Barrett, Esqr., of Edmonson; Robert Clarke, Esqr., of Estill; Hon. George Robertson, Gen. Leslie Combs, Gen. John M. M'Calla, Col. Richard Spurr, Hon. Robert Wickliffe, Rev. Robert J. Breckinridge, D.D., and John C. Breckinridge, William S. Waller, John Bradford, James Logue, Samuel D. M'Cullough, and Fielding R. Bradford, Esqrs., of Fayette; C. C. Lane, and W. S. Botts, Esqrs, of Fleming; Edwin Trimble, and Daniel Hager, Esqrs., of Floyd; Gov. William Owsley, Hon. Benjamin Monroe, Hon. James Harlan, Gen. Peter Dudley, Col. James Davidson, Orlando Brown, John W. Finnell, William D. Reed, H. I. Bodley, and A. S. Mitchell, Esqrs., of Franklin; Major J. W. Gibson, and R. A. Hatcher, Esqr., of Fulton; Rev. Benjamin Fuller, of Gallatin; A. J. Brown, Esqr., of Garrard; John W. M'Cann, Esqr., of Grant; Jack Thomas, Esqr., of Grayson; G. W. Montague, Esqr., of Greene; W. L. Poage, Esqr., of Greenup; D. L. Adair, Esqr., of Hancock; Dr. Samuel B. Young, and Thomas D. Brown, Esqr., of Hardin; E. V. Unthank, Esqr., of Harlan; Gen. L. B. Desha, and J. V. Bassett, Esqr., of Harrison;

---

* It is due to Mr. Smiley to state, that the Sketch of the Methodist Episcopal Church, was prepared by him upon a few days' notice.

Robert D. Murray, and John Bowman, Esqrs., of Hart; Dr. Owen Glass, O. H. Hillyer, and J. E. M'Callister, Esqrs., of Henderson; W. B. Edmunston, and N. E. Wright, Esqrs., of Hickman; Samuel Woodson, Esqr., of Hopkins; Hon. Henry Pirtle, Tal. P. Shaffner, Esqr., and Dr. Bullitt, of Jefferson; R. E. Woodson, Esqr., of Jessamine: John House, Esqr., of Johnson; Hon. James T. Morehead, and J. W. Menzies, Esqr., of Kenton; B. H. Ohler, Esqr., of Knox; John Duncan, and William Beelar, Esqrs., of Larue; G. F. Hatcher, Esqr., of Lawrence; W. B. Hampton, Esqr., of Letcher; R. G. Carter, Esqr., of Lewis; J. Campbell, Esqr., of Lincoln; William Gordon, Esqr., of Livingston; M. B. Morton, and Albert G. Rhea, Esqrs., of Logan: Abner Oldham, Esqr., Col. John Speed Smith, and Col. David Irvine, of Madison; Nicholas S. Ray, Esqr., and Captain Edmund A. Graves, of Marion; Henry Hand, Esqr., of Marshall; William Fairleigh, Esqr., of Meade; Hon. Adam Beatty, Col. James C. Pickett, Dr. J. M. Duke, R. H. Collins, and Joseph B. Boyd, Esqrs., of Mason; William H. Jones, Esqr., of M'Cracken; Gen. Robert B. M'Afee, Captain Samuel Daveiss, Dr. C. Graham, and James M'Afee, Esqr., of Mercer; William Butler, Esqr., of Monroe; Richard Apperson, Esqr., of Montgomery; James Elliott, Esqr., of Morgan; Charles F. Wing, Esqr., of Muhlenburg; Hon. Charles A. Wickliffe, G. Clayton Slaughter, and A. G. Botts, Esqrs., of Nelson; Charles Henderson, H. D. Taylor, and Stephen Stateler, Esqrs., of Ohio; G. Armstrong, Esqr., of Oldham; J. W. Bacon, Esqr., of Owen; William Williams, Esqr., of Owsley; S. Thomas Hauser, Esqr., of Pendleton; John D. Mims, Esqr., of Pike; E. Kelley, Esqr., of Pulaski; Col. Elisha Smith, of Rockcastle; Joseph T. Rowe, Esqr., of Russell; John T. Steppe, Esqr., and Rev. Howard Malcom, D.D., of Scott; Thomas J. Throop, I. Shelby Todd, and John H. Todd, Esqrs., and Rev. Abraham Cook, of Shelby; John Hoy, Esqr., of Simpson; Ralph Lancaster, Esqr., of Spencer; W. H. Wells, and R. E. Glenn, Esqrs., of Todd; Kain A. M'Caughan, and Robert Baker, Esqrs., of Trigg; W. Samuels, Esqr., of Trimble; J. W. Cromwell, Esqr., of Union; Hon. A. W. Graham, Hon. Joseph R. Underwood, and Loyd Berry, Esqr., of Warren; W. B. Booker, Esqr., of Washington; W. Simpson, Esqr., of Wayne; W. S. Cooke, and Squire Gatliffe, Esqrs., of Whitley; Major Herman Bowmar, of Woodford.—Also, to Thomas B. Stevenson, Esqr., Dr. J. R. Buchanan, and Rev. Thornton A Mills, of Cincinnati.

INDEX TO THE OUTLINE HISTORY.

INDEX TO COUNTIES, CITIES, TOWNS, AND VILLAGES.

The names of the Counties are in *Small Capitals.*

GENERAL INDEX.

A CHRONOLOGICAL TABLE

OF IMPORTANT EVENTS IN THE HISTORY OF KENTUCKY.

1750—Dr. Walker, of Virginia, visits the north-eastern portion of Kentucky. Another account says, that it was in 1758; and a third, places it in 1747, and says, he visited the eastern and south-eastern parts.

1751—Christopher Gist sent out, by the Ohio Company, to explore the Western Company, descends the Ohio river to the Falls.

1765, June 8—Col. George Croghan, a British officer, in descending the Ohio from Fort Pitt, is taken prisoner by the Indians, below the Wabash.

1766—Col. James Smith visits Kentucky.

1767—John Finley visits Kentucky on a trading expedition.

1769—Finley again in Kentucky, accompanied by Daniel Boone, and others. This party built a wigwam, to shelter them from the storms, and remained two years, traversing the northern and middle regions.

December 22—Boone and Stuart taken prisoners by the Indians.

1770—The "Long Hunters," from Holston, on Clinch river, led by Col. James Knox, explore the middle and southern regions of the State.

Gen. Washington descends the Ohio, as far as the north-eastern part of Kentucky.

1773. Sept. 25—Boone, and others, start to settle Kentucky. Oct. 10—Are attacked by Indians, and turn back.

May 29 — Capt. Thomas Bullitt, and the M'Afees, descend the Ohio river. Bullitt and others proceed to the Falls, and survey land below the Falls to Salt river, and up the same to Bullitt's lick.

July 16—The M'Afees, and others of the company, separated from Bullitt at the mouth of the Kentucky river; which they ascended as far as where Frankfort now stands, and surveyed six hundred acres there.

Gen. Thompson, of Pennsylvania, makes some surveys upon the north fork of Licking river.

1774—James Harrod, late in the spring, ascended the Kentucky river, and built the first cabin in the State, on the spot where Harrodsburg now stands.

1775. March 17—Col. Richard Henderson, Nathaniel Hart, and others, conclude the Wataga treaty with the Cherokees, by which, for £10,000 sterling, they acquired the territory between the Ohio, the Kentucky, or Louisa river, the Cumberland mountains, and the Cumberland river. Virginia refused to recognize the purchase, but compromised it by grants of land.

Lord Dunmore issues a proclamation against the Transylvania Company of purchasers.

April 1—Fort at Boonsborough begun, and finished June 14th. Settlements made, and stations built, also, at Harrodsburg, at the Boiling Spring, and at St. Asaph's, in Lincoln county.

May 23—Pursuant to a call by Henderson, representatives, chosen by the people of Transylvania, met at Boonsborough, agreed upon a proprietary government, and passed nine laws. They adjourned to meet again in September, but never met.

September—Boone. and others, bring their wives and children to Kentucky.

George Rogers Clark visits Kentucky, but returns before winter.

Simon Kenton builds a cabin, and plants corn, near where Washington stands, in Mason county.

1776—Clark moves to Kentucky early, this year.

June 6—At a general meeting at Harrodsburg, Clark and Gabriel Jones were chosen members of the Virginia Assembly, and required to present the petition, drawn up, asking admission as citizens, and efficient protection.

August 23 — Clark procures five hundred pounds of powder from the Council of Virginia, which he takes from Pittsburgh, down the Ohio, to Limestone.

December 6—Kentucky county established out of Fincastle county, by Virginia.

December 25 — Col. John Todd, and his party, while on their way to Limestone, for the powder secreted there, defeated near the Blue Licks, and Gabriel Jones killed. Clark takes the powder, in safety, to Harrodsburg.

December 29 — M'Clelland's Fort, on Elkhorn, attacked by Indians.

1777, March 7 — Harrodsburg attacked by the savages.

April 15—First attack on Boonsborough.

Burgesses chosen to represent the county of Kentucky in the legislature of Virginia.

May—Logan's station attacked.

Major Clark's spies in the Illinois country.

September—First court at Harrodsburg.

October 1—Clark starts to Virginia.

December 10 — Clark opens his plan, for conquering Illinois. to Gov. Patrick Henry.

1778, January 2—Col. Clark appointed to lead an expedition against the British posts in Illinois.

February 7—Boone taken prisoner at the Blue Licks.

May 25—Disastrous attack, by Indians, on a boat ascending Salt river.

June 24—Col. Clark established a fort on Corn Island, before leaving the Falls of the Ohio, for Illinois.

July 4—Clark took Kaskaskia, and, two days after, Cahokia.

August 1—Vincennes voluntarily submitted to the Americans.

August 8—Boonsborough besieged.

October—Louisville settled.

Virginia grants Henderson and Company 200,000 acres on the Ohio, below Green river.

December—Governor Hamilton took Vincennes.

1779, Feb. 24—Vincennes surrendered to Colonel Clark.

April 1—Blockhouse built at Lexington.

July—Col. Bowman's expedition against Chillicothe.

October—Col. Rogers and Captain Benham defeated by Indians, near the mouth of Licking.

Virginia land commissioners open their session at St. Asaph's.

1780, January—The "hard winter;" game frozen in the forest, and cattle around the stations. Corn sold at $50 to $175.

May—Virginia grants land in Kentucky for educational purposes.

June 22—Col. Byrd, of the British army, with six field-pieces, and six hundred Canadians and Indians, compels the surrender of Ruddell's station; and, immediately after, of Martin's station.

July—Gen. Clark, at the head of 1000 men, destroyed the Piqua towns on the Miami.

November 1—The county of Kentucky divided into the three counties of Lincoln, Fayette, and Jefferson.

1781—County lieutenants and surveyors appointed.

1782, March 22—Desperate battle near the Little Mountain, known as Estill's defeat.

August 14—Bryant's station besieged by five hundred Indians, under Simon Girty.

August 19—The disastrous battle of Blue Lick, in which one hundred and sixty, or one hundred and eighty-two white men were defeated by the Indians, with the loss of sixty killed and seven taken prisoners.

September—Another expedition of Gen. Clark against the Miami towns. No large body of Indians thenceforward invaded Kentucky.

1783. March—Kentucky formed into one district, and a District Court established.

Danville founded.

A store opened, at Louisville, by Daniel Brodhead.

1784, Feb.—Gen. James Wilkinson came to Lexington, as the leader of a large commercial company, formed in Philadelphia.

An informal meeting of the people, held at Danville, on the state of the district.

Dec. 27—First Convention held at Danville; separation from Virginia discussed, but referred to a second convention.

Blockhouse erected at Limestone, or Maysville.

1785, May 23—Second convention adopted an address to the Assembly of Virginia, and one to the people of Kentucky, together with strong resolutions in favor of separation.

Aug. 8—Third convention assembled. and adopted two new addresses, conceived in bolder terms than before.

1786, January—First act of Virginia favoring a separation by Kentucky, on certain conditions.

September—Fourth convention met, but without a quorum, and continued its meetings by adjournment. until January, 1787; when a quorum attended, expressed their feelings in favor of separation, and called another convention. to be held in the fall.

October—Expedition of Gen. Clark against the Wabash Indians; returns without effecting anything.

Second act of Virginia, postponing the separation of Kentucky until Jan. 1st, 1789.

Col. Logan's expedition against the Shawanese.

Gen. Clark's seizure of Vincennes, and other movements against the Spaniards.

1787, May—Meeting at Danville, in relation to the navigation of the Mississippi.

June—Gen. Wilkinson descends, with the first cargo from Kentucky, to New Orleans, and obtained a permit to import tobacco for the Spanish king's stores.

August 18—The Kentucky Gazette established at Lexington.

Sept. 17—Fifth convention unanimously decided in favor of separation, on the terms offered by Virginia.

1788, June 28—Convention of Virginia decided, by a vote of eighty-eight to seventy-eight, in favor of adopting the Constitution of the United States; the Kentucky delegation voting eleven against it, and three in its favor.

July 3—Congress refers the subject of the admission of Kentucky into the Union to the new government.

July 28—Sixth convention meets, and adjourns without other action than calling another convention, with full discretionary powers.

Spanish intrigues, in Kentucky, during this year.

Nov. 4—Seventh convention meets.

Dr. Connolly in Kentucky, as a British agent.

Dec. 24—The founders of Cincinnati leave Maysville.

Dec. 27—Third act of Virginia in favor of separation.

1789, Jan.—No votes given, for electors of President and Vice-president of the United States, in the District of Kentucky.

Feb. 12—Correspondence between Gen. George Washington and Col. Thos. Marshall, respecting British and Spanish intrigues in Kentucky.

July 20—Eighth convention assembled, and remonstrated against the conditions of separation contained in the third act of Virginia.

Dec. 18—Fourth act of separation passed by Virginia, complying with the wishes of Kentucky.

1790, July 26—Ninth convention assembled, accepted the terms of Virginia, and fixed June 1st, 1792, for the independence of the State of Kentucky.

Oct.—Colonel Trotter leads the Kentuckians, at Harmar's defeat.

Dec.—Kentuckians petition Congress to fight Indians in their own way.

Local Board of War appointed in Kentucky.

1791, Feb. 4—Congress agree to admit Kentucky on the 1st of June, 1792.

May 23—Gen. Scott's expedition against the Indians on the Wabash.

August 1—Gen. Wilkinson marched against the Eel river Indians.

1792, April 3—Convention met to draft the first Constitution of Kentucky.

May—Colonel John Hardin, and Major Trueman, killed by the Indians, while on a peace mission to them.

Nov. 6—Major John Adair attacked, near Fort St. Clair, by Little Turtle.

Frankfort chosen as the capital of the State.

1793, Oct. 24—Gen. Scott joins Gen. Wayne, near Fort Jefferson, with 1000 mounted volunteers from Kentucky.

Nov. 1—Genet, the French minister, sent agents to Kentucky, to organize an expedition against New Orleans, and the then Spanish possessions.

Democratic societies established in Kentucky.

1794, July 26—Gen. Scott again joins Wayne, with 1600 men, from Kentucky.

August 20—Gen. Wayne defeated the Canadians and Indians, at the battle of the Fallen Timber, with very gratifying effect.

1795. July—Thomas Power sent, by Gov. Carondelet, of Louisiana, to concert with the people of Kentucky, a commercial treaty for the navigation of the Mississippi; in consequence of which, Judge Sebastian met Col. Gayoso at New Madrid The agreement was, however, defeated by the Spanish treaty.

1796, August—First paper-mill in the west.

1797, July 12—Thomas Power sent, by Gov. Carondelet, to concert a separation of Kentucky from the Union.

Oct.—Occupying claimant law passed.

1798, Nov. 16—Nullifying resolutions passed, with regard to the Alien and Sedition laws.

Death, except for murder, abolished in Kentucky.

1799, July 22—Convention assembled for forming a new constitution.

Internal improvements talked of.

Nov. 14—The nullifying resolutions of last year affirmed.

1800, June 1—The present Constitution goes into operation.

1801—Circuit Court system established.

1802, January—An Insurance Company, with banking powers, chartered.

The right of deposit, for American produce, at New Orleans, suspended.

1805—Aaron Burr twice visits Kentucky.

1806, Nov. 11—Burr brought before the District Court of Kentucky, but for want of testimony, the grand jury was dismissed.

Dec. 2—Burr is indicted, but the grand jury return, "not a true bill."

Dec. 6—Judge Sebastian convicted of being a pensioner of Spain; resigns his office.

1807—Bank of Kentucky chartered.

1809—The limitation in actions in ejectment, prolonged from seven to twenty years.

1811, Nov. 7—Battle of Tippecanoe, in which Col. Jo. Hamilton Daveiss, and other distinguished Kentuckians, fell.

1812—Gen. Harrison appointed major-general of the Kentucky troops.

Oct.—Gen. Hopkins' expedition against the Indians on the Wabash.

Dec.—Battle of Mississiniway.

1813. Jan. 10—The Kentuckians, under General Winchester, reach the Maumee.

Jan. 18—British defeated at Frenchtown.

Jan. 22—Disastrous battle of the river Raisin, and massacre of the Americans.

May 5 — Gen. Clay reaches Fort Meigs; eight hundred Kentuckians, under General Dudley, killed or taken prisoners.

July 31—Fort Stephenson besieged.

Oct. 5—Victory of the Thames.

Nov. 25—The capitol, at Frankfort, consumed by fire.

1815, Jan 8—Victory at New Orleans.

April 6—The Ohio river higher than it had been since 1793.

Oct. 15—A steamboat built at Louisville.

1816, Oct. 14—Gov. Madison died, soon after his inauguration.

1817, July—Much excitement in reference to the succession of the Lieut. Governor, in case of the death of the governor.

Dec. 12—Shock of an earthquake felt throughout the State.

1817–18—Forty independent banks chartered.

1818, Feb.—Gen. George Rogers Clark died, near Louisville.

Oct. 19—A treaty with the Chickasaw Indians, for all their claims in Tennessee and Kentucky, containing about 7,000,000 acres, for an annuity of $20,000 for fifteen years.

1819–20—Right of replevin extended from three to twelve months.

The relief excitement commenced.

1820–21—Commonwealth's bank chartered.

The Legislature controlled the directors of the old Bank of Kentucky.

1823—The Court of Appeals decided the replevin laws unconstitutional.

1824–25—New Court of appeals organized.

1833–34—Bank of Kentucky, Northern Bank of Kentucky, and Bank of Louisville chartered.

1835, February—Internal improvement system adopted.

1837—Banks suspend specie payments.

1839—Second suspension of specie payments.

1842—Relief excitement.

OUTLINE HISTORY.

CHAPTER I.

KENTUCKY was first explored by the Anglo-Saxon race, about the middle of the eighteenth century. It then formed a vast hunting-ground, upon which the savage tribes of the south and of the north killed the elk and buffalo, and occasionally encountered each other in bloody conflict. No permanent settlements existed within its borders. Its dark forests and cane thickets separated the Cherokees, Creeks, and Catawbas of the south, from the hostile tribes of Shawanees, Delawares, and Wyandots of the north. Each, and all of these tribes, encountered the Anglo-American pioneer, and fiercely disputed the settlement of the country.

It is certain, however, that these were not the original occupants of the country lying between the Alleghany mountains and the Mississippi river. Geological monuments of deep interest, but as yet imperfectly investigated, speak in language not to be mistaken, of a race of men who preceded the rude tribes encountered by Boone and Finley. Their origin, language, and history, are buried in darkness which, perhaps, may never be dispelled; but the scanty vestiges which they have left behind them, enable us to affirm, with confidence, that they far surpassed the rude tribes which succeeded them, in arts, in civilization, and in knowledge. They had certainly worked the copper mines of the west, and were in possession of copper tools for working in wood and stone. Their pipes, and household utensils elaborately fashioned, of clay, are far above the rude and clumsy contrivances of their successors; while their large fortifications, constructed of solid masonry, and artificially contrived for defence and convenience, show that they had foes to resist, and that they had made considerable progress in the military art.

How long they occupied the country, whence they came, whither they have gone, or whether they perished within the crumbling walls which alone speak of their existence, the present state of our knowledge does not enable us to decide. The historical facts *with certainty* to be inferred from the data which exist,

2   (17)

are few and meagre. In relation to time, we can only affirm that the fortifications and cemeteries, which have been examined, are *certainly* more than eight hundred years old, but how much older they may be can only be conjectured. Time, and future investigation, may throw some additional light upon the history of this ancient race; but at present we can only say that they lived, that they struggled against enemies, that they made progress in arts and civilization, and that the places which once knew them, now know them no more.

Neglecting the obscure visit of Dr. Walker to the north-eastern portion of Kentucky in 1758, and the equally obscure, but more thorough examination of the country by Finley in 1767, we may regard the company headed by Daniel Boone in 1769, and by Knox in 1770, as the earliest visits to Kentucky worthy of particular attention. Boone's party remained two years in the State, and traversed its northern and middle regions with great attention. The party led by Colonel James Knox, called the Long Hunters, came one year later, and remained about the same time. Both parties were in the country together, but never met. Boone was a native of Pennsylvania, but had emigrated to North Carolina. Knox's party was from Holston, on Clinch river, and thoroughly explored the middle and southern regions of Kentucky. Boone's party was harassed by the Indians, and one of their number, James Stuart, was killed. Boone himself at one time fell into their hands, but escaped. In 1771, they returned from their long hunting excursion, and spread throughout the western settlements of Virginia and North Carolina the most glowing accounts of the inexhaustible fertility of the soil.

The bounty in lands, which had been given to the Virginia troops who had served throughout the old French war, were to be located upon the western waters, and within less than two years after the return of Boone and Knox, surveyors were sent out to locate these lands upon the Ohio river. In 1773, Captain Thomas Bullitt, who had distinguished himself in the expedition against fort Du Quesne, led a party of surveyors down the Ohio to the Falls, where a camp was constructed and roughly fortified to protect them from the Indians. During this expedition many surveys were executed in Kentucky, and large portions of the country explored with a view to future settlement. Three brothers from Virginia, James, George and Robert M'Afee, accompanied Bullitt to the mouth of Kentucky river. There they left him, and in company with several others ascended the Kentucky to the forks, exploring the country and making surveys in various places.

In the summer of 1774, other parties of surveyors and hunters followed; and during this year James Harrod erected a log cabin upon the spot where Harrodsburg now stands, which rapidly grew into a station, probably the oldest in Kentucky. During this year, Colonel Richard Henderson purchased from the Cherokee Indians the whole country south of Kentucky river. His purchase was subsequently declared null and void by the legislature of Virginia, which claimed the sole right to purchase land from the Indians within the bounds of the royal charter; but great activity was displayed by Henderson in taking possession of his new empire, and granting land to settlers, before the act of the Virginia legislature overturned all his schemes. Daniel Boone was employed by him to survey the country, and select favorable positions; and, early in the spring of 1775, the foundation of Boonsborough was laid, under the title of Henderson. From the 22d of March to the 14th of April, Boone was actively engaged in constructing the fort, afterwards called Boonsborough, during which time his party was exposed to four fierce attacks from the Indians. By the middle of April the fort was completed, and within two months from that time his wife and daughters joined him, and resided in the fort,—the first white women who ever stood upon the banks of the Kentucky river. From this time, Boonsborough and Harrodsburg became the nucleus and support of emigration and settlement in Kentucky. In 1775, the renowned pioneer, Simon Kenton, erected a log cabin, and raised a crop of corn in the county of Mason, upon the spot where the town of Washington now stands, and continued to occupy the spot until the fall of that year, when he removed to Boonsborough. The limits allotted to this Historical sketch will not admit of details of individual adventures; these may be found under their appropriate heads in other portions of the work.

In the month of September of this year, and three months after the arrival of Mrs. Boone and her daughters, the infant colony was enriched by the arrival of three more ladies, Mrs. Denton, Mrs. M'Gary, and Mrs. Hogan, who, with their husbands and children, settled at Harrodsburg. Early in the spring of 1776, Colonel Richard Calloway brought his wife and two daughters to Boonsborough, and in March of the same year, Colonel Benjamin Logan brought his wife and family to Logan's fort, about one mile west of the present town of Stanford, in Lincoln county, where he, with a few slaves, had raised a crop of corn in 1775.

During this summer, an incident occurred which powerfully impressed upon the minds of the women of Kentucky the dangers which beset them in their frontier home: while a daughter of Daniel Boone and two of the Miss Calloways were amusing themselves within a short distance of the fort, a party of Indians suddenly rushed upon them, and bore them off as captives. They were rapidly pursued by Colonel Floyd and Daniel Boone, with a party of eight men, and at the distance of forty miles from the fort, were overtaken, dispersed, and the girls recovered. During this summer, Colonel George Rogers Clark for the first time made his appearance in Kentucky. He visited the different stations, but made no location; he spent much of his time in the woods, alone and hunting, and encouraged the young pioneers much by his presence and example.

In the winter of this year, Kentucky was formed into a county by the legislature of Virginia, and thus became entitled to a separate county court, to justices of the peace, a sheriff, constables, coroner, and militia officers. Law, with its imposing parapharnalia, (upon a small scale,) for the first time reared its head in the forests of Kentucky. In the spring of 1777, the court of quarter sessions held its first sitting at Harrodsburgh, attended by the sheriff of the county and its clerk, Levi Todd. The first court of Kentucky was composed of John Todd, John Floyd, Benjamin Logan, John Bowman, and Richard Calloway.

They had scarcely adjourned when the infant republic was rocked to its centre by an Indian invasion. Harrodsburg, Boonsborough, Logan's fort were all in succession furiously assailed. The hunters and surveyors were driven in from the woods, and compelled to take refuge within the forts. Much injury was done; but the forts withstood their utmost efforts, and after sweeping through Kentucky like a torrent for several weeks, the angry tide slowly rolled back to the north, leaving the agitated settlers to repair their loss as they best could. They were reinforced during the summer by forty-five men from North Carolina, and, in September, by one hundred more under Colonel Bowman, from Virginia. During this summer, Colonel Benjamin Logan distinguished himself by a display of the most noble and elevated qualities of the human heart. Details will be found in another part of this work; our limits forbid them here.

The year 1778 was rendered memorable in Kentucky by two great military events, in which she was deeply interested. The one, was the invasion of the country by an army of Indians and Canadians, under the command of Captain DuQuesne, a Canadian officer; the other, was the brilliant expedition of Colonel George Rogers Clark against the English posts of Vincennes and Kaskaskias. We will give a brief summary of each in their order.

In the month of February, Boone, at the head of thirty men, was at the lower Blue Licks, engaged in making salt, when he was surprised by two hundred Indians, on their march to attack Boonsborough, and himself and party taken prisoners. They surrendered upon terms of capitulation, which were faithfully observed by the Indians, and were all carried to Detroit. Here his companions were delivered up to the English commandant, but Boone was reserved by the Indians and taken to Chillicothe. His captors treated him with great kindness, and permitted him to hunt, with but little restraint upon his motions. While at Chillicothe, he saw three hundred and fifty Indians assembled, armed and painted, for a hostile expedition against Boonsborough, which had only been suspended, not relinquished, by his capture in the spring. He immediately effected his escape, and lost no time in returning to Boonsborough, where he gave the alarm throughout all Kentucky. Instant preparations were made to receive the enemy; the distant settlements were abandoned, the forts were put upon the war establishment, and all anxiously expected the approach of the enemy. The escape of Boone, however, had disconcerted the enterprise, and it was delayed for several weeks.

Impatient of the slow advance of the enemy, Boone, at the head of thirty men, of whom Simon Kenton was one, projected an expedition against one of the Indian towns on Paint Creek; and while in the enemy's country, he obtained certain information that the Indian army had passed him, and was already on its march to Boonsborough. Countermarching with great rapidity, he halted not, day or night, until he reached Boonsborough with his men; and scarcely had he done so, when Captain Du Quesne made his appearance at the head of five hundred Indians and Canadians. This was such an army as Kentucky had never yet beheld, and it produced an immense sensation. The garrison of Boonsborough consisted of fifty men; Harrodsburg and Logan's fort were strongly menaced by detachments, and could afford them no assistance. The attack commenced; and every artifice was resorted to in order to deceive, to intimidate, or subdue the garrison, but all proved ineffectual. The attack continued during nine days, and was resisted with steady fortitude. On the tenth day the enemy decamped, having lost thirty men killed and a much greater number wounded. The garrison sustained a loss of two killed and four wounded; the loss of the country, however, in stock and improvements, was great.

The expedition of Colonel George Rogers Clark belongs more properly to the history of the United States than to that of Kentucky; it will be referred to, therefore, with great brevity. When Clark was in Kentucky, in the summer of 1776, he took a more comprehensive survey of the western country than the rude pioneers around him; his keen military eye was cast upon the northwestern posts, garrisoned by British troops, and affording inexhaustible supplies of arms and ammunition to the small predatory bands of Indians which infested Kentucky. He saw plainly that they were the true fountains from which the thousand little annual rills of Indian rapine and murder took their rise, and he formed the bold project of striking at the root of the evil.

The revolutionary war was then raging, and the western posts were too remote from the great current of events to attract, powerfully, the attention of either friend or foe; but to Kentucky they were objects of capital interest. He unfolded his plan to the executive of Virginia, awakened him to a true sense of its importance, and had the address to obtain from the impoverished legislature a few scanty supplies of men and munitions for his favorite project. Undismayed by the scantiness of his means, he embarked in the expedition with all the ardor of his character. A few State troops were furnished by Virginia, a few scouts and guides by Kentucky, and, with a secrecy and celerity of movement never surpassed by Napoleon in his palmiest days, he embarked in his daring project.

Having descended the Ohio in boats to the Falls, he there

landed thirteen families who had accompanied him from Pittsburgh, as emigrants to Kentucky, and by whom the foundation of Louisville was laid. Continuing his course down the Ohio, he disembarked his troops about sixty miles above the mouth of that river, and, marching on foot through a pathless wilderness, he came upon Kaskaskias as suddenly and unexpectedly as if he had descended from the skies. The British officer in command, Colonel Rochdublare, and his garrison, surrendered to a force which they could have repelled with ease, if warned of their approach; but never, in the annals of war, was surprise more complete. Having secured and sent off his prisoners to Virginia, Clark was employed for some time in conciliating the inhabitants, who, being French, readily submitted to the new order of things. In the meantime, a storm threatened him from Vincennes. Governor Hamilton, who commanded the British force in the northwest, had actively employed himself during the fall season in organizing a large army of savages, with whom, in conjunction with his British force, he determined not only to crush Clark and his handful of adventurers, but to desolate Kentucky, and even seize fort Pitt. The season, however, became so far advanced before he had completed his preparations, that he determined to defer the project until spring, and in the meantime, to keep his Indians employed, he launched them against the frontiers of Pennsylvania and Virginia, intending to concentrate them early in the spring, and carry out his grand project.

Clark in the meantime lay at Kaskaskias, revolving the difficulties of his situation, and employing his spies diligently in learning intelligence of his enemy. No sooner was he informed of the dispersion of Hamilton's Indian force, and that he lay at Vincennes with his regulars alone, than he determined to strike Vincennes as he had struck Kaskaskias. The march was long, the season inclement, the road passed through an untrodden wilderness, and through overflowed bottoms; his stock of provisions was scanty, and was to be carried upon the backs of his men. He could only muster one hundred and thirty men; but, inspiring this handful with his own heroic spirit, he plunged boldly into the wilderness which separated Kaskaskias from Vincennes, resolved to strike his enemy in the citadel of his strength, or perish in the effort. The difficulties of the march were great, beyond what even his daring spirit had anticipated. For days his route led through the drowned lands of Illinois; his stock of provisions became exhausted, his guides lost their way, and the most intrepid of his followers at times gave way to despair. At length they emerged from the drowned lands, and Vincennes, like Kaskaskias, was completely surprised. The governor and garrison became prisoners of war, and, like their predecessors at Kaskaskias, were sent on to Virginia. The Canadian inhabitants readily submitted, the neighboring tribes were overawed, and some of them became allies, and the whole of the adjacent country became subject to Virginia, which employed a regiment of State troops in maintaining and securing their conquest. A portion of this force was afterwards permanently stationed at Louisville, where a fort was erected, and where Clark established his head-quarters.

The year 1779 was marked, in Kentucky, by three events of unequal importance. About the 1st of April a solitary block-house, with some adjacent defences, the forlorn hope of advancing civilization, was erected by Robert Patterson, upon the spot where the city of Lexington now stands ; the singularly unfortunate expedition of Colonel Bowman, against the Indian town of Chillicothe, was undertaken and carried out ; and the celebrated land law of Kentucky was passed by the Virginia legislature.

Bowman's expedition consisted of the flower of Kentucky. Colonel Benjamin Logan was second in command, and Harrod, Bulger, Bedinger, and many other brave officers, held subordinate commands. The march was well conducted, the surprise was complete, the plan of attack well concerted, and the division led by Logan performed its part well. Yet the whole failed by reason of the hesitation, the imbecility, or the panic of the commander-in-chief. Logan's division, left unsupported by Bowman, was compelled to make a disorderly retreat to the main column, and the rout quickly became general. All would have been lost but for the daring bravery of some of the subordinate officers, who charged the enemy on horseback, and covered the retreat ; but the failure was as complete as it was unexpected and disgraceful.

Our limits forbid an analysis of the land law. It was doubtless well intended, and the settlement and pre-emption features were just and liberal. The radical and incurable defect of the law, however, was the neglect of Virginia to provide for the general survey of the country at the expense of government, and its subdivision into whole, half, and quarter sections, as is now done by the United States. Instead of this, each possessor of a warrant was allowed to locate the same where he pleased, and was required to survey it at his own cost ; but his entry was required to be so special and precise that each subsequent locator might recognize the land already taken up, and make his entry elsewhere. To make a good entry, therefore, required a precision and accuracy of description which such men as Boone and Kenton could not be expected to possess ; and all vague entries were declared null and void. Unnumbered sorrows, lawsuits, and heart-rending vexations, were the consequence of this unhappy law. In the unskillful hands of the hunters and pioneers of Kentucky, entries, surveys, and patents, were piled upon each other, overlapping and crossing in endless perplexity. The full fruits were not reaped until the country became more thickly settled.

In the meantime the immediate consequence of the law was a flood of immigration. The hunters of the elk and buffalo were now succeeded by the more ravenous hunters of land; in the pursuit, they fearlessly braved the hatchet of the Indian and the privations of the forest. The surveyor's chain and compass were seen in the woods as frequently as the rifle; and during the years 1779-80-81, the great and all-absorbing object in Kentucky was to enter, survey, and obtain a patent, for the richest sections of land. Indian hostilities were rife during the whole of this period, but these only formed episodes in the great drama.

The year 1780 was distinguished by the vast number of emigrants who crowded to Kentucky for the purpose of locating land warrants; Indian hostility was proportionably active, and a formidable expedition, consisting of Indians and English, under Colonel Bird, threatened Kentucky with destruction. For the first time, cannon were employed against the stockade forts of Kentucky; and Ruddle's and Martin's stations were completely destroyed, and their garrisons taken. The impatience of the Indians then compelled the colonel to retire, without pushing his successes further.

In the fall of this year, Colonel Clark, at the head of his State troops stationed at Louisville, reinforced by all the disposable force of Kentucky, invaded the Indian country in Ohio, and having defeated the Indians in a pitched battle, laid waste their villages and destroyed their corn fields, with inexorable severity, in retaliation of Bird's expedition in the spring.

In November of this year, Kentucky was divided into three counties, to which the names of Fayette, Lincoln, and Jefferson were given. They had now three county courts, holding monthly sessions, three courts of common law and chancery jurisdiction, sitting quarter-yearly, and a host of magistrates and constables. No court, capable of trying for capital offences, existed in the country, or nearer than Richmond. The courts of quarter-session could take notice only of misdemeanors.

The year 1781 was distinguished by a very large emigration, by prodigious activity in land speculation, and by the frequency of Indian inroads, in small parties. Every portion of the country was kept continually in alarm, and small Indian ambushes were perpetually bursting upon the settlers. Many lives were lost, but the settlements made great and daily advances, in defiance of all obstacles. The rich lands of Kentucky were the prize of the first occupants, and they rushed to seize them with a rapacity stronger than the fear of death.

The year 1782 was uncommonly prolific in great events. Indian hostility was unusually early and active. In the month of May, a party of twenty-five Wyandots invaded Kentucky, and committed shocking depredations in the neighborhood of Estill's station. Captain Estill hastily collected a party of equal force, and pursued them rapidly. He overtook them upon Hinckstone's fork of Licking, near Mount-Sterling, and the best fought battle of the war there occurred. The creek ran between the parties, forbidding a charge but at perilous disadvantage, and the two

lines, forming behind trees and logs, within half rifle shot, stood front to front for hours, in close and deadly combat. One-third on each side had fallen, and the fire was still vivid and deadly, as at the opening of the combat. Estill, determined to bring it to a close, ordered Lieutenant Miller to turn their flank with six men, and attack them in the rear. While Miller was making a small detour to the right, for the purpose, most probably, of executing his orders in good faith (for there are various constructions placed upon his conduct), the Indian commander became aware of the division of his adversary's force, and,—with that rapid decision which so often flashed across Napoleon's battle-fields, and whether exhibited upon a great or a small scale, mark the great commander,—determined to frustrate the plan, by crossing the creek with his whole force and overwhelming Estill, now weakened by the absence of Miller. This bold thought was executed with determined courage, and after a desperate struggle, Estill was totally overpowered, and forced from the ground with slaughter. Himself, and nearly all his officers, were killed; and it was but a poor consolation that an equal loss had been inflicted on the enemy. This brilliant little fight is deeply written in the annals of Kentucky, and will long be remembered, for the exquisite specimen of the military art, exhibited in miniature, by the Indian commander. It created a sensation, at the time, far beyond its real importance, and was rapidly followed by stunning blows, from the same quarter, in rapid succession.

A party of Wyandots, consisting of twenty men, encountered Captain Holder, at the head of seventeen Kentuckians, near the upper Blue Licks, and defeated him with loss.

But these small parties were the mere pattering drops of hail, which precede the tempest. In the month of August, an army of five hundred Indian warriors, composed of detachments from all the north-western tribes, rapidly and silently traversed the northern part of Kentucky, and appeared before Bryant's station, as unexpectedly as if they had risen from the earth. The garrison, although surprised, took prompt measures to repel the enemy. By the daring gallantry of the women, the fort was supplied with water from a neighboring spring. Two of the garrison burst through the enemy's lines, and gave the alarm to the neighboring stations, while those who remained, by means of a well-conceived and successful *ruse*, gave a bloody repulse to the only assault which the Indians ventured to make upon the fort. A party of sixteen horsemen, with great gallantry and good fortune, forced their way through the Indians, and entered the fort unhurt. More than double that number, on foot, made a similar effort, but failed, and sustained considerable loss.

In the meantime, the garrison remained under cover, and kept up a deliberate and fatal fire upon such Indians as showed themselves. The enemy became discouraged, and, apprehensive of bringing the whole force of the country upon them, by farther delay, broke up their camp, on the second night of the siege, and retreated by the buffalo-trace, leading to the lower Blue Lick. By the next day, at noon, one hundred and sixty men had assembled at Bryant's station, burning with eagerness to encounter the invaders. Colonels Todd, Trigg, and Daniel Boone; majors Harland, M'Bride, and Levi Todd; captains Bulger and Gordon, with forty-five other commissioned officers, including the celebrated M'Gary, assembled in council, and hastily determined to pursue the enemy, without waiting for Colonel Logan, who was known to be collecting a strong force in Lincoln, and who might be expected to join them in twenty-four hours.

If Major M'Gary is to be believed, he remonstrated against this rash precipitation, and urged a delay of one day for reinforcements, but so keen was the ardor of officer and soldier, that his dissent was drowned, in an impatient clamor for instant battle; and in an evil hour, on the 18th of August, the line of march was taken up, and the pursuit urged with a keenness which quickly brought them up with the retreating foe. Before noon, on the 19th, they reached the southern bank of Licking, and for the first time beheld their enemy. A few Indians were carelessly loitering upon the rocky ridge, which bounded the prospect to the north. These warriors seemed nowise disconcerted by the presence of so large a body of Kentuckians, but after gazing upon them for a few moments with cool indifference, very leisurely disappeared beyond the ridge.

This symptom was not to be mistaken by the youngest woodsman in the ranks. The enemy was before them in force, and a battle against fearful odds, or a rapid retreat, became inevitable. A dozen officers rode to the front and exchanged opinions. Boone, who was best acquainted with the ground, declared with confidence that the Indian army lay in ambuscade about one mile beyond the river, which there ran in an irregular ellipsis, and offered peculiar advantages to the Indians, if the Kentuckians should advance by the buffalo trace. He advised either a retreat upon Logan, or a division of their force, for the purpose of making a flank attack upon each wing of the Indian army, of whose position he had no doubt. All further deliberation, however, was broken up by M'Gary, who suddenly spurred his horse into the stream, waved his hat over his head, and shouted aloud, " Let all who are not cowards follow me." Of the gallant band of one hundred and sixty, there was not one who could endure this taunt. The electric cord was struck with a rude hand, and the shock was as universal as it was violent. The horsemen dashed tumultuously into the stream, each striving to be foremost. The footmen were mingled with them in one rolling and irregular mass. They struggled through a deep ford as they best could, and without stopping to reform their ranks on the northern shore, pressed forward in great disorder, but in a fierce mood, to close with their concealed enemy. The stinging taunt of M'Gary had struck deep, and every thought save that of confronting death without fear, was for the moment banished from their minds.

M'Gary still led the van, closely followed by Boone, Harland and M'Bride. Suddenly a heavy fire burst upon them in front, and the van halted and endeavored to obtain cover and return the fire. The centre and rear hurried up to support their friends, and the bare and rocky ridge was soon crowded with the com batants. The ravines flanked them on each side, from which came a devouring fire, which rapidly wasted their ranks. There was no cover for the Kentuckians, and nearly one half of their force was on horseback. The Indians had turned each flank, and appeared disposed to cut off their retreat. The rear fell back to prevent this, the centre and van followed the movement, and a total rout ensued. The pursuit was keen and bloody, and was pressed with unrelenting vigor. Todd, Trigg, Harland, M'Bride, Bulger, and Gordon, were killed on the field of battle. M'Gary, although more deeply involved in the ranks of the enemy than any other officer, was totally unhurt; sixty officers and men were killed in the battle or pursuit, and seven prisoners were taken. The number of wounded was never ascertained. Some of the fugitives reached Bryant's station on the night after the battle, and were there met by Colonel Logan, at the head of four hundred and fifty men. Logan remained at Bryant's until the last of the survivors had arrived, and then continued his march to the battle ground. The bodies of the dead were collected and interred, and having satisfied himself that the Indians had crossed the Ohio and were beyond his reach, he returned to Bryant's station and disbanded his troops.

It was an established custom in Kentucky at that time, never to suffer an Indian invasion to go unpunished, but to retaliate upon their villages and corn fields, the havoc, which their own settlements had experienced. Colonel George Rogers Clark, stationed permanently at Louisville, declared that he would lead his regiment of State troops against the Indian villages in Ohio, and invited the militia of Kentucky to accompany him. The call was promptly answered. One thousand riflemen rendezvoused at the mouth of Licking, and under the command of Clark, penetrated into the heart of the Indian country. No resistance was offered. Their towns were reduced to ashes, their corn cut up, and the whole country laid waste with unsparing severity. Having completely destroyed every thing within their reach, the detachment returned to Kentucky.

CHAPTER II.

THE certainty that actual hostilities between Great Britain and America had ceased, and that a treaty of peace would be formally ratified in the spring, led to an universal expectation that Indian hostilities would cease, and in expectation of that event, there was a vast accession of emigrants in the fall of 1782. Peace followed in 1783, as was expected, and Indian hostilities for a time were suspended; but an unhappy failure on both sides fully and fairly to execute the treaty, finally resulted in the renewal of the Indian war with treble violence.

By the terms of the treaty, England was bound to carry away no slaves, and to surrender the north-western posts in her possession within the boundaries of the United States. On the other hand, Congress had stipulated, that no legal impediments should be opposed to the collection by British merchants, of the debts due them from citizens of the United States. None of these stipulations were faithfully executed, as they were understood by the parties severally interested. Slaves taken during the war were removed by the British fleet. Virginia became indignant and passed a law which prohibited the collection of British debts, and England refused to deliver up the western posts, until the obnoxious laws were repealed. Congress, in helpless imbecility, was unable to control the sovereign States, and the posts were withheld until Jay's treaty, more than ten years after peace had been ratified.

The Indians at first, however, assumed a pacific attitude, and the year 1783 passed away without hostilities. In the meantime, the settlements advanced with great rapidity. Simon Kenton, after an interval of nine years, reclaimed his settlement at Washington, and in 1784 erected a block house where Maysville now stands, so that the Ohio river became the northern frontier of Kentucky. The general course of emigration henceforth was down the Ohio to Maysville, and thence by land to the interior.

In the spring of 1783, Kentucky was erected into a district, and a court of criminal as well as civil jurisdiction, coextensive with the district, was erected. The court held its first session in Harrodsburg, in the spring of 1783, and was opened by John Floyd and Samuel M'Dowell, as judges, John May being clerk, and Walker Daniel prosecuting attorney. Seventeen culprits were presented by the grand jury; nine for keeping tippling houses, and eight for fornication. From these presentments, we may form some opinion of the vices most prevalent in Kentucky at that time. During the summer, a log court-house and jail, " of hewed or sawed logs nine inches thick," was erected on the spot where Danville now stands; during this summer, a retail store of dry goods was opened at Louisville, and the tone of society became visibly more elevated.

In 1784, General James Wilkinson emigrated to the country, and settled in Lexington. This gentleman occupied a distinguished position in the early civil conflicts of Kentucky, and became the leader of a political party; he had distinguished himself in the war of independence, and was aid-de-camp to Gates at Saratoga. For distinguished services in that campaign, and upon the particular recommendation of Gates, he had been promoted by Congress to the rank of brigadier-general. Friends and enemies have agreed in ascribing to him the qualities of courage, energy, address, and eloquence; of a somewhat meretricious and inflated character. A graceful person, amiable manners, liberal hospitality, with a ready and popular elocution, when added to his military fame, ensured him popularity with the mass of the people. He came to Kentucky with the avowed object of improving his circumstances, which were somewhat embarrassed; he was understood to be connected with an eastern mercantile company, and not to be averse to any speculation which might improve his fortune. He soon became deeply involved in the fiercest political controversies of the day, and has left his countrymen divided in opinion as to whether he acted from patriotic and honorable motives, or was a selfish and abandoned adventurer, ready to aid any project which promised to advance his interests.

In the summer of 1784, some depredations were committed by the Indians upon the southern frontier, and Colonel Benjamin Logan had received intelligence that a serious invasion was contemplated, and publicly summoned such citizens as could conveniently attend, to meet at Danville on a particular day, and consult as to what measures should be taken for the common defence.

The alarm in the end proved unfounded; but in the meantime a great number of the most distinguished citizens assembled at Danville, under a belief that Indian hostilities upon a large scale were about to be renewed, and would continue until the northwestern posts were surrendered by the British. Upon an examination of the laws then in existence, their most eminent lawyers decided that no expedition could lawfully and effectually be carried out against the Indian tribes; the power of impressment had ceased with the war, and in a state of peace could not legally be exercised. Nor was there any power known to the law capable of calling forth the resources of the country, however imminent the danger; all of their legislation came from Richmond, distant many hundred miles, and separated from Kentucky by desert mountains and interminable forests traversed by roving bands of Indians.

The necessity of a government independent of Virginia was deeply and almost unanimously felt. But how was this to be accomplished? It is interesting to trace the origin, progress, and consummation of independence in this infant community—the first established west of the mountains; and when we reflect upon the bloodshed and violence which has usually attended such political changes in the old world, we are profoundly struck with the good sense, moderation, and patience, under powerful temptation, which marked the conduct of Kentucky.

The first step taken marks the simplicity and integrity of the movers. The assembly, having no legal authority, published a recommendation, that each *militia company* in the district should on a certain day elect one delegate, and that the delegates thus chosen should assemble in Danville, on the 27th December, 1784. The recommendation was well received, the elections held, and the delegates assembled. Samuel M'Dowell was elected president, and Thomas Todd, clerk. A great number of spectators were in attendance, who maintained the most commendable order, and the *convention*, as they styled themselves, debated the question of *separation* from the parent State with all the gravity and decorum of a deliberative body.

A division of opinion was manifest, but none, save legal and constitutional means, were even hinted at by the warmest advocate for separation; order and law reigned without a rival. A very great majority were in favor of a petition to the legislature of Virginia, and through them to Congress, for the passage of an act, in the manner provided by the constitution, by which Kentucky might become an independent member of the confederacy. A resolution was passed, by a large majority, declaratory of the views of the convention. But as no clear determination, upon that subject, had been expressed by the people previous to their election, they did not consider themselves authorized to take any steps to carry their resolution into effect, further than to recommend that, in the spring election of delegates, from the several counties, to the Virginia legislature, the people should also elect twenty-five delegates to a convention, to meet at Danville, in May, 1785, and finally determine whether separation was expedient. They also apportioned the delegates among the several counties, with great fairness, according to the supposed population. The people peaceably conformed to the recommendation of their delegates, and elected the members as prescribed by the convention.

In the meantime, the subject was gravely and earnestly discussed in the primary assemblies, and, in some parts of the country, with passionate fervor. A great majority were in favor of constitutional separation—none other was then thought of. On the 23d of May, 1785, this second convention assembled and adopted five resolutions. They decided that constitutional separation from Virginia was expedient,—that a petition to the legislature be prepared,—that an address to the people of Kentucky be published, and that delegates to another convention be elected in July, and assemble at Danville in August following, to whom the petition, address, and proceedings of the present convention be referred for final action.

The people, thus involved in a labyrinth of conventions, to which no end could be seen, nevertheless quietly conformed, elected a new batch of delegates in July, who assembled in August, being the third convention which had already assembled, while scarcely any progress had been made in carrying into effect the object of their meeting. In the meantime, Indian hostility became more frequent, and the exasperation of the people daily increased. The petition and address, with the other proceedings of the convention of May, were referred to the present, and underwent considerable change. The petition was drawn in language less simple, the address to the people of Kentucky was more exciting, impassioned, and exaggerated. No printing press, as yet, existed in the country, but copies of the address and petition were zealously multiplied by the pen, and widely dispersed among the people. The chief-justice of the District Court, George Muter, and the attorney-general, Harry Innis, were deputed to present the petition to the legislature of Virginia. This was accordingly done, and in January, 1786, the legislature passed an act, with great unanimity, in conformity to the wishes of Kentucky, annexing, however, certain terms and conditions sufficiently just and fair, but which necessarily produced some delay. They required a fourth convention, to assemble at Danville in September, 1786, who should determine whether it were the will of the district to become an independent State of the confederacy, upon the conditions in the act enumerated, and well known under the denomination of the Compact with Virginia. And if the convention should determine upon separation, they were required to fix upon a day posterior to the 1st of September, 1787, on which the authority of Virginia was to cease and determine forever ; provided, however, that previous to the 1st day of June, 1787, the Congress of the United States should assent to said act, and receive the new State into the Union.

The great mass of the citizens of Kentucky received this act with calm satisfaction, and were disposed peaceably to conform to its provisions. But two circumstances, about this time, occurred, which tended to create unfavorable impressions, in Kentucky, towards the government of the Union. The one was the utter inability of Congress to protect them from the north-western tribes, by compelling a surrender of the posts, or otherwise. The other was a strong disposition, manifested by the delegates in Congress from the seven north-eastern States, to yield, for twenty years, the right to navigate the Mississippi to the ocean. The one inspired contempt; the other awakened distrust, which might rapidly ripen to aversion. Hostilities had ceased with Great Britain, but hatred and resentment blazed as fiercely between the people of the two nations, as if the war was still raging. The retention of the posts kept alive Indian hostility against Kentucky, while the eastern States enjoyed profound peace.

Congress had, after long delay, made treaties with the Indians, which were totally disregarded by the latter, as far as Kentucky was concerned, and the violation of which the former was totally unable to chastise. Repeated efforts were made by General Henry Lee, of Virginia, to obtain a continental force of seven hundred, or even three hundred men, to protect the western frontier; but the frantic jealousy of the central power cherished by the sovereign States, at a time when that central power grovelled in the most helpless imbecility, peremptorily forbade even this small force to be embodied, lest it might lead to the overthrow of State rights. In the meantime, Kentucky was smarting under the scourge of Indian warfare ; had no government at home, and their government beyond the mountains, however sincerely disposed, was totally unable to protect them, from a radical and incurable vice in its constitution.

To this cause of dissatisfaction came the astounding intelligence, in the succeeding year, that several States in Congress had voted to barter away the right to navigate the Mississippi, in consideration of commercial advantages to be yielded by Spain to the eastern States, in which Kentucky could have no direct interest. There was neither printing press nor post office in Kentucky, and the people were separated by an immense wilderness from their eastern brethren. Intelligence came slowly, and at long intervals. In passing through so many hands, it was necessarily inaccurate, exaggerated and distorted, according to the passions or whims of its retailers. Never was harvest more ripe for the sickle of the intriguer ; and it soon became manifest, that schemes were in agitation which contemplated a severance of Kentucky from Virginia by other than constitutional means, and which vaguely, and cautiously, seemed to sound the way for a total severance of Kentucky from the Union.

In the elections which took place in the spring of 1786, for the fourth convention, directed by the legislature of Virginia, General James Wilkinson became a candidate to represent the county of Fayette. With all the address, activity, and eloquence of which he was master, he strove to ripen the public mind for an immediate declaration of independence, without going through the slow formalities of law, which the exigencies of the country, in his opinion, would not permit them to await. He was the first public man who gave utterance to this bold sentiment; and great sensation was produced in the county of Fayette, by its promulgation. A violent opposition to his views quickly became manifest, and displayed such strength and fervor, as drew from him an explanation and modification, which lulled the force of present opposition, but left an indelible jealousy in the breasts of many, of the general's ulterior intentions. He was elected to the convention. There was but little excitement in the other counties, who chose the prescribed number of delegates, with the intention of patiently awaiting the formalities of law.

In the meantime, Indian depredations became so harassing, that the people determined upon a grand expedition against the Indian towns, notwithstanding the treaties of Congress, and absence of legal power. A thousand volunteers under General Clark rendezvoused at Louisville, with the determination thoroughly to chastise the tribes upon the Wabash. Provisions and ammunition were furnished by individual contribution, and were placed on board of nine keel boats, which were ordered to proceed to Vincennes by water, while the volunteers should march to the same point by land.

The flotilla, laden with provisions and munitions of war, encountered obstacles in the navigation of the Wabash, which had not been foreseen, and was delayed beyond the time which had been calculated. The detachment moving by land reached the point of rendezvous first, and awaited for fifteen days the arrival of the keel boats. This long interval of inaction gave time for the unhealthy humors of the volunteers to ferment, and proved fatal to the success of the expedition. The habits of General Clark had also become intemperate, and he no longer possessed the undivided confidence of his men. A detachment of three hundred volunteers broke off from the main body, and took up the line of march for their homes. Clark remonstrated, entreated, even shed tears of grief and mortification, but all in vain. The result was a total disorganization of the force, and a return to Kentucky, to the bitter mortification of the commander-in-chief, whose brilliant reputation for the time suffered a total eclipse.

This expedition led to other ill consequences. The convention which should have assembled in September, was unable to muster a quorum, the majority of its members having marched under Clark upon the ill-fated expedition. A number of the delegates assembled at Danville at the appointed time, and adjourned from day to day until January, when a quorum at length was present, and an organization effected. In the meantime, however, the minority of the convention who had adjourned from day to day, had prepared a memorial to the legislature of Virginia, informing them of the circumstances which had prevented the meeting of the convention, and suggesting an alteration of some of the clauses of the act, which gave dissatisfaction to their constituents, and recommending an extension of the time within which the consent of Congress was required. This produced a total revision of the act by the Virginia legislature, whereby another convention was required to be elected in August of 1787, to meet at Danville, in September of the same year, and again take into consideration the great question, already decided by four successive conventions, and requiring a majority of two-thirds to decide in favor of separation, before the same should be effected. The time when the laws of Virginia were to cease, was fixed on the 1st day of January, 1789, instead of September, 1787, as was ordered in the first act; and the 4th of July, 1788, was fixed upon as the period, before which Congress should

3

express its consent to the admission of Kentucky into the Union.

This new act became known in Kentucky shortly after the fourth convention, after a delay of three months, had at length rallied a quorum, and had with great unanimity decided upon separation. They then found themselves deprived of all authority, their recent act nullified, their whole work to begin anew, and the time of separation adjourned for two years, and clogged with new conditions. An ebullition of impatience and anger was the unavoidable result. They seemed, by some fatality, to be involved in a series of conventions, interminable as a Cretan labyrinth, tantalizing them with the prospect of fruit, which invariably turned to ashes, when attempted to be grasped.

While such was the temper of the public mind, the navigation of the Mississippi was thrown into the scale. Shortly after the convention adjourned, a number of gentlemen in Pittsburgh, styling themselves a "committee of correspondence," made a written communication to the people of Kentucky, informing them, "that John Jay, the American secretary for foreign affairs, had made a proposition to Don Gardoqui, the Spanish minister, near the United States, to cede the navigation of the Mississippi to Spain for twenty years, in consideration of commercial advantages to be enjoyed by the eastern States alone."

On the 29th of March, a circular letter was addressed to the people of Kentucky, signed by George Muter, Harry Innis, John Brown, and Benjamin Sebastian, recommending the election of five delegates from each county to meet at Danville in May, and take into consideration the late action of Congress upon the subject of the Mississippi. The letter contemplated the formation of committees of correspondence throughout the west, and a "decent, but spirited," remonstrance to Congress against the cession, which they evidently supposed in great danger of being consummated. There is nothing objectionable in either the language or object of this circular, and, considering the impression then prevailing in the west as to the intentions of Congress, it may be regarded as temperate and manly in its character. The most ignorant hunter in the west could not be blind to the vital importance of the interest which, (as they supposed,) was about to be bartered away for advantages to be reaped by their eastern brethren alone; and although the ferment was violent for a time, yet regular and constitutional remedies were only proposed by the circular or adopted by the citizens.

The delegates were elected as proposed, but before they assembled the true state of affairs in Congress was more accurately understood, and the convention, after a brief session, and after rejecting various propositions, which *looked* towards increasing and prolonging the excitement of the people upon this agitating subject, quietly adjourned, without taking any action whatever upon the subject.

This negotiation belongs properly to the history of the United

States; but it is impossible to understand the early political history of Kentucky, without briefly adverting to some of its most prominent features. No sooner did it become evident that the war, however protracted, must finally end in the establishment of American independence, than the friendly courts of France and Spain began to exhibit the most restless jealousy as to the western limits of the infant republic. Spain was then an immense land-holder upon the northern part of the continent, claiming all east of the Mississippi, lying south of the 31st degree of north latitude, and all west of the Mississippi to the Pacific. France had large islands in the West Indies. The object of both was to make the Alleghany the western limit, if possible; if not, at least to bound them by the Ohio, leaving Kentucky, Tennessee, and Mississippi, to indemnify his Catholic majesty for the expenses of the war.

These views were early disclosed by the two allied powers, and urged with all the skill and power of a long practiced and tortuous diplomacy. On the contrary, they were steadily and manfully opposed by Jay and the elder Adams, the American ministers abroad, who succeeded in securing to their country the boundary of the Mississippi, as far south as latitude 31, the full extent of the ancient English claim. Baffled upon the subject of boundary, Spain still clung to the navigation of the Mississippi, and anxiously strove to retain the exclusive right to its navigation, and to obtain from the United States a cession of all right thereto. This was firmly resisted by Jay during the war, when his instructions gave him a large discretion, and when pecuniary aid was lavishly proffered by Spain if this right was ceded, and no less pertinaciously adhered to by him after the war.

In 1786, Don Gardoqui, the Spanish ambassador, opened a negotiation with Jay, the secretary for foreign affairs, at New York. Jay's instructions from Congress forbade him to make any concessions upon the subject of the Mississippi, and under these instructions the negotiation began. Jay reported to Congress that his opinion of the question remained unaltered, but that by relinquishing the right for twenty years they could obtain great and important advantages, more than equivalent to the disadvantages of the said cession, which, in his opinion, (so little did he anticipate the rapid growth of the west,) would be of little importance for twenty years.

The seven north-eastern States voted to rescind the instructions above alluded to, restricting him upon the subject of the Mississippi. This was violently opposed by Virginia, and the other States, and as the votes of nine States were necessary to the success of the resolution, and it was obviously impossible to obtain so many votes for the measure, the subject was entirely relinquished. Virginia, in the meantime, by an unanimous vote of her legislature, had instructed her delegates in Congress *never* to accede to any such proposition; and she was warmly supported by the other non-concurring States. As soon as these facts were thoroughly understood by the convention, they quietly adjourned, without action of any kind. There was left upon the public mind, however, a restless jealousy of the intentions of the north-eastern States, which could, at any time, be fanned into a flame, and of which political aspirants eagerly availed themselves, whenever it suited their purposes. The name of Jay became peculiarly odious in Kentucky, which odium was not diminished by his celebrated treaty, concluded many years afterwards.

In the meantime, the delegates to the fifth convention, in conformity to the last act of Virginia, were quietly elected, and a newspaper, entitled the "Kentucky Gazette," printed by John Bradford, of Lexington, having been established, the pent up passions of the various political partisans found vent in its pages. During this summer, General Wilkinson descended the Mississippi with a cargo of tobacco, for New Orleans, avowedly upon a mercantile adventure alone. But those who had been startled by the boldness of the general's project, of separation from Virginia, coupling this trip with the recent agitation of the question of the navigation of the Mississippi, and the unsettled state of the public mind in relation to the Spanish pretensions, did not scruple to charge him with ulterior projects, other than commercial in their tendency. The delegates, in the meantime, assembled in Danville, and again repeated the uniform decision of their predecessors, by an unanimous vote.

A copy of their proceedings was sent to the executive of Virginia, and the editor of the Gazette was requested to publish them, for the information of the people. An address to Congress was adopted, perfectly respectful in its character, praying that honorable body to receive them into the Union. The representatives from Kentucky to the Virginia legislature, were also requested to exert their influence to have a delegate to Congress, elected from the district of Kentucky, who should sit with the delegation from Virginia. They decided that the power of Virginia should cease on the 31st of December, 1788, and made provision for the election of still another convention—it was hoped the last—to assemble, in the ensuing year, at Danville, in order to form a constitution. The legislature of Virginia cordially assented to the suggestion of the convention, in relation to the appointment of a delegate from Kentucky, to Congress, and Mr. John Brown, a representative from Kentucky to the Virginia legislature, was elected, by that legislature, a delegate to Congress, taking his seat with the other representatives from Virginia. This gentleman was one of the most eminent lawyers of Kentucky, possessed of talents, influence, and popularity. He was charged with the delivery of the petition of the convention to Congress, and lost no time in presenting himself before that body.

The great convention, which gave birth to the American constitution, had concluded their labors, in Philadelphia, in September, 1787, and the public mind was so much excited upon the subject of the new constitution, that the old Congress could scarcely be kept alive until the new government should be organized. A quorum of the members could not be rallied, during the winter, and although the act of the Virginia legislature required their assent before the 4th of July, 1788, it was not until the 3d of July that the question of the admission of Kentucky was taken up. The federal constitution had then been adopted by ten States, and it was certain that the new government would quickly go into operation. The old Congress declined to act upon the petition of Kentucky, and referred the question to the new government, whenever the same should be organized.

Thus was Kentucky again baffled in her most ardent wish, and flung back to the point from which she had started, more than four years before. Her long array of conventions had in vain decided, again and again, that it was expedient to separate from Virginia, and become an independent member of the confederacy. Mr. Brown communicated the intelligence to his constituents; and his own views upon the subject are clearly contained in two letters, the one to Samuel M'Dowell, who had acted as president of nearly all the Kentucky conventions, the other to George Muter. In these letters he attributes the refusal of Congress, to act upon the petition of Kentucky, to the jealousy of the New England States, of any accession to the southern strength, in Congress, and he inclines to the opinion that the same causes will have equal weight with the new government. He gives the result of various private interviews between himself and Don Gardoqui, the Spanish minister—speaks of the promises of that minister, of peculiar commercial advantages to Kentucky, connected with the navigation of the Mississippi, *if she will erect herself into an independent government; but these advantages, he says, can never be yielded to her by Spain, so long as she remains a member of the Union!* He communicates this information *in confidence*, and with the permission of Don Gardoqui, to a few friends, not doubting that they will make a prudent use of it. He gives his own opinion decidedly in favor of immediate independence, without waiting for the result of another application to Congress, under the new government.

It is worthy of observation, that in July 1787, Harry Innis, attorney-general of Kentucky, wrote to the executive of Virginia, giving it as his opinion that Kentucky would form an independent government in two or three years, as *Congress did not seem disposed to protect them, and under the present system she could not exert her strength.* He adds, " I have just dropped this hint to your excellency for matter of reflection !" Coupling these passages with the early and bold declaration of Wilkinson upon the same subject, we cannot for a moment doubt, that the project of unconstitutional separation from Virginia and the union was seriously entertained by some of the statesmen of Kentucky, including Wilkinson, Brown, and Innis, as the prominent and leading characters. Whether this project was horrid and damnable, as characterized by Marshall, or innocent and patriotic, as esteemed by Mr. Butler, may be left to nice casuists in political morality to decide. But that the scheme was seriously entertained cannot fairly be denied, and truth and fidelity require that the historian should not attempt to conceal it.

Before the result of the application to Congress could be known in Kentucky, the public mind was powerfully directed to the importance of the navigation of the Mississippi by the return of General Wilkinson from New Orleans, and the intelligence that he had obtained for himself the privilege of shipping tobacco to New Orleans, and depositing it in the king's stores, at the price of ten dollars per hundred weight. He immediately offered to purchase tobacco to any amount, and dilated eloquently upon the advantages that would result to Kentucky, even from the partial trade which he had succeeded in opening, but explained that a commercial treaty might be formed with Spain, which would throw open their ports to the whole western country, if the west were erected into an independent government, capable of treating with a foreign power. In the meantime Indian hostility never slumbered, but murders upon the frontier were incessant. The old confederation was about to expire, despised abroad and scarcely respected at home, and early in the spring Kentucky was called upon to elect delegates to the Virginia convention, which was called to adopt or reject the federal constitution. Nearly every leading man in Kentucky, and an immense majority of the people, were warmly anti-federal; yet three of the Kentucky delegation, one from Fayette and two from Jefferson, voted in favor of its adoption. The member from Fayette was no other than the veteran historian of Kentucky, Humphrey Marshall, who certainly voted against the opinion of a majority of his constituents.

On the 28th of July the sixth convention assembled at Danville. But scarcely had they organized and commenced business when the intelligence was communicated to them, that Congress had declined to act upon the petition of Kentucky, and had referred the whole subject to the new government. Anger and disappointment were strongly expressed in all quarters. The party which with invincible firmness had uniformly adhered to "law and order," now received a rude shock. The party which vaguely and cautiously advocated immediate independence, contrary to law, became more bold and open in urging their project. The trade to New Orleans, recently opened by Wilkinson, was made to loom largely before the public eye, and unfolded visions of future wealth which dazzled the imagination. The old confederation was contemptible, from its helpless imbecility, and the new government, yet in embryo, was odious and unpopular. A proposition to form a constitution without further delay was warmly advocated, and it was proposed in convention that the question should be submitted to each militia company in the district, and that the captain of said company should report the result of the vote. This proposition awakened the most passionate opposition, and was voted down by a large majority. Yet the ambiguous character of the resolutions finally adopted, displays the balanced condition of parties in the convention, and that neither could fully carry out their designs. They finally resolved that a seventh convention be elected in October, and assemble in November, with general power to take the best steps for securing *admission into the union*, and also *the navigation of the Mississippi;* that they have power to form a constitution, and do generally whatever may seem necessary to the best interests of the district. We clearly recognize the finger of each party in the above resolution, and may infer that each felt their inability to carry out decisive measures.

As the time for the election of the seventh convention approached, a publication appeared in the Gazette, signed by George Muter, the chief justice of the district court, which, in a concise and clear manner points out the particular clauses in the laws of Virginia and the articles of confederation, which would be violated by the formation of an independent government, in the manner proposed by the party of which Wilkinson was the leader. This publication was universally attributed to Colonel Thomas Marshall, of Fayette, the father of the late chief justice Marshall. This gentleman had emigrated with his family to Kentucky in 1785, had been appointed surveyor of Fayette county, and had taken an active part in the early struggle of parties in Kentucky. His opposition to the project of independence, contrary to law, was early, decided, and uncompromising, and two tickets were now formed in the county of Fayette, for the approaching convention. Colonel Marshall was at the head of one, and General Wilkinson of the other. The old English party names of "Court," and "Country," were given to them by the wits of the day, and the canvass was conducted with a zeal and fervor proportioned to the magnitude of the questions involved in the issue. The election lasted for five days, and it soon became evident, that the ticket headed by Marshall was running ahead. During the election, Wilkinson so far modified his tone, as to declare that his action in the convention should be regulated by the instructions of his constituents; and by the strength of his personal popularity, he was elected. Fayette was entitled to five representatives, of whom four were elected from the ticket headed by Marshall, and Wilkinson alone was elected, of the opposite party.

In November the delegates assembled at Danville, and proceeded to business. The resolution of Congress, transmitted by Mr. Brown, was first referred to the committee of the whole, without opposition. A motion was then made to refer the resolution of the last convention, upon the subject of the Mississippi navigation, to the committee also, in order that the whole subject might be before them. The restless jealousy of the "law and order party" took alarm at this proposition, and a keen and animated debate arose upon the question of reference. Wilkinson, Brown, Innis, and Sebastian, were in favor of the reference, while it was warmly opposed by Marshall, Muter, Crockett, Allen, and Christian. The reference was carried by a large majority. Regarding this as an unfavorable indication of the temper of the convention, Colonel Crockett left his seat on Saturday, and on Monday returned, with a remonstrance, signed by nearly five hundred citizens, against violent or illegal separation from their eastern brethren. This bold step undoubtedly made a deep impression upon the convention, and gives a lively indication of the strong passions awakened by the discussion.

In the debate upon the question of reference, Wilkinson and Brown had glanced at the project of illegal separation, in a manner which showed that they were doubtful of the temper of the convention. General Wilkinson, after dwelling upon the vital importance of the navigation to Kentucky, and the improbability that Spain would ever grant it to Congress, concluded, with emphasis, "*that there was one way, and only one, of obtaining this rich prize for Kentucky, and that way was so guarded by laws, and fortified by constitutions, that it was difficult and dangerous of access.*" He added, "that Spain might concede to Kentucky alone, what she would not concede to the United States," and "that there was information within the power of the convention, upon this subject, of the first importance, which, he had no doubt, a gentleman in the convention would communicate." He sat down, and looked at Mr. Brown; the eyes of all the members traveled in the same direction, expressive of very different emotions. Mr. Brown arose, and remarked, "that he did not consider himself at liberty to disclose the private conferences held with Don Gardoqui, but this much he would say, in general, *that provided they were unanimous, everything that they could wish for was within their reach.*" He then resumed his seat. General Wilkinson again arose, and read a long manuscript essay upon the navigation of the Mississippi, giving the sheets to Sebastian, as they were read. This essay was addressed to the Spanish intendant. A motion was made to give the thanks of the convention to the general, for the essay, which was unanimously concurred in.

A resolution, offered by Edwards, and seconded by Marshall, might be regarded as a test of the temper of the convention. It was " to appoint a committee to draw up a decent and respectful address, to the legislature of Virginia, for obtaining the independence of Kentucky, agreeably to the late resolution and recommendation of Congress." No opposition was made, and the committee was appointed, of whom Wilkinson was one, and the only one of his party, on the committee. In due time the committee reported, an amendment was moved, which resulted in the postponement of the whole matter to a future day. In the interval, General Wilkinson brought forward a preamble and resolution, which, after lamenting the divisions and distractions which appeared in the convention, and urging the necessity of unanimity, proposed the appointment of a committee to draw up an appeal to the people, for instructions as to their future action, upon the great subjects before them. The committee was appointed, of which he was chairman. He quickly reported an address to the people, which was referred to the committee of the whole.

Before this was acted upon, the address to the Virginia legislature, which had been postponed, came up. The address was temperate, respectful, and clearly repelled the idea of any but constitutional measures. It prayed the good offices of the parent State, in procuring their admission into the Union, and if adopted, was decisive of the temper of the convention. It was finally adopted. Wilkinson's address to the people was never afterwards called up. The adoption of the address to Virginia gave it a quiet deathblow, from which it did not attempt to recover. An address to Congress was also voted, and was drawn up by Wilkinson. The convention then adjourned, to meet again at a distant day.

In the meantime the legislature of Virginia assembled, and, having received information of the refusal of Congress to act upon the application of Kentucky for admission, they passed a third act, requiring the election, in Kentucky, of a seventh convention, to assemble at Danville, in July 1789, and go over the whole ground anew. They gave this convention ample powers to provide for the formation of a State government. Two new conditions were inserted in this act, which gave serious dissatisfaction to Kentucky; but, upon complaint being made, they were readily repealed, and need not be further noticed. In other respects, the act was identical with its predecessors. An English agent, from Canada, during this winter, visited Kentucky, and called upon Colonel Marshall, and afterwards upon Wilkinson. His object seems to have been to sound the temper of Kentucky, and ascertain how far she would be willing to unite with Canada, in any contingency which might arise. The people, believing him to be a British spy, as he undoubtedly was, gave certain indications, which caused him to leave the country, with equal secrecy and dispatch.

In the meantime the people quietly elected delegates to the seventh convention, as prescribed in the third act of separation, which, in July, 1789, assembled in Danville. Their first act was to draw up a respectful memorial to the legislature of Virginia, remonstrating against the new conditions of separation, which, as we have said, was promptly attended to by Virginia, and the obnoxious conditions repealed by a new act, which required another convention to assemble in 1790. In the meantime the new general government had gone into operation; General Washington was elected president, and the convention was informed, by the executive of Virginia, that the general government would lose no time in organizing such a regular force as would effectually protect Kentucky from Indian incursions. This had become a matter of pressing necessity, for Indian murders had become so frequent, that no part of the country was safe.

The eighth convention assembled in July, 1790, and formally accepted the Virginia act of separation, which thus became a compact, between Kentucky and Virginia. A memorial to the President of the United States and to Congress, was adopted, and an address to Virginia, again praying the good offices of the parent State in procuring their admission into the Union. Provision was then made for the election of a ninth convention, to assemble in April, 1791, and form a State constitution. The convention then adjourned. In December, 1790, President Washington strongly recommended to Congress to admit Kentucky into the Union. On the 4th of February, 1791, an act for that purpose had passed both Houses, and received the signature of the President.

We have thus detailed as minutely as our limits would permit, the long, vexatious, and often baffled efforts, of the infant community of the West, to organize a regular government, and obtain admission into the Union. And it is impossible not to be struck with the love of order, the respect for law, and the passionate attachment to their kindred race, beyond the mountains, which characterized this brave and simple race of hunters and farmers. The neglect of the old confederation, arose, no doubt, from its inherent imbecility, but never was parental care more coldly and sparingly administered. Separated by five hundred miles of wilderness, exposed to the intrigues of foreign governments, powerfully tempted by their own leading statesmen, repulsed in every effort to obtain constitutional independence, they yet clung with invincible affection to their government, and turned a deaf ear to the syren voice, which tempted them with the richest gifts of fortune, to stray away from the fold in which they had been nurtured. The spectacle was touching and beautiful, as it was novel in the history of the world.

CHAPTER III.

No sooner was the new federal government organized than its attention was anxiously turned to the exposed condition of the western frontier. A useless effort to obtain peace for Kentucky, was quickly followed by a military force such as the west had never seen under the federal government, but which was still utterly inadequate to the wants of the country.

General Harmar, at the head of three hundred and fifty regulars, was authorized to call around his standard fifteen hundred militia from Pennsylvania and Virginia. A considerable part of this force rendezvoused at Cincinnati, in September, 1790, and marched in hostile array upon the Miami towns. The result was most disastrous. Two large detachments, composed both of regulars and militia, were successively surprised, and routed with dreadful slaughter. The regulars were absolutely destroyed, and the militia sustained enormous loss. Harmar returned with loss of reputation, and the events of the campaign were such as to impress Kentucky with the belief that regulars were totally unfit for Indian warfare. They zealously endeavored to impress this truth upon the mind of the President, and were not a little discontented that he adhered to his own opinion in opposition to theirs.

To satisfy them as much as possible, however, a local board of war was appointed in Kentucky, composed of General Scott, Shelby, Innis, Logan, and Brown, who were authorized to call out the militia, into the service of the United States, whenever they thought proper, to act in conjunction with regular troops. Under the direction of this board, an expedition of eight hundred mounted men under General Scott, under whom Wilkinson served as second in command, was got up against the north-western tribes. Some skirmishing ensued, some prisoners were taken, and about fifty Indians killed. No loss of any amount was sustained by the detachment, but no decisive or permanent impression was made upon the Indians.

Warned, by the disastrous campaign of Harmar, of the necessity of employing a greater force, the general government employed two thousand regular troops, composed of cavalry, infantry, and artillery, in the ensuing campaign. The command was given to General St. Clair, the governor of the north-western territory. This gentleman was old and infirm, and had been very unfortunate in his military career, during the Revolutionary war. He was particularly unpopular in Kentucky, and no volunteers could be found to serve under him. One thousand Kentuckians were drafted, however, and reluctantly compelled to serve under a gouty old disciplinarian, whom they disliked, and in conjunction with a regular force, which they regarded as doomed to destruction in Indian warfare. The consequence was that desertions of the militia occurred daily, and when the battle day came there were only about two hundred and fifty in camp.

The army left Cincinnati about the 1st of October, and encamped upon one of the tributaries of the Wabash on the evening of the 3d of November. Encumbered by wagons and artillery, their march through the wilderness had been slow and painful. His Kentucky force had dwindled at every step, and about the 1st of November a whole regiment deserted. The general detached a regiment of regulars after them, to protect the stores in the rear, and, with the residue of his force, scarcely exceeding one thousand men, continued his march to the encampment upon the tributary of the Wabash. Here he was assailed, at daylight, by about twelve hundred Indians, who surrounded his encampment, and, lurking under such cover as the woods afforded, poured a fire upon his men, more destructive than the annals of Indian warfare had yet witnessed. His troops were raw, but his officers were veterans, and strove for three hours, with a bravery which deserved a better fate, to maintain the honor of their arms. Gallant and repeated charges were made with the bayonet, and always with temporary success. But their nimble adversaries, although retreating from the bayonet, still maintained a slaughtering fire upon the regulars, which swept away officers and men by scores in every charge. A retreat was at length ordered, which quickly became a rout, and a more complete overthrow was never witnessed. The remnant of the troops regained fort Jefferson, twenty-nine miles from the battle ground, on the night after the battle, and thence retreated to Cincinnati, in somewhat better order.

This dreadful disaster produced great sensation throughout the United States, and especially in Kentucky. A corps of mounted volunteers assembled with great alacrity, for the purpose of relieving St. Clair, who was at first supposed to be besieged in fort Jefferson, but upon the receipt of more correct intelligence, they were disbanded.

In December, 1791, the ninth and last convention was elected, who assembled at Danville in April following, and formed the first constitution of Kentucky. George Nicholas, who had eminently distinguished himself in the Virginia convention which adopted the federal constitution, was elected a member of the Kentucky convention from the county of Mercer, and took an active and leading part in the formation of the first constitution. This constitution totally abandoned the aristocratic features of the parent State, so far as representation by counties was concerned, and established *numbers* as the basis. Suffrage was universal, and sheriffs were elected triennially by the people.

But while these departures from the constitution of Virginia displayed the general predominance of the democratic principle in Kentucky, there are strong indications that the young statesmen of the west, were disposed to curb the luxuriance of this mighty element, by strong checks. The executive, the senate, and the judiciary, were entirely removed from the direct control of the people. The governor was chosen by electors, who were elected by the people for that purpose every fourth year. The members of the senate were appointed by the same electoral college which chose the president, and might be selected indifferently from any part of the State. The judiciary were appointed as at present, and held their offices during good behavior. The supreme court, however, had original and final jurisdiction in all land cases. This last feature was engrafted upon the constitution, by Colonel Nicholas, and was most expensive and mischievous in practice. The constitution was adopted, and the officers elected, in May, 1792. Isaac Shelby was elected governor, a brave and plain officer, who had gallantly served in the Revolutionary war, and distinguished himself at Kings' Mountain, and Point Pleasant. Alexander Bullitt was chosen speaker of the senate, and Robert Breckenridge of the house of representatives. The governor met both branches of the legislature in the senate chamber, and personally addressed them in a brief speech, in reply to which they voted an address. James Brown was the first secretary of state, and George Nicholas the first attorney-general. John Brown and John Edwards (heretofore political opponents,) were elected, by joint ballot, senators to Congress. They fixed upon Frankfort as the future seat of government, by a process somewhat singular. Twenty-five commissioners were first chosen by general ballot; then the counties of Mercer and Fayette, the rival competitors for the seat of government, alternately struck five names from the list until the commissioners were reduced to five. These last were empowered to fix upon the capital.

The legislature was busily engaged, during its first session, in organizing the government. The judiciary and the revenue principally engaged their attention. Acts passed, establishing the supreme court, consisting of three judges, county courts, and courts of quarter session, the latter having common law and chancery jurisdiction over five pounds, and a court of oyer and terminer composed of three judges, having criminal jurisdiction, and sitting twice in the year. Taxes were imposed upon land, cattle, carriages, billiard tables, ordinary licenses and retail stores.

In the meantime Indian depredations were incessant, and General Washington, to the infinite distress of Kentucky, persevered in the employment of a regular force, instead of mounted militia, in the north-west. St. Clair was superseded and General Wayne became his successor. A regular force, aided by militia, was again to be organized, and a final effort made to crush the hostile tribes. General Wilkinson received a commission in the regular service, and joined the army of Wayne. In December, 1792, Colonel John Hardin, of Kentucky, who had commanded detachments under Harmar, was sent as a messenger of peace to the hostile tribes, and was murdered by them. Boats were intercepted at every point on the Ohio, from the mouth of Kenawha to Louisville, and in some cases their crews murdered. Stations upon the frontiers, were sometimes boldly attacked, and were kept perpetually on the alert. Yet the President was compelled, by public opinion, in the east, to make another fruitless effort for peace with these enraged tribes, during the pendency of which effort, all hostilities from Kentucky were strictly forbidden. Great dissatisfaction and loud complaints against the mismanagement of government were incessant. In addition to the Indian war, the excise law told with some effect upon the distilleries of Kentucky, and was peculiarly odious. Kentucky had been strongly anti-federal at the origin of the government, and nothing had occurred since to change this original bias.

Early in the spring of 1793, circumstances occurred which fanned the passions of the people into a perfect flame of disaffection. The French Revolution had sounded a tocsin which reverberated throughout the whole civilized world. The worn out despotisms of Europe, after standing aghast for a moment, in doubtful inactivity, had awakened at length into ill-concerted combinations against the young republic, and France was engaged in a life and death struggle, against Britain, Spain, Prussia, Austria, and the German principalities. With this war the United States had, strictly, nothing to do, and the best interests of the country clearly required a rigid neutrality; which President Washington had not only sagacity to see, but firmness to enforce by a proclamation, early in 1793. The passions of the people, however, far outran all consideration of prudence or interest, and displayed themselves in favor of France, with a frantic enthusiasm which threatened perpetually to involve the country in a disastrous war with all the rest of Europe. The terrible energy which the French Republic displayed, against such fearful odds, the haughty crest with which she confronted her enemies, and repelled them from her frontier on every point, presented a spectacle well calculated to dazzle the friends of democracy throughout the world. The horrible atrocities which accompanied these brilliant efforts of courage, were overlooked in the fervor of a passionate sympathy, or attributed, in part, to the exaggerations of the British press.

The American people loved France as their ally in the Revolution, and now regarded her as a sister republic contending for freedom against banded despots. The sympathy was natural, and sprang from the noblest principles of the heart, but was not on that account, less threatening and disastrous to the future happiness and prosperity of the country. Washington, fully aware of the danger, boldly and firmly strove to restrain the passions of his countrymen from overt acts of hostility to the powers at war with France, and in so doing, brought upon himself a burst of passion, which put his character to the most severe test. In no part of the world did the French fever blaze more brightly than in Kentucky. Attributing to English perfidy in refusing to surrender the western posts, the savage murders, which desolated their frontier, they hated that nation with the same fierce fervor with which they loved France. The two passions fanned each other, and united with the excise and the Indian war in kindling a spirit of disaffection to the general government, which, more than once, assumed a threatening aspect.

Citizen Genet, the ambassador of the French Republic, landed at Charleston in the spring of 1793, and was received with a burst of enthusiasm, which seems completely to have turned his brain. His progress through the country to New York, was like the triumphant march of a Roman conqueror. Treating the President's proclamation of neutrality with contempt, he proceeded openly to arm and equip privateers, and to enlist crews in American ports to cruize against the commerce of England and Spain, as if the United States were openly engaged in the war, as an ally of France. Four French agents were sent by him to Kentucky, with orders to enlist an army of two thousand men, appoint a generalissimo, and descending the Ohio and Mississippi in boats, attack the Spanish settlements at the mouth of the Mississippi, and bring the whole of that country under the dominion of the French republic. The troops and officers were to receive the usual pay of French soldiers, and magnificent donations of land in the conquered provinces.

There was a cool impudence in all this which startled the minds of many, but the great mass were so thoroughly imbued with the French fever, that they embraced the project with ardor, and regarded the firm opposition of Washington with open indignation, expressed in the strongest terms. General George Rogers Clark accepted the office of Generalissimo, with the high sounding title of "Major General in the armies of France and Commander in Chief of the French Revolutionary Legions on the Mississippi," and great activity was displayed in enlisting men and officers for the expedition. Upon the first intelligence of this extraordinary project, the President caused Governor Shelby to be informed of it, and explaining to him the mischief which would result to the United States, requested him to warn the citizens against it. The governor replied, that he did not believe that any such project was contemplated in Kentucky, "That her citizens were possessed of too just a sense of the obligations due to the general government to embark in such an enterprise."

In the meantime democratic societies, somewhat in imitation of the terrible Jacobin clubs of France, were established in the east, and rapidly extended to Kentucky. There were established during the summer of 1793, one in Lexington, another in Georgetown, and a third in Paris. Their spirit was violently anti-federal. The navigation of the Mississippi, the excise, the Indian war, the base truckling to England, the still baser desertion of France, in the hour of her terrible struggle with the leagued despotism of the old world, became subjects of passionate declamation in the clubs, and violent invectives in the papers. The protracted negotiation then in progress with Spain, relative to the navigation of the Mississippi, although pressed by the executive, with incessant earnestness, had as yet borne no fruit. The sleepless jealousy of the west, upon that subject, was perpetually goaded into distrust of the intentions of the general government. It was rumored that their old enemy, Jay, was about to be sent to England, to form an alliance with that hated power, against their beloved France; and it was insinuated that the old project, of abandoning the navigation of the Mississippi, would be revived the moment that the power in Congress could be obtained. Under the influence of all these circumstances, it would have been difficult to find a part of the United States in which antifederal passions blazed more fiercely than in Kentucky. The French emissaries found their project received with the warmest favor. The free navigation of the Mississippi forever, would be the only direct benefit accruing to Kentucky, but French pay, French rank, and lands *ad libitum*, were the allurements held out to the private adventurers.

In November, 1793, there was a second communication from the President to the governor. This stated that the Spanish minister, at Washington, had complained of the armament preparing in Kentucky, mentioned the names of the Frenchmen engaged in it, of whom Lachaise and Depeau were chief, and earnestly exhorted the governor to suppress the enterprise, by every means in his power, suggesting legal prosecution, and, in case of necessity, a resort to the militia. The governor of the north-western territory (the unfortunate St. Clair), about the same time, communicated to Governor Shelby, that extraordinary preparations seemed to be going on for the enterprise. Two of the French emissaries also wrote to the governor, and we are tempted to give the letter of Depeau in full. Here it is:

" CITIZEN GOVERNOR,

It may appear quite strange to write to you on a subject, in which, although it is of some consequence. With confidence from the French ambassador I have been dispatched with more Frenchmen to join the expedition of the Mississippi. As I am to procure the provision I am happy to communicate to you, whatever you shall think worthy of my notice, as I hope I have in no way *disoblige* you; if I have, I will most willingly ask your pardon. For no body can be more than I am, willing for your prosperity and happiness. As some strange reports *has* reached my ears that your *excellence* has positive orders to arrest all citizens inclining to our assistance, and as my remembrance know by your conduct, in justice you will satisfy in this uncommon request. Please let me know as I shall not make my supply till your excellence please to honor me with a small answer. I am your well wisher in remaining for the French cause, a true citizen Democrat.   CHARLES DEPEAU."

"*Postscript.* Please to *participate* some of these hand bills to that noble society of democrats. I also enclose a paper from Pittsburgh."

The governor replied to citizen Depeau in a grave and formal manner, reciting, at length, the information and instructions he had received from the department of state, and concluding with the remark, that his official position would compel him to pay some attention to them. As to whether he "participated" the handbills to the "noble society of democrats," the voice of history is, unfortunately, silent.

About the same time General Wayne wrote to the Governor, advising him that the regular cavalry, then wintering in Kentucky, under the command of Major Winston, would be subject to his orders, and that an additional force should be furnished, if necessary, to repress any illegal expedition from Kentucky. The reply of the governor to the secretary of state, is somewhat curious, and shows that the views of the brave and plain old soldier had become somewhat warped, from their original simplicity, by the nice distinctions and quibbling subtleties of his legal advisers. The following extracts from his reply are given.

"I have great doubts, even if they (General Clark and the Frenchmen,) attempt to carry this plan into execution, (provided they manage the business with prudence,) whether there is any legal authority to restrain or to punish them, at least before they have actually accomplished it. For if it is lawful for any one citizen of this state to leave it, it is equally so for any number of them to do it. It is also lawful for them to carry with them any quantity of provisions, ammunition and arms. And if the act is lawful in itself, there is nothing but the intention with which it is done which can make it unlawful. But I know of no law which inflicts a punishment upon intention only, or any criterion by which to decide what would be sufficient evidence of that intention." Again he says, "Much less would I assume power to exercise it against men whom I consider as *friends* and *brethren*, in favor of a man, whom I view as an *enemy* and a *tyrant*. I shall also feel but little inclination to take an active part in punishing or restraining my fellow citizens for a *supposed intention only*, to gratify or remove the fears of the minister of a prince who openly withholds from us an invaluable right, and who secretly instigates against us a most savage and cruel enemy."

These extracts are given as powerfully illustrative of the times. The course of reasoning and passions disclosed in them, were not peculiar to Governor Shelby, but were shared by a vast majority of the citizens of every class. Upon receiving this answer, the President gave orders to General Wayne to occupy fort Massac with artillery, and to take such other steps as might be necessary to arrest this mad expedition.

In the mean time, the democratic societies resorted to every method of inflaming the popular mind upon the subject of the navigation of the Mississippi, and the jealousy of the east,

4

which they contended was the true cause of the failure of the general government to procure it for them. They had invited a general meeting of the people in Lexington, in the spring of 1794, where resolutions were adopted of a violent character, breathing the deepest hostility to the general government, and inviting the citizens of the different counties to hold meetings and elect delegates to a *convention*, whose object was not precisely defined, but which looked in the old direction of separation. Just at this time, however, the intelligence came that citizen Genet had been recalled, that his acts were disavowed by the French government, and all his proceedings disapproved. At once, Messieurs Lachaise and Depeau lost all authority, General Clark was stripped of his magnificent title, and the splendid vision of conquest in the south, which had dazzled the eyes of the Kentuckians, vanished into air. The project of a convention, so fiercely demanded by the late resolutions, fell still-born, and a reasonable degree of tranquility was restored to the public mind.

In the mean time preparations for another campaign against the Indians, were incessantly urged by the President. During the summer of 1793, a powerful regular force had been concentrated at Cincinnati, and a requisition was made on Governor Shelby for one thousand mounted riflemen. None would volunteer, and a draft was again resorted to. The reinforcement reached Wayne in October, and during its stay, had an opportunity of witnessing the energy and discipline infused into the regular force by its gallant commander.

The season was too far advanced for active operations, and the Kentucky contingent was dismissed until the following spring. A much better opinion of the efficiency of a regular force was diffused through the country by the return of the mounted men, and in the following spring, fifteen hundred volunteers took the field with alacrity under the command of General Scott, and joined the regular force under Wayne. That intrepid commander, after one more ineffectual effort to obtain peace, marched into the heart of the hostile country, and on the morning of the 20th of August, attacked them in a formidable position which they occupied near the rapids of the Miami. A dense forest, for miles had been overthrown by a tempest, and the Indians occupied this forest, upon which neither cavalry nor artillery could make any effectual impression. Wayne ordered the mounted riflemen to make a circuit far to the left and operate upon the right flank and rear of the enemy, while the regular infantry was formed, under the eye of the commander in chief, directly in front of the fallen timber. After allowing time for the mounted men to take their designated position, the general ordered the regulars to make a rapid charge with the bayonet upon the Indian position, without firing a shot until the enemy should be roused from their covert, and then to deliver a general fire. This order was promptly executed, and resulted in a total route of the enemy. The conquering troops pressed their advantage, and never was victory more complete. The action was fought almost under the guns of a British fort, and the routed enemy fled in that direction. It was with the utmost difficulty that a collision was prevented, as the Kentucky troops were violently incensed against the British, who undoubtedly furnished the Indians with arms and ammunition. All the houses and stores around the fort were destroyed, notwithstanding the spirited remonstrances of the British commandant, but further hostilities were avoided.

This brilliant success was followed by the most decisive results. A long series of defeats had injured the credit of the government, and the Indian tribes of the east and south, gave indications of a disposition to co-operate with their brethren in the north-west. But the shock of the victory at the Rapids, was instantly felt in all quarters. A treaty was made with the hostile tribes, which was observed until the war of 1812, while the Six Nations of the east, and the Cherokees in the south, instantly became pacific, even to servility.

The effect in Kentucky was scarcely less propitious. A better feeling towards the general government was instantly visible, which manifested itself by the election of Humphrey Marshall, in the ensuing winter, to the Senate of the United States, over the popular and talented John Breckinridge; Marshall being a determined federalist, and his competitor a republican or democrat.

During this winter an attempt was made by the legislature to remove by address two of the judges of the supreme court, George Muter and Benjamin Sebastian. Their crime was a decision in an important land suit, flagrantly illegal, and which would have been most mischievous in its consequences, if adhered to. The effort, as usual, failed, but the court revised its opinion and changed its decision. By another act, the courts of quarter session were abolished, as well as the court of oyer and terminer, and the district courts established in their places. All the judges expired with their courts. Original jurisdiction in land cases was also taken away from the supreme court, and conferred upon the district courts. An act also passed obliging every white male, over sixteen, to kill a certain number of *crows* and *squirrels* annually, which is too characteristic of the times to be omitted.

The good humor created by Wayne's victory was sadly disturbed by the intelligence received in the spring of 1795, that Jay had concluded a treaty with Great Britain, which, if ratified, would produce the immediate surrender of the north-western posts, and insure peace, tranquillity, and rapid appreciation of property in Kentucky. Yet so much more powerful is passion than interest, that the intelligence of this treaty was received with a burst of fury, throughout Kentucky, that knew no bounds. The people regarded it as a base desertion of an ancient friend struggling

134316

with a host of enemies, and a cowardly truckling to England, from cold blooded policy, or a secret attachment to aristocratic institutions. Their senator, Marshall, with that firmness of purpose which eminently distinguished him through life, had voted for the conditional ratification of the treaty, against the wishes of a vast majority of his constituents. This determined exercise of his own judgment, exposed him to popular odium, and even personal violence upon his return, from which he made a narrow escape.

A treaty with Spain was also concluded in October, 1795, by which the right to navigate the Mississippi to the ocean, was conceded to the United States, together with a right of deposit at New Orleans, which, in effect, embraced all that Kentucky desired. Peace with the Indians, the surrender of the posts, the navigation of the Mississippi, had at length been obtained, by the incessant exertions of the general government, for Kentucky.

But pending the negotiation with Spain, an intrigue was commenced, between the agents of that power and certain citizens of Kentucky, which was not fully disclosed to the country until the year 1806, and the full extent of which is not even yet certainly known. In July, 1795, the Spanish governor, Carondelet, dispatched a certain Thomas Power to Kentucky, with a letter to Benjamin Sebastian, then a judge of the Court of Appeals of Kentucky. In this communication he alludes to the *confidence* reposed in the judge by his predecessor, General Miro, and the *former correspondence* which had passed between them. He declared that his Catholic majesty was willing to open the Mississippi to the *western country*, and to effect that object, and to negotiate a treaty, in relation to this and other matters, Sebastian was requested to have agents chosen by the people of Kentucky, who should meet Colonel Gayoso, a Spanish agent, at New Madrid, when all matters could be adjusted. Judge Sebastian communicated this letter to Judge Innis, George Nicholas and William Murray, the latter a very eminent lawyer of Kentucky, of the federal party, and they all agreed that Sebastian should meet Gayoso at New Madrid, and hear what he had to propose. The meeting accordingly took place, and the outline of a treaty was agreed to, but before matters were concluded, intelligence was received of the treaty concluded with Spain by the United States, by which the navigation was effectually and *legally* secured. The Spanish governor broke up the negotiation, much to the dissatisfaction of Sebastian, who concluded that the *regular* treaty would not be ratified, and preferred carrying out the *irregular* negotiation then commenced.

All communication then ceased, so far as is known, until 1797. The commissioners were busily engaged in marking the line of boundary between Spain and the United States, as fixed by the treaty, when Carondelet again opened the negotiation. His former agent, Thomas Power, again appeared in Louisville, with a letter to Sebastian, and a request that Sebastian would disclose its contents to Innis, Nicholas and Murray. Sebastian positively refused to hold any intercourse with Murray, but instantly showed the letter to Judge Innis. The scheme unfolded in this letter was, " to withdraw from the federal union and form an independent western government. To effect this object it was suggested that these gentlemen should, by a series of eloquently written publications, dispose the public mind to withdraw from any further connection with the Atlantic States. In consideration of the devotion of their time and talents to this purpose, it was proposed that the sum of one hundred thousand dollars should be appropriated to their use, by his Catholic majesty. Should any one *in office*, in Kentucky, be deprived thereof, on account of his connection with Spain, the full value of said office was to be paid to him by his majesty." This article was inserted at the suggestion of Sebastian.

To effect these great objects, it was proposed that twenty pieces of field artillery, with a large supply of small arms and munitions of war, together with one hundred thousand dollars in money, should instantly be furnished to Kentucky by the King of Spain, as his majesty's quota in aid of the enterprise. Fort Massac was to be seized instantly, and the federal troops were to be dispossessed of all posts upon the western waters. The only stipulation for the benefit of his Catholic majesty was an extension of his northern boundary, to the mouth of the Yazoo, and thence due east to the Tombigbee. For this miserable pittance of desert territory, this corrupt and worn out despotism was willing to violate its faith recently plighted in a solemn treaty, and, by treachery and intrigue, to sow the seeds of discord and revolution, where all was peace and confidence. Such was the morality of courts in the eighteenth century.

This proposal was received by Sebastian with great coolness, and submitted to Innis for his opinion. The testimony of Innis himself is all that we have to rely on, as to the manner in which he received the proposition. He declares that he denounced the proposal as dangerous and improper, and gave it as his opinion that it ought to be rejected. Sebastian concurred in this opinion, but desired Innis to see Colonel Nicholas, and have a written answer prepared for Power, declaring that whatever they concurred in would be approved by him. Innis saw Nicholas, who wrote a refusal couched in calm but decisive language, which was signed by them both, and delivered to Power, through the medium of judge Sebastian. No disclosure was made by either of the parties of this proposal from the Spanish government. Power, in the mean time, visited Wilkinson, who still held a command in the regular army, and then was stationed in garrison at Detroit. Power's ostensible object in visiting Wilkinson was to deliver to him a letter of remonstrance from Governor Carondelet, against the United States taking immediate possession of the posts on the Mississippi. His real object was, no doubt, to sound him upon the Spanish proposition. Power afterwards reported to Carondelet, that Wilkinson received him coldly, informed him that the governor of the north-west had orders from the President to arrest him, and send him on to Philadelphia, and that there was no way for him to escape, but to permit himself to be conducted, under guard, to fort Massac, whence he could find his way to New Madrid. He states that in their first conference Wilkinson observed, bitterly, " We are both lost, without deriving any benefit from your journey." He pronounced the Spanish proposal a chimerical project, that the west having obtained, by the late treaty, all that they desired, had no motive to form any connection with Spain. That the best thing Spain could do, would be honestly to comply with the treaty; that his personal *honor* forbade him to listen to the project; *that the late treaty had overturned all his plans, and rendered his labors for ten years useless;* that he had destroyed his *ciphers,* and complained that his secret had been divulged; that he might be named governor of Natchez, and he might *then,* perhaps, have power to realize his political projects.

In this report to Carondelet, Power represents Sebastian as speaking to him in a more encouraging tone of the prospect of a union of Kentucky with Spain. Sebastian expressed the opinion that, in case of a war with Spain, Kentucky might be induced to take part against the Atlantic States. In conclusion, Power gives his own opinion, that nothing short of a war with France or the denial of the navigation of the Mississippi could induce Kentucky to separate herself from the eastern States. After visiting Wilkinson, instead of returning to Louisville, as he had at first intended, he was sent, by Wilkinson, under escort of Captain Shaumbergh, of the United States' army, to fort Massac, and thence returned to New Madrid. At Massac he received from Sebastian the letter of Nicholas and Innis. Nothing certainly was known of the particulars of this transaction, until 1806, when it became public that Sebastian had received a pension of two thousand dollars from Spain, from about 1795 to 1806.

After the English and Spanish treaties had been ratified, Washington retired from office, and John Adams, greatly to the dissatisfaction of Kentucky, was elected President of the United States. The eyes of the people became henceforth directed to the general government, and they participated fiercely in the old party struggle of federalist and republican, or democrat. If the administration of Washington was unpopular, that of Adams was absolutely odious, in Kentucky. In no part of the Union were his measures denounced with more bitterness, nor his downfall awaited with more impatience.

The only domestic question which excited much interest, was the propriety of calling a convention to revise the old constitution. The people were becoming weary of seeing the governor and senate removed so far from their control, and equally weary of the sheriffs, which popular suffrage had given them. According to the provisions of the constitution, a poll was opened in

May, 1797, and the votes of the citizens taken for or against a convention. There were 5446 votes given for a convention, out of 9814 votes regularly returned. But five counties did not return the whole number of their votes, and the result was doubtful.

A second vote was given in May, 1798, and there were returned 8804 for a convention, out of 11,853 votes returned. But no less than ten counties failed to return the whole number of their votes, and eight counties did not vote at all on the subject. It is certain that there was not a majority for a convention upon the first vote, and probably not upon the second. By the constitution, a majority of all the legal votes was required two years in succession, or else a majority of two-thirds of the legislature. So far as the vote of the people was concerned the convention had failed, but the legislature, believing such to be the will of their constituents, called a convention, by a constitutional majority, in the session of 1798—9.

This session was rendered memorable, also, by the passage of certain resolutions declaratory of the powers of the general government, and the rights and privileges of the States. At the opening of the session, Governor Garrard, who had succeeded Shelby, in his address to the legislature, denounced severely, the acts recently passed by congress, commonly known as the alien and sedition laws. Early in the session a series of resolutions, which were originally drawn up by Mr. Jefferson, were presented to the house by John Breckenridge, the representative from Fayette, and almost unanimously adopted. The only member who spoke against them, and steadily voted, generally alone, against the whole series, was that William Murray, to whom, in conjunction with others, the letter of Carondelet was directed, and with whom Sebastian refused to hold any communication on the subject. These resolutions, taken in connection with those passed at the succeeding session, in substance declare, " That the constitution of the United States is a compact between the several States, *as States*, each sovereign State being an integral party to that compact. That as in other compacts between equal sovereigns, who have no common judge, each party has the right to interpret the compact for itself, and is bound by no interpretation but its own. That the general government has no final right in any of its branches, to interpret the extent of its own powers. That these powers are limited, within certain prescribed bounds, and that all acts of the general government, not warranted by its powers, may properly be nullified by a State, within its own boundaries." These resolutions are remarkable, as clearly expressing the political views of Mr. Jefferson, at the time, and as containing, not merely the germ, but the fully developed doctrine of *nullification*, which has since become so celebrated, and which has since been so heartily and strongly denounced, not only by Kentucky, but almost every other State in the Union.

A copy of the resolutions was sent to each State in the Union, and were assented to by none, save Virginia. Some of her sister sovereigns handled the Kentucky doctrine with great roughness, and exposed its falsehood with merciless severity. The resolutions were approved by Governor Garrard, and thus fastened upon Kentucky the mark of nullification, until the session of 1832, when the true doctrine was strongly proclaimed.

In the spring of 1799 the members of the convention were elected, and in July that body assembled, and adopted the present constitution. In June, 1800, the new constitution went into operation. James Garrard was re-elected governor, and Alexander Bullitt lieutenant-governor. Never was a government changed with so little sensation. But the indifference of Kentucky to a change of government did not extend to national affairs. The defeat of Adams and the election of Jefferson, the downfall of the federalists, and the exaltation of the republican or democratic party, produced a whirlwind under which the Union rocked to its foundation. Kentucky, with great unanimity, supported Jefferson, and no State exulted more in his election.

In the winter session of 1801, the legislature of Kentucky repealed the act establishing district courts, and established the circuit courts as they now exist. At the same session an insurance company was chartered in Lexington, to which banking powers were given, by a clause, which was not thoroughly understood by the members who voted for it, and thus was the first bank chartered in Kentucky. The political party which then controlled Kentucky held banks in horror, and never would have passed the bill, had they understood its provisions.

CHAPTER IV.

In the year 1802, Kentucky, in common with the whole western country, was thrown into a ferment, by the suspension of the American right of deposit at New Orleans, which had been guarantied by the Spanish treaty for three years, with the further provision, that at the end of three years, should the right of deposit at New Orleans be withheld, some other place should be afforded, for the same purpose, near the mouth of that river. This right was now refused by Morales, the Spanish intendant, and no equivalent place of deposit was granted. The treaty was evidently violated, and the commerce of the west struck at in its most vital point. The excitement increased, when it was understood that Louisiana had been ceded to France, and that this important point was held by Napoleon, then first consul of the republic.

A motion was made in the senate of the United States to authorize President Jefferson instantly to take and hold possession of New Orleans; but milder counsels prevailed, and Mr. Monroe was dispatched to France, in order to arrange this difficulty with the first consul. He found Napoleon on the eve of a rupture with Great Britain, and fully impressed with the utter impossibility of retaining so distant and so assailable a colony as Louisiana, while Great Britain ruled the seas. He determined to place it beyond the reach of the English navy, by selling it to the Americans, before the English could equip an expedition against it, which he plainly saw would be one of the first measures adopted, after the rupture of the peace of Amiens. The American minister expected to negotiate for a place of deposit at the mouth of the river, and was informed that for the trifling sum of fifteen millions he could purchase a magnificent empire.

No time was lost in closing this extraordinary sale, as Bonaparte evidently apprehended that Louisiana would be taken by the British fleet, within six months after hostilities commenced. And thus the first *great annexation* of territory to the United States was accomplished. The Floridas, Oregon, Texas, have followed, and the end is not yet.

In 1804, Christopher Greenup was elected governor of Kentucky, and Mr. Jefferson was re-elected President of the United States, without any organized opposition. So popular and brilliant had been his administration.

Aaron Burr, who had been elected Vice President in 1801, had lost the confidence of his party, and was at variance with the President. In 1805, this extraordinary man first made his appearance in Kentucky, and visited Lexington and Louisville. He then passed on to Nashville, St. Louis, Natchez, and New Orleans, and again returned to Lexington, where he remained for some time. General Wilkinson, at this time, commanded the United States' troops in Louisiana, and the affairs of the United States with Spain were in an unsatisfactory state. That miserable power resented the purchase of Louisiana, by the United States, and assumed a sulkiness of demeanor somewhat resembling that of Mexico in more modern times. In the spring of 1806, their forces advanced to the Sabine, in somewhat hostile array, and General Wilkinson had orders to be upon the alert, and repel them if they should cross that barrier. Such was the aspect of affairs, when in 1806, colonel Burr again appeared in the west, spending a large portion of his time at Blannerhasset's Island, on the Ohio river, but being seen in Lexington, Nashville and Louisville.

This extraordinary man having quarreled with the President, and lost caste with the republican party, endeavored to retrieve his political fortunes by becoming a candidate for the office of governor, in New York, in opposition to the regular democratic candidate. He was supported by the mass of the federalists and a small section of the democrats who still adhered to him.

He lost his election chiefly by the influence of Hamilton, who scrupled not to represent him as unworthy of political trust, and deprived him of the cordial support of the federalists. Deeply stung by his defeat, Burr turned fiercely upon his illustrious antagonist, and killed him in a duel. Hamilton was idolized by the federalists, and even his political adversaries were not insensible to his many lofty and noble qualities. Burr found himself abandoned by the mass of the democrats, regarded with abhorrence by the federalists, and banished from all the legitimate and honorable walks of ambition. In this desperate state of his political fortunes, he sought the west, and became deeply involved in schemes as desperate and daring as any which the annals of ill regulated ambition can furnish.

The ground work of his plan, undoubtedly, was to organize a military force upon the western waters, descend the Mississippi, and wrest from Spain an indefinite portion of her territory adjoining the Gulf of Mexico. The southwestern portion of the United States, embracing New Orleans and the adjacent territory, was, either by force or persuasion, to become a part of the new empire, of which New Orleans was to become the capital, and Burr the chief, under some one of the many names, which, in modern times, disguise despotic power under a republican guise. These were the essential and indispensable features of the plan. But if circumstances were favorable, the project was to extend much farther, and the whole country west of the Alleghenies was to be wrested from the American Union, and to become a portion of this new and magnificent empire.

Mad and chimerical as this project undoubtedly was, when the orderly and law-respecting character of the American people is considered, yet the age in which it was conceived had witnessed wonders, which had far outstripped the sober calculations of philosophy and surpassed the limits of probable fiction. When the historian, Gibbon, was closing his great work upon the decline and fall of the Roman empire, he expressed the opinion that the age of great and startling revolutions had passed away, never to return; that mankind had become sobered down by centuries of experience, to a tame and moderate level, which would not admit of those brilliant materials for history which the past had afforded. Scarcely had this opinion been recorded, when the great drama opened in France, and for twenty-five years, the world stood aghast at the series of magnificent and wonderful pageants, which moved before them in the wild confusion of a feverish dream. Kings became beggars, and peasants became kings. Ancient kingdoms disappeared, and new and brilliant republics sprung up in their places. Names, boundaries, ranks, titles, religions, all were tossed about like withered leaves before the wind. A lieutenant in a French regiment had mounted to the throne of western Europe, and drummers, corporals and privates, had become dukes, princes, and kings.

It was not wonderful, then, that a man like Burr, ostracised in the east, and desperate in his fortunes, abounding in talent, energy, and courage, should have determined in the new world, like the Corsican in the old, to stand the hazard of the die, for empire or a grave. The unsettled relations then existing with Spain afforded a specious cloak to his enterprise, and enabled him to give it a character suitable to the temper of the persons whom he addressed. To the daring youth of the west, desirous of military adventure, he could represent it as an irregular expedition to be undertaken upon private account, against the possessions of a nation with whom the United States would shortly be at war. It was upon land what privateering was upon the ocean. He could hint to them that the United States' government would *connive* at the expedition, but could not *openly countenance* it until hostilities actually commenced. There is little doubt that many concurred in the enterprise, without being aware of its *treasonable* character, while it is certain that to others the scheme was exposed in its full deformity.

In the prosecution of his object, he applied himself with singular address to any one who could be useful to him in forwarding the great scheme. Blannerhasset's Island lay directly in his path, and he fixed his keen eye upon the proprietor as one who could be useful to him. This unfortunate man was an Irish gentleman, reputed to be of great wealth, married to a beautiful and accomplished woman, secluded and studious in his habits, devoted to natural science, and as unfitted for the turbulent struggle of active ambitious life, as Burr was for those simple and quiet pursuits, in which his victim found enjoyment and happiness. Blannerhasset's wealth, though, could be employed to advantage. Burr opened the correspondence by a flattering request to be permitted to examine Blannerhasset's grounds and garden, which had been improved at great expense. Once admitted, he employed all the address and eloquence of which he was master, in turning the whole current of Blannerhasset's thoughts, from the calm sedentary pursuits in which he had hitherto delighted, to those splendid visions of empire, greatness and wealth, with which his own ardent imagination was then so fiercely glowing. No better evidence of Burr's power need be desired, than the absolute command which he obtained over the will and fortune of this man. He moulded him to his purpose, inspired him with a frantic enthusiasm in his cause, and obtained complete command of all that Blannerhasset had to offer.

The scheme of separation from the Atlantic States had been too much agitated in Kentucky, not to have left some materials for Burr to work upon, and that he neglected no opportunity of rallying the fragments of the old party, may be readily believed. There is no doubt that General Adair concurred in his scheme, so far as an expedition against the Spanish provinces was concerned; and it is certain that Burr himself calculated upon the co-operation of Wilkinson, and held frequent intercourse with him. During the summer of 1806, the public mind in Kentucky, became agitated by rumors of secret expeditions and conspiracies, in which Burr and others were implicated, but all was wrapped in mystery and doubt.

At length a paper entitled the "Western World," published in Frankfort, by Wood & Street, came out with a series of articles, in which the old intrigue of Sebastian with Power, and the present project of Burr, were blended, in a somewhat confused manner, and some round assertions of facts were made, and some names implicated which created no small sensation. Sebastian, then a judge of the supreme court, was boldly asserted to be an intriguer with Spain, and a pensioner of the Spanish crown. Innis, then a judge of the federal court; Brown, a senator in Congress from Kentucky; Wilkinson, a general in the regular army, were all implicated. Burr was plainly denounced as a traitor, and the whole of his scheme was unfolded. There was a mixture of truth and error in these articles, which no one was then able to separate, and the public mind was completely bewildered at the number of atrocious plots which were exposed, and at the great names implicated. The friends of some of the parties violently resented the articles, and pistols and dirks were resorted to, to silence the accusation. But the paper sturdily adhered to its charges, and an address was prepared and published, to the legislature elected in 1806, praying an inquiry into the conduct of Sebastian, which was circulated among the people for signatures, and was signed by a great number, particularly in the county of Woodford.

In the meantime Colonel Joseph Hamilton Daviess, the attorney for the United States, appeared in open court, before Judge Innis on the 3d of November, and moved for process to compel the attendance of Burr, before the court, to answer to a charge of a high misdemeanor, in organizing a military expedition against a friendly power, from within the territory and jurisdiction of the United States. This motion was grounded upon the oath of the attorney, setting forth with great accuracy the preparations then being made by Burr, and imputing to him designs which subsequent events proved to have been well understood by the attorney. This startling affidavit created immense sensation at the time. Burr was then popular in Kentucky, and was caressed and countenanced by her most eminent citizens. Daviess was greatly admired, for those splendid powers of eloquence which he possessed, in a degree rarely if ever surpassed, but labored under the odium of being an incurable federalist, and equally bold and eloquent in expressing his opinions. Nine-tenths of the public at the time, were startled at the boldness of the accusation, and seem to have attributed it to the well known hatred of the federalists to Colonel Burr. Be the cause, however, what it might, the public feeling was strong in favor of Burr, and against the attorney, who was boldly and manfully discharging his duty. Judge Innis took time to consider the application, and after two days, overruled the motion.

Colonel Burr was in Lexington at the time, and was informed of the motion made by Daviess, in an incredibly short space of time after it was made. He entered the court-house shortly after Innis had over-ruled the motion, and addressed the judge with a grave and calm dignity of manner, which increased if possible the general prepossession in his favor. He spoke of the late motion as one which had greatly surprised him, insinuated that Daviess had reason to believe that he was absent, upon business of a private but pressing nature, which it was well known required his immediate attention, that the judge had treated the application as it deserved, but as it might be renewed by the attorney in his absence, he preferred that the judge should entertain the motion *now*, and he had voluntarily appeared in order to give the gentleman an opportunity of proving his charge. Nowise disconcerted by the lofty tranquillity of Burr's manner, than which nothing could be more imposing, Daviess promptly accepted the challenge, and declared himself ready to proceed as soon as he could procure the attendance of his witnesses. After consulting with the marshal, Daviess announced his opinion that his witnesses could attend on the ensuing Wednesday, and with the acquiescence of Burr, that day was fixed upon by the court for the investigation.

Burr awaited the day of trial with an easy tranquillity, which seemed to fear no danger, and on Wednesday the court-house was crowded to suffocation. Daviess upon counting his witnesses, discovered that Davis Floyd, one of the most important, was absent, and with great reluctance, asked a postponement of the case. The judge instantly discharged the grand jury. Colonel Burr then appeared at the bar, accompanied by his counsel, Henry Clay and Colonel Allen. The first of these gentlemen had emigrated to Kentucky from Virginia, in 1798, and had early attracted attention by the boldness with which he had advocated a provision in the new constitution for the gradual emancipation of slaves in Kentucky, then as now a subject of great delicacy. He had already given indications of those extraordinary powers of eloquence, and that daring boldness of character, which have since shone out with such surpassing splendor. Allen was a lawyer of character and celebrity, whose early and lamentable death, in the war with Great Britain, we shall have occasion hereafter to notice. Colonel Burr arose in court, expressed his regret that the grand jury had been discharged, and inquired the reason. Colonel Daviess replied, and added that Floyd was then in Indiana, attending a session of the territorial legislature. Burr calmly desired that the cause of the postponement might be entered upon the record, as well as the reason why Floyd did not attend. He then with great self-possession, and with an air of candor difficult to be resisted, addressed the court and crowded audience, upon the subject of the accusation. His style was without ornament, passion or fervor; but the spell of a great mind, and daring but calm spirit, was felt with singular power by all who heard him.   He hoped that the good people of Kentucky would dismiss their apprehensions of danger from him, if any such really existed.   There was really no ground for them, however zealously the attorney might strive to awaken them. He was engaged in no project, inimical to the peace or tranquillity of the country, as they would certainly learn, whenever the attorney should be ready, which he greatly apprehended would never be.   In the mean time, although private business urgently demanded his presence elsewhere, he felt compelled to give the attorney one more opportunity of proving his charge, and would patiently await another attack.

Upon the 25th of November, Colonel Daviess informed the court, that Floyd would attend on the 2d December following, and another grand jury was summoned to attend on that day. Colonel Burr came into court, attended by the same counsel as on the former occasion, and coolly awaited the expected attack. Daviess, with evident chagrin, again announced that he was not ready to proceed, that John Adair had been summoned and was not in attendance, and that his testimony was indispensable to the prosecution.   He again asked a postponement of the case, for a few days, and that the grand jury should be kept enpannelled until he could compel the attendance of Adair by attachment.

Burr upon the present occasion remained silent, and entirely unmoved by any thing which occurred.   Not so his counsel. A most animated and impassioned debate sprung up, intermingled with sharp and flashing personalities between Clay and Daviess.   Never did two more illustrious orators encounter each other in debate.   The enormous mass, which crowded to suffocation, the floor, the galleries, the windows, the plat-form of the judge, remained still and breathless for hours, while these renowned, and immortal champions, stimulated by mutual rivalry and each glowing with the ardent conviction of right, encountered each other in splendid intellectual combat.   Clay had the sympathies of the audience on his side, and was the leader of the popular party in Kentucky.   Daviess was a federalist, and was regarded as persecuting an innocent and unfortunate man, from motives of political hate.   But he was buoyed up by the full conviction of Burr's guilt, and the delusion of the people on the subject, and the very infatuation which he beheld around him, and the smiling security of the traitor, who sat before him, stirred his great spirit to one of its most brilliant efforts.   All, however, was in vain.   Judge Innis refused to retain the grand jury, unless some business was brought before them; and Daviess, in order to gain time, sent up to them an indictment against John Adair, which was pronounced by the grand jury "not a true bill."   The hour being late, Daviess then moved for an attachment to compel the attendance of Adair, which was resisted by Burr's counsel, and refused by the court, on the ground that Adair was not in contempt until the day had expired.   Upon the motion of Daviess the court then adjourned until the ensuing day.

In the interval, Daviess had a private interview with the judge, and obtained from him an expression of the opinion that it would be allowable for him as prosecutor to attend the grand jury in their room, and examine the witnesses, in order to explain to them the connexion of the detached particles of evidence, which his intimate acquaintance with the plot would enable him to do, and without which the grand jury would scarcely be able to comprehend their bearing. When the court resumed its sitting on the following morning, Daviess moved to be permitted to attend the grand jury in their room. This was resisted by Burr's counsel as novel and unprecedented, and refused by the court. The grand jury then retired, witnesses were sworn and sent up to them, and on the fifth of the month they returned, as Daviess had expected " not a true bill." In addition to this, the grand jury returned into court a written declaration, signed by the whole of them, in which from all the evidence before them they completely exonerated Burr from any design inimical to the peace or well being of the country. Colonel Allen instantly moved the court that a copy of the report of the grand jury should be taken and published in the newspapers, which was granted. The popular current ran with great strength in his favor, and the United States' attorney for the time was overwhelmed with obloquy.

The acquittal of Burr was celebrated in Frankfort, by a brilliant ball, numerously attended; which was followed by another ball, given in honor of the baffled attorney, by those friends who believed the charge to be just, and that truth for the time had been baffled by boldness, eloquence, and delusion. At one of these parties the editor of the " Western World," who had boldly sounded the alarm, was violently attacked, with the view of driving him from the ball room, and was rescued with difficulty.

These events are given as striking indications of the tone of public feeling at the time. Before Mr. Clay took any active part as the counsel of Burr, he required of him an explicit disavowal, *upon his honor*, that he was engaged in no design contrary to the laws and peace of the country. This pledge was promptly given by Burr, in language the most broad, comprehensive and particular. "*He had no design,*" he said, "*to intermeddle with, or disturb the tranquillity of the United States, nor its territories, nor any part of them. He had neither issued nor signed, nor promised a commission, to any person, for any purpose. He did not own a single musket, nor bayonet, nor any single article of military stores, nor did any other person for him, by his authority or knowledge. His views had been explained to several distinguished members of the administration, were well understood and approved by the government. They were such as every man of honor, and every good citizen, must approve. He considered this declaration proper as well to counteract the chimerical tales circulated by the malevolence of his enemies, as to satisfy Mr. Clay, that he had not become the counsel of a man in any way unfriendly to the laws, the government, or the well being of his country.*"

Thoroughly to appreciate the daring coolness and effrontery

of this extraordinary man, as well as the fearful risk, which he faced with such imperturbable self-possession, the reader should understand, what was the real attitude in which he then stood. This declaration was made on the 1st December, 1806, at Frankfort. On the 29th of July preceding, he had written to Wilkinson, "I have obtained funds, and have actually commenced the enterprise. Detachments from different points and on different pretences will rendezvous on the Ohio on the 1st November. Every thing internal and external favors views ————. Already are orders given to contractors to forward six months provisions to any point Wilkinson may name. The project is brought to the point so long desired. Burr guarantees the result with his life and honor, with the lives, the fortunes, of hundreds—the best blood of the country. Wilkinson shall be second only to Burr. Wilkinson shall dictate the rank of his officers. Burr's plan of operations is to move down rapidly from the Falls by the 15th November, with the first five or ten hundred men, in light boats now constructing, to be at Natchez between the 5th and 15th of December, there to meet Wilkinson, ☞ there to determine, whether it will be expedient in the first instance, to SEIZE on, or pass by Baton Rouge!!"

Before the date of this letter he had fully unfolded his project to General Eaton, which was to revolutionize the western country, establish an empire, with New Orleans as the capital, and himself the chief. On the 24th July, 1806, General Dayton, one of Burr's firmest adherents, wrote to General Wilkinson in cypher, "Are you ready? Are your numerous associates ready? Wealth and Glory! Louisiana and Mexico!!" So much for Burr's intentions. Now for the risk of detection, which he braved with such undaunted composure.

On the 25th of November, one week before his declaration to Mr. Clay, President Jefferson issued his proclamation, denouncing the enterprise, and warning the west against it. On the 1st of December, a messenger from the President arrived at the seat of government of Ohio, and instantly procured the passage of a law by which ten of Colonel Burr's boats, laden with provisions and military stores, were seized on the Muskingum, before they could reach the Ohio. At the very moment that he appeared in court, an armed force in his service occupied Blannerhasset's island, and boats laden with provisions and military stores, were commencing their voyage down the river, and passed Louisville, on the 16th of December. Scarcely was the grand jury discharged, and the ball which celebrated his acquittal, concluded, when the President's proclamation reached Kentucky, and a law was passed in hot haste, for seizing the boats which had escaped the militia of Ohio, and were then descending the river. Burr had left Frankfort about the 7th, and had gone to Nashville. The conclusion of his enterprise belongs to the history of the United States. But that portion of the drama which was enacted in Kentucky has been detailed with some minuteness, as affording a rich and rare example, of cool and calculating impudence, and of truth, loyalty and eloquence most signally baffled and put to shame, by the consummate art and self-possession, of this daring intriguer.

The Kentucky legislature assembled, and the petition for an inquiry into the conduct of Sebastian was presented. A vigorous effort was made to stifle the inquiry, but in vain. The film had fallen from the public eye, and the people were not to be deluded twice, in such rapid succession. The inquiry was sturdily pressed. Sebastian resigned his office, hoping thus to stifle further examination; but the legislature refused to notice his resignation, and the examination proceeded. Judge Innis was the principal witness, and apparently with great reluctance disclosed what has already been detailed as to the secret intrigue with Power. Other evidence made it evident, that he had enjoyed a pension of two thousand dollars per annum, from Spain, since 1795. The public mind was violently agitated, by the sudden disclosure of these plots, and conspiracies, and in the minds of many Judge Innis was deeply implicated. Being a judge of the federal court, however, the legislature of Kentucky had no authority to investigate his conduct. At the succeeding session, however, it passed a resolution recommending an inquiry into the conduct of the judge, by the Congress of the United States, which was had, and resulted in his acquittal.

The foreign relations of the United States were now becoming critical. The attack of the English frigate Leopard, upon the Chesapeake, exasperated the American people almost beyond control, and was nowhere more fiercely resented than in Kentucky. Mr. Madison succeeded Mr. Jefferson, in 1808, and General Scott was elected governor of Kentucky. The breach between the United States and Great Britain grew daily wider, and Kentucky became deeply engrossed in national politics. Great numbers of resolutions, replete with patriotism, and not a little marked by passion, were adopted by her legislature.

The only act of a purely domestic nature which deserves attention, is the charter of the Bank of Kentucky, with a capital of $1,000,000, which was passed at the session of 1807. In the session of 1808–9, the limitation in actions of ejectment, was changed from twenty to seven years, where the defendant actually resided upon the land, and claimed under an adverse entry or patent, and the new limitation was made available in all suits at law, or in equity for the recovery of land. This celebrated act has quieted all litigation upon original conflicting claims, and was introduced by Humphrey Marshall.

No circumstances of domestic interest claim the attention of the historian, in a brief outline like the present, until the war which broke out between the United States and Great Britain in 1812. The general history of that war belongs to the historian of the United States, but no history of Kentucky, however brief and general, can pass unnoticed, those stirring incidents in the

5

north-west and south-west, in which Kentucky acted so prominent a part. The principal causes of the war should also be briefly and generally adverted to. As has been repeatedly stated, the angry feelings occasioned by the war of Independence, were not quieted by the peace of 1783. Mortification and resentment rankled in the breasts of the parties long after the war had terminated, and the convulsions of the French revolution so violently agitated the civilized world, that it became very difficult for a nation like the United States to remain undisturbed by the terrible struggle, of which the earth and the ocean were made the theatre.

Being the second maritime power in the world, the United States became the carrier on the ocean, of a large portion of the commerce of Europe. Many English seamen, tempted by the high wages given by American merchants, were employed in our commercial marine; and England claimed and exercised the right of impressing her own seamen wherever they might be found. The enormous navy which she maintained, required to be supported by constant impressment; and under color of seizing her own citizens, she was constantly in the habit of stopping American merchantmen, and selecting from the crew such men, as her subordinate officers chose to consider English, Irish or Scotch, and who were, frequently, native American citizens. Redress could seldom be obtained, and never except after interminable delay and vexation. All Americans upon the ocean thus became liable to be seized at the discretion of any British officer, and forced, under the discipline of the lash, to waste their lives in the most unhealthy climates, and in the most degraded stations. This grievance was the subject of protracted and bitter remonstrance, from the administration of Washington to the opening of the war; but Great Britain constantly refused to abandon the right, or rather the exercise of the power. In truth her extraordinary efforts by land and sea, called for all the resources of men and money, which could be made available, in any part of the world; and the sixty thousand splendid and unequaled seamen, which manned the American marine, totally unprotected, save by diplomatic remonstrance, afforded too rich a resource to be abandoned.

To the embittering grievance of impressment, was added in 1806 and 1807, a series of paper blockades, by means of which, not only American seamen, but American merchandize afloat, became subject to seizure and confiscation upon the high seas, under circumstances, which left the American government no choice but to abandon the ocean entirely, or submit to a wholesale plunder upon the seas, destructive to their prosperity, and intolerable to national pride. By these orders in council the whole French empire, with its allies and dependencies, then embracing nearly all of Europe, were declared in a state of blockade. Any American vessel bound to, or returning from any port in any of these countries, without first stopping at an English port and obtaining a license to prosecute the voyage, was declared a lawful prize. This was in retaliation of Napoleon's Berlin and Milan decrees, wherein he had declared the British islands, their dependencies and allies in a state of blockade, and had rendered every vessel liable to confiscation, which either touched at a British port, or was laden in whole or in part with British produce. This decree, however, was in retaliation of a previous decree, passed by the English government in 1806, whereby the whole imperial coast, from Brest to the Elbe, was declared in a state of blockade.

All these decrees were haughty and high handed violations of national law, which allows of no mere paper blockades, and requires the presence of a sufficient force, to render them legal. Between these haughty belligerents, no American vessel could be free from liability to confiscation. If they were bound on a voyage to any European port, they must touch at an English port, and obtain a license, or become a lawful prize to some one of the thousand British cruisers which vexed the ocean. If they touched at an English port, or were laden in whole or in part with British merchandise, they were confiscated by the imperial edict, as soon as they reached a continental port. Both decrees were equally hostile to American commerce; but the English had set the first example, and the practical operation of their orders in council was far more destructive than Napoleon's decree. One thousand American vessels, richly laden, became the prize of the British cruisers; irritating cases of impressment were constantly occurring; the language of American diplomacy became daily more angry and impatient, that of England daily more cold and haughty, and in June, 1812, the American Congress declared war.

By engaging in war, at that time, the United States unavoidably became the ally of Napoleon Bonaparte, who at that time governed Europe with a rod of iron, repressing all freedom, and grinding the hearts of the people, by a system of plunder, and violence, which had already begun to react. The federalists, since the days of Washington, had regarded the French revolution with aversion, and looked upon Bonaparte with undisguised horror. The great strength of this party lay in the New England States, where the strict religious principles of the Old Puritans had taken deep root, and where revolutionary France was regarded as a power equally hostile to religion, to freedom and morality. They looked upon the war with deep aversion, and opposed it by all means in their power. Such is the force of passion, that this party, composed perhaps of the great mass of intelligence and property, and embracing a majority of the religious and moral strength of the country, were so far blinded by their hatred to Napoleon, and French principles, as to become almost insensible to the equally lawless, and intolerable despotism, with which Great Britain scourged the ocean. While it cannot be denied that the love of the democratic party for France, which originally sprung from gratitude, and a love of liberty, was so far blind and perverted, that they heartily sympathised with Napoleon, and rejoiced in his triumphs. Both claimed to be entirely independent and American, yet the affections of the one leaned strongly to England, and those of the other to France.

Our country was then a second rate power. England and France were the giant champions of the hostile principles, which warred with each other for twenty-five years, and the whole civilized world ranged themselves under one or the other of the hostile banners. England was the champion of the ancient institutions of Europe, which consisted of religion intimately interwoven with aristocracy. France attacked both, with a fury which strengthened each by the alliance of the other. Both united were far too strong for the most virtuous democracy which has ever yet existed; far less could they be overthrown by a democracy, trampling upon all freedom, and reveling in universal violence and plunder. He who understands mankind, will not wonder that the great mass of property and religion throughout the world, hated France, and sided with England; nor will he be surprised that the ardent passions which originally embraced the French cause, from gratitude and sympathy with freedom, should still cling to their first love, after the original character of the contest had gradually changed, and the milk-white lamb of 1789, struggling for life against despotism, had been transformed into the ten-horned monster of 1812, trampling under foot the liberties of the world.

Under this state of parties the war commenced. In Kentucky the federal party was so extremely weak, and the popular passion for the war blazed with such fury, that scarcely any opposition was perceptible. But in the New England States, where it predominated, it displayed itself with a strength and fervor, which seriously embarrassed the government, and has excited against the party generally, a degree of odium from which it will not easily recover.

The first events of the war, upon land, were such as might naturally be expected, from a nation essentially pacific, mercantile and agricultural. An invasion of Upper Canada by Hull, resulted in the surrender of his army, and the loss of the whole territory of Michigan. An attempt to invade Canada upon the Niagara frontier, resulted in a total failure, attended with some disgrace and an immense clamor. By the loss of Michigan, all American control over the numerous Indian tribes of the northwest, was lost, and they poured down, from the great lakes, upon our extended frontier, in great numbers.

The war spirit in Kentucky blazed forth with unprecedented vigor. Seven thousand volunteers at once offered their services to the government, and fifteen hundred were on the march for Detroit, when the intelligence of Hull's surrender induced them to halt. This disastrous news was received with a burst of indignant fury, which no other event has ever excited in Kentucky. The author of this sketch was then a child, and well recollects hearing the news discussed by a company of married ladies, who unanimously pronounced Hull a traitor, and with great vehemence declared that he ought to be gibbeted, or crucified—ordinary hanging being far too mild a punishment for so monstrous a traitor.

The military ardor of the men seemed rather increased than diminished by the disaster, and a call of the governor for fifteen hundred volunteers, to march against the Indian villages of northern Illinois, was answered by more than two thousand volunteers, who assembled at Louisville under General Hopkins, and marched into the Indian country, until their provisions became scarce, and their ardor had become cooled by the protracted fatigue and hardships to which they were exposed, when, without having encountered the enemy, they suddenly abandoned their general and returned home, in defiance of all remonstrances.

The residue of the Kentucky volunteers were placed under the orders of General Harrison, the governor of the Indiana territory, and since elected to the presidency. This gentleman had long been governor of Indiana, and in the preceding year had fought a bloody battle, at Tippecanoe, with the Indians, in which the brave and eloquent Daviess had lost his life. The last act of Governor Scott's administration, was to confer upon him the rank of major general in the Kentucky militia, and shortly after the same rank was given him by the President, in the regular service, with the chief command in the north-west. The plan of the campaign, as laid at Washington city, was to assemble under this general, the militia of Ohio, Kentucky, Virginia, and Pennsylvania, with such regular troops as could be raised, to retake Detroit, overawe the north-western tribes, and conquer Upper Canada.

The secretary of war evidently regarded this as a simple and easy undertaking, and the autumn and winter of 1812–13 was spent in ill-digested, awkward and unsuccessful efforts to carry out this plan. The face of the country presented obstacles to the march of an army, with the necessary baggage and supplies, which seem to have been totally overlooked by the secretary. The country to be traversed was little better than a wilderness of swamps and marshes, which, in the rainy season, were almost impassable. The command of the lake, so essential to a well digested plan, was entirely overlooked, and was in the possession of the enemy. Volunteers were furnished in great numbers, and muskets in abundance, but the commissariat's and quartermaster's departments were in a state of total anarchy. The men were full of courage, and ardently desired to fight; the government was sincerely anxious to furnish them with what was necessary; but every department was raw, inexperienced, and inefficient. Delays, disappointments, and blunders without number occurred. The ardor of the volunteers expended itself in inglorious struggles with hunger, disease, and intolerable hardships and privations, and one of the finest of the Kentucky regiments, commanded by the brave and unfortunate Allen, was with much difficulty restrained from disbanding and returning home. The money expended in miserable and abortive efforts to drag provisions and ammunition through a marshy wilderness of nearly two hundred miles, would have nearly equipped a fleet sufficient to maintain the command of the lake, and the sums wasted in the quartermaster's department, would nearly have furnished transports for a sufficient force to have seized Malden. But the secretary had planned the campaign as if this swampy wilderness was a high and healthy region, traversed thickly by the best turnpike roads, and acted as if totally ignorant that such a body of water as lake Erie was in existence.

After a series of plans hastily conceived, partially executed, and then as hastily abandoned, after forced marches undertaken through horrible roads, without adequate object, and terminating in nothing, sometimes upon half rations, and a part of the time upon no rations at all, the army at length found itself about the 1st of January, with the left wing at fort Defiance under General Winchester, and the right at Upper Sandusky under Harrison. The left wing was composed almost entirely of Kentucky volunteers, and the right of militia from Ohio, Pennsylvania and Virginia. The immediate object was to advance to the Rapids, and thence to make a march upon Detroit. The left wing took the lead, and the Kentuckians, with Wells' regiment of regulars, reached the Rapids on the 10th. Here they halted, and by order were to wait the arrival of Harrison.

On the 14th, however, they received intelligence that two companies of Canadian militia and about two hundred Indians were at Frenchtown on the river Raisin, within striking distance, and instantly a burning thirst for battle, seized both officers and soldiers. Frenchtown was about thirty-eight miles from the Rapids, and only eighteen miles from the British garrison of Malden. The lake was frozen hard, and the march over the ice from Malden could be made in a few hours. The British could in a few hours throw two thousand men upon Frenchtown, and no support was nearer than Upper Sandusky, at least five days march distant. Yet a detachment of nine hundred and ninety Kentucky militia, was thrust forward, within the very jaws of the British garrison, to strike at this detachment of Indians and Canadians. Colonel Lewis commanded the detachment, and under him were Colonel Allen, Majors Graves and Madison. A forced march within less than two days brought them in view of the enemy, whom they attacked with the greatest bravery; Major Reynolds commanded the British, and made a spirited defence, from the picketed enclosures and houses near the village, but was driven from all his defences, under a continual charge, for more than two miles, with some loss.

This battle was fought on the 18th January. Prompt intelligence of the action was sent to General Winchester, on the night after the battle, which reached him on the morning of the 19th. On that evening he commenced his march with a reinforcement of two hundred and fifty regulars under Colonel Wells, leaving three hundred men to guard the camp. On the evening of the 20th he reached Frenchtown, and found Colonel Lewis still in possession of the town, and encamped within a large picketed enclosure, which afforded an excellent protection against musketry, but none against artillery. There was room within the enclosure to the left of Colonel Lewis, for the whole of the regulars; but Winchester encamped in open ground on the right, having his right flank within musket shot of some detached houses and enclosures which were not occupied. On the 21st all remained quiet, and the general determined on the following day, to throw up some works for the protection of the regulars, declining to avail himself of the picketing on the left of Lewis, from an absurd regard to military etiquette, which entitled regulars to the post of honor on the right.

On the evening of the 21st, he learned that a large force was at Malden, apparently preparing for a march,—yet he sottishly slighted the intelligence, and on that evening gave permission to Colonel Wells to return to the Rapids, and fixed his own headquarters nearly a mile from the camp, at the house of Colonel Navarre. The night was intensely cold, and no picket was posted in advance, upon the road by which the enemy might be expected. At day-light on the morning of the 22d the camp was suddenly attacked by about two thousand British and Indians, in two divisions. The British regulars under Proctor advanced against the picketing with a rapid and firm step, and under a heavy fire of cannon and musketry, and were received by the Kentuckians, with a torrent of fire, which did vast execution. Thirty of the British regulars fell dead within musket shot of the lines, and three times that number of wounded were borne to the rear. The survivors retreated in great disorder, and contented themselves with a heavy cannonade from six field pieces, against the picketing.

In the meantime, the Indians and Canadians attacked Wells' regiment, encamped in the open ground, with savage yells, and a slaughtering fire, from the cover of the houses, and enclosures which flanked them. After a brief action of only a few minutes, this regiment gave way in total confusion. Winchester came up from his distant quarters in time to witness the flight of this regiment, and strove to rally it within cover of the picketing occupied by the Kentuckians; but the panic was so complete that no order could be heard, and these unhappy men fled through a deep snow along the road by which they had advanced from the Rapids, thirty-six hours before. They were pursued by four times their number of Indians, and an indiscriminate and almost total butchery ensued. Colonels Allen and Lewis left the picketing, and exerted themselves bravely, to rally and re-form the fugitives, but Allen was killed and Lewis taken, as was also the commander-in-chief. Many Kentuckians of every grade united in the effort to rally the fugitives, and bring them within the shelter of the picketing, among whom were Woolfolk, Simpson and Meade, all of whom were killed. Scarcely a man of the fugitives escaped death or captivity, and not a Kentuckian who had sallied from the picketing, returned. While this dreadful butchery was enacted within sight and hearing of both armies, the Kentuckians, now commanded by Majors Madison and Graves, remained within their enclosure, and for four hours kept the enemy at bay. During this time six field pieces played upon them incessantly, from various positions, and at length their ammunition was reduced to a single keg of cartridges. Proctor then summoned them, through General Winchester, to surrender, offering honorable conditions, and ample protection to the wounded. After considerable parley, the terms were accepted, and the whole detachment became prisoners of war. The conditions were faithfully kept, so far as the officers and men, who were unhurt, was concerned, but inhumanly violated with regard to the wounded. These were left in Frenchtown, *without a guard,* as had been stipulated, under the care of the American surgeons, attended by a single British officer and a few interpreters. A number of drunken Indians entered the town on the morning after the battle, and the helpless wounded were murdered with circumstances of shocking barbarity. The wounded officers, Major Graves, Captains Hart and Hickman, were tomahawked, and two houses crowded with wounded officers and men, were set on fire, and consumed, with their helpless inmates. This dreadful crime is chargeable to the gross negligence, if not wilful connivance of Proctor, and is an indelible stain upon the honor of the British arms.

The brave and veteran Shelby had succeeded Scott as governor of Kentucky, and upon the intelligence of the dreadful disaster at Raisin, was authorized, and requested by the legislature of Kentucky, to take the field in person, at the head of the reinforcements which volunteered their services in profusion, to supply the places of their countrymen who had fallen, or been led into captivity. Four regiments instantly tendered their services, commanded by the colonels, Dudley, Boswell, Cox and Caldwell; the whole forming a strong brigade under General Clay.

A portion of this force was pushed forward by forced marches to reinforce Harrison, who was now nearly destitute of troops (their time of service having expired), and was lying at the Rapids, exposed to a *coup de main,* from the enemy who lay within striking distance at Malden, and might by a little activity, repeat the terrible blow of the Raisin, upon the banks of the Maumee. The war had not lasted six months, there was but one regular British regiment in Upper Canada, and the United States had already lost the whole territory of Michigan, and instead of taking the offensive, was occupying a weak defensive position, within her own territory, the enemy being strongest upon the point of operations, and having complete command of the lake.

Harrison employed himself during the winter in fortifying his position below the Rapids, which was called camp Meigs, in honor of Governor Meigs, of Ohio. It consisted of an area of about seven acres, enclosed by strong pickets, deeply sunk in the ground, and with block houses at the angles. It could not resist regular approaches, or heavy artillery, but was available against light artillery and sudden attacks, and enabled him to await the arrival of reinforcements. Proctor gave him ample time to receive reinforcements and strengthen himself by fortifications, making no movement of consequence until late in April, although able at any time to throw a superior force upon his adversary.

On the 12th of April, the advanced guard of the Kentucky reinforcement reached camp Meigs, and on the 26th of that month the British flotilla, having on board battering cannon, and abundant supplies for a siege, appeared upon the lake at the mouth of Maumee river. Shortly afterwards his gun boats ascended the river to within two miles of the fort, the cannon were disembarked, and batteries were thrown up, both above and below the fort. A vast force of Indians, under the celebrated Tecumseh, attended the British army, and cut off communication with the interior. A heavy fire was opened from the British batteries on the 1st of May, which was returned at intervals from the fort, their supply of cannon balls being very limited, and their twelve pounders being principally supplied with balls from the enemy.

On the 4th of May, General Clay, with the residue of the Kentucky brigade, had reached fort Defiance. The present General Leslie Combs, of Lexington, then a captain, gallantly volunteered to carry to the garrison the news of Clay's approach, and at the head of five men, attempted to descend the river in a canoe, for that purpose. But the swarms of Indians who infested the woods defeated the attempt, and after the loss of nearly all his men, he was compelled to return. Lieutenant David Trimble had better success, and Harrison was informed that Clay's brigade was descending the river from fort Defiance to his aid, and would probably arrive on the 5th at daylight. General Harrison then sent orders to Clay by captain Hamilton, who ascended the river in a canoe, to land eight hundred men upon the northern shore, opposite the fort, to carry the British batteries, there placed, to spike the cannon and destroy the carriages, after which they were immediately to regain their boats and cross over to the fort. The residue of the brigade was ordered to land upon the southern shore, and fight their way through the Indians to the fort.

Nothing was more easy than the execution of these orders, had the troops been well drilled, and had the object of Harrison, which was simply to silence the batteries, been distinctly understood by the officers. The batteries were slightly guarded, the mass of British infantry was in the camp two miles below, and the Indian force was on the opposite side of the river. Had the order been given to a captain and one hundred regulars, it would probably have been successfully executed. Clay received the order from Hamilton, and directed him to communicate it to Colonel Dudley, who was charged with its execution. Dudley received the order, and landed with the troops in the first twelve boats, upon the northern shore as directed. He does not seem to have thoroughly understood the object of Harrison, and he never communicated to his subordinates the precise nature of his orders. The great mass knew nothing more, than they were to fight an enemy on the northern shore, and were totally ignorant that when the cannon were spiked and the carriages destroyed, their object was accomplished. They accordingly rushed upon the batteries, which were abandoned in disorder by the artillerymen, and the real object of the expedition was in a moment accomplished. A small force of Indians and Canadians, however, showed themselves upon the skirts of the wood, and opened a straggling fire, which was eagerly returned by the Kentuckians, and the retreating enemy was hotly followed up, in considerable disorder, for nearly two miles. The detachment was dispersed in small parties, no general command was retained over it, and no one seems to have understood, that they were expected to retreat rapidly to their boats as soon as the cannon were spiked. The consequences were such as might have been predicted. Proctor came up with a British force and intercepted their retreat, the Indians crossed over in great numbers and reinforced the retreating party, which had decoyed the Kentuckians into the woods, and the whole detachment, with the exception of about one hundred and fifty men, was killed or taken. The prisoners were taken within the walls of the old British fort, below, under a very slender guard, and while huddled together in this place, the Indians amused themselves in shooting them down and scalping them. This cruel sport continued for some time, until it was interrupted by the arrival of Tecumseh at full gallop, who instantly and with great indignation, put a stop to the massacre. A sortie was made about the same time from the fort, against a battery on the southern shore of the river, in which a company of Kentucky militia brilliantly distinguished themselves, but sustained great loss.

On the whole, the 5th of May was disastrous to the American army. The movement on the northern bank was too critical and delicate to be performed by a corps of undisciplined volunteers, unless under the most precise instructions, thoroughly understood, by officers and men. The force was far too great for the object contemplated, which might have been accomplished by one fourth of the number, and was too small to defend itself against a force which was within forty minutes' march of the batteries, and was sure to be aroused, if there was the least delay. The news of the capture of fort George by General Dearborn, however, alarmed Proctor, and the little effect produced by his fire, together with the large force which had reinforced Harrison, induced him to abandon the siege, and return to Malden. The force under Proctor, including Indians, was probably 3200 men.

Harrison's force exclusive of Clay's reinforcement was about 1200, and including Clay's brigade about 2500 rank and file fit for duty. Colonel Richard M. Johnson, then a member of Congress, had early in the spring, raised a regiment of mounted gunmen, who now joined General Harrison, and were engaged during the early part of the summer in distant, harassing, and fruitless expeditions against the Indian villages of the north-west. Proctor remained quiet at Malden, organizing an Indian force for a second invasion of Ohio. Harrison remained at Upper Sandusky, busily engaged in preparing for decisive operations in the fall.

The secretary had now practically learned the importance of commanding lake Erie. Lieutenant Perry of the navy, had been detached, from the squadron under command of Chauncey on lake Ontario, to superintend the equipment of a fleet on lake Erie, and take the command of it when ready for service. The plan of the present campaign, was sensible and military. It was simply to obtain command of the lake, and by means of a cheap and rapid water communication, to pour a superior force upon Upper Canada, and finish the war in the north-west by a single blow. All depended upon the result of the naval battle, to be fought with ships, which in June, existed in the shape of green timber growing upon the shore of lake Erie. Money however was lavishly, and now wisely expended, and under the active exertions of Perry, two brigs of twenty guns each, and seven smaller vessels, by the middle of summer began to assume the appearance of a fleet. All difficulties both of building and launching, were successfully overcome, and by the close of summer, Perry was ready to engage the enemy.

In the meantime Harrison had called upon the veteran Shelby, for a force not exceeding two thousand infantry. The governor instantly issued a proclamation, inviting volunteers to meet him at Newport, and announcing that he would lead them in person against the enemy. Four thousand mounted volunteers responded to the call, who after some hesitation were accepted by Harrison, and proceeded without delay to the scene of operations.

In the meantime a second feeble and abortive effort was made by Proctor to take camp Meigs, which failed disgracefully, after vast expense had been incurred in collecting stores and Indian auxiliaries, and the result of which displayed that imbecility had passed over to the enemy, and that energy and wisdom were beginning to prevail in the American conduct of affairs. Having failed to make any impression upon camp Meigs, Proctor attempted to carry fort Stephenson, a small picketed stockade, garrisoned by Colonel Croghan of Kentucky with one hundred and fifty men, and so totally indefensible that Harrison had ordered Croghan to evacuate it, and rejoin the main army. It was completely invested, however, before these orders could be obeyed, and successfully resisted the attack of fifteen hundred men. Only one assault was attempted, which was bravely repulsed with a slaughter which induced Proctor hastily to decamp and return to

Malden, after one of the feeblest and most disgraceful expeditions, which has ever disgraced the British arms.

The crisis of the campaign had now arrived, and on the morning of the 10th of September, the flotilla of lieutenant Perry engaged the British fleet under captain Barclay, a British officer of great experience, who had fought under Nelson at Trafalgar. The number of men in the respective squadrons was nearly equal; the British vessels carried sixty-three guns, and the American fifty-four; the British had six vessels, and the American nine. But seven of the American vessels were mere gun boats, carrying most of them only one gun, and none of them more than three, while the remaining two, named the Lawrence and Niagara, carried twenty guns each. A great proportion of the British armament consisted of long guns, while the two American brigs were armed almost exclusively with carronades. If the British official report is to be trusted, however, the weight of metal in a close action would be immensely in favor of the American fleet, as most of their guns were thirty-two and twenty-four pounders, while the great majority of the British guns, were nine, six and four pounders, and only a few as high as twenty-four and eighteen. A detachment of one hundred and fifty of the Kentucky volunteers served on board of Perry's fleet as marines, and upon this new element acquitted themselves with the greatest bravery.

The action began between eleven and twelve o'clock, with scarcely a breath of air to stir the bosom of the lake. Perry in the Lawrence, accompanied by two of the small vessels, bore down upon the enemy, but was not closely followed by lieutenant Elliot in the Niagara, and the rest of the small vessels. For two hours Perry remained exposed to the fire of the whole British fleet, by which his vessel was cut to pieces, and three-fourths of his crew killed and wounded. Elliot during this time was never within less than half a mile of the enemy, and the residue of the fleet was not nearer than a mile and a half, save the two small vessels which accompanied him. By two o'clock Perry's vessel was totally disabled, but the rest of his fleet was but little injured. The lake was so smooth, that the distant gun boats, from their long twenty-four and thirty-two pounders, threw their shot with great precision, and had made themselves felt in the action; but Elliot's brig, which formed so essential a part of the force, and which was armed almost exclusively with carronades had as yet annoyed the enemy but little, and had fought principally with two twelve pounders, the only long guns she had. At two o'clock, Perry left the Lawrence under command of her lieutenant, and in an open boat, rowed to the Niagara. Upon Perry's expressing dissatisfaction at the manner in which the gun boats were managed, Elliot volunteered to bring them up. He left the Niagara in a boat for that purpose, and passed swiftly down the line, ordering them to cease firing, and by the combined use of their sweeps and sails, to press forward into close action.

Instantly a new impulse was given to the whole line. The well known signal for close action, was now seen flying from the Niagara, and after a delay of fifteen minutes, to enable the gun boats to come up, Perry bore down upon the British line, passed through it, and delivered a raking fire of grape and cannister, from both broadsides, at half pistol shot distance. The dreadful cries from the Queen Charlotte and Lady Prevost, which followed this close and murderous discharge, announced the fatal accuracy with which it had been delivered. The gun boats were now within pistol shot, and a tremendous cannonade, accompanied by the shrill clear notes of many bugles from the English vessels, announced that they expected to be boarded, and were summoning their boarders to repel the anticipated assault. No boarding, however, was attempted. The superior weight of the American mettle, was now telling, in close fight, when the full power of their carronades was felt, and in fifteen minutes the enemy surrendered, with the exception of two of their smallest vessels, which attempted to escape. The attempt proved fruitless, and the whole fleet of the enemy became the prize of the captors. When the smoke cleared away, so that the hostile fleets could be distinctly seen, they were found intermingled, within half pistol shot. The signal for close action was still flying from the mast head of the American commodore, and the small vessels were still sternly wearing their answering flag of intelligence and obedience. The loss on both sides, owing to the dreadful slaughter on board the Lawrence, was nearly equal. The American loss was twenty-seven killed and ninety-six wounded, considerably more than half of which was sustained by the crew of the Lawrence.

This victory, never surpassed in splendor, however it may have been in magnitude, was decisive of the fate of the campaign. It gave to Harrison the complete command of the lake, and the power of throwing an overwhelming force into the rear of Proctor, if he should attempt to maintain his position at Detroit and Malden. Such, however, was by no means his intention. No sooner did he learn that Harrison, at the head of a small regular force, and the powerful reinforcement of Kentuckians under Shelby, was crossing the lake, and about to operate upon his rear, than he abandoned his position with great precipitation, and commenced a rapid retreat, in the first stages of which he was deserted by more than one half of his Indian auxiliaries. The gallant Tecumseh, at the head of more than a thousand warriors, however, remained faithful in adversity, and accompanied him, as is believed under a promise that the first favorable ground should be selected for a battle. No time was lost in availing himself of his complete command of the lake. The horses of the Kentuckians were left upon the American shore, under a guard reluctantly draughted for that indispensable but inglorious service, and enclosed within an ample grazing ground, while their comrades were joyfully wafted to the hostile shore, where

they debarked on the 27th of September.   Proctor had retreated
on the 24th of the same month.

After detaching General McArthur to resume possession of Detroit, which had now been under British dominion for thirteen
months, General Harrison, at the head of the Kentucky infantry,
about one hundred and twenty regulars, and Colonel Johnson's
regiment of mounted gunmen, commenced pursuit of Proctor.
He came up with him on the 5th of October, upon the banks of
the Thames, near the old Moravian village, where a decisive battle was fought.   The ground occupied by the British, was the
river bottom, about three hundred yards wide, and thickly set with
beech trees.   Their left rested upon the river and their right upon
a swamp, which ran parallel to the river, and covered their right
flank.   Beyond this swamp their line was prolonged by their
Indian allies under Tecumseh.   There were probably about five
hundred British regulars, rank and file, upon the ground, and from
1000 to 1500 Indians.   The force of Harrison, including the handful of regulars and friendly Indians, was probably 3500 men.
The English, however, presented a narrow front, and were well
secured upon each flank, and the ground was extremely favorable to their Indian allies.   Harrison's line of battle was formed of
five brigades of Kentucky volunteers, under the generals Trotter,
King, Chiles, Allen and Caldwell, the three first composing the
division of Major General Henry; the two last commanded by
Major General Desha.   The division of Henry was formed in
three lines, fronting the British regulars—that of Desha was
formed at right angles to Henry facing the swamp, from which
the Indian torrent was expected to burst.   The venerable Shelby
took his station at the point where the lines intersected.   Colonel
Johnson's regiment had originally been intended to turn the flank
of the Indians, and operate in the rear, as in Wayne's battle, but
General Harrison was informed by Colonel Wood, of the engineers, that the British regulars were deployed as skirmishers in
loose order, and he instantly determined to charge them with
the mounted gun men.

Colonel Johnson, finding that the whole of his regiment could
not act with effect upon the English troops, directed his brother
to charge the English with one battalion, while he charged the Indians with the other.   The charge upon the British was completely
successful, and the whole regiment threw down their arms and
surrendered.   The charge upon the Indians, from the nature of
the ground, and the more vigorous resistance, proved unsuccessful.
The horsemen recoiled in disorder, and dismounting, commenced
an irregular skirmish with the Indians.   Colonel Johnson, who
had gallantly led a forlorn hope of twenty men, was desperately
wounded, and borne off before the close of the action.   A vigorous
fire was kept up by the Indians for a considerable time after the
English had surrendered, but the fall of the brave Tecumseh, and
the overwhelming force opposed to them, soon compelled them to
a flight.   Proctor fled early in the engagement, and was pursued

for several miles by several American officers—John Chambers and Charles S. Todd, aids to General Harrison, together with majors Wood and Payne. All was vain, however. The victory was decisive, and closed the hostilities, so long protracted, in the north-west. They continued with increasing fury upon the eastern and southern borders of the Union, but as Kentucky had no direct share in the campaign of 1814–15, save in the crowning victory at New Orleans, it is inconsistent with the plan of this sketch to notice any but the last event.

CHAPTER V.

The battle of New Orleans was the most brilliant event of the last war. It created a deep sensation at the time, and the vast political consequences which have resulted from it, have engraved it deeply and indelibly upon the minds of the American people. The overthrow of Napoleon in 1814, had rendered disposable a large part of that veteran British force, which had marched under Wellington, through six campaigns of uninterrupted victory, in Spain. New Orleans at that time, contained about 17,000 inhabitants, and was then as now, the great emporium of the Mississippi valley, and its possession by a hostile force would inflict incalculable evil, upon the whole country west of the Alleghenies.

At the close of 1814, a force of from eight to twelve thousand veteran and incomparable British troops, was placed under the command of Sir Edward Packenham, the brother-in-law of Wellington, and an officer who in a subordinate station, had brilliantly distinguished himself at the battle of Salamanca. His orders were to seize and hold New Orleans, and in pursuance of that object he effected a landing at the mouth of the Mississippi on the 22d of December, after destroying a flotilla of six gun boats, which attempted to prevent the disembarkation of this mighty armament. Such was the principal maritime force, which the American government had prepared to resist this invasion. The land forces were upon a similar beggarly scale. General Andrew Jackson, of Tennessee, since so celebrated throughout the civilized world, was the American commander-in-chief, and when the vanguard of the British force encamped a few miles below the city, he had only two regiments of regular troops, amounting to less than seven hundred men, and about 3000 citizens, without discipline, and poorly provided with arms, to meet the bronzed veterans of the Peninsula. A division of Kentucky militia was descending the Mississippi, under General Thomas, to aid in the defence, but had not yet arrived, and when it did come, was almost entirely

without arms or ammunition, nor were there any adequate magazines in the city, from which they could be supplied. Several
boat loads of arms and munitions of war had been shipped at
Pittsburgh, and were then struggling through the shoals of the
Ohio; but when they might be expected to arrive, if ever, was
matter of conjecture. Such was the preparation for defence.

In the meantime their formidable enemy was upon them,
within two hours' march of the city, which was entirely unfortified, and filled with consternation. On the very night of their
landing, Jackson promptly marched to meet them. The British
force present under arms was about 4500 men. The force with
which Jackson made the attack was about 2500, having left one
brigade of Tennessee militia under General Carroll, and a corps
of Louisiana militia under Governor Claiborne in the rear, to
guard against any attempt which might be made by the residue
of the British force. The American schooner Caroline, commanded by Lieutenant Henly, of the navy, was ordered to drop
down the river until abreast of the British camp, and co-operate
with the land forces in the attack. The British troops were encamped upon the very verge of the river, which was high at the
time, and only prevented by the levee from overflowing the encampment. The Caroline floated slowly down the river, and attracted no notice from the enemy, who had no suspicion of her
character. When abreast of the encampment, which was lit up by
numerous fires, the Caroline dropped her anchor and brought her
broadside to bear. The enemy in crowded masses, were before
her, their blood-red uniforms, and gilded accoutrements, glaring
in the light of an hundred fires. Her guns loaded with grape
and musket balls, were discharged within half range, upon this
dense mass, with fatal accuracy. The enemy was completely
surprised by this attack, and great confusion ensued. The Caroline poured in repeated broadsides, in rapid succession, which
was answered by vollies of musketry, quickly followed by showers of Congreve rockets, one of which exploded directly over her
deck. A portion of the British force sought shelter behind the
levee, while the residue were withdrawn from the bank, and the
fires completely extinguished. A dense fog now settled over the
river and encampment, which added to the darkness of the night.

For some time the silence was broken only by the regular broadsides of the schooner, and the equally regular discharges of the
mortar battery. But other sights and sounds quickly followed.
A tremendous roar of musketry, was soon heard, about one half
mile back from the river, and the horizon in that direction was
lit up for a mile in extent by a stream of fire. Scarcely had this
occurred, when another burst of musketry, intermingled with the
sharper reports of rifles, in irregular but heavy vollies, upon the
very verge of the river, and above the late encampment, announced to the British commander that Jackson was upon him
in two divisions, and that in the murky mist, where the fight was
waged, discipline must yield to native daring. The British

troops, accustomed to the regular battles, and splendid evolutions of the Peninsula, were entirely out of their element in this wildcat fight, in the mud and darkness, of the Mississippi. They were ignorant of the number of their enemies, and totally ignorant of the ground. Great confusion on both sides ensued. The American troops occasionally fired upon each other, and the British did the same. An English officer who was present describes it as a desperate and bloody struggle in the dark, where wounds were given by swords, knives, bayonets, butts of guns, musket and rifle balls in profusion, amidst shouts, cries, and curses, which might have awakened the dead.

After a vehement struggle of two hours, the parties separated as if by mutual consent, and sullenly retired to their respective camps. The British remained under arms until daylight, not knowing when or from what quarter the attack might be renewed, and during the long winter night, the silence was broken only by the cries of the miserable wounded, who were left in their blood, as they had fallen, over the whole theatre of the battle. The American loss, in killed, wounded and prisoners, was two hundred and thirteen. The English loss was nearly five hundred. The force present on the field, under Jackson, in this battle, was composed of Coffee's brigade of Tennesseeans, the seventh and forty-fourth regiments of regulars, a company of riflemen, a company of marines, two battalions of city volunteers, and a regiment of Mississippi volunteer dragoons, who were not actually engaged. Upon retiring from the British camp, Jackson instantly ordered up Carroll's brigade of Tennesseeans, directing Governor Claiborne alone to hold the position in the rear, intending with this reinforcement to renew the attack. Carroll promptly obeyed the order, and in one hour after midnight was upon the ground ready for action.

Jackson in the meantime had ascertained the force of the enemy from the prisoners taken in the battle, and further learned that they would be reinforced in the morning by two additional regiments. He declined renewing the attack, therefore; and withdrawing his force from the immediate vicinity of the enemy, he formed them behind a shallow ditch, which crossed the bottom at right angles to the river, connecting the river with a swamp. The bottom was rather more than one thousand yards broad. The earth had been thrown out of the ditch upon the upper side and formed a natural, but low breast work. This was greatly strengthened by an additional quantity of earth thrown upon it, from the upper side, leaving a shallow trench on the upper side of the breastwork, in which the men stood, and which in rainy weather, was more than ankle deep in mud and water. The ditch was extended some distance into the swamp, which was nearly impassable beyond it. Coffee's brigade had charge of the flank resting upon the swamp. Carroll's brigade and the regulars were posted in the centre, and the Louisiana militia had charge of the river quarter. The troops were incessantly employed in

6

strengthening the lines, and the arrival of the Kentucky militia was anxiously expected.

On the morning after the night skirmish, Sir Edward Packenham, with two more regiments of the British force arrived, and no good reason can be given for his tardiness and delay in availing himself of his overpowering superiority. He certainly had from five to seven thousand men present under arms, and it is equally certain that General Jackson had not much more than half that number, fit for duty. When Jackson retired behind the ditch, then offering no serious defence, there was nothing to prevent Packenham's advancing upon him. Kentucky had not then appeared, and the British were in full force, save two regiments which had not yet come up. Napoleon would have seized the golden opportunity, and would have pressed the retiring militia so closely as to have given no leisure for that formidable breastwork, against which courage and discipline toiled in vain.

No movement of consequence was made by the British from the 24th to the 28th of December, which precious interval was improved by Jackson in incessant labor upon his works, and in the most active exertions to procure arms from the city and neighborhood, and have them prepared by workmen, who were employed day and night, in fitting them for service. The right bank of the river also engaged Jackson's attention, which was completely open to the British, and as they had destroyed the schooner Caroline with hot shot, they had complete command of the river below. Jackson threw up some hasty works on the right bank, and manned them with a few hundred militia, badly armed; but there was nothing on the right bank capable of even delaying Packenham's march, so late as the 8th of January.

On the 28th, after the loss of four days, Packenham moved forward, with a heavy mass against the front of the American lines, while a smaller column under Lieutenant Colonel Rennie, a gallant Scotch officer, attempted to turn the left of the line, where it rested upon the swamp. The demonstration in front under Packenham was repulsed by a converging fire of artillery from the whole line, for Jackson had availed himself of the ample time given him by the enemy, to mount some heavy guns taken from ships, along his line, and they were worked by the officers and seamen of the Caroline, with a skill and accuracy that told fearfully upon the advancing column. The demonstration of Rennie upon the left flank, if made with a large force and properly supported, would probably have been successful. He found the swamp passable, although with difficulty, and succeeded in turning the left of the line. He was there met by a portion of Coffee's brigade, with whom he skirmished, until he was recalled by Packenham.

This demonstration called Jackson's attention more particularly to his left. The breastwork was extended farther into the swamp, and platforms were constructed in the water, upon which the men could stand, and by which they could readily pass to the extremity of the line. Baffled in this tardy and feeble effort to advance, Packenham then commenced regular approaches, as if he were attacking a Spanish town strongly fortified, and after several days' labor, opened a battery of heavy artillery against the earthen breastwork. His guns were ineffectual, however, and were quickly dismounted by the American artillery. It seems then suddenly to have occurred to Packenham, that the opposite bank of the river afforded a passage to the city, and was but slightly defended, and he instantly determined to employ his whole force, in deepening the canal that led from the British fleet to the Mississippi, in order to bring up the boats from the fleet, and thus command both banks of the river. This proved a herculean undertaking, and was not completed until the evening of the 6th of January.

In the meantime a division of Kentucky militia, commanded by General Thomas, more than 2000 strong, arrived in camp, and two additional regiments of Louisiana militia arrived. The Kentucky troops could at first, only muster five hundred muskets, and the Louisiana reinforcements were miserably armed. But the men were hardy and brave, and immense exertions were made to arm them, which were partially successful. Even on the day of battle, however, there were six hundred men under Jackson ready and anxious to fight, who could not procure a musket, to defend their country. Never was there a more striking contrast between the activity, energy, and inexhaustible resources of a general, and the imbecility of a government.

Having now allowed his enemy time to receive all his reinforcements, to entrench himself behind formidable works, to manufacture and repair arms for his naked troops,—having first directed his enemy's attention to the vulnerable point in his line of defence, by a weak demonstration, and then given him ten days to strengthen it, Packenham at last determined to attack. Having now fifty boats at command, one would suppose that he would prefer advancing by the right bank, which was unfortified, rather than by the left, which bristled with entrenchments. Both would lead to within reach of the city, and by the former rout, he would turn those terrible lines, before which he had halted seventeen days, and render all Jackson's labor useless. With his ample corps of sappers and miners, he might have bridged the Mississippi, in the time employed in deepening the canal. Even after the boats arrived, twenty-four hours would have transported his whole force to the opposite shore. He determined, however, to make a demonstration with only 1400 on the right bank, and with the residue of his force, to assail the terrible lines in front. Orders were given to that effect, on the evening of the 7th. Colonel Thornton was to cross the river with 1400 men at midnight, and assail General Morgan, who commanded on the right bank, at day light. At the same time the main body, in three columns, on the left bank, was to assail Jackson's line. Packenham would lead the centre column in person. Lieutenant

Colonel Rennie the left column, which was to assault the line upon the river ; and Lieutenant Colonel Jones, the right column, which was destined to turn the left of the line through the swamp, and attack the rear of the centre.

The preparation in the American lines, was of the most formidable kind. The right of the line resting on the river, was strengthened by an advanced redoubt, and that whole quarter was defended by the Louisiana militia and the regulars. Carroll's Tennessee brigade and about 1100 Kentucky militia, formed the centre; and Coffee's brigade of Tennesseeans guarded the left flank, extending far into the swamp. General Thomas being sick, General Adair commanded the Kentuckians, who formed a corps *de reserve*, and were directed to march to the assailed point, and strengthen the line there. It was well understood that an attack would be made on the morning of the 8th, and the Kentucky troops were marched to the lines before day, and halted about fifty yards in rear of the centre, until the grand point of attack should be disclosed. It was intended that the line should have a depth of ten files at the point of attack, so that the stream of fire should be incessant. The front rank alone would fire, as fast as the nine ranks behind could pass forward their loaded muskets, receiving those discharged, in their places. When the point of attack had been clearly disclosed, the Kentucky troops were ordered to close up, with Carroll's brigade of Tennesseeans, upon whom it was evident, the storm was about to burst.

Two rockets thrown into the air were the signals to move forward, and the three columns, the veterans of six glorious campaigns, covered with renown as with a garment, and hitherto victorious in every field, rushed against an earthern breastwork, defended by men who had hurried from the plough and the workshop, to meet the invaders of their country. The fog lay thick and heavy upon the ground, but the measured step of the centre column was heard long before it became visible, and the artillery opened upon them, directed by the sound of the mighty host, which bore forward as one man to the assault. At the first burst of artillery, the fog slowly lifted, and disclosed the centre column advancing in deep silence, but with a swift and steady pace.

The field was as level as the surface of the calmest lake, and the artillery ploughed through the column, from front to rear, without for a moment slackening its pace or disordering the beautiful precision of its formation. Its head was pointed against the centre of the Kentucky and Tennessee line, where ten ranks of musketry stood ready to fire as soon as it came within one hundred and fifty yards; the musketry opened along a front of four hundred yards, and converged upon the head of the column, with destructive effect. There was not a moment's pause in the fire. The artillery along the whole line discharged showers of grape, the roll of musketry was in one deep uninterrupted thunder, like the roar of an hundred water falls, and the central breastwork for four hundred yards, was in a bright and long continued blaze, which dazzled the eye. Yet still the heroic column bore forward, into the very jaws of death, but no longer maintained the beautiful accuracy of its formation. The head of the column actually reached the ditch, and were there killed or taken. The residue paused and seemed bewildered for a moment, and then retired in disorder under the same exterminating torrent of fire, which had greeted their advance. Their commander Packenham had perished; Generals Gibbs and Keane, the next in command, had also fallen. A host of inferior officers had shared the same fate, and their organization for the time was destroyed.

General Lambert now succeeded to the command, and rallied the column for a second effort. The officers who had survived the terrible burst of fire from the lines, were seen busily reforming the ranks and encouraging the men. In a few minutes all traces of disorder disappeared, and again the column moved forward, with as rapid a step, and proud a front as at first. Again the artillery tore its ranks with grape shot, until it came within range of small arms, when the same uninterrupted thunder of musketry ensued. The column did not again persevere in advance with the heroic fortitude which marked the first effort. They broke and fled in confusion, before arriving within one hundred yards of the lines, and no efforts of their officers could induce them again to advance.

The river column, under Lieutenant-colonel Rennie, advanced against the redoubt with a resolution which nothing but death could control. The same fatal fire of artillery and musketry enveloped its ranks. But through all it persevered in advance, and mounted the walls of the redoubt with loud cheers, compelling its defenders to retire to the breastwork. The redoubt was commanded by the breastwork, and the British troops were exposed to a destructive fire, which proved fatal to their gallant commander and most of the inferior officers. They maintained their ground, at an enormous loss, until the central column was discomfited, when they gave way and retired in confusion.

The column under Colonel Jones had no better success. They found the left flank greatly strengthened since the 28th, and extending so far into the swamp, that it could not be turned. They were greeted with the same deadly fire from Coffee's brigade, which had proved fatal to the other columns, and were withdrawn to the shelter of the wood, about the time that Packenham's division was repulsed. The battle was over upon the left bank, and deep silence succeeded the intolerable roar, which had just tortured the senses. Enormous masses of smoke, hovered a few feet above the breastwork, and slowly drifted over the bloodstained field. Horrid piles of carcasses marked the rout of the centre column, which thickened as it approached the lines. The hostile ranks were cowering behind a ditch, within half range of the artillery, unwilling to advance or retreat. Upon the right bank the battle was still going on.

Previously to the morning of the 8th, General Morgan had been detached to the opposite bank with about 1000 militia. Some slight defences were hastily thrown up, and a shallow ditch formed part of the line, easily passable at every point. Before day of the 8th, one hundred and eighty Kentucky militia, and a regiment of Louisiana militia, were thrown over to reinforce Morgan, raising his force to about 1700 men. The position, although weak in other respects, was well garnished with artillery, and if occupied by well trained troops, could easily have resisted Thornton's attack. As it was, however, the militia gave way, and the British veterans drove Morgan's whole force before them. Although scarcely a tenth of Morgan's force was composed of Kentuckians, and although the Kentuckians formed the strength of that central force which repulsed Packenham, yet the flight of one hundred and eighty Kentuckians upon the right bank, is conspicuously set forth in General Jackson's official report, while the steady bravery of 1100 men under Adair, upon the left bank, is left to be gathered from other sources.

The further proceedings before New Orleans, belong to the biographer of Jackson, or the historian of the war. But it would be improper to dismiss this subject, without some observations upon the force of the respective armies. Some American writers rate the British force at 14,000, and state Jackson's force at 4000. Some British writers estimate Jackson's force at 25,000, and sink their own to one-fifth of that number. General Jackson states his force at 4698 rank and file, present upon the field. Major Pringle, of the British army, states that the field return, on the day preceding the battle, shows that the three columns which attacked Jackson's lines on the left bank, numbered precisely 5493 rank and file. This he admits is exclusive of Thornton's force, 1400 rank and file, and also exclusive of the cavalry, two squadrons, the artillery, the sappers and miners, the engineers, etc. Permitting each party to state his own force, and taking their accounts as true, it will appear that Jackson had 4698 rank and file, a portion without arms, and of course not engaged, while the British had 6893 rank and file, actually employed, and the cavalry, the artillery, the sappers and miners, about 1000 rank and file in all, stood idle. The British certainly had nine regiments of grenadiers, one of cavalry, a large body of marines, a corps of artillery, a corps of sappers, engineers, etc. Two of the regiments, the fifth and ninety-third, are known to have exceeded a thousand men; two more, the eighty-fifth and ninety-fifth, were less than three hundred strong; while three more, the seventh, twenty-first and forty-third, averaged eight hundred apiece. It is probable that each party may somewhat understate his force, but these statements are the best data for forming an opinion. The British loss, by their own account, was

2070, but by the American inspector general, was reported as 2600. Peace had actually been agreed upon at Ghent, several weeks before the battle, and was soon afterwards ratified. The war opened with disgrace, and terminated with glory. It is impossible to regard the military operations of Jackson before New Orleans, without being struck with the extraordinary firmness, vigor, prudence and activity, displayed upon the one side; and the singular tardiness, and absence of the higher military qualities, conspicuous in all Packenham's movements. Every moment of time was precious to Jackson, and was improved by him, with that activity, and energy, which is the precursor of success. On the morning of the 24th December, Packenham was within two hours' march of the city, and three-fourths of his whole force was present under arms. Jackson was before him, with a greatly inferior force, and on that day retired behind the shallow ditch, which he afterwards made impregnable by sixteen days' labor. Why did not Packenham follow him closely? *He waited four days, until joined by the residue of his force, and then advanced.* During these four days, the shallow ditch had been deepened, the earthen pile had been trebled in height and thickness, and heavy cannon had been procured from the shipping and mounted upon the works. Yet still the breastwork could have been turned on its right, as Rennie's demonstration showed. Ten more days, however, were given to make every thing impregnable, and to receive large reinforcements from Kentucky and Louisiana. The British bravery and discipline certainly shown out with a brilliant splendor, which was never surpassed on their proudest fields. But we look in vain for the *mind* of a commander.

CHAPTER VI.

AFTER the close of the war, the civil history of Kentucky is memorable by the dreadful monetary derangement, which led to the passage of the relief laws, and gave rise to the most embittered and violent conflict of parties, which has ever occurred in Kentucky.

In 1816, George Madison was elected governor, and Gabriel Slaughter lieutenant governor. Madison died a few months after his election, and the question agitated Kentucky, whether the lieutenant governor became governor during the four years, or whether a new election could be ordered by the legislature. The question was settled after an animated conflict, against the power of the legislature to order a new election, and Slaughter became governor until 1820.

In the meantime the financial affairs of the civilized world were in a painful state of disorder. The long wars of the French revolution had banished gold and silver from circulation as money, and had substituted an inflated paper currency, by which nominal prices were immensely enhanced. At the return of peace, a restoration of specie payments, and the return of Europe to industrial pursuits, caused a great fall in the nominal value of commodities, accompanied by bankruptcy upon an enormous scale. In Kentucky the violence of this crisis was enhanced by the charter of forty independent banks, with an aggregate capital of nearly ten million of dollars, which were by law permitted to redeem their notes with the paper of the bank of Kentucky, instead of specie.

These banks were chartered at the session of 1817–18. The bank of Kentucky had then resumed specie payments, and was in good credit. In the summer of 1818, the state was flooded with the paper of these banks. Their managers were generally without experience or knowledge of finance, and in some instances, destitute of common honesty. The consequences were such as might have been anticipated. Speculation sprung up in all directions. Large loans were rashly made and as rashly expended. Most of these bubbles exploded within a year, and few were alive at the end of two years. In the meantime the pressure of debt became terrible, and the power to replevy judgments was extended by the legislature from three to twelve months by an act passed at the session of 1819–20. During the summer of 1820, the cry for further relief became overwhelming, and vast majorities of both houses, were pledged to some measure which should relieve the debtor from the consequences of his rashness. The reign of political quackery was in its glory. The sufferings of the patient were too acute, to permit him to listen to the regular physician who prescribed *time, industry* and *economy*, as the only honest and just remedy. He turned eagerly to the quacks, who promised him instantaneous relief, by infallible nostrums and specifics, *without pain—without self-denial, and without paying the penalty which nature always imposes, upon any gross violation of her laws.*

General Adair had been elected governor of Kentucky in 1820, and heartily concurred with the legislature in the acts passed at the ensuing session. The great cry of the people was for money, and their heaviest complaint was debt. Therefore, the legislature of 1820--21, chartered the bank called the Bank of the Commonwealth, which was relieved from all danger of suspension, by not being required even to redeem its notes in specie. Its paper was made payable and receivable in the public debts and taxes, and certain lands owned by the state, south of Tennessee river, were pledged for the final redemption of its notes. Its business was to pour out paper in profusion, in order *to make money plenty.* But how was debt to be relieved? Easily. The creditor was required to receive this bank paper in payment of his debt, and if he refused to do so, the debtor was authorized to replevy the debt for the space of two years.

But these were not the only acts of this mad session. They had already one bank, the old Bank of Kentucky, then in good credit, its paper redeemable in specie, and its stock at par or nearly so. By the terms of its charter, the legislature had the power of electing a number of directors, which gave the control of the board. This power was eagerly exercised during this winter. An experienced conservative president and board were turned out by the legislature, and a president and board elected who stood pledged before their election, to receive the paper of the Bank of the Commonwealth, in payment of the debts due the Bank of Kentucky. This was no doubt intended to buoy up their darling bank, and sustain the credit of its paper. But the effect was instantly to strike down the value of the stock of the Bank of Kentucky to one half its nominal value, and to entail upon it an eternal suspension of specie payments.

The paper of the new bank sunk rapidly to one half its nominal value, and the creditor had his choice of two evils. One was to receive one half his debt in payment of the whole, and the other was to receive nothing at all for two years, and at the end of that time, to do the best he could,—running the risk of new delays at the end of that time, and of the bankruptcy of his securities. Great was the indignation of the creditor, at this wholesale confiscation of his property, and society rapidly arranged itself into two parties, called relief and anti-relief. With the first party, were the great mass of debtors, and some brilliant members of the bar, such as John Rowan, William T. Barry and Solomon P. Sharpe. A great majority of the voting population swelled its ranks, and it was countenanced by the governor, and furnished with plausible arguments by the eminent lawyers already named, to whom may be added the name of Bibb. With the anti-relief party, were ranged nearly all the mercantile class, a vast majority of the bar and bench, and a great majority of the better class of farmers. The mass of property and intelligence, was drawn up in array, against the mass of numbers, and an angry conflict commenced in the newspapers, upon the stump, in the taverns and highways, which gradually invaded the most private and domestic circles. Robert Wickliffe, of Fayette, George Robertson, since chief justice of Kentucky, then an eminent lawyer of Garrard, and Chilton Allen, an eminent lawyer of Clark, were early engaged in the conflict, and were regarded as leaders of the anti-relief party.

The question of the power of the legislature to pass the act, was raised at an early day, and was quickly brought before the circuit courts. Judge Clarke, of Clarke county, boldly decided the act unconstitutional, in the first case which came before him, and brought upon himself a tempest of indignation, which thoroughly tested the firmness of his character. He was summoned to appear before a called session of the legislature, which was convened in the spring of 1822, and violent efforts were made to intimidate, or remove him by address. The gallant judge defended his opinion with calm reason, and invincible firmness, and partly from a want of a constitutional majority, partly perhaps from the suggestion, that the legislature should await the decision of the supreme court of Kentucky upon the subject, the legislative storm blew over, leaving the judge as it found him. He adhered steadily to his decision, and was quickly supported by Judge Blair of Fayette, in an opinion replete with learning, temper and eloquence. Great was the indignation of the party at this refractory spirit displayed by the inferior judiciary.

But all awaited the decision of the supreme court. That high tribunal was then occupied by John Boyle, chief justice, and William Owsley and Benjamin Mills, associate judges. These gentlemen had passed the meridian of life, and had been drilled for a long series of years, to the patient and abstract severity of judicial investigation. In simplicity and purity of character, in profound legal knowledge, and in Roman-like firmness of purpose, the *old court* of appeals of Kentucky have seldom been surpassed. The question came directly before them in the case of Lapsley *vs.* Brashear, at the fall term 1823, and their decision was awaited, with intense anxiety by all parties. Terrible denunciations of popular vengeance in advance, if they dared to thwart the will of a vast majority of the people, were intended to warp their judgments or operate upon their fears. They had maintained an unbroken silence until called upon to act, but when the case came directly before them, the judges delivered their opinion, *seriatim*, and at length, and calmly concurred with their brethren of the circuit court, that the act of the legislature was in violation of the constitution of the United States, and totally void. The clause of the constitution with which the act conflicted, was that which prohibited the states from passing any law impairing the obligation of contracts. In the article on the court of appeals, in the following pages, a concise summary of the reasoning of the court is given.

The opinion created an immense sensation in the State, and the conflict of parties was renewed with redoubled fury. Clark and Blair were completely forgotten, and the great popular party of Kentucky, prepared to sweep from their path, and make an example to future ages of the three calm and recluse students, who had dared to set up reason against rage, and the majesty of truth and law, against the popular will. The *great majority*, had been accustomed to make and to unmake, to set up and to pull down at its sovereign will and pleasure. Presidents, governor, senators, representatives, had long been the creatures of its power, and the flatterers of its caprice. James the first had not a more exalted notion of his divine prerogative than the *great majority* had of its undoubted right to govern. The power of the judiciary had heretofore been so unobtrusive, that its vast extent and importance had escaped attention, and the masses were startled to find that three plain citizens, could permanently arrest the action, and thwart the wishes of that majority, before which presidents, governors and congresses, bowed with implicit submission. Many good honest citizens looked upon it, as monstrous, unnatural, unheard of in a republican government. It shocked all the notions of liberty and democracy which had grown with their growth, and violently wounded that sense of importance allied to arrogance, which always attends a long exercise of unresisted power.

The judiciary, by the constitution, held their offices during good behavior. Nothing less than two-thirds of both houses could remove them. Could they hope to obtain this majority? The canvass of 1824, was conducted with the hope of obtaining this result. General Joseph Desha was the candidate of the relief party for the office of governor, and canvassed the state with that energy and partizan vehemence, for which he was remarkable. He was elected by an overwhelming majority. A vast majority of both houses were of the relief party. The governor and the legislature met in December, with passions heated by the fierce canvass through which they had passed, and the unsparing wounds which they had received from their enemies. The sword was fairly drawn, and the scabbard had been thrown away by both parties. So exasperated were the passions, that the minority was as little disposed to ask quarter, as the majority was to give it. The three judges were summoned before the legislative bar, and calmly assigned reasons at length, for their decision. These reasons were replied to, with great speciousness and subtlety; for the great talents of Rowan, Bibb and Barry, were at the command of the relief party, and their manifestos were skillfully drawn. A vote was at length taken, and the constitutional majority of two-thirds could not be obtained. The minority exulted in the victory of the judges.

But their adversaries were too much inflamed to be diverted from their purpose, by ordinary impediments. The edict of "Delenda est Carthago," had gone forth, and the party rapidly recovering from their first defeat, renewed the assault in a formidable direction, which had not been foreseen, and when success was clearly within their reach. The majority could not remove the judges by impeachment or address, because their majority although large, was not two-thirds of each house. But they could repeal the act by which the court of appeals had been organized, and could pass an act organizing the court anew. The judges would follow the court as in the case of the district court and court of quarter sessions, and a bare majority would suffice to pass this act. A bill to this effect was drawn up, and debated with intense excitement, during three days, and three protracted night sessions. Wickliffe, denounced the party, with fierce and passionate invective, as trampling upon the constitution, deli-

berately, knowingly and wickedly. Rowan replied with cold and
stately subtlety, perplexing when he could not convince, and sedulously confounding the present act, with the repeal of the district court and with the action of Congress, in repealing the
federal circuit court system, and displacing its judges by a bare
majority. On the last night, the debate was protracted until
past midnight. The galleries were crowded with spectators as
strongly excited as the members. The governor and lieutenant
governor M'Afee were present upon the floor, and mingled with
the members. Both displayed intense excitement, and the governor was heard to urge the calling of the previous question.
Great disorder prevailed, and an occasional clap and hiss, was
heard in the galleries. The bill was passed by a large majority
in the house of representatives, and by a nearly equal majority
in the senate.

No time was lost in organizing the new court, which consisted
of four judges. William T. Barry was chief justice, and John
Trimble, James Haggin and Reginald Davidge, were associate
justices. Francis P. Blair was appointed clerk, and took forcible possession of the records of Achilles Sneed, the old clerk.
The old court in the meantime, denied the constitutionality of
the act, and still continued to sit as a court of appeals, and decide such causes as were brought before them. A great majority
of the bar of Kentucky recognized them as the true court, and
brought their causes by appeal before their tribunal. A great
majority of the circuit judges, obeyed their mandates, as implicitly as if no reorganizing act had passed. A certain proportion of cases, however, were taken up to the new court, and some
of the circuit judges obeyed their mandates exclusively, refusing
to recognize the old court. A few judges obeyed both, declining
to decide which was the true court.

This judicial anarchy could not possibly endure. The people
as the final arbiter was again appealed to by both parties, and
the names of relief and anti-relief became merged in the title of
old court and new court. Great activity was exerted in the canvass of 1825, and never were the passions of the people more
violently excited. The result was the triumph of the old court
party by a large majority in the popular branch of the legislature, while the senate still remained attached to the new court;
the new popular impulse not having had time to remould it.

In consequence of this difference between the political complexion of the two houses, the reorganizing act still remained
unrepealed, and the canvass of 1826, saw both parties again arrayed in a final struggle for the command of the senate. The
old court party again triumphed, and at the ensuing session of
the legislature the obnoxious act was repealed, the opinion of
the governor to the contrary notwithstanding, and the three old
judges re-established, de facto as well as de jure. Their salaries
were voted to them, during the period of their forcible and illegal removal, and all the acts of the new court have ever been

treated as a nullity. This is one of the most signal triumphs of law and order over the fleeting passions, which for a time overcome the reason of the most sober people, which is recorded in the annals of a free people. It is honorable to the good sense of the people of Kentucky, and strikingly displays their inherent attachment to sober and rational liberty.

The new court party acquiesced in the decision of the people, and abandoning state politics, they strove to forget their defeat in a new issue of a national character, in which the state became as deeply excited in the year 1827, as it had been in its domestic policy. Adams had been elected president in 1824, by the vote of Mr. Clay, and by his influence in the house of representatives over the delegates from Kentucky and Missouri. Jackson had been his strongest competitor, and was personally more popular in the west than Adams. Mr. Clay received the appointment of secretary of state from Adams, and of course became identified with his administration. The ancient dislike to New England, was still strong in Kentucky, and the new court party in mass threw themselves into the opposition to Adams' administration, and boldly denounced Mr. Clay as an apostate from the ancient republican party, although Mr. Adams for nearly twenty years had been a member of that party, and had formed a distinguished part of president Monroe's administration.

The great mass of the old court party, warmly and passionately sustained Clay in his vote, and adhered to the administration of which he formed the life and soul. The old issues in 1827 were completely forgotten, and national politics were discussed with an ardor unknown in Kentucky since the war fever of 1812. It quickly became obvious that in this new issue, the old court party were losing their preponderance in the state. The unpopular name of Adams told heavily against them, and the sword of Jackson and the glory of New Orleans, were thrown into the scale.

Both parties prepared for the great contest of 1828 in Kentucky, with intense interest. Their gubernatorial election came off in August, and the old court party, which had now assumed the name of "National Republican," selected General Thomas Metcalfe as their candidate for governor, while the opposite party adopted the popular name of "Democratic Republicans," selected William T. Barry, the late chief justice of the new court, as their candidate. Metcalfe had commenced life as a stone mason, and by the energy of his character, had risen to honor and distinction. He had been a representative in congress for nearly ten years, and was possessed of great personal popularity. After an active canvass Metcalfe was elected by a small majority, but the opposite party carried their lieutenant governor and a majority of the legislature, and it was obvious that they had a majority of the votes in their ranks.

At the November election Jackson carried the state by a majority of eight thousand, and Adams was beaten in the United

States by an overwhelming vote. Although Clay was not directly involved in this issue, yet the weight of the popular verdict fell heavily upon him. The party that had supported Adams in the United States instantly rallied upon Clay, and organized for another struggle in 1832, against Jackson, who would certainly be a candidate for re-election. With Clay directly before the people, the "National Republican" party in Kentucky, felt confident of regaining their ascendency in the State. His brilliant eloquence, his courage, his energy of character, his indomitable spirit, made him a fit competitor for Jackson, who possessed some of the same qualities in an equal degree. During the conflicts of 1829 and 1830, the Jackson supremacy was maintained in the legislature, and in the delegates to Congress, but in the fall of 1831, the "Clay party" as it was called by many, obtained a majority in the legislature, and this was strikingly made manifest to the Union by the election of Clay to the senate of the United States. A majority of the congressional delegation, however, were still of the "Democratic" or Jackson party, and it was uncertain which party had obtained a majority of the popular vote.

The great contest of 1832 came on. Jackson and Clay were competitors for the presidency, and Kentucky had to choose a successor to Metcalfe in the gubernatorial chair. Judge Buckner was the candidate selected by the "Nationals," and Breathitt by the "Democrats" or Jackson party. Great efforts were made by both parties, and Breathitt was elected by more than one thousand votes. Immense rejoicings upon one side, and bitter mortification upon the other, were occasioned by this result. But the "Nationals" instantly called a convention, which was numerously attended, and organized for a decisive struggle in November, with a spirit exasperated, but not cowed by their recent defeat. The "Democrats" or "Jackson party" also held a convention, and it became obvious that the preliminary trial of strength in August, was only a prelude to the decisive conflict which was to come off in November. The intervening months were marked by prodigious activity on both sides, and the excitement became so engrossing, that all ages and both sexes, were drawn into the vortex. The result was a signal and overwhelming triumph of the "National Republicans." The popular majority exceeded seven thousand, and the party which then triumphed has held uninterrupted possession of political power in the State ever since. But although the triumph of Clay was signal in Kentucky, he was totally defeated by Jackson in the general election, and that popular chieftain was re-elected by a great majority.

National politics have almost entirely engrossed the attention of Kentucky since the termination of the great relief struggle. Her domestic history since 1827, is so closely interwoven with that of the general government, that it would be impossible to give a satisfactory view of the subjects which engrossed the attention of the people, without entering into details forbidden by the plan of an outline sketch like the present. A few events belonging exclusively to her domestic history may be briefly noticed.

The fate of the Commonwealth's Bank, and the replevin laws connected with it, was sealed by the triumph of the old court party. The latter were repealed, and the former was gradually extinguished by successive acts of the legislature, which directed that its paper should be gradually burned, instead of being reissued. In a very few years its paper disappeared from circulation, and was replaced by the paper of the United States' Bank, of which two branches had been established in Kentucky, the one at Lexington and the other at Louisville. It was the policy of the great Jackson party of the United States to destroy this institution entirely, and the re-election of Jackson in 1832, sealed its doom. It became obvious to all that its charter would not be renewed, and the favorite policy of that party was to establish state banks throughout the Union, to supply its place.

As soon as it became obvious that the charter of the bank of the United States would not be renewed, the legislature of Kentucky, at its sessions of 1833 and 1834, established the Bank of Kentucky, the Northern Bank of Kentucky, and the Bank of Louisville, the first with a capital of $5,000,000, the second with a capital of $3,000,000, the third with a capital of $5,000,000. The result of this simultaneous and enormous multiplication of state banks throughout the United States, consequent upon the fall of the National Bank, was vastly to increase the quantity of paper money afloat, and to stimulate the wildest spirit of speculation. The nominal prices of all commodities rose with portentous rapidity, and states, cities and individuals, embarked heedlessly and with feverish ardor in schemes of internal improvement, and private speculation, upon the most gigantic scale. During the years of 1835 and 1836, the history of one State is the history of all. All rushed into the market to borrow money, and eagerly projected plans of railroads, canals, slack-water navigation and turnpike roads, far beyond the demands of commerce, and in general without making any solid provision for the payment of the accruing interest, or reimbursement of the principal. This fabric was too baseless and unreal to endure.

In the spring of 1837, all the banks of Kentucky and of the Union suspended specie payments. Kentucky was then in the midst of a scheme of internal improvement, upon which she was spending about $1,000,000 annually, embracing the construction of turnpike roads and the improvement of her rivers, and she was eagerly discussing railroad projects upon a princely scale. Her citizens were generally involved in private speculations, based upon the idea that the present buoyant prices would be permanent, and both public and private credit had been strained to the utmost.

In this state of things the legislature of 1837 met, and legalized the suspension of the banks, refusing to compel them to

resume specie payments, and refusing to exact the forfeiture
of their charters. A general effort was made by banks, government and individuals, to relax the pressure of the crisis, as much
as possible, and great forbearance and moderation was exercised
·by all parties. The effect was to mitigate the present pressure,
to delay the day of reckoning, but not to remove the evil. Specie
disappeared from circulation entirely, and the smaller coin was
replaced by paper tickets, issued by cities, towns and individuals,
having a local currency, but worthless beyond the range of their
immediate neighborhood. The banks in the meantime were conducted with prudence and ability. They forbore to press their
debtors severely, but cautiously and gradually lessened their circulation and increased their specie, until after a suspension of
rather more than one year, they ventured to resume specie payment. This resumption was general throughout the United
States, and business and speculation again became buoyant.
The latter part of 1838 and nearly the whole of 1839, witnessed
an activity in business, and a fleeting prosperity, which somewhat resembled the feverish ardor of 1835 and 1836. But the
fatal disease still lurked in the system, and it was the hectic
flush of an uncured malady, not the ruddy glow of health,
which deluded the eye of the observer.

In the autumn of 1839, there was a second general suspension
of specie payments, with the exception of a few eastern banks.
It became obvious that the mass of debt could not much longer
be staved off. Bankruptcies multiplied in every direction.   All
public improvements were suspended; many states were unable
to pay the interest of their respective debts, and Kentucky was
compelled to add fifty per cent. to her direct tax, or forfeit her integrity.   In the latter part of 1841, and in the year 1842, the tempest so long suspended, burst in full force over Kentucky. The
dockets of her courts groaned under the enormous load of law-
suits, and the most frightful sacrifices of property were incurred
by forced sales under execution.   All at once the long forgotten
cry of relief again arose from thousands of harassed voters, and
a new project of a Bank of the Commonwealth, like the old one,
was agitated, with a blind and fierce ardor, which mocked at the
lessons of experience, and sought present relief at any expense.

This revival of the ancient relief party, assumed a formidable
appearance in the elections of 1842, but was encountered in the
legislature with equal skill and firmness. The specific measures
of the relief party were rejected, but liberal concessions were
made to them in other forms, which proved satisfactory to the
more rational members, and warded off the fury of the tempest
which at first threatened the most mischievous results. The
middle term of the circuit courts was abolished. The magistrates were compelled to hold four terms annually, and forbidden
to give judgment save at their regular terms. The existing banks
were required to issue more paper, and give certain accommodations for a longer time and a regular apportionment. These con-

cessions proved satisfactory, and at the expense of vast suffering, during the years 1843 and 1844, society gradually assumed a more settled and prosperous state.

In order to preserve a record of the succession of chief magistrates, we may observe that judge James Clark, was elected governor in 1836, Robert P. Letcher in 1840, and judge William Owsley in 1844. The first will be recollected as the circuit judge who first had the hardihood to pronounce the relief law unconstitutional. The last was a member of the old court of appeals. Their successive election to the first office within the gift of the people, was a late and well merited reward for the signal services which they had rendered their country, at a period when all the conservative features of the constitution, were tottering beneath the fury of a revolutionary tempest. Governor Letcher had long occupied a seat in congress, and had inflexibly opposed the great Jackson party of the Union in its imperious sway.

General Harrison was before the people as a presidential candidate, during the years 1836 and 1840, when both Clark and Letcher were elected, and was warmly supported by that party in Kentucky, which successively bore the name of "Anti-relief," "Old Court," "National Republican" and "Whig." When Owsley was a candidate in 1844, Clay was again before the people as a candidate for the presidential chair, and was opposed by James K. Polk, of Tennessee, a member of the old Jackson party, which had assumed the popular title of "Democratic Republican." Clay was supported as usual in Kentucky, with intense and engrossing ardor, and obtained its electoral vote by a majority exceeding nine thousand. He was supported by the whig party of the Union, with a warmth of personal devotion, which has seldom been witnessed, and was never surpassed in the annals of popular government. Parties were so equally balanced, that the result was in doubt to the last moment, and was finally decided by the state of New York, which out of nearly 500,000 votes cast, gave Polk a plurality over Clay of less than 6000.

The great national issue involved in this election, was the annexation of Texas to the United States. Polk was the champion of the party in favor of annexation, and Clay opposed it as tending to involve the country in foreign war and internal discord. This tendency was vehemently denied by the adversaries of Clay, and annexation was accomplished by the election of Polk. Foreign war has already followed in the train, and internal discord seems slowly upheaving its dismal front, among the States of the confederacy.

With the year 1844, we close this sketch. The war with Mexico which grew out of the policy then adopted, is still raging, and the spirit of indefinite territorial aggrandizement which then triumphed, has not yet developed its consequences. A brief record of the past is here presented. The darkening

7

shadows of coming events, present a dim and troubled prospect, which we leave to the pencil of the future historian.

~~~~~~~~~~~~~~~~~~~~~~~

In the foregoing " Outline History," reference has necessarily been made and considerable space devoted to the political transactions that occurred in Kentucky previously to her admission into the Union as an independent State. That there were at that time two rival parties for popular favor, is obvious from what has been already written ; and that their rivalship was characterized by great and bitter personal animosity, is no less true. Angry and fierce contests, and crimination and recrimination marked the period, and the temper of the times can be clearly discerned from the nature of the charges brought on one side, and the manner in which they were repelled by the other. Mr. McCLUNG, the writer of the Outline History, has given a summary of the facts, as stated by the two historians, Mr. Marshall and Mr. Butler, as he understands them, but declines to draw any conclusion from them—leaving that to the reader's judgment. The principal allegation against the Honorable JOHN BROWN, then a conspicuous member of Congress, and three times subsequently thereto elected a senator in Congress from the State of Kentucky, is, that in a letter to Judge Muter, he communicated the substance of an interview between himself and Gardoqui in *confidence*, and that he afterwards in a convention held at Danville, maintained an ominous silence on the same subject. This seeming secrecy and reserve were held to be evidences of a criminal purpose, and as such are commented upon with great acrimony by the first named historian.

Since the preparation of the outline history, and after it had passed through the hands of the stereotypist, attention has been called to the following letter from Mr. Madison, which discloses the fact that so far from its being the wish of Mr. Brown to conceal the interview with Gardoqui, or invest it with mystery, he communicated it at the time to Mr. Madison himself, then a member of Congress from Virginia, and known to be one of the profoundest statesmen and purest patriots in the country ; and that whatever of reserve may have appeared in his communications or manner to others, was in accordance with the advice of Mr. Madison himself. It is due to the truth of history that the letter of Mr. Madison should be inserted here. In the opinion of the author of this work, it is a triumphant vindication of the motives of Mr. Brown, and he believes it will be generally so considered.

Copy of a letter from James Madison, ex-president of the United States, to Mann Butler, Esq., (as published in Appendix to second edition of Butler's History of Kentucky, page 518.)

" MONTPELIER, October 11, 1834.

" DEAR SIR : I have received your letter of the 21st ult., in which you wish to obtain my recollection of what passed between Mr. Brown and me in 1788 on the overtures of Gardoqui, 'that if the people of Kentucky would erect themselves into an Independent State, and appoint a proper person to negotiate with him, he had authority for that purpose, and would enter into an arrangement with them for the exportation of their produce to New Orleans.'

" My recollection, with which reference to my manuscript papers accord, leaves no doubt that the overture was communicated to me by Mr. Brown. Nor can I doubt that, as stated by him, I expressed the opinion and apprehension that a knowledge of it in Kentucky, might, in the excitement there, be mischievously employed. This view of the subject evidently resulted from the natural and known impatience of the people on the waters of the Mississippi, for a market for the products of their exuberant soil; from the distrust of the Federal policy, produced by the project for surrendering the use of that river for a term of years; and from a coincidence of the overture in point of time, with the plan on foot for consolidating the Union by arming it with new powers, an object, to embarrass and defeat which, the dismembering aims of Spain would not fail to make the most tempting sacrifices, and to spare no intrigues.

"I owe it to Mr. Brown, with whom I was in intimate friendship when we were associated in public life, to observe, that I always regarded him, whilst steadily attentive to the interests of his constituents, as duly impressed with the importance of the Union, and anxious for its prosperity. I pray you to accept with my respects, my cordial salutations.

Signed   "JAMES MADISON."

" MANN BUTLER, Esq."

WESTERN HUNTER.

SKETCH

COURT OF APPEALS.

THE Constitution of Kentucky—like that of the United States, and those, also, of all the States of the Anglo-American Union—distributes among three departments of organic sovereignty, all the political powers which it recognises and establishes. And to effectuate, in practice, the theoretic equilibrium and security contemplated by this fundamental partition of civil authority, it not only declares that the Legislature shall exercise no other power than such as may be legislative—the Judiciary no other than that which is judicial—nor the Executive any other than such as shall be executive in its nature; but it also, to a conservative extent, secures the relative independence of each of these depositaries of power. If courts were permitted to legislate, or the legislature were suffered not only to prescribe the rule of right, but to decide on the constitutional validity of its own acts, or adjudicate on private rights, no citizen could enjoy political security against the ignorance, the passions or the tyranny of a dominant party: And if judges were dependent for their offices on the will of a mere legislative majority, their timidity and subservience might often add judicial sanction to unconstitutional enactments, and thereby, instead of guarding the constitution as honest and fearless sentinels, they would help the popular majority to become supreme, and to rule capriciously, in defiance of all the fundamental prohibitions and guaranties of the people's organic law. As the legislature derives its being and authority from the constitution, which is necessarily supreme and inviolable, no legislative act prohibited by any of its provisions, can be *law ;* and, consequently, as it is the province of the judiciary, acting as the organ of the judicial function of popular sovereignty, to declare and administer the law in every judicial case, it must be the duty, as well as privilege, of every court to disregard every legislative violation of the constitution, as a nullity, and thus maintain the practical supremacy and inviolability of the fundamental law. But the will to do so, whenever proper, is as necessary as the power; and, therefore, the constitution of Kentucky provides that the judges of the Court of Appeals, and also of inferior courts, shall be entitled to hold their offices during good behavior; and, moreover, provides that no judge shall be subject to removal otherwise than by impeachment, on the trial of which there can be no conviction, without the concurrence of two-thirds of the Senate—or by the address of both branches of the legislature, two-thirds of each branch concurring therein.

The first constitution of Kentucky, which commenced its operation on the 1st of June, 1792, also prohibited the legislature from reducing a judge's salary during his continuance in office. But the present constitution, adopted in 1799, contains no such prohibition. It is not difficult to perceive which of these constitutions is most consistent with the avowed theory of both as to judicial independence; for, certainly, there can be no sufficient assurance of judicial indepen dence, when the salary of every judge depends on the will of a legislative majority of the law-making department.

But to secure a permanent tribunal for adjudicating on the constitutionality of legislative acts, the existing constitution of Kentucky, like its predecessor in this respect, *ordained and established* "A SUPREME COURT," and vested it with ultimate jurisdiction. Section one and two of the 4th article reads as follows :

"SEC. 1. The judicial power of this commonwealth, both as to matters of law and equity, *shall* be vested in one Supreme Court, which *shall* be styled the Court of Appeals, and in such inferior courts as the General Assembly may, from time to time, erect and establish.

"SEC. 2. The Court of Appeals, except in cases otherwise provided for in this constitution shall have appellate jurisdiction only, which shall be co-extensive with the state, under such restrictions and regulations, not repugnant to this constitution, as may, from time to time, be prescribed by law."

As long as these fundamental provisions shall continue to be authoritative, there must be in Kentucky a judicial tribunal with appellate jurisdiction "co-extensive with the State," and co-ordinate with the legislative and executive departments. And this tribunal being established by the constitution, the legislature can neither abolish it nor divest it of appellate jurisdiction. The theoretic co-ordinacy of the organic representatives of the three functions of all political sovereignty, requires that the judicial organ, of the last resort, shall be as permanent and inviolable as the constitution itself. The great end of the constitution of Kentucky, and of every good constitution, is *to prescribe salutary limits to the inherent power of numerical majorities.* Were the political omnipotence of every such majority either reasonable or safe, no constitutional limitations on legislative *will* would be necessary or proper. But the whole tenor of the Kentucky constitution implies that liberty, justice and security, (the ends of all just government,) require many such fundamental restrictions : And not only to prescribe such as were deemed proper, but more especially *to secure their efficacy,* was the ultimate object of the people in adopting a constitution : And, to assure the integrity and practical supremacy of these restrictions, they determined that, as long as their constitution should last, there should be a tribunal, the judges of which should be entitled to hold their offices as long as the tribunal itself should exist and they should behave well and continue competent, in the judgment of as many as one-third of each branch of the legislature, on an address, or of one-third of the senate, on an impeachment : And, to prevent evasion, they have provided that, whilst an incumbent judge of the Appellate Court may be removed from his office by a concurrent vote of two-thirds, neither the appellate tribunal, nor the office itself, shall be subject to legislative abolition.

There is a radical difference in the stability of the supreme and inferior courts. The first is constitutional—the last is only statutory. As the constitution itself establishes the Court of Appeals, this tribunal can be abolished by a change of the constitution alone. But as the circuit courts are established by statute, the supreme power, that is, a legislative majority, may repeal it, and thereby abolish these courts ; and, of course, the office of judge ceases with the abolition of his court. It would be certainly incompatible with the genius of the constitution to abolish the circuit courts, merely to get clear of the incumbent judges : Yet, as the power to abolish exists, the motive of the abolition cannot judicially affect the validity of the act. And, as the organization of inferior courts is deferred, by the constitution, to legislative experience and discretion ; and as, moreover, a new system of such courts may often be usefully substituted for one found to be ineligible, the legislature ought not to be restrained from certain melioration, by a fear of shaking the stability of the judiciary. The constitutional inviolability of the Court of Appeals, which may rectify the errors of the inferior tribunal, may sufficiently assure judicial independence and rectitude.

The fundamental immutability of the Court of Appeals, and the value of the durable tenure by which the judges hold their offices, have been impressively illustrated in the history and results of *"the relief system,"* and resulting *"old and new court,"* which agitated Kentucky almost to convulsion for several years—the most pregnant and memorable in the annals of the State. That system of legislative *"relief,"* as it was miscalled, was initiated in 1817–18, by retrospective prolongations of replevins, of judgments and decrees—and it was matured, in 1820, by the establishment of the Bank of the Commonwealth, without either capital or the guaranty of state credit, and by subsidiary enactments extending replevins to two years in all cases in which the creditor should fail to endorse on his execution his consent to take, at its nominal value, local bank paper greatly depreciated. The object of the legislature, in establishing such a bank, and in enacting such co-operative statutes as those just alluded to, was to enable debtors to pay their debts in much less than their value, by virtually compelling creditors to accept much less, or incur the hazards of indefinite and vexatious delays.

The constitutionality of the Bank of the Commonwealth, though generally doubted, was sustained by many judicial recognitions by the Court of Appeals of Kentucky, and finally by an express decision in which the then judges (Robertson, chief justice, and Underwood and Nicholas, judges) without expressing their own opinions, deferred to those incidental recognitions by their predecessors, and also to the opinion of the Supreme Court of the United States, in the case of Craig vs. Missouri, in which that court defined a "*bill of credit*," prohibited by the national constitution, to be a bill issued, as currency, by a State and *on the credit of the State*. The notes of the Bank of the Commonwealth, though issued by and in the name of the State of Kentucky, were not issued on the credit of the State, but expressly on the exclusive credit of a nominal capital dedicated by the charter—and this known fact produced the rapid depreciation of those notes; and, consequently, the same Supreme Court of the United States, affirmed the said decision of the Appellate Court of Kentucky, as it was compelled to do by its own authority, in Craig vs. Missouri, unless it had overruled so much of that decision as declared that it was an indispensable characteristic of a prohibited "bill of credit," that it should be issued *on the credit of the State*. There is much reason for doubting the correctness of these decisions by the national judiciary—and, if they be maintained, there is good cause for apprehending that the beneficent policy of the interdiction of State bills of credit may be entirely frustrated, and the constitutional prohibition altogether paralysed or eluded.

When the validity of the statutes retrospectively extending replevins, was brought before the Court of Appeals, the three judges then constituting that court, (Messrs. Boyle, chief justice, and Owsley and Mills, judges,) delivered separate opinions, all concurring in the conclusion that those statutes, *so far as they retroacted on contracts depending for their effect on the law of Kentucky*, were inconsistent with that clause in the federal constitution, which prohibits the legislatures of the several states in the union from passing any act "*impairing the obligation of contracts*," and also, of course, with the similar provision in the constitution of Kentucky, inhibiting any such enactment by the legislature of this State. A more grave and eventful question could not have been presented to the court for its umpirage. It subjected to a severe, but decisive ordeal, the personal integrity, firmness and intelligence of the judges, and the value of that degree of judicial independence and stability contemplated by the constitution. The question involved was new and vexed; and a majority of the people of the State had approved, and were, as *they* seemed to think, vitally interested in maintaining their constituent power to enact such remedial statutes.

Under this accumulated burthen of responsibility, however, the court being of the opinion that the acts impaired the obligation of contracts made in Kentucky antecedently to their date, honestly and firmly so decided, without hesitation or dissent. The court argued, 1st. That every valid contract had two kinds of obligation—the one moral, the other *legal* or civil; that the fundamental interdicts applied to the *legal* obligation only, because, as moral obligations are as immutable as the laws of God, and depend on the consciences of men, and therefore cannot be impaired by human legislation or power—consequently, it would be ridiculously absurd to suppose that the constitution intended to interdict that which, *without any interdiction*, could not be done. 2d. That, as moral obligation results from the sanctions of natural law, so civil obligation arises from the sanctions of human law; that, whenever the laws of society will not uphold nor enforce a contract, that contract possesses no civil obligation, but may be alone morally obligatory; that the obligation, whether moral or civil, is the chain, tie, or ligature, which binds, coerces, persuades, or *obliges* the obligor; that all *civil* obligation, therefore, springs from and is regulated by the punitory or remedial power of human law; that the destruction or withdrawal of all such power, must annihilate all merely civil obligation; that, consequently, that which impairs such power must, to the same extent, impair such obligation; and, that, whatever renders the remedial agency of the law less certain, effectual or valuable, impairs it; and, also, necessarily impairs, therefore, the obligation which it creates. 3d. That the civil obligation of a contract depends on the law of the place when and where it is made; and that any subsequent legislation that essentially impairs the legal remedy for maintaining or enforcing that contract, must, consequently, so far, impair its legal obligation. 4th. That, if a retroactive extension of replevin from three months to two years, would not impair the obligation of a contract made under the shorter replevin law, the like prolongation to one hundred years would not impair the obligation; and, if this would not, the abrogation of all legal remedy could not. 5th. *That it is impossible that legislation can destroy or impair the legal obligation of contracts, otherwise than by operating on the legal remedies for enforcing them;* and, that, consequently, any legislation retro-actively and essentially deteriorating legal remedy, as certainly and essentially impairs the legal obligation of all contracts on which it so retroacts: And, finally, therefore, that the retrospective extension of replevin in Kentucky, was unconstitutional and void.

Unanswerable and conclusive as this mere skeleton of the court's argument may be, yet the decision excited a great outcry against the judges. Their authority to disregard a legislative act as unconstitutional was, by many, denied, and they were denounced as *"usurpers,—tyrants,—kings."* At the succeeding session of the legislature, in the fall of 1823, a long, verbose, and empty preamble and resolutions, for addressing them out of office, were reported by John Rowan, to which the judges responded fully and most effectually. But after an able and boisterous debate, the preamble and resolutions were adopted by a majority less than two-thirds. The judges—*determined to stand or fall by the constitution*—refused to abdicate. At the next session of the legislature, in 1824, there then being a still larger majority against the judges and their decision,—*but not quite two-thirds,*—the dominant party now became furious and reckless, passed an act, mis-entitled " an act to *reorganize* the Court of Appeals ;" the object and effect of which, if sustained, were to abolish the "*old*" constitutional "*court*," and substitute a "*new*" legislative "*court.*" The minority in that legislature united in a powerful protest against the "reorganizing act," which, on the presentation of it to the house of representatives by George Robertson, by whom it was written, was, unceremoniously, ordered to be entered on the journal of that house, *without being read.* A copy, however, which was read in the senate, was refused a place on the journal of that body,—and a "new court " senator, coming into the other house immediately afterwards, and there learning that the protest had, unheard, been admitted to the journal of that house, told Mr. Rowan that it was "*the devil,*" and if embalmed in the record, would blow "the new court party *sky high.*" Whereupon, a reconsideration was moved, and the memorable document was kicked out of that house also.. But it could not be strangled. It lived and triumphed. It was published as an unanswerable text, and rallied and electrified the friends of the constitution, order, and justice.

The "new court " (consisting of William T. Barry, chief justice, and James Haggin, John Trimble, and Rezin H. Davidge, judges,) took unauthorized possession of the papers and records in the office of the Court of Appeals, appointed Francis P. Blair, clerk, and attempted to do business and decide some causes, their opinions on which, were published by Thomas B. Monroe, in a small duodecimo volume, which has never been regarded or read as authority. The judges of the constitutional Court of Appeals were thus deprived, without their consent, of the means of discharging official duties properly; and, the people not knowing whether the "old " or the "new court" was the constitutional tribunal of revision, some appealed to the one, and some to the other. In this perplexing crisis of judicial anarchy, the only authoritative arbiter was the ultimate sovereign— *the freemen of the State at the polls.* To that final and only tribunal, therefore, both parties appealed; and no period, in the history of Kentucky, was ever more pregnant, or marked with more excitement, or able and pervading discussion, than that which immediately preceded the annual elections in the year 1825.

The portentous agony resulted in the election, to the house of representatives, of a decisive majority in favor of the "old court," and against the constitutionality of the "new court." But only one-third of the senators having passed the ordeal of that election, a small "*new court*" majority still remained in the senate; and, disregarding the submission of the question to the votes of the people, that little majority refused to repeal the "reorganizing act," or acknowledge the existence of the "old court." This unexpected and perilous contumacy, brought the antagonist parties to the brink of a bloody revolution. For months the commonwealth was trembling on the crater of a heaving volcano. But the considerate prudence of the "old court party" prevented an eruption, by forbearing to resort to force to restore to the "old court" its papers and records, which the minority guarded, in Blair's custody, by military means—and, also, by appealing, once more, to the constituent body, in a printed manifesto prepared by George Robertson, signed by the members constituting the majority of the popular branch of the legislature, and exposing the incidents of the controversy and the conduct of the defeated party. The result of this last appeal was a majority in the senate, and an augmented majority in the house of representatives in favor of repealing as unconstitutional, the "act to reorganize the Court of Appeals." That act was accordingly repealed in the session of 1826-7, by "an act to remove the unconstitutional obstructions which have been thrown in the way of the Court of Appeals," passed by both houses the 30th December, 1826—*the governor's objections notwithstanding*. The "new court" vanished, and the "old court," redeemed and reinstated, proceeded, without further question or obstruction, in the discharge of its accustomed duties.

As soon as a *quietus* had been given to this agitating controversy, John Boyle, who had adhered to the helm throughout the storm in a forlorn hope of saving the constitution, resigned the chief-justiceship of Kentucky, and George M. Bibb, a distinguished champion of the "relief" and "new court" parties, was, by a *relief* governor and senate, appointed his successor. Owsley and Mills retained their seats on the appellate bench until the fall of 1828, when they also resigned, and, being re-nominated by Gov. Metcalfe, who had just succeeded Gov. Desha, they were rejected by a relief senate, and George Robertson and Joseph R. Underwood (both "anti-relief" and "old court") were appointed to succeed them. Then Bibb forthwith resigned, and there being no chief justice until near the close of 1829, these two judges constituted the court, and, during that year, declared null and void all the acts and decisions of the "new court," and disposed of about one thousand cases on the docket of the Court of Appeals. In December, 1829, Robertson was appointed chief justice, and Richard A. Buckner judge of the Court of Appeals. And thus, once more, "*the old court*" was complete, homogeneous and peaceful, and the most important question that could engage the councils or agitate the passions, of a state, was settled finally, and settled right.

This memorable contest between the constitution and the passions of a popular majority—between the judicial and legislative departments—proves the efficacy of Kentucky's constitutional structure, and illustrates the reason and the importance of that system of judicial independence which it guaranties. It demonstrates that, if the appellate judges had been dependent on a bare majority of the people or their representatives, the constitution would have been paralyzed, justice dethroned, and property subjected to rapine, by tumultuary passions and numerical power. And its incidents and results not only commend to the gratitude of the living and unborn, the proscribed judges and the efficient compatriots who dedicated their time and talents for years to the rescue of the constitution, but also, impressively illustrate the object and efficacy of the fundamental limitations in the will of the majority—that is, the ultimate prevalence of reason over passion—of truth over error—which, in popular governments, is the sure offspring, *only*, of time and sober deliberation, which it is the object of constitutional checks to ensure.

As first and now organized, the Court of Appeals consists of three judges, one of whom is commissioned "*chief justice of Kentucky*." In the year 1801, the number was increased to four, and Thomas Todd (who had been clerk of that court, and in the year 1807 was appointed a judge of the Supreme Court of the United States) was the first who was appointed fourth judge. In the year 1813, the number was prospectively reduced to three; and, all the incumbents having immediately resigned, two of them (Boyle and Logan) were instantly re-commissioned, and Robert Trimble, who was commissioned by Gov. Shelby, having declined to accept, Owsley, who had been one of the four judges who had resigned, was afterwards also re-commissioned ; and ever since that time, the court has consisted of three judges only.

All the judges have always received equal salaries. At first the salary of each judge was $666.66. In the year 1801, it was increased to $833.33 ; in the year 1806, to $1000 ; in the year 1815, to $1500 ; in the year 1837, to $2000 ; and in the year 1843, it was reduced to $1500. During the prevalence of the paper of the Bank of the Commonwealth, the salaries were paid in that currency, which was so much depreciated as, for some time, to reduce the value of each salary to about $750.

The following is a chronological catalogue of the names of all who have been judges of the Appellate Court of Kentucky:

CHIEF JUSTICES.

Harry Innis,	com.	June 28, 1792	John Boyle,	com.	M'ch 20, 1810
George Muter,	"	Dec. 7, 1792	George M. Bibb,*	"	Jan. 5, 1827
Thomas Todd,	"	Dec. 13, 1806	George Robertson,	"	Dec. 24, 1829
Felix Grundy,	"	April 11, 1807	E. M. Ewing,	"	April 7, 1843
Ninian Edwards,	"	Jan. 5, 1808	Thos. A. Marshall,	"	June 1, 1847
George M. Bibb,	"	May 30, 1809	*Resigned Dec. 23, 1828.		

JUDGES.

Benj. Sebastian,	com.	June 28, 1792	William Owsley,	com.	April 8, 1810
Caleb Wallace,	"	June 28, 1792	John Rowan,	"	Jan. 14, 1819
Thomas Todd,	"	Dec. 19, 1801	Benjamin Mills,	"	Feb. 16, 1820
Felix Grundy,	"	Dec. 10, 1806	George Robertson,	"	Dec. 24, 1828
Ninian Edwards,	"	Dec. 13, 1806	Jos. R. Underwood,	"	Dec. 24, 1828
Robert Trimble,	"	April 13, 1807	Richard A. Buckner,	"	Dec. 21, 1829
William Logan,*	"	Jan. 11, 1808	Samuel S. Nicholas,	"	Dec. 23, 1831
George M. Bibb,	"	Jan. 31, 1808	Ephraim M. Ewing,	"	March 5, 1835
John Boyle,	"	April 1, 1809	Thos. A. Marshall,	"	M'ch 18, 1835
William Logan,	"	Jan. 20, 1810	Daniel Breck,	"	April 7, 1843
James Clark,	"	M'ch 29, 1810	James Simpson,	"	June 7, 1847

*Resigned January 30, 1808.

Of the chief justices, Muter, Boyle, and Robertson were in commission, collectively, about 41 years—Muter for about 11, Boyle 16, and Robertson nearly 14 years; and of all the justices of the court, Logan, Mills, and Owsley held their stations longest.

In the year 1803, Muter, very poor and rather superannuated, was induced to resign by a promise of an annuity of $300, which, being guarantied by an act of the legislature in good faith, was complained of as an odious and unconstitutional "provision," and was taken away by a repealing act of the next year.

Under the first constitution of 1792, the appellate judges were required to state in their opinions such facts and authorities as should be necessary to expose the principle of each decision. But no mode of reporting the decisions was provided by legislative enactment until 1815, when the governor was authorized to appoint a reporter. Previously to that time, James Hughes, an eminent "land lawyer," had, at his own expense, published a volume of the decisions of the old District Court of Kentucky whilst an integral portion of Virginia, and of the Court of Appeals of Kentucky, rendered in suits for land—commencing in 1785 and ending in 1801 : Achilles Sneed, clerk of the Court of Appeals, had, in 1805, under the authority of that court, published a small volume of miscellaneous opinions, copied from the court's order book; and Martin D. Hardin, a distinguished lawyer, had, in 1810, published a volume of the decisions from 1805 to 1808, at the instance of the court in execution of a legislative injunction of 1807, requiring the judges to select a reporter. George M. Bibb was the first reporter appointed by the Governor. His reports, in four volumes, include opinions from 18— to

18—. Alexander K. Marshall, William Littell, Thomas B. Monroe, John J. Marshall, James Dana, and Benjamin Monroe were, successively, appointed, and reported afterwards. The reports of the first, are in three volumes—of the second, in six—of the third, in seven—of the fourth, in seven—of the fifth, in nine—and the last, who is yet the reporter, has published seven volumes. Consequently, there are now forty-six volumes of reported decisions of the Court of Appeals of Kentucky. Of these reports, Hardin's, Bibb's, and Dana's are most accurate—Littell's, Thomas B. Monroe's and Ben. Monroe's next. Those of both the Marshall's are signally incorrect and deficient in execution. Dana's in execution and in the character of the cases, are generally deemed the best. Of the decisions in Dana, it has been reported of Judge Story that he said they were the best in the Union—and of Chancellor Kent, that he said he knew no state decisions superior to them. And that eminent jurist, in the last edition of his Commentaries, has made frequent reference to opinions of chief justice Robertson, and has commended them in very flattering terms.

The comprehensive jurisdiction of the court imposes upon it duties peculiarly onerous. An act of Assembly of 1796, confers on this Appellate Court jurisdiction of appeal or writ of error, "in cases in which the inferior courts have jurisdiction." A writ of error may be issued to reverse a judgment or decree for one cent; but, by an act of 1796, no appeal can be prosecuted to reverse a judgment or decree, unless it relate to a franchise or freehold, or (if it do not) unless the amount of it, "exclusive of costs," be at least $100. But in cases of decretal divorces, and in fines for riots and routs, the legislature has denied to the court any revising jurisdiction. Still, although it has no original jurisdiction excepting only in the trial of clerks, and although it has no criminal jurisdiction in any case of felony, the average number of its annual decisions has, for many years, been about five hundred. The court is required to hold two terms in each year—one commencing the first Monday in May, the other the first Monday in September; and no term is allowed to be less than forty-eight juridical days. By a rule of court, any party may appear either by himself or his counsel, and in person or by brief. And a majority of the cases have been decided without oral argument.

A statute of 1816 enacted, that "all reports of cases decided in England since the 4th of July, 1776, should not be read in court or cited by the court." The object of this strange enactment was to interdict the use of any British decision since the declaration of American independence. The statute, however, literally imports, not that no such decision shall be read, but that "all" shall not be. And this self-destructive phraseology harmonises with the purpose of the act—that is, to smother the light of science and stop the growth of jurisprudence. But for many years, the Court of Appeals inflexibly enforced the statute—not in its letter, but in its aim. In the reports, however, of J. J. Marshall, and Dana, and Ben. Monroe, copious references are made (without regard to this interdict) to post-revolutionary cases and treatises in England, and now that statute may be considered dead.

The Appellate Court of Kentucky has generally been able, and always firm, pure, and faithful. It has been illustrated by some names that would adorn any bench of justice or age of jurisprudence. And it might have been oftener filled by such jurists, had not a suicidal parsimony withheld from the judges an adequate compensation for the talents, learning, labor, and responsibility which the best interests of the commonwealth demand for the judicial service, in a court appointed to guard the rights and the liberties of the people, and to settle conclusively the laws of the commonwealth.

HISTORICAL SKETCH

OF THE

BAPTIST CHURCH.

The Baptists were the pioneers of religion in Kentucky. They came with the earliest permanent settlers. In 1776, William Hickman, sr., commenced here his labors in the Gospel ministry.* He was the first to proclaim " the unsearchable riches of Christ," in the valley of the Kentucky. He was on a tour of observation merely, and after a stay of several months, returned to Virginia, remained several years, and then located in this state, where he labored faithfully in the field of the gospel for more than fifty years. In 1779, John Taylor, Joseph Reding, Lewis Lunsford, (the Patrick Henry of the pulpit), and several other ministers of Virginia, visited Kentucky. They found many of their brethren, but owing to the constant alarm from savage depredations, and the other stirring incidents peculiar to new settlements amid the wilds of a strange and unbroken forest, there seemed to be but little concern manifested for religion. These ministers had but few opportunities for preaching. They did preach, however, at a few of the stations. Their object was chiefly to see the country, with reference to subsequent settlement. They found it destitute of almost everything except grass for their horses, and meat from the woods, procured at the risk of life. They could do but little more than feast their eyes upon the luxuriant soil, which the Indians had resolved should never be cultivated.† These ministers, except Reding, returned to Virginia, but some of them, a few years later, took permanent residence in Kentucky.

In 1780, many Baptists removed to this state, chiefly from Virginia; but it was not until the next year, that there was an organized church. This was the Gilbert's creek church. When Lewis Craig left Spottsylvania county, Va., most of his large church there came with him. They were constituted when they started, and were an organized church on the road—wherever they stopped, they could transact church business. They settled at Craig's station on Gilbert's creek, a few miles east of where the town of Lancaster, Garrard county, is now situated.‡ There were now a number of efficient ministers in Kentucky.

In 1782, several other churches are known to have been constituted, viz: Severn's valley,‖ (now Elizabethtown), and Nolynn, both now in Hardin county. Also Cedar creek, now in Nelson county.§

In 1783, the first Baptist church and the first worshiping assembly of any order, was organized on South Elkhorn, five miles south of Lexington, by Lewis Craig, principally out of members dismissed from the church on Gilbert's creek. This church was for forty years one of the most prosperous churches in the state; but its candlestick has been removed.**

After the close of the American Revolution, a flood of Baptists poured into Kentucky, chiefly from Virginia, and churches began to spring up every where in the wilderness. It was still a time of great peril. Before houses of worship were erected, the worshipers would assemble in the forest, each man with his gun; sentinels would be placed to guard against surprise from the Indians, while the minister, with a log or stump for his pulpit, and the heavens for his sounding board, would dispense the word of life and salvation.

> " The groves were God's first temples. Ere man learned
> To hew the shaft, and lay the architrave,
> And spread the roof above them, ere he framed
> The lofty vault, to gather and roll back
> The sound of anthems, in the darkling wood,

---

* John Taylor's History of Ten Churches, p. 48.   ‖ Benedict, vol. 2, p. 542.
† Benedict's History of the Baptists, vol. 2, p. 228.   § Asplund's Register of 1790, p. 32.
‡ History of Ten Churches, p. 42.   ** History of Ten Churches, p. 50.

Amidst the cool and silence, he knelt down,
And offered to the Mightiest solemn thanks
And supplications."*

In 1785, three associations were organized, viz.: The ELKHORN, comprising all the regular Baptist churches then north of the Kentucky and Dix rivers; the SALEM, comprising all the churches of the same order south of those rivers; and the SOUTH KENTUCKY, comprising all the separate Baptist churches in the State. These associations, which were constituted of some three or four churches each, increased with great rapidity. In 1790, there were attached to them 42 churches and 3105 members; viz.: Elkhorn, 15 churches and 1389 members; Salem, 8 churches and 405 members: and South Kentucky, 19 churches and 1311 members. The population of Kentucky at that period was about 73,000. So there was one Baptist to about every twenty-three inhabitants. Besides, there were many churches not yet associated; and many members just moved into the state, who were not yet attached to the churches. There were, too, at this period, 42 ordained ministers and 21 licentiates; or one ordained minister to every 1825 of the inhabitants. This was a tolerably fair proportion of Baptist leaven to the whole lump of people.†

Among the ministers of that day, were John Gano, Ambrose Dudley, John Taylor, Lewis Craig, William Hickman, Joseph Reding, William E. Waller, Augustine Eastin, Moses Bledsoe, John Rice, Elijah Craig, William Marshall, and other kindred spirits—men of ardent piety, untiring zeal, indomitable energy of character, of vigorous and well-balanced intellects, and in every way adapted to the then state of society. Pioneers to a wilderness beset with every danger and every privation, they were the first ministers of the brave, the daring, and noble spirits who first settled and subdued this country—such men as the Boones, the Clarkes, the Harrods, the Bullitts, the Logans, the Floyds, and the Hardins would respect and venerate, and listen to with delight and profit. It has been the good fortune of the writer to hear some of these venerable ministers preach. Some of them survived many years the men of their own generation. But age seemed to bring to them few of its infirmities. They retained almost to the last the vigor of their manhood's prime: and although they could not be called *literary* men, they were nevertheless distinguished for their intelligence, for commanding talents, for profound acquaintance with the doctrines of the Bible, and were possessed of a knowledge of men and things, which eminently qualified them to be teachers and guides of the people.

In 1793, an attempt was made to bring about a union between the Regular and Separate Baptists, which failing of success, sundry churches of the South Kentucky association withdrew from that body, and organized the TATE'S CREEK association.‡ The oldest churches in this association were organized at the dates following: Tate's creek, now in Madison county, 1785;§ White Oak, in the same county, 1790;‖ and Cedar creek, now Crab Orchard, Lincoln county, 1791.§

In 1798, the number of churches in the Elkhorn association being 33, and its territory extending from the Holstein on the south, to Columbus, Ohio, on the north; and from the mouth of Beargrass on the west, to the Virginia line on the east, it was deemed expedient to dismiss the churches north of Licking river for the purpose of forming a new organization; and accordingly the BRACKEN association was constituted. The oldest churches in this association are, Limestone creek** (now extinct), near the present city of Maysville, and Washington, both constituted in 1785; and Mayslick church, constituted 1791.††

The general harmony of the denomination was undisturbed, and their progress steady and healthful. In 1799, commenced what is known to this day as the *Great Revival*, which continued through several years. During its prevalence, the accessions to the churches in every part of the state were unprecedented. The Baptists escaped almost entirely those extraordinary and disgraceful scenes produced by the *jerks*, the *rolling* and the *barking exercises*, &c., which extensively obtained among some other persuasions of those days. The work among the

---

* Bryant.   ‖ Benedict. vol. 2, p. 540.
† Asplund's Register, p. 33.   § Asplund. p, 32.   ** Ibid.
‡ Benedict, vol. 2., p. 238.   †† Benedict, *ut supra*.

Baptists was deep, solemn, and powerful; but comporting with that decency and order so emphatically enjoined in the scriptures. During this revival, large additions were made to the churches in every quarter of the State. The Elkhorn association, at its annual meeting in 1801, reported an addition of 3011 members by baptism during the current year; and in 1802, an accession of twelve churches was reported, making the whole number of members, 5310. So numerous were the churches, and so extensive still were the boundaries, it was thought advisable again to divide the association, and accordingly those churches lying along the Ohio river, west of the Bracken association, were dismissed and organized into the NORTH BEND association.

To the South Kentucky, the accessions were almost equal to those of the Elkhorn association. It too became of such unwieldy dimensions, as to demand a division. It was accordingly separated into two bodies, in 1802; the part north of the Kentucky river being denominated the NORTH DISTRICT association, and the part south of the river, the SOUTH DISTRICT association.

The Tate's creek association reported in 1801, the addition of 1148 members by baptism. The Salem association also shared largely in the blessings of this revival. It received upwards of 2000 members. Its boundaries were extended north of Salt river, where enough churches were gathered to justify the organization of the LONG RUN association in 1803.*

The GREEN RIVER association, lying in what are now Warren, Barren, Green, and Adair counties, was constituted in 1800, about the beginning of the Great Revival in that section of the state. It contained at first, nine churches, eight ministers, and about three hundred and fifty members. The very first year of its existence, it increased to more than one thousand members, and in 1804, it contained 38 churches, and comprised so much territory that it was deemed sound policy to divide it into three bodies. The middle portion of the churches retained the old name of the association: those of the northern portion were organized into the RUSSEL'S CREEK association: and those of the southern portion, into the STOCKTON'S VALLEY association.†

This revival had the happy effect to bring about a union between the REGULAR and SEPARATE Baptists. These distinctive names were imported from Virginia, and mean the same as those of *Particular* and *General* Baptists in England—the former meaning those who hold to Calvinistic, and the latter those holding Arminian sentiments. Several unsuccessful efforts had been made to effect a union between the Regular and Separate Baptists in Kentucky; but the Great Revival removed all obstacles. Melted into love by its influences, these kindred parties then mingled into one. In 1801, terms of union previously agreed upon by a committee appointed for the purpose, were ratified by the two parties in their respective associations. The names Regular and Separate were henceforth to be laid aside, and that of the *United Baptists* used in their stead. Thus was consummated the " General Union."

But the harsh note of discord was heard just as the sweet melody of revival and brotherly love began to subside, and ere they had ceased. In 1796, James Garrard, a Baptist minister and a member of Cooper's run church, Bourbon county, was elected Governor of Kentucky. He appointed to the office of secretary of state, Harry Toulmin, who had been a follower of Dr. Priestly in England, and a minister of the Unitarian persuasion. Mr. Toulmin was a gentleman of talents and erudition.‡ It was owing perhaps to the intimacy existing between Gov. Garrard and Secretary Toulmin, arising in part from their official relations, that the former became tinctured with Unitarian sentiments. Be that as it may, it is certain that in 1802, Mr. Garrard and the pastor of Cooper's run church, Augustine Eastin, a minister of considerable eminence, began to propagate Arian, or rather, Socinian sentiments. The majority of Cooper's run church, and several neighboring churches to which Mr. Eastin preached, espoused the doctrines of Garrard and their ministers. Every effort was made to reclaim these individuals and churches. The Elkhorn association promptly attended to the case, but failing to effect their return to the old paths, reluctantly dropped them from connection and correspondence. It may be recorded to the credit of this association, and of

---

the Baptists, that although Garrard and Eastin were much beloved, and of powerful influence, yet they could take but a very inconsiderable fraction with them, which declined gradually and noiselessly away. Unitarianism could never obtain favor with the Baptists.[*]

About the same time, in the South District association, a very popular minister, John Bayley, embraced the sentiments of the Restorationists. He was generally believed to be a very pious man, and the majority of the association was devotedly attached to him; and insisted, that although he preached this doctrine, yet he did it in such a manner as not to offend the most delicate ear. The minority, however, thought differently, refused all fellowship for him and his adherents, and claimed to be the association. The neighboring associations acknowledged their claim : the other party could not obtain any countenance from the associations in the General Union, and again assumed the old name of the South Kentucky association of Separate Baptists.[†]

About 1804, Carter Tarrant, David Barrow, John Sutton, Donald Holmes, Jacob Gregg, George Smith, and other ministers of less note, with many of their members, declared for the abolition of slavery; alledging that no fellowship should be extended to slaveholders, as slavery, in every branch of it, both in principle and practice, was a sinful and abominable system, fraught with peculiar evils and miseries, which every good man ought to abandon and bear testimony against. They called themselves " Friends of Humanity," but are known in the records of those times by the name of " Emancipators." The associations generally declared it " improper for ministers, churches, or associations to meddle with the emancipation of slavery, or any other political subject; and advised them to have nothing to do with it in their religious capacity." These resolutions gave great offence to the "Friends of Humanity ;" and they withdrew from the General Union of Baptists, and in 1807, formed an association of their own, called " The Baptized Licking-Locust Association, Friends to Humanity." They were quite numerous at first, but they soon dwindled—consumed in the fires of their own zeal. Not a vestige of them remains.[‡]

In 1809, a respectable and highly influential portion of the ministers and churches of the Elkhorn association withdrew, not only from that body, but from the General Union of Baptists in the state, and organized the " LICKING ASSOCIATION OF PARTICULAR BAPTISTS." This schism had its foundation in a personal difficulty between Jacob Creath and Thomas Lewis, *about a negro trade !* The former was pastor, and the latter a member of the Town-fork church, a few miles west of Lexington. The matter was not suffered to remain in the church where it properly belonged ; it became a topic of general conversation, and of the printing press ; other churches became involved in it; it gathered other matters in its progress ; when finally, it was thrust upon the association, and schism ensued.[||]

But notwithstanding these adverse events, the course of the Baptists was onward. They were refreshed with many revival seasons. In 1812, they had 13 associations, 285 churches, 183 ministers, and 22,694 members. The population of the state at that time was rising 400,000. So that the proportion of the Baptists to that of the inhabitants was about one to twenty.[§]

During the next twenty years, no event transpired among the Baptists deemed of sufficient consequence to claim a notice in this brief sketch, except the schism produced by what is generally known as the " reformation," begun and carried on by Alexander Campbell. This is not the place nor the occasion to discuss the principles involved in that unfortunate controversy. Suffice it to say, that in 1829, and for several years thereafter, until 1832, a great many divisions in associations and churches occurred. But in spite of all this, the Baptists stood firm, and still retained their accustomed ratio to the population of the state. In 1832, after this storm had spent its fury, after the greatest secession from the Baptist ranks ever known in their history in Kentucky, they had 33 associations, 484 churches, 236 ordained ministers, and 34,124 members. The population of the state, by the census of 1830, was 687,917—so that the Baptists still retained their proportion of about one to twenty of the inhabitants.[**]

[*] Benedict, vol. 2, p. 231. [||] Benedict, vol. 2, p. 233–4.
[†] Ib., 241. [§] Benedict, vol. 2., p. 545. and Bap. Mem'l. Feb. 1846, p. 54.
[‡] Baptist Herald of 1814, p. 80. [**] Baptist Memorial, *ut supra*, p. 55.

The depletion proved to be sanative. The increase of the Baptists since then has been unprecedented. Disturbed by no serious discord, if we except the clamor raised against missionary and other benevolent efforts, they have been blessed with many remarkable instances of divine favor. In the next ten years they had doubled their numbers! But it is not in this way alone that they have been the most blessed. They have been aroused to every good work. They have engaged, with considerable zeal, in the cause of missions, foreign and domestic. They have now a GENERAL ASSOCIATION, for the purpose of aiding weak churches, and of supplying the destitute portions of the state with the gospel. They have also a state society for foreign missions; and a state bible society for the circulation of the holy scriptures in all lands. The board of the American Indian mission association is located in Louisville. They have a weekly newspaper and a monthly magazine published in the state. The subject of education, too, has engrossed a large share of their attention. The Georgetown college is under their patronage, and is one of the most respectable and flourishing literary institutions in the West. The Western Theological institute of the Baptists is situated in Covington. We have not the means of arriving at the *precise* number of Baptists now (March 1847), in the state; but there are in the General Union, 42 associations, 685 churches, and at least 65,000 members. To these add the 7,085 anti-missionary Baptists, many of whom claim to be United Baptists, and differ from the great body of their brethren only in relation to the propriety of missionary and kindred institutions, and we have the present grand total of the Baptists in Kentucky, 72,085 members, which we are sure falls under the actual number. The proportion of the Baptists to the population of the state may safely be set down at one to eleven. Thus it will be seen that the Baptists have steadily and rapidly increased—that they have come triumphantly through every trial. Hitherto hath the Lord helped them.

In looking over the list of the early Baptist ministers, the pioneers of the gospel in our state, we cannot choose *one* for a biographical sketch, agreeably to the suggestion of the compiler of this work. Out of a host equally deserving, it would be invidious to make a selection. Besides, the brief space that remains for us, would not allow of justice to any one of them. We will therefore let it suffice to submit some characteristic anecdotes and sketches of several of them.

WILLIAM HICKMAN, as the first preacher in Kentucky, claims of course, the first attention. He commenced his ministry in this state. Then he returned to Virginia, and for several years labored there with great success. In 1784, he became a permanent resident in the state. Here he encountered peculiar trials. The country was sparsely populated, while tribes of wandering savages were continually making depredations on the property and lives of the settlers. But Mr. Hickman was not silent because of danger. He traveled extensively, and even in the most distant and exposed settlements, and at the peril of his life, bore the tidings of salvation. Elder John Taylor said of him in 1822, " Though now about 76 years of age, he walks and stands erect as a palm tree, being at least six feet high, and of rather slender form. His whole deportment is solemn and grave, and is much like Caleb, the servant of the Lord, who at fourscore years of age was as capable to render service in war, as when young. This veteran can yet perform a good part in the gospel vineyard. His style of preaching is plain and solemn, and the sound of it like thunder in the distance; but when he becomes animated, it is like thunder at home, and operates with prodigious force on the consciences of his hearers." He was pastor a number of years to the church at the " Forks of Elkhorn." He baptised, it is thought, as many persons as any minister that ever labored in the state.

LEWIS CRAIG was the founder of the first worshipping congregation in Kentucky. He had been a valiant champion of the cause in Virginia. He was several times imprisoned in that state for preaching the gospel. The first time, he was arrested in company with several other ministers. The prosecuting attorney represented them to be a great annoyance to the county by their zeal as preachers. " May it please your worships," said he, " they cannot meet a man upon the road, but they must ram a text of scripture down his throat." As they passed on to prison, through the streets of Fredericksburgh, they united in singing the lines,

" Broad is the road that leads to death," &c.

They remained in prison one month, and while there, Mr. C. preached through the grate to large crowds, and was the means of doing much good. Once after this, he was imprisoned three months. Mr. Taylor says of him, " He was in the gospel ministry near sixty years, and was about eighty-seven when he gave up the ghost. As an expositor of scripture, he was not very skillful, but dealt closely with the heart. He was better acquainted with men than with books. He never dwelt much on doctrine, but most on experimental and practical godliness. Though he was not called a great preacher, perhaps there was never found in Kentucky so great a gift of exhortation as in Lewis Craig : the sound of his voice would make men tremble and rejoice. The first time I heard him preach, I seemed to hear the sound of his voice for many months. He was of middle stature, rather stoop shouldered, his hair black, thick set and somewhat curled, a pleasant countenance, free spoken, and his company very interesting; a great peace-maker among contending parties. He died suddenly, of which he was forewarned, saying, I am going to such a house to die ; and with solemn joy he went on to the house, and with little pain, left the world."

JOHN TAYLOR was well qualified to labor as a pioneer, having learned by previous hazards in Virginia, to endure hardness as a good soldier of Jesus Christ. When first settled in Kentucky, he itinerated for ten years with much credit to himself, and profit to the cause. He had a fine constitution and much bodily strength; was as bold as a lion, yet meek as a lamb. In preaching, he attempted nothing but scriptural plainness. The weapons of his warfare were wielded with much power. No man knew better than he, how to reprove, rebuke, and exhort, with all long suffering and doctrine. When he used the rod of correction, all were made to tremble. He was very efficient as a preacher. His judicious zeal, strong faith, and remarkable industry, qualified him to be useful to many souls. He was always cheerful, yet solemn, and willing to preach when requested. His whole demeanor, at home and abroad, was uniformly Christian-like. The labors of his ministry extended from the Kentucky to the Ohio river. It was his custom to visit six or eight associations every year. His great skill in discipline and faithfulness in preaching endeared him to all the followers of Christ. He lived to see his children and his children's children rise up and call him blessed. He died in his 82d year.*

JOHN GANO settled in Kentucky in 1787. He was one of the most eminent ministers in his day. He was a native of New Jersey. He spent many years as an itinerant, traveling over the United States, from New England to Georgia. He was pastor for about twenty-five years in the city of New York, and his labors were greatly blessed. During the revolutionary war, he was chaplain in the army, and by his counsels and prayers greatly encouraged the American soldiery in those times of peril *which tried men's souls.* Many interesting anecdotes are related of him, several of which we will quote from Benedict. One morning, while in the army and on his way to pray with the regiment, he passed by a group of officers, one of whom (who had his back towards him) was uttering his profane expressions in a most rapid manner. The officers, one after another, gave him the usual salutation. " Good morning, Doctor," said the swearing Lieutenant. " Good morning, sir," replied the chaplain ; "you pray early this morning." " I beg your pardon, sir." " O, I cannot pardon you : carry your case to your God."

One day he was standing near some soldiers who were disputing whose turn it was to cut some wood for the fire. One profanely said, he would be d——d if he cut it. But he was soon afterwards convinced that the task belonged to him, and took up the axe to perform it. Before, however, he could commence, Mr. Gano stepped up and asked for the axe. " O ! no," said the soldier, " the chaplain shan't cut wood." " Yes," replied Mr. Gano, " I must." " But why ?" asked the soldier. " The reason is," answered Mr. G., "I just heard you say that you would be d——d if you cut it, and I had much rather take the labor off your hands, than that you should be made miserable forever."

While he resided in New York, he was introduced to a young lady as the

---

* Lives of Virginia Baptist Ministers, p. 220.

daughter of a very prominent citizen. "Ah!" replied he. "and I can tell a good match for her, and he is an only son." The young lady understood his meaning; she was, not long after, united to this Son, and has, for about forty years, been an ornament to his cause.

Dr. Furman, of Charleston, S. C., who knew him intimately, says: "As a minister of Christ, he shone like a star of the first magnitude in the American churches, and moved in a widely extended field of action. For this office, God had endowed him with a large portion of grace, and with excellent gifts. He *believed*, and therefore *spake*." Having discerned the excellence of gospel truths, and the importance of eternal realities, he felt their power on his own soul, and accordingly he inculcated and *urged* them on the minds of his hearers with persuasive eloquence and force. He was not deficient in doctrinal discussion, or what rhetoricians style the demonstrative character of a discourse; but he excelled in the pathetic—in pungent, forcible addresses to the heart and conscience. The careless and irreverent were suddenly arrested, and stood awed before him, and the insensible were made to feel. * * * * He lived to a good old age; served his generation according to the will of God; saw his posterity multiplying around him; his country independent, free, and happy; the church of Christ, for which he felt and labored, advancing; and thus he closed his eyes in peace; his heart expanding with the sublime hope of immortality and heavenly bliss. Like John, the harbinger of our Redeemer, "he was a burning and a shining light, and many rejoiced in his light." Resembling the sun, he arose in the church with morning brightness, advanced regularly to his station of meridian splendor, and then gently declined with mild effulgence, till he disappeared, without a cloud to intercept his rays, or obscure his glory."

Such were some of the early ministers of Kentucky. They are but examples of the dispositions, and talents, and high moral worth of their companions and compeers, a sketch of whom we must omit, and who aided these to unfurl the banner of the cross in the valley of the Kentucky, and to maintain it against every danger and privation. The Christians of this State may as proudly refer to their ancestors, in all that is noble and elevating in man, as may the politician. If theirs were mighty in battle and wise in counsel, ours were no less so, and in a nobler sense, because in a higher and holier enterprise.

HISTORICAL SKETCH

OF THE

CHRISTIAN CHURCH.

BACON COLLEGE.

THIS institution, located at Harrodsburg, Ky., was chartered by the commonwealth of Kentucky in the winter of 1836–7. Though it has not yet completed the tenth year of its existence, and has had to contend with no ordinary difficulties, it has already secured an enviable reputation, and is making steady progress in gaining the confidence of the public. The course of studies is equal to that which is generally adopted in the best regulated American colleges; and the officers, without exception, have had long and successful experience in the business of teaching. The following is a list of the

FACULTY.

James Shannon, President, and Professor of Intellectual, Moral, and Political Science.

Samuel Hatch, Professor of Chemistry, Natural Philosophy, Geology, &c.

Henry H. White, Professor of Mathematics and Civil Engineering.

George H. Matthews, Professor of Ancient Languages.

E. Askew, Teacher of the Preparatory Department.

During the last session, one hundred and thirteen students were received into Bacon college, from the states of Kentucky, Virginia, Georgia, Alabama, Mississippi, Lousiana, Indiana, Ohio, and New York. About the same number have already been received the present session, with a reasonable prospect of a large increase. Tuition for the college year of ten months is forty dollars, with an extra charge for fuel of one dollar each half session.

Boarding can be had in respectable families, in the town and its vicinity, at rates varying from one dollar and seventy-five cents to two dollars per week; so that the whole cost of boarding and tuition for the college year of forty-two weeks need not exceed one hundred and fifteen dollars.

The session begins on the first Monday in September, and ends on the last Friday in June, which is the annual commencement.

Connected with the Institution, are two literary and debating societies, each of which has a respectable library. Whole number of volumes in the libraries pertaining to the college about sixteen hundred.

In Bacon college the authority of Christianity is fully recognized; but nothing that savors in any degree of a sectarian character is either taught or required. The institution was established by the Christian churches of Kentucky, and from them it derives its principal support. Efficient aid has also been received, at various times, from men of liberal and enlightened minds, who are not members of any religious society.

At a general meeting of the Christian Churches in Kentucky, held at Harrodsburg, in May, 1834,

An agent was appointed to visit the churches, ascertain the number of members in each congregation, and collect such other information as he might deem important, and report the result at the next general meeting. The following extract is taken from this

REPORT.

" I find in the state 380 congregations, with an aggregate number of 33,830 members; average number 83 and a fraction.

" Number of additions reported for twelve months prior to receiving the report from each church, 3,678; number since reported, 206; total number of additions reported, 3,884. It must be remarked, however, that these additions go back as far as June 1st, 1843; yet, as the report is for 12 months prior to collecting the items from each church, my returns, with the exception of the 206, show but the increase for one year. It must also be remarked, that many of the churches report no increase at all, owing mainly to the fact, that the information was collected from individuals unacquainted with this item. I have no doubt, could the increase have been obtained from all the churches, it would exceed four thousand.

" Number of elders reported, 666; number of deacons, 676; number of preachers, evangelist and local, 195.

" Of the 380 churches, 163 meet for worship every Lord's day; and, in many places, three times on Lord's day, and several times through the week; 68 meet semi-monthly, 6 tri-monthly, 92 monthly, and 51 did not report this item. A large majority of those that meet monthly and semi-monthly, would meet every Lord's day, but are prevented in consequence of holding houses of worship in partnership with others.

" I deem it important to state, that 136 of these churches have been organized within the last four and a half years."

As the average time that has elapsed, since the foregoing information was collected, exceeds two years, a moderate estimate of the increase to the present date (Dec. 1846), will give an aggregate number of 41,186. This calculation is based upon the hypothesis, that the annual increase for the last two years has barely equalled the ascertained increase for twelve months prior to the collection of the statistics embodied in the report. It is confidently believed that this estimate falls considerably below the truth.

The churches aforesaid are unanimous in repudiating human creeds and unscriptural names; believing that the Bible is ordained of God to be the only authoritative, as it is *the only infallible* rule of faith and practice; and that all unscriptural names, and all ecclesiastical organizations, not established by the inspired Apostles, are unlawful, and, in their very nature, sectarian and divisive.

Influenced by these views, they call themselves Christians, or Disciples of Christ, and feel religiously bound to repudiate all names, that are not applied in the New Testament to those, who "have been baptized into Christ," and have thus "put on Christ." To believe what God says, and to do what he commands, they regard as the sum total of human duty; nor do they believe that any man is authorized to hope for an admission into the everlasting kingdom of our Lord and Savior Jesus Christ, except as he is using his best powers, day by day, to purify himself from all filthiness of the flesh and spirit, and to perfect holiness in the fear of God. When the believer obeys God's commands, *then*, but not till then, do they conceive, that he has a right to appropriate God's promises. Consequently, when the penitent believer confesses Christ before men, and from the heart bows to his authority, being baptized in obedience to his command, he has a right to appropriate to himself all those promises that are made to baptized believers as such; but he has, even then, no right to hope for a continuance of the divine favor, except so far as he makes it the business of his life to know the will of God, and to do that will in all things.

For all purposes of discipline and government, they regard the individual church as the highest, and indeed the only ecclesiastical organization recognized in the New Testament. "As for associations, conferences, conventions, &c., presuming to act under the sanctions of a divine warrant, or claiming to be a court of Jesus Christ, or to decide on any matters of conscience, or to do any act or deed interfering with, or in opposition to, the perfect independenc of each individual congregation, or at all legislating for the churches in any district of the country,"—they regard it as "altogether foreign to the letter and spirit—to the precepts and examples—to the law and to the testimony of the Christian books." One and all, they profess to be engaged in persevering efforts for the union of all saints, by the restoration of unsectarian Christianity in faith and practice, as it is found, pure and unpolluted, on the pages of the New Testament.

Among the host of worthies, living and dead, who have co-operated hitherto in this grand enterprise, the name of Alexander Campbell stands deservedly pre-eminent. Others may have preceded him, and no doubt did, in repudiating human creeds and adopting the bible as the only and all-sufficient rule of faith and practice; of union, communion, and co-operation among the followers of the Lamb. Others may have been more successful, and no doubt were, as proclaimers of the Gospel, in making proselytes to the cause, and adding members to the various churches. But, as a master spirit, exciting investigation, overturning antiquated prejudices, enlightening the master spirits of the age, and setting them to work, each in his own sphere, it is the deliberate opinion of a mighty host, that, in the current reformation of the nineteenth century, Alexander Campbell has no equal. On this subject the venerable and beloved Barton W. Stone, in 1843, and shortly before his death, remarks—"I will not say there are no faults in brother Campbell; but that there are fewer, perhaps, in him, than any man I know on earth; and over these few my love would draw a veil, and hide them from view forever. I am constrained, and willingly constrained to acknowledge him the greatest promoter of this reformation of any man living. The Lord reward him!"

The writer of this article applied to President Campbell for facts and documents, that might furnish the basis of a short biographical sketch, and received for reply the following information—"Averse to autobiography, and to giving a man's biography while living, I have left the task for one who may survive me."

A few leading facts, however, may be noted for the information of the reader. Alexander Campbell was born, about the year 1787 or 8, in the county of Down, in the north of Ireland, where he spent the first fourteen years of his life, and was then removed to Scotland, the land of his fathers, to complete his education for the Presbyterian ministry. In 1809 he came to America with his father, Elder Thomas Campbell, who is still living. Naturally of an independent and investigating mind, he soon became convinced that infant sprinkling is unscriptural, and was forthwith baptized upon a profession of his faith. Prosecuting his inquiries still farther, he soon discovered that he had imbibed many other doctrines unauthorised by the Scriptures, and contrary to them. All such he relinquished without delay, having nobly resolved, that he would sacrifice every thing for the truth, but the truth for nothing.

In allusion to this part of his life, he remarks, in the conclusion of the Christian Baptist—" Having been educated as Presbyterian clergymen generally are, and looking forward to the ministry as both an honorable and useful calling, all my expectations and prospects in future life were, at the age of twenty-one, identified with the office of the ministry. But scarcely had I begun to make sermons, when I discovered that the religion of the New Testament was one thing, and that of any sect which I knew was another. I could not proceed. An unsuccessful effort by my father to reform the presbytery and synod to which he belonged, made me despair of reformation. I gave it up as a hopeless effort, but did not give up speaking in public assemblies upon the great articles of Christian faith and practice. In the hope, the humble hope, of erecting a single congregation, with which I could enjoy the social institutions, I labored. I had not the remotest idea of being able to do more than this; and, therefore, betook myself to the occupation of a farmer, and for a number of years attended to this profession for a subsistence, and labored every Lord's day to separate the truth from the traditions of men, and to persuade men to give up their fables for the truth—with but little success I labored."

In 1816 he was urged by some of the most influential Baptists in New York and Philadelphia, to settle in one of those cities, but declined—alledging in justification of his course, that he did not think the church in either city would submit to the primitive order of things; and rather than produce divisions among them, or adopt their order, he " would live and die in the backwoods."

In August 1823, soon after the Debate with MacCalla, he commenced the publication of the " Christian Baptist," a monthly pamphlet, the design of which was " to restore a pure speech to the people of God—to restore the ancient order of things in the Christian kingdom—to emancipate the conscience from the dominion of human authority in matters of religion—and to lay a foundation—an imperishable foundation, for the union of all Christians, and for their co-operation in spreading the glorious gospel throughout the world."

In the debate aforesaid, Mr. Campbell contended that " baptism was a divine institution, designed for putting the legitimate subject of it in actual possession of the remission of his sins." In January 1828, he remarks, " It was with much hesitation I presented this view of the subject at that time, because of its perfect novelty. I was then assured of its truth, and, I think, presented sufficient evidence of its certainty. But having thought still more closely upon the subject, and having been necessarily called to consider it more fully, as an essential part of the Christian religion, I am still better prepared to develop its import."

From the time of the debate, *baptism for the remission of sins* seems to have been but little agitated, if at all publicly, till 1827. In that year Walter Scott and John Secrest began to preach in the bounds of the Mahoning association, Ohio, the apostolic doctrine of remission, recorded in Acts 2d, 38. The effect was astounding to the advocates of the worn-out and powerless systems of human origin. During the last six months of the year, Elder Secrest immersed with his own hands *for the remission of sins,* " five hundred and thirty persons."

The writer has not the means of ascertaining exactly how many were immersed during the year by the pious, indefatigable, and talented Walter Scott. It is certain, however, that he converted and baptized a mighty host—more, perhaps, than any other uninspired man ever did in the same length of time.

The Mahoning association, at their meeting of that year, determined to employ Brother Scott for the whole of his time the next twelve months, preaching and teaching in the bounds of the association. This appointment was highly commended by Bro. Campbell in the " Christian Baptist" for October following.

The editor remarks, " Brother Walter Scott, who is now in the field, accepted of the appointment ; and few men on this continent understand the ancient order of things better than he. His whole soul is in the work." The results of this appointment, and the success of the pleadings for the ancient gospel were everywhere triumphant. Soon a host of able advocates in various parts embraced the same views, and began to propagate them with zeal and success—especially in Kentucky and Ohio. The clergy became alarmed. The work of proscription and anathema commenced ; and, in a short time, the advocates of the same gospel that was preached by Peter on the day of Pentecost, and by all the apostles, were driven out of the Baptist communion, and reluctantly compelled to establish separate churches, that they might enjoy the liberty wherewith Christ had made them free. Sons, whilst they read the record, in a more enlightened and Christian age, will blush for the bigotry and intolerance of their sires.

At the completion of the 7th volume of the Christian Baptist, in 1830, the Editor thus writes—" I had but very humble hopes, I can assure the public, the day I wrote the first essay, or the preface for this work, that I could at all succeed in gaining a patient hearing. But I have been entirely disappointed. The success attendant on this effort has produced a hope, which once I dared not entertain, that a blissful revolution can be effected. It has actually begun, and such a one as cannot fail to produce a state of society, far surpassing, in the fruits of righteousness, and peace, and joy, any result of any religious revolution, since the great apostacy from Christian institutions."

In 1830, the Millennial Harbinger was begun, and has continued to be issued monthly down to the present time. These periodicals, aided by several others, and by a numerous host of zealous and indefatigable advocates, have spread the principles of this reformation with a rapidity that has perhaps no parallel in the history of the world, except the progress of primitive Christianity in the times of the apostles. Already do the " Christian Churches" in these United States number, as it is confidently believed, more than 200,000 members ; and the cause is successfully pleaded, not merely in the Canadas, in England, Scotland, and Wales, but also in almost every part of the civilized world.

While A. Campbell was thus laboring in the western part of Virginia, and even before he made his appearance on the public stage, another distinguished actor, impelled by a kindred spirit, was shaking time-honored religious systems to their very center in the heart of Kentucky. I mean that much calumniated, but great and good man

BARTON WARREN STONE.

The subject of this sketch was born in Maryland on the 24th day of December, 1772. His father dying while he was very young, his mother in 1779, with a large family of children and servants, moved into what was then called the backwoods of Virginia—Pittsylvania county, near Dan river. Here he went to school for four or five years to an Englishman, named Sommerhays, and was by him pronounced a finished scholar. In February, 1790, he entered a noted academy in Guilford, North Carolina, under the care of Dr. David Caldwell, determined, as he himself says, to " acquire an education, or die in the attempt." His design at that time was to qualify himself for a barrister.

When he first entered the academy, about thirty or more of the students had embraced religion under the labors of James McGready, a Presbyterian preacher of great popularity and zeal. In about a year from this time, after a long and painful "experience," he became a member of the Presbyterian church, and turned his thoughts to the ministry.

In 1793, at the close of his academic course, he commenced the study of divinity under the direction of Wm. Hodge, of Orange county, North Carolina. Here Witsius on the Trinity was put into his hands. The metaphysical reasonings of this author perplexed his mind, and he laid the work aside as unprofitable and unintelligible. He heard of Dr. Watts' treatise on the Glory of Christ; sought after and obtained the work ; read it with pleasure, and embraced its views. The venerable Henry Patillo, on whom it devolved, at the next meeting of the Presbytery, to examine the candidates on the subject of theology, had himself embraced Watts' views of the Trinity. As might reasonably be expected under such circumstances, the examination on this topic was short, and embraced no peculiarities of the system.

In April, 1796, he was licensed by the Orange Presbytery, North Carolina, and shortly afterwards directed his course westward (preaching at various points on the route), to Knoxville and Nashville, in Tennessee, and thence to Bourbon county, Kentucky, where about the close of the year 1796 he settled within the bounds of the congregations of Cane-ridge and Concord. Here he labored with great zeal, acceptance and success; about eighty members having been added to his church in a few months!!

In the fall of '98, he received a unanimous call from those congregations to become their settled pastor, which call he accepted. A day was set apart by the presbytery of Transylvania for his ordination. Having previously notified the leading members of the presbytery with respect to his difficulties on the subject of the Trinity, also on the doctrines of election, reprobation, and predestination, *as taught in the Confession of Faith*, when he was asked, "Do you receive and adopt the Confession of Faith, as containing the system of doctrine taught in the Bible?" he answered aloud, so that the whole congregation might hear—"I do, as far as I see it consistent with the word of God." No objection being made, he was ordained.

Early in 1801, "the Great Revival" commenced in Tennessee, and in the southern part of Kentucky, under the labors of James McGready, and other Presbyterian ministers. Determined to hear and judge for himself, Barton W. Stone hastened to a great Presbyterian camp-meeting in Logan county, Kentucky, where for the first time he witnessed those strange exercises of falling, jerking, dancing, &c.

Filled with the spirit of the revival, he returned to his congregations—related what he had seen and heard, and, with great earnestness and zeal, dwelt on the universality of the gospel, and urged the sinner to believe now, and be saved. The effects were immediate and powerful; the "*exercises*" made their appearance; a series of meetings followed; the work spread in all directions; multitudes united with the different churches; and, for a time, party creeds, names, and feelings, seemed to be buried in Christian love and union.

The "Great Caneridge Meeting" commenced in August following, and continued some six or seven days. From twenty to thirty thousand were supposed to be collected. Many had come from Ohio, and other remote parts, who, on their return, diffused the spirit in their respective neighborhoods. Methodist and Baptist Preachers united heartily in the work, and the salvation of sinners seemed to be the great object of all.

About this time, Robert Marshall, John Dunlavy, Richard McNemar, B. W. Stone, and John Thompson, all members of the synod of Kentucky, renounced the dogmas of Calvinism, and taught wherever they went, that Christ died for all—that the divine testimony was sufficient to produce faith—and that the spirit was received, not in order to faith, but *through faith*. The sticklers for orthodoxy, seeing the powerful effects of these doctrines, were for a time afraid to oppose. At length the friends of the Confession determined to arrest the progress of these anti-calvinistic doctrines, and put them down. The presbytery of Springfield, in Ohio, first took McNemar under dealings; and from that presbytery the case came before the synod of Lexington, Ky., in September, 1803.

So soon as they discovered, from the tone of the synod, that its decision in McNemar's case would be adverse, the five drew up a protest against the proceedings, and a declaration of their independence, and withdrawal from the jurisdiction of that body. Immediately after their withdrawal from the synod, they constituted themselves into a presbytery, which they called the Springfield presbytery. They had not, however, worn this name more than one year, before they saw that it savored of a party spirit. With the man-made creeds they threw it overboard, and took the name *Christian*—the name given to the disciples by divine appointment first at Antioch. "From this period" (says Stone), "I date the commencement of that reformation, which has progressed to this day." (1843). Soon after their withdrawal from the synod, they were joined by Matthew Houston and David Purviance.

In 1805, Houston, McNemar, and Dunlavy joined the Shakers; and in 1807,

Marshall and Thompson, after vainly attempting to enslave their associates a second time to a creed, returned back into the bosom of the Presbyterian church. Meanwhile the subject of baptism had begun to arrest the attention of the churches. Many became dissatisfied with their infant sprinkling. The preachers baptized one another, and crowds of the private members came, and were also baptized. The congregations generally submitted to it, and yet the pulpit was silent on the subject.

About the same time, Barton W. Stone and some others began to conclude that baptism was ordained for the remission of sins, and ought to be administered in the name of Jesus Christ to all believing penitents. At a great meeting at Concord, he addressed mourners in the words of Peter, (Acts ii, 38), and urged upon them an immediate compliance with the exhortation. He informed us, however, that " into the spirit of the doctrine he was never fully led, until it was revived by Bro. Alexander Campbell some years after."

Although Elder Stone repudiated the orthodox views on the subject of the Trinity, Sonship, and Atonement, he never acknowledged the sentiments with which he was so frequently charged by his opponents. And in the latter part of his life, he often regretted that he had allowed himself to be driven in self-defence to speculate on these subjects as much as he had done. In the near prospect of death he averred, that he had never been a Unitarian, and had never regarded Christ as a created being.

He died in the triumphs of faith, on the 9th day of November, 1844, universally beloved and regretted by all who knew him. A worthy Methodist preacher in Jackson, Louisiana, once remarked to the writer of this article, in the presence of two old-school Presbyterian clergymen—" I know Barton W. Stone well, having lived neighbor to him for a considerable time in Tennessee. A lovelier man, or a better Christian, in my judgment, never lived; and he is no more a Unitarian, than those brethren there are"—addressing himself at the same time to the two preachers. The person who, from a regard to truth and justice, bore this honorable testimony, was Mr. Finley, son of Dr. Finley, (a former president of the University of Georgia), and brother of the Secretary of the American Colonization Society.

Stone justly occupies a high rank as a scholar, a gentleman, and a Christian. In the department of poetry, his talents fitted him to shine, had they been cultivated. There can hardly be found, in the English language, a lovelier, sweeter hymn, than one from his pen, written during the revivals about the beginning of the present century, and universally admired by the Christian world ever since. Be it known to the orthodox calumniators of Barton W. Stone, and to all men who have souls to feel the power either of religion or of poetry, that he is the author of that soul-inspiring hymn, in which the orthodox world has so greatly delighted for nearly half a century, viz.,

"The Lord is the fountain of goodness and love."

A short account of the union between Stone's friends and those of Alexander Campbell, in 1832, shall close this hasty and imperfect sketch. In 1843, B.W. Stone writes thus:—" I saw no distinctive feature between the doctrine he (A. Campbell) preached, and that which we had preached for many years, except on baptism for the remission of sins. Even this I had once received and taught, as before stated, but had strangely let it go from my mind, till Brother Campbell revived it afresh. *   *   *   " He boldly determined to take the Bible alone for his standard of faith and practice, to the exclusion of all other books as authoritative. He argued that the Bible presented sufficient evidence of its truth to sinners, to enable them to believe it, and sufficient motives to induce them to obey it—that until they believed and obeyed the gospel, in vain they expected salvation, pardon, and the Holy Spirit—that now is the accepted time, and now is the day of salvation."

"These truths we had proclaimed and reiterated through the length and breadth of the land, from the press and from the pulpit, many years before A. Campbell and his associates came upon the stage, as aids of the good cause. Their aid gave a new impetus to the reformation which was in progress, especially among the Baptists in Kentucky; and the doctrines spread and greatly increased in the west. The only distinguishing doctrine between us and them was, that they preached baptism for remission of sins to believing penitents. This doctrine had not generally obtained amongst us, though some few had received it, and practised accordingly. They insisted also on weekly communion, which we had neglected." * * *

"Among others of the Baptists who received, and zealously advocated the teaching of A. Campbell, was John T. Johnson, than whom there is not a better man. We lived together in Georgetown, had labored and worshipped together. We plainly saw, that we were on the same foundation, in the same spirit, and preached the same gospel. We agreed to unite our energies to effect a union between our different societies. This was easily effected in Kentucky; and in order to confirm this union, we became co-editors of the Christian Messenger. This union, I have no doubt, would have been as easily effected in other states as in Kentucky, had not there been a few ignorant, headstrong bigots on both sides, who were more influenced to retain and augment their party, *than to save the world* by uniting according to the prayer of Jesus."

The biographer of Elder Stone informs us, that the union was consummated in the following manner:

"A meeting of four days was held at Georgetown, embracing the Christmas of 1831, and another at Lexington of the same length, embracing the New Year's day of 1832. The writer had the happiness to be in attendance at both these meetings.

"At these meetings the principles of our union were fully canvassed, which were such as we have stated. We solemnly pledged ourselves to one another before God, to abandon all speculations, especially on the Trinity, and kindred subjects, and to be content with the plain declarations of scripture on those topics, on which there had been so much worse than useless controversy. Elder John Smith and the writer were appointed by the churches, as evangelists to ride in this section of Kentucky, to promote this good work. In that capacity we served the churches three years. Thousands of converts to the good cause was the result of the union and co-operation of the churches, and their many evangelists during that period ; and I look back to those years as among the happiest of my life."

As the short space allowed to this article precludes the possibility of doing it justice, the reader who desires further information, is referred to the Christian Baptist, and to the " Biography of Barton W. Stone," by Elder John Rogers, of Carlisle, Kentucky—an excellent work just out of press.

HISTORICAL SKETCH

OF THE

CUMBERLAND PRESBYTERIAN CHURCH.

The Cumberland Presbyterian church was organized in Tennessee in 1810, by the constitution of the Cumberland Presbytery. One of the leading ministers, however, resided in Kentucky at the time of the organization. In 1813 the original presbytery was divided into three presbyteries, one of which included those ministers and congregations that adhered to the Cumberland presbytery in its difficulties with the Presbyterian church. There are now two synods in the state, the Green river and the Kentucky synods. The number of ordained ministers in the two synods is sixty-five; of licentiates, thirty; of candidates for the ministry, twenty-five. The whole number of communicants is estimated at 7000.

The operations of the church have been mainly confined to the south-western portion of the state. Many of its ministers and members were pioneers in that section of country. They found much of the country physically and morally in a state of nature. Their labors, sacrifices, and self-denial were necessarily very great; but it will be seen from the preceding statistics that they did not labor in vain. The early ministers of the Cumberland Presbyterian church were remarkable for a bold, manly, and impressive eloquence. They were western men in the full sense of the expression. Without the training of the schools, they were nevertheless reared up and brought into the ministry under circumstances well calculated to develop all their energies. With indomitable perseverance, and without worldly compensation, they performed an important part in converting a "wilderness," a moral desolation, into a "fruitful field." They were men for the country and the times. Long will they live in the memory of that generation in which they labored, and long in south-western Kentucky will their influence be felt after a short-lived generation shall have passed away.

HISTORICAL SKETCH

OF THE

EPISCOPAL CHURCH.

THE convention of the diocese of Kentucky was organized in 1830. Its first bishop was consecrated Oct. 31st, 1832.

There are about 20 clergymen in the diocese, 13 of whom are officiating in as many organized parishes. There are six missionary stations, and sixteen church edifices. The whole number of families is about 600, and of communicants 650.

Shelby college was organized in 1836, and transferred to the Episcopal church in 1841. It has graduated two very small classes. Its presidency is now temporarily vacant.

The Theological Seminary was chartered in 1834. It has an excellent library of above three thousand volumes, and funds to the amount of $12,000. Its library is now deposited in the library room of Shelby college.

The Rev. JOHN LYTHE, of the Episcopal church, or church of England, came early to Kentucky. When Col. Henderson established his proprietary government in 1775, Mr. Lythe was a delegate from the Harrodsburgh station or settlement to the legislative assembly. The delegates met on the 23d of May, 1775, and the assembly being organized, "divine service was performed by the Rev. Mr. Lythe, one of the delegates from Harrodsburg." In the records of this legislative assembly, we note the following proceedings:

"The Rev. Mr. Lythe obtained leave to bring in a bill *to prevent profane swearing and Sabbath breakng.* After it was read the first time, it was ordered, says the journal, ' to be re-committed; and that Mr. Lythe, Mr. Todd, and Mr. Harrod be a committee *to make amendments.*'

" Mr. Todd, Mr. Lythe, Mr. Douglas, and Mr. Hite were appointed a committee to draw up a contract between the proprietors and the people of the colony."

On the day succeeding the adjournment of the legislature of Transylvania, (for so this legislative council was termed,) " divine service," the same journal records, " was performed by the Rev. Mr. Lythe, of the church of England." And it was under the shade of the same magnificent elm, that the voices of these rude hunters rose in accents of prayer and thanksgiving to the God of their fathers—

that the verdant groves of the land of the savage and the buffalo, first rang with the anthems of the Christian's worship, and echoed back the message of the Redeemer of the world. It was fit it should be so, for

" The groves were God's first temples."[*]

We know nothing further of the Rev. John Lythe, except what is contained in these extracts of the proceedings of the " Legislature of Transylvania." He was doubtless the first minister of the gospel who penetrated the wilds of Kentucky; and, from the fact that he was elected to the legislative assembly—that he officiated as chaplain—and that his name appears on some important committees, he must have been a man of some note.

The Rev. JAMES MOORE was the first minister of the Episcopal church of the United States, who permanently located in Kentucky. He emigrated to the State in 1792, from Virginia, and was at that time a candidate for the ministry in the Presbyterian church. His trial sermons not being sustained by the Transylvania presbytery, Mr. Moore became displeased with what he considered rigorous treatment, and in 1794 sought refuge in the bosom of the Episcopal church. Soon afterwards he became the first rector of Christ's church in Lexington. In 1798, he was appointed acting president of Transylvania university, and professor of Logic, Metaphysics, Moral Philosophy, and Belles-Lettres. This situation he held for several years, during which Transylvania enjoyed a good degree of prosperity. Mr. Moore was distinguished for sound learning, devoted piety, courteous manners, and liberal hospitality.

The Rev. BENJAMIN ORR PEERS was born in Loudon county, Virginia, in the year 1800. His father, the late Major Valentine Peers, of Maysville, (a soldier of the revolutionary army) emigrated to Kentucky in 1803, when the subject of this brief notice was only three years old. Mr. Peers received the first rudiments of an academical education in the Bourbon academy, and completed his scholastic course at Transylvania university, while under the administration of Dr. Holley. He studied theology at Princeton. After completing his course in that institution, he connected himself with the Episcopal church, having previously belonged to the Presbyterian. He located in Lexington, where he established the Eclectic Institute, which became, under his supervision, one of the most valuable institutions of learning in the west. During the time he was at the head of the Eclectic Institute, and subsequently, he spent much time, labor, and money in the cause of common school education, and was instrumental in arousing the public attention to the importance of the subject—the present common school system of Kentucky being the result of the popular will thus brought to bear upon the question.

Mr. Peers, while at the head of the Eclectic Institute, was chosen president of Transylvania university, which position he accepted, in opposition to the advice of many warm friends, and which he held but a very brief period. At the time of his decease, in the year 1842, at Louisville, he was editor of the Episcopal Sunday School Magazine at New York, and, also, editor of the Sunday School publications of the church. He was distinguished not only for his zealous devotion to the cause of general education, but for his sound learning and ardent piety. His published writings were not extensive—the work on *Christian Education* appears to have been his favorite. He fell early, but fell at the post of duty.

---

*Gov. Morehead's Boonesborough Address.

METHODIST EPISCOPAL CHURCH.

THE early history* of Methodism in Kentucky, is, to a certain extent, obscure and indefinite, arising partly from the want of proper documents, and partly from the difficulty of collecting those that are in existence.

The most authentic and reliable information in regard to the origin and progress of Methodism in the United States, is to be gathered from the minutes of the several annual conferences; but these, consisting mainly of statistical accounts, are rather meager and unsatisfactory. Yet brief as these records are, they throw a steady and continuous light upon the rise and progress of Methodism in Kentucky, down to the present time. From these conference documents we gather the fact, that the first traveling preachers appointed to labor in the State of Kentucky, were

JAMES HAW AND BENJAMIN OGDEN.

These two men were appointed to travel the entire State in the year 1786, and were the *first regular itinerant ministers*, who, under the control of the Methodist Episcopal church, commenced the work of spreading " Scriptural holiness over these lands."

At the time of their appointment, it appears that there were no regular societies in existence in Kentucky, as is evidenced by the entire absence of statistical information in the minutes. James Haw and Benjamin Ogden were, therefore, the first to collect the scattered Methodist emigrants of the " Dark and Bloody Ground" into classes, and organize them into societies. The first Methodist Episcopal church organized in Kentucky, was in the cabin of Thomas Stevenson, about two and a half miles south-west of Washington, Mason county, by Benjamin Ogden, some time during the year 1786.

1787. The appointments for this year were

Kentucky—James Haw, Elder. Thomas Williamson, Wilson Lee.

Cumberland—Benjamin Ogden.

The numbers in society, reported at the close of this year were, whites, 90, colored, none.

1788. Kentucky—Francis Poythress, James Haw, Elders.

Lexington ct.—Thomas Williamson, Peter Massie, Benjamin Snelling.

Cumberland—D. Combs, B. McHenry.

Danville—Wilson Lee.

Numbers at the close of this year, whites, 479, colored, 64.

Lexington circuit embraced the northern part of the State; Cumberland circuit, the few societies which were in the lower end of the State and middle Tennessee: Danville circuit the center of Kentucky south of the Kentucky river.

1789. The same number of ministers were sent this year to the Kentucky work as on the previous year, and the arrangement of the circuits remained same.

The summer and fall of '89 and spring of '90, was a season of gracious revival; the "desert was made to rejoice, and the wilderness and the solitary place to blossom as the rose." The word of God, among the early settlers, was accompanied "with the demonstration of the Spirit and power," and the numerical strength of the church was more than doubled.

The numbers in society at the close of this year were, whites, 1037, colored, 51.

1790. Conference was held this year for the first time in Kentucky, on the 26th of April, at Masterson's station, about five miles west of Lexington.

This conference was the first attended in the west by Bishop Asbury. The

---

* For the facts in these sketches, we are indebted mainly to the Rev. William Burke, of Cincinnati, and to the published minutes of conference; many of the sketches of pioneer ministers are in the language of the minutes.

conference was composed of twelve preachers, the bishop, and Hope Hull, the traveling companion of the bishop. At the close of the conference, which was held this year in Charleston, South Carolina, Bishop Asbury, attended by Hope Hull, started on his journey to Kentucky, to meet the western preachers in conference. In his journal, the bishop speaks of his trip in the following language. "After crossing the Kentucky river," he says, "I was strangely outdone for want of sleep, having been greatly deprived of it during my journey through the wilderness, which is like being at sea in some respects, and in others worse. Our way is over mountains, steep hills, deep rivers, and muddy creeks, a thick growth of reeds for miles together, and no inhabitants but wild beasts and savage men. Sometimes, before I was aware, my ideas would be leading me to be looking out ahead for a fence, and I would, without reflection, try to recollect the houses we should have stopped at in the wilderness. I slept about an hour the first night, and about two the last. We ate no regular meal—our bread grew short, and I was very much spent."

Speaking of the preachers who were then traveling in the wilds of Kentucky, the bishop says: "I found the poor preachers indifferently clad, with emaciated bodies, and subject to hard fare, but I hope rich in faith." At the winding up of the first visit, he says: "My soul has been blessed among these people, and I am exceedingly pleased with them. I would not for the worth of all the place, have been prevented in this visit." The following appointments were made at this conference:

1790. F. Poythress, presiding elder.
Lexington circuit—Henry Birchett, David Haggard.
Limestone   "   S. Tucker, J. Lillard.
Danville   "   Thomas Williamson, Stephen Brooks.
Madison   "   B. McHenry, Benjamin Snelling.
Cumberland   "   Wilson Lee, James Haw, Peter Massie.

A brief sketch of the life and labors of the men who composed this first conference, and who are emphatically the pioneer ministers of the Methodist Episcopal church, may not be out of place.

FRANCIS ASBURY, the presiding bishop, stands among that hardy and laborious band supremely pre-eminent,—"In labors more abundant than they all." Landing from England, on the shores of our country, on the 27th of October, 1771, from that hour until the termination of his pilgrimage, his clear and manly voice was heard upon all occasions, lifting itself up against sin, and in favor of the gospel of Christ. The trump of the gospel, when applied to his lips, gave no uncertain sound; his mind was clear, discriminating, and logical; he was rich— by the "word of God dwelling in him richly in all wisdom;" he was great—by the spirit of glory and of God which rested upon him; and for the space of forty-five years, he moved as an "angel" among the churches, "feeding the flock of Christ," and building the believer up in his most holy faith. Perhaps no man, since the settlement of America, has traveled as extensively, and labored as untiringly, overcoming so many serious obstacles, as the apostolic Asbury. His foot-prints have been left wide and deep upon "the sands of time." He preached "Jesus and the resurrection" along the sea-board, from Maine to Georgia—from the Atlantic out west, until, from the rude cabin of the frontier squatter, the unbroken forest re-echoed back the burden of his embassy. Of this first visit to Kentucky, in his journal he says: "I rode about three hundred miles to Kentucky in six days, and back by way of Tennessee, about five hundred miles, in nine days. O! what exertions for man and beast." While performing these journies, too, the bare earth for days was his bed, and his only covering the protecting wing of his "ministering angel." After spending fifty-five years in the ministry, forty-five of which were spent in America, he was transferred by the Great Superintendent to the church above, on the 21st of March, 1816. His name unstained—his labors and hardships unsurpassed—the name of Francis Asbury will be remembered in all the greenness of affection, while the pure doctrines of Methodism have a votary.

FRANCIS POYTHRESS was admitted into the traveling connection at a conference held in Baltimore, on the 21st of May, 1776. In 1778, he was sent out to Kentucky in the capacity of elder. As a preacher, few in those days excelled him.

His voice clear and musical; his knowledge of the scriptures vast and accurate; his sermons bedewed with his tears in his closet, fell as the dews of life upon the hearts of his congregation; sinners trembled before the Lord, and the keen flash of the Spirit's sword was felt passing all through the soul, discerning by its brightness, " the thoughts and intents of the heart." In the visit Bishop Asbury made to Kentucky in 1790, a single note made in his journal pours a flood of light upon the secret of his success. He says: " I met the preachers in conference," and adds: "Brother Poythress is much alive to God." Sermons anointed with the spirit of God, and baptized in the blood of the Lamb, will always " burn as fire in dry stubble." Brother Poythress continued to travel in the west, mainly in Kentucky, until the spring of 1800, when he attended the general conference held in Baltimore, at which conference he was appointed to a district in North Carolina, including circuits from the sea shore to the summit of the Blue Ridge. The excessive draughts made upon his mind and body, by the labor of this district, unsettled his mental balance, so that during the summer he became partially deranged.

In the fall of 1800, he returned to Kentucky to his sister's, the widow Prior, who then resided in Jessamine county, about three miles from Nicholasville, where he remained a confirmed lunatic until his death.

HENRY BIRCHETT was born in Brunswick county, State of Virginia. He continued between five and six years in the ministry, a gracious, happy, useful man, who freely offered himself for four years' service in the dangerous stations of Kentucky and Cumberland. Birchett was one among the worthies who cheerfully left safety, ease, and prosperity, to seek after and suffer faithfully for souls. His meekness, love, labors, prayers, tears, sermons, and exhortations, were not soon forgotten. He died in peace, in Cumberland circuit, on the western waters, in February, 1794.

DAVID HAGGARD came out with Birchett, as a volunteer from the Virginia conference, to do battle in the hard service of Kentucky. He was appointed as colleague with Birchett on the Lexington circuit in 1790, and traveled a few years in Kentucky with considerable acceptability, when he joined O'Kelley's* party, returned to the east, and died in connection with the New Lights.

JAMES HAW was admitted into the traveling connection at a conference held on the 17th of April, 1782, at " Ellis's preaching house," in Sussex county, Virginia, and appointed to labor as one of the first two ministers in Kentucky, in 1786, where he continued to travel until 1791, when he located and settled in Sumner county, Tennessee. In 1795, he joined O'Kelly's party. In 1800, he attached himself to the Presbyterian church, joined in with the Cumberland Presbyterians when they separated from the mother church, and finally died in their communion, a few years after, on his farm in Sumner county.

PETER MASSIE entered the connection in 1789, and traveled successively the Danville, Cumberland, and Limestone circuits. At the close of '91, he departed for a purer clime. The published account briefly states that, " He labored faithfully in the ministry for upwards of three years, confirmed and established in the grace of God, and useful. An afflicted man, who desired and obtained a sudden death, by falling from his seat and expiring December 19th, 1791, at Hodge's station, five miles south of Nashville." He was the first who fell in the harness on the western waters.

SAMUEL TUCKER was appointed from the Baltimore conference of 1790, to Limestone circuit (now Maysville). Leaving his friends and all behind, he started to preach Jesus on the work assigned him, but in descending the Ohio river, at or near the mouth of Brush creek, about thirty miles below Portsmouth, the boat in which he was descending was attacked by Indians, and the most of the crew were killed; but he continued to defend the boat with his rifle, until it floated out into the stream, beyond the reach of the Indians pursuing. He arrived at Limestone, and there died of his wounds. His remains now lie in the cemetery in Maysville, unhonored—the spot unknown.

* O'Kelly separated from the Methodist Episcopal church on the subject of episcopacy and the elective franchise, in November, 1792.

BENJAMIN SNELLING was admitted into connection in 1788, and sent to travel the Lexington circuit that year. He continued in Kentucky but a short time, and then returned to the east, and after remaining some time, he returned to Kentucky, settled in Bath county, where he finally died.

JOSEPH LILLARD was born in Kentucky, not far from Harrodsburg, and admitted into the traveling connection at the first conference held in Kentucky, at Masterson's station, April 26th, 1790. He was appointed that year to Limestone circuit. He traveled but a few years, and died near Harrodsburgh, in a located relation.

BARNABAS MCHENRY embraced religion and attached himself to the Methodist Episcopal church in the infancy of Methodism in the United States. Believing it to be his duty to preach the gospel, he joined the traveling connection in 1787. In 1788, he was sent to Cumberland circuit, and continued to labor in the various circuits of Kentucky, faithfully and successfully, until 1796, when, in consequence of the loss of health, he located. In 1819, he was re-admitted into the traveling connection; but his strength not being sufficient for the labors of an effective man, he was, in 1821, returned superannuated. This relation he sustained until death by cholera, June 16th, 1833, relieved him of all his infirmities. As an old apostle of Methodism, he was fond of the doctrines of the church, and took delight in teaching them to others. He lived in the enjoyment of the blessing of sanctification, and died in peace, going up from earth to take a position of nearer concernment in the lofty worship of heaven.

WILSON LEE was born in Sussex county, Delaware, November, 1761, and admitted into the traveling connection in 1784. He was sent out to labor in Kentucky in 1787, and continued to labor in the different appointments assigned him, as a man of God esteemed very highly, for his work's sake, until 1792. From that conference he was transferred to the east, where he continued to labor until he finished his course, by the rupture of a blood vessel, in Anne Arundel county, Maryland, October 11th, 1804. Wilson Lee was a preacher of no ordinary acceptability, correct in the economy of himself and others. As an elder and presiding elder he showed himself a workman that needed not to be ashamed. Professing the sanctifying grace of God, he carried about him the air and port of one who had communion with heaven; his life and conversation illustrated the religion he professed. He was neat in his dress, affable in his manners, fervent in his spirit, energetic in his ministry, and his discourses were fitted to the characters and cases of his hearers. His labors and his life were laid down together. It may be truly said, that he hazarded his life upon all the frontier stations he filled, from the Monongahela to the Cumberland river, all through Kentucky, in many of which stations there were savage cruelty and frequent deaths. He had to ride from station to station, and from fort to fort, sometimes with, and sometimes without a guide.

BENJAMIN OGDEN was born in New Jersey in 1764. In early life he was a soldier of the revolution, which gave distinction and independence to his country. He embraced religion in 1784, at the age of 20. Progressing like Timothy in the knowledge of religion, he united himself with the traveling connection in 1786, and received his first appointment to the then wilderness of Kentucky, in connection with James Haw, as a missionary : and to him belongs the honor of organizing the first Methodist Episcopal church in Kentucky, in the house of Thomas Stevenson, of Mason county. Ill health compelled him to desist from traveling in 1788, remaining in a located relationship for nearly thirty years. In 1817, he re-entered the traveling connection, but soon sunk again under the pressure of ill health—but earnestly desirous to be more extensively useful than he could be in that relation, he attempted the work of an itinerant again in 1824, and continued an effective man until 1827, when he was placed upon the superannuated list, and remained so until his death in 1834. Benjamin Ogden was a man of good natural intellect, and various attainments as a Christian minister. He was especially well instructed in the principles, and deeply imbued with the spirit of his vocation, as a primitive Methodist preacher. After a long life of laborious toils and effective service in the furtherance of the gospel, this venerable servant of God and his church—one of the first two missionaries who penetrated the vast valleys of the Mississippi—was released by death from his militant charge—expiring in all the calmness and confidence of faith and hope, went to his reward.

JOHN PAGE was admitted into the traveling connection at Holstein on the 15th of May, 1791. He came over with Bishop Asbury to Kentucky, and was stationed on the Lexington circuit. Traveled Danville circuit in '93—Salt river in '94—Limestone in '95—Green circuit, Holstein conference in '96—Hinkston in '97—Salt river and Shelby in '98—Cumberland in '99—Holstein, Russell, and New river in 1800—Cumberland in 1801—ditto in 1802. In 1803, he was appointed as presiding elder on the Cumberland district. In 1804 he located. Sometime afterwards he joined in a superannuated relation, and now lives on the Cumberland river, in Tennessee, near the mouth of Caney fork.

BENJAMIN NORTHCOTT was admitted on trial at the second conference that was held in Kentucky, at Masterson's station, May 1st, 1792, and appointed that year to Lexington circuit. In 1793 he was sent to Limestone circuit. This year he married and settled in the neighborhood of Flemingsburg, where he now lives—a preacher of holiness—illustrating the same in life.

JAMES O'CULL was admitted on trial at Uniontown, Pennsylvania, July 28th, 1791, and appointed with Barnabas McHenry to Cumberland circuit, (comprehending middle Tennessee). From Cumberland he returned back to Kentucky, married near Lexington, and afterwards settled on the North fork of Licking river, in Mason county, Kentucky, where a few years past he left for the "land that is afar off, where the King is seen in his beauty."

JOHN RAY was admitted on trial in 1791, and appointed to Limestone circuit. Traveled Green circuit in '93—New river circuit, Virginia, in '94—Bedford, Virginia, in '95—Amherst, Virginia, in '96—Tar river circuit, North Carolina, in '97—Roanoke, North Carolina, in '98—Tar river circuit in '99—Caswell circuit, North Carolina, in 1800. Located in 1801, and returning to Kentucky, settled near Mount Sterling, where he lived a number of years, after which he was readmitted into the Kentucky conference, and a few years past moved to Indiana, and there passed from earth to the spirit land.

WILLIAM BURKE was born in Loudon county, Va., on the 13th of January, 1770, and was received into the traveling connection in 1791, at McKnight's, on Tar river, North Carolina, and appointed to West New river, in Virginia. Met again in conference in the next year in the rich valley of Holstein, near the salt works, on the 15th May, and appointed to Green circuit, in the Western Territory (now East Tenn.). Met again in conference at Nelson's on the 13th of April, 1793, at which conference he volunteered for Kentucky, came out and attended the conference held at Masterson's station on the 6th of May, 1793, and was appointed that year to Danville circuit. Met again in conference at Bethel Academy, in Jessamine county, on the 15th of April, 1794, and appointed to Hinkston circuit. During the year traveled Hinkston, Salt river, and Lexington. As a faithful, effective, and laborious itinerant, William Burke continued to travel various circuits and districts in Kentucky, Tennessee, North Carolina, and Ohio, until 1808, when he was changed from effective to a supernumerary relation, and appointed to Lexington circuit. In 1809 he was appointed to the Green river district, and continued in that extensive and laborious work, until conference met in Cincinnati, October 1st, 1811, when he was appointed to the Miami circuit, including Cincinnati. In 1812, from the conference which met that year in Chillicothe, he was appointed to Cincinnati station, the *first* station west of the mountains. In the fulfilling of that work, he lost his voice entirely, and was placed in a supernumerary relation for several years. He then superannuated, which relation he now sustains to the Kentucky conference. As a preacher, William Burke stood among the first in his day. Possessing a cultivated and accurate memory, he stored it richly with Bible truths, and joining with his biblical knowledge a deep acquaintance with human nature, he was enabled to adapt his sermons to the varied characters of his hearers; nor did he fail, whenever a fit occasion offered, to rebuke sin boldly in high places. Possessing a large, muscular frame, he had a great deal of native physical courage, and this, added to high moral purpose, made him one of the most fearless and at the same time most effective men in planting the gospel of Jesus Christ in a new country. There are thousands in Kentucky, who yet remember the voice of William Burke pealing the thunders of Sinai around them, and then softly wooing the melted heart to the foot of the cross. He is still living in Cincinnati, his faculties unimpaired, and his attachment to the cause of Christ undiminished. Long may he be spared to guide by his discriminating counsel the ark of Methodism.

Methodism, planted as we have seen in Kentucky, as late as 1786, grew rapidly up to 1790 in numbers. In that year, at the conference held at Masterson's station, the numbers reported were

	Whites.	Colored.
Lexington	424	32
Limestone	66	—
Danville	322	26
Madison	212	8
Cumberland	241	41
	1265	107

Limestone circuit was taken from Lexington, and Madison from Danville circuit, this year. When we take into consideration the fact that the country was at that time sparsely populated, the increase of numbers is somewhat surprising. In a little more than three years from the hour that the first missionary of the Methodist Episcopal church began to preach among them a *free, present, and full salvation*, we find that a church has sprung up, embracing within its pale a membership of nearly 1400. Well might the hardy pioneers of that day say "behold what God has wrought." The increase of membership in Kentucky appears to have been steady and uniform in its growth.

In 1791 there were...................... *Whites* 1459   *Colored* 94
In 1792 " .... " 2059   " 176

Bishop Asbury, in his journal, speaks of attending the Kentucky conference this year, which was held on the 26th of April, at Masterson's station, and says, "Vast crowds of people attended public worship,—the spirit of matrimony is prevalent here; in one circuit both preachers are settled—the land is good—the country new—and indeed all possible facilities to the comfortable maintainance of a family are afforded to an industrious, prudent pair."

In 1795 there were whites 2262, colored 99.

This year FRANCIS ACUFF, for three years a traveling preacher, was called home to his reward. He was a young man of genius and improvable talents : he was brought up in Sullivan county, Tennessee, and died in August, 1795, near Danville in Kentucky, in the twenty-fifth year of his age. Bishop Asbury, speaking of his death says, "Francis Acuff from a fiddler, became a christian—from a christian a preacher—from a preacher I trust a glorified saint."

In 1800, the ordained preachers who had been traveling in the west, were requested by Bishop Asbury, to attend the general conference held that year in Baltimore, in order that their fields of labor might be changed, and new preachers sent out to the western work. Consequently the majority of the old traveling preachers were recalled from the west, and an almost entirely new supply sent out.

The minutes for 1800 stand thus—

NO'S. IN CONNECTION.

	Whites.	Colored.
Scioto and Miami—Henry Smith	467	1
Limestone—William Algood	417	20
Hinkstone—William Burke	283	4
Lexington—Thomas Allen	273	15
Danville—Hezekiah Harriman	339	67
Salt river and Shelby—John Sale	167	7
Cumberland—William Lambeth	247	40
Green—James Hunter	434	22
Holstein, Russell and New river, } John Watson, John Page	621	64
	3248	240

9

No presiding elder being appointed that year, the first five circuits named above, were taken oversight of by William Burke. Harriman and Sale, being the only other elders in the entire western country, took charge of the remainder. The time of the meeting of the conference was changed this year from spring to the fall, and met in October at Bethel academy. Bishops Asbury and Whatcoat attended at this conference. William McKendree was appointed presiding elder for Ohio, Kentucky, Tennessee and part of Western Virginia.

WILLIAM McKENDREE, whose name is in all the churches, and who was like an illuminated torch sent down for awhile from the upper sanctuary, to burn in the golden candlesticks of God's house on earth,—came out with Asbury and Whatcoat in the fall of 1800 from the Virginia conference, and at the conference held that year at Bethel in October, was appointed presiding elder for all the western country, comprehending in his district the whole of Kentucky and part of three other states, viz: Ohio, Virginia and Tennessee. He continued traveling as elder over that immense scope of country for two years, when the district was divided into three parts—Holstein district, Cumberland district and Kentucky district. McKendree remained presiding elder of the Kentucky district for three years, when he was appointed to Cumberland district in the fall of 1806, and continued traveling in that work, until the general conference of 1808, held that year in Baltimore, when he was elected bishop, and in that relation he continued for twenty-five years, visiting successively all the states in the Union, often made the instrument in the hands of the Holy Spirit of breathing fresh life into the churches, and then again like the youthful David, of smiting some proud defier of Israel low. As a christian, William McKendree combined solemnity and cheerfulness together in such a manner as to command the reverence and esteem of all about him. As a preacher of the gospel, his sermons were replete with the sweet story of the cross—mingling together the sublime discoveries of faith and the sweet anticipations of hope, in such a manner as to captivate and entrance the hearts of his hearers. He departed for a home in Heaven in 1833. He sleeps sweetly.

From the conference of 1800, the church continued steadily to advance both in numbers and spirituality. The summer and fall of this year witnessed the commencement of those gracious outpourings of the Holy Spirit, which soon obtained the appellation of "THE GREAT REVIVAL." This work, commencing in Tennessee and the lower parts of the state of Kentucky, gradually spread upwards into the interior of the State, leavening the country all around; camp meetings attended by convening thousands, and continuing for days and nights and sometimes weeks together, took the place of the ordinary stated ministrations, and the water flowing from the smitten rock of Horeb, rolled its life-giving current to thousands of souls thirsting for salvation. In May 1801, the work broke out in Madison county, Kentucky, and at a meeting on Cabin creek, the scene was awful beyond description—the novelty of the manner of worship—"the ranges of tents—the fires reflecting light amidst the branches of the towering trees—the candles and lamps illuminating the encampment—hundreds moving to and fro, with lights and torches like Gideon's army; the preaching, praying, singing and shouting, all heard at once rushing from different parts of the ground, like the sound of many waters, was enough to swallow up all the powers of contemplation." Meeting after meeting followed in quick succession until the 6th of August, 1801, when "the great general camp meeting" was held at Cane Ridge, about 7 miles from Paris (Bourbon county). This meeting was the climax of all the rest, rendered wonderful by the almost incredible numbers that attended, as well as by the extraordinary scenes and developments there witnessed. "The concourse in attendance was most prodigious, being computed by a revolutionary officer who was accustomed to estimate encampments, to amount to not less than 20,000 souls." Although there were many extravagances and irregularities connected with and growing out of these protracted and highly excited meetings, yet good men of all denominations, now concur in the opinion "That the spirit of God was really poured out, and that many sincere converts were made." The evidence of the genuine nature of the work being seen in the humble, loving and holy walk of those who were the subjects of this work.

The first Methodist meeting-house erected in Kentucky, was a log one, put up at Masterson's station, in the Lexington circuit, in 1787 or '88.

The next house of worship, was erected at Poplar Flats, in Salt river circuit, about 1790, called Ferguson's chapel.

About the same time, a log meeting-house was erected in Jessamine county, near Bethel Academy, called Lewis' meeting house.

In Danville circuit, a log meeting-house called Procter's chapel, was erected in Madison county, about the same time. In the fall of 1793, the second meeting-house in Danville circuit, was built in Garrard county, called Burke's chapel.

The first in Limestone circuit was Bracken meeting-house.

The first *brick* church built in Kentucky, was at Flemingsburg, and the second in Shelby county, called the brick chapel.

The limits assigned to this sketch forbid a more extended history of the Methodist Episcopal church. From the statistical accounts of the church, however, it will be seen that from that period up to the present time, her march has been steady and onward.

There were within the limits of the Kentucky conference

	Whites.	Colored.
In 1800	1626	115
" 1810	5513	243
" 1820	11,887	1199
" 1830	22,074	4682
" 1840	30,939	6321
" 1845	39,756	9362

From the above statistics it will be seen that the Methodist Episcopal church, has a little more than doubled its numbers every ten years, until the year 1830. In the spring of 1846, the church in Kentucky was divided into two conferences, the upper called "THE KENTUCKY CONFERENCE," the lower called "THE LOUISVILLE CONFERENCE." The first session of the Kentucky conference was held in September, 1846, at Covington.

The first session of the Louisville conference was held in October, at Hopkinsville.

The numbers embraced in the bounds of the Kentucky conference were in the fall of 1846,

	Whites.	Colored.
	21,559	5,151

Traveling Preachers	90
Local "	240
Total	27,040

In the Louisville conference there are about.......................... 25,000

52,040

Add the ratio of increase up to this time from the conferences of 1846, and it will be about..................... 2,371

54,411

These statistical accounts will close this imperfect sketch of the rise and progress of Methodism in Kentucky. Though later than some others in entering into this interesting field, yet with her characteristic energy, from the hour that she first planted her banner in "Kentucky's tangled wilderness," down to the present time, she has been first with the foremost, entering heartily into every benevolent plan having for its object the amelioration or evangelization of our race. Tens of thousands have already risen up and called her "blessed," and if she will continue to stand by the ancient land-marks, which have guided her thus far, generations yet unborn, feeling her influence and bowing before the force and purity of her doctrines, will say of her what has been said by an eloquent divine, "across the waters," that "*Methodism is christianity in earnest.*"

HISTORICAL SKETCH

PRESBYTERIAN CHURCH.

In the year 1783, the Rev. David Rice immigrated to Kentucky, and was the first Presbyterian minister who crossed the mountains. He gathered the scattered Presbyterians into regular congregations, at Danville, Cane run, and the forks of Dick's river. He was followed the next year by the Rev. Adam Rankin, who gathered the church at Lexington, and the Rev. James Crawford, who settled at Walnut Hill. In the year 1786, the Rev. Thomas Craighead, and the Rev. Andrew McClure were added to the number. These ministers were shortly after organized into a presbytery under the name of the presbytery of Transylvania; a euphonious and classical epithet for the backwoods. All the above named persons were from Virginia, except Mr. Craighead, who was of North Carolina.

The presbytery of Transylvania met in the court house at Danville, on Tuesday, October 17, 1786. Mr. Rice presided as moderator, by appointment of the General Assembly of the Presbyterian church. Mr. McClure acted as clerk. The following ministers were present: Rev. David Rice, Adam Rankin, Andrew McClure, James Crawford, and Terah Templin, recently ordained by a commission of Hanover presbytery. There were five ruling elders present, as representatives of as many churches, viz: Messrs. Richard Steele, David Gray, John Bovel, Joseph Reed, and Jeremiah Frame.

There were at this time twelve congregations in a more or less perfect state of organization, viz.: Cane River, Concord (Danville), the forks of Dick's run, New Providence (McAfee's station), Mount Zion (Lexington), Mount Pisgah, Salem, Walnut Hill, Hopewell, Paint Lick, Jessamine creek, Whitley's station, and Crab Orchard.

By the year 1802, the number of Presbyterians had so multiplied, as to call for the erection of a synod. Accordingly, on Tuesday, October 14, 1802, the synod of Kentucky held its first meeting, in the Presbyterian church in Lexington. Mr. Rice preached the opening sermon, and was elected moderator. Mr. Marshall was chosen clerk. The number of members present was thirty; of whom seventeen were ministers, and thirteen elders. The total number of ministers within the bounds was thirty-seven. The synod was composed of the three presbyteries of Transylvania, West Lexington, and Washington, in Ohio. During the sessions, Cumberland presbytery was set off from Transylvania, embracing the south-western portion of the State, and part of Tennessee. Thus it will be seen, that the territorial jurisdiction of the synod was co-extensive with the settlement of the entire region west of the mountains.

The members of the synod were as follows:

Of the presbytery of Transylvania, *Ministers present*, David Rice, Samuel Finley, Matthew Houston, Samuel Robertson, Archibald Cameron. *Elders*, Andrew Wallace, James Bigham, Court Voris, (Voorhees). *Ministers absent*, Thomas Craighead, Terah Templin, James Balch, James McGready, William Hodge, John Bowman, William McGee, John Rankin, Samuel Donald, William Mahon, Samuel McAdow, John Howe, James Vance, Jeremiah Abel.

Of the presbytery of West Lexington, *Ministers present*, James Crawford, Samuel Shannon, Isaac Tull, Robert Marshall, James Blythe, James Welch, Joseph P. How, Samuel Rannels, John Lyle, William Robinson. *Elders*, James Bell, Robert Maffet, Malcolm Worley, William Scott, Joseph Walker, William McConnel, Samuel Hayden, William Henry. *Absent*, Rev. Barton W. Stone.

Of the presbytery of Washington, *Ministers present*, James Kemper, John P. Campbell, Richard McNemar, John Thompson, John Dunlavy. *Elders*, Robert Gill, John Campbell. *Ministers absent*, John E. Finley, Matthew G. Wallace.

The limits of the synod were reduced, in 1814, by the erection of the synod of Ohio; and in 1817, by the erection of the synod of Tennessee; since which time its boundaries have corresponded with those of the State. It consists at present of six presbyteries: Transylvania, West Lexington, Louisville, Muhlenburg, Ebenezer, and Bowling Green; comprising seventy-nine ministers, one hundred and forty churches, and eight thousand and forty-eight communicants. This statement does not embrace the members of twenty-seven churches, which failed to report the number of their communicants to the General Assembly of 1846, and which are supposed to contain about fifteen hundred communicants; making the whole number in the State about nine thousand and five hundred. In 1838, there were several ministers and churches which separated from the synod, and formed a new synod, which is commonly designated the New School synod, and which embraces three presbyteries, fourteen ministers, twenty-one churches, and nine hundred and fifty-four members.

The contributions, during the year 1845-6, to the General Assembly's Boards of Education and Missions, foreign and domestic, exceeded $13,000, independently of all that has been done for Center College, which is under its control, and has an endowment of over $70,000.

The Rev. DAVID RICE (or "Father Rice," as that venerable man was familiarly known), was born in Hanover county, Va., December 20, 1733. He was converted under the preaching of President Edwards, and studied Theology under Rev. John Todd. In the struggle for national independence, he took a warm and zealous part, and did not esteem it unbecoming his clerical profession to harangue the people on their grievances at county meetings.

In 1783, he removed to Kentucky, and identified his fortunes with the infant colony. Besides his active duties as a minister of the gospel, and the organization of many churches, he was zealously engaged in advancing the cause of education. He was the first teacher in the Transylvania seminary, and for several years the chairman of its board of trustees; and when that seminary, after its removal to Lexington, fell under deistical influence, he took an active part in raising up a rival in the Kentucky academy. The public estimation in which he was held, may be inferred from his election as a member of the convention which met in Danville in 1792, to frame a state constitution. He exerted his influence in that convention, but without success, for the insertion of an article providing for the gradual extinction of slavery in Kentucky.

Previous to Mr. Rice's arrival in Kentucky, marriages had been solemnized by the magistrates; but after that event, the people made it a point to procure the services of a clergyman. On the 3d of June, 1784, he married a couple at McAfee's station, and on the 4th, preached the funeral sermon of Mr. James M'Cann, sen., the first sermon ever preached on the banks of Salt river.

Father Rice's talents were of a plain, practical cast—not of a commanding order. His judgment was sound, his disposition conservative, and his deportment exemplary. He spent much time in prayer. In the pulpit, his manner was solemn and impressive; in his intercourse with society, dignified and grave. His person was slender, but tall and active, and even at the age of seventy, he exhibited an astonishing degree of alertness. He died in Green county, on the 18th of June, 1816, in the 83d year of his age. His last words were—"Oh, when shall I be free from sin and sorrow!"*

Rev. JAMES CRAWFORD removed with his family to Kentucky in 1784. Like most of the pioneer Presbyterian ministers, he was from Virginia. He settled at Walnut Hill, where he gathered and organized a flourishing church. Although laboring under feeble health, he was zealous and active in the cause of his Master, and numerous converts were added to the church through his instrumentality. He was a plain looking man, of very grave demeanor; not a popular preacher, but highly useful and instructive. He died in March, 1803.

The Rev. TERAH TEMPLIN, having been licensed by the Hanover (Va.) pres-

---

* This sketch. as well as most of those which follow, is abridged from "The History of the Presbyterian Church of Kentucky," by the Rev. Robert Davidson, D. D.,—a work eloquently and classically written, and displaying very extensive research—published at New York early in the present year.

bytery in 1780, soon after came to Kentucky, where he received ordination in
1785. He located in Washington county, on the south side of the Kentucky
river, where he organized several churches, and did the work of an evangelist
faithfully. He also organized several churches, and supplied destitute congregations in Livingston county. He died October 6, 1818, at the advanced age of
seventy-six. Faithful to the attachment of his early years, which had been prematurely sundered, he never married. His talents were respectable, his manner
solemn and impressive, and his deportment exemplary, guileless, and unassuming.

The Presbyterian ministry of Kentucky was reinforced, in 1786, by the accession of the Rev. Thomas B. Craighead, and Rev. Andrew McClure. Mr.
Craighead was a native of North Carolina. Shortly after his arrival in Kentucky,
he was called to the pastoral charge of the Shiloh congregation in Sumner
county, Tenn. Here, being opposed to the extravagancies of the times, and suspected of favoring Pelagianism, he became unpopular. In 1805, a commission
was appointed by the synod of Kentucky, which was directed to investigate the
correctness of the report of his unsoundness. The investigation which succeeded, a long and protracted one, resulted in the suspension of Mr. Craighead
from the gospel ministry. He made several ineffectual efforts to have the suspension removed, but did not succeed until the year 1824, when he was enabled
to make so good a vindication of himself, and to explain his views so much to
the satisfaction of the General Assembly, that they restored him to his ministerial standing. Not long after this event, he departed this life in Nashville, aged
about seventy years. For some time before his death, he had suffered under the
combined misfortunes of poverty and blindness. Mr. Craighead was of a tall
but spare figure, not less than six feet in height. He excelled as an extempora-
neous orator—his eloquence being of that fervid kind which captivates and car-
ries away the hearer in spite of himself. The Hon. John Breckinridge said of
him, that his discourses made a more lasting impression upon his memory than
those of any other man he had ever heard.

The Rev. Andrew McClure, who removed to Kentucky in company with Mr.
Craighead, in 1787, organized the Salem and Paris churches ; and in 1789 took
charge of the latter, where he remained till his decease in 1793, in the 39th year
of his age.

In 1784, the Rev. Adam Rankin, of Augusta county, Va. came to Kentucky,
and settled in Lexington. He immediately became the pastor of Mount Zion
church, and subsequently, in conjunction, of that of Pisgah, about eight miles
south-west of Lexington. In 1792, he separated from the Presbyterian church,
on account of psalmody, carrying with him a majority of his congregation, and
retaining possession of the church edifice in Lexington. The portion adhering
to the Presbyterian communion erected a new building ; and in 1795, called
the Rev. James Welch to the pastoral charge.

Eight Missioners of the Synod entered Kentucky in the following order, viz:
Robert Marshall in 1791; Carey H. Allen and William Calhoon in 1792 ; John
P. Campbell and Samuel Rannells in 1794 ; Robert Stuart and Robert Wilson
in 1798 ; and John Lyle in 1800.

Rev. Robert Marshall was a native of Ireland, emigrating to Pennsylvania
in his 12th year. He enlisted in the American army when sixteen years of age,
and was in six general engagements in the revolutionary war, one of which was
the hard-fought battle of Monmouth, where he narrowly escaped with his life, a
bullet grazing his locks. He was licensed by Redstone presbytery to preach
the gospel, and after his removal to Kentucky, was ordained, in 1793, pastor of
Bethel and Blue spring churches. He was an active leader in the great revival
of 1800, and carried away by the torrent of enthusiasm that swept over Kentucky.
In 1803, he embraced the views of the New Lights, but afterwards saw his error,
and, in 1811, returned to the bosom of the church. In 1812, he was reinstated
in the pastoral charge of the Bethel church, where he continued till his decease
in 1833, at the advanced age of 73. As a preacher, Mr. Marshall was clear,

logical, systematic, and adhered closely to his text. He was occasionally calm, mild and persuasive; but more generally warm, vehement, and even startling in his language and manner, particularly when he attempted to rouse and impress his audience.

Rev. CAREY H. ALLEN, on the 11th of October, 1794, was ordained pastor of Paint Lick and Silver creek churches. He was a mirthful, fun loving, pleasant companion, and a great wit and satirist. Sanguine and impulsive, his sallies partook occasionally of no little eccentricity. On his way to Kentucky, he put up for the night at a house where the young people had assembled to dance. The handsome stranger was invited to join them, and no denial would be taken. At length he suffered himself to be led to the musician—"Stop! I am always in the habit," said he, "when I enter on any business that I am unaccustomed to, first to ask the blessing of God upon it. Now, as I find myself in new and unexpected circumstances, I beg permission to implore the Divine direction in the matter." Suiting the action to the word, he dropped on his knees, and poured forth a prayer in his characteristic impassioned manner: then, springing to his feet he followed the prayer with a powerful and eloquent exhortation. Mute with astonishment at such an unlooked-for interruption, the company stood spellbound. They were enchained by eloquence such as they had never listened to before; the orator's burning words sank into their souls, and found an echo in their consciences: death and judgment flashed their terrors before their eyes; and they felt how unprepared they were to meet their God. Bursting into tears, they besought him to tell them what they must do to be saved. He remained and preached in the neighborhood a few days; and several hopeful conversions were the happy result of a measure which many would consider of questionable propriety, and which it must be admitted, in less skillful hands, might have proved a signal failure. Mr. Allen was a man of highly popular talents, impassioned eloquence and ardent zeal. He was remarkably fluent—his style original and forcible—and he never failed to make a powerful impression wherever he went. After a brief ministry of less than two years, he was carried off by consumption amid flattering prospects of usefulness, on the 5th of August, 1795.

The Rev. JOHN POAGE CAMPBELL, M. D., unquestionably the most brilliant in this constellation of missionaries, was born in Augusta county, V , in 1767, and removed to Kentucky with his father when fourteen years of age. He graduated at Hampden Sidney in 1790, and in 1792 was licensed to preach. Such was the esteem in which he was held, that he was at once associated with his preceptor, (Dr. Moses Hoge), as co-pastor of Lexington, Oxford, New Monmouth and Timber Ridge congregations. In 1795, he took up his abode in Kentucky, and his first charge was the churches of Smyrna and Flemingsburg. He afterwards exercised his ministry in various places, among which were Danville, Nicholasville, Cherry Spring, Versailles, Lexington, and Chillicothe; and in 1811, he officiated as chaplain to the legislature. Dr. Campbell possessed an acute and discriminating mind; was an accurate and well read theologian; an able polemic; and decidedly the most talented, popular, and influential minister of his day. His pen was very prolific. His published writings were numerous and able, among them—Strictures on Stone's Letters on the Atonement—Essays on Justification—Letters to Craighead—A Sermon on Christian Baptism—The Pelagian Detected, a Reply to Craighead—An Answer to Jones, and Review of Robinson's History of Baptism, &c., &c. Dr. Campbell was married three times, and on his demise, left a family of nine children. His death occurred on the 4th of November, 1814, at the age of 53, in the vicinity of Chillicothe, Ohio.

The Rev. SAMUEL RANNELLS was born in Hampshire county, Va., December 10th, 1765. He was licensed in 1794, and the next spring visited Kentucky as one of the synod's missionaries. In 1796, he was ordained over the united churches of Paris and Stonermouth, which charge he retained for twenty-two years, until his death, March 24th, 1817, in the 52d year of his age. He was a man of eminent piety, of exemplary conduct, and of respectable talents—remarkably gifted in prayer, and a zealous and indefatigable minister.

The Rev. ROBERT STUART came to Kentucky in 1798. In December of the same year, he was appointed Professor of Languages in Transylvania University, but resigned in the year following. During the year 1803, he preached to the church of Salem; and in 1804, took charge of Walnut Hill church, about six miles east of Lexington, which he continued to retain for nearly forty years. He has performed much laborious service in the church—is a man of rare prudence and discretion—and is esteemed by all who know him, as " an Israelite indeed, in whom there is no guile." This venerable father still lives, in the 75th year of his age, while most of his early companions in the ministry of Kentucky, have gone to their rest.

The Rev. ROBERT WILSON was descended from ancestors whom persecution had driven from the north of Ireland to western Virginia. He entered Kentucky as a missionary in 1798, and on the expiration of his engagement, married and settled in Washington, Mason county, where he remained till his death, October 31, 1822, in the fiftieth year of his age. He was an amiable and estimable man, possessing great equanimity of temper, and remarkable throughout his whole ministerial career, for his active, humble and devoted piety. While his labors were signally blessed among his own flock, it was through his unwearied exertions that the churches of Augusta and Maysville were organized; and those of Smyrna and Flemingsburg owed to him their preservation when languishing without a pastor.

The Rev. JOHN LYLE was a native of Rockbridge county, Va. born on 20th October, 1769. He was licensed to preach the gospel in 1795. In 1797, he came to Kentucky as a missionary, and in 1800 took charge of Salem church, where he remained for several years. Mr. Lyle subsequently removed to Paris, where he established a female academy, which became one of the most flourishing in the state, embracing from 150 to 200 pupils. In 1809, he declined teaching, but continued in the active discharge of his ministerial labors until 1825, on the 22d of July of which year he departed this life. He bore a prominent part in the trying scenes through which the church was called to pass during the early period of his ministry. He was a man of sound judgment and studious habits; his manner, in the pulpit, feeling and earnest, and his matter sensible. As an evidence of the blessed fruits of his faithful, earnest and affectionate style of preaching, on one occasion, at Mount Pleasant, the Rev. William L. McCalla noted the names of thirty-three persons impressed by the sermon, thirty-one of whom afterward became respectable members of the church.

REV. ARCHIBALD CAMERON. [A sketch of this distinguished divine, prepared by a friend, but too long for insertion under this head, will be found under the head of Shelby county.]

Rev. JOSEPH P. HOWE came from North Carolina in 1794, and was ordained in July, 1795, over Little Mountain (Mount Sterling) and Springfield. He was a good man—prayed and sang well—and took a conspicuous part in the Great Revival. He died in 1830.

Rev. JAMES WELCH, from Virginia, was ordained pastor of the Lexington and Georgetown churches, in 1796, in which charge he continued till 1804. He was obliged to practice medicine for the support of his family. In 1799, he was appointed professor of ancient languages in the Transylvania University, which station he filled for several years.

Revs. MATTHEW HOUSTON, JOHN DUNLAVY, and RICHARD McNEMAR, who came to Kentucky about the close of the last century, became Shakers—the latter still living.

Rev. JOHN HOWE was installed pastor of Beaver creek and Little Barren, in April, 1798. He is still living, and has been for many years connected with the church at Greensburg.

Many other ministers came to Kentucky about the close of the last century, among them the Rev. WILLIAM ROBINSON, who, in 1804, was dismissed to Washington Presbytery; Rev. SAMUEL FINLEY, from South Carolina; Rev. JAMES VANCE, from Virginia; Rev. JAMES KEMPER, and Rev. SAMUEL B. ROBERTSON, and Rev. JOHN BOWMAN, and Rev. JOHN THOMPSON, from North Carolina.

Rev. JAMES BLYTHE, D. D., was among the early and distinguished preachers in the field. He was born in North Carolina in 1765, and came to Kentucky, as a licentiate, in 1791. In July, 1793, he was ordained pastor of Pisgah and Clear creek churches. To these churches he ministered, as pastor or stated supply, for upwards of forty years. Dr. Blythe took an active part in the establishment of the Kentucky academy. When that institution, in 1798, was merged in the University of Transylvania, he was appointed professor of Mathematics, Natural Philosophy, Astronomy, and Geography; and, subsequently, on the resignation of Mr. Moore, fulfilled for twelve or fifteen years the duties of acting president.

On the election of Dr. Holly, as president, in 1818, Dr. Blythe was transferred to the chair of Chemistry in the medical department, which situation he retained till 1831, when he resigned.

As a preacher, Dr. Blythe was full of energy and animation, in his earlier career; in his latter years, he yielded more to the softer emotions. His native strength of character, prompt decision, and practical turn, enabled him to acquit himself creditably in every situation; while, in deliberative bodies, and the courts of the church, these qualities gave him a marked ascendency, to which his portly figure and commanding appearance contributed not a little. He died in 1842, aged seventy-seven years.

In the year 1820, died the Rev. JAMES McCHORD. He was born in Baltimore in 1785, and removed to Lexington when five years of age. His education was liberal, and at an early age he proceeded to read law with the Hon. Henry Clay. Becoming pious, he devoted his life to the ministry. He was chosen the first pastor of the second Presbyterian church of Lexington in 1815, which situation he held till the year 1819, when he removed to Paris. His published writings were considerable, among them two volumes of sermons. Mr. McChord was a remarkably brilliant man—possessing a rapid and comprehensive intellect, a glowing and gorgeous style, and an exuberant imagination. His successors in the second or McChord church, were able and eloquent men—the Rev. John Breckinridge in 1823; Rev. John C. Young in 1829; Rev. Robert Davidson in 1832; Rev. John D. Matthews in 1841; and Rev. John H. Brown, in 1844.

The Rev. GIDEON BLACKBURN was one of the most eloquent divines of the west; and his early history presents a most remarkable instance of perseverance in the face of difficulties. Left an orphan and penniless when about eleven years of age (being defrauded out of the handsome patrimony of twenty thousand dollars), a kind school-master gave him instruction gratuitously; and he obtained a situation in a saw-mill, where he tended the saw from dark till day-light, studying by a fire of pine-knots. In this way he earned a dollar every night, and made rapid proficiency in his studies. Thus he struggled on till ready to enter college. To defray this new expense, he labored as a surveyor for four months; frequently sleeping in a cane-brake to avoid the Indians, and having no shelter from the rain but a blanket. He received for his pay fourteen horses, valued at forty dollars a-piece. These he took to Maryland and sold for fifteen hundred dollars; with which he discharged all his debts, and went through Dickinson college. Thus early enured to hardships, he was admirably fitted for the arduous duties of a missionary to the Cherokee Indians, to which he was appointed by the general assembly in 1803, when 31 years of age. In 1827, he was appointed President of Centre College at Danville, which situation he filled till 1830, when he was succeeded by the Rev. Dr. Young. The last years of his life were spent in Illinois.

The Rev. JOHN McFARLAND and the Rev. DAVID NELSON were clergymen of a high order of talent. The former died, while pastor of the Paris church, in 1828; the latter departed this life, in Illinois, in 1844.

The Rev. Thomas Clelland, D. D., is among the few surviving ministers who took part in the great Revival commencing in 1800. He was born in Maryland in 1777, and came to Kentucky when very young. He has been for nearly half a century, an active, laborious and remarkably successful herald of the cross. His printed works have been numerous and popular. At the age of three score and ten, there seems to be but little abatement of his mental and physical energies.

The Rev. John Breckinridge, D. D., was the sixth of nine children of the Hon. John Breckinridge, (of whose life a sketch will be found under the head of Breckinridge county). He was born at Cabell's-Dale, on North Elkhorn, on the 4th day of July, 1797; and died at the same place on the 4th day of August, 1841, having just completed his 44th year. Some account has been given of his paternal ancestors, in the notice of his father; and of his maternal, in that of his elder brother, Joseph Cabell Breckinridge. His father died when he was nine years old; and from that time, he was reared under the care of his widowed mother, and brother Cabell, who was his guardian. His education was conducted at the best schools which Kentucky afforded, and completed at Princeton college, N. J., where he spent about three years as a pupil, and graduated with great distinction in the autumn of 1818, having just completed his 21st year. He was destined by his family for the profession of the law. During his residence in Princeton college, he became a subject of divine grace, and united himself with the Presbyterian church, to which his paternal ancestors had been attached from the period of the reformation of the sixteenth century, in Scotland; and determined, against the earnest wishes of all his immediate family—not one of whom was at that time a professor of religion—to devote himself to the gospel ministry, and, as it is believed, to the work of foreign missions. The providential dealings of God constantly frustrated this latter intention, but the former was carried into effect; and after spending several years more in Princeton, as a student of the theological seminary there, and part of the time as a tutor in the college, he was licensed and ordained a minister of Jesus Christ, in the Presbyterian church of the United States.

In 1822, he was chaplain of the House of Representatives of the Congress of the United States. In 1823, he settled in Lexington, Ky., as pastor of the McChord church of that place. In 1826, he removed to the city of Baltimore, as co-pastor of the late Rev. Dr. Glendy; and afterwards, as sole pastor of the second Presbyterian church in that city. In 1831, he removed to the city of Philadelphia, as secretary and general agent of the board of education of the Presbyterian church. In 1836, the general assembly of that church elected him a professor in the theological seminary at Princeton, New Jersey, to which place he then removed. Upon the organization of the board of foreign missions by the Presbyterian church, he was elected its secretary and general agent, and continued at the head of the operations of that board from about 1838 to 1840. At the period of his death, he was the pastor elect of the Presbyterian church in the city of New Orleans, and president elect of the university of Oglethorpe, in Georgia.

He was a man of extraordinary gifts. To great gentleness and refinement of manners and feelings, he added remarkable correctness and vigor of purpose and force of will. Ardent and intrepid, as ever man was, he was also patient of labor, calm and wary in the formation of his designs, and indomitable in the resolution with which he pursued his objects. His success in life was, of necessity, striking and universal; and at the period of his death, though he had scarcely attained the meridian of life, he was probably as universally known, and as universally admired and loved, as any minister of the gospel in America had ever been. A more generous, disinterested and benevolent man, never lived. His talents were of a high order; and in the midst of a life of incessant activity, he acquired very extensive learning in his immediate profession, and was justly and highly distinguished for the compass and elegance of his general attainments. As a public speaker, and especially as a pulpit orator, few of his generation equalled him—and taken for all in all, hardly one excelled him. So greatly was he admired and loved, and so high was the public confidence in him, that calls and invitations to churches, colleges, and every sort of public employment, suitable to his calling as a christian minister, were continually pressed upon him from every section of the United States. His connection with the great movements and controversies of his age, so far as they bore a moral or religious aspect, was close and constant. A few hours before his death, and almost as his last words, he uttered these sublime words : "I am a poor sinner, who have worked hard, and had constantly before my mind one great object—THE CONVERSION OF THE WORLD." It was a true and an honest synopsis of his life and labors.

One of the most extraordinary and scandalous events that ever occurred, was the attempt made five years after the death of this good and great man, by certain Roman Catholics of St. Louis and elsewhere, to prove that he had died a convert to their religion—a religion which he spent many years of his life in the most ardent efforts to confute and expose—and in regard to which, the evidence was perfectly conclusive that, to the end of his life, he thought the worse of it, as he more and more examined it.

In personal appearance, he was a man of the middle stature—lightly, but finely and elegantly made—and possessed of great strength and activity. His features wore an habitual aspect of mingled gentleness, sadness, and almost severity. His eyes and hair were light hazle. He was twice married—the first time, to a daughter of the Rev. Dr. Miller, of New Jersey ; the second time, to a daughter of Colonel Babcock, of Connecticut. His second wife, and three children by the first, and one by the second marriage, survive him.

HISTORICAL SKETCH

OF THE

EARLY ROMAN CATHOLIC CHURCH, IN KENTUCKY;

WITH BRIEF BIOGRAPHICAL NOTICES OF THE PRINCIPAL CATHOLIC MISSIONARIES, WHO HAVE SUCCESSIVELY LABORED IN THIS STATE.

THE glowing accounts of the surpassing beauty and fertility of Kentucky, furnished by the early pioneers on their return to the bosom of their families in North Carolina and Virginia, created a deep sensation throughout the western borders of these states, and awakened a spirit of adventure, which soon extended to Maryland and other adjoining states. Large bodies of emigrants began to pour into the newly discovered and but half explored wilderness, inhabited till then only by wild beasts and by roving bands of savages. The daring spirit of Boone, Harrod and Logan was soon communicated to large masses of population ; and the consequence was, that in less than a quarter of a century from its first discovery or exploration, Kentucky had a sufficient population to be admitted as one of the independent states of this great confederacy; the second that was added to the venerable THIRTEEN, which had fought the battles of independence.

Maryland shared abundantly in the enthusiasm which had already set one-fourth of the adjacent populations in motion towards the west. The Catholics who settled in Kentucky, came principally from this state, which had been founded by Lord Baltimore, and a band of colonists professing the Roman Catholic religion. Bold, hardy, adventurous and strongly attached to their faith, but tolerant towards those of other denominations, the Catholic emigrants to Kentucky, proved not unworthy of their ancestors, who had been the first to unfurl on this western continent, the broad banner of universal freedom, both civil and religious.* They cheerfully underwent the labors, privations and dangers,

---

* Bancroft in his History of the United States, (Vol. I. Maryland), awards this praise to the Catholic colonists of Maryland; and so do our other historians, *passim.*

to which all the early emigrants were exposed; and they made common cause with their brethren in providing for the security of their new homes in the wilderness, and in repelling Indian invasions. Several of their number were killed or dragged into captivity on their way to Kentucky; others passed through stirring adventures, and made hair-breadth escapes.

The first Catholic emigrants to Kentucky, with whose history we are acquainted, were Dr. Hart and William Coomes. These came out in the spring of 1775, and settled at Harrod's station. Here Dr. Hart engaged in the practice of medicine; and the wife of William Coomes opened a school for children. Thus in all probability, the first practising physician and the first school teacher of our infant commonwealth were both Roman Catholics. A few years later they removed with their families to Bardstown, in the vicinity of which most of the Catholic emigrants subsequently located themselves. Previously to their removal, however, they were both actively employed in the defence of Harrod's Station during its memorable siege by the Indians in 1776–77. William Coomes was with the party which first discovered the approach of the savages; one of his companions was shot dead at his side; and he made a narrow escape with his life.

In the year 1785 a large colony of Catholics emigrated to Kentucky from Maryland, with the Haydens and Lancasters, and settled chiefly on Pottinger's creek, at a distance of from ten to fifteen miles from Bardstown. They were followed in the spring of the next year, by another colony led out by captain James Rapier, who located himself in the same neighborhood. In 1787, Thomas Hill and Philip Miles brought out another band of Catholic emigrants, and they were followed in 1788, by Robert Abell, and his friends; and in 1790–91, by Benedict Spalding and Leonard Hamilton, with their families and connexions. The last named colonists settled on the Rolling Fork, a branch of Salt river, in the present county of Marion.

In the spring of the year 1787, there were already about fifty Catholic families in Kentucky. They had as yet no Catholic clergyman to administer to their spiritual wants: and they felt the privation most keenly. Upon application to the Very Rev. John Carroll, of Baltimore, then the ecclesiastical superior of all the Catholics in the United States, they had the happiness to receive as their first pastor the Rev. Mr. Whelan, a zealous and talented Irish priest, who had served as chaplain in the French navy, which had come to our assistance in the struggle for independence. He remained with his new charge till the spring of 1790, when he returned to Maryland by the way of New Orleans.

After his departure, the Catholics of Kentucky were again left in a destitute condition for nearly three years; when they were consoled by the appearance among them of the Rev. Stephen Theodore Badin, who was sent out as their pastor by bishop Carroll, of Baltimore, in the year 1793. This excellent, learned, zealous and indefatigable religious pioneer of our state, still lingering in venerable old age above the horizon of life, labored with unremitting zeal among the Catholics of our state for more than thirty years, and even after this long term of service, though worn down with previous exertion, and induced to travel and take some relaxation for his health, he still continued to work at intervals in the vineyard which he had so dearly loved and so long cultivated.

His adventures and hardships would fill a volume; and the varied incidents of his remarkable life cannot even be alluded to in this brief sketch. Wherever there was sickness or spiritual destitution; wherever error or vice was to be eradicated, and virtue inculcated; wherever youth was to be instructed and trained to religious observances; wherever, in a word, his spiritual ministrations were most needed, there he was sure to be found laboring with all his native energy, for the good of his neighbor. Difficulties and dangers, which would have appalled a heart less stout and resolute, were set at naught by this untiring man. He traversed Kentucky on horseback hundreds of times on missionary duty; and he spent nearly half his time in the saddle. Through rain and storm, through hail and snow; along the beaten path and through the trackless wilderness, by day and by night, he might be seen going on his errand of mercy; often for years together, alone in the field, and always among the foremost to labor, even when subsequently joined by other zealous Catholic missionaries. He was intimate with the most distinguished men of Kentucky in the early times, and his politeness, learning, affability and wit, made him always a welcome guest at their tables.

When he first came to Kentucky in 1793, he estimated the number of Catholic families in the state at *three hundred ;* he has lived to see this number swell to more than *six thousand.* When he first entered on this missionary field, there was not a Catholic church in the entire commonwealth, and there were few, if any, Catholic schools; at present there are more than forty churches, besides a great number of missionary stations, about forty Catholic priests, one religious establishment for men, two colleges for young men, four female religious institutions, eleven academies for girls, five or six charitable institutions : besides an ecclesiastical seminary, and some minor schools. The entire Catholic population of the State, may be now estimated at thirty thousand.

After having remained alone in Kentucky for nearly four years, Rev. M. Badin was joined by another zealous Catholic missionary, like himself a native of France; the Rev. M. Fournier, who reached the State in February, 1797. Two years later—in February, 1799, the two missionaries were cheered by the arrival of another, the Rev. M. Salmon, likewise a Frenchman. But these two last named clergymen did not long survive the arduous labors of the mission. M. Salmon after a serious illness contracted by exposure, was suddenly killed by a fall from his horse near Bardstown, on the 9th of November, 1799; and the Rev. M. Fournier died soon after on the Rolling Fork, probably from the rupture of a blood-vessel.

Their places were filled by the Rev. Mr. Thayer, a native of New England, who had once been a Congregational minister in Boston, but had from conviction become a Catholic, and had been promoted to the ministry in our church. He arrived in Kentucky in 1799 ; having been sent out, like the rest, by bishop Carroll, of Baltimore, the venerable patriarch of the Catholic church in America ; and he remained in the State till 1803. After his departure, M. Badin was again left alone for about two years,—until the year 1805.

This year is memorable in our religious annals, as marking the arrival among us of one among the most active and efficient of our early missionaries—the Rev. Charles Nerinckx, a native of Belgium, who, like many others of our first missionaries, had been compelled to leave Europe in consequence of the disturbances caused by the French Revolution. Strong, healthy, robust, and full of faith and religious zeal, he was admirably suited to endure the hardships necessarily connected with our early missions. He shrank from no labor, and was disheartened by no difficulties. He labored without cessation, both bodily and mentally, for nearly twenty years, and he died on a missionary excursion to Missouri, in 1824. He erected in Kentucky no less than ten Catholic churches, in the building of which he often worked with his own hands. Two of these were of brick, and the rest of hewed logs.

For many years he had charge of six large congregations, besides a great number of minor stations, scattered over the whole extent of the State. Like M. Badin, he spent much of his time on horseback, and traveled by night as well as by day. On his famous horse *Printer*, he very often traveled sixty miles in the day; and to save time, he not unfrequently set out on his journeys at sunset. He often swam swollen creeks and rivers, even in the dead of winter; he frequently slept in the woods : and on one occasion, in what is now Grayson county, he was beset by wolves during a whole night, when he was saved, under the divine protection, by his presence of mind in sitting on his horse and keeping his persecutors at bay by hallooing at the top of his voice. Exact in enforcing discipline, he was more rigid with himself than with any one else. He cared not for his bodily comfort, and was content with the poorest accommodations. He delighted to visit the poor, and to console them in their afflictions; while children and servants were the special objects of his pastoral solicitude.

In order to promote female piety and education, this good man founded the Sisterhood of Loretto, in April, 1812. The objects of this establishment were; to enable those young ladies who wished to retire from the world, and to devote themselves wholly to prayer and the exercises of charity, to be useful to themselves and to others, by diffusing the blessings of a Christian education among young persons of their own sex, especially among the daughters of the poor. They were also to receive and rear up orphan girls, who, if left on the cold charities of the world, might have gone to ruin themselves, and have become an

occasion of ruin to others.   The institution succeeded even beyond his most san
guine expectations.   Within the twelve years which elapsed from its establishment to the death of its founder, the number of sisters who devoted themselves
to this manner of life had already increased to more than a hundred; and they
had under their charge more than two hundred and fifty girls, distributed through
six different schools, besides many orphans, whom they fed, clothed, and educated
gratuitously.   The institution now reckons about one hundred and eighty members; and besides the mother house, which is at Loretto, in Marion county, it has
eight branch establishments, five of which are in Kentucky, and three in Missouri.   All of these have female schools attached to them, in which young ladies
are taught not only the elements of English education, but also the varied accomplishments which fit them for the most refined society.

In the spring of the year 1806, a new band of Catholic missionaries came to
Kentucky, and established themselves at St. Rose's, near Springfield.   They were
the Rev. Messrs. Edward Fenwick,* Thomas Wilson, Wm. Raymond Tuite, and
R. Anger; the first a native ot Maryland, and the three last Englishmen.   They
were all of the order of St. Dominic.   They took charge of a considerable portion of the Catholic missions, and labored with great zeal and efficiency in the
vineyard.   Connected with their institution were a theological seminary and a
college for young men, both of which continued to flourish for many years.

About a mile from St. Rose's, there was also established, at a later period, the
still flourishing female institution of St. Magdalene's, conducted by sisters of
the third order of St. Dominic, which has now a branch establishment at Somerset, Ohio.   This latter institution, the permanent establishment of which is
mainly due to the enlightened zeal of Bishop Miles, of Nashville, has done great
good in promoting the diffusion of female education among all classes of our
population.

In the fall of the year 1805, the Trappists came to Kentucky with the Rev.
Urban Guillet, their superior; and they remained in the State, at their establishment on Pottinger's creek, near Rohan's knob, for about four years, when they
removed to Missouri, and subsequently to Illinois.   They were a body of religious
monks who devoted themselves to fasting and prayer, and lived retired from the
world.   They were, however, of great assistance to the infant Catholic missions
of Kentucky, not only by the influence of their prayers and good example, but
also by their efforts to promote education, especially among the children of the
poor.   They established a school for boys, in which manual labor and instruction in the mechanical arts were combined with a religious training and the
teaching of the ordinary rudiments of an English education.

In the year 1811, the Catholics of our State were cheered by the arrival among
them of their first bishop, the Rt. Reverend Dr. Flaget, who had been consecrated
in Baltimore by Bishop Carroll, on the 4th of November of the previous year.
This venerable missionary pioneer, now in his eighty-fourth year, had been
already in the west, having been stationed for two years at Post Vincennes, as
early as 1792, shortly after his arrival in the United States from France, his
native country.   When he passed Cincinnati in that year, there were only four
rude cabins in this now flourishing city; and Louisville was but little farther advanced.   How different is the entire west now, from what it was on occasion of
his first visit, or even on that of his second in 1811 !   What was then an unreclaimed wilderness, filled with wild beasts and still fiercer savages, is now a
smiling garden of civilization.

We cannot attempt to write even a rapid sketch of the life and labors of Bishop
Flaget in Kentucky, during the last thirty-six years; a volume would be necessary to do full justice to his excellent and admirable character.   The incidents
of his life are familiar to all the Catholics of the State; while the many benevolent and literary institutions he has reared, are the best monuments to his memory.   Suffice it to say, that he has ever blended the active benevolence and
charity of the Christian missionary with the amiable politeness of the accomplished gentleman.   He had and still has a multitude of warm friends, even
among the dissenting communions: he never had one enemy.

Among the companions of Bishop Flaget, when he came to take up his

---

* Subsequently the first bishop of Cincinnati.

permanent abode in Kentucky, were the Rev. J. B. M. David, and the Rev. G. J. Chabrat—the latter not yet a priest; both of whom afterwards were successively appointed his coadjutors. The latter was the first priest ordained by Bishop Flaget in Kentucky.

The Rev. Mr. David, or, as he was familiarly called, *Father David*, was consecrated bishop in the newly dedicated cathedral of Bardstown, on the 15th of August, 1819 ; and he died on the 12th of July, 1841, in the eighty-first year of his age. He was the founder of the theological seminary of Bardstown, and of the order of Sisters of Charity, in Kentucky. In the former institution, founded in 1811, were educated most of the clergymen now on the missions of Kentucky, many of them under his own eye. The society of Sisters of Charity was commenced at St. Thomas, four miles from Bardstown, in November, 1812 ; and the number of its members increased apace, until it was soon able to send out new colonies to different parts of the State. The society now has four branch establishments under the general supervision of the parent institution at Nazareth, near Bardstown ; it has more than seventy-five members ; it educates annually about five hundred young ladies, and has charge of an infirmary and orphan asylum, in the latter of which there are at present about seventy orphan girls, rescued from want, and trained to virtue and learning.

Among the most zealous and efficient deceased Catholic clergymen of our State, we may reckon the Rev. William Byrne and the Rev. G. A. M. Elder; the former an Irishman, and the founder of St. Mary's college, in Marion county ; the latter a Kentuckian, and the founder of St. Joseph's college, in Bardstown. These two institutions, which have continued to flourish ever since, and which have been of immense advantage to the cause of education in Kentucky, stand forth the fittest and most durable monuments to their memory. Having been for many years bound together by ties of the closest Christian friendship, they were both ordained together in the cathedral of Bardstown, by Bishop David, on the 18th of September, 1819.

As an evidence of the unconquerable energy of these two men, we may remark, that the two institutions which they respectively founded, and in the welfare of which they felt so lively an interest, were both reduced to ashes under their very eyes,—St. Mary's college at two different times ; and that they were immediately rebuilt by their founders, who, far from being discouraged by the afflicting disaster, seemed in consequence of it to be clothed, on the contrary, with new vigor and resolution. No difficulties terrified them ; no obstacles were deemed by them insurmountable. The State never contributed one dollar to either of these institutions, nor were they erected by the wealth of their founders or the liberal contributions of individuals. The persevering industry and untiring energy of two men, wholly unprovided with pecuniary means, and yet determined to succeed at all hazards, built up, rebuilt, and maintained those two institutions of learning. They and their associates asked no salary, no worldly retribution for their labors ; and the entire proceeds of the institutions thus went towards paying the debts contracted for the erection of them. So great was the confidence reposed in the two founders by all classes of the community, that they had credit, to an unlimited amount ; and it is almost needless to add, that not one of their creditors ever lost a dollar by the trust reposed in their integrity and ability to meet all their liabilities.

The Rev. William Byrne died of the cholera, at St. Mary's college, on the 5th of June, 1833 ; and his friend followed him on the 28th of September, 1838. The latter died at St. Joseph's college, of an affection of the heart, which he had contracted many years before, while a student at Emmetsburgh college, Maryland. Both fell victims of their zeal in the discharge of the duties of their office ; both died in the arms of their dearest friends, in the institutions which they had reared, and which they left behind them as their sepulchral monuments.

Here we must close this hasty and imperfect sketch. The narrow limits by which we were confined, prevented us from speaking of several other things worthy of notice in our religious history ; while we have on purpose abstained from saying much of those who are still living, whose biographies will be more appropriately written when they shall be no more.

MISCELLANEOUS STATISTICS.

GOVERNORS, LIEUTENANT GOVERNORS AND SECRETARIES OF THE COMMONWEALTH.

I. Isaac Shelby, the first governor, took the oath of office on the 4th of June, 1792, under the first constitution. James Brown, secretary of state.

II. James Garrard took the oath of office June 1, 1796. Harry Toulman, secretary. The present constitution was formed 1799.

III. James Garrard, being eligible, was again elected governor; Alexander S. Bullitt, lieutenant governor; Harry Toulman secretary—1800.

IV. Christopher Greenup, governor; John Caldwell, lieutenant governor; John Rowan, secretary—1804.

V. Charles Scott, governor; Gabriel Slaughter, lieutenant governor; Jesse Bledsoe, secretary—1808.

VI. Isaac Shelby, governor; Richard Hickman, lieutenant governor; Martin D. Hardin, secretary—1812.

VII. George Madison, governor; Gabriel Slaughter, lieutenant governor; Charles S. Todd, secretary—1816. Governor Madison died at Paris, Kentucky, on the 14th October, 1816, and on the 21st of the same month, Gabriel Slaughter, lieutenant governor, assumed the duties of executive. John Pope, and after him, Oliver G. Waggoner, secretary.

VIII. John Adair, governor; William T. Barry, lieutenant governor; Joseph Cabell Breckinridge, and after him, Thomas B. Monroe, secretary—1820.

IX. Joseph Desha, governor; Robert B. M'Afee, lieutenant governor; William T. Barry, succeeded by James C. Pickett, secretary—1824.

X. Thomas Metcalfe, governor; John Breathitt, lieutenant governor; George Robertson, succeeded by Thomas T. Crittenden, secretary—1828.

XI. John Breathitt, governor: James T. Morehead, lieutenant governor; Lewis Sanders, jr., secretary. Governor Breathitt died on the 21st of February, 1834, and on the 22d of the same month, James T. Morehead, the lieutenant governor, took the oath of office as governor of the state. John J. Crittenden, William Owsley and Austin P. Cox, were successively, secretary—1832.

XII. James Clark, governor; Charles A. Wickliffe, lieutenant governor; James M. Bullock, secretary. Governor Clark departed this life on the 27th September, 1839, and on the 5th of October, Charles A. Wickliffe, lieutenant governor, assumed the duties of Governor—1836.

XIII. Robert P. Letcher, governor; Manlius V. Thomson, lieutenant governor; James Harlan, secretary—1840.

XIV. William Owsley, governor; Archibald Dixon, lieutenant governor; Benjamin Hardin, George B. Kinkead and William D. Reed, successively, secretary—1844.

LIST OF SENATORS IN CONGRESS, FROM 1792 TO 1847.

	In. Out.		In. Out.
Adair, John	1805–06	Edwards, John	1792–95
Barry, William T	1814–16	Hardin, Martin D	1816–17
Bibb, George M	{ 1811–14	Johnson, Richard M	1819–29
	{ 1829–35	Logan, William	1819–20
Bledsoe, Jesse	1813–15	Marshall, Humphrey	1795–1801
Breckinridge, John	1801–05	Morehead, James T	1841–47
Brown, John	1792–95	Pope, John	1807–13
	{ 1806–07	Rowan, John	1825–31
Clay, Henry	{ 1810–11	Talbot, Isham	{ 1815–19
	{ 1831–42		{ 1820–25
	{ 1817–19	Thurston, John Buckner	1805–10
Crittenden, John J	{ 1835–41	Underwood, Joseph R	1847–53
	{ 1842–49	Walker, George	1814–15

(144)

LIST OF REPRESENTATIVES IN CONGRESS.

Name	In. Out.
Adair, John	1831–33
Allan, Chilton	1831–37
Anderson, Richard C.	1817–21
Anderson, S. H.	1839–41
Andrews, L. W.	1839–43
Barry, William T.	1810–11
Beatty, Martin	1833–35
Bedinger, George M.	1803–07
Bell, Joshua F.	1845–47
Boyd, Linn	1835–37 / 1839–47
Boyle, John	1803–09
Breckenridge, J. D.	1821–23
Brown, William	1819–21
Buckner, Richard A.	1823–29
Bullock, Wingfield	1820–21
Butler, William O.	1839–43
Caldwell, G. A.	1843–45
Calhoun, John	1835–39
Campbell, John	1837–38
Chambers, John	1828–29 / 1835–39
Chilton, Thomas	1827–31 / 1833–35
Christie, Henry	1809–11
Clark, James	1813–16 / 1825–31
Clay, Henry	1811–14 / 1815–21 / 1823–25
Coleman, Nicholas D.	1829–31
Daniel, Henry	1827–33
Davis, Amos	1833–35
Davis, Garret	1839–47
Davis, Thomas T.	1797–1803
Desha, Joseph	1807–19
Duval, William P.	1813–15
Fletcher, Thomas	1816–17
Fowler, John	1797–1807
French, Richard	1835–37 / 1843–45
Gaither, Nathan	1829–33
Graves, William J.	1835–41
Green, Willis	1839–45
Greenup, Christopher	1792–97
Grider, Henry	1843–47
Hardin, Benjamin	1815–17 / 1819–23 / 1833–37
Harlan, James	1835–39
Hawes, Albert G.	1831–37
Hawes, Richard	1837–41
Hawkins, Joseph W.	1814–15
Henry, Robert P.	1823–27
Hopkins, Samuel	1813–15
Howard, Benjamin	1807–10
Johnson, Francis	1821–27
Johnson, James	1825–26
Johnson, Richard M.	1807–19 / 1829–37

Name	In. Out.
Johnson, John T.	1821–25
Kincaid, John	1829–33
Lecompte, Joseph	1825–33
Letcher, Robert P.	1823–33
Love, James	1833–35
Lyon, Chittenden	1827–35
Lyon, Matthew	1803–11
Marshall, Thomas A.	1831–35
Marshall, Thomas F.	1841–43
Martin, John P.	1845–47
McHatton, Robert	1826–29
McHenry, John H.	1845–47
McKee, Samuel	1809–17
McLean, Alney	1815–17 / 1819–21
Menifee, Richard H.	1837–39
Metcalfe, Thomas	1819–29
Montgomery, Thomas	1813–15 / 1821–23
Moore, Thomas P.	1823–29 / 1833–34
Murray, John L.	1828–39
New, Anthony	1811–13 / 1817–19 / 1821–23
Ormsby, Stephen	1811–17
Orr, Alexander D.	1792–97
Owsley, Bryan Y.	1841–43
Pope, John	1837–43
Pope, P. H.	1833–35
Quarles, Tunstall	1817–20
Robertson, George	1817–21
Rowan, John	1807–09
Rumsey, Edward	1837–39
Sanford, Thomas	1803–07
Sharpe, Solomon P.	1813–17
Smith, John S.	1821–23
Southgate, William W.	1837–39
Speed, Thomas	1817–19
Sprigg, James C.	1841–43
Stone, James	1843–45
Taul, Micah	1815–17
Thompson, John B.	1841–47
Thompson, Philip	1823–25
Tibbatts, John W.	1843–47
Tompkins, Christopher	1831–35
Trimble, David	1817–27
Triplett, Philip	1839–43
Trumbo, Andrew	1845–47
Underwood, Joseph R.	1835–43
Walker, David	1817–20
Walton, Matthew	1803–07
White, David	1823–25
White, John	1835–45
Wickliffe, Charles A.	1823–33
Williams, Sherrod	1835–41
Woodson, Samuel H.	1820–23
Yancey, Joel	1827–31
Young, Bryan Y.	1845–47
Young, William F.	1825–27

MEMBERS OF THE CONVENTION HELD IN DANVILLE, ON THE 23d DAY OF MAY, 1785.

Samuel McDowell, *President.*
George Muter,
Christopher Greenup,
James Speed,
Robert Todd,
James Beard,
Matthew Walton,
James Trotter,
Ebenezer Brooks,
Caleb Wallace,
Richard Terrell,
. . . Clarke,
Robert Johnson,
John Martin,

Benjamin Logan,
Willis Green,
Harry Innis,
Levi Todd,
Isaac Cox,
Richard Taylor,
Richard Steele,
Isaac Morrison,
James Garrard,
John Edwards,
George Wilson,
. . . Payne,
James Rogers,
. . . Kincheloe.

MEMBERS OF THE CONVENTION WHICH ASSEMBLED AT DANVILLE, IN AUGUST, 1785.

Samuel McDowell, *President.*
George Muter,
Christopher Irvine,
William Kennedy,
Benjamin Logan,
Caleb Wallace,
John Coburn,
James Carter,
Richard Terrell,
George Wilson,
Isaac Cox,
Andrew Hines,
James Rogers,

Harry Innis,
John Edwards,
James Speed,
James Wilkinson,
James Garrard,
Levi Todd,
John Craig,
Robert Patterson,
Benjamin Sebastian,
Philip Barbour,
Isaac Morrison,
Matthew Walton.

MEMBERS OF THE CONVENTION IN 1787, HELD IN DANVILLE.

Jefferson County.
Richard Easton,
Alexander Breckinridge,
Michael Lackasang,
Benjamin Sebastian,
James Meriwether.
Nelson County.
Joseph Lewis,
William McClung,
John Caldwell,
Isaac Cox,
Matthew Walton.
Fayette County.
Levi Todd,
John Fowler,
Humphrey Marshall,
Caleb Wallace,
William Ward.
Bourbon County.
James Garrard,
John Edwards,

Benjamin Harrison,
Edward Lyne,
Henry Lee.
Lincoln County.
Benjamin Logan,
John Logan,
Isaac Shelby,
William Montgomery,
Walker Baylor.
Madison County.
William Irvine,
John Miller,
Higgerson Grubbs,
Robert Rodes,
David Crews.
Mercer County.
Samuel McDowell,
Harry Innis,
George Muter,
William Kennedy,
James Speed.

MEMBERS OF THE CONVENTION IN 1788, HELD IN SAME PLACE.

Jefferson County.
Richard Taylor,
Richard C. Anderson,
Alexander S. Bullitt,
Abraham Hite,
Benjamin Sebastian.

Nelson County.
Isaac Morrison,
John Caldwell,
Philip Phillips,
Joseph Burnett,
James Bard.

Fayette County.
James Wilkinson,
Caleb Wallace,
Thomas Marshall,
William Ward,
John Allen.
Bourbon County.
James Garrard,
John Edwards,
Benjamin Harrison,
John Grant,
John Miller.
Lincoln County.
Benjamin Logan,
Isaac Shelby,

William Montgomery,
Nathan Houston,
Willis Green.
Madison County.
William Irvine,
George Adams,
James French,
Aaron Lewis,
Higgerson Grubbs.
Mercer County.
Samuel M'Dowell,
John Brown,
Harry Innis,
John Jouitt,
Christopher Greenup.

NAMES OF THE KENTUCKY MEMBERS OF THE VIRGINIA CONVENTION WHICH RATIFIED THE PRESENT CONSTITUTION OF THE UNITED STATES.

Fayette County.
Humphrey Marshall,
John Fowler.
Jefferson County.
Robert Breckinridge,
Rice Bullock.
Lincoln County.
John Logan,
Henry Pauling.
Nelson County.
John Steele,
Matthew Walton.

Mercer County.
Thomas Allen,
Alexander Robertson.

Madison County.
Green Clay,
William Irvine.

Bourbon County.
Henry Lee,
John Edwards.

The names of the following members of the Virginia legislature, from Kentucky, are given in Governor Morehead's Boonsborough address, viz:

John Brown, Benjamin and John Logan, Esquire Boone, Swearingen, Thomas, John and Robert Todd, James Harrod, William M'Clung, John Steele, James Garrard, John Edwards, John Jewitt, William Pope and Richard Taylor.

MEMBERS OF THE CONVENTION OF 1792, WHICH FORMED THE FIRST CONSTITUTION OF KENTUCKY; HELD IN DANVILLE.

Fayette County.
Hubbard Taylor,
Thomas Lewis,
George S. Smith,
Robert Fryer,
James Crawford.
Jefferson County.
Richard Taylor,
John Campbell,
Alexander S. Bullitt,
Benjamin Sebastian,
Robert Breckinridge.
Bourbon County.
John Edwards,
James Garrard,
James Smith,
John McKenny,
Benjamin Harrison.
Nelson County.
William Keen,
Matthew Walton,
Cuthbert Harrison,
Joseph Hobbs,
Andrew Hynes.
Madison County.
Charles Kavendor,
Higgerson Grubbs,

Thomas Clay,
Thomas Kennedy,
Joseph Kennedy.
Mercer County.
Samuel Taylor,
Jacob Froman,
George Nicholas,
David Rice,
Samuel McDowell.
Lincoln County.
Benjamin Logan,
John Bailey,
Isaac Shelby,
Benedict Sayre,
William Montgomery.
Woodford County.
John Watkins,
Richard Young,
William Steele,
Caleb Wallace,
Robert Johnston.
Mason County.
George Lewis,
Miles W. Conway,
Thomas Waring,
Robert Rankin,
John Wilson.

MEMBERS OF THE CONVENTION WHICH FRAMED THE PRESENT CONSTITUTION OF KENTUCKY; ASSEMBLED AT FRANKFORT, AUGUST 17, 1799.

Jefferson County.
Alexander S. Bullitt, *President,*
Richard Taylor.
Bourbon County.
John Allen,
Charles Smith,
Robert Wilmot,
James Duncan,
William Griffith,
Nathaniel Rogers.
Bracken County.
Philip Buckner.
Campbell County.
Thomas Sanford.
Clarke County.
Robert Clarke,
R. Hickman,
William Sudduth.
Christian County.
Young Ewing.
Fayette County.
John Breckenridge,
John McDowell,
John Bell,
H. Harrison,
B. Thruston,
Walter Carr.
Franklin County.
Henry Innis,
John Logan.
Fleming County.
George Stockton.
Garrard County.
William M. Bledsoe.
Green County.
William Casey.
Harrison County.
Henry Coleman,
William E. Boswell.
Jessamine County.
John Price.

Lincoln County.
William Logan,
N. Huston.
Logan County.
John Bailey,
Reuben Ewing.
Mason County.
Philemon Thomas,
Thomas Marshall, Jr.
Joshua Baker.
Mercer County.
Peter Brunner,
John Adair,
Thomas Allen,
Samuel Taylor
Madison County.
Green Clay,
Thomas Clay,
William Irvine.
Montgomery County.
Jilson Payne.
Nelson County.
John Rowan,
Richard Prather,
Nicholas Minor.
Shelby County.
Benjamin Logan,
Abraham Owen.
Scott County.
William Henry,
Robert Johnson.
Woodford County.
Caleb Wallace,
William Steele.
Washington County.
Felix Grundy,
Robert Abell.
Warren County.
Alexander Davidson.

NAMES OF REPRESENTATIVES AND ELECTORS OF SENATE FOR 1792, UNDER THE FIRST CONSTITUTION.

Bourbon County.

REPRESENTATIVES.
George M. Bedinger,
John Waller,
Charles Smith,
James Smith,
John M'Kenney.

ELECTORS.
John Edwards,
Benjamim Harrison,
Thomas Jones,
Andrew Hood,
John Allen.

Fayette County.

William Russel,
John Hawkins,
Thomas Lewis,
Hubbard Taylor,
James Trotter,
Joseph Crockett,
James M'Millan,
John McDowell,
Robert Patterson.

William Campbell,
Edward Payne,
John Martin,
Abraham Bowman,
Robert Todd,
John Bradford,
John Morrison,
Gabriel Madison,
Peyton Short.

Jefferson County.

REPRESENTATIVES.	ELECTORS.
Richard Taylor,	Alexander S. Bullitt,
Robert Breckinridge,	Richard C. Anderson,
Benjamin Roberts.	John Campbell.

Lincoln County.

William Montgomery,	John Logan,
Henry Pawling,	Benjamin Logan,
James Davis,	Isaac Shelby,
Jesse Cravens.	Thomas Todd.

Madison County.

Higgerson Grubbs,	William Irvine,
Thomas Clay,	Higgerson Grubbs,
John Miller.	Thomas Clay.

Mason County.

Alexander D. Orr,	Robert Rankin
John Wilson.	George Stockton.

Mercer County.

Samuel Taylor,	Christopher Greenup,
John Jouitt,	Harry Innis,
Jacob Frowman,	Samuel McDowell,
Robert Mosby.	William Kennedy.

Nelson County.

William King,	Walter Beall,
William Abell,	John Caldwell,
Matthew Walton,	William May,
Edmund Thomas,	Cuthbert Harrison,
Joseph Hobbs,	Adam Shepherd,
Joshua Hobbs.	James Shepherd.

Woodford County.

John Watkins,	John Watkins,
Richard Young,	George Muter,
William Steele,	Richard Young
John Grant.	Robert Johnson.

SENATORS ELECTED BY THE ELECTORS IN 1792.

John Campbell, Jefferson county.	John Allen, Bourbon county.
John Logan, Lincoln county.	Robert Johnson, Woodford county.
Robert Todd, Fayette county.	Alexander D. Orr, Mason county.
John Caldwell, Nelson county.	EXTRA SENATORS.
William McDowell, Mercer county.	Alexander S. Bullitt, Jefferson county.
Thomas Kennedy, Madison county.	Peyton Short, Fayette county.

A LIST OF DISTINGUISHED CITIZENS OF KENTUCKY, WHO HAVE FILLED HIGH AND RESPONSIBLE STATIONS UNDER THE UNITED STATES' GOVERNMENT, OR UNDER THE GOVERNMENT OF OTHER STATES.

GOVERNORS AND LIEUTENANT GOVERNORS OF STATES.

Names.	From whence.	Where stationed.
Ninian Edwards,	Logan county,	Governor of Illinois.
Benjamin Howard,	Fayette county,	Governor of Missouri.
William Clarke,	Jefferson county,	Governor of Missouri.
John Pope,	Washington county,	Governor of Arkansas.
S. T. Mason, jr.	Fayette county,	Governor of Michigan.
Joseph M. White,	Franklin county,	Governor of Florida.
Richard K. Call,	Logan county,	Governor of Florida.
Lilburn W. Boggs,	Fayette county,	Governor of Missouri.
John M'Lean,	Logan county,	Governor of Illinois.
Henry Dodge,	Jefferson county,	Governor of Wisconsin.
James B. Ray,	Boone county,	Governor of Indiana.
Mr. Carlin,	Nelson county,	Governor of Illinois.
John Dunklin,	Mercer county,	Governor of Missouri.
C. W. Bird,	Fayette county,	Secretary North-west Territory
James Brown,	Lexington,	Lieutenant Governor of Louisiana.

Names.	From whence.	Where stationed.
Robert Crittenden,	Logan county,	Acting Governor of Arkansas.
Mr. Step,	Scott county,	Lieutenant Governor of Indiana.
Mr. Ewing,	Logan county,	Lieutenant Governor of Illinois.
Mr. Hubbard,	Warren county,	Lieutenant Governor of Illinois.
Ratliffe Boon,	Mercer county,	Lieutenant Governor of Indiana.
John Chambers,	Mason county,	Governor of Iowa.
John Floyd,	Jefferson county,	Governor of Virginia.

AMBASSADORS, FOREIGN MINISTERS, ETC.

Henry Clay,	Lexington,	Minister Extraordinary to Ghent.
James Brown,	Lexington,	Minister to France.
Richard C. Anderson,	Louisville,	Minister to Colombia.
Wm. T. Barry,	Lexington,	Minister to Spain,
James Shannon,	Lexington,	Chargé to Central America.
Ninian Edwards,	Logan county,	Minister to Mexico.
Thomas P. Moore,	Mercer county,	Chargé to Bogota.
Robert B. M'Afee,	Mercer county,	Chargé to Bogota.
Anthony Butler,	Logan county,	Chargé to Mexico.
Peter W. Grayson,	Fayette county,	Minister Plen. Texas to U. S.
Charles S. Todd,	Shelby county,	Minister to Russia.
James C. Pickett,	Mason county,	Chargé to Peru.
Robert Wickliffe, jr.	Fayette county,	Chargé to Sardinia.

VICE PRESIDENT.

Richard M. Johnson,	Scott county,	Vice President of United States.

HEADS OF DEPARTMENT AND OFFICERS UNITED STATES' GOVERNMENT.

John Breckinridge,	Fayette county,	Attorney General United States.
Henry Clay	Lexington,	Secretary of State United States.
William T. Barry,	Lexington,	Post Master General United States.
Amos Kendall,	Franklin county,	Post Master General United States.
Robert Johnson,	Franklin county,	As't. Post Master Gen. United States.
James Boyle,	Russellville,	Major General United States Army.
George Croghan,	Jefferson county,	Major General United States Army.
Thomas S. Jesup,	Fayette county,	Major General United States Army.
D. M'Reynolds,	Russellville,	Surgon General United States Army.
John McLean,	Mason county,	Post Master General United States.
Zachary Taylor	Jefferson county,	Major General United States Army.
Isaac Shelby,	Lincoln county,	Secretary of War United States.
Felix Grundy,	Nelson county,	Attorney General United States.
John J. Crittenden,	Frankfort,	Attorney General United States.
George M. Bibb,	Louisville,	Secretary of Treasury United States.
Charles A. Wickliffe,	Nelson county,	Post Master General United States.

JUDGES UNITED STATES OR OTHER HIGH COURTS.

John McLean,	Mason county,	Supreme Court United States.
C. W. Bird,	Fayette county,	United States Judge, Ohio.
Judge Lewis,	Jessamine county,	Supreme Court Louisiana.
Francis L. Turner,	Fayette county,	Supreme Court Louisiana.
Joseph E. Davis,	Logan county,	Supreme Court Mississippi.
E. Turner,	Fayette county,	Supreme Court Mississippi.
Thomas P. Davis,	Madison county,	United States Judge, Indiana.
B. Johnson,	Scott county,	United States Judge, Arkansas.
N. Pope,	Jefferson county,	United States Judge, Illinois.
Henry Humphreys,	Lexington,	Supreme Court Texas,
Thomas Todd,	Frankfort,	Supreme Court United States.

UNITED STATES' SENATORS.

Thomas Reed,	Mercer county,	From Missouri.
James Brown,	Lexington,	From Louisiana.
John M'Lean,	Logan county,	From Illinois.
Dr. Linn,	Jefferson county,	From Missouri.

Josiah S. Johnston,	Mason county,	From Louisiana.
John M. Robinson,	Scott county,	From Illinois.
J. Norvell,	Lexington,	From Michigan.
D. R. Atchison,	Fayette county,	From Missouri.
E. A. Hannegan,	Mason county,	From Indiana.

PRESIDENTS OF COLLEGES.

Robert G. Wilson,	Mason county,	President University, Athens, Ohio.
Robert Bishop,	Lexington,	President University, Oxford, Ohio.
James Blythe,	Lexington,	President S. Hanover College, Ia.
John P. Durbin,	Augusta,	President Dickinson College, Penn.
David Nelson,	Danville,	President Theo. Seminary, Illinois.
John Chamberlin,	Danville,	President Oakland College, Miss.
William H. M'Guffey,	Paris,	President Cincinnati College, Ohio.
Robert J. Breckinridge,	Lexington,	President Jefferson College, Penn.

POPULATION OF KENTUCKY.

FROM THE YEAR 1790 TO THE YEAR 1840, INCLUSIVE.

Years.	Total.	Blacks.	Increase, Whites.	Increase, Blacks.
1790	73,677	12,430		
1800	220,959	43,344	147,282	30,914
1810	406,511	80,560	185,552	37,217
1820	564,317	120,732	147,806	40,171
1830	688,844	165,350	124,527	44,618
1840	779,828	182,258	110,981	16,908

The population of Kentucky in 1847, with the same rate of increase as shown in the foregoing table to have taken place from 1830 to 1840, amounts to 847,860. In 1850, if the ratio of increase continue the same, the population of Kentucky will be 881,863.

POPULATION OF COUNTIES AND COUNTY TOWNS, 1840.

Counties.	Census of 1840.				County Towns.	Pop. 1840.
	Whites.	Free Col'd.	Slaves.	Total Pop.		
Adair	6,769	92	1,605	8,466	Columbia	486
Allen	6,375	19	935	7,329	Scottsville	215
Anderson	4,372	21	1,059	5,452	Lawrenceburg	
Barren	13,147	76	4,065	17,288	Glasgow	505
Bath	7,708	104	1,951	9,763	Owingsville	251
Boone	7,824	27	2,183	10,034	Burlington	
Bourbon	7,845	308	6,325	14,478	Paris	1,197
Breathitt	2,076		119	2,195		
Bracken	6,083	151	819	7,053	Augusta	786
Breckinridge	7,239	14	1,691	8,944	Hardinsburg	634
Bullitt	4,996	18	1,320	6,334	Shepherdsville	
Butler	3,379	4	515	3,898	Morgantown	
Caldwell	8,091	103	2,171	10,365	Princeton	
Calloway	8,870	13	911	9,794	Wadesborough	165
Campbell	4,921	4	289	5,214	Newport	
Carroll	3,212	23	731	3,966		
Carter	2,711	8	186	2,905		
Casey	4,371	37	531	4,939	Liberty	135
Christian	9,491	99	5,997	15,587	Hopkinsville	1,581
Clark	6,755	145	3,902	10,802	Winchester	1,047
Clay	3,954	150	503	4,607	Manchester	
Clinton	3,674	1	188	3,863		
Cumberland	4,571	34	1,485	6,090	Burkesville	
Daviess	6,327	44	1,960	8,331	Owensborough	
Edmonson	2,579	1	334	2,914	Brownsville	112
Estill	4,960	17	558	5,535		
Fayette	10,885	599	10,710	22,194	Lexington	6,997
Fleming	11,158	118	1,992	13,268	Flemingsburg	591
Floyd	6,103	15	184	6,302	Prestonsburg	84
Franklin	6,337	234	2,849	9,420	FRANKFORT,	1,917

Counties.	Census of 1840.				County towns.	Pop. 1840.
	Whites.	Free Col'd.	Slaves.	Total.		
Gallatin	3,361	38	604	4,003	Warsaw	600
Garrard	7,110	87	3,283	10,480	Lancaster	480
Grant	3,838	6	348	4,192	Williamstown	
Graves	6,644	4	817	7,465	Mayfield	
Grayson	4,262		199	4,461	Litchfield	
Greene	10,263	119	3,830	14,212	Greensburg	58?
Greenup	5,479	64	754	6,297	Greenup	
Hancock	2,039	3	539	2,581	Hawesville	420
Hardin	13,829	46	2,482	16,357	Elizabeth	979
Harlan	2,928	8	79	3,015	Harlan C. H.	
Harrison	8,995	93	3,384	12,472	Cynthiana	798
Hart	5,978	44	1,009	7,031	Munfordsville	274
Henderson	6,181	48	3,319	9,548	Henderson	
Henry	7,637	29	2,349	10,015	New Castle	528
Hickman	7,345	8	1,615	8,968	Columbus	
Hopkins	7,417	31	1,723	9,171	Madisonville	51
Jefferson	26,987	763	8,596	36,346	Louisville	21,210
Jessamine	5,780	144	3,472	9,396	Nicholasville	632
Kenton	7,031	34	751	7,816	Covington	2,026
Knox	5,022	164	536	5,722	Barbourville	224
Laurel	2,964	6	109	3,079		
Lawrence	4,652	1	77	4,730	Louisa	
Lewis	5,873	27	406	6,306		
Lincoln	6,582	155	3,450	10,187	Stanford	263
Livingston	7,338	99	1,588	9,025	Salem	233
Logan	8,479	310	4,826	13,615	Russellville	1,196
Madison	10,860	82	5,413	16,355	Richmond	822
Marion	8,340	80	2,612	11,032	Lebanon	546
Mason	11,138	272	4,309	15,719	Maysville	2,741
McCracken	4,064	27	654	4,745	Paducah	
Meade	4,366	5	1,409	5,780	Brandenburg	
Mercer	13,061	373	5,286	18,720	Harrodsburg	1,254
Monroe	5,811	12	703	6,526	Tompkinsville	188
Montgomery	6,409	188	2,735	9,332	Mount Sterling	585
Morgan	4,539	3	61	4,603	West Liberty	
Muhlenburg	5,755	13	1,196	6,964	Greenville	
Nelson	8,878	116	4,643	13,637	Bardstown	1,492
Nicholas	7,310	182	1,253	8,745	Carlisle	256
Ohio	5,747	22	823	6,592	Hartford	309
Oldham	4,858	145	2,377	7,380	La Grange	233
Owen	6,915	36	1,281	8,232	New Liberty	227
Pendleton	4,013	5	437	4,455	Falmouth	
Perry	2,923	23	143	3,089	Perry C. H.	
Pike	3,469	13	85	3,567	Pikeville	92
Pulaski	8,583	18	1,119	9,620	Somerset	238
Rockcastle	3,023	9	377	3,409	Mount Vernon	209
Russell	3,828	4	406	4,238	Jamestown	
Scott	8,220	109	5,339	13,668	Georgetown	1,511
Shelby	11,256	157	6,355	17,768	Shelbyville	1,335
Simpson	5,004	40	1,493	6,537	Franklin	
Spencer	4,650	20	1,911	6,581	Taylorsville	398
Todd	6,070	42	3,879	9,991	Elkton	470
Trigg	5,614	50	2,052	7,716	Cadiz	
Trimble	3,787	20	673	4,480	Bedford	148
Union	4,909	36	1,728	6,673	Morganfield	
Warren	11,078	161	4,207	15,446	Bowling Green	
Washington	7,900	38	2,658	10,596	Springfield	598
Wayne	6,754	15	630	7,399	Monticello	142
Whitley	4,508	19	146	4,673	Whitley C. H.	
Woodford	5,816	172	5,752	11,740	Versailles	1,044
Total	590,253	7,317	182,258	779,828		

POPULATION OF THE PRINCIPAL TOWNS.

	1810.	1820.	1830.	1840.	1847.
Louisville	1,357	4,012	10,352	21,210	40,000
Lexington	4,226	5,279	6,104	6,996	8,000
Maysville	335	1,130	2,040	2,741	5,000
Frankfort	1,099	1,679	1,680	1,916	2,500
Covington					6,000

SITUATION, BOUNDARIES, AND EXTENT.

The State of Kentucky is situated between 36 degrees 30 minutes, and 39 degrees 10 minutes, north latitude; and between 81 degrees 50 minutes, and 89 degrees 26 minutes, west longitude—and includes all that portion of territory which lies south and westward of a line, beginning on the Ohio river, at the mouth of the Great Sandy river, and running up the same, and the main and north-easterly branch thereof, to the great Laurel ridge or Cumberland mountains; thence south-west along said mountains, to a line of North Carolina. It is bounded north by Illinois, Indiana, and Ohio; east by Virginia; south by Tennessee; and west by the Mississippi river and State of Missouri. It is three hundred miles in length from east to west, and one hundred and fifty miles in mean breadth; and contains 42,600 square miles, or about twenty-seven millions of acres.

FACE OF THE COUNTRY, ETC.

The face of the country is quite diversified, presenting every variety of surface as well as quality of soil. The region around Lexington, including the entire counties of Bourbon, Fayette. Woodford, and portions of Franklin, Jessamine, Clarke, Montgomery, Bath, Nicholas, Harrison, and Scott, comprises the largest body of fine land in Kentucky—the surface being agreeably undulating, and the soil black and friable, producing the sugar-tree, blue and black ash, black and honey locust, elm, hickory, black walnut, mulberry, buckeye, pawpaw, &c. Portions of the uplands of Boone, Grant, Mason, and Fleming, in the north, and Mercer, Madison, Boyle, Lincoln, Garrard, Shelby, Washington, Laurel, Green, Nelson, &c., in the middle district, together with a number of counties south of Green river, comprise remarkably rich, and doubtless as productive bodies of land as that which has been most appropriately termed the garden of Kentucky, but more circumscribed in their extent.

Capt. Imlay, an officer of the Revolutionary army, and an early witness of the settlement of Kentucky, caused to be published in 1793, in New York, "a topographical description of the western territory of North America," comprised in a series of letters to a friend in England. In these letters, the following glowing description is given of the country, as it was presented to his view in the spring season of the year:

"Everything here assumes a dignity and splendor I have never seen in any other part of the world. You ascend a considerable distance from the shore of the Ohio, and when you would suppose you had arrived at the summit of a mountain, you find yourself upon an extensive level. Here an eternal verdure reigns, and the brilliant sun of latitude 39°, piercing through the azure heavens, produces in this prolific soil an early maturity which is truly astonishing.

"Flowers full and perfect, as if they had been cultivated by the hand of a florist, with all their captivating odors, and with all the variegated charms which color and nature can produce here, in the lap of elegance and beauty, decorate the smiling groves. Soft zephyrs gently breathe on sweets, and the inhaled air gives a voluptuous glow of health and vigor, that seems to ravish the intoxicated senses. The sweet songsters of the forest appear to feel the influence of the genial clime, and in more soft and modulated tones warble their tender notes in unison with love and nature. Every thing here gives delight; and, in that wild effulgence which beams around us, we feel a glow of gratitude for the elevation which our all bountiful Creator has bestowed upon us.

"You must forgive what I know you will call a rhapsody, but what I really experienced after traveling across the Alleghany mountain in March, when it was covered with snow, and after finding the country about Pittsburgh bare, and not recovered from the ravages of the winter. There was scarcely a blade of grass to be seen; every thing looked dreary, and bore those marks of melancholy which the rude hand of frost produces. I embarked immediately for Kentucky, and in less than five days landed at Limestone, where I found nature robed in all her charms."

In Filson's " Discovery, Settlement and present state of Kentucky," published as a supplement to " Imlay's Description," and written in 1784, the following no less glowing description of the country is given:

"The country is in some parts nearly level; in others not so much so; in others again hilly, but moderately—and in such places there is most water. The levels are not like a carpet, but interspersed with small risings and declivities, which form a beautiful prospect. The soil is of a loose, deep, black mould without sand, in the first rate lands about two or three feet deep, and exceedingly luxuriant in all its productions. The country in general may be considered as well timbered, producing large trees of many kinds, and to be exceeded by no country in variety. Those which are peculiar to Kentucky are the sugar tree, which grows in all parts, and furnishes every family with great plenty of excellent sugar. The honey-locust is curiously surrounded with large thorny spikes, bearing broad and long pods in the form of peas, has a sweet taste, and makes excellent beer. The coffee tree greatly resembles the black-oak, grows large, and also bears a pod, in which is enclosed coffee. The pawpaw tree does not grow to a great size, is a soft wood, bears a fine fruit, much like a cucumber in shape and size, and tastes sweet." Of the "fine cane, on which the cattle feed and grow fat," he says: "This plant in general grows from three to twelve feet high, of a hard substance, with joints at eight or ten inches distance along the stalk, from which proceed leaves resembling those of the willow. There are many canebrakes so thick and tall, that it is difficult to pass through them. Where no cane grows, there is an abundance of wild rye, clover and buffalo grass, covering vast tracts of country, and affording excellent food for cattle. The fields are covered with an abundance of wild herbage not common to other countries. Here are seen the finest crown-imperial in the world, the cardinal flower, so much extolled for its scarlet color, and all the year, excepting the winter months, the plains and valleys are adorned with a variety of flowers of the most admirable beauty. Here is also found the tulip-bearing laurel tree, or magnolia, which is very fragrant and continues to blossom and seed for several months together. The reader by casting his eye upon the map, and viewing round the heads of Licking from the Ohio, and round the heads of Kentucky, Dick's river, and down Green river to the Ohio, may view in that great compass of above one hundred miles square, the most extraordinary country on which the sun has ever shone."

This is a glowing description of Kentucky AS SHE WAS, robed in primeval beauty. The hand of man has been laid upon the forest, and the wild grandeur of nature succeeded by the arts of a civilized people. Kentucky AS SHE IS, presents attractions which are found in but few, if any other regions of the world. Situated in the very centre of the American confederated states, beyond the reach of foreign intrusion—she is rich in a genial climate, rich in a prolific soil, rich in her agricultural products, rich in her beautiful farms and grazing lands, rich in the magnificent scenery and abundant ores of her mountains ; and, above all and beyond all, rich in a population at once industrious, enterprising, hospitable, intelligent and patriotic.

PRINCIPAL RIVERS.

The principal rivers of Kentucky, are the Ohio, Mississippi, Tennessee, Cumberland, Kentucky, Green, Licking, Big and Little Sandy, Salt and the Rolling Fork of Salt river. The Ohio flows along the whole northern boundary of the State for six hundred and thirty-seven miles, following its windings. The Mississippi washes the Kentucky shore from the mouth of the Ohio, to a point below New Madrid, for the distance of one hundred miles. Big and Little Sandy rivers lie in the eastern extremity of the State, the former being its eastern boundary. Cumberland and Tennessee intersect the western extremity ; the former rises in the eastern part of the State, and passes into the State of Tennessee, after which it returns and flows through Kentucky into the Ohio river. The Kentucky, Licking, Salt and Rolling Fork of Salt rivers, flow through the interior of the State. The principal creeks are generally mentioned under the head of the counties in which they rise, or through which they flow.

GEOLOGICAL FORMATION.

The geological formations of Kentucky, in common with those of the other western States generally, belong to that great system which extends from the Alleghanies on the east, across the Mississippi, and perhaps to the Rocky mountains on the west. Throughout this vast territory, the primary fossiliferous or protozoic and lower secondary, or carboniferous rocks prevail. These comprehend a great number of distinct formations, very unequally developed in different parts of this wide valley, producing a great variety in the mineral and agricultural wealth and resources of different sections. Almost all these rocks contain organic remains, although they are found much more abundantly in some strata and localities than in others. We are not, however, to suppose that they are indiscriminately dispersed through the whole series. Here, as in every other part of the world, each formation is distinguished more or less by peculiar species or varieties. There are, however, indubitable proofs that the whole of these strata were once covered by the waters of the ocean, and that the remains which are found in them, and in many places almost compose them, all belong to marine species.

These rocks all belong to the class which are termed sedimentary, and were gradually deposited upon the bottom of the ocean. The shells and skeletons which they contain, no doubt once belonged to the inhabitants of this ocean, and as the animals died and decayed, their harder and more lasting coverings sank to the bottom, and were gradually covered up by clay and sand, and other layers of shells, until at length under a heavy pressure of superincumbent strata, and by a slow and long continued chemical action, they were converted into solid rocks: and now that the waters of the ocean have retired, are exposed to our view as the lasting records of the earth's history during ages long anterior to our own.

When these deposites were made, it is beyond the power of science to determine. Geologically speaking, it was very early.

The strata over nearly the whole surface of Kentucky lie nearly horizontal, with scarcely any dislocations. They have, however, a slight dip. This dip seems to be in every direction from a point near Cincinnati on the Ohio river, as a centre. At this point we see the lowest surface rocks of the State exposed. As we go up the river, we meet with the other strata in succession, cropping out as it is termed, but sinking beneath other rocks as they extend eastward, and rising generally again to the surface on the western slope of the Alleghanies. If from Cincinnati we travel down the river, we meet with the same succession of rocks, but dipping to the west. If from the same point we penetrate into the interior of the State, we find the rocks dipping to the south. Cincinnati seems thus to have been a centre of elevation when this broad valley was lifted above the waters of the ocean.

But it is necessary to be somewhat more minute in our description of the various formations. We will begin with the lowest or oldest, and describe them in the order of their superposition.

FIRST FORMATION—THE BLUE LIMESTONE.

The blue limestone is the lowest rock exposed on the surface in Kentucky. It is, as its name indicates, a limestone. It, however, generally contains a good deal of clay, and in some places a large amount of magnesia. It underlies an immense extent of territory, reaching continuously in all likelihood, though not every where exposed, from the Alleghanies on the east, to at least two hundred miles west of the Mississippi, and probably to the foot of the Rocky mountains. Over much the greater part of this territory it is covered by superincumbent strata. In Kentucky and Ohio it forms the surface rock, over an area extending about one hundred and seventy miles north and south, and one hundred and twenty-five miles east and west. It is somewhat oval in its shape, and reaches from Danville, near the centre of Kentucky, across the Ohio river to Dayton, and from the town of Madison in Indiana, to a short distance above Maysville. This formation is of great though unknown thickness, probably not less than one thousand feet, and is composed of many strata of limestone alternating with layers of clay. The rock is generally found in thin seams, and easily quarried, and well adapted for building purposes. In some places, however, it becomes very thick, and massive, and where the water courses have cut their channels through it, is left exposed in high and perpendicular cliffs. This is very conspicuous on the banks of the Kentucky at Frankfort, and for some miles above. Here the river is confined by high and perpendicular walls of solid rock. The stream no doubt once flowed on the surface level of the country, but for ages has the water been slowly and silently but steadily cutting its way through the hard rock, until the bed of the river is now four or five hundred feet beneath the surface of the surrounding country. That there was once no natural valley here, but that the channel has been formed by the action of the running water itself, we have this proof: The layers of rock, on the opposite sides of the river, exactly correspond. Opposite to a thick bed you find one of the same thickness and character. So of a thinner layer, and of the seams of clay which separate the different beds. Besides this, we find near the surface, far above the present level of the bed of the river, in many places, manifest marks of the action of water, giving indubitable proof, that it once occupied a channel not near so deep as at present.

It is in these cliffs of the Kentucky river, and in the adjacent country that we find what is termed the Kentucky marble. This presents quite a different appearance from that of the common limestone, ordinarily. As has been stated, the layers are much thicker, the rock is less crystalline, more brittle, breaks with a concoidal fracture, and is barren of organic remains. It is used as a building stone, and is the material of which the State-house in Frankfort is constructed. It is susceptible of a good polish, and is sometimes used for tomb stones, and monuments, though liable to scale when exposed to the action of the weather. It is almost too coarse to be suitable for finer ornamental purposes. It is said to contain a large per cent. of magnesia.

SECOND FORMATION—THE CLIFF LIMESTONE.

If we travel up the Ohio river, from Cincinnati, until we get to about the dividing line between the counties of Mason and Lewis, we meet with the formation overlying the blue limestone. If we travel down the river we first meet the same formation at Madison, Indiana. It takes its name of "Cliff Limestone" from the high cliffs which are usually found on the water courses where this formation prevails. It differs in its structure, color and general appearance, from the blue limestone. It is generally found in thicker layers, and has less clay, but more sand in its composition. As a surface rock it covers but a small area in Kentucky. It forms a narrow belt entirely surrounding the space occupied by the underlying rock. At its broadest point in Kentucky, this belt is not more than twenty or thirty miles, and entirely disappears in the centre of the State. On the east and west it dips under the other strata. On the west it is the surface rock, between Madison and Louisville. On the east it occupies a somewhat narrower strip of country. But towards the north it spreads out over an immense extent of territory, and becomes much thicker. It is the rock over which the waters pour at the falls of Niagara, and it is the same rock that causes the falls of the Ohio at Louisville. Towards the north-west, in Illinois and Iowa, this rock attains a thickness of six or seven hundred feet, and is the great lead-bearing rock of those states. In Kentucky it is perhaps too thin ever to furnish any rich veins of ore.

THIRD FORMATION—SLATE OR SHALE.

The slate rests upon the cliff limestone, and is seen immediately on crossing this formation in traveling either up or down the Ohio from Cincinnati. It has a dip exactly corresponding to that of the preceding rock, and like it, occupies a narrow semi-circular belt of country lying just outside of the cliff limestone. Crossing the Ohio in Lewis county, where it is not more than ten or twelve miles broad, and passing in a south-west direction to the centre of the State, a few miles south of Danville, it makes a sweep round towards the north-west, and re-crosses the Ohio at Louisville. Indeed this slate may be traced on the surface from the north-eastern part of Illinois, in a south-east direction, through Illinois, Indiana, and to the centre of Kentucky, where it bends to the north, and runs through the whole length of Ohio, until it strikes the western end of Lake Erie, and thence east along the southern margin of that lake, into the interior of New York, where bending south again, it runs along the western slope of the Alleghanies; and throughout this vast circuit, is in no place more than fifteen or twenty miles broad, on the surface, though it underlies an immense region. In the eastern part of the State it is between two and three hundred feet thick.

The slate is highly bituminous, and burns readily when thrown on the fire. Throughout its whole extent, it abounds in iron pyrites (sulphate of iron) and in iron ores, and over the whole territory it occupies mineral springs are very numerous.

FOURTH FORMATION—SANDSTONE.

The slate is everywhere accompanied by an overlying sandstone, or freestone, as it is sometimes termed. This sandstone may be traced through that same vast extent of territory, in which it has just been mentioned the slate can be followed; and in Kentucky comes to the surface in a narrow semi-circular belt of country completely surrounding the slate. It gives rise to a low range of hills termed "knobs," which may be traced, from Louisville around south of Danville, to the Ohio river again in Lewis county. In some cases this rock, when exposed to the weather, becomes soft and crumbles to pieces. But if care be taken to select specimens entirely free from clay, it forms a firm and durable material for architectural. purposes. It is readily cut into any desired shape, and is extensively used for columns, tombstones and other purposes. But of the finer qualities great numbers of grindstones are manufactured. Near Portsmouth it is about three hundred and fifty feet thick; below Louisville, two hundred and eighty; and it seems to grow thinner as it extends towards the west, though it is not known to what distance it reaches. It has the same dip with the preceding rocks. It underlies the whole of the eastern part of Kentucky, and is the rock which furnishes the salt springs in this State and Virginia.

FIFTH FORMATION—OR CAVERNOUS LIMESTONE.

Immediately above the sandstone we meet with another formation of limestone. It is termed the " Cavernous limestone" because in it are found those numerous caves, which abound in Kentucky, and of which the Mammoth Cave, is the most remarkable yet discovered. The mouth of this cave is in Edmonston county, on the banks of Green river. It is said to have been explored to the distance of ten miles from its mouth, without having yet reached its termination; and the aggregate length of all the branches already discovered, is more than forty miles. It is the most remarkable cave known, for its vast extent. Its various branches sometimes swell out into vast arches a hundred feet high, and into vaulted rooms or domes, some of which are said to be more than three hundred feet from floor to roof. In it are several springs of fresh and mineral waters, even a river as it is called, but which is more like a pool of water, as scarcely any current can be detected, and which is most probably fed by the Green river, as it rises and falls with the water in that stream. In this river or pool are found "blind fish," without the slightest appearance of eyes. They are not more than four or five inches long, but from their snowy whiteness can be seen at considerable depths, darting through the transparent water. They are often caught with nets.

Stalactites and stalagmites abound in some parts of the cave; and in at least one room the roof and sides are covered with the most brilliant incrustations of gypsum, (sulphate of lime), which looks like it had been carved by the hand of art. But no description can convey any adequate idea of the impression the endless variety in the cave makes upon the beholder.

But this is only one of a thousand or perhaps ten thousand caves found in this rock. Throughout the whole section of country where this formation prevails, sink holes, sinking springs, and underground streams are constantly to be met with. These sink holes are probably produced by the falling in of the roofs of the caves, and the springs and streams pour into them, and often run for great distances under ground.

The rock of this formation is almost a pure limestone, and when burned makes most beautiful lime. It is manufactured and sent down the Ohio and Mississippi rivers, in considerable quantities, for the southern markets. It is generally compact, and can be quarried in thick blocks, and forms an excellent building material. It is sometimes oolitic in its structure, and in many places is covered with fragments of flint or hornstone.

This cavernous limestone forms the surface rock for a large section, perhaps a fourth or fifth of Kentucky. Its boundary may be traced as follows : Beginning at the Tennessee line near Thompsonville in Monroe county, and proceeding in a north-east direction to Mt. Vernon ; thence westward, to the head waters of the southern branch of Rolling Fork, and thence along this stream to where it empties into the Ohio, we mark its eastern limits. It occupies all the State west of this boundary, except the portion occupied by the lower coal field, which will be described, and which rests upon this rock. The dip of this rock is towards the south and west in Kentucky. It thins out towards the east, but becomes thicker towards the west, and attains a great thickness in Missouri and Illinois. In Kentucky the country underlaid by this rock, is termed the "Barrens." The name is probably not derived from the poverty of the soil, for this is of a medium quality, and sometimes very good; but from the scarcity of the timber. The barrens are said to have been once a vast prairie, and are now covered by scarcely any timber except a small scrubby oak, termed black-jack. It is impossible to assign the cause of this peculiar feature of this remarkable region.

SIXTH FORMATION—THE CONGLOMERATE COAL SERIES.

Resting on the cavernous limestone we find a conglomerate or pudding stone. It is composed of coarse pebbles of quartz, and fine grains of sand, rounded and cemented together by a silicious cement. It underlies the coal series in both the eastern and western fields in Kentucky, and is generally regarded as a member of the coal formation. It forms a kind of basin or trough in which the coal beds were deposited, and comes to the surface in a border completely surrounding the coal fields. In Kentucky it is found in two narrow strips,—in one extending from the Ohio river in Greenup county, in a south-west direction to where the Cumberland river crosses the Tennessee line; in the other, forming a margin to the lower coal field extending from the Ohio in the western part of Meade county, south and west until it nearly reaches the southern limits of the State, at a point near the dividing line between the counties of Todd and Christian, and thence bending to the north-west, recrosses the Ohio in Crittenden county. The rock is very firm, and is sometimes used for millstones to grind Indian corn. It varies in thickness from eighty to two or three hundred feet, though perhaps no where so thick as this in Kentucky.

The Coal series.—Immediately over the conglomerate we find what may be more properly termed the coal formation. The whole series is made up of various combinations of layers of shale and sandstone, with thinner strata of limestone, hornstone and iron ore alternating with coal beds.

In Kentucky there are two distinct and separate coal fields. The one in the eastern part of the State, termed the coal field of the upper Ohio, includes the whole of that section of the State, which lies to the east of a line beginning on the Ohio river, at Greenupsburg, and running in a south-west direction by Irvine on the Kentucky, Somerset, the county seat of Pulaski, and Jamestown, to the Tennessee line. This is a part of the great coal field, the largest in the world, occupying a very large district in western Pennsylvania and Virginia, a portion of Ohio, and the eastern part of Kentucky, and extending down into Tennessee, and probably into Alabama.

The other coal field is in the Green river country, and is a part of the great field covering a large portion of Illinois, considerable sections in Kentucky and Indiana, and even extending into Missouri and Iowa. Mr. Mather, who, under the direction of the Legislature, made a geological reconnoisance of Kentucky, in 1838, in his report says: "The boundary of the lower Ohio coal formation may be indicated, by an irregular line drawn from near the mouth of the Wabash, so as to include Henderson, Davies, Hancock, Ohio, and most of Union, Hopkins, Muhlenburg, Butler, Edmonston, Grayson, and a small portion of Breckinridge. Hart, and Warren counties."

In both fields the strata dip from the border towards the center, and the rocks which we observe passing under the coal formation as we ascend the Ohio, come again to the surface before we reach the Alleghanies, forming a kind of basin or trough, in which the coal has been deposited.

In Kentucky the coal fields are supposed to cover ten or twelve thousand square miles, and but a small part of each field is included within the limits of this State. In England, the largest coal field does not embrace more than twelve hundred square miles, or the one-tenth of the coal district of Kentucky. In many places several workable beds of coal are found. But as yet, mining operations have been carried on only to a very limited extent, and generally a seam is opened where the coal is found cropping out on a hill side, and only the most accessible coal procured. The nearly horizontal position of the beds in Kentucky, the dip being just sufficient for drainage, if the vein is opened on the right side of a hill, renders the operation of mining very easy. There are several varieties of coal, but all of them bituminous. Mr. Mather in his report mentions three kinds.

" 1st. The common bituminous or caking coal.

" 2nd. A similar coal which does not cake, and adhere in lumps when burning, but each piece keeps separate and distinct.

" 3d.   coal."

He adds " All these coals burn well and give out much heat ; but the two latter are far more pleasant for domestic use, and do not emit that kind of smoke from which flakes of soot, like lampblack, are diffused through the air."

The coal of Kentucky is very accessible. The Cumberland, the Licking, the Kentucky, and the two Sandies, penetrate almost every part of the eastern field, and Green river runs right through the center of the western ; and upon the bosom of these streams is a large amount of coal annually carried to the towns on their banks. The amount annually raised from all the mines in Kentucky, cannot be accurately stated. Mr. Mather states it at three millions of bushels.

METALS AND OTHER USEFUL MINERALS.

Iron. There are several varieties of iron ore found in Kentucky. In several localities the bog ore is found as a deposit from mineral springs. But this is comparatively unimportant. In addition to this, however, there is

1st. The ore of the coal measures. This ore is found in layers, or else in courses of nodules, in the shales or sandstones of the coal fields, and is generally an hydrated peroxide of iron. When found in layers, it is readily broken into rectangular blocks ; otherwise it is taken from the mine in round lumps of various sizes.

2d. The ore found in connection with the limestone underlying the coal measures. This ore is very abundant, and is extensively worked for furnaces.

3d. *The ore of the slate formation.* This ore too, is very abundant, and is found, either in continuous strata, or in layers of nodules in the slate (formation three). It seems to be a calcareous and argillaceous carbonate of iron. In many places where the slate has been crumbled to pieces, and been washed away, it is found abundantly on the surface. All the above ores are worked more or less extensively for the furnaces in various sections of the State.

" In the coal fields of eastern and western Kentucky, there appears to be an almost inexhaustible supply of iron. Over an area of twelve thousand square miles, there may be probably an average thickness of one yard of iron ore in the coal formation alone, without counting the slate and limestone regions, where there is probably as much more. Each cubic yard of this ore will yield on an average one ton of bar iron, or five thousand tons to the acre, or 3,200,000 tons to the square mile, or 38,400,000,000 on the twelve thousand square miles ; a quantity sufficient to supply a ton of iron annually to every individual in the United States (estimating our population at fifteen million of people) for 2,560 years."

It will be remembered that as much more is supposed to belong to the limestone and slate formation.

Like the coal, the iron in every part of Kentucky is very accessible. It is spread over a wide district, penetrated in every direction by navigable streams, and everywhere accompanied by the fuel necessary for its reduction. As yet the mining business may be said hardly to have commenced, but it is destined to be the source of great future wealth to the State.

LEAD.

In a variety of localities, veins of lead ore have been found in the blue limestone (formation one), but no where yet in such abundance as to justify mining operations. The cliff limestone (No. two), and the cavernous limestone (No. five), especially the former, seem to be the great lead-bearing rocks of our country, and neither of them appear to be sufficiently developed in Kentucky, to furnish any rich veins of this metal. It is more than probable, that as long as there is such an inexhaustible supply of lead from the mines further west, it will never be worked in Kentucky.

SALT.

It has already been mentioned that the sandstone (formation fourth), which overlies the slate, seems to furnish the salt springs of this State and Virginia, and perhaps of Ohio and New York. This rock underlies the coal measures, forming a kind of basin in which they were deposited, and over the whole area salt water may be reached by boring to this rock. The water is generally stronger near the center of the basin, as for example in the eastern part of Kentucky, and western part of Virginia, though it is sometimes necessary to bore to the depth of a thousand feet, before the salt-bearing stratum can be reached.

The amount of salt annually manufactured at the various salines of the State, may be estimated from 500,000 to 1,000,000 of bushels.

SALTPETER, GYPSUM, HYDRAULIC LIME.

Saltpeter is found in most of the caves, which are so numerous in the cavernous limestone. It exists in the caves as a nitrate of lime, and is converted into saltpeter (nitrate of potassa), by leaching through wood ashes. It is not largely manufactured.

Gypsum or plaster of Paris and hydraulic limestone, are found in several places. It has already been mentioned that Gypsum forms a complete coating or incrustation, over the walls in some branches of the Mammoth Cave. The hydraulic limestone is in some places found imbedded in the slate, and doubtless a more accurate survey of the State, will serve to discover both these materials in many localities where they are not now imagined to exist.

MINERAL SPRINGS.

Mineral and medicinal springs abound in Kentucky, especially in those sections adjacent to and underlaid by the slate. The gradual decomposition of the sulphuret of iron in this rock, probably affords the sulphuretic hydrogen of the sulphur waters, and sulphuric acid, which combining with oxide of iron, soda, magnesia, etc., form the various salts held in solution by these waters.

Sulphur, chalybeate and Epsom springs, are all very common, and in the watering seasons are much resorted to by invalids.

At the Blue Licks, near the bank of the Licking river, is a sulphur spring containing besides a variety of other ingredients a large amount of common salt, whose waters are highly prized and much used for medicinal purposes. It is annually resorted to by hundreds, for pleasure or health; and large quantities of the water is barreled and sent off through the country, where it meets a ready market. It rises in the blue limestone, though it probably has its origin in the slate.

This, however, is not the only instance of a mineral spring in this formation. At Drennon's Lick, at Big Bone Lick, and in a number of other places in the blue limestone, water is found which is said not to be very dissimilar to that of the Blue Licks.

At Harrodsburg, near the center of the State, are numbers of springs whose predominate ingredient seems to be sulphate of magnesia or Epsom salt. And near Crab Orchard, thirty miles from this place, are several more springs of the same kind, together with sulphur and chalybeate waters. Both of these places are much visited in the watering season. But besides these, a great variety of valuable waters are known; as for example, the springs in Rockcastle, Estill, Bath and Lewis counties.

ORGANIC REMAINS.

Organic remains abound more or less in all the strata of the state. Sufficiently minute examinations have not, however, been made to ascertain the number and variety of species belonging to the different formations. In the lower rocks (formations one and two), fossil remains are exceedingly abundant. The blue limestone in many places seems to be almost entirely composed of the shells of marine animals. "Among the most common are delthyris, atrypa, orthis, stophomena, trilobites, orthocerotites, corallines, cyathophylla, encrinites and a number of other radiata."

In formation two, fossils are perhaps not so numerous, but larger and more distinct than in the preceding rock. Many genera are common to both, though generally shells prevail most in formation one, and radiata in two. The pentamerus, trilobites, cyathophylla, catenipora, retepora, lithodendron, etc., are very abundant in this rock.

Formations third and fourth, the slate and sandstone are barren of organic remains.

Formation fifth is a limestone, and is much richer in fossils. In some places miscroscopic shells are exceedingly abundant.

In the conglomerate, which underlies the coal beds, only a few traces of fossil plants can be discovered. The coal itself is now generally understood to be of vegetable orgin, and the impressions of plants are always more or less distinctly traceable in all the varieties of it.

But besides these remains disseminated so profusely through some of these rocks, there are others of a very different epoch, and in some respects of a much more interesting character. These are the bones of extinct quadrupeds.

In many places on the surface of the rocks already described, and as appears of a much more recent date, there has been deposited, a deep marshy soil, occupying the natural valleys of the country. In these marshy grounds, and especially in the neighborhood of " Licks," to which the animals seem to have been attracted, are often found the bones of several species of extraordinary but now extinct quadrupeds. The most remarkable locality is in Boone county, at Big Bone Lick. Here a large number of bones, perfectly sound and well preserved, have been dug up. And while perhaps in no case has a complete skeleton been found, yet it has been computed that to furnish the specimens carried off from this place alone, there would be required of the

Mastodon maximus, -	100	individuals.
Elephas primigenius,	20	"
Megalonyx Jeffersonia,	1	"
Bos bombifrous, - -	2	"
Bos pallasii, - -	1	"

Some of these animals, especially the mastodon, must have been of extraordinary size, and while there can be no doubt that they are now extinct, there can be as little, that geologically speaking, they were very recently tenants of the earth. The nearly complete skeleton of a mastodon found in the State of New York, and put up by Mr. Peale in the museum in Philadelphia, measures fifteen feet in length, and is nearly eleven feet high. This animal must once have roamed through this whole country, as its remains are found in many States, and many localities. How long since it became extinct, or why it perished, is unknown to us.

SOILS.

Perhaps it may be proper to add a few words in regard to the connection between the geology and soils of different sections of the State. It is well known that the soil takes its character from the underlaying rock; that it is formed by its decomposition, and varies with it. In Kentucky, the blue limestone, or formation one, forms the richest soil. That beautiful section of country,—the garden of the State—embracing Fayette, Bourbon, Woodford, Scott, Jessamine, and the counties between them and the Ohio river, is underlaid by this rock. The soil over this section is not everywhere equally fertile, but altogether is the best in the State.

Formation second and formation fifth are both limestone, and form good soils. The former is, as has already been mentioned, developed only to a very limited extent in this State. The latter covers a much larger territory. The " Barrens " are underlaid by it. The soil is good, and in some places of an excellent quality.

The slate and sandstone generally form poor soils. In some places, however, a proper mixture of limestone with the clay of the slate, forms an excellent soil. The soil over the coal measures is generally poor, though it varies much in its qualities.

EARLY MANNERS AND CUSTOMS.

The plan of this work would be incomplete, if it did not contain some account of the spirit and manners of society in the primitive ages of Kentucky history. The following sketch of early life is drawn from various sources; but we are principally indebted to " Doddridge's Notes."

The household offices were performed by the women; the men cultivated the soil, hunted the game and brought in the meat, built the houses, garrisoned the

11

forts, and freely exposed themselves to danger and privations in defence of the settlements.

Most of the articles in common use were of domestic manufacture. There might have been incidentally a few things brought to the country for sale in a private way, but there was no store for general supply. Utensils of metal, except offensive weapons, were extremely rare, and almost entirely unknown. The table furniture usually consisted of wooden vessels, either *turned* or *coopered*. Iron forks, tin cups, &c., &c., were articles of rare and delicate luxury. The food was of the most wholesome and nutritive kind. The richest meat, the finest butter, and best meal that ever delighted man's palate, were here eaten with a relish which health and labor only know. The hospitality of the people was profuse and proverbial.

The dress of the settlers was of primitive simplicity. The hunting shirt was worn universally. Many of these garments are still in use in the back settlements, and their appearance is familiar to almost every reader in the west. This backwoods costume was peculiarly adapted to the pursuits and habits of the people, and has been connected with so many thrilling passages of war and wild adventure, that the Kentucky hunting shirt is famous throughout the world. The hunting shirt was usually made of linsey, sometimes of coarse linen, and a few of dressed deer skins. The bosom of this dress was sewed as a wallet, to hold a piece of bread, cakes, jerk, tow for wiping the barrel of the rifle, and any other necessary for the hunter or warrior. The belt, which was always tied behind, answered several purposes besides that of holding the dress together. In cold weather, the mittens, and sometimes the bullet bag occupied the front part of it. To the right side was suspended the tomahawk, and to the left the scalping knife in its leathern sheath. The shirt and jacket were of the common fashion. A pair of drawers, or breeches and leggins were the dress of the thighs and legs, and a pair of moccasins answered for the feet much better than shoes. These were made of dressed deer skin. They were generally made of a single piece, with a gathering seam along the top of the foot, and another from the bottom of the heel, without gathers, as high as the ankle joint. Flaps were left on each side to reach some distance up the leg. Hats were made of the native fur; the buffalo wool was frequently employed in the composition of cloth, as was also the bark of the wild nettle.

The forts in which the inhabitants took refuge from the fury of the savages, consisted of cabins, block houses, and stockades. A range of the former commonly formed at least one side of the fort. Divisions or partitions of logs separated the cabins from each other. The walls on the outside were ten or twelve feet high, the slope of the roof being invariably inward. A few of these cabins had puncheon floors, but the greater part were earthen.

The block houses were built at the angles of the fort. They projected about two feet beyond the outer walls of the cabins and stockades. Their upper stories were about eighteen inches every way larger in dimensions than the under one, leaving an opening at the commencement of the second story to prevent the enemy from making a lodgment under their walls. A large folding gate made of thick slabs closed the fort on the side nearest the spring. The stockades, cabins, and blockhouse walls were furnished with ports at proper heights and distances. The entire extent of the outer wall was made bullet proof. The whole of this work was made without the aid of a single nail or spike of iron, which articles were not to be had.

The inhabitants generally married young. There was no distinction of rank, and very little of fortune. The first impression of love generally resulted in marriage, and a family establishment cost but a little labor and nothing else.

A Kentucky wedding in early times was a very picturesque affair, and was an event which excited the general attention of the whole community in which it occurred. The following description of the proceedings had on these interesting occasions, is taken almost verbatim from the account of one who had been present at many of these joyful assemblies:

In the morning of the wedding day, the groom and his attendants assembled at the house of his father, for the purpose of proceeding to the mansion of his bride, which it was desirable to reach by noon, the usual time of celebrating the nuptials, which ceremony must at all events take place before dinner. Let the reader imagine an assemblage of people, without a store, tailor, or mantua maker within an hundred miles ; an assemblage of horses, without a blacksmith or saddler within a like distance. The gentlemen dressed in shoe packs, moccasins, leather breeches, leggins, linsey hunting shirts, and all home made. The ladies in linsey petticoats and linsey or linen bedgowns, coarse shoes, stockings, handkerchiefs, and buckskin gloves. If there were any buckles, rings, buttons, or ruffles, they were relics of old times. The horses were caparisoned with old saddles, old bridles or halters, and pack saddles, with a bag or blanket thrown over them ; a rope or string as often constituted the girth as a piece of leather.

The march, in double file, was often interrupted by the narrowness or obstructions of the horse path, for roads there were none; and these difficulties were often increased by the jocularity, and sometimes by the malice of neighbors, by felling trees and tying grape vines across the way. Sometimes an ambuscade was formed by the way side, and an unexpected discharge of several guns took place, so as to cover the wedding company with smoke. Let the reader imagine the scene which followed this discharge : the sudden spring of the horses, the shrieks of the girls, and the chivalric bustle of their partners to save them from falling. Sometimes, in spite of all that could be done to prevent it, some were thrown to the ground. If a wrist, elbow, or ancle happened to be sprained, it was tied with a handkerchief, and little more was thought or said about it.

Another ceremony took place before the party reached the house of the bride, after whisky was introduced, which was at an early period. When the party had arrived within a mile of the house, two young men would single out to run for the bottle. The worse the path the better, as obstacles afforded an opportunity for the greater display of intrepidity and horsemanship. The start was announced by an Indian yell ; logs, brush, muddy hollows, hills, and glens were speedily passed by the rival ponies. The bottle was always filled for the occasion, and the first who reached the door was presented with the prize, with which he returned in triumph to the company. The contents of the bottle were distributed among the company.

The ceremony of the marriage preceded the dinner, which was a substantial backwoods feast of beef, pork, fowls, and sometimes venison and bear meat roasted and boiled, with plenty of potatoes, cabbage, and other vegetables. After dinner the dancing commenced, and generally lasted till next morning. The figures of the dances were three and four handed reels, or square sets and jigs.

About nine or ten o'clock, a deputation of young ladies stole off the bride and put her to bed. This done, a deputation of young men in like manner stole off the groom and placed him snugly by the side of his bride. The dance still continued, and if seats happened to be scarce, every young man when not engaged in the dance, was obliged to offer his lap as a seat for one of the girls, and the offer was sure to be accepted. In the midst of this hilarity, the bride and groom were not forgotten. Pretty late in the night, some one would remind the company that the new couple must stand in need of some refreshments ; ' black betty,' which was the name of the bottle, was called for and sent up stairs, but often ' black betty' did not go alone. Sometimes as much bread, beef, pork and cabbage was sent along with her, as would afford a good meal for half a dozen hungry men. The young couple were compelled to eat and drink more or less of whatever was offered them.

The marriage being over, the next thing in order was to " settle " the young couple. A spot was selected on a piece of land of one of the parents for their habitation. A day was appointed shortly after their marriage, for commencing the work of building the cabin. The fatigue party consisted of choppers, whose business it was to fell the trees and cut them off at the proper length. A man with a team for hauling them to the place, and arranging them properly assorted at the sides and ends of the building, a carpenter if such he might be called, whose business it was to search the woods for a proper tree for making clapboards for the roof. The tree for this purpose must be straight grained and from three to four feet in diameter. The boards were split four feet long with a large froe, and as wide as the timber would allow. They were used without planing or shaving. Another division were employed in getting puncheons for the floor of the cabin ; this was done by splitting trees about eighteen inches in diameter, and hewing the face of them with a broadaxe. They were half the length of the floor they were intended to make. The materials being prepared, the neighbors collected for the raising. The roof and sometimes the floor were finished on the same day the house was raised. A third day was commonly spent by the carpenters in leveling off the floor and making a clapboard door and table. This last was made of a split slab and supported by four round legs set in auger holes. Some three legged stools were made in the same manner. Pins stuck in the logs at the back of the house supported clapboards which served as shelves for the table furniture. A single fork placed with its lower end in a hole in the floor and the upper end fastened to a joist, served for a bedstead, by placing a pole in the fork with one end through a crack in the logs of the wall. This front pole was crossed by a shorter one within the fork, with its outer end through another crack. From the front pole through a crack between the logs of the end of the house, the boards were placed which formed the bottom of the bed. A few pegs around the wall for a display of the coats of the women and the hunting shirts of the men, and two small forks or bucks' horns to a joist for the rifle and shot pouch, completed the carpenter's work.

The cabin being finished, the ceremony of house warming took place before the young people were permitted to move into it. This was a dance of a whole night's continuance, made up of the relations of the bride and groom and their neighbors. On the day following the young people took possession of their new mansion.

At house raisings, log rollings, and harvest parties, every one was expected to do his duty faithfully. A person who did not perform his share of labor on these occasions, was designated by the epithet of "Lawrence," or some other title still more opprobrious; and when it came to his turn to require the like aid from his neighbors, the idler soon felt his punishment in their refusal to attend to his calls.

Although there was no legal compulsion to the performance of military duty, yet every man of full age and size was expected to do his full share of public service. If he did not, "He was hated out as a coward." Thefts were severely punished.

With all their rudeness, these people were hospitable, and freely divided their rough fare with a neighbor or stranger, and would have been offended at the offer of pay. In their settlements and forts they lived, they worked, they fought and feasted or suffered together in cordial harmony. They were warm and constant in their friendships; but bitter and revengeful in their resentments. Instances of seduction and bastardy did not frequently happen. Indeed, considering the chivalrous temper of the people, the former could not take place without great personal danger from the brothers or relations of the victim of seduction, family honor being then estimated at a high rate. There was no other vestige of the Christian religion than a faint observation of Sunday, and that merely as a day of rest for the aged and a play day for the young.

ADAIR COUNTY

ADAIR was formed in the year 1801. It is situated in the south middle part of the state, and lies on the waters of Russell's creek and Little Barren river, which flow into Green river: Is bounded on the north by Green county; east, by Casey and Russell; south, by Cumberland; and west, by Barren. Contains 209,551 acres of land; average value per acre, $2,54. Total value of taxable property in the county, in 1846, $1,228,776; number of voters, 1408; number of children between five and sixteen years, 1844; total population in 1830, 8,220—in 1840, 8,466.

COLUMBIA is the county seat of Adair. It is a handsome and thriving town, distant about 150 miles from Frankfort, and 620 from Washington city; contains the usual public buildings for county purposes; two churches, occupied by four denominations; two schools, seven stores and groceries, five doctors, seven lawyers, one tavern, six mechanical shops;—population, 500.

NEATSVILLE, a small village in this county, contains a population of about 50.

BREEDINGS, another village, contains a population of 20.

Principal articles of export of Adair:—tobacco, hogs, horses and cattle. Face of the country, hilly; soil, second rate, based principally on slate and limestone. Green river runs through the northern portion of the county. Principal tributaries on the north, White-oak and Case's creeks; on the south, Russell's creek and its tributaries. The east fork of Little Barren river passes through the west end of the county.

General JOHN ADAIR, in honor of whom this county received its name, was born in South Carolina, in the year 1757. His character was formed in the trying times and amidst the thrilling incidents of the Revolution. At an early age, he entered the army as a volunteer, was made prisoner by the British, and as usual, treated with savage cruelty, having been thrown into prison and subjected to every species of insult and hardship that the ingenuity of his captors could devise.

In 1786 he emigrated to Kentucky, and settled in Mercer county. In the border war which raged with so much fury on the north-western frontier, General (then Major,) Adair was an active and efficient officer, and frequently engaged with the Indians. One incident of this nature merits a relation. On the sixth of November 1792, Major Adair, at the head of a detachment of mounted volunteers, from Kentucky, while encamped in the immediate vicinity of Fort St. Clair, twenty-six miles south of Greenville, near where Eaton, the county seat of Preble county, Ohio, now stands, was suddenly and violently attacked by a large party of Indians, who rushed on the encampment with great fury. A bloody conflict ensued, during which Major Adair ordered Lieutenant Madison, with a small party to gain the right flank of the enemy, if possible, and at the same time gave an order for Lieutenant Hall to attack their left, but learning that that officer had been slain, the Major with about twenty-five of his men made the attack in person, with a view of sustaining Lieutenant Madison.

The pressure of this movement caused the enemy to retire. They were driven about six hundred yards, through and beyond the American camp, where they made a stand, and again fought desperately. At this juncture about sixty of the Indians made an effort to turn the right flank of the whites. Major Adair foreseeing the consequences of this manœuvre, found it necessary to order a retreat. That movement was effected with regularity, and as was expected, the Indians pursued them to their camp, where a halt was made, and another severe battle was fought, in which the Indians suffered severely, and were driven from the ground. In this affair six of the whites were killed, five wounded, and four missing. Among the wounded were Lieutenant (afterwards Governor) George Madison, and Colonel Richard Taylor, the father of the present Major General Zachary Taylor, the hero of Palo Alto, Monterey. Buena Vista, &c.

The Indians on this occasion, were commanded by the celebrated Little Turtle. Some years afterwards, in 1805–6, when General Adair was Register of the land office in Frankfort, Captain William Wells, Indian agent, passed through that place, on his way to Washington city, attended by some Indians, among whom was the chief, Little Turtle. General Adair called on his old antagonist, and in the course of the conversation, the incident above related, being alluded to, Gen. Adair attributed his defeat to his having been taken by surprise. The little Turtle immediately remarked with great pleasantness, " a good general is never taken by surprise."

In 1807, Major Adair's popularity underwent a temporary obscuration from his supposed connection with the treasonable enterprise of Burr. His conduct and opinions became the subject of much speculation, and the public got to regard him with an eye of some suspicion. But it is now generally believed that General Adair's course in that affair was predicated upon an opinion that Colonel Burr's plans were approved by the government, which at that time contemplated a war with Spain. General Adair's opinions and associations at that day, placed him with the federal party, among whom he stood deservedly high.

In the campaign of 1813 he accompanied Governor Shelby into Canada, as an aid, and was present in that capacity at the battle of the Thames. His conduct during this campaign was such as to draw from his superior officers an expression of their approbation, and his name was honorably mentioned in the report to the war department. Governor Shelby afterwards conferred upon him the appointment of adjutant general of the Kentucky troops, with the brevet rank of brigadier general, in which character he commanded the Kentuckians in the glorious battle of New Orleans. The acrimonious controversy between him and General Jackson, growing out of the imputations cast by the latter on the conduct of the Kentucky troops on that eventful day, is fresh in the recollection of all.

In 1820, he was elected governor of Kentucky, in opposition to Judge Logan, Governor Desha, and Colonel Butler. He was often a member of the State legislature, and on several occasions was speaker of that body. In 1805 he was elected to the senate of the United States, from Kentucky, for the term of one year. In 1831 he was elected to congress, and served in the house of representatives from 1831 to 1833, inclusive.

General Adair, in all the situations, military and civil, to which he was elevated by his countrymen, discharged his duties in such a manner as to command the respect and confidence of his fellow citizens. He was a brave soldier, an active, vigilant and efficient officer—a politician of sound principles and enlarged views, and an ardent patriot. Among the early pioneers of Kentucky, he deservedly occupies a prominent place and a high rank. He died on the 19th of May, 1840, at the advanced age of 83 years.

ALLEN COUNTY.

ALLEN county was formed in the year 1815, and named in honor of Colonel JOHN ALLEN. It is situated in the southern part of the State, and lies on the waters of Big Barren river: Bounded on the north by Warren; east by Barren and Monroe; south by the Tennessee line, and west by Simpson county. Scottsville, the county seat, is about one hundred miles from Frankfort.

Statistics.—The Auditor's report for 1846, gives to this county 177,242 acres of land; average value of land per acre, $2,84; total valuation of taxable property, $1,200,645. Number of voters 1,272; number of children between five and sixteen years old, 2,047. Population in 1830, 6,486; in 1840, 7,329—increase in ten years, eight hundred and forty-three.

Towns.—There are two towns in Allen—Scottsville, the county seat, and Port Oliver. SCOTTSVILLE contains the court house and the usual public buildings, four churches, four stores, three taverns, five lawyers, three doctors, eight mechanical trades. Established in 1817, and called for General Winfield Scott, of the United States' army. PORT OLIVER is situated ten miles from Scottsville, on Barren river, and contains one store and tavern. Salt works are in operation in the latter place, which manufacture three hundred bushels of salt per week.

Inscriptions.—On the Sulphur fork of Bay's fork of Big Barren river, at or near the Sulphur Lick, the following words were found cut in the bark of a beech tree—"James M'Call dined here on his way to Natchez, June the 10th, 1770." On Barren river, about nine miles from Scottsville, on the lands of Colonel S. E. Carpenter, near where his mill now stands, the following is inscribed on a large beech tree—"*Ichabod Clark, mill site,* 1779." On the other side of the tree, this inscription is found—"Too sick to get over," date and name not mentioned.

Caves.—There are a number of caves in the county, but few of them have been explored to any extent. In the year 1844, two shells were found in one of these caves, resembling a conch shell. One of these shells is about eighteen inches long, has been sawed or cut lengthwise in the middle, having a small hole bored in the little end, so as to be hung up by a string; the other or bowl end, answering a good purpose for a water vessel.

Antiquities.—In the west end of the county, about thirteen miles from Scottsville, and seventeen from Bowling-green, is one of the most remarkable of the remains of those ancient fortifications, belonging to a people unknown, of whom our country exhibits so many traces. The fortification alluded to is at once romantic and impregnable, presenting one of the strongest military positions in the world. At this place, Drake's creek makes a horse-shoe bend—running one mile, and then with a gradual bend, returning to within thirty feet of the channel where the bend may be said to commence. The partition which divides the channels of the creek at this point, is of solid limestone, thirty feet thick at the base, two hundred yards in length, forty feet high, and six feet wide at the top. The top is almost perfectly level, and covered with small cedar trees. The area included within the bend of the creek, is to the east of this narrow pass, and contains about two hundred acres of land, rising from the creek in a gradual ascent of one hundred feet, where it forms a bold promontory. The top of this is leveled and forms a square area containing about three acres, enclosed with walls and a ditch. The outer ditch is still perceptible, and the walls are now about three feet high around the whole circuit of the fort. In the rear of this, are to be seen many small mounds. This is by nature one of the strongest military positions in the world; the only approach to the fort, being over the narrow cause-way above mentioned—tall cliffs intercepting all access from the opposite banks of the stream.

At the west side of the narrow pass, and immediately at its termination, there is a hill similar to the one on the east. Here is to be seen a small mound forty feet in circumference and four feet high. Upon excavating one side of this mound, a stone coffin was dug up two and a half feet long, one foot wide and one foot deep, with a stone covering—the top of the coffin projecting one inch beyond the sides. Upon opening the coffin, the arm and thigh bones of an infant were found in it. This coffin

being removed, others of larger dimensions were to be discovered, but were not removed. Many very large human bones
have been exhumed from mounds in this county—some of the
thigh bones measuring from eight to ten inches longer than the
race of men now inhabiting the country.

This county received its name from Col. JOHN ALLEN, who fell in the disastrous battle of the river Raisin. He was born in Rockbridge county, Virginia, the
30th of December, 1772.   His father, James Allen, emigrated to Kentucky in
the fall of the year 1780, and settled at Dougherty's station, on Clarke run,
about one and a half miles below the present town of Danville.   Here he formed
an acquaintance with Joseph Daviess, the father of Col. Joseph Hamilton Daviess.   Becoming impatient of the close confinement of the station, these fearless
and ardent men removed farther down the creek, and erecting a small station,
lived there for three years.   At the expiration of this period, Mr. Daviess purchased a tract of land three or four miles west of Danville, and removed to it.
In 1784, the father of John Allen removed to Nelson county, and settled on
Simpson's creek, seven and a half miles from Bardstown. In 1786, the subject
of this notice attended a school in Bardstown, kept by a Mr. Shackleford, where
he acquired a slight knowledge of the classics.   This school was succeeded by
one under the charge of Dr. James Priestly, with whom young Allen finished his
education.   At this school, Joseph H. Daviess, John Rowan, Felix Grundy,
Archibald Cameron, John Pope, and John Allen, all distinguished in after life,
formed one class.
In the year 1791, John Allen commenced the study of the law in the office of
Col. Archibald Stewart, of Stanton, Va. He pursued his legal studies with great
assiduity for about four years, and in 1795, he returned to Kentucky and settled
in Shelbyville, where he continued to practice law till 1812.   As a lawyer, he
ranked with the first men of his profession.
On the breaking out of the war in 1812, he raised a regiment of riflemen, for
the campaign under Harrison in the north-west.   Part of this regiment was in
the battle of Brownstown, on the 18th of January, 1813.   In the fatal battle of
the river Raisin, Col. Allen's regiment formed the left wing of the American
force.   The termination of this affair is too well known to require recapitulation
here; and among the many noble and chivalrous Kentuckians who there found a
bloody grave, there was none whose loss was more sensibly felt or deeply deplored than Col. Allen.   Inflexibly just, benevolent in all his feelings, and of
undaunted courage, he was a fine specimen of the Kentucky gentleman of that
day, and his name will not soon pass away from the memory of his countrymen.

ANDERSON COUNTY.

ANDERSON county was formed in 1827, and named for the Hon.
Richard C. Anderson. It is situated in the middle portion of the
state; the Kentucky river forming its northern boundary, and
Salt river entering its southern border from Mercer, penetrating
near the center, when it takes a different direction, and flows out
on the western border, passing through Spencer, and uniting with
the Rolling Fork in Bullitt county. The county is bounded on the
north by Franklin; east by the Kentucky river; south by Mercer
and Washington; and west by Spencer county. The tributaries
of Salt river are Crooked, Fox, Stoney, and Hammond creeks;
while Bailey's run, Little Benson, and Gilbert's creek fall into the
Kentucky river. The surface is generally rolling, though some

portions are level, rich, and very productive—the hills producing fine tobacco and grasses. The staple products are wheat, corn, hemp, and tobacco; the articles of export, horses, mules, cattle, and hogs.

The auditor's report for 1846, gives to this county 101,891 acres of land; average value of land per acre, $5,66; total valuation of taxable property, $1,137,922; number of white males over twenty-one years of age, 1,001; number of children between five and sixteen years old, 1,401. Population in 1830, 4,542; in 1840, 5,452.

LAWRENCEBURG, the county seat of Anderson, is situated on the turnpike road leading from Louisville to Harrodsburg, fifty-five miles from the former, and twenty from the latter place; three and a half miles from lock and dam No. five, and twelve miles from Frankfort. Contains four stores, four groceries, two taverns, a handsome court house and other public buildings; Reformed or Christian, Presbyterian and Baptist churches; one seminary; five lawyers; four doctors; one each, carpenter, hatter, gunsmith, and blacksmith shops—population 350. Established in 1820, and called after Capt. James Lawrence, of the U. S. navy, whose last words on board the Chesapeake, it will be remembered, were, " Don't give up the ship." This place was first settled by an old Dutchman by the name of Coffman, who was killed by the Indians. When his good wife first heard of his melancholy fate, she exclaimed in the bitterness of her affliction, " I always told my old man that these savage *Ingens* would kill him; and I'd rather lost my best cow at the pail than my old man."

RICHARD CLOUGH ANDERSON, JR., (in honor of whom the county of Anderson was named,) was born at Louisville, in the *then* district of Kentucky, on the 4th day of August, 1788. His father was Richard C. Anderson, Sr., who served with great gallantry, as an officer, throughout the revolutionary war, at the conclusion of which he was a lieutenant colonel. His mother was Elizabeth Clark, a sister of the celebrated General George Rogers Clark.

Mr. Anderson was sent at an early age to Virginia for his education; and after being graduated at William and Mary college, studied law under Judge Tucker. Upon his return to Kentucky he commenced the practice of his profession; and, possessing all the qualities, intellectual, moral and social, necessary to insure success, soon took a high stand at the bar, as an able counsellor, and as an eloquent advocate. His popular talents would not permit him long to devote himself to private pursuits. The solicitations of friends and a natural ambition, drew him, in a very short time, into the service of the public. He commenced his career, as a politician, in the popular branch of the State legislature, in which he served several years, with distinguished credit to himself, and with the marked approbation of his constituents. He was accordingly elected to congress, in 1817, by a handsome majority over his opponent—the old incumbent. In congress he continued four years, during which time he participated in the splendid debates of that most interesting period, with an ability and success, which reflected no slight honor on his character as an orator and a statesman. His reported speeches, during this period, are admirable for their terseness, beauty of arrangement, closeness of argument, and unambitious elegance of diction; but they now lack the charm of that distinct and melodious elocution—that graceful and manly and persuasive manner—which gave interest and attractiveness to their delivery. In 1822, declining a re-election to congress, under the belief that his services were more needed in the councils of his own State, than in those of the nation, he again entered the State legislature, and was chosen speaker of the house of representatives. The duties of this office he discharged, in that most excited period of our State history, with a courtesy, propriety, discretion and ability, that caused him to be regarded, by many of that day, as the perfect model of a presiding officer. This was the origin of the angry controversy existing between the old and new court parties, to the former of which Mr. Anderson belonged. In January, 1823, Mr. Anderson was appointed, by President Monroe, the first minister plenipotentiary to the Republic of Colombia. Upon his arrival at Bogota—the capital—with his family, he was received with every demonstration of honor and respect. He resided there but a very short time, before he came to be regarded, by the authorities of the republic, rather as a friend and counsellor than as a stranger. His intercourse with the principal officers of state, was of the most agreeable and confidential character. In 1824 he negotiated the treaty between the two republics, which was ratified among the last acts of President Monroe's administration. In 1825 he lost his wife—an admirable and estimable lady, to whom he was most tenderly attached. This loss induced him to return home for a short time, in order to place his children—two daughters and a son—with his friends in Kentucky. In October of that year, he revisited Bogota, accompanied by his brother, now Captain Robert Anderson of the U. S. Army, and remained until July, 1826, when he was instructed by President Adams to repair to Porto Bello, to join Mr. Sergeant, who had been appointed together with himself, an envoy extraordinary and minister plenipotentiary to the congress to be assembled at Panama. On his way to Carthagena, his intended place of embarkation, he fell sick at Turbaco, a small village some twelve miles distant from that city, where, on the 24th day of July, his disease terminated in death. He was succeeded in his mission to Colombia, by the late ex-president of the United States, General William H. Harrison.

Thus prematurely ended a brilliant career of usefulness and honor, and of still higher promise. The writer of this slight sketch heard one of the most distinguished men of our country declare, that Mr. Anderson's death alone in all probability, prevented his reaching the highest office in the Union. A brief but discriminating notice by the editor, in the National Intelligencer, of August 29th, 1826, renders the following just tribute to his worth and memory. "The United States in general, and his native State of Kentucky in particular, have sustained a great loss in the death of this distinguished gentleman. On his former visit to Colombia he lost his excellent wife—which bereavement he did not long survive.

"Mr. Anderson was one of the most amiable of men, and most discreet of politicians. A career of a few years in congress disclosed his valuable qualities. He possessed in an eminent degree, a clear discriminating mind, combined with the most conciliatory and persuasive address, the effect of which has often been seen on the floor of the house of representatives, and afterwards on that of the popular branch of the legislature of Kentucky, in the midst of the greatest contentions, like oil stilling the agitated waves of the ocean. In this point of his character, it is sufficient praise to say, he nearly resembled the late lamented WILLIAM LOWNDES. In brief, without offence be it said, the country could not boast a *better* man than Richard C. Anderson."

Mr. Anderson was so actively engaged in professional and political pursuits, that he had but little leisure for literature. He was fondly addicted, however, to reading, and devoted most of his spare time to books—principally of biography and history. His writings are few, but those few are characterised by strong sense, sober reasoning and sagacious insight. He was the author of the article in the North American Review, for October, 1826, on the constitution of Colombia—an article well worthy of perusal for its general excellence, as well as for the statesman-like suggestions it contains, relative to our own constitution. He was also engaged on a larger work, upon the political institutions and history of Colombia, the completion of which was unfortunately frustrated by his untimely death. Besides these, a fragmentary journal, of the last few years of his life still exists, possessing great interest, from the judicious observations upon books, and the shrewd remarks upon men and events, with which it is interspersed.

In making an estimate of the character of Mr. Anderson, in his public and private relations, it may be truly said of him, that while in private life he was without a vice, in his public career he was equally without a reproach.

BALLARD COUNTY.

BALLARD county was formed out of parts of M'Cracken and Hickman in 1842, and named in honor of Capt. BLAND BALLARD. It is situated in the extreme western part of the state, and bounded on the north by the Ohio river; on the west, by the Mississippi; on the east by the counties of Graves and M'Cracken, and on the south by the county of Hickman. The lands in the northern part of the county are barren; in the southern, well timbered,—both regions undulating. The bottoms of the Ohio and Mississippi are extensive,—soil, a mixture of black loam and sand, and very productive. The principal creek is Mayfield; heads in Tennessee, passes through Calloway and Graves counties, thence through the center of Ballard, running north-west, and empties into the Mississippi at Fort Jefferson. Humphrey's creek heads in Mc-Cracken, passes through the north-east corner of Ballard, and empties into the Ohio below the Grand Chain. This county contains, according to the auditor's report for 1846, 243,675 acres of land; average value per acre, $1,80; total value of taxable property, $632,131; number of white males over twenty-one years old, 706; number of children between five and sixteen years old, one thousand. Principal productions of the county, tobacco, hemp, corn, and oats. Stock raising is also beginning to attract the attention of farmers.

The towns of the county are Blandville, Lovelaceville, and Milbourn. BLANDVILLE is the county seat, and contains a court house and other public buildings; two churches (United Baptist and Methodist), two schools, four stores, three taverns, nine lawyers, seven doctors, nine mechanical trades—population four hundred. Called for the christian name of Captain *Bland* Ballard, for whom the county was named.

LOVELACEVILLE is a small village, named in honor of Mr. Lovelace, containing one United Baptist church, one Methodist church, one school, one store, one tavern, two physicians, two mechanical trades—population forty.

MILBOURN contains two churches (Methodist and Christian), two schools, two stores, one tavern, three physicians, three mechanical trades—population ninety.

CAPTAIN BLAND BALLARD, in honor of whom this county was named, was born near Fredericksburg, Virginia, on the 16th of October, 1761, and is now in his 87th year. He came to Kentucky in 1779, and joined the regular militia which was kept up for the defence of the country; and after serving on Bowman's campaign in 1779, accompanied the expedition led by Gen. Clark against the Pickaway towns in Ohio in 1781, on which occasion he received a severe wound in the hip, from the effects of which he is suffering at this day. At the time of the wound, he was near bleeding to death before he could procure surgical aid. In 1782, he was on the campaign led by Gen. Clark, with Floyd and Logan as colonels, that destroyed the Pickaway towns. In 1786 he was a spy for General Clark in the expedition to the Wabash, rendered abortive by the mutiny of the soldiers. In the summer of 1791, he served as a guide under Generals Scott and

Wilkinson, and was present under General Wayne at the decisive battle on the 20th of August, 1794.

When not engaged in regular campaign, he served as hunter and spy for General Clark, who was stationed at Louisville, and in this service he continued for two years and a half. During this time he had several rencounters with the Indians. One of these occurred just below Louisville. He had been sent in his character of spy to explore the Ohio from the mouth of Salt river to the falls, and from thence up to what is now the town of Westport. On his way down the river, when six or eight miles below the falls, he heard, early one morning, a noise on the Indiana shore. He immediately concealed himself in the bushes, and when the fog had scattered sufficiently to permit him to see, he discovered a canoe filled with three Indians, approaching the Kentucky shore. When they had approached within range, he fired and killed one. The others jumped overboard, and endeavored to get their canoe into deep water, but before they succeeded, he killed a second, and finally the third. Upon reporting his morning's work to General Clark, a detachment was sent down, who found the three dead Indians and buried them. For this service General Clark gave him a *linen shirt*, and some other small presents. This shirt, however, was the only one he had for several years, except those made of leather; of this shirt the pioneer hero was doubtless justly proud.

While on a scout to the Saline Licks, on one occasion, Ballard, with one companion, came suddenly upon a large body of Indians, just as they were in the act of encamping. They immediately charged, firing their guns and raising the yell. This induced the Indians, as they had anticipated, to disperse for the moment, until the strength of the assailing party could be ascertained. During this period of alarm, Ballard and his companion mounted two of the best horses they could find, and retreated for two days and nights, until they reached the Ohio, which they crossed upon a raft, making their horses swim. As they ascended the Kentucky bank, the Indians reached the opposite shore.

At the time of the defeat on Long Run, he was living at Lynn's station on Beargrass, and came up to assist some families in moving from Squire Boon's station, near the present town of Shelbyville. The people of this station had become alarmed on account of the numerous Indian signs in the country, and had determined to move to the stronger stations on the Beargrass. They proceeded safely until they arrived near Long Run, when they were attacked front and rear by the Indians, who fired their rifles and then rushed on them with their tomahawks. Some few of the men ran at the first fire, of the others, some succeeded in saving part of their families, or died with them after a brave resistance. The subject of this sketch, after assisting several of the women on horseback who had been thrown at the first onset, during which he had one or two single handed combats with the Indians, and seeing the party about to be defeated, he succeeded in getting outside of the Indian line, when he used his rifle with some effect, until he saw they were totally defeated. He then started for the station, pursued by the Indians, and on stopping at Floyd's Fork, in the bushes, on the bank, he saw an Indian on horseback pursuing the fugitives ride into the creek, and as he ascended the bank near to where Ballard stood, he shot the Indian, caught the horse and made good his escape to the station. Many were killed, the number not recollected, some taken prisoners, and some escaped to the station. They afterwards learned from the prisoners taken on this occasion, that the Indians who attacked them were marching to attack the station the whites had deserted, but learning from their spies that they were moving, the Indians turned from the head of Bullskin and marched in the direction of Long Run. The news of this defeat induced Colonel Floyd to raise a party of thirty-seven men, with the intention of chastising the Indians. Floyd commanded one division and captain Holden the other, Ballard being with the latter. They proceeded with great caution, but did not discover the Indians until they received their fire, which killed or mortally wounded sixteen of their men. Notwithstanding the loss, the party under Floyd maintained their ground, and fought bravely until overpowered by three times their number, who appealed to the tomahawk. The retreat, however, was completed without much further loss. This occasion has been rendered memorable by the magnanimous gallantry of young Wells (afterwards the Colonel Wells of Tippecanoe), who saved the life of Floyd, his personal enemy, by the timely offer of his horse at a moment when the Indians were near to Floyd, who was retreating on foot and nearly exhausted.

In 1788, the Indians attacked the little Fort on Tick creek (a few miles east of Shelbyville), where his father resided. It happened that his father had removed a short distance out of the fort, for the purpose of being convenient to the sugar camp. The first intimation they had of the Indians, was early in the morning, when his brother Benjamin went out to get wood to make a fire. They shot him and then assailed the house. The inmates barred the door and prepared for defence. His father was the only man in the house, and no man in the fort, except the subject of this sketch and one old man. As soon as he heard the guns he repaired to within shooting distance of his father's house, but dared not venture nearer. Here he commenced using his rifle with good effect. In the meantime the Indians broke open the house and killed his father, not before, however, he had killed one or two of their number. The Indians, also, killed one full sister, one half sister, his step-mother, and tomahawked the youngest sister, a child, who recovered. When the Indians broke into the house, his step-mother endeavored to effect her escape by the back door, but an Indian pursued her and as he raised his tomahawk to strike her, the subject of this sketch fired at the Indian, not, however, in time to prevent the fatal blow, and they both fell and expired together. The Indians were supposed to number about fifteen, and before they completed their work of death, they sustained a loss of six or seven.

During the period he was a spy for General Clark, he was taken prisoner by five Indians on the other side of the Ohio, a few miles above Louisville, and conducted to an encampment twenty-five miles from the river. The Indians treated him comparatively well, for though they kept him with a guard they did not tie him. On the next day after his arrival at the encampment, the Indians were engaged in horse racing. In the evening two very old warriors were to have a race, which attracted the attention of all the Indians, and his guard left him a few steps to see how the race would terminate. Near him stood a fine black horse, which the Indians had stolen recently from Beargrass, and while the attention of the Indians was attracted in a different direction, Ballard mounted this horse and had a race indeed. They pursued him nearly to the river, but he escaped, though the horse died soon after he reached the station. This was the only instance, with the exception of that at the river Raisin, that he was a prisoner. He was in a skirmish with the Indians near the Saline Licks, Colonel Hardin being the commander; the Colonel Hardin who fought gallantly under Morgan at the capture of Burgoyne, and who fell a sacrifice to Indian perfidy in the northwest; the father of General M. D. Hardin, and grand-father of the Col. Hardin of Illinois, whose heroic death at Buena Vista was worthy of his unsullied life.

In after life Major Ballard repeatedly represented the people of Shelby county in the legislature, and commanded a company in Colonel Allen's regiment under General Harrison in the campaign of 1812–13. He led the advance of the detachment, which fought the first battle of the river Raisin—was wounded slightly on that day, and severely by a spent ball on the 22d January. This wound, also, continues to annoy his old age. On this disastrous occasion he was taken prisoner, and suffered severely by the march through snow and ice, from Malden to Fort George.

As an evidence of the difficulties which surrounded the early pioneer in this country, it may be proper to notice an occasion in which Major Ballard was disturbed by the Indians at the spot where he now resides. They stole his only horse at night. He heard them when they took the horse from the door to which he was tied. His energy and sagacity was such, that he got in advance of the Indians before they reached the Ohio, waylaid them, three in number, shot the one riding his horse, and succeeded not only in escaping, but in catching the horse and riding back in safety.

The generation now on the sphere of action, and the millions who are to succeed them in the great valley, will have but an imperfect idea of the character and services of the bold patriotic men, who rescued Kentucky from the forest and the savage. The subject of this sketch, however, is a fine specimen of that noble race of men, and when his gray hairs shall descend to an honorable grave, this short biography may serve, in some degree, to stimulate the rising generation to emulate his heroic patriotism.

BARREN COUNTY.

BARREN county was formed in 1798, and takes its name from what is generally termed the *barrens* or *prairies* which abound in the region of country in which it is located. It is bounded north by Hart; east by Adair and Green; south by Monroe, and west by Warren. Glasgow, the county seat, is about one hundred miles from Frankfort. The county embraces almost every description of soil and surface. From Glasgow north and northeast for about ten miles, the land is level and the soil rich; beyond it is generally hilly and poor: the remainder of the county is mostly rolling, but with a productive soil. The sub-soil is of clay, founded on limestone. Fine springs abound; and being well timbered and watered with several large creeks, saw and grist mills have been erected in abundance. The staple products are tobacco, corn, wheat, rye and oats. Tobacco is the most important article of export from this county—about twenty-five hundred hogsheads being the average annual product. Horses, mules, and hogs, are also raised for export. There are three salt furnaces in operation in the county, making from thirty to forty bushels each per day.

In 1846, the number of acres of land reported was 359,941; average value per acre $3,34; total value of taxable property, $3,191,500 : number of white males over twenty-one years of age, 2,769 ; number of children between five and sixteen years of age, 3,341.

The towns of Barren are Glasgow, Chaplinton, Edmonton and Frederick. GLASGOW, the seat of justice, is situated on the turnpike road leading from Louisville to Nashville, one hundred and twenty-six miles from Frankfort---contains three meeting houses, in which seven denominations worship, viz : Methodists, Episcopalians, Reformers, Old and New School Presbyterians, Cumberland Presbyterians and United Baptists ; two academies, male and female ; one school, thirteen stores, two groceries, eleven lawyers, five doctors, two tanneries, with a large number of mechanical trades. Was established in 1809, and named after the old city of Glasgow, in Scotland. Population six hundred. *Chaplinton*, a small village on Big Barren river, contains a store, a post-office, etc. *Edmonton*, a small village eighteen miles south-east of Glasgow, contains one school, one store, one tannery, one doctor, post-office, etc. *Frederick*, situated seventeen miles north-east from Glasgow—contains one school, two doctors, one tannery, etc.

There are a number of mineral springs in Barren, which are considered efficacious in many diseases; but none have been as yet, much resorted to. There is a white sulphur spring on the east fork of Little Barren river, sixteen miles east of Glasgow, the waters from which, as they flow off, form quite a respectable branch, and is supposed to be the largest stream of mineral water in the Green river country. There is a well on Buck creek, fourteen miles nearly.west of

Glasgow, which was commenced for salt water, but at the depth of thirty feet or more, a very large stream of medical water was struck (sulphur, magnesia, etc.), which rises about four feet above the surface of the earth through a large pipe, and runs off in a branch of considerable size. This is becoming a place of considerable resort. There are, also, several smaller springs within a few miles of Glasgow, which are thought to be very beneficial to invalids.

The Indians in the early settlement, made but few incursions into this county. Edmund Rogers, one of the first surveyors and pioneers, was compelled on several occasions, to abandon his surveys from the signs or attacks of Indians. On one occasion when in hot pursuit of him, they overtook and killed one of his company—and he imputes his escape alone to the time occupied in dispatching the unfortunate individual who fell into their hands.

EDMUND ROGERS, one of the pioneers of the Green river country, was born in Caroline county, Virginia, on the 5th of May, 1762. He served as a soldier in the memorable campaign of 1781, in his native State, which resulted in the capture of Cornwallis. He was in the battles of Green Springs, Jamestown, and at the siege of York. For these services he refused to apply for a pension, although entitled under the acts of congress. It was the love of his country's liberty and independence, and no pecuniary reward, which induced him to fight her battles. He emigrated to Kentucky in 1783, and became intimate with most of the early pioneers. He possessed a remarkable memory, and could detail with accuracy up to the time of his death, all the important events of the Indian wars and early settlement of Kentucky. He had enjoyed better opportunities to learn the history of these transactions than most persons, in consequence of his intimacy with General George Rogers Clark (his cousin), and captain John Rogers (his brother), and captain Abraham Chapline, of Mercer, in whose family he lived for years.

Mr. E. Rogers was the longest liver of that meritorious and enterprising class of men who penetrated the wilderness of Kentucky, and spent their time in locating and surveying lands. It is confidently believed that he survived all the surveyors of military lands south of Green river. He began business as a surveyor in the fall of 1783, in Clark's or the Illinois grant as it was called, on the north side of the Ohio river, opposite to Louisville. In the spring of 1784, his operations were changed to the military district in this State, on the south side of Green river. He made most of the surveys on Little and Big Barren rivers and their tributary streams. Muldrough's hill was the boundary of the settlements towards the south-west in Kentucky, when Mr. Rogers commenced surveying in the military district. He settled upon a tract of land, upon which he afterwards laid out the town of Edmonton in Barren county, in the year 1800. He married Mary Shirley in 1808. She died in 1835, leaving seven daughters and one son. In 1840 owing to his advanced age, he broke up house keeping and removed with his single daughters to the house of his son John T. Rogers, where he died on the 28th day of August, 1843. His remains were taken to his own farm and buried by the side of his wife near Edmonton.

In purity of life and manly virtues, Mr. Rogers had but few equals. His intercourse with mankind was characterized by great benevolence and charity, and the strictest justice. He was ever ready to lend a helping hand to the needy and deserving. He raised and educated his nephew, the honorable Joseph Rogers Underwood.

He was not ambitious of distinction. He accepted the office of justice of the peace shortly after he settled in Barren county, at the solicitation of his neighbors. Perceiving as he thought, an act of partiality on the part of the court, he resigned his commission at the first court he ever attended, and thereafter persisted in his resolution to hold no office.

Mr. Rogers believed that the distinctions made among men, arising from the offices they filled, without regard to their intellectual and moral attainments and qualifications, were unjust. He therefore spurned official stations and those who filled them, when he thought genuine merit was overlooked, and the shallow and presumptuous promoted. He believed that the fortunes of men, were controled by things apparently of little moment, and that there was in regulating and governing the affairs of this world, if not of the whole universe, a chain of causes and effects or consequences, in which every link was just as important as every other in the eyes of God, although in the estimation of men, they were regarded as very different in importance. To his philosophic mind, he saw what mankind usually call great things, springing as results from very little things, and he was not disposed to concede that the *effect* was entitled to more consideration than the *cause*. He admitted a controling providence, which operated in a manner inscrutable to man; and hence he never despised what were called *little things*, and never became greatly excited with passionate admiration for what were called *great things*. He admitted there were two great principles at work in the earth, one of good, the other of evil. His affections and his actions were all with the good.

In illustration of his idea that apparent trifles were important affairs, he often told the writer that the most consequential events of his life, had been the result of his falling off a log and getting wet, in attempting to cross a creek. This happened the day he left Pitman's station to go into the wilderness south of Green river. He got his papers wet, and was induced to return to the station to dry them, and then to take a new start. Upon his return, he met with a stranger who had a large number of land warrants, and made a contract with him for their location. Under this contract he secured the land around Edmonton where he lived, and upon these facts he reasoned thus: "If I had not fallen into the creek, I should not have turned back; if I had not returned to the station, I should not have made the contract by which I obtained the land on which I settled; if I had not got that land, I should not have lived upon it; if I had not lived there, I should have been thrown into a different society, and most probably would never have seen the lady I married, and of course would not have had the wife and children I have; and as a further consequence, the very existence and destiny of those children and their descendants through all coming generations, and the influence they may exercise in families, neighborhoods and counties, depended upon my falling from the log."

Mr. Rogers and his brother captain John Rogers, made a very singular contract. It was firmly agreed between them, that he who died first, should return from the world of spirits, and inform the other what was going on there. This engagement between the brothers, was most seriously entered into. Mr. Rogers has often told the writer, that there could be no such thing as visits from the spirits of the dead, and holding intercourse with the living; for said he, if such a thing could be, I know my brother John would have kept and fulfilled his promise. He discountenanced every thing of a superstitious character.

The motto upon which Mr. Rogers acted through life, was "to do justice, love mercy and walk humbly before God." He often repeated these words as containing man's whole duty.

His last illness was of short duration. He was in his perfect mind to the last breath. About an hour before he expired he was seen to smile, and being asked what occasioned it, he said, "he was thinking of the vain efforts of three of the best physicians in the country, to save the life of an old man when his time had come." He died with perfect composure and without a struggle.

Inscription.—Mr. Butler, in his History of Kentucky, states, upon the authority of Judge Underwood, that Edmund Rogers had discovered on a beech tree, standing upon the margin of the east fork of the south branch of Little Barren river, before there was any settlement south of Green river, the following inscription: "James M'Call, of Mecklenburg county, North Carolina, June 8th, 1770." These words were cut in very handsome letters, with several initials of other names.

ANTIQUITIES.—The most remarkable mounds in the county, are situated at the mouth of Peter's creek, on Big Barren river. Twelve miles south-west from Glasgow, on the turnpike leading to Nashville, and immediately in the fork of the river and creek, there are a large number of small mounds, which closely resemble each other in size and shape. They now appear to be two or three feet high, of an oval form, about fifty yards apart, forming a circle of from four to five hundred yards in circumference, and presenting strong indications of having had huts or some other kind of buildings upon them. About the center of the circle of small mounds, is situated a large mound, twenty or thirty feet high, and from ninety to one hundred feet in diameter. Without the circle, about one hundred yards distant, is another large mound, about the same dimensions of the one within the circle of small ones. Upon these mounds trees are growing, which measure five feet in diameter. Some two hundred yards from these mounds, are a number of small mounds, which contain bones, teeth, and hair of human beings, in a perfect state of preservation. These bones are found in graves about three feet long, and from one to one and a half feet wide, all lined with flat stones. In the neighborhood, for half a mile or more, are found many of these graves. There is a large warehouse standing on the mound which is within the circle of small mounds.

There is a cave in the bluff of the river, about three miles above Glasgow, which contains a large number of bones ; but it is of small dimensions, and no correct description has been obtained of it. On Skegg's creek, about five miles south-west of Glasgow, there is a small cave, in which human bones have been found, but they appeared to be those of infants altogether. One bone was found, which seemed to be that part of the skull bone about the crown of the head ; it was made round, about two and a half inches in diameter, scolloped on the edges, and carved on the outside. Whether this was made for an ornament, or for eating out of, could not well be determined, although it was sufficiently large to be used as a spoon.

BATH COUNTY.

Bath county was organized in 1811, and is situated in the eastern part of the State, and lies on Licking river. It is bounded on the north and east by Fleming, south by Morgan, and west by Montgomery. It received its name from the great number of medicinal springs which abound in the county. The celebrated Olympian or Mud Lick springs are situated here, which contain a variety of waters, such as salt, black and red sulphur, and chalybeate of iron. Four miles east of these springs is the White Sulphur.

Lands reported for the county in 1846, 205,261 acres ; average value per acre, $8,63; total valuation of taxable property, $3,006,835. White males over twenty-one years old, 1,732 ; children between five and sixteen years old 2,420. Population in 1830, 8,799—in 1840, 9,763.

Licking river washes the entire north-east boundary of the county, and it is watered by several fine streams, flowing through various portions of it. The surface is diversified—hilly, undulating, and level. The soil north and west of Slate creek, is rich and fertile, being based upon limestone ; south and east the county abounds in iron and coal, and the soil is not so good. Immediately around Sharpsburg, for several miles, the surface is gently undulating, and the lands highly cultivated, rich, and very productive. The principal articles of production and commerce, are cattle, mules, hogs, corn, and wheat. There are two iron furnaces and one forge in the county, manufacturing about two thousand tons of iron per year.

The towns of the county are, Owingsville, Sharpsburg, Wyoming, and Bethel. Owingsville is the seat of justice, and contains two churches, two taverns, a fine court house, post office, five stores and groceries, three doctors, seven lawyers, two schools

12

one blacksmith shop, one tailor, one saddler, &c. Incorporated in 1829, and named in honor of Col. Thomas Dye Owings. Population three hundred.

SHARPSBURG is situated on the Maysville and Mount Sterling turnpike road, thirty-eight miles from the former, and twelve from the latter place, and twelve miles west of Owingsville. It contains three churches, one tavern, four stores, six doctors, two saw mills, one bagging factory, one male and one female school, two wool factories, and ten mechanical shops. Established in 1825, and named for Moses Sharp.

WYOMING, a small village at the mouth of Slate creek, contains two stores, two taverns, two cabinet shops, one blacksmith shop, two grist and saw mills.

BETHEL, a small village on the main route from Maysville to Mount Sterling, contains a post office, one store, one tavern, two saddler's shops, blacksmith and hat shops—thirty inhabitants.

The following interesting incident in the early settlement of Bath county, is related in McClung's "Sketches of Western Adventure," a work published by the author of these notes in the year 1832 :

"In the month of August, 1786, Mr. Francis Downing, then a mere lad, was living in a fort, where subsequently some iron works were erected by Mr. Jacob Myers, which are now known by the name of Slate creek works, and are the property of Colonel Thomas Dye Owings. About the 16th, a young man belonging to the fort, called upon Downing, and requested his assistance in hunting for a horse which had strayed away on the preceding evening. Downing readily complied, and the two friends traversed the woods in every direction, until at length, towards evening, they found themselves in a wild valley, at the distance of six or seven miles from the fort. Here Downing became alarmed, and repeatedly assured his elder companion, (whose name was Yates), that he heard sticks cracking behind them, and was confident that Indians were dogging them. Yates, being an experienced hunter, and from habit grown indifferent to the dangers of the woods, diverted himself freely at the expense of his young companion, often inquiring, at what price he rated his scalp, and offering to ensure it for a sixpence.

"Downing, however, was not so easily satisfied. He observed, that in whatever direction they turned, the same ominous sounds continued to haunt them, and as Yates still treated his fears with the most perfect indifference, he determined to take his measures upon his own responsibility. Gradually slackening his pace, he permitted Yates to advance twenty or thirty steps in front of him, and immediately afterwards descending a gentle hill, he suddenly sprung aside, and hid himself in a thick cluster of whortleberry bushes. Yates, who at that time was performing some woodland ditty to the full extent of his lungs, was too much pleased with his own voice to attend either to Downing or the Indians, and was quickly out of sight. Scarcely had he disappeared, when Downing, to his unspeakable terror, beheld two savages put aside the stalks of a canebrake, and look out cautiously in the direction which Yates had taken.

"Fearful that they had seen him step aside, he determined to fire upon them, and trust to his heels for safety, but so unsteady was his hand, that in raising his gun to his shoulder, she went off before he had taken aim. He lost no time in following her example, and after running fifty yards, he met Yates, who, alarmed at the report, was hastily retracing his steps. It was not necessary to inquire what was the matter. The enemy were in full view, pressing forward with great rapidity, and "devil take the hindmost," was the order of the day. Yates would not outstrip Downing, but ran by his side, although in so doing he risked both of their lives. The Indians were well acquainted with the country, and soon took a path that diverged from the one which the whites followed, at one point, and rejoined it at another, bearing the same relation to it, that the string does to the bow

"The two paths were at no point distant from each other more than one hundred yards, so that Yates and Downing could easily see the enemy gaining rapidly upon them. They reached the point of re-union first, however, and quickly came to a deep gully which it was necessary to cross, or retrace their steps. Yates cleared it without difficulty, but Downing, being much exhausted, fell short, and falling with his breast against the opposite brink, rebounded with violence, and fell at full length upon the bottom. The Indians crossed the ditch a few yards below him, and eager for the capture of Yates, continued the pursuit, without appearing to notice Downing. The latter, who at first had given himself up for lost, quickly recovered his strength, and began to walk slowly along the ditch, fearing to leave it, lest the enemy should see him. As he advanced, however, the ditch became more shallow, until at length it ceased to protect him at all.

"Looking around cautiously, he saw one of the Indians returning, apparently in quest of him. Unfortunately, he had neglected to reload his gun, while in the ditch, and as the Indian instantly advanced upon him, he had no resource but flight. Throwing away his gun, which was now useless, he plied his legs manfully in ascending the long ridge which stretched before him, but the Indian gained on him so rapidly that he lost all hope of escape. Coming at length to a large poplar which had been blown up by the roots, he ran along the body of the tree upon one side, while the Indian followed it upon the other, doubtless expecting to intercept him at the root. But here the supreme dominion of fortune was manifest.

"It happened that a large she bear was suckling her cubs in a bed which she had made at the root of the tree, and as the Indian reached that point first, she instantly sprung upon him, and a prodigious uproar took place. The Indian yelled, and stabbed with his knife; the bear growled and saluted him with one of her most endearing " hugs ;" while Downing, fervently wishing her success, ran off through the woods, without waiting to see the event of the struggle. Downing reached the fort in safety, and found Yates reposing after a hot chase, having eluded his pursuers, and gained the fort two hours before him. On the next morning, they collected a party and returned to the poplar tree, but no traces either of the Indian or bear were to be found. They both probably escaped with their lives, although not without injury."

BOONE COUNTY.

Boone county was formed in 1798, and named in honor of Colonel Daniel Boone. It is situated in the most northern part of the state, in a well known bend of the Ohio river, called North Bend. The average length of the county is about twenty miles, from north to south, and its average breadth about fourteen miles. It is bounded on the east by Kenton, on the south by Grant and Gallatin counties, and on the north and west by the Ohio river, which flows along its border about forty miles, dividing it from the states of Ohio and Indiana. The surface of the county is generally hilly, but still there is a considerable quantity of level land in it, and nearly all the land is tillable. On the Ohio river there are found considerable bodies of level land called bottoms, the soil of which is very productive ; farther out from the river the land is good second rate. The taxable property in this county in 1846 was $3,332,138 ; number of acres of land, 153,330 ; average value of land per acre $14,39 ; white males over 21 years of age 1,959 ; children between 5 and 16 years of age, 2,104 : population in 1830, 9,012 ; in 1840, 10,034. The staple productions are Indian corn, tobacco, oats, wheat whisky, flour, apples, and hogs; timothy and blue grass grow luxuriantly in almost all parts of the county. The Covington and Lexington turnpike road runs about ten miles through this county. The principal streams and creeks are Woolper, Middle creek, Gunpowder and Big Bone creek, which is at its mouth and some distance up the south boundary of the county.

The principal towns are Burlington, the seat of justice, situated six miles S. S. W. from the nearest point of the Ohio river; Florence, on the Covington and Lexington turnpike road; Union; Walton; Verona; Hamilton, on the Ohio river; Petersburg, on the Ohio, and Francisville.

BURLINGTON, the seat of justice, is situated fourteen miles from Cincinnati and seventy miles from Frankfort,—contains four churches : Baptist, Methodist, Presbyterian and Reformed ; Morgan's Academy, with an endowment of $5,000 and sixty students ; two schools, seven lawyers, five doctors, five stores, two taverns, one shoe and boot store, one wool factory, eight mechanics' shops, one tobacco factory, and a population of four hundred. It was incorporated in 1824. *Florence* contains two churches, three doctors, two stores, two taverns, two schools, four mechanics' shops, and a population of two hundred. It was incorporated in 1830. *Francisville* contains one church, one tobacco factory, and one store. *Hamilton* contains one school, one tavern, three stores, two doctors, and a population of two hundred. *Petersburg* contains two schools, one tobacco factory, one steam distillery and flouring mill, two churches, one tavern, two doctors, and a population of two hundred and fifty. *Springtown*, below Covington, is a fishing place with seventy-five inhabitants. *Union* contains two churches, one store, one doctor, and fifty inhabitants. *Walton* contains one tavern and two tobacco factories, and has a population of fifty.

Amongst the *antiquities* of this county is the site of an aboriginal burying ground, whose history is hid in the darkness of past ages, now covered by the flourishing town of Petersburg. In digging cellars for their houses, the inhabitants have excavated pieces of earthenware vessels and Indian utensils of stone, some of them curiously carved. A little above the town, on the bank of the river, are the remains of an ancient fortification. All that is now visible is an embankment or breastwork, about four feet high, and extending from the abrupt bank of the Ohio to the almost precipitous bank of Taylor's creek, including between the river and the creek an area of about twenty or twenty-five acres of ground.

At the mouth of Woolper creek, about twelve miles nearly west from Burlington, is a singular chasm in a hill, which has been cleft from top to bottom. The part split off is separated by an interval of ten or twelve feet from the main body of the hill, thus forming a zigzag avenue through it from the low land or bottom on the Ohio river to Woolper creek. The north side of this chasm is a perpendicular wall of rock seventy or eighty feet high, composed of pebble stones.

In this county is situated the celebrated *Big Bone Lick*, about twelve miles a little west of south from Burlington, and one mile and a half east from Hamilton, on the Ohio river. The lick is situated in a valley which contains about one hundred acres, through which flows Big Bone creek. There are two principal springs, one of which is almost on the northern margin of the creek; the other is south of the creek, and at the base of the hills which bound the valley. There is a third spring of smaller size some considerable distance north of the creek, which flows from a well sunk many years ago, when salt was manufactured at this lick. The valley is fertile, and surrounded by irregular hills of unequal elevation, the highest being on the west, and attaining an altitude of five hundred feet. The back water from the river, at times, ascends the creek as far as the lick, which, by the course of the stream, is more than three miles from its mouth. At a very early day the surrounding forest had no undergrowth, the ground being covered with a smooth grassy turf, and the lick spread over an area of about ten acres. The surface of the ground within this area was generally depressed three or four feet below the level of the surrounding valley. This depression was probably occasioned as well by the stamping of the countless numbers of wild animals, drawn thither by the salt contained in the water and impregnating the ground, as by their licking the earth to procure salt. There is no authentic account of this lick having been visited by white men before the year 1773. In that year James Douglass, of Virginia, visited it, and found the ten acres constituting the lick bare of trees and herbage of every kind, and large numbers of the bones of the mastodon or mammoth, and the arctic elephant, scattered upon the surface of the ground. The last of these bones which thus lay upon the surface of the earth, were removed more than forty years ago; but since that time a considerable number have been exhumed from beneath the soil, which business has been prosecuted as zealously by some, as others are wont to dig for hidden treasures. Some of the teeth of these huge animals would weigh near ten pounds, and the surface on which the food was chewed was about seven inches long and four or five broad. A correspondent informs us that he had seen dug up in one mass, several tusks and ribs, and thigh bones, and one skull, besides many other bones. Two of these tusks, which belonged to different animals, were about eleven feet in length, and at the largest end six or seven inches in diameter; two others were seven or eight feet long. The thigh bones were four or five feet in length, and a straight line drawn from one end of some of the ribs to the other would be five feet; the ribs were between three and four inches broad. These dimensions correspond with what Mr. Douglass has said of the ribs which he used for tent poles when he visited the lick in 1773. Our correspondent thinks the skull above mentioned certainly belonged to a young animal, and yet the distance across the forehead and between the eyes was two feet, and the sockets of the tusks eighteen inches deep. The tusks which have been stated to be seven or eight feet long exactly fitted these sockets. This lick is the only place in which these gigantic remains have been found in such large quantities, and deserves to be called the *grave yard of the mammoth*. The first collection of these fossil remains was made by Dr. Goforth in 1803, and in 1806 was intrusted by him to the English traveler, Thomas Ashe, (the slanderer of our country), to be exhibited in Europe, who, when he arrived in England, sold the collection and pocketed the money. The purchaser afterwards transferred parts of this collection to the Royal College of Surgeons in London, to Dr. Blake of Dublin, and Professor Monroe of Edinburgh, and a part was sold at auction. The next collection was made by order of Mr. Jefferson, while he was president of the American Philosophical Society, about the year 1805, and was divided between that society and M. Cuvier, the distinguished French naturalist. A third collection was made in 1819, by the Western Museum society. In the year 1831 a fourth collection was made by Mr. Finnell. This was first sold to a Mr. Graves for $2,000, and taken by him to the eastern states, and there sold for $5,000.

It has before been intimated that salt was once manufactured at this lick; but since the year 1812 no effort of that kind has been made, as it requires five or six hundred gallons of the water to make a single bushel of salt.

The springs at this place have been considerably frequented on account of their medicinal virtues; but at this time no accommodation of any sort for visiters is kept there, and but very inadequate accommodation is to be found any where in the neighborhood.

The distinguished pioneer Colonel DANIEL BOONE, (in honor of whom Boone county was named, and who was the first white man who ever made a permanent settlement within the limits of the present State of Kentucky), was born in Bucks county, Pennsylvania, on the right bank of the Delaware river, on the 11th of February, 1731. Of his life, but little is known previous to his emigration to Kentucky, with the early history of which his name is, perhaps, more closely identified than that of any other man. The only sources to which we can resort for information, is the meagre narrative dictated by himself, in his old age,—and which is confined principally to that period of his existence passed in exploring the wilderness of Kentucky, and which, therefore, embraces but a comparatively small part of his life; and the desultory reminiscences of his early associates in that hazardous enterprise. This constitutes the sum total of our knowledge of the personal history of this remarkable man, to whom, as the founder of what may without impropriety be called a *new empire*, Greece and Rome would have erected statues of honor, if not temples of worship.

It is said that the ancestors of Daniel Boone were among the original Catholic settlers of Maryland ; but of this nothing is known with certainty, nor is it, perhaps, important that anything should be. He was eminently the architect of his own fortunes; a self formed man in the truest sense—whose own innate energies and impulses, gave the moulding impress to his character. In the years of his early boyhood, his father emigrated first to Reading, on the head waters of the Schuylkill, and subsequently to one of the valleys of south Yadkin, in North Carolina, where the subject of this notice continued to reside until his fortieth year. Our knowledge of his history during this long interval, is almost a perfect blank; and although we can well imagine that he could not have passed to this mature age, without developing many of those remarkable traits, by which his subsequent career was distinguished, we are in possession of no facts out of which to construct a biography of this period of his life. We know, indeed, that from his earliest years he was distinguished by a remarkable fondness for the exciting pleasures of the chase;—that he took a boundless delight in the unrestrained freedom, the wild grandeur and thrilling solitude of those vast primeval forests, where nature in her solemn majesty, unmarred by the improving hand of man, speaks to the impressionable and unhacknied heart of the simple woodsman, in a language unknown to the dweller in the crowded haunts of men. But, in this knowledge of his disposition and tastes, is comprised almost all that can absolutely be said to be known of Daniel Boone, from his childhood to his fortieth year.

In 1767, the return of Findley from his adventurous excursion into the unexplored wilds beyond the Cumberland mountain, and the glowing accounts he gave of the richness and fertility of the new country, excited powerfully the curiosity and imaginations of the frontier backwoodsmen of Virginia and North Carolina, ever on the watch for adventures ; and to whom the lonely wilderness, with all its perils, presented attractions which were not to be found in the close confinement and enervating inactivity of the settlements. To a man of Boone's temperament and tastes, the scenes described by Findley, presented charms not to be resisted ; and, in 1769, he left his family upon the Yadkin, and in company with five others, of whom Findley was one, he started to explore that country of which he had heard so favorable an account.

Having reached a stream of water on the borders of the present State of Kentucky, called Red river, they built a cabin to shelter them from the inclemency of the weather, (for the season had been very rainy), and devoted their time to hunting and the chase, killing immense quantities of game. Nothing of particular interest occurred until the 22d December, 1769, when Boone, in company with a man named Stuart, being out hunting, they were surprised and captured by Indians. They remained with their captors seven days, until having by a rare and powerful exertion of self-control, suffering no signs of impatience to escape them, succeeded in disarming the suspicions of the Indians, their escape was effected without difficulty. Through life, Boone was remarkable for cool, collected self-possession, in moments of most trying emergency, and on no occasion was this rare and valuable quality more conspicuously displayed than during the time of this captivity. On regaining their camp, they found it dismantled and deserted. The fate of its inmates was never ascertained, and it is worthy of remark, that this is the last and almost the only glimpse we have of Findley, the first pioneer.

A few days after this, they were joined by Squire Boone, a brother of the great pioneer, and another man, who had followed them from Carolina, and accidentally stumbled on their camp. Soon after this accession to their numbers, Daniel Boone and Stuart, in a second excursion, were again assailed by the Indians, and Stuart shot and scalped; Boone fortunately escaped. Their only remaining companion, disheartened by the perils to which they were continually exposed, returned to North Carolina; and the two brothers were left alone in the wilderness, separated by hundreds of miles from the white settlements, and destitute of everything but their rifles. Their ammunition running short, it was determined that Squire Boone should return to Carolina for a fresh supply, while his brother remained in charge of the camp. This resolution was accordingly carried into effect, and Boone was left for a considerable time to encounter or evade the teeming perils of his hazardous solitude alone. We should suppose that his situation now would have been disheartening and wretched in the extreme. He himself says, that for a few days after his brother left him, he felt dejected and lonesome, but in a short time his spirits recovered their wonted equanimity, and he roved through the woods in every direction, killing abundance of game and finding an unutterable pleasure in the contemplation of the natural beauties of the forest scenery. On the 27th of July, 1770, the younger Boone returned from Carolina with the ammunition, and with a hardihood almost incredible, the brothers continued to range through the country without injury until March, 1771, when they retraced their steps to North Carolina. Boone had been absent from his family for near three years, during nearly the whole of which time he had never tasted bread or salt, nor beheld the face of a single white man, with the exception of his brother and the friends who had been killed.

We, of the present day, accustomed to the luxuries and conveniences of a highly civilized state of society—lapped in the soft indolence of a fearless security—accustomed to shiver at every blast of the winter's wind, and to tremble at every noise the origin of which is not perfectly understood—can form but an imperfect idea of the motives and influences which could induce the early pioneers of the west to forsake the safe and peaceful settlements of their native States, and brave the unknown perils, and undergo the dreadful privations of a savage and unreclaimed wilderness. But, in those hardy hunters, with nerves of iron and sinews of steel, accustomed from their earliest boyhood to entire self-dependence for the supply of every want, there was generated a contempt of danger and a love for the wild excitement of an adventurous life, which silenced all the suggestions of timidity or prudence. It was not merely a disregard of danger which distinguished these men, but an actual insensibility to those terrors which palsy the nerves of men reared in the peaceful occupations of a densely populated country. So deep was this love of adventure, which we attribute as the distinguishing characteristic of the early western hunters, implanted in the breast of Boone, that he determined to sell his farm, and remove with his family to Kentucky.

Accordingly, on the 25th of September, 1771, having disposed of all his property, except that which he intended to carry with him to his new home, Boone and his family took leave of their friends, and commenced their journey west. In Powell's valley, being joined by five more families and forty men, well armed, they proceeded towards their destination with confidence; but when near the Cumberland mountains, they were attacked by a large party of Indians. These, after a severe engagement, were beaten off and compelled to retreat; not, however, until the whites had sustained a loss of six men in killed and wounded. Among the killed, was Boone's eldest son. This foretaste of the dangers which awaited them in the wilderness they were about to explore, so discouraged the emigrants, that they immediately retreated to the settlements on Clinch river, a distance of forty miles from the scene of action. Here they remained until 1774. During this interval, Boone was employed by Governor Dunmore, of Virginia, to conduct a party of surveyors through the wilderness, to the falls of the Ohio, a distance of eight hundred miles. Of the incidents attending this expedition, we have no account whatever. After his return, he was placed by Dunmore in command of three frontier stations, or garrisons, and engaged in several affairs with the Indians. At about the same period, he also, at the solicitation of several gentlemen of North Carolina, attended a treaty with the Cherokees, known as the treaty of Wataga, for the purchase of the lands south of the Kentucky river. It was in connection with this land purchase, and under the auspices of Colonel Richard Henderson, that Boone's second expedition to Kentucky was made. His business was to mark out a road for the pack horses and waggons of Henderson's party. Leaving his family on Clinch river, he set out upon this hazardous undertaking at the head of a few men, in the early part of the year 1775, and arrived, without any adventure worthy of note, on the 22nd of March, in the same year, at a point within fifteen miles of the spot where Boonesborough was afterwards built. Here they were attacked by Indians, and it was not until after a severe contest, and loss on the part of the whites of four men in killed and wounded, that they were repulsed. The attack was renewed the next day, and the whites sustained a loss of five more of their companions. On the first of April, they reached the southern bank of the Kentucky river, and began to build a fort, afterwards known as Boonesborough. On the 4th, they were again attacked by the Indians, and lost another man ; but, notwithstanding the dangers to which they were continually exposed, the work was prosecuted with indefatigable diligence, and on the 14th of the month finally completed. Boone instantly returned to Clinch river for his family, determined to remove them to this new and remote settlement at all hazards. This was accordingly effected as soon as circumstances would permit. From this time, the little garrison was exposed to incessant assaults from the Indians, who appeared to be perfectly infuriated at the encroachments of the whites, and the formation of settlements in the midst of their old hunting grounds ; and the lives of the emigrants were passed in a continued succession of the most appalling perils, which nothing but unquailing courage and indomitable firmness could have enabled them to encounter. They did, however, breast this awful tempest of war, and bravely, and successfully, and in defiance of all probability, the small colony continued steadily to increase and flourish, until the thunder of barbarian hostilities rolled gradually away to the north, and finally died in low mutterings on the frontiers of Ohio, Indiana, and Illinois. The summary nature of this sketch will not admit of more than a bare enumeration of the principal events in which Boone figured, in these exciting times, during which he stood the center figure, towering like a colossus amid that hardy band of pioneers, who opposed their breasts to the shock of that dreadful death struggle, which gave a yet more terrible significance, and a still more crimson hue, to the history of the old dark and bloody ground.

In July, 1776, the people at the Fort were thrown into the greatest agitation and alarm, by an incident characteristic of the times, and which singularly illustrates the habitual peril which environed the inhabitants. Two young ladies, a Miss Boone and a Miss Calloway, were amusing themselves in the neighborhood of the fort, when a concealed party of Indians suddenly rushed from the surrounding coverts and carried them away captives. The screams of the terrified girls instantly aroused the inmates of the garrison; but the men being generally dispersed in their usual avocations, Boone hastily pursued with a small party of only eight men. The little party, after marching hard during the night, came up with the Indians early in the next day, the pursuit having been conducted with such silence and celerity that the savages were taken entirely by surprise, and having no preparations for defence, they were routed almost instantly, and without difficulty. The young girls were restored to their gratified parents without having sustained the slightest injury or any inconvenience beyond the fatigue of the march and a dreadful fright. The Indians lost two men, while Boone's party was uninjured.

From this time until the 15th of April, the garrison was constantly harassed by flying parties of savages. They were kept in continual anxiety and alarm ; and the most ordinary duties could only be performed at the risk of their lives. " While plowing their corn, they were way-laid and shot; while hunting, they were pursued and fired upon; and sometimes a solitary Indian would creep up near the fort during the night, and fire upon the first of the garrison who appeared in the morning." On the 15th of April, a large body of Indians invested the fort, hoping to crush the settlement at a single blow ; but, destitute as they were of scaling ladders, and all the proper means of reducing fortified places, they could only annoy the garrison, and destroy the property ; and being more exposed than the whites, soon retired precipitately. On the 4th of July following, they again appeared with a force of two hundred warriors, and were repulsed with loss. A short period of tranquility was now allowed to the harassed and distressed garrison; but this was soon followed by the most severe calamity that had yet befallen the infant settlement. This was the capture of Boone and twenty-seven of his men in the month of January 1778, at the Blue Licks, whither he had gone to make salt for the garrison. He was carried to the old town of Chillicothe, in the present state of Ohio, where he remained a prisoner with the Indians until the 16th of the following June, when he contrived to make his escape, and returned to Boonsborough.

During this period, Boone kept no journal, and we are therefore uninformed as to any of the particular incidents which occurred during his captivity. We only know, generally, that, by his equanimity, his patience, his seeming cheerful submission to the fortune which had made him a captive, and his remarkable skill and expertness as a woodsman, he succeeded in powerfully exciting the admiration and conciliating the good will of his captors. In March, 1778, he accompanied the Indians on a visit to Detroit, where Governor Hamilton offered one hundred pounds for his ransom, but so strong was the affection of the Indians for their prisoner, that it was unhesitatingly refused. Several English gentlemen, touched with sympathy for his misfortunes, made pressing offers of money and other articles, but Boone steadily refused to receive benefits which he could never return.

On his return from Detroit, he observed that large numbers of warriors had assembled, painted and equipped for an expedition against Boonsborough, and his anxiety became so great that he determined to effect his escape at every hazard. During the whole of this agitating period, however, he permitted no symptom of anxiety to escape; but continued to hunt and shoot with the Indians as usual, until the morning of the 16th of June, when, making an early start, he left Chillicothe, and shaped his course for Boonsborough. This journey, exceeding a distance of one hundred and fifty miles, he performed in four days, during which he ate only one meal. He was received at the garrison like one risen from the dead. His family supposing him killed, had returned to North Carolina; and his men, apprehending no danger, had permitted the defences of the fort to fall to decay. The danger was imminent; the enemy were hourly expected, and the fort was in no condition to receive them. Not a moment was to be lost: the garrison worked night and day, and by indefatigable diligence, everything was made ready within ten days after his arrival, for the approach of the enemy. At this time one of his companions arrived from Chillicothe, and reported that his escape had determined the Indians to delay the invasion for three weeks. The attack was delayed so long that Boone, in his turn, resolved to invade the Indian country; and accordingly, at the head of a select company of nineteen men, he marched against the town of Paint Creek, on the Scioto, within four miles of which point he arrived without discovery. Here he encountered a party of thirty warriors, on their march to join the grand army in its expedition against Boonsborough. This party he attacked and routed without loss or injury to himself; and, ascertaining that the main body of the Indians were on their march to Boonsborough, he retraced his steps for that place with all possible expedition. He passed the Indians on the 6th day of their march, and on the 7th reached the fort. The next day the Indians appeared in great force, conducted by Canadian officers well skilled in all the arts of modern warfare. The British colors were displayed and the fort summoned to surrender. Boone requested two days for consideration, which was granted. At the expiration of this period, having gathered in their cattle and horses, and made every preparation for a vigorous resistance, an answer was returned that the fort would be defended to the last. A proposition was then made to treat, and Boone and eight of the garrison, met the British and Indian officers, on the plain in front of the fort. Here, after they had went through the farce of pretending to treat, an effort was made to detain the Kentuckians as prisoners. This was frustrated by the vigilance and activity of the intended victims, who springing out from the midst of their savage foemen, ran to the fort under a heavy fire of rifles, which fortunately wounded only one man. The attack instantly commenced by a heavy fire against the picketing, and was returned with fatal accuracy by the garrison. The Indians then attempted to push a mine into the fort, but their object being discovered by the quantity of fresh earth they were compelled to throw into the river, Boone cut a trench within the fort, in such a manner as to intersect their line of approach, and thus frustrated their design. After exhausting all the ordinary artifices of Indian warfare, and finding their numbers daily thinned by the deliberate and fatal fire from the garrison, they raised the siege on the ninth day after their first appearance, and returned home. The loss on the part of the garrison, was two men killed and four wounded. Of the savages, twenty-seven were killed and many wounded, who, as usual, were carried off. This was the last siege sustained by Boonsborough.

In the fall of this year, Boone went to North Carolina for his wife and family, who, as already observed, had supposed him dead, and returned to their kindred. In the summer of 1780, he came back to Kentucky with his family, and settled at Boonsborough. In October of this year, returning in company with his brother from the Blue Licks, where they had been to make salt, they were encountered by a party of Indians, and his brother, who had been his faithful companion through many years of toil and danger, was shot and scalped before his eyes. Boone, after a long and close chase, finally effected his escape.

After this, he was engaged in no affair of particular interest, so far as we are informed, until the month of August, 1782, a time rendered memorable by the celebrated and disastrous battle of the Blue Licks. A full account of this bloody and desperate conflict, will be found under the head of Nicholas county, to which we refer the reader. On this fatal day, he bore himself with distinguished gallantry, until the rout began, when, after having witnessed the death of his son, and many of his dearest friends, he found himself almost surrounded at the very commencement of the retreat. Several hundred Indians were between him and the ford, to which the great mass of the fugitives were bending their way, and to which the attention of the savages was particularly directed. Being intimately acquainted with the ground, he together with a few friends, dashed into the ravine which the Indians had occupied, but which most of them had now left to join in the pursuit. After sustaining one or two heavy fires, and baffling one or two small parties who pursued him for a short distance, he crossed the river below the ford by swimming, and returned by a circuitous route by Bryant's station.

Boone accompanied General George Rogers Clark, in his expedition against the Indian towns, undertaken to avenge the disaster at the Blue Licks ; but beyond the simple fact that he did accompany this expedition, nothing is known of his connection with it : and it does not appear that he was afterwards engaged in any public expedition or solitary adventure.

The definitive treaty of peace between the United States and Great Britain, in 1783, confirmed the title of the former to independence, and Boone saw the standard of civilization and freedom securely planted in the wilderness. Upon the establishment of the court of commissioners in 1779, he had laid out the chief of his little property to procure land warrants, and having raised about twenty thousand dollars in paper money, with which he intended to purchase them, on his way from Kentucky to the city of Richmond, he was robbed of the whole, and left destitute of the means of procuring more. Unacquainted with the niceties of the law, the few lands he was enabled afterwards to locate, were, through his ignorance, swallowed up and lost by better claims. Dissatisfied with these impediments to the acquisition of the soil, he left Kentucky, and in 1795, he was a wanderer on the banks of the Missouri, a voluntary subject of the king of Spain. The remainder of his life was devoted to the society of his children, and the employments of the chase—to the latter especially. When age had enfeebled the energies of his once athletic frame, he would wander twice a year into the remotest wilderness he could reach, employing a companion whom he bound by a written contract to take care of him, and bring him home alive or dead. In 1816, he made such an excursion to Fort Osage, one hundred miles distant from the place of his residence. "Three years thereafter," says Gov. Morehead, "a patriotic solicitude to preserve his portrait, prompted a distinguished American artist to visit him at his dwelling near the Missouri river, and from him I have received the following particulars : He found him in a small, rude cabin, indisposed, and reclining on his bed. A slice from the loin of a buck, twisted round the rammer of his rifle, within reach of him as he lay, was roasting before the fire. Several other cabins, arranged in the form of a parallelogram, marked the spot of a dilapidated station. They were occupied by the descendants of the

To

Judge John Cobren

Sant Louis

October the 5th 1809

Dear Sir

The Later I Recd from you Respecting
Squire Boones Sustenate Was Long coming
to hand and my Not beeing able to go to
fort Lewis I Dunn the Bisness before Col
feebey and Sent it on by Lewis Bryan
in Closed in a Later to your Self and one

to Squire Boone Derecting him to Deliver
it to you him Self these Laters Could Not
Reach you before you Left home if that —
Wilnot Son pleas Wright to me at Soft
Charles and I will Make out another and
Send it to you before Courts adjornes as
I have the form you Sent me I am well

in health But Deep in Mankquery and Not able to Come Down I Shall Say Nothing about our petistion but Leve it all to your Self I am Dear is youres Daniel Boone

Judge Colman

pioneer. Here he lived in the midst of his posterity. His withered energies and locks of snow, indicated that the sources of existence were nearly exhausted." He died of fever, at the house of his son-in-law, in Flanders, Calloway county, Mo., in the year 1820, at the advanced age of 89 years. The legislature of Missouri was in session at St. Louis when the event was announced; and a resolution was immediately passed, that, in respect for his memory, the members would wear the usual badge of mourning for twenty days, and an adjournment was voted for that day.

It has been generally supposed that Boone was illiterate, and could neither read nor write, but this is an error. There is now in the possession of Mr. Joseph B. Boyd, of Maysville, an autograph letter of the old woodsman, a *fac simile* of which is herewith published.

The following vigorous and eloquent portrait of the character of the old pioneer, is extracted from Gov. Morehead's address, delivered at Boonsborough, in commemoration of the first settlement of Kentucky:

" The life of Daniel Boone is a forcible example of the powerful influence which a single absorbing passion exerts over the destiny of an individual. Born with no endowments of intellect to distinguish him from the crowd of ordinary men, and possessing no other acquirements than a very common education bestowed, he was enabled, nevertheless, to maintain through a long and useful career, a conspicuous rank among the most distinguished of his cotemporaries; and the testimonials of the public gratitude and respect with which he was honored after his death, were such as are never awarded by an intelligent people to the undeserving. * * * * He came originally to the wilderness, not to settle and subdue it, but to gratify an inordinate passion for adventure and discovery— to hunt the deer and buffalo—to roam through the woods—to admire the beauties of nature—in a word, to enjoy the lonely pastimes of a hunter's life, remote from the society of his fellow men. He had heard, with admiration and delight, Finley's description of the country of Kentucky, and high as were his expectations, he found it a second paradise. Its lofty forests—its noble rivers—its picturesque scenery— its beautiful valleys—but above all, the plentifulness of " beasts of every American kind"—these were the attractions that brought him to it. * * * * * He united, in an eminent degree, the qualities of shrewdness, caution, and courage, with uncommon muscular strength. He was seldom taken by surprise—he never shrunk from danger, nor cowered beneath the pressure of exposure and fatigue. In every emergency, he was a safe guide and a wise counsellor, because his movements were conducted with the utmost circumspection, and his judgment and penetration were proverbially accurate. Powerless to originate plans on a large scale, no individual among the pioneers could execute with more efficiency and success the designs of others. He took the lead in no expedition against the savages—he disclosed no liberal and enlarged views of policy for the protection of the stations; and yet it is not assuming too much to say, that without him, in all probability, the settlements could not have been upheld, and the conquest of Kentucky might have been reserved for the emigrants of the nineteenth century. * * * * * His manners were simple and unobtrusive—exempt from the rudeness characteristic of the backwoodsman. In his person there was nothing remarkably striking. He was five feet ten inches in height, and of robust and powerful proportions. His countenance was mild and contemplative—indicating a frame of mind altogether different from the restlessness and activity that distinguished him. His ordinary habiliments were those of a hunter—a hunting shirt and moccasins uniformly composing a part of them. When he emigrated to Louisiana, he omitted to secure the title to a princely estate, on the Missouri, because it would have cost him the trouble of a trip to New Orleans. He would have traveled a much greater distance to indulge his cherished propensities as an adventurer and a hunter. He died, as he had lived, in a cabin, and perhaps his trusty rifle was the most valuable of his chattels.

Such was the man to whom has been assigned the principal merit of the discovery of Kentucky, and who filled a large space in the eyes of America and Europe. Resting on the solid advantages of his services to his country, his fame will survive, when the achievements of men, greatly his superiors in rank and intellect, will be forgotten."

(For an account of the removal of the mortal remains of Boone and his wife from Missouri to Kentucky, and their re-interment at Frankfort, see Franklin county.)

BOURBON COUNTY.

BOURBON county was formed in the year 1785, and is one of the nine organized by the Virginia legislature before Kentucky became an independent State. It was named in compliment to the Bourbon family of France—a prince of that family, then upon the throne, having rendered the American colonies most important aid, in men and money, in the great struggle for independence. The county is bounded north by Harrison, east by Montgomery, south by Clarke, and west by Fayette. It lies in the heart of the garden of Kentucky—the surface gently undulating, the soil remarkably rich and productive, based on limestone, with red clay foundation. Hemp, corn and wheat are cultivated in the county, and grasses, generally, grow in great luxuriance; but stock appears to be the staple article of commerce. Horses, mules, cattle and hogs, in great numbers, are annually exported. The *Bourbon cattle* are unsurpassed in beauty, or in the fine quality of their meat, by any in the United States.

The taxable property of Bourbon in 1846 was valued at $9,-475,752; 175,017 acres of land in the county; average value per acre, $33,66; number of white males over twenty-one years of age, 1,712; number of children between five and sixteen years old, 1,470; population in 1830, 18,434—in 1840, 14,478.

PARIS, the principal town and county seat of Bourbon, is situated on the turnpike road from Maysville to Lexington, about forty-three miles from Frankfort. It is a neat and pleasant town, and is a place of considerable business and importance: Containing a handsome court-house, with cupalo and clock, six churches—Baptist, Reformed, Old School Presbyterian, New School Presbyterian, Episcopal, and Methodist,—an academy and several private schools, a branch of the northern bank of Kentucky, three taverns, seven dry goods stores, six grocery stores, fifteen lawyers, eight physicians, three bagging factories, a large flouring, saw and fulling mills, forty or fifty mechanics' shops, and about 1,500 inhabitants. Paris contains one newspaper office—the "*Western Citizen*"—the oldest newspaper, except the Kentucky Gazette, in the State. The establishment is now owned by Messrs. Lyle & Walker, but was formerly, for a period of more than twenty years, owned by JOEL R. LYLE, Esq., still living in the neighborhood of Paris, and who is among the few editors of Kentucky who have been able to retire from the press with a handsome competency.

The town was established by the Virginia legislature in 1789, under the name of *Hopewell*, by which it was known for several years. It was also called Bourbonton, after the county in which it lies, but finally received its present name from the city of Paris in France, in the plenitude of good feeling which then existed towards that nation.

VIEW OF MAIN STREET, PARIS, KY.

MOUNT LEBANON, KY., RESIDENCE OF GOV. GARRARD

Millersburg is situated on Hinkston, on the Maysville and Lexington road, eight miles from Paris and thirty-eight from Maysville: Contains five hundred inhabitants, four churches—Methodist, Reformed, Baptist and Presbyterian—five stores, four doctors, two taverns, one flouring mill, two saw mills, and a number of mechanics' shops. Established in 1817, and named after the owner of the land, Mr. Miller. *Centreville* is a small village situated on the road from Paris to Georgetown, with sixty inhabitants, one tavern, two stores, one wool factory, and several mechanics. *Clintonville* lies nine miles south of Paris, and contains two churches, one tavern, two stores, one doctor, and several mechanics. *Jacksonville* lies nine miles north west of Paris, with two stores, two mechanics, and thirty inhabitants. *North Middleton* is a small town in the east part of Bourbon, ten miles from Paris, containing two churches and an academy, three stores, one tavern, two doctors, a large number of mechanics, and three hundred and seventy-five inhabitants. *Ruddell's Mills*, situated on Hinkston creek, seven miles from Paris, contains two churches, three stores, one tavern, twelve mechanics' shops, and one hundred inhabitants.

The lands in Bourbon are in a high state of cultivation, being all enclosed, and the woodland well set in grass. The soil of the "Caneridge lands" is of a reddish color, which is supposed to be more durable than the black loam, and not so easily affected either by a dry or wet season. Primitive limestone, without any apparent organic remains, occurs in this section of the county in huge masses.

The only salt spring in the county is on the farm of Joseph Wilson, Esq., in the Caneridge neighborhood. It was formerly worked, and is said to be more strongly impregnated than the waters of the Blue Licks. Sulphur and chalybeate springs are common in the county. Lead ore is occasionally found in small quantities, as also an inferior species of iron ore.

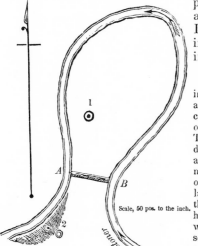

Scale, 50 pos. to the inch.

The line *A B*, in the annexed drawing, represents an ancient ditch across a narrow neck of land intercepted in a bend of Stoner, about one and a fourth miles below Paris. The peninsula thus cut off by the ditch, embraces an area of about fifty acres. The figures 1 and 2 represent mounds of earth. The first is situated on the lowest bench of the bottom land, and the other is on the top of the cliff. The mound in the bottom has been opened, and human bones were discovered therein. An old settler of the county has informed me, that a well defined cause-way,

13

or smaller ditch, was perceptible at the period of the first settlement in the county, which extended from this ditch one and a half miles west to another large mound, on an elevated piece of ground. This latter mound is one of a range or chain of mounds, that extend quite across the county, in a north-west by west direction, than which, for telegraphic purposes, their position could hardly have been better selected by the most skillful engineer. Indeed, it is conjectured by some, that beacons were sometimes kindled on their summits, as coals have been found just below the surface, and occasionally, human bones, stone hatchets, spears, arrow points and a peculiar kind of ware.

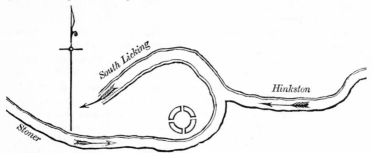

This draft represents an ancient circular fortification with embrasures at the cardinal points, near the junction of Stoner's and Hinkston's forks of Licking, six miles north of Paris, near to which is the village of Ruddell's mills, formerly called Ruddell's station. No tradition points to the period when, or by whom this entrenchment was made; but being situated upon low ground, subject to overflow, there is reason to suppose, that it has been constructed within the last hundred and fifty years; for if it had been formed anterior to this period, all vestiges of its configuration would have been destroyed by the action of the confluent waters.

Three miles further up Hinkston's fork, there is a similar fortification, with the addition of two mounds ; one within, and the other without the circle. Stone axes, hatchets, chisels, dirks, spear and arrow points of flint, also a hatchet of iron, very much corroded with rust, have been found here.

On all of the principal water courses in the county, Indian graves are to be found, sometimes single, but most frequently, several grouped together. Single graves are usually indicated by broad flat stones, set in the ground edgewise around the skeleton ; but where a number have been deposited together, rude stone walls were erected around them, and these having fallen inwards, the rocks retain a vertical position, sometimes resembling a rough pavement. Many of these piles appear to be in various stages of decomposition, according to the lapse of time they have been thus exposed to the action of the elements. From the deliberate care that seems to have been bestowed upon their dead, and other indications, it is manifest that at no very remote period, the territory of Bourbon had a native Indian population. In proof of this, the vestiges of a large Indian town are still perceptible near where Pretty-run empties into Strode's creek, on the farm of Peter Hedge. The centre of the site is distinguished by three small mounds ranged in a line ; and flanked on either side by the remains of double rows of lodges or huts; and at the distance of about one hundred rods to the eastward, on a bluff of Stoner, was their regular burial ground. At the western extremity of the village, on a slight elevation of black earth or mould, the bones of almost every species of wild animal are to be found, those of the buffalo, the bear and the deer being the most common.

At a short distance from this, on a similar elevation, is where either the funeral pyre or the stake, for the purpose of torturing prisoners was erected, as it is at the spot that coals, ashes and calcined human bones have been found ; sad vestiges of their cruel orgies. A variety of ornaments, such as bears' tusks and claws with holes drilled through them, stone medals, shells, etc.; fragments of vases with handles, stone axes, and implements of warfare, have been found in profusion. The growth of the timber on the site, and in its immediate vicinity, fixes within reasonable certainty the period, when the village ceased to be inhabited. This timber is of the same varieties with that of the primitive stock on the hills, with this singular difference, that the former invariably grew two or three trees from the same roots, and when a portion of them were cut down by the present owner, they exhibited the uniform age of ninety years, counting the annulations. The current supposition is this, that the original growth was cut down by the inhabitants of the village, and after they made their exit, that two or three sprouts had sprung up from the still living roots, among the ruined wigwams, and thus exhibiting a cotemporaneous growth at the present day. However this may be, it is evident that this aboriginal town had a tragic end. In every direction the bones and teeth of its unfortunate inhabitants, corresponding to every age, have been discovered just beneath the surface of the soil; sometimes lying across each other within the foundation of their huts, but most numerously in the bottom below the site of the town, whither perhaps the tide of battle rolled, and the devoted inhabitants met their fate at the hands of some hostile band.

In excavating a place for a building in this town a few years since, two or three large bones were found fifteen feet below the surface, in a fissure between two rocks. They were not as large as the bones of the mammoth, but were larger than those of any known species of living animal of this continent.

Five miles below Paris, on Stoner, a cave has been recently discovered, containing a number of skeletons in a good state of preservation. The crania is of Indian conformation, and one of them appears to have been pierced by a rifle ball. It is highly probable that these are the relics of some of the hostile Indians that were killed in the siege of Hinkston's station, a few miles below, as it is well remembered the same band of British and Indians encamped in the vicinity of this cave after the reduction of Hinkston's station, while on their march to attack Martin's station, which was located on Stoner, about three miles below Paris.

At a period when there were but few settlers in the county, a band of Indians, numbering about twenty, ventured into it, for the purpose of stealing horses. A party of a dozen hunters followed their trail, and overtook them on Stoner, a few miles above Paris, and fired a volley of rifle balls into their camp, which killed one of their number and wounded two or three more. The Indians then fled; but after a short interval, contrary to their usual custom, they came back, and fired in turn upon the hunters while they were engaged in securing their stolen horses. Both parties then took trees, and the fight was continued obstinately for a long time. Finally the ammunition of the whites failed, and being nearly all wounded, they were obliged to leave the Indians masters of the field. In this skirmish, which was the last that took place in Bourbon, it was supposed the Indians lost half their number in killed and wounded. The hunters lost but one killed, (Frank Hickman, it is believed was his name), whose skeleton was afterwards identified by the initials on his knee buckles.

In June, 1780, Martin's station, in this county, was captured by a large body of Canadians and Indians, under Colonel Byrd, an officer of the British army. For the particulars of the expedition, and the capture of Ruddell's and Martin's stations, see Harrison county.

On the night of the 11th of April, 1787, the house of a widow, named Shanks, on Cooper's run, in this county, became the scene of an adventure of thrilling interest. She occupied what is generally called a double cabin, in a lonely part of the county, one room of which was tenanted by the old lady herself, together with two grown sons, and a widowed daughter, at that time suckling an infant, while the other was occupied by two unmarried daughters from sixteen to twenty years of age, together with a little girl not more than half grown. The hour was 11 o'clock at night. One of the unmarried daughters was still busily engaged at the loom, but the other members of the family, with the exception of one of the sons, had retired to rest. Some symptoms of an alarming nature had engaged the attention of the young man for an hour before anything of a decided character took place.

The cry of owls was heard in the adjoining wood, answering each other in rather an unusual manner. The horses, which were enclosed as usual in a pound near the house, were more than commonly excited, and by repeated snorting and galloping, announced the presence of some object of terror. The young man was often upon the point of awakening his brother, but was as often restrained by the fear of incurring ridicule and the reproach of timidity, at that time an unpardonable blemish in the character of a Kentuckian. At length hasty steps were heard in the yard, and quickly afterwards, several loud knocks at the door, accompanied by the usual exclamation, "who keeps house?" in very good English. The young man, supposing from the language, that some benighted settlers were at the door, hastily arose, and was advancing to withdraw the bar which secured it, when his mother, who had long lived upon the frontiers, and had probably detected the Indian tone in the demand for admission, instantly sprung out of bed, and ordered her son not to admit them, declaring that they were Indians. She instantly awakened her other son, and the two young men seizing their guns, which were always charged, prepared to repel the enemy. The Indians finding it impossible to enter under their assumed characters, began to thunder at the door with great violence, but a single shot from a loop hole, compelled them to shift the attack to some less exposed point; and, unfortunately, they discovered the door of the other cabin, which contained the three daughters. The rifles of the brothers could not be brought to bear upon this point, and by means of several rails taken from the yard fence, the door was forced from its hinges, and the three girls were at the mercy of the savages. One was instantly secured, but the eldest defended herself desperately with a knife which she had been using at the loom, and stabbed one of the Indians to the heart, before she was tomahawked.

In the meantime the little girl, who had been overlooked by the enemy in their eagerness to secure the others, ran out into the yard, and might have effected her escape, had she taken advantage of the darkness and fled, but instead of that the terrified little creature ran around the house wringing her hands, and crying out that her sisters were killed. The brothers, unable to hear her cries, without risking every thing for her rescue, rushed to the door and were preparing to sally out to her assistance, when their mother threw herself before them and calmly declared that the child must be abandoned to its fate; that the sally would sacrifice the lives of all the rest without the slightest benefit to the little girl. Just then the child uttered a loud scream, followed by a few faint moans, and all was again silent. Presently the crackling of flames was heard, accompanied by a triumphant yell from the Indians, announcing that they had set fire to that division of the house which had been occupied by the daughters, and of which they held undisputed possession.

The fire was quickly communicated to the rest of the building, and it became necessary to abandon it, or perish in the flames. In the one case there was a possibility that some might escape; in the other, their fate would be equally certain and terrible. The rapid approach of the flames cut short their momentary suspense. The door was thrown open, and the old lady, supported by her eldest son, attempted to cross the fence at one point, while her daughter carrying her child in her arms, and attended by the younger of the brothers, ran in a different direction. The blazing roof shed a light over the yard but little inferior to that of day, and the savages were distinctly seen awaiting the approach of their victims. The old lady was permitted to reach the stile unmolested, but in the act of crossing, received several balls in her breast, and fell dead. Her son, providentially, remained unhurt, and by extraordinary agility, effected his escape.

The other party succeeded also in reaching the fence unhurt, but in the act of crossing, were vigorously assailed by several Indians, who throwing down their guns, rushed upon them with their tomahawks. The young man defended his sister gallantly, firing upon the enemy as they approached, and then wielding the butt of his rifle with a fury that drew their whole attention upon himself, and gave his sister an opportunity of effecting her escape. He quickly fell, however, under the tomahawks of his enemies, and was found at day-light, scalped and mangled in a shocking manner. Of the whole family, consisting of eight persons, when the attack commenced, only three escaped. Four were killed upon the spot, and one (the second daughter) carried off as a prisoner.

The neighborhood was quickly alarmed, and by daylight about thirty men were assembled under the command of Colonel Edwards. A light snow had fallen during the latter part of the night, and the Indian trail could be pursued at a gallop. It led directly into the mountainous country bordering upon Licking, and afforded evidences of great hurry and precipitation on the part of the fugitives. Unfortunately, a hound had been permitted to accompany the whites, and as the trail became fresh and the scent warm, she followed it with eagerness, baying loudly and giving the alarm to the Indians. The consequences of this imprudence were soon displayed. The enemy finding the pursuit keen, and perceiving that the strength of the prisoner began to fail, instantly sunk their tomahawks in her head, and left her, still warm and bleeding, upon the snow.

As the whites came up, she retained strength enough to wave her hands in token of recognition, and appeared desirous of giving them some information with regard to the enemy, but her strength was too far gone. Her brother sprung from his horse and knelt by her side, endeavoring to stop the effusion of blood, but in vain. She gave him her hand, muttered some inarticulate words, and expired within two minutes after the arrival of the party. The pursuit was renewed with additional ardor, and in twenty minutes the enemy was within view. They had taken possession of a steep narrow ridge, and seemed desirous of magnifying their numbers in the eyes of the whites, as they ran rapidly from tree to tree, and maintained a steady yell in their most appalling tones. The pursuers, however, were too experienced to be deceived by so common an artifice, and being satisfied that the number of the enemy must be inferior to their own, they dismounted, tied their horses, and flanking out in such a manner as to enclose the enemy, ascended the ridge as rapidly as was consistent with a due regard to the shelter of their persons.

The firing quickly commenced, and now for the first time they discovered that only two Indians were opposed to them. They had voluntarily sacrificed themselves for the safety of the main body, and had succeeded in delaying pursuit until their friends could reach the mountains. One of them was instantly shot dead, and the other was badly wounded, as was evident from the blood upon his blanket, as well as that which filled his tracks in the snow for a considerable distance. The pursuit was recommenced, and urged keenly until night, when the trail entered a running stream and was lost. On the following morning the snow had melted, and every trace of the enemy was obliterated. This affair must be regarded as highly honorable to the skill, address, and activity of the Indians, and the self devotion of the rear guard is a lively instance of that magnanimity of which they are at times capable, and which is more remarkable in them, from the extreme caution, and tender regard for their own lives, which usually distinguishes their warriors.

A few weeks after this melancholy affair, a very remarkable incident occurred in the same neighborhood. One morning, about sunrise, a young man of wild and savage appearance suddenly arose from a cluster of bushes in front of a cabin, and hailed the house in a barbarous dialect, which seemed neither exactly Indian nor English, but a collection of shreds and patches, from which the graces of both were carefully excluded. His skin had evidently once been white—although now grievously tanned by constant exposure to the weather. His dress in every respect was that of an Indian, as were his gestures, tones, and equipments, and his age could not be supposed to exceed twenty years. He talked volubly but uncouthly, placed his hand upon his breast, gestured vehemently, and seemed very earnestly bent upon communicating something. He was invited to enter the cabin, and the neighbors quickly collected around him.

He appeared involuntarily to shrink from contact with them; his eyes rolled rapidly around with a distrustful expression from one to the other, and his whole manner was that of a wild animal, just caught, and shrinking from the touch of its captors. As several present understood the Indian tongue, they at length gathered the following circumstances, as accurately as they could be translated, out of a language which seemed to be an "omnium gatherum" of all that was mongrel, uncouth, and barbarous. He said that he had been taken by the Indians, when a child, but could neither recollect his name, nor the country of his birth. That he had been adopted by an Indian warrior, who brought him up with his other sons, without making the slightest difference between them, and that under his father's roof he had lived happily until within the last month.

A few weeks before that time, his father, accompanied by himself and a younger brother, had hunted for some time upon the waters of the Miami, about forty miles from the spot where Cincinnati now stands, and after all their meat, skins, &c., had been properly secured, the old man determined to gratify his children by taking them upon a war expedition to Kentucky. They accordingly built a bark canoe, in which they crossed the Ohio near the mouth of Licking, and having buried it, so as to secure it from the action of the sun, they advanced into the country and encamped at the distance of fifteen miles from the river. Here their father was alarmed by hearing an owl cry in a peculiar tone, which he declared boded death or captivity to themselves, if they continued their expedition; and announced his intention of returning without delay to the river.

Both of his sons vehemently opposed this resolution, and at length prevailed upon the old man to disregard the owl's warning, and conduct them, as he had promised, against the frontiers of Kentucky. The party then composed themselves to sleep, but were quickly awakened by their father, who had again been warned in a dream that death awaited them in Kentucky, and again besought his children to release him from his promise, and lose no time in returning home. Again they prevailed upon him to disregard the warning, and persevere in the march. He consented to gratify them, but declared he would not remain a moment longer in the camp which they now occupied, and accordingly they left it immediately, and marched on through the night, directing their course towards Bourbon county.

In the evening they approached a house, that which he had hailed, and in which he was now speaking. Suddenly, the desire of rejoining his people occupied his mind so strongly as to exclude every other idea, and seizing the first favorable opportunity, he had concealed himself in the bushes, and neglected to reply to all the signals which had been concerted for the purpose of collecting their party when scattered. This account appeared so extraordinary, and the young man's appearance was so wild and suspicious, that many of the neighbors suspected him of treachery, and thought that he should be arrested as a spy. Others opposed this resolution, and gave full credit to his narrative. In order to satisfy themselves, however, they insisted upon his instantly conducting them to the spot where the canoe had been buried. To this the young man objected most vehemently, declaring, that although he had deserted his father and brother, yet he would not betray them.

These feelings were too delicate to meet with much sympathy from the rude borderers who surrounded him, and he was given to understand that nothing short of conducting them to the point of embarcation, would be accepted as an evidence of his sincerity. With obvious reluctance he at length complied. From twenty to thirty men were quickly assembled, mounted upon good horses, and under the guidance of the deserter, they moved rapidly towards the mouth of Licking. On the road, the young man informed them that he would first conduct them to the spot where they had encamped when the scream of the owl alarmed his father, and where an iron kettle had been left concealed in a hollow tree. He was probably induced to do this from the hope of delaying the pursuit so long as to afford his friends an opportunity of crossing the river in safety.

But if such was his intention, no measure could have been more unfortunate. The whites approached the encampment in deep silence, and quickly perceived two Indians, an old man and a boy, seated by a fire, and busily employed in cooking some venison. The deserter became much agitated at the sight of them, and so earnestly implored his countrymen not to kill them, that it was agreed to surround the encampment, and endeavor to secure them as prisoners. This was accordingly attempted, but so desperate was the resistance of the Indians, and so determined were their efforts to escape, that the whites were compelled to fire upon them, and the old man fell mortally wounded, while the boy, by an incredible display of address and activity, was enabled to escape. The deserter beheld his father fall, and throwing himself from his horse, he ran up to the spot where the old man lay, bleeding but still sensible, and falling upon his body, besought his forgiveness for being the unwilling cause of his death, and wept bitterly.

His father evidently recognized him, and gave him his hand, but almost instantly afterwards expired. The white men now called upon him to conduct them at a gallop to the spot where the canoe was buried, expecting to reach it before the Indian boy, and intercept him. The deserter in vain implored them to compassionate his feelings. He urged that he had already sufficiently demonstrated the truth of his former assertions, at the expense of his father's life, and earnestly entreated them to permit his younger brother to escape. His companions, however, were inexorable. Nothing but the blood of the young Indian wou!d satisfy them, and the deserter was again compelled to act as a guide. Within two hours they reached the designated spot. The canoe was still there, and no track could be seen upon the sand, so that it was evident that their victim had not yet arrived.

Hastily dismounting, they tied their horses and concealed themselves within close rifle shot of the canoe. Within ten minutes after their arrival, the Indian appeared in sight, walking swiftly towards them. He went straight to the spot where the canoe had been buried, and was in the act of digging it up, when he received a dozen balls through his body, and leaping high into the air, fell dead upon the sand. He was instantly scalped and buried where he fell, without having seen his brother, and probably without having known the treachery by which he and his father had lost their lives. The deserter remained but a short time in Bourbon, and never regained his tranquility of mind. He shortly afterwards disappeared, but whether to seek his relations in Virginia or Pennsylvania, or whether disgusted by the ferocity of the whites, he returned to the Indians, has never yet been known. He was never heard of afterwards.*

CAPTAIN GARRARD'S TROOP.

We copy the "Muster roll of a troop of volunteer state dragoons, for twelve months, under command of Captain William Garrard, of Major James V. Ball's squadron, in the service of the United States from date of the last muster (October 31, 1812), to the 31st December, 1812, inclusive," with the remarks appended to each name. The roll is certified as correct, and the remarks as "accurate and just," by the officers. The roll will awaken old reminiscences, and will be examined by many of our readers with great interest.

OFFICERS.

William Garrard, Captain, frost bitten.
Edmund Basye, 1st Lieut. do. and wounded.
David M. Hickman, 2d do., wounded.
Thos. H. McClanahan, Cornet, frost bitten.
Chas. S.Clarkson,1st Serg't, sick on furlough.
William Barton, 2d do., do.
John Clark, 3d do., died Nov. 15, 1812.
Benj.W. Edwards,4th do., Serg't Major.

James Benson, 1st Corporal, sick on furlough.
Wm. Walton, 2nd do., frost bitten.
Jesse Todd, 3d do., sick, absent.
Jno. S. Bristow, 4th do., frost bitten.
Joseph McConnell, Farrier, wounded Dec. 18.
Ephraim Wilson, Trumpeter, frost bitten.
William Daviss, Saddler, do., resigned Nov. 20.

PRIVATES.

John Finch, frost bitten, appointed Sergeant.
William Beneer, present fit for duty.
David B. Langhorn, frost bitten.
John Wynne, sick, absent.
William Mountjoy, frost bitten.
Samuel Henderson, do.
Henry Wilson, wounded Dec. 18th, 1812.
William Jones, sick on furlough.
John Terrill, frost bitten.
Walter Woodyard, do.
Moses Richardson, do., wounded 18th Dec.
Jacob Shy, frost bitten.
Lewis Duncan, sick on furlough.
Robert Thomas, frost bitten.
Jacob Counts, absent on furlough.
John Snoody, frost bitten.
Thomas Bedford, killed in action 18th Dec.
James Finch, frost bitten and sick.
Walker Thornton, present fit for duty.
Thomas Eastin, wounded on the 18th Dec.
Gerrard Robinson, sick on furlough.
William M. Baylor, frost bitten.
Alexander Scott, do.
William Scott, do., wounded Dec. 18.
James Clark, do., sick.
Roger P. West, burnt by the explosion of powder.
Frederick Loring, frost bitten.
Thomas Barton, do.

Samuel J. Caldwell, frost bitten and sick.
John Baseman, do.
Jesse Bowlden, do.
John Funston, do.
James Johnston, do.
John Layson, do.
Will. B. Northcutt, do.
Jonathan Clinkenbeard, do.
Thomas Webster, wounded on the 18th Dec.
Abel C. Pepper, frost bitten and sick.
Beverly Brown, killed in action 18th Dec.
Edward Waller, fit for duty.
Gustavus E. Edwards, wounded, frost bitten.
Stephen Barton, do. do.
Stephen Bedford, do.
John M. Robinson, do.
Jacob Sharrer, sick on furlough.
Isaac Sanders, rejoined 26th November.
James Brown, frost bitten.
Henry Towles, sick on furlough.
John Metcalfe, frost bitten.
Stephen Owen, do.
James Conn, sick on furlough.
Jacob Thomas, frost bitten.
William Allentharp, not yet joined the troop.
Nathaniel Hill, do.
Strother J. Hawkins, wounded, frost bitten.
Edward McGuire, sick on furlough.
Troy Waugh, servant, frost bitten.

* Sketches of Western Adventure.

The number of horses marked as killed, on the roll. is eight, and eight as wounded.

This county was the residence of Governor JAMES GARRARD, whose biographical sketch will be found under the head of Garrard county. The monument to his memory, erected by the state of Kentucky, contains the following inscription:

"This marble consecrates the spot on which repose the mortal remains of Colonel JAMES GARRARD, and records a brief memorial of his virtues and his worth. He was born in the county of Stafford, in the colony of Virginia, on the 14th day of January, 1749. On attaining the age of manhood, he participated with the patriots of the day in the dangers and privations incident to the glorious and successful contest which terminated in the independence and happiness of our country. Endeared to his family, to his friends, and to society, by the practice of the social virtues of Husband, Father, Friend and Neighbor; honored by his country, by frequent calls to represent her dearest interests in her Legislative Councils; and finally by two elections, to fill the chair of the Chief Magistrate of the State, a trust of the highest confidence and deepest interest to a free community of virtuous men, professing equal rights, and governed by equal laws; a trust which, for eight successive years, he fulfilled with that energy, vigor, and impartiality which, tempered with christian spirit of God-like mercy and charity for the frailty of men, is best calculated to perpetuate the inestimable blessings of Government and the happiness of Man. An administration which received its best reward below, the approbation of an enlightened and grateful country, by whose voice, expressed by a resolution of its general assembly in December, 1822, THIS MONUMENT of departed worth and grateful sense of public service, was erected, and is inscribed. He departed this life on the 19th day of January, 1822, as he had lived, a sincere and pious christian, firm, constant and sincere in his own religious sentiments, tolerant for those who differed from him; reposing in the mercy of God, and the merits of his Redeemer, his hopes of a glorious and happy Immortality."

This county has been the nursery of many prominent, and some very distinguished men, particularly at the bar and on the bench. It was the residence of Judge Robert Trimble, of the supreme court of the United States, (see Trimble county)—of Judge Mills, of the court of appeals of Kentucky—and of Judge Bledsoe, who was remarkable for his forensic powers. Captain William and General James Garrard, were active soldiers in the war of 1812—both frequent representatives in the legislature, and the former for many years clerk of the Bourbon county court. Several distinguished pioneer divines were also residents of this county, who are noticed under proper heads.

The Honorable Thomas Corwin, the able and eloquent senator of Ohio, and the Rev. John P. Durbin, D. D., late president of Dickinson college, and one of the most eloquent divines in the United States, are both natives of Bourbon county.

Colonel James Smith, whose interesting narrative of his captivity in western Pennsylvania and residence among the Indians, was published many years since, and transferred, in an abridged form, to the "Sketches of Western Adventure," settled in Bourbon, seven miles above Paris, in 1788. Having been prominent in his native State, as an Indian fighter, a member of the Pennsylvania convention, and a member of her legislature, his public and private worth became speedily known in Bourbon; and in the first year of his residence, he was elected a member of the convention, that sat at Danville, to confer about a separation from the State of Virginia. From that period until 1799, with an intermission of two years only, according to his narrative, he continued to represent Bourbon county, either in convention or as a member of the general assembly. A few extracts from the narrative of Colonel Smith are subjoined.

On the second evening succeeding his capture, (in the year 1755), Colonel Smith arrived with his captors at fort Du Quesne, now Pittsburgh. When within half a mile of the fort, they raised the scalp halloo, and fired their guns. The garrison was instantly in commotion, the cannon were fired, the drums were beaten, and the French and Indians ran out in great numbers to meet the party and partake of their triumph. Smith was instantly surrounded by a multitude of savages, painted in various colors, and shouting with delight. They rapidly formed in two long lines, and brandishing their hatchets, ramrods, switches, etc., called aloud upon him to run the GAUNTLET.

"Never having heard of this Indian ceremony before, he stood amazed for some time, not knowing what to do; one of his captors explained to him, that he was to run between the two lines, and receive a blow from each Indian as he passed, concluding his explanation by exhorting him to "run his best," as the faster he run the sooner the affair would be over. This truth was very plain; and young Smith entered upon his race with great spirit. He was switched very handsomely along the lines, for about three-fourths of the distance, the stripes only acting as a spur to greater exertions, and he had almost reached the opposite extremity of the line, when a tall chief struck him a furious blow with a club upon the back of the head, and instantly felled him to the ground. Recovering himself in a moment, he sprung to his feet and started forward again, when a handful of sand was thrown in his eyes, which, in addition to the great pain, completely blinded him. He still attempted to grope his way through; but was again knocked down and beaten with merciless severity. He soon became insensible under such barbarous treatment, and recollected nothing more, until he found himself in the hospital of the fort, under the hands of a French surgeon, beaten to a jelly, and unable to move a limb. Here he was quickly visited by one of his captors, the same who had given him such good advice, when about to commence his race. He now inquired, with some interest, if he felt "very sore." Young Smith replied, that he had been bruised almost to death, and asked what he had done to merit such barbarity. The Indian replied that he had done nothing, but that it was the customary greeting of the Indians to their prisoners; that it was something like the English "how d'ye do?" and that now all ceremony would be laid aside, and he would be treated with kindness."

Smith was still a captive and at fort Du Quesne, when General Braddock was defeated, the same year, and nearly the whole of his army cut down, or dragged into captivity, and reserved for a more painful death.

"About sunset, [on the day of battle] he heard at a distance the well known scalp halloo, followed by wild, quick, joyful shrieks, and accompanied by long continued firing. This too surely announced the fate of the day. About dusk, the party returned to the fort, driving before them twelve British regulars, stripped naked and with their faces painted black! an evidence that the unhappy wretches were devoted to death. Next came the Indians displaying their bloody scalps, of which they had immense numbers, and dressed in the scarlet coats, sashes, and military hats of the officers and soldiers. Behind all came a train of baggage horses, laden with piles of scalps, canteens, and all the accoutrements of British soldiers. The savages appeared frantic with joy, and when Smith beheld them entering the fort, dancing, yelling, brandishing their red tomahawks, and waving their scalps in the air, while the great guns of the fort replied to the incessant discharge of rifles without, he says, that it looked as if h—ll had given a holiday, and turned loose its inhabitants upon the upper world. The most melancholy spectacle was the band of prisoners. They appeared dejected and anxious. Poor fellows! They had but a few months before left London, at the command of their superiors, and we may easily imagine their feelings, at the strange and dreadful spectacle around them. The yells of delight and congratulation were scarcely over, when those of vengeance began. The devoted prisoners—British regulars—were led out from the fort to the banks of the Alleghany, and to the eternal disgrace of the French commandant were there burnt to death, one after another, with the most awful tortures. Smith stood upon the battlements and witnessed the shocking spectacle. The prisoner was tied to a stake with his hands raised above his head, stripped naked, and surrounded by Indians. They would touch him with red hot irons, and stick his body full of pine splinters and set them on fire, drowning the shrieks of the victim in the yells of delight with which they danced around him. His companions in the meantime stood in a group near the stake, and had a foretaste of what was in reserve for each of them. As fast as one prisoner died under his tortures, another filled his place, until the whole perished. All this took place so near the fort, that every scream of the victims must have rung in the ears of the French commandant!"

Colonel Smith has an article in his pamphlet on the manners and customs of the Indians, their traditions and religious sentiments, their police or civil government, ect. The following extracts must suffice:

"Their traditions are vague, whimsical, romantic, and many of them scarce worth relating; and not any of them reach back to the creation of the world. They tell of a squaw that was found when an infant, in the water, in a canoe made of bull-rushes; this squaw became a great prophetess and did many wonderful things; she turned water into dry land, and at length made this continent, which was, at that time, only a very small island, and but a few Indians in it. Though they were then but few, they had not sufficient room to hunt; therefore this squaw went to the water side, and prayed that this little island might be enlarged. The great Being then heard her prayer, and sent great numbers of water tortoises and muskrats, which brought with them mud and other materials, for enlarging this island, and by this means, they say, it was increased to the size that it now remains; therefore, they say, that the white people ought not to encroach upon them, or take their land from them, because their great grand-mother made it. They say that, about this time, the angels or the heavenly inhabitants, as they call them, frequently visited them and talked with their forefathers; and gave directions how to pray, and how to appease the great Being when he was offended   They told them they were to offer sacrifice, burnt tobacco, buffalo and deer bones; but that they were not to burn bear or raccoon bones in sacrifice.

"The Indians, generally, are of opinion that there are a great number of inferior Deities, which they call *Carreyugaroona*, which signifies the Heavenly inhabitants. These beings, they suppose, are employed as assistants in managing the affairs of the universe, and in inspecting the actions of men: and that even the irrational animals are engaged in viewing their actions, and bearing intelligence to the gods. The eagle, for this purpose, with her keen eye, perched on the trees around their camp in the night; therefore, when they observe the eagle or the owl near, they immediately offer sacrifice, or burn tobacco, that they may have a good report to carry to the gods. They say that there are also great numbers of evil spirits, which they call *Onasahroona*, which signifies the inhabitants of the Lower Region. These spirits are always going after them, and setting things right, so that they are constantly working in opposition to each other. Some talk of a future state, but not with any certainty: at best, their notions are vague and unsettled. Others deny a future state altogether, and say that after death they neither think nor live.

"I have often heard of Indian kings, but never saw any. How any term used by Indians in their own tongue, for the chief man of a nation, could be rendered king, I know not. The chief of a nation is neither the supreme ruler, monarch or potentate: He can neither make war or peace, league or treaties: He cannot impress soldiers or dispose of magazines: He cannot adjourn, prorogue or dissolve a general assembly, nor can he refuse his assent to their conclusions, or in any manner control them. With them, there is no such thing as hereditary succession, title of nobility or royal blood, even talked of. The chief of a nation, even with the consent of his assembly, or council, cannot raise one shilling of tax off the citizens, but only receive what they please to give as free and voluntary donations. The chief of a nation has to hunt for his living, as any other citizen."

BENJAMIN MILLS was born in the county of Worcester, on the eastern shore of Maryland, January 12th, 1779. While he was quite young, his family emigrated to the vicinity of Washington, Pennsylvania, where he obtained his education, and engaged in the study of medicine. While yet a youth, he was called to the presidency of Washington Academy, an institution which was soon after erected into Washington College, and which has sent from its walls a number of prominent public men. Having removed with his father to Bourbon county, Kentucky, and relinquished the study of medicine for that of the law, in 1805 or '06, he commenced in Paris the practice of the latter profession. His abilities and diligence soon ensured him, in his own and the adjacent counties, an extensive practice. For several years he was elected to represent the county of Bourbon in the legislature, and in 1816 failed of an election to the senate of the United States, in competition with Isham Talbot, Esq., by only three votes. In 1817, to relieve himself from an oppressive and injurious practice of the law, he accepted the appointment of judge in the Montgomery circuit. In the succeeding year, by the unanimous request of the Fayette bar, he was transferred to that circuit. In 1820, he was elevated to a seat on the bench of the court of appeals, which he filled with great firmness, through a period of extraordinary excitement with reference to the judiciary of the State, till he retired in 1828. Having resigned this post, he removed from Paris to Frankfort, to engage again in the practice of the law in the higher courts of the State. Success commensurate with his wishes again crowned his labors, till the morning of the 6th of December, 1831, when, by an apoplectic stroke, his mortal existence was terminated.

As a man, Judge Mills was never remarkably popular. Though kind and faithful in every relation of life, he aimed, by a course of firm and inflexible integrity, rather to command the approbation than to win the affections of his fellow men. He was, to a very great exent, a self-made man, and affords a fine example of the ennobling tendency of republican institutions, and an encouragement to all meritorious young men who are struggling in obscurity and poverty.

As a practitioner of the law, by a profound and thorough knowledge of its principles, and the most approved forms of practice, he soon rose to eminence. As a public speaker, he was clear, logical and forcible; but not possessing a fine voice, and seldom using the ornaments of rhetoric, he was less admired as an orator than many others.

As a legislator, he was zealous and active in the promotion of wise, and the resistance of injudicious measures. Some of the most valuable provisions of the statutes of the state, had their origin in his conceptions. His efforts on the exciting new election question in 1816, will be remembered by those familiar with the politics of that day, as having a great influence in settling a construction of the constitution, which, in several instances since, has been acquiesced in with happy effects by the people of the state.

As a circuit judge, he conducted the business of the courts with uncommon industry and energy. The promptness and general accuracy of his decisions, and the perfect impartiality of his administration of justice, gained for him the respect of the orderly portion of the community.

While on the bench of the court of appeals, his official acts tended not only to enlighten, but to enlarge the sphere of his profession, and to establish a system of legal polity alike favorable to the country and honorable to himself. His written opinions furnish abundant proofs of the clearness of his perceptions, the depth of his legal researches, the strength of his memory, his power of analysis, and the steadiness and sternness of his integrity.

For the last twelve years of his life, he was a member of the Presbyterian church, and for a considerable portion of that time a ruling elder. His life, during this period, was in a high degree consistent with his profession; and the extent of his charities in the support of all the great benevolent enterprises of the day, was surprising to those who knew how limited were his means.

Jesse Bledsoe was born on the 6th of April, 1776, in Culpepper county, Virginia. His father, Joseph Bledsoe, was a Baptist preacher. His mother's maiden name was Elizabeth Miller. In early life, Judge Bledsoe's health was delicate, and from weakness in his eyes, could not be sent regularly to school. When his health and sight were restored, which was not until he had become quite a large boy, (having emigrated with an elder brother to the neighborhood of Lexington, Kentucky), he went to Transylvania seminary, and by the force of talent and assiduous industry, became a fine scholar. Few men were better or riper classical scholars; and to the day of his death it was his pleasure and delight to read the Grecian orators and poets in their original tongue. After finishing his collegiate course, he studied law, and commenced its practice with success and reputation.

Judge Bledsoe was repeatedly elected to the house of representatives of the Kentucky legislature, from the counties of Fayette and Bourbon; and was also a senator from the latter county. He was secretary of state, of Kentucky, under Gov. Charles Scott; and during the war with Great Britain, was elected a senator in the congress of the United States from the state of Kentucky, for an unexpired term, serving in that capacity for two or three years. In 1822, he was appointed by Gov. Adair, a circuit judge in the Lexington district, and removed to Lexington, where he received the appointment of professor of law in the Transylvania University. He held the offices of judge and professor for five or six years, when he resigned both, and again commenced the practice of law.

In 1833, he removed to Mississippi, and in the fall of 1835 or spring of 1836, he emigrated to Texas, and commenced gathering materials for a history of the new republic. In May, 1836, he was taken sick in that portion of Texas near the line of the United States, and not far from Nacogdoches, where he died.

At an early age, he married the eldest daughter of Colonel Nathaniel Gist, and his widow is still living in Frankfort.

Judge Bledsoe possessed a strong and powerful intellect, and was surpassed in popular and forensic eloquence by but few men of his day.

John Allen was born in James City county, Va., in 1749. When the revolutonary war broke out, he joined the American army, and devoted all his energies to the service of his country. He rose to the rank of major, and acted for some time as commissary of subsistence. At a tea party in Charleston, South Carolina, which was attended by British and American officers, the conduct of the former towards the latter became very insulting; and an officer named Davis repeated the insult so frequently as to provoke Major Allen to strike him with his sword, which instantly broke up the party. In the course of the war, Major Allen was taken prisoner by the same officer, (Davis), and what was most remarkable in the history of the times, was treated by him with special kindness.

In 1781, Major Allen married Miss Jane Tandy, of Albermarle county, Virginia, and engaged in the practice of the law, having studied his profession with Colonel George Nicholas, then of Charlottesville. He emigrated to Kentucky in 1786, in company with Judge Sebastian, and located in Fayette county. In 1788, he removed to Bourbon, and settled in Paris, then containing but a few log cabins—the ground upon which the town is now reared being then a marsh, springs of water bursting from the earth in great profusion. After the organization of the State government, Major Allen was elected one of the commissioners to select a site for the permanent seat of government. During the first term of Gov. Garrard, under the old constitution, Major Allen was appointed judge of the Paris district court, the duties of which he discharged with general acceptance. In 1802, after the adoption of the present constitution, and during the second term of Gov. Garrard, he was appointed judge of the circuit court, including in his district the county of Bourbon.

Judge Allen died in the year 1816, having devoted a large portion of his long life to the service of his country, and leaving behind him a name which will be held in grateful remembrance by his posterity. He had born to him twelve children—nine sons and three daughters. His widow still survives, and resides in Paris, being now four score years of age, and enjoying a degree of health which rarely falls to the lot of one of her years.

BOYLE COUNTY.

Boyle county was formed from parts of Mercer and Lincoln in 1841, and named for the Hon. John Boyle, for many years chief justice of the state. It is bounded on the north by Mercer, east by Garrard, south by Casey and Lincoln, and west by Marion. Danville, the county seat, is forty miles from Frankfort. The soil of this county is very deep and rich, and generally lies well for cultivation. The products are principally stock and hemp. The citizens are generally independent in their circumstances well educated and intelligent. Number of acres of land in the county, 147,045 ; average value per acre, $12,22 ; taxable property in 1846, $3,852,123 ; number of white males over twenty-one years of age, 1,119 ; number of children between the ages of five and sixteen years, 1,372. The county was organized since the census of 1840 was taken.

The towns of Boyle are Danville and Perryville. DANVILLE is situated three miles west from Dick's river, forty miles south by west from Frankfort, and thirty-five miles from Lexington—latitude thirty-seven degrees thirty minutes north. It contains a new and capacious court-house and other public buildings, six churches—Presbyterian, Methodist, Baptist, Reformed or Christian, Episcopal and African,—a branch bank of the Bank of Kentucky, twelve dry goods stores, one book and drug store, two hotels, ten physicians, nine lawyers, one weekly newspaper, (the Kentucky Tribune), several mills and factories, and about forty mechanics' shops and manufacturing establishments. Centre College, the Deaf and Dumb Asylum, and a fine Female Seminary, are also situated in Danville. Danville was established by the Virginia legislature in 1787, and was for many years the seat of government of Kentucky. The first court-house and jail built in Kentucky was erected here, and here the first constitution of the state was formed; but owing to some freak of fortune, the seat of government was moved to Lexington in 1792, where it enjoyed but a brief sojourn, and was removed from thence to Frankfort. The town was laid out by Mr. Walker Daniel, who gave it its name. Population about 2,000. PERRYVILLE is a small village twelve miles west of Danville—contains one Presbyterian church and one Cumberland Presbyterian church, seven physicians, two taverns, five stores, one wool factory, and eight mechanical trades. Established in 1817.

The Deaf and Dumb Asylum located at Danville was chartered in 1822, and went into operation the spring following. The plan of instruction pursued in this institution is based upon the system invented and successfully used by the Abbe Sicard, of Paris, in France, with such improvements as experience has pointed out. The average number of pupils is about thirty. Two instructors attend them all the time. The other officers of the institution are a physician, superintendent and matron, in whose family all the pupils reside and receive their constant attention. The terms of admission are $105 per year for board and tuition to those who can afford to pay; but ample provision has been made by the state for those who are in indigent circumstances, which fact must be certified to by a magistrate in the county where they reside. Persons in comfortable circumstances at home, but unable to educate their children without ruinous sacrifices, receive the public assistance, in part or in whole, as may be necessary. The buildings consist of two substantial plain brick houses, which are ample and comfortable, situated in a retired part of the town, with a superintendent who is eminently qualified to discharge the duties of his station. The number of pupils in the institution from January 1, 1846, to January 1, 1847, was fifty-three, and provis on is made by law for the support of forty indigent pupils.

CENTRE COLLEGE, DANVILLE, KY.

CENTRE COLLEGE is located in Danville, a pleasant town near the centre of the state, with a very intellectual and intelligent population. The college was chartered by the legislature of Kentucky in 1819. Jeremiah Chamberlain, D. D., the first president, went into office in 1823. In 1824, the board of trustees, according to an arrangement with the Presbyterian synod of Kentucky, procured an act of the legislature modifying its charter so as to secure to the synod, on its payment of twenty thousand dollars to the funds of the institution, the right of appointing the board of trustees. This condition having, in 1830, been completely fulfilled on the part of the synod, all the members of the board have since that period been appointed by the synod, as their terms of office, from time to time, have expired. One third of the board are appointed each year.

Dr. Chamberlain resigned his office in 1826, and the Rev. Gideon Blackburn, D. D., succeeded him in 1827, the office having, in the meantime, been temporarily filled by the Rev. David C. Proctor. On the resignation of Dr. Blackburn in 1830, JOHN C. YOUNG, D. D., the present president, was elected.

The number of students varied in the earlier period of the existence of the institution, from fifty to one hundred and ten, and a very large proportion of those in attendance were pursuing only a partial and irregular course. In 1830, the number of students had been reduced to 33 of all classes, including those in the grammar school, as well as those in the college proper. Since that period, the number has been, with slight temporary variations, steadily, but slowly increasing, until it has ranged, during the last three years, from one hundred and sixty-five to one hundred and eighty-five. The number of those pursuing a full course, has increased in a much greater ratio. The graduating classes, formerly very small, have been steadily enlarging. The graduates of the first twelve years amounted to 55. This number the last ten years has enlarged to 224. About 1200 students have been connected with the institution, nearly all of whom have received all their higher education from its instructions.

The synod determined to raise $100,000 as a permanent endowment. Funds have been already contributed, by the liberality of various individuals, which, as vested by the board, yield an annual income of about $3,000. Of this amount, twelve thousand dollars were given by Mr. Samuel Laird, of Fayette county, to endow a professorship. Measures have been adopted which, it is hoped, will secure the full amount contemplated by the synod.

The course of instruction varies but slightly from that pursued by those colleges which have the oldest and most established reputation. An equal amount of the ancient languages and mathematics is taught. In the natural sciences, the want of equal facilities for illustration and experiment renders the course somewhat less complete than theirs; while, on the other hand, in the moral and mental sciences, it is somewhat more extensive.

The moral and religious culture of the youth under their care, has been always regarded by the officers of the college, as their most important object. Their aim is not to inculcate the peculiarities of any religious sect, but to fix in the minds and hearts of their pupils those great and controlling truths of revelation, which influence the happiness, and shape the character of men for time and eternity; and while no parent of any other religious denomination has ever had his son proselyted here, many have rejoiced to find him return, at the close of his college course, deeply impressed with those religious principles which give strength and consolation to man in the duties and trials of life. The college has been remarkable for many years, for the moral and religious habits of its students, and for the rare occurrence of such disorders as are frequent in many institutions.

The tuition fee is thirty dollars per session of ten months. The ordinary charges in town, for board, washing, lodging, fuel and lights, vary from two dollars to two dollars and fifty cents per week; and in the country, at from one to two miles distant, from one dollar and twenty-five cents to two dollars per week. Young men pursuing their studies with a view to the ministry, and receiving aid from any society, pay only ten dollars per annum for tuition.

In the libraries connected with the college, there are between five thousand and six thousand volumes, and among them, some rare and valuable works. The course of study embraces the customary period of four years; and instruction is given in all the branches of learning usually taught in the colleges of the country. There is but one term during the year, with a short vacation in the spring.

Commencement on the third Thursday in July.   The session begins on the third Thursday in September.

Among the early settlers of Danville, was a young man, named Tom Johnson, possessed of a good education and some genius, and withal a poet.   He became, however, an inveterate drunkard, his intemperance hurrying him to a premature grave.   On one occasion, when Tom's poetical inspirations were quickened by his devotions at the shrine of Bacchus, he came into Gill's tavern to procure his dinner; but too many hearty eaters had been in advance of him at the table, and Tom found nothing but bones and crumbs.   He surveyed the table for some minutes quite philosophically, and then offered up the following prayer:

> "O ! Thou who blest the loaves and fishes,
> Look down upon these empty dishes;
> And that same power that did them fill,
> Bless each of us, but d—n old Gill."

A man in the neighborhood, bearing the christian name of *John*, had become largely indebted to the merchants and others of Danville, and like many of the present day, left for parts unknown.   Tom consoled the sufferers by the following impromptu effusion:

> "John ran so long and ran so fast,
> No wonder he ran out at last;
> He ran in debt, and then to pay,
> He distanc'd all, and ran away."

WALKER DANIEL, a young lawyer from Virginia, came to Boyle, then Lincoln, in 1781, and entered upon the practice of his profession.   His only competitor at that period, was Christopher Greenup, afterwards governor of the State.   Mr. Daniel was the original proprietor of the town of Danville, and succeeded in laying the foundation of an extensive fortune.   He was killed by the Indians in August, 1784, after the short residence of three years.   From an old pioneer of Mercer, we learn that Mr. Daniel was a young gentleman of rare talents, and gave promise of great distinction.

JOHN BOYLE, for more than sixteen years chief justice of Kentucky, was born of humble parentage, October 28, 1774, in Virginia, at a place called "Castle Woods," on Clinch river, in the then county of Bottetourt, near Russell or Tazewell.   His father emigrated, in the year 1779, to Whitley's station in Kentucky, whence he afterwards moved to a small estate in the county of Garrard, where he spent the remainder of his days.

Young Boyle's early education, notwithstanding the limited means of obtaining scholastic instruction, was good, and his knowledge of what he learned thorough. In the rudiments of the Greek and Latin languages, and of the most useful of the sciences, the Rev. Samuel Finley, a pious Presbyterian minister of Madison county, was his instructor.   Energetic and ambitious, Mr. Boyle readily settled upon the law as the calling most congenial to his feelings, and most certain and gratifying in its rewards.   He studied under the direction of Thomas Davis, of Mercer county, then a member of congress, and whom he succeeded as the representative of the district.

In the year 1797, just after he had entered upon his professional career, he married Elizabeth Tilford, the daughter of a plain, pious, and frugal farmer, and moved to the town of Lancaster.   In the following year, upon an out-lot of the town, which he had purchased, he built a small log house, with only two rooms, in which not only himself, but *three* other gentlemen—*who successively followed him as a national representative, and one of whom succeeded him in the chief justiceship, and another served a constitutional term in the gubernatorial chair of Kentucky,* —began the sober business of conjugal life.   Here the duties of his profession engrossed his attention until 1802, when he was elected, without opposition, to the house of representatives of the United States.

As a member of congress, Mr. Boyle was vigilant, dignified, and useful, commanding at once the respect and confidence of the Jeffersonian, the then dominant party, with which he acted, and the hearty approbation of a liberal constituency.   He was twice re-elected without competition, and refused a fourth canvass, because a political life was less congenial to his taste, than the practice of his profession amid the sweets of his early home.   The same feeling compelled him to decline more than one federal appointment, tendered him by President Jefferson. President Madison, among his earliest official acts, appointed him the first governor of Illinois, a position doubly alluring, and which Mr. Boyle conditionally accepted.   On his return to Kentucky, he was tendered a circuit judgeship, and afterwards a seat upon the bench of the court of appeals.   The latter he accepted, and entered upon its onerous and responsible duties on the 4th of April, 1809. Ninian Edwards, then chief justice of the court, solicited and obtained the relinquished governorship.

On the 3d of April, 1810, Judge Boyle was promoted to the chief justiceship, which he continued to hold until the 8th of November, 1826.   The decisions of the court, while he was upon the bench, are comprised in fifteen volumes of the State Reports, from 1st Bibb to 3d Monroe, and are marked with firmness and purity.

Chief Justice Boyle was the head of the " Old Court " of appeals, during the intensely exciting contest of three years duration, between the " Relief " or " New Court," and the " Anti-Relief " or " Old Court " parties.   The notes of " The Bank of the Commonwealth," issued upon a deficient capital, were necessarily quite fluctuating in value—at one time depreciating more than fifty per cent.   A serious revulsion in the monetary interests of the State, opened the way for a system of popular legislation, designed to satisfy temporarily the cry for relief.   The two years replevin law—prolonging from three months to two years the right of replevying judgments and decrees on contracts, unless the creditor would accept Commonwealth bank money at par—was the crowning project of the system.   The court of appeals unanimously decided the statute unconstitutional, so far as it was designed to be retroactive—a step that brought upon them the full torrent of popular abuse and indignation.   The relief party carried the day at the election soon after, (1823), and on the meeting of the legislature, an address was voted—by less than *two-thirds*, as the constitution required, to remove by address—calling upon the governor to remove the appellate judges, and setting forth their decision as unauthorised, ruinous and absurd.   This bold effort at intimidation failing in its end, at the succeeding session the majority, grown more determined as the echo of the popular will became louder, "re-organized" the court of appeals, or abolished the court established by the constitution, and instituted a *new court*, for which purpose commissions were issued to other persons.   Matters now reached a crisis, and Kentucky was required either to take her stand by the broad fundamental law which had so powerfully contributed to her progress, or to yield to the inconstant, unreasonable and selfish clamor that rang hoarsely through the State.   The struggle was, as it were, for the life of the State—involving the stability of a constitutional government, and the efficiency and independence of an enlightened judiciary.   In August, 1826, the appeal to the ballot box decided the contest.   The " Old Court" party triumphed, and confidence was gradually restored in the ability, integrity and purity of Chief Justice Boyle and his associates.

In the November following, the earliest day at which it could be done consistently with his determination to ride out the judicial storm the memorable decision of the court had brewed, Boyle resigned the chief justiceship of Kentucky. But his services upon the bench were too highly appreciated to be dispensed with. The federal government, anticipating his resignation, tendered him the office of district judge of Kentucky, which he accepted, and was induced to hold, although his better judgment prompted him to give it up, until his death, which occurred on the 28th day of January, 1835.   His estimable lady preceded him a year and a half, having fallen a victim to that scourge of the nations, the cholera, in 1833.

The appointment of associate justice of the supreme court of the United States was twice within his reach ; but he loved retirement, and distrusted his qualifications for a position so responsible.   Upon the death of Judge Todd, he refused to be recommended as his successor; and, subsequently, expressed the same unwillingness upon the demise of Judge Trimble, of the same court.

For one year, in the latter part of his life, he was sole professor in the Transylvania law school.   Numbers of young men followed him to the quiet of his home, where his pleasures were divided between teaching law, miscellaneous reading, and the cares of his family and farm.

AUGUSTA COLLEGE, AUGUSTA, KY.

His dying ejaculation—"*I have lived for my country*"—is the best eulogium that could be written upon his life and public services. In all the relations of father, friend, representative and judge, his conduct and conversation marked him as a man, tender and sympathising, generous and disinterested, faithful and vigilant, deliberative and incorruptible.

BRACKEN COUNTY.

BRACKEN county was formed in 1796, lies in the northern part of the state, on the Ohio river, and bounded as follows: North by the Ohio river, east by Mason, west by Pendleton, south-west by Harrison, and south-east by Nicholas. Brooksville is the county seat—Augusta the principal town and landing place or depot. The lands of the county are high, and the surface rolling and hilly, such as usually border on the Ohio river, the south-west resting upon the Licking river. The upper part, bordering on Mason, is rich and fertile. The staples are tobacco, wheat, corn and pork. The finest "*Mason county tobacco*" is raised in Bracken; the wheat crops are good, and the land, when new, produces good corn.

Number of acres of land in Bracken 124,844; taxable property in 1846, $1,750,242; average value of land per acre, $7,99; number of white males over twenty-one years of age, 1,421; number of children between five and sixteen years old, 1,675. Population in 1830, 6,392—in 1840, 7,053.

AUGUSTA lies on the Ohio river, six miles below the Mason line, and immediately below the mouth of Bracken creek. The town includes three hundred acres of land, and is one of the most beautiful situations on the Ohio river, with a fine harbor. It is eighteen miles below Maysville, and forty-five miles above Cincinnati—has three lawyers, four physicians, and contains three brick churches, (Methodist, Presbyterian and Baptist), the town hall, a large brick building fifty feet square, the spacious and elegant edifice of the Augusta college, large steam saw and merchant mills, an extensive tannery, ten stores and groceries, one book and drug store, three tobacco warehouses, a large number of mechanics' shops, and 1,200 inhabitants. A letter from Gen. JOHN PAYNE, who has resided many years in Augusta, and who was an active, brave, and efficient officer under Harrison at the Mississinaway towns, and on the north-west frontier during the last war with Great Britain, gives the following interesting account of the ancient remains discovered in that place:

The bottom on which Augusta is situated, is a large burying ground of the *ancients*. A post hole cannot be dug without turning up human bones. They have been found in great numbers, and of all sizes, every where between the mouths of Bracken and Locust creeks, a distance of about a mile and a half. From the cellar under my dwelling, sixty by seventy feet, one hundred and ten skeletons were taken. I numbered them by the *skulls*; and there might have been many more, whose skulls had crumbled into dust. My garden was a cemetery; it is full of bones, and the richest ground I ever saw. The skeletons were of all sizes, from seven feet to the infant. David Kilgour (who was a tall and very large

14

man) passed our village at the time I was excavating my cellar, and we took him down and applied a thigh bone to his—the owner, if well proportioned, must have been some ten or twelve inches taller than Kilgour, and the lower jaw bone would slip on over his, skin and all. Who were they? How came their bones there? Among the Indians there is no tradition that any town was located near here, or that any battle was ever fought near here. When I was in the army, I inquired of old Crane, a Wyandott, and of Anderson, a Delaware, both intelligent old chiefs, (the former died at camp Seneca in 1813,) and they could give no information in reference to these remains of antiquity. They knew the localities at the mouths of Locust, Turtle and Bracken creeks, but they knew nothing of any town or village near there. In my garden, Indian arrow heads of flint have been found, and an earthen ware of clay and pounded muscle. Some of the largest trees of the forest were growing over these remains when the land was cleared in 1792.

Augusta College, one of the best literary institutions of the west, is located here. It is under the patronage of the Methodist Episcopal church, and was the first college ever established by that denomination in the world. The college was founded in 1822—has six professorships, and a preparatory and primary school attached to it. The number of students varies from one hundred to one hundred and fifty. The library contains 2,500 volumes. Commencement on Thursday after the first Wednesday in August. Rev. Joseph S. Tomlinson, D. D. President.

BROOKSVILLE, the seat of justice, is nine miles from Augusta, and about sixty-five miles from Frankfort—contains a commodious brick court-house and other public buildings; three taverns, three stores, three lawyers, two physicians, and four mechanics' shops. Population about seventy-five. Named after David Brooks. *Powersville*, is a small village, three miles south of Brooksville, containing but few inhabitants. *Germantown*, a handsome village, lies on the line between Mason and Bracken,—the greatest portion in Bracken.

The soil of Bracken is based on yellow clay, with limestone foundation. Timber, in some parts, sugar tree, buckeye, black walnut and hickory; in others, white and black oak. Gold has been found in the county, and it is believed by some of the most intelligent citizens that, upon a strict examination, by competent persons, this precious metal might be found in great abundance.

This county derived its name from two creeks: Big and Little Bracken, and these creeks were called for an old hunter, named Bracken, who settled on the banks of one of them, and is supposed to have been killed by the Indians at an early period of the settlement of Kentucky.

BREATHITT COUNTY.

BREATHITT county was formed in 1839, and called after the late Governor Breathitt. It is situated in the eastern part of the State, on the head waters of the Kentucky river; and is bounded on the north by Morgan county; east by Floyd; south by Perry, and west by Owsley. Jackson is the county seat and only town. The surface is hilly, interspersed with rich and productive vallies—the soil based on red clay, with sandstone foundation. The county abounds in bituminous coal, large quantities of which are sent to market annually, down the Kentucky river. Iron ore is also found in abundance; and salt is manufactured to some extent. The principal articles of export are coal, timber, beeswax and ginseng. Taxable property of the county in 1846, $323,479. Number of acres of land in Breathitt 162,121 ; number of white males over twenty-one years, 528 ; number of children between the ages of five and sixteen years, 868. Population in 1840, 2,195.

JACKSON, the county seat, received its name in honor of the late president Jackson. It contains the county buildings, one Methodist church, one Reformed church, two schools, five stores and groceries, two taverns, three lawyers, one doctor and five mechanical trades. Population, 150.

JOHN BREATHITT, late governor of Kentucky, (for whom this county was called) was a native of the state of Virginia. He was the eldest child of William Breathitt, and was born on the ninth day of September, 1786, about two miles from New London, near the road leading to Lynchburg. His father removed from Virginia, and settled in Logan county, Kentucky, in the year 1800, where he raised a family of five sons and four daughters. The old gentleman was a farmer, possessed of a few servants and a tract of land, but not sufficiently wealthy to give his children collegiate educations. The schools of his neighborhood (for it should be remembered the Green river country was a wilderness in 1800), afforded but few opportunities for the advancement of pupils. John, the subject of this notice, made the best use of the means for improvement placed within his reach, and by diligent attention to his books, made himself a good surveyor. Before he arrived at age, he received an appointment as deputy surveyor of the public lands, and in that capacity, surveyed many townships in the state of Illinois, then a territory of the United States.

John Breathitt taught a country school in early life, and by his industry and economy, as teacher and surveyor, he acquired property rapidly, consisting mostly in lands, which were easily obtained under the acts of the assembly appropriating the public domain. After his earnings had secured a capital capable of sustaining him a few years, he resolved to read law, which he did under the direction of the late Judge Wallace. He was admitted to the bar as a qualified attorney, in February, 1810. His industry and capacity for business, soon secured him a lucrative practice ; and from this time he rapidly advanced in public estimation.

In 1810 or '11, he was elected to represent the county of Logan in the house of representatives of the general assembly, and filled the same office for several years in succession. In 1828, he was elected lieutenant governor of the commonwealth, the duties of which station he filled with great dignity and propriety. In 1832, he was elected governor, but did not live to the end of his official term. He died in the governor's house, in Frankfort, on the 21st of February, 1834.

It is not the design of the writer to notice the political principles, official acts, and measures of policy recommended or executed by Governor Breathitt. These may be found among the archives and records of the country, and their consideration here would swell this article to the magnitude of a lengthy work. It may not, however, be improper to say, that Governor Breathitt acted with the democratic party, and espoused with warmth the election of General Jackson to the presidency in 1828 and 1832.

Governor Breathitt had two wives, both of whom he survived. The first was Miss Whitaker, daughter of William Whitaker of Logan county ; and the second was Miss Susan M. Harris, daughter of Richard Harris, of Chesterfield county, Virginia. By his first wife he left a son and daughter, and by his last a daughter.

Governor Breathitt, in all his transactions, was considerate and cautious. Rashness was no part of his character. He was nevertheless, firm, and pursued his objects with great assiduity, after resolving upon the course he intended to pursue. He did not commit himself in favor of any measure, without beforehand weighing the consequences with much deliberation.

As a husband, father, friend and neighbor, it is not too much to say that Governor Breathitt had no superior. In all the relations of life, he was actuated by a spirit of indulgence and benevolence. The comfort and happiness of others, with him were objects of pre-eminent solicitude. His affection and kindness to his relations, manifested itself in an eminent degree, by the assistance he gave his father, and the liberal expenditures he made in educating his brothers and sisters. To associates of his profession, he was uniformly courteous, and ever ready to give the younger members of the bar aid and instruction.

BRECKINRIDGE COUNTY.

THE county of BRECKINRIDGE was formed in the year 1799, and was named in honor of the Hon. John Breckinridge. It is situated in the western-middle part of the State, and bounded on the north by the Ohio river, on the east by Hardin, on the south by Grayson, and on the west by Hancock county.

The face of the country is generally rolling, high, dry, and finely watered. The climate is pleasant and healthy; the soil fertile, with a basis of red clay and limestone. The principal water courses are, Sinking creek, the North Fork of Rough creek, main Rough creek, and Clover creek.

The principal products of the county are tobacco, corn, wheat, and oats. Four thousand five hundred hogsheads of tobacco are annually raised and exported. The total wealth of the county in 1846, according to the auditor's report, was $1,933,364. Number of acres of land, 309,926. The population in 1830 was 7,345— in 1840 it was 8,944; showing an increase of population in ten years of 1,599.

The principal towns are Hardinsburg, Cloverport, Stephensport, Hudsonville, Constantine, and Jackeysburg.

Hardinsburg is the seat of justice, and was named in honor of Captain William Hardin, a distinguished Indian fighter. It was laid out in town lots in 1782; incorporated in 1800, and contains a population of eight hundred inhabitants.

Cloverport is the second town in the county; it is a place of considerable importance as a shipping point, and contains a population of seven hundred inhabitants. Its immediate neighborhood abounds in extensive banks of coal of fine quality. Four miles from Cloverport are the Breckinridge, Tar, and White Sulphur Springs, which are becoming one of the most fashionable watering places in the State.

Stephensport is a neat and handsome village, of some commercial importance, situated on the Ohio river, at the mouth of Sinking creek. It contains a population of two hundred inhabitants, and was incorporated in 1825. The remaining towns are Hudsonville, Constantine, and Jackeysburg.

Breckinridge county possesses a very remarkable curiosity, in Sinking creek, a considerable stream, which supplies a sufficiency of water to drive machinery during the entire year. Six or seven miles from its source, the creek suddenly sinks beneath the earth, showing no trace of its existence for five or six miles, when it re-appears above ground, and flows into the Ohio. On this creek is to be seen a natural rock mill-dam, eight feet high, and forty feet wide, which answers all the purposes of a dam to a mill which has been erected at the place by a Mr. Huston. Near the creek is a large cave, called Penitentiary cave, which has never been fully explored. Some of the apartments are said to rival, in the splendor and magnificence of their scenery, the celebrated Mammoth cave in Edmonson county. In one of the rooms, about one hundred yards from the mouth of the cave, the roof is from sixty to seventy feet high, and on the floor there are three natural basins or troughs of cool, clear water, of very remarkable construction and appearance, fifteen feet in length, four feet wide, and twelve inches deep. These basins are elevated above the level of the floor in the form of troughs, and it is remarkable that the stone which forms the sides and ends of the basins, do not exceed in thickness the blade of a table knife.

One of the earliest settlers in that portion of Kentucky which now forms the county of Breckinridge, was Capt. WILLIAM HARDIN, a noted hunter and Indian fighter—a man of dauntless courage and resolution—cool, calm, and self-possessed in the midst of most appalling dangers, and perfectly skilled in all the wiles and arts of border warfare. Soon after Capt. Hardin had erected a station in what is now the county of Breckinridge, intelligence was received that the Indians were building a town on Saline creek, in the present state of Illinois. Hardin, not well pleased that the savages should establish themselves in such close vicinity to his little settlement, determined to dislodge them. He soon had collected around him a force of *eighty* select men; the hardiest and boldest of those noted hunters whose lives were passed in a continual round of perilous adventure.

When this force reached the vicinity of the lick, they discovered Indian signs, and approaching the town cautiously, they found it in the possession of three warriors who had been left to guard the camp. Hardin ordered his men to fire on them, which they did, killing two. The third attempted to make his escape, but he was shot down as he ran. He succeeded, however, in regaining his feet, and ran fifty yards, leaped up a perpendicular bank, six feet high, and fell dead.

In the mean time, Hardin, correctly supposing that the main body of the Indians were out on a hunting expedition, and would shortly return, made immediate preparation for battle. He accordingly selected a place where a few acres of timbered land were surrounded on all sides by the prairie. Here he posted his men with orders to conceal themselves behind the trees, and reserve their fire until the Indians should approach within twenty-five yards. Soon after the little band had taken their position, they discovered the Indians rapidly approaching on their trail, and numbering apparently between eighty and one hundred men. When the savages had arrived within one hundred yards of the position of the Kentuckians, one of the men, in his impatience to begin the battle, forgot the order of the captain, and fired his gun. Immediately the Indians charged, and the fight commenced in earnest.

At the first fire, Captain Hardin was shot through the thighs. Without, however, resigning his command, or yielding to the pain of his wound, he sat down on a large log, and during the whole action, continued to encourage his men and give forth his orders, with as much coolness, promptitude, and self-possession, as if engaged in the most ordinary avocation. This more than Spartan firmness and resolution, was not, however, anything very remarkable in the early history of Kentucky. Every battle field furnished many examples of similar heroism. The iron men of those times, seem, indeed, to have been born insensible to fear, and impregnable to pain. The coolness, courage, and unyielding determination of

Hardin, in this trying situation, no doubt contributed greatly to the success of the day; and after a severe contest, in which some thirty of the savages fell, they were finally repulsed. The loss of the whites, in killed and wounded, was very considerable. During the action the parties were frequently engaged hand to hand.

This battle was never reported to the government, and it seems to have escaped the notice of the historians of early times in Kentucky; though it was, unquestionably, one of the most fiercely contested battles ever fought in the west.

The Honorable JOHN BRECKINRIDGE, [for whom this county was named], was the second son of Colonel Robert Breckinridge, of Augusta county, Virginia, and was born on a farm, upon a part of which the town of Staunton now stands, on the 2d day of December, 1760. His paternal ancestors were what were then called "Scotch Irish," that is, they were Presbyterians—from the north of Ireland, immediately—but originally from Scotland. After the restoration of Charles II., they were hotly persecuted in Ayreshire, their original seat, and being driven out from thence, spent half a century in the highlands of Breadalbane, and removed thence to Ireland, and early in the last century to Virginia; a portion of the persecuted remnant of the Scotch Covenanters, who suffered so long and so heroically for liberty and the reformed religion. His paternal and maternal grand fathers both lie buried in the grave yard of the Tinkling Springs congregation, in the county of Augusta, of which both of them were ruling elders. His mother, Lettice Preston, was the oldest child of John Preston and Elizabeth Patton, and was the second wife of his father. General James Breckinridge, of Virginia, was his younger, and a full brother; General Robert Breckinridge, of Kentucky, was his elder, and a half brother.

At a very early age, he was carried by his father to the neighborhood of Fincastle, in Bottetourt county, Virginia, whither he removed, and where he died, when his son was about eleven years of age; leaving a widow, and seven children, in circumstances which we should now consider narrow: and exposed, upon what was then almost the extreme limit of the white settlements, to all the dangers of an Indian frontier; and this only a few years before the commencement of our long and bloody struggle for National Independence, which was ended about the time the subject of this notice arrived at man's estate.

Raised in the midst of dangers, hardships, and privations; the tradition of his family replete only with tales of suffering and exile, for conscience sake; and a widowed mother and orphan family—of which he became the head at the age of early boyhood—the objects of his constant care; it is by no means strange that his powerful character and uncommon talents, should have been early and remarkably developed. A calm, simple, correct man—gentle to those he loved—stern and open to those he could not trust—always true, always brave, always self dependent, it is just in such a way, that such circumstances would mould and develop such a nature as his. But it is not so easy to ascertain how it was, that in his circumstances, there should have been implanted in him, from earliest childhood, a thirst for knowledge that seemed to the end of his life, insatiable; nor could anything less than the highest mental endowments, directed with energy that never flagged, explain the extent, the variety, and the richness of the acquisitions which he was enabled to make. His education, both preparatory and professional, was privately conducted, and so far as is now known, chiefly without other aid than books, except about two years, which he spent at the college of William and Mary, in Virginia. During the latter part of his attendance at this ancient seat of learning, and when he was about nineteen years of age, he was elected to the Virginia house of burgesses, from the county of Bottetourt, without his having even suspected that such a matter was in agitation. On account of his youth, the election was twice set aside, and it was only on the third return, and against his own wishes and remonstrances, that he took his seat. From this time to the period of his death, he lived constantly, as a lawyer and a statesman, in the public eye.

In the year 1785 he married Mary Hopkins Cabell, a daughter of Colonel Joseph Cabell, of Buckingham county, Virginia; and settled in the county of Albemarle, and practised law in that region of Virginia, until the year 1793, in the spring of which he removed to Kentucky, and settled in Lexington; near to which place, at "Cabell's Dale," in the county of Fayette, he resided till the period of his death, which occurred on the 14th December, 1806, when he had just completed his 46th year.

As a lawyer, no man of his day excelled him, and very few could be compared with him. Profoundly acquainted with his profession, highly gifted as a public speaker, laborious and exact in the performance of all his professional duties and engagements—these great qualities, united to his exalted private character, gave him a position at the bar, which few men ever attained, or ever deserved; and enabled him, besides the great distinction he acquired, to accumulate a large fortune. An event extremely characteristic attended the disposition of his estate: for on his death bed, he absolutely refused to make a will, saying that he had done his best to have such provisions made by law for the distribution of estates, as seemed to him wise and just, and he would adhere to it for his own family. At the end of forty years, it is not unworthy to be recorded, that his wisdom and foresight, in this remarkable transaction, did not lose their reward.

As a statesman, very few men of his generation occupied a more commanding position, or mingled more controllingly with all the great questions of the day; and not one enjoyed a more absolute popularity, or maintained a more spotless reputation. He took a leading, perhaps a decisive part in all the great questions of a local character that agitated Kentucky, from 1793 to 1806, and whose settlement still exerts a controlling influence upon the character of her people and institutions. The constitution of 1798–99, which is still preserved unaltered, was more the work of his hands than of any one single man. The question of negro slavery, as settled in that constitution, upon a middle and moderate ground,—the ground which Kentucky still occupies—the systematizing, to some extent, the civil and criminal codes—the simplification of the land law—the law of descents—the penitentiary system—the abolition of the punishment of death, except for wilful murder and treason—all these, and many other important subjects, of a kindred nature, fell under his moulding labors at the forming period of the commonwealth, and remain still nearly as they were adjusted half a century ago. In those vital questions that involved the destiny of the whole west, and threatened the plan if not the continuance of the Union itself, no man took an earlier or more decided stand. It is capable of proof, that the *free navigation* of the Mississippi river, and subsequently the purchase of Louisiana (which latter act, though it covered Mr. Jefferson with glory, he hesitated to perform, upon doubts both as to its policy and constitutionality), were literally forced upon the general government by demonstrations from the west, in which the mind and the hand of this great patriot and far-sighted statesman were conspicuous above all.

As a statesman, however, he is best known as one of the leading men—perhaps in the west, the undoubted leader of the old democratic party; which came into power with Mr. Jefferson, as president, under whose administration he was made attorney general of the United States. He was an ardent friend, personal and political, of Mr. Jefferson; he coincided with him upon the great principles of the old democracy; he concerted with him and Mr. Madison, and others of kindred views, the movements which brought the democratic party into power; he supported the interests of that party with pre-eminent ability, in the legislature of Kentucky, and in the senate of the United States; and died as much beloved, honored and trusted by it, as any man he left behind. Some twenty years after his death, it began to be whispered, and then to be intimated in a few newspapers, that the Kentucky resolutions of 1798–9, which he offered, and which was the first great movement against the alien and sedition laws—and the general principles of the party that passed them, were in fact the production of Mr. Jefferson himself, and not of John Breckinridge; and it is painful to reflect that Mr. Jefferson did certainly connive at this mean calumny upon the memory of his friend. The family of Mr. Breckinridge have constantly asserted that their father was the sole and true author of these resolutions, and constantly defied the production of proof to the contrary: and there seems to be no question that they are right.

In stature, John Breckinridge was above the middle size of men; tall, slender and muscular; a man of great power and noble appearance. He had very clear gray eyes, and brown hair, inclining to a slight shade of red. He was extremely grave and silent in his ordinary intercourse ; a man singularly courteous and gentle, and very tenderly loved by those who knew him. His family consisted of nine children: two of them only, with his venerable widow, still live; but his descendants are numerous, both of his own and other names.

BULLITT COUNTY.

Bullitt county was established in 1796, and named for Lieutenant Governor Bullitt. It is situated in the north-west middle part of the state, its extreme western boundary extending to near the mouth of Salt river, and is watered by that stream and its tributaries. Bounded on the north by Jefferson ; east by Spencer ; south by Nelson, and on the west by Hardin and Meade,—the Rolling fork of Salt river washing its south-west border. This county is generally fertile, though the surface is rolling ; the scenery is variegated and beautiful, the hills covered with tall pine and laurel, and abounding in iron and other ores, and salt and mineral waters. The valuation of taxable property in 1846, $1,801,972; number of acres in the county, 162,004; average value per acre, $5,56; number of white males over twenty-one years of age, 1,206; children between five and sixteen years of age, 1,313. Hogs, cattle and sheep, are the principal articles of commerce ; a great number of the former being driven to Louisville annually. There are in the county, three woolen factories, four steam merchant mills, a number of blast iron furnaces, and a rolling mill and forges, making superior iron and nails.

The towns in Bullitt, are, Shepherdsville, Mount Washington and Pittstown. *Shepherdsville*, the county seat, is situated on Salt river, seventy-four miles from Frankfort—contains one Methodist church, (a handsome brick building, appropriated to the use of Bullitt academy,) four stores, two groceries, five doctors, seven lawyers, three taverns and twenty mechanics' shops. Incorporated in 1793. Population about four hundred. Mount Washington, formerly Vernon, a beautiful town, incorporated in 1822, contains three churches, two schools, six stores and groceries, five doctors, one lawyer, two taverns, and twelve mechanical trades. Population about seven hundred. *Pittstown* is a small village, situated at the junction of the Rolling fork and main Salt river, nine miles from Shepherdsville.

The Paroquet Springs, a fine and popular watering place—the grounds beautifully improved, with rooms sufficient for the accommodation of six hundred persons—is situated half a mile above Shepherdsville, in this county. The water contains salt, iron, magnesia and salts. Bullitt's old licks, where the first salt works were erected in Kentucky, lie about three miles from Shepherdsville.

The first forts and stations erected in the county, were called Fort Nonsense, Mud Garrison, Breashear's Station, Clear's Station and Whitaker's Station ; which were severally the scenes of a number of conflicts with the Indians, who resorted to the licks to hunt the game, and make salt. Near Bullitt's lick, on a high knob, which is called "Cahill's knob," the Indians whipped to death an old man whom they caught while chopping wood for the salt works.

HENRY CRIST was born in the state of Virginia, in the year 1764. During the revolutionary war, his father, with a numerous family, emigrated to the western part of Pennsylvania, from whence young Henry and other ardent youths of the neighborhood, made frequent and daring excursions into the western wilderness; sometimes into what is now the state of Ohio, sometimes to Limestone, (now Maysville,) and finally to the falls of the Ohio, which place he first visited in 1779. The buffalo and deer had clearly indicated to the early settlers, those places where salt water was to be found. The great difficulty of importing salt, the increasing demand and high price of the article, encouraged the attempt to manufacture here at a very early day. Salt was made at Bullitt's lick, now in Bullitt county, near seventy years ago.

In Crist's excursions to the west, he had become acquainted and associated with an enterprising Dutchman, named Myers, a land agent and general locator, and in whose name more land has been entered than in that of almost any other man in the west. This pursuit of locator of lands, brought Crist at a very early day to Bullitt's lick, where he took a prominent and active part in some of those scenes which have contributed to the notoriety of that renowned resort of all who lived within fifty miles around in the first settlement of the country. Here the first salt was made in Kentucky, and here from five hundred to a thousand men were collected together in the various branches of salt making, as well as buying of, selling to, and guarding the salt makers, when Louisville and Lexington could boast but a few hovels, and when the buffalo slept in security around the base of Capitol hill.

In May, 1778, a flat boat loaded with kettles, intended for the manufacture of salt at Bullitt's lick, left Louisville with thirteen persons, twelve armed men and one woman, on board. The boat and cargo were owned by Henry Crist and Solomon Spears; and the company consisted of Crist, Spears, Christian Crepps, Thomas Floyd, Joseph Boyce, Evans Moore, an Irishman named Fossett, and five others, and a woman, whose names the writer cannot now recollect, though he has heard Crist often repeat them. The intention of the party was to descend the Ohio, which was then very high, to the mouth of Salt river, and then ascend the latter river, the current of which was entirely deadened by back water from the Ohio, to a place near the licks, called *Mud Garrison*, which was a temporary fortification, constructed of two rows of slight stockades, and the space between filled with mud and gravel from the bank of the river hard by. The works enclosed a space of about half an acre, and stood about midway between Bullitt's lick and the falls of Salt river, where Shepherdsville now stands. These works were then occupied by the families of the salt makers, and those who hunted to supply them with food, and acted also as an advanced guard to give notice of the approach of any considerable body of men.

On the 25th of May, the boat entered Salt river, and the hands commenced working her up with sweep-oars. There was no current one way or the other—while in the Ohio, the great breadth of the river secured them against any sudden attack, but when they came into Salt river, they were within reach of the Indian rifle from either shore. It became necessary, therefore, to send out scouts, to apprise them of any danger ahead. In the evening of the first day of their ascent of the river, Crist and Floyd went ashore to reconnoitre the bank of the river ahead of the boat. Late in the evening they discovered a fresh trail, but for want of light, they could not make out the number of Indians. They remained out all night, but made no further discoveries. In the morning, as they were returning down the river towards the boat, they heard a number of guns, which they believed to be Indians killing game for breakfast. They hastened back to the boat and communicated what they had heard and seen.

They pulled up the river until about eight o'clock, and arrived at a point eight miles below the mouth of the Rolling fork, where they drew into shore on the north side of the river, now in Bullitt county, intending to land and cook and eat their breakfast. As they drew into shore, they heard the gobbling of turkeys (as they supposed) on the bank where they were going to land, and as the boat touched, Fossett and another sprang ashore, with their guns in their hands, to shoot turkeys. They were cautioned of their danger, but disregarding the admonition, hastily ascended the bank. Their companions in the boat had barely lost sight of them, when they heard a volley of rifles discharged all at once on the bank immediately above, succeeded by a yell of savages so terrific as to induce a belief that the woods were filled with Indians. This attack, so sudden and violent, took the boat's company by surprise; and they had barely time to seize their rifles and place themselves in a posture of defence, when Fossett and his companion came dashing down the bank, hotly pursued by a large body of Indians. Crist stood in the bow of the boat, with his rifle in his hand. At the first sight of the enemy, he brought his gun to his face, but instantly perceived that the object of his aim was a white man, and a sudden thought flashed across his mind, that the enemy was a company of surveyors that he knew to be then in the woods, and that the attack was made in sport, &c., let his gun down, and at the same time his white foeman sunk out of his sight behind the bank. But the firing had begun in good earnest on both sides. Crist again brought his rifle to his face, and as he did so the white man's head was rising over the bank, with his gun also drawn up and presented. Crist got the fire on him, and at the crack of his rifle the white man fell forward dead. Fossett's hunting companion plunged into the water, and got in safely at the bow of the boat. But Fossett's arm was broken by the first fire on the hill. The boat, owing to the high water, did not touch the land, and he got into the river further toward the stern, and swam round with his gun in his left hand, and was taken safely into the stern. So intent were the Indians on the pursuit of their prey, that many of them ran to the water's edge, struck and shot at Fossett and his companion while they were getting into the boat, and some even seized the boat and attempted to draw it nearer the shore. In this attempt many of the Indians perished; some were shot dead as they approached the boat, others were killed in the river, and it required the most stubborn resistance and determined valor to keep them from carrying the boat by assault. Repulsed in their efforts to board the boat, the savages with drew higher up the bank, and taking their stations behind trees, commenced a regular and galling fire, which was returned with the spirit of brave men rendered desperate by the certain knowledge that no quarter would be given, and that it was an issue of victory or death to every soul on board.

The boat had a log-chain for a cable, and when she was first brought ashore, the chain was thrown round a small tree that stood in the water's edge, and the hook run through one of the links. This had been done before the first fire was made upon Fossett on shore. The kettles in the boat had been ranked up along the sides, leaving an open gangway through the middle of the boat from bow to stern. Unfortunately, the bow lay to shore, so that the guns of the Indians raked the whole length of the gangway, and their fire was constant and destructive. Spears and several others of the bravest men had already fallen, some killed and others mortally wounded. From the commencement of the battle, many efforts had been made to disengage the boat from the shore, all of which had failed. The hope was that, if they could once loose the cable, the boat would drift out of the reach of the enemy's guns; but any attempt to do this by hand would expose the person to certain destruction. Fossett's right arm was broken, and he could no longer handle his rifle. He got a pole, and placing himself low down in the bow of the boat, commenced punching at the hook in the chain, but the point of the hook was turned from him, and all his efforts seemed only to drive it further into the link. He at length discovered where a small limb had been cut from the pole, and left a knot about an inch long; this knot, after a number of efforts, he placed against the point of the hook, and, jerking the pole suddenly towards him, threw the hook out of the link. The chain fell, and the boat drifted slowly out from the bank; and by means of an oar worked over head, the boat was brought into the middle of the river, with her side to the shore, which protected them from the fire of the Indians. The battle had now lasted upwards of an hour. The odds against the crew was at least ten to one. The fire had been very destructive on both sides, and a great many of the Indians had been killed; but if the boat had remained much longer at the shore, it was manifest that there would have been none of the crew left to tell the tale of their disaster.

The survivors had now time to look round upon the havoc that had been made of their little band. Five of their companions lay dead in the gangway—Spears,

Floyd, Fossett and Boyce were wounded—Crepps, Crist and Moore remained unhurt. It was evident that Spears' wound was mortal, and that he could survive but a few moments. He urged the survivors to run the boat to the opposite side of the river, and save themselves by immediate flight, and leave him to his fate. Crepps and Crist positively refused.

But the boat was gradually nearing the southern shore of the river. At this time the Indians, to the number of forty or fifty, were seen crossing the river above, at a few hundred yards distance, some on logs, and some swimming and carrying their rifles over their heads. The escape of the boat was now hopeless, as there was a large body of Indians on each side of the river. If the boat had been carried immediately to the opposite side of the river as soon as her cable was loosed, the survivors might have escaped; but to such minds and hearts, the idea of leaving their dying friends to the mercy of the Indian tomahawk was insupportable. The boat at length touched the southern shore—a hasty preparation was made to bear the wounded into the woods—Floyd, Fossett and Boyce got to land, and sought concealment in the thickets. Crepps and Crist turned to their suffering friend, Spears, but death had kindly stepped in and cut short the savage triumph. The woman now remained. They offered to assist her to shore, that she might take her chance of escape in the woods; but the danger of her position, and the scenes of blood and death around her, had overpowered her senses, and no entreaty or remonstrance could prevail with her to move. She sat with her face buried in her hands, and no effort could make her sensible that there was any hope of escape.

The Indians had gained the south side of the river, and were yelling like blood-hounds as they ran down towards the boat, which they now looked upon as their certain prey. Crepps and Crist seized a rifle apiece, and ascended the river bank: at the top of the hill they met the savages and charged them with a shout. Crepps fired upon them, but Crist, in his haste, had taken up Fossett's gun, which had got wet as he swam with it into the boat on the opposite side— it missed fire. At this time Moore passed them and escaped. The Indians, when charged by Crepps and Crist, fell back into a ravine that put into the river immediately above them. They parted, and met no more. The Indians, intent on plunder, did not pursue them, but rushed into the boat. Crist heard one long, agonizing shriek from the unfortunate woman, and the wild shouts of the savages, as they possessed themselves of the spoils of a costly but barren victory.

Crepps, in the course of the next day, arrived in the neighborhood of Long lick, and being unable to travel farther, laid down in the woods to die. Moore alone escaped unhurt, and brought in the tidings of the defeat of the boat. The country was at once roused. Crepps was found, and brought in, but died about the time he reached home. Crist described Crepps as a tall, fair haired, handsome man: kind, brave, and enterprising, and possessed of all those high and striking qualities that gave the heroic stamp to that hardy race of pioneers amongst whom he had lived and died. He had been the lion of the fight. By exposing himself to the most imminent peril, he inspirited his companions with his own contempt of danger. He and Crist had stood over Fossett, and kept the Indians treed while he disengaged the cable; and his coolness during the long, bloody struggle of the day, had won the admiration of Crist himself—than whom a more dauntless man had never contended with mortal foe. Crepps left a young wife and one son, then an infant. His wife was *enceinte* at the time of his death —the posthumous child was a daughter, and is the wife of the Hon. Charles A. Wickliffe. The son died shortly after he arrived at man's estate.

Crist was so disabled by the wound that he could not walk. The bones of his heel were crushed. He crept into a thicket and laid down—his wound bled profusely. He could not remain here long. His feet were now of no use to him. He bound his moccasins on his knees, and commenced his journey. Piece by piece his hat, hunting shirt, and vest were consumed to shield his hands against the rugged rocks which lay in his way. He crawled on all day up the river, and at night crossed over to the north side upon a log that he rolled down the bank. He concealed himself in a thicket and tried to sleep—but pain and exhaustion and loss of blood had driven sleep from his eyes. His foot and leg were much swollen and inflamed. Guided by the stars he crept on again—between midnight and day he came in sight of a camp fire, and heard the barking of a dog. A number of Indians rose up from around the fire, and he crept softly away from the light. He laid down and remained quiet for some time. When all was still again, he resumed his slow and painful journey. He crawled into a small branch, and kept on down it for some distance upon the rocks, that he might leave no trace behind him. At daylight, he ascended an eminence of considerable height to ascertain, if possible, where he was, and how to shape his future course; but all around was wilderness. He was aiming to reach Bullitt's lick, now about eight miles distant, and his progress was not half a mile an hour. He toiled on all day—night came on—the second night of his painful journey. Since leaving the small branch the night before, he had found no water—since the day before the battle he had not tasted food. Worn down with hunger, want of sleep, acute pain, and raging thirst, he laid himself down to die. But his sufferings were not to end here—guided again by the stars, he struggled on. Every rag that he could interpose between the rugged stones and his bleeding hands and knee (for he could now use but one), was worn away. The morning came —the morning of the third day; it brought him but little hope; but the indomitable spirit within him disdained to yield, and during the day he made what progress he could. As the evening drew on, he became aware that he was in the vicinity of Bullitt's lick; but he could go no further; nature had made her last effort, and he laid himself down and prayed that death would speedily end his sufferings.

When darkness came on, from where he lay he could see the hundred fires of the furnaces at the licks all glowing; and he even fancied he could see the dusky forms of the firemen as they passed to and fro around the pits, but they were more than a half mile off, and how was he to reach them? He had not eaten a morsel in four days, he had been drained of almost his last drop of blood, the wounded leg had become so stiff and swollen that for the last two days and nights he had dragged it after him; the flesh was worn from his knee and from the palms of his hands. Relief was in his sight, but to reach it was impossible. Suddenly he heard the tramp of a horse's feet approaching him, and hope sprang up once more in his breast. The sound came nearer and still more near. A path ran near the place where he lay, a man on horse-back approached within a few rods of him, he mustered his remaining strength, and hailed him; but to his utter surprise and dismay, the horseman turned suddenly and galloped off towards the Licks. Despair now seized him. To die alone of hunger and thirst, in sight of hundreds and of plenty, seemed to him the last dregs of the bitterest cup that fate could offer to mortal lips. O! that he could have fallen by the side of his friends in the proud battle! That he could have met the Indian tomahawk, and died in the strength of his manhood; and not have been doomed to linger out his life in days and nights of pain and agony, and to die by piecemeal in childish despair. While these thoughts were passing in his mind, the horseman (a negro), regained the Licks and alarmed the people there with the intelligence that the Indians were approaching. On being interrogated, all the account he could give was, that some person had called to him in the woods a half mile off, and called him by the wrong name. It was manifest it was not Indians; and forthwith a number of men set out, guided by the negro, to the place. Crist's hopes again revived, when he heard voices, and saw lights approaching. They came near and hailed. Crist knew the voice, and called to the man by name. This removed all doubt, and they approached the spot where he lay. A sad and mournful sight was before them. A man that had left them but a few days before, in the bloom of youth, health and buoyant spirits, now lay stretched upon the earth, a worn and mangled skeleton, unable to lift a hand to bid them welcome. They bore him home. The ball was extracted; but his recovery was slow and doubtful. It was a year before he was a man again.

The woman in the boat was carried a prisoner to Canada. Ten years afterwards, Crist met her again in Kentucky. She had been redeemed by an Indian trader, and brought into Wayne's camp on the Maumee, and restored to her friends. She informed Crist that the body of Indians which made the attack on the boat, numbered over one hundred and twenty, of whom about thirty were killed in the engagement. This account was confirmed by Indians whom Crist met with afterwards, and who had been in the battle. They told Crist that the boat's crew fought more like devils than men, and if they had taken one of them prisoner, they would have roasted him alive. Crist was afterwards a member of the Kentucky legislature, and in 1808 was a member of Congress. He died at his residence in Bullitt county, in August, 1844, aged eighty years.

ALEXANDER SCOTT BULLITT was born in Prince William county, Virginia, in the year 1761. His father, Cuthbert Bullitt, was a lawyer of some distinction, and practiced his profession with success until he was appointed a judge of the supreme court of Virginia, which office he held at the time of his death. In 1784, six years before the father's death, the subject of this sketch emigrated to Kentucky, then a portion of Virginia, and settled on or near the stream called Bullskin, in what is now Shelby county. Here he resided but a few months, being compelled by the annoyances to which he was subjected by the Indians, to seek a less exposed situation. This he found in Jefferson county, in the neighborhood of Sturgus' station, where he entered and settled upon the tract of land on which he continued to reside until his death. In the fall of 1785, he married the daughter of Col. W. Christian, who had removed from Virginia the preceding spring. In April, 1786, Colonel Christian, with a party of eight or ten men, pursued a small body of Indians, who had been committing depredations on the property of the settlers in the neighborhood of Sturgus' station. Two of the Indians were overtaken about a mile north of Jeffersonville, Indiana, and finding escape impossible, they turned upon their pursuers, and one of them fired at Colonel Christian, who was foremost in the pursuit, and mortally wounded him. Next to Colonel Christian, was the subject of this sketch and Colonel John O'Bannon, who fired simultaneously, bringing both Indians to the ground. Under the impression that the Indians were both dead, a man by the name of Kelly incautiously approached them, when one of them who, though mortally wounded, still retained some strength and all his thirst for blood, raised himself to his knees, and fired with the rifle which had not been discharged, killed Kelly, fell back and expired.*

In the year 1792, Colonel Bullitt was elected by the people of Jefferson county a delegate to the convention which met in Danville, and framed the constitution of Kentucky. After the adoption of the constitution, he represented the county in the legislature, and was president of the senate until 1799, when he was again chosen a delegate to the convention to amend the constitution, which met in Frankfort. Of this convention he was chosen president. The year following this convention, (1800,) he was elected lieutenant governor of the state, in which capacity he served one term. After this, his county continued to send him to the legislature, of which body he served either as a representative or senator, until about 1808, when he retired from public life, and resided on his farm in Jefferson county until his death, which occurred on the 13th of April, 1816.

BUTLER COUNTY.

BUTLER county was organized in the year 1810. It is situated in the south-west part of the State, and lies on both sides of Green river. It is bounded on the north by Ohio and Grayson; east by Warren; south by Logan, and west by Muhlenburg. The taxable property of the county in 1846, as reported by the auditor, is $501,483; number of acres of land, 163,441; average value per acre, $1,45; white males over twenty-one years, 793; children between the ages of five and sixteen years, 1,162. Population in 1830, 3,055; in 1840, 3,898. The surface is hilly; the soil second rate, but productive. Besides Barren river, which flows through

---

*This account, which is believed to be substantially correct, differs in some particulars from that given in the biographical sketch of Colonel Christian.

the county, it is watered by a number of fine mill streams. Tobacco is the principal staple.

The towns of the county are—Morgantown, Lockport and
Roduster. MORGANTOWN is the seat of justice, and is situated on
the left or southern bank of Green river, one hundred and forty-
one miles from Frankfort—contains a court-house and jail, post
office, one school, two lawyers, three doctors, six different trades,
and one hundred and ten inhabitants. Incorporated in 1813.
Lockport is a small village, containing thirty inhabitants, situated
on the Green river, at lock and dam No. 4. *Roduster* is also a
very small village, containing about thirty inhabitants.

This county received its name in honor of General BUTLER, of Pennsylvania,
an officer of the revolutionary war, who distinguished himself, on more than one
occasion, in a remarkable manner. He commanded the right wing of the American army under General St. Clair, in the memorable and disastrous battle with
the Indians on one of the tributaries of the Wabash, near the Miami villages, in
the now state of Ohio. He was wounded early in the action, and before his
wounds could be dressed, an Indian who had penetrated the ranks of the regiment, ran up to the spot where he lay, and tomahawked him before his attendants
could interpose. The desperate savage was instantly killed.

CALDWELL COUNTY.

CALDWELL county was formed in 1809, and named in honor of
Gen. John Caldwell. It is situated on the waters of the Cumberland and Tennessee rivers—bounded on the north by Crittenden
and Hopkins; east by Christian; south by Trigg; and west by
the Tennessee river. The portion of the county lying between
the Twigg and Crittenden lines, is a beautiful plain, being level
and productive, except between the Cumberland and Tennessee,
which is broken and poor, but abounds with ore; and there are
already in operation in that section, five large iron establishments, and one furnace for smelting lead. The portion of the
county bordering on the Trade water, (a navigable stream,) is
generally undulating. Coal has been found on Flinn's fork, but
has not yet been worked. The principal exports are tobacco,
corn, pork, and iron.

The valuation of taxable property in 1846, was $2,157,206;
number of acres of land, 304,935; number of white males over
twenty one years of age, 1,935; children between five and sixteen years of age, 2,253. Population in 1830, 8,832—in 1840,
10,365.

The towns of Caldwell are, Princeton, Fredonia, and Eddyville.
PRINCETON, the county seat, is about 230 miles from Frankfort—
contains four churches (Episcopal, Methodist, Presbyterian and
Cumberland Presbyterian), Cumberland college, one academy,
two schools, ten stores and groceries, four taverns, seven lawyers,
seven doctors, and twenty mechanical shops and manufactories.
Incorporated in 1820—population twelve hundred. *Fredonia* is a

smail town, twelvé miles west of Princeton, and contains one Presbyterian church, one school, two stores, two doctors, and four mechanical trades—population one hundred. *Eddyville* is situated on the Cumberland river, at the mouth of Eddy creek, from which it takes its name—contains one church edifice, two schools, ten stores and groceries, four warehouses, two taverns, three doctors, and fourteen mechanical shops. Incorporated in 1812—population six hundred.

THE CUMBERLAND COLLEGE is located in the vicinity of Princeton, and under the control and management of the Cumberland Presbyterian church. The institution was organized in 1825, as a manual labor school; but the mode of conducting it has been changed, and it is now a literary institution only, the manual labor system not having operated well. Like most institutions of learning in the west, it has had many and trying reverses. In 1842 it was in a great measure abandoned by the church. In 1844, the Green river synod assumed the charge of the college, and undertook to endow and perpetuate it. Its operations, in the mean time, had been carried on by enterprising individuals. The institution is located one mile from the court house. The site is beautiful, and susceptible of the highest degree of improvement. There are two neat and substantial brick buildings, one of them newly erected, for dormitories and public purposes, besides a president's house. The college library consists of several hundred volumes. There is also a respectable philosophical and chemical apparatus. The faculty of the institution consists of a president, two professors, and a tutor. The average number of students is sixty. The whole number of graduates since the establishment of the college is fifty-two.

Gen. JOHN CALDWELL, in honor of whom this county received its name, was a native of Prince Edward county, Virginia. He removed to Kentucky in 1781, and settled near where Danville now stands. He took an active part in the conflicts with the Indians, and rose by regular steps from the rank of a common soldier to that of a major general in the militia. He served as a subaltern in the campaign against the Indians in 1786, under Gen. George Rogers Clark. He was a prominent man of his day—esteemed in private and political, as he was in military life. He was a member, from Nelson county, of the conventions held in Danville in 1787 and 1788. In 1792, he was elected from the same county a senatorial elector, under the first constitution; and in the college of electors, he was chosen the senator from Nelson. He took his seat in the senate at the session of 1792–3. He was elected lieutenant governor of the State in 1804, and during his term of service removed to the lower part of the State. He died at Frankfort in the year 1807 or 1808, while the legislature was in session.

CALLOWAY COUNTY.

CALLOWAY county was formed in 1821, and is situated in the south-western part of the State, immediately below and on the waters of the Tennessee river—bounded on the north by Marshall, east by the Tennessee river, south by the State line of Tennessee, and west by the county of Graves. The surface of more than half of the county is level bottoms, interspersed with enough timber for farming purposes, though the broken and hilly portion has the densest population. The staple products are tobacco, corn, and small grain.

Value of taxable property in 1846, $860,004; number of acres of land in the county, 235,736 ; average value per acre, $1,78 ; number of white males over twenty-one years of age, 1,191 ; children between five and sixteen years old, 1,966. Population in 1840, 9,794.

There are three towns, Murray, New Concord, and Wadesborough, in Calloway. Murray, the county seat, is about two hundred and fifty miles from Frankfort—contains a handsome brick court-house and jail, a Christian church, four stores, two taverns, three lawyers, three doctors, five mechanics' shops, with 200 inhabitants—named after the Hon. J. L. Murray. *New Concord* is a small village in the south-eastern part of the county, containing two doctors, one store, one tavern, a few mechanics' shops, with 60 inhabitants. *Wadesborough* was formerly the county seat —contains one store, two taverns, one doctor, one smith, one tanyard—population 70. Named after Mr. Banister Wade.

This county was called after Col. Richard Calloway, who removed with his family to Kentucky in 1776. He speedily became an efficient actor in the affairs of the infant settlements, and his services were numerous and valuable. As early as 1777, he and John Todd were elected the first burgesses to the general assembly of Virginia; while, in the spring of the same year, he had been appointed a justice of the peace. In 1779, he, with others, under an act of the Virginia legislature, was appointed a trustee to lay off the town of Boonsborough. The trustees declined to act; others were appointed. Mr. Morehead, in his eloquent Boonsborough address, classes Col. Calloway among the law-givers and defenders of the frontier. His career in the new settlements, however, was short. Like a great many other daring spirits of the times, he was killed before he had an opportunity of very greatly distinguishing himself.

CAMPBELL COUNTY.

Campbell county was formed in 1794, and named in honor of Colonel John Campbell. It is situated in the north part of the State, and lies on the Ohio, immediately above Licking river: Bounded on the north and east by the Ohio river; south by Pendleton, and west by Licking river, which separates it from Kenton. .Alexandria, the county seat, is about eighty miles from Frankfort. The face of the country is diversified—the river bottoms being level, rich and productive, while the uplands are undulating or hilly. The staple products are corn, wheat, tobacco and pork.

The taxable property of Campbell in 1846, was valued at $1,668,757 ; number of acres of land in the county, 77,208 ; average value per acre, $11,56 ; total number of white males over twenty-one years of age, 1,472 ; children between five and sixteen years old, 1,444. Population in 1840, 5,214.

Newport is the principal town of Campbell. It is situated on a beautiful bottom on the Ohio, immediately above the junction of the Licking with that noble river, and opposite the city of Cincinnati. It contains five churches of different denominations, one seminary of learning, five private schools, five lawyers, five physicians, six stores, twenty-three groceries, two lodges of Masons, one lodge of Odd Fellows, one division of the Sons of Temperance, one rolling mill, one cotton factory, one rope walk, one silk factory, three blacksmith shops, twelve carpenter and joiners' shops, two tailor and two saddler shops, two taverns, one court-house, one market-house—with two hundred and fifty brick and one hundred and seventy-five frame houses. Population about 4,000. Newport is rapidly increasing in population and wealth, and her trade and manufacturing establishments have more than doubled within the short period of five years.

ALEXANDRIA is the county seat of Campbell, situated about thirteen miles from Newport, and about eighty miles from Frankfort. It contains a court-house and the usual public buildings, with a small population.

The county of Campbell, as originally organized, comprised the territory at present embraced by Campbell, Pendleton, Boone, Kenton and part of Grant. The justices of the first quarter session court of the new county, were—Washington Berry, president, Captain John Craig and Charles Daniel, sen. The county court justices, were—Robert Benham, Thomas Kennedy, John Hall, John Bush, John Cook, John Ewing and Thomas Corwin. The first courts of the county met, by law, at Wilmington, on Licking river, about twenty-two miles from Newport, but the county seat was afterwards located at Newport.

James Taylor (the present venerable General James Taylor of Newport), was elect ⟨ ⟩ the first clerk of both the county and quarter sessions court, and Captain Nathan Kelly the first sheriff of the county. When the county of Kenton was stricken off from Campbell, the county seat was removed to Alexandria.

In the autumn of 1779, two keel boats, laden with military stores, bound from New Orleans to Pittsburgh, under the command of Colonel Rogers, were ascending the Ohio river; and when near the sand-bar, above where the city of Cincinnati now stands, called four mile bar—they discovered a number of Indians on rafts and in canoes coming out of the mouth of the Little Miami river, which stream was then very high, and shot its waters, together with the Indian craft, nearly across the river. Colonel Rogers immediately landed his boats, and the crew, to the number of seventy men, advanced secretly through the woods and willows that grew thickly on the sand bar which here joined the Kentucky shore, expecting to attack the Indians, when they should land, by surprise. Before, however, Rogers had succeeded in reaching the point where he presumed he would encounter the savages, he found himself suddenly surrounded by a force of more than treble his numbers. The Indians instantly poured in a close discharge of rifles, and then throwing down their guns, fell upon the survivors with the tomahawk! The panic was complete, and the slaughter prodigious. Major Rogers, together with forty-five of his men, were almost instantly destroyed. The survivors made an effort to regain their boats, but the five men who had been left in charge of them, had immediately put off from shore in the hindmost boat, and the enemy had already gained possession of the other. Disappointed in the attempt, they turned furiously upon the enemy, and aided by the approach of darkness, forced their way through their lines, and with the loss of several severely wounded, at length effected their escape to Harrodsburgh.

Among the wounded was Capt. Robert Benham. Shortly after breaking through the enemy's line, he was shot through both hips, and the bones being shattered,

15

he instantly fell to the ground. Fortunately, a large tree had recently fallen near the spot where he lay, and with great pain, he dragged himself into the top, and lay concealed among the branches. The Indians, eager in pursuit of the others, passed him without notice, and by midnight all was quiet. On the following day, the Indians returned to the battle ground, in order to strip the dead and take care of the boats. Benham, although in danger of famishing, permitted them to pass without making known his condition, very correctly supposing that his crippled legs would only induce them to tomahawk him on the spot, in order to avoid the trouble of carrying him to their town.

He lay close, therefore, until the evening of the second day, when perceiving a racoon descending a tree, near him, he shot it, hoping to devise some means of reaching it, when he could kindle a fire and make a meal. Scarcely had his gun cracked, however, when he heard a human cry, apparently not more than fifty yards off. Supposing it to be an Indian, he hastily reloaded his gun, and remained silent, expecting the approach of an enemy. Presently the same voice was heard again, but much nearer. Still Benham made no reply, but cocked his gun, and sat ready to fire as soon as an object appeared. A third halloo was quickly heard, followed by an exclamation of impatience and distress, which convinced Benham that the unknown must be a Kentuckian. As soon, therefore, as he heard the expression, "whoever you are, for God's sake answer me," he replied with readiness, and the parties were soon together.

Benham, as we have already observed, was shot through both legs. The man who now appeared, had escaped from the same battle, *with both arms broken!* Thus each was enabled to supply what the other wanted. Benham, having the perfect use of his arms, could load his gun and kill game with great readiness, while his friend, having the use of his legs, could kick the game to the spot where Benham sat, who was thus enabled to cook it. When no wood was near them, his companion would rake up brush with his feet, and gradually roll it within reach of Benham's hands, who constantly fed his companion, and dressed *his* wounds as well as his own—tearing up both their shirts for that purpose. They found some difficulty in procuring water at first; but Benham at length took his own hat, and placing the rim between the teeth of his companion, directed him to wade into the Licking up to his neck, and dip the hat into the water by sinking his own head. The man who could walk, was thus enabled to bring water by means of his teeth, which Benham could afterwards dispose of as was necessary.

In a few days, they had killed all the squirrels and birds within reach, and the man with broken arms was sent out to drive game within gunshot of the spot to which Benham was confined. Fortunately, wild turkies were abundant in those woods, and his companion would walk around, and drive them towards Benham, who seldom failed to kill two or three of each flock. In this manner they supported themselves for several weeks, until their wounds had healed so as to enable them to travel. They then shifted their quarters, and put up a small shed at the mouth of the Licking, where they encamped until late in November, anxiously expecting the arrival of some boat, which should convey them to the falls of the Ohio.

On the 27th of November, they observed a flat boat moving leisurely down the river. Benham instantly hoisted his hat upon a stick, and hallooed loudly for help. The crew, however, supposing them to be Indians—at least suspecting them of an intention to decoy them ashore, paid no attention to their signals of distress, but instantly put over to the opposite side of the river, and manning every oar, endeavored to pass them as rapidly as possible. Benham beheld them pass him with a sensation bordering on despair, for the place was much frequented by Indians, and the approach of winter threatened them with destruction, unless speedily relieved. At length, after the boat had passed him nearly half a mile, he saw a canoe put off from its stern, and cautiously approach the Kentucky shore, evidently reconnoitering them with great suspicion.

He called loudly upon them for assistance, mentioned his name, and made known his condition. After a long parley, and many evidences of reluctance on the part of the crew, the canoe at length touched the shore, and Benham and his friend were taken on board. Their appearance excited much suspicion. They were almost entirely naked, and their faces were garnished with six weeks growth of beard. The one was barely able to hobble on crutches, and the other could manage to feed himself with one of his hands. They were taken to Louisville, where their clothes (which had been carried off in the boat which deserted them) were restored to them, and after a few weeks confinement, both were perfectly recovered.

Benham afterwards served in the north-west throughout the whole of the Indian war, accompanied the expeditions of Harmar and Wilkinson, shared in the disaster of St. Clair, and afterwards in the triumph of Wayne. Upon the return of peace, he bought the land upon which Rogers had been defeated, and ended his days in tranquility, amid the scenes which had witnessed his sufferings.

The county of Campbell received its name in honor of Colonel JOHN CAMPBELL, a native of Ireland. He came to Kentucky at an early period. Having received a grant of four thousand acres of land from the commonwealth of Virginia, which was located immediately below, and adjoining the grant on which Louisville stands, Col. Campbell became an extensive landed proprietor, and a very wealthy man. He was a member of the convention which formed the first constitution of Kentucky, from Jefferson county. During the same year, he was elected one of the electors of the senate from Jefferson, and in the electoral college was chosen the senator from Jefferson county, in the new State legislature. He was a large man, of fine personal appearance, and strong mind, but rough in his manners. He never married, and having died intestate, his large estate passed into the hands of many heirs.

General JAMES TAYLOR, one of the pioneers of Kentucky, resides in Newport. He has attained his seventy-eighth year, and is remarkably active and sprightly for a man of his age. His venerable consort, to whom he has been united for upwards of half a century, and who came to Kentucky in the midst of Indian troubles, still retains much of the vigor of her youth, and attends strictly to her household affairs. The mansion of these venerable pioneers, "*Belleview*," one of the most beautiful and costly in Kentucky, has long been distinguished for elegant hospitality.

Mrs. Taylor removed to Kentucky in 1784, in company with a large party of emigrants, among them the Rev. Augustine Eastin, of Bourbon county, who married an elder sister. In their progress through the wilderness, and after they had made their encampment for the night, the party of Mr. Eastin were overtaken about night-fall by a large body of emigrants, who were seeking new homes in Kentucky. Mr. Eastin advised the party to encamp with him, as Indian signs had been discovered through the day, and there were strong reasons to apprehend an attack. The party, however, disregarded the warning, and having traveled about a mile further, made their encampment. From some unexplained cause—probably incredulous of danger—they retired to rest without stationing a single sentinel to guard their camp, or warn them of the approach of an enemy. In the midst of the night, when the fatigued and jaded travelers were wrapped in the most profound sleep, the savages attacked them, and killed and scalped more than half of the company, numbering altogether about forty persons. A man, his wife, and two children, of this company, became separated at the instant of alarm. The mother, with her youngest child, effected her escape to the woods, and made her way back to the camp of Mr. Eastin. The father also escaped, and in a short time afterwards reached the settlements; the eldest child was slain. Two weeks after the arrival of Mr. Eastin's party in Kentucky, the husband and wife were re-united, each supposing, up to the period of their meeting, the other to be dead.

Gen. James Taylor is a native of Virginia, having been born at Midway, in Caroline county, on the 19th day of April, 1769. He was a quarter-master general of the north-western army in the late war, and was active in the discharge of the important duties which devolved upon him. When Gen. Hull surrendered Detroit to the British forces under General Brock, in August, 1812, General Taylor and Major (now General) Jesup, with other officers, were called upon to assist in drawing up the articles of capitulation; but they all indignantly refused any participation in an act so disgraceful to the American arms. General Taylor had previously taken an active part in the plan concerted by the field officers to displace General Hull, and confer the command of the fortress on General McArthur. Had the latter, with his command, reached Detroit in time, the plan would have been consummated. In the course of a long life, General Taylor has accumulated a very large estate, and is probably one of the most extensive landed proprietors of the west.

CARROLL COUNTY.

CARROLL county was formed in the year 1838, and named in honor of CHARLES CARROLL of Carrollton. It lies on the Ohio and Kentucky rivers—bounded north by the Ohio river, east by Gallatin, south by Owen and Henry, and west by Trimble county. The hills bordering the rivers are lofty, and in some places precipitous; back of them the surface of the county is rolling, and the soil of good quality. The staple products are corn, small grain, and Irish potatoes.

The taxable property of the county, according to the auditor's report of 1846, amounts to $1,310,213; number of acres of land in the county, 75,525; number of white males over twenty-one years of age, 884; number of children between five and sixteen years old, 1,094. Population in 1840, 3,966.

CARROLLTON, (formerly Port William), the seat of justice, is about fifty miles from Frankfort. It is situated on the Ohio, immediately above the mouth of the Kentucky river—contains a fine brick court-house and jail, three churches, (Methodist, Presbyterian and Reformed), seven stores and groceries, four taverns, four lawyers, three physicians, one academy, one common school, two piano forte manufacturers, thirty mechanical trades, embracing every variety, two corn mills, one steam saw mill, one wool carding factory, and one rope walk with six spindles, working twenty tons of hemp per week. Population 800. It was incorporated as Port William in 1794; but received its present name from " Carrollton," the residence of Charles Carroll.

GHENT is a neat village, also situated on the Ohio river, opposite the town of Vevay in Indiana. It contains one Baptist, one Methodist, and one Reformed church, one tavern, five stores and groceries, two physicians, one tobacco factory, and seven mechanics' shops—population 300. Named after the city of Ghent in Europe, where the treaty of peace between Great Britain and the United States was signed. *Preston* is a small village situated below the mouth of the Kentucky, and opposite Carrollton—contains a store and tavern and about 100 inhabitants. Named after Col. Preston, of Virginia, who owned the land on which it is erected.

In March, 1785, a body of Indians surrounded the house of Mr. Elliott, situated at the mouth of Kentucky river, and made a furious assault upon it. The members of the family generally made their escape; but Mr. Elliott was killed and his house burnt by the savages. In 1786 or '87, Captain Ellison built a block house on the point at the confluence of the Kentucky and Ohio river, and was successively driven from his post in the two succeeding summers, by a superior

Indian force. In 1789–90, General Charles Scott built a block house on the second bank, in an elevated position, and fortified it by picketing. This post was occupied until 1792, when the town of Port William (now Carrollton) was first laid out. The Indians were then troublesome.

ANTIQUITIES.—About one-fourth of a mile from the Kentucky river, on the second bank of the Ohio, and about one hundred yards from the latter river, there are the remains of a fortification, of a circular form, about one hundred and twenty feet in diameter, situated on level ground. About two miles from the mouth of the Kentucky, there are also the remains of what must have been a formidable fortification, situated on an eligible point, and of quadrangular form. The heavy embankment on which it was erected, is evidently of artificial construction, and must have been made at great labor and expense. It includes about an acre of ground, and is so graded as to throw the water from the centre in every direction. On the west and north of the fort, the paths, or roads leading to the water, and which were doubtless used for the general purpose of ingress and egress, are still distinctly marked and visible.

There are a number of mounds in the county, but generally of small size. In 1837, one was examined, in which was found the skull and thigh bones of a human being of very large frame, together with a silver snuff box, made in the shape of an infant's shoe. On an elevated hill, a short distance from the Kentucky river, in opening a stone quarry, the jaw bone and a large number of human teeth were found ; and on the points of the ridges, generally, similar discoveries have been made. About four miles from Carrollton, on the Muddy fork of White run, in the bed of the creek, on a limestone rock, is the form of a human being, in a sitting posture ; and near by, is the form of one lying on his back, about six feet long, and distinctly marked.

This county received its name in honor of CHARLES CARROLL, of Carrollton, one of the signers of the declaration of Independence, and the last of that immortal band of patriots who descended to the tomb. Mr. Carroll was born at Annapolis, Maryland, on the 8th of September, 1737, O. S. He received his literary education in France, and studied law in England. In 1764, he returned to Maryland, a finished scholar and an accomplished gentleman. He married in 1768. He soon became a distinguished advocate of popular rights, and ultimately an ardent and devoted friend of the independence of the American colonies. At one time the delegates from Maryland in the continental congress were instructed to vote against the declaration of independence ; but through his influence the decision was reversed, and under new instructions on the 4th of July, 1776, the votes of the Maryland delegation were given for independence. Mr. Carroll having been appointed a delegate, on the 18th of July took his seat in Congress. On the same day a secret resolution was adopted, directing the declaration to be engrossed on parchment, and signed by all the members, which was accordingly done on the 2nd of August. As Mr. Carroll had not given a vote on the adoption of that instrument, he was asked by the president if he would sign it ; " most willingly," he replied, and immediately affixed his name to that "record of glory," which has endeared him to his country, and rendered his name immortal. He subsequently aided in the formation of the constitution of Maryland, was a member of congress, a member of the state senate, and a member of the senate of the United States. He retired from public employments in 1801, and spent the remainder of his days in private life. On the 14th of November, 1832, at the advanced age of 95, he was gathered to his fathers.

An anecdote is told of Carroll, illustrative of the fearlessness and firmness of the man, which may not be out of place here. Immediately after he placed his name to the declaration of independence, one of his friends jocularly remarked that if the British got hold of him, they would not know whether it were he, or the Charles Carroll of Massachusetts, who had signed the declaration ; consequently, they would be at a loss which to hang as the rebel. " In order," says he, " that there may be no mistake about that, I will save them the trouble of hanging two of us," and instantly affixed his residence to his name, and by which he was ever afterwards known as " Charles Carroll of Carrollton."

CARTER COUNTY.

CARTER county was formed in 1838, and called in honor of Colonel WILLIAM G. CARTER, the then senator in the state legislature from the counties of Lewis, Greenup and Lawrence. It is situated in the extreme eastern portion of the State, and is watered by Big and Little Sandy rivers and Tygart's creek: Bounded on the north by Greenup and Lewis; east by Big Sandy river, which divides Kentucky from Virginia; south by Lawrence, and west by Fleming. GRAYSON, the county seat, is about one hundred and ten miles from Frankfort—contains a fine brick court-house and other public buildings, two stores, four lawyers, two doctors, and several mechanics. Named after Colonel Robert Grayson.

The taxable property of Carter in 1846, was assessed at $433,856; number of acres of land, 246,977; average value per acre, $1,13; number of white males over twenty-one years is given at 878; and number of children between five and sixteen years old, 1,194. Population in 1840, was 2,905.

The surface of this county, like most of the eastern counties, is very much broken; and except in the bottoms of the rivers and the numerous small streams by which it is watered, the lands are not well adapted for agricultural purposes. The hills, however, abound in stone coal and iron ore; and the mineral resources of the county, when fully developed, will prove an inexhaustible source of wealth. to its population. Salt, in considerable quantities, has been annually manufactured, at the Sandy Salines, for nearly half a century.

CASEY COUNTY.

CASEY county was organized in 1806, and named in memory of Colonel WILLIAM CASEY. It is situated in the middle part of the State, and lies on the head waters of Green river and the Rolling Fork of Salt river: Bounded on the north by Boyle; east by Lincoln; south by Pulaski, and west by Adair. LIBERTY is the seat of justice, which stands on the bank of Green river, about sixty-five miles from Frankfort. The surface is high and broken—corn, wheat, oats and potatoes, the principal productions.

Assessed taxable property in 1846, $719,257; number of acres of land in the county 175,118; average value per acre, $2,16; number of white males over twenty-one years of age, 961; number of children between five and sixteen years old, 1,425. Population in 1830, 4,342—in 1840, 4,939.

LIBERTY contains a court-house and public offices, three

churches, one school, five stores and groceries, three taverns, two lawyers, three doctors, seven mechanics' shops—population 200. Incorporated 1830.

Colonel WILLIAM CASEY, in honor of whom this county received its name, was a native of Frederick county, Virginia. In company with two or three families, he removed to Kentucky in the early part of the winter of 1779–80; and during the intensely cold weather of that memorable winter, lived in a camp on the Hanging fork of Dick's river. He remained there until the year 1791; when under the influence of that spirit of adventure and change which marked the era in which he lived, he struck his tent, and removed to Russell's creek, a tributary of Green river. Here, at a distance of fifty miles from any white settlement, in conjunction with several families who pushed their fortunes with him, he located and built a station. Though feeble in numbers, the hardy band of pioneers by whom he was surrounded, and who reposed in him unbounded confidence as a leader, maintained themselves, gallantly and victoriously, against several attacks of the Indians. His station was subsequently reinforced by several families, whose presence was instrumental in preventing any further assault on the part of the Indians. In one of the incursions, however, of a small band of savages, Mr. John Tucker, a Methodist preacher, together with his wife, were cruelly murdered.

CHRISTIAN COUNTY.

CHRISTIAN county was formed in the year 1796, and named in honor of Colonel WILLIAM CHRISTIAN. It lies in the south-western part of the State, adjoining the Tennessee line: Bounded on the north by Hopkins and Muhlenburg; east by Todd; south by the State of Tennessee, and west by Trigg. HOPKINSVILLE, the seat of justice, is about two hundred miles from Frankfort.

The auditor reports the valuation of the taxable property of Christian for 1846, at $4,855,552; number of acres of land in the county, 377,147; average value per acre, $5,08; number of white males over twenty-one years of age, 2,149; number of children between five and sixteen years old, 2,548. Population in 1830, 12,694—in 1840, 15,587.

This county is twenty-two miles wide and thirty-two long, containing an area of seven hundred and four miles, and is the eleventh county in the State in point of wealth. The southern division of the county is generally composed of rich, fertile, level bottoms, and produces fine crops of tobacco, corn, wheat, rye, oats, and grass. The northern division is broken, and in some portions almost mountainous, with a soil less fertile, but sufficiently rich to sustain a large population—finely timbered, well watered, and abounding in inexhaustible beds of coal and iron ore. The general basis of the soil is a red clay, founded on cavernous limestone; and like most of the southern counties, abounds in sinks, caves and caverns. The situation of the county is elevated, and the surface of the country has a descending inclination in all directions from the centre, as it contains the head waters of Pond, Trade Water, Little, and the west fork of

Red rivers : The first emptying into Green river, the second into the Ohio, and the two last into Cumberland river. Mineral and Sulphur springs abound, and many invalids visit them during the watering season. The staple products are corn, wheat, oats and tobacco—not less than 3,500 hogsheads of the latter article being exported annually; while coal from the mines, in large quantities, finds its way to market.

There are five towns in Christian—Hopkinsville, Belleview, Garrettsburg, Lafayette and Oaktown. HOPKINSVILLE is the county seat; situated near the centre of the county, on Little river, in a gently undulating, fertile valley, and presents a neat and flourishing appearance: Contains a large and commodious court-house, market-house, branch of the Bank of Kentucky, six churches, (Baptist, Presbyterian, Christian, Cumberland Presbyterian, Methodist and Episcopalian), a part beautiful and well finished edifices; two male and two female academies; one printing office, (the Hopkinsville Gazette), eighteen dry-goods stores, three drug stores, five groceries, three hotels, with nineteen lawyers, thirteen physicians, and the following mechanics' shops, viz : four blacksmiths, four saddlers, seven tailors, six carpenters, four cabinet and chair makers, two tinners, two hatters, five shoe and boot makers, four wagon and carriage makers, two silversmiths, three house and sign painters, one gun smith, two tanneries, one barber, one carding factory, and three large tobacco factories. Population 2,000. Immediately in the vicinity of the town is a beautiful botanic garden and nursery, containing six acres, and supplied with choice fruit, shrubbery, plants, etc., together with a fine fish pond, well stocked with fish, the water of which is conveyed five hundred yards through pipes, and flowing up in the centre, forms a beautiful fountain. This garden is a place of very general resort. Hopkinsville was laid out in 1799, on the lands of Mr. Bartholomew Wood, and called Elizabethtown, by which name it was known for several years. It was incorporated in 1806, by its present name, in honor of General Samuel Hopkins.

Belleview is a small village, ten miles from Hopkinsville, containing a Baptist church, post-office, store, grocery and tailor's shop. *Garrettsburg* is fourteen miles south from Hopkinsville, and contains a Baptist church, a lawyer, a doctor, two stores, one grocery and five mechanics' shops. *Lafayette* is situated in the south-west corner of the county, eighteen miles from Hopkinsville, and one mile from the Tennessee state line—contains one Presbyterian, one Cumberland Presbyterian, one Methodist Episcopal, one Methodist Protestant, and one Reformed or Christian church; eight stores and groceries, three physicians, one tavern, post-office and eleven mechanics' shops. *Oaktown* lies thirteen miles south-east of Hopkinsville, on the Clarksville road, and contains a post-office, two stores, a blacksmith and tailor.

Christian county contains several exceedingly interesting natural curiosities. 1st. Two of the forks of the Little river sink and disappear entirely in the earth for many miles, when they emerge and flow on about their usual width. 2d. The *Pilot Rock*, a rare curiosity, is situated about twelve miles from Hopkinsville, rather north of an east direction. The rock rests upon elevated ground, and is about two hundred feet in height. Its summit is level, and covers about half an acre of ground, which affords some small growth and wild shrubbery. This rock attracts great attention, and is visited by large numbers of persons, particularly in the summer months. Its elevated summit, which is reached without much difficulty, affords a fine view of the surrounding country for many miles, presenting a prospect at once picturesque, magnificent and beautiful. 3d. Situated in the northern extremity of this county, near "Harrison's tanyard," about twenty miles from Hopkinsville, is a *Natural Bridge*, somewhat similar, but on a reduced scale, to the celebrated rock bridge in Virginia, which was considered by Mr. Jefferson the greatest natural curiosity in the world. The bridge in question crosses a deep ravine, is thirty feet in height, with a span of sixty feet, and a magnificent arch. The surface is perfectly level, and the general width about five feet. The scenery in the vicinity of the bridge is remarkably romantic, and presents great attractions to the lovers of the picturesque in nature.

The first settlement in the county was made in 1785, by John Montgomery and James Davis, from Virginia, on the west fork of Red river, where they built a block house. At or near this block house, was a large cave, which served as a hiding place for themselves and families against the attacks of marauding parties of Indians.

Col. WILLIAM CHRISTIAN, in honor of whom this county received its name, was a native of Augusta county, Virginia. He was educated at Stanton, and when very young, commanded a company attached to Col. Bird's regiment, which was ordered to the frontier during Braddock's war. In this service, he obtained the reputation of a brave, active and efficient officer. Upon the termination of Indian hostilities, he married the sister of Patrick Henry, and settled in the county of Bottetourt. In 1774, having received the appointment of colonel of militia, he raised about three hundred volunteers, and by forced marches, made a distance of two hundred miles, with the view of joining the forces under General Lewis, at the mouth of the Great Kenhawa. He did not arrive, however, in time to participate in the battle of Point Pleasant, which occurred on the preceding day, the 10th of October, 1774. In 1775, he was a member of the general state convention of Virginia. In the succeeding year, when hostilities had commenced between Great Britain and the American colonies, he received the appointment of colonel in the Virginia line of the regular army, and took command of an expedition, composed of 1200 men, against the Cherokee Indians. No event of moment occurred in this expedition, the Indians having sued for peace, which was concluded with them. After his return from this expedition, Colonel Christian resigned his command in the regular service, and accepted one in the militia, at the head of which he kept down the *tory* spirit in his quarter of Virginia throughout the revolutionary struggle. Upon the conclusion of the war, he represented his county in the Virginia legislature for several years, sustaining a high reputation for his civil as well as his military talents.

In 1785, Colonel Christian emigrated to Kentucky, and settled on Bear-grass. The death of Colonel Floyd, who was killed by an Indian in 1783, rendered his location peculiarly acceptable to that section of the state, where a man of his intelligence, energy and knowledge of the Indian character, was much needed. In April of the succeeding year, 1786, a body of Indians crossed the Ohio and stole a number of horses on Bear-grass, and with their usual celerity of movement, recrossed the river, and presuming they were in no further danger of pursuit, leisurely made their way to their towns. Colonel Christian immediately raised a party of men, and crossed the Ohio in pursuit of the marauders. Having found their trail, by a rapid movement he overtook them about twenty miles from the river, and gave them battle. A bloody conflict ensued, in which Colonel Christian and one man of his party were killed, and the Indian force totally destroyed.[*] His death created a strong sensation in Kentucky. He was brave, intelligent and remarkably popular.

---

[*]Vide Marshall's History, vol. 1, page 228. This account varies in some of its particulars from that which appears in the biographical sketch of Lieutenant Governor Bullitt, who belonged to the party of Colonel Christian. See Bullitt county.

CLARK COUNTY.

CLARK county was established in 1793, by an act of the legislature, and named in honor of General GEORGE ROGERS CLARK. It is situated in the middle section of the State, and lies on the waters of the Kentucky and Licking rivers. It is bounded on the north by Bourbon county, on the east by Montgomery, on the south by the Kentucky river, which separates it from Madison and Estill counties, and on the west by Fayette county. One half of the western half of Clark county is very productive, the soil being as good as any in Kentucky ; a fourth of the county is very much broken, but fertile ; the remaining portion is very poor oak land. The exports consist principally of hemp, cattle, horses, mules, and hogs.

The aggregate value of taxable property in Clark county in 1846 was $5,904,832; number of acres of land in the county, 167,055 ; average value per acre, $20,56 ; number of white males over twenty-one years of age, 1,666; number of children between five and sixteen years old, 1,931. Population in 1830, 13,052—in 1840, 10,302.

The towns are Winchester, Kiddville, Colbysville, Schollville, and Webster. *Winchester* is the county seat, situated on the Lexington and Mount Sterling road, and forty five miles distant from Frankfort. It contains a Methodist, Presbyterian and Reformed Baptist church, a public seminary, a female academy, twelve stores, six grocery stores, ten lawyers, six physicians, two hemp factories, and a large number of mechanical shops. It has a population of about 700 souls. The other villages, above named, are small, and contain but few inhabitants.

Clark county was settled at a very early period in the history of Kentucky; it being separated from Boonsborough, the first point settled in the State, only by the Kentucky river, which forms the southern boundary of the county. Strodes Station, a point of considerable importance in the early Indian wars, was situated about two miles from Winchester, the present seat of justice. In the year 1780 it was besieged by a large body of Indians, who attempted to cut off the supply of water from the garrison. But, foiled in this effort, the savages were repulsed and forced to retreat. In the pursuit which followed, a white man by the name of Van Swearingen, a man of noted courage, was killed. This was the only loss sustained by the garrison during the siege.

When this county was first settled, some ancient corn-fields were discovered about twelve miles east of Winchester. It was supposed that these fields had been cultivated by the Indians, many years prior to the period of the first entrance of the whites into this territory.

At the present time Clark county is noted for its fine stock, its highly cultivated farms and beautiful grass pastures. Captain Isaac Cunningham, a citizen of this county, who died in 1842, was the pioneer of the grazing business in Kentucky, from which he amassed a large fortune. He was a man of great integrity of character, an ardent patriot, and held in high esteem by all who knew him. At the battle of the Thames he commanded a company of Kentucky volunteers, which did good service during the engagement.

The two Howard's creeks in Clark county derived their names from the venerable John Howard, a well known citizen of Kentucky, who died some years ago in Fayette county. He was the father of the late Governor Benjamin Howard, and of the first wife of Robert Wickliffe, Sen'r., Esq. He held a pre-emption of one thousand acres of land at the mouth of each of these creeks.

In this county repose the remains of two governors of Kentucky—Charles Scott and the late James Clarke. Monuments have been erected over the graves of both by the legislature.

Among the noted citizens of Clark, was the late venerable HUBBARD TAYLOR. He emigrated to the county at a very early period, was a senator for a number of years in the Kentucky legislature, and on several occasions was chosen as one of the presidential electors. He was distinguished for his patriotism, his hospitality and public spirit. He died in the year 1842, beloved and mourned by all who knew him.

General RICHARD HICKMAN, a lieutenant governor of the St. e, and acting governor during the absence of Governor Shelby in the campaign of 1813, was also a citizen of this county. He was highly esteemed by his c. untrymen for his intelligence and many virtues.

Colonel WILLIAM SUDDUTH, was one of the earliest settlers in Clark county, and the last surviving member of the convention which framed the present constitution of Kentucky. He was a gallant soldier under Wayne in the campaign of 1793. For thirty years he was the county surveyor of Clark. He was a man of intelligence, with the manners of an accomplished gentleman. He died at the residence of one of his sons in Bath county, in the year 1845, having nearly attained his eightieth year.

The Hon. CHILTON ALLAN, who for many years served as representative in congress from Kentucky, with a high reputation for ability and efficiency, is a citizen of this county. He is a profound lawyer, a statesman of enlarged and liberal views, a sound politician, a devoted patriot, and a man of remarkably pure and elevated moral character.

Among the most distinguished citizens of Clark county was the Hon. JAMES CLARKE, late governor of the commonwealth. Our materials for a sketch of his life are exceedingly meagre, and we can attempt nothing more than a bare enumeration of the most prominent incidents in his career. He was the son of Robert and Susan Clarke, and was born in 1779, in Bedford county, Virginia, near the celebrated Peaks of Otter. His father emigrated from Virginia to Kentucky at a very early period, and settled in Clark county, near the Kentucky river. The subject of this notice received the principal part of his education under Dr. Blythe, afterwards a professor in Transylvania university. He studied law with his brother, Christian Clarke, a very distinguished lawyer of Virginia. When he had qualified himself to discharge the duties of his profession, he returned to Kentucky, and commenced the practice of the law in Winchester, in 1797.

He remained here, however, but a short time, before he set out in search of a more eligible situation, and traveled through what was then the far west, taking Vincennes and St. Louis in his route; but failing to find a place to suit his views, he returned to Winchester, where, by his unremitting attention to business, and striking displays of professional ability, he soon obtained an extensive and lucrative practice.

At this period of his life, he was several times elected a member of the State legislature, in which body he soon attained a high and influential position. In 1810, he was appointed a judge of the court of appeals, and acted in that capacity for about two years. In 1812, he was elected to congress, and served from the 4th of March, 1813, until March, 1816. In 1817 he received an appointment as judge of the circuit court, for the judicial district in which he resided, which station he filled with great ability, and to the general satisfaction of the public, till the year 1824, when he resigned. During his term of service as judge, occurred that great and exciting struggle between the relief and anti-relief parties, which has left its traces on the political and social condition of Kentucky, in deep and indelible characters, to be seen even at the present day. In May, 1823, Mr. Clarke rendered an opinion in the Bourbon circuit court, in which he decided that the relief laws were unconstitutional. This decision produced great excitement, and was the cause of his being arraigned and impeached before the legislature. But, notwithstanding the temporary dissatisfaction it excited in the breasts of the relief party, there was probably no act of his life which inspired his fellow citizens with greater confidence in his integrity, firmness, independence, and patriotism, than this decision. It was given just before the election, and he must have foreseen the temporary injury it would inflict upon the party with which he acted, and which he regarded as the bulwark of the constitution. But his was a nature which knew not the possibility of making a compromise between his principles and policy.

In 1825, he was elected to congress to fill the vacancy occasioned by Mr. Clay's appointment as secretary of state, and continued to represent the Fayette district in that body until 1831. In 1832, he was elected to the senate of Kentucky, and was chosen speaker in the place of Mr. Morehead, who was then acting as governor, in the place of Governor Breathitt, deceased. He was elected governor of Kentucky in August, 1836, and died on the 27th of August, 1839, in his sixtieth year.

Governor Clarke was endowed by nature with great strength of mind, and a fine vein of original wit. His literary attainments were respectable, ranking in that respect with most of his cotemporaries of the legal profession at that day. A fine person, a cheerful and social disposition, an easy address, and fascinating manners, made him the life of every circle in which he mingled. He was full of fun, fond of anecdotes, and could tell a story with inimitable grace. To these qualities, so well calculated to display the amiable traits of his character in their most attractive light, he added all those stern and manly virtues which inspire confidence and command respect. His death made a vacancy in the political and social circles of Kentucky, which was very sensibly felt and universally deplored.

General GEORGE ROGERS CLARK, whose name is deservedly celebrated in the early history of Kentucky, and conspicuously prominent in the conquest and settlement of the whole west, was born in the county of Albemarle, in the State of Virginia, on the 19th of November, 1752. Of his early years and education, but little is known. In his youth, he engaged in the business of land surveying, which appears to have presented to the enterprising young men of that day, a most congenial and attractive field for the exercise of their energies. It is worthy of remark, that many of the most opulent and influential families of Kentucky were founded by men engaged in this pursuit. How long Clark continued in this vocation, is unknown. He commanded a company in Dunmore's war, and was engaged in the only active operation of the right wing of the invading army, against the Indians. At the close of this war, he was offered a commission in the English service, but, upon consultation with his friends, he was induced by the troubled aspect of the relations between the colonies and Great Britain, to decline the appointment.

In the spring of 1775, he came to Kentucky, drawn hither by that love of adventure which distinguished him through life. He remained in Kentucky during the spring and summer of this year, familiarizing himself with the character of the people and the resources of the country, until the fall, when he returned to Virginia. During this visit, he was temporarily placed in command of the irregular militia of the settlements; but whether he held a commission is not known. In the spring of the following year (1776), he again came to Kentucky, with the intention of making it his permanent home; and from this time forth, his name is closely associated with the progress of the western settlements in power and civilization.

His mind had been very early impressed with the immense importance of this frontier country to the security of the parent State of Virginia, as well as to the whole confederacy; and his reflections on this subject led him to perceive the importance of a more thorough, organized, and extensive system of public defence, and a more regular plan of military operations, than the slender resources of the colonies had yet been able to effect. With the view of accomplishing this design, he had been in Kentucky but a few months, when he suggested to the settlers the propriety of convening a general assembly of the people at Harrodstown (now Harrodsburgh), to take steps towards forming a more definite and certain connection with the government and people of Virginia, than as yet existed. The immediate necessity for this movement grew out of the memorable and well known conflict between Henderson & Co., and the legislature of Virginia, relative to the disputed claim of jurisdiction over a large portion of the new territory. The excitement which arose out of this dispute, and the prevailing uncertainty whether the south side of Kentucky river appertained to Virginia or North Carolina, (the latter claiming by virtue of Henderson's purchase of the Cherokees at the treaty of Wataga), added very greatly to the perplexity of the settlers, and rendered it necessary that the disposition of Virginia should be distinctly ascertained. The proposed meeting was accordingly held at Harrodstown on the 6th of June, 1776, at which Clark and Gabriel Jones were chosen members of the assembly of Virginia. This, however, was not precisely the thing contemplated by Clark. He wished that the people should appoint *agents*, with general powers to *negotiate* with the government of Virginia, and in the event that that commonwealth should refuse to recognize the colonists as within its jurisdiction and under its protection, he proposed to employ the lands of the country as a fund to obtain settlers and establish an independent State. The election had, however, gone too far to change its object when Clark arrived at Harrodstown, and the gentlemen elected, although aware that the choice could give them no seat in the legislature, proceeded to Williamsburg, at that time the seat of government. After suffering the most severe privations in their journey through the wilderness, the delegates found, on their arrival in Virginia, that the legislature had adjourned, whereupon Jones directed his steps to the settlements on Holston, and left Clark to attend to the Kentucky mission alone.

He immediately waited on Governor Henry, then lying sick at his residence in Hanover county, to whom he stated the objects of his journey. These meeting the approbation of the governor, he gave Clark a letter to the executive council of the state. With this letter in his hand he appeared before the council, and after acquainting them fully with the condition and circumstances of the colony, he made application for five hundred weight of gun-powder for the defence of the various stations. But with every disposition to assist and promote the growth of these remote and infant settlements, the council felt itself restrained by the uncertain and indefinite state of the relations existing between the colonists and the state of Virginia, from complying fully with his demand. The Kentuckians had not yet been recognised by the legislature as citizens, and the proprietary claimants, Henderson & Co., were at this time exerting themselves to obtain from Virginia, a relinquishment of her jurisdiction over the new territory. The council, therefore, could only offer to *lend* the gun-powder to the colonists as *friends*, not *give* it to them as *fellow citizens*. At the same time they required Clark to be personally responsible for its value, in the event the legislature should refuse to recognize the Kentuckians as citizens, and in the meantime to defray the expense of its conveyance to Kentucky. Upon these terms he did not feel at liberty to accept the proffered assistance. He represented to the council that the emissaries of the British were employing every means to engage the Indians in the war; that the people in the remote and exposed stations of Kentucky might be exterminated for the want of a supply which he, a private individual, had at so much hazard and hardship sought for their relief, and that when this frontier bulwark was thus destroyed, the fury of the savages would burst like a tempest upon the heads of their own citizens. To these representations, however, the council remained deaf and inexorable; the sympathy for the frontier settlers was deep, but the assistance already offered was a stretch of power, and they could go no farther. The keeper of the public magazine was directed to deliver the powder to Clark; but having long reflected on the situation, prospects and resources of the new country, his resolution to reject the assistance on the proposed conditions, was made before he left the council chamber. He determined to repair to Kentucky, and as he had at first contemplated, exert the resources of the country for the formation of an *independent state*. He accordingly returned the order of the council in a letter, setting forth his reasons for declining to accept their powder on these terms, and intimating his design of applying for assistance elsewhere, adding, "*that a country which was not worth defending, was not worth claiming.*" On the receipt of this letter the council recalled Clark to their presence, and an order was passed on the 23d of August, 1776, for the transmission of the gun-powder to Pittsburg, to be there delivered to Clark or his order, for the use of the people of Kentucky. This was the first act in that long and affectionate inter-change of good offices, which subsisted between Kentucky and her parent state for so many years; and obvious as the reflection is, it may not be omitted, that on the successful termination of this negotiation, hung the connection between Vir-ginia and the splendid domain she afterwards acquired west of the Alleghany mountains.

At the fall session of the legislature of Virginia, Messrs. Jones and Clark laid the Kentucky memorial before that body. They were of course not admitted to seats, though late in the session they obtained, in opposition to the exertions of Colonels Henderson and Campbell, the formation of the territory which now com-prises the present state of that name, into the county of Kentucky. Our first political organization was thus obtained through the sagacity, influence and exer-tions of George Rogers Clark, who must be ranked as the earliest founder of this commonwealth. This act of the Virginia legislature first gave it form and a political existence, and entitled it under the constitution of Virginia to a repre-sentation in the assembly, as well as to a judicial and military establishment.

Having obtained these important advantages from their mission, they received the intelligence that the powder was still at Pittsburg, and they determined to take that point in their route home, and bring it with them. The country around Pittsburg swarmed with Indians, evidently hostile to the whites, who would no doubt seek to interrupt their voyage. These circumstances created a necessity for the utmost caution as well as expedition in their movements, and they accord-ingly hastily embarked on the Ohio with only seven boatmen. They were hotly pursued the whole way by Indians, but succeeded in keeping in advance until they arrived at the mouth of Limestone creek, at the spot where the city of Mays-ville now stands. They ascended this creek a short distance with their boat, and concealed their cargo at different places in the woods along its banks. They then turned their boat adrift, and directed their course to Harrodstown, intending to return with a sufficient escort to ensure the safe transportation of the powder to its destination. This in a short time was successfully effected, and the colonists were thus abundantly supplied with the means of defence against the fierce ene-mies who beset them on all sides.

The space allotted to this brief sketch, will not admit of a detailed narrative of the adventures of Major Clark after his return to Kentucky. Let it suffice to say, that he was universally looked up to by the settlers as one of the master spirits of the time, and always foremost in the fierce conflicts and desperate deeds of those wild and thrilling days.

Passing over that series of private and solitary adventures in which he em-barked after he returned from Virginia, and in which he appears to have taken a peculiar pleasure, but of which no particulars have been preserved, we shall pro-ceed at once to notice his successful expedition against the British posts of Kas-kaskia and Vincennes; one of the most important events, if we estimate it by its consequences, immediate and remote, in the early history of the west. It was at the same time marked by incidents of romantic and thrilling interest, and a striking display of the qualities of courage, perseverance and fortitude, which bring to mind the heroic deeds of antiquity.

The war in Kentucky previous to this time had been a true *border war*, and conducted in the irregular and desultory manner incident to that kind of hostili-ties. Nearly all the military operations of the period resembled more the preda-tory exploits of those sturdy cattle-drovers and stark moss-troopers of the Scottish Highlands, whose valorous achievements have been immortalized by the graphic pen of the author of Waverley, than the warfare of a civilized people. Every man fought, pretty much, " *on his own hook*," and waged the war in a fashion to suit himself. He selected his own ground, determined upon the time, place, and manner of attack, and brought the campaign to a close whenever his own incli-nations prompted. The war indeed was sustained, and its " sinews supplied," by the adventurous spirit of private individuals. The solitary backwoodsman would sharpen his hunting knife, shoulder his rifle, and provide himself with a small quantity of parched corn as a substitute for bread, and thus equipped for service, start on an expedition into the Indian country, without beat of drum or note of warning. Arrived on the hostile soil, he would proceed with the caution of a panther stealing on his prey, until he reached the neighborhood of a village, when concealing himself in the surrounding thickets, he would lie in wait until an opportunity presented of shooting an Indian and stealing a horse, when he would return to the cultivation of his farm and the ordinary pursuits of his business. Even those more ambitious enterprises which occasionally diversified this personal warfare, were the result rather of the spontaneous combination of private individuals, than of any movement by the state. The perseverance and gallantry of the backwoodsman was left to sustain itself, with little assistance from the power of Virginia, at that time engaged in the tremendous struggle of the war of Independence, which demanded all her energies and taxed all her resources. The State had not disposable means to act on so remote a frontier, nor does she appear to have been distinctly aware of the important diversion of the Indian force, which might be made by supporting the exertions of Kentucky. As little did she perceive the rich temptations offered to her military ambition in the British posts in the west. Yet every Indian engaged on the frontier of Kentucky, was a foe taken from the nearer frontier of the parent state. And in those remote and neglected garrisons of Kaskaskia, Vincennes and Detroit, was to be found the source of those Indian hostilities, which staid the advancing tide of emigration, and deluged the whole west in the blood of women and children.

These combined views, however, began to acquire weight with the Virginia statesmen, with the progress of the revolution, and the rapid increase of emigration to Kentucky; and they were particularly aided and enforced by the impressive representations of Major Clark. To his mind they had been long familiar, and his plans were already matured. He was thoroughly acquainted with the condition, relations and resources of the country, and with that instinctive genius which stamps him as the most consummate of the western commanders, he saw at a glance the policy required to develop the nascent strength and advantages of the infant settlements. At a glance, he discovered what had so long escaped the perspicacity of the Virginia statesmen, that the sources of the Indian devastations were Detroit, Vincennes and Kaskaskia. It was by the arms and clothing supplied at these military stations that the merciless ferocity of these blood thirsty warriors was stimulated to the commission of those fearful ravages which "drenched the land to a mire." If they could be taken, a counter influence would be established over the Indians, and the streams of human blood, which deluged the fields of Kentucky, would be dried up.

So strongly had the idea of reducing these posts taken possession of the mind and imagination of Major Clark, that in the summer of 1777, he dispatched two spies to reconnoitre and report their situation. On their return they brought intelligence of great activity on the part of the garrisons, who omitted no opportunity to promote and encourage the Indian depredations on the Kentucky frontier. They reported further, that although the British had essayed every art of misrepresentation, to prejudice the French inhabitants against the Virginians and Kentuckians, by representing these frontier people, as more shocking barbarians than the savages themselves, still there were to be seen strong traces of affection for the Americans among many of the inhabitants.

In December, 1777, Major Clark submitted to the executive of Virginia a plan for the reduction of these posts. The result was a full approbation of the scheme, and the governor and council entered into the undertaking so warmly that every preliminary arrangement was soon made. Clark received two sets of instructions: one public, directing him to proceed to Kentucky for its defence; the other secret, ordering an attack on the British post at Kaskaskia. Twelve hundred pounds were advanced to defray the expenses of the expedition, and orders issued to the Virginia commandant at fort Pitt, to supply Clark with ammunition, boats, and all other necessary equipments. The force destined for the expedition, consisting, after a rigid selection, of only four companies, rendezvoused at Corn Island, opposite the falls of the Ohio, and having fully completed their preparations, they embarked in boats on the Ohio. Landing on an island at the mouth of the Tennessee river, they encountered a party of hunters who had recently came from Kaskaskia, and from them they obtained the most important intelligence relative to the state of things at that post. They reported that the garrison was commanded by one M. Rocheblave; that the *militia* were kept in a high state of discipline,; that spies were stationed on the Mississippi river, and all Indian hunters directed to keep a sharp look out for the Kentuckians. They stated further that the fort which commanded the town was kept in order as a place of retreat, but without a regular garrison, and the military defences were attended to as a matter of form, rather than from any belief in its necessity to guard against an attack. The hunters thought that by a sudden surprise the place might be easily captured, and they offered their services as guides, which were accepted. The boats were dropped down to a point on the Illinois shore, a little above the place where fort Massac was afterwards built, and there concealed, and the little army took up its line of march through the wilderness. Their commander marched at their head, sharing in all respects the condition of his men. On the evening of the 4th of July, 1778, the expedition arrived in the neighborhood of the town, where it lay until dark, when the march was continued. That night the town and fort were surprised and captured without the effusion of a drop of blood. M. Rocheblave, the British governor, was taken in his chamber, but very few of his public papers were secured, as they were secreted or destroyed by his wife, whom the Kentuckians were too polite to molest. In the course of a few days, Clark had, by his wise and prudent policy, entirely dissipated the alarm, and gained the affections of the French inhabitants, and his conquest was thus confirmed, and the ascendency of the Virginia government firmly rooted in the feelings of the people. Having effected this most desirable revolution in the sentiments of the inhabitants, he next turned his attention to the small French village of Cahokia, situated about sixty miles higher up the Mississippi. He accordingly dispatched Major Bowman, with his own and part of another company, to effect the reduction of this small post, at that time a place of considerable trade, and a depot for the distribution of arms and ammunition to the Indians, a considerable body of whom were encamped in the neighborhood when the Americans approached. The expedition was accompanied by several Kaskaskia gentlemen, who volunteered their services to assist in the reduction of the place. The expedition reached the town without being discovered. The surprise and alarm of the inhabitants was great, but when the Kaskaskia gentlemen narrated what had occurred at their own village, the general consternation was converted into hurras for freedom and the Americans. The people took the oath of allegiance, and in a few days the utmost harmony prevailed.

The expedition thus far had met with full success, but Vincennes still remained in the possession of the British, and until it should share the fate of Kaskaskia, Clark felt that there was no safety for his new conquest. His uneasiness was great. His situation was critical. His force was too small to garrison Kaskaskia and Cahokia, and leave him a sufficient power to attempt the reduction of Vincennes by open assault. At length he communicated his perplexity to a Catholic priest, M. Gibault, who agreed to attempt to bring the inhabitants over whom he had pastoral charge into the views of the American commander. This, through the agency and influence of the priest, was effected with little difficulty. The inhabitants threw off their allegiance to the British, the garrison was overpowered and expelled, and the American flag displayed from the ramparts of the fort.

Having thus succeeded beyond his most sanguine expectations, in his designs against the power of the British in the west, Clark next turned his attention to conciliate the various Indian tribes inhabiting this region. This great purpose, after a long and tedious series of negotiations, in which the character of the American commander unfolded itself under its most powerful aspect, was finally accomplished, the hostility of many of the tribes pacified, and their prejudices disarmed. The summary nature of this sketch will not admit of a particular account of the incidents attending this great enterprise, though the narrative would be replete with interest, as it was in this wild and dangerous diplomacy that the genius of Colonel Clark displayed its most commanding attributes. Success in this politic intercourse with the untutored savage of the wilderness, depends far more on the personal qualities of the negotiator, than on the justice of the cause or the plausibility of his reasoning. The American Indian has an unbounded admiration for all those high and heroic virtues which enter into the character of the successful warrior, and the terror of Clark's name had spread far and wide. To these advantages he added that of a thorough knowledge of the Indian character. in all its peculiarities, its strength, and its weakness. He knew when to be mild and conciliating—when to be stern and uncompromising. The tact and promptitude with which he adapted his conduct to the exigency of the occasion has become proverbial. His address was wonderful—the fertility of his resources inexhaustible, and his influence among those wild and unsophisticated children of the woods grew so predominant, that they gave whate'er he asked.

Colonel Clark now began to entertain great fears for the safety of Vincennes. No intelligence had been received from that post for a long time; but on the 29th of January 1779, Colonel Vigo brought intelligence that Governor Hamilton of Detroit had marched an expedition against the place in December, and again reduced the inhabitants and the fort, and re-established the British power. The expedition had been fitted out on a large scale, with the view of recapturing Kaskaskia, and making an assault along the whole line of the Kentucky frontier. But owing to the advanced period of the season, Governor Hamilton had postponed the further execution of this grand scheme of conquest until spring, when he contemplated reassembling his forces.

Having received this timely intelligence of the British governor's designs, Colonel Clark with characteristic promptitude and decision, determined to anticipate him, and strike the first blow. He accordingly made immediate preparation for an expedition against Vincennes. He commenced his march through the wilderness with a force of one hundred and seventy-five men, on the 7th of February, having previously dispatched Captain Rogers with a company of forty-six men and two four-pounders, in a boat, with orders to force their way up the Wabash, station themselves a few miles below the mouth of White river, suffer nothing to pass, and wait for further orders. For seven days the land expedition pursued its toilsome course over the drowned lands of Illinois, exposed to every privation that could exhaust the spirits of men, when it arrived at the Little Wabash. But now the worst part of the expedition was still before them. At this point the forks of the stream are three miles apart, and the opposite heights of land five miles distant even in the ordinary state of the water. When the expedition arrived, the intervening valley was covered with water three feet in depth. Through this dreadful country the expedition was compelled to make its way until the 18th, when they arrived so near Vincennes that they could hear the morning and evening guns at the fort. On the evening of the same day they encamped within nine miles of the town, below the mouth of the Embarrass river. Here they were detained until the 20th, having no means of crossing the river; but on the 20th the guard brought to and captured a boat, in which the men and arms were safely transported to the other shore. There was still, however, an extensive sheet of water to be passed, which on sounding proved to be up to the arm-pits. When this discovery was made, the whole detachment began to manifest signs of alarm and despair, which Colonel Clark observing, took a little powder in his hand, mixed some water with it, and having blackened his face, raised an Indian war whoop and marched into the water. The effect of the example was electrical, and the men followed without a murmur. In this manner, and singing in chorus, the troops made their way through the water, almost constantly waist deep, until they arrived within sight of the town. The immense exertion required to effect this march may not be described. The difficulty was greatly heightened by there being no timber to afford support to the wearied soldiers, who were compelled to force their way through the stagnant waters, with no aid but their own strength. When they reached the dry land the men were so exhausted, that many of them fell, leaving their bodies half immersed in the water. Having captured a man who was shooting ducks in the neighborhood of the town, by him Clark sent a letter to the inhabitants, informing them that he should take possession of the town that night. So much did this letter take the town by surprise, that the expedition was thought to be from Kentucky; in the condition of the waters they did not dream that it could be from Illinois. The inhabitants could not have been more astonished if the invaders had arisen out of the earth.

On the evening of the 23d the detachment set off to take possession of the town. After marching and countermarching around the elevations on the plain, and displaying several sets of colors, to convey to the garrison as exaggerated an idea as possible of their numbers, they took position on the heights back of the village. The fire upon the fort immediately commenced, and was kept up with spirit. Our

16

men would lie within thirty yards of the fort, untouched by its guns, from the awkward elevation of its platforms; while no sooner was a port-hole opened than a dozen rifles would be directed at it, cutting down every thing in the way. The garrison became discouraged, and could not stand to their guns, and in the evening of the next day the British commandant finding his cannon useless, and apprehensive of the result of being taken at discretion, sent a flag asking a truce of three days. This was refused, and on the 24th of February, 1779, the fort was surrendered and the garrison became prisoners of war. On the 25th it was taken possession of by the Americans, the stars and stripes were again hoisted, and thirteen guns fired to celebrate the victory.

In a few days Colonel Clark returned to Kaskaskia. Soon after this Louisville was founded, and he made it his head-quarters. In 1780 he built Fort Jefferson, on the Mississippi. In the course of this year he led an expedition against the Indians of Ohio, the occasion of which was as follows: on the 1st of June, 1780, the British commander at Detroit, assembled six hundred Canadians and Indians, for a secret expedition under Colonel Byrd, against the settlements in Kentucky. This force, accompanied by two field pieces, presented itself on the 22d, before Ruddell's station, which was obliged to capitulate. Soon after Martin's station shared the same fate, and the inhabitants, loaded with the spoil of their own dwellings, were hurried off towards Canada.

A prompt retaliation was required, and when Col. Clark called on the militia of Kentucky for volunteers to accompany his regiment against the Indians, they flocked to his standard without delay. The point of rendezvous was the mouth of Licking river, where the forces assembled. They were supplied with artillery, conveyed up the river from the Falls. When all assembled, the force amounted to near a thousand men. The secrecy and dispatch which had ever attended the movements of this efficient commander, continued to mark his progress on this occasion. The Indian town was reached before the enemy had received any intimation of their approach. A sharp conflict ensued, in which seventeen of the savages were slain, with an equal loss on the part of the whites. The Indians then fled, the town was reduced to ashes, and the gardens and fields laid waste. Col. Clark returned to the Ohio and discharged the militia, and the Indians, reduced to the necessity of hunting for the support of their families, gave the whites no farther trouble that season.

For a long time the ever active mind of Clark had been revolving a scheme for the reduction of the British post at Detroit, and in December of the year 1780, he repaired to Richmond, to urge the government to furnish him with means to execute this long cherished design. His views were approved; but before the necessary arrangements could be completed, a British force from New York, under Arnold, carried hostilities into the heart of the State. Clark took a temporary command under Baron Steuben, and participated in the active operations of that officer against the marauding traitor.

After several months had been spent in indefatigable efforts to raise a force of two thousand men, for the enterprise against Detroit, the several corps destined for the service were designated, and ordered to rendezvous on the 15th of March, 1781, at the falls of the Ohio, and Clark was raised to the rank of a brigadier general; but unexpected and insuperable difficulties arose, and the ardent genius of the commander was confined to defensive operations. This appears to have been the turning point in the fortunes of the hardy warrior. He had set his heart on destroying the British influence throughout the whole North-Western Territory. Could he have had the means which he required, his advancement in rank would no doubt have been gratifying; but without a general's command, a general's commission was of no value. Dangers and hardships would have been disregarded; but with his small force to be stationed on the frontier to repel the inroads of a few predatory bands of Indians, when he was eager to carry the war to the lakes, was more than he could bear, and it preyed upon his spirit. From this time forth his influence sensibly decreased, and the innate force and energy of his character languished and degenerated.

He was a lion chained, but he was still a lion, and so the enemy found him in 1782. When the news of the disastrous battle of the Blue Licks reached him, he took immediate measures to rouse the country from that benumbed torpor of anguish and despondency in which this great calamity had plunged it, and to carry the war once more into the enemy's country. In September, a thousand mounted riflemen assembled on the banks of the Ohio, at the mouth of Licking, and moved against the Indian towns on the Miami and Scioto. The Indians fled before them, and not more than twelve were killed or taken. Five of their towns were reduced to ashes, and all of their provisions destroyed. The effect of this expedition was such that no formidable party of Indians ever after invaded Kentucky.

In 1786, a new army was raised to march against the Indians on the Wabash, and Clark, at the head of a thousand men, again entered the Indian territory. This expedition proved unfortunate, and was abandoned.

Several years elapsed before the name of General Clark again appeared in connection with public affairs. When Genet, the French minister, undertook to raise and organize a force in Kentucky for a secret expedition against the Spanish possessions on the Mississippi, George Rogers Clark accepted a commission as major general in the armies of France, to conduct the enterprise. But, before the project was put in execution, a counter revolution occurred in France, Genet was recalled, and Clark's commission annulled. Thus terminated his public career.

General Clark was never married. He was long in infirm health, and severely afflicted with a rheumatic affection, which terminated in paralysis, and deprived him of the use of one limb. After suffering under this disease for several years, it finally caused his death in February, 1818. He died and was buried at Locust Grove, near Louisville.

CLAY COUNTY.

Clay county was formed in 1806, and named in honor of General Green Clay. It lies on the south fork of the Kentucky river—and is bounded north by Owsley; east by Breathitt and Perry; south by Knox; and west by Laurel. The face of the country is generally hilly and mountainous—the principal products, corn, wheat and grass; the latter growing spontaneously, in great abundance, on the mountains and in the valleys. Coal is abundant, and is used generally by the inhabitants for fuel. Salt is manufactured at fifteen furnaces in the county, producing it is supposed, from 150,000 to 200,000 bushels per annum, and of the very best quality. About nine miles from Manchester, there is a spring which produces an abundant supply of gas.

The taxable property in Clay county in 1846, was assessed at $513,303; number of acres in the county, 154,370; average value per acre, $1,55; number of white males over twenty-one years of age, 738; children between five and sixteen years of age, 1,180. Population in 1830, 3,549—in 1840, 4,607.

Manchester is the seat of justice, and only town in the county—about eighty miles from Frankfort. It is situated near Goose creek, and contains the usual public buildings, one seminary, one Methodist church, one Reformed church, two taverns, two stores, two groceries, two lawyers, two physicians, and seven or eight mechanics' shops. Population 100. Named for the great manufacturing town of England.

General Green Clay, in honor of whom this county was named, was born in Powhattan county, Virginia, on the 14th August, 1757. He was the son of Charles Clay, and descended from John Clay, a British grenadier, who came to

Virginia during Bacon's rebellion, and declined returning when the king's troops were sent back. Whether this ancestor was from England or Wales, is not certainly known, but from the thin skin and ruddy complexion of his descendants, the presumption is that Wales was his birth place. Green Clay came to Kentucky when but a youth. His education was exceedingly limited. To read, write, and cypher, a slight knowledge of the principles of grammar, together with the rudiments of surveying, constituted his entire stock of scholastic learning. With some men, richly endowed by nature, these are advantages sufficient to insure distinction, or to command a fortune, both of which the subject of this notice effected. The first few years after his arrival in Kentucky, were spent in examining the country, and aiding to expel the savages. He then entered the office of James Thompson, a commissioned surveyor, where he more thoroughly studied the principles and acquired the art of surveying. In executing the work assigned him by his principal, who soon made him a deputy, he became minutely acquainted with the lands in the upper portion of the (then) county of Kentucky. The power (at that time unrestrained), to enter and survey lands, wherever ignorance of a prior location, or a wish to lay a warrant might incline, rendered the titles to land exceedingly doubtful and insecure. Many entries were made on the same land by different individuals, producing expensive litigation, and often occasioning the ruin of one of the parties. Entering and surveying lands at an early day was attended with great danger. The country one vast wilderness, with the exception of a few forts which at rare intervals dotted its surface, was infested by innumerable hordes of savage warriors, wiley and full of stratagem, breathing vengeance against the invaders—rendered the location of lands a perilous employment. Surveying parties consisted generally of not more than four—the surveyor, two chain carriers and a marker—hence more reliance was placed in caution and vigilance than in defence by arms.

Clay soon established a character for judgment, industry and enterprise, which drew to him a heavy business. His memory of localities was remarkable, and enabled him to revisit any spot he had ever seen, without difficulty. His position in the office—his access to books—his retentive memory—his topographical knowledge—enabled him to know when lands were unappropriated. Hence his services were much sought, by all who wished to locate lands in the region of country where he resided. Whilst the great body of land in Kentucky was being appropriated, it was the custom for the holders of warrants to give one half to some competent individual to enter and survey the quantity called for by the warrant. Much of this business was thrown into Clay's hands ; and he thus acquired large quantities of land. He also applied all his slender resources to increase this estate. An anecdote is related which evinces the high estimation in which he held this species of estate,.and the sagacity and foresight of the young surveyor. Having gone to Virginia, soon after the surrender of Cornwallis, at a time when the continental paper money was so depreciated that five hundred dollars were asked for a bowl of rum-toddy, he sold his riding horse to a French officer for twenty-seven thousand dollars of the depreciated currency, and invested it in lands. The lands thus purchased, are at this day worth half a million of dollars.

After the land in the middle and upper parts of the State had been generally entered and appropriated, Clay went below, and on the Ohio and Mississippi rivers entered and surveyed large tracts of land for some gentlemen of Virginia. These surveys were made at a time when the Indians were in the exclusive occupancy of those regions, and so perilous was the business that his chain carriers and marker deserted him, without notice, before his work was entirely completed. Some of his field notes had become defaced, and after being thus abandoned by his companions, he was detained some weeks, revisiting the corners and other objects to renew and finish his notes. His danger in this lone undertaking was great; but notwithstanding all difficulties, so accurately did he accomplish his work, that subsequent surveyors have readily traced the lines, and found the corner trees and other objects called for. During this period he traveled mostly in the night, and slept during the day in thick cane brakes, hollow logs, and the tops of trees. Notwithstanding his heavy engagements in the land business, he devoted several years of his life to politics. Before the erection of Kentucky into a State, he was elected a delegate to the general assembly of Virginia. He was a member of the convention which formed the present constitution of Kentucky. After the admission of Kentucky into the union, he represented Madison county many years in each branch of the legislature. He took a prominent and leading part in all the important legislative measures of his day. The records of the country bear abundant evidence of his great industry, strict attention, capacious intellect, and uniform patriotism. He was particularly observant of the local and personal interests of his immediate constituents, without permitting them to interfere with his general duties as a law maker and statesman. When the last war between Great Britain and the United States was declared, he was a major general in the militia of Kentucky. Determined to lend his service to his country, in this, her second struggle for independence, he adjusted his private affairs preparatory to an absence from home. After the defeat of General Winchester, and the wanton butchery of our troops, who had surrendered under promise of safety and good treatment, the first call for volunteers was responded to from Kentucky, who had been a principal sufferer in that bloody catastrophe, by a general rush to the scene of hostilities. It was necessary to succor fort Meigs, and reinforce General Harrison, to enable him to retake Detroit and invade Canada. For this emergency Kentucky furnished three thousand troops, and placed them under the command of General Green Clay, with the rank of brigadier general.✗ General Clay made all haste to the scene of action, and arrived at fort Meigs on the 4th of May, 1813, cutting his way through the enemy's lines into the fort. It does not consist with the character of this work to narrate the incidents attending this celebrated siege. They belong to the public history of the country, where they may be found related at large. Suffice it to say, that General Clay inspired General Harrison with such confidence in his eminent military abilities, that when that great warrior left fort Meigs, he placed that post under the command of General Clay. In the autumn of 1813, the garrison was besieged by a force of fifteen hundred British and Canadians, and five thousand Indians under Tecumseh; but fearing to attempt its capture by storm, and failing in all their stratagems to draw the garrison from their entrenchments, the enemy soon raised the siege. After this, nothing of special interest occurred until the troops of the garrison were called out to join the army prepared for the invasion of Canada. The term of service of the Kentuckians expiring about this time, they were discharged; but General Clay accompanied the army as far as Detroit, when he returned to his residence in Madison county. He devoted the remaining years of his life to agricultural pursuits, and the regulation of his estate.

General Clay was more robust than elegant in person—five feet eleven inches in height—strong and active—of remarkable constitution—rarely sick, and capable of great toil—submitting to privations without a murmur. No country ever contained, according to its population, a greater number of distinguished men than Kentucky. At an early day, and among the most distinguished, General Clay was a man of mark. He was a devoted husband—a kind and affectionate father—a pleasant neighbor—and a good master. He died at his residence on the 31st of October, 1826, in the seventy-second year of his age.

CLINTON COUNTY.

CLINTON county was formed in 1835, from Wayne and Cumberland, and called for Governor DE WITT CLINTON, of New York. It is situated in the southern part of the State, and bounded on the north by Russell, east by Wayne, south by the Tennessee line, and west by Cumberland. Albany is the seat of justice, about 126 miles from Frankfort.

The taxable property in Clinton, as given in the auditor's report for 1846, is $445,909; number of acres of land in the county

86,610; average value per acre, $2,68; number of white males in the county over twenty-one years of age, 739; number of children between five and sixteen years old, 1,235. Population in 1840, 3,863.

ALBANY, the county seat, contains a court-house and other public buildings, a United Baptist church, one school, three stores, two taverns, three lawyers, two doctors, fifteen mechanics' shops, and one hundred and thirty inhabitants. *Seventy-Six* is a small village, containing a lawyer, post office, tannery, saw and grist mill, and twenty-five inhabitants.

A spur of the Cumberland mountain, called Poplar mountain, penetrates this county, and terminates about two miles west of its centre. In its windings, this mountain makes a beautiful curve, and the valley on the eastern side and within the curve, called Stockton's valley, is fertile limestone land. The elevation of Poplar mountain above the valley is from one thousand to fifteen hundred feet. Coal in abundance, and of the best quality, is found in the mountain, in strata of about four feet. On the top of this mountain, about four miles from Albany, there are three chalybeate springs, which have been visited more or less for eight or ten years. These waters, combined with the purity of the atmosphere, have proved of immense benefit to invalids who have resorted there for their health. From these mountain springs, a most extensive and magnificent view of the surrounding country is presented. On a clear morning the fog seems to rise on the water courses in the distance, and stand just above the trees, when the eye can trace the beautiful Cumberland river in its windings for at least one hundred miles, and may distinctly mark the junction of its tributaries, in a direct line, for thirty miles. The springs are about ten or twelve miles from the Cumberland, and it is believed that, in the hands of an enterprising proprietor, they would soon become a place of great resort. The elevation of the mountain, and the consequent purity of the atmosphere—the beauty and magnificence of the scenery and prospect daily presented to the eye of the visitor, combined with the medicinal virtues of the water, a good host, and intelligent and refined association, would make these springs a most desirable point for a summer excursion.

On Indian creek, about three miles from the mountain springs, there is a perpendicular fall of ninety feet. Above the great falls, for the distance of about two hundred yards, the fall of the stream is gradual, and several fine mills have been erected on it. There are three large springs in the county: one on the south, and two at Albany, which send forth volumes of water sufficiently large to turn a grist mill or other machinery. Wolf river runs through a part of the county, and the Cumberland touches it on the north-west. The face of the country is undulating in some portions of the county; in others, hilly and broken. Besides coal, iron ore abounds, and plaster of Paris, it is reported, has been recently discovered in the hills.

DE WITT CLINTON, whose name this county bears, was a native of New York, and one of the most distinguished men in the United States. He was born at Little Britain, in Orange county, on the 2d of March, 1769. He was educated at Columbia college, and studied law with the Hon. Samuel Jones. He early imbibed a predilection for political life, and the first office he held was that of private secretary to his uncle George Clinton, then governor of New York. In 1797, Mr. Clinton was elected a member of the New York legislature, where he espoused the political sentiments of the republican or democratic party. Two years after, he was elected to the State senate. In 1801, he received the appointment of United States' senator, to fill a vacancy, where he served for two sessions. After that period, he was chosen mayor of New York, and remained in this position, with an intermission of but two years, until 1815. In 1817, he was elected, almost unanimously, governor of his native State—the two great parties having combined for the purpose of raising him to that dignity. He was re-elected in 1820, but declined a candidacy in 1822. In 1824, he was again nominated and elected to the office of governor, and in 1826 was re-elected by a large majority. He died suddenly, while sitting in his library, on the 11th of February, 1828, before completing his last term of office. Mr. Clinton was the projector and the active and untiring friend of the canal system of New York, which has been instrumental in adding so largely to the wealth and population of that great State. He was a man of very superior literary attainments—extensively versed in the physical sciences, and a fine classical and belles-lettres scholar. He was a member of most of the literary and scientific institutions of the United States, and an honorary member of many of the learned societies of Great Britain and the continent of Europe. His moral character was excellent, and his personal appearance commanding, being tall and finely proportioned.

CRITTENDEN COUNTY.

CRITTENDEN county was formed in 1842, and named for the Hon. JOHN J. CRITTENDEN. It is situated in the western part of the State, on the Ohio river—bounded on the north by that river, east by Hopkins, south by Caldwell, and west by Livingston. Coal abounds in the county, and lead and iron ores are found in inexhaustible quantities. In the vicinity of the mines the surface is hilly, but the greater portion of the county is level or gently undulating, and very productive. The principal articles of export are coal, tobacco, corn, wheat, oats, and pork.

The taxable property in 1846 was valued at $666,014; number of acres of land in the county, 162,960 ; average value, $2,09; number of white males over twenty-one years of age, 948 ; number of children between the ages of five and sixteen years, 1,316.

MARION, the seat of justice for Crittenden, contains a new brick court-house and other public buildings, six stores and groceries, one tavern, two houses of entertainment, four lawyers, three doctors, and four mechanics' shops—population 120. Organized in 1842, and named in honor of General Francis Marion. *Clementsburg* is a very small village, situated on the Ohio river.

JOHN JORDAN CRITTENDEN, in honor of whom this county was named, was born in the county of Woodford, within a few miles of the town of Versailles, on the 10th of September, 1786. He is the son of John Crittenden, a revolutionary officer, who emigrated to Kentucky soon after the conclusion of the war. The character of the father may be judged of from the virtues of the children; and applying this rule to the present instance, no man could wish a prouder eulogium than is due to the elder Mr. Crittenden. His four sons, John, Thomas, Robert, and Henry, were all distinguished men—the three first were eminent at the bar, and in public life; and the last, who devoted himself to agricultural pursuits, was nevertheless so conspicuous for talent that his countrymen insisted on their right occasionally to withdraw him from the labors of the farm to those of the public councils. They were all remarkable for those personal qualities that constitute the perfect gentleman. Brave and gallant as the sire from whom they descended, accomplished in mind and manners, men without fear and without reproach, they have made their name a part and parcel of the glory of this commonwealth.

Of the early boyhood of Mr. Crittenden, there is but little that needs to be recorded in as hurried a sketch as this must necessarily be. He received as good an education as could be obtained in the Kentucky schools of that day, and completed his scholastic studies at Washington academy, in Virginia, and at the college of William and Mary, in the same State. On his return to Kentucky, he became a student of law in the office of the honorable George M. Bibb, and under the care of that renowned jurist, he became thoroughly prepared for the practice of his profession. At that period the Green River country was the attractive field for the enterprize of the State, affording to the youth of Kentucky similar inducements to those that the west still continues to offer to the citizens of the older States. Mr. Crittenden commenced the practice of the law in Russellville, in the midst of a host of brilliant competitors. He went there unknown to fame—he left it with a fame as extended as the limits of this great nation. All the honors of his profession were soon his, and while his accurate and thorough knowledge of the law gained for him hosts of clients, his brilliant oratory filled the land with his praise, and the pride of that section of the State demanded that he should serve in the legislative assembly. He was accordingly elected to the legislature from the county of Logan, in 1811; and that noble county conferred the same honor upon him, in six consecutive elections. In 1817, and while a representative from Logan, he was elected speaker of the house of representatives, having thus attained the highest distinction in the popular branch of the legislature of his native State. That same honest pride which had impelled the Green River people to press him into public life, had spread throughout the State, and the *people of Kentucky* resolved to place him where the eyes of the nation might be upon him—confident that he would win honor for himself and advance the fame of those he represented. He was accordingly, in 1817, elected a senator in the congress of the United States, and although the youngest member of that body, no sooner had occasion presented, when it was meet for him to speak, than by the universal acclaim of the American people, he was hailed as among the foremost of our orators—as a fit colleague for Henry Clay himself—and as one who must take rank with our ablest statesmen. His private affairs requiring his unremitted attention, he withdrew from this theatre where he was winning golden opinions from all, to enter more vigorously upon the practice of his profession. In order that he might be enabled to do this in the most favorable manner, he removed to Frankfort, in 1819, at which place the federal court and supreme court of the State are held. But here, again, the same popular love and enthusiasm followed him, and he was compelled to yield a reluctant assent to the wishes of his friends, who desired him to serve them in the legislature. He was elected from Franklin, in 1825—a period memorable in the history of Kentucky. In the Old and New Court controversy, no man occupied a more conspicuous point than Mr. Crittenden, and as the advocate of the laws and constitution of Kentucky, and in the maintenance of a sound private and public faith, no man was more distinguished. He was three times elected to the legislature from Franklin, and during one of the periods, he was again chosen speaker of the house of representatives.

The troubles of that period having subsided, and the public service not requiring the sacrifice of his time and business, he again returned to private life, but was permitted a very short respite from the political arena: for, in 1835, he was once more sent to the senate of the United States, and held the office by re-election until the coming in of the administration of President Harrison. By that patriot president he was appointed attorney general of the United States, and the appointment was hailed by men of all parties as the most appropriate that could have been made. The melancholy death of the president brought into power an administration that forfeited the respect of honorable minds. Mr. Crittenden left it, and resigned his office in a note which he sent to the President, that has been considered an admirable specimen of the manner in which a lofty mind can retire from place, when its possession cannot be held with self respect. But only a few months had elapsed before we find him again in the Senate of the United States, by another election from Kentucky, where he now stands, unrivalled in debate—the acknowledged leader of the great whig party, in an assemblage where the talent of a nation is concentrated. He has been *five* times elected to the senate of the United States from Kentucky—an honor of which no other citizen can boast. The history of congress, while he has been a member, cannot be written without his name standing forth in conspicuous prominence, for he has been truly great upon every question that has been of sufficient importance to interest the public mind. It may be said of him, that he never shrank from public duty, but was always ready to defend his principles and opinions as became a man.

He was an advocate for the last war, and was willing to show his faith by his works, and to volunteer in the service of his country. He served in two campaigns—was aid to Gen. Ramsey in the expedition commanded by Gen. Hopkins, and was aid to Governor Shelby, and served in that capacity with distinguished gallantry at the battle of the Thames. There are not a few of his countrymen who entertain the hope that the highest office in the gift of the American people will at no distant day be conferred upon him. Should it be so, the destinies of the republic will be confided to one whose head and heart qualify him for the great office.

CUMBERLAND COUNTY.

CUMBERLAND county was formed in the year 1798, and called after *Cumberland* river, which runs through the county from one extremity to the other. It is situated in the southern part of the state, adjoining the state of Tennessee—bounded on the north by Adair and Russell; east by Clinton; south by the Tennessee line, and west by Monroe county. The Cumberland river passes through the county from north-east to south-west, and the hills which bound it, with occasional exceptions, are quite lofty, affording as beautiful scenery as any river in the west. The surface of the county and its staple products, are similar to those of the surrounding counties.

The taxable property in Cumberland in 1846, was assessed at $998,886; number of acres of land in the county, 120,996; average value $3.58; number of white males in the county over twenty-one years of age, the same year, 949; number of children between five and sixteen years of age, 1,205. Population in 1840, 6,090.

BURKSVILLE, the seat of justice of Cumberland, (so called in honor of one of the original proprietors,) is about one hundred and twenty miles from Frankfort, and situated on the north bank of the Cumberland river. Besides the usual public buildings, it contains a flourishing academy, six stores and groceries, two taverns, four lawyers, five physicians, twelve mechanics' shops, and a Reformed church. Population 350.

The *American Oil* well is situated three miles above Burksville, on the bank of the Cumberland river. About the year 1830, while some men were engaged in boring for salt-water, and after penetrating about one hundred and seventy-five feet through a solid rock, they struck a vein of oil, which suddenly spouted up to the height of fifty feet above the surface. The stream was so abundant and of such force, as to continue to throw up the oil to the same height for several days. The oil thus thrown out, ran into the Cumberland river, covering the surface of the water for several miles. It was readily supposed to be inflammable, and upon its being ignited, it presented the novel and magnificent spectacle of a "*river on fire*," the flames literally covering the whole surface for miles, reaching to the top of the tallest trees on the banks of the river, and continued burning until the supply of oil was exhausted. The salt borers were greatly disappointed, and the well was neglected for several years, until it was discovered that the oil possessed valuable medicinal qualities. It has since been bottled up in large quantities, and is extensively sold in nearly all the states of the Union.

About fourteen miles from Burksville, on the Cumberland river, and not far from Creelsburg in Russell county, is situated what is termed the "*Rock House*," a lofty arch of solid rock, forty feet in height, fifty or sixty feet in breadth, about the same in length, and a tall cliff overhanging it.   In high stages of the water, a portion of the river rushes through the aperture with great violence down a channel worn into the rock, and pours into the river again about a mile and a half below.   In ordinary stages of the water, the arch, or as generally termed, the "Rock House," is perfectly dry.

Not far from the oil well, at the junction of Big and Little Renick's creeks, there is a beautiful cataract or fall in the latter of about fifteen or twenty feet.   At the point where these streams empty into the Cumberland, there was, in the first settlement of the county, a severe battle between the whites and Indians, in which the former were the victors.   The rock-bound graves of the latter can yet be seen on the ground, a lasting monument of the valor they exhibited in defence of their wigwams, their fires and their hunting grounds.   Other battles also took place in the county, but the particulars cannot be gathered.

DAVEISS COUNTY.

Daveiss county was formed in 1815, and was so called after the gallant Joseph H. Daveiss, who fell at the battle of Tippecanoe. It lies upon the Ohio and Green rivers :   Bounded north by the Ohio river; east by Hancock and Ohio; south by Muhlenburg and Hopkins, and west by Henderson.   The lands are generally level, fertile and well adapted to the production of corn and tobacco, its principal exports.   Hemp has been cultivated for a few years past as an experiment, and the crops produced compare well in quantity and quality with those in the best hemp region. Grasses also succeed well, and there is an increased attention to stock raising in the county.   The lands are heavily timbered, consisting of sugar tree, locust, hackberry, walnut, dogwood, beech and poplar.

The taxable property of Daveiss in 1846, was valued at $2,558,592; number of acres of land in the county, 306,651; average value of lands per acre, $4,20 ; number of white males over twenty-one years of age, 1,674 ; number of children between five and sixteen years old, 1,928.   Population in 1830, 5,218—in 1840, 8,331—increase in ten years, 3,113.

The towns of the county are Owenborough, Bon Harbor, Nottsville and Yelvington.   Owenborough, the seat of justice, is situated on the Ohio river at the Yellow Banks, about one hundred and thirty miles from Frankfort.   Contains a handsome court-house, Baptist, Cumberland Presbyterian and Catholic churches, an academy and common school, ten dry good stores, three groceries, four taverns, six lawyers and four physicians, with a population of about 1,000.   A considerable trade is carried on by this town with the interior of the country, especially during a suspension of navigation on Green river; and the tobacco stemming business is extensively carried on here.   Bon Harbor is a small village, three miles below Owenborough, on the Ohio river, where there is an eddy formed by a bar, which serves as an excellent harbor for steam boats and other craft.   This place bids fair to become quite a manufacturing town. *Nottsville* is a small village, thirteen miles from Owenborough, on the Hardinsburg road. *Yelvington* is a small village, eleven miles from Owenborough, on the Hawesville road.

Daveiss county abounds in mineral resources, especially coal, which is found in vast quantities. The only mine which is in successful operation, is that known as the "Bon Harbor coal mine," lying about three miles below the county seat, and three-fourths of a mile from the Ohio river. There is a railroad from the mine to the river, at the terminus of which, the owners of the mine have erected one of the largest cotton and woollen manufactories in the west. At this point there has been a town laid off, and several very handsome houses built. The population, composed principally of operatives, already numbers two or three hundred.

There are several medicinal springs in the county, which are frequented by those in the immediate vicinity. The tar and sulphur springs in the neighborhood of the "Old Vernon settlements" on Green river, are deservedly the most popular.

Colonel JOSEPH HAMILTON DAVEISS, (for whom this county was named,) was the son of Joseph and Jean Daveiss, and was born in Bedford county, Virginia, on the 4th of March, 1774. The parents of Mr. Daveiss, were both natives of Virginia; but his father was of Irish, his mother of Scotch descent; and the marked peculiarities of each of those races were strongly developed in the character of their son. The hardy self-reliance, the indomitable energy, and imperturbable coolness, which have from earliest time distinguished the Scotch, were his; while the warm heart, free and open hand, and ready springing tear of sensibility, told in language plainer than words, that the blood of Erin flowed fresh in his veins. When young Daveiss was five years old, his parents removed to Kentucky, then an almost unbroken wilderness, and settled in the then county of Lincoln, in the immediate vicinity of the present town of Danville. An incident which attended their journey to Kentucky, although trifling in itself, may be related, as exhibiting in a very striking light the character of the mother, to whose forming influence was committed the subject of this notice. In crossing the Cumberland river, Mrs. Daveiss was thrown from her horse, and had her arm broken. The party only halted long enough to have the limb bound up, with what rude skill the men of the company possessed; and pursued their route, she riding a spirited horse and carrying her child, and never ceasing her exertions to promote the comforts of her companions when they stopped for rest and refreshment. The parents of young Daveiss, in common with the very early settlers of Kentucky, had many difficulties to encounter in raising their youthful family, especially in the want of schools to which children could be sent to obtain the rudiments of an English education. It was several years after their settlement in Kentucky, before the subject of this sketch enjoyed even the advantages of a common country school. Previous to this time, however, his mother had bestowed considerable attention in the education of her sons, by communicating such information as she herself possessed. At the age of eleven or twelve, he was sent to a grammar school taught by a Mr. Worley, where he continued for about two years, learned the Latin language, and made considerable progress in his English education. He subsequently attended a grammar school taught by a Dr. Brooks, at which he remained a year, making considerable advances in a knowledge of the Greek language. At school he evinced unusual capacity, being always at the head of his class. He was particularly remarkable for his talent for declamation and public speaking, and his parents felt a natural anxiety to give him as many advantages as their limited resources would permit. There being at that time no college in the country, he was placed under the charge of a Dr. Culbertson, where he completed his knowledge of the Greek tongue. At this time, the sudden death of a brother and sister occasioned his being recalled from school, and he returned home to assist his father in the labors of the farm. There is a tradition that young Daveiss was not particularly distinguished by his devotion to agricultural pursuits, frequently permitting the horses of his plough to graze at leisure, in a most unfarmerlike way, while he, stretched supinely on his back on some luxurious log, indulged in those delicious dreams and reveries so sweet to young and aspiring ambition.

In the autumn of 1792, Major Adair, under government orders, raised some companies of mounted men, to guard the transportation of provisions to the forts north of the Ohio river, and Daveiss, then in his 18th year, volunteered in the service, which it was understood would be from three to six months duration. Nothing of particular interest occurred in the course of this service, except on one occasion, when Major Adair had encamped near fort St. Clair. Here he was surprised, early in the morning, by a large body of Indians, who, rushing into the camp just after the sentinels had been withdrawn from their posts, killed and wounded fourteen or fifteen of the men, and captured and carried away about two hundred head of horses. These were taken within the Indian lines and tied. After the whites had sought shelter in the neighborhood of the fort, young Daveiss, discovering his own horse at some distance hitched to a tree, resolved to have him at all hazards. He accordingly ran and cut him loose, and led him back to his companions amid a shower of balls. This exploit nearly cost him his life; a ball passing through his coat, waistcoat, and cutting off a small piece of his shirt. He, however, saved his horse, which was the only one retaken out of the two hundred.

When his term of service expired, he returned home, and spent some time in reviewing his classical studies. He ultimately concluded to study law, and accordingly entered the office of the celebrated George Nicholas, then the first lawyer in Kentucky. Daveiss entered a class of students consisting of Isham Talbott, Jesse Bledsoe, William Garrard, Felix Grundy, William Blackbourne, John Pope, William Stuart, and Thomas Dye Owings, all of whom were subsequently distinguished at the bar and in the public history of the country. Nicholas was very profoundly impressed with the striking indications of genius of a high order, manifested by Daveiss while under his roof; and so high an opinion did he form of the power of his character and the firmness of his principles, that at his death, which occurred but a few years after, he appointed him one of his executors. He was a most laborious and indefatigable student; he accustomed himself to take his repose upon a hard bed; was fond of exercise in the open air, habituating himself to walking several hours in each day; he was accustomed in the days when he was a student, to retire to the woods with his books, and pursue his studies in some remote secluded spot, secure from the annoyance and interruption of society. In connection with his legal studies, he read history and miscellaneous literature, so that when he came to the bar, his mind was richly stored with various and profound knowledge, imparting a fertility and affluence to his resources, from which his powerful and well trained intellect drew inexhaustible supplies. He commenced the practice of the law in June, 1795; in August he was qualified as an attorney in the court of appeals; and in his first cause had for an antagonist his old preceptor, over whom he enjoyed the singular gratification of obtaining a signal triumph.

At the session of 1795–6, the legislature passed a law establishing district courts. One of these courts was located at Danville, one at Lexington, and one at Bardstown. Daveiss settled at Danville, and soon commanded a splendid business, not only in that, but in all the courts in which he practiced. He continued to reside in Danville until the abolition of the district courts, and the substitution of circuit courts in their place. He then removed to Frankfort, to be enabled more conveniently to attend the court of appeals and the federal court, having been appointed United States' attorney for the State of Kentucky. In the year 1801 or '2, he went to Washington city, being the first western lawyer who ever appeared in the supreme court of the United States. He here argued the celebrated cause of Wilson vs. Mason. His speech is said to have excited the highest admiration of the bench and bar, and placed him at once in the foremost rank of the profession. During this trip he visited the principal cities of the north and east, and formed an acquaintance with many of the most distinguished men of America, with several of whom he continued to correspond until the period of his death. In 1803, he was united in marriage to Anne Marshall, the sister of the chief justice of the United States. After he had resided in Frankfort a few years, he removed to Owensburg, Daveiss county, to be able to attend more closely to the interests of a large property he had acquired in that region. In 1809, he removed to Lexington, and resumed the practice of the law. During the short period of two years previous to his death, there was hardly a cause of importance litigated in the courts where he practiced, that he was not engaged on one side or the other. We should have noticed before, his prosecution of Aaron Burr for treason, whilst acting as attorney for the United States. He had noticed the movements of this person for some time before he commenced a prosecution, and became satisfied from his observations that he had some unlawful design in view; and, considering it to be his duty to arrest his movements, he caused him to be apprehended and brought before the court; but, from a failure of evidence, the prosecution was ultimately abandoned.

In the fall of 1811, Colonel Daveiss joined the army of General Harrison, in the campaign against the Indians on the Wabash. He received the command of major, the duties of which station he discharged promptly, and to the entire satisfaction of his superior officer. On the 7th of November, 1811, in the celebrated battle of Tippecanoe, he fell in a charge against the Indians, made at his own solicitation. He survived from 5 o'clock in the morning until midnight, retaining to the last the full command of all his faculties.

Colonel Daveiss was near six feet high, with an athletic and vigorous form, combining with his high intellectual endowments, a remarkably commanding and impressive personal appearance. His bearing was grave and dignified. His manner bland and courteous to those he loved, but haughty and repulsive in the extreme to those he disliked. As an orator, he had few equals and no superiors. The late Judge Boyle, the Hon. John Pope, and the Hon. Samuel M'Kee, all competent judges, and associates of Daveiss at the bar, frequently declared that he was the most impressive speaker they ever heard. As a colloquialist, he was unequalled, and the life of every circle in which he was thrown. His death occasioned a shock in the public mind throughout the State.

EDMONSON COUNTY.

EDMONSON county was formed in 1825, and named for Captain JOHN EDMONSON. It is situated in the south-west middle section of the State, and lies on both sides of Green river—bounded on the north and north-west by Grayson, east by Hart and Barren, and south and south-west by Warren. The face of the county is generally undulating, and in some places quite hilly. There are several sulphur springs in the county, with ores of various kinds, and an inexhaustible supply of stone coal. The staple products are corn and oats.

The taxable property of the county in 1846, was valued at $401,127; number of acres of land in the county, 124,038; average value of land per acre, $1,97; number of white males over twenty-one years old, 604; number of children between five and sixteen years of age, 955. Population in 1830, 2,642—in 1840, 2,914.

BROWNSVILLE, the seat of justice and only town in Edmonson, is one hundred and thirty miles from Frankfort—contains a Baptist and a Methodist church, an academy, two stores, two taverns, two lawyers, two doctors, (and three in the vicinity), and eight mechanics' shops. Population 150. Established in 1828, and named in honor of General Jacob Brown.

There are three natural curiosities in this county: the "Dismal Rock," the "Indian Hill," and the "Mammoth Cave." Dismal Rock is a perpendicular rock on Dismal creek, one hundred and sixty-three feet high. The Indian Hill lies one mile from Brownsville—is circular at its base, and one mile in circumference—its altitude eighty-four feet, and, except on one side, which is easy of ascent on foot, perpendicular. The remains of a fortification are seen around the brow, and a number of mounds and burial places are scattered over the area. A spring of fine water issues from the rock near the surface.

The MAMMOTH CAVE.—In Edmonson county is situated, perhaps the greatest natural wonder of the world, the celebrated *Mammoth Cave.* In no other place has nature exhibited her varied powers on a more imposing scale of grandeur and magnificence. The materials of the following sketch of this cave, are derived, principally, from a small publication issued by Morton & Griswold, of Louisville, entitled "Rambles in the Mammoth Cave, during the year 1844, by a Visitor." This publication contains, we believe, the most complete and accurate description of this subterranean palace that has yet appeared, and gives the reader a very vivid conception of that amazing profusion of grand, solemn, picturesque and romantic scenery, which impresses every beholder with astonishment and awe, and attracts to this cave crowds of visitors from every quarter of the world.

The cave is situated equi-distant from the cities of Louisville and Nashville, (about ninety miles from each,) and immediately on the nearest road between those two places. Green river is distant from the cave only half a mile, and since the improvements effected in the navigation of that stream, by the construction of locks and dams, steam boats can at all seasons ascend to Bowling-green, twenty miles below the cave, and during a great part of the year to the cave itself. For a distance of two miles from the cave, by the approach from the south-east, the country is level. It was, until recently, a prairie, on which however the oak, chestnut, and hickory are now growing; and there being no underbrush, its smooth verdant openings present here and there, a close resemblance to the parks of the English nobility. Emerging from these beautiful woodlands, the visitor is presented with a view of the hotel and adjacent grounds. The hotel is a large edifice, two hundred feet long, by forty-five wide, with piazzas sixteen feet wide, extending the whole length of the building above and below. The accommodations at this hotel are kept up in superior style.

The cave is about two hundred yards from the hotel, and is approached through a romantic and beautiful dell, shaded by a forest of trees and grape-vines. Passing by the ruins of some old salt-petre furnaces, and large mounds of ashes, and turning abruptly to the right, the visitor is suddenly startled by a rush of cold air, and beholds before him the yawning mouth of the great cavern, dismal, dark and dreary. Descend some thirty feet, by rude steps of stone, and you are fairly under the arch of this "nether world." Before you, in looking towards the entrance, is seen a small stream of water, falling from the face of the rock, upon the ruins below, and disappearing in a deep pit; behind you, all is gloom and darkness. Proceeding onward about one hundred feet, the progress of the explorer is arrested by a door, set in a rough stone wall, which stretches across and completely blocks up the entrance to the cave. Passing through this door, you soon enter a narrow passage, faced on the left by a wall, built by the miners to confine the loose stones thrown up in the course of their labors, and descending gradually a short distance along this passage, you arrive at the great vestibule or ante-chamber of the cave. This is a hall of an oval shape, two hundred feet in length by one hundred and fifty wide, with a roof as flat and level as if finished by the trowel, and from fifty to sixty feet high. Two passages, each a hundred feet in width, open into it at its opposite extremities, but at right angles to each other; and as they run in a straight course for five or six hundred feet, with the same flat roof common to each, the appearance presented to the eye is that of a vast hall in the shape of the letter L, expanded at the angle, both branches being five hundred feet long by one hundred wide. The passage to the right hand is "Audubon Avenue." That in the front, the beginning of the grand gallery or the main cavern itself. The entire extent of this prodigious space is covered by a single rock, in which the eye can detect no break or interruption, save at its borders, which are surrounded by a broad sweeping cornice, traced in horizontal panel work, exceedingly noble and regular. Not a single pier or pillar of any kind contributes to support it. It needs no support; but is

"By its own weight made steadfast and immoveable."

At a very remote period, this chamber seems to have been used as a cemetery; and there have been disinterred many skeletons of gigantic dimensions, belonging to a race of people long since vanished from the earth. Such is the vestibule of the Mammoth cave. The walls of this chamber are so dark that they reflect not one single ray of light from the dim torches. Around you is an impenetrable wall of darkness, which the eye vainly seeks to pierce, and a canopy of darkness, black and rayless, spreads above you. By the aid, however, of a fire or two which the guides kindle from the remains of some old wooden ruins, you begin to acquire a better conception of the scene around you. Far up, a hundred feet above your head, you catch a fitful glimpse of a dark gray ceiling, rolling dimly away like a cloud, and heavy buttresses, apparently bending under the superincumbent weight, project their enormous masses from the shadowy wall. The scene is vast, and solemn and awful. A profound silence, gloomy, still and breathless, reigns unbroken by even a sigh of air, or the echo of a drop of water falling from the roof. You can hear the throbbings of your heart, and the mind is oppressed with a sense of vastness, and solitude, and grandeur indescribable.

Leaving this ante-chamber by an opening on the right, the visitor enters Audubon avenue, which is a chamber more than a mile long, fifty or sixty feet wide, and as many high. The roof or ceiling of this apartment, exhibits the appearance of floating clouds. Near the termination of this avenue, a natural well twenty-five feet deep, and containing the purest water, has been within the last few years discovered. It is surrounded by stalagmite columns, extending from the floor to the roof, upon the incrustation of which, when lights are suspended, the reflection from the water below and the various objects above and around, gives to the whole scene an appearance most romantic and picturesque. This spot, however, being difficult of access, is but seldom visited. The Little Bat room cave—a branch of Audubon avenue, is on the left as you advance, and not more than three hundred yards from the great vestibule. It is a little over a quarter of a mile in length, and is chiefly remarkable for its pit of two hundred and eighty feet in depth; and as being the resort, in winter, of immense numbers of bats. During this season of the year, tens of thousands of these are seen hanging from the walls, in apparently a torpid state, but no sooner does spring open than they disappear.

From the Little Bat Room, and Audubon Avenue, the visitor returns into the vestibule, from whence, by another passage, at right angles to that just mentioned, he enters the grand gallery or main cavern. This is a vast tunnel, extending for many miles, averaging throughout fifty feet in width by as many in height. This noble subterranean avenue, the largest of which we have any knowledge, is replete with interest from its varied characteristics and majestic grandeur. Proceeding down this main cave a quarter of a mile, the visitor comes to the Kentucky cliffs, so called from a fancied resemblance to the cliffs on the Kentucky river, and descending gradually about twenty feet, enters the *Church*. The ceiling here is sixty-three feet high, and the *church* itself, including the recess, is about one hundred feet in diameter. Eight or ten feet above the *pulpit*, and immediately behind it, is the *organ* loft, which is sufficiently capacious for an organ and choir of the largest size. This *church* is large enough to contain thousands, a solid projection of the wall seems to have been designed as a pulpit, and a few feet back is a place well calculated for an organ and choir. In this great temple of nature, religious service has been frequently performed, and it requires but a slight effort on the part of the speaker to make himself heard by the largest congregation.

Leaving the church, the visitor is brought to the ruins of the old nitre works, leaching vats, pump frames, &c., &c., and looking from thence some thirty feet above, will see a large cave, connected with which is a narrow gallery, sweeping across the main cave, and losing itself in a cave which is seen above, upon the right. This latter cave is the Gothic Avenue, which no doubt was at one time connected with the cave opposite, and on the same level, forming a complete bridge over the main cave, but has been broken down and separated by some great convulsion. The cave on the left, which is filled with sand, has been penetrated but a short distance. The Gothic Avenue, to which the visitor ascends from the main cave by a flight of stairs, is about forty feet wide, fifteen feet high, and two miles long. The ceiling in many places is as smooth and white as if formed by the trowel of the most skillful plasterer. In a recess on the left hand, elevated a few feet above the floor, two mummies, long since taken away, were to be seen in 1813. They were in good preservation—one was a female, with her extensive wardrobe placed before her. Two of the miners found a mummy in Audubon avenue in 1814; but having concealed it, it was not found until 1840, when it was so much injured and broken to pieces by the weights which had been placed upon it, as to be of no value. There is no doubt that by proper efforts discoveries might be made which would throw light on the history of the early inhabitants of this continent. A highly scientific gentleman of New York, one of the early visitors to the cave, says in his published narrative:

"On my first visit to the Mammoth Cave in 1813, I saw a relic of ancient times which requires a minute description. This description is from a memorandum made in the cave at the time.

"In the digging of saltpetre earth in the short cave, a flat rock was met with by the workmen, a little below the surface of the earth, in the cave: this stone was raised, and was about four feet wide, and as many long; beneath it was a square excavation about three feet deep, and as many in length and width. In this small nether subterranean chamber sat in solemn silence one of the human species, a female, with her wardrobe and ornaments placed at her side. The body was in a state of perfect preservation, and sitting erect. The arms were folded up, and the hands were laid across the bosom; around the two wrists was wound a small cord, designed, probably, to keep them in the posture in which they were first placed; around the body and next thereto were wrapped two deer skins. These skins appeared to have been dressed in some mode different from what is now practiced by any people of whom I have any knowledge. The hair of the skins was cut off very near the surface. The skins were ornamented with the imprints of vines and leaves, which were sketched with a substance perfectly white. Outside of these two skins was a large square sheet, which was either wove or knit. The fabric was the inner bark of a tree, which I judge from appearances to be that of the linn tree. In its texture and appearance, it resembled the south sea island cloth or matting; this sheet enveloped the whole body or head. The hair on the head was cut off within an eighth of an inch of the skin, except near the neck, where it was an inch long. The color of the hair was a dark red; the teeth were white and perfect. I discovered no blemish upon the body, except a wound between two ribs, near the back bone; and one of the eyes had also been injured. The finger and toe nails were perfect and quite long. The features were regular. I measured the length of one of the bones of the arm with a string, from the elbow to the wrist joint, and they equalled my own in length, viz:—ten and a half inches. From the examination of the whole frame I judged the figure to be that of a very tall female, say five feet ten inches in height. The body, at the time it was discovered, weighed but fourteen pounds, and was perfectly dry; on exposure to the atmosphere, it gained in weight, by absorbing dampness, four pounds. Many persons have expressed surprise that a human body of great size should weigh so little, as many human skeletons, of nothing but bone, exceed this weight.

"Recently some experiments have been made in Paris, which have demonstrated the fact of the human body being reduced to ten pounds, by being exposed to a heated atmosphere for a long period of time. The color of the skin was dark, not black; the flesh was hard and dry upon the bones. At the side of the body lay a pair of moccasins, a knapsack, and an indispensable, or reticule. I will describe these in the order in which I have named them. The moccasins were made of wove or knit bark, like the wrapper I have described. Around the top was a border to add strength, and perhaps as an ornament. These were of middling size, denoting feet of a small size. The shape of the moccasins differs but little from the deer skin moccasins worn by the northern Indians. The knapsack was of wove or knit bark, with a deep strong border around the top, and was about the size of knapsacks used by soldiers. The workmanship of it was neat, and such as would do credit as a fabric, to a manufacturer of the present day. The reticule was also made of knit or wove bark. The shape was much like a horseman's valise, opening its whole length on the top. On the side of the opening, and a few inches from it, were two rows of loops, one row on each side. Two cords were fastened to one end of the reticule at the top, which passed through the loop on one side, and then on the other side, the whole length, by which it was laced up and secured. The edges of the top of the reticule were strengthened with deep fancy borders. The articles contained in the knapsack and reticule were quite numerous, and were as follows; one head cap, made of wove or knit bark, without any border, and of the shape of the plainest night cap; seven head dresses, made of the quills of large birds, and put together somewhat in the way that feather fans are made, except that the pipes of the quills are not drawn to a point, but are spread out in straight lines with the top. This was done by perforating the pipe of the quill in two places, and running two cords through the holes, and then winding round the quills and the cord fine thread, to fasten each quill in the place designed for it. These cords extended some length beyond the quills on each side, so that on placing the feathers erect, the cords could be tied together at the back of the head. This would enable the wearer to present a beautiful display of feathers standing erect, and extending a distance above the head, and entirely surrounding it. These were most splendid head dresses, and would be a magnificent ornament to the head of a female at the present day. Several hundred strings of beads; these consisted of very hard, brown seed, smaller than hemp seed, in each of which a small hole had been made, and through the whole a small three corded thread, similar in appearance and texture to seine twine; these were tied up in bunches, as a merchant ties up coral beads when he exposes them for sale. The red hoofs of fawns, on a string supposed to be worn around the neck as a necklace. These hoofs were about twenty in number, and may have been emblematic of innocence. The claw of an eagle, with a hole made in it through which a cord was passed, so that it could be worn pendant from the neck. The jaw of a bear, designed to be worn in the same manner as the eagle's claw, and supplied with a cord to suspend it around the neck. Two rattlesnake skins; one of these had fourteen rattles; these skins were neatly folded up. Some vegetable colors done up in leaves. A small bunch of deer sinews, resembling cat-gut in appearance. Several bunches of thread and twine, two and three threaded, some of which were nearly white. Seven needles, some of which were of horn and some of bone; they were smooth, and appeared to have been much used. These needles had each a knob or whorl on the top, and at the other end were brought to a point like a large sail needle. They had no eyelets to receive a thread. The top of one of these needles was handsomely scolloped. A hand piece made of deer-skin, with a hole through it for the thumb, and designed probably to protect the hand in the use of the needle, the same as thimbles are now used. Two whistles, about eight inches long, made of cane, with a joint about one third the length; over the joint is an opening extending to each side of the tube of the whistle; these openings were about three quarters of an inch long, and an inch wide, and had each a flat reed placed in the opening. These whistles were tied together with a cord wound round them.

"I have been thus minute in describing this mute witness from the days of other times, and the articles which were deposited within her earthen house. Of the race of people to whom she belonged when living we know nothing; and as to conjecture, the reader who gathers from these pages this account, can judge of the matter as well as those who saw the remnant of mortality in the subterranean chambers in which she was entombed. The cause of the preservation of her body, dress, and ornaments, is no mystery. The dry atmosphere of the cave, with the nitrate of lime, with which the earth that covers the bottom of these nether palaces is so highly impregnated, preserves animal flesh, and it will neither putrify nor decompose when confined to its unchanging action. Heat and moisture are both absent from the cave, and it is these two agents acting together which produce both animal and vegetable decomposition and putrefaction.

"In the ornaments, &c., of this mute witness of ages gone, we have a record of olden-time, from which, in the absence of a written record, we may draw some conclusions. In the various articles which constituted her ornaments, there were no metallic substances. In the make of her dress, there is no evidence of the use of any other machinery than the bone and horn needles. The beads are of a substance, of the use of which for such purposes we have no account among people of whom we have any written record. She had no warlike arms. By what process the hair on her head was cut short, or by what process the deer skins were shorn, we have no means of conjecture. These articles afford us the same means of judging of the nation to which she belonged, and of their advances in the arts, that future generations will have in the exhumation of a tenant of one of our modern tombs, with the funeral shroud &c. in a state of like preservation; with this difference, that with the present inhabitants of this section of the globe, but few articles of ornament are deposited with the body. The features of this ancient member of the human family much resembled those of a tall, handsome, American woman. The forehead was high, and the head well formed."

In this chamber (the Gothic Avenue), there are to be seen a number of stalagmite pillars reaching from the floor to the ceiling, once white and translucent, but now black and begrimed with smoke. In this chamber, too, there are a number of stalactites, one of which, called the Bell, on being struck, gave forth a sound like the deep bell of a cathedral; but was broken several years ago by a

visitor, and now tolls no longer.   In this chamber, also, are Louisa's Bower and
Vulcan's Furnace.   In the latter, there is a heap not unlike cinders in appearance,
and some dark colored water.   Here, too, are the Register Rooms, where on a
ceiling as smooth and white as if finished by art,·thousands of names have been
traced by the smoke of a candle.   In this neighborhood the visitor reaches the
Stalagmite Hall or Gothic Chapel, an elliptical chamber, eighty feet long by fifty
feet wide.   Stalagmite columns, of enormous size, nearly block up the two ends;
and two rows of pillars of smaller dimensions, reaching from the floor to the ceiling,
and equi-distant from the wall on either side, extend the entire length of the hall.
This apartment is one of surprising grandeur and magnificence, and when brilliantly lighted up by the lamps, presents a scene inspiring the beholder with feelings of solemnity and awe.   The Devil's Arm Chair is a large stalagmite column,
in the centre of which is formed a capacious and comfortable seat.   Near the foot
of the Chair is a small basin of sulphur water.   In this Avenue are situated
Napoleon's Breast Work, the Elephant's Head, and the Lover's Leap.   The latter
is a large pointed rock, projecting over a dark and gloomy hollow, thirty feet
deep.   Descending into the hollow, immediately below the Lover's Leap, the
visitor enters, to the left, a passage or chasm in the rock, three feet wide and fifty
feet high, which leads to the lower branch of the Gothic Avenue.   At the entrance of this lower branch, is a large flat rock called Gatewood's Dining Table,
to the right of which is a cave, in which is situated the Cooling Tub,—a beautiful basin of six feet wide and three deep—into which a small stream of the purest water pours from the ceiling and afterwards flows into the Flint Pit.   Cir-
cling round Gatewood's Dining Table, which almost blocks up the way, the
visitor passes Napoleon's Dome, the Cinder Banks, the Crystal Pool, the Salts
Cave, etc., and descending a few feet, and leaving the direct course of the cave,
enters on the right Annett's Dome,—a place of great seclusion and grandeur.
Through a crevice in the wall of this Dome is a beautiful waterfall—issuing in a
stream of a foot in diameter from a high cave in the side of the dome, and passing off by a small channel into the Cistern, a large pit directly in the pathway
of the cave, which is usually full of water.   Near the end of this lower branch
of the Gothic Avenue, there is a crevice in the ceiling over the last spring,
through which the sound of water may be heard falling in a cave or open space
above.

Returning from the Gothic Avenue, again into the main cave, which continues
to increase in interest as he advances, the visitor is met at every step by something to elicit his admiration and wonder.   At a small distance from the stairs
which descend from the Gothic Avenue into the main cave, is situated the Ball
Room, so called from its singular adaptation to such assemblages.   Here is an
orchestra fifteen feet high, large enough to accommodate a hundred musicians,
with a gallery extending back to the level of the high embankment near the
Gothic Avenue; and the cave is here wide, straight, and perfectly level for several
hundred feet.   By the addition of a plank floor, seats and lamps, a ball room
might be furnished, more grand and magnificent than any other on earth.   Next
in order is Willie's Spring, a beautiful fluted niche in the left hand wall, caused
by the continual attrition of water trickling down into the basin below.   Proceeding onwards the visitor passes the Well Cave, Rocky Cave, etc. etc., and ar-
rives at the Giant's Coffin, a huge rock on the right, thus named from its singular resemblance to a coffin.   At this point commence those incrustations which,
assuming every imaginable shape on the ceiling, afford full scope to the fancy,
to picture what it will, whether of "birds, or beasts or creeping things." About a
hundred yards beyond the Coffin, the cave makes a majestic curve, and sweeping
round the Great Bend, resumes its general course.   Here, by means of a Bengal
light, this vast amphitheatre may be illuminated and a scene of enchantment exposed to the view.   No language can describe the splendor and sublimity of the
scene.   Opposite to this point is the entrance to the Sick Room Cave, so called
from the sudden sickness of a visitor, brought on by smoking cigars in one of its
remote nooks.   Immediately beyond this there is situated a row of cabins for
consumptive patients.   These are well furnished, and would, with good and comfortable accommodations, pure air and uniform temperature, cure the pulmonary
consumption.   The atmosphere of the cave is always temperate and pure.

Next in the order of succession, is the Star Chamber.   This is a very remarkable avenue, and presents the most perfect optical illusion; in looking up to the ceiling, which is very high, the spectator seems to see the very firmament itself, studded with stars,—and afar off, a comet, with its long, bright tail. Not far from this Star Chamber, may be seen in a cavity in the wall on the right, and about twenty feet above the floor, an oak pole, about ten feet long and six inches in diameter, with two round sticks of half the thickness, and three feet long, tied on to it transversely, at about four feet apart. One end of this pole rests on the bottom of the cavity, and the other reaching across and forced firmly into a crevice about three feet above. It has been supposed that on this pole was once placed a dead body,—similar contrivances being used by some Indian tribes, on which to place their dead. This pole was first discovered in 1841. Ages have rolled away since it was placed here, and yet it is perfectly sound. In this neighborhood there are Side Cuts, as they are called; caves opening on the sides of the avenues, and after proceeding some distance, entering them again. Some of these side cuts exceed half a mile in length, but they are generally short.

The visitor next enters the Salts room, the walls and ceiling of which are covered with salts hanging in crystals. In this room are the Indian houses under the rocks,—small spaces or rooms completely covered—some of which contain ashes and cane partly burnt. The Cross rooms is a grand section of this avenue; the ceiling presenting an unbroken span of one hundred and seventy feet, without a column to support it. In this neighborhood are the Black Chambers, in which are to be seen many curious and remarkable objects. The Humble Chute is the entrance to the Solitary chambers, in going into which you must crawl on your hands and knees some fifteen or twenty feet under a low arch. In the Solitary cave is situated the Fairy Grotto; here an immense number of stalactites are seen at irregular distances, extending from the roof to the floor, of various sizes and of the most fantastic shapes—some straight, some crooked, some large and hollow, forming irregularly fluted columns; and some solid near the ceiling, and divided lower down, into a great number of small branches like the roots of trees, exhibiting the appearance of a coral grove. Lighted up by lamps, this grove of stalactites exhibits a scene of extraordinary beauty. Returning from the Fairy Grotto, you re-enter the main cave at the Cataract, and come next to the chief city or Temple, which is thus described by Lee in his notes on the Mammoth Cave:

"The Temple is an immense vault, covering an area of two acres, and covered by a single dome of solid rock, one hundred and twenty feet high. It excels in size the cave of Staffa; and rivals the celebrated vault in the Grotto of Antiparos, which is said to be the largest in the world. In passing through from one end to the other, the dome appears to follow like the sky in passing from place to place on the earth. In the middle of the dome there is a large mound of rocks rising on one side nearly to the top, very steep, and forming what is called the *mountain*. When first I ascended this mound from the cave below, I was struck with a feeling of awe, more deep and intense than any thing I had ever before experienced. I could only observe the narrow circle which was illuminated immediately around me, above and beyond was apparently an unlimited space, in which the ear could catch not the slightest sound, nor the eye find an object to rest upon. It was filled with silence and darkness; and yet I knew that I was beneath the earth, and that this space, however large it might be, was actually bounded by solid walls. My curiosity was rather excited than gratified. In order that I might see the whole in one connected view, I built fires in many places with the pieces of cane which I found scattered among the rocks. Then taking my stand on the mountain, a scene was presented of surprising magnificence. On the opposite side, the strata of gray limestone breaking up by steps from the bottom, could scarcely be discerned in the distance by the glimmering. Above was the lofty dome, closed at the top by a smooth oval slab beautifully defined in the outline, from which the walls sloped away on the right and left, into thick darkness. Every one has heard of the dome of the mosque of St. Sophia, of St. Peter's and St. Paul's; they are never spoken of but in terms of admiration, as the chief works of architecture, and among the noblest and most stupendous examples of what man can do when aided by science; and yet, when compared with the dome of this temple, they sink into comparative insignificance. Such is the surpassing grandeur of nature's works."

A narrow passage behind the Giant's coffin leads to a circular room one hundred feet in diameter, with a low roof called the Wooden Bowl, in allusion to its figure, or as some say, from a wooden bowl having been found here by some old miner. This Bowl is the vestibule of the Deserted Chambers. On the right are the Steeps of Time, down which descending about twenty feet, and almost perpendicularly for the first ten, the visitor enters the Deserted

Chambers, which present features extremely wild and terrific. For two hundred yards the ceiling is rough and broken, but further on it is white, smooth and waving, as if worn by water. At Richardson's Spring the imprint of moccasins and of children's feet of some bygone age, are to be seen. There are more pits in the Deserted Chambers than in any other part of the cave; among the most remarkable of these, are the Covered Pit, the Side-saddle Pit and the Bottomless Pit. One of the chief glories of the cave is Gorin's Dome. This dome is of solid rock, with sides apparently fluted and polished, and two hundred feet high. The range of the Deserted Chambers is terminated by the Bottomless Pit. This pit is somewhat in the shape of a horse-shoe, having a tongue of land twenty-seven feet long, running out into the middle of it. Beyond the Bottomless Pit is the Winding Way, and Persico Avenue.

Persico Avenue averages about fifty feet in width, with a height of about thirty feet; and is said to be two miles long. It unites in an eminent degree the beautiful and the sublime, and is highly interesting throughout its entire extent. For a quarter of a mile from the entrance the roof is beautifully arched, about twelve feet high and sixty wide. The walking here is excellent, a dozen persons might run abreast for a quarter of a mile to Bunyan's Way, a branch of the avenue leading to the river. At this point the avenue changes its features of beauty and regularity for those of wild grandeur and sublimity, which it preserves to the end. The roof becomes lofty and imposingly magnificent, its long pointed or lancet arches, reminding the spectator of the rich and gorgeous ceilings of the old Gothic cathedrals. Not far from this point the visitor descending gradually a few feet, enters a tunnel of fifteen wide, the ceiling twelve or fourteen feet high, perfectly arched and beautifully covered with white incrustations, and soon reaches the Great Crossings. The name is not unapt, because two great caves cross here. Not far from here is the Pine-apple Bush, a large column composed of a white soft crumbling material, with bifurcations extending from the ceiling. The Winding Way is one hundred and five feet long, eighteen inches wide, and from three to seven feet deep, widening out above sufficiently to admit the free use of one's arms. It is throughout tortuous, forming a perfect zig-zag.

Relief Hall, at the termination of the Winding Way, is very wide and lofty, but not long; it terminates at River Hall, a distance of one hundred yards from its entrance. Here two routes present themselves. The one to the left conducts to the Dead Sea and the Rivers, and that to the right to the Bacon Chamber, the Bandit's Hall, the Mammoth Dome, &c., &c., &c. The Bacon Chamber is a pretty fair representation of a low ceiling, thickly hung with canvassed hams and shoulders. The Bandit's Hall is a vast and lofty chamber, the floor covered with a mountainous heap of rocks, rising amphitheatrically almost to the ceiling. From the Bandit's Hall diverge two caves, one of which, the left, leads you to a multitude of domes; and the right to one which, par excellence, is called the *Mammoth Dome*. This dome is near four hundred feet high, and is justly considered one of the most sublime and wonderful spectacles of this most wonderful of caverns. From the summit of this dome there is a waterfall. Foreigners have been known to declare, on witnessing an illumination of the great dome and hall, that it alone would compensate for a voyage across the Atlantic.

The River Hall is a chamber situated at the termination of Relief Hall, which has been already mentioned, and through which the visitor must pass in approaching the greatest wonders of the cave, the Dead Sea and the Rivers. We despair of giving any adequate description of this subterranean lake and rivers. "The River Hall descends like the slope of a mountain; the ceiling stretches away—away before you, vast and grand as the firmament at midnight." Proceeding a short distance, there is on the left "a steep precipice, over which you can look down, by the aid of blazing missiles, upon a broad black sheet of water, eighty feet below, called the Dead Sea. This is an awfully impressive place, the sights and sounds of which do not easily pass from memory. He who has seen it, will have it vividly brought before him by Alfieri's description of Filippo. 'Only a transient word or act gives us a short and dubious glimmer that reveals to us the abysses of his being—daring, lurid, and terrific as the throat of the infernal pool.' Descending from the eminence by a ladder of about twenty feet, we find ourselves among piles of gigantic rocks, and one of the most picturesque sights in the world is to see a file of men and women passing along those wild and scraggy paths, moving slowly—slowly that their lamps may have time to illuminate their sky-like ceiling and gigantic walls,—disappearing behind high cliffs—sinking into ravines—their lights shining upwards through fissures in the rocks—then suddenly emerging from some abrupt angle, standing in the bright gleam of their lights, relieved by the towering black masses around them. As you pass along, you hear the roar of invisible water falls; and at the foot of the slope the river Styx lies before you, deep and black, overarched with rocks. Across (or rather down) these unearthly waters, the guide can convey but four passengers at once. The lamps are fastened to the prow, the images of which are reflected in the dismal pool. If you are impatient of delay, or eager for new adventure, you can leave your companions lingering about the shore and cross the Styx by a dangerous bridge of precipices over head. In order to do this you must ascend a steep cliff, and enter a cave above, three hundred yards long, from an egress of which you find yourself on the bank of the river, eighty feet above its surface, commanding a view of those in the boat, and those waiting on the shore. Seen from this height, the lamps in the canoe glare like fiery eyeballs; and the passengers sitting there so hushed and motionless look like shadows. The scene is so strangely funereal and spectral, that it seems as if the Greeks must have witnessed it, before they imagined Charon conveying ghosts to the dim regions of Pluto. If you turn your eye from the parties of men and women whom you left waiting on the shore, you will see them by the gleam of their lamps, scattered in picturesque groups, looming out in bold relief from the dense darkness around them."

Having passed the Styx, the explorer reaches the banks of the river Lethe. Descending this about a quarter of a mile, he lands, and enters a level and lofty hall called the Great Walk, which stretches to the banks of the Echo, a distance of three or four hundred yards. The Echo is wide and deep enough, at all times, to float a steamer of the largest class. At the point of embarkation the arch is very low; but in two boats' lengths, the vault of the cave becomes lofty and wide. The novelty, the grandeur, the magnificence of the surrounding scenery here, elicits unbounded admiration and wonder. The Echo is three quarters of a mile long. It is in these rivers that the extraordinary white eyeless fish are caught. There is not the slightest indication of an organ similar to an eye to be discovered.

Beyond the Echo there is a walk of four miles to Cleveland's Avenue, in reaching which the visitor passes through El Ghor, Silliman's Avenue, and Wellington's Gallery, to the foot of the ladder which leads up to Mary's Vineyard, the commencement of Cleveland's Avenue. Proceeding about a hundred feet from this spot, you reach the base of the hill on which stands the Holy Sepulchre. Cleveland's avenue is about three miles long, seventy feet wide, and twelve or fifteen feet high—more rich and gorgeous than any ever revealed to man, abounding in formations which are no where else to be seen, and which the most stupid cannot behold without feelings of admiration. But a detailed description of these wonders would not consist with the plan of this work. In this Avenue are situated Cleveland's Cabinet, the Rocky Mountains, Croghan's Hall, Serena's Arbor, &c. &c. There is in this vast cave another avenue, more than three miles long, lofty and wide, and at its termination there is a hall which the guide thinks larger than any other in the cave. It is as yet without a name.

Captain JOHN EDMONSON, from whom this county derived its name, was a native of Washington county, Virginia. He settled in Fayette county, Kentucky, in the year 1790. He raised a company of volunteer riflemen, and joined Col. John Allen's regiment in the year 1812, and fell in the disastrous battle of the river Raisin, the 22d of January, 1813.

ESTILL COUNTY.

ESTILL county was formed in 1808, and named in honor of Captain James Estill. It is situated in the eastern middle part of the State, and lies on both sides of the Kentucky river. Bounded on the north by Montgomery, east by Breathitt, south by Clay, and west by Madison. The face of the country is generally broken and mountainous—the settlements being mostly confined to the valleys on the water courses. The growth of the bottom land is oak, walnut, hickory, cherry, and sugar tree; that of the upland, oak and poplar, and along the river banks, some pine and cedar. Iron ore and coal are found in great abundance in the mountains.

The taxable property of the county in 1846 was valued at $633,-834; number of acres of land in the county, 189,765; average value of lands per acre, $2.15; number of white males over twenty-one years old, 903; number of children between five and sixteen years of age, 1,361. Population in 1830, 4,618—in 1840, 5,535.

The *Red River Iron Works* is located in this county. It is an extensive establishment, wielding a heavy capital, and employing a large number of hands. A large quantity of bar iron and nails are manufactured at the works. The proprietors and all the operatives in this establishment are *temperance men*, ardent spirits having been altogether banished from its precincts. The Estill steam furnace is situated ten miles east, and Miller's creek salt works eight miles above Irvine. Three or four miles from the county seat, hydraulic lime has been found in great quantities.

IRVINE, the seat of justice, is seventy miles south-east of Frankfort. It is located on a beautiful site on the northern bank of the Kentucky river—contains a brick court-house and jail, and seminary; (the court-house and seminary being used for religious worship,) four lawyers, four physicians, four stores and seven mechanics' shops. Population two hundred. Established in 1812, and named in honor of Colonel William Irvine, who is noticed under the head of Madison county.

Capt. JAMES ESTILL, in honor of whom this county received its name, was a native of Augusta county, Virginia. He removed to Kentucky at an early period, and settled on Muddy creek, in the present county of Madison, where he built a station which received the name of Estill's station. In 1781 in a skirmish with the Indians, he received a rifle-shot in one of his arms, by which it was broken. In March, 1782, with a small body of men, believed to be about twenty-five, he pursued a similar number of Wyandotts across the Kentucky river, and into Montgomery county, where he fought one of the severest and most bloody battles on record, when the number of men on both sides is taken into the account.* Captain Estill and his gallant Lieutenant, South, were both killed in the retreat which succeeded. Thus fell (says Mr. Morehead in his Boonsborough address), in the ripeness of his manhood, Captain James Estill, one of Kentucky's bravest and most beloved defenders. It may be said of him with truth, that if he did not achieve the victory, he did more—he deserved it. Disappointed of success—vanquished—slain, in a desperate conflict with an enemy of superior strength and equal valor, he has nevertheless left behind him a name of which his descendants may well be proud—a name which will live in the annals of Kentucky, so long as there shall be found men to appreciate the patriotism and self-devotion of a martyr to the cause of humanity and civilization.

The Rev. JOSEPH PROCTOR, of this county, was one of the intrepid band of Captain Estill, in the bloody battle noticed under the Montgomery head. His coolness and bravery throughout the battle, were unsurpassed. A savage warrior having buried his knife in Captain Estill's breast, Proctor instantly sent a ball from his rifle through the Wyandott's heart. His conduct after the battle, elicited the warmest approbation. He brought off the field of battle his wounded friend, the late Colonel William Irvine, of Madison, who is noticed under the head of that county.

In an engagement with the Indians at Pickaway towns, on the Great Miami, Proctor killed an Indian chief. He was a brave soldier, a stranger to fear, and an ardent friend to the institutions of his country. He made three campaigns into Ohio, with the view of suppressing Indian hostilities; and fought side by side

*See a full account of this battle under the head of Montgomery county.

with Boone, Calloway and Logan. He joined the Methodist Episcopal church in a fort in Madison county, under the preaching of the Rev. James Hawkes; and was ordained in 1809, by Bishop Asbury. He was an exemplary member of the church for sixty-five years, and a local preacher upwards of half a century. He died at his residence on the 2d of December, 1844, and was buried with military honors.

FAYETTE COUNTY.

FAYETTE county was formed in 1780 by the State of Virginia, and is one of the three original counties that at one time comprised the whole district of Kentucky—and included all that territory beginning at the mouth of the Kentucky river, and extending up its middle fork to the head, and embracing the northern and eastern portion of the present State. It received its name as a testimonial of gratitude to GEN. GILBERT MORTIER DE LA FAYETTE —the gallant and generous Frenchman who volunteered as the CHAMPION OF LIBERTY on this side of the Atlantic, and proved to the world, that although a nobleman by descent, he was a republican in principle, and was more ennobled by nature than by all the titles of hereditary rank.

Fayette county is situated in the middle portion of the State, and lies on the waters of the Kentucky and Elkhorn. It is bounded on the north by Scott, east by Bourbon and Clark, south by Madison and Jessamine, and west by Woodford; being twenty-five miles from north to south, mean breadth eleven miles, and containing 275 square miles. It is fair table land—all the streams rise and flow from the centre of the county, and empty into their common receptacle, the Kentucky river. The centre of the garden of Kentucky, the surface of this county is very gently undulating, and the soil is probably as rich and productive as any upon which the sun ever shone. It is properly a stock raising county —horses, mules, cattle, and hogs, in large numbers, being annually exported; but corn and hemp are produced in great abundance—the latter being generally manufactured in the county.

The taxable property of the county in 1846, was valued at $16,007,020 (second in amount only to Jefferson, including the city of Louisville); number of acres of land in the county, 193,-061; average value of land per acre, $33.95; number of white males over twenty-one years of age, 2,883; children between five and sixteen years old, 2,233. Population in 1830, 25,174; in 1840, 22,194.

LEXINGTON, the county seat of Fayette, is a remarkably neat and beautiful city, situated on the Town fork of Elkhorn river, 25 miles south-east from Frankfort, 64 miles south-west from Maysville, 77 miles south-east from Louisville, 85 miles from Cincinnati, and 517 from Washington city. Latitude 38° 02' north; longitude 84° 26' west. It was founded in the year 1776. About the first of April, 1779, a block house was built on the site now occupied by Mr. Leavy's store, and the settlement commenced under the influence of Col. Robert Patterson, joined by Messrs. McConnels, Lindseys, and James Masterson. Major John Morrison removed his family soon after from Harrodsburg, and the lady of that gentleman was the first white female that graced the infant settlement. Being settled during the revolution,* it received its name in commemoration of the battle of Lexington, where the first blood was shed in the great cause of human liberty. Lexington was incorporated by Virginia in 1782, and was for several years the seat of government of the State. The first improvements consisted of three rows of cabins, the two outer serving as a part of the walls of the fortification, which extended from the corner now known as Leavy's corner, to James Masterson's house on Main street. The block house commanded the public spring, and a common field included the site of the present court house.

The streets of Lexington are laid out at right angles, and are well paved. Main street is one mile and a quarter long. Few towns are more delightfully situated. Its vicinity has a softness and beauty about it, and the city itself presents an appearance of neatness, that rarely fails to strike a stranger's eye with admiration. Many of the private residences, and several of the public edifices, are fine specimens of architectural taste; while the surrounding country, rich and highly cultivated, is dotted over with elegant mansions. (See note on p. 265.)

TRANSYLVANIA UNIVERSITY, LEXINGTON, KY.

VIEW OF LUNATIC ASYLUM, LEXINGTON, KY

The public buildings are—a court house; a masonic hall erected by the grand lodge of Kentucky; Morrison College, and Medical Hall, both imposing and costly edifices belonging to Transylvania University; eleven churches, embracing one Episcopal, two Presbyterian, one Methodist, one Catholic, one Reformed or Christian, one Baptist, one Independent Methodist, one Seceder, and two African; a city free school, established in 1834, and amply endowed, containing from three to five hundred scholars; the city hospital and work house is a plain brick building, erected in 1836; the Lunatic Asylum, first erected by the city, but afterwards taken under the care of the State, and greatly enlarged, containing upwards of two hundred rooms, and capable of accommodating from three to four hundred patients; the Northern Bank of Kentucky, a beautiful and finely finished edifice; and the Orphan Asylum, erected in the year 1833, for the benefit of the destitute orphans who were deprived of their parents by cholera, which raged so fearfully in that year.

There are two newspapers published in the city, which are ably edited and widely circulated, viz:—The "*Kentucky Gazette*," established in 1787, by the brothers, John and Fielding Bradford, the first number having been issued on the 18th of August, with the title of "Kentucke Gazette.† This is the oldest newspaper west of the Alleghany mountains, with the exception of the Pittsburgh Gazette. The "*Lexington Observer and Reporter*," originally called the "Lexington Reporter," was established by William W. Worsley, nearly forty years since, and is now published semi-weekly and weekly.

There are in Lexington between thirty-five and forty of each of the two professions—law and medicine, sixty or seventy stores and groceries—many of them wholesale, four book stores, six drug stores, ten taverns, and about seventy mechanical and manufacturing establishments, embracing blacksmiths, saddle and harness makers, painters, tailors, carriage makers, silver smiths, gun smiths, platers, copper and tin manufacturers, boot and shoe makers, iron and brass founders, carpenters, cabinet makers, hatters, and morocco, looking glass and brush manufacturers. Capital invested in dry goods, $1,500,000—groceries, $700,000 —manufactures and banks, $12,000,000. Taxable property in the city, $3,039,-608, in 1845. Annual importations same year, $897,445; stock in trade, $470,-568. The manufacture of hemp is carried on very extensively in Lexington and the county of Fayette. In the city there are fifteen hemp establishments, working six hundred hands, running ninety looms, and making annually 2,500,000 yards of bagging, and 2,000,000 pounds of rope. In the suburbs of the city there are four factories, manufacturing 680,000 yards of bagging and 400,000 pounds of rope. In the remainder of the county there are fourteen factories, working three hundred hands, running fifty looms, and turning out 1,250,000 yards bagging and 1,000,000 pounds of rope. Thus, in the city and county, there are thirty-three bagging and rope establishments, working one thousand and fifty hands, running one hundred and sixty-five looms, and making 4,430,000 yards of bagging and 3,400,000 pounds of rope. Population of Lexington in 1845—whites, 4,999; blacks, 3,179; total, 8,178. The population in 1847 is supposed to be about 9,000.

TRANSYLVANIA UNIVERSITY was established by the legislature of Kentucky in 1798, by the amalgamation of the two institutions known by the name of the Transylvania Seminary and Kentucky Academy. Until within a few years, it was properly a State institution. In the year 1842 it passed under the supervision of the Kentucky conference of the Methodist Episcopal church, and is now, like all the other colleges of the State, a denominational institution. It has passed through many vicissitudes, but is at present in a flourishing condition, and bids fair, under the patronage of the Methodist Episcopal church south, to rival its palmiest days.

Morrison College (the literary department of Transylvania University) has six professors and teachers, with about three hundred students, including the pre-

---

* In the year 1775, intelligence was received by a party of hunters, who were accidentally encamped on one of the branches of Elkhorn, that the first battle of the revolution had been fought in the vicinity of Boston, between the British and provincial forces, and in commemoration of the event, they called the spot of their encampment Lexington. No settlement was then made. The spot is now covered by one of the most beautiful cities on the continent.—*Governor Morehead's Address.*

† The first and about half of the second volume of the Gazette was printed with the name of the "Kentucke Gazette." Afterwards the *y* was substituted for the *e* in *Kentucky.*

MASONIC HALL, LEXINGTON, KY.

MEDICAL HALL, LEXINGTON, KY.

paratory department. The Rev. Henry B. Bascom, D. D., is president. The alumni numbers about 650. The number of volumes in the library 4,500.

The Medical School is under the supervision of eight trustees, and was founded in 1818. It has eight professors, and an average, for several years, of about one hundred and seventy-five students. The number of graduates, up to January, 1847, exceeded fifteen hundred. Connected with the institution is a fine museum, a very valuable library, and an extensive chemical apparatus for experimenting. The professors are able and generally distinguished men, and the institution, until recently, has had no rival in the west.

The Law School, like the Medical college, is connected with the Transylvania University. . This department has three professors, (Judges Robertson, Woolley and Marshall), who are distinguished for their learning and legal acquirements.

The Lunatic Asylum is one of the noblest institutions of Kentucky, and reflects immortal honor upon the city which founded and the commonwealth which sustains it. The buildings are very extensive and commodious, the rooms large and well ventilated, warmed by flues which conduct the heated air through the house. The grounds connected with the asylum embrace an area of thirty acres, and are handsomely improved and ornamented with a variety of beautiful shrubbery. The garden is cultivated entirely by the patients themselves, and affords sufficient vegetables for the supply of the institution. Dr. ALLEN, who has been for many years the superintendent, is eminently qualified for the important and very responsible position he occupies; and the cures effected under his supervision and treatment, bear as large a proportion to the number admitted as appear in the reports of any other insane institution in the United States. The admirable adaptation of the architectural arrangements—the complete classification of the patients—the moral and well-educated attendants, and the judicious system of treatment pursued by the superintendent, happily adapted to every form of the disease, ensure the attainment of as complete success as is possible in this branch of the medical art, and must be felt and acknowledged by all who have had an opportunity to observe the excellent plan upon which the institution is conducted.

ATHENS is a small but handsome village, situated ten miles from Lexington, on the Boonsborough road, and in sight of Boone's station—surrounded by a rich and fertile country, with an intelligent, industrious and moral community. It has two churches, two physicians, one lawyer, three stores, one school and twenty mechanics' shops—population 350.

Bryant's station, about five miles north-east of Lexington, was settled by the Bryants in 1779. In 1781, Bryant's station was much harassed by small parties of Indians. This was a frontier post, and greatly exposed to the hostilities of the savages.* It had been settled in 1779 by four brothers from North Carolina, one of whom, William, had married a sister of Colonel Daniel Boone. The Indians were constantly lurking in the neighborhood, waylaying the paths, stealing their horses, and butchering their cattle. It at length became necessary to hunt in parties of twenty or thirty men, so as to be able to meet and repel those attacks, which were every day becoming more bold and frequent.

One afternoon, about the 20th of May, William Bryant, accompanied by twenty men, left the fort on a hunting expedition down the Elkhorn creek. They moved with caution, until they had passed all the points where ambuscades had generally been formed, when, seeing no enemy, they became more bold, and determined, in order to sweep a large extent of country, to divide their company into two parties. One of them, conducted by Bryant in person, was to descend the Elkhorn on its southern bank, flanking out largely, and occupy as much ground as possible. The other, under the orders of James Hogan, a young farmer in good circumstances, was to move down in a parallel line upon the north bank. The two parties were to meet at night, and encamp together at the mouth of Cane run.

Each punctually performed the first part of their plans. Hogan, however, had traveled but a few hundred yards, when he heard a loud voice behind him ex-

---

* McClung's Sketches.

claim in very good English, "stop, boys!" Hastily looking back, they saw several Indians, on foot, pursuing them as rapidly as possible. Without halting to count numbers, the party put spurs to their horses, and dashed through the woods at full speed, the Indians keeping close behind them, and at times gaining upon them. There was a led horse in company, which had been brought with them for the purpose of packing game. This was instantly abandoned, and fell into the hands of the Indians. Several of them lost their hats in the eagerness of flight; but quickly getting into the open woods, they left their pursuers so far behind, that they had leisure to breathe and inquire of each other, whether it was worth while to kill their horses before they had ascertained the number of the enemy.

They quickly determined to cross the creek, and await the approach of the Indians. If they found them superior to their own and Bryant's party united, they would immediately return to the fort; as, by continuing their march to the mouth of Cane run, they would bring a superior enemy upon their friends, and endanger the lives of the whole party. They accordingly crossed the creek, dismounted, and awaited the approach of the enemy. By this time it had become dark. The Indians were distinctly heard approaching the creek upon the opposite side, and after a short halt, a solitary warrior descended the bank and began to wade through the stream.

Hogan waited until he had emerged from the gloom of the trees which grew upon the bank, and as soon as he had reached the middle of the stream, where the light was more distinct, he took deliberate aim and fired. A great splashing in the water was heard, but presently all became quiet. The pursuit was discontinued, and the party remounting their horses, returned home. Anxious, however, to apprize Bryant's party of their danger, they left the fort before daylight on the ensuing morning, and rode rapidly down the creek, in the direction of the mouth of Cane. When within a few hundred yards of the spot where they supposed the encampment to be, they heard the report of many guns in quick succession. Supposing that Bryant had fallen in with a herd of buffalo, they quickened their march in order to take part in the sport.

The morning was foggy, and the smoke of the guns lay so heavily upon the ground that they could see nothing until they had approached within twenty yards of the creek, when they suddenly found themselves within pistol shot of a party of Indians, very composedly seated upon their packs, and preparing their pipes. Both parties were much startled, but quickly recovering, they sheltered themselves, as usual, and the action opened with great vivacity. The Indians maintained their ground for half an hour with some firmness, but being hard pressed in front, and turned in flank, they at length gave way, and being closely pursued, were ultimately routed, with considerable loss, which, however, could not be distinctly ascertained. Of Hogan's party, one man was killed on the spot, and three others wounded, none mortally.

It happened that Bryant's company had encamped at the mouth of Cane, as had been agreed upon, and were unable to account for Hogan's absence. That, about daylight, they had heard a bell at a distance, which they immediately recognized as the one belonging to the led horse which had accompanied Hogan's party, and which, as we have seen, had been abandoned to the enemy the evening before. Supposing their friends to be bewildered in the fog, and unable to find their camp, Bryant, accompanied by Grant, one of his men, mounted a horse, and rode to the spot where the bell was still ringing. They quickly fell into an ambuscade, and were fired upon. Bryant was mortally, and Grant severely wounded, the first being shot through the hip and both knees, the latter through the back.

Being both able to keep the saddle, however, they set spurs to their horses, and arrived at the station shortly after breakfast. The Indians, in the mean time, had fallen upon the encampment, and instantly dispersed it, and while preparing to regale themselves after their victory, were suddenly attacked, as we have seen, by Hogan. The timidity of Hogan's party, at the first appearance of the Indians, was the cause of the death of Bryant. The same men who fled so hastily in the evening, were able the next morning, by a little firmness, to vanquish the same party of Indians. Had they stood at first, an equal success would probably have attended them, and the life of their leader would have been preserved.

On the night of the 14th of August, 1782, this station was surrounded by a body of Indians from various tribes, composed of about six hundred warriors, headed by the notorious renegade, Simon Girty. The fort was situated on the right of the present road from Maysville to Lexington, immediately on the southern bank of Elkhorn, and contained about forty cabins, placed in parallel lines, connected by strong palisades, and garrisoned by about forty or fifty men. On the succeeding morning the enemy showed themselves, but so secret and stealthy had been their approach, that not the slightest suspicion existed that the savages were in the neighborhood. Had the Indians showed themselves only a few hours later, they would have found the fort occupied only by old men, women and children, as the effective force of the garrison had determined to march on that morning to the assistance of Hoy's station, from which a messenger had arrived the evening before, with the intelligence of Holder's defeat. As it was, most of the garrison was under arms, and those out of the fort, generally, succeeded in regaining the station.

The garrison was supplied with water from a spring at some distance from the fort, on its north-west side—an error common to most of the stations,—and in a long continued siege, necessarily resulting in dreadful suffering for want of water. Near this spring a considerable body of the Indians were placed in ambush— Girty and the Indian chiefs making their arrangements for the assault under the erroneous opinion, superinduced from the military preparations within, that their approach had been discovered by the garrison.

Another party was ordered to take position in full view of the garrison—to display itself at a given time and open a fire upon them, with the hope of enticing them to an engagement outside of the walls. If this stratagem proved successful, the remainder of the forces were so disposed as to sieze the opportunity which the withdrawal of the garrison afforded, to storm one of the gates and take forcible possession of the fort. Unapprised of the danger without, the garrison having completed their preparations for the intended excursion, threw open the gates, when a sudden firing announced the presence of an enemy, and the gates were instantly closed. The yells and screams of the Indians which accompanied the discharge of rifles, struck terror to the hearts of the women and children, and startled even the men ; but with the latter it was momentary only. Among the inhabitants of the station there were men of experience, of tried bravery, and intimately acquainted with the wiles of their Indian foemen. Such men might be startled, but never intimidated—and their resources and courage rose with the occasion which called them into requisition. Every effort was made to protect the station.* The gates, the bastions, the loopholes were manned—the breaches in the palisades were repaired, and messengers were forthwith dispatched to the adjoining stations to communicate intelligence of the siege, and to procure assistance.

---

* Mr. McClung has preserved a singular anecdote of female intrepidity connected with this siege, which we append :

" The more experienced of the garrison felt satisfied that a powerful party was in ambuscade near the spring, but at the same time they supposed that the Indians would not unmask themselves, until the firing on the opposite side of the fort was returned with such warmth, as to induce the belief that the feint had succeeded.

"Acting upon this impression, and yielding to the urgent necessity of the case, they summoned all the women, without exception, and explaining to them the circumstances in which they were placed, and the improbability that any injury would be offered them, until the firing had been returned from the opposite side of the fort, they urged them to go in a body to the spring, and each of them bring up a bucket full of water. Some of the ladies, as was natural, had no relish for the undertaking, and asked why the men could not bring water as well as themselves ? observing that *they* were not bullet proof, and that the Indians made no distinction between male and female scalps !

" To this it was answered, that women were in the habit of bringing water every morning to the fort, and that if the Indians saw them engaged as usual, it would induce them to think that their ambuscade was undiscovered, and that they would not unmask themselves for the sake of firing at a few women, when they hoped, by remaining concealed a few moments longer, to obtain complete possession of the fort. That if *men* should go down to the spring,

The arrangements to meet the enemy being complete, thirteen young men were sent out of the fort to attack the decoy party, with orders to fire with great rapidity, and make as much noise as possible, but not to pursue the enemy too far, while the rest of the garrison took post on the opposite side of the fort, cocked their guns, and stood in readiness to receive the ambuscade as soon as it was unmasked. The firing of the light parties on the Lexington road was soon heard, and quickly became sharp and serious, gradually becoming more distant from the fort. Instantly Girty sprang up at the head of his five hundred warriors, and rushed rapidly upon the western gate, ready to force his way over the undefended palisades. Into this mass of dusky bodies, the garrison poured several rapid volleys of rifle balls with destructive effect. Their consternation may be imagined. With wild cries they dispersed on the right and left, and in two minutes not an Indian was to be seen. At the same time, the party who had sallied out on the Lexington road, came running into the fort at the opposite gate, in high spirits, and laughing heartily at the success of their manœuvre.

A regular attack, in the usual manner, then commenced, without much effect on either side, until two o'clock in the afternoon, when a new scene presented itself. Two men of the garrison, Tomlinson and Bell, who had been mounted upon fleet horses, and sent at full speed to Lexington, announcing the arrival of the Indians and demanding reinforcements, found the town occupied only by women and children, and a few old men, the rest having marched at the intelligence of Holder's defeat, to the general rendezvous at Hoy's station. The couriers instantly followed at a gallop, and overtaking them on the road, informed them of the danger to which Lexington was exposed during their absence. The whole party, amounting to sixteen horsemen, and more than double that number on foot, with some additional volunteers from Boone's station, instantly countermarched, and repaired with all possible expedition to Bryant's station. They were entirely ignorant of the overwhelming numbers opposed to them, or they would have proceeded with more caution. By great exertions, horse and foot appeared before Bryant's at two in the afternoon, and pressed forward with precipitate gallantry to throw themselves into the fort. The Indians, however, had been aware of the departure of the two couriers, who had, in fact, broken through their line in order to give the alarm, and expecting the arrival of reinforcements, had taken measures to meet them.

To the left of the long and narrow lane, where the Maysville and Lexington road now runs, there were more than one hundred acres of green standing corn. The usual road from Lexington to Bryant's, ran parallel to the fence of this field, and only a few feet distant from it. On the opposite side of the road was a thick wood. Here more than three hundred Indians lay in ambush, within pistol shot of the road, awaiting the approach of the party. The horsemen came in view at a time when the firing had ceased, and every thing was quiet. Seeing no enemy and hearing no noise, they entered the lane at a gallop, and were instantly saluted with a shower of rifle balls from each side, at the distance of ten paces.

At the first shot, the whole party set spurs to their horses, and rode at full speed through a rolling fire from either side, which continued for several hundred yards, but owing partly to the furious rate at which they rode, partly to the clouds of dust raised by the horses' feet, they all entered the fort unhurt. The men on foot were less fortunate. They were advancing through the corn-field, and might

the Indians would immediately suspect that something was wrong, would despair of succeeding by ambuscade, and would instantly rush upon them, follow them into the fort, or shoot them down at the spring. The decision was soon over.

" A few of the boldest declared their readiness to brave the danger, and the younger and more timid rallying in the rear of these veterans, they all marched down in a body to the spring, within point blank shot of more than five hundred Indian warriors ! Some of the girls could not help betraying symptoms of terror, but the married women, in general, moved with a steadiness and composure that completely deceived the Indians. Not a shot was fired. The party were permitted to fill their buckets, one after another, without interruption, and although their steps became quicker and quicker, on their return, and when near the gate of the fort, degenerated into a rather unmilitary celerity, attended with some little crowding in passing the gate, yet not more than one-fifth of the water was spilled, and the eyes of the youngest had not dilated to more than double their ordinary size."—*See M'Clung's Sketches, page 62.*

have reached the fort in safety, but for their eagerness to succor their friends. Without reflecting, that from the weight and extent of the fire, the enemy must have been ten times their number, they ran up with inconsiderate courage, to the spot where the firing was heard, and there found themselves cut off from the fort, and within pistol shot of more than three hundred savages.

Fortunately the Indian guns had just been discharged, and they had not yet leisure to re-load. At the sight of this brave body of footmen, however, they raised a hideous yell, and rushed upon them, tomahawk in hand. Nothing but the high corn and their loaded rifles, could have saved them from destruction. The Indians were cautious in rushing upon a loaded rifle, with only a tomahawk, and when they halted to load their pieces, the Kentuckians ran with great rapidity, turning and dodging through the corn in every direction. Some entered the wood and escaped through the thickets of cane, some were shot down in the corn-field, others maintained a running fight, halting occasionally behind trees and keeping the enemy at bay with their rifles; for, of all men, the Indians are generally the most cautious in exposing themselves to danger. A stout, active young fellow, was so hard pressed by Girty and several savages, that he was compelled to discharge his rifle, (however unwilling, having no time to re-load it,) and Girty fell. It happened, however, that a piece of thick sole-leather was in his shot-pouch at the time, which received the ball, and preserved his life, although the force of the blow felled him to the ground. The savages halted upon his fall, and the young man escaped.

Although the skirmish and the race lasted for more than an hour, during which the corn-field presented a scene of turmoil and bustle which can scarcely be conceived, yet very few lives were lost. Only six of the white men were killed and wounded, and probably still fewer of the enemy, as the whites never fired until absolutely necessary, but reserved their loads as a check upon the enemy. Had the Indians pursued them to Lexington, they might have possessed themselves of it without resistance, as there was no force there to oppose them; but after following the fugitives for a few hundred yards, they returned to the hopeless siege of the fort.

It was now near sunset, and the fire on both sides had slackened. The Indians had become discouraged. Their loss in the morning had been heavy, and the country was evidently arming, and would soon be upon them. They had made no impression upon the fort, and without artillery could hope to make none. The chiefs spoke of raising the siege and decamping; but Girty determined, since his arms had been unavailing, to try the efficacy of negotiation. Near one of the bastions there was a large stump, to which he crept on his hands and knees, and from which he hailed the garrison.

He highly commended their courage, but assured them, that further resistance would be madness, as he had six hundred warriors with him, and was in hourly expectation of reinforcements, with artillery, which would instantly blow their cabins into the air; that if the fort was taken by storm, as it certainly would be, when their cannon arrived, it would be impossible for him to save their lives; but if they surrendered at once, he gave them his honor, that not a hair of their heads should be injured. He told them his name, inquired whether they knew him, and assured them that they might safely trust to his honor.

The garrison listened in silence to his speech, and many of them looked very blank at the mention of the artillery, as the Indians had, on one occasion, brought cannon with them, and destroyed two stations. But a young man by the name of Reynolds, highly distinguished for courage, energy, and a frolicsome gaiety of temper, perceiving the effect of Girty's speech, took upon himself to reply to it. To Girty's inquiry, "whether the garrison knew him?" Reynolds replied, "That he was very well known; that he himself had a worthless dog, to which he had given the name of 'Simon Girty,' in consequence of his striking resemblance to the man of that name; that if he had either artillery or reinforcements, he might bring them up and be d—d; that if either himself, or any of the naked rascals with him, found their way into the fort, they would disdain to use their guns against them, but would drive them out again with switches, of which they had collected a great number for that purpose alone; and finally, he declared that *they* also expected reinforcements; that the whole country was marching to their assistance; and that if Girty and his gang of murderers remained twenty-four hours longer before the fort, their scalps would be found drying in the sun upon the roofs of their cabins."

Girty took great offence at the tone and language of the young Kentuckian, and retired with an expression of sorrow for the inevitable destruction which awaited them on the following morning. He quickly rejoined the chiefs; and instant preparations were made for raising the siege. The night passed away in uninterrupted tranquility, and at daylight in the morning, the Indian camp was found deserted. Fires were still burning brightly, and several pieces of meat were left upon their roasting sticks, from which it was inferred that they had retreated a short time before daylight.

In 1780, Transylvania Seminary, the first literary institution of the west, was established by the legislature of Virginia. One-sixth of the surveyor's fees, formerly conferred on the college of William and Mary, with eight thousand acres of the first land in the then county of Kentucky, which should be confiscated, were granted for the endowment and support of the seminary. This institution was the nucleus of literature and sound learning in Kentucky, which can now boast of a greater number of colleges than any other State in the American union.

Early in the spring of 1780, Mr. ALEXANDER McCONNELL, of Lexington, Ky., went into the woods on foot, to hunt deer. He soon killed a large buck, and returned home for a horse, in order to bring it in. During his absence, a party of five Indians, on one of their usual skulking expeditions, accidentally stumbled on the body of the deer, and perceiving that it had been recently killed, they naturally supposed that the hunter would speedily return to secure the flesh. Three of them, therefore, took their station within close rifle shot of the deer, while the other two followed the trail of the hunter, and waylaid the path by which he was expected to return. McConnell, expecting no danger, rode carelessly along the path, which the two scouts were watching, until he had come within view of the deer, when he was fired upon by the whole party, and his horse killed. While laboring to extricate himself from the dying animal, he was seized by his enemies, instantly overpowered, and borne off as a prisoner.

His captors, however, seemed to be a merry, good natured set of fellows, and permitted him to accompany them unbound ; and, what was rather extraordinary, allowed him to retain his gun and hunting accoutrements. He accompanied them with great apparent cheerfulness through the day, and displayed his dexterity in shooting deer for the use of the company, until they began to regard him with great partiality. Having traveled with them in this manner for several days, they at length reached the banks of the Ohio river. Heretofore, the Indians had taken the precaution to bind him at night, although not very securely ; but on that evening he remonstrated with them on the subject, and complained so strongly of the pain which the cords gave him, that they merely wrapped the buffalo tug loosely around his wrists, and having tied it in an easy knot, and attached the extremities of the rope to their own bodies, in order to prevent his moving without awakening them, they very composedly went to sleep, leaving the prisoner to follow their example or not, as he pleased.

McConnell determined to effect his escape that night, if possible, as on the following night they would cross the river, which would render it much more difficult. He, therefore, lay quiet until near midnight, anxiously ruminating upon the best means of effecting his object. Accidentally casting his eyes in the direction of his feet, they fell upon the glittering blade of a knife, which had escaped its sheath, and was now lying near the feet of one of the Indians. To reach it with his hands, without disturbing the two Indians, to whom he was fastened, would be impossible, and it was very hazardous to attempt to draw it up with his feet. This, however, he attempted. With much difficulty he grasped the blade between his toes, and after repeated and long continued efforts, succeeded at length in bringing it within reach of his hands.

To cut his cords, was then but the work of a moment, and gradually and silently extricating his person from the arms of the Indians, he walked to the fire and sat down. He saw that his work was but half done. That if he should attempt to return home, without destroying his enemies, he would assuredly be

---

*M'Clung's Sketches.

pursued and probably overtaken, when his fate would be certain. On the other hand, it seemed almost impossible for a single man to succeed in conflict with five Indians, even although unarmed and asleep. He could not hope to deal a blow with his knife so silently and fatally, as to destroy each one of his enemies in turn, without awakening the rest. Their slumbers were proverbially light and restless; and if he failed with a single one, he must instantly be overpowered by the survivors. The knife, therefore, was out of the question.

After anxious reflections for a few minutes, he formed his plan. The guns of the Indians were stacked near the fire; their knives and tomahawks were in sheathes by their sides. The latter he dared not touch for fear of awakening their owners; but the former he carefully removed, with the exception of two, and hid them in the woods, where he knew the Indians would not readily find them. He then returned to the spot where the Indians were still sleeping, perfectly ignorant of the fate preparing for them, and taking a gun in each hand, he rested the muzzles upon a log within six feet of his victims, and having taken deliberate aim at the head of one, and the heart of another, he pulled both triggers at the same moment.

Both shots were fatal. At the report of the guns, the others sprang to their feet, and stared wildly around them. McConnell, who had run instantly to the spot where the other rifles were hid, hastily seized one of them and fired at two of his enemies, who happened to be in a line with each other. The nearest fell dead, being shot through the centre of the body; the second fell also, bellowing loudly, but quickly recovering, limped off into the woods as fast as possible. The fifth, and only one who remained unhurt, darted off like a deer, with a yell that announced equal terror and astonishment. McConnell, not wishing to fight any more such battles, selected his own rifle from the stack, and made the best of his way to Lexington, where he arrived safely within two days.

Shortly afterwards, Mrs. Dunlap, of Fayette, who had been several months a prisoner amongst the Indians on Mad river, made her escape, and returned to Lexington. She reported that the survivor returned to his tribe with a lamentable tale. He related that they had taken a fine young hunter near Lexington, and had brought him safely as far as the Ohio; that while encamped upon the bank of the river, a large party of white men had fallen upon them in the night, and killed all his companions, together with the poor defenceless prisoner, who lay bound hand and feet, unable either to escape or resist!!*

Higbee's grist mill, near Lexington, was erected in the fall of 1785, and is believed to have been the first of that kind which went into operation in the bounds of Kentucky.

The second dry goods store in Kentucky, was opened in Lexington by General James Wilkinson, in the spring of the year 1784.

The first Kentucky Almanac was published by the Messrs. Bradford, in 1788. In the same year, the first grammar school was opened at Lexington, where the Greek and Latin languages, with other branches, were taught—price of tuition, four pounds in cash or produce. The first dancing school was opened in Lexington in April, 1788. Mr. West was the first watch maker, who settled in Lexington in August, 1788. He constructed a steam boat on a small scale, which, in the year 1794, in the presence of hundreds of citizens, he tried on the Town fork of Elkhorn, previously dammed up for the purpose, and it is said that it moved through the water with great velocity.† This is believed by many to have been the first successful application of steam to navigation. Mr. West also invented the machine now used for cutting nails.

Levi Todd, who first located at Harrodsburg, settled a station in this county, about ten miles south-west from Lexington, in the year 1779. This gentleman

---

* M'Clung's Sketches.

† A letter from Lexington says Mr. West was a gunsmith, and that he was the father of the celebrated artist, William West, now of London. His miniature steamboat had no fly wheels; but to overcome the dead point, the piston rod was made to strike metallic springs at every return motion given by the steam. The experiment on Elkhorn was made in 1798. A large steam boat, constructed after the plan of Mr. West, was advertised in the Kentucky Gazette of April 23, 1816, to start from the "mouth of Hickman creek," in Jessamine county, for New Orleans, and no doubt was entertained but that it would be able to stem the current of the Mississippi. What became of the "large steam boat," the writer does not know. The identical miniature engine, or rather, the cylinder, piston rod, frame work, supply, and escape pipe, can now be seen in the museum of the Adelphi society of Transylvania university.

afterwards removed to Lexington, as a place of greater safety, and became distinguished among the early settlers.

From the files of the Kentucky Gazette, which we have been permitted to examine, the following extracts are made:

" Lexington, April 26, 1790.

Friday the 10th instant was appointed for the examination of the students of the Transylvania seminary, by the trustees. In the presence of a very respectable audience, several elegant speeches were delivered by the boys, and in the evening a tragedy acted, and the whole concluded with a farce. The several masterly strokes of eloquence, throughout the performance, obtained general applause, and were acknowledged by a universal clap from all present. The good order and decorum observed throughout the whole, together with the rapid progress of the school in literature, reflects very great honor on the president."

Lexington, February 26, 1791.

" The following posts on the frontiers are to be immediately occupied by the guards, for the defence of the district, viz.:

Posts.	No. of men.	Posts.	No. of men.
Three Islands	20	Mouth of Salt river	19
Locust creek	13	Hardin's settlement	12
Iron works	17	Russel's creek	15
Forks of Licking	12	Sovereign's valley	10
Big bone Lick	13	Widow Wiljohn's	5
Tanner's	5	Estill's station	10
Drennon's lick	10	Stevenson's	10
Mouth Kentucky	19	Lackey's	8
Patten's creek	10	Noke's lick	9

December 1, 1787.

" Whereas, the subscribers to the proposals for establishing a society, to be called the " Kentucky society for promoting useful knowledge," were prevented from meeting on the fourth Monday in September last, according to appointment, and it is probable that a meeting of the subscribers cannot, in any short time be had, and absolutely necessary that something should be done for the benefit of the society, without further loss of time, it is proposed by sundry subscribers that a select committee, curator, and treasurer, shall be forthwith chosen by the subscribers, in the (only) manner which their dispersed situation will at present admit of. The committee, curator, and treasurer to act in their several capacities, till a meeting of the subscribers can be had.

" Each subscriber is therefore requested to forward to Mr. Thomas Speed, at Danville, before the fifth day of February next, a list of such gentlemen as he chooses to constitute a select committee; and also the names of such gentlemen as he wishes to be appointed curator and treasurer.

" It is proposed that such gentlemen as are found on the said first day of February next, to have a majority of such votes in their favor, as have *then* came to hand, shall be a select committee, and act as curator and treasurer, till a meeting as above mentioned can be had.

" A list of all the subscribers is hereunto subjoined; and it is necessary to observe that the select committee is to consist of seven members, including the chairman, who is to be chosen by the committee."

George Muter,	John Jouett,	John Coburn,
Samuel McDowell,	Thomas Allen,	George Gordon,
Harry Innes,	Robert Todd,	Alexander D. Orr,
James Speed,	Joseph Crockett,	Robert Barr,
William McDowell,	Ebenezer Brooks,	Horace Turpin,
Willis Green,	T. Hall,	Robert Johnson,
Thomas Todd,	Caleb Wallace,	John Craig,
Thomas Speed,	William Irvine,	James Garrard,
Gabriel J. Johnson,	Charles Scott,	Isaac Shelby,
Joshua Barbee,	Levi Todd,	David Leitch,
Stephen Ormsby,	James Parker,	H. Marshall,
J. Overton, jun.,	Alexander Parker,	Christopher Greenup.
J. Brown,	John Fowler,	

Education.—Notice is hereby given, that on Monday the 28th of January next, a school will be opened by Messrs. Jones & Worley, at the royal spring in Lebanon town, Fayette county, where a commodious house, sufficient to contain fifty or sixty scholars, will be prepared. They will teach the Latin and Greek languages, together with such branches of the sciences as are usually taught in public seminaries, at twenty-five shillings a quarter for each scholar, one half to be paid in cash, the other in produce at cash price. There will be a vacation of a month in the spring and another in the fall, at the close of each of which, it is expected that such payments as are due in cash, will be made. For diet, washing and house-room, for a year, each scholar pays three pounds in cash, or five hundred weight of pork on entrance, and three pounds cash on the beginning of the third quarter. It is desired that as many as can would furnish themselves with beds; such as cannot may be provided for here to the number of eight or ten boys, at thirty-five shillings a year for each bed. ELIJAH CRAIG.

N. B. It would be proper for each boy to have his sheets, shirts, stockings, &c. marked, to prevent mistakes.

Lebanon, December 27, 1787.

Lexington, June 4, 1791.

On Wednesday the 25th ult. seven Indians killed a family about twelve miles from Danville, consisting of a man, his wife and five children. They were pursued by a party of men, overtaken, one killed and another wounded.

About the same time they took a prisoner with a number of horses from the neighborhood of Fort Washington, on the north-west side of Ohio.

Lexington, March 10, 1792.

On Monday evening last the Indians stole ten or twelve horses from near Grant's mill, on North Elkhorn; and on Tuesday night burnt a dwelling house, together with all the household furniture belonging to the proprietors, they having left their houses late in the evening.

July 28, 1792.

Notice is hereby given, that the commissioners for fixing the permanent seat of government, will attend at Brent & Love's tavern in Lexington, on the first Monday in August next, and the succeeding day, to receive proposals from any persons authorized to make offers concerning the business of their commission, and will proceed from thence to view any place or places which will be thought most eligible.

Lexington, January 5, 1789.

A large company will meet at the Crab Orchard, on the 29th inst. in perfect readiness to make an early start through the wilderness the next morning.

Richmond, Va. October 24, 1788.

I propose attending the General Court in the District of Kentucky, as an Attorney, and shall be at the next March term, if not prevented by some unforeseen event. GEORGE NICHOLAS.

Col. JOHN PATTERSON was among the early settlers of Lexington. He came to Kentucky shortly after the old pioneer Boone made his location here. He bought all the property on the hill, in the western limits of the city, a large portion of which is now very tastefully and beautifully improved. Colonel Patterson commanded a company in the disastrous battle of the Blue Licks. In the retreat from the battle field an incident occurred, as rare as it was magnanimous and noble. Young Reynolds, whom the reader will remember for his rough and humorous reply to Girty at the siege of Bryant's station, after bearing his share in the action with distinguished gallantry, was galloping, with several other horsemen, in order to reach the ford. The greater portion of the fugitives having preceded them, their situation was extremely critical and dangerous. About half way from the battle-ground to the river, the party overtook Colonel (then Captain) Patterson, on foot, infirm in consequence of former wounds received from the Indians, and so exhausted by recent exertions, as to be unable to keep up with his companions in flight. The Indians were close after him, and every moment shortened the distance between them. Reynolds, upon coming up with this brave officer, instantly sprung from his horse, aided Patterson to mount into the saddle, and continued his own flight on foot. From his remarkable vigor and activity, he was enabled to outstrip his pursuers, and reach the opposite side of the river in safety. Here, finding that the water absorbed by his buckskin breeches, had rendered them so tight and heavy as to impede his flight, he sat down for the purpose of pulling them off, and was overtaken by a party of Indians, and made prisoner. The pursuit was continued, and Reynolds, strictly guarded, was compelled to follow on. A small body of the flying Kentuckians, however, soon attracted their attention, and he was left in charge of three Indians, who, eager in pursuit, in turn committed him to one of their number. Reynolds and his guard moved on at a slow pace, the former unarmed, the latter armed with a rifle and tomahawk. At length the Indian stopped to tie his moccasin, when Reynolds instantly sprung upon him, knocked him down with his fist, and quickly disappeared in the thicket which surrounded them. For this act of noble generosity, Colonel Patterson afterwards made him a present of two hundred acres of first rate land. There is a moral beauty in this incident which cannot fail to elicit the admiration of every reader.

BENJAMIN HOWARD was an early adventurer to this county. He made a settlement at Boonsborough in 1775. He was a firm and decided whig in the revolution; and was a volunteer at the battle of Guilford. While in the act of taking a wounded man from the field, he was attacked by Tarleton's light horse, and received five wounds, three of which were pronounced mortal by the surgeon who dressed them. He was a native of Virginia, and completed his education with the celebrated Dr. Samuel Daviess, afterwards president of Princeton college. He was a devoted christian, having lived an exemplary member of the Presbyterian church for upwards of *eighty* years. His only son, Governor Benjamin Howard, of Missouri, died at St. Louis in 1814. Mr. Howard out-lived all his family, except his second daughter, and died at the advanced age of 103, at the residence of Maj. Woolley (who married a grand-daughter) in Lexington.

NATHAN BURROWS was also among the first settlers of Lexington. About the year 1796, he introduced into Kentucky the manufacture of hemp—being the pioneer in that branch of manufactures; but through the unworthiness of agents, he never reaped any advantage from it. He afterwards established a manufactory of mustard in Lexington, and produced the unrivalled article which still bears his name. He died in 1841.

ANDREW MCCALLA, the father of Rev. William L. and General John M. McCalla, was another of the pioneers of Lexington. He spent most of his life in acts of charity and kindness. He was the projector, and main stay in its infancy, of the lunatic asylum. He died at a good old age.

JOHN BRADFORD was born in Fauquier county, Virginia, in the year 1749. He married Eliza James, daughter of Captain Benjamin James, of said county, in the year 1761, and had five sons and four daughters. He served for a short time in the revolutionary army, and came to Kentucky for the first time in the fall of the year 1779. He was in the battle with the Indians at Chillicothe. In the year 1785, he removed his family to Kentucky, and settled about four miles north of Lexington, on Cane run. In the year 1787, he, in conjunction with his brother, Fielding Bradford, (a venerable man, who now lives about two miles nearly north from Georgetown), established the "Kentucke Gazette," the first number of which was published in Lexington on the 11th of August in that year; under which title it was continued until the 14th of March, 1789, when it was changed to the "Kentucky Gazette," in consequence of the legislature of Virginia requiring certain advertisements to be inserted in the Kentucky Gazette. Fielding Bradford remained a partner until the 31st of May, 1788, when he withdrew from the concern; after which it was continued by John Bradford until the 1st of April, 1802, when he conveyed the establishment to his son, Daniel Bradford, who continued the publication of the Gazette for many years, and is still residing in Lexington, an acting magistrate of Fayette county.

The first number of the Gazette was published on a sheet of demi paper—the second on a half sheet of the same size; but owing to the difficulty of procuring paper, it was soon after reduced to a half sheet fools-cap, and thus published for several months. It has been reported that the type on which the paper was issued, were cut out of dog-wood by Mr. Bradford. This is not true, except as to particular *sorts*, which fell short, and also as to a few large letters, although he was a man of uncommon mechanical ingenuity.

ROBERT WICKLIFFE, sen., one of the pioneer lawyers of Fayette, is still living near the city of Lexington, in a green old age. He has represented the county for many years, in both branches of the legislature of Kentucky, and has discharged creditably and honorably, several other important public trusts. He has borne an active and conspicuous part in all the leading questions which have agitated the State for nearly or quite half a century. When the State was rocked as with an earthquake, by the discussions on the *relief* and *new court* questions, Mr. Wickliffe was among the most active and efficient champions of the constitutional judiciary. He is universally acknowledged to be one of the ablest land lawyers in the State; and has, by his industry and devotion to his profession, amassed immense wealth.

One of the most noted citizens of Fayette, is GEN. LESLIE COMBS. He is a lawyer of high repute in his profession; and, during the late war with Great Britain, was a brave and gallant soldier under Harrison. While out on the northwestern frontier, he was highly distinguished as a brave, vigilant, and efficient officer. He was attached to the force under General Green Clay, which went to the relief of Fort Meigs in May, 1813. He volunteered at the head of five men, in an open canoe, to carry to Harrison the intelligence of Clay's approach, through swarms of hostile savages, who occupied every known avenue to the beleaguered fort. In this daring attempt he narrowly escaped death, and lost nearly all his men. He took part with distinguished courage, in the disastrous attack made upon the British batteries by Colonel Dudley, and was severely wounded, and taken prisoner, in that affair. He has repeatedly represented the county of Fayette in the legislature of Kentucky, and always with ability. At the session of 1846–7, he was chosen speaker of the house of representatives, and presided over that body, during its sittings, with dignity and tact.

Colonel JAMES MORRISON, one of the most wealthy and influential citizens of Lexington in his day, was born in Cumberland county, Pennsylvania, in the year 1755. The son of an Irish emigrant, his native strength of mind gradually elevated him far above his humble origin. He served for six years in the army of the revolution, and distinguished himself as one of Morgan's select corps of riflemen. After the war, he went into business at Pittsburgh, and rose to be sheriff of the county. In 1792, he removed to Lexington, then presenting an inviting field to the adventurous and enterprising. Here he filled, in succession, the high and important trusts of land commissioner, representative in the legislature, supervisor of the revenue, navy agent, contractor for the north-western army during the war of 1812, quarter-master general, president of the Lexington branch of the United States bank, and chairman of the board of trustees of Transylvania university. Col. Morrison was a man of commanding appearance; stern but courteous; of great decision of character, native talent, wide experience, and considerable reading.* He acquired immense wealth, which he disbursed in elegant hospitality, judicious patronage of deserving young men, and the promotion of letters. He died in the 68th year of his age, at Washington city, April 23, 1823, whither he had gone to obtain the settlement of a large claim against the government.

WILLIAM TAYLOR BARRY.—Among the many distinguished men who have reflected honor upon the west, the subject of this sketch ranks high for great abilities and lofty virtues. No man who has figured so largely in the well-contested arena of western politics, ever left it with fewer enemies, or a larger number of admiring and devoted friends. He was born in the State of Virginia, on the day of   178 , of reputable parentage, and early in life removed to Lexington, Kentucky, which continued to be his residence until he removed to

---

* Dr. Davidson's History of the Presbyterian church.

Washington in 1829, to form a part of President Jackson's cabinet. In 1835, he was appointed minister to Spain. He sailed for his destination by the way of Liverpool, but on his arrival at that city, he was arrested by disease, which, in a short time, consigned him to a premature grave, where his remains still rest.

Major Barry was eminent as a lawyer, and pre-eminently eloquent as an advocate. During his professional career, he came in contact with men of the highest order of talents and merit; and among those who formed the pride and strength of the bar in Kentucky between the years 1800 and 1825, he held an equal rank with the foremost. Those who were witnesses of the struggles at the bar in interesting and important causes, between Major Barry and such men as Mr. Clay, Judge Bledsoe, and many others of similar grade, all unite in expression of admiration for the man and the orator.

In Kentucky, the legal profession has always furnished a large proportion of its legislators. The ardent patriotism, the high order of talents which distinguished him, as well as his benevolence of disposition, early pointed him out as a popular favorite. The fiery eloquence with which he stirred the minds of the multitude, gave him a controlling influence with the people, which was increased and secured by his many private virtues. He was accordingly early called to occupy places in the legislature of the State, by large majorities; and at length, in 1820, he was elected lieutenant governor. During his legislative career, he was the zealous advocate of every public measure calculated to benefit the people. His report upon the subject of public education, is still referred to by the statesmen of Kentucky, as their guide on that all important subject. While holding the latter office, the division of parties, called old and new court, took place in Kentucky, which was accompanied by more violence than any which ever agitated the State. It divided the bar and the bench, as well as the people; and those who, from this era, look back upon its struggles, may well doubt the correctness of a triumph over constitutional principles which were sustained by a Barry, a Rowan, a Bledsoe, and a Haggin.

When the series of outrages which England offered to this country, previous to 1812, were rousing the public indignation, Major Barry warmly advocated the cause of his country, and by his ready eloquence, greatly aided in bringing the public mind to the issue which national honor and national safety alike demanded. After the declaration of war, he advocated its vigorous prosecution. When Governor Shelby led his countrymen in 1813, to take vengeance on England and her savage allies for the massacre of the river Raisin and fort Meigs, Major Barry held the responsible station of one of his aids. In that post he served during the severe and glorious campaign which terminated in the capture of the British army, the death of Tecumseh, and the conquest of a large portion of Upper Canada. His courage and conduct in that campaign, secured to him the approbation of his veteran commander, and the affection of his comrades.

In the change of parties which Mr. Clay's adherence to Mr. Adams in 1825, produced in Kentucky, Major Barry adhered to the democratic party, in whose ranks he remained without deviation until his death. He became, in fact, its head and leader in Kentucky, and contended, with his characteristic zeal and ability, for its principles and measures. Being a candidate for the office of governor in 1828, he canvassed the State, and in pursuance of the custom of Kentucky, he addressed numerous public meetings of the citizens. Although he failed in his election, being defeated by a majority of less than seven hundred votes, he acquired additional reputation by the contest, and aided greatly in producing the triumph of the democratic party in the presidential election which followed, when the vote of Kentucky was given to General Jackson, against Mr. Adams, by nearly eight thousand majority. The bitter feelings which were created by the old and new court contest, which prevented many democrats from supporting him, alone prevented his election to the office of governor.

Upon General Jackson's accession to the executive office, he called Major Barry to the office of postmaster general, which he continued to hold until unable, from physical debility, to discharge its onerous duties. In the hope to retrieve his health, and to place him in a situation where his high qualities might be made eminently honorable to himself, as well as useful to his country, the president appointed him to the office of ambassador to Spain. But the decrees of a higher power had gone forth, and the amiable, the generous and the exalted Barry was destined to close in a foreign land, a life which had been honorably devoted to the service of his country.

Major Barry was twice married. His first wife was Miss Overton, daughter of the late John Overton, of Fayette county. Of their children, only one, Mrs. Taylor, wife of James Taylor, Esq. of Newport, Kentucky, survives. His second wife was Miss Mason, of Virginia, sister of General John T. Mason. Of that marriage, one son only survives.

A portion of his fellow citizens of Lexington have erected a plain, unpretending monument to his memory, which, by unanimous consent of the county court, was placed in the public square. But a more interesting monument of his virtues will be found in the heart of every one who knew him as he was, and could judge him without the bias of party prejudice.

JOSEPH CABELL BRECKINRIDGE was the second child and eldest son of the late Hon. John Breckinridge, and was born in Albemarle county, Virginia, the 24th day of July, 1788. Some account has been given of his paternal ancestors in the notice of his father. His mother, Mary Hopkins Cabell, was the daughter of Colonel Joseph Cabell, of Buckingham county, Virginia, whose name he bore; and of Mary Hopkins, the daughter of Arthur Hopkins, an Irish gentleman, who emigrated to Virginia early in the eighteenth century, and was the ancestor of a very numerous family of his own and other names, scattered over the middle and southern states. William Cabell, the great grand father of the subject of this notice, was an Englishman by birth, but emigrated to Virginia at an early period, and at the commencement of the American revolution, his four sons, who were all born in America, embarked with great ardor in that struggle, and were all colonels in the Virginia militia. William Cabell and several of his sons, amongst them Joseph, were by profession physicians. The family was originally Italian, and the name Capellari, changed in France to Capel, and became in English, Cabell. This modification of names in the various languages of Europe, is extremely common in families of ancient origin. There is a tradition in this family that they are remotely descended from a Catawba Indian chief, whose name was Davis, from whom various other families (Floyd, Burke, Venable, Williams, Morgan, &c.) are also descended; and in this branch of the Breckinridge family, the evidences of its truth have been carefully collected.

In 1793, when Joseph was in his fifth year, his parents removed to Lexington, Kentucky. The country was newly settled, and the facilities even for elementary instruction by no means ample. At the age of fourteen, he was sent to a grammar school in his native state, and after the usual preparatory studies, entered one of the lower classes in the college of Princeton, New Jersey, where he graduated with distinguished honor in 1810. While a student there, he formed an attachment for, and soon afterwards married Miss Mary Clay Smith, daughter of Dr. Samuel Stanhope Smith, president of the college, and grand daughter of Dr. John Witherspoon, a former president, and a whig statesman of the revolution.

The premature and lamented death of his father in 1806, had, for a time, interrupted his studies, and called him to Kentucky, to become, in his boyhood, the head of a large family, and to prepare for the chief labor in managing an extensive and complicated estate. The responsibilities of this new position, gave him even at this early period, a certain prudence and grave maturity of character which accompanied him through life; and the duties it involved, were faithfully and ably performed.

Upon his return to Kentucky, Mr. Breckinridge devoted himself to the various duties thrown upon him by the death of his father, and to the study of the law. But before he completed his profession, the troubles on the north-western frontier called forth the gallantry and patriotism of Kentucky, and among many other brave men, he volunteered his services to his country, and served one campaign as aid-de-camp to General Samuel Hopkins. Soon afterwards he was admitted to the bar, and commenced the practice of law in Lexington.

He had been but a short time before the public, when he began to attract, in a remarkable degree, its notice and regard. His engaging manners and exalted character, irresistibly drew to him the respect and affection of his fellow men. He was a stranger to deceit in every form; no one ever suspected him of duplicity; he was open, frank, and true; generous and confiding, perhaps to a fault;

and possessed the unbounded confidence of all who knew him. Such qualities naturally fitted him for public life; and, accordingly, at a very early age, he was elected to the legislature from Fayette county, by the largest majority ever given there. His legislative career was highly honorable to himself and useful to the State. The urbanity of his manners, united to his vigorous talents, and high, steady character, gave him uncommon power and influence. He filled the chair of speaker of the house, with an impartiality and dignity that commanded the approbation of all parties.

Though as far as possible removed from the brawling partisan, and without one quality of the demagogue in his character, Mr. Breckinridge always took a deep interest in public affairs, and his hereditary principles were those of the republican party of '98, which brought Mr. Jefferson into power. The national theatre, in his day, presented comparatively a quiet scene; for the greater part of his public life was passed in what was called the " era of good feeling"—during the adminis- tration of Mr. Monroe—that interval of peace between the violent party contests of our earlier and later history. In the politics of his own State, it was the rare good fortune of Mr. Breckinridge to command the confidence of both parties; and when Gen. Adair was elected governor of Kentucky, the voice of the public, and of the governor himself, designated him for the office of secretary of state. He accepted the appointment, and removed to Frankfort with his family in the spring of 1821, where he continued to reside, attending to his lucrative practice and the duties of his office, until the fall of 1823, when he was seized with a malignant fever then raging in the town, which baffled the skill of his physicians, and of which he died on the 1st of September.

Thus was lost to his family, his friends, and his country, at the early age of thirty-five years, Joseph Cabell Breckinridge—a man who, from his first appear- ance on the theatre of affairs, had been steadily growing in the affection and gratitude of his countrymen—whose life had given a sure guarantee of true greatness—and whose noble character and genuine talents promised, in any sphere, to reflect honor on his state. At the bar, his eloquence, which was of a high and persuasive order, united to his extensive professional attainments, placed him in the front rank. The few compositions and published speeches which the pressure of his other avocations allowed him to throw off, show remarkable pu- rity and force of style. Perhaps, in his day, he had no superior as a writer in the west. His mind was of that long maturing kind, which is late in attaining the utmost force and cultivation to which it is susceptible; and at his death, his powers were expanding into greater strength, and he seemed but upon the thresh- hold of his fame. In social intercourse, his influence on those around him was remarkable. There was a certain individuality about him, not to be forgotten, even by a casual observer—which arose, in part, from his extraordinary personal advantages, but chiefly from a lofty tone of character, which impressed itself on all his conduct. At his death, his position was fixed; no dispute arose concern- ing it; the public sentiment was settled and unanimous. And when his coun- trymen were called to mourn his loss, all joined their according testimony to the perfect nobility of his nature, and the steadfast uprightness of his life.

In person, Mr. Breckinridge was somewhat above the middle height, with a form of remarkable symmetry. His complexion was fair, his eyes and hair dark. His whole appearance was strikingly graceful and manly, and he was esteemed one of the most accomplished gentlemen of his day.

For a number of years before his death, he was a professor of religion, and was one of the founders and ruling elders of the second Presbyterian church in Lex- ington. He carried his religious character wherever he went, and died as he had lived, a christian gentleman. His life is worthy of study, and his example of imitation. He left a numerous family, of whom his widow, an only son, and several daughters, still survive.

HENRY CLAY, the son of a Baptist clergyman of respectable standing, was born in Hanover county, Virginia, on the 12th of April, 1777. His father died when young Henry had attained his fifth year, and the care of superintending his education devolved on his widowed mother. She appears to have been a lady of sterling worth, singular intelligence, and masculine vigor of intellect. Though left in very reduced circumstances, she was enabled, by prudence, economy, and energy, to raise her large family in comfort, and to place her sons in the way to assume stations of respectability and honor in society. Mr. Clay has never ceased to cherish a tender and profound affection and reverence for the memory of this fond mother, and has frequently expressed his sense of the inestimable advantage derived from this early maternal training.

The boyhood of Henry Clay was furnished with few of those facilities for obtaining a literary education, which are now accessible to almost all. His mind was left to develop its powers and attain its growth through the force of its own innate energies, with but little aid from books or competent instructors. Those rich treasures of intellectual wealth, which are to be found in well selected libraries and properly organized schools, were to him a sealed fountain. The extent of his boyish attainments in literature, consisted of the common elements taught in a country school of the most humble pretensions. Even these slender advantages were but sparingly enjoyed, and the future orator and statesman was compelled, by the straitened circumstances of his family, to devote a considerable portion of his time to manual labor in the field. The subsequent brilliant achievements of that master mind, derive increased lustre from the contemplation of the obstacles thus early interposed to its progress, and no more honorable testimony can be offered to the ardour, energy, and invincibility of that towering intellect and imperial spirit, than the severe trials which at this period it encountered, and over which it triumphed. It is probable that this early familiarity with the sternest realities of life, contributed to give to his mind that strong practical bias, which has subsequently distinguished his career as a statesman : while there can be no doubt that the demands thus continually made upon his energies, tended to a quick development of that unyielding strength of character which bears down all opposition, and stamps him as one of the most powerful spirits of the age.

At the age of fourteen, he was placed in a small drug store in the city of Richmond, Virginia. He continued in this situation but a few months, and in 1792 entered the office of the clerk of the high court of chancery. While in this office he attracted the attention of chancellor Wythe, who, being very favorably impressed by his amiable deportment, uniform habits of industry, and striking displays of intelligence, honored him with his friendship, and employed him as an *amanuensis*. It was probably through the advice of chancellor Wythe that he first conceived the design of studying law, and he has himself borne testimony to the fact, that his intercourse with that great and good man exercised a decided and very salutary influence in the development of his mental powers, and the formation of his character.

In the year 1796, he went to reside with Robert Brooke, Esq., attorney general of Virginia. While in the family of this gentleman, his opportunities for acquiring a knowledge of the profession to which he had determined to devote his life, were greatly improved, and he appears to have cultivated them with exemplary assiduity. The year 1797 seems to have been devoted by Mr. Clay exclusively to the study of his profession. It is worthy of remark, that this was the first year in which his necessities permitted him to pursue an uninterrupted system of study, and so eagerly did he avail himself of the privilege, and such was the ardor and vivacity of his mind, that near the close of the year he obtained from the Virginia court of appeals a license to practice. Of course the acquisitions made in the science of law, in the course of these irregular and broken efforts to master that intricate and complex system, were somewhat desultory and crude, and it is not the least striking evidence of the wonderful resources of Mr. Clay's genius, that he was enabled, notwithstanding these disadvantages, to assume so early in life a high rank in his profession, at a bar distinguished for the number, ability and profound erudition of its members.

Upon obtaining his license, Mr. Clay, then in the twenty-first year of his age, came to Lexington, Kentucky. He did not, however, immediately enter upon the duties of his profession, but spent several months in reviewing his legal studies, and forming an acquaintance with the people. His appearance at this period is represented to have been that of a man in feeble health. Delicate in his person, slow and languid in all his movements, his whole air and bearing was pervaded by a lassitude, which gave no promise of that untiring energy, which has since so singularly marked his extraordinary history.

When Mr. Clay entered upon the duties of his profession, the Lexington bar was noted for talent, numbering among its members some of the first lawyers that have ever adorned the legal profession in America. He commenced the practice under circumstances somewhat discouraging, and as appears from his own statement, with very moderate expectations. His earliest efforts, however, were attended with complete success; his reputation spread rapidly, and, to use his own language, he " immediately rushed into a lucrative practice." This unusual spectacle, so rare in the legal profession, is to be ascribed mainly to Mr. Clay's skill as an advocate. Gifted by nature with oratorial genius of a high order, his very youth increased the spell of that potent fascination which his splendid elocution and passionate eloquence threw over the public mind, and led the imagination a willing captive to its power. It was in the conduct of criminal causes, especially, that he achieved his greatest triumphs. The latitude customary and allowable to an advocate in the defence of his client, the surpassing interest of the questions at issue, presented an occasion and a field which never failed to elicit a blaze of genius, before which the public stood dazzled and astonished.

A large portion of the litigation at that day, in Kentucky, grew out of the unsettled tenure by which most of the lands in the country were held. The contests arising out of those conflicting claims, had built up a system of land law remarkable for its intricacy and complexity, and having no parallel in the whole range of the law of real property. Adapted to the exigencies of the country, and having its origin in the necessities of the times, it was still remarkable for its logical consistency and sound principle. Kentucky, at that day, could boast some of the most profound, acute and subtle lawyers in the world. And it is no slight tribute to the talents and acquirements of Mr. Clay, to say that, among those strong and deeply learned men, he stood among the foremost.

When Mr. Clay first arrived in Kentucky, the contest between the old federal and democratic parties was violent and bitter. Any one acquainted with the ardent, frank, open and somewhat boisterous and extravagant character of the Kentuckians at that period, will not require to be told that neutrality in politics, even had Mr. Clay been disposed to pursue that equivocal line of conduct, was for him utterly out of the question, and would not have been tolerated for a moment. He, accordingly united himself with the Jeffersonian or democratic party, with whose principles his own sentiments entirely harmonized. He was prominent at a very early day among those who denounced the most obnoxious measures of the Adams administration, and was especially conspicuous for the energy, eloquence and efficiency with which he opposed the alien and sedition laws.

In 1803 he was elected to represent the county of Fayette in the most numerous branch of the state legislature. He was re-elected to that body at every session, until 1806. The impression made upon his associates must have been of the most favorable character, since, in the latter year, he was elected to the senate of the United States, to serve out the unexpired term of General Adair. He was elected for one session only.

During this session, Mr. Clay, as a member of the senate, had occasion to investigate the extent of the power of congress to promote internal improvements, and the result of his examination was a full conviction that the subject was clearly within the competency of the general government. These views he has never changed; and profoundly impressed with the policy of promoting such works, he at the same session gave his cordial support to several measures of that character. When it is remembered how long and earnestly Mr. Clay has labored to engraft this upon the settled policy of the government, and that it was almost the first subject upon which he was called to act when he entered the senate, it will be difficult to produce a similar example of consistency and firm persistence in the pursuit of a cherished object, and presents a refreshing contrast to the zigzag track of some other American statesmen of great eminence. It is difficult to resist the conclusion that to the man who could thus steadily persevere, against an overwhelming tide of opposition, through all changes of party, and all vicissitudes of personal fortune, in the advocacy of a principle, frequently obnoxious, there must have been something in the aspect of truth herself, independent of all extraneous considerations, irresistibly lovely and attractive.

At the close of the session, Mr. Clay returned to Kentucky and resumed the

practice of his profession. At the ensuing election in August, he was returned
as the representative from Fayette to the legislature. When the legislature
assembled, he was elected speaker of the house. In this station he was distinguished for the zeal, energy and decision with which he discharged its duties.
He continued a member of the legislature until 1809, when he tendered his resignation, and was elected to the senate of the United States for two years, to fill
the vacancy occasioned by the resignation of Mr. Thruston. During his continuance in the legislature he had produced the deepest impression of his abilities,
and won the warm regard and full confidence of his associates. How completely
he had established himself in the favorable opinion of that body, may be inferred
from the fact that he was elected to the office before named, by a vote of two-thirds.
He retired, accompanied by expressions of ardent admiration for his talents, high
esteem for his services, and sincere regret for his loss.

The principal matters which came before the senate during Mr. Clay's second
term of service, related to the policy of encouraging domestic manufactures : the
law to reduce into possession, and establish the authority of the United States
over the territory between the Mississippi and Perdido rivers, comprehending the
present states of Mississippi, Alabama and Florida ; and the question of a re-
charter of the bank of the United States. In the discussions which arose on each
of these questions, Mr. Clay bore a conspicuous part, fully sustaining the high
reputation for ability with which he entered the senate.

His speech in favor of giving the preference to articles of American growth and
manufacture, in providing supplies for the army and navy, was remarkable, as
being the first occasion in which he developed to the national legislature, those
peculiar views in reference to the policy of building up a system of home industry,
which he had at an earlier day sought to impress on the legislation of Kentucky.
Up to this period, this subject, which has since, and mainly through the instrumentality of Mr. Clay, become so prominent and exciting a question in American
politics, had attracted little or no attention, and when the principle of protection
and encouragement was at this session brought forward for the first time, and
attempted to be embodied in legislative enactments, the resistance it encountered
was violent, bitter, and determined. Mr. Clay's speech in favor of the proposition,
was the first he delivered upon re-entering the senate, and is remarkable as having
distinctly shadowed forth the outlines of that magnificent system of "protection,"
of which he has been styled the "father," and which has since become a cherished object of American policy with our soundest statesmen. To the admirers
of Henry Clay it is a source of gratification that the majority of those great principles of internal polity, which his subsequent life has been devoted to build up
and defend, are clearly announced and distinctly to be traced in the first acts of
his public career ; thus presenting in his history as a politician, a consistency and
singleness of purpose, as rare as it is honorable to his character as a man, and his
foresight as a statesman.

His speech delivered at the same session, on the " *line of the Rio Perdido*," in
which he undertook to investigate and trace the title of the United States to the
territory which comprises the present states of Mississippi, Alabama and Florida,
is a masterpiece of legislative logic, distinguished for the clearness of its statements, and the cogent closeness of its reasoning.

At the session of 1810–11, the question of a re-charter of the bank of the United
States was brought before the senate, and became the subject of a debate, noted
in our congressional history, for its intemperate violence and splendid displays of
eloquence. On this occasion Mr. Clay was found opposed to the re-charter of the
bank, and maintained his views in a speech of great ingenuity and power. He
afterwards, in 1816, saw reason to change his opinions, and since then has been
firm in the support he has given to that institution. The explanation of this inconsistency is to be sought in the peculiar views held by American statesmen at
that day, in reference to the construction of the constitution. The grand subject
of difference in *principle* between the old federal and democratic parties, related to
the interpretation of that instrument. The federalists were the advocates of a
free construction, granting to the general government the utmost latitude in the
exercise of its powers. It is probable that in the heat of party controversy they
carried their principles to an extreme, perhaps a dangerous length. The democrats, on the other hand, were strict constructionists ; opposed to deriving

powers to congress by implication, and confining the government to the exercise of such as were expressly and in terms granted in the constitution. In
looking back now with the calm eye of the historian to those troubled times, it
is probable that both of the great parties of the day pushed their principles to an
impolitic length, and that greater moderation would have approximated each nearer
to the truth. The question of a re-charter of the bank of the United States, was
the one of all others calculated to develop the peculiar views, and array the
ancient prejudices of those powerful parties in deadly opposition. The power to
incorporate a bank was one which could be obtained by implication only, and the
arguments adduced in its favor assailed the constitutional system of the democrats
in its most sacred principles. Mr. Clay was a Jeffersonian democrat, and had
been educated in all the peculiar views of that school. He had entered public
life at a period when the contest between the parties was most furious and determined ; and he had, with the ardour and energy of his nature, espoused most of
the doctrines of the party with which he acted ; consequently, when the question
of re-chartering the bank came up, he was found among the ablest and most determined opponents of that measure. His speech, delivered on the occasion, is
remarkable for the force with which it arrays the objections to the bank, and may
be consulted by any one desirous of obtaining a clear knowledge of the principles
of his party at that day in reference to the powers vested in congress by the constitution. In 1816, time, and the intervening experience of the war, had, with
its usual meliorating effect, modified the opinions of men on this as on other subjects. Mr. Clay became convinced of the necessity of a bank to regulate the
financial affairs of the government and country, and with the manly frankness
characteristic of his nature, yielded to that institution his friendship and support.
   When, at the expiration of the term of service for which he had been elected,
Mr. Clay retired from the senate, he left behind him a character for general
ability and sound statesmanship, which few men of the same age have ever attained.
   In 1811, the same year in which he retired from the senate, he was elected by
the people of the Fayette district to represent them in the house of representatives of the United States. In 1813 he was re-elected, and continued a member
of the house until he was sent to Europe as one of the commissioners to negotiate a treaty of peace with Great Britain. During the whole of this period, he
filled the speaker's chair in the house, having received the high and unusual compliment of being chosen to that responsible station the first day on which he appeared in his seat in congress.
   Mr. Clay, consequently, presided over the twelfth and thirteenth congresses,
and participated largely in those measures adapted to vindicate the honor and
assert the rights of the country, against the usurpations and aggressions of Great
Britain. He gave a warm and hearty co-operation in all those efforts that were
made to put the country in a state of defence, and contributed as much, if not
more, by his sleepless energy and unrivalled eloquence, to infuse a proper spirit
into the deliberations of congress, than any other man. His speeches on the
subject of our difficulties with Great Britain, exhibit some of the most brilliant
specimens of parliamentary eloquence extant, and their effect at the time, in
arousing the country to a sense of its wrongs, and a determination to redress them,
is said to have been unequalled. As strange as it may sound in the ears of the
present generation, there was a large and respectable party, at that period, both
in and out of congress, which was averse to war with Great Britain, and disposed to submit to almost any outrage rather than distract her efforts to put down
the power of Napoleon, then in the midst of his extraordinary career. It was in
opposition to what he considered the parricidal efforts of these men, that the
transcendent genius of the Kentucky statesman displayed its most brilliant, powerful, and commanding attributes. He was the life and soul of the war party in
congress—the master spirit around whom all the boldness and chivalry of the
nation rallied in that dark hour, when the gloom of despondency hung heavy on
every brow, and the generous pride of a free people drooped under the withering
sense of the unavenged insult that had been offered to the national honor. In
1814, he resigned his place in congress, to accept an appointment as commissioner
and minister plenipotentiary to Ghent. At this period, the control which he had

acquired in congress was unlimited. In the house, it was probably equal to that he had obtained a few years before in the Kentucky legislature.

In 1814, having been appointed in conjunction with Messrs. John Q. Adams, James A. Bayard, Albert Gallatin, and Jonathan Russell, a commissioner to meet commissioners appointed on the part of Great Britain, he proceeded to Europe. On the sixth of August, the plenipotentiaries of both nations met in the ancient city of Ghent, prepared to proceed to business. The plan of this sketch does not require, nor would it admit of a detailed account of the negotiations, extending through several months, which finally resulted in a treaty of peace between the two nations. These are to be found related at large, in the public histories of the time, and to them we refer the reader for a full knowledge of those transactions. Let it suffice to say, that, on this, as on all other occasions, Mr. Clay mingled controllingly in the deliberations of his distinguished colleagues, and exercised a very commanding influence over the course of the negotiation. There is, indeed, reason to believe, that, but for his firmness and tact, the right to the exclusive navigation of the Mississippi river would have been surrendered for a very inconsiderable equivalent. His colleagues in the negotiation have always borne the most honorable testimony to the ability and comprehensive knowledge displayed by Mr. Clay in those memorable transactions, and he returned to the United States with a reputation materially enhanced.

When the commissioners had closed their diplomatic labors, Mr. Clay visited Paris, and subsequently London, forming an acquaintance with many of the most distinguished characters on the continent and in England. In 1815, he left the shores of Europe, and returned to America, which continent he has not since left, except on one occasion, when he made a brief visit to the island of Cuba for the benefit of his health.

He found upon his arrival in Kentucky, that, during his absence, he had been nominated by his friends and elected to congress; but, as there arose doubts respecting the legality of his election, he resigned, and the canvass was opened anew. This resulted as the previous vote, in his being returned by an overwhelming majority. He was re-elected in succession to every congress that assembled, until the session of 1820–21, when he retired to repair the inroads made in his private fortune by his long devotion to public affairs. During this period, he was thrice elected speaker of the house, and presided over the deliberations of that body during the whole period which intervened between 1815 and 1821.

On his re-entrance into congress, Mr. Clay was called to defend the treaty, in the formation of which he had participated so largely, against the animadversions of his old enemies, the Federalists. That treaty was made the subject of unbridled criticism, by those who had opposed the war, and with the magical astuteness of hatred, they discovered objectionable features in every clause. In the course of the discussions which thus arose, he had frequent occasion to review the origin, progress, and termination of the war, which task he performed with masterly ability, exposing the inconsistency and malignity of his adversaries to deserved odium. He met them at every point, and never failed to make their rancorous virulence recoil on their own heads with tremendous effect.

During the time of this, Mr. Clay's second incumbency in the house of representatives, many questions were presented for its deliberation of surpassing interest, and closely touching the permanent welfare of the republic. The finances of the country were found to be in a condition of ruinous embarrassment; the nation was deeply involved in debt, and the little money left in the country was being continually drained away to pay for foreign importations. It was in this gloomy conjuncture of affairs that the session of 1815–16 opened, and congress was called to the arduous task of repairing the breaches which thus yawned in the public prosperity. In all those measures recommended by Mr. Madison's administration, with a view to the accomplishment of this end, Mr. Clay heartily co-operated. Among other things, he gave his support to a proposition to reduce the direct tax of the United States. He advocated, as has been already stated, the incorporation of a United States' bank. This he justified on the ground that such an institution was necessary to the financial department of the government, and to maintain a healthy condition of the circulating medium. At the same session a law was passed, establishing a tariff for revenue and protection. The principle of protection was distinctly avowed and clearly developed. To this measure, of course,

Mr. Clay gave all the support of his great talents and commanding influence. On this occasion John C. Calhoun was found arrayed on the side of protection, and Daniel Webster in the opposition. But

" *Tempora mutantur, et nos mutamur cum illis.*"

The position and sentiments of these gentlemen are now entirely reversed. Mr. Calhoun has become the great nullifier, and Mr. Webster is universally recognized as one of the most powerful champions of protection.

In 1820 the subject of a protective tariff again came before Congress, and Mr. Clay gave an ardent support to a bill introduced for the purpose of increasing the measure of protection. Nor did he relax his efforts until he finally had the satisfaction of seeing the system for which he had been so long struggling fully established. This firmness and constancy in the pursuit of a favorite object constitutes one of the prominent features in Mr. Clay's character, and has given to his career as a politician a consistency rarely to be observed among that fickle and ever changing tribe. There is an iron tenacity and obduracy of purpose evinced in his life, which knows not to yield to opposition or obstacles, however formidable. With a foresight rarely equaled, his measures were founded in a profound knowledge of the condition, resources and wants of the nation, and hence he has but seldom had occasion to change his opinions on any subject.

In March, 1818, a resolution was introduced declaring that Congress had power to construct post-roads and canals, and also to appropriate money for that object. This resolution encountered a most formidable array of opposition. Mr. Madison, previous to his retirement from the presidential chair, had vetoed a bill for the promotion of internal improvements, and in succeeding him, Mr. Monroe manifested a disposition to " follow in his footsteps." But nothing daunted by the overwhelming opposition against which he had to contend, and the discouraging fact that the administrations of Jefferson, Madison and Monroe were all against the policy, Mr. Clay continued to urge upon Congress the adoption of his system, from a profound conviction that it was intimately connected with the progress of the country in all those elements which promote the general good. The resolution was adopted by a vote of ninety to seventy-five. It was a triumph, and a signal one, over opposition that had been accumulating during two previous administrations, and which, in the existing one, was directed against him with all the violence and impetuosity that power, patronage, and energy could impart to it. It was a moment of proud satisfaction to the indefatigable statesman, when he beheld the last vestige of opposition disappear beneath his feet. The system of internal improvements has been since erected so much under his supervision and through his direct instrumentality, as to give him the title of "its father."

The recognition of the South American republics by the government of the United States, a measure which was almost entirely attributable to the indefatigable exertions, personal influence and powerful eloquence of Mr. Clay, while it shed lustre on the Monroe administration, surrounded the brow of the great statesman with a halo of true glory which grows brighter with the lapse of time.

At the session of 1816–17 the subject of the Seminole war was brought before Congress, and Mr. Clay, in the course of his speech on that occasion, found it necessary to speak with some severity of the conduct of General Jackson. This was the origin of that inveterate hostility on the part of the old general towards the great Kentuckian, the consequences of which were deeply felt in after years.

The only remaining measure of importance with which Mr. Clay's name is connected in the history of those times, was the great and exciting question which arose on the application of Missouri for admission into the union. Probably at no period of our history has the horoscope of our country's destiny looked so dark and threatening. The union was convulsed to its centre. An universal alarm pervaded all sections of the country and every class of the community. A disruption of the confederacy seemed inevitable—civil war, with its attendant horrors, seemed to scowl from every quarter, and the sun of American liberty appeared about to set in a sea of blood. At this conjuncture every eye in the country was turned to Henry Clay. He labored night and day, and such was the excitement of his mind, that he has been heard to declare that if the settlement of the controversy had been suspended three weeks longer, it would have cost him his life. Happy was it for America that he was found equal to the emergency, and that the tempest of desolation which seemed about to burst upon our heads was, through his agency, permitted to pass away harmless. At the close of the session of congress in 1821, Mr. Clay retired, and resumed the practice of his profession. He did not again enter congress until 1823.

Upon resuming his place in congress at the commencement of the session of 1823-4, Mr. Clay was elected speaker, over Mr. Barbour of Virginia, by a considerable majority. He continued speaker of the house until he entered the cabinet of Mr. Adams, in 1825. During this time, the subject of the tariff again came before congress, and was advocated by Mr. Clay in one of the most masterly efforts of his life. His speech on the occasion, was distinguished for the thorough knowledge of the subject which it displayed ; for its broad, comprehensive and statesmanlike views, and for its occasional passages of impressive and thrilling eloquence. He also advocated a resolution, introduced by Mr. Webster, to defray the expenses of a messenger to Greece, at that time engaged against the power of the Turks in an arduous and bloody struggle for independence. A spectacle of this kind never failed to enlist his profoundest sympathies, and elicit all the powers of his genius.

Toward the close of the year 1824, the question of the presidency was generally agitated. As candidates for this office, Messrs. J. Q. Adams, Andrew Jackson, Henry Clay and W. H. Crawford had been brought forward by their respective friends. Mr. Clay had been nominated by the Kentucky legislature as early as 1822. The people failing to make a choice, the election was thrown into the house. Mr. Clay, being the lowest on the list, was excluded from the house by the constitutional provision, which makes it the duty of congress to select one of the three highest candidates. His position in the house now became exceedingly delicate as well as important. He had it in his power, by placing himself at the head of the party who went with him in the house, to control its choice of the three candidates before it. When the election came on, he cast his vote for Mr. Adams, who thus became president of the United States. This vote of Mr. Clay has been made the subject of much calumny and misrepresentation. At the time, it was charged that he had been bought up by the offer of a seat in the cabinet. Efforts were made to produce evidence to this effect, but it was attended by signal failure. Of late years the charge was reiterated by General Jackson, the defeated candidate, which led to an investigation of the whole affair. The result of this was the exposure of one of the darkest conspiracies ever formed, to ruin the character of an individual. Our limits forbid an attempt to array the evidence on this subject, and we must content ourselves with the remark, that there is probably not one man of intelligence now in the Union, who gives to the charge of " bargain and corruption," the slightest credit.

During Mr. Adams' administration, Mr. Clay occupied a seat in his cabinet, as secretary of state. The various official documents prepared by him while in this office, are among the best in our archives. While secretary of state, he negotiated many treaties with the various foreign powers with whom this country maintained relations, in which he approved himself as superior as a diplomatist, as he had been before unrivalled as a legislator and orator. He was a universal favorite with the foreign ministers, resident at Washington, and contributed much, by his amenity and suavity of deportment, to place the negotiations on a footing most favorable to his own country.

At the expiration of Mr. Adams' term of office, Mr. Clay retired to Ashland, his seat near Lexington. He continued engaged in the avocations of his profession until 1831, when he was elected to the senate of the United States for the term of six years. About the same time, in a national convention at Baltimore, he was nominated to the presidency in opposition to General Jackson.

The subjects brought before the senate during this term of Mr. Clay's service, were of the most important and exciting character. The subjects of the tariff, the United States' bank, the public lands, &c., embracing a system of legislative policy of the most comprehensive character and the highest importance, constantly engaged the attention of the country and of congress. During the period signalized by the agitation of these great questions, probably the most exciting in the political annals of America, no man filled a larger space in the public eye than Mr. Clay. He was the centre of a constellation of genius and talent, the most brilliant that has ever lighted this western hemisphere. Although defeated when the election for president came on, that circumstance appeared but to increase the devotion of his friends, and perhaps the star of Henry Clay never blazed with a lustre so bright, so powerful, and far-pervading, as at this moment, when all the elements of opposition, envy, hatred, malice, and detraction, conglomerated in lowering masses, seemed gathering their forces to extinguish and obscure its light forever.

It was at this period that the lines were drawn between those two great and powerful parties, which, assuming to themselves the respective *noms de guerre* of Whig and Democratic, lighted up those flames of civil contention which have kept this country in a state of confusion ever since. At the head of these two parties, towering in colossal strength above their followers, stood two of the most remarkable men of the age. One of these two great men has since descended to the tomb. Like all strong and decided characters, it was his fortune to be pursued with a relentless hatred by his enemies, and rewarded with a love, admiration, and devotion equally boundless, uncalculating, and indiscriminating on the part of his friends. He was unquestionably a man of great virtues and high qualities; but the coloring of his character was marred by shades of darkness, which appeared yet more repulsive from their strong contrast to those traits of brightness and nobility which, gleaming out through the habitual sternness of his nature, shed a redeeming glory over his life. He left the traces of his mind engraved in deep and enduring marks upon the history of his time, and, whatever may be the sentence pronounced by posterity upon his character, truth will say that when Andrew Jackson died, he left no braver heart behind him. He was brave to the definition of bravery: deterred by no danger, moral or physical. A man of impetuous impulses, of strong will and indomitable firmness—he was one of those characters that seem born to command. Such was the man whose powerful hand, gathering up the scattered fragments of many factions and parties, and moulding their heterogeneous elements into one combined, consistent and firm knit mass, seemed resolved to direct its concentrated energies to the destruction of any institution, the subversion of any principle, and the prostration of any individual, that jarred with his feelings, his prejudices or his interests.

It was in opposition to this great leader, and this powerful party, that Mr. Clay was called to act upon his entrance into the senate in 1831. It was an exigency which demanded all his energy and all his talents. We shall not pretend to say that the conduct of Mr. Clay in these bitter and exciting controversies, was free from the influence of passion. On the contrary, passion constitutes one of the strong forces of his character, and is stamped on every action of his life. Perhaps, with the exception of Andrew Jackson, there was not a man in America so remarkable for the fierce and unyielding power of his will, and the deep and fervent impetuosity of his passions, as Henry Clay. It is the characteristic of all decided men. Mr. Clay had no love for his great antagonist, either personal or political. The hostility between them was deep, bitter, and irremediable; and of them it may be truly said, that,

"Like fabled gods, their mighty war
Shook realms and nations in its jar."

Our limits will not allow us to give more than a mere summary of the great questions and events which made up the history of those busy times. They belong to the public history of the country, and to that source the reader must resort for particulars.

General Jackson's veto of the bill to re-charter the Bank of the United States, while it clearly indicated the unsparing temper in which this war of parties was to be prosecuted, produced an effect on the financial condition of the country, which resulted in the most disastrous consequences to trade, commerce, and business in all its branches. The establishment of the pet bank system but aggravated and hastened the evil, and in those first measures of General Jackson's second term of service, were sown the seeds which, at a future day, were reaped in a harvest of woe and desolation. As in 1816, Mr. Clay advocated the re-charter of the bank, and denounced the veto in unmeasured terms. He predicted the consequences which would result from the measure, and subsequent events verified his anticipations.

In relation to the tariff, South Carolina had assumed a hostile attitude. She declared her intention to resist the execution of the revenue laws within her borders, and prepared to maintain herself in this resistance by force of arms. Jackson, on the contrary, swore by the Eternal, that the revenue laws should be enforced at all hazards, and threatened to hang Mr. Calhoun and his coadjutors as high as Haman. The national horizon began to look bloody, and peaceable men to tremble. At this juncture, Mr. Clay again stepped forward as mediator. Although wedded to the protective system, by his conviction of its utility, and its close connection with the progress of the country in arts, wealth, and civilization, he was not the man to jeopardize the existence of the union, or sacrifice the peace of his country to the preservation of any favorite system of policy. He accordingly introduced, and after great efforts succeeded in passing, a compromise measure, which, without yielding the principle of protection, but deferring to the exigencies of the times, pacified the troubled elements of contention, and restored harmony to a distracted people. Perhaps one motive which governed Mr. Clay in his anxiety to pass the compromise act, was his just alarm at the rapidly increasing power of the executive, which, about this period, began to assume a most portentous aspect. He was doubtful of the prudence of entrusting in the hands of President Jackson, the power necessary to enforce the collection of the revenue by hostile measures. He considered that the power and patronage of the executive had already attained a magnitude incompatible with the public liberty. Subsequent developments justified his apprehensions.

Mr. Clay's land bill, introduced into congress about this time, embodying a system for the gradual disposition of the unappropriated public domain of the United States, although it has been the subject of rancorous contention, comprehends perhaps the most wise, federal, and judicious plan for accomplishing that object, that has yet been devised. We have not space for a detail of the principles and particulars of this celebrated measure. They belong to the public history of the nation, and would be out of place in this sketch.

In 1836, Mr. Van Buren became President of the United States, and Mr. Clay was re-elected to the senate. Mr. Van Buren's administration was taken up principally with the disputes relative to the currency. The pet bank system having failed, and a general derangement and prostration of all the business relations and facilities of the country having followed in its train, an attempt was made to rescue the government from the embarrassment in which it had involved the nation, by the establishment of the sub-treasury system. Up to this period, the power of the executive had gone on steadily increasing, until it had absorbed every department of the government. This is the feature which distinguishes the Jackson and Van Buren administrations from all which preceded them. It was against this tendency of politics and legislation that the whigs, under the lead of Mr. Clay, were called to combat, and it finally got to be the engrossing subject of controversy. The sub-treasury was intended to consummate, complete, and rivet that enormous system of executive power and patronage, which had commenced under General Jackson, and attained its maximum during the administration of his obsequious follower and slavish imitator, Martin Van Buren. The debates in congress on this exciting question, are among the ablest in our history, and it is scarcely necessary to say, that among those who opposed on the floor of the senate, by the most gigantic efforts of human intellect, the creation of this dangerous money power in the government, Mr. Clay was with the foremost and most able. The sub-treasury, however, was established, and the system of executive patronage under which the majesty of law and the independence of official station disappeared, was complete.

In 1840, General Harrison, the whig candidate for the presidency, was elected by one of those tremendous and irresistible popular movements, which are seen in no other country besides this. During the canvass, Mr. Clay visited Hanover county, the place of his nativity, and while there addressed an assembly of the people. It was one of the ablest speeches of his life, and contained a masterly exposition of the principles and subjects of controversy between the two parties.

After the election of General Harrison, when congress assembled, it set itself to work to repair the ravages made in the prosperity and institutions of the country

19

by twelve years of misgovernment. Unfortunately, however, the work had scarcely commenced before death removed the lamented Harrison from the scene of his usefulness, and Mr. Tyler, the vice-president, succeeded to his place. Then followed, in rapid succession, veto after veto, until all hope of accomplishing the objects for which the whigs came into power, were extinct.

During this period, Mr. Clay labored night and day to bring the president into an accommodating temper, but without success. He seemed resolved to sever all connection between himself and the party which brought him into power. He will go down to posterity with the brand of *traitor* stamped upon his brow, and take his place with the Arnolds of the revolution.

On the 31st of March, 1842, Mr. Clay executed his long and fondly cherished design of retiring to spend the evening of his days amid the tranquil shades of Ashland. He resigned his seat in the senate, and presented to that body the credentials of his friend and successor, Mr. Crittenden. The scene which ensued was indescribably thrilling. Had the guardian genius of congress and the nation been about to take his departure, deeper feeling could hardly have been manifested than when Mr. Clay arose to address, for the last time, his congressional compeers. All felt that the master spirit was bidding them adieu; that the pride and ornament of the senate, and the glory of the nation was being removed, and all grieved in view of the void that would be created. When Mr. Clay resumed his seat, the senate unanimously adjourned for the day.

In May, 1844, the national whig convention nominated Mr. Clay as a candidate for president of the United States. The nominee of the democratic party was Colonel James K. Polk, of Tennessee. The canvass was probably one of the most exciting ever witnessed in this country. In addition to the old issues, a new one was formed on the proposition to annex the republic of Texas to the American union. This question, intimately involving the exciting subject of slavery, gave to the presidential canvass a new character and an unforeseen direction. It would be out of place here, although not without interest and instruction, to trace and analyze the causes which operated to defeat the whigs. Suffice it to say, that Mr. Polk was made president. Texas became one of the United States. War ensued with Mexico; and the armies of the United States swept the fertile provinces of that sister republic from the mouth of the Rio Grande to the western base of the Rocky mountains. Governments were abrogated, and new ones established in their place, by the fiat of subordinate militia officers; and throughout the whole extent of that rich and beautiful region, scenes were enacted which carry the mind back to the days of romance, and revive the memory of those bloody national tragedies which have crimsoned the pages of European and Asiatic history.

Since the presidential election of 1844, Mr. Clay has lived in retirement at Ashland, engaged in the practice of his profession. He is now in the seventieth year of his age, and the full enjoyment of all his faculties. Few men have ever lived who could look back over a career so various, so full of strange vicissitude and stirring incident. And fewer still have lived, who could find in such retrospect, so little to condemn or regret; so many subjects of pleasing reflection and allowable self-gratulation. May the evening of his days be as bright and tranquil and pleasant, as their meridian has been brilliant, glorious and successful.

Mr. Clay entered the legislature of Kentucky in 1803. He returned from the senate of the United States in 1842. During a period of forty years, he has mingled actively and with a controlling influence in the politics of the country. Probably no man has lived during this time, who has made an impression upon legislation so deep and enduring, or who has exercised so strong an influence in shaping the course of public sentiment. He entered public life when the nation was yet in its early infancy. Our institutions were new and comparatively untried. Our principles were in a state of formation; and those gigantic elements of wealth and power, with which providence has blessed this magnificent land, were still undiscovered and remained to be developed. More than half of the country was covered with an unbroken forest. Those rich and wide spread regions, which, stretching from the Alleghany to the Rocky mountains, and from the head waters of the Mississippi and Missouri to the sands of the Mexican Gulf, are now the seat of many powerful states and opulent communities, then lay dark and silent, the home of the panther, the bear, and the prowling savage. Before the public men of that day was spread the grandest field that ever invited the attention or presented a fitting theatre to the genius of a statesman. Those immense resources were to be developed, and those noble elements combined and moulded into all those fair forms of public prosperity which modern civilization presents for the admiration of the patriot, philanthropist and philosopher. For forty years this great work has been steadily progressing. Those gloomy forests have been subdued and converted into the garden spot of the world. Civilization has penetrated their dark glades, and arts and knowledge have humanized their most savage retreats. Temples to the living God now lift their lofty spires in every direction throughout that smiling region, and splendid cities rear their glittering domes where the sombre forest waved its rustling foliage. Over this region, so late a howling solitude, there is now spread a population of many millions; active, industrious and intelligent; moral, religious and refined; carrying forward the arts to the highest perfection, and sending forth the products of their industry and ingenuity into every country of the earth.

With the progressive advance of this wonderful development of national greatness, Mr. Clay has been contemporary: and in the wise and judicious legislation, under whose fostering care the great work has gone steadily forward, the traces of his powerful hand are to be seen at every step. Endowed by nature with genius of high and commanding attributes—eloquent and brilliant—ardent and ambitious—he possesses all those qualities which, in a democratic country and under popular institutions, confer power and extended influence. From his earliest manhood he has been placed in the most responsible stations; and from the control which he has always exercised over the party with which he was connected, has given a direction to its energies, and communicated the coloring of his own views to its principles and opinions.

The question, then, as to the light in which his character will be estimated by posterity—whether as a true statesman, comprehensive, sagacious and far-sighted —a patriot, pure, and undefiled, exerting his God-given faculties in singleness of heart to build up the fortunes and secure the liberties of his country; or as a mere intriguing politician, absorbed in the pursuit of his own selfish ambition, becomes one of great interest and general importance. It cannot be disguised that, if the principles upon which this man's conduct has been founded, are false, and hollow, and corrupt, there is much of that which is noblest, highest and most excellent in our own history, liable to the same reproach. For it is these principles, and the spirit of this man, working out through many obstacles its cherished designs, that now stand before the world embodied in the forms of laws, opinions and institutions, which give a character to the age.

In early life Mr. Clay acted with that party which was known as the democratic, and of which Thomas Jefferson was the acknowledged leader and animating spirit. His first public efforts after his arrival in Kentucky were directed against the alien and sedition laws: and upon most subjects he continued to think and act with the democratic party, while it retained an organized existence, and until the party lines were broken up and obliterated under the administration of James Monroe. But, although agreeing in sentiment with his party upon the majority of those questions which formed the grounds of the controversy between it and its great antagonist, it is due to Mr. Clay to say that he never sacrificed the right of private judgment, or yielded up his freedom of action. Thus, upon some questions, in which he believed the principles of the party to be inimical to the true interests of the country, he separated without hesitation from the majority of his political friends. As a noted example of this perfect independence with which he exercised the right of judging for himself, we may mention his course in relation to the great subject of internal improvements. It is well known that from his first entrance into the senate of the United States in 1806, he was an ardent advocate of the policy of extending the patronage and protection of government to works of this kind. And yet, the administrations of Jefferson, Madison, and Monroe, and the majority of the democratic party, were hostile to the policy. The power to promote internal improvements was among those implied powers, which the creed of democracy almost utterly disclaimed. On the question of the United States' bank, again, in 1811, Mr. Clay acted with his party, as he did not believe the necessity for such institution to be such, as would justify a resort to implied powers. On this subject, in 1811, he participated fully in the jealousy with which his party viewed all corporations. Power, in any shape, was the great bugbear of democracy at that day; and the power which resided in independent corporations of individuals, was honored with a peculiar share of aversion. The democrats of 1811 viewed the incorporation of the United States' bank with much the same feeling with which the whigs, at a later day, looked upon the establishment of the sub-treasury.

On the subject of the tariff, Mr. Clay had the happiness to act in concert with his party; as it is well known that Jefferson, Madison, and Monroe, with a majority of their followers, were all friendly to the policy.

When the modern whig and democratic parties were organized, Mr. Clay was found with the whigs. The principles and leading characteristics of this party, corresponded very closely with those of the old democratic or Jeffersonian party, with such modification as time, experience and the altered circumstances of the country, had inevitably produced. Both were distinguished by the same jealousy of executive power; which may be said to have formed the basis upon which the organization of each reposed.

Upon the subject of slavery, Mr. Clay has always been a sound conservative. For many years, he acted as president of the American colonization society; and while deprecating the acknowledged evils of African slavery, and prepared to co-operate in any plan by which it could be gradually and safely banished from the country, he has invariably opposed, with firmness, the wild fanatic schemes of modern abolitionism.

Upon an impartial review of his career as a politician, it may be pronounced that Mr. Clay's principles have approached as near the standard of true democracy, as those of any public man in our history; equally removed from the fanaticism and radicalism of the demagogue, as from the bigotry of aristocratic prejudice.

The personal characteristics of Mr. Clay are obvious to the most superficial observer. That he is a man of vast powers, has never been contested. As an orator, he has had few equals. As a statesman, he has been remarkable for the enlargement of his views, and for his far sighted sagacity. His political information is extensive and accurate. He is a man of proud spirit and dauntless courage; ardent, impetuous, self-willed, and withal ambitious; a man of intense convictions and burning passions. These qualities have made him as much feared and hated by his adversaries as he is admired and beloved by his friends. It has fallen to the lot of few men to live a life so crowded with incidents, events and passages of stirring interest and deep excitement. From his earliest youth, he has been accustomed to mingle in those scenes which develop the deepest and strongest faculties of our nature, both of good and evil. And in view of all, it may be said that few men, looking back over the same career, could find so few actions which merit reproach. Posterity, removed by time and distance from the influence of passions and interests which now obscure the judgments of men, will look calmly at the great epic of his life, and with stern impartiality award to each particular act the meed of praise or odium of censure, and summing up the events of his varied career, pronounce upon his character, and write his epitaph.

Ashland, the residence of Mr. Clay, comprising the house, grounds and park, is situated a mile and a half south-east of the court-house in Lexington, on the south-west side of the turnpike road leading to Richmond. The whole estate of Ashland consists of five or six hundred acres of the best land in Kentucky. Ashland proper was projected for an elegant country seat. The house is a spacious brick mansion, without much architectural pretensions, surrounded by lawns and pleasure grounds. The grounds are interspersed with walks and groves, and planted with almost every variety of American shrubbery and forest trees. As the domicil of the great American statesman, Ashland is one of the household words of the American people.

Mr. Clay is one of the most enterprising and successful farmers in Kentucky, and has contributed much to improve the quality of the stock of the country. Mrs. Clay, we understand, derives from the produce of her dairy alone a very considerable revenue.

Colonel WILLIAM DUDLEY, well known in American history from the bloody

ASHLAND, RESIDENCE OF HENRY CLAY, KY.

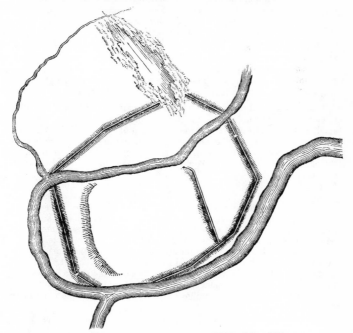

ANCIENT FORT, FAYETTE CO., KY.

and disastrous defeat sustained by the Kentuckians under his command, at fort Meigs during the late war, was a citizen of Fayette county. He was a native of Spottsylvania county, Virginia, and emigrated to Kentucky at an early age. He was for many years a leading magistrate of Fayette county, and was much respected by all who knew him. In the north-western campaign of 1813, under General Harrison, he held the command of a colonel in the Kentucky troops, and on the 5th of May was sent, at the head of a detachment, to spike a battery of cannon which had been erected by the British army, at that time besieging fort Meigs. He succeeded in spiking the guns, but attempting to follow up his advantage, by attacking some troops in the vicinity, was surrounded by the Indians and defeated with terrible slaughter. Colonel Dudley was shot in the body and thigh, and thus disabled. When last seen, he was sitting in the swamp, defending himself against the Indians, who swarmed around him in great numbers. He was finally killed, and his corpse mutilated in a most shocking manner. He was a brave and accomplished officer, and but for his rashness, a fault too common at that day among Kentuckians, his military character would have stood high.

Among the distinguished men who have made Fayette county their residence, was the late RICHARD H. MENIFEE, whose premature death cast a gloom over the whole State. It has been the fortune of but few men, of the same age, to leave behind them a reputation so brilliant. Born in obscurity, and forced to struggle in early life against an array of hostile influences sufficient to have crushed any common spirit, he had, at the period of his early death, attained an eminence which fixed upon him the eyes of all America, as one of our most promising statesmen. He was a native of Bath county, and in early life taught a school to supply himself with the means of obtaining a profession. His success at the bar was rapid and brilliant. He was barely eligible, when he was elected to represent the county of Montgomery in the Kentucky legislature. In this body he established a character for ability which spread his name through the State. At twenty-seven years of age, he was elected to Congress. His efforts on the floor of the house, bearing the impress of high genius and commanding talent, soon placed him in the front rank of debaters, at a time when Congress was remarkable for the number of its able men. At the close of his term of service, he removed to Lexington, and devoted himself to the practice of his profession. Business flowed in upon him, and he was rapidly amassing a fortune, which would have enabled him to re-enter public life, and accomplish those ardent desires cherished from his early boyhood, when his career was prematurely checked by death. He died at his residence in Lexington, in 1840, in the thirty-first year of his age.

COL. WILLIAM R. M'KEE was a resident, and Lieutenant Colonel HENRY CLAY, Jun., a native, of Fayette. These officers fell while bravely fighting at the head of the second Kentucky regiment, at Buena Vista, in Mexico.

There are several remains in the northern part of Fayette county, which appear to be vestiges of ancient Indian fortifications. Thirty years ago, there was a small and very intricate one on the plantation of the late Col. William Russell; but it was examined in the summer of 1846, and found to be nearly obliterated. There are three, two of them still very distinct, near the dividing line between the old military surveys of Dandridge and Meredith, of which a brief description may be interesting. The most easterly of those is on the estate of C. C. Moore, Esq. It is on the top of a high bluff, on the west side of North Elkhorn, in the midst of a very thick growth, mostly of sugar trees. The area within a deep and broad circular ditch, is about a quarter of an acre of ground. The ditch is still deep enough, in some places, to hide a man on horseback. The dirt taken from the ditch, is thrown outward; and there is a gateway where the ditch was never dug, some ten feet wide, on the north side of the circle. Trees, several hundred years old, are growing on the bank and in the bottom of the ditch, and over the area which it encloses, and the whole region about it. A hundred yards, or thereabout, from this work, down a gentle slope, and near a large spring branch, there was, about the commencement of this century, a circular ditch enclosing a very small area, probably not above ten feet wide, within the inner margin of the ditch, which was broad, flat, and obscure at that time; at present it is hardly visible. This is also on Mr. Moore's estate. Going still westward from this spot, you cross a branch, ascend a sharp slope, and come upon an elevated and beautiful forest along the old military line spoken of above; and at the distance of a quarter of a mile from the work first described, is a work of considerable extent. It commences on the Meredith estate, and runs over on the Cabell's Dale estate (the Breckinridge property), and contains perhaps ten acres of land. The shape of the area is not unlike that of the moon, when about two-thirds full. The dirt from the ditch enclosing this area, is thrown sometimes out, sometimes in, and sometimes both ways. There is no water within a hundred yards of this work; but there are several very fine springs a few hundred yards off; and North Elkhorn is within that distance in a north-eastern direction. An ash tree was cut down in the summer of 1845, which stood on the bank of this ditch, which, upon being examined, proved to be four hundred years old. The ditch is still perfectly distinct throughout its whole extent, and in some places is so deep and steep as to be dangerous to pass with a carriage. It is difficult, perhaps impossible, to ascertain when, by whom, or for what purpose, these works were made. Many of them seem wholly incapable of military use of any kind; and it is probable they may have been connected with the national religion, or possibly the national shows and sports of the original makers of them. In one of the fields of the Cabell Dale estate, an immense mass, perhaps several bushels, of flint arrow heads, have been picked up within the last half century, over an area of an acre or two of ground; and on the same estate, in a southerly direction from the work first described, are several ancient tumuli of considerable extent.

SINGULAR INCIDENT.—Mr. McClung, in his "Sketches of Western Adventure," relates the following incident, which, from its singularity, will doubtless be read with interest:

"In 1781, Lexington was only a cluster of cabins, one of which, near the spot where the court house now stands, was used as a school house. One morning in May, McKinley, the teacher, was sitting alone at his desk, busily engaged in writing, when hearing a slight noise at the door, he turned his head, and beheld, what do you suppose, reader? A tall Indian in his war paint, brandishing his tomahawk or handling his knife? No! an enormous cat, with her fore-feet upon the step of the door, her tail curled over her back, her bristles erect, and her eyes glancing rapidly through the room, as if in search of a mouse.

McKinley's position at first completely concealed him, but a slight and involuntary motion of his chair, at sight of this shaggy inhabitant of the forest, attracted puss's attention, and their eyes met. McKinley having heard much of the powers of "the human face divine," in quelling the audacity of wild animals, attempted to disconcert the intruder by a frown. But puss was not to be bullied. Her eyes flashed fire, her tail waved angrily, and she began to gnash her teeth, evidently bent upon serious hostility. Seeing his danger, McKinley hastily arose and attempted to snatch a cylindrical rule from a table which stood within reach, but the cat was too quick for him.

"Darting upon him with the proverbial activity of her tribe, she fastened upon his side with her teeth, and began to rend and tear with her claws like a fury. McKinley's clothes were in an instant torn from his side, and his flesh dreadfully mangled by the enraged animal, whose strength and ferocity filled him with astonishment. He in vain attempted to disengage her from his side. Her long sharp teeth were fastened between his ribs, and his efforts served but to enrage her the more. Seeing his blood flow very copiously from the numerous wounds in his side, he became seriously alarmed, and not knowing what else to do, he threw himself upon the edge of the table, and pressed her against the sharp corner with the whole weight of his body.

"The cat now began to utter the most wild and discordant cries, and McKinley, at the same time, lifting up his voice in concert, the two together sent forth notes so doleful as to alarm the whole town. Women, who are always the first in hearing or spreading news, were now the first to come to McKinley's assistance. But so strange and unearthly was the harmony within the school house, that they hesitated long before they ventured to enter. At length the boldest of them rushed in, and seeing McKinley bending over the corner of the table, and writhing his body as if in great pain, she at first supposed that he was laboring under a severe fit of the colic; but quickly perceiving the cat, which was now in the agonies of death, she screamed out, "why good heaven! Mr. McKinley, what is the matter?"

"I have caught a cat, madam!" replied he, gravely turning round, while the sweat streamed from his face under the mingled operation of fright, and fatigue, and agony. Most of the neighbors had now arrived, and attempted to disengage the dead cat from her antagonist;

but, so firmly were her tusks locked between his ribs, that this was a work of no small difficulty. Scarcely had it been effected, when McKinley became very sick, and was compelled to go to bed. In a few days, however, he had entirely recovered, and so late as 1820, was alive, and a resident of Bourbon county, Kentucky, where he has often been heard to affirm, that he, at any time, had rather fight two Indians than one wild cat."

FLEMING COUNTY.

FLEMING county was formed in 1798, and named in honor of Colonel JOHN FLEMING. It is situated in the north-east part of the State, on Licking river—bounded on the north by Mason and Lewis; east by Carter; south by Bath, and west by Nicholas. The face of the country is variegated, and the soil as diversified as that of any county in Kentucky. The western portion of the county, in the centre of which is situated the county seat, is rolling or undulating, abounding in limestone and very productive for grasses, hemp and corn, and a part well adapted for wheat. The eastern and north-eastern portion of the county, embracing an extensive territory, is generally mountainous, interspersed with large creeks and fertile bottoms, adapted to corn, wheat, clover and tobacco—abounding in mineral-waters—among which the Fox Springs and Phillips Springs are improved as watering places; watered by main Licking, Fleming, Fox and Triplett creeks. Its principal exports consist of cattle, hogs and hemp.

Taxable property in 1846, $3,422,370; number of acres of land in the county 280,681; average value of lands per acre, $6,96; number of white males over twenty-one years of age, 2,325; number of children between five and sixteen years old, 2,810. Population in 1830, 13,493—in 1840, 13,268.

The towns of Fleming, are Flemingsburg, Poplar Plains, Mount Carmel, Elizaville, Hillsborough and Sherburn. FLEMINGSBURG is the county-seat and principal town, situated on the Maysville and Mount Sterling turnpike road, seventeen miles from the former place, and seventy-nine miles from Frankfort. It contains a large and handsome brick court house, with a fine cupola, bell and clock; five churches, (Presbyterian, Baptist, Methodist, Reformed or Christian, and Seceder). One Academy, one collegiate institution, six physicians, twelve lawyers, six stores, three hotels, one printing office, (Fleming Flag,) market house and jail, a branch of the Louisville bank, one hat store, one drug store, twenty mechanics' shops, and one large steam flouring mill. Established in the year 1812. Population 800. Derived its name from the Fleming family.

Elizaville is five miles from Flemingsburg, and contains three stores, one tavern, three physicians, one tannery, one manufactory of saleratus, pearlash, &c., one school and five mechanics' shops. *Hillsborough* contains two stores, one tavern, post office and blacksmith shop. Population forty. *Mount Carmel* is seven miles north of Flemingsburgh, and contains two stores, one tavern, one Methodist church, one school house, two doctors, two tanneries, one wool factory, five mechanical trades. Population 120. Incorporated in 1825. *Poplar Plains* is situated five miles southeast of Flemingsburg—incorporated in 1831, contains two stores, one tavern, post office, tannery, woolen factory and oil mill, two doctors and six mechanics' shops. Population, 100. *Sherburn* is a small village and mills on Licking river, containing a store, post office, tailor's shop, blacksmith shop and tavern. Population about 40.

The *Geological statistics* of Fleming county are not in general of a rich or varied character. It rests principally upon the upper strata of the blue limestone series, belonging, with its accompaniments, to the transition formation : though in the eastern part, it is in some places overlaid with a very silicious limestone, probably the equivalent of the cliff limestone; and in the " knobs " rises into the black slate, capped with old red sandstone. Except where the rocks and clays occupy the surface, (which is but a small portion,) the soil is very productive, much of it being good hemp land ; but no important metals are to be found. There are several small deposites of iron ore, not valuable or extensive to work, as far as examined. One of these, however, lying near the Licking river, is a remarkable and rare deposite. The oxide of iron, incorporated with sand, is formed into regular tubes, from the size of a pistol barrel to several inches in diameter, the cylinder being from a half to one and a half inches thick. It is impossible to estimate the length of these *fulgurites*, as the fragments have been fractured at both ends by the ploughshare.

There is likewise a large deposite of clay near Poplar Plains, suitable for potter's ware. The other minerals are small quantities of sulphurate of iron, calcarious spar, barytes and petroleum or " mineral tar." The disintegrating limestone presents about seventy-five species of fossils, some of them in great abundance and perfection, the hill sides of the undulating surface exposing them to observation. The soil has but a small proportion of sand in its composition, clay and lime predominating.

GEORGE STOCKTON, who, in his infancy, had been taken prisoner, together with a sister, by the Indians in Virginia, and carried to New York, there remained until he became so much attached to the Indian manner of living, that the desire to see his friends and family could scarcely overcome his reluctance to part with those whom association had made dear.

After he had grown up, he accompanied his tribe on a trading expedition to Pennsylvania, and there determined to visit his friends in Virginia. A fondness for forest life had so entertwined itself with his very nature, that he could ill support the dull uniformity of society, and he soon set out for Kentucky, to enjoy the glorious solitude and freedom of the woods. He settled at Stockton's station, in sight of Flemingsburg, in 1787.

Robert Stockton and Beacham Rhodes set out from Stockton's station in the winter of 1789, for the purpose of hunting on the waters of Fox's creek and its tributaries, then the favorite resorts of the buffalo, deer, bear, &c. Regarding the season of the year, it was not considered any adventure fraught with great danger, as the Indians rarely visited Kentucky except in the seasons when the necessaries of life were more easily obtained. The hunters pitched their camp upon the bank of Fox's creek, and enjoyed several days of successful hunting and exciting sport. On the night of the 15th February, after a day of unusual excitement and fatigue, the hunters, replenishing their fire, rolled themselves up in their blankets, and stretching themselves (with their two fine dogs) upon the ground, after the manner of the hunters of that day, without other "means and appliances," were soon soundly asleep. About the middle of the night, they were aroused by the simultaneous discharge of two guns. Stockton sprung to his feet only to fall lifeless to the earth. Rhodes, though severely wounded in the hip by two balls from the same gun, succeeded (whilst the dogs made fiercely at the Indians) in crawling beyond the light of the fire. Stationing himself behind a tree, he calmly awaited the re-appearance of the Indians, resolved to sell his life at the cost of one of theirs. The Indians, doubtless, suspecting his purpose, were wise enough to mount the horses of the hunters, and made for the Kentucky river, where one of them was afterwards killed. The Indians not appearing, Rhodes determined, if possible, to conceal himself before day should dawn. With this hope, he crawled into the creek, and that his trail might not be discovered, kept in the water until about a half a mile from camp he came to a large pile of brush and logs which the creek had drifted. In this he remained secreted (in momentary expectation of hearing the Indians) all day. At night he set out on a painful journey towards home, and on the seventh day after his wound, reached Fleming creek, having *crawled* a distance of fourteen miles. The creek was considerably swollen, and in his wounded and exhausted state, presented an insuperable barrier to his further progress. Fortunately, however, he was found by another hunter, who aided him in reaching his home. The friends of Stockton, instantly collecting, started for the camp, where they found

> " His faithful dog, in life his firmest friend,
> The first to welcome, foremost to defend,
> Whose honest heart was still his master's own,
> Who labor'd, fought, lived and breathed for him alone,"—

guarding his body, though so weak from starvation, as to be unable to walk. A circle of torn earth all around the body of Stockton, marked the rage and disappointment of wolves and panthers, and told how watchful and firm had been the protection of the dog. Stockton was buried where he fell, and his grave, marked with a large slab, is yet to be seen in going from Flemingsburg to Carter courthouse, one mile beyond Phillips' springs. The friends of Stockton carried home the dog, and after several weeks, the other dog, which had followed the horses, also returned.

Zadock Williams, whilst working in a tobacco field, in sight of Stockton's station, was shot by an Indian in the year 1790. There were no men in the fort at the time; and the old settlers, to this day, speak with wonder at the *efforts* of an old negro woman upon a horn, with which she alarmed the residents of a fort five or six miles distant. The Indians, probably terrified at such prodigious blasts, made off.

The three forts or stations in the county, (Stockton's, Cassiday's and Fleming's,) had in their service two brothers, named Stuart, whose duty it was (dressed after the Indian fashion) to keep a look out, and give timely notice of the presence of hostile Indians. It was understood by all the settlers, that no one was to fire a gun within hearing of either fort, unless at an Indian. In returning at Cassiday's station in the evening, one of the brothers was overcome by the temptation to shoot a large owl. Michael Cassiday and John Clifford, who were at the fort, supposing the gun to be fired by an Indian, seized their rifles and issued forth into the woods to reconnoitre. They soon observed the two brothers approaching, but owing to the dusk of the evening and their Indian dress, did not recognize them. Old man Cassiday, who was proverbial for his resolution and bravery, pushed on until within gun shot, fired, and one of the brothers fell to the ground. Clifford, in the mean time, was exerting all his ingenuity and stratagem to get a shot at the other brother, until he finally made himself heard. The three then went to the wounded man, and found him with but just enough life to tell Cassiday his death was the result of his own folly in firing his gun within hearing of the fort, forgave him, and expired. The surviving brother afterwards declared, that he was once or twice upon the point of shooting Clifford, to save his own life.

Michael Cassiday, the individual mentioned in the foregoing narrative, was a native of Ireland, whence he emigrated to the United States in his youth. At the breaking out of the revolutionary war, he enlisted and served for several years in the ranks of the army. After leaving the army, he came to Kentucky, and attached himself to Strode's station, in what is now Clark county, and from thence removed to this county, and settled at Cassiday's station. He was remarkably small in stature, little if at all exceeding five feet, and there are many amusing stories told of his contests with Indians, who looked upon him as a boy.

Upon one occasion, while encamped in the woods with two other friends, (Bennett and Spor), three Indians attacked their camp, and killed Bennett and Spor at the first fire. Cassiday sprung to his feet, but was soon overpowered and made prisoner. The Indians, supposing him to be a boy, and proposing to relieve the tedium of the night, selected the smallest of their number to *carve* him up with a large butcher knife, for their diversion. Cassiday, whose fiery spirit little predisposed him to suffer an unresisting martyrdom, grappled his antagonist, and flung him several times with great violence to the earth, greatly to the amusement of the other Indians, who laughed immoderately at their companion's defeat by one seemingly so disproportioned in strength. The two Indians, finding that it was growing a serious matter, came to the rescue of their companion, and with several strokes of their war clubs, felled Cassiday to the ground. Fortunately, Cassiday fell with his hand upon the knife which his competitor had let fall, and rising, brandished it with such fierceness that the Indians gave back, when he, stepping to one side, darted rapidly into the woods. The darkness of the night enabled him to elude his pursuers until he came to a deep pool of water, overhung by a large sycamore. Under the roots of this tree, up to his neck in the water, he remained concealed until the Indians, flashing their torches around him in every direction, gave up in despair. He carried to his grave the marks of the Indian clubs, to testify with what good will they were given. Colonel Thomas Jones, who was at the burial of the two men, (Bennett and Spor), yet lives near Flemingsburg.

Upon another occasion, whilst hunting on Cassiday's creek, in what is now Nicholas county, he very unexpectedly found himself in close proximity to a powerful Indian, in a place quite free from timber. Each observed the other at the same time, and both leveled their guns. But Cassiday, to his consternation, found that his pocket handkerchief was tied round the lock of his gun, so as to prevent its being cocked, and he feared to untie it, lest the Indian perceiving it, should fire. They remained pointing their guns at each other in this manner for some time. The Indian not firing, Cassiday suspected that something was the matter with his gun also, and began to take off his handkerchief, when the Indian fled to a tree. Cassiday followed in full speed, and taking a circuit so as to bring the Indian in view, fired and wounded him in the shoulder. Drawing his knife, he made towards the wounded Indian, in whose gun he now perceived the ramrod. When Cassiday approached, the Indian (lying on the ground) extended his hand, crying "brother!" Cassiday told him he was "a d—d mulatto hypocrite, and he shouldn't *claim kin* with him. Saint Patrick! but he would pummel him well." After a desperate conflict with the Indian, who, though deprived of the use of his right arm, proved no contemptible foe, and whose nakedness afforded no tangible hold, Cassiday succeeded in dispatching him.

Cassiday was in upwards of thirty Indian fights, and such and so many was his 'hair breadth 'scapes,' that he was commonly said to have a *charmed* life. He served in the legislature repeatedly, lived respected and died regretted, at his station, in the year 1829.

Colonel JOHN FLEMING, after whom Fleming county was called, was born in Virginia; and in company with Major George Stockton, emigrated to Kentucky in the year 1787, descending the Ohio river in a canoe, and settled at Stroud's station. He afterwards removed to Fleming county, and settled Fleming's station in the year 1790, where he remained till his death in the year 1794. The witnesses of his life, like the fabled leaves of the Sybil's prophecy, have been so scattered by the hand of death, that it is impossible to collect the history of any save the following incidents:

Some twenty Indians having stolen horses, and made prisoners of two children near Strode's station, in Clark county, in the year 1791, were pursued by about fifteen whites, and overtaken on a creek, since called *Battle run*, in Fleming county. A sharp contest ensued, in which the loss was about equal on either side; but the whites, being outnumbered, were forced to give way.

Col. John Fleming, the settler of Fleming's station, was severely wounded in the engagement, and in the retreat, being hotly pursued by an Indian, directed one of the men who was flying past him, to point his gun at the Indian and compel him to tree, until he could reload his gun. The man replied that his gun was not loaded. Fleming quickly remarked, "the Indian don't know that;" whereupon the man did as directed, with the effect that Fleming foresaw. Whilst the Indian was intent upon the manœuvres of the man, Fleming succeeded in loading his gun. The pursuit becoming alarming, the man fled. The Indian, supposing Fleming to be too badly wounded to be dangerous, made confidently towards him with uplifted tomahawk. Fleming, supporting his gun upon a log, waited until the Indian came very near, when, firing, he fell headlong almost against the log behind which Fleming was lying.

Fleming's mare, which had broken loose during the fight, came galloping by, recognized the voice of her master, went to him, received him on her back, and carried him gallantly off the field. He reached the large pond near Sharpsburg, where, exhausted from the loss of blood, and burning with thirst, he, with a fellow fugitive, encamped. Such was his fever from his wound, that, to allay his insatiate thirst, he kept his friend constantly engaged throughout the night in bringing water. Next morning, he was sufficiently recovered to resume his way, and arrived safely at the station.

In the family of Major George Stockton was a slave named Ben. Ben was a "regular" negro, devoted to his master—hated an Indian with an enmity passing Randolph's aversion to sheep—loved to moralize over a dead one—got into a towering rage, and swore "magnificently" when a horse was missing—handled his rifle well, though somewhat foppishly—and hopped and danced and showed his teeth with infinite satisfaction, at the prospect of a chase of the "*yaller varmints.*" His master had every confidence in his resolution and prudence, and in fact Ben was a great favorite with all the hunters, adding much to their stock of fun on dull expeditions.

A party of Indians having stolen horses from some of the upper stations, were pursued by a party of whites, who called at Stockton's station for reinforcements. Ben, among others, gladly volunteered. The Indians were overtaken at Kirk's springs, in Lewis county. The whites dismounting, secured their horses, and advanced to the attack. Only eight or ten Indians could be seen, and they retreated rapidly over the mountain. The whites followed, but in descending the mountain, discovered, from an attempt to out-flank them, that the retreating Indians were but a part of the enemy remaining behind to decoy them into an ambuscade, prepared at the base of the mountain. Various indications plainly showed that the Indians were greatly superior in number, and the whites were ordered to retreat. Ben was told of the order by a man near him, but was so intently engaged, that he did not hear. The man, in a louder tone, warned him of his danger. Ben turned upon him a reproving look, with indescribable grimaces and ludicrous gesticulations, admonishing silence, and springing forward, set off at a furious rate down the mountain. The man, unwilling to leave him, started after, and reached his side in time to see him level his rifle at a huge Indian down the mountain, tiptoe on a log, peering with outstretched neck into the thick woods. Ben's rifle cracked, and the Indian, bounding high in air, fell heavily to the earth. A fierce yell answered this act of daring, and "the Indians, (said Ben) skipped from tree to tree thick as grass-hoppers." Ben, chuckling with huge self-satisfaction, bawled out, " take dat to 'member Ben—de 'black white man ; " and set off in earnest after his retreating party.

The following interesting incident of a well known and highly esteemed citizen of Fleming (which occurred after St. Clair's defeat in November, 1791), is related in M'Clung's Sketches of Western Adventure:

The late WILLIAM KENNAN, of Fleming county, at that time a young man of eighteen, was attached to the corps of rangers who accompanied the regular force. He had long been remarkable for strength and activity. In the course of the march from fort Washington, he had repeated opportunities of testing his astonishing powers in that respect, and was universally admitted to be the swiftest runner of the light corps. On the evening preceding the action, his corps had been advanced, as already observed, a few hundred yards in front of the first line of infantry, in order to give seasonable notice of the enemy's approach. Just as day was dawning, he observed about thirty Indians within one hundred yards of the guard fire, advancing cautiously towards the spot where he stood, together with about twenty rangers, the rest being considerably in the rear.

Supposing it to be a mere scouting party, as usual, and not superior in number to the rangers, he sprang forward a few paces in order to shelter himself in a spot of peculiarly rank grass, and firing with a quick aim upon the foremost Indian, he instantly fell flat upon his face, and proceeded with all possible rapidity to reload his gun, not doubting for a moment, but that the rangers would maintain their position, and support him. The Indians, however, rushed forward in such overwhelming masses, that the rangers were compelled to fly with precipitation, leaving young Kennan in total ignorance of his danger. Fortunately, the captain of his company had observed him when he threw himself in the grass, and suddenly shouted aloud, "Run Kennan! or you are a dead man!" He instantly sprang to his feet, and beheld Indians within ten feet of him, while his company was already more than one hundred yards in front.

Not a moment was to be lost. He darted off with every muscle strained to its utmost, and was pursued by a dozen of the enemy with loud yells. He at first pressed straight forward to the usual fording place in the creek, which ran between the rangers and the main army, but several Indians who had passed him before he arose from the grass, threw themselves in the way, and completely cut him off from the rest. By the most powerful exertions, he had thrown the whole body of pursuers behind him, with the exception of one young chief, (probably Messhawa), who displayed a swiftness and perseverance equal to his own. In the circuit which Kennan was obliged to take, the race continued for more than four hundred yards. The distance between them was about eighteen feet, which Kennan could not increase nor his adversary diminish. Each, for the time, put his whole soul into the race.

Kennan, as far as he was able, kept his eye upon the motions of his pursuer, lest he should throw the tomahawk, which he held aloft in a menacing attitude, and at length, finding that no other Indian was immediately at hand, he determined to try the mettle of his pursuer in a different manner, and felt for his tomahawk in order to turn at bay. It had escaped from its sheath, however, while he lay in the grass, and his hair had almost lifted the cap from his head, when he saw himself totally disarmed. As he had slackened his pace for a moment the Indian was almost in reach of him, when he recommenced the race, but the idea of being without arms, lent wings to his flight, and for the first time, he saw himself gaining ground. He had watched the motions of his pursuer too closely, however, to pay proper attention to the nature of the ground before him, and he suddenly found himself in front of a large tree which had been blown down, and upon which brush and other impediments lay to the height of eight or nine feet.

The Indian (who heretofore had not uttered the slightest sound) now gave a short quick yell, as if sure of his victim. Kennan had not a moment to deliberate. He must clear the impediment at a leap or perish. Putting his whole soul into the effort, he bounded into the air with a power which astonished himself, and clearing limbs, brush, and every thing else, alighted in perfect safety upon the other side. A loud yell of astonishment burst from the band of pursuers, not one of whom had the hardihood to attempt the same feat. Kennan, as may be readily imagined, had no leisure to enjoy his triumph, but dashing into the bed of the creek (upon the banks of which his feat had been performed) where the high banks would shield him from the fire of the enemy, he ran up the stream until a convenient place offered for crossing, and rejoined the rangers in the rear of the encampment, panting from the fatigue of exertions which have seldom been surpassed. No breathing time was allowed him, however. The attack instantly commenced, and as we have already observed, was maintained for three hours, with unabated fury.

When the retreat commenced, Kennan was attached to Major Clarke's battalion, and had the dangerous service of protecting the rear. This corps quickly lost its commander, and was completely disorganized. Kennan was among the hindmost when the flight commenced, but exerting those same powers which had saved him in the morning, he quickly gained the front, passing several horsemen in the flight. Here he beheld a private in his own company, an intimate acquaintance, lying upon the ground, with his thigh broken, and in tones of the most piercing distress, implored each horseman who hurried by to take him up behind him. As soon as he beheld Kennan coming up on foot, he stretched out his arms and called loud upon him to save him. Notwithstanding the imminent peril of the moment, his friend could not reject so passionate an appeal, but seizing him in his arms, he placed him upon his back, and ran in that manner for several hundred yards. Horseman after horseman passed them, all of whom refused to relieve him of his burden.

At length the enemy was gaining upon him so fast, that Kennan saw their death certain, unless he relinquished his burden. He accordingly told his friend, that he had used every possible exertion to save his life, but in vain; that he must relax his hold around his neck or they would both perish. The unhappy wretch, heedless of every remonstrance, still clung convulsively to his back, and impeded his exertions until the foremost of the enemy (armed with tomahawks alone,) were within twenty yards of them. Kennan then drew his knife from its sheath and cut the fingers of his companion, thus compelling him to relinquish his hold. The unhappy man rolled upon the ground in utter helplessness, and Kennan beheld him tomahawked before he had gone thirty yards. Relieved from his burden, he darted forward with an activity which once more brought him to the van. Here again he was compelled to neglect his own safety in order to attend to that of others.

The late governor Madison, of Kentucky, who afterwards commanded the corps which defended themselves so honorably at Raisin, a man who united the most amiable temper to the most unconquerable courage, was at that time a subaltern in St. Clair's army, and being a man of infirm constitution, was totally exhausted by the exertions of the morning, and was now sitting down calmly upon a log, awaiting the approach of his enemies. Kennan hastily accosted him, and enquired the cause of his delay. Madison, pointing to a wound which had bled profusely, replied that he was unable to walk further, and had no horse. Kennan instantly ran back to a spot where he had seen an exhausted horse grazing, caught him without difficulty, and having assisted Madison to mount, walked by his side until they were out of danger. Fortunately the pursuit soon ceased, as the plunder of the camp presented irresistible attractions to the enemy. The friendship thus formed between these two young men, endured without interruption through life. Mr. Kennan never entirely recovered from the immense exertions which he was compelled to make during this unfortunate expedition. He settled in Fleming county, and continued for many years a leading member of the Baptist church. He died in 1827.

FLOYD COUNTY.

FLOYD county was established in 1799, and named in honor of Colonel JOHN FLOYD. It is situated in the eastern extremity of the State, and lies on the waters of Big Sandy river,—bounded on the north by Johnson; east by the Virginia line; south by Pike, and west by Breathitt. PRESTONSBURG is the seat of justice, about one hundred and sixty miles from Frankfort. The mean width of the county is about thirty miles; the surface mountainous, in some places reaching an elevation of five hundred feet, and abounding in rich and inexhaustible strata of stone-coal. The principal crop is corn, though wheat, oats and flax are also cultivated. The mountains afford excellent range for sheep, hogs and cattle. Three thousand hogs are annually driven to market from this county, and wool is beginning to be an article of exportation. Seventeen miles from Prestonsburg, there is a spring called the " Burning Spring," which constantly emits a thick sulphurous vapor, and instantly ignites on the application of fire.

Valuation of taxable property in Floyd county in 1846, $485,-

878 ; number of acres of land in the county, 96,732 ; average value of land per acre, $2,89 ; number of white males over twenty-one years old, 812 ; number of children between the ages of five and sixteen years, 1490. Population in 1840, 6,302.

Prestonsburg is situated on Big Sandy river, about seventy miles from its mouth—contains a brick court house, jail and other public buildings, one seminary, six stores, two groceries, two taverns, four lawyers, three doctors, three tan-yards and six mechanics' shops. Incorporated in 1818, and called in honor of Col. John Preston, of Virginia, who owned the land. Population 200.

Colonel JOHN FLOYD, in honor of whom this county received its name, was a native of Virginia, as were most of the pioneers of Kentucky. Towards the close of the year 1773, as stated both by Butler and Marshall, or in 1774, according to the authority of Mr. Nathaniel Hart, Sen., late of Woodford county, he came to Kentucky on a surveying excursion, as a deputy of Colonel William Preston, principal surveyor of Fincastle county, of which the region in Virginia, west of the mountains, was then a part. He made many surveys on the Ohio, and belonged to the party that was re-called by Dunmore, in consequence of the dangers attending the performance of their official duties. Colonel Floyd returned in 1775, and became a conspicuous actor in the stirring scenes of the times. Alternately a surveyor, a legislator and a soldier, his distinguished qualities rendered him at once an ornament and a benefactor of the infant settlements. No individual among the pioneers was more intellectual or better informed ; none displayed, on all occasions that called for it, a bolder and more undaunted courage. His person was singularly attractive. With a complexion unusually dark, his eyes and hair were deep black, and his tall spare figure was dignified by the accomplishments of a well bred Virginia gentleman. Connecting himself with the fortunes of the Transylvania company, he became their principal surveyor, and was chosen a delegate from the town of St. Asaph to the assembly that met at Boonesborough on the 24th of May, 1775, to make laws for the infant colony. He accompanied Boone in the pursuit and rescue of his daughter and her companions, whom the savages had decoyed and captured in July, 1776, and his cotemporaneous account of that thrilling occurrence, does equal credit to his soldiership and pen. In all the stations, civil and military, to which he was called, he acquitted himself with honor, and came at last to a violent death, by the hands of the savages, in 1783.

FRANKLIN COUNTY.

FRANKLIN county was formed in the year 1794, and named in honor of the distinguished patriot and statesman, Dr. BENJAMIN FRANKLIN. It lies on both sides of the Kentucky river, and is bounded on the north by Owen; east by Scott ; south by Anderson and Woodford ; and west by Shelby. The face of the country is diversified: a small portion gently undulating ; another part, intersected by the small streams which flow into the Kentucky, uneven and hilly ; while tall cliffs, in many places quite precipitous, rear their heads along the meandering course of that river through the county. The staple products of the county are wheat, corn and oats. Hemp is cultivated to a limited extent.

Number of acres of land, reported by commissioners, as lying in Franklin, 120,731 ; average value per acre in 1846, $11,47 ;

value of taxable property, $4,004,223 ; number of white males over 21 years of age, 1692 ; number of children between five and sixteen years old, 1537. Population in 1830, 9,251—in 1840, 9,420.

FRANKFORT is the seat of justice for Franklin county, and the capital of the state of Kentucky, being 25 miles from Lexington, and 550 miles from Washington city. It is beautifully situated on the Kentucky river, 60 miles above its mouth, and in the midst of the wild and romantic scenery which renders that stream so remarkable. From the summits of the overhanging cliffs which encircle the plains beneath like the ramparts of a mighty fortress, the city of Frankfort and the town of South Frankfort, with their public edifices and private residences, their spires and gardens, intermingled and occupying both banks, the meadows around, and the graceful stream itself as it sweeps through the verdant valley, are all mapped out to the eye in a single view of varied and picturesque beauty. The state house, with the public offices on either side of it, is situated on a slight eminence about midway between the river, which it fronts, and the northern termination of the valley. It is a large and very handsome structure, built of Kentucky marble, with a portico in front, supported by six columns of the Ionic order. The senate and representative halls are in the second story—the former a capacious room, handsomely finished, with a portrait of General Washington, large as life, immediately in the rear of the speaker's chair, and portraits of General Lafayette and Colonel Daniel Boone on the right and left. The senate chamber is a smaller room, also very neatly finished, and having a full length portrait of General William Henry Harrison suspended over the president's chair. The rooms on the lower story, are appropriated to the state library, court of appeals, federal court, &c. The public offices are plain, but neat and substantial buildings. The public grounds embrace an area of some four or five acres, and are studded with a variety of handsome shrubs and forest trees. In front of the capitol is a beautiful fountain, supplied with water conveyed through iron pipes from a large spring some distance from the city. The governor's house is a large, plain building of brick. The other public buildings are—a court house, Presbyterian, Baptist, Methodist and Episcopal churches, an academy, and a banking house for the branch bank of Kentucky.

Frankfort contains, also, two newspaper establishments—the "Frankfort Commonwealth," and "Kentucky Yeoman,"—both weeklies, but the former published daily, as well as weekly, during the session of the legislature ; twenty lawyers, twelve physicians, twelve dry goods' stores, two book stores, six grocery stores, two drug stores, two hardware stores, two jewelry stores, four commission houses, four taverns, three bagging factories, with a large number of manufacturing establishments and mechanic shops. Population in 1840, 1,917—in 1847, supposed to be about 2,600. The place is well supplied with water, of an

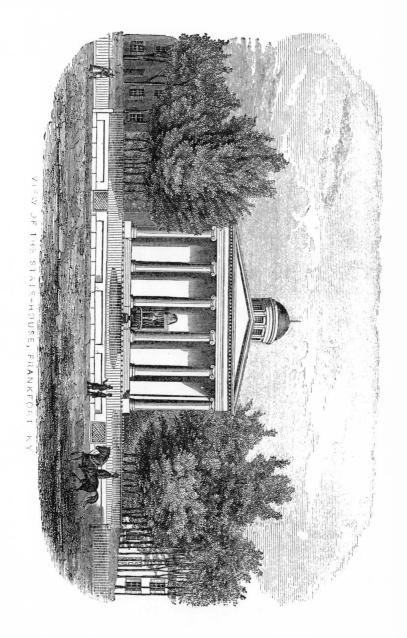

VIEW OF THE STATE-HOUSE, FRANKFORT, KY.

éxcellent quality, conducted through pipes from a spring some one or two miles from the city. The improvement of the Kentucky river has greatly advanced the commercial importance of Frankfort, which must continue to grow with the increasing population and wealth of the surrounding country.

Frankfort was established by the Virginia legislature in 1786, though the first survey of 600 acres was made by Robert M'Afee on the 16th July, 1773. The seat of government was located here in 1792, and the first session of the assembly was held 1793. The public buildings not being ready, the legislature assembled in a large frame house belonging to Major James Love, which is yet seen on the bank of the river in the lower part of the city.

The *State's Prison* or *Penitentiary*, is located at Frankfort. The penitentiary system was established in Kentucky in 1798; the legislature which adopted it being moved by feelings of the most benevolent character. The prisoners were, for some years, allowed to appropriate to their own use, the excess of their earnings, above the costs of prosecution and after making restitution to those they had injured. This system was repealed in 1805. Under the operation of subsequent acts of the legislature, no revenue was derived to the state from the penitentiary; indeed, for twenty years, it was a dead expense. In the year 1825, Mr. Joel Scott was appointed agent and keeper by act of assembly, who entered upon his duties in the nature of a contract with the state, stipulating to pay to the state one half the profits, and guarantying they should not fall below a specified sum. To him is due the credit of introducing the Auburn system, under which the Kentucky penitentiary has long been the most prosperous institution of the kind in the United States or the world. He was appointed for two terms of five years each, but relinquished the last year of his last term on account of ill health. The average number of prisoners during his term of nine years, was about 85, and the clear average earnings of the prison, over and above expenses, was $70,000.

Dr. T. S. Theobalds succeeded Mr. Scott in 1834, upon the same terms. He conducted the institution on the same general principles, but changing somewhat the employment of the prisoners, and introducing additional machinery. The heaviest branch of business is the manufacture of bagging and rope. During his first term, the earnings above expenses, were about $80,000; during the second, ending March, 1844, about $120,000. The number of prisoners from 1834 to 1839, ranged from eighty to one hundred and forty; and from the latter year to 1846, from one hundred and forty to one hundred and eighty. The present keepers (Messrs. Craig and Henry) were appointed for five years, on the same terms as their predecessors, except that they stipulate to pay the state two-thirds of the net profits earned, at the same time guarantying a certain annual profit of not less than $5,000.

The distinguishing disciplinary feature of the institution is silence by day and solitary confinement by night. The convicts are employed in associated labor by day, but not allowed to talk together except about the business in hand. They have two meals a day, of plain, coarse, but wholesome fare, each eating as much as he likes of bread, various meats, vegetables and soups. They have divine service every Sabbath, and the ignorant are taught letters and learning; and those who can read, are required to choose books for perusal from a good library of moral books, provided by the State. Their heads are shaved every Saturday, a disagreeable punishment, but deemed a necessary safeguard. Their hair is allowed to grow four months before expiration of sentence. On discharge, each prisoner is entitled to five dollars cash, and a comfortable suit of new clothes. The auditor, treasurer, land register and attorney general of the State, are inspectors, required by law to examine the institution, condition of the prisoners, their treatment, clothing, food, &c. monthly. The buildings of the penitentiary are extensive, and well arranged alike for the security and comfort of the convicts. The office of the keeper is an elegant building of cut stone, ornamented with two hexagonal gothic towers.

20

FEMALE HEROISM.—The facts in the following account of an attack on Innis settlement, near Frankfort, in April, 1792, are derived from the Rev. Abraham Cook, a venerable minister of the Baptist church, himself a pioneer, now upwards of eighty years of age, and the brother of Jesse and Hosea Cook, the husbands of the two intrepid and heroic females whose bravery is here recorded:

Some five or six years previous to the occurrence of the event named, a settlement was commenced on South Elkhorn, a short distance above its junction with the North fork, which, though not very strong, was considered a sort of asylum from Indian invasion. About Christmas in the year 1791, two brothers, Jesse and Hosea Cook and their families, their brothers-in-law, Lewis Mastin and family, and William Dunn and part of his family, with William Bledsoe and family, moved to Main Elkhorn, about three miles from the above named place, and formed a settlement in a bottom there, known as Innis' bottom. A man by the name of Farmer, with his family, shortly after made a settlement a short distance lower down the creek; and an overseer and three negroes had been placed on an improvement of Colonel Innis' a short distance above. The new settlement was between three and four miles from Frankfort, at that time containing but a few families. It was composed of newly married persons, some with and others without children. They had been exempt from Indian depredations up to the 28th of April, 1792, although a solitary Indian on horseback, had passed it in the night, during the preceding winter. The two Cooks settled in cabins close together; Mastin and Bledsoe occupied double cabins some three hundred yards from the Cooks; the cabin of Dunn was about three hundred yards from those above named, and Farmer's about the same distance below the Cooks: while Innis' overseer and negroes were located about three-fourths of a mile above.

On the day above mentioned (the 28th of April, 1792), an attack was made on three several points of the settlement, almost simultaneously, by about one hundred Indians. The first onset was made upon the Cooks. The brothers were near their cabins, one engaged in shearing sheep, the other looking on. The sharp crack of rifles was the first intimation of the proximity of the Indians; and that fire was fatal to the brothers—the elder fell dead, and the younger was mortally wounded, but enabled to reach the cabin. The two Mrs. Cooks, with three children, (two whites and one black), were instantly collected in the house, and the door, a very strong one, made secure. The Indians, unable to enter, discharged their rifles at the door, but without injury, as the balls did not penetrate through the thick boards of which it was constructed. They then attempted to cut it down with their tomahawks, but with no better success. While these things occurred without, there was deep sorrow, mingled with fearless determination and high resolve within. The younger Cook, mortally wounded, immediately the door was barred, sunk down on the floor, and breathed his last; and the two Mrs. Cooks were left the sole defenders of the cabin, with the three children. There was a rifle in the house, but no balls could be found. In this extremity, one of the women got hold of a musket ball, and placing it between her teeth, actually bit it into two pieces. With one she instantly loaded the rifle. The Indians, failing in their attempts to cut down the door, had retired a few paces in front, doubtless to consult upon their future operations. One seated himself upon a log, apparently apprehending no danger from within. Observing him, Mrs. Cook took aim from a narrow aperture and fired, when the Indian gave a loud yell, bounded high in the air, and fell dead. This infuriated the savages, who threatened (for they could speak English) to burn the house and all the inmates. Several speedily climbed to the top of the cabin, and kindled a fire on the boards of the roof. The devouring element began to take effect, and with less determined and resolute courage within, the certain destruction of the cabin and the death of the inmates, must have been the consequence. But the self possession and intrepidity of these Spartan females were equal to the occasion. One of them instantly ascended to the loft, and the other handed her water, with which she extinguished the fire. Again and again the roof was fired, and as often extinguished. The water failing, the undaunted woman called for some eggs, which were broken and the contents thrown upon the fire, for a time holding the flames at bay. Their next resource was the bloody waistcoat of the husband and brother-in-law, who lay dead upon the floor. The blood with which this was profusely saturated, checked the progress of the flames—but, as they appeared speedily to be gather-

ing strength, another, and the last expedient   *   *   *   *   *   *
proved successful. The savage foe yielded, and the fruitful expedients of female
courage triumphed.   One Indian, in bitter disappointment, fired at his unseen
enemy through the boards, but did not injure her, when the whole immediately
descended from the roof.

About the time the attack commenced, a young man named McAndre, escaped
on horseback in view of the Indians, who, it was supposed, would give the alarm
to the older neighboring settlement. As soon as they descended from the house-
top, a few climbed some contiguous trees, and instituted a sharp look-out. While
in the trees, one of them fired a second ball into the loft of the cabin, which cut to
pieces a bundle of yarn hanging near the head of Mrs. Cook, but without doing
further injury. Soon after, they threw the body of the dead Indian into the adjacent creek, and precipitately fled.

A few moments after the Cooks were attacked, Mastin, in conversation with Mc-
Andre near his cabin, was fired upon and wounded in the knee; but not so badly
as to disable him. He commenced a rapid retreat to his house, but received a
second shot, which instantly killed him. McAndre escaped on horseback, and
carried with him to the old settlement one of Mastin's small children. Dunn and
two of his sons, one aged sixteen and the other nine years, the only members of
the family then in the bottom, not having been observed by the Indians when the
attack commenced, escaped to the woods and separated. The old man made his
way safely to the older settlement, but the boys were afterwards discovered by
the Indians, and both murdered. One of the negroes at Innis's quarter, being
sick, was killed, and the two others taken captive, (the overseer being absent).
Of the captives, one died among the Indians, and the other returned to his master. The survivors of this infant colony were taken to the older settlement, and
found all the kindness and hospitality so characteristic of pioneer life.

The alarm was quickly communicated to the adjacent settlements, and before
night-fall, a body of from seventy-five to one hundred men were in hot pursuit of
the retreating foe. The main body of the Indians, however, reached the Ohio
and crossed it safely, in advance of the Kentuckians. A small party who had
lingered behind and stolen some negroes and horses from another settlement, were
overtaken on the succeeding morning, a short distance from the Ohio, by a portion of the pursuing force, among them the venerable William Tureman, of the
city of Maysville, then a youth. The whites fired, and the hindmost Indian fell,
severely wounded. One of the whites imprudently rushed his horse through the
tall grass to the spot where the Indian fell, when the latter raised his rifle and
shot him through the heart. He then rose to his feet, and attempted to reach the
thicket to which his companions had retreated, but was fired upon and killed,
some fifteen or twenty balls having been lodged in his body.

REMAINS OF DANIEL BOONE.—At its session of 1844–45, the legislature of Kentucky adopted measures to have the mortal remains of the celebrated pioneer,
DANIEL BOONE, and those of his wife, removed from their place of burial on the
banks of the Missouri, for the purpose of interment in the public cemetery at
Frankfort. There seemed to be a peculiar propriety in this testimonial of the
veneration borne by the commonwealth for the memory of the illustrious dead ;
and it was fitting that the soil of Kentucky should afford the final resting place
of his remains, whose blood in life had so often been shed to protect it from the
fury of savage hostility. It was as the beautiful and touching manifestation of
filial affection shown by children to the memory of a beloved parent; and it was
right that the generation who were reaping in peace the fruits of his toils and dangers, should desire to have in their midst, and decorate with the tokens of their love,
the sepulchre of this primeval patriarch, whose stout heart watched by the cradle
of this now powerful commonwealth, in its weak and helpless infancy, shielding
it with his body from all those appalling dangers which threatened its safety and
existence.

The consent of the surviving relations of the deceased having been obtained, a
commission was appointed, under whose superintendence the removal was effected ; and the 13th of September, 1845, was fixed upon as the time when the ashes
of the venerable dead, would be committed with fitting ceremonies to the place
of their final repose. It was a day which will be long remembered in the history

of Franklin.   The deep feeling excited by the occasion, was evinced by the assembling of an immense concourse of citizens from all parts of the State; and the ceremonies were most imposing and impressive. A procession, extending more than a mile in length, accompanied the coffins to the grave. The hearse, decorated with evergreens and flowers, and drawn by four white horses, was placed in its assigned position in the line, accompanied as pall bearers, by the following distinguished pioneers, viz. Colonel Richard M. Johnson, of Scott: General James Taylor, of Campbell; Captain James Ward, of Mason; General Robert B. McAfee, and Peter Jordan, of Mercer; Waller Bullock, Esq., of Fayette; Captain Thomas Joyce, of Louisville; Mr. Landon Sneed, of Franklin; Colonel John Johnston, of the State of Ohio; Major Z. Williams, of Kenton; and Colonel William Boone, of Shelby. The procession was accompanied by several military companies, and by the members of the Masonic Fraternity, and the Independent Order of Odd Fellows, in rich regalia. Arrived at the grave, the company was brought together in a beautiful hollow near the grave, ascending from the center on every side. Here the funeral services were performed. The hymn was given out by the Rev. Mr. Godell, of the Baptist church; prayer by Bishop Soule, of the Methodist Episcopal church; oration by the Honorable John J. Crittenden; closing prayer by the Rev. J. J. Bullock, of the Presbyterian church; and benediction by the Rev. P. S. Fall, of the Christian church. The coffins were then lowered into the graves. The spot where the graves are situated, is as beautiful as nature and art combined can make it. It is designed to erect a monument on the place.

Honorable John Brown.—The present high rank that Kentucky occupies in the Union, is but a continuation and expansion of the impulse first given by those who rescued the land from the dominion of the savages. No country was ever settled by men of more distinct character from the great mass, and the infusion of those traits was so common to the population of the early emigrants, that it will take centuries to eradicate it from their descendents. More of the gallant officers of the American revolution, and their no less gallant soldiers, found a retreat in Kentucky, than in any other part of America ; and they brought with them to the west, the young men of enterprise and talent and courage who, like Sidney, were determined to "find or to make" a way to distinction. Among the pioneers of Kentucky, no one acted a more conspicuous part than the gentleman whose name is at the head of this notice, and a brief sketch of his life is not only appropriate, but indispensable, to a work having for its object an elucidation of the history of the State.

Mr. Brown was born at Staunton, Virginia, on the 12th day of September, 1757. He was the son of the Rev. John Brown and Margaret Preston. His father was eminently distinguished as a Presbyterian minister of piety and learning, a graduate of Princeton college, and pastor for forty-four years of the church at Providence meeting house in Rockbridge. The mother was a woman of remarkable energy of character and vigor of mind—the second daughter of John Preston and Elizabeth Patton, and sister of William Preston, of Mrs. Breckinridge, Mrs. Smith and Mrs. Howard, from whom are descended the Prestons, the Breckinridges, the M'Dowells, the Harts, and many other distinguished females in Kentucky and Virginia. The children were reared in the hardy nurture of the western borderers, and having no patrimony in expectancy, were habituated to depend on their own energies for success in life. A good education was all that they could look for, and this was carefully bestowed. John, being the eldest, was sent to Princeton, at which place he was a student when the American army made its memorable retreat though the Jerseys. The college was broken up, and he joined the troops and crossed the Delaware with them, and remained with the army under Washington for some time as a volunteer. He subsequently was a member of a volunteer company from Rockbridge, which company was under the command of the Marquis de Lafayette. He completed his education at William and Mary college—assisted the celebrated Dr. Waddill for two years as a teacher in his school—read law in the office of Mr. Jefferson, and removed to Kentucky in 1782, arriving directly after the battle of the Blue Licks ; and from that date to the period of his death he was a citizen of the western country.

From the commencement of our political history, Mr. Brown was called to act a prominent part. He was elected a member of the Virginia legislature from the district of Kentucky, and was, by the legislature of that state, appointed a representative to the "*old Congress*," in 1787, and also in 1788. In 1789 and 1791, he was elected by the people of Kentucky a representative to the first and second Congress, under the present constitution. After Kentucky became a state, he was three times consecutively elected a senator in the Congress of the United States, and continued in the senate until 1805, when he retired to private life. It was his fortune as a politician, to live to be nearly, if not the very, last survivor of the old Congress; and he was the first member of the Congress of the United States ever sent from the great valley of the Mississippi ! He came to it in his youth, and it was a vast and dangerous wilderness—he lived to see it under the dominion of eleven powerful and independent sovereignties, teeming with a population of more than seven millions of people, and holding the balance of power in the national confederacy. Coming into public life at the close of the Revolution, he was brought into an intimate association with many of the most prominent actors of that eventful period, and enjoyed the personal friendship of General Washington, Mr. Adams, Mr. Jefferson, Mr. Madison and Mr. Monroe. General Washington honored him, in conjunction with General Charles Scott, Benjamin Logan, Harry Innis and Isaac Shelby, with important commissions of a military trust, with power to enlist men, commission officers, and carry on war at home and abroad. He was the projector of several of the military expeditions into the Indian countries, and accompanied one of the most successful of them as a volunteer, lending the influence of his example to enforce his official exhortations. He was a most distinguished actor in all the events that attended the admission of Kentucky into the Union, and the securing for the west the navigation of the Mississippi ; and the efforts of no one individual contributed more to bring about those results. In the celebrated controversy between Mr. Jefferson and Colonel Burr for the presidency, he, then a senator from Kentucky, advocated the claims of Mr. Jefferson with zealous ardor. Mr. Jefferson pressed upon him, during his administration, the acceptance of several highly important and lucrative offices, all of which he declined. The intimacy and friendship which existed between them, commencing while he was a student in the office of that world-renowned statesman, continued without interruption throughout life. When Mr. Monroe became president, he also addressed him a letter, wishing to know in what manner his administration could testify its regard for his character and early public service; but he declined all preferment. With the public men of the west, he was on terms of the most endearing friendship. With General George Rogers Clark, Governor Shelby and Governors Scott and Madison, and with Judges Innis and Todd, and Colonels Nicholas and Breckinridge, and their illustrious associates, he held the most confidential intercourse, and their attachment, commenced in periods of danger and under circumstances of trial, never wavered. This eminent man—eminent as a patriot, as a statesman and citizen—lived to the advanced age of 80 years, and died at his residence in Frankfort on the 29th of August, 1837. His accomplished wife, the daughter of the Rev. John Mason, of the city of New York, and sister of the Rev. John M. Mason, both distinguished divines, survived him but a few months.

Honorable JAMES BROWN, a brother of the Honorable John Brown, was a distinguished lawyer in Kentucky, and a cotemporary at the bar of the Honorable Henry Clay, (both of whom married daughters of Colonel Thomas Hart), and also of George Nicholas, Mr. Murray, John Breckinridge, and others, and was distinguished, even in such competition, as an able lawyer and eloquent speaker. He was appointed first secretary of state of Governor Shelby. Upon the purchase of Louisiana, he removed to New Orleans, was associated with Mr. Livingston in the compilation of the civil code, was several times elected to the senate of the United States, and subsequently received the appointment of minister to France, in which capacity he resided many years in the city of Paris, admired for his ability as a diplomatist, and beloved for his munificent hospitality. He died in the city of Philadelphia in 1836.

Dr. SAMUEL BROWN, also another brother of the Hon. John Brown, was a graduate of Edinburgh, and very distinguished for his medical writings, and for many years filled, with great credit to himself and usefulness to the institution, the chair of professor of theory and practice of medicine in the Transylvania University. He died in Alabama.

Dr. PRESTON W. BROWN, the youngest of the brothers, was a graduate of the school of medicine in Philadelphia, and favorably known to the profession as a successful practitioner of medicine in Kentucky. He died in Jefferson county in 1826.

Governor GEORGE MADISON was born in Virginia, about the year 1763. His career was one of distinction in arms as well as the cabinet. He was one of the soldiers of the American revolution. Before he was of age, whilst yet a boy, he threw himself in the ranks, and with a gallant bearing passed through the scenes of his country's first and great struggle for independence. He was also engaged in the battles which were fought by the early settlers of Kentucky with the Indians of the north-western territory. At the head of his company, Captain Madison was wounded at St. Clair's defeat in 1791; and he was again wounded in the attack upon the camp of Major John Adair, by the Indians, in 1792. Major Adair, in his report of that battle to Brigadier General Wilkinson, speaking of Captain Madison, whom he had ordered to take a party and gain the right flank of the enemy, says:—" Madison's bravery and conduct *need no comment; they are well known.*" This was his reputation in military life—to speak in favor of his courage was considered superfluous—all who saw him in the field, both men and officers, knew him to be brave—that knowledge came, as if by intuition, to all who beheld him—his looks, his words, his whole demeanor on the field, were emphatically those of a *soldier.* No hero ever shed his blood in the cause of his country more freely than George Madison; when called into her service, there seemed no limit to his patriotism, no bounds to his zeal in her behalf. It did in truth appear as if he considered himself—all he had, and all he could do—a free gift, a living sacrifice, to be offered up on the altar of his country.

Having passed through two wars with honor and distinction, and having settled permanently in Kentucky at a very early period, he was soon called upon to take part in the civil administration of the State. On the 7th of March, 1796, he was appointed by Governor Shelby auditor of public accounts, to fill the vacancy occasioned by the resignation of William McDowell, which office he held for more than twenty years. During the whole of this period, his official duties, and his position at the seat of government, threw him in constant personal intercourse with persons from every quarter of the State; and the influence which he thus acquired, and the universal confidence and love with which he inspired all who knew him, were so unbounded throughout Kentucky, that there was no office within the gift of the people which he could not easily have attained, without the slightest solicitation.

In the summer of 1812, a requisition was made on the State of Kentucky to aid in an expedition against Canada and the Indians of the north-western territory, who, at that time, were in alliance with the British. In obedience to the call of the government, Colonel John Allen raised a volunteer regiment of Kentuckians, and George Madison, then auditor of public accounts, accepted the office of second major under him, at the earnest solicitation of Captains Hickman, Ballard and others, who had served with him in previous campaigns against the Indians, and knew, therefore, how to appreciate his skill as an officer. At the memorable battle of the river Raisin, which occurred in January, 1813, in which that regiment suffered so severely, and in which Colonel Allen, Captains Simpson, McCracken, Hickman, and a host of others fell, Madison behaved with exemplary firmness and courage. He was in immediate command of the force that stood within the pickets, and by his calm and collected bearing, and his desperate resolution, exacted terms of capitulation from General Proctor, the commander of the British and Indians, by which his men and all the wounded were to be thrown under the immediate protection of the British commander, and saved from the violence of savage cruelty. Accordingly, Madison and such of the Americans as were able to march, were removed to Malden, whence he and the other officers were sent to Quebec. The non-commissioned officers and privates were shortly afterwards discharged on parole, and permitted to return to the United States. In consequence of the shameful violation by Proctor of the terms of capitulation entered into with Madison—in permitting the Indians to massacre our wounded men left at the river Raisin—a retaliation was apprehended, and Madison and our other officers were kept in confinement at Quebec as hostages.

In the year 1816, having resigned his office as auditor of public accounts, Major Madison was urged from every section of the state to become a candidate for governor. So loud and so general was the call made on him, that he consented to run. Colonel James Johnson, who had distinguished himself at the battle of the Thames, was announced as the opposing candidate. Colonel Johnson had not, however, been engaged very long in the canvass, before he found it impossible to resist the popularity of Major Madison. He accordingly retired during the very heat of the canvass, and declined the race, declaring that it was utterly futile for him or any body else to run against a man so universally popular and beloved, as he found his opponent to be. He was not, however, permitted to enjoy very long the high honor conferred upon him by the State with such marked distinction. He died on the 14th day of October, 1816, and left a whole people to mourn over his loss with a sorrow as deep as was the love which they had borne him.

Col. SOLOMON P. SHARP.—In a work designed to perpetuate a knowledge of the remarkable events that have transpired in Kentucky, and the memory of distinguished men who have given renown to the State, the name of Colonel Solomon P. Sharp deserves a conspicuous place. It was the fortune of this able man to illustrate, by his own career, the noble tendency of our republican institutions, and to teach to his youthful countrymen the important lesson that each may, and must be, the architect of his own fortunes, and that there is no station to which the humblest may not aspire. He was born of a parentage that brought him no aid but that which an unsullied name can give. His father had been a soldier of the Revolution, and one of the gallant but obscure borderers who gained the memorable victory at King's mountain. The war being over, he moved from Washington county, in Virginia, first to the neighborhood of Nashville, Tennessee, and in a short time afterwards to the vicinity of Russellville, Kentucky. It was at the latter place that Colonel Sharp grew up to manhood, having been but a very small child at the period of his father's removal to the Green river country. At that early day, that region was almost a desert, and but few advantages were possessed by the young for mental improvement. The simplest rudiments of education were all that even the most favored could expect, and even these were only to be obtained by alternate interchange between the labors of the farm and the employments of the school room. Still, such was the nursery of many of the most distinguished men of Kentucky; and in that school they acquired a vigor of constitution and independence in thought, action and speech, that gave them throughout life, a force of character which enabled them to leave their impress on the times in which they lived.

Col. Sharp, at the early age of nineteen, had, in the midst of innumerable and, to any but a brave spirit, insurmountable difficulties, gained admittance to the bar. He entered the profession unknown, without the influence of friends or fortune, his sole dependence being on his own energies. But, in a short time, he stood forth before all observers as a youth of uncommon promise, and, in his earliest professional efforts, he displayed powers of reasoning, of research and of eloquence that drew upon him the admiration and esteem of the whole community. As a reasoner, his powers were remarkable, clear, discriminating and logical; in debate, he had few equals and no superiors. His style of speech was of the conversational order—plain and concise—he was always understood; and those who heard him, felt that they were taking part in unravelling the propositions which he sought to make manifest. He seldom turned aside from his subject, unless to relieve the mind from the tenseness of the argument; and when this was necessary, he never lacked a playful sally or happy illustration to suit his purpose. Without any thing like redundancy, he never hesitated for a word, and was strictly fluent from the force of his own thought, and he never became excited that he had not a convinced and sympathising auditory.

At the earliest period permissible by the constitution, he was elected a member of the Kentucky legislature, and on the political theatre displayed talents of such rare order that, at twenty-four years of age, he might have been considered one of the first public men in Kentucky. He was again and again honored by a seat in the legislature, until, by the general voice of the district in which he lived, he was transferred to the Congress of the United States, and for two successive terms, embracing the most interesting period of the administration of Mr. Madison, he occupied the very front rank among the most eminent politicians of that day. He was the room mate and intimate friend of the Hon. John C. Calhoun, of South Carolina ; and stood side by side with him, in the support of the administration of Mr. Madison. The high estimation in which he was held by that distinguished statesman, is attested by his having been heard to declare, more than once, that " he was the ablest man of his age that had ever crossed the mountains."

Enticing as were these early political honors to a youth of honorable ambition, and holding out, as they did, the prospect of still further advancement, Col. Sharp relinquished them all with cheerfulness, in order that he might devote himself with more assiduity to the labors of his profession. Having married the daughter of Colonel John M. Scott, of Frankfort, and his reputation as a lawyer being commensurate with the State, he determined to remove to the seat of government, where the supreme court of the State, and the federal court of the district of Kentucky held their sessions. Before these two distinguished tribunals —distinguished for the great learning of the presiding justices, and the unsurpassed ability of the lawyers who practiced before them, Colonel Sharp was the acknowledged equal of the most eminent, and acquired a practice as extensive and lucrative as any practitioner at the bar, and the docket of the court of appeals of that day, shows his name to almost every litigated case, from the first day of his location in Frankfort.

He was selected by Governor Adair as peculiarly qualified for the important office of attorney general, and he discharged its duties to the perfect satisfaction of the country. This was the highest honor of the legal profession that a practitioner could enjoy, and there was but one step more for legal ambition, and that was a seat upon the bench. He did not attain the age when lawyers, in full practice, are willing to retire and leave the field of active and profitable labor to younger competitors ; but there is no question, judging of the future from the past, that he would have been called to occupy a distinguished place in the highest courts of judicature, at a little later period.

It was in the midst of a career like this, fruitful of honors, of public usefulness and domestic happiness, that he fell by the hand of an assassin, on the night of the — November, 1825, in the thirty-eighth year of his age. The peculiar atrocity of the deed created a thrill of horror throughout the land, for it was attended with circumstances of most fiend-like barbarity. The legislature, of which Colonel Sharp was at that time a member, being in session, offered a reward of three thousand dollars for the detection and apprehension of the murderer, and passed resolutions testifying the public condolence and sympathy with the afflicted family, and the great loss the State had sustained in his untimely death.

ISHAM TALBOT was born in the county of Bedford, and State of Virginia, in the year 1773. While quite a youth, his father emigrated with his family to Kentucky, and settled near Harrodsburg, in Mercer county. The means of acquiring an education, at that early day, were necessarily limited, and each individual in the pursuit of knowledge, had to rely, in a great degree, on the resources of his own intellect and will. Young Talbot was sent to the best schools of Harrodsburg ; but he acquired, without the aid of teachers, a respectable knowledge of the ancient and some of the modern languages.

On arriving at manhood, he studied law with Colonel George Nicholas, and commenced the practice of his profession in the town of Versailles, in Woodford county. He soon afterwards removed to Frankfort, and entered the lists when Clay, and Daveiss, and Bibb, and Bledsoe, and Rowan adorned the bar; and public opinion of that day and this, has regarded Mr. Talbot as one of the brightest in that galaxy of illustrious names.

In 1812, he was elected to the senate of Kentucky from the county of Franklin, which office he continued to hold until his election, in 1815, to the senate of the United States, to fill the vacancy occasioned by the resignation of Jesse Bledsoe. In 1820, he was re-elected to the senate, and served in that body till the 4th of March, 1825. Mr. Talbot's career in the senate is a part of the history of our common country, and the reports of the debates of that body bear ample proofs of his eloquence and patriotism. He died at Melrose, his residence near Frankfort, on the 21st of September, 1837.

Hon. HARRY INNES. The subject of this sketch was born in 1752, in Caroline county, Virginia. His father, the Rev. Robert Innes, of the Episcopal church, was a native of Scotland, and married Catharine Richards, of Va., by whom he had three sons, Robert, Harry, and James. The eldest was a physician, and Harry and James read law with Mr. Rose, of Va. Harry was a schoolmate of the late President Madison. James was attorney general of Virginia, and one of the most eloquent debaters in the convention which adopted the present constitution of the United States. During the administration of President Washington, he was deputed to Kentucky as a special envoy to explain to Governor Shelby and the legislature, the measures in progress by the government of the United States to secure the navigation of the Mississippi.

In 1776-7, whilst the lead mines became objects of national solicitude and public care for procuring a supply necessary to the revolutionary contest, the subject of this sketch was employed by the committee of public safety in Virginia, to superintend the working of Chipil's mines. His ability, zeal and fidelity in that employment, commanded the thanks of that committee. In 1779, he was elected by the legislature of Virginia a commissioner to hear and determine the claims to unpatented lands in the district including Abingdon. That duty he performed to public satisfaction. In 1783, he was elected by the legislature of Virginia, one of the judges of the supreme court for the district of Kentucky, and on the third day of November of that year, he entered upon the duties of his commission at Crow's station, near Danville, in conjunction with the Hon. Caleb Wallace and Samuel M'Dowell. In 1787, he was elected by the legislature of Virginia, attorney general for the district of Kentucky, in the place of Walker Daniel, who fell a victim to the savage foe. In 1785, he entered upon the duties of that office, in which he continued until he was appointed, in 1787, judge of the court of the United States for the Kentucky district, the duties of which he discharged until his death, September, 1816.

Upon the erection of Kentucky into an independent state in 1792, he was offered, but declined, the office of chief justice. He was president of the first electoral college for the choice of governor and lieutenant governor under the first constitution. In April, 1790, he was authorized by the secretary of war, (General Knox,) to call out the scouts for the protection of the frontier; and, in 1791, he was associated with Scott, Shelby, Logan and Brown, as a local board of war for the western country, to call out the militia on expeditions against the Indians, in conjunction with the commanding officer of the United States, and to apportion scouts through the exposed parts of the district. In all these responsible capacities the conduct of Judge Innes was without reproach, and raised him, most deservedly high, in the public esteem, and received the repeated thanks of General Washington for the discharge of high trusts. As a judge, he was patient to hear, diligent to investigate and impartial to decide. These qualities were especially requisite in his position as the sole judge, until 1807, of the court of the United States for the district of Kentucky, whose decisions were final, unless reversed by the supreme court of the United States.

As a neighbor, as an agriculturist, and as a polished gentleman in all the relations of private and social life he was a model of his day and generation : and although his public career in the west, amidst its earliest difficulties, had always been one of high trust and confidence under all the changes of government, his conduct in reference to the efforts to secure the navigation of the Mississippi, was the subject of envenomed calumny at a subsequent period, when the peculiar condition of affairs in the early transactions in Kentucky was not fully appreciated. The proudest refutation of these misrepresentations, is found, however, in the repeated evidence of the approbation of Washington ; and the after intrigues attempted by Powers, as agent of the Spanish governor, but so promptly rejected by Innes and Nicholas, did not impair the public confidence in their devotion to the freedom and happiness of their country, of which a satisfactory proof is afforded in the refusal of Congress in 1808 to institute any measures for the impeachment of Judge Innes. The negotiations proposed by the Spanish agents, and listened to by the early patriots of Kentucky, had reference solely to commercial arrangements between the people occupying the same great valley. They occurred at a time when the Kentucky pioneers had, by personal exertion and peril, without aid from the mother state, conquered the forest and the roaming savage ; when neither Virginia nor the general government afforded them adequate protection, nor permitted them to exert their strength ; and, yet, no serious design was ever entertained in Kentucky of separating from the Union or accepting the protection of Spain. The favorable progress of the subsequent negotiations entered into by the general government, rendering private efforts to secure the navigation of the Mississippi unnecessary, a corresponding reply by Innes and Nicholas was sent to Powers, and particularly rejecting the tempting monied offers made by that agent. In the language of Judge Hall, one of the most profound and polished writers of the west: "The motives of these early patriots stand unimpeached. They were actuated only by a zeal for the public good, and their names will hereafter stand recorded in history among those which Kentucky will be proud to honor. She has reared many illustrious patriots, but none who have served her more faithfully through a period of extraordinary embarrassment and peril, than Brown, Innes and Nicholas."

Judge Innes married, in early life, a daughter of Colonel Calloway, of Bedford county, Virginia, by whom he had four daughters, two of whom survive. Shortly after his removal to Kentucky, (having lost his first wife), he intermarried with Mrs. Shields, by whom he had one child, the present Mrs. Crittenden, wife of the Hon. John J. Crittenden. The venerable relict of Judge Innes survives, at the age of eighty-seven—a noble specimen of the old school, in dignified courtesy and varied intelligence.

The Hon. THOMAS TODD, formerly chief justice of the State of Kentucky, and late one of the associate justices of the supreme court of the United States, was the youngest son of Richard Todd. He was born on the 23d of January, 1765, in the county of King and Queen, on York river, in the State of Virginia. His father was descended from one of the most respectable families in the colony, his ancestors being among the early emigrants from England. His mother was Elizabeth Richards. At the age of eighteen months, his father died, leaving a considerable estate, which, by the laws of primogeniture of that day, descended to the eldest son, William, afterwards high sheriff of Pittsylvania county in that State. This event rendered it necessary that his mother should exert herself to provide for the support and education of her orphan son. She repaired, for this purpose, to Manchester, opposite to Richmond, and, by the proceeds of a boarding house under her care and management, she was enabled to give, at her death in 1776, a handsome patrimony to her son, in the care of his guardian and her executor, Dr. McKenzie, of that place. By the aid of his friends, Thomas Todd received a good English education, and advanced considerably in a knowledge of the Latin language, when his prospects were clouded by the unexpected embarrassments of his guardian, which terminated in the loss of the patrimony bequeathed him by his mother.

At a tender and unprotected age, he was again thrown upon the world to depend for his support, education and character, upon his own efforts. To these contingencies, which seemed at the time to be remediless misfortunes, may be traced that energy and enterprise which afterwards signalized his character. During the latter period of the revolutionary war, he served a tour of duty for six months as a substitute ; and often, in after life, referred to the incident as being the first money he ever earned. He was afterwards a member of the Manchester troop of cavalry, during the invasion of Virginia by Arnold and Philips. He was shortly afterwards invited by his relative, the late Harry Innes, of Kentucky, who was a cousin of his mother, to reside in his family, then in Bedford county. By his friendship at that early period—a friendship cemented by forty years of affectionate intercourse through life—he obtained a knowledge of surveying, and of the duties of a clerk. In 1785, Judge Innes visited Kentucky ; and having resolved to remove his family the following year, committed them to the care of his young friend, who arrived at Danville in the spring of 1786. Mr. Todd's pecuniary means were so limited, that, whilst residing in the family of Judge Innis at Danville, he was engaged during the day in teaching the daughters of his friend, and at night prosecuting the study of the law by fire-light.

This was an interesting period in the history of Kentucky. The people were actively engaged in measures to procure a separation from the parent State; and such was the opinion entertained of his character for business, that he was chosen clerk of all the conventions held from that period until 1792, for the purpose of erecting the former into an independent member of the Union.

He commenced the practice of law very soon after he came to the State, and made his first effort at Madison old court-house. His horse, saddle and bridle, and thirty-seven and a half cents in money, constituted his whole means at the commencement of the court: at the close of the term, he had made enough to meet his current expenses, and returned to Danville with the bonds for two cows and calves, the ordinary fees of that day. The high judicial stations he afterwards occupied with such reputation to himself, and such benefit to the country, are a proud commentary on the spirit of our institutions; and form the noblest incentives to industry and perseverance in the prosecution of a profession.

Mr. Todd was appointed clerk of the federal court for the district of Kentucky, the duties of which he performed until the separation from Virginia, when he was appointed clerk of the court of appeals, under the new constitution. He held this office until December, 1801, when he was appointed by Governor Garrard fourth judge of the court of appeals; an office created, it is believed, with the special object of adding some younger man to the bench, already filled by judges far advanced in life. In this station he continued until the resignation of Judge Muter, in 1806, when he was appointed, during the administration of Governor Greenup, to be chief justice. During the session of Congress of 1806–7, the increase of business and of population in the western States, and the necessity of bringing into the supreme court some individual versed in the peculiar land law of those States, induced Congress to extend the judiciary system, by constituting Kentucky, Tennessee and Ohio as the seventh circuit, and adding another member to the supreme court. In filling this new office, Mr. Jefferson adopted a mode somewhat different from that pursued in latter times. He requested each delegate from the States composing the circuit to communicate to him a nomination of their first and second choice. Judge Todd was the first or second upon the nomination of every delegate, although to some of them he was personally unknown. His appointment was the first intimation to him that he had been thought of for the office. In this high and arduous station he continued until his death, February 7th, 1826.

In 1788, he married Elizabeth Harris, a niece of William Stewart, from Pennsylvania, an early adventurer to Kentucky, who fell in the battle of the Blue Licks. Five of their offspring, three sons and two daughters, arrived to maturity; only two survived him, the youngest daughter and the second son, Colonel C. S. Todd, advantageously known as an officer of the late war, and as the first public agent of the United States in Colombia, South America. In 1811, Mrs. Todd died, and in 1812, Judge Todd married the widow of Major George Washington, a nephew of General Washington, and the youngest sister of Mrs. Madison, wife of the late president. He left one daughter and two sons by this marriage.

Mr. Todd possessed, in an eminent degree, the respect and esteem of his friends. His stability and dignity of character, united with manners peculiarly amiable, left a deep impression on all with whom he had intercourse. His deportment on the bench, as well as in the social circle, secured him universal veneration. The benevolence of his character was manifested in the patronage and support he extended to many indigent young friends and near relations, whole families of whom he advanced in life by his friendly influence and means. There is one incident of this sort, which, being connected in some degree with his official career, deserves to be mentioned.

In 1805–6, some influential members of the legislature of Kentucky prevailed on chief justice Muter to resign, upon an assurance of being allowed a pension during life. He had devoted his property and the prime of his days to his country in the revolutionary war, and was now in indigent circumstances and far advanced in life. The pension was granted by the legislature at the next session, but repealed at the second session after the grant. In the mean time Judge Todd had succeeded his old friend as chief justice; and about the time the legislature repealed the pension, he was appointed a judge of the supreme court of the United States, with a salary more than double that of the chief justice of Kentucky. He proposed to his friend Muter to come and reside with him, especially as a better adverse claim had deprived Muter of his home. The offer was accepted; and Muter, who had commanded a ship of war during the revolution, with the rank of Colonel; and who had, without reproach, presided in the civil tribunals of the State from its early settlement, spent the remainder of his days upon the bounty of judge Todd. As a testimony of his gratitude and affection, Muter having no family, made Todd his heir and residuary legatee, though at the time his debts greatly exceeded his available means. But, as though heaven had decreed that an act so generous in an individual, when contrasted with the ingratitude of the State, should not go unrewarded even in this world, the revolutionary claims of Judge Muter have been acknowledged by congress, and the proceeds have descended to the widow and younger children of Judge Todd.

The land law of Kentucky, originally an act of the assembly of Virginia of 1789, forms a peculiar system, and has been established chiefly upon principles of law and equity contained in decisions of the appellate court. To this result the labors of Judge Todd eminently contributed, as well in the state court as in the supreme court of the United States. His opinions had a prevailing influence in the decisions of the state authorities; and his decisions on the circuit were rarely reversed in the supreme court at Washington—an exalted tribunal, whose character is illustrated by the genius and attainments of Marshall, Story, Washington and Trimble. He was cherished with peculiar regard by his associates in the state and national tribunals; his judgment and acquaintance with the principles of the land law having, in one instance in particular, (the Holland company of New York,) rescued the reputation of the supreme court from the effects of an erroneous decision, which, at one time, nearly all of the judges would have pronounced, against his advice.

Mr. Todd entered upon the duties of judge of the supreme court at the age of forty-two; the station required an experienced head upon a younger man's shoulders. He possessed at that time, the abilities to act under the system which made it the duty of the judge to sit twice a year in the three western states, and once a year at Washington; but no constitution could long survive under the operation of this incongruous system; and the last years of Judge Todd were worn down with the duties of his office. A dyspepsia, which impaired his general health, gradually reduced his strength; and for the last two years of his life he rarely attended court.

Judge Todd's person was finely proportioned, and his face a model of beauty and intelligence. The soundness of his judgment, the dignity of his manners, and the probity of his conduct, made him the esteemed associate of Shelby and other patriotic statesmen who adorned the early annals of the state; as well as of those who, in latter days, have shed imperishable lustre on the genius and character of the first republic in the wilderness of the great west. Posterity will long venerate the name of a citizen, who, among such contemporaries, by the force of his talents and the integrity of his heart, rose to the first offices of his country.

" Mr. Justice Todd possessed many qualities admirably fitted for the proper discharge of judicial functions. He had uncommon patience and candor in investigation; great clearness and sagacity of judgment; a cautious but steady energy; a well balanced independence; a just respect for authority; and, at the same time, an unflinching adherence to his own deliberate opinions of the law. His modesty imparted a grace to an integrity and singleness of heart, which won for him the general confidence of all who knew him. He was not ambitious of innovations upon the settled principles of the law; but was content with the more unostentatious character of walking in the trodden paths of jurisprudence—*super antiquas vias legis.* From his diffident and retiring habits, it required a long acquaintance with him justly to appreciate his judicial as well as his personal merits. His learning was of a useful and solid cast; not perhaps as various or as comprehensive as that of some men; but accurate and transparent, and applicable to the daily purposes of the business of human life. In his knowledge of the local law of Kentucky, he was excelled by few; and his brethren drew largely upon his resources to administer that law, in the numerous cases which then crowded the docket of the supreme court from that judicial circuit. What he did not know, he never affected to possess; but sedulously sought to acquire. He was content to learn without assuming to dogmatise. Hence he listened to arguments for the purpose of instruction, and securing examination; and not merely for that of confutation, or debate. Among his associates he enjoyed an enviable respect, which was constantly increasing as he became more familiarly known to them. His death was deemed by them a great public calamity; and in the memory of those who survived him, his name has ever been cherished with a warm and affectionate remembrance."

No man ever clung to the constitution of the United States with a more strong and resolute attachment. And in the grave cases which were agitated in the supreme court of the United States during his judicial life, he steadfastly supported the constitutional doctrines which Mr. Chief Justice Marshall promulgated in the name of the court. It is to his honor, and it should be spoken, that, though bred in a different political school from that of the chief justice, he never failed to sustain those great principles of constitutional law on which the security of the Union depends. He never gave up to party, what he thought belonged to the country.

For some years before his death, he was sensible that his health was declining, and that he might soon leave the bench, to whose true honor and support he had been so long and zealously devoted. To one of his brethren, who had the satisfaction of possessing his unreserved confidence, he often communicated his earnest hope that Mr. Justice Trimble might be his successor, and he bore a willing testimony to the extraordinary ability of that eminent judge. It affords a striking proof of his sagacity and foresight; and the event fully justified the wisdom of his choice. Although Mr. Justice Trimble occupied his station on the bench of the supreme court for a brief period only, yet he has left on the records of the court enduring monuments of talents and learning fully adequate to all the exigencies of the judicial office. To both these distinguished men, under such circumstances, we may well apply the touching panegyric of the poet:

" Fortunati ambo !
Nulla dies unquam memori vos eximet ævo."

HUMPHREY MARSHALL, Esq., the father of the present Thomas A. Marshall of the court of appeals, and of the late John J. Marshall, of Louisville, was one of the early pioneers of Kentucky, and for many years was a distinguished citizen of Franklin county. He came to Kentucky about the year 1780, and from his undisputed talents soon assumed a high rank and a conspicuous position among the public men of the State. For many years no man was more actively engaged in the contests which agitated the political circles of Kentucky; and however great the prejudice excited against him in the breasts of some, by party feeling, he was never denied the possession of brilliant talents and commanding force of character. He was a member of the convention of 1787 which assembled at Danville, preliminary to the formation of a constitution for the state. He was a prominent and influential member of the legislature for many years, and in 1795 he was elected to the senate of the United States, for the term of six years, ending on the 4th of March, 1801. Mr. Marshall was a federalist, and held to all the principles and measures of that party in their fullest extent. In 1824, he published a history of Kentucky, the first ever published. This work bears evident marks of high talent, and although occasionally marred by the introduction of the personal prejudices of the author, is a most delightful and entertaining production. He died a few years ago, at an advanced age, at the residence of his son Thomas A. Marshall, in Lexington.

BENJAMIN FRANKLIN, from whom Franklin county received its name, one of the most eminent philosophers of modern times, and a distinguished statesman of the revolution, was born in the city of Boston on the 17th of January, 1706. His father was a tallow chandler and soap boiler, one of those English non-conformists who emigrated to the wilderness of America to enjoy religious freedom. Benjamin was the fifteenth of seventeen children; and being intended for the ministry, was sent to a common grammar school at the age of eight years. The design, however, of educating him for the ministry his father was compelled, by his straitened circumstances, to abandon. Young Benjamin was taken from school and employed in cutting wicks, filling moulds, and running errands. Disgusted with this occupation, he was soon after placed with his brother to learn the printing business. His apprenticeship does not appear to have been pleasant, and after he had been with his brother some time, he availed himself of an opportunity which presented itself to terminate the connection between them, and went to Philadelphia. Here he obtained employment as a compositor, and having attracted the notice of Sir William Keith, the governor of Pennsylvania, was induced by his promises to go to England for the purpose of purchasing types to establish himself in business. Deceived in the promises of Sir William Keith, he found himself in London without money, friends, or employment. But he soon succeeded in getting business, and became a model of industry and temperance. While in London he continued to devote his leisure hours to study. After a residence of eighteen months in London, he returned to Philadelphia, in the capacity of clerk in a dry goods shop; but he soon returned to his trade, and in a short time formed an establishment in connection with a person who supplied the necessary capital. They printed a newspaper, which was managed with much ability, and acquired Franklin much reputation. It is impossible to trace all the steps of his progress to distinction. His industry, frugality, temperance, activity, intelligence; his plans for improving the condition of the province; and his municipal services, made him an object of attention to the whole community. His advice was asked by the governor and council on all important occasions, and he was elected a member of the provincial assembly. He engaged actively in various literary pursuits, and was the founder of the university of Pennsylvania, and of the American philosophical society, and one of the chief promoters of the Pennsylvania hospital. In the scientific world he is highly distinguished for his experiments and discoveries in electricity. In 1751 he was appointed deputy post master general. In 1757, the disputes with the mother country occasioned him to be sent to Great Britain as the agent of the province of Pennsylvania. While in Great Britain, Oxford and the Scotch universities conferred on him the degree of LL. D., and the royal society elected him a fellow. In 1762, he returned to America; but in 1764 was again sent to England as a representative, not of a single province, but of the whole colonies. On the 3d of February, 1766, he was examined before the house of commons in relation to the stamp act. In 1775 he returned to America, and was immediately elected to Congress. He was a member of the committee appointed to prepare the declaration of independence, and his name is attached to that instrument as one of the signers. In 1776 he was sent as minister to France. He remained in France until the close of the war, and was one of the commissioners to negotiate a treaty of peace with Great Britain. In 1785 he returned to the United States. On his return to his native country, before he was permitted to retire to the bosom of his family, he filled the office of governor of Pennsylvania, and served as a delegate in the convention of 1787, which formed the federal constitution. He died April 17th, 1790, with his faculties unimpaired, and in the full enjoyment of all his powers, after a career of usefulness and honor which it has fallen to the lot of few men to run.

FULTON COUNTY.

Fulton county was formed in 1845, and named in honor of Robert Fulton. It is situated in the extreme south-west corner of the State, lying on the Mississippi river—bounded on the north by Hickman, east by Graves, south by the Tennessee line, and west by the Mississippi river. Hickman, formerly Mills' Point, is the county seat. The face of the country east and south of

Hickman is level and fertile; while in the south-west it is broken and only tolerably fertile. In the west, the land is low, and subject to inundation for a distance of twenty-five miles along the river bank—but is very rich and, in dry seasons particularly, remarkably productive. The staples of the county are corn, hay and tobacco, the latter cultivated to great perfection—the exports are tobacco, cotton, corn, wheat, horses, mules, cattle, hogs, sheep, turkies, &c.

The taxable property of Fulton in 1846 was valued at $758,603; number of acres of land in the county, 87,177; average value of lands per acre, $3,97; number of white males over twenty-one years of age, 624; number of children between six and fifteen years old, 764.

HICKMAN, the county seat, and only town of Fulton, has a population of five hundred inhabitants, is situated on the Mississippi river, thirty-five miles below the mouth of the Ohio, and 320 miles from Frankfort—contains two churches, (one Episcopal and one free for all denominations), twelve stores, including several forwarding and commission houses, two drug stores, two taverns, four physicians, two dentists, six lawyers, one rectifying house, one tan yard, one plough factory, twenty other mechanical shops, and one newspaper (the Commercial Standard). This place was established by act of the Legislature in 1834—then called "Mills' Point"—and changed to its present name in 1837, in honor of Colonel Hickman, who fell at the river Raisin. It was originally settled by Mr. Mills in 1819. The exports of Hickman in 1845, as furnished by an intelligent citizen, were—three thousand hogsheads of tobacco, two thousand bales of cotton, two hundred thousand bushels of corn, fifty thousand bushels wheat, thirty thousand dozen chickens and turkies; also, a great number of horses, mules, cattle, sheep, and hogs.

Fulton county received its name in honor of ROBERT FULTON, the celebrated engineer. He was born in Little Britain, in the State of Pennsylvania, in 1765. In his infancy he was put to school in Lancaster, where he acquired the rudiments of a common English education. Here his peculiar genius manifested itself at a very early age. All his hours of recreation were passed in the shops of mechanics, or in the employment of his pencil. At the age of seventeen years, he went to Philadelphia, and entered under a portrait and landscape painter, where he remained until he was twenty-one. In his twenty-second year, he went to England, where he was received with great kindness by his celebrated countryman, Benjamin West, who was so pleased with his promising genius and his amiable qualities, that he took him into his house, where he continued an inmate for several years, devoting his time to painting. At this period he formed many valuable acquaintances, among others with the Duke of Bridgewater, so famous for his canals, and Lord Stanhope, a nobleman celebrated for his love of science, and particularly for his attachment to the mechanic arts. Even at that early period, he had conceived the idea of propelling vessels by steam, and he speaks in some of his manuscripts of its practicability. In May, 1794, he obtained from the British government a patent for a double inclined plane, to be used for transportation; and in the same year he submitted to the British society for the promotion of arts and commerce, an improvement of his invention on mills for sawing marble, for which he received the thanks of the society, and an honorary medal. In 1797 he went to Paris, where he lived seven years in the family of Joel Barlow, during which time he studied the higher mathematics, physics, chemistry,

and perspective. While there, he projected the first panorama that was exhibited
in Paris. He returned to America in 1806. At what time Fulton's attention was
first directed to the subject of steam navigation is not known; but in 1793 he
had matured a plan in which he had great confidence. While in Paris, he, in
conjunction with others, built a small boat on the Seine, which was perfectly successful. On his arrival at New York in 1806, he and Robert Livingston engaged in building a boat of what was then deemed very considerable dimensions.
This boat began to navigate the Hudson in 1807; its progress through the water
was at the rate of five miles an hour. In 1811 and 1812, two steam boats were
built under Fulton's directions, as ferry boats for crossing the Hudson river, and
soon after one on the East river, of the same description. We have not space for
the details of Fulton's connection with the project of the grand Erie canal; of
his plans and experiments relative to submarine warfare—of the construction of
the steam frigate which bore his name—of the modifications of his submarine
boat; of his vexatious and ruinous lawsuits and controversies with those who
interfered with his patent rights and exclusive grants. He died February 24th,
1815. In person he was about six feet high, slender, but well proportioned, with
large dark eyes, and a projecting brow. His manners were easy and unaffected.
His temper was mild, and his disposition lively. He was fond of society. He
expressed himself with energy, fluency, and correctness, and as he owed more to
experience and reflection than to books, his sentiments were often interesting from
their originality. In all his domestic and social relations, he was zealous, kind,
generous, liberal, and affectionate. He knew of no use for money but as it was
subservient to charity, hospitality, and the sciences. But the most conspicuous
trait in his character was his calm constancy in his industry, and that indefatigable patience and perseverance, which always enabled him to overcome difficulties.

GALLATIN COUNTY.

GALLATIN county was formed in 1798, and named in honor of
Albert Gallatin. It is situated in the northern part of the state,
and lies on the Ohio river—bounded on the north by the Ohio
river; east by Boone and Grant; south by Owen, and west by
Carroll. Eagle is the principal creek of the county. The surface
of the county is generally hilly, but well timbered—the growth
being principally poplar, walnut, ash, beech, sugar-tree, oak and
hickory. The soil is generally productive,—corn, wheat and tobacco are the staples.

The taxable property of Gallatin in 1846, was valued at $1,024,-
232; number of acres of land in the county 59,231; average value
of lands in 1846, $9,71; number of white males over twenty-one
years of age, 827; number of children between five and sixteen
years old, 886. Population in 1840, 4,003.

The towns of the county are Warsaw and Napoleon. WARSAW,
the county seat, is situated on a beautiful bottom, four miles long
and one mile wide, and distant fifty-seven miles from Frankfort;
contains a large court house and the requisite public offices, one
Baptist and one Reformed church, seven stores, five groceries, two
taverns, five lawyers, four physicians, one newspaper printing
office, (the Warsaw Herald,) three schools, two pork-houses, one
tobacco factory, a large flouring mill and steam distillery, and
twenty mechanical shops. Population 700. Established in 1831,

and formerly known by the name of Fredericksburg. Warsaw is a healthy location, and enjoys a large trade—the exports exceeding $150,000 per annum. *Napoleon* is a small village, seven miles east of Warsaw, and contains a Baptist church, a tavern, a store and two doctors. Population 60.

ALBERT GALLATIN was born at Geneva, in Switzerland, on the 29th of January, 1761. In his infancy he was left an orphan; but under the kind protection of a female relative of his mother, received a thorough education, and graduated at the University of Geneva, in 1779. His family were wealthy and highly respectable. Without the knowledge or consent of his family, Albert when only nineteen, with a young comrade, left home to seek glory and fortune, and freedom of thought, in the infant republic of America. He was recommended by a friend to the patronage of Dr. Franklin, then in Paris. He arrived in Boston in July 1780, and soon after proceeded to Maine, where he purchased land, and resided there until the close of 1781. While here he served as a volunteer under Colonel John Allen, and made advances from his private purse for the support of the garrison. In the spring of 1782, he was appointed instructor in the French language at Harvard University, where he remained about a year. Going to Virginia in 1783 to attend to the claims of a European house for advances to that State, he fell in with Patrick Henry, who treated him with marked kindness and respect, and under whose advice he sought his fortune in the new and wild country then just opening on the Ohio. In December 1785 he purchased a large tract of land in Fayette county, Pennsylvania, where he made his residence. His talents for public life soon became extensively known, and in 1789, he was elected to a seat in the convention to amend the constitution of Pennsylvania. In 1793, he was elected to the United States' senate; but lost his seat on the ground that he had not been nine years a legally naturalized citizen of the United States. He soon after married a daughter of Commodore Nicholson. In 1794 he was elected to congress. While in congress, where he continued three terms, he was distinguished as a leader of the democratic party. In 1801 Mr. Jefferson appointed him secretary of the treasury, which post he filled with pre-eminent ability for several years. In 1813 he was made one of the commissioners to negotiate the treaty of Ghent; and was afterwards associated with Messrs. Clay and Adams at London, in negotiating the commercial treaty with Great Britain. He continued in Europe as ambassador at Paris until 1823, when he returned to America. In 1826, he was appointed a minister to England. On his return, he made his residence in New York, where he still lives. His career has been alike honorable to himself, to his adopted county, and to his native land.

GARRARD COUNTY.

GARRARD county was formed in the year 1796, and named for Governor JAMES GARRARD. It is situated in the middle section of the State, and lies on the east side of Dick's river: bounded on the north by the Kentucky river, which separates it from Jessamine; east by Madison; south by Lincoln; and west by Boyle and Mercer. The face of the country is diversified—gently undulating or hilly—but all productive for grains or grasses. The staple products are, corn, wheat, rye and oats—the principal exports, horses, mules, cattle, hogs and sheep.

The taxable property of the county in 1846, was valued at $3,445,820; number of acres of land in the county 140,190; av-

21

erage value of lands per acre, $12,40; number of free white males over twenty-one years of age, 1596; number of children between five and sixteen years old, 1956. Population in 1840, 10,480.

The towns of the county are Lancaster, Bryantsville, Tetersville and Fitchport. LANCASTER, the seat of justice, is situated two and one half miles from Dick's river, and about fifty miles from Frankfort—contains a fine court-house and jail, four churches, (Methodist, Baptist, Presbyterian and Reformed,) two taverns, one seminary, one female academy, eight physicians, ten lawyers, eight stores, one drug and book store, twenty mechanic shops, one carding and bagging factory, and 700 inhabitants : established in 1798. *Bryantsville* and *Fitchport* are small villages, situated on the Lexington turnpike road, the one nine and the other twelve miles west of north from Lancaster. *Tetersville* is also a small village, and lies six miles east of north from Lancaster.

About twelve miles east of Lancaster, on Paint Lick creek, there is an area of ground, embracing about ten acres, which bears the name of " *White Lick*." The ground is deeply indented with ravines, and marks resembling the tracks of wagon wheels, newly made, are now plainly visible, and have been visible since the settlement of the country some sixty years since. After a heavy rain, the water which flows into the creek from this area gives the stream a white appearance, resembling milk, for several miles.

JAMES GARRARD (in honor of whom this county received its name) was born on the —— of —— 17—, in the county of Stafford, in the (then) colony of Virginia. At a very early period in the revolutionary struggle, he engaged in the public service, and in the capacity of a militia officer, shared in the dangers and honors of that memorable war. While in service, he was called by the voice of his fellow citizens to a seat in the Virginia legislature, where he contributed, by his zeal and prudence, as much, or perhaps more than any other individual, to the passage of the famous act securing universal religious liberty.

He was an early emigrant to Kentucky, and was exposed to all the perils and dangers incident to the settlement and occupation of the country. He was repeatedly called by the voice of his fellow citizens to represent their interests in the legislature of the state : and finally, by two successive elections, was elected to the chief magistracy of the commonwealth, a trust which, for eight years, he discharged with wisdom, prudence and vigor.

As a man, Governor Garrard had few equals ; and in the various scenes and different stations of life, he acted with firmness, prudence and decision. At an early age, he embraced and professed the religion of Christ, giving it, through life, the preference over all sublunary things. In the private circle he was a man of great practical usefulness, and discharged with fidelity and tenderness the social and relative duties of husband, parent, neighbor and master. He died on the 19th of January, 1822, at his residence, Mount Lebanon, in Bourbon county, in the seventy-fourth year of his age.

GEORGE ROBERTSON, (late chief justice of Kentucky).—Alexander Robertson, the father of the subject of this brief memoir, was descended from a parentage that emigrated from the north of Ireland to Virginia about the year 1737. Mrs. Margaret Robertson, the wife of Alexander, was the daughter of William Robinson, who also emigrated, a few years later, from the north of Ireland to the same colony. They were early emigrants to the wilderness of Kentucky, then infested by savages, arriving at Gordon's station December 24, 1779, during "*the hard winter*." Near this spot Mr. Robertson permanently settled himself, where he built " the first fine house in Kentucky." He was a man of strong mind, sterling moral qualities, and popular with his fellow citizens. He was elected a member of the Virginia federal convention, which he attended at Richmond, June, 1788, and having been also elected a member of the Virginia legislature, he remained there the ensuing winter, in discharge of his legislative duties. In 1792, he was elected by the people the first sheriff of Mercer county, under the original constitution of Kentucky. He died in 1802. Mrs. Robertson was a woman of extraordinary strength of intellect, of most exemplary character, illustrating in practical life all the social and christian virtues. She died at the residence of her son-in-law, ex-governor Letcher, in Frankfort, in 1846, at a very advanced age.

George Robertson, the youngest son of these parents, was born in 1790. After attaining a good English education, he was placed (August, 1804) under the tuition of Joshua Fry, through whose instruction he acquired a knowledge of the Latin and French languages and geography. He next entered Transylvania, (November, 1805), where he remained till August, 1806, when he quitted that institution with the purpose of graduating at Princeton; but his plan was frustrated by the failure of friends to furnish expected funds. He then devoted about six months to learning with Rev. Samuel Finley, who conducted a classical school at Lancaster, and about six months more to assisting him in teaching. The winter of 1807–8 was employed in miscellaneous reading, chiefly historical. In the spring of 1808, he went to Lancaster to study law under the direction of Martin D. Hardin; but failing to procure eligible boarding, he returned immediately and resided with his brother-in-law, Samuel McKee, then and afterwards an eminent member of Congress. Here he read law till September, 1809, when Judges Boyle and Wallace, of the court of appeals, granted him licence to practice. In November of the same year, he married Eleanor, a daughter of Dr. Bainbridge, of Lancaster, being then but a few days over nineteen years of age, and she less than sixteen. They commenced the world very poor; but being patient and prudent, and refusing to go in debt, though they suffered much privation and anxiety, were happy. After about two years, he attained a fine practice, and it has been said that the most he acquired had been earned when, at the age of twenty-six, (1816), he was elected a representative to Congress, against formidable opposition. He was re-elected twice afterwards, without opposition; though he served but two terms (four years) of the three, resigning the last without taking his seat, in order, by resuming his practice, to complete the independence of his family.

During his service, he was chairman of the land committee, and was a member of the judiciary and internal improvement committees. He drew and introduced the bill to establish a territorial government in Arkansas. On that bill, the question of interdicting slavery was introduced and elaborately discussed. The restriction was carried by one vote. A reconsideration was had, and the bill finally passed, divested of the restriction, by the casting vote of the speaker, Mr. Clay.

He was the author of the present system of selling public lands, in lieu of the old system and two dollars minimum; his object being to redeem the west, then owing $20,000,000, from subjugation—by cash payments, to prevent monopolies in the hands of speculators—by reducing the quantity which might be entered to eighty acres, to enable poor men to buy and cultivate—and thus to destroy a pestilent debt system and promote the settlement and independence of the west. Upon considerations of expediency, the bill, though projected and drafted by him, was first carried through the senate.

Shortly after his retirement from Congress, Governor Adair tendered him, successively, the appointments of attorney general of Kentucky and judge of the Fayette, &c., circuit court, which, as also that of a law professorship in Transylvania University, tendered about the same time by the authorities, were respectively declined, his purpose being strongly fixed to pursue his profession vigorously a few years, to secure a competence for his family.

But in 1822, the people of Garrard elected him, *nolens volens*, a representative in the general assembly, in view of the agitating relief questions, which produced such political convulsions throughout the State. Having embarked, he felt bound to ride out the storm, and he remained in the legislature until that fearful contest was settled in 1826–7. He was elected speaker of the house of representatives in 1823, and was re-elected every session afterwards while he remained in the legislature, except the revolutionary session of 1824. During all this memorable period in the annals of Kentucky, his time was principally devoted to writing and speaking on the great questions involved, of course neglecting his professional interests. Sundry of his speeches were extensively published, and are regarded as powerful productions of a masterly intellect, being often quoted for sound principles and conclusive reasoning.

He wrote the celebrated protest of 1824, signed by the anti-relief party in the legislature, to the effect of which the final triumph of that party has been, in a great degree, not unjustly ascribed ; for it is certain that it prevented their disbandment at the time, electrified the people, and furnished the text themes on which they were rallied to the rescue of the constitution. He was also the author of the manifesto signed by the majority in 1825–6.

During his service in the legislature, he delivered speeches on several important questions, distinguished for depth of thought, force of argument, and profound knowledge of the principles of the constitution and laws.

Of his anonymous productions of that period, those under the signature of "*Plebeian*," may now be avowed.

Though he never sought an office, appointments were frequently tendered him. President Monroe offered him that of governor of Arkansas, and afterwards, in July, 1824, Richard C. Anderson, then minister at Bogota, having expressed a desire to return home if Mr. Robertson would take his place, the mission to Colombia was offered him, which being declined, Mr. Anderson determined to remain. In 1828, President Adams tendered him the mission to Peru, which was not accepted.

On the election of Thomas Metcalfe as governor of Kentucky, he provisionally accepted the appointment of secretary of state, the duties of which he discharged for a short time.

After the rejection of the nomination of Judges Mills and Owsly to the bench of the court of appeals, he was confirmed as a judge of that court, and subsequently commissioned chief justice, which elevated station he held until the first of April, 1843, when he resigned it, again returning to the bar.

Of his Herculean labors on the bench and his judicial abilities, the authorized reports of the decisions furnish the amplest testimonials.

He still retains the professorship of constitutional law, which he has held for many years, in Transylvania university ; and in this connexion it may not be inappropriate to mention that the honorary degree of LL. D. has been conferred on him by two colleges—Centre and Augusta.

Of his miscellaneous writings, speeches, addresses, &c. as well as his professional lectures, affording evidences as they do, of profound investigation of the most important and difficult principles, with which the greatest intellects alone can successfully grapple, it should be presumed that an authorized collection will be published, at no distant day, for the instruction and gratification of his countrymen.

On the character of the man and his works, the writer of this meagre sketch hereby regrets that the circumscribed limits allotted to personal biography in this book, precludes any enlargement. One remark, at least, will however be indulged; and that is, that the life, labors and character of GEORGE ROBERTSON, present an emulous example to his young countrymen, whether regarded as citizen, jurist, professor or statesman.

The following romantic incident is related by Judge Robertson, in his anniversary address, at Camp Madison, in Franklin county, on the 4th of July, 1843 :

"On the long roll of that day's reported slain [the fatal battle of the Blue Licks,] were the names of a few who had, in fact, been captured, and, after surviving the ordeal of the gauntlet, had been permitted to live as captives. Among these was an excellent husband and father who, with eleven other captives, had been taken by a tribe and painted black as the signal of torture and death to all. The night after the battle, these twelve prisoners were stripped and placed in a line on a log—he to whom we have specially alluded being at one extremity of the devoted row. The cruel captors, then beginning at the other end, slaughtered eleven, one by one ; but when they came to the only survivor, though they raised him up, also, and drew their bloody knives to strike under each uplifted arm, they paused, and after a long pow-wow, spared his life—why, he never knew. For about a year none of his friends, excepting his faithful wife, doubted his death. She, hoping against reason, still insisted that he lived and would yet return to her. Wooed by another, she, from time to time, postponed the nuptials, declaring that she could not divest herself of the belief that her husband survived. Her expostulating friends finally succeeding in their efforts to stifle her affectionate instinct, she reluctantly yielded, and the nuptial day was fixed. But, just before it dawned, the crack of a rifle was heard near her lonely cabin—at the familiar sound, she leaped out, like a liberated fawn, ejaculating as she sprang—"*that's John's gun !*" It was John's gun, sure enough ; and, in an instant, she was, once more, in her lost husband's arms. But, nine years afterwards, that same husband fell in "St. Clair's defeat,"—and the same disappointed, but persevering lover, renewed his suit—and, at last, the widow became his wife. The scene of these romantic incidents was within gun-shot of my natal homestead ;* and with that noble wife and matron I was myself well acquainted."

GRANT COUNTY.

GRANT county was formed in 1820, and named for Colonel JOHN GRANT. It is situated in the northern part, and watered by Eagle creek—bounded on the north by Boone ; east by Pendleton ; west by Gallatin and Owen ; and south by Owen. Grant was stricken off the western portion of Pendleton, called the "Dry Ridge," and forms a parallelogram twenty-two by twenty-two and a half miles. The face of the country, generally, is undulating ; the north portion very rich ; the south rather thin land, but well timbered. The staple products of the county are, wheat, corn, tobacco and sugar—hogs are exported in great numbers.

The taxable property of Grant in 1846, was valued at $928,191 ; number of acres of land in the county, 155,260 ; average value of land per acre, $4,60 ; number of white males over twenty-one years of age, 1,016 ; number of children between five and sixteen years old, 1,405. Population in 1840, 4,192.

The towns of Grant, are Williamstown, Crittenden and Downingville. WILLIAMSTOWN, the seat of justice, is situated on the turnpike road from Covington to Lexington, fifty-six miles from Frankfort—contains a brick court-house, four churches, Methodist, Baptist, Presbyterian and Reformed, two hotels, four stores, four lawyers, four doctors, one masonic lodge, and twenty mechanics' shops. Established in 1825. Population 350. *Crittenden,* (called for the Hon. John J. Crittenden,) lies ten miles north of Williamstown, on the same road, and has three churches, (Methodist, Reformed and Presbyterian,) one hotel, five stores, three doctors and eight mechanics' shops. Established in 1831. Population 250. *Downingville* is a small village, situated ten miles west from Williamstown, and contains one tavern, one doctor, one lawyer, one store, a school, a few mechanics, and thirty inhabitants.

---

* In Garrard county, Kentucky.

The dry ridge which runs through the county, is a rib of the great Cumberland mountain, and divides the waters of Licking from those of the Kentucky river, the terminus of which is at Covington, not a break intercepting its course. Near the line of Pendleton, about seven miles from Williamstown, there are some fine mineral springs, the waters of which are composed of iron, magnesia and salts.

A remarkable occurrence took place in Grant county, in the year 1841. *Smith Mayes* and *Lyman Crouch* had been apprehended and committed to jail for the robbery and murder of William S. Utterback, a short distance from Williamstown, on the Paris road. On the 10th of July, in the year named, about three hundred and fifty persons, from neighboring counties, came to the jail, forced it open, took out the prisoners, run them off to the place where the murder was committed, and hung them till they were dead on a gallows erected for the purpose. Mayes and Crouch, after being pronounced dead, were cut down and buried under the gallows.*

Mr. John M'Gill, who published a small gazetteer of Kentucky in 1832, states that this county was named in honor of Colonel JOHN GRANT, who was born and raised near the Shallow ford of the Yadkin river, North Carolina. He came to Kentucky in the year 1779, and settled a station within five miles of Bryant's station, in the direction where Paris now stands. When the Indians captured Martin's and Ruddell's stations, he removed back to North Carolina, and thence to Virginia. In the year 1784, he again moved to Kentucky, and settled at his old station. He erected salt works on Licking river; but moved from that place to the United States' saline, in Illinois. He afterwards returned to his residence on the Licking, where he remained until he died. He served his country faithfully and ably in the field and council.

On the other hand, J. Worthing McCann, Esq., a very intelligent citizen of Grant, and a resident at the time the county was organized, states that Grant was named after SAMUEL GRANT, who was killed by the Indians near the Ohio river, in the present State of Indiana, in the year 1794. This gentleman, Mr. M'Cann, further states, that Samuel Grant was a brother of General Squire and Colonel John Grant. Major William K. Wall, of Harrison, who has been a practitioner at the Grant bar ever since the formation of the county, concurs in the opinion of Mr. McCann, that the county was named in honor of SAMUEL Grant, and not Colonel John Grant, his brother, as stated by Mr. McGill.

GRAVES COUNTY.

GRAVES county was formed in 1823, and named after Major BENJAMIN GRAVES. It is situated in the south-west part of the State. Bounded on the north by M'Cracken, east by Calloway and Marshall, south by Tennessee, and west by Ballard and Hickman. Staple products, corn, tobacco, and live stock.

The taxable property of the county in 1846, was valued at $1,136,400; number of acres of land in the county 339,194; average value of land per acre $1,90; number of white males over 21 years of age, 1,570; number of children between five and sixteen years old, 2,582. Population in 1840, 7,465.

The towns of the county are MAYFIELD and FARMINGTON—the former the seat of justice, 284 miles from Frankfort, containing

---

* Mr. Utterback recovered of his wounds, and is still alive.

a court house, five lawyers, four doctors, four stores, several mechanics' shops, and about one hundred inhabitants. *Farmington* has two doctors, three stores, and a number of mechanics—population not given.

Major BENJAMIN GRAVES, in honor of whom this county received its name, was a native of Virginia, and emigrated to Kentucky when quite young. He resided in Fayette county, and was engaged in agricultural pursuits. He was an amiable, shrewd, and intelligent man, and represented Fayette county for several years in the legislature of the State. In 1812, when war was declared by the United States against Great Britain, he was among the first to volunteer his services in defence of his country's rights. He received the appointment of Major in Colonel Lewis' regiment, and proved himself an active, vigilant, and gallant officer. He was killed in the ever memorable battle of Raisin, where his blood mingled with much of the best blood of Kentucky.

GRAYSON COUNTY.

The county of GRAYSON was formed in 1810, and named in honor of Colonel WILLIAM GRAYSON. It is situated in the west middle part of the State, and is bounded by Breckinridge and Hardin counties on the north; east by Hart; south by Edmonson; and west by Ohio county. The face of the county is generally level and the land about second rate. Wheat, corn, oats, grass and tobacco, are the principal productions.

The total value of taxable property in this county in 1846, was $539,165; number of acres of land in the county, 130,222—average value of land per acre, $1,33; number of white males over twenty-one years of age, 1013; number of children between five and sixteen years of age, 1,506: population in 1840 was 4,461.

The principal water courses are Rock creek, Big and Little Clifty creeks, Pleasant Run, Cave creek, Bear creek and Caney creek. On the two last named creeks the bottoms are rich and fertile.

Like most of the counties of Kentucky, this abounds in mineral waters. There are an immense number of white sulphur springs, about one hundred of which are included in a small tract of land not more than a quarter of an acre in extent. These springs are situated within four miles of Litchfield, and are said to be more strongly impregnated with sulphur than any in the United States. Some of these springs are very cold, and some very warm, and it is said that many remarkable cures have been effected by the use of the waters.

The principal towns are Litchfield and Millerstown. LITCHFIELD is the seat of justice, and is distant 110 miles from Frankfort. It contains a court-house and other public buildings, one school, three stores, one grocery, two taverns, two doctors, two lawyers, one saddler, one gunsmith, one blacksmith, one shoemaker, one tannery: population 130. The town was named after David Leitch, who patented the land on which it stands. *Millerstown* is a small village, containing a population of 50 inhabitants.

Colonel WILLIAM GRAYSON, for whom this county was named, was a native of Virginia. He was first elected a member of Congress in 1784. He was a member of the Virginia convention which was called to ratify the constitution of the United States. In this illustrious assembly his talents rendered him conspicuous. He opposed the adoption of the constitution. After the adoption of the constitution he was elected in conjunction with Richard H. Lee to represent his native State in the senate of the United States. He died March 12th, 1790, while on his way to Congress.

GREENE COUNTY.

GREENE county was formed in the year 1792, and named in honor of General NATHANIEL GREENE, of revolutionary memory. It is situated in the middle section of the State, and lies on the waters of Greene river—bounded north by Marion ; east and south by Adair ; and west by Hart. The principal creeks are—Robinson's, Meadow, Pittman's, Bush and Russell. The surface of the country is generally undulating; in some places quite broken and hilly. The soil is based on red clay and limestone. Tobacco is the principal staple of the county ; but horses, mules, cattle and hogs are exported to some extent. There are two salt works, manufacturing a considerable quantity of salt, and one extensive iron foundry in operation in the county.

The taxable property of the county in 1846 was valued at $3,122,570 ; number of acres of land in the county, 281,957—average value of land per acre, $3,96 ; number of white males over twenty-one years old, 2,331 ; number of children between five and sixteen years old, 3,193 : population in 1840, 14,212.

The towns of the county are Greensburg, Campbellsville, Saloma and Somerville. GREENSBURG is the principal town and seat of justice. It is situated on the northern bank of Greene river, about ninety miles from Frankfort : contains a court house and other public buildings ; Methodist, Presbyterian and Baptist churches, one school, ten stores and groceries, two taverns, twelve lawyers, six physicians, and about thirty mechanics' shops : established in 1795—population about 700.

Campbellsville is about twelve miles north-east of Greensburg—contains a Methodist, a Baptist and a Reformed church, five stores, one tavern, two lawyers, four physicians, and thirty mechanics' shops ; established in 1817. *Saloma* is situated fourteen miles north of Greensburg—contains two stores, one tavern, two doctors and twelve mechanics' shops. *Somerville* is a small village six miles west of Greensburg—contains one tavern, one lawyer, one store and three mechanics' shops : established in 1817.

Major General NATHANIEL GREENE, for whom this county was named, was born May the 22d, 1742, in the town of Warwick, Rhode Island. His father was an anchor smith, and at the same time a Quaker preacher, whose ignorance, combined with the fanaticism of the times, made him pay little attention to the worldly learning of his children, though he was very careful of their moral and religious instruction. The fondness for knowledge, however, of the young Greene, was such that he devoted all the time he could spare to its acquisition, and employed all his trifling gains in purchasing books. His propensity for the life of a soldier was early evinced by his predilection for works on military subjects. He made considerable proficiency in the exact sciences; and after he had attained his twentieth year, he added a tolerable stock of legal knowledge to his other acquirements. In 1770, he was elected a member of the State legislature, and in 1774 enrolled himself as a private in a company called the Kentish guards. After the battle of Lexington, Rhode Island raised what was termed an army of observation, and chose Greene as commander, with the title of major general. This sudden elevation from the ranks to an important command, may give some idea of the estimation in which his military talents were held. He accepted a commission from Congress as brigadier general, although under the State he held that of major general, preferring the former, as it promised a larger sphere of action, and the pleasure of serving under the immediate command of Washington. When the American army went to New York, the division posted on Long Island was under Greene's command; but at the time of the unfortunate affair with the enemy, he was suffering under severe sickness, and General Sullivan was in command. When he had recovered his health, he joined the retreating army, having been previously raised to the rank of major general, and was appointed to command the troops in New Jersey, destined to watch the movements of a strong detachment of the British, which had been left on Staten island, December 26th, 1776. When Washington surprised the English at Trenton, Greene commanded the left wing of the American forces. In the battle of Brandywine, Greene commanded the vanguard, together with Sullivan, and it became his duty to cover the retreat, in which he fully succeeded. He commanded the left wing of the American forces in the disastrous attempt on Germantown. At the battle of Monmouth, he led the right of the second line, and mainly contributed to the partial success of the Americans. When General Washington, alarmed for the safety of the garrisons on the North river, repaired to West Point, he left Greene in command of the army in New Jersey. On the 23d of June, he was attacked by Clinton, but the enemy were repulsed with loss. October 6th he was appointed to the command of West Point. On the 14th of the same month he was appointed to succeed General Gates in the chief command of the southern army. The ability, prudence and firmness which he here displayed, have caused him to be ranked in the scale of our revolutionary generals, second only to Washington. In this command he continued till the close of the war. When peace released him from his duties, he returned to Rhode Island; and his journey thither, almost at every step, was marked by some private or public testimonial of regard. He died June 19th, 1786, in his forty-fourth year, in consequence of an inflammation of the brain, contracted by exposure to the rays of an intense sun.

" BIG JOE LOGSTON."—About the year 1790, an individual, known as " Big Joe Logston," removed from near the source of the north branch of the Potomac to Kentucky, and resided many years in the family of Andrew Barnett, in Greene county. He subsequently removed to Illinois. Big Joe seems to have been a rare chap. Mr. Felix Renick has given some anecdotes of him in the Western Pioneer, in which he says—" No Kentuckian could ever, with greater propriety than he, have said, 'I can out-run, out-hop, out-jump, throw down, drag out, and whip any man in the country.' " The following account is given by Mr. Renick of a desperate fight between Joe and two Indians:

" The Indians made a sudden attack, and all that escaped were driven into a rude fort for preservation, and, though reluctantly, Joe was one. This was a new life to him, and did not at all suit his taste. He soon became very restless, and every day insisted on going out with others to hunt up the cattle. Knowing the danger better, or fearing it more, all persisted in their refusal to go with him. To indulge his taste for the woodman's life, he turned out alone, and rode till the after part of the day without finding any cattle. What the Indians had not killed, were scared off. He concluded to return to the fort. Riding along a path which led in, he came to a fine vine of grapes. He turned into the path and rode carelessly along, eating his grapes, and the first intimation he had of danger, was the crack of two rifles, one from each side of the road. One of these balls passed through the paps of his breasts, which, for a male, were remarkably prominent, almost as much so as that of many nurses. The ball just grazed the skin between the paps, but did not injure the breast bone. The other ball struck his horse behind the saddle, and he sunk in his tracks. Thus was Joe eased off his horse in a manner more rare than welcome. Still he was on his feet in an instant, with his rifle in his hands, and might have taken to his heels; and I will venture the opinion, that no Indian could have caught him. That, he said, was not his sort. He had never left a battle ground without leaving his mark, and he was resolved that *that* should not be the first. The moment the guns fired, one very athletic Indian sprang towards him with tomahawk in hand. His eye was on him, and his gun to his eye, ready, as soon as he approached near enough to make a sure shot, to let him have it. As soon as the Indian discovered this, he jumped behind two pretty large saplings, some small distance apart, neither of which were large enough to cover his body, and to save himself as well as he could, he kept springing from one to the other.

"Joe, knowing he had two enemies on the ground, kept a look out for the other by a quick glance of the eye. He presently discovered him behind a tree loading his gun. The tree was not quite large enough to hide him. When in the act of pushing down his bullet, he exposed pretty fairly his hips. Joe, in the twinkling of an eye, wheeled and let him have his load in the part so exposed. The big Indian then, with a mighty "ugh!" rushed towards him with his raised tomahawk. Here were two warriors met, each determined to conquer or die —each the Goliah of his nation. The Indian had rather the advantage in size of frame, but Joe in weight and muscular strength. The Indian made a halt at the distance of fifteen or twenty feet, and threw his tomahawk with all his force, but Joe had his eye on him, and dodged it. It flew quite out of the reach of either of them. Joe then clubbed his gun, and made at the Indian, thinking to knock him down. The Indian sprang into some brush or saplings, to avoid his blows. The Indian depended entirely on dodging, with the help of the saplings. At length Joe, thinking he had a pretty fair chance, made a side blow with such force, that, missing the dodging Indian, the gun, now reduced to the naked barrel, was drawn quite out of his hands, and flew entirely out of reach. The Indian now gave an exulting "ugh!" and sprang at him with all the savage fury he was master of. Neither of them had a weapon in his hands, and the Indian, seeing Logston bleeding freely, thought he could throw him down and dispatch him. In this he was mistaken. They seized each other, and a desperate struggle ensued. Joe could throw him down, but could not hold him there. The Indian being naked, with his hide oiled, had greatly the advantage in a ground scuffle, and would still slip out of Joe's grasp and rise. After throwing him five or six times, Joe found that, between loss of blood and violent exertions, his wind was leaving him, and that he must change the mode of warfare, or lose his scalp, which he was not yet willing to spare. He threw the Indian again, and without attempting to hold him, jumped from him, and as he rose, aimed a fist blow at his head, which caused him to fall back, and as he would rise, Joe gave him several blows in succession, the Indian rising slower each time. He at length succeeded in giving him a pretty fair blow in the burr of the ear, with all his force, and he fell, as Joe thought, pretty near dead. Joe jumped on him, and thinking he could dispatch him by choking, grasped his neck with his left hand, keeping his right free for contingencies. Joe soon found that the Indian was not so dead as he thought, and that he was making some use of his right arm, which lay across his body, and on casting his eye down, discovered the Indian was making an effort to unsheath a knife which was hanging at his belt. The knife was short, and so sunk in the sheath, that it was necessary to force it up by pressing against the point. This the Indian was trying to effect, and with good success. Joe kept his eye on it, and let the Indian work the handle out, when he suddenly grabbed it, jerked it out of the sheath, and sunk it up to the handle into the Indian's breast, who gave a death groan and expired.

"Joe now thought of the other Indian, and not knowing how far he had succeeded in killing or crippling him, sprang to his feet. He found the crippled Indian had crawled some distance towards them, and had propped his broken back against a log and was trying to raise his gun to shoot him, but in attempting to do which he would fall forward and had to push against his gun to raise himself again. Joe seeing that he was safe, concluded that he had fought long enough for healthy exercise that day, and not liking to be killed by a crippled Indian, he made for the fort. He got in about nightfall, and a hard looking case he was—blood and dirt from the crown of his head to the sole of his foot, no horse, no hat, no gun, with an account of the battle that some of his comrades could scarce believe to be much else than one of his big stories, in which he would sometimes indulge. He told them they must go and judge for themselves.

"Next morning a company was made up to go to Joe's battle ground. When they approached it, Joe's accusers became more confirmed, as there was no appearance of dead Indians, and nothing Joe had talked of but the dead horse. They however found a trail as if something had been dragged away. On pursuing it they found the big Indian, at a little distance, beside a log, covered up with leaves. Still pursuing the trail, though not so plain, some hundred yards farther, they found the broken backed Indian, lying on his back with his own knife sticking up to the hilt in his body, just below the breast bone, evidently to show that he had killed himself, and that he had not come to his end by the hand of an enemy. They had a long search before they found the knife with which Joe killed the big Indian. They at last found it forced down into the ground below the surface, apparently by the weight of a person's heel. This had been done by the crippled Indian. The great efforts he must have made, alone, in that condition, show, among thousands of other instances, what Indians are capable of under the greatest extremities."

The concluding paragraph of Mr. Renick's sketch of Logston, must have reference to the frontier of Illinois, and not of Kentucky, as we have the best authority for saying that Joe left Greene county for the then territory of Illinois. The following is the paragraph:

"Some years after the above took place, peace with the Indians was restored. That frontier, like many others, became infested with a gang of outlaws, who commenced stealing horses and committing various depredations. To counteract which, a company of regulators, as they were called, was raised. In a contest between these and the depredators, Big Joe Logston lost his life, which would not be highly esteemed in civil society. But in frontier settlements, which he always occupied, where savages and beasts were to be contested with for the right of soil, the use of such a man is very conspicuous. Without such, the country could never have been cleared of its natural rudeness, so as to admit of the more brilliant and ornamental exercises of arts, sciences and civilization."

GREENUP COUNTY.

Greenup county was formed in 1803, and named in honor of Governor Christopher Greenup. It is situated in the north-east corner of the State, and lies on the waters of the Ohio, and the Big and Little Sandy rivers: Bounded on the north by the Ohio river; east by Virginia, south by Carter, and west by Lewis county. Greenup is rich in mineral resources—her iron ore being of a very superior character, and the supply inexhaustible, while coal is found in great abundance. There are ten blast furnaces now in the county, in successful operation, employing a heavy capital and a large number of hands. The water power of the county is not excelled in the State.

The taxable property of Greenup in 1846, was valued at $1,031,601; number of acres of land in the county, 256,027; average value of land per acre $2,20; number of white males over twenty-one years old, 1,404; number of children between five and sixteen years of age, 1,012. Population in 1830, 5,853; do. in 1840, 6,297.

The towns of Greenup are, Greenupsburg, Catlettsburg, Linn and Springville. Greenupsburg, the seat of justice, is one hundred and thirty-two miles from Frankfort—situated on the Ohio river, immediately above the mouth of Little Sandy river, on an elevated and beautiful bottom: contains a large brick court-house and other public buildings, one church, one school, three physicians, four lawyers, eight stores, six groceries and sixteen mechanics' shops : population 250 : established in 1818. *Catletts-burg* is a small village situated immediately below the mouth of Big Sandy, on the Ohio river, containing a tavern, post-office and store, and some four or five families. *Linn* is a small manufacturing village, and contains two churches, two stores, two tanyards, and a large number of shoe-makers, which fact induced the change of its name from Liberty to *Linn.* *Springville* is a small village on the Ohio, in the lower part of the county—contains a foundry and bedstead manufactory, gun shop, venetian blind manufactory, plow factory, tan yard and post office : Population, 130.

On a beautiful bottom of the Ohio, in this county, and between the river and a spur of the adjacent cliff, is an old fortification—embracing, within the enclosure, about ten acres of land, in a square form, with two wings—one about three-fourths of a mile long, extending to the Ohio river on the north ; the other about half a mile long, and extending to a tributary on the south. The following diagram will enable the reader to comprehend the above description more fully :

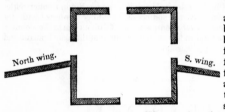

North wing.   S. wing.

The walls around the ten acres are constructed of earth—the breadth on top is twelve feet, at bottom thirty, and in height ten feet. The openings are twelve feet wide; the wings about six feet high. The ground within is a level plain, and covered with trees of the largest class—beech, sugar-tree, poplar, &c. The walls are covered with trees also. When or by whom this fortification was constructed, must forever remain a mystery.

Governor CHRISTOPHER GREENUP was born about the year 1750, in the then colony of Virginia. When the American revolution occurred, he was in the prime of youth. It was not in his nature to see his country engaged in such a struggle, without engaging in it himself. He accordingly devoted his youth to her cause, and was one of the soldiers and heroes of that great conflict ; and passed through its scenes of trial and hardship, acting well his part, and winning no small share of that honor which crowned the triumph of the American arms. In the bloody war which took place between the pioneers of the west and the Indian tribes, he also bore a part, and brought into active service against that formidable foe, the skill which he had acquired during the revolution. To the dangers of such a warfare he freely exposed his life, and risked, with a manly and brave heart, all its perils. After thus gaining for himself considerable distinction in arms, he settled in Kentucky, and on the 4th of March, 1783, was sworn in as an attorney at law in the old court for the district of Kentucky, established by an act of the Virginia legislature. On the 18th day of March, 1785, he was appointed the clerk of that court, which office he held during the existence of the court. In 1792, he was elected a member of Congress, and served as such until the year 1797. After this he filled the office of clerk of the senate of Kentucky to within a short time of his election as governor, which occurred in August, 1804. For four years, he discharged the duties of this office with high honor and credit both to himself and the State over which he presided. At the expiration of his gubernatorial term, he was elected to the legislature from the county of Franklin. In 1812, he acted as a justice of the peace for the same county. He served also many years as a director in the old bank of Kentucky ; and, after a long life of public service to his country, he died on the 27th of April, 1818, in the 69th year of his age.

Whilst he filled the highest executive office of the State, it may be said of him that no one ever discharged its duties with a more scrupulous regard for the public good. Prompt, assiduous and faithful in the labors which claimed his own personal attention as governor, he required the same of all who were under his immediate control and influence. In his appointments to office, he always reserved and exercised the right to select those only whom he knew to be qualified, and in whom *he himself* reposed confidence. In this he was never governed or swayed by the number or character of the petitioning friends of an applicant for office. It was to the man himself he looked, and that, too, through his own and not the eyes of another. His great object in making choice of public officers having been always to promote those only who were the most worthy and the best qualified, it was a source of the highest gratification to him afterwards, to know himself, and to see all convinced, that he had accomplished it. Often has he been heard in conversation to dwell, with pride, on the appointments of men to office, who afterwards proved themselves, by their public services, to have been worthy of them. And it may not be improper to say, that of none did he speak more frequently, and with a prouder satisfaction, than of his appointment of William M'Clung as judge of the Mason circuit court, of Robert Trimble as judge of the court of appeals, and of Robert Alexander as president of the bank of Kentucky. In consequence of Judge M'Clung's connection with a family in Kentucky who were looked upon as leading federalists in the State, his appointment to office was at first unpopular. Time, however, convinced the community, as they acknowledged to the governor, that he had appointed a man of the highest integrity, firmness and capacity.

A circumstance occurred while he was in office, calculated to illustrate very forcibly the character of Governor Greenup as a man of high sense of justice, and who felt always the full force of moral obligations in the administration of civil government. Before the resignation of Judge Muter as one of the judges of the court of appeals, it was known that, although a correct and honest man, who performed the duties of his office to the best of his abilities, he had become superannuated; and owing to this fact, he was induced to resign his seat, with a promise that a pension should be allowed him during the remainder of his life, in consideration of his public services. The legislature accordingly passed an act, shortly after his resignation, allowing him a small pension. Some time afterwards, however, an effort was made in the legislature to repeal this act, which ultimately proved successful. Governor Greenup, however, esteeming it an act of injustice, and a breach of the public faith, with a degree of decision and high moral courage worthy of himself and his fame, interposed his constitutional prerogative, and vetoed the bill.

HANCOCK COUNTY.

HANCOCK county was formed in 1829, and called after JOHN HANCOCK, president of the continental Congress. It is situated in the west middle part of the State, and lies on the Ohio river—bounded on the north by the Ohio, east by Breckinridge, west by Daveiss, and south by Grayson and Ohio counties. The surface of the county is diversified. Along the Ohio river, the bottom varies in width from one to seven miles, and the lands are level and remarkably rich and productive. The face of the country back of the river hills is undulating, and the lands second rate. The staple products are wheat, corn, oats, tobacco, &c. The hills abound in coal of a fine quality, and the article must ultimately become one of extensive export.

The taxable property of Hancock in 1846, was valued at $633,-972; number of acres of land in the county, 67,458; average value of land per acre, $3,69; number of white males over twenty-one years old, 543 ; children between five and sixteen years, 705. Population in 1840, 2,581.

The towns of the county are Hawesville and Lewisport HAWESVILLE, the seat of justice, is situated on the Ohio river, about one hundred and fifty miles from Frankfort. It contains the usual public buildings, a Baptist and a Methodist church, a public and a private school, five lawyers, five physicians, ten stores, one tavern, thirty mechanics' shops, and thirty coal diggers. Population 500. There are three coal banks worked here, which supply the town and steam boats with fuel. Named after the late Richard Hawes, who was the original proprietor. *Lewisport* is a small village on the Ohio river, containing one school, one tavern, three stores and two doctors, with a population of 200.

About four miles above Hawesville, and about three-fourths of a mile from the Ohio river, there is a natural curiosity which is worthy of note—it is a NATURAL FORTIFICATION, being a circular table of land, surrounded on all sides by a cliff of from fifty to one hundred and twenty-five feet in height, generally projecting at the top, and impossible of ascent, except in one place, where it seems to have slided over and formed an inclined plane. A string of fence of twenty poles, renders it impossible of ingress or egress to stock, and makes it a fine park for deer. By a little work in digging, it might be rendered impregnable ; and if it were so situated as to command some water course or strait, or exposed point on the frontier, might be made valuable to the country. Where located, it is thought to be a favorable site for an armory or garrison, as a communication could be easily opened to the Ohio river, by a rail road three-quarters of a mile long.

On the Ohio river, some five miles above Hawesville, there is a mound or general burial place of the dead. The site is one of romantic and picturesque beauty, beneath an overhanging cliff of considerable height, which almost entirely shelters this repository of bones. The thick timber and undergrowth surrounding it, gives a sombre and melancholy appearance to the scene, well befitting the resting place of the unknown dead. The bodies seem not to have been deeply interred, for the surface is covered with bones ; and with a stick they may be disinterred in numbers, or kicked up with the foot. The mound has never been explored, but in the external examinations, no other bones have been discovered but those of human beings.

About one hundred yards from the mound, there is a spring, issuing from a ledge of rock, from which is discharged a bituminous matter, similar in smell and consistency to common tar. This spring is some seven or eight miles from the " Tar Spring " in Breckinridge county, and is supposed to be a continuation of the same stream.

JOHN HANCOCK, in honor of whom this county received its name, was born at Quincy, near Boston, and graduated at Harvard University in 1754. On the sudden demise of an uncle in 1764, he succeeded to his large fortune and business, both of which he managed with great judgment and munificence. As a member of the provincial legislature, his zeal and resolution against the royal governor and the British ministry, rendered him so obnoxious to them, that, in the proclamation of General Gage, after the battle of Lexington, and before that of Bunker Hill, offering pardon to the rebels, he and Samuel Adams were specially excepted, their offences being "of too flagitious a nature to admit of any other consideration than that of condign punishment." This circumstance gave additional celebrity to these two patriots. Mr. Hancock was president of the provincial Congress of Massachusetts, until he was sent as a delegate to the general Congress at Philadelphia in 1775. Soon after his arrival there, he was chosen to succeed Peyton Randolph as president, and was the first to affix his signature to the declaration of independence. He continued to fill the chair until 1779, when he was compelled by disease to retire from Congress. He was then elected governor of Massachusetts, and was annually chosen from 1780 to 1785. After an interval of two years, he was again re-elected, and continued to hold the office until his death, which occurred on the 8th of October 1793, at the age of fifty-six years In the interval, he acted as president of the state convention for the adoption of the federal constitution, for which he finally voted. His talents were rather useful than brilliant. He seldom spoke, but his knowledge of business, and keen insight into the characters of men, rendered him a superior presiding officer. In private life, he was eminent for his hospitality and beneficence.

HARDIN COUNTY.

HARDIN county was formed in 1792, and named after Colonel JOHN HARDIN. It is situated in the west middle part of the State, and lies on the waters of Salt river—bounded on the north by Bullitt and Meade ; east by Nelson and Larue ; south by Grayson, and west by Breckinridge. It presents the different varieties of surface, viz : rolling, hilly and flat. In its northern and western portions, being hilly and thin land ; in its eastern and southern portions, it is rolling, with rich alluvial soil ; and in its central portion, presents a flat and sandy surface, which, in the common *parlance* of the country, is called "*barrens.*" The staple products are corn and tobacco.

The taxable property of Hardin in 1846 was valued at $2,781,-397 ; number of acres of land in the county, 314,604 ; average value of land per acre, $3,69 ; number of white males over twenty-one years of age, 2,278 ; number of children between five and sixteen years old, 3,062. Population in 1840, 16,357.

There are five towns in Hardin, viz : Elizabethtown (the county seat,) West Point, Stephensburg, Red Mill and Big Spring ; the latter place located in the corner of three counties—Breckinridge, Meade and Hardin. ELIZABETHTOWN was laid off fifty odd years ago, by Mr. Hynes (the same gentleman who laid off Bardstown) and was so called from the christian name of his wife. It is pleasantly situated on Valley creek, immediately on the great thoroughfare from Nashville to Louisville. It has a population of twelve hundred inhabitants, the houses generally of brick, and handsomely constructed ; contains a Methodist, Presbyterian and Baptist church, six physicians, eight lawyers, six mercantile houses, a male and female seminary, and twelve mechanics' shops. Distance from Frankfort, seventy-five miles. *West Point* is situated at the mouth of Salt river, twenty-four miles from Elizabethtown. Located here, are four physicians, four mercantile houses, and recently there has been an extensive *boat yard* established, which is doing a flourishing business.

About the year 1781, a band of Indians came into Hardin county, and after committing numerous depredations and killing some women and children, were pursued by the whites. During the pursuit a portion of the Indians, who were on stolen horses, took a southerly direction so as to strike the Ohio about where Brandenburg is now situated ; while the other party, who were on foot, attempted to cross the Ohio at the mouth of Salt river.   The whites pursued each party, the larger portion following the trail of the horses—the smaller the foot party. Among the latter was the hero of this sketch, Peter Kennedy.   Young Kennedy was noted for his fleetness of foot, strength of body and wary daring.   He was selected as their leader.   They pursued the Indians to within a mile of the river, the Indians awaiting them in ambush.   The Indians were ten in number, the whites six.   As they were led on by their daring leader in an effort to overtake them before they could reach the river, all of his comrades were shot down, and he was left to contend single handed with ten fierce and savage Indians.   This was an odds calculated to make the bravest tremble ; but young Kennedy was determined to sell his life as dearly as possible.   With one bound he reached a tree, and awaited his opportunity to wreak vengeance upon the savage foe. The savages, with their usual wariness, kept their cover ; but at last one, more impatient than the remainder, showed his head from behind a tree.   As quick as thought, Kennedy buried a rifle ball in his forehead, and instantly turned to flee ; but no sooner did he abandon his cover, than nine deadly rifles were levelled at him and instantly fired, and with the fire a simultaneous whoop of triumph, for the brave Kennedy fell, pierced through the right hip with a ball.   Disabled by the wound, and unable to make further resistance, he was taken prisoner and immediately borne off to the Wabash, where the tribe of the victorious party belonged.

The wound of Kennedy was severe, and the pain which he suffered from it, was greatly aggravated by the rapid movement of the Indians.   The arrival of the party was hailed with the usual demonstrations of Indian triumph—but Kennedy, owing to his feeble and suffering condition, was treated with kindness. His wound gradually healed, and as he again found himself a well man, he felt an irrepressible desire for freedom.   He determined to make his escape, but how to effect it was the question.   In this state of suspense, he remained for two years ; well knowing that, however kindly the Indians might treat a prisoner when *first* captured, an unsuccessful attempt to escape would be followed by the infliction of death, and that, too, by the *stake*.   But still Kennedy was willing to run this risk, to regain that most inestimable of gifts—freedom.   The vigilance of the Indians ultimately relaxed, and Kennedy seized the opportunity, and made good his escape to this side of the Ohio.

Hitherto Kennedy had rapidly pressed forward without rest or nourishment, for he knew the character of the savages, and anticipated a rapid pursuit.   Hungry and exhausted, he was tempted to shoot a deer which crossed his path, from which he cut a steak, cooked it, and had nearly completed his meal, when he heard the shrill crack of an Indian rifle, and felt that he was again wounded, but fortunately not disabled.   He grasped his gun and bounded forward in the direction of Gooden's station, distant nearly thirty miles.   Fortunately, he was acquainted with the localities, which aided him greatly in his flight.   The chase soon became intensely exciting.   The fierce whoop of the Indians was met with a shout of defiance from Kennedy.   For a few minutes at the outset of the chase, the Indians appeared to gain on him ; but he redoubled his efforts, and gradually widened the distance between the pursuers and himself.   But there was no abatement of effort on either side—both the pursuers and pursued put forward all their energies.   The yell of the savages as the distance widened, became fainter and fainter—Kennedy had descended in safety the tall cliff on the Rolling fork, and found himself, as the Indians reached the summit, a mile in advance.

Here the loud yell of the savages reverberated along the vallies of that stream, but so far from damping, infused new energy into the flight of Kennedy. The race continued, Kennedy still widening the distance, to within a short distance of Gooden's station, when the Indians, in despair, gave up the chase.   Kennedy arrived safely at the station, but in an exhausted state.   His tale was soon told.   The men in the station instantly grasped their rifles, and under the direction of Kennedy, sallied forth to encounter the savages.   The scene was now changed.   The pursuers became the pursued.   The Indians, exhausted by their long continued chase, were speedily overtaken, and *not one returned to their tribe to tell of the fruitless pursuit of Kennedy!*   Kennedy lived in Hardin to a very old age, and left a numerous and clever progeny.

About the middle of September, 1782, a roving band of Indians made their appearance in Hardin county, and committed several depredations. Silas Hart, whose keen penetration and skill as an Indian fighter, had extorted from them the name of *Sharp-Eye*, with other settlers, pursued them; and in the pursuit, Hart shot their chief, while several others of the party were also killed. Only two of the Indians made good their escape. These conveyed to the tribe the intelligence of the chieftain's death. Vengeance was denounced by them against Sharp-Eye and his family, for the death of the fallen chief, and speedily did the execution follow the threat! A short time thereafter, a band of Indians, led by a brother of the slain chieftain, secretly and silently made their way into the neighborhood of Elizabethtown, where they emerged from their hiding places, and commenced their outrages. The neighborhood was instantly aroused, and Hart, always ready to assist in repelling the savage foe, was the first upon their *trail*. The whites followed in rapid pursuit for a whole day, but were unable to overtake them. As soon as they had turned towards their homes, the Indians, who must have closely watched their movements, turned upon *their trail*, and followed them back to the settlements. Hart arrived at his home (five miles from Elizabethtown) about dark in the evening, and slept soundly through the night, for he had no apprehension of further Indian depredations. On the succeeding morning, just as the family were seating themselves to partake of their frugal meal, the band of Indians, who had been prowling round the house all night, suddenly appeared at the door, and the brother of the fallen chief shot Hart dead! The son of Hart, a brave youth only twelve years old, the instant he saw his father fall, grasped his rifle, and before the savage could enter the door, sent a ball through his heart—thus avenging, almost as quick as thought, a beloved parent's death. The Indians then rushed to the door in a body, but the first who entered the threshhold, had the hunting knife of the gallant boy plunged to the hilt in his breast, and fell by the side of his leader. A contest so unequal, could not, however, be maintained. The youth, with his mother and sister, were overpowered and hurried off to the Wabash as captives. The sister, from the feebleness of her constitution, was unable to bear the fatigue of a forced march, and the Indians dispatched her after proceeding a few miles. The mother and son were intended for a more painful and revolting death.

Upon the arrival of the party at the Wabash towns, preparations were made for the sacrifice, but an influential squaw, in pity for the tender years, and in admiration of the heroism of the youth, interposed and saved his life. The mother was also saved from the stake, by the interposition of a chief, who desired to make her his wife. The mother and son were ultimately redeemed by traders, and returned to their desolate home. Mrs. Hart (who has often been heard to declare, that she would have preferred the stake to a union with the Indian chief) subsequently married a man named *Countryman*, and lived in Hardin to a very advanced age, having died but a few years since. Young Hart, now well stricken in years, is believed to be an inhabitant of the State of Missouri.

In the year 1790, Mr. Frederick Bough arrived in Kentucky, and being on the 13th of October in that year, in company with a young man of his acquaintance, near Jacob Vanmeter's fort, in Hardin county, fell in with a party of Indians. As they approached, he observed to his companion that he thought he saw an Indian; but the young man ridiculed the idea, and coolly replying, " you are a fool for having such thoughts," kept on his way. They soon discovered a party of Indians within ten yards of them. The young man, exclaiming, " Good God! there they are!" fled with the utmost precipitation, but taking the direction *from* the fort, was soon caught by one of the savages, and barbarously killed. Mr. Bough, in running towards the fort, was fired at by the whole party in pursuit; which consisted of four, and was hit by three of them. One ball struck him in the left arm, another on the right thigh, and the third, passing through his waistcoat and shirt, grazed the skin of his left side. He was still, however, able to run, but, in attempting to cross a creek on his way to the fort, he stuck in the mud, when one of the Indians caught him, pulled him out, and felt of his arm to see if it was broken. Finding it was not, he pulled out a strap with a loop at the end, for the purpose of confining Mr. Bough; but he, suddenly jerking away his hand, gave the savage a blow on the side of the head, which knocked him down. By this time two other Indians came up, the fourth having gone in-

22

pursuit of the horses. Mr. Bough kicked at the one he had knocked down, but missed him. Just at that moment one of the other Indians aimed a blow at his head with a tomahawk, but in his eagerness struck too far over, and hit only with the handle, which, however, nearly felled Mr. Bough to the ground; but he, instantly recovering himself, struck at the tomahawk and knocked it out of his antagonist's hand. They both grasped at it, but the Indian being quickest, picked it up, and entered into conversation with his companion. The latter then struck Mr. Bough with a stick, and as he stepped forward to return the blow, they all retreated, (probably fearing an attack by a party from the fort), and suddenly went off, leaving one of their blankets and a kettle, which Mr. Bough took with him to the fort. [The foregoing particulars were communicated to the editor of the Western Review, in 1821, by Mr. Bough himself, then residing in Bath county.]

Colonel JOHN HARDIN was born in Fauquier county, Virginia, October 1st, 1753. His parents were poor, and compelled to labor for their livelihood. Martin Hardin, the father, removed from Fauquier county to George's creek, on the Monongahela, when John was about twelve years of age. He had already learned the use of the rifle. The new settlement was quite a frontier. Old Mr. Hardin thought it was in Virginia; but it turned out, when the line was settled and run, that he was in Pennsylvania. In their new situation, hunting was an occupation of necessity; and it was not long before Indian hostilities commenced, and war was added to the former motive for carrying the rifle. Young Hardin, finding even in the first of these, scope for the exercise of his active, enterprising disposition, and not being called to any literary occupation, for there were no schools, hunting became his sole pursuit and chief delight. With his rifle he traversed the vales, or crossed the hills, or clambered the mountains, in search of game, insensible of fatigue, until he became one of the most expert of the craft. The rapidity and exactness with which he pointed his rifle, made him what is called a "dead shot."

In the expediton conducted by Gov. Dunmore against the Indians in 1774, young Hardin served in the capacity of ensign in a militia company. In the ensuing August, he volunteered with Captain Zack Morgan, and during an engagement with the savages, was wounded while in the act of aiming his rifle at the enemy. The better to support his gun, he had sunk on one knee, and whilst in this position, the ball struck his thigh, on the outer side, ranged up it about seven inches, and lodged near the groin, whence it never was extracted. The enemy were beaten and fled. Before he had recovered from his wound, or could dispense with his crutches, he joined Dunmore on his march to the Indian towns. Soon after the peace which ensued, Hardin turned his attention towards Kentucky, as to a scene for new adventure; and had actually prepared for a journey hither, but this was abandoned, probably on account of the increasing rumors of an approaching war with Great Britain. The American Congress having determined to raise a military force, Hardin applied himself to the business of recruiting, and with such success that he was soon enabled to join the continental army with the command of a second lieutenant. He was afterwards attached to Morgan's rifle corps, which was generally on the lines; and with which he served until his resignation of his commission as first lieutenant, in December 1779. In the meantime he acquired and held a high place in the esteem of General Daniel Morgan, by whom he was often selected for enterprises of peril, which required discretion and intrepidity to ensure success. A few anecdotes have been preserved, which illustrate very forcibly the coolness, courage, and eminent military talents of Hardin, and which are for that reason related. While with the northern army, he was sent out on a reconnoitering excursion with orders to capture a prisoner, for the purpose of obtaining information. Marching silently in advance of his party, he found himself on rising the abrupt summit of a hill, in the presence of three British soldiers and a Mohawk Indian. The moment was critical, but without manifesting the slightest hesitation he presented his rifle and ordered them to surrender. The British immediately threw down their arms—the Indian clubbed his gun. They remained motionless, while he continued to advance on them; but none of his men having come up to his assistance, he turned his head a little to one side and called to them to come on. At this time the Indian warrior observing his eye withdrawn from, him, reversed his gun with a rapid motion, with the intention of shooting. Hardin caught the gleam of light which was reflected from the polished barrel of the gun, and readily devising its meaning, brought his own rifle to a level, and without raising his piece to his face, gained the first fire, and gave the Indian a mortal wound, who however was only an instant too late, sending his ball through Hardin's hair. The rest of the party were marched into camp, and Hardin received the thanks of General Gates. Before he left the army he was offered a Major's commission in a regiment about to be raised; but he declined, alleging that he could be of more service where he then was. In 1779 he resigned and returned home. It appears that in 1780, the year after leaving the army, he was in Kentucky, and located lands on treasury warrants, for himself and some of his friends. In April 1786, he removed his wife and family to Nelson, afterwards Washington county, in Kentucky. In the same year he volunteered under General Clark for the Wabash expedition, and was appointed quartermaster. In 1789, among other depredations, a considerable party of Indians stole all his horses, without leaving him one for the plow. They were pursued, but escaped, by crossing the Ohio. In the course of this year he was appointed county lieutenant with the rank of colonel, which gave him the command of the militia of the county. As the summer advanced he determined to cross the Ohio, and scour the country for some miles out in order to break up any bands of Indians that might be lurking in the neighborhood. With two hundred mounted men he proceeded across the river, and on one of the branches of the Wabash, fell on a camp of about thirty Shawanees, whom he attacked and defeated, with a loss of two killed and nine wounded. Two of the whites were wounded—none killed or taken. From these Indians Colonel Hardin recovered two of the horses and some colts which had been stolen in the spring; and it is worthy of remark, that no more horses were stolen from that neighborhood during the war. There was no expedition into the Indian country, after Hardin settled in Kentucky, that he was not engaged in; except that of General St. Clair, which he was prevented from joining by an accidental wound received while using a carpenter's adze. In the spring of the year 1792, he was sent by General Wilkinson with overtures of peace to the Indians. He arrived on his route towards the Miami villages attended by his interpreter, at an Indian camp about a day's journey from the spot where Fort Defiance was afterwards built. Here he encamped with the Indians during the night, but in the morning they shot him to death. He was a man of unassuming manners and great gentleness of deportment; yet of singular firmness and inflexibility. For several years previous to his death he had been a member of the Methodist church.

In March, 1794, a party of Indians made an incursion into Hardin county, and stole a number of horses. Captain William Hardin, with his usual alacrity, raised a small company and pursued them. The marauders were overtaken, and in the skirmish which ensued, Captain Hardin was wounded, but the Indians dispersed and the horses were recovered.

HARLAN COUNTY.

HARLAN county was formed in 1819, and named after Major SILAS HARLAN. It is situated in the extreme south-eastern part of the state, and lies on the head waters of Cumberland river. It is bounded on the north by Perry; east and south by Virginia; and west and northwest by Knox county. Harlan is a high, rugged and mountainous county. On the southern border lies the great Stone or Cumberland mountain, surmounted by a stupendous rock, one mile long, and 600 feet high. On the northern border lies the Pine mountain, ranging nearly east and west, and separates this from Letcher, Perry and Owsley counties. In the eastern part of the county lies the Black mountain, which is probably an arm of the Cumberland.

The taxable property of Harlan in 1846, was assessed at $302,245 ; number of acres of land in the county, 214,990 ; average value per acre, $1.98 ; white males over twenty-one years of age, 593 ; number of children between five and sixteen years old, 1,000 : population in 1840, 3,040.

Mount Pleasant is the county seat and only town of Harlan—one hundred and sixty-eight miles from Frankfort. It contains a court house and other public buildings,—(preaching occasionally in the court-house by the Baptists and Methodists),—a tailor, hatter, blacksmith, and a tavern : population about 50. It received its name from the high mound or Indian grave yard on which it is built. From this mound have been taken a large quantity of human bones, pots curiously made of blue earth and muscle shells, and dried in the sun.

Major Silas Harlan, in honor of whom this county received its name, was born in Berkley county, Virginia, near the town of Martinsburg. He came to Kentucky in 1774, and took a very active part in the battles and skirmishes with the Indians. He commanded a company of spies under General George Rogers Clark, in the Illinois campaigns in 1779, and proved himself a most active, energetic and efficient officer. General Clark said of him, that "he was one of the bravest and most accomplished soldiers that ever fought by his side." About the year 1778, he built a stockade fort on Salt river, 7 miles above Harrodsburg, which was called "Harlan's station." He was a major at the battle of the Blue Licks, and fell in that memorable contest at the head of the detachment commanded by him. He was never married. In stature he was about six feet two inches high, of fine personal appearance, and was about thirty years old when he was killed. He was universally regarded as a brave, generous and active man —beloved by his associates, and all who knew him.

HARRISON COUNTY.

Harrison county was formed in 1793, and named after Colonel Benjamin Harrison. It is situated in the north middle section of the State, lies on both sides of South Licking river, and is bounded on the north by Pendleton ; east by Nicholas ; south by Bourbon ; and west by Scott county. Main Licking river runs through the northern portion of the county ; and the principal creeks are, Cedar, West, Beaver and Richland, emptying into Main Licking; Indian, Lilas, Mill, Twin and Raven, which put into South Licking. The face of the country is irregular. About one half of the county is gently undulating, rich and very productive—the other portion hilly and less productive—but the whole well adapted for grazing. Soil based on red clay, with limestone foundation. The principal productions are, hemp, corn, wheat, and live stock, consisting of horses, mules, cattle, sheep and hogs.

The taxable property of Harrison in 1846, was valued at

$4,576,526; number of acres of land in the county, 202,601; average value of land per acre, $12.80; number of white males over twenty-one years old, 2,034; number of children between five and sixteen years old, 2,533. Population in 1830, 13,180— in 1840, 12,472.

The towns and villages of the county are Cynthiana, Broadwell, Claysville, Colemansville, Havelandville and Leesburg. CYNTHIANA, the county seat and chief town, is situated on the right bank of the south fork of Licking, thirty-seven miles from Frankfort. It contains the usual county buildings, three churches, (Methodist, Presbyterian and ——), five physicians, ten lawyers, thirteen stores, six groceries, two taverns, one academy, two common schools, one drug store, one auction store, one rope walk and bagging factory, one wool factory, one job printing office, two tanneries, one masonic lodge, 30 mechanics' shops, market house, &c., Population about 1,000. Incorporated in 1802, and named after *Cynthia* and *Anna*, two daughters of Mr. Robert Harrison, the original proprietor.

Claysville is situated at the mouth of Beaver creek, on Main Licking—contains a Republican church, two taverns, one physician, three stores, one merchant mill, three tobacco factories, one woolen factory and fulling mill, two warehouses, and about fifty inhabitants. Formerly called Marysville, but changed in 1821 to its present name, in honor of Henry Clay. *Colemansville* is thirteen miles north-west of Cynthiana—contains four stores and groceries, one church, one tavern, four physicians, eight mechanics' shops, and about one hundred inhabitants. Incorporated in 1831, and called after Robert Coleman, the original proprietor. *Havelandville* is a small manufacturing town, owned by a gentleman named Haveland, containing a cotton mill, and a large number of small residences. *Leesburg* is situated ten miles west of Cynthiana, and contains three churches (Episcopal, Reformed, and Republican), five stores and groceries, one tavern, one wool factory, seven mechanics' shops, and one bagging factory and rope walk.

In the summer of 1780, a formidable military force, consisting of six hundred Indians and Canadians, under the command of Colonel Byrd, an officer of the British army, accompanied by six pieces of artillery, made an incursion into Kentucky. The artillery was brought down the Big Miami, and thence up Licking as far as the present town of Falmouth, at the forks of Licking, where, with the stores and baggage, it was landed, and where Colonel Byrd ordered some huts to be constructed, to shelter them from the weather. From this point Colonel Byrd took up his line of march for Ruddell's station, with one thousand men. Such a force, accompanied by artillery, was resistless to the stockades of Kentucky, which were altogether destitute of ordnance. The approach of the enemy was totally undiscovered by our people until, on the 22d of June, 1780, the report of one of the field pieces announced their arrival before the station. This is the more extraordinary, as the British party were twelve days in marching from the Ohio river to Ruddell's station, and had cleared a wagon road the greater part of the way. This station had been settled the previous year, on the easterly bank of the south fork of Licking river, three miles below the junction of Hinkston and Stoner's branches of the same stream. A summons to surrender at discretion to his Britannic majesty's arms, was immediately made by Col. Byrd—to which demand Captain Ruddell answered, that he could not consent to surrender but on certain conditions, one of which was, that the prisoners should be under the protection of the British, and not suffered to be prisoners to the Indians. To these terms Colonel Byrd consented, and immediately the gates were opened to him. No sooner were the gates opened, than the Indians rushed into the station, and each Indian seized the first person they could lay their hands on, and claimed them as their own prisoner. In this way the members of every family were separated from each other; the husband from the wife, and the parents from their children. The piercing screams of the children when torn from their mothers—the distracted throes of the mothers when forced from their tender offspring, are indescribable. Ruddell remonstrated with the colonel against this barbarous conduct of the Indians, but to no effect. He confessed that it was out of his power to restrain them, their numbers being so much greater than that of the troops over which he had control, that he himself was completely in their power.

After the people were entirely stripped of all their property, and the prisoners divided among their captors, the Indians proposed to Colonel Byrd to march to and take Martin's station, which was about five miles from Ruddell's; but Col. Byrd was so affected by the conduct of the Indians to the prisoners taken, that he peremptorily refused, unless the chiefs would pledge themselves in behalf of the Indians, that all the prisoners taken should be entirely under his control, and that the Indians should only be entitled to the plunder. Upon these propositions being agreed to by the chiefs, the army marched to Martin's station, and took it without opposition. The Indians divided the spoils among themselves, and Colonel Byrd took charge of the prisoners.

The ease with which these two stations were taken, so animated the Indians, that they pressed Colonel Byrd to go forward and assist them to take Bryant's station and Lexington. Byrd declined going, and urged as a reason, the improbability of success; and besides, the impossibility of procuring provisions to support the prisoners they already had, also the impracticability of transporting their artillery by land, to any part of the Ohio river—therefore the necessity of descending Licking before the waters fell, which might be expected to take place in a very few days.

Immediately after it was decided not to go forward to Bryant's station, the army commenced their retreat to the forks of Licking, where they had left their boats, and with all possible dispatch got their artillery and military stores on board and moved off. At this place the Indians separated from Byrd, and took with them the whole of the prisoners taken at Ruddell's station. Among the prisoners was Captain John Hinkston, a brave man and an experienced woodsman. The second night after leaving the forks of Licking, the Indians encamped near the river; every thing was very wet, in consequence of which it was difficult to kindle a fire, and before a fire could be made it was quite dark. A guard was placed over the prisoners, and whilst part of them were employed in kindling the fire, Hinkston sprang from among them and was immediately out of sight. An alarm was instantly given, and the Indians ran in every direction, not being able to ascertain the course he had taken. Hinkston ran but a short distance before he lay down by the side of a log under the dark shade of a large beech tree, where he remained until the stir occasioned by his escape had subsided, when he moved off as silently as possible. The night was cloudy, and very dark, so that he had no mark to steer by, and after traveling some time towards Lexington, as he thought, he found himself close to the camp from which he had just before made his escape. In this dilemma he was obliged to tax his skill as a woodsman, to devise a method by which he should be enabled to steer his course without light enough to see the moss on the trees, or without the aid of sun, moon, or stars. Captain Hinkston ultimately adopted this method: he dipped his hand in the water, (which almost covered the whole country), and holding it upwards above his head, he instantly felt one side of his hand cold; he immediately knew that from that point the wind came—he therefore steered the balance of the night to the cold side of his hand, that being from the west he knew, and the course best suited to his purpose. After traveling several hours, he sat down at the root of a tree and fell asleep.

A few hours before day, there came on a very heavy dense fog, so that a man could not be seen at twenty yards distance. This circumstance was of infinite advantage to Hinkston, for as soon as daylight appeared, the howling of wolves, the gobbling of turkeys, the bleating of fawns, the cry of owls, and every other wild animal, was heard in almost every direction. Hinkston was too well acquainted with the customs of the Indians, not to know that it was Indians, and not beasts and birds that made these sounds—he therefore avoided approaching the places where he heard them, and notwithstanding he was several times within a few yards of them, with the aid of the fog he escaped, and arrived safe at Lexington, and brought the first news of that event.

The Indians not only collected all the horses belonging to Ruddell's and Martin's stations, but a great many from Bryant's station and Lexington, and with their booty crossed the Ohio river near the mouth of Licking, and there dispersed. The British descended Licking river to the Ohio, down the Ohio to the mouth of the Big Miami, and up the Miami as far as it was then navigable for their boats, where they hid their artillery, and marched by land to Detroit. The rains having ceased, and the weather being exceeding hot, the waters fell so low, that they were able to ascend the Miami but a short distance by water.

The following account of an adventure at Higgins' block-house, near Cynthiana, is from the notes of Mr. E. E. Williams, of Covington, Ky., an actor in the events which he records :

After the battle of the Blue Licks, and in 1786, our family removed to Higgins' block-house on Licking river, one and a half miles above Cynthiana. Between those periods my father had been shot by the Indians, and my mother married Samuel Van Hook, who had been one of the party engaged in the defence at Ruddell's station in 1780, and on its surrender was carried with the rest of the prisoners to Detroit.

Higgins' fort, or block-house, had been built at the bank of Licking, on precipitous rocks, at least thirty feet high, which served to protect us on every side but one. On the morning of the 12th of June, at day light, the fort, which consisted of six or seven houses, was attacked by a party of Indians, fifteen or twenty in number. There was a cabin outside, below the fort, where William M'Combs resided, although absent at that time. His son Andrew, and a man hired in the family, named Joseph McFall, on making their appearance at the door to wash themselves, were both shot down—M'Combs through the knee, and McFall in the pit of the stomach. McFall ran to the block-house, and M'Combs fell, unable to support himself longer, just after opening the door of his cabin, and was dragged in by his sisters, who barricaded the door instantly. On the level and only accessible side, there was a corn-field, and the season being favorable, and the soil rich as well as new, the corn was more than breast high. Here the main body of the Indians lay concealed, while three or four who made the attack attempted thereby to decoy the whites outside of the defences. Failing in this, they set fire to an old fence and corn-crib, and two stables, both long enough built to be thoroughly combustible. These had previously protected their approach in that direction. Captain Asa Reese was in command of our little fort. " Boys," said he, " some of you must run over to Hinkston's or Harrison's." These were one and a half and two miles off, but in different directions. Every man declined. I objected, alleging as my reason, that he would give up the fort before I could bring relief; but on his assurance that he would hold out, I agreed to go. I jumped off the bank through the thicket of trees, which broke my fall, while they scratched my face and limbs. I got to the ground with a limb clenched in my hands, which I had grasped unawares in getting through. I recovered from the jar in less than a minute, crossed the Licking, and ran up a cow-path on the opposite side, which the cows from one of those forts had beat down in their visits for water. As soon as I had gained the bank, I shouted, to assure my friends of my safety, and to discourage the enemy. In less than an hour, I was back, with a relief of ten horsemen, well armed, and driving in full chase after the Indians. But they had decamped immediately, upon hearing my signal, well knowing what it meant, and it was deemed imprudent to pursue them with so weak a party—the whole force in Higgins' block-house hardly sufficing to guard the women and children there. McFall, from whom the bullet could not be extracted, lingered two days and nights in great pain, when he died, as did M'Combs, on the ninth day, mortification then taking place.

This county was named in honor of Colonel BENJAMIN HARRISON, who removed to Kentucky from Pennsylvania at an early day. He was a member of the convention which met at Danville in 1787, from Bourbon county; was a member of the convention which met the succeeding year (1788) at the same place; and was also a member, from Bourbon, of the convention which formed the first constitution of Kentucky, and which assembled at Danville in 1792. In the same year, after the adoption of the constitution, he was elected a senatorial elector from Bourbon county. In 1793, he was elected a representative from Bourbon county, being a member of the legislature when the county of Harrison was formed.

HART COUNTY.

HART county was formed in 1819, and named after Captain NATHANIEL HART. It is situated in the south-west middle part of the State, and lies on both sides of Greene river. Bounded on the north by Larue, east by Greene, south by Barren, and west by Grayson and Edmonson. The face of the country, except along the river bottoms, is rolling, and in some parts hilly and broken; but the soil, generally, is very productive. Tobacco, cattle, horses, sheep, and hogs, form the principal articles of exportation; though corn, wheat, and oats, are raised in great abundance. Greene river is navigable for steamboats as high as Munfordville, during a portion of the year. Nolin river, which borders a portion of the county, is navigable for flat boats in high water, and will afford throughout the year fine water power for any number of manufacturing establishments.

The taxable property of Hart, in 1846, was valued at $1,122,-265; number of acres of land in the county, 176,564; average value of land per acre, $3.15; number of white males over twenty-one years of age, 1,259; number of children between five and sixteen years old, 1,692. Population in 1840, 7,031.

The towns of Hart are—MUNFORDVILLE, situated on the north bank of Greene river, 105 miles from Frankfort, and 75 miles from Louisville: contains the usual county buildings, and an academy (the court house and academy used for religious worship), five stores, two taverns, four lawyers, four physicians, and twelve mechanics' shops—population three hundred: named after R. J. Munford, former proprietor. *Woodsonville* is a small village on the south side of Greene river, opposite Munfordville, containing a Baptist church, two stores, post office, &c.—population about fifty: named after Thomas Woodson, sen. *Monroe* is a small village, fourteen miles east of Munfordville—population about thirty: named after President Monroe. *Leesville* is a small village, twelve miles north of Munfordville—population about twenty. The *Bear Wallow* is a very noted place in the Barrens, where there was a great resort of hunters, at an early period, in quest of the bears which were attracted there to wallow and drink at a spring. A fine tavern, with the sign of the "Bear," is all that remains of the place.

There are a number of natural curiosities, such as caves, sinks, springs, &c., in Hart county. About three and a half miles from Munfordville, near Greene river, there is a large spring, which possesses this remarkable singularity. A short distance below the head of this spring, a milldam has been erected; and at certain hours in the day, the water rises to the height of twelve or fifteen inches above its ordinary level, flows over the dam for some time, and then falls to its usual stand, resembling very greatly the ebb and flow of the ocean tides. The flood occurs about the hour of twelve o'clock each day—recurs at the same hour on every day, and is marked by the utmost uniformity in the time occupied in its ebb and flow. Six miles east of Munfordville, in the level barrens, there is a hole in the earth which attracts no little attention. The hole is circular, of some sixty or seventy feet in diameter, and runs down in a funnel shape to the depth of twenty-five or thirty feet, where the diameter is diminished to ten or twelve feet. Below that point it has never been explored, and sinks to an unknown depth. On throwing a rock into this hole or pit, its ring, as it strikes the sides, can be heard for some time, when it gradually dies away, without being heard to strike anything like the bottom. It is supposed that more than a hundred cart loads of rocks have been thrown into this pit, by the persons visiting it. Six or seven miles north north-east from the county seat, is the "Frenchman's Knob," so called from the circumstance that a Frenchman was killed and scalped upon it. Near the top of this knob, there is a hole or sink which has been explored to the depth of 275 feet, by means of letting a man down with ropes, without discovering bottom! There are also a number of caves in the county, from a half to two miles in length; but being in the neighborhood of the *Mammoth Cave*, they excite but little attention.

Captain NATHANIEL G. T. HART, (in honor of whom this county received its name,) was the son of Colonel Thomas Hart, who emigrated at an early day from Hagerstown, Maryland, to Lexington, which place became his residence, and has continued to be that of most of his descendants. Captain Hart was born at Hagerstown, and was but a few years old when his father came to Kentucky. The Hon. Henry Clay and the Hon. James Brown, so long minister at the French court, were his brothers-in-law, having married his sisters. Under the first named gentleman, Captain Hart studied the profession of law, and practiced for some time in Lexington. Shortly before the war of 1812, he had engaged in mercantile pursuits, and was rapidly making a large fortune. In the year 1812, being then about twenty-seven years of age, he commanded a volunteer company called the "*Lexington Light Infantry;*" and Kentucky being in that year called upon for volunteers for the war in the north-west, he, with his company, enrolled themselves in the service of their country. His command rendezvoused at Georgetown in the fall of 1812, and from thence proceeded to the seat of war. He served through the winter campaign of 1812–13, a portion of the time as a staff officer. At the battle of Raisin, on the 22d January, 1813, he commanded his company, and received a wound in the leg. When taken prisoner, he found an old acquaintance among the British officers. This was a Captain *Elliott*, who had previously been in Lexington, and during a severe illness there remained at the house of Colonel Hart, and was attended by Captain Hart and the family. On meeting Captain Hart he expressed himself delighted at the opportunity to return the kindness he had received, and promised to send his carryall to take Captain Hart to Malden. Captain Hart relied implicitly upon his promise, but the carryall was never sent, and he never saw Captain Elliott again. He started from Raisin on horseback under the care of an Indian, whom he employed to take him to Malden; but had proceeded only a short distance, when they met other Indians, who had been excited by the hope of a general massacre of the prisoners, and Captain Hart was then tomahawked.

He left a wife, who was Miss Ann Gist, (a member of one of the most respectable families of the county,) and two sons. His wife died a short time after he did, and but one of his sons is now living. This is Henry Clay Hart, who now resides in Paris, Bourbon county, and who was a midshipman in the navy and commanded a gun in the attack made by the frigate Potomac on the fort at Qualla Battoo in the island of Sumatra, with great credit. The Lexington light infantry, commanded by Captain Hart at the Raisin, exists to this day; and its flag lately waved on the battle field at Buena Vista as the regimental flag of the Kentucky cavalry.

HENDERSON COUNTY.

HENDERSON county was formed in 1798, and named in honor of Colonel RICHARD HENDERSON. It is situated in the south-west part of the State, on the Ohio river, Greene river forming a portion of its eastern border, and then passing through the upper part, in a north-west direction, empties its waters into the Ohio,—bounded north by the Ohio river; east by Daveiss; south by Hopkins, and west by Union. This county is watered by the Ohio and Greene rivers, and inhabited by an industrious and enterprising people. The soil is generally very productive—adapted to the cultivation of corn and tobacco, which are the chief articles of production— between 75 and 100,000 bushels of the former, and about 7,000,- 000 pounds of the latter being annually exported.

About sixty thousand acres of land in this county is of the alluvial kind, and remarkable for its fertility. It includes seventy miles of the "bottoms" on the Ohio, and forty miles on Green river. The grasses succeed extremely well in many places; and horses, cattle and hogs are raised in great numbers. There are some indications of iron ore, and extensive beds of coal, of good quality, are found in the county. It contains, also, immense quantities of timber, of the best and most desirable kinds.

Valuation of taxable property in Henderson, in 1846, $3,161,- 640; number of acres of land lying in the county, 273,159; average value per acre, $4.79; number of white males over twenty-one years of age, 1,569; number of children between five and seventeen years old, 1,961. Population in 1840, 9,548.

HENDERSON, the county seat of Henderson county, is situated on the Ohio river, twelve miles below the town of Evansville, and about one hundred and seventy miles from Frankfort. It is a thriving town, having a population of about fifteen hundred; and from its position, is an important shipping point for the produce of the Greene river country. One or two packet boats ply regularly between this town and Louisville. The court-house is a handsome structure; and the Baptists, Presbyterians, Cumberland Presbyterians, Methodists and Episcopalians, have each respectable and commodious houses of worship. There are four schools, two male, and two female; eight stores, three wholesale groceries, one drug store, four taverns, eight lawyers, eight doctors, five large tobacco factories, employing from fifty to sixty hands each, with about fifty mechanics' shops, in the various branches. Incorporated in 1812.

Cairo is a small village, containing one store, one doctor, one school, a tobacco stemmery, and four mechanics' shops. *Hibbardsville* contains a free church, one school, two stores, one doctor, six mechanics' shops, and about 30 inhabitants. *Steamport* is a small village on Greene river, containing two stores, one tavern, one doctor, one tobacco factory, three mechanics' shops, and about 30 inhabitants.

General SAMUEL HOPKINS, (see Hopkins county) who commanded one of the divisions of the army in the last war with England, was a citizen of Henderson. Audubon, the ornithologist, resided here for several years. The Rev. James McGready, an eminent Presbyterian minister, who greatly distinguished himself in what is called in the Greene river country, "the great revival of eighteen hundred," closed his earthly career in this county: and Major Barbour, who fell while gallantly fighting for his country, in the late battle of Monterey, was raised and educated here.

Colonel RICHARD HENDERSON, from whom Henderson county received its name, was a native of North Carolina. The date of his birth is not known. His parents were poor, and young Henderson grew to maturity before he had learned to read or write. These rudiments of education he had to acquire by his own unaided exertions.

While yet a young man, he was appointed a constable; and subsequently promoted to the office of under sheriff. Having devoted his leisure time to the perusal of such law books as he could procure, he obtained a license to practice law in the inferior or county courts, and in due time was admitted to the bar of the superior court. Here he soon became distinguished for his skill as an advocate, for the uniform success which attended his efforts, and his general and accurate knowledge of the principles and details of his profession. He soon established a high reputation as a lawyer, was promoted to the bench, and received the appointment of associate chief judge of the province of North Carolina, with a salary adequate to the dignity of the office.

A man of great ambition and somewhat ostentatious, he soon became involved in speculations which embarrassed him in his pecuniary relations, and cramped his resources. Bold, ardent and adventurous, he resolved to repair the ravages made in his private fortune, by engaging in the most extensive scheme of speculation ever recorded in the history of this country. Having formed a company for that purpose, he succeeded in negotiating with the head chiefs of the Cherokee nation a treaty, (known as the treaty of Wataga,) by which all that tract of country lying between the Cumberland river, the mountains of the same name, and the Kentucky river, and situated south of the Ohio, was transferred, for a reasonable consideration, to the company. By this treaty Henderson and his associates became the proprietors of all that country which now comprises more than one half of the state of Kentucky. This was in 1775. They immediately proceeded to establish a proprietory government, of which Henderson became the President, and which had its seat at Boonesborough. The new country received the name of Transylvania. The first legislature assembled at Boonesborough, and held its sittings under the shade of a large elm tree, near the walls of the fort. It was composed of Squire Boone, Daniel Boone, William Coke, Samuel Henderson, Richard Moore, Richard Calloway, Thomas Slaughter, John Lythe, Valentine Harmond, James Douglass, James Harrod, Nathan Hammond, Isaac Hite, Azariah Davis, John Todd, Alexander S. Dandridge, John Floyd, and Samuel Wood. These members formed themselves into a legislative body, by electing Thomas Slaughter, chairman, and Matthew Jewett, clerk. This cismontane legislature, the earliest popular body that assembled on this side of the Apalachian mountains, was addressed by Colonel Henderson, on behalf of himself and his associates, in a speech of sufficient dignity and of excellent sense. A compact was entered into between the proprietors and the colonists, by which a free, manly, liberal government was established over the territory. The most important parts of this Kentucky Magna Charta, were, 1st. That the election of delegates should be annual. 2d. Perfect freedom of opinion in matters of religion. 3d. That Judges should be appointed by the proprietors, but answerable for mal-conduct to the people; and that the convention have the sole power of raising and appropriating all moneys, and electing their treasurer. This epitome of substantial freedom and manly, rational government, was solemnly executed under the hands and seals of the three proprietors acting for the company, and Thomas Slaughter acting for the colonists.

The purchase of Henderson from the Cherokees was afterwards annulled by act of the Virginia legislature, as being contrary to the chartered rights of that State. But, as some compensation for the services rendered in opening the wilderness, and preparing the way for civilization, the legislature granted to the proprietors a tract of land twelve miles square, on the Ohio, below the mouth of Greene river.

After the failure of his attempt to establish an independent government west of the mountains, little or nothing is known of the subsequent life of Henderson. We are even ignorant of the time of his death. He was a man of a high order of talents, and entitled to a distinguished place among the early pioneers.

~~~~~~~~~~~~~~~~

HENRY COUNTY.

HENRY county was formed in 1798, and called after the celebrated PATRICK HENRY. It is situated in the north middle portion of the State, and lies on the Kentucky river. Bounded on the north by Carroll, east by Owen, separated by the Kentucky, south by Shelby, and west by Oldham. The surface of the county is generally undulating—in some portions quite hilly. South of the Little Kentucky creek, which empties into the Kentucky river, the lands (generally termed the sugar lands) are remarkably rich and fertile, producing as fine hemp as any lands in the State. In the oak lands, fine tobacco is grown, and the beech lands yield large quantities of corn. The staples are, wheat, corn, hemp, and tobacco.

Valuation of taxable property in Henry county in 1846, $4,135,673; number of acres of land in the county, 174,680; average value of land per acre, $12.45; number of white males over twenty-one years of age, 1,827; number of children between five and sixteen years old, 2,110; population in 1840, 10,015.

The towns of the county are, New Castle, Franklinton, Hendersonville, Lockport, Pleasuresville, and Port Royal. NEW CASTLE, the seat of justice, is situated near Drennon's creek, about twenty-six miles from Frankfort: contains an excellent court house and other public buildings, four churches (Baptist, Methodist, Presbyterian, and Reformed), six taverns, nine dry goods stores and groceries, one drug store, one shoe and boot store, four doctors, four lawyers, a seminary and female academy, one tannery, one oil mill, twenty mechanics' shops, and seven hundred inhabitants.

Franklinton is a small village, eight miles east of New Castle—contains one store and grocery, one free church, one tavern, and four mechanics. *Hendersonville* lies six miles west of New Castle, and contains one tavern, two stores, one church, and two mechanics. *Lockport* is situated on the Kentucky river, at lock and dam number two—contains two stores, two taverns, one doctor, three tobacco warehouses—and is the principal landing for Henry county. *Pleasuresville* lies six miles from New Castle, and contains one church, two taverns, four stores, two doctors, and six mechanics' shops. *Port Royal* is ten miles north-east from New Castle, and one mile from the Kentucky river—contains two stores, one tavern, one doctor, one tan yard, and four mechanics' shops.

DRENNON'S LICK, a medicinal spring of black and salt sulphur, is a place of considerable resort during the watering season. The accommodations are good. This lick was esteemed a valuable hunting ground of the Indians before the settlement of Kentucky—the deer and other game resorting to it in great numbers.

PATRICK HENRY, from whom this county derives its name, was one of the great lights of the revolution, and an extended sketch of his life belongs more properly to the history of the American republic. He was born in Hanover county, Virginia, on the 29th of May, 1736, and his early years gave no promise of the distinction which he acquired in subsequent life. His education was limited, embracing the common English branches, with a smattering of Latin, and a pretty good knowledge of mathematics, for which he manifested some degree of fondness. He was married at the early age of eighteen, and engaged successively, but most unsuccessfully, in the mercantile. agricultural, and again in the mercantile business. When his family had been so reduced in circumstances, as to be in want of even the necessaries of life, he turned his attention to the law, and after six weeks' study, obtained license to practice. It was then, and not till then, that his star arose and took position among the bright galaxy of the day. His genius first displayed itself in the contest between the clergy and the people of Virginia, in an effort of popular eloquence, to which Mr. Wirt has given immortality. His second brilliant display was before a committee of the house of burgesses, on a contested election case—and here the successive bursts of eloquence in defence of the right of suffrage, from a man so very plain and humble in his appearance, struck the committee with astonishment. In 1765, he was elected a member of the house of burgesses, and prepared and was instrumental in passing through that body, a series of resolutions against the stamp act, and the scheme of taxing America by the British parliament. It was in the midst of the debate which arose on these resolutions, that Mr. Henry exclaimed : " Cæsar had his Brutus, Charles the First his Cromwell, and George the Third "—" Treason ! " cried the speaker—" Treason ! treason ! " echoed from every part of the house. Henry faltered not for an instant; but taking a loftier attitude, and fixing on the speaker an eye of fire, he finished his sentence with the firmest emphasis—" *may profit by their example.* If *this* be treason, make the most of it." From this period, Mr. Henry became the idol of the people of Virginia, and his influence was felt throughout the continent, as one of the great champions of civil liberty.

He continued a member of the house of burgesses till the commencement of the revolution—was one of the standing committee of correspondence, and a member of the Virginia delegation in the first general Congress which met in Philadelphia in September, 1774. He acted a short time in a military capacity, but felt that his influence in civil life was more important to his country. Resigning his military command, he was chosen first governor of the commonwealth of Virginia, and successively elected to that office while eligible. In 1786, he resigned the office of governor. He subsequently declined the appointment of the legislature as a member of the convention which framed the constitution of the United States ; but was a member of the Virginia convention which assembled to ratify that instrument, and, as is generally known, arrayed all his great powers of eloquence against its ratification. He became afterwards, however, a firm friend of the constitution, and of the federal system of government established by that instrument. In 1791, he retired from public life—in 1794 from the bar, and on the 6th of June, 1797, he closed his brilliant and eventful career on earth, leaving a large family in affluent circumstances.

Patrick Henry was a natural orator of the highest order, combining imagination, acuteness, dexterity and ingenuity, with the most forcible action and extraordinary powers of utterance. As a statesman, he was bold and sagacious, and his name is brilliantly and lastingly connected with those great events which resulted in the emancipation of his country.

HICKMAN COUNTY.

HICKMAN county was formed in 1821, and named in honor of Captain PASCHAL HICKMAN. It is situated in the extreme south-west part of the state, and lies on the Mississippi river: Bounded on the north by Ballard; east by Graves; south by Fulton; and west by the Mississippi river. The territory embraces about 220 square miles—the face of the country is generally level or gently undulating—The Iron Banks and Chalk bluffs, washed by the Mississippi, being the only elevations which can properly be called hills in the county, and their altitude does not exceed 100 to 150 feet, with a gradual ascent. The soil is a black mould, very rich, but based upon sand. Corn and tobacco are grown in abundance, the latter of superior quality. The timber is heavy and of good quality, and the county finely watered by many mill streams, together with the Bayou de Chien.

Valuation of taxable property in 1846, $627,820; number of acres of land in the county, 150,124; average value of land per acre, $2.78; number of white males over twenty-one years of age, 660; number of children between five and sixteen years old, 986. Population in 1840, including Fulton, since stricken off, 8,968.

The towns of the county are Clinton and Moscow. CLINTON, the seat of justice, was established in 1831, and is about three hundred miles from Frankfort. It contains four stores, two taverns, six lawyers, three doctors, one large school, one tannery, eight mechanics' shops, and 275 inhabitants. *Moscow* is a small village, six miles from Clinton—contains two stores, two doctors, one tobacco stemmery, one lawyer, four or five mechanics' shops, and a population of 100.

This county was named in memory of Captain PASCHAL HICKMAN, a native of Virginia. When very young, he emigrated to Kentucky with his father, the Rev. William Hickman, and settled in Franklin county. He served in most of the campaigns against the Indians, in which he was distinguished for his activity, efficiency and bravery. In 1812, he was commissioned a captain, raised a volunteer company, and joined Colonel John Allen, who commanded the first regiment of Kentucky riflemen. He was in the memorable battle of the river Raisin, where he was severely wounded, and like many kindred Kentucky spirits, was inhumanly butchered in cold blood, by the savage allies of his Britannic majesty.

HOPKINS COUNTY.

HOPKINS county was formed in 1806, and called for General SAMUEL HOPKINS. It is situated in the western part of the State, lying on the waters of Greene river—bounded on the north by Henderson; east by Pond river, which separates it from Muhlenburg; south by Christian; and west by Caldwell. The largest portion of land in the county is good, producing, in great

abundance, tobacco, corn and oats—though tobacco is the principal export. The hills abound in inexhaustible coal mines, and
some iron ore has been discovered. Greene river, which forms the
northern boundary of the county, is always navigable for steamboats—and Pond river is navigable for flat boats to within eleven
or twelve miles of Madisonville, rendered so by locks and dams
on Greene river. Value of taxable property in 1846, $1,633,280 ;
number of acres of land in the county, 303,302 ; average value of
land per acre, $2.30 ; number of white males over twenty-one
years of age, 1,719 ; number of children between five and sixteen years old, 2,548. Population in 1840, 9,171.

The towns of the county are, Madisonville, Ashbysburg and
Providence. MADISONVILLE, the seat of justice, is about two hundred miles from Frankfort : contains a handsome brick court-
house and other public buildings, two churches, (Christian and
Methodist, the latter worshipped in, also, by the Cumberland
Presbyterians), one academy, one female school for small girls,
three common schools, five stores, four taverns, six lawyers, twelve
doctors, (including three of the botanical order), in and near
the town, with a large number of mechanics—population 450.
Incorporated in 1812, and named for James Madison. *Ashbysburg*
is a small village on Greene river, containing one store, post office,
and about fifty inhabitants—named for General Stephen Ashby.
Providence contains two stores, one tavern, post office, and 100
inhabitants.

About four or five miles from Madisonville, on a high and rocky hill, are the
remains of what is supposed to be a fortification. The wall is of stone, and contains an area of ten acres. No one living can tell when or by whom it was built.

General SAMUEL HOPKINS (whose name this county bears) was a native of
Albermarle county, Virginia. He was an officer of the revolutionary army, and
bore a conspicuous part in that great struggle for freedom. Few officers of his
rank performed more active duty, rendered more essential services, or enjoyed
in a higher degree the respect and confidence of the commander-in-chief. He
fought in the battles of Princeton, Trenton, Monmouth, Brandywine, and Germantown—in the last of which he commanded a battalion of light infantry, and
received a severe wound, after the almost entire loss of those under his command
in killed and wounded. He was lieutenant-colonel of the tenth Virginia regiment at the siege of Charleston, and commanded that regiment after Colonel Par-
ker was killed, to the close of the war. The following anecdote is told of him :
At the surrender of Charleston, on the 20th of May, 1780, he was made a prisoner of war. After a short detention on an island, he and his brother officers, his
companions in misfortune, were conducted in a British vessel round the coast to
Virginia. During the voyage, which was a protracted one, the prisoners suffered
many privations, and much harsh treatment, being often insulted by the Captain.
Hopkins became indignant at the cruelty and insolence of the captain of the vessel, and determined, at all hazards, to resent the harsh treatment to which himself
and brother officers had been subjected. On receiving his day's allowance, which
consisted of a mouldy biscuit, he deliberately crumbled it up into a wad, and
then, presenting it to the captain, demanded of him whether he thought *that* was
sufficient to keep soul and body together. The petty tyrant was taken by surprise,
and had no reply. " Sir," continued Hopkins, " the fortune of war has frequently
placed British soldiers in my power, and they have never had cause to complain
of my unkindness or want of hospitality. That which I have extended to others,
I have a right to demand for my companions and myself in similar circumstances.
And now, sir, (he continued with great emphasis), unless we are hereafter

treated as gentlemen and officers, I will raise a mutiny and take your ship." This determined resolution had the desired effect. His companions and himself, during the remainder of the voyage, were treated with kindness and respect.

In 1797, General Hopkins removed to Kentucky and settled on Greene river. He served several sessions in the legislature of Kentucky, and was a member of Congress for the term commencing in 1813, and ending in 1815. In October, 1812, he led a corps of two thousand mounted volunteers against the Kickapoo villages upon the Illinois; but being misled by the guides, after wandering in the prairies for some days to no purpose, the party returned to the capital of Indiana, notwithstanding the wishes and commands of their general officers. Chagrined at the result of this attempt, in the succeeding November, General Hopkins led a band of infantry up the Wabash, and succeeded in destroying several deserted Indian villages, but lost several men in an ambuscade. His wily enemy declining a combat, and the cold proving severe, he was forced again to retire to Vincennes, where his troops were disbanded.

After the close of this campaign, General Hopkins served one term in Congress, and then retired to private life on his farm near the Red banks.

About twenty miles from the town of Henderson, at a point just within the line of Hopkins county, where the roads from Henderson, Morganfield and Hopkinsville intersect, there is a wild and lonely spot called "*Harpe's Head.*" The place derived its name from a tragical circumstance, which occurred there in the early part of the present century. The bloody legend connected with it, has been made the foundation of a thrilling border romance, by Judge Hall, of Cincinnati, one of the most pleasing writers of the west. The narrative which follows, however, may be relied on for its strict historical truth and accuracy, the facts having been derived from one who was contemporary with the event, and personally cognizant of most of the circumstances. The individual to whom we allude is the venerable James Davidson, of Frankfort, the present treasurer of Kentucky. Colonel Davidson was a distinguished soldier in the last war with Great Britain, and has filled the office of treasurer for many years. His high character for veracity is a pledge for the truth of any statement he may make.

In the fall of the year 1801 or 1802, a company consisting of two men and three women arrived in Lincoln county, and encamped about a mile from the present town of Stanford. The appearance of the individuals composing this party was wild and rude in the extreme. The one who seemed to be the leader of the band, was above the ordinary stature of men. His frame was bony and muscular, his breast broad, his limbs gigantic. His clothing was uncouth and shabby, his exterior weatherbeaten and dirty, indicating continual exposure to the elements and designating him as one who dwelt far from the habitations of men, and mingled not in the courtesies of civilized life. His countenance was bold and ferocious, and exceedingly repulsive, from its strongly marked expression of villainy. His face, which was larger than ordinary, exhibited the lines of ungovernable passion, and the complexion announced that the ordinary feelings of the human breast were in him extinguished. Instead of the healthy hue which indicates the social emotions, there was a livid unnatural redness, resembling that of a dried and lifeless skin. His eye was fearless and steady, but it was also artful and audacious, glaring upon the beholder with an unpleasant fixedness and brilliancy, like that of a ravenous animal gloating on its prey. He wore no covering on his head, and the natural protection of thick coarse hair, of a fiery redness, uncombed and matted, gave evidence of long exposure to the rudest visitations of the sunbeam and the tempest. He was armed with a rifle, and a broad leathern belt, drawn closely around his waist, supported knife and tomahawk. He seemed, in short, an outlaw, destitute of all the nobler sympathies of human nature, and prepared at all points for assault or defence. The other man was smaller in size than him who led the party, but similarly armed, having the same suspicious exterior, and a countenance equally fierce and sinister. The females were coarse, sunburnt, and wretchedly attired.

The men stated in answer to the enquiry of the inhabitants, that their names were Harpe, and that they were emigrants from North Carolina. They remained at their encampment the greater part of two days and a night, spending the time in rioting, drunkenness and debauchery. When they left they took the road leading to Greene river. The day succeeding their departure, a report reached the neighborhood that a young gentleman of wealth from Virginia, named Lankford, had been robbed and murdered on what was then called, and is still known as the "*Wilderness Road*," which runs through the Rock-castle hills. Suspicion immediately fixed upon the Harpes as the perpetrators, and Captain Ballenger, at the head of a few bold and resolute men, started in pursuit. They experienced great difficulty in following their trail, owing to a heavy fall of snow, which had obliterated most of the tracks, but finally came upon them while encamped in a bottom on Greene river, near the spot where the town of Liberty now stands. At first they made a show of resistance, but upon being informed that if they did not immediately surrender they would be shot down, they yielded themselves prisoners.

They were brought back to Stanford, and there examined. Among their effects were found some fine linen shirts, marked with the initials of Lankford. One had been pierced by a bullet and was stained with blood. They had also a considerable sum of money, in gold. It was afterwards ascertained that this was the kind of money Lankford had with him. The evidence against them being thus conclusive, they were confined in the Stanford jail, but were afterwards sent for trial to Danville, where the district court was in session. Here they broke jail, and succeeded in making their escape.

They were next heard of in Adair county, near Columbia. In passing through that county, they met a small boy, the son of Colonel Trabue, with a pillow case of meal or flour, an article they probably needed. This boy it is supposed they robbed and then murdered, as he was never afterwards heard of. Many years afterwards human bones, answering the size of Colonel Trabue's son at the time of his disappearance, were found in a sink hole near the place where he was said to have been murdered.

The Harpes still shaped their course towards the mouth of Greene river, marking their path by murders and robberies of the most horrible and brutal character. The district of country through which they passed was at that time very thinly settled, and from this reason their outrages went unpunished. They seemed inspired with the deadliest hatred against the whole human race, and such was their implacable misanthropy, that they were known to kill where there was no temptation to rob. One of their victims was a little girl, found at some distance from her home, whose tender age and helplessness would have been protection against any but incarnate fiends. The last dreadful act of barbarity, which led to their punishment and expulsion from the country, exceeded in atrocity all the others.

Assuming the guise of Methodist preachers, they obtained lodgings one night at a solitary house on the road. Mr. Stagall, the master of the house, was absent, but they found his wife and children, and a stranger, who, like themselves, had stopped for the night. Here they conversed and made inquiries about the two noted Harpes who were represented as prowling about the country. When they retired to rest, they contrived to secure an axe, which they carried with them into their chamber. In the dead of night they crept softly down stairs, and assassinated the whole family, together with the stranger, in their sleep, and then setting fire to the house, made their escape.

When Stagall returned, he found no wife to welcome him; no home to receive him. Distracted with grief and rage, he turned his horse's head from the smouldering ruins, and repaired to the house of Captain John Leeper. Leeper was one of the most powerful men of his day, and fearless as powerful. Collecting four or five other men well armed, they mounted and started in pursuit of vengeance. It was agreed that Leeper should attack "Big Harpe," leaving "Little Harpe" to be disposed of by Stagall. The others were to hold themselves in readiness to assist Leeper and Stagall, as circumstances might require.

This party found the women belonging to the Harpes attending to their little camp by the road side; the men having gone aside into the woods to shoot an unfortunate traveler, of the name of Smith, who had fallen into their hands, and whom the women had begged might not be dispatched before their eyes. It was this halt that enabled the pursuers to overtake them. The women immediately gave the alarm, and the miscreants mounting their horses, which were large, fleet and powerful, fled in separate directions. Leeper singled out the Big Harpe, and being better mounted than his companions, soon left them far behind. Little

23

Harpe succeeded in escaping from Stagall, and he, with the rest of his companions, turned and followed on the track of Leeper and the Big Harpe. After a chase of about nine miles, Leeper came within gun shot of the latter and fired. The ball entering his thigh, passed through it and penetrated his horse, and both fell. Harpe's gun escaped from his hand and rolled some eight or ten feet down the bank. Reloading his rifle, Leeper ran up to where the wounded outlaw lay weltering in his blood, and found him with one thigh broken, and the other crushed beneath his horse. Leeper rolled the horse away, and set Harpe in an easier position. The robber begged that he might not be killed. Leeper told him that he had nothing to fear from him, but that Stagall was coming up, and could not probably be restrained. Harpe appeared very much frightened at hearing this, and implored Leeper to protect him. In a few moments Stagall appeared, and without uttering a word, raised his rifle and shot Harpe through the head. They then severed the head from the body, and stuck it upon a pole where the road crosses the creek, from which the place was then named and is yet called *Harpe's Head*. Thus perished one of the boldest and most noted freebooters that has ever appeared in America. Save courage, he was without one redeeming quality, and his death freed the country from a terror which had long paralyzed its boldest spirits.

The Little Harpe, when next heard from, was on the road which runs from New Orleans, through the Choctaw grant, to Tennessee. Whilst there, he became acquainted with and joined the band of outlaws led by the celebrated Mason. Mason and Harpe committed many depredations upon the above mentioned road, and upon the Mississippi river. They continued this course of life for several years, and accumulated great wealth. Finally, Mason and his band became so notorious and troublesome, that the governor of the Mississippi territory offered a reward of five hundred dollars for his head. Harpe immediately determined to secure the reward for himself. Finding Mason one day in a thick canebrake, counting his money, he shot him, cut off his head, and carried it to the village of Washington, then the capital of Mississippi. A man who had been robbed about a year before by Mason's band, recognized Harpe, and upon his evidence, he was arrested, arraigned, tried, condemned, and executed. Thus perished the "Little Harpe," who, lacking the only good quality his brother possessed, courage, was if any thing, more brutal and ferocious.

JEFFERSON COUNTY.

JEFFERSON county was formed in 1780, by the Virginia legislature, (being one of the three original counties which composed the district of Kentucky), and named in honor of THOMAS JEFFERSON, distinguished, at that day, as the author of the declaration of independence, and one of the ablest and most efficient members of the continental Congress. This county is situated in the northwest middle part of the State—bounded on the north by Oldham and the Ohio river, on the east by Shelby, on the south by Bullitt and Spencer, and on the west by the Ohio river. LOUISVILLE city is the seat of justice, about fifty miles from Frankfort.

Besides the Ohio river, which, in an extended and beautiful curve, borders half of the northern and the entire southern portion of the county, Jefferson is watered by Beargrass, a stream noted in the early settlement of the State, which enters the Ohio at Louisville, and by Pond's and Floyd's creeks—the latter emptying its waters into Salt river. The face of the country is diversified, presenting, for many miles around, and including the city of Louisville, an almost unbroken level plain, rich, productive and highly cultivated; while the up-lands are undulating or hilly, with a soil inferior, generally, to the bottom-lands, but producing fine wheat, oats and corn. The staples of Jefferson are hemp, wheat, corn, oats and potatoes. Horses, cattle and hogs, in large numbers, are also raised, and the county is dotted with fine gardens for the supply of the Louisville market with vegetables.

Number of acres of land in Jefferson county, 200,680; average value per acre, $28.12; value of taxable property in 1846, $22,-940,533; number of white males over twenty-one years old, 7,547; number of children between five and sixteen years old, 6,326. Population in 1830, 10,090—in 1840, 36,346.

The city of LOUISVILLE is situated at the Falls of the Ohio, immediately at the junction of Beargrass with that river. It is 1,480 miles, by water, from New-Orleans, 607 from Pittsburgh, 350, by land, from St. Louis, 53 miles from Frankfort: latitude 38 deg., 3 min. north; longitude 85 deg., 30 min. west from Greenwich, and 8 deg., 45 min. west from Washington city. It is built on an elevated plain, 70 feet above low water mark, and very gently declining towards its southern border; is regularly laid out on a plan similar to that of Philadelphia, having eight broad and beautiful streets, running east and west, and parallel with the river, from one and a half to two miles in length, and from sixty to one hundred and twenty feet in breadth—these are intersected at right angles by more than thirty cross streets, all sixty feet wide. The streets are generally well paved, and the side walks wide and convenient. The public buildings are a city hall and court-house not yet complete, a city and county jail, on the most approved model, a marine hospital, a medical institute, an asylum for the blind, an edifice for the university of Louisville, thirty churches, viz : four Baptist, one Christian, six Methodist (one of which is German), one Seamen's Bethel, four Presbyterian, three Episcopal, one Unitarian, two Universalist, two Roman Catholic (one of which is German), four churches for colored people (three Methodist and one Baptist), one Free church, one Jewish synagogue, five banking houses, four market houses, one city work-house, one hospital, two orphan asylums, one Magdalen asylum, under the care of the Sisters of the Good Shepherd, four large city school-houses, twenty-four schools, six of which are grammar schools, three for males and three for females. Some of these buildings are splendid structures, and would do credit to any city of the United States. The city hall is a noble building, admirably planned, and presenting a beautiful exterior. It is not yet complete. The first Presbyterian and St. Paul's (Episcopal), churches are fine specimens of architectural beauty.

RELIGIOUS AND BENEVOLENT INSTITUTIONS.—Thirty churches, of the various denominations of Christians, including one of the Jews, a depository of the American Sunday School Union, the Louisville Bible Society, and the Young Men's

Tract Society, five Masonic lodges, one Royal Arch Chapter, one Encampment of Knights Templars, six lodges of Odd Fellows, one grand lodge of Odd Fellows, and one grand encampment, ten divisions of the Sons of Temperance, three Temples of Honor, and one grand division Sons of Temperance of Kentucky.

The MEDICAL INSTITUTE ranks high among the *public institutions* of Louisville. It was organized in 1837, by an ordinance of the city council, which appropriated $50,000 for the library, chemical apparatus, and suitable buildings. The first course of lectures was delivered to 80 students, the second to 120; the third class numbered 204, the fourth 208, the fifth 262, the sixth 189, the seventh 242, the eighth 283, the ninth 342, and the tenth 349 students. The college edifice is a commodious, well arranged, and handsome building; and the professors are learned and able men.

The *Asylum for the Blind* is a noble institution, established by the State of Kentucky in 1842. A spacious building has been erected for this institution, by the joint contributions of the State and benevolent citizens of Louisville. The institution already embraces between forty and fifty students, of both sexes. The course of instruction embraces the elementary and higher branches of the English language, ancient and modern languages, and music, vocal and instrumental. The students are instructed also, in the various kinds of handicraft, by which they will be enabled to gain an honorable support, after leaving the institution.

The *University of Louisville* is yet in its infancy; but from the liberality of its endowment, and the character of the people among whom it is located, there can be no doubt that it is destined to take a high rank among the literary institutions of the west. The first course of lectures in the *law department*, was delivered last winter to about thirty students.

The *Marine Hospital* is another important public institution, located at Louisville. It was established in 1820, by a grant from the State of $40,000—and designed as a refuge for sick and infirm mariners.

The *Kentucky Historical Society*, which has its location in Louisville, was incorporated by the legislature in 1838. It is an institution of great value—the object of its organization being, to collect and preserve the public and private records which are calculated to elucidate the history of the west, but more particularly, of Kentucky.

The other public institutions of Louisville, consist of—the Bank of Kentucky, with a capital of $5,000,000; Bank of Louisville, capital $2,000,000; Branch of the Northern Bank of Kentucky, capital $600,000; Louisville Gas Company, capital $1,200,000; Mechanics' Savings Institute, $100,000; ten insurance companies; and the Mercantile Library Association, with a library of four thousand volumes.

The trade of Louisville is very extensive, and to those who have not made themselves acquainted with statistics of this character, would appear almost incredible. In the two articles of sugar and coffee, the sales, during the year 1847, it is believed, will amount to several millions of dollars; while the total export and import trade will fall but little short of $50,000,000.* The houses engaged in the dry goods, commission, drug, hardware, grocery, fruit, and produce business, number upwards of six hundred, employing a capital of about $6,000,000. Besides the houses engaged in the business named, there are seven book stores, seven iron stores, ten lumber yards, twelve founderies for the construction of steamboat and mill machinery, one brass foundry, one rolling and slitting mill, two steam bagging factories, producing about two million yards cotton bagging annually, six cordage and rope factories, one cotton factory, one woolen factory, four flouring mills, four lard oil factories, one white lead factory, one burr millstone factory, several extensive potteries, six tobacco stemmeries, two tobacco inspection houses, two glass cutting establishments, one oil cloth factory, two

*In May, 1815. the first trip of a steamboat was made from New Orleans to Louisville and Pittsburgh; the second and third trips in 1817. In 1841, there were 369 steamboats on the western and south-western waters, measuring, in the aggregate, more than fifty thousand tons. In 1847. the number of boats and tonnage is believed to be double that of 1841. In the immense trade carried on by these boats, Louisville largely participates.

FIRST PRESBYTERIAN CHURCH, LOUISVILLE, KY.

ST. PAUL'S CHURCH, LOUISVILLE, KY.

surgical instrument manufactories, two lithographic engravers, one large paper mill, one star candle factory, four pork houses, three piano manufactories, three breweries, one ivory clock manufactory, six tanneries, ten soap and candle factories, four planing machines, city gas works, two scale beam factories, two glue factories, three ship yards, one nail manufactory. There are, also, extensive manufactories of sheet iron, brass, copper, tin ware, silver ware, saddlery and harness, cabinet ware, chairs, plows, carriages, wagons, hats, boots and shoes, clocks, clothing, &c., &c., with a large number of building mechanics.

The city is well supplied with hotels and boarding-houses of a high character. The professions of law, medicine, and divinity, are well filled with able and distinguished men—there being, in the city, about one hundred lawyers, ninety physicians, and upwards of thirty ministers of the gospel.

There are twelve newspapers and periodicals—political, commercial, religious, temperance, medical, emancipation, and agricultural—some of them old establishments and of high repute, published in the city. The *Louisville Journal,** published daily, tri-weekly, and weekly; the *Morning Courier*, daily, tri-weekly, and weekly; the *Evening Express*, daily; the *Louisville Democrat*, daily, tri-weekly, and weekly; the *Journal of Commerce*, weekly; the *Presbyterian Herald*, weekly; the *Baptist Banner*, weekly; the *Catholic Advocate*, weekly; the *Spirit of the Age*, weekly; the *Examiner*, weekly; the *Western Journal of Medicine and Surgery*, monthly; and the *Southern Methodist Quarterly Review*.

There are several extensive job printing offices in the city; and the book printing establishment of Messrs. Morton & Griswold, is one of the most extensive in the western country.

The want of public squares in Louisville is deeply felt. According to the original plan, a strip of land nearly two hundred feet in width, lying south of Greene street, and extending the whole length of the city, was reserved for a public promenade. If this plan had been followed, and some of the magnificent forest trees had been suffered to remain, Louisville would have presented beauties which the most splendid buildings in the world could not give. Health, pleasure, taste and even morality are improved by fine promenades and public squares. No one can tell how much of the literary eminence of Athens is due to the " groves of Academus." There is yet an opportunity for Louisville to have a good promenade, though she can have no central public square. If Broadway were properly graded and set with trees, it would prove one of the most beautiful streets in the world. If the street were extended to " Preston's Wood" on the east, and this wood were properly improved, it would be a delightful place of resort.

The population of Louisville, in 1780, comprised only thirty souls; in 1800, population six hundred; in 1810, population one thousand three hundred; in 1820, four thousand; in 1830, ten thousand and ninety; in 1840, twenty-one thousand; in 1843, twenty-eight thousand; in 1845, thirty-two thousand; and in 1847, it is estimated at forty thousand.

Those who approach Louisville from the east, will probably arrive in the night. When within a few miles of the city, the boat winds round an island, and a long row of brilliant gas lights presents itself to the view. The effect of this is very fine, and a considerable time elapses before the appearance of buildings mars the beauty of the scene. But those who approach by daylight, have a much more varied and beautiful prospect. A view taken from the Kentucky shore, just above the city, is one of the most charming on which the eye can rest. Before you are the Falls, Corn Island, and, in the distance, New Albany; on the left is a view of part of Louisville; on the right, below Jeffersonville, appear some of the forest trees of Indiana. The river here has the appearance of a lake, for it winds around in such a manner that its course is concealed. The upper part of this apparent lake, is smooth and tranquil : while the lower part is in violent commotion from the dashing of the water over the rocks. In looking at the upper part, the river seems to you to be collecting its energies for some violent exertion. After a moment's hesitation, after taking breath, as it were, it rushes furiously upon the im-

---

* George D. Prentice, who has been for many years connected with the Journal as a proprietor and the principal editor, stands unrivalled as a political writer, a wit. and a satirist, and has written some poetical articles of exceeding beauty. Among the poets of Louisville, it is proper to mention the name, also, of Mrs. Amelia Welby, whose exquisite productions, under the signature of "AMELIA," have given her a high rank among American poets. Fortunatus Cosby, and his son, Robt. T. Cosby, have also written many poetical articles of great merit.

PRISON, LOUISVILLE, KY.

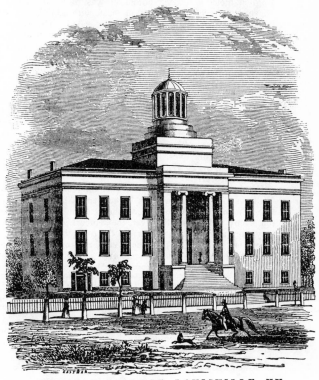

MEDICAL COLLEGE, LOUISVILLE, KY.

pediments in its way, like an army charging upon the foe. In the back-ground the blue hills crown the view, the long line curving itself as if to embrace the city.

Three-quarters of a century have not elapsed since Louisville was selected as a site for a town. Captain Thomas Bullitt, of Virginia, uncle of the late Alexander Scott Bullitt, who was the first lieutenant-governor of Kentucky, is said to have laid off the town in August, 1773.* This was before the first log cabin was built in Kentucky. For several years after this, the silence of the forest was undisturbed by the white man. The place was occasionally visited by different persons, but no settlement was made until 1778. In the spring of this year, a party, consisting of a small number of families, came to the Falls with George Rogers Clark, and were left by him on an island near the Kentucky shore, now called Corn island. The name is supposed to have been derived from the circumstance that the settlers planted their first Indian corn on this island.

These settlers were sixty or seventy miles distant from any other settlement, and had nothing but their insular position to defend them from the Indians. The posts in the Wabash country, occupied by the British, served as points of support for the incursions of the savages. After these had been taken by Clark, the settlers were inspir d with confidence, and, in the fall of 1778, removed from the island to the site now occupied by Louisville. Here a block house was erected,† and the number of settlers was increased by the arrival of other emigrants from Virginia.

In 1780, the legislature of Virginia passed " an act for establishing the town of Louisville,‡ at the falls of Ohio." By this act, "John Todd, jr., Stephen Trigg, George Slaughter, John Floyd, William Pope, George Meriwether, Andrew Hynes, James Sullivan, gentlemen," were appointed trustees to lay off the town on a tract of one thousand acres of land, which had been granted to John Connolly by the British government, and which he had forfeited by adhering to the English monarch. Each purchaser was to build on his own lot " a dwelling house, sixteen feet by twenty, at least, with a brick or stone chimney, to be finished within two years from the day of sale." On account of the interruptions caused by the inroads of the Indians, the time was afterwards extended. The state of the settlers was one of constant danger and anxiety. Their foes were continually prowling around, and it was risking their lives to leave the fort.

The settlement at the Falls was more exposed than those in the interior, on account of the facility with which the Indians could cross and re-cross the river, and the difficulties in the way of pursuing them. The savages frequently crossed the river, and after killing some of the settlers, and committing depredations upon property, recrossed and escaped. In 1780, Colonel George Slaughter arrived at the Falls with one hundred and fifty state troops. The inhabitants were inspired with a feeling of security which led them frequently to expose themselves with too little caution. Their foes were ever on the watch, and were continually destroying valuable lives. Danger and death crouched in every path, and lurked behind every tree. We give here some illustrations of the incidents connected with Indian warfare.

In March, 1781, several parties entered Jefferson county, and killed Colonel William Lynn, and Captains Tipton and Chapman. Captain Whittaker and fifteen men pursued and traced them to the foot of the Falls. Supposing that the enemy had crossed the river, they embarked in canoes to follow them. While they were making their way across the river, they were fired upon by the Indians, who were still on the Kentucky side, and nine were killed or wounded. The rest returned and defeated the enemy. In the next month a party that had made

---

*Captain Bullitt was a man of great energy and enterprise, as he showed on several important occasions. He served in the French war, and was engaged in the battle which resulted in Braddock's defeat, and in other actions. He was a captain in the regiment that was commanded by Washington. On one occasion, two detachments from Colonel Washington's regiment were out upon the frontiers to surprise a party of French troops from Fort Du Quesne. Instead of falling in with the French, the two detachments met each other, and, the day being very foggy, each party supposed the other to be the enemy, and a warm firing was commenced on both sides. Captain Bullitt was one of the first that discovered the mistake, and ran in between the two parties, waving his hat, and calling upon them to cease firing.

†A larger fort was built in 1782, and called Fort Nelson, in honor of Gov. Nelson, of Virginia.

‡The name was given to the place in honor of the ill-fated French monarch, Louis XVI. whose troops were at that time assisting the Americans in the war against England.

VIEW OF MAIN STREET, LOUISVILLE, KY.

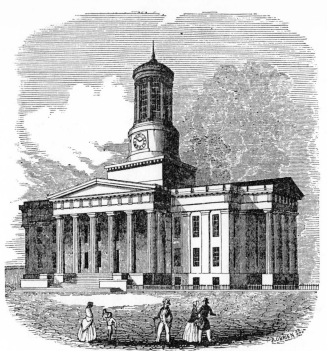

JEFFERSON COURT-HOUSE, LOUISVILLE, **KY**.

UNIVERSITY OF LOUISVILLE, KY

a settlement under Squire Boone, near the place where Shelbyville now stands, became alarmed by the appearance of Indians, and resolved to remove to the neighborhood of Louisville. On the way, the party, consisting of men, women and children, encumbered with the charge of household goods and cattle, were attacked by a large company of Indians that had pursued them, and were defeated and dispersed. Colonel John Floyd, on receiving intelligence of this event, raised a company of twenty-five men, and hastened to pursue the enemy. He divided his men and proceeded with great caution; but this did not prevent his falling into an ambuscade. The Indians, whose force is said to have been three times as great as his, completely defeated him, killing about half his men, and losing nine or ten. Colonel Floyd himself lost his horse, and was retreating on foot, nearly exhausted, and closely pursued, when Captain Samuel Wells seeing him, rode up and gave him his horse, running by his side to support him. These two gentlemen had been unfriendly towards each other, but this noble act made them friends for life.*

In 1793, a party of Indians fired on a flat boat descending the river, but without serious injury to those on board. On the succeeding day, they captured a boy at Eastin's mill, and conveyed him to the Ohio. Here, by a strange freak, they gave him a tomahawk, knife and pipe, and set him at liberty, unhurt.†

In those days, the dress and furniture were of the simplest kind. Many who are now proud of their ancestors, would be ashamed of them if they were to appear before them in the costliest dress of the early times. It is amusing to imagine the consternation of a belle at a fashionable party, if her ancestors should present themselves before her—the grandfather in coon-skin cap and buckskin breeches, and his wife dressed out for the occasion in her best attire of linsey-woolsey. The very fan of the belle would tremble, as if participating in the shame and confusion, and the odor of the smelling-bottle would rise in indignant steam.

In 1783, Daniel Brodhead began a new era, by exposing goods from Philadelphia for sale in Louisville. The merchandise had been brought from Philadelphia to Pittsburgh in wagons, and thence to Louisville in flat boats. The belles of our "forest-land" then began to shine in all the magnificence of calico, and the beaux in the luxury of wool hats.

After the old county of Kentucky had been divided, in November, 1781, into three counties—Jefferson, Fayette and Lincoln—Jefferson included all the part of the old county lying south of the Kentucky river, north of Greene river, and west of Big Benson, and Hammond's creek. The county court of each county was composed of the most respectable citizens of such county, and appointed its own clerk. The limits of its authority were rather undefined. The county court of Jefferson sat also as a court of oyer and terminer. In regard to capital offences, it acted merely as an examining court when white persons were concerned, but tried and condemned slaves to death. "At a called court held for Jefferson county on the 10th day of August, 1785, for the examination of negro Peter, the property of Francis Vigo, committed to the jail of this county on suspicion of stealing, present, James F. Moore, William Oldham, Richard Taylor and David Meriwether, gent."—Peter was found guilty, valued at eighty pounds, current money, and condemned to be executed on the 24th day of that month. On the 21st day of October, 1786, "negro Tom, a slave, the property of Robert Daniel," was condemned to death for stealing "two and three-fourths yards of cambric, and some ribbon and thread, the property of James Patten." The following appears on the early records of the court:

"The court doth set the following rates to be observed by ordinary keepers in this county, to wit: whiskey fifteen dollars the half pint; corn at ten dollars the gallon; a diet at twelve dollars; lodging in a feather bed, six dollars; stablage or pasturage one night, four dollars."

These seem to be very extravagant prices; but we suppose travelers took care to pay in continental money. These were the times when a hat was worth five hundred dollars. The following is an inventory rendered to the court of the property of a deceased person:

---

* Marshall I, 115. See also biographical sketch of Colonel Floyd.   † Ibid. II, 81.

" To a coat and waistcoat £250, an old blue do. and do. £50 . . . 300
" To pocket book £6, part of an old shirt £3 9
" To old blanket, 6s.; 2 bushels salt £480 . . . . 480 6

£789 6."

The following is recorded May 7th, 1784 :—" George Pomeroy being brought before the court, charged with having been guilty of a breach of the act of assembly, entitled ' divulgers of false news,' on examining sundry witnesses, and the said Pomeroy heard in his defence, the court is of opinion that the said George Pomeroy is guilty of a breach of the said law, and it is therefore ordered that he be fined 2000 pounds of tobacco for the same. And it is further ordered that the said George Pomeroy give security for his good behavior, himself in £1000, with two securities in £500, and pay costs, &c."

This may seem like making rather too serious a matter of divulging false news. It is certain that if all who are guilty of this crime in our day were punished, it would add very materially to the business of the courts. The history of this matter is rather curious. Tom Paine wrote a book ridiculing the right of Virginia to the lands of Kentucky, and urging Congress to assume possession of the whole country. Two Pennsylvanians, whose names were Pomeroy and Galloway, had imbibed the principles of this production, and came to Kentucky to propagate them—Pomeroy to the Falls, and Galloway to Lexington. Galloway produced considerable disturbance at Lexington. " Several of the good people," says Mr. H. Marshall, " yielded so far to his persuasions as to commence chopping and improving upon their neighbors' lands, with the *pious* intent of appropriating them, under an act of Congress, which, they were assured, was soon to be promulgated." It was decided that he must be punished. After this determination had been made, an old law of Virginia was fortunately found which inflicted a penalty, in tobacco, at the discretion of the court, upon the " propagation of false news, to the disturbance of the good people of the colony." Galloway was fined one thousand pounds of tobacco. As it was impossible to procure so much tobacco in Kentucky at that time, he had a prospect of spending some time in prison. At length it was intimated to him that if he would leave the country, justice would be satisfied. He instantly caught at the offer. Mr. Marshall says that at the Falls, no one minded Paine's disciple. The extract from the records shows that he was mistaken, and that Pomeroy was fined twice as much tobacco as Galloway was ordered to pay.

Into the original log cabins the light entered by the open door, or by any opening it could find. One of the first settlers would almost as soon have thought of bringing some " bright particular star " into his dwelling to illuminate it, as of introducing light through a glass window. In the progress of time, however, the owner of a certain shop or " store " procured some glass, and inserted a few panes in his house. A young urchin who had seen glass spectacles on the noses of his elders, saw this spectacle with astonishment, and, running home to his mother, exclaimed, " O ma! there is a house down here with specs on!" This may be considered a very precocious manifestation of the power of generalization in the young Kentuckian.

The first brick house was built in 1789, by Mr. Kaye, on the square on which the court house now stands.

The beginning of the nineteenth century found Louisville with a population of 600 in the midst of her ponds. In 1810, the number had increased to 1,357.

In 1811 and 1812, occurred that succession of earthquakes which shook a great part of our continent. The first shock was felt at Louisville, December 16, 1811, a few minutes after two o'clock in the morning, and continued three and a half or four minutes. For one minute, the shock was very severe. Several gentlemen of Louisville were amusing themselves at a social party, when one of their acquaintances burst into the room and cried out, " Gentlemen, how can you be engaged in this way, when the world is so near its end!" The company rushed out, and from the motion of objects around them, every star seemed to be falling. " What a pity," exclaimed one of them, " that so beautiful a world should be thus destroyed!" Almost every one of them believed that mother earth, as she heaved and struggled, was in her last agony. For several months, the citizens of Louisville were in continual alarm. The earth seemed to have no rest, except the uneasy rest of one disturbed by horrid dreams. Each house generally had a key suspended over the mantle piece, and by its oscillations the inmates were informed of the degree of danger. If the shock was violent, brick houses were immediately deserted. Under the key usually lay a bible. In the opinion of a distinguished citizen of Louisville, who has related to us many incidents of those exciting times, the earthquake had a beneficial influence upon public morals. Usually, we believe, times of great danger and excitement have had a contrary effect. Thucydides tells us that during the prevalence of the plague at Athens, men became more reckless and wicked, more eager in grasping at the pleasures which they saw so rapidly flitting by them. When the great plague raged in Italy, if we may judge from the character of the ladies and gentlemen in Boccaccio's Decameron, the morals were any thing but good. The plague in London, also, was accompanied by a corruption of morals.

In 1812, the legislature passed an act authorising the paving of Main street from Third to Sixth. No city in the Union had greater need of pavements. The horses had to draw the wagons through the business part of the city, as Sisyphus rolled "the huge round stone" up the hill,

> "With many a weary step, and many a groan."

In 1819, Dr. McMurtrie published his "Sketches of Louisville." The number of inhabitants was then more than four thousand, and was rapidly increasing. Society was becoming more refined. Dr. McMurtrie complains a good deal of that characteristic of all new cities, too great a devotion to the accumulation of wealth; and adds, with considerable rotundity of style: "There is a circle, small 'tis true, but within whose magic round abounds every pleasure that wealth, regulated by taste, can bestow. There the ' red heel' of Versailles may imagine himself in the very emporium of fashion, and, whilst leading beauty through the mazes of the dance, forget that he is in the wilds of America."

In speaking of the diseases of the place, Dr. M. mentions "a bilious remitting fever, whose symptoms are often sufficiently aggravated to entitle it to the name of *yellow fever*," and predicts the appearance of yellow fever itself, "unless greater attention be paid to cleanliness in every possible way." " During the months of July, August and September," says he, " so strongly are the inhabitants of this and the adjacent towns predisposed to this disease, by the joint influence of climate and the miasm of marshes, and decayed and decaying vegetable matter, that they may be compared to piles of combustibles, which need but the application of a single spark to rouse them into flame." The yellow fever did not make its appearance as Dr. M. predicted, but in 1822 a fever raged which seemed to threaten almost the depopulation of the town. It prevailed in some degree over the whole western country, but in Louisville it was particularly virulent. Almost every house seemed to become a hospital. In a family, consisting of twenty persons, nineteen were sick at one time. In one family, perhaps in more, every individual died.

After that visitation, Louisville began to be more healthy. At that time, where now stand some of the finest buildings in the city, large ponds flourished in perpetual green, and the croaking of frogs was not less ominous of death than had been the yell of the savage. That period, like all others, had its conservative party—"its party of the present,"—who wished every thing to remain as it was, and were opposed to depriving the frogs of the possessions which they had held "time whereof the memory of man runneth not to the contrary." They would as soon have thought of interfering with the music of the spheres as with that of the ponds. But other counsels began to prevail, and the inhabitants of the waters were obliged to retire before advancing civilization, as the inhabitants of the woods had done before them. Louisville had been called " the grave yard of the west;" but it began to change its character. Dr. M. says—" To affirm that Louisville is a healthy city, would be absurd." The affirmation may now be made without any fear of the charge of absurdity. Louisville is now acknowledged by all who are acquainted with the matter, to be one of the most healthy cities in the world. There is nothing to make it unhealthy. There are no hills to confine the air until it becomes putrid. The course of the breeze is as unobstructed as is that of the winds that revel over the surface of the ocean. The water is cool and pure and abundant. Ten years after the fever had made its dreadful ravages, the cholera appeared; but so gently did the destroying angel lay his hand upon the city, that the appearance of this scourge of the world scarcely forms an epoch in her history.

The attention of the people was directed, at a very early period, to plans for overcoming the obstructions to navigation presented by the " Falls." In 1804, the legislature of Kentucky incorporated a company to make a canal round the Falls. Nothing was done, however, for many years. The Louisville and Portland canal company was incorporated in 1825, and the canal was finished in 1833. The completion of the canal produced a great change in the business of the city. The " forwarding and commission" business, the operations in which formed so great a part of the mercantile transactions of Louisville, and had given employment to so many persons, was, in a great measure, destroyed. Much of the capital and industry of the city was obliged to seek new channels, and the transition state was one of great embarrassment. But a more healthy condition of things succeeded.

In the latter part of April, 1784, the father of the late Judge Rowan, with his family and five other families, set out from Louisville in two flat-bottomed boats, for the Long Falls of Greene river.* The intention was to descend the Ohio river to the mouth of Greene river, and ascend that river to the place of destination. At that time there were no settlements in Kentucky, within one hundred miles of the Long Falls of Greene river (afterwards called Vienna). The families were in one boat, and their cattle in the other. When the boats had descended the Ohio about one hundred miles, and were near the middle of it, gliding along very securely, as it was thought, about ten o'clock of the night, a prodigious yelling of Indians was heard, some two or three miles below, on the northern shore ; and they had floated but a short distance further down the river, when a number of fires were seen on that shore. The yelling continued, and it was concluded that they had captured a boat which had passed these two about mid-day, and were massacreing their captives. The two boats were lashed together, and the best practicable arrangements were made for defending them. The men were distributed by Mr. Rowan to the best advantage, in case of an attack—they were seven in number, including himself. The boats were *neared* to the Kentucky shore, with as little noise by the oars as possible ; but avoided too close an approach to that shore, lest there might be Indians there also. The fires of the Indians were extended along the bank at intervals, for half a mile or more, and as the boats reached a point about opposite the central fire, they were discovered, and commanded to *come to*. All on board remained silent, for Mr. Rowan had given strict orders that no one should utter any sound but that of his rifle, and not that until the Indians should come within powder burning distance. They united in a most terrific yell, rushed to their canoes, and gave pursuit. The boats floated on in silence—not an oar was pulled. The Indians approached within less than a hundred yards, with a seeming determination to board. Just at this moment, Mrs. Rowan rose from her seat, collected the axes, and placed one by the side of each man, where he stood with his gun, touching him on the knee with the handle of the axe, as she leaned it up by him against the side of the boat, to let him know it was there, and retired to her seat, retaining a hatchet for herself. The Indians continued hovering on the rear, and yelling, for nearly three miles, when, awed by the inference which they drew from the silence observed on board, they relinquished farther pursuit. None but those who have a practical acquaintance with Indian warfare, can form a just idea of the terror which their hideous yelling is calculated to inspire. Judge Rowan, who was then ten years old, states that he could never forget the sensations of that night, or cease to admire the fortitude and composure displayed by his mother on that trying occasion. There were seven men and three boys in the boats, with nine guns in all. Mrs. Rowan, in speaking of the incident afterwards, in her calm way, said—"we made a *providential escape*, for which we ought to feel grateful."

Col. Richard C. Anderson (the father of the Hon. Richard C. Anderson, a sketch of whose life will be found under the head of Anderson county), was a

---

* Dr. D. Drake's Oxford Address.

citizen of Jefferson—a member of the first electoral college, and for several years a member of the legislature.

Colonel RICHARD TAYLOR, the father of General Zachary Taylor, came to Kentucky at a very early period, and settled in Jefferson county. He was a member of the conventions of 1792 and 1799, which formed the first and second constitutions of Kentucky, and was often a member of the legislature.

Commodore TAYLOR, a distinguished officer of the American navy, resided in Louisville for many years before his death.

Colonel G. R. CLARK FLOYD, son of Col. John Floyd, (for whom Floyd county was called), a native of this county, commanded the fourth regiment of infantry at the battle of Tippecanoe, and was highly complimented by the commanding general for his gallantry and good conduct on that occasion.

Colonel JOHN FLOYD, of Virginia, also a native of Jefferson, and son of Colonel John Floyd. He removed to Virginia when twenty-one years of age, and is the only Kentuckian who ever became Governor of the Ancient Dominion.

Colonel WILLIAM POPE was an early and estimable citizen of Louisville, and was the ancestor or relative of the extensive connection of the same name in Louisville and Jefferson county.

Judge FORTUNATUS COSBY, also a citizen of Louisville, was an eminent lawyer, several times a member of the legislature, and judge of the circuit court. He lived to the age of eighty-one, and died in the year 1846.

Colonel GEIGER, also a citizen, was distinguished at the battle of Tippecanoe, and lived to an advanced age, honored and esteemed by all who knew him.

Honorable STEPHEN ORMSBY was a judge of the circuit court, and a member of Congress from 1811 to 1817. He was highly esteemed as a man and as a public servant, and lived to an advanced age.

THOMAS and CUTHBERT BULLITT were two of the first merchants of Louisville —distinguished for their probity and business qualifications, and amassed large estates for their descendents.

THOMAS PRATHER was also one of the first merchants of Louisville, and a most remarkable man. Possessed of a strong intellect, bland and courteous manners, a chivalric and high moral bearing, with superior business qualifications, and an integrity and probity of character which became proverbial—riches flowed in upon him like water, and he distributed his wealth with a beneficent hand, in benefactions which will prove a perpetual memorial of his liberality. He was president of the old bank of Kentucky, and when that institution suspended specie payments, he resigned the office, with this remark :—" I can preside over no institution which declines to meet its engagements promptly and to the letter ! "

JOHN ROWAN was an able jurist and statesman, and one of the most distinguished men in the western country. He was a native of Pennsylvania. His father, William Rowan, having sustained in the cause of liberty heavy losses, at the close of the revolutionary war came to Kentucky in the hope of repairing the ravages made in his private fortune. Kentucky was then a wilderness, the choice hunting ground of many hostile tribes of savages—the field of hazardous adventure, the scene of savage outrage, the theatre of ceaseless war, an arena drenched in blood and reeking with slaughter. In the month of March, 1783, the father of John Rowan settled in Louisville, then an insignificant village. In the spring of 1784, when John was eleven years old, his father, with five other families, made a settlement at the Long Falls of Greene river, then about one hundred miles from any white settlement. This region was resorted to by a band of the Shawnee tribe of Indians, as a hunting ground, and Mr. Rowan and his neighbors had many encounters with their savage foes. Young Rowan was soon distinguished for his bravery and for his remarkable energy and sprightliness. He spent several years of his boyhood in this wild and adventurous life, developing his physical powers in the manly and athletic sports and exercises common to the country, and insensibly communicating to his mind and character, a maturity and firmness inseparable from the habits of self reliance and fortitude, generated by a continual familiarity with danger.

At the age of seventeen, he entered a classical school kept at Bardstown, by a Dr. Priestly. In this school were educated many of those men who have since figured conspicuously in the history of Kentucky, and on the broader theatre of national politics. Here John Rowan was remarkable among his fellows for the facility with which he mastered the most difficult branches. He obtained an accurate and critical knowledge of the classical tongues, seemingly without an effort, and soon learned to appreciate the unrivalled beauty and sublimity of those wonderful productions of ancient genius, which have been the admiration of all ages. In his old age, he used to refer with much liveliness, to the pleasure he experienced at this period of his life, when he first learned to appreciate the beauty of the Greek writers, in retiring to the summit of a wild cliff, and there reading aloud to the rocks, woods and waters, the Iliad of Homer.

At this school, he received an education much superior to what we might now suppose could be afforded by the institutions of the country at that early day. In addition to this, he enjoyed the advantage of access to instructive and well selected libraries; and his acquirements in general information were commensurate with the development of his uncommon faculties, which now began to attract the attention of men of the best talents in the country.

Guided by the advice of his friends he went, upon leaving this school, to Lexington, and commenced the study of the law. In 1795, he was admitted to the bar, and soon attained a high rank in his profession. Kentucky, even at that day, held many men eminent for talent, learning and eloquence; yet he was considered among the foremost. As an advocate, in criminal cases, he had few equals in the state.

The Virginia act of 1779, constituting the basis of the celebrated land laws of Kentucky, though originally drawn and reported to the legislature by George Mason, one of Virginia's most able statesmen, was so amended before its passage, as to destroy all system in the procuring of patents, and the consequence was much litigation in Kentucky, arising out of conflicting land claims. Many of our most eminent lawyers acquired great wealth by buying up contested claims, and from contingent fees. In these things, Mr. Rowan never indulged, conceiving them to be inimical to the high moral tone which should be preserved by the profession, and tempting to oppression of the occupants of lands.

At an early age, he was called into public life, and was a member of the convention that formed the present constitution of Kentucky, in 1799. He was appointed secretary of state in 1804, and in 1806 was elected to Congress from a district in which he did not reside. He took his seat in 1807, and served during the 11th Congress.

He was frequently a member of the State legislature, and in 1819, was appointed a judge of the court of appeals. While on the bench, he delivered a learned and forcible opinion on the power of Congress to charter the bank of the United States in 1816. Not relishing the close confinement of the bench, in 1821 he resigned his seat. In 1823, he was appointed by the legislature, in conjunction with Henry Clay, a commissioner to defend what were called the occupying claimant laws of the State, before the supreme court of the United States. The uncertainty of land titles under the Virginia laws before alluded to, had led to the enactment of laws by the Kentucky legislature, more favorable to the occupant than the common law of England. These statutes were attacked before the supreme court, upon the ground that they violated the compact between Virginia and Kentucky. The petition of the commissioners was drawn by Judge Rowan, and is deemed the ablest vindication of those laws ever published.

In 1824, he was elected to the senate of the United States, in which body he served for six years. On the 10th of April, 1826, he delivered a speech of great ability, on a bill further to amend the judiciary system of the United States. In 1828, he made a learned and powerful speech on the subject of imprisonment for debt, under process issued from the courts of the United States. It had been abolished in Kentucky in 1821, and yet he had seen it practiced by process from the federal courts in this State, in defiance of public sentiment.

The last public office Mr. Rowan filled was that of commissioner to adjust the claims of citizens of the United States against Mexico, under the convention of Washington of the 11th of April, 1839. In this office he labored with great assiduity; and when, upon an adjournment of the commission, he made a visit to his family in Kentucky, and from a temporary indisposition, was unable to return to Washington at the time appointed for the reassembling of the commissioners, he resigned his appointment. Upon the organization of the Kentucky Historical Society in 1838, he was elected president of that institution, and held the office until the period of his death. He died, after a short illness, at his residence in Louisville, on the 13th of July, 1843, in the seventieth year of his age.

Judge Rowan was a man devoted in his friendships and exceedingly urbane in his manners; kind and hospitable in all his relations. He possessed an imposing person and dignified bearing. His colloquial powers were of the highest order, and made him the life of every company in which he mingled.

Among the distinguished men, whom Jefferson county enrolls with her worthies, a prominent place belongs to Major General ZACHARY TAYLOR, of the United States' army. Although not a Kentuckian by birth, he was brought by his parents to this State when only nine months old, and received his first impressions of the world amid the hardy hunters, the tall forests and romantic scenery of the dark and bloody ground.

His father, Colonel Richard Taylor, was a Virginian, and a distinguished soldier in the continental army during the war of the revolution. He received a commission in the first regiment of troops raised by the " Old Dominion," on the breaking out of the war. He continued in the service until the army was disbanded, and retired with the rank of lieutenant colonel. He was distinguished for his intrepid courage and imperturbable coolness in battle; and possessed the faculty, so invaluable in a military leader, of inspiring his followers with the same dauntless spirit that animated his own terrible and resistless charge. After his removal to Kentucky, he was engaged in frequent contests with the Indians, until his name became a word of terror in every wig-wam from the Ohio to the lakes.

In 1785, he removed with his family to Kentucky, and settled near the Falls of the Ohio. His son Zachary was at that time 9 months old. He was brought up and educated in the neighborhood, and grew up to manhood with the yell of the savage and the crack of the rifle almost constantly ringing in his ears. General Zachary Taylor may be literally said to have been cradled in war, nor have the deeds of his subsequent life done discredit to his early training. He is a true son of the " land of blood," and has proved, in many stricken fields of death, how pure are the ancestral currents that flow through his veins.

He manifested, at an early age, a decided predilection for the profession of arms, and in 1808 was appointed a first lieutenant in the 7th regiment of U. S. infantry. Not long after, he joined the army at New Orleans, then under the command of General Wilkinson. In 1810 he was united in marriage to Miss Margaret Smith, of Maryland, a lady in all respects worthy of his affections. In the following November, he was promoted to the rank of captain. In 1811, he was placed in command of Fort Knox on the Wabash, in the vicinity of Vincennes. From this station he was ordered to the east, a short time before the battle of Tippecanoe. In 1812 he received orders to take command of Fort Harrison, a post situated on the Wabash, seventy-five miles above Vincennes, and fifty miles beyond the frontier settlements. This was a most important trust for one of his age. But subsequent events proved the sagacity of the appointment.

While in command of Fort Harrison, Captain Taylor became the hero of one of the most desperate conflicts fought during the war. This frontier post was nothing more than a slight stockade, which had been thrown up by General Harrison in 1811, while on his march to Tippecanoe. The defences were of the most simple and primitive kind. The whole was built of unseasoned timber; and was formed on three sides by single rows of pickets; the fourth side consisting of a range of log huts, appropriated as barracks for the soldiers, and terminated at either extreme by a block house. When Captain Taylor assumed the command of this rude fortification, it was exceedingly ill provided either for comfort or defence, and was garrisoned by a single broken company of infantry.

The situation of the fort was unhealthy, and the officers and men suffered greatly from disease. On the 1st of September the number of men fit for duty did not exceed *fifteen;* and several of these were greatly disabled from recent indisposition. Captain Taylor was the only officer in the fort, and he was slowly recovering from a severe attack of the fever.

The Indians, in their frequent visits to the fort, had learned its weakness; and from reliable information received from his spies, Captain Taylor was induced to expect an attack. The crisis was most momentous. The Indian force on the Wabash was strong and increasing; and demonstrations were visible of a hostile disposition in the whole north-western tribes. The frontier posts of Detroit, Michillimacinac and Chicago had already yielded to the prowess of the combined arms of the British and Indians, and the destruction of Fort Harrison would have removed the only obstacle to havoc and desolation along the whole border of Indiana.

On the 3d of September, 1812, two men were murdered by the Indians within a few hundred yards of the fort. Late on the evening of the 4th, between thirty and forty Indians arrived from the Prophet's town, bearing a white flag. They were principally chiefs, and belonged to the various tribes that composed the Prophet's party. Captain Taylor was informed that the principal chief would make him a speech the next morning, and that the object of their visit was to get something to eat. The plot was well conceived, and boldly executed; but it was instantly detected by the eagle eye of the young commander, and he redoubled his exertions to put the fort in a proper state defence. The arms were examined and found to be in good order, and each man was furnished with sixteen rounds of cartridges. The guard was strengthened, and a non-commissioned officer ordered to walk around the inside of the garden during the night. These precautions were not uncalled for; the extreme darkness of the night rendering it difficult to discover the approach of the foe.

The premeditated attack, so craftily arranged, was made as expected. About eleven o'clock, Captain Taylor was awakened by the firing of one of the sentinels. He immediately ordered the men to their posts, and the firing became general on both sides. In the midst of the uproar, it was discovered that the Indians had set fire to the lower block house. Without a moment's hesitation, Captain Taylor directed buckets to be brought, and the fire to be extinguished. But it was much easier to give the order, than to have it executed. The men appeared to be paralyzed and stupified. The alarm of fire had thrown the garrison into the greatest confusion, in the midst of which all orders were unheard or disregarded. Unfortunately, there was a quantity of whiskey among the contractor's stores deposited in the block house, which having caught fire, caused the flames to spread with great rapidity, and rage with irresistible fury. During this time the Indians were not idle, but kept up an incessant and rapid discharge of rifles against the picketing, accompanied by a concert of the most infernal yells that ever issued from the throat of man, beast or devil. The fire soon ascended to the roof of the block house, and threatened to wrap the whole fort in a sheet of flame. The men gave themselves up for lost, and ceased to pay any attention to the orders. Disorder was at its height, and the scene became terrific. The fire raged and surged, and roared—the Indians howled and yelled—dogs barked—the wounded groaned; and high above all, arose the shriek of woman in her terror, sending its keen and thrilling accents through the mingled sounds of battle—the surrounding forest, bathed in bloody light, returned a fiery glare, yet more appalling from the intense darkness of the night; and all combined made up a time of awful terror, before which the stoutest heart quailed and quaked. In the midst of this pandemonium stood the youthful hero, like a living rock, firm and collected, rapid and decisive, at a single glance intuitively determining the order of the defence, animating his comrades to confidence and constancy, and by the irresistible force of example, imparted a spirit of determined and courageous perseverance even to the weaker sex. The roof of the block house was thrown off; the other buildings were kept wet, and by the greatest exertions the flames kept under. The opening made in the line of the defences by the burning of the block house, was supplied by a temporary breastwork; and after keeping up a constant fire until about six o'clock in the morning, the Indians retired. The loss of the garrison, in this affair, was only one man killed, and two wounded. That of the Indians was very considerable.

24

The brilliant and successful defence of Fort Harrison, made such an impression on the spirits of the tribes, that it arrested the march of the Indian forces, and preserved the lives of hundreds of women and children. The demonstrations of joy in Kentucky, upon the receipt of the intelligence, were universal. Captain Taylor, for this affair, was promoted to the rank of Major by brevet. It was the first brevet conferred during the war; and never was similar reward more justly merited.

Major Taylor continued actively engaged in various departments of service in the west, constantly extending the sphere of his reputation and influence, until 1814, when he was placed temporarily at the head of the troops in Missouri, until the arrival of General Howard, the commanding officer; and was busily employed on that frontier till the month of August. The territory of Missouri, at that time, had been almost entirely abandoned by the government, and was consequently peculiarly exposed to Indian depredations. This rendered the service in which Captain Taylor was engaged, one of peculiar hardship and hazard. The British having taken Fort Shelby, at Prairie du Chien, had concentrated on the Upper Mississippi a combined force of regulars and Indians, preparatory to a descent on the American settlements. To encounter this force and protect the extensive frontier of Indiana, Illinois, and Missouri, and keep in order the western and north-western tribes, General Howard had only ten companies of rangers, badly organised, and one hundred and twenty efficient regular troops.

The crisis was important and the urgency pressing. No time was to be lost; and on the 22d of August, Major Taylor was sent with a detachment of three hundred and twenty men and a few pieces of artillery to the Indian villages at the mouth of Rock river, with instructions to destroy the villages, cut up the corn, disperse the inhabitants, and erect a fort in a situation to command the Mississippi. If he should find it impracticable to reach his point of destination, he had orders to take up a position at the junction of the Des Moines and Mississippi rivers, and there establish a fortification.

When Major Taylor arrived at the mouth of Rock river, after a difficult voyage up the Mississippi against a strong and rapid current, and through a region swarming with hostile savages, he found a detachment of British troops, well supplied with artillery, and an immense body of Indians armed and equipped for war, ready to receive him. Unable to return the fire of the British artillery with effect, and finding it impossible to accomplish the main purpose of his expedition, the American commander, after skirmishing some time with the Indians, dropped his boats down to the rapids of the Des Moines, and there, in pursuance of his orders, proceeded to erect a fort on a scite to command the Mississippi and the mouth of the Des Moines. This was attended with peculiar hazard, and almost incredible privation and toil; but the resolution and skill of the commander surmounted every obstacle, and enabled him to complete the work. It received the name of Fort Johnson, and from its position in the heart of the Indian country, became a post of great importance to the safety and tranquillity of the frontier.

In October, Major Taylor was recalled to St. Louis by the sudden death of General Howard; and in November, accompanied Colonel Russell several hundred miles up the Missouri, to relieve a small settlement much exposed to Indian depredations. In December he was transferred to Vincennes, and assumed the command of the troops in Indiana, where he remained until the termination of the war. A short time before the conclusion of peace, he had been promoted to a majority in the 26th regiment of infantry, and ordered to join the regiment at Plattsburg: but when the army was disbanded, he was retained on the peace establishment with only the rank of captain. Declining to come into this arrangement, he resigned his commission, and retired to his farm near Louisville.

In 1816, he was reinstated in the army with his original rank, and placed in command of Fort Crawford, at the mouth of Fox river, which empties in Green Bay. He continued in the command of various posts in the west until the breaking out of the Black Hawk war in 1832, when he was again called into active service. In 1832 he was promoted to the rank of colonel, and served under General Atkinson in his various campaigns against the Indians. It is scarcely necessary to say that, in this service, he fully sustained his high military reputation. He commanded the regulars in the bloody and decisive battle of the Wisconsin, which resulted in the capture of Black Hawk and the Prophet, and terminated the war.

In 1836, Colonel Taylor was ordered to Florida, at that time the scene of a bloody war between the United States and the Seminole and other tribes of southern Indians. This war, perhaps, was the most extraordinary in which the United States was ever engaged. It had been protracted from year to year at an immense expense of blood and treasure, unsignalized by any decided advantage; and when Colonel Taylor was transferred to that theatre, there appeared no better prospect of its termination than at its first commencement. Our best and bravest officers had sunk under the hardships of a service in which no glory was to be won, and which presented no inducement to skill and courage, but patriotism. In this vexatious and exhausting service, Colonel Taylor soon became distinguished for zeal, energy, activity and indomitable hardihood. The uniform policy of the Indians had been to avoid battle; directing their operations against small detachments and isolated individuals, thus destroying our force in detail, without incurring the hazard of a defeat. This plan of carrying on the war, Colonel Taylor resolved to terminate, and bring the Indians to a battle at all hazards.

On the 19th of December, 1836, he learned that the savages under the noted chiefs Alligator and Sam Jones, had selected a situation deemed impregnable, where they had determined to await an attack. Upon the receipt of this intelligence, he struck into the wilderness, with about a thousand men, and twelve days' rations, with the intention of assailing the enemy in their strong hold. On the 25th of December, he arrived at the place where the Indians were posted, on the lake Okeechobee. The Indian line was formed in a dense hammock, the only approach to which was by a swamp three-quarters of a mile wide, covered with a growth of grass five feet high, and knee deep in mud and water. Undismayed by the obstacles which opposed his advance, Colonel Taylor resolved to make the attack without delay. The boldness and hardihood of the man, were never more signally displayed than on this occasion. The advantages were all against him; and any man of less nerve would have hesitated long before ordering an attack on such a position under such circumstances. But it is one of the peculiar characteristics of this officer never to yield to difficulties, however formidable. He had marched his troops for five days through an almost impassable wilderness, and encountered incredible privation and toil, to bring his enemy to battle; and now that he had found him, he was not the man to abandon the design of his expedition. A large portion of his troops were raw volunteers, untried in battle, and upon whom he could place only a precarious dependence. But he had with him a body of five hundred regulars, with whom he was well acquainted, and upon whom he knew he could rely.

At half past twelve o'clock the troops were formed in order of battle and advanced to the attack. To the volunteers, at their own request, the post of honor was assigned in front. Before the men could close with the enemy, they had to pass the swamp spoken of above, and struggle through the tangled morass, within point blank shot of seven hundred concealed and practiced Indian marksmen. Upon receiving the fire of the Indians, the volunteers broke their line and fled with precipitation. Opening their ranks to let the retreating soldiers pass through, the regulars immediately closed up, and pressed forward firmly in the face of the tempest of balls which hailed from the thicket in front, and cheered on by their officers, faltered not until they had passed the swamp, and drove the Indians from their coverts at the point of the bayonet. The savages fought with desperation, and contested every inch of ground with a cool, determined bravery, worthy of trained soldiers. Slowly and sullenly they retired, step by step, before the steady and overwhelming charge of the regulars, and when their line was broken and the battle lost, they still continued to pour upon the advancing troops, from every bush and thicket and covert, a shower of balls which loaded the earth with heaps of dead. The struggle lasted from half past twelve o'clock until three, P. M., and was terribly severe throughout the whole time. The slaughter among the officers was immense. Colonel Taylor himself was constantly exposed to the most imminent danger; but refusing to dismount from his horse, which rendered him a conspicuous mark for the enemy's rifles, he continued to ride through that tornado of balls, which hurtled in the air like hail stones, as calmly as if on parade. This battle was the most successful of the war. The victory was complete, and contributed more than any other event, to subdue the spirit of the tribes and dispose them for peace. The Indian force in this engagement was seven hundred strong, while the detachment commanded by Colonel Taylor numbered only about five hundred effective men. The loss was very severe; more than one-fourth of the whole number engaged being killed and wounded.

For this affair, Colonel Taylor was promoted to the rank of Brigadier General by brevet, and made his head quarters at Tampa Bay. The Indians were so much broken in spirit by their defeat, that they did not afford him another opportunity of meeting them in a general battle, and the residue of his time in Florida passed without his being engaged in any affair of striking interest.

In 1841, General Taylor was transferred to the command of the second department on the Arkansas, where he remained until the difficulties with Mexico presented a new and broader field for the display of those powers which had been developed by a long career of arduous and devoted service, and were now matured. The battles of Palo Alto, Resaca de la Palma, Monterey and Buena Vista, fought since the commencement of this war, while they have given new lustre to the American arms, have made General Taylor known to the civilized world as one of the first commanders of the age.

Government having determined to establish an army of observation on the southwestern frontier, General Taylor was selected for that command. He was directed to take a position between the Nueces and the Rio Grande; and in August, 1845, established his camp at Corpus Christi. Here he remained until the 11th of March, 1846, when he was instructed to march his force to the east bank of the Rio Grande. At the Rio Colorado, he was encountered by the Mexican authorities, and informed that an attempt to cross that river would be followed by actual hostilities. He crossed, nevertheless; and leaving his army on its march, advanced with a body of dragoons to Point Isabel, near the mouth of the Rio Grande, where he established a camp, and received supplies for his army. Having rejoined the main body of his army, General Taylor proceeded to take up a position on the eastern bank of the Rio Grande, opposite Matamoras, which he fortified. This post subsequently received the name of Fort Brown.

The communication between Fort Brown and Point Isabel, having been interrupted by the interposition of large forces of Mexicans between those points, General Taylor, on the 1st of May, leaving a small but determined force in possession of Fort Brown, marched the main body of his army to Point Isabel, determined to open the communication. On the 3d of May, he reached Point Isabel without interruption; and on the 7th of the same month started again for Fort Brown. He had with him a force of less than 2,300 men; two eighteen pounders, drawn by oxen; and Ringgold's and Duncan's batteries of light artillery.

At a place called Palo Alto, about twelve miles from Point Isabel, he encountered, on the 8th of May, a force of 6000 Mexican regulars, provided with ten pieces of artillery, and supported by a considerable body of rancheros.

The Mexicans were drawn up in a line of battle, extending a mile and a half across the plain, and outflanking the American army at either extreme. The lancers were posted in advance on the left, their arms glittering in the meridian sun, and presenting a most brilliant and martial appearance. The rest of the line was formed by the infantry and artillery.

The right of the American line of battle was composed of the third, fourth and fifth regiments of regular infantry, and Ringgold's artillery, under the command of Colonel Twiggs. The two eighteen pounders, under Lieutenant Churchill, occupied the centre; while the left of the line was formed by the eighth infantry and Duncan's artillery, under Colonel Belknap.

The action was commenced by the Mexican artillery, which opened its fire while the American army was yet at some distance. The engagement soon became general, and was fought almost entirely by the artillery. Ringgold's battery opened with terrible effect on the Mexican left, scattering that brave array of cavalry as if it had been smitten by the thunder of heaven. They soon recovered, however, and making a detour, attempted to fall on the American rear, but were met by the infantry, in squares, and repelled with immense slaughter. While Ringgold's battery, supported by the infantry, was sweeping every thing before it on the right, Duncan, on the left, was hurling his fierce volleys into the reeling columns of the foe, who melted away at every discharge, as the Alpine forest is swept before the terrible path of the avalanche; and in the centre, the two eighteen pounders kept up a steady and destructive fire. And now, while the ground quaked and trembled under the incessant roar of the artillery, and the air was all a flame from the unremitting flashes of the guns, the prairie took fire, and the flames, gathering force and fury as they flew, rolled their devouring billows over the field, and wrapped the two armies in an impervious canopy of smoke. This, for a time, stayed the contest. But Duncan and his men, dashing through the flames, which curled ten feet high, showed themselves like spirits from the infernal deep, on the Mexican flank, and opening a furious fire, scattered the terror stricken columns in every direction. This terminated the contest. The Mexicans retreated to the chapparal, and the Americans encamped on the field of battle. The Mexican loss in this affair was two hundred killed and four hundred wounded : that of the Americans was four killed and thirty-seven wounded. Of the killed, three were officers, among whom were Major Ringgold and Captain Page.

That night the enemy retired four miles, and having received a reinforcement of two thousand men, selected a strong position at Resaca de la Palma, with a ravine in front, guarded by a pond on one flank and a chapparal on the other : and having placed eight pieces of artillery in a situation to command the approaches, determined to await the advance of the Americans. Contrary to the advice of his officers, General Taylor, notwithstanding the immense superiority of the force opposed to him, determined to continue his march to Fort Brown, and early the next morning the army again advanced against the foe.

As soon as the presence of the enemy was ascertained, the artillery of Lieutenant Ridgely was moved to the front, and opened its fire upon that of the Mexicans. The infantry was pressed forward on the right, and after a desperate struggle, succeeded in penetrating through the chapparal, and gaining the flank ; while on the left, our troops gained a decided advantage. But, in the meantime, the enemy's centre kept up a deadly and destructive fire, which arrested the advance of the Americans, and rendered the fortunes of the day for some time doubtful. Though Ridgely's artillery continued to make terrible havoc in the ranks of the foe, the Mexicans still kept up a well directed fire, which swept our lines and did fearful execution. At this crisis, General Taylor ordered Captain May to charge the battery with his dragoons. Without a moment's hesitation, the gallant May and his fearless horsemen dashed forward through the tempest of fire and iron which the well worked artillery of the Mexicans hurled in one unbroken torrent over the plain, and though he lost many of his followers by the discharge with which his advance was met, he faltered not, but, with trumpets ringing merrily, and gleaming sabres, swept on like a tornado, before which the firm lines of the enemy wavered and broke, and fled. This advantage was followed up by a fierce onslaught from the infantry, at the point of the bayonet. The enemy's centre was broken, and the fortune of the day decided. The victory was complete as it was wonderful. General Taylor brought into action but seventeen hundred wearied men, against a force of at least six thousand, well disciplined, officered and conditioned. The enemy had every advantage of position, and maintained it valiantly and well, and nothing but hard fighting wrested the victory from them. Our loss in the battle was one hundred and ten killed and wounded. That of the enemy was probably ten fold, though never precisely ascertained. On the 18th of May, General Taylor took possession of Matamoras without resistance.

Though his instructions required his advance into the interior of the country, General Taylor was forced to delay his operations for some time, from having no supplies and no adequate means of transportation. At length, these obstacles being removed, the army was set in motion and advanced upon Monterey. This was a place strong by nature, amply fortified, and maintained by an army of 7,000 troops of the line and 3,000 irregulars. To reduce this strong-hold, General Taylor had a force, comprising 425 officers and 6,220 men. Against the forty-two pieces of cannon of the Mexicans, he arrayed but one ten inch mortar, two twenty-four pound howitzers, and four light field batteries of four guns each, the mortar being the only piece suitable to the operations of a siege. With these fearful odds against him, he invested the city.

Having established his camp three miles from the defences of the city, reconnoissances were made, and it was found possible to turn the enemy's position, and gain the heights in his rear. General Worth was detached upon this duty, which, having been performed, he was to carry the enemy's works on that side of the town. The operations soon became two-fold—the assailing party of Worth being independent of the command of Taylor, whose principal efforts were to divert the attention of the enemy, while Worth proceeded to the execution of his orders.

The order was issued on the 19th of September, and the next day, at two o'clock, Worth commenced his advance, and succeeded in reaching a position above the Bishop's palace. The next morning, the battle commenced in earnest. Pressing forward, Worth encountered the enemy in force, and drove them before him with slaughter. Gaining the Saltillo road, he cut off the communications, and carrying two heights west of the Saltillo road, from one of them he was enabled, with his guns, to command the Bishop's palace. In the meantime, a determined assault was made upon the town from below, by the force under General Taylor. It would be useless to attempt a description, in the narrow limits of this sketch, of the series of terrific and bloody contests which ensued. Our loss was very heavy, from the character of the enemy's defences, and the daring ardor of our troops. General Taylor's purpose of diverting attention from Worth, was, however, attained; one of their advanced works was carried at the point of the bayonet, and a strong footing secured in the town. This was on the third day after the commencement of active operations. On the fourth, Worth was victorious at every point. The Bishop's palace was taken, while the troops under Taylor pressed upon the city, the lower part of which was evacuated that night. On the fifth day of the siege, the troops under Taylor advanced from square to square, every inch of ground desperately disputed, until they reached within a square of the Plaza; while Worth pressed onward, on the opposite side of the city, carrying all before him. At length, matters being ripe for such a movement, preparations were made for a concerted storm of the enemy's position on the next day. The morning, however, brought an offer of capitulation, which resulted in the surrender of the city. Our loss in the affair was about five hundred killed and wounded; but the victory secured the possession of an immense territory and a vast amount of military spoils.

Making his head quarters at Monterey, General Taylor proceeded to occupy Saltillo and Paras, while the Mexicans fell back upon San Luis Potosi.— Santa Anna was recalled to Mexico, and placed at the head of the government and army. Before December he had 20,000 men under his command, well organized; and with this force, he determined to crush Taylor at a blow, and redeem the conquered provinces. While these preparations were going on, the government of the United States, for the purpose of an attack on Vera Cruz, withdrew from General Taylor the most effective portion of his forces, leaving him with an extended line of territory to defend, a formidable foe in front, and with only a small force, principally untried volunteers, to encounter the enemy. Rejecting the advice of the department, to retire to Monterey, and there defend himself, General Taylor determined to encounter Santa Anna at an advanced position, and selected Buena Vista for that purpose. This field was admirably chosen, and the hero, with his little band, there awaited the shock of his powerful adversary. Santa Anna brought into the field 20,000 men, to encounter which General Taylor had a force of 334 officers, and 4,425 men.

On the 22d of February, the Mexicans arrived in sight of the American position, and made immediate preparations for the attack. Vaunting his immense superiority, and the impossibility of a successful resistance, Santa Anna summoned General Taylor to surrender. This was politely but firmly declined. It was followed by an attack, late in the evening, upon the extreme right of the Americans, and an attempt to gain our flank. The skirmishing was continued until dark. During the night the enemy threw a body of light troops on the mountain side, with the intention of outflanking the American left; and at an early hour the next morning, the engagement commenced at this point. It continued, without intermission, through the day, until night separated the combatants. Well and nobly did the little band sustain itself against the overwhelming numbers opposed to them. Our limits, however, will not permit us to give the details of this battle, the most desperate ever fought on the American continent. On the part of the Mexicans, it was conducted with consummate skill, and maintained with courage and obstinacy. Overpowering masses of troops were poured upon our weakest points, and at several periods of the battle, their success seemed almost inevitable. But the American commander was found equal to every crisis. Calm, collected, and resolved, he rose superior to the danger of his situation, and wrested victory from defeat. It is admitted by all who were present, that no man but General Taylor could have won the victory of Buena Vista. The battle raged with variable fortunes for ten hours. At length night put an end to the conflict. The Americans slept upon the field of victory, and the foe, shattered and disheartened, retired, and the next day were in full retreat for San Luis Potosi. Our loss was 267 killed, and 456 wounded ; that of the enemy was 2,000.

The battle of Buena Vista closed the war in that quarter of Mexico ; and since that period, General Taylor has found no enemy able or willing to encounter him.

The prominent qualities of General Taylor's mind and character may be gathered from the preceding narrative of the events of his life. He owes nothing to the patronage of the great, or the partiality of the powerful, but independent and self-reliant, has fought his way up to the lofty eminence which he now occupies in the minds and hearts of his countrymen. His own counsels have directed, his own energies sustained him. His vigor of character, his power of will, and fertility of resources, have swept every obstacle from before him, and he will hereafter live in the most cherished affections of our people, and on the brightest pages of our country's history.

Jefferson county received its name from THOMAS JEFFERSON, of Virginia, the distinguished author of the Declaration of Independence, and the Virginia Bill of Rights. He entered public life at a very early age; was a distinguished patriot and statesman of the revolution ; and was foremost in the assertion of his country's liberties against the usurpations of Great Britain. He was elected Vice President of the United States under Mr. Adams—was secretary of state under Washington, and twice elected President of the United States. He was for many years abroad as Minister to France, and left a reputation in that country second only to Franklin. For forty years no man filled a larger space in the public eye, and his memory is still cherished with fond veneration by a large portion of the American people. •

JESSAMINE COUNTY.

JESSAMINE county, which was formed in 1798, is situated in the middle section of the State, and lies on the Kentucky river, which borders its territory on the south-east, south, and south-west. Bounded on the north by Fayette ; east by Madison ; south by Garrard ; and west by Mercer and Woodford. That portion of Jessamine which is comprised within the boundary appropriately termed the "garden of Kentucky," presents a slightly undulating surface, and a black, friable, and remarkably rich soil—producing luxuriant crops of hemp, corn, and grass. Hemp is the staple, but large numbers of horses, mules, cattle and hogs are annually exported. A part of the county is hilly, but is also productive. The whole is in a high state of cultivation, indicating a rapid advance in agricultural improvement.

Value of taxable property in Jessamine in 1846, $4,275,384 ; number of acres of land in the county, 102,324 ; average value of lands per acre, $22.52 ; number of white males over twenty-one years of age, 1,353 ; number of children between five and sixteen years old, 1,515. Population in 1840, 10,015.

NICHOLASVILLE, the county seat, is situated twenty miles south-west of Lexington, thirty seven miles from Frankfort, and five hundred and forty-six miles from Washington city : contains a fine court-house, and clerks' offices and prison ; four churches, (Methodist, Baptist, Reformed and Presbyterian,) one male and one female academy, two schools, four taverns, eight lawyers, six physicians, eight stores and groceries, four bagging factories, twenty mechanics' shops, and about 700 inhabitants. Established in 1812, and named in honor of Colonel GEORGE NICHOLAS. Situated in the heart of a fine country, and surrounded by a rich and intelligent population, Nicholasville is necessarily a place of considerable business. *North Liberty* is a small village, established in 1813.

The county of Jessamine derived its name from *Jessamine creek*, which rises in the northern part of the county, and flows through it southwardly to the Kentucky river. The creek has been generally supposed to have obtained its name from the profusion of flowers which grew upon its banks at an early day ; but such is not the fact. It was called in honor of a young lady named *Jessamine* Douglass, whose father settled at the head of the creek, and entered a quantity of land, including the land of Jessamine creek. In honor of his beautiful but unfortunate daughter, he gave the creek the name of *Jessamine.* This creek is of good size, and as large at its source as at its termination. It rises at two points about ten feet from each other. At one point, it gushes from between two large smooth rocks, and is very deep ; at the other point it boils up from a bed of gravel.

JOHNSON COUNTY.

JOHNSON county was formed in 1842, and named in honor of Colonel RICHARD M. JOHNSON. It is situated in the extreme eastern portion of the state, on the waters of Sandy river : Bounded on the north by Lawrence ; east by Pike, and Sandy river ; south by Floyd ; and west by Morgan county. The surface of the county is hilly, interspersed with fertile vallies—the soil sandy, based upon sand-stone. Exports—horses, cattle, hogs, lumber of various kinds, and coal. Several mineral springs are found in the county. The south fork of Big Sandy is navigable for flat boats and small steam boats several months in the year.

Number of acres of land in Johnson county, 89,669 ; average value per acre, $1.84 ; taxable property in 1846, valued $266,074 ; white males over twenty-one years of age, 506 ; children between five and seventeen years old, 920. Organized since the census of 1840.

PAINTVILLE, the county seat, is situated on Paint creek, about 140 miles from Frankfort—contains a handsome brick court-house, five stores, two taverns, two lawyers, two doctors, twelve mechanics' shops, and manufacturing establishments. Population, 125.

A copper cross, about one inch and a half long, with an image extended on it, and also a crescent about an inch in diameter, made of copper, and having either pearl or imitation of pearl on it, was found at the mouth of Paint creek, in this county, about seven years ago, by a gentleman when plowing his corn. On the cross were the letters " *Santa Maria.*"

Colonel RICHARD M. JOHNSON, the third son of Colonel Robert Johnson, of Scott county,* was born in Kentucky in the autumn of 1781. The literary institutions of Kentucky were then in their infancy, and the facilities for thorough education, exceedingly limited. Richard remained with his father until the age of fifteen, receiving only such instruction as the nature of circumstances would allow. At this age he left his father's house, intent upon advantages superior to those afforded in that vicinity, and entered a country school, where he acquired a knowledge of grammar, and the rudiments of the Latin language. Afterwards he entered Transylvania University, where, by unremitted industry, he made rapid progress in the acquisition of classic and scientific knowledge.

Upon quitting the university, he entered upon the study of the law, under the guidance and instruction of that celebrated jurist and statesman, Colonel George Nicholas. On the decease of this gentleman, which took place a few weeks after his young student had entered his office, the subject of this biography placed himself under the instruction of the Hon. James Brown, late a senator in Congress from Louisiana, and subsequently a minister from the United States to the court of France, but then a distinguished member of the Kentucky bar. With this eminent citizen he finished his preparatory studies, and at the early age of nineteen entered upon the arduous duties of his profession.

In his vocation as a lawyer, he was eminently successful, and displayed the same active energy of mind and benevolence of heart, which have since so eminently distinguished him in higher and more responsible stations. He despised injustice and oppression, and never omitted an occasion to render his services, without prospect of reward, where honest poverty or injured innocence was found struggling against the oppressions of wealth. The inability of a client to pay a fee, never deterred him from attending sedulously to his cause, no matter how intricate and laborious were the services. By these means, even at so early an age, he secured to himself the just reward of his virtues, and the approbation and esteem of the public.

Scarcely had he been fairly installed in the duties of his profession, before an opportunity was afforded for the development of that high and chivalrous patriotism which has since identified him with some of the noblest feats of American valor, and given his name to immortality. In 1802, the port of New Orleans, in violation of an existing treaty, was closed against the United States by the Spanish intendant. The occurrence gave rise to immense excitement throughout America, especially in the valley of the Ohio and Mississippi, and a rupture between Spain and the United States, likely to end in war, was the consequence. Richard M. Johnson, then only in his twentieth year, with many other young men of his neighborhood, promptly volunteered his services to pass down the western waters and make a descent on New Orleans, in the event of war. In a few days, chiefly through his exertions, a large company was enrolled, and he was chosen to the command. The speedy adjustment of the dispute with Spain, deprived him and the brave youths under his command, of the opportunity of signalizing themselves and the State upon the field of battle.

Before he had attained the age of twenty-one, at which period the constitution of Kentucky fixes the eligibility of the citizen to a seat in the legislature, the citizens of Scott county elected him, by acclamation, to a seat in that body. As a member of the legislature, he acquitted himself with great credit, and to the entire satisfaction of his constituents. Having served two years in that station, at the age of twenty-four he was elected a representative in the Congress of the United States ; and in October, 1807, being then just twenty-five, took his seat in that body.

He entered upon the theatre of national politics, at a period when party excitement ran high, and attached himself to the republican party, more from a uniform and fixed devotion to the principles of democracy, than from any purely selfish policy. He was immediately placed upon some of the most important committees, and at the second session of the term for which he was elected, was ap-

---

* See a sketch of Colonel Robert Johnson, under the head of Scott county.

pointed chairman of the committee of claims, at that time among the most important of the house committees. His zealous and faithful devotion to business, and the distinction which he had acquired in Congress and throughout the Union, as a genuine friend of the liberty and happiness of his country, increased his popularity at home, and insured his re-election by his constituents, who from that period to the present time, have never failed to manifest their devoted attachment to him, whenever he was a candidate for office, either under the State or national government.

In 1811, our relations with Great Britain were such as, in the opinion of many, to render an appeal to arms inevitable. Richard M. Johnson was among those who were convinced that no other alternative remained to the people of the United States; and accordingly, after supporting, with great energy, all the preparatory measures which the crisis demanded, in June, 1812, gave his vote for the declaration of war. This important measure was shortly afterwards followed by an adjournment of Congress, when he hastened home, raised the standard of his country, and called around him many of the best citizens of his neighborhood, some of whom, schooled in the stormy period of the early settlement of the State, were veteran warriors, well suited for the service for which they were intended. With this battalion, composed of three companies, he hastened to the frontier, and when arrived at St. Mary's on the 13th of September, his force, by general order, was augmented by a battalion of mounted volunteers, and he elected to the command of the regiment thus formed. A portion of the regiment only, during that season, had any opportunity of an engagement; and this was a party of the mounted battalion, under Major Suggett, which, in communicating with Fort Wayne, besieged by a superior force, encountered an equal number of the enemy, whom it routed, killing an Indian chief of some distinction. After an active campaign of about ten months, Colonel Johnson returned home for the purpose of proceeding to Washington to re-enter Congress, having added to his reputation as a statesman, that of an energetic and patriotic soldier.

In the winter following while in attendance upon Congress, he rendered material aid to the president, in arranging the plan of campaign for the ensuing summer, and his views being adopted, were subsequently carried out, and contributed essentially to the successes which followed upon the frontier. Colonel Johnson was authorized by the secretary of war to raise, organize and hold in readiness, a regiment of mounted volunteers, to consist of one thousand men. Accordingly upon the adjournment of Congress in March, he hastened home, and in a few weeks secured from among the most respectable and patriotic citizens of the state, the full complement of volunteers, to the organization and discipline of whom he gave his most sedulous attention. In this important part of his military duty, he had the valuable aid of his skillful and intrepid brother, Lt. Col. James Johnson, whose military talents, decision and courage in the hour of battle, have entitled him to a full share of the glory acquired by the regiment. Colonel Johnson, with his accustomed energy, lost no time in repairing with his command to the frontier of Ohio, then the theatre of operations. His regiment soon acquired a name that attracted the admiration of the country. Never did soldiers perform their arduous duties with more alacrity and cheerfulness, nor were the services of any more useful and extensive. In making inroads upon the enemy, and in various skirmishes, their success was always complete.

In October, 1813, the decisive crisis in the operations of the north-western army arrived—the battle of the Thames, which led to a termination of hostilities in that quarter, was fought and won. The distinguished services of Colonel Johnson, and his brave regiment, in that sanguinary engagement, have scarcely a parallel in the heroic annals of our country. The British and Indians, the former under the command of General Proctor, and the latter under that of Tecumseh, the celebrated Indian warrior, had taken an advantageous position, the British in line between the river Thames and a narrow swamp, and the Indians in ambush on their right, and west of the swamp, ready to fall upon the rear of Colonel Johnson, should he force a retreat of the British. Colonel Johnson, under the orders of the commander in chief, divided his regiment into two battalions, one under the command of his gallant brother James, and the other to be led by himself. Col. Johnson with his battalion passed the swamp and attacked the Indians, at the same moment that his brother James fell upon and routed the British regulars.

The contest for a while between Colonel Johnson's battalion and the Indians, was obstinate and bloody, the slaughter great, but success complete. The gallant Colonel was in the very midst and thickest of the fight, inspiring by his presence and courage the utmost confidence of his brave followers, and though perforated with balls, his bridle arm shattered, and bleeding profusely, he continued to fight until he encountered and slew an Indian chief who formed the rallying point of the savages. This chief was supposed to be the famous Tecumseh himself, upon whose fall the Indians raised a yell and retreated. The heroic Colonel, covered with wounds, twenty-five balls having been shot into him, his clothes, and his horse, was borne from the battle ground, faint from exertion and loss of blood, and almost lifeless. Never was victory so complete or its achievement so glorious. Fifteen hundred Indians were engaged against the battallion of Col. Johnson, and eight hundred British regulars against that of his brother. Both forces were completely routed, and an effectual end put to the war upon the northern frontier, distinguished as it had been by so many murderous cruelties upon the part of the savage allies of the British.

The war in that quarter being now ended, in a short time the army took up its march homeward; but Colonel Johnson being unable to continue with his regiment, was carried to Detroit, from whence after a short confinement he departed for home. After a distressing journey, during which he endured the most painful suffering, he reached his home in Kentucky early in November. In February 1814, still unable to walk, he reached Washington city, and resumed his seat in Congress. Every where upon the route, and at the metropolis, he was met with the most enthusiastic and cordial greetings of a grateful people. Even his political opponents, deeply sensible of his sincerity, his patriotism and his valor, cordially united in doing honor to the man who had at so much sacrifice, rendered such glorious service to the country. Congress by joint resolution, made appropriate acknowledgment of his gallant deeds, and directed him to be presented with a suitable testimonial of his services.

He continued to serve his constituents in Congress until the year 1819, when he voluntarily retired, carrying with him the esteem of the whole nation. But his native state, of which he was justly the idol, would not suffer him to remain in retirement. The people of Scott county immediately returned him to the state legislature, and that body elected him to the United States' senate. An honor so exalted, from a source so honored, he could not resist; and accordingly in December 1819 he took his seat in the United States' senate, and after serving his term was unanimously re-elected, a circumstance which serves to show how well he preserved the confidence of the people of his native state, and how deeply he was enshrined in their affections.

His career as a legislator, was scarcely less brilliant and useful, than that in which he distinguished himself as a warrior. His speeches and reports, are monuments of his wisdom and liberality as a statesman. The whole nation will bear evidence to his zeal and industry in support of all measures calculated to promote the end of free government—the happiness of the people. No man labored more indefatigably, in behalf of private claimants, than did Colonel Johnson; and so scrupulously faithful was he in the discharge of his duty towards all who applied for his services, that he never failed while in congress to attend to a single application that was made to him. The old soldiers of the revolution, the invalids of the last war, and thousands of other persons, all over the Union, who had claims to urge upon the government, had no truer or surer friend in Congress than Col. Johnson, as many of them now enjoying the bounty of the government through his instrumentality, can bear most grateful testimony.

In 1836 he was made Vice President of the United States, and presided over the senate with great dignity for the term of four years, at the expiration of which, he retired to his farm in Scott county, Kentucky, where he has with the exception of a single term in the legislature, remained in private life ever since, devoting himself with praiseworthy assiduity to the reparation of his private fortune, somewhat impaired by a too liberal hospitality and constant attention for so long a period to public affairs.

KENTON COUNTY.

KENTON county was formed in 1840, by a division of Campbell county, and named in honor of the distinguished pioneer, General SIMON KENTON. It is situated in the northern part of the State, and lies on the Ohio and Licking rivers : Bounded on the north by the Ohio river; east by Licking river and Campbell county ; south by Pendleton ; and west by Boone. Covington is the principal town, and Independence the seat of justice, the former about eighty and the latter seventy-four miles from Frankfort. The bottom lands of Kenton county are rich and very productive. The up-lands are undulating or hilly, but grow fine wheat, corn and tobacco, which are the principal products of the county. The county is dotted with fine gardens, which the markets of Cincinnati and Covington render very profitable to the owners. The lands along the Lexington road, and between it and Dry creek, are of a very superior quality—and many of the farmers have engaged in the dairy business, more or less extensively.

Number of acres of land in Kenton county, 92,402 ; average value of lands per acre in 1846, $14.95 ; number of white males over twenty-one years of age, 2,429 ; number of children between five and sixteen years old, 2,050. Total valuation of taxable property in 1846, $2,882,155.

The city of COVINGTON is situated on the Ohio river, opposite the city of Cincinnati, and immediately below the mouth of Licking river, separated from Newport by that river. It is built upon a beautiful plain, several miles in extent, and the streets have been so planned as to present the appearance of a continuation of those of Cincinnati. The public buildings are,—a large city hall, two Methodist, one Presbyterian, one Baptist, one Reformed or Christian, one Episcopal, and two Catholic churches —two female academies, one common and two classical schools, and the Western Baptist Theological college. There are two printing offices in the city, which publish weekly papers—the " Licking Valley Register" and the "Covington Intelligencer." Covington also contains sixteen lawyers, ten physicians, twenty dry goods stores, fifty produce and grocery stores, thirty-five tobacco manufactories, one rolling mill, employing one hundred hands and manufacturing two thousand tons of iron annually, one large cotton manufactory, one silk factory, one hemp factory with eighteen looms and one hundred and twenty hands, one steam flouring mill, one printing ink manufactory, three coverlet manufactories, one saw mill, three rope walks, and a large number of other manufacturing establishments and mechanics' shops. The population of Covington, amounting now to upwards of six thousand, is increasing with great rapidity.

The Western Baptist Theological College is a richly endowed institution, and is now in a flourishing condition. The Rev. Dr. PATTISON is the president.

ORR'S FEMALE ACADEMY, COVINGTON, KY.

BAPTIST THEOLOGICAL, SEMINARY, COVINGTON, KY

The Female Seminary of the Rev. Mr. ORR, has steadily grown in public favor, and is now one of the best literary institutions of the kind in the State. It is located near the Licking river, in a retired and pleasant situation—the building spacious and well arranged, and the grounds very tastefully ornamented.

Covington is destined to be the second city of Kentucky in population and wealth. Although separated from Cincinnati by the Ohio river, the facilities of communication by steam ferry boats are such as to induce many business men in that place to make Covington their residence. This disposition will increase as Cincinnati grows, and the difficulty of obtaining private residences near the centre of trade becomes greater.

Independence, the county seat, is situated ten miles from Covington—contains the county buildings, one church, a post-office, and several dwellings, stores and shops.

There is a well on the farm of Ellison Williams, which was formerly called the *Hygean* well, and was once kept as a watering place, but not much resorted to. Mr. Williams was a pioneer of Kentucky and a companion of Boone. He is a sprightly old man, and relates many interesting anecdotes of pioneer life. When the remains of Boone were brought to Kentucky, and re-interred in the public cemetery at Frankfort, this venerable pioneer was one of the pall-bearers.

The *Lettonian Springs*, a weak sulphur, is situated four miles from Covington, on the Bank Lick road. The springs are well kept, and being a pleasant ride from Covington, they have become a place of considerable resort in the watering season.

Dry Creek, in this county, is remarkable for the fact, that, after a heavy rain, it is so flush and high, that it cannot be forded, but in a few hours it runs *dry*, or so nearly so, that hogs will be seen where it was deepest, turning up the rocks in search of craw-fish.

Captain CRUISE encamped with his company (belonging to Wayne's army) on the creek bearing his name, in 1784. He strayed from camp, and was found dead, the next day, in the creek, bearing marks of savage violence. He was buried by his company on this creek, which rises in Boone, and running across Kenton, empties into Licking, about twenty miles above its mouth. The old residents disagree about the spot " where they buried Cruise." The testimony, as to his grave, is so contradictory, that gentlemen land-jobbers have several times gone there in order to find it, but without success. Their patents called for Cruise's grave as a beginning. The old settlers, it is thought, may have had some *design* in making it uncertain "where they buried Cruise."

Kenton county takes its name from one of the most celebrated pioneers of the west. General SIMON KENTON was born of obscure parents, in Fauquier county, Virginia, May 15th, 1755. His father was an Irishman; his mother of Scotch descent. The poverty of his parents caused his education to be neglected, most unfortunately for his future prosperity. His life, until he was sixteen years of age, appears to have run smoothly enough, distinguished by no uncommon events from that of the neighboring boys. About that age, however, a calamity befell him, which, apart from its irreparable nature, in the opinion of all young gentlemen of sixteen, gave a direction to his whole future life. He lost his sweetheart; not by *death*, or anything of that kind—for that could have been endured—but by means of a more favored rival. The successful lover's name was William Veach. Kenton, in utter despair and recklessness, having gone uninvited to the wedding, and thrust himself between the happy pair (whom he found seated cosily on a bed), was pounced upon by Veach and his brothers, who gave him, in the language of such affairs, "what he wanted." They, however, had mistaken his *wants*, for, meeting with William Veach a short time afterwards, in a retired place, he informed him that he was not satisfied. A severe fight ensued, which, after varied success, terminated in the complete discomfiture of Veach. In the course of the contest, Kenton succeeded in entangling his antagonist's long hair in a bush, which put him entirely in his power. The desperate young man beat his rival with a severity altogether foreign to his subsequent amiable character. His violence appeared to be fatal; the unhappy man, bleeding at mouth and nose, attempted to rise, and fell back insensible. Kenton was alarmed; he raised him up, spoke kindly to him, and receiving no answer, believed him dead! He dropped his lifeless body and fled to the woods. Now, indeed, he thought himself ruined beyond redemption. He had lost the girl he loved, and had killed his former friend and companion, and therefore the society of civilized man must be not only repulsive, but dangerous. The Alleghanies, and the wilderness of the unexplored west offered him a secure asylum, and he plunged at once into the woods. Traveling by night, and lying concealed by day, after many sufferings he arrived at Ise's ford, on Cheat river, some time in April 1771. Here he changed his name to "Simon Butler." Thus, at the age of sixteen, this man, who, in the hands of the Almighty, was so instrumental in redeeming the great west from the savage, and opening the way for the stream of civilization which has since poured over its fertile plains, desolate in heart, and burdened with crime, was thrown upon his own resources, to struggle with the dangers and privations of the wilderness.

After some months' stay on Cheat river, Kenton, having earned a good rifle by his labor, joined a party, with whom he proceeded to Fort Pitt. Here, while hunting in the employ of the small garrison at that place, he made the acquaintance and formed a friendship with Simon Girty, afterwards so infamous as a renegado. In the fall of 1771, he fell in with George Yeager and John Strader. Yeager it was who first mentioned to Kenton the "cane land," called by the Indians, Kain-tuck-ee, and fired his imagination with his descriptions of its soil and scenery, and the numbers and extent of the game.

In company with Yeager and Strader, Kenton proceeded down the Ohio river as far as the mouth of the Kentucky river, looking for the cane, which, according to Yeager, covered the country. It is a remarkable fact, that cane nowhere grew on the banks of the Ohio, above the mouth of the Kentucky river, although the interior was covered with it. The party, not finding land answering the description of Yeager, returned up the Ohio to the mouth of Big Kenawha; examining the creeks and rivers on the southern shore without success. Abandoning the search, in the winters of 1771–2, they built a camp on a branch of the great Kenawha, and hunted and trapped with considerable success. Here they lived a free and unrestrained life, and a very happy one, engaged in the pursuits of the hunter, until the spring of 1773. The troubles with the mother country beginning to thicken about this time, the Indians were excited against the colonists. One evening in March, while the three hunters were quietly reposing in their rude camp, they were fired upon by the Indians. Yeager was killed, and Kenton and Strader fled to the woods. Night setting in, they effected their escape, though barefooted and naked, having on nothing but their shirts, and without food; they suffered dreadfully, during the six days they wandered, famished, and torn by the briars through the wilderness. On the sixth day they often laid down to die, so completely were they exhausted. Their feet had become so sore that they were unable to perform but six miles during the day. At last they reached the Ohio, where they found a party of hunters, who fed and clothed them. With this party Kenton returned up to the mouth of Little Kenawha. Here he employed himself with Dr. Briscoe, until he had bought a rifle, and other necessaries. In the summer, he joined a party going down the Ohio in search of Captain Bullitt. The party, not finding Bullitt, and alarmed by the Indians, abandoned their canoes at the Three Islands, and under the guidance of Kenton proceeded by land through Kentucky to Virginia.

Kenton spent the winters of 1773–4, on the Big Sandy, with a hunting-party, and in the spring, when the war broke out with the Indians, he retreated into Fort Pitt, with the other settlers. When Lord Dunmore raised an army to punish the Indians, Kenton volunteered, and was actively employed as a spy, both under the expedition of Dunmore and that of Colonel Lewis. In the fall, he was discharged from the army, and returned, with Thomas Williams, to his old hunting-ground, on Big Sandy river, where they passed the winter. In the spring of 1775, having disposed of their peltries to a French trader, whom they met on the Ohio, for such necessaries as their mode of life required, they descended the Ohio in search, once more, of the "cane land." Although Yeager was now dead, the impressions left upon the mind of Kenton, by his glowing descriptions of Kain-tuck-ee, which Yeager had visited with the Indians, when a boy and a prisoner, were still fresh and strong; and he determined to make another effort to find the country. For this purpose, he and Williams were now descending the Ohio. Accident at last favored them. While gliding along down "la belle riviere" (as the French had christened it), night overtook the young adventurers, and they were compelled to land. They put in with their canoe, at the mouth of Cabin creek, situated in the present county of Mason, and about six miles above Maysville. Next morning, while hunting some miles back in the country, the ardently-sought "cane" burst upon Kenton's view, covering land richer than any he had ever seen before. Overjoyed at this piece of good fortune, he returned, in haste, to communicate the joyful intelligence to Williams. Sinking their canoe, the pioneers, par excellence, of north Kentucky, struck into their new domain. In the month of May, 1775, within a mile of the present town of Washington, in Mason county, having built their camp, and finished a small clearing, they planted about an acre of land, with the remains of the corn bought from the French trader. The spot chosen by them, for their agricultural attempt, was one of the most beautiful and fertile in the State of Kentucky. Here, in due season, they ate the first roasting ears, that ever grew by the care of a white man, on the north side of the Kentucky river.

Before this they had discovered the upper and lower Blue Licks, and the immense herds of buffalo, elk, &c., that frequented those places, covering the hills and valleys of the Licking. The land was a hunters' paradise, and our adventurers were completely happy in their new and undisputed home. They soon had cause, however, to apprehend that others would contend with them for the mastership of the soil. Happening one day at the lower Blue Licks, they discovered two white men. Approaching them with due caution, they found them friendly, and learned that they had wandered without guns and food thus far into the country, their canoe having been upset in a squall on the Ohio. Fitzpatrick and Hendricks (so these strangers were named) were invited by Kenton to join his station near Washington. Hendricks acceded to the proposal, but Fitzpatrick insisted upon returning to Virginia. Accordingly Kenton and Williams (having left Hendricks at the Licks) accompanied Fitzpatrick to the Ohio, gave him a gun, and took leave of him on the other side from where Maysville now stands. Returning quickly as possible, they were surprised and not a little alarmed to find the camp where they had left Hendricks abandoned and in disorder. Looking around they observed a smoke in a low ravine, and at once comprehended the whole affair. They were satisfied that a party of Indians had captured their friend, and they at once fled to the woods. Next morning cautiously approaching the still smoking fire, they discovered that the savages had departed, and with feelings that may be easily imagined, they found, what they did not doubt were the skull and bones of the unfortunate Hendricks. He had been burned to death, while they were so cowardly flying. Filled with shame and remorse that they had so basely abandoned him to his fate without an effort to rescue him, they went back to their camp near Washington. They had the good fortune themselves to escape the notice of the Indians who prowled through the country. In the fall, Kenton, leaving Williams at the camp, took a ramble through his rich domain. Every where he saw abundance of game, and the richest and most beautiful land. At the lower Blue Licks he met with Michael Stoner, who had come to Kentucky with Boone the year before. He now learned that himself and Williams were not the only whites inhabiting the cane land. Taking Stoner to his camp, and gathering up his property, he and Williams accompanied him to the settlements already formed in the interior. Kenton passed the winter of '75–6 at Hinckston's station, in the present county of Bourbon, about forty miles from his corn patch. In 1776, the Indians enraged at the encroachments made upon their hunting grounds, and urged on by the British, made frequent incursions into Kentucky, and became so troublesome that the weaker stations were abandoned. The settlers at Hinckston's station took shelter in McClelland's fort, situated where Georgetown now stands, Kenton accompanying them. Major George Rogers Clark having prevailed upon the Virginia legislature to afford the pioneers some assistance, arrived in company with a lawyer named Jones, at the Three Islands, late in the winter, with a considerable quantity of powder and lead. They concealed it on the lower island and proceeded to McClelland's station, in order to obtain a party to bring it off to the settlements. McClelland's station being too weak to furnish a sufficient escort, Clark, piloted by Kenton, set out for Harrodsburg. Unfortunately, during their absence, Jones prevailed on ten men to accompany him to the place where the ammunition was concealed. They set out, and on Christmas day, 1776, they were encountered by the Indian chief Pluggey and defeated. Jones and William Grayson were killed, and two of the party taken prisoners. The remainder escaped into the station, where Clark and Kenton soon arrived with some men from Harrodsburgh, who immediately returned on the news of this disaster. On the morning of January 1st, 1777, Pluggey and his warriors appeared before the fort. McClelland and his men sallied out and were repulsed by the Indians. McClelland himself and two of his men being slain and four wounded. The Indians immediately withdrew, and in a few days the ammunition was safely brought away from its concealment. McClelland's was immediately afterwards abandoned, and the settlers in great gloom, and amidst the lamentations of the women and children, departed for Harrod's station. Here Kenton also took up his abode. In the spring, Major Clark, who now had command of the settlements, sent Kenton, John Haggin, and four others to Hinckston's to break out some flax and hemp. Haggin was in front, and observed a party of Indians encamped around Hinckston's. He rode back and informed the party of the fact. Kenton, who was as prudent as he was brave, counseled a retreat. Haggin swore that nobody but a coward would run without one fire. Kenton immediately dismounted from his horse, and all the party followed his example but a young Dutchman, who appeared to have more sense than any of his companions. In the meantime the Indians, always wide awake, had seen Haggin, and following him, now opened a fire on the whites, who quickly took to their heels, Haggin valiantly leading the van, and abandoned their horses to the Indians, all but the sensible Dutchman, who having kept his seat, cantered off much at his ease. Kenton directed his party to retreat into Harrodsburgh, while he put the garrison at Boone's station on their guard. Arriving before the fort, he determined not to attempt to enter it before dark, knowing the custom of the wily savage to ambush the stations, and thus shoot whoever might attempt to enter or depart. Accident befriends many a man, but the due exercise of one's five wits, is a much more safe reliance. When he did enter the fort, he found the men carrying in the bodies of two of their friends, who had been killed two or three hours before, on the very same path by which he entered. His caution had saved his life. The red man was now furious at the occupation of his beloved Kain-tuck-ee by the long knife. The incursions into the country by the exasperated foe were frequent and bloody, and every station was hotly besieged, Boonesborough sustaining three. To watch the Indians and give timely notice of their approach, six spies were appointed, for the payment of whom Major Clark pledged the faith of Virginia. Boone appointed Kenton and Thos. Brooks; Harrod, Samuel Moore, and Bates Collier; and Logan, John Conrad and John Martin. These spies performed good service. It was the custom for two each week, by turns, to range up and down the Ohio, and about the deserted stations, looking for Indian signs, &c. By this means, the settlers had timely notice during the year of the approach of the enemy, but once. On this occasion, Kenton and two others, early one morning, having loaded their guns for a hunt, were standing in the gate of Boonesborough, when two men in the fields were fired on by the Indians. They immediately fled, not being hurt. The Indians pursued them, and a warrior overtook and tomahawked one of the men within seventy yards of the fort, and proceeded leisurely to scalp him. Kenton shot the daring savage dead and immediately with his hunting companions gave chase to the others. Boone, hearing the noise, with ten men hastened out to the assistance of his spies. Kenton turned and observed an Indian taking aim at the party of Boone—quick as thought he brought his rifle to his shoulder, pulled the trigger first, and the red man bit the dust. Boone, having advanced some distance, now discovered that his small party, consisting of fourteen men, was cut off

25

from the fort by a large body of the foe, which had got between him and the gate. There was no time to be lost; Boone gave the word—"right-about—fire—charge!" and the intrepid hunters dashed in among their adversaries, in a desperate endeavor to reach the fort. At the first fire from the Indians, seven of the fourteen whites were wounded, among the number the gallant Boone, whose leg was broken, which stretched him on the ground. An Indian sprang on him with uplifted tomahawk, but before the blow descended, Kenton, every where present, rushed on the warrior, discharged his gun into his breast, and bore his leader into the fort. When the gate was closed and all things secure, Boone sent for Kenton :—" Well, Simon," said the old pioneer, "you have behaved yourself like a man to-day—indeed you are a fine fellow." This was great praise from Boone, who was a silent man, little given to compliment. Kenton had deserved the eulogium : he had saved the life of his captain and killed three Indians, *without having time to scalp any one of them.* There was little time to spare, we may well believe, when Kenton could not stop to take a scalp.

The enemy, after keeping up the siege for three days, retired. Boonesborough sustained two other sieges this year, (1777), in all of which the youthful Kenton bore a gallant and conspicuous part.

Kenton continued to range the country as a spy until June, 1778, when Major Clark came down the Ohio from Virginia with a small force, and landed at the Falls. Clark was organizing an expedition against Okaw or Kaskaskia, and invited as many of the settlers at Boonesborough and Harrodsburgh as desired, to join him. The times were so dangerous that the women. especially, in the stations objected to the men going on such a distant expedition. Consequently, to the great mortification of Clark, only Kenton and Haggin left the stations to accompany him. This expedition, so honorable to the enterprise of Virginia and the great captain and soldiers composing it, and so successful and happy in its results, is elsewhere fully described (see Clark county—life of General Clark). After the fall of Kaskaskia, Kenton returned to Harrodsburgh, by way of Vincennes, an accurate description of which, obtained by three days' secret observation, he sent to Clark, who subsequently took that post.

Kenton, finding Boone about to undertake an expedition against a small town on Paint creek, readily joined him. Inaction was irksome to the hardy youth in such stirring times; besides; he had some melancholy reflections that he could only escape from in the excitement of danger and adventure.

The party, consisting of nineteen men, and commanded by Boone, arrived in the neighborhood of the Indian village. Kenton, who, as usual, was in advance, was startled by hearing loud peals of laughter from a cane brake just before him. He scarcely had time to *tree*, before two Indians, mounted upon a small pony, one facing the animal's tail and the other his head, totally unsuspicious of danger and in excellent spirits, made their appearance. He pulled trigger, and both Indians fell, one killed and the other severely wounded. He hastened up to scalp his adversaries, and was immediately surrounded by about forty Indians. His situation, dodging from tree to tree, was uncomfortable enough, until Boone and his party coming up, furiously attacked and defeated the savages. Boone immediately returned to the succor of his fort, having ascertained that a large war party had gone against it. Kenton and Montgomery, however, resolved to proceed to the village to get 'a shot' and steal horses. They lay within good rifle distance of the village for two days and a night without seeing a single warrior ; on the second night, they each mounted a fine horse and put off to Kentucky, and the day after the Indians raised the siege of Boonesborough, they cantered into the fort on their stolen property.

This little speculation, unfortunately, appears to have whetted the appetite of Kenton and Montgomery for horse flesh. Accordingly, in September of the same year, (1778), in company with George Clark, they proceeded to Chillicothe on a similar expedition. Arriving in the night, they found a pound of horses, and succeeded in haltering seven, not without much noise. They mounted in haste, hotly pursued by the enraged savages. Riding all night and next day, they struck the Ohio at the mouth of Eagle creek, a few miles below Maysville. The wind was high and the river exceedingly rough, so that the frightened horses refused to cross, after several ineffectual efforts to compel them. Here they rashly waited until the next day, hoping that the wind would abate ; but, although the next day the wind did subside, the horses could by no means be forced into the river, owing to the fright they had received the day before. Satisfied that longer delay would be dangerous, they each mounted a horse, abandoning the remaining four. But after turning them loose, with an indecision unworthy of the leader at least, it was determined that they would have all or none. They now separated to hunt up the horses they had just unhaltered. Kenton had not ridden far before he heard a whoop behind him. Instead of putting spurs to his horse and galloping off like a sensible man, he deliberately dismounted from his horse, tied him, and crept back in the direction of the noise. At the top of the bank he saw two Indians and a white man, all mounted. It was too late to retreat—he raised his rifle, took aim, and—it flashed ! Now, at last, he took to his heels, the Indians dashing after him with a yell. He gained some fallen timber, and thus was in a fair way to elude his mounted pursuers, when, upon emerging into the open woods, he beheld an Indian galloping around the brush within a few rods of him. The game was up, and for the first time he was a prisoner in the hands of the savages, furious at the attempt to steal their property.

While the Indians were yet beating and upbraiding him as a " hoss steal," Montgomery very foolishly came to his assistance, fired without effect, and fled. Two of the Indians gave chase, and in a few moments returned with his bleeding scalp. Clark, the only one of the three having his five wits in a healthy condition, laid whip and escaped.

Bitterly now did Kenton expiate his horse stealing offences. It was a crime not easily to be pardoned by the very *virtuous* tribe into whose hands he had fallen. After beating him until their arms were too tired to indulge that gratifying recreation any longer, they secured him for the night. This was done by first placing him upon his back on the ground. They next drew his legs apart, and lashed each foot firmly to two saplings or stakes driven in the earth. A pole was then laid across his breast, and his hands tied to each end, and his arms lashed with thongs around it, the thongs passing under his body so as to keep the pole stationary. After all this, another thong was tied around his neck, and the end of it secured to a stake in the ground, his head being stretched back so as not *entirely* to choke him. In this original manner he passed the night, unable to sleep, and filled with the most gloomy forebodings of the future. In the morning he was driven forward to the village.

The plan of this work forbids a particular account of Kenton's adventures during his long captivity, running through a period of more than eight months. The cruelties he suffered at the hands of the Indians—his narrow escapes from death in an hundred forms—his alternate good and bad fortune, and his final successful flight, form one of the most romantic adventures anywhere furnished by the incidents of real life, seeming more like an invention of the novelist, than a veracious narrative. He was eight times compelled to run the gauntlet, three times tied to the stake, once brought to the brink of the grave by a blow from an axe; and throughout the whole time, with brief intervals, subjected to great hardship and privations. Once his old friend, Simon Girty, the infamous hater of his race, interposed and saved him for a short space from the flames. Being again condemned to the stake in spite of the influence of Girty, Logan the celebrated Mingo, (whose wrongs had not obliterated the nobility of his nature,) exerted his influence in his behalf, and prevailed upon a Canadian trader, named Druyer to purchase him from his owners. Druyer succeeded in obtaining him as a prisoner of war, upon a promise of returning him, which he of course never intended to fulfil. Kenton was now taken by his new friend and delivered over to the British commander at Detroit. Here he remained working for the garrison, on half pay, until the summer of 1779, when he effected his escape, by the assistance of Mrs. Harvey, the wife of an Indian trader. Kenton, at this time but twenty-four years of age, according to one who served with him, "was fine looking, with a dignified and manly deportment, and a soft, pleasing voice, and was wherever he went a favorite among the ladies." This lady had become interested in him, and upon his solicitation, promised to assist him and two other Kentuckians, prisoners with him, to procure rifles, ammunition, &c., without which a journey through the wilderness could not be performed. Engaging in their cause with all the enthusiasm of her sex, she only awaited an opportunity to perform her promise. She had not long to wait. On the 3d of June, 1779, a large concourse of Indians assembled at Detroit to take "a spree." Preparatory to getting drunk, they stacked their guns near Mrs. Harvey's house, who as soon as it was dark stole silently out to the guns, selected three of the best looking, and quickly hid them in her garden in a patch of peas. Avoiding all observation, she hastened to Kenton's lodgings and informed him of her success. She told him, at midnight to come to the back of her garden, where he would find a ladder, by means of which he could climb over and get the guns. She had previously collected such articles of food, clothing, ammunition, &c., as would be necessary in their adventure. These she had hid in a hollow tree well known to Kenton, some distance out of town. No time was now to be lost, and the prisoners at once set about getting things in order for their flight. At the appointed hour Kenton with his companions appeared at the designated spot, discovered the ladder and climbed into the garden, where he found Mrs. Harvey sitting by the guns awaiting his arrival. To the eyes of the grateful young hunter, no woman ever looked so beautiful. There was little time however for compliments, for all around could be heard the yells of the drunken savages, the night was far advanced, and in the morning both guns and prisoners would be missed. Taking an affectionate leave of him, with many tender wishes for his safety, she now urged him to be gone. Heaping thanks and blessings on her, he left her and re-joined his companions. Kenton never saw her afterwards, but he never forgot her; for, more than half a century afterwards, when the wilderness and the savages who peopled it, were alike exterminated before the civilizing march of the Anglo Saxon, the old pioneer, in words that glowed with gratitude and admiration, delighted to dwell on the kindness, and expatiate on the courage and virtue of his benefactress, the fair trader's wife. In his reveries, he said he had seen her "a thousand times sitting by the guns in the garden."

After leaving Detroit the fugitives, departing from the usual line of travel, struck out in a western direction towards the prairies of the Wabash. At the end of thirty-three days, having suffered incredible hardships, the three adventurers, Kenton, Bullitt and Coffer, safely arrived at Louisville some time in July '79.

Here he stayed but a short time to recruit his strength. He had been long a prisoner and thirsted for action and adventure. Shouldering his rifle he set out through the unbroken wilderness to visit his old companion in arms, Major Clark, then at Vincennes. This post he found entirely quiet, too much so for him. He had been treading the wilderness and fighting the savages since his sixteenth year, and was yet too young and strong to be contented with a life of inaction. He had no family or connection to bind him to a particular spot here in the west, and by a deed utterly repugnant to his generous nature, he was exiled as he yet believed, from his home and friends in the east; it was therefore his destiny, as it was his wish, to rove. Striking again into the pathless wilderness then lying between Vincennes and the falls of the Ohio, he soon reached the latter place, whence he immediately proceeded to Harrod's station, where he was joyfully welcomed by his old companions.

The winter of 1779–80 was a peaceful one to the Kentuckians, but in the spring the Indians and British invaded the country, having with them two pieces of cannon, by means of which two stations, Martin's and Ruddell's, fell into their hands; whereupon the allied savages immediately retreated.

When General Clark heard of the disaster, he hastened from Vincennes to concert measures for present retaliation and the future safety of the settlements. Clark was no doubt one of the greatest men ever furnished by the west, of no ordinary military capacity. He believed the best way to prevent the depredations of the Indians, was to carry the war into their own country, burning down their villages and destroying their corn, and thus give them sufficient employment to prevent their incursions among the settlements on the south side of the river. Accordingly an expedition consisting of 1100 of the hardiest and most courageous men that the most adventurous age of our history could furnish, inured to hardships and accustomed to the Indian mode of fighting, assembled at the mouth of the Licking. Kenton commanded a company of volunteers from Harrod's station, and shared in all the dangers and success of this little army. Commanded by Clark, and piloted by one of the most expert woodsmen and the greatest spy of the west, Simon Kenton, the Kentuckians assailed the savages in their dens with complete success. Chillicothe, Pickaway and many other towns were burnt, and the crops around them destroyed. At Pickaway, the Indians were brought to a stand. Here where he had run the gauntlet and afforded the Indian squaws and warriors so much *fun*, two years before, Kenton now at the head of his gallant company, had the satisfaction of dashing into the thickest of the fight and repaying with usury the blows he had received at their hands. After an obstinate resistance the savages were defeated and fled in all directions, leaving their killed and wounded on the field. (See life of Clark.)

This was the first invasion of Ohio by the Kentuckians in any force, and the red man long remembered it. For two years the stations enjoyed comparative peace, and Kenton passed away his time as a hunter, or spy, or with surveying parties, heavily enough until the fall of 1782. Then for the first time he heard that his old father yet lived, and learned the joyful intelligence that he had not killed his old playmate and friend William Veach. It is impossible to describe his feelings upon hearing this news. For eleven years he wandered in the wilderness filled with remorse for his rash, though unpremeditated crime, the brand of murder upon his heart if not upon his brow, isolated from his home and friends, about whom he dare not even inquire, and his very name forbidden to him. At length after expiating his crime by these long sufferings, unexpectedly the weight of murder is removed from his mind—his banishment from home and family revoked, and his long abandoned name restored. Kenton was Simon Butler now no longer, and he felt like a new man.

In the fall of 1782 General Clark, to revenge the disaster of the Blue Licks, led another army 1500 strong against the Indian towns, which spread destruction far and wide through their country. (See life of Clark.) Kenton again commanded a company on this occasion, and was again the pilot for the army, as his knowledge of the country was unsurpassed, and his skill in woodcraft unequalled. It was upon the return of this expedition opposite the mouth of the Licking, Nov. 4th, 1782, that the pioneers composing it, entered into the romantic engagement, that fifty years thereafter, the survivors "should meet and talk over the affairs of the campaign," and the dangers and hardships of the past. It was first suggested by Captain M'Cracken of the Kentucky light horse, who was then dying* from the mortification of a slight wound received in the arm while fighting, immediately by the side of Kenton in the attack on Piqua town. To carry out the request of the dying soldier, Colonel Floyd, from the Falls of the Ohio, brought forward a resolution, and the semi-centennial meeting was determined upon. All around was the unbroken wilderness; but as they bore the dying M'Cracken down the hill above Cincinnati, the future stood revealed to his fast closing eyes, the cities and villas peopled with tens of thousands, crowning the valley and the hill tops, the noise of abounding commerce in the streets and on the rivers—building rising upon building—palace and temple and all the magnificent panorama of fifty years, passed in review before him. The desire to link one's name with all this greatness was pardonable in him who had shed his blood in the struggle to achieve it. The interesting day that was to witness the re-union of the surviving heroes of '82, fell upon the 4th of November, 1832. At that time many were still surviving, among the rest General Simon Kenton. As the day drew near, the old hero was deeply affected at the prospect of meeting his old brothers in arms, as well as solicitous to keep the solemn appointment. To encourage a large attendance he published an interesting and feeling " address to the citizens of the western country." It is a fair type of his kind heart, dictated to a friend who wrote it for him, and signed with his own hand. The following is the only extract the limits of this work will permit us to make.

" Fellow citizens !—Being one of the first, after Colonel Daniel Boone, who aided in the conquest of Kentucky, and the west, I am called upon to address you. My heart melts on such an occasion; I look forward to the contemplated meeting with melancholy pleasure; it has caused tears to flow in copious showers. I wish to see once more before I die, my few surviving friends. My *solemn promise*, made fifty years ago, binds me to meet them. I ask not for myself; but you may find in our assembly some who have never received any pay or pension, who have sustained the cause of their country, equal to any other service; who in the decline of life are poor. Then, you prosperous sons of the west, forget not those old and gray-headed veterans on this occasion; let them return to their families with some

---

* He died as the troops descended the hill where Cincinnati now stands, and was buried near the block-house at the mouth of the Licking, on the Kentucky side.

little manifestation of your kindness to cheer their hearts. I add my prayer. may kind heaven grant us a clear sky, fair and pleasant weather—a safe journey and a happy meeting, and smile upon us and our families, and bless us and our nation on the approaching occasion.

Simon Kenton

URBANA, Ohio, 1832.

The day at last came so long looked for by our "old fathers of the west," and the terrible cholera, more barbarous than the savages, who fifty years before battled the pioneers, spread death far and wide over the west, sparing neither age nor sex. Cincinnati was wrapt in gloom, yet many of the veteran patriots assembled, and the corporation voted them a dinner. General Kenton, in spite of his ardent desire, was unable from sickness and old age, to attend. He met his beloved companions no more until he met them in the spirit land.

After the volunteers disbanded at the mouth of Licking, Kenton returned to Harrod's station. He had acquired many valuable tracts of land, now becoming of importance, as population began to flow into the country with a rapid increase, as the sounds of savage warfare grew fainter in the distance. He settled on his lands on Salt river, and being joined by a few families in 1782–3, he built some rude block-houses, cleared land, and planted corn. His settlement thrived wonderfully. In the fall, having gathered his corn, he determined to visit his father, ascertain his circumstances, and bring him to Kentucky. He had not seen his family for thirteen years, a period to him full of dangers, sufferings and triumphs. Who can paint the joy of the returning adventurer, young in years, but old in deeds and reputation, on reaching home, to find that his aged father "yet lived." The reunion was joyful to all, especially so to his friends, who had long considered him dead. He visited with delight the friends and the scenes of his early childhood, so different from his boisterous manhood, and the gauntlet, the stake, and the fierce foray, and the wild war-whoop were to him as the confused image of some uneasy dream. Veach and the ungracious fair one, his first love, were still living; he saw them, and each forgot the old feud.

He gathered up his father and family and proceeded as far as Red Stone Fort, journeying to Kain-tuck-ee, where his old father died, and was buried on the winding banks of the Monongahela, without marble or inscription to mark the last resting place of the father of the great pioneer. Kenton, with the remainder of his father's family, reached his settlement in safety in the winter of 1784.

Kentucky was now a flourishing territory, and emigrants came flocking in to appropriate her fertile lands. Kenton determined to occupy his lands, around his old camp, near Maysville, remarkable for their beauty and fertility. This part of Kentucky was still uninhabited, and infested by the Indians. In July, 1784, collecting a small party of adventurers, he went to his old camp, one mile from Washington, in Mason county. The Indians being too troublesome, the party returned to Salt river. In the fall of the same year Kenton returned, built some block-houses, and was speedily joined by a few families. In the spring of '85, many new settlements were made around Kenton's station, and that part of the country soon assumed a thriving appearance, in spite of the incursions of the savages. In 1786, Kenton sold (or according to M'Donald), GAVE Arthur Fox and William Wood one thousand acres of land, on which they laid out the town of Washington; "Old Ned Waller" had settled at Limestone (Maysville) the year before.

The Indians were too badly crippled, by Clark's last expedition, to offer any considerable opposition to the settlers; nevertheless, they were exceedingly troublesome, during their many small predatory incursions, and plied the fashionable trade of horse-stealing with praiseworthy activity. To put a stop to such proceedings, on the part of their red neighbors, an expedition, seven hundred strong, composed of volunteers from all the surrounding stations, assembled at Washington under the command of Colonel Logan. Fighting, in those days, cost our affectionate "Uncle Sam" very little, as every man paid his own war expenses.

Kenton commanded a company from his settlement, and, as usual, piloted the way into the enemy's country. The expedition fell upon Mochacheek and Pickaway very suddenly, defeated the Indians with considerable loss, burnt four other towns, without resistance, and returned to Washington with only ten men killed and wounded.

Notwithstanding this successful blow, the Indians, all next year, kept the inhabitants around Kenton's station in perpetual alarm. Kenton again called on the stations to rendezvous at Washington, for the purpose of punishing the Indians, by "carrying the war into Africa;" a trick he had learned from his old commander, General Clark. It was essentially to the interest of the interior stations to see Kenton's well sustained, as thereby the savages were kept at a distance from them. They were, consequently, always ready to render their more exposed brethren any assistance required. Several hundred hardy hunters, under Colonel Todd, assembled again at Washington. Kenton again commanded his company, a gallant set of young men, trained by himself, and piloted the expedition. Near Chillicothe a detachment, led by majors Hinkston and Kenton, fell upon a large body of Indians, about day-break, and defeated them before Todd came up. Chillicothe was burned down, and the expedition returned without losing a man.

The pioneers had now become formidable to the Indians, and kept them at bay. Kenton's station was a frontier for the interior settlements, and manfully beat back the foe, in his incursions into the State. The country around Washington was fast filling up, and bid fair soon to be in a condition to set the Indian at defiance. Kenton, universally esteemed and beloved, was acknowledged to be the chief man in the community. His great experience and reputation as a frontier man; his superior courage and skill in the fight, as well as the extent of his possessions, rendered him conspicuous. In all the incursions made into the country of the enemy, and the many local contests that took place with the Indians, Captain Kenton was invariably the leader selected by the settlers.

From 1788 to 1793, many small but bloody conflicts came off around the settlements in Mason county, in which the Indians were severely punished by Captain Kenton and his volunteers. In 1793 the Indians made the last incursion into this, or perhaps any other part of Kentucky. On that occasion (see Mason county) Kenton ambushed them at the place where they crossed the Ohio, killed six of the party, and dispersed the remainder. They never afterwards invaded the long contested shore of their beloved hunting ground. After a desperate and sanguinary struggle of more than twenty years, Kain-tuck-ee, "the dark and bloody ground," was lost to the red man forever. The Saxon, in his insatiable thirst for land, had felled her forests, driven out her elk and buffalo, ploughed up her virgin sod, polluted her soil with the unfamiliar city and village, and in the blood of the red man written his title to the country, which he held with a grasp of iron. Cornstalk, Blackfish, Logan, Little Turtle, Elinipsico, Meshawah, the young Tecumseh, and the thousand north-western braves, bled in vain. Equal courage, superior intellect, and the destiny of the Saxon, overthrew the heroism, the perseverance, and the despair of the sons of the forest.

In 1793, General Wayne came down the Ohio to prepare for his successful expedition. Kenton, at that time a major, joined Wayne with his battalion, and proceeded to Greenville, where he was conspicuous among the hardy hunters composing the army, on account of his superior reputation, courage, skill, and activity. He was not in the battle of the Fallen Timber, having been discharged with his battalion the winter previous. The Indians, being defeated by Wayne, and their power completely broken, sued for peace, which was granted, and the war was over.

Kentucky and the west, after the peace of Greenville, rushed forward with rapid strides in the career of population and wealth. Emigrants came pouring over the Alleghanies into the fertile valley of the Ohio, to occupy the beautiful "land of the cane." These lands rose rapidly in price and importance, and Kenton was now thought to be one of the wealthiest men in his State, and deserved to be so, for he had purchased his wealth by many a bloody conflict, and by many incredible hardships. But behold the gratitude of his countrymen!

The crafty offsprings of peace, who slept in the lap of eastern ease and security, while this noble pioneer was enduring the hardships of the wilderness, and braving the gauntlet, and stake, and tomahawk of the Indian to redeem the soil of the west, creep in when the fight, and toil, and danger are past, and by dishonorable trick, miserable technicality, and cunning procedure, wrest the possessions bought at such a terrible price from the gallant, unlettered, simple hearted man, unversed in the rascality of civilization. He lost his lands acre after acre, the superior skill of the speculator prevailing over the simplicity and ignorance of the hunter. What a burning, deep disgrace to the west, that the hero who had suffered so much and fought so well to win the soil of his glorious "cane land" from the savage, should, when the contest was ended, be compelled to leave it to those who never struck a blow in its defence! Together with Boone and numerous other brave old frontier men, who bore "the heat and burden of the day," Kenton, like an old shoe, was kicked aside when he was no longer of any use, or had become too antiquated for the fashion of the times. Kentucky treated her earliest and staunchest defenders scarcely so well as *they* treated their dogs—after running down the game, she denied them the very offal.

The fate of General Simon Kenton was still more hard than that of the other simple hearted fathers of the west. His body was taken for debt upon the covenants in deeds to lands, which he had, in effect, given away, and for twelve months he was imprisoned, upon the very spot where he first built his cabin in '75—where he planted the first corn ever planted on the north of the Kentucky river by the hand of any white man—where he ranged the pathless forest in freedom and safety—where he subsequently erected his foremost station house, and battled the Indians in an hundred encounters, and, nearly alone, endured the hardships of the wilderness, while those who then reaped the fruits of his former sufferings were yet unborn, or dwelt afar in the lap of peace and plenty.

In 1802, beggared by law-suits and losses, he moved into Ohio, and settled in Urbana. He was no longer young, and the prospect of spending his old age in independence, surrounded by plenty and comfort, which lightened the toils and sufferings of his youth, was now succeeded by cheerless anticipations of poverty and neglect. Thus, after thirty years of the prime of his life, spent faithfully in the cause of Kentucky and the west, all that remained to him was the recollection of his services, and a cabin in the wilderness of Ohio. He himself never repined, and such was his exalted patriotism, that he would not suffer others to upbraid his country in his presence, without expressing a degree of anger altogether foreign from his usual mild and amiable manner. It never occurred to his ingenuous mind that *his* country could treat any body, much less him, with neglect, and his devotion and patriotism continued to the last unimpaired.

In 1805, he was elected a brigadier general in the Ohio militia, and in 1810 he joined the Methodist Episcopal church. It is a consoling fact, that nearly all the "old fathers of the west" devoted the evening of their stormy lives to the service of their Maker, and died in the triumphs of the Christian faith. In 1813, the gallant old man joined the Kentucky troops under Governor Shelby, into whose family he was admitted as a privileged member, and was in the battle of the Thames. This was his last battle, and from it the old hero returned to obscurity and poverty in his humble cabin in the woods. He remained in Urbana till 1820, when he moved to the head of Mad river, Logan county, Ohio, in sight of Wapatomika, where he had been tied to the stake by the Indians when a prisoner in their hands. Here he was harassed by judgments and executions from Kentucky, and to prevent being driven from his cabin by his white *brethren*, (as formerly by the savages) to the forest for a shelter, he was compelled to have some land entered in the name of his wife and children. He still had many tracts of mountain land in Kentucky of little value, which, however, were forfeited to the State for taxes. In 1824, then seventy years of age, he undertook a journey to Frankfort, in tattered garments and on a sorry horse, to endeavor to get the legislature, then in session, to release the claim of the State on his mountain lands.

Here, where he had roved in an unbroken wilderness in the early day, now stood a flourishing city, but he walked up and down its streets, an object of curiosity to the boys, a stranger, recognized by no one. A new generation had arisen to people and possess the land which he had defended, and his old friends and companions were gone. At length General Thomas Fletcher, from Bath county, saw and knew him, and by his means the old pioneer was clothed in a decent suit, and entertained in a kind and becoming manner. When it became known that

Simon Kenton was in the town, numbers speedily assembled to see the celebrated warrior and hunter, and testify their regard for him. He was taken to the capitol and placed in the speaker's chair, "and then was introduced the second great adventurer of the west, to a crowded assembly of legislators, judges, officers of the government, and citizens generally." This the simple hearted old man was wont to call " the proudest day " of his life. His lands were at once released, and shortly afterwards, by the exertions of Judge Burnet and General Vance of Congress, a pension of two hundred and forty dollars a year was obtained for him, securing his old age from absolute want.

Without any further reward from his government, or particular notice from his fellow-citizens and contemporaries, General Kenton lived in his quiet and obscure home to the age of eighty-one, beloved and respected by all who knew him. In April, 1836, in sight of the place where the Indians, fifty-eight years before, proposed to torture him to death, he breathed his last, surrounded by his family and neighbors, and supported by the consolations of the gospel.

The following is a description of the appearance and character of this remarkable man, by one who often shared with him in the dangers of the forest and the fight:

" General Kenton was of fair complexion, six feet one inch in height. He stood and walked very erect; and, in the prime of life, weighed about one hundred and ninety pounds. He never was inclined to be corpulent, although of sufficient fullness to form a graceful person. He had a soft, tremulous voice, very pleasing to the hearer. He had laughing, gray eyes, which appeared to fascinate the beholder, and dark auburn hair. He was a pleasant, good-humored, and obliging companion. When excited, or provoked to anger, (which was seldom the case), the fiery glance of his eye would almost curdle the blood of those with whom he came in contact. His rage, when roused, was a tornado. In his dealing, he was perfectly honest; his confidence in man, and his credulity, were such, that the same man might cheat him twenty times; and if he professed friendship, he might cheat him still."

The thing which strikes us most forcibly, in contemplating the lives of the great leading men, who pioneered the march of civilization to the west, is their complete simplicity of character. Some have not hesitated to pronounce this stupidity, but we can not agree with them. The pioneers of the west, in addition to a plentiful lack of education and mental discipline, were certainly children in their knowledge of the great book of human nature. Still the courage, skill, sagacity, perseverance and endurance exhibited in their life of privation and danger, prove them to have been men of no ordinary mould, and the same intellectual and physical forces called into action in any other sphere of life, expressed with the same energy, would have rendered their possessors distinguished.

We can easily see how unfit for civilized life, were Boone and Kenton, suddenly transposed from an almost primitive and savage state of society, unsophisticated and simple-minded as they were. The great questions of property, regulated by law, and liberty, regulated by policy, in their profound mysteries, were to them as sealed books : they had not studied them ; but for more than twenty years, battling with the savages, and enduring bitter privations with constant and necessary activity, they lived in the free wilderness, where action was unfettered by law, and where property was not controlled by form and technicality, but rested on the natural and broader foundation of justice and convenience. They knew how to beat back the invader of their soil, or repel the aggression of the private wrong-doer—they knew how to bear down a foe in the open field, or circumvent him by stratagem, or destroy him by ambush. But they knew not how to swindle a neighbor out of his acres, by declaration, demurrer, plea and replication, and all the scientific pomp of chicanery—they knew not how *damages* could salve a private injury or personal wrong, or how the verdict of a jury could remove the poison from the tongue of the slanderer, or medicine the incurable wounds inflicted by the seducer. Hence, in the broad and glorious light of civilization, they were stupid. Their confidence in men, their simplicity, their stupidity, by whatever name proper to call it, rendered them an easy prey to selfish and unprincipled speculators. Certain it is, that hundreds arose to prey upon the simple Fathers of the West; and they were driven out in their old age yet farther into the wilderness. Instead of seeing their children possess and people the beautiful land won by their fathers, after so long and terrible a conflict, we see them, like their sires, on the borders of civilization, beating back the savage, themselves ever driven back by that wave of population which follows on their steps, by a strange decree, the exterminators of the red man, soon thereafter, themselves to be exterminated.

It is now perhaps too late, to repair the injustice done to these old heroes by the west; yet one act remains to Kentucky, demanded alike by gratitude and a just sense of honor. It is to gather up the sacred remains of Simon Kenton, from their last, obscure resting place, and placing them in the cemetery of her capital, in the bosom of that beloved soil which he was among the first and stoutest to defend; to erect a monument over his grave, commemorating throughout all succeeding years the services and virtues of her Great Pioneer. Will it ever be done?

BANK LICK is a beautiful stream, emptying into the Licking river, five miles from its confluence with the Ohio, in Kenton county. This stream received its name from the early settlers, and its banks have, doubtless, been trodden by Boone and Kenton. The engraving represents a scene on this stream, about a mile above its junction with the Licking. The picture is by Frankenstein, a young artist of Cincinnati.

VIEW OF BANK LICK, KENTON CO., KY.

Among the prominent citizens of Kenton county, is the Honorable JAMES T. MOREHEAD, late Senator in the Congress of the United States. He enjoys a reputation for ability and eloquence, which is co-extensive with the limits of the Union, and ranks among the first public men of the State. He was born on the 24th May, 1797, near Shepherdsville, in the county of Bullitt. When he was three or four years old, his father removed to Russellville, Logan county, where he enjoyed the advantages of the village schools. In the spring of 1813, he was sent to Transylvania University, where he continued until 1815. The University was then under the charge of Dr. Blythe, as principal, Rev. Mr. Bishop, professor of moral philosophy, and Mr. Ebenezer Sharpe, professor of languages. On his return to Russellville, Mr. Morehead commenced the study of the law under the Honorable H. P. Brodnax, then one of the circuit court judges; and he continued it in the office of the Honorable J. J. Crittenden, who was then living at Russellville. In the spring of 1818, Mr. Morehead settled at Bowling Green, and commenced the practice of law. In August, 1828, he was elected to the legislature from the county of Warren, and was re-elected in 1829–1830. In the winter of 1831-2, while attending the convention at Baltimore which nominated Mr. Clay for the presidency and John Sergeant for vice president, he was nominated by the state convention that met at Frankfort as candidate for lieutenant governor. He was elected to this office in August, 1832. He presided over the senate until the death of Governor Breathitt, in February, 1834, and succeeded that gentleman in the administration of the government. In his first message to the legislature, he recommended an enlarged system of internal improvements, which the legislature, on the 28th of February, 1835, provided for by "an act for the internal improvement of the State of Kentucky," creating a board of internal improvement, of which Mr. Morehead was made *ex-officio* the president. In the fall of 1836, he resumed the practice of the law in Frankfort. In March, 1837, he was commissioned by Governor Clark, as the agent of the State, for the sale of the bonds for internal improvement purposes. In August, 1837, he was elected to the legislature in Franklin county. In the spring of 1838, he was appointed by Governor Clark, president of the board of internal improvements. In the winter of the next year, he was selected by the legislature, in conjunction with Colonel J. Speed Smith, of Madison, as a commissioner to the State of Ohio, to obtain the passage of a law for the protection of the property of the citizens of Kentucky in their slaves. The mission was entirely successful. Mr. Morehead remained in the board of internal improvement until the latter part of February, 1841, when he was elected to the senate of the United States for the term of six years. In the senate, as a debater, few men ranked higher than Governor Morehead. An announcement that he was to speak, never failed to fill the lobbies and galleries with spectators. As a speaker, he is remarkably fluent and energetic, with a manner eminently graceful and dignified. His political information is extensive, and his opinions as a statesman, sound and conservative. Governor Morehead is now living in Covington, engaged in the practice of his profession.

~~~~~~~~~~~~~~~~~

KNOX COUNTY.

KNOX county was formed in 1799, and named in honor of General HENRY KNOX. It is situated in the southeastern part of the State, and lies on both sides of the Cumberland river: Bounded on the north by Laurel and Clay; northeast by Clay; southeast by Harlan; south by Tennessee line; and west by Whitley. The Pine mountain, a spur of the great Cumberland, skirts this county on the southeast. The face of the country, except on the river bottoms, is hilly and mountainous—the staple products, corn and oats, though other grains are produced, and horses, cattle, hogs and sheep are raised in considerable numbers.

Valuation of taxable property in 1846, $767,326; number of acres of land in the county, 150,308; average value of land per acre, $2.74; number of white males over twenty-one years of age, 1,027; number of children between five and sixteen years old, 1,688.   Population in 1840, 5,722.

BARBOURSVILLE, the county seat and only town, is situated on the right bank of the Cumberland river, about one hundred and fifty miles from Frankfort.   It contains three churches, one school, court-house, five stores and groceries, one tavern, three lawyers, two physicians and six mechanical trades—population 225.   Established in 1812.

The State road from Frankfort to the State of Tennessee, crosses at the Cumberland ford in this county, thence passes out of the State at the Cumberland Gap. The Pine mountain, which is situated on the border of this county, presents to the eye all the grandeur and sublimity of nature in her wildest and most romantic aspect, through which the Cumberland river seems to have forced its way, the cliffs on either side, consisting of almost interminable heaps of limestone, rising to the height of thirteen hundred feet. In the vicinity of this cliff, there is a cave of considerable magnitude.

Three miles from Barboursville, on the north bank of the Cumberland, there are the remains of an ancient fortress, around which a circular ditch is discernible, enclosing about four acres of ground.

It was through the Cumberland Gap, in this county, that the distinguished pioneer, Daniel Boone, first penetrated Kentucky.

General HENRY KNOX, in honor of whom this county received its name, was a native of Massachusetts, having been born at Boston, on the 25th July, 1750. He received a good education, and at an early period of his life was a bookseller. At the age of eighteen, he was chosen one of the officers of a company of grenadiers, and evinced a fondness and ability for the military profession. At the battle of Bunker Hill he served as a volunteer; and soon after undertook the perilous task of procuring from the Canada frontier some pieces of ordnance, greatly needed by the American army, which he successfully accomplished. For this daring feat, he received the most flattering testimonials from the commander-in-chief and congress, and was soon after entrusted with the command of the artillery department, with the rank of a brigadier general. In the battles of Trenton and Princeton, Germantown and Monmouth, he displayed peculiar skill and bravery; and subsequently contributed greatly to the capture of Cornwallis at Yorktown. Immediately after this event, he was created a major-general. He was subsequently one of the commissioners to adjust the terms of peace—was deputed to receive the surrender of New York from the English forces—and afterwards appointed commander at West Point, where he executed the delicate and difficult task of disbanding the army, which he executed with extraordinary address. In 1785, he was appointed secretary at war, the duties of which office he discharged with general approbation until the year 1794, when he retired to his estate, in the then district, but now State of Maine. In 1798, when the state of our affairs with France indicated a rupture, he was again appointed to a command in the army; but the re-establishment of amicable relations with that power, enabled him soon to return to his retirement. He died October 25, 1806, at his seat in Thomaston, Maine, at the age of 56. General Knox was as amiable in private, as he was eminent in public life. But few men in the stirring times in which he lived, possessed in a higher degree those traits of character which dignify and ennoble human nature.

LARUE COUNTY.

LARUE county was formed in 1843, and named for JOHN LARUE. It lies on Salt river, in the middle portion of the State : Bounded on the north by Hardin and Nelson ; east by Nelson and Washington ; south by Hart and Greene ; and southwest and northwest by Hart and Hardin. The surface is generally undulating, a portion rolling or hilly—the celebrated Muldrow's hill skirting the county on the north. The soil is good in the more level portion—the hills producing fine grasses, and well adapted for sheep culture. Principal products, corn, tobacco and hogs. The Rolling fork of Salt river, and Nolin and Otter creeks, are the principal streams.

Value of taxable property in 1846, $727,344 ; number of acres of land in the county, 123,157 ; average value of land per acre, $3.58 ; number of white males over twenty-one years of age, 872 ; number of children between five and sixteen years old, 1,207.

The towns of the county are—Hodgenville, the county seat, and Levelwood. HODGENVILLE is about ninety miles from Frankfort, and is a pleasant place, of some business—containing a neat court-house with the usual county buildings, and has five lawyers, two physicians, six stores, with a number of mechanics' shops.

About one mile above Hodgenville on the south side of Nolin creek, there is a *knoll* which may be appropriately termed a natural curiosity. It is about thirty feet above the level of the creek, and contains about two acres of ground, the top of which is level, and a comfortable house has been erected upon it. Benjamin Lynn and others, early pioneers of the county, encamped on this knoll. In a hunting excursion, shortly after they made their encampment, Lynn got lost. The remainder of the company returned to camp, and not finding their companion, some one remarked, " Here is the *Nole* (knoll) but *No Lynn*, from which circumstance the creek which runs near the knoll took its name—*Nolin*." They immediately started in search of Lynn, and traveled a south course about fifteen miles, and found where he had encamped on a creek, from which circumstance they called the creek *Lynn-camp* creek. [The creek lies within the present county of Hart.] Philip Phillips erected a fort about one fourth of a mile from the knoll, on the north side of Nolin, about the year 1780 or '81, where the first settlement of the county was made. Phillips was from Pennsylvania, and a surveyor.

JOHN LARUE, for whom the county was named, emigrated with a considerable company, from Virginia, and settled in Phillips' fort. When they left the fort, Larue bought and settled the land which includes the *knoll*. Robert Hodgen, his brother-in-law, bought and settled the land on which Hodgenville has been erected. They were both noted for their uprightness and sterling moral worth— both of them members of the Baptist church, and beloved for their unobtrusive and devoted piety. Benjamin Lynn was a minister of the same church, and also distinguished for his zeal and piety.

On the farm of Mr. John Duncan, about five miles from Hodgenville, on the Big South fork of Nolin, there are several mounds. Two of these have been opened, and found to contain human bones, beads of ivory or bone, and a quantity of sea shells. Near the mounds, there appear to be the remains of a town or fortification, and within the area covered by this relic of antiquity, several curi-

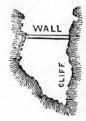

ous articles have been found, among them the image of a bird, cut out of a rock, with several holes drilled through it. On one of the bluffs of the Rolling Fork, where the creek makes a short elbow, is to be seen a stone wall, now three or four feet high. The wall at the elbow extends across the level land, from cliff to cliff, somewhat in the shape of the annexed drawing, and must have constituted, at the time of its construction, an impregnable fortress. The cliff is about two hundred feet high, and so precipitous that an invading army could not possibly scale it, where there was any show of resistance.

LAUREL COUNTY.

LAUREL county was formed in 1825, and derived its name from the river Laurel, which runs partly through the county—and the river is supposed to derive its name from the quantity of laurel growing upon its banks. The face of the country is elevated and generally rolling—the staple products corn and oats.

Value of taxable property in 1846, $333,099; number of acres of land in the county, 184,595; average value of land per acre, $1.10; number of white males over twenty-one years of age, 714; number of children between five and sixteen years old, 1,133. Population in 1840, 3,079.

The towns of the county are London and Hazlepatch. LONDON, the seat of justice, is one hundred and two miles from Frankfort —contains a court-house and jail, post-office, tavern, one physician, two lawyers, a store, and a few mechanics' shops. *Hazlepatch* is a small village, containing a post office and a few houses.

Boone's old trace, which ran through this county, is yet perceivable, passing immediately over the spot where the court-house is built. A quantity of iron ore has been discovered in the county, and some appearances of lead. Swift's old mine is supposed to be in this county. Coal is found in great abundance, and several fine chalybeate springs have been discovered. The water power is unsurpassed. There are the remains of some old Indian towns in the county, among which vessels apparently used for cooking, and other implements, have been found.

LAWRENCE COUNTY.

LAWRENCE county was formed in 1821, and named after Captain JAMES LAWRENCE, of the United States' navy. It is situated in the eastern portion of the State, lying on the waters of Big Sandy river—bounded on the north by Carter, west by Morgan, south by Johnson, and on the east by Big Sandy river, the separating line between Virginia and Kentucky. The surface is hilly and broken, but the soil fertile, producing wheat, corn, oats, rye, and all kinds of vegetables, in abundance. The county is well watered and the timber fine, such as beech, poplar, chesnut, black and white walnut, and oak of various kinds. Steamboats have ascended the Big Sandy as far as Piketon, in Pike county. The soil along the whole valley of the Big Sandy is remarkably rich, while the hills abound in coal and iron ore. The county contains many natural curiosities, a description of which, it is to be regretted, has not been received.

Value of taxable property in 1846, $394,535; number of acres of land in the county, 131,587; average value of land per acre, $1.75; number of white males over twenty-one years of age, 850; number of children between five and sixteen years old, 1,467. Population in 1840, 3,079.

LOUISA, the county seat and only town in Lawrence, is located at the forks of Big Sandy, about one hundred miles from Frankfort. It contains a court-house, church, post-office, four stores, two doctors, two lawyers, and several mechanics' shops. Established in 1822.

RICHARD APPERSON, Esq. of Mount Sterling, has in his possession one of the oldest patents probably now in Kentucky. It was issued by the crown of Great Britain in 1772, to John Fry, for 2084 acres of land, embracing the town of Louisa, in this county. Nearly one-third of the land lies on the Virginia side of Big Sandy river. The survey upon which the patent issued was made by General Washington between 1767 and 1770, inclusive, and upon the beginning corner he cut the initials of his name. Nearly every corner was found well marked. It has not heretofore been generally known that George Washington was ever in Kentucky. Another survey was made by him for John Fry, on Little Sandy river, eleven miles from its mouth, and in the present county of Greenup. The town of Louisa, and the whole of the lands included in the patent, are held under the title of Fry.

In the year 1789, Charles Vancouver settled in the forks of Big Sandy, and employed ten men to build a fort and cultivate some corn. This settlement lasted but a year, as the Indians in a few weeks after Vancouver took possession, stole all the horses, and continued to be troublesome.

JAMES LAWRENCE, (in honor of whom this county received its name,) a distinguished American naval commander, was born in New Jersey in 1781. In 1798, he entered the navy as a midshipman. In 1801 he was promoted, and in 1803, during the Tripoli war, was sent out to the Mediterranean as first lieutenant of the schooner Enterprise. While there, he performed a conspicuous part in the destruction of the Philadelphia frigate, which had been captured by the Tripolitans—and took an active part in the subsequent bombardment of the city of Tripoli. In 1806, he returned to the United States as first lieutenant of the John Adams. In 1812, after war was declared between Great Britain and the United States, Lawrence was appointed to the command of the sloop of war, Hornet. In February 1813, off the Brazil coast, the Hornet fell in with the fine British sloop Peacock, which she captured after a furious action of fifteen minutes. The Peacock was so much cut up in the short action, that she sunk before all the prisoners could be removed. For this gallant action, Lawrence received the thanks of Congress, with the present of a sword; and his return to the United States was welcomed with the applause due to his conduct. Shortly after his return, he was ordered to Boston, to take command of the frigate Chesapeake, confessedly one of the worst ships in the navy. He had been but a short time there, when the British frigate Shannon, Captain Brooke, appeared before the harbor and challenged the Chesapeake to combat. Lawrence did not refuse the challenge, although his ship was not in condition for action. On the 1st of June, 1813, he sailed out of the harbor and engaged his opponent. After the ships had exchanged several broadsides, and Lawrence had been wounded in the leg, he called his boarders, when he received a musket ball in his body. At the same time the enemy boarded, and after a desperate resistance, succeeded in taking possession of the ship. Almost all the officers of the Chesapeake were either killed or wounded. The last exclamation of Lawrence, as they were carrying him below, after the fatal wound, was, "Don't give up the ship." He died on the fourth day after the action, and was buried with naval honors at Halifax.

LETCHER COUNTY.

LETCHER county was formed in 1842, and named after Governor Robert P. Letcher. It is situated in the extreme eastern section of the State, on the head waters of the Kentucky river—bounded north by Floyd; east by Pike and the Virginia line; south by Harlan, and west by Perry. The face of the country is hilly and mountainous—the Cumberland and Black mountains bordering the south-east, while the Pine mountain passes through a portion of the county. The principal articles of export are, cattle, horses, hogs, ginseng and wool.

Value of taxable property in 1846, $126,989; number of acres of land in the county, 52,507; average value of land per acre, $1.71; number of white males over twenty-one years of age, 320; number of children between five and sixteen years old, 590.

WHITESBURG, the county seat, is about one hundred and fifty miles from Frankfort—contains a Methodist and a Baptist church, court house and jail, one school, three stores and groceries, one tavern, one lawyer, one doctor, and three or four mechanics' shops, and about fifty inhabitants. Named after Mr. C. White, a member of the legislature.

ROBERT P. LETCHER, in honor of whom this county was named, is a native of Garrard county. In his youth he received a good education, and studied law. He represented his native county frequently in the legislature of Kentucky, and in 1822 was elected to Congress. He continued a member of Congress from 1823 to 1833. He was always a firm and consistent whig, and the last term he served in Congress, he received the vote of the entire whig party for speaker. Returning to Kentucky, he devoted his attention to the practice of his profession, and was subsequently elected to the legislature, of which body he was long a useful and influential member. In 1838 he was chosen speaker of the house of representatives, in which office he was distinguished for the energy, promptitude and ability with which he discharged its various duties. In 1840 he was selected as the whig candidate for governor, and when the election came on, received the largest majority ever obtained by any candidate for that office. Upon retiring from the gubernatorial chair, Governor Letcher resumed the practice of his profession in Frankfort, where he now resides. As a popular electioneerer, Governor Letcher has no superior in the State. He has a pleasing manner and fine address, tells an anecdote with inimitable grace and humor, and is a general favorite with the people as a stump orator. In his domestic and social relations, he is kind, hospitable, and generous—a man of stern integrity, and uniformly correct in all his business transactions.

ESCULAPIA SPRINGS, KY.

LEWIS COUNTY.

Lewis county was formed in 1806, and named after Captain Meriwether Lewis. It is situated in the north-eastern section of the State, lying upon the Ohio river—bounded north by the Ohio; east by Greenup; south by Fleming, and west by Mason. The surface of the county is generally hilly; but the western portion is fertile and productive, while the vallies of the Ohio river, and Kinnoekonnick and Cabin creeks, are very rich. The products are, corn, wheat, rye and oats. The exports, horses, cattle and hogs, principally.

Value of taxable property in 1846, $967,740; number of acres of land in the county, 191,789; average value of land per acre, $3.70; number of white males over twenty-one years of age, 1,229; number of children between five and sixteen years old, 1,417. Population in 1840, 6,306.

The towns of Lewis, are Clarksburg, Concord, Vanceburg, Middleburg and Poplar Flat. CLARKSBURG, the county seat, is about ninety miles from Frankfort—contains a good brick court-house and public offices, two lawyers, one physician, one tavern, one blacksmith, tan-yard and shoe-shop. Population about fifty,—called for General George Rogers Clark. *Vanceburg* is situated on the Ohio river, twenty miles above Maysville, and three miles from Clarksburg: contains three taverns, three stores, two physicians, and five or six mechanical trades. Population 150. Incorporated in 1827. *Concord* is situated, also, on the Ohio, about 14 miles below Vanceburg—contains four stores, two taverns, two doctors, post office, one school, one free church, and six or eight mechanical trades. Population 125. *Middleburg* and *Poplar Flat* are very small places, with post offices.

Near Vanceburg, in this county, is a large quarry of slate stone; and immediately at the water's edge at a common stage of the river, at the same place, is a quarry of white limestone rock, which produces remarkably white lime, and is said to contain from fifty to sixty per cent. of magnesia. Free white or sand stone is found in great abundance on the Ohio, a few miles above Vanceburg, where there is also a large quarry of alum rock. On Salt Lick creek, near Vanceburg, there is a copperas bed, from which the people of the county supply themselves with that article; and one mile distant, there is an extensive blue clay bank, suitable for stone ware ard fire brick. There are also in the neighborhood, two salt wells, three hundred feet deep, which afford a large quantity of water, from which this part of the state was formerly supplied with salt.

Esculapia or Sulphur Springs.—This celebrated watering place in Lewis county, is situated in a romantic valley, surrounded by tall hills of easy ascent, from which the view is picturesque and enchanting. The improvements have been greatly extended within a few years, and now afford ample accommodations for two hundred visitors. There are two springs, one of white sulphur, the other chalybeate, said to be equal, if not superior, to the waters of a similar kind in Virginia.

This county was named in honor of Captain MERIWETHER LEWIS, the companion of Clark in the celebrated exploring expedition over the Rocky Mountains. He was born near Charlottesville, in Virginia, in 1774. At twenty years of age,

26

he acted as a volunteer, in the suppression of the whisky insurrection, and after-wards received an appointment in the regular service. In 1801, Mr. Jefferson appointed him his private secretary, which situation he held till 1803, when, with William Clark, he started on his exploring expedition to the Rocky Mountains. Mr. Jefferson, in recommending him for this service, gave him a high character for courage, firmness and perseverance, an intimate knowledge of the Indian character, fidelity, intelligence, and all those peculiar combinations of qualities that eminently fitted him for so arduous an undertaking. They were absent three years, and were highly successful in accomplishing the objects contemplated in their tour. Shortly after his return, in 1806, he was appointed governor of the territory of Louisiana. On his arrival at St. Louis, the seat of administration, he found the country torn by dissension; but his moderation, impartiality and firmness soon brought matters into a regular train. He was subject to constitutional hypochon-dria, and while under the influence of a severe attack, shot himself on the bor-ders of Tennessee, in 1809, at the age of 36. The account of the expedition, written by him, was published in 1814.

LINCOLN COUNTY.

LINCOLN county was formed in 1780, and was one of the three original counties organized in the district of Kentucky by the legislature of Virginia. It was named in honor of General BEN-JAMIN LINCOLN, a distingushed officer of the revolutionary army. The original territory of Lincoln, which comprised nearly one-third of the State, has been reduced, by the formation of new counties, to comparatively small dimensions; but it is still a com-pact and well-formed county: Bounded on the north by Boyle and Garrard; east by Garrard and Rockcastle; south by Pulaski; and west by Casey. The exports of the county are, horses, mules, cattle, hogs and wool; while wheat, corn, oats and rye are exten-sively cultivated.

Number of acres of land in Lincoln county, 178,557; average value per acre, $9.26; total valuation of taxable property in 1846, $3,490,144; number of white males over twenty-one years of age, 338; number of children between five and sixteen years old, 1,679. Population in 1830, 11,012—in 1840, 10,187.

The towns of the county are—Stanford, Crab Orchard, Hus-tonville, Waynesburg and Walnut Flat. STANFORD, the county seat, is fifty-one miles from Frankfort—and contains a court-house, one Presbyterian and one Christian church, one academy, seven stores and groceries, three taverns, eight lawyers, four physi-cians and twelve mechanics' shops: population 400. *Crab Or-chard* has one church, one academy, eight stores and groceries, two taverns, two physicians and eight mechanics' shops: popu-lation 350. *Hustonville* contains one church, one school, four stores, one tavern, two physicians and six mechanics' shops: pop-ulation, 200. *Waynesburg* is a small village, with three stores, three mechanics' shops, and one doctor: population 40. *Walnut Flat* has a republican church, one tavern and five mechanics' shops: population 60.

The Knob Licks, in this county, is a locality of some curiosity. What are called *Knobs*, are detached hills of a soft clay slate formation, in some instances the slate having been decomposed and abraded to a considerable depth by the action of the elements, leaving large hollows on the side of the hills, intersected in every direction with ravines, and entirely destitute of vegetation. The greatest height of these knobs is about two hundred feet, and the highest has a base of some one hundred and fifty yards in diameter.

In the year 1775, Col. BENJAMIN LOGAN, a sketch of whose life will be found under the head of "Logan county," arrived at St. Asaph's, about a mile west of the present town of Stanford, and established a fort, called Logan's fort. On the 20th of May, 1777, this fort was invested by a force of a hundred Indians; and, on the morning of that day, as some of the females belonging to it were engaged, outside of the gate, in milking the cows, the men who acted as the guard for the occasion were fired upon by a party of the Indians, who had concealed themselves in a thick canebrake. One man was shot dead, another mortally wounded, and a third so badly, as to be disabled from making his escape; the remainder made good their retreat into the fort, and closed the gate. Harrison, one of the wounded men, by a violent exertion, ran a few paces and fell. His struggles and exclamations attracted the notice, and awakened the sympathies, of the inmates of the station. The frantic grief of his wife gave additional interest to the scene. The enemy forbore to fire upon him, doubtless from the supposition that some of the garrison would attempt to save him, in which event they were prepared to fire upon them from the canebrake. The case was a trying one; and there was a strong conflict between sympathy and duty, on the part of the garrison. The number of effective men had been reduced from fifteen to twelve, and it was exceedingly hazardous to put the lives of any of this small number in jeopardy; yet the lamentations of his family were so distressing, and the scene altogether so moving, as to call forth a resolute determination to save him, if possible. Logan, always alive to the impulses of humanity, and insensible to fear, volunteered his services, and appealed to some of his men to accompany him. But so appalling was the danger, that all, at first, refused. At length, John Martin consented, and rushed, with Logan, from the fort; but he had not gone far, before he shrunk from the imminence of the danger, and sprung back within the gate. Logan paused for a moment, then dashed on, alone and undaunted—reached, unhurt, the spot where Harrison lay—threw him on his shoulders, and, amidst a tremendous shower of rifle balls, made a safe and triumphant retreat into the fort.

The fort was now vigorously assailed by the Indian force, and as vigorously defended by the garrison. The men were constantly at their posts, whilst the women were actively engaged in moulding bullets. But the weakness of the garrison was not their only grievance. The scarcity of powder and ball, one of the greatest inconveniences to which the settlers were not unfrequently exposed, began now to be seriously felt. There were no indications that the siege would be speedily abandoned; and a protracted resistance seemed impracticable, without an additional supply of the munitions of war. The settlements on Holston could furnish a supply—but how was it to be obtained? And, even if men could be found rash and desperate enough to undertake the journey, how improbable was it that the trip could be accomplished in time for the relief to be available. Logan stepped forward, in this extremity, determined to take the dangerous office upon himself. Encouraging his men with the prospect of a safe and speedy return, he left the fort under cover of the night, and, attended by two faithful companions of his own selection, crept cautiously through the Indian lines without discovery. Shunning the ordinary route through Cumberland Gap, he moved, with incredible rapidity, over mountain and valley—arrived at the settlement on the Holston—procured the necessary supply of powder and lead—immediately retraced his steps, and was again in the fort in ten days from the time of his departure. He returned alone. The necessary delay in the transportation of the stores, induced him to entrust them to the charge of his companions; and his presence at St. Asaph's was all-important to the safety of its inhabitants. His return inspired them with fresh courage; and, in a few days, the appearance of Col. Bowman's party compelled the Indians to retire.

In the fall of the year 1779, Samuel Daviess, who resided in Bedford county,

Virginia, moved with his family to Kentucky, and lived for a time at Whitley's station, in Lincoln. He subsequently moved to a place called Gilmer's Lick, some six or seven miles distant from said station, where he built a cabin, cleared some land, which he put in corn next season, not apprehending any danger from the Indians, although he was considered a frontier settler. But this imaginary state of security did not last long; for on a morning in the month of August, in the year 1782, having stepped a few paces from his door, he was suddenly surprised by an Indian's appearing between him and the door, with tomahawk uplifted, almost within striking distance. In this unexpected condition, and being entirely unarmed, his first thought was, that by running around the house, he could enter the door in safety; but, to his surprise, in attempting to effect this object, as he approached the door he found the house full of Indians. Being closely pursued by the Indian first mentioned, he made his way into the corn field, where he concealed himself, with much difficulty, until the pursuing Indian had returned to the house.

Unable as he was to render any relief to his family, (there being five Indians), he ran with the utmost speed to the station of his brother James Daviess—a distance of five miles. As he approached the station—his undressed condition told the tale of his distress, before he was able to tell it himself. Almost breathless, and with a faltering voice, he could only say, his wife and children were in the hands of the Indians. Scarcely was the communication made, when he obtained a spare gun, and the five men in the station, well armed, followed him to his residence. When they arrived at the house, the Indians, as well as the family, were found to be gone, and no evidence appeared that any of the family had been killed. A search was made to find the direction the Indians had taken; but owing to the dryness of the ground, and the adroit manner in which they had departed, no discovery could be made. In this state of perplexity, the party, being all good woodsmen, took that direction in pursuit of the Indians, which they thought it most probable they would take. After going a few miles, their attention was arrested by the howling of a dog, which afterwards turned out to be a house-dog that had followed the family, and which the Indians had undertaken to kill, so as to avoid detection, which might happen from his occasionally barking. In attempting to kill the dog, he was only wounded, which produced the howling that was heard. The noise thus heard satisfied them that they were near the Indians, and enabled them to rush forward with the utmost impetuosity. Two of the Indians being in the rear as spies, discovering the approach of the party, ran forward where the other Indians were with the family—one of them knocked down the oldest boy, about eleven years old, and while in the act of scalping him, was fired at, but without effect. Mrs. Daviess, seeing the agitation and alarm of the Indians, saved herself and sucking child by jumping into a sink hole. The Indians did not stand to make fight, but fled in the most precipitate manner. In that way the family was rescued by nine o'clock in the morning, without the loss of a single life, and without any injury but that above mentioned. So soon as the boy had risen on his feet, the first word he spoke was, " *curse that Indian, he has got my scalp.*"

After the family had been rescued, Mrs. Daviess gave the following account of the manner in which the Indians had acted. A few minutes after her husband had opened the door and stepped out of the house, four Indians rushed in, whilst the fifth, as she afterwards found out, was in pursuit of her husband. Herself and children were in bed when the Indians entered the house. One of the Indians immediately made signs, by which she understood him to enquire how far it was to the next house. With an unusual presence of mind, knowing how important it would be to make the distance as far as possible, she raised both hands, first counting the fingers of one hand then of the other—making a distance of eight miles. The Indian then signed to her that she must rise; she immediately got up, and as soon as she could dress herself, commenced showing the Indians one article of clothing and then another, which pleased them very much: and in that way delayed them at the house nearly two hours. In the mean time, the Indian who had been in pursuit of her husband returned, with his hands stained with poke berries, which he held up, and with some violent gestures and waving of his tomahawk, attempted to induce the belief, that the stain on his hands was the blood of her husband, and that he had killed him. She was enabled at once to discover the deception, and instead of producing any alarm on her part, she was satisfied that her husband had escaped uninjured.

After the savages had plundered the house of every thing that they could conveniently carry off with them, they started, taking Mrs. Daviess and her children—seven in number—as prisoners, along with them. Some of the children were too young to travel as fast as the Indians wished, and discovering, as she believed, their intention to kill such of them as could not conveniently travel, she made the two oldest boys carry them on their backs. The Indians, in starting from the house, were very careful to leave no signs of the direction they had taken, not even permitting the children to break a twig or weed as they passed along. They had not gone far, before an Indian drew his knife and cut off a few inches of Mrs. Daviess' dress, so that she would not be interrupted in traveling.

Mrs. Daviess was a woman of cool deliberate courage, and accustomed to handle the gun, so that she could shoot well, as many of the women were in the habit of doing in those days. She had contemplated, as a last resort, that if not rescued in the course of the day, when night came on and the Indians had fallen asleep, she would deliver herself and children by killing as many of the Indians as she could—thinking that in a night attack as many of them as remained would most probably run off. Such an attempt would now seem a species of madness; but to those who were acquainted with Mrs. Daviess, little doubt was entertained, that if the attempt had been made, it would have proved successful.

The boy who had been scalped was greatly disfigured, as the hair never after grew upon that part of his head. He often wished for an opportunity to avenge himself upon the Indians for the injury he had received. Unfortunately for himself, ten years afterwards, the Indians came to the neighborhood of his father and stole a number of horses. Himself and a party of men went in pursuit of them, and after following them for some days, the Indians finding that they were likely to be overtaken, placed themselves in ambush, and when their pursuers came up, killed young Daviess and one other man; so that he ultimately fell into their hands when about twenty-one years old.

The next year after, the father died; his death being caused, as it was supposed, by the extraordinary efforts he made to release his family from the Indians.

An act of courage subsequently displayed by Mrs. Daviess is calculated to exhibit her character in its true point of view.

Kentucky, in its early days, like most new countries, was occasionally troubled by men of abandoned character, who lived by stealing the property of others, and after committing their depredations, retired to their hiding places, thereby eluding the operation of the law. One of these marauders, a man of desperate character, who had committed extensive thefts from Mr. Daviess as well as from his neighbors, was pursued by Daviess and a party whose property he had taken, in order to bring him to justice. While the party were in pursuit, the suspected individual, not knowing any one was pursuing him, came to the house of Daviess, armed with his gun and tomahawk—no person being at home but Mrs. Daviess and her children. After he had stepped in the house, Mrs. Daviess asked him if he would drink something—and having set a bottle of whisky upon the table, requested him to help himself. The fellow, not suspecting any danger, set his gun up by the door, and while drinking, Mrs. Daviess picked up his gun, and placing herself in the door, had the gun cocked and levelled upon him by the time he turned around, and in a peremptory manner ordered him to take a seat, or she would shoot him. Struck with terror and alarm, he asked what he had done. She told him he had stolen her husband's property, and that she intended to take care of him herself. In that condition, she held him a prisoner, until the party of men returned and took him into their possession.

Sallust says: "The actions of the Athenians doubtless were great, yet I believe they are somewhat less than fame would have us conceive them." Not so with the pioneers of Kentucky. But we may say of their exploits, as this author says of the actions of the Romans: "History has left a thousand of their more brilliant actions unrecorded, which would have done them great honor, but for want of eloquent historians."

In the fall of 1779, William Montgomery the elder, the father-in-law of General Logan, with his family, and son-in-law, Joseph Russell, and his family, moved from Virginia to Kentucky, and took refuge in Logan's fort. Here they remained but a few months, when, apprehending no danger from Indians, the old man, with his sons, William, John, Thomas and Robert, and his son-in-law, Russell, built four log cabins on the head waters of Greene river, about twelve miles in a south-west direction from Logan's fort, to which they removed in the latter part of the winter or early in the spring of 1780. They had, however, been there but a short time, when the savages discovered and attacked the cabins. In one of the cabins lived William Montgomery the elder and wife, and his sons Thomas and Robert, and daughters Jane and Betsey, with two younger children, James and Flora. Mrs. Montgomery with her youngest child, Flora, were then at Logan's fort; and Thomas and Robert were absent spying. William Montgomery, jr., his wife and one child, the late Judge Thomas Montgomery, son of a former wife, and a bound boy, occupied another. John Montgomery, then but lately married, occupied a third; and Joseph Russell, his wife and three children, the fourth. These were all the white persons, but there were, besides, several slaves.

In the month of March, 1780, at night, a small body of Indians surrounded the cabins, which were built close to each other, and rather in a square. On the succeeding morning, between daylight and sunrise, William Montgomery the elder, followed by a negro boy, stepped out at the door of his cabin. They were immediately fired at and both killed by the Indians, the boy's head falling back on the door-sill. Jane, the daughter, then a young woman, afterwards the wife of Col. William Casey, late of Adair county, sprang to the door, pushed out the negro's head, shut the door and called for her brother Thomas' gun. Betsey, her sister, about twelve years of age, clambered out at the chimney, which was not higher than a man's head, and took the path to Pettit's station, distant about two and a half miles. An Indian pursued her for some distance, but being quite active, she was too fleet for him, and reached the station in safety. From Pettit's a messenger was immediately dispatched to Logan's fort.

From some cause or other, probably the call of Jane for her brother's rifle, which was doubtless overheard by the Indians, they did not attempt to break into the cabin. William Montgomery, jr., on hearing the first crack of a gun, sprang to his feet, seized a large trough which had been placed in his cabin to hold sugar-water, placed it against the door, and directing the apprentice boy to hold it, grasped his rifle, and through a crevice over the door, fired twice at the Indians, in rapid succession, before they left the ground, killing one and severely wounding another. John Montgomery was in bed, and in attempting to rise, was fired upon through a crack, and mortally wounded, his door forced open, and his wife made prisoner. Joseph Russell made his escape from his cabin, leaving his wife and three children to the mercy of the savages. They, with a mulatto girl, were also made prisoners.

The Indians commenced an early retreat, bearing off their wounded companion, and taking with them their captives. A few minutes after their departure, and when they were barely out of sight, the Indian who had pursued Betsey Montgomery returned, and being ignorant of what had occurred in his absence, mounted a large beech log in front of the younger William Montgomery's door, and commenced hallooing. Montgomery, who had not yet ventured to open his door, again fired through the crevice, and shot him dead.

As soon as the messenger reached Logan's fort, General Logan, with his horn, sounded the well known note of alarm, when, in a few minutes, as if by magic, a company of some twelve or fifteen men, armed and equipped for battle, were at his side. They instantly commenced their march, passed the cabins where the attack had been made, and took the trail of the Indians. By the aid of some signs which Mrs. Russell had the presence of mind to make, by occasionally breaking a twig and scattering along their route pieces of a white handkerchief which she had torn in fragments, Logan's party found no difficulty in the pursuit. After traveling some distance, they came upon the yellow girl, who had been tomahawked, scalped and left for dead; but who, on hearing the well-known voice of General Logan, sprang to her feet, and afterwards recovered.

The Indians, as was known to be their habit when expecting to be pursued, had a spy in the rear, who was discovered by Logan's party at the same instant he got his eyes upon them, and a rapid march ensued. In a few minutes they came in sight of the savages, when Logan ordered a charge, which was made with a shout, and the Indians fled with great precipitancy, leaving their wounded companion, who was quickly dispatched. A daughter of Mrs. Russell, about twelve years of age, upon hearing Logan's voice, exclaimed in ecstacy, "*there's uncle Ben*," when the savage who had her in charge struck her dead with his tomahawk. The remainder of the prisoners were recaptured without injury. As the force of the Indians was about equal to that of the whites, Gen. Logan, now encumbered with the recaptured women and children, wisely determined to return immediately; and reached the cabins, in safety, before dark on the same day.

The particulars of the foregoing narrative have been received from the Montgomery family—but principally from Mrs. Jane Casey, who was an actor in the drama.

In the spring of the year 1784, three young men—Davis, Caffree and M'Clure —pursued a party of southern Indians, who had stolen horses from Lincoln county; and were resolved, if they could not previously overtake them, to proceed as far as their towns on the Tennessee river, and make reprisals. They had reached, as they supposed, within a few miles of the Indian town called *Chickamongo*, when they fell in with three Indians, traveling in the same direction with themselves. By signs the two parties agreed to travel together; but each was evidently suspicious of the other. The Indians walked upon one side of the road and the whites upon the other, watching each other attentively. At length, the Indians spoke together in tones so low and earnest, that the whites became satisfied of their treacherous intentions, and determined to anticipate them. Caffree being a very powerful man, proposed that he himself should seize one Indian, while Davis and McClure should shoot the other two. He accordingly sprung upon the nearest Indian, grasped his throat firmly, hurled him to the ground, and, drawing a cord from his pocket, attempted to tie him. At the same instant, Davis and McClure leveled their rifles at the others. McClure fired and killed his man, but Davis' gun missed fire. Davis, McClure, and the Indian at whom the former had flashed, immediately took trees, and prepared for a skirmish, while Caffree remained upon the ground with the captured Indian, both exposed to the fire of the others. In a few seconds, the savage at whom Davis had flashed, shot Caffree as he lay upon the ground, and gave him a mortal wound, and was instantly shot in turn by McClure, who had reloaded his gun. Caffree, becoming very weak, called upon Davis to come and assist him in tying the Indian, and instantly afterwards expired. As Davis was running up to the assistance of his friend, the Indian, now released by the death of his captor, sprung to his feet, and seizing Caffree's rifle, presented it menacingly at Davis, whose gun was not in order for service, and who ran off into the forest, closely pursued by the Indian. McClure hastily reloaded his gun, and taking up the rifle which Davis had dropped, followed them for some distance into the forest, making all those signals which had been concerted between them, in case of separation. All, however, was vain; he saw nothing more of Davis, nor could he ever afterwards learn his fate. As he never returned to Kentucky, however, he probably perished.

McClure, finding himself alone in the enemy's country, and surrounded by dead bodies, thought it prudent to abandon the object of the expedition and return to Kentucky. He accordingly retraced his steps, still bearing Davis' rifle in addition to his own. He had scarcely marched a mile, before he saw advancing, from the opposite direction, an Indian warrior, riding a horse with a bell around its neck, and accompanied by a boy on foot. Dropping one of the rifles, which might have created suspicion, McClure advanced with an air of confidence, extending his hand and making other signs of peace. The opposite party appeared frankly to receive his overtures, and dismounting, seated himself upon a log, and drawing out his pipe, gave a few puffs himself, and then handed it to McClure.

In a few minutes another bell was heard, at the distance of half a mile, and a second party of Indians appeared upon horseback. The Indian with McClure now coolly informed him by signs, that when the horsemen arrived, he (McClure) was to be bound and carried off as a prisoner, with his feet tied under the horse's belly. In order to explain it more fully, the Indian got astride of the log, and locked his legs together underneath it. McClure, internally thanking the fellow for his excess of candor, determined to disappoint him, and while his enemy was busily engaged in riding the log and mimicking the actions of a prisoner, he very quietly blew his brains out, and ran off into the woods. The Indian boy instantly mounted the belled horse, and rode off in an opposite direction.

McClure was fiercely pursued by several small Indian dogs, that frequently ran between his legs and threw him down. After falling five or six times, his eyes became full of dust, and he was totally blind. Despairing of escape, he doggedly lay upon his face, expecting every instant to feel the edge of the tomahawk. To his astonishment, however, no enemy appeared; and even the Indian dogs, after tugging at him for a few minutes, and completely stripping him of his breeches, left him to continue his journey unmolested. Finding every thing quiet, in a few moments he arose, and taking up his gun, continued his march to Kentucky. He reached home in safety.

In the year 1784 or 5, near the Crab Orchard, in Lincoln county, a very singular adventure occurred at the house of a Mr. Woods. One morning he left his family, consisting of a wife, a daughter not yet grown, and a lame negro man, and rode off to the station near by, not expecting to return till night. Mrs. Woods being a short distance from her cabin, was alarmed by discovering several Indians advancing towards it. She instantly screamed loudly in order to give the alarm, and ran with her utmost speed, in the hope of reaching the house before them. In this she succeeded, but before she could close the door, the foremost Indian had forced his way into the house. He was instantly seized by the lame negro man, and after a short scuffle, they both fell with violence, the negro underneath. Mrs. Woods was too busily engaged in keeping the door closed against the party without, to attend to the combatants; but the lame negro, holding the Indian tightly in his arms, called to the young girl to take the axe from under the bed and dispatch him by a blow on the head. She immediately attempted it; but the first attempt was a failure. She repeated the blow and killed him. The other Indians were at the door, endeavoring to force it open with their tomahawks. The negro rose and proposed to Mrs. Woods to let in another, and they would soon dispose of the whole of them in the same way. The cabin was but a short distance from the station, the occupants of which having discovered the perilous situation of the family, fired on the Indians and killed another, when the remainder made their escape.

In 1793, a number of families removing to Kentucky, were attacked near the Hazle Patch, on the Cumberland road, by a strong party of Indians. A portion of the men fought bravely, and several of them were killed. The others ran away, and left the women and children to be made captives. The fate of the prisoners is not mentioned by the historian.*

In the year 1780, Captain Joseph Daveiss, (the father of Colonel Joseph H. and Captain Samuel Daveiss,) residing at that time on Clark's run, while breaking up the ground in a field lying near the creek, turned up fourteen conch shells, quite smooth, and of a larger size than any now imported into the country. Seven of these shells were in a perfect state of preservation—the others somewhat decomposed. A portion of them were used, for many years, by the family of Captain Daveiss, for summoning the hands to their meals.

In the month of May, 1781, a hail storm passed over this section of Kentucky, of a remarkable character. The hail, which fell in great quantities, was generally about the size of hen's eggs, but some measured *nine* inches in circumference. The dark cloud, which overhung the heavens, the vivid flashes of lightning, the terrible rattling of hail, and the deafening roar of thunder, produced general consternation. The destruction was complete to the growing crops, while a large portion of the young animals, both domestic and wild, in the route of the storm were destroyed.

In the year 1786, Colonel John Logan, of Lincoln county, received intelligence that one of the inhabitants of the county, by the name of Luttrell, had been killed by the Indians on Fishing creek. He immediately collected a small

---

* Marshall.

VIEW OF SMITHLAND, KY.

militia force, repaired to the place of the outrage, and getting upon the trail, pursued the Indians across the Cumberland river into their own territory. Here he overtook the marauders, and a conflict ensued, in which the Indians were speedily defeated—several of their number being killed and the remainder dispersed. Colonel Logan retook the property which the Indians had carried off from the white settlements, with all the furs and skins belonging to the camp, and returned home in triumph.

General BENJAMIN LINCOLN, in honor of whom this county received its name, was a native of Massachusetts, and an eminent American revolutionary general. In 1776, when he had attained his 42d year, the council of Massachusetts appointed him a brigadier general, and soon after a major-general of militia. The congress subsequently, by the recommendation of General Washington, conferred on him the appointment of major-general of the continental forces. He served as second in command under General Gates, at the capture of Burgoyne's army, where he was severely wounded. In 1778, he was designated by Congress to conduct the war in the southern states. He continued in command of the southern army until the capture of Charleston in 1780, where he was made a prisoner of war. In 1781, having been previously exchanged, he commanded a division at Yorktown, and was honored by General Washington with the office of receiving and directing the distribution of the conquered troops. In October of the same year, he was appointed by Congress secretary of war, which situation he held till 1784, when he retired to his farm. He was afterwards instrumental in suppressing the insurrection of Shays in Massachusetts; and filled several important appointments under the national and state governments. He was also a member of several learned societies. He died in 1810, aged 77 years.

LIVINGSTON COUNTY.

LIVINGSTON county was formed in 1798, and named for the Hon. Robert R. Livingston, of New York. It is situated in the extreme western part of the State, lying on the Cumberland, Tennessee and Ohio rivers—bounded on the north by Crittenden and the Ohio river; on the east by Crittenden and Caldwell; on the south by Marshall, and on the west by the Ohio river. SALEM, the seat of justice; Smithland, the chief town—the former about two hundred miles from Frankfort. The general appearance of the county is undulating, but hilly and broken in places, interspersed with sandstone and limestone, and mostly well timbered—river bottoms remarkably rich. Staple products, Indian corn, tobacco, Irish potatoes and oats. Exports, horses, cattle, sheep and hogs.

This county abounds in iron-ore, of excellent quality; and veins of bituminous coal have been found, but not worked to any extent. Possessing very superior advantages, from the border and central navigation—the Ohio river bounding it about forty miles on the north-west, the Tennessee about twenty-seven miles on the south-west, and the Cumberland passing through it—the facilities for the export of its raw materials, manufactures, stock and agricultural products, are equal to any county in the State.

Number of acres of land in Livingston, 146,996; average value per acre, $2.97; valuation of taxable property in 1846, $1,052,-409; number of white males over twenty-one years of age, 873;

number of children between five and sixteen years old, 947. Population in 1840, 9,025.

Smithland is situated on the Ohio river, at the mouth of the Cumberland,—contains a population of about 1000; with two churches, Episcopal and Methodist; two schools; fourteen stores, besides several small groceries; four taverns, eight lawyers, seven physicians; the most extensive tannery in the west; one foundry, finishing and steam engine shop, and thirty mechanics' shops. *Salem* has a population of about one hundred—with two stores, one tavern, one school and two physicians.

ROBERT R. LIVINGSTON, a distinguished American statesman, was born in the city of New York in 1746. He studied and practiced law with great success. He was a member of the first general Congress; was one of the committee which prepared the declaration of independence; in 1780 was appointed secretary of foreign affairs, and throughout the revolution signalized himself by his zeal and efficiency in the cause. He was for many years chancellor of his native state, and in 1801, was appointed by president Jefferson minister to France. He was a general favorite at the French capital, and in conjunction with Mr. Monroe conducted the treaty which resulted in the cession of Louisiana to the United States. After his return from Europe, he devoted his life chiefly to the cause of agricultural and general science—was president of the New York society for the promotion of the fine arts, and also of the society for the promotion of agriculture. He died in 1813, with the reputation of an able statesman, a learned lawyer, and a most useful citizen.

LOGAN COUNTY.

LOGAN county was formed in 1792, and named in honor of Gen. BENJAMIN LOGAN, a distinguished pioneer. It is situated in the southern section of the State—bounded on the north by Muhlenburg and Butler; east by Warren and Simpson; west by Todd, and south by the Tennessee line. RUSSELLVILLE is the county seat, one hundred and eighty miles from Frankfort. Red river passes through the southern part of the county, nearly parallel with the state line, and the whole is finely watered with large mill streams, over which have been erected about twenty substantial bridges. The surface is beautifully diversified by ranges of hills, covered with timber, with an occasional Indian mound to arouse the imagination to scenes of former ages. There are several mineral springs in the county, some of which have become places of considerable resort. Wheat, oats, corn and tobacco are the staple products.

Number of acres of land in Logan county, 306,129; average value of land per acre, $5.49; total valuation of taxable property in 1846, $4,479,903; number of white males over twenty-one years of age, 2 050; number of children between five and sixteen years old, 2,588. Population in 1840, 13,615.

RUSSELLVILLE is situated near the centre of the county, on the head waters of Muddy river, and on the state road from Louisville to Nashville. It contains a good court-house, one Baptist, one Methodist Episcopal, and one Union church; one academy and three schools, eight lawyers, ten physicians, seventeen dry goods stores, three groceries, three taverns, two drug-stores, one iron store, one oil mill, one wool carding establishment, one printing office (the "Russellville Herald"), and about fifty mechanics' shops. Population 1200. Established in 1810, and named for General WILLIAM RUSSELL, a distinguished officer of the revolutionary army, and owner of the land. *Adairville* is a handsome village, thirteen miles south of Russellville, and contains one school, three physicians, four stores, two groceries, one tavern, and twelve mechanical shops. Established in 1812, and named in honor of General John Adair. *Keasburg* is a small village about sixteen miles south-west from Russellville, containing one Union church, three doctors, two schools, four stores, two taverns and nine or ten mechanics' shops,—named after the proprietor, John Keas. *South Union* is a small Shaker village, quite neat and attractive, about fifteen miles from Russellville.

The only historical incident we have from Logan county, is contained in the following short paragraph from Marshall's History, volume 2, page 81: "In January, 1793, the Indians stole horses in Logan county; were pursued, and one of them killed, after he wounded one of the pursuers."

General BENJAMIN LOGAN, from whom Logan county received its name, was among the earliest and most distinguished of those bold pioneers who, penetrating the western wilds, laid the foundation of arts, civilization, religion and law, in what was then the howling wilderness of Kentucky. It is among the proudest of those distinctions which have exalted the character of our venerable commonwealth, that she numbers among her founders, men beneath whose rough and home spun hunting shirts resided qualities of heroism which would have made them prominent in Greece and Rome. As the eye wanders along the serried ranks of those stern and iron men, who stand so firm and fearless amid the gloom of the overhanging forest, it is arrested by a commanding form which towers conspicuous among them all—tall, athletic, dignified—a face cast in the finest mould of manly beauty, dark, grave and contemplative, and which, while it evinces unyielding fortitude and impenetrable reserve, invites to a confidence which never betrays. Such was Benjamin Logan.

His parents were Irish. When young, they removed to Pennsylvania, and there intermarried. Shortly afterwards they removed to Augusta county, in the then colony of Virginia, where Benjamin Logan was born. At the age of fourteen he lost his father, and found himself prematurely at the head of a large family. Neither the circumstances of the country, then newly settled, nor the pecuniary resources of his father, had been favorable to the education of the son; nor is it to be supposed that the widowed mother had it more in her power, whatever her inclination might have been, to bestow upon him a literary education. His mind was not only unadorned by science, but almost unaided by letters; and in his progress through life, he rather studied men than books.

His father died intestate, and as a consequence of the laws then in force, the lands descended to him by right of primogeniture, to the exclusion of his brothers and sisters. He did not, however, avail himself of this advantage, but with his mother's consent, sold the land not susceptible of a division, and distributed the proceeds among those whom the law had disinherited. To provide for his mother a comfortable residence, he united his funds to those of one of his brothers, and with the joint stock purchased another tract of land on a fork of James river, which was secured to the parent during her life, if so long she chose to reside on it, with the remainder to his brother in fee. Having seen his mother and family comfortably settled, he next determined to provide a home for himself.

He accordingly removed to the Holston river, purchased lands, married, and commenced farming.

At an early age he had evinced a decided predilection for military life, and when only twenty-one had accompanied Colonel Beauquette in his expedition against the Indians of the north, in the capacity of sergeant. In 1774 he was with Dunmore in his expedition to the north-west of Ohio.

In 1775 he determined to come to Kentucky, and accompanied by only two or three slaves, set out to see the lands and make a settlement. In Powell's valley he met with Boone, Henderson and others, also on their way to Kentucky. With them he traveled through the wilderness; but not approving of their plan of settlement, he separated from them on their arrival in Kentucky, and turning his course westwardly, after a few days' journey, pitched his camp in the present county of Lincoln, where he afterwards built his fort. Here, during the same year, he and William Galaspy raised a small crop of Indian corn. In the latter end of June he returned to Holston to his family. In the fall of the year he removed his cattle and the residue of his slaves to the camp; and leaving them in the care of Galaspy, returned to his home alone, with the intention of removing his family. These journeys, attended with considerable peril and privation, evince the hardihood and energy of his mind, as well as his bodily vigor and activity. He removed his family to Kentucky in 1776.

The year 1776 is memorable in the early history of Kentucky as one of peculiar peril. The woods literally swarmed with the Indians, who seemed excited to desperation by the formation of settlements in their old hunting grounds, and abandoned themselves to the commission of every species of outrage. Savage ingenuity seemed stimulated to the utmost to devise new modes of annoyance to the settlers, and Mr. Logan judged it prudent to place his wife and family behind the more secure defences of Harrodsburgh, where they would be less exposed to danger than in his own remote and comparatively undefended station. He himself remained with his slaves, and attended to the cultivation of his farm. The year passed without his being engaged in any adventure of consequence.

In the spring of the year 1777 Mrs. Logan returned to her husband, and having been reinforced by the arrival of several white men, he determined to remain and maintain himself at all hazards. His resolution was soon put to the test. On the 20th of May, 1777, one hundred Indians appeared before the fort, and having fired on the garrison, then engaged in the fields, commenced a regular siege. This, in the end, proved to be one of the most determined and well sustained investments ever executed by Indian hostility and enterprise. The garrison were in continual danger for several weeks, and many incidents occurred which even at this distance of time, makes the blood curdle. Never did the high and manly qualities of courage, sagacity and fortitude, for which Mr. Logan was so eminently distinguished, display themselves more gloriously than during those terrible days, when his little garrison was beset for weeks by those howling devils of the forest. A full account of this siege will be found under the head of Lincoln county, to which the reader is referred for particulars.

During this same year, (1777), while on one of his excursions, in search of Indian signs, he discovered a camp of Indians, at the Big Flat lick, about two miles from his station. He immediately returned, and raising a party of men, attacked them with great resolution. The Indians fled, without much loss on their part and none on his. He was again at the same lick,—it being the resort of game as well as of Indians,—when he received a fire from a concealed party of Indians, which broke his right arm and wounded him slightly in the breast. The savages then rushed upon him, and so near was he falling in their hands, that they at one time had hold of his horse's tail. No sooner had his wounds healed, than he resumed his active course of life—shunning no danger, when to incur it was for the benefit of his country or his friends.

In the year 1779, an expedition was set on foot against the Indian town of Chillicothe. In this expedition, Logan served as second in command; Col. Bowman commanded in chief. The detachment amounted to one hundred and sixty men; consisted entirely of volunteers, accustomed to Indian warfare; and was well officered, with the exception of its commander. The following account of the expedition, is from the graphic pen of Mr. McClung—(see his interesting Sketches of Western Adventure, page 113):

"They left Harrodsburg in July, and took their preliminary measures so well, that they arrived within a mile of Chillicothe, without giving the slightest alarm to the enemy. Here the detachment halted at an early hour in the night, and, as usual, sent out spies to examine the condition of the village. Before midnight they returned, and reported that the enemy remained unapprised of their being in the neighborhood, and were in the most unmilitary security. The army was instantly put in motion. It was determined that Logan, with one half of the men, should turn to the left and march half way around the town, while Bowman, at the head of the remainder, should make a corresponding march to the right; that both parties should proceed in silence, until they had met at the opposite extremity of the village, when, having thus completely encircled it, the attack was to commence.

"Logan, who was bravery itself, performed his part of the combined operation, with perfect order, and in profound silence; and having reached the designated spot, awaited with impatience the arrival of his commander. Hour after hour stole away, but Bowman did not appear. At length daylight appeared. Logan, still expecting the arrival of his colonel, ordered the men to conceal themselves in the high grass, and await the expected signal to attack. No orders, however, arrived. In the mean time, the men, in shifting about through the grass, alarmed an Indian dog, the only sentinel on duty. He instantly began to bay loudly, and advanced in the direction of the man who had attracted his attention. Presently a solitary Indian left his cabin, and walked cautiously towards the party, halting frequently, rising upon tiptoes, and gazing around him.

"Logan's party lay close, with the hope of taking him without giving the alarm; but at that instant a gun was fired in an opposite quarter of the town, as was afterwards ascertained, by one of Bowman's party, and the Indian, giving one shrill whoop, ran swiftly back to the council house. Concealment was now impossible. Logan's party instantly sprung up from the grass, and rushed upon the village, not doubting for a moment that they would be gallantly supported. As they advanced, they perceived Indians of all ages and of both sexes running to the great cabin, near the centre of the town, where they collected in full force, and appeared determined upon an obstinate defence. Logan instantly took possession of the houses which had been deserted, and rapidly advancing from cabin to cabin, at length established his detachment within close rifle shot of the Indian redoubt.

"He now listened impatiently for the firing which should have been heard from the opposite extremity of the town, where he supposed Bowman's party to be, but, to his astonishment, every thing remained quiet in that quarter. In the mean time, his own position had become critical. The Indians had recovered from their panic, and kept up a close and heavy fire upon the cabins which covered his men. He had pushed his detachment so close to the redoubt, that they could neither advance nor retreat without great exposure. The enemy outnumbered him, and gave indications of a disposition to turn both flanks of his position, and thus endanger his retreat.

"Under these circumstances, ignorant of the condition of his commander, and cut off from communication with him, he formed the bold and judicious resolution, to make a moveable breastwork of the planks which formed the floor of the cabins, and, under cover of it, to rush upon the stronghold of the enemy and carry it by main force. Had this gallant determination been carried into effect, and had the movement been promptly seconded, as it ought to have been, by Bowman, the conflict would have been bloody, and the victory decisive. Most probably not an Indian would have escaped, and the consternation which such signal vengeance would have spread throughout the Indian tribes, might have repressed their incursions for a considerable time. But before the necessary steps could be taken, a messenger arrived from Bowman, with orders 'to retreat!'

"Astonished at such an order, at a time when honor and safety required an offensive movement on their part, Logan hastily asked if Bowman had been overpowered by the enemy? No! Had he ever beheld an enemy? No! What, then, was the cause of this extraordinary abandonment of a design so prosperously begun? He did not know: the colonel had ordered a retreat! Logan, however reluctantly, was compelled to obey. A retreat is always a dispiriting movement, and with militia, is almost certain to terminate in a complete rout. As soon as the men were informed of the order, a most irregular and tumultuous scene commenced. Not being buoyed up by the mutual confidence which is the offspring of discipline, and which sustains regular soldiers under all circumstances, they no longer acted in concert.

" Each man selected the time, manner, and route of his retreat for himself. Here a solitary Kentuckian would start up from behind a stump, and scud away through the grass, dodging and turning to avoid the balls which whistled around him. There a dozen men would run from a cabin, and scatter in every direction, each anxious to save himself, and none having leisure to attend to their neighbors. The Indians, astonished at seeing men rout themselves in this manner, sallied out of their redoubts and pursued the stragglers, as sportsmen would cut up a flock of wild geese. They soon united themselves to Bowman's party, who, from some unaccountable panic of their commander, or fault in themselves, had stood stock still near the spot where Logan had left them the night before.

" All was confusion. Some cursed their colonel; some reproached other officers: one shouted one thing; one bellowed another; but all seemed to agree that they ought to make the best of their way home, without the loss of a moment's time. By great exertions on the part of Logan, well seconded by Harrod, Bulger, and the present Major Bedinger, of the Blue Licks, some degree of order was restored, and a tolerably respectable retreat commenced. The Indians, however, soon surrounded them on all sides, and kept up a hot fire, which began to grow fatal. Colonel Bowman appeared totally demented, and sat upon his horse like a pillar of stone, neither giving an order, nor taking any measures to repel the enemy. The sound of the rifle shots had, however, completely restored the men to their senses, and they readily formed in a large hollow square, took trees, and returned the fire with equal vivacity. The enemy were quickly repelled, and the troops recommenced their march.

" But scarcely had they advanced half a mile, when the Indians re-appeared, and again opened a fire upon the front, rear, and both flanks. Again, a square was formed and the enemy repelled; but scarcely had the harassed troops recommenced their march, when the same galling fire was opened upon them from every tree, bush and stone, capable of concealing an Indian. Matters now began to look serious. The enemy were evidently endeavoring to detain them, until fresh Indians could come up in sufficient force to compel them to lay down their arms. The men began to be unsteady, and the panic was rapidly spreading from the colonel to the privates. At this crisis, Logan, Harrod, Bedinger, &c., selected the boldest, and best mounted men, and dashing into the bushes on horseback, scoured the woods in every direction, forcing the Indians from their coverts, and cutting down as many as they could overtake.

" This decisive step completely dispersed the enemy, and the weary and dispirited troops continued their retreat unmolested. They lost nine killed and a few others wounded."

No other affair of importance occurred, until the rash and disastrous battle of the Blue Licks, in which Logan was unable to participate, although in full march for that place at the head of a well appointed force when he received intelligence of the defeat of his countrymen. He immediately retraced his steps to Bryant's station, where he remained until the following day, when he proceeded to the battle ground for the purpose of burying the dead. Having performed this duty, he disbanded his men and returned home.

He remained quietly engaged in agricultural pursuits until the summer of 1788, when he conducted an expedition against the north-western tribes, which as usual terminated in burning their villages and cutting up their corn, serving to irritate but not to subdue the enemy.

From this time until the period of his death, General Logan devoted himself to the cultivation of his farm, and engaged actively in the civil and political contests which had begun to occupy a large share of public attention. He was a member of the convention of 1792, which formed the first constitution of Kentucky, and when in 1799, a convention was called for the purpose of remodeling that instrument, he was a delegate from the county of Shelby, and assisted in the formation of the present constitution. He was repeatedly a member of the State legislature, and it is scarcely necessary to add, stood high in the esteem and confidence of his legislative compeers. After having discharged faithfully and with ability all the duties of the man, the soldier, the patriot, and statesman, he died at an advanced age, full of years and full of honors, beloved and mourned by all who knew him.   General Logan was the father of the Honorable William Logan, twice a judge of the court of appeals.

Closely connected with the history of General Benjamin Logan is that of a young Indian, distinguished for his high qualities of bravery, generosity, and all those rude virtues which at times impart such nobility to the character of the American aborigines.   He was taken prisoner by General Logan in 1786, when a youth.   On parting with him to send him back to his people, the general had given him his name, which he retained to the end of his life.   Before the treaty of Greenville he had distinguished himself as a warrior, though still very young.   His mother was a sister to the celebrated Tecumseh and the Prophet.   His death occurred under very tragical circumstances—for an account of which we are indebted to M'Afee's history of the late war.

Shortly after General Tupper's expedition to the Miami Rapids in 1812, Logan was sent by General Harrison with a small party of his tribe to reconnoitre in the direction of the Rapids.   He met with a superior force of the enemy near that place, by which he was so closely pursued that his men were obliged to disperse for safety in their retreat.   Logan and two of his companions, Captain John and Bright Horn, arrived safe at General Winchester's camp, where he faithfully reported the incidents of the excursion.   But there were certain persons in the army who suspected his fidelity, and reproached him with being friendly to and with communicating intelligence to the enemy.   The noble spirit of Logan could not endure the ungenerous charge.   With the sensibility of a genuine soldier, he felt that his honor should be not only pure and firm, but unsuspected.   He did not, however, demand a court of enquiry—following the natural dictate of a bold and generous spirit, he determined to prove by unequivocal deeds of valor and fidelity, that he was calumniated by his accusers.

On the 22d of November, he set out the second time, accompanied by only the two persons before named, determined either to bring in a prisoner or a scalp, or to perish himself in the attempt.   When he had gone about ten miles down the north side of the Miami, he met with a British officer, the eldest son of Colonel Elliott, accompanied by five Indians.   As the party was too strong for him, and he had no chance to escape, four of them being mounted, he determined to pass them under the disguise of friendship for the British.   He advanced with confident boldness and friendly deportment to the enemy—but unfortunately one of them was Winnemac, a celebrated Potawatamie chief, to whom the person and character of Captain Logan were perfectly well known.   He persisted however in his first determination, and told them he was going to the Rapids to give information to the British.   After conversing some time he proceeded on his way, and Winnemac, with all his companions, turned and went with him.   As they traveled on together, Winnemac and his party closely watched the others, and when they had proceeded about eight miles, he proposed to the British officer to seize and tie them.   The officer replied that they were completely in his power; that if they attempted to run, they could be shot; or failing in that, the horses could easily run them down.   The consultation was overheard by Logan; he had previously intended to go on peaceably until night, and then make his escape; but he now formed the bold design of extricating himself by a combat with double his number.

Having signified his resolution to his men, he commenced the attack by shooting down Winnemac himself.   The action lasted till they had fired three rounds apiece, during which time Logan and his brave companions drove the enemy some distance, and separated them from their horses.   By the first fire Winnemac and Elliott fell; by the second a young Ottawa chief lost his life; and another of the enemy was mortally wounded about the conclusion of the combat, at which time Logan himself, as he was stooping down, received a ball just below the breast bone; it ranged downwards, and lodged under the skin on his back.   In the mean time Bright Horn was also wounded by a ball which passed through his thigh.   As soon as Logan was shot he ordered a retreat; himself and Bright Horn, wounded as they were, jumped on the horses of the enemy and rode to Winchester's camp, a distance of twenty miles, in five hours.   Captain John, after taking the scalp of the Ottowa chief, also retreated in safety, and arrived at the camp the next morning. After lingering with his wounds, Logan expired at Winchester's camp on the third day after his arrival. He was buried with all the honors due to his rank.

~~~~~~~~~~~~~~~~~~~~~~~~~~~~~~

MADISON COUNTY.

MADISON county was formed in 1785, and named in honor of JAMES MADISON, president of the United States. It is situated in the middle portion of the State, and lies on the waters of Kentucky river, which skirts it on the north and west—bounded on the north by Fayette and Clark, east by Estill, south by Laurel and Rockcastle, and west by Rockcastle, Garrard and Jessamine. Madison is one of the largest counties in the State, with a diversified surface—the greater portion being gently undulating, with a rich and productive soil—while other portions are level and hilly, and not so productive. The principal streams are Downing, Muddy, Silver, Tate, and Otter creeks, all named by Daniel Boone, and flowing into the Kentucky river. The exports of the county consist of horses, mules, cattle, and hogs, the latter being raised in vast quantities. Indian corn and tobacco are extensively cultivated, but the hemp and wheat crops are limited to domestic consumption.

Number of acres of land in Madison county, 277,608; average value per acre in 1846, $12; total valuation of taxable property in 1846, $6,935,495; number of white males over twenty-one years of age, 2,594; number of children between five and sixteen years of age, 2,943. Population in 1840, 16,385.

The towns of Madison are Richmond and Boonsborough. RICHMOND, the county seat, lies fifty miles from Frankfort. It is a handsome town, with a thriving and intelligent population of some 1,000 or 1,200 souls, and surrounded by a beautiful country and a rich and enlightened community—contains a court-house, four churches, (Baptist, Presbyterian, Methodist and Christian), twelve lawyers, eleven doctors, two female schools, one academy, a public library, fourteen dry goods stores, six grocery stores, two taverns, two newspapers, (the Richmond Chronicle and Review), a branch of the bank of Kentucky, one rope factory, and about forty mechanics' shops. This place was first settled by John Miller in 1785, but was not incorporated until 1809.

Boonsborough is a small and dilapidated village, situated on the western bank of the Kentucky river. There is nothing in its *appearance* calculated to impress the beholder; but the *name* and the *locality* have become *classical*. It was here that Daniel Boone, the great pioneer, built the first fort ever erected in Kentucky, and made the commencement of a permanent settlement; and it was here there was convened, more than seventy years ago, the

OLD FORT AT BOONSBOROUGH, 1775.

27

first legislative assembly of the great valley of the west.* This fort was built in 1775, having been commenced on the 1st of April, and completed on the 14th of June. An engraving of the fort, from a drawing of Colonel Henderson, is here given.

It was situated adjacent to the river, with one of the angles resting on its bank near the water, and extending from it in the form of a parallelogram. The length of the fort, allowing twenty feet for each cabin and opening, must have been about two hundred and sixty, and the breadth one hundred and fifty feet.† In a few days after the work was commenced, one of the men was killed by the Indians.

There are several mineral springs and mounds in Madison, but none of sufficient interest to require particular notice in this work. There is a black sulphur spring, highly impregnated with salt, at Boonsborough. This was a great resort of buffalo, deer and other animals, when Kentucky was first explored, and no doubt Boone was induced, from this fact, to select that place for the location of his fort. One of the mounds has been partially explored, but no relics discovered. A large fire must have been burned near the base before the mound was reared, as the coals are so well preserved as to show clearly the wood from which they were burned.

In the summer of 1775, after the completion of the fort at Boonsborough, Daniel Boone returned to Clinch river for his family. He brought them to the new fort as soon as the journey could be performed, and Mrs. Boone and her daughters were the first white women who ever stood upon the banks of the Kentucky river.‡ They were soon reinforced by the arrival of three more families, at the head of which were Mrs. McGary, Mrs. Hogan and Mrs. Denton.

Boonsborough soon became the central object of Indian hostilities. On the 24th of December, 1775, the garrison was suddenly attacked by a party of Indians, and one of the number killed.

On the 7th of July, 1776, a much more alarming incident occurred. A daughter of Daniel Boone, in company with Miss Betsey and Miss Frances Calloway, the first and last named about thirteen years of age, the other grown, while amusing themselves in a canoe, were captured by a party of Indians, in sight of the fort. The screams of the terrified girls quickly alarmed the families in the garrison; but as it was near night fall, and the canoe on the opposite side of the river, pursuit was not commenced in time to follow more than five miles during the night. By day-light next morning, a party consisting of Daniel Boone, Col. Floyd and six others, got upon their track, and continued the pursuit. The exceeding caution of the Indians, rendered it difficult for the pursuing party to keep on their trail ; but, notwithstanding, they pressed forward in the direction they supposed the Indians would take, with almost incredible rapidity. Having trav-

---

* See biographical sketch of Colonel Henderson.

† A fort in these rude military times, consisted of pieces of timber sharpened at the end and firmly lodged in the ground: rows of these pickets enclosed the desired space, which embraced the cabins of the inhabitants. A block-house or more, of superior care and strength, commanding the sides of the fort, with or without a ditch, completed the fortifications, or stations, as they were called. Generally the sides of the interior cabins formed the sides of the fort. Slight as this advance was in the art of war, it was more than sufficient against attacks of small arms, in the hands of such desultory warriors, as their irregular supply of provisions necessarily rendered the Indians. Such was the nature of the military structures of the pioneers against their enemies. They were ever more formidable in the cane-brakes and in the woods, than before even these imperfect fortifications.—*Butler's History, page* 28.

‡ See sketch of Daniel Boone.

eled about thirty-five miles, they struck a buffalo trace, where they found the tracks quite plain. The pursuit was urged on with great keenness, and at the further distance of ten miles, they came in sight of the savages, just as they were kindling a fire to cook. Both parties saw each other at the same instant. Four of the whites fired, and then charged so suddenly and furiously upon the Indians, that they were compelled to retreat with a single shot gun without ammunition, and without time to tomahawk their captives. The girls sustained no other injury than excessive fright and fatigue. Two of the Indians were killed. The party were so much elated with the recovery of the frightened and jaded little girls, that they did not pursue the Indians, but immediately retraced their steps, and safely arrived at Boonsborough on the succeeding day.

The infant settlement at Boonsborough continued to be incessantly harassed by flying parties of Indians; and on the 15th of April, 1777, a simultaneous attack was made on Boonsborough, Harrodsburg and Logan's fort, by a large body of the enemy. But being destitute of artillery and scaling ladders, they could produce no decided impression on the fort. Some loss was sustained by Boonsborough in men, and the corn and cattle of the settlers were partially destroyed, but the Indians suffered so severely as to retire with precipitation.

On the 4th of July, following, Boonsborough was again attacked by about two hundred warriors. The onset was furious, but unsuccessful. The garrison, less than half the number of the assailants, made a vigorous defence, repulsing the enemy with the loss of seven warriors known to have been killed, and a number wounded. The whites had one man killed and two wounded. The siege lasted two days and nights, when the Indians made a rapid and tumultuous retreat.

Some time in June, 1777, Major Smith with a party of seventeen men, followed a small body of Indians from Boonsborough to the Ohio river, where they arrived in time to kill one of the number, the remainder having crossed over. As they returned, about twenty miles from the Ohio, they discovered another party of about thirty Indians, lying in the grass, but were themselves unobserved. They immediately dismounted, tied their horses and left nine men to take care of them. Smith, with the remaining eight men of his party, crept forward until they came near the Indians. At this moment, one of the Indians passed partly by Smith, in the direction of the horses. He was shot by one of the whites. He gave a loud yell, and his friends supposing he had killed some wild animal, burst out in a noisy fit of laughter. At that instant Smith and his party fired on the savages and rushed upon them. The fire was returned, but the Indians speedily gave way and fled. Smith had one man (John Martin) wounded.*

On the 9th of September, 1778, a third attack was made upon Boonsborough. The enemy appeared in great force—the Indians, numbering at least five hundred warriors, armed and painted in their usual manner, were conducted by Canadian officers, well skilled in the usages of modern warfare. As soon as they were arrayed in front of the fort, the British colors were displayed, and an officer, with a flag, was sent to demand the surrender of the fort, with a promise of quarter and good treatment in case of compliance, and threatening "the hatchet," in case of a storm. Boone requested two days for consideration, which in defiance of all experience and common sense, was granted. This interval, as usual, was employed in preparation for an obstinate resistance. The cattle were brought into the fort, the horses secured, and all things made ready against the commencement of hostilities.

Boone then assembled the garrison, and represented to them the condition in which they stood. They had not now to deal with Indians alone, but with British officers, skilled in the art of attacking fortified places, sufficiently numerous to *direct*, but too few to *restrain* their savage allies. If they surrendered, their lives might and probably would be saved; but they would suffer much inconvenience, and *must* lose all their property. If they resisted and were overcome, the life of every man, woman and child would be sacrificed. The hour was now come in which they were to determine what was to be done. If they were inclined to surrender, he would announce it to the officer; if they were resolved to maintain the fort, he would share their fate, whether in life or death. He had scarcely finished, when every man arose and in a firm tone announced his determination to defend the fort to the last.

* Notes on Kentucky.

Boone then appeared at the gate of the fortress and communicated to Captain Duquesne the resolution of his men. Disappointment and chagrin were strongly painted upon the face of the Canadian at this answer; but endeavoring to disguise his feelings, he declared that Governor Hamilton had ordered him not to injure the men if it could be avoided, and that if nine of the principal inhabitants of the fort would come out into the plain and treat with them, they would instantly depart without farther hostility. The insidious nature of this proposal was evident, for they could converse very well from where they then stood, and going out would only place the officers of the fort at the mercy of the savages, not to mention the absurdity of supposing that this army of warriors would " *treat*," but upon such terms as pleased them, and no terms were likely do so short of a total abandonment of the country.

Notwithstanding these obvious objections, the word " treat," sounded so pleasantly in the ears of the besieged, that they agreed at once to the proposal, and Boone himself, attended by eight of his men, went out and mingled with the savages, who crowded around them in great numbers, and with countenances of deep anxiety. The treaty then commenced and was soon concluded. What the terms were, we are not informed, nor is it a matter of the least importance, as the whole was a stupid and shallow artifice. This was soon made manifest. Duquesne, after many, very many pretty periods about the " *bienfaisance et humanité*" which should accompany the warfare of civilized beings, at length informed Boone, that it was a custom with the Indians, upon the conclusion of a treaty with the whites, for two warriors to take hold of the hand of each white man.

Boone thought this rather a singular custom, but there was no time to dispute about etiquette, particularly, as he could not be more in their power than he already was; so he signified his willingness to conform to the Indian mode of cementing friendship. Instantly, two warriors approached each white man, with the word " brother " upon their lips, but a very different expression in their eyes, and grappling him with violence, attempted to bear him off. They probably (unless totally infatuated) expected such a consummation, and all at the same moment sprung from their enemies and ran to the fort, under a heavy fire, which fortunately only wounded one man.

The attack instantly commenced by a heavy fire against the picketing, and was returned with fatal accuracy by the garrison. The Indians quickly sheltered themselves, and the action became more cautious and deliberate. Finding but little effect from the fire of his men, Duquesne next resorted to a more formidable mode of attack. The fort stood on the south bank of the river, within sixty yards of the water. Commencing under the bank, where their operations were concealed from the garrison, they attempted to push a mine into the fort. Their object, however, was fortunately discovered by the quantity of fresh earth which they were compelled to throw into the river, and by which the water became muddy for some distance below. Boone, who had regained his usual sagacity, instantly cut a trench within the fort in such a manner as to intersect the line of their approach, and thus frustrated their design.

The enemy exhausted all the ordinary artifices of Indian warfare, but were steadily repulsed in every effort. Finding their numbers daily thinned by the deliberate but fatal fire of the garrison, and seeing no prospect of final success, they broke up on the ninth day of the siege and returned home. The loss of the garrison was two men killed and four wounded. On the part of the savages, thirty-seven were killed and many wounded, who, as usual, were all carried off. This was the last siege sustained by Boonsborough. The country had increased so rapidly in numbers, and so many other stations lay between Boonsborough and the Ohio, that the savages could not reach it without leaving enemies in the rear.*

Besides Boonsborough, there were several other forts or stations in Madison —among them, Hoy's, Irvine's, Estill's and Hart's, or White Oak stations. The latter station was situated about a mile above Boonsborough, in the same bottom of the river, and was settled in 1779. The settlers were composed principally of families from Pennsylvania—orderly, respectable people, and the men good soldiers. But they were unaccustomed to Indian warfare, and the conse-

---

* McClung's sketches of Western Adventure.

quence was, that, of some ten or twelve men, all were killed but two or three.[*] During the fall or winter of 1781–2, Peter Duree, the elder, the principal man of the connexion, determined to settle a new fort between Estill's station and the mouth of Muddy creek. Having erected a cabin, his son-in-law, John Bullock and his family, and his son Peter Duree, his wife and two children removed to it, taking a pair of hand-mill stones with them. They remained for two or three days shut up in their cabin, but their corn meal being exhausted, they were compelled to venture out, to cut a hollow tree in order to adjust their hand-mill. They were attacked by Indians—Bullock, after running a short distance, fell. Duree reached the cabin, and threw himself upon the bed. Mrs. Bullock ran to the door to ascertain the fate of her husband—received a shot in the breast, and fell across the door sill. Mrs. Duree, not knowing whether her husband had been shot or had fainted, caught her by the feet, pulled her into the house and barred the door. She grasped a rifle, and told her husband she would help him to fight. He replied that he had been wounded and was dying. She then presented the gun through several port holes in quick succession—then calmly sat by her husband and closed his eyes in death. After waiting several hours, and seeing nothing more of the Indians, Mrs. Duree sallied out in desperation to make her way to the White Oak Spring, with her infant in her arms, and a son three or four years of age, following her. Afraid to pursue the trace, she entered the woods, and after running till she was nearly exhausted, she came at length to the trace. She determined to follow it at all hazards, and having advanced a few miles further, she met the elder Mr. Duree, with his wife and youngest son, with their baggage, on their way to the new station. The melancholy tidings induced them, of course, to return. They led their horses into an adjoining canebrake, unloaded them, and regained the White Oak Spring fort before daylight.

About the same time, an attack was made on Estill's station, three miles south of Richmond, by a party of about twenty-five Wyandots. They killed one man, took a negro prisoner, and disappeared. Captain Estill was the commander of the station, and he immediately raised about an equal number of men and pursued them. He overhauled them at the Little Mountain, where the bloody battle was fought recorded under the head of Montgomery county.

In August, 1792, seven Indians attacked the dwelling house of Mr. Stephenson, in Madison county. They approached the house early in the morning, before the family had risen, forced open the door, and fired into the beds where the members of it lay. Mrs. Stephenson was severely wounded, having her thigh and arm broken; but the rest of the family escaped unhurt. Mr. Stephenson sprang from his bed, seized his rifle, and returned the fire of the savages. Two young men, living with him, came to his assistance, and a severe conflict ensued. The assailants, although double the number of the defenders of the house, were ultimately expelled, having one of their number killed and several wounded. Mr. Stephenson was badly wounded, and one of the young men killed in the contest.

NATHANIEL HART, the elder, came to Kentucky in 1775, being among the first pioneers to the State. He was born in the year 1734, in Hanover county, Virginia. His father having died while he was young, his mother removed with the family to North Carolina. In 1760, Mr. Hart married, and engaged for several years in the mercantile business. In 1770 and 1771, he commanded a company in North Carolina in suppressing an insurrection, the object of which was to shut up the courts of justice and prostrate government itself. For his gallant and spirited behaviour while in the discharge of the arduous and hazardous duties which devolved upon him, he was handsomely complimented by the officers of the government. Shortly after this, Captain Hart, who had listened to the glowing descriptions which Boone gave of the beauty and fertility of the soil of Kentucky, was fired with the idea of forming a permanent settlement in a region presenting so many attractions to the adventurer. Accordingly, through his instrumentality, a company was formed composed of his own and four other families, with Colonel Henderson as its legal head, for the purpose of undertaking

---

[*] Letter of Nathaniel Hart, Sen., to Governor Morehead.

the purchase and settlement of the wilderness of Kentucky. As soon as the company was organized, Captain Hart set out alone on a trip to the Cherokee towns, on Holston, to ascertain, by a previous conference with the Indians, whether the purchase could be effected. After a propitious interview, he returned to North Carolina, taking with him a delegation of the Indian chiefs, who remained to escort the company back to the treaty ground, when, on the 17th of March, 1775, they negotiated the purchase of Transylvania from the Indians, and immediately departed for the Kentucky river. From this period Captain Hart spent most of his time in Kentucky, although he did not attempt to bring his family out till the fall of 1779. In August, 1782, as he was carelessly riding out in the vicinity of the fort, he was killed and scalped by a small party of Indians, who made their escape, although warmly pursued by Colonel Boone. His widow survived him about two years. Their descendants all reside in Kentucky.

In the final settlement of the affairs of Henderson & Co., the company allowed Captain Hart two hundred pounds for the extraordinary services rendered and risk incurred by him in the settlement of Kentucky.

Capt. CHRISTOPHER IRVINE, with his younger brother, the late Col. William Irvine, removed to Kentucky in 1778 or 1779, and settled in the present county of Madison, near where the town of Richmond now stands. In 1786, Capt. Irvine raised a company, and joined an expedition under Gen. Logan against the Indians in the northern part of Ohio. While on this expedition, he met his death in rather a singular manner. In a skirmish which took place, an Indian, who had been severely wounded,—a brave and fearless fellow,—made great efforts to effect his escape. Capt. Irvine and a part of his company gave pursuit, and were enabled to trail him by the blood which flowed from his wound, and stained the high grass through which he passed. The Indian discovered his pursuers, and when the foremost approached within rifle shot, he fired and killed him. He retreated again, and in his wounded state, loaded his rifle as he ran. Another of Capt. Irvine's company getting considerably in advance of his companions in the chase, the wounded Indian again turned, shot him dead, and resumed his retreat, reloading his rifle as he fled. The delay produced by the fatal effect of his fire, enabled him to get some distance ahead of his pursuers. Capt. Irvine, after losing two of his men by the fire of the Indian, became very much excited, and, contrary to the earnest advice of his party, determined to lead in the pursuit. He gave chase, and in a few minutes was within a short distance of the Indian, when the latter, with but too fatal an aim, fired a third time, and killed him. One of his men, who was close upon his heels, instantly sprang to the place where the Indian had concealed himself, and found him again loading his rifle! As quick as thought, he struck the Indian to the ground, and beat out his brains with the breech of his gun.

Capt. Irvine was a man of high character and standing—intrepid, energetic, and daring—with a strong and vigorous intellect—popular in the community, and beloved and admired by his pioneer companions. His widow married Gen. Richard Hickman, of Clark county, afterwards lieutenant-governor of Kentucky. *Irvine*, the county seat of Estill county, was named in honor of Capt. C. Irvine, and his brother, Col. William Irvine.

Col. WILLIAM IRVINE came to the county with his brother, and built a station, called *Irvine's Station*, near where Richmond stands. Col. Irvine was in the hard-fought and bloody battle at Little Mountain, known as "*Estill's defeat*," in the year 1782. About the close of the action, while Joseph Proctor, Irvine, and two others, were endeavoring to cover the retreat of the whites, Irvine was severely wounded, by a bullet and two buck shot entering his body a little above the left groin. The Indian who shot him, saw him fall, and, leaving the tree behind which he was sheltered, made a rapid advance with the view of tomahawking and scalping him. Irvine, as he approached, raised and presented his gun, which had just been fired, and was then empty, when the savage rapidly retreated to his tree for protection. Proctor, who was about fifty yards off, seeing the disabled condition of Irvine, called to him to mount, if he could, Capt. Estill's horse, (the owner having been previously killed), and retreat to a given point on the trace, about three miles distant,—promising him that he would, from that point, conduct him to his station in Madison. This assurance was given by Proctor under the conviction that, from the severity of Irvine's wounds, combined with the great loss of blood, he would be unable to proceed further on the retreat than the point designated. Irvine determined to follow the advice of Proctor; but the Indian who had wounded him, appeared resolved to baffle all his efforts to make his escape. As Irvine attempted to mount, the Indian would abandon his shelter, and make towards him with his tomahawk, when the former would raise and present his empty gun, and the latter as quickly retreat to his tree. This was repeated four times in succession. On the fifth trial, Irvine succeeded in mounting the horse, and safely reached the place designated by Proctor. Upon his arrival, he was exceedingly faint from loss of blood, but had sufficient presence of mind to diverge from the main trace, and shield himself in a thicket near by. Here he dismounted, and holding on to his horse's bridle, laid himself against a log to die. In a short time, Proctor and his two companions reached the place of rendezvous, and the former, true to his promise, determined to search for Irvine; the latter objected, under the apprehension that the Indians were in close pursuit. Proctor, however, persisted in the search, and, in a few minutes, discovered, through the bushes, the white horse rode by Irvine. He approached cautiously, and with a stealthy step, fearing an Indian ambuscade. Irvine, notwithstanding, caught the sound of his footsteps, and suffered all the horrors of death, under the impression that the footsteps were those of an enemy and not a friend. He was, however, speedily undeceived. Proctor bound up his wounds, and relieving his burning thirst by a supply of water from a contiguous branch, mounted him on horseback, and placing one of the men behind to hold him, safely conveyed him to Bryant's station, where they arrived on the succeeding day. Col. Irvine suffered severely from his wounds, and did not fully recover his health for several years. The bullet and shot were never extracted, and he carried them with him to his grave. He died in 1820, thirty-eight years after receiving his wound.

Colonel Irvine was a man of estimable character and high standing. When Madison county was established, he was appointed clerk of the quarter session and county courts, and after the quarter session court was abolished, was made clerk of the circuit court. These offices (clerk of the county and circuit courts) he held until his death. While clerk of the former courts, and before the separation of Kentucky, he was elected to the legislature of Virginia—was a member of several conventions held at Danville, preparatory to the introduction of Kentucky into the Union, and was a member from Madison, of the convention which formed the present constitution of Kentucky. He was repeatedly elected an elector of president and vice-president of the United States. No man had a stronger hold upon the affections of the people, and but few have gone to the grave more generally lamented.

Col. JOHN SPEED SMITH, is a citizen of Madison county, and has been long noted as one of the most prominent politicians in the State. He is a man of decided talents, and exercises great influence over those with whom in public life he is associated. He has repeatedly served in the legislature of Kentucky, and presided over that body as speaker. During Monroe's administration he was for two years a member of Congress. During J. Q. Adams' administration he was appointed by the president, secretary of legation to the United States' mission sent to the South American Congress, which was to assemble at Tacubaya. Gen. Jackson when president, appointed him district attorney for the United States for the district of Kentucky. In the winter of 1839, he was appointed by the legislature of Kentucky in conjunction with the Honorable James T. Morehead, a commissioner to the state of Ohio to obtain the passage of a law for the protection of the slave property of Kentucky. The mission was entirely successful. Colonel Smith is now living in Madison, which he represents in the senate. In the campaign of 1813 he served as aid-de-camp to General Harrison, and proved himself a brave, vigilant and efficient officer.

JAMES MADISON, the fourth president of the United States, in honor of whom this county received its name, was born in Port Royal, a town on the south side of the Rappahannock, in Virginia, on the 5th of March, 1751. The house of his parents, however, was in Orange county, where he always resided. Mr. Madison received the very best education the country afforded, having graduated at Princeton college, during the presidency of the celebrated Dr. Witherspoon. Upon leaving college, he studied law, not, however, with a view of making it a profession. In 1776 he was elected to the legislature of Virginia. At the succeeding county election he was not returned, but when the legislature assembled he was appointed a member of the council of State, which place he held until he was elected to Congress in 1779. Whilst a member of the council of State, he formed an intimate friendship with Patrick Henry and Thomas Jefferson, which was never afterwards interrupted. He continued in Congress from 1780 till the expiration of the allowed term computed from the ratification of the articles of confederation in 1781. During the years 1780–81–82–83, he was a leading, active and influential member of that body, and filled a prominent part in all its deliberations. In the years 1784–85–86, he was elected a delegate to the State legislature. In 1786 he was a member of the convention at Annapolis, which assembled preliminary to the convention at Philadelphia, which formed the federal constitution. Of the latter convention he was also a member, and assisted to frame the present constitution of the United States. He continued a member of the old Congress by re-appointment until its expiration in 1786. On the adoption of the constitution, he was elected to Congress from his district, and continued a member from 1789 till 1797. He was the author of the celebrated resolution against the alien and sedition laws passed by the Virginia legislature in 1798. When Mr. Jefferson was elected president in 1801, he appointed Mr. Madison secretary of state, in which office he continued during the eight years of Jefferson's administration. In 1809, on the retirement of Mr. Jefferson, he was elected president, and administered the government during a period of eight years. At about sixty years of age, he retired from public life, and ever afterwards resided on his estate in Virginia, except about two months, while at Richmond as a member of the convention in 1829, which sat there to remould the constitution of the State. His farm, his books, his friends, and his correspondence, were the sources of his enjoyment and occupation during the twenty years of his retirement. On the 28th of June, 1836, he died, as serene, philosophical and calm in the last moments of his existence as he had been in all the trying occasions of life. When they received intelligence of his death, the Congress of the United States adopted a resolution appointing a public oration to commemorate his life, and selected the Hon. John Q. Adams to deliver it.

MARION COUNTY.

MARION county was formed in 1834, and named after General FRANCIS MARION, a distinguished partizan officer of the revolutionary war It is situated in the central portion of the state, and lies on the head waters of the Rolling fork of Salt river: Bounded on the north by Washington ; east by Boyle and Casey; south by Greene ; and west by Larue. The face of the country, in the greater portion of Marion, is gently undulating ; but there are several chains of hills or " knobs," as they are called, running partially or entirely through the county. The soil, generally, is of a superior quality and very productive ; but in a small portion of the county is comparatively poor. Horses, mules and hogs are exported in large quantities—and tobacco and corn are extensively cultivated. Iron ore, in small quantities, is found in the hills of the county.

Number of acres of land in Marion, 194,117; average value per acre, $5.93; total value of taxable property in the county in 1846, $2,650,401; number of white males over twenty-one years of age, 1,648; number of children between five and sixteen years old, 2,092. Population in 1840, 11,032.

There are four towns in Marion, viz : Lebanon, the seat of justice, Bradfordsville, New Market and Raywick. LEBANON is a handsome town, about sixty miles from Frankfort—containing a court-house, three churches, (Roman Catholic, Methodist, and Presbyterian,) one male and one female seminary, six physicians, eight lawyers, three taverns, fourteen stores and groceries, one steam saw mill, fifteen mechanics' shops, and about 750 inhabitants : Incorporated in 1815, and took its name from the surrounding growth of cedars. *Bradfordsville* is a small village, nine miles south of Lebanon, containing two churches, (Methodist and Christian,) one tavern, and 120 inhabitants : Named after Peter Bradford. *New Market* lies six miles south of Lebanon, on the Rolling fork—contains a Presbyterian church, tavern, store and post-office, with about 50 inhabitants. *Raywick* is also situated on the Rolling fork, twelve miles west of Lebanon—containing 80 inhabitants, a Catholic church, post-office, &c. Named for Messrs. *Ray* and *Wick*-liffe.

ST. MARY'S COLLEGE, a Roman Catholic institution, is situated five miles from Lebanon, in this county. The college buildings are extensive and handsome, and the domain embraces about seven hundred acres of first rate land. W. S. MURPHY, president, assisted by eight instructors. Number of students about one hundred and twenty-five. Library contains 5,000 volumes. Commencement on the last week in July.

GENERAL FRANCIS MARION, one of the most celebrated partizan officers of the revolution, was born near Georgetown, in South Carolina, in 1732. In early life he engaged in sea-faring, but from the solicitations of his mother, was soon induced to abandon it. He then engaged in agricultural pursuits. In the year 1775, he was elected to the provincial Congress of South Carolina. In the same year he was made captain in the second regiment of troops raised by South Carolina on the breaking out of the war. He bore a conspicuous part in the engagement which ensued in the attack made on Sullivan's Island, by the British. He had been previously promoted to the rank of major, and for his conduct in this affair was made a lieutenant colonel. Upon the arrival of Count D'Estaing, Marion, with the second regiment, joined General Lincoln before Savannah. The united French and American forces, after a siege of three weeks, assaulted the works, and suffered a repulse with an immense loss. The fatal battle of Camden left South Carolina in the possession of the British, with Marion, Horry, and only thirty men to oppose their victorious and disciplined hosts. On hearing the result of the battle of Camden, Marion collected his little band of patriots around him, and having addressed them, they took an oath never to serve a tyrant, or be the slaves of Great Britain, and to fight to the last for liberty.

From this time until the close of the war in South Carolina, he continued actively engaged, with variable success against the British. In this dangerous and exciting service, he proved himself one of the most efficient partizan officers of whom history gives any account. His little party continually received accessions from the resolute and decided whigs, and in 1780 he was made a brigadier general, and was invested with the command of the military district extending from Charleston to Camden, and along the coast eastward to Georgetown. He commanded the front line of General Greene's army in the successful and decisive battle of the Eutaw. In this battle his marksmen did great execution, and behaved with their accustomed gallantry. General Marion's services in this action received the particular acknowledgments of Congress. In 1782 he was elected to the senate of the State; but in February of the same year he rejoined his regiment. He served in the convention which framed the constitution of the State, in 1790, after which he declined all public service. He died on the 27th February, 1795. In person he was below the middle size, thin and swarthy. His nose was aquiline, his chin projecting, his forehead was high, and eyes dark and piercing.

MARSHALL COUNTY.

MARSHALL county was formed in 1841, and named in honor of JOHN MARSHALL, chief justice of the United States. It is situated in the western part of the State, lying on the Tennessee river, which skirts it on the north and east—bounded on the north by Livingston, east by Caldwell, south by Calloway, and west by Graves and M'Cracken. Indian corn and tobacco are the staple products.

Number of acres of land in Marshall, 162,193; average value per acre, $1.62; total value of taxable property in the county in 1846, $405,107; number of white males over twenty-one years of age, 827; number of children between five and seventeen years old, 1,326.

BENTON, the seat of justice and only town in the county, contains three stores, one grocery, one tavern, one lawyer, one doctor, one tan-yard, and a blacksmiths' shop—population not given. Named after the Hon. Thomas H. Benton.

JOHN MARSHALL, chief justice of the United States, was born in Virginia, on the 24th of September, 1755; and as early as the summer of 1775, received a commission as lieutenant of a company of minute men, and was shortly afterwards engaged in the battle of Great Bridge, when the British troops under Lord Dunmore were repulsed with great gallantry. He was subsequently engaged in the memorable battles of Brandywine, Germantown, and Monmouth, and in 1780 obtained a license to practice law. He returned to the army shortly after, and continued in the service until the termination of Arnold's invasion.

In the spring of 1782, he was elected a member of the State legislature, and in the autumn of the same year a member of the executive council. He married in 1783. In 1788 he was elected to represent the city of Richmond in the legislature, and continued to occupy that station during the years 1789, 1790, 1791, and upon the recall of Mr. Monroe as minister to France, President Washington solicited Mr. Marshall to accept the appointment as his successor, but he respectfully declined. In 1799 he was elected and took his seat in Congress, and in 1800 was appointed secretary of war.

On the 31st of January, 1801, he became chief justice of the supreme court of the United States, which distinguished station he continued to fill with unsullied dignity and pre-eminent ability until the close of his mortal career. He died at Philadelphia on the 6th of July, 1837.

MASON COUNTY.

MASON county was established in 1789, being formed out of all that part of the then county of Bourbon which lay to the northeast of Licking river, and was bounded by the main stream of Licking, from its mouth to its source; thence, by a direct line to the nearest point on the State line of Virginia, and county line of Russell; thence, along said line, to Big Sandy river, down that river to the Ohio, and down the Ohio to the mouth of Licking: comprehending all the present counties of Bracken, Campbell, Carter, Fleming, Greenup, Johnson, Lawrence, and Lewis, and parts of Floyd, Morgan, Nicholas, Pendleton, and Pike.

It was named in honor of GEORGE MASON, a distinguished statesman of Virginia, whom Mr. Jefferson described as a man " of the first order of wisdom among those who acted on the theatre of the revolution; of expansive mind, profound judgment, cogent in argument, learned in the lore of our former constitution, and earnest for the republican change on democratic principles. His eloquence was neither flowing nor smooth, but his language was strong, his manner most impressive, and strengthened by a dash of biting sarcasm, when provocation made it seasonable." Mr. Mason was the framer of the constitution of Virginia, and a member of the convention which formed the federal constitution, although he did not sign that instrument. He opposed it in the Virginia convention, believing that its tendency would be to monarchy. He also opposed the slave trade with great zeal. He died at his country seat, Gunston Hall, on the Potomac, in the autumn of 1792, aged sixty-seven years.

The present county of Mason lies in the northern section of the State, and is bounded on the north by the Ohio river, east by the counties of Lewis and Fleming, south by Fleming and Nicholas, and west by Bracken. Bordering the Ohio river with a bold range of hills, it runs back into the interior, maintaining, generally, the same high and healthy elevation, and presenting a surface usually uneven—sometimes abrupt and broken—most frequently gently undulating—but always a varied and beautiful landscape. It is intersected by the north fork of Licking river; by Lawrence, Lee's, Limestone, Beasley's and Cabin creeks; and is otherwise abundantly watered by smaller streams and springs. The soil rests upon limestone, and is deep, rich, and highly productive, except in the north-eastern and south-western angles of the county. The staple productions are Indian corn, hemp, and tobacco;—wheat, barley, rye, horses, hogs, beef cattle and sheep being produced also in considerable quantities. Its agriculture is good, and steadily improving; it is probably the most extensive hemp-growing county in the state; and " Mason county tobacco " is famous for its excellence, in the markets of Europe. The county is small in extent and compact in shape, skirting about seventeen miles on the Ohio, and running back about the same distance; it measures 236 square miles, and contains 151,017 acres, averaging, according to the commissioner's returns for the year 1846, $22.78 per acre, and giving an aggregate value of $3,439,960. In that year, its taxable wealth amounted to $6,-968,326; the number of white males over twenty-one years old to 2,875; and the number of white children, between five and sixteen years old, to 2,967. In 1840, its entire population was 15,719.

The towns of Mason are Washington, Mayslick, Minerva, Dover, Germantown, Lewisburg, Orangeburg, Helena, Murphysville, Mount Gilead, Sardis, and the city of Maysville.

In the spring of 1775, Simon Kenton passed down the Ohio river, and landed at the mouth of a small creek called, afterwards, Limestone, and which runs through the present city of Maysville. The morning after, he shouldered his rifle and went back into the hills to look for game. After traveling two or three miles, to his great joy he found abundance of cane growing upon the richest land he had ever seen. Finding a spring of good water, he and his companion, a young man by the name of Thomas Williams, made themselves a comfortable camp, and, with their tomahawks, cleared a small piece of ground. Their clearing was finished in May, and from the remains of some corn which they had got from a French trader, for the purpose of parching, they obtained seed, and planted, perhaps, the first corn ever planted in that country, on the north side of the Kentucky river. Here, tending their corn with their tomahawks, they remained the undisputed masters of all they could see, till they had the pleasure of eating roasting ears, and of seeing their corn come to perfection. This place, which was called Kenton's station, is about one mile from where the town of Washington stands, and is now owned and cultivated by Mr. Thomas Forman.

In 1784, after an absence of several years, Kenton returned; and from this period may be dated the real commencement of the village.

WASHINGTON is the present county seat, and was established as a town in 1786 by the Virginia legislature, but was laid out the year previous, by William Wood, a Baptist preacher, and Arthur Fox, Sr. It seems to have improved very rapidly after its establishment, for Judge Goforth, the first justice of the peace for the county of Hamilton, Ohio, states in his journal under date 8th of January 1790, as published in the first volume of Cist's Miscellany, page 173, that Washington at that date had 119 houses. In the years 1797–8, the "Kentucky Palladium," one of the earliest papers in the State, was published in Washington by Hunter & Beaumont, who afterwards removed to Frankfort. For many years Washington was the principal place of trade for a very large scope of country around, comprehending many of the present northern counties, and at one time it contained fifteen or twenty flourishing mercantile houses; but within the last thirty years it has greatly declined, owing principally to its proximity

to the city of Maysville, which has, during that time, sprung into
considerable importance as the commercial agency of this section of the State. Washington is beautifully situated in the
heart of a rich and highly cultivated country, three and a half
miles from Maysville, and contains a court-house and public offices, three churches, (Baptist, Methodist and Presbyterian,) four
retail dry goods stores, four grocery stores, two taverns, three rope
walks, one of which is in operation, ten mechanics' shops and a
post-office. There are five lawyers and four physicians living in
the place, and a population of between six and seven hundred.

Mayslick, situated twelve miles from Maysville, on the Lexington turnpike road, in a fine section of the county, was named
after Mr. May, of Virginia, the former proprietor of the soil, and
a famous *lick* near the place ; and contains two churches (Baptist
and Christian), four stores, one tavern, a rope-walk and seven
mechanics' shops. There are four physicians resident in the village, and a population of about 400.

The village of *Minerva* lies in the lower part of the county,
about ten miles west of Maysville, in the centre of the tobacco
region ; and contains two churches (Baptist and Methodist), one
tavern, two dry goods stores, six mechanics' shops, and four
physicians. *Dover*, four miles from Minerva and ten or twelve
from Maysville, is situated on the Ohio river, and is a thriving
village, with two churches (Methodist and Christian), two taverns,
six stores and groceries, three large tobacco warehouses, a large
brick flour-mill, one steam saw-mill, and ten mechanics' shops.
It has three resident physicians and a population of five or six
hundred. This is a place of considerable business, being the
point whence much of the tobacco raised in the counties of Mason and Bracken is shipped. *Germantown*, seven or eight miles
south of Dover, lies partly in Mason and partly in Bracken county,
the smaller portion lying in Mason. It has two churches, two
taverns, five stores, several mechanics' shops, three physicians,
and a population of two or three hundred. *Orangeburg* is eight
miles from Maysville, *Lewisburg* seven miles, (on the Flemingsburg turnpike road,) *Mount Gilead* eleven or twelve miles, and all
in the eastern section of the county ; *Helena* is about eleven miles
south-east from Maysville ; *Murphysville* about nine miles south,
and *Sardis* fourteen miles south from Maysville. They are all
small country villages, with one or two stores each, a church, a
few mechanics, a physician, and a population varying from fifty
to one hundred.

Maysville, known for many years as *Limestone*, from the creek
of that name which empties in the Ohio at that place, is situated
on the Ohio river, sixty miles above Cincinnati, and was named
after John May, the owner of the land, and an intelligent and
highly respectable gentleman from Virginia. In 1784 the first
settlement at this place was made, and a double log cabin and
block house built by Edward Waller, John Waller and George
Lewis, of Virginia. Colonel Daniel Boone resided there in the

year 1786. During his residence there, a party of seventy-five Indians came to the mouth of Fishing Gut, on the Ohio river, opposite Maysville, to treat for the exchange of prisoners. Colonel Boone, Jacob Boone, Colonel Sharpe and Colonel Logan went over to meet them. The wife of Colonel Sharpe was one of the prisoners released. Colonel Boone killed a fat beef, and the Indians had a feast and a dance. They were under the chief Blue Jacket, of the Shawanee tribe, and were so delighted with Col. Boone and the entertainment he gave them, that they made a solemn pledge to him that if ever they met with a citizen of Maysville in suffering or captivity, they would do all in their power to relieve him. This pledge they religiously kept. Samuel Blackburn, of Maysville, was afterwards taken prisoner, the Indians having ascertained that he was from Maysville, treated him with every mark of attention, released him from captivity and restored him to his friends.

In 1788 the town was established. In 1790 the first school was opened in Maysville by Israel Donaldson, who had been held in captivity for a long time by the Indians. It was the principal

CITY HALL, MAYSVILLE, KY.

point where the immigrants to Kentucky landed, and through which the merchandize and supplies for the interior passed. There also, as well as at Logan's Gap, four miles below, the predatory bands of the warlike Indians of the north-west frequently crossed the Ohio in their hostile incursions into the white settlements of the interior. Its frontier and exposed position retarded its progress for many years, and kept it in the rear of towns altogether inferior to it in natural commercial advantages; and it was not until about the year 1815 that its steady and permanent improvement may be said to have fairly commenced.

Maysville was incorporated as a city in 1833, is well and compactly built, contains a handsome and imposing public edifice called the City Hall, five churches (Presbyterian, Baptist, Christian, Methodist Episcopal south, and Catholic), and one building in progress for the Methodist Episcopal church; two seminaries, one (that of Rand & Richeson), very large, well established and flourishing; two public free schools, seven private schools, six taverns, one large new and substantial stone jail, one hospital and alms house, one bank with a capital of $450,000, two printing offices, each publishing weekly and tri-weekly papers, the "Maysville Eagle" the fourth oldest paper in the state, and the "Maysville Herald" recently established, two steam cotton factories, one large power loom bagging factory with an actual capital paid in of $80,000, one wool carding factory, two founderies, five rope-walks, two steam saw-mills, one large steam flour-mill, one tallow and candle factory, twelve plow factories, three wagon factories, two coach manufactories, two stone cutting establishments, five tin-ware manufactories, three tobacco manufactories and warehouses, one saddle-tree manufactory, one large tannery, four saddle, harness and trunk manufactories, three wooden ware manufactories, twelve storage and commission ware houses, fourteen wholesale groceries, thirty retail groceries, three wholesale dry goods stores, twenty-three retail dry goods stores, two wholesale and retail hard-ware houses, one wholesale and retail China, glass and queensware store, one cotton store, five stove and hollow-ware stores, two iron stores, three drug stores, three shoe stores, two book stores, two hat stores, three pork houses, four lumber yards, twelve lawyers, eleven physicians, three resident dentists, one Daguerrean artist, three principal cabinet makers, three jewelers, one gunsmith, ten blacksmith shops, fourteen carpenters' shops, five principal stonemasons, five principal bricklayers, two mattress makers, eight shoe shops, one hatters' shop, fifteen principal milliners and mantua makers, ten principal tailors, five bakeries and confectionaries, eight painters, glaziers and paper hangers, five coopers' shops, and five livery stables.

The progress of Maysville has been slow but steady. The capital she now wields, which is very considerable, has been gradually realized and accumulated within the city, by her own citizens, by a long course of persevering and enterprising industry. Within the last six years her improvement has been much

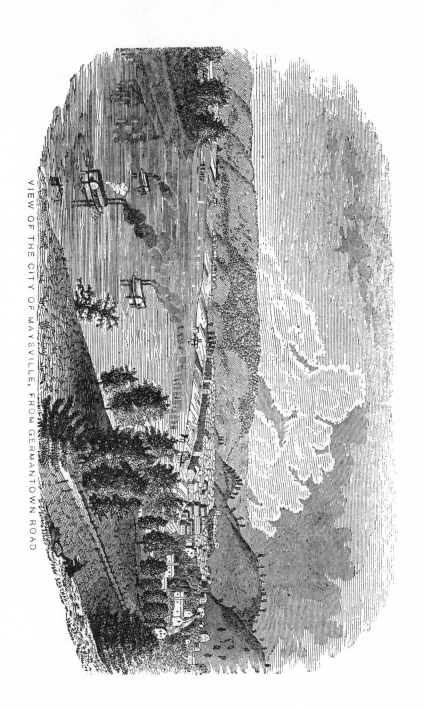

VIEW OF THE CITY OF MAYSVILLE, FROM GERMANTOWN ROAD

more rapid than for years back. Twenty years ago her whole grocery business did not equal the half of what is singly done by several of the larger houses, and within the last two years that branch has more than doubled, so that during the present year (1847) more than half a million will be realized for groceries. The sales of hardware, which in 1838 amounted to not more than $15,000, will this year reach $75,000. A few years since, there was but a single tinware manufactory and stove ware-house, now there are *five* large establishments, doing a lucrative and greatly extended business. Maysville is the largest hemp market in the United States, and this year her purchases will amount to 6,500 tons. She is the point of reception, storage and transhipment of all the merchandise and produce imported and exported by the north-eastern section of Kentucky. And although the slackwater improvements on the Kentucky river had the effect for a time of diverting the trade of some of the midland counties, yet her superior position and facilities, united to the energy of her citizens, are compelling its return. As a corporation, she has expended *seventy thousand dollars* in the con-struction of the different turnpike roads which concentrate upon her as a terminus, in addition to the individual subscriptions of her citizens. In the midst of one of the most extended, imposing and attractive landscapes of the 'beautiful river,' surrounded by a fertile and highly cultivated country directly dependant upon and tributary to her, herself the commercial agent for north-eas-tern Kentucky, with great manufacturing advantages from her proximity to many of the most important of the raw materials, and from her facilities of transportation, Maysville, with a labori-ous, substantial, energetic and enterprising population of near 5,000, must continue, with an increasing progression, to advance in prosperity, population and wealth.

The early settlement of Mason county was, like that of many other sections of the state, attended with great hardship, danger and suffering ; and being a border county, and one through which the daring and bloody incursions of the Indians of the north were made, the adventurous pioneers who settled it were necessarily exposed to constant and peculiar hazards. And it is to be regretted that so few authentic accounts of the romantic and thrilling adventures of those hardy heroes of the west have been preserved to us by legend or tradition.

As early as 1785, many families came down the Ohio river in boats, landed at Maysville, and continued their route to such parts of the country as pleased them. Among them, Colonel Thomas Marshall, formerly commander of the third Vir-ginia regiment on continental establishment, subsequently colonel of the regiment of Virginia artillery, embarked with a numerous family on board a flat boat, and descended the Ohio without any incident of note until he passed the mouth of the Kenawha. Here about ten o'clock at night, he was hailed from the northern shore by a man who announced himself as James Girty, the brother of the noto-rious Simon Girty. The boat dropped slowly down within one hundred and fifty yards of the shore, and Girty making a corresponding movement on the beach, the conference was kept up for several minutes. He began by mentioning his name, and enquiring that of the master of the boat.

Having been satisfied upon this head, he assured him that he knew him well, respected him highly, &c., &c., and concluded with some rather extraordinary remarks : " He had been posted there," he said, " by the order of his brother Simon, to warn all boats of the danger of permitting themselves to be decoyed

28

ashore. The Indians had become jealous of him, and he had lost that influence which he formerly held amongst them. He deeply regretted the injury which he had inflicted upon his countrymen, and wished to be restored to their society. In order to convince them of the sincerity of his regard, he had directed him to warn all boats of the snares spread for them. Every effort would be made to draw passengers ashore. White men would appear upon the bank; and children would be heard to supplicate for mercy. But," continued he, "do you keep the middle of the river, and steel your heart against every mournful application you may receive." The colonel thanked him for his intelligence, and continued his course. He arrived safely at Maysville, and settled in that part of the then county of Fayette which afterwards became the county of Mason. Colonel Marshall was a gentleman of high standing in Virginia. He had been a member of the general assembly in 1774, and was one of the band of patriots, who with Washington and Henry, resolved to resist the assumptions of the British government at the hazard of all that was dear to men. He attached himself in 1775 to the army, and in the capacity of major was conspicuous for his gallantry in the battle of the Great Bridge on the 9th of December, 1775. He also distinguished himself as colonel in the battles of Brandywine and Germantown.

About the same time, Captain JAMES WARD, lately a highly respectable citizen of Mason county, Kentucky, was descending the Ohio, under circumstances which rendered a rencounter with the Indians peculiarly to be dreaded. He, together with half a dozen others, one of them his nephew, embarked in a crazy boat, about forty-five feet long and eight feet wide, with no other bulwark than a single pine plank, above each gunnel. The boat was much encumbered with baggage, and seven horses were on board. Having seen no enemy for several days, they had become secure and careless, and permitted the boat to drift within fifty yards of the Ohio shore. Suddenly, several hundred Indians showed themselves on the bank, and running down boldly to the water's edge, opened a heavy fire upon the boat. The astonishment of the crew may be conceived.

Captain Ward and his nephew were at the oars when the enemy appeared, and the captain knowing that their safety depended on their ability to regain the middle of the river, kept his seat firmly, and exerted his utmost powers at the oar, but his nephew started up at sight of the enemy, seized his rifle, and was in the act of leveling it, when he received a ball in the breast, and fell dead in the bottom of the boat. Unfortunately, his oar fell into the river, and the captain, having no one to pull against him, rather urged the boat nearer to the hostile shore than otherwise. He seized a plank, however, and giving his own oar to another of the crew, he took the station which his nephew had held, and unhurt by the shower of bullets that flew around him, continued to exert himself, until the boat had reached a more respectable distance. He then, for the first time, looked around him in order to observe the condition of the crew.

His nephew lay in his blood, perfectly lifeless; the horses had been all killed or mortally wounded. Some had fallen overboard; others were struggling violently, and causing their frail bark to dip water so abundantly, as to excite the most serious apprehensions. But the crew presented the most singular spectacle. A captain, who had served with reputation in the continental army, seemed now totally bereft of his faculties. He lay upon his back in the bottom of the boat, with hands uplifted and a countenance in which terror was personified, exclaiming in a tone of despair, " Oh Lord! Oh Lord!" A Dutchman, whose weight might amount to about three hundred pounds, was anxiously engaged in endeavoring to find shelter for his bulky person, which, from the lowness of the gunnels, was a very difficult undertaking. In spite of his utmost efforts, a portion of his posterial luxuriance appeared above the gunnel, and afforded a mark to the enemy, which brought a constant shower of balls around it.

In vain he shifted his position. The hump still appeared, and the balls still flew around it, until the Dutchman, losing all patience, raised his head above the gunnel, and in a tone of querulous remonstrance, called out, " oh now! quit tat tamned nonsense, tere, will you!" Not a shot was fired from the boat. At one time, after they had partly regained the current, Captain Ward attempted to bring his rifle to bear upon them, but so violent was the agitation of the boat, from the furious struggles of the horses, that he could not steady his piece within twenty yards of the enemy, and quickly laying it aside, returned to the oar. The Indians followed them down the river for more than an hour, but having no canoes, they did not attempt to board; and as the boat was at length transferred to the opposite side of the river, they at length abandoned the pursuit and disappeared. None of the crew, save the young man already mentioned, were hurt, although the Dutchman's seat of honor served as a target for the space of an hour, and the continental captain was deeply mortified at the sudden, and, as he said, " unaccountable " panic which had seized him. Captain Ward himself was protected by a post, which had been fastened to the gunnel, and behind which he sat while rowing.

In the early part of 1790, JOHN MAY, from whom the city of Maysville derived its name, and who had frequently before visited Kentucky, embarked at Kelly's station, on the Kenawha river, for Maysville, in company with his clerk, Mr. Charles Johnston, and Mr. Jacob Skyles, also a gentleman of Virginia, who had with him a stock of dry goods for Lexington. They arrived without accident at Point Pleasant, where they were joined by a man named Flinn, and two sisters named Fleming, natives of Pittsburg. After leaving Point Pleasant, when near the mouth of the Scioto, they were awakened at daylight on the morning of the 20th of March, by Flinn, whose turn it was to watch, and informed that danger was at hand. All instantly sprung to their feet, and hastened upon deck without removing their night caps or completing their dress. The cause of Flinn's alarm was quickly evident. Far down the river a smoke was seen, ascending in thick wreaths above the trees, and floating in thinner masses over the bed of the river. All instantly perceived that it could only proceed from a large fire ; and who was there to kindle a fire in the wilderness which surrounded them ? No one doubted that Indians were in front, and the only question to be decided was, upon which shore they lay, for the winding of the river, and their distance from the smoke, rendered it impossible at first to ascertain this point. As the boat drifted on, however, it became evident that the fire was upon the Ohio shore, and it was instantly determined to put over to the opposite side of the river. Before this could be done, however, two white men ran down upon the beach, and clasping their hands in the most earnest manner, implored the crew to take them on board.

They declared that they had been taken by a party of indians in Kennedy's bottom, a few days before; had been conducted across the Ohio, and had just effected their escape. They added, that the enemy was in close pursuit of them, and that their death was certain, unless admitted on board. Resolute in their purpose, on no account to leave the middle of the stream, and strongly suspecting the supplicants of treachery, the party paid no attention to their entreaties, but steadily pursued their course down the river, and were soon considerably ahead of them. The two white men ran down the bank, in a line parallel with the course of the boat, and their entreaties were changed into the most piercing cries and lamentations upon perceiving the obstinacy with which their request was disregarded. Instantly the obduracy of the crew began to relax. Flinn and the two females, accustomed from their youth to undervalue danger from the Indians, earnestly insisted upon going ashore and relieving the white men, and even the incredulity of May began to yield to the persevering importunity of the supplicants. A parley took place. May called to them from the deck of the boat, where he stood in his nightcap and drawers, and demanded the cause of the large fire, the smoke of which had caused so much alarm. The white men positively denied that there was any fire near them. This falsehood was so palpable, that May's former suspicions returned with additional force, and he positively insisted upon continuing their course without paying the slightest attention to the request of the men. This resolution was firmly seconded by Johnston and Skyles, and as vehemently opposed by Flinn and the Miss Flemings, for, contrary to all established rules of policy, the females were allowed an equal vote with the males on board of the boat.

Flinn urged that the men gave every evidence of real distress which could be required, and recounted too many particular circumstances attending their capture and escape, to give color to the suspicion that their story was invented for the occasion, and added, that it would be a burning shame to them and theirs forever, if they should permit two countrymen to fall a sacrifice to the savages, when so slight a risk on their part would suffice to relieve them. He acknowledged that they had lied in relation to the fire, but declared himself satisfied that it was only because they were fearful of acknowledging the truth, lest the crew should suspect that Indians were concealed in the vicinity. The controversy became warm, and, during its progress, the boat drifted so far below the men, that they appeared to relinquish their pursuit in despair.

At this time, Flinn made a second proposal, which, according to his method of reasoning, could be carried into effect, without the slightest risk to any one but himself. They were now more than a mile below the pursuers. He proposed that May should only touch the hostile shore long enough to permit him to jump out. That it was impossible for Indians (even admitting that they were at hand) to arrive in time to arrest the boat, and even should any appear, they could immediately put off from shore and abandon him to his fate. That he was confident of being able to outrun the red devils, if they saw him first, and was equally confident of being able to see them as soon as they could see him. May remonstrated upon so unnecessary an exposure; but Flinn was inflexible, and in an evil hour the boat was directed to the shore.

They quickly discovered, what ought to have been known before, that they could not float as swiftly after leaving the current as while borne along by it, and they were nearly double the time in making the shore, that they had calculated upon. When within reach, Flinn leaped fearlessly upon the hostile bank, and the boat grated upon the sand. At that moment, five or six savages ran up out of breath, from the adjoining wood, and instantly seizing Flinn, began to fire upon the boat's crew. Johnston and Skyles sprung to their arms, in order to return the fire, while May, seizing an oar, attempted to regain the current. Fresh Indians arrived, however, in such rapid succession, that the beach was quickly crowded by them, and May called out to his companions to cease firing and come to the oars. This was instantly done, but it was too late.

Seeing it impossible to extricate themselves, they all lay down upon their faces, in such parts of the boat as would best protect them from the horses, and awaited, in passive helplessness, the approach of the conquerors. The enemy, however, still declined boarding, and contented themselves with pouring in an incessant fire, by which all the horses were killed, and which at length began to grow fatal to the crew. One of the females received a ball in her mouth, which had passed immediately over Johnston's head, and almost instantly expired. Skyles, immediately afterwards, was severely wounded in both shoulders, the ball striking the right shoulder blade, and ranging transversely along his back. The fire seemed to grow hotter every moment, when, at length May arose and waved his nightcap above his head as a signal of surrender. He instantly received a ball in the middle of the forehead, and fell perfectly dead by the side of Johnston, covering him with his blood.

Now, at last, the enemy ventured to board. Throwing themselves into the water, with their tomahawks in their hands, a dozen or twenty swam to the boat, and began to climb the sides. Johnston stood ready to do the honors of the boat, and presenting his hand to each Indian in succession, he helped them over the side to the number of twenty. Nothing could *appear* more cordial than the meeting. Each Indian shook him by the hand, with the usual salutation of "how de do," in passable English, while Johnston encountered every visitor with an affectionate squeeze, and a forced smile, in which terror struggled with civility. The Indians then passed on to Skyles and the surviving Miss Fleming, where the demonstrations of mutual joy were not quite so lively. Skyles was writhing under a painful wound, and the girl was sitting by the dead body of her sister.

Having shaken hands with all of their captives, the Indians proceeded to scalp the dead, which was done with great coolness, and the reeking scalps were stretched and prepared upon hoops for the usual process of drying, immediately before the eyes of the survivors. The boat was then drawn ashore, and its contents examined with great greediness. Poor Skyles, in addition to the pain of his wounds, was compelled to witness the total destruction of his property, by the hands of these greedy spoilers, who tossed his silks, cambric, and broadcloth into the dirt with the most reckless indifference. At length they stumbled upon a keg of whisky. The prize was eagerly seized, and every thing else abandoned.

The Indian who had found it, instantly carried it ashore, and was followed by the rest with tumultuous delight. A large fire nearly fifty feet long was quickly kindled, and victors and vanquished indiscriminately huddled around it.

On the next morning the Indians arose early and prepared for another encounter, expecting as usual that boats would be passing. It happened that Captain Thomas Marshall, of the Virginia artillery, afterwards a citizen of Mason, and son of Colonel Marshall, in company with several other gentlemen, was descending the Ohio, having embarked only one day later than May. About twelve o'clock on the second day after May's disaster, the little flotilla appeared about a mile above the point where the Indians stood. Instantly all was bustle and activity. The additional oars were fixed to the boat, the savages instantly sprung on board, and the prisoners were compelled to station themselves at the oars, and were threatened with instant death unless they used their utmost exertions to bring them along side of the enemy. The three boats came down very rapidly, and were soon immediately opposite their enemy's. The Indians opened a heavy fire upon them, and stimulated their rowers to their utmost efforts.

The boats became quickly aware of their danger, and a warm contest of skill and strength took place. There was an interval of one hundred yards between each of the three boats in view. The hindmost was for a time in great danger. Having but one pair of oars, and being weakly manned, she was unable to compete with the Indian boat, which greatly outnumbered her both in oars and men. The Indians soon came within rifle shot, and swept the deck with an incessant fire, which rendered it extremely dangerous for any of the crew to show themselves. Captain Marshall was on board of the hindmost boat, and maintained his position at the steering oar in defiance of the shower of balls which flew around him. He stood in his shirt sleeves with a red silk handkerchief bound around his head, which afforded a fair mark to the enemy, and steered the boat with equal steadiness and skill, while the crew below relieved each other at the oars.

The enemy lost ground from two circumstances. In their eagerness to overtake the whites, they left the current, and attempted to cut across the river from point to point, in order to shorten the distance. In doing so, however, they lost the force of the current, and soon found themselves dropping astern. In addition to this, the whites conducted themselves with equal coolness and dexterity. The second boat waited for the hindmost, and received her crew on board, abandoning the goods and horses, without scruple, to the enemy. Being now more strongly manned, she shot rapidly ahead, and quickly overtook the foremost boat, which, in like manner, received the crew on board, abandoning the cargo as before, and having six pair of oars, and being powerfully manned, she was soon beyond the reach of the enemy's shot. The chase lasted more than an hour. For the first half hour, the fate of the foremost boat hung in mournful suspense, and Johnson, with agony, looked forward to the probability of its capture. The prisoners were compelled to labor hard at the oars, but they took care never to pull together, and by every means in their power endeavored to favor the escape of their friends.

At length the Indians abandoned the pursuit, and turned their whole attention to the boats which had been deserted. The booty surpassed their most sanguine expectations. Several fine horses were on board, and flour, sugar, and chocolate in profusion. Another keg of whisky was found, and excited the same immoderate joy as at first.

Flinn was subsequently burnt by his fiendish captors at the stake, with all the aggravated tortures that savage cruelty could devise. Skyles, after running the gauntlet, and having been condemned to death, made his escape and reached the white settlements in safety. The remaining Miss Fleming was rescued by an Indian chief, at the very time when her captors had bound her to a stake and were making preparations to burn her alive, and conducted safely to Pittsburg. Johnston was ransomed by a Frenchman at Sandusky, at the price of six hundred silver brooches, and returned in safety to his family.

In April, 1791, Colonel Timothy Downing, a citizen of Mason county, returning from Lexington, where he had been on a trading expedition with two horses, riding one and leading the other, which was laden with cotton goods, was captured near the Blue Licks by a party of Shawanee Indians. They crossed with him into Ohio at Logan's Gap, where he was given in charge to two of the party, an old Indian and his son. After two day's traveling, the Indians with Downing encamped for the night. He had been treated very kindly by them during their march, and before supper the old Indian came up to him—" tie to-night, after to-night, no more tie ;" Downing replied—" no tie 'till after supper." This was assented to. The old Indian then directed him to hand a drink of water; and Downing, whilst getting the water, picked up a tomahawk, which he concealed. It had been raining during the day, and the young Indian was busy before the fire, drying a shirt, which had been taken from Downing; and whilst the old Indian, not suspecting any thing, was drinking the water he had handed him, Downing cleft his skull with the tomahawk and pitched him into the fire. It was neces- sary to kill the old Indian, but as they had been kind to him, he did not wish to hurt the young Indian. His object was to take him prisoner. But the instant he struck his father, the young Indian sprung upon his back with the most horri- ble yells, and confined him so that it was difficult to extricate himself from his grasp. It was not more than four or five miles to the main camp, and as soon as Downing was released from his struggles, he made for his horses, and the young Indian, who was badly wounded in the encounter, for the camp. He caught one of his horses and mounted him, and struck off into the woods, hoping that the other horse would follow. But the night was very dark, and he never saw any thing of his second horse. He was a bad woodsman, and before he got far from the scene of his exploits, he heard the eager yells of Indians in hot pursuit of him. But the darkness of the night favored his escape, and he succeeded in eluding his pursuers. A day or two afterwards Kenton, at the head of a party in pursuit of the Indians, came upon the camp whence Downing had escaped, discovered the old Indian, who had been buried with twenty-five yards of the cloth wrapped around him, and found also Downing's shirt, with blood on it. No Indians were to be seen, and the party returned. Kenton took the shirt to Mrs. Downing, who recognized it at once as her husband's, whom she concluded to have been murdered by the Indians. Downing, in the meantime, after travel- ing all night after his escape, found himself on a creek, which he followed to its junction with the Scioto river, and finally struck the Ohio below the mouth of the Scioto, just as a flat boat was passing down. He immediately hailed it, but the boat very prudently made for the Kentucky shore, evidently suspecting an In- dian decoy. He followed it two miles before he could prevail on the owners of it to send a boat to his relief. He finally succeeded ; a man came in a canoe, with his rifle, and told him as he approached that if he saw an Indian, he would shoot him (Downing) dead in his tracks. He was taken on board, landed at Maysville, and rejoiced his family, who were mourning him as dead, by his sud- den return. He resided then where Mr. Robert Downing, of Mason county, now lives, and after reaching an advanced age, died some fifteen or sixteen years ago.

In the month of April, 1792, a number of horses belonging to Captain Luther Calvin of Mason county, were stolen by the Indians ; and, as usual, a strong party volunteered to go in pursuit of the enemy and recover the property. The party consisted of thirty-seven men, commanded by Captains Calvin and Ken- ton, and was composed chiefly of young farmers, most of whom had never yet met an enemy. Captain Charles Ward, late deputy sheriff of Mason county, was one of the volunteers, and was at that time a mere lad, totally unacquainted with Indian warfare. They rendezvoused upon the Kentucky shore, immediately opposite Ripley, and crossing the river in a small ferry boat, pursued the trail for five or six miles with great energy. Here, however, a specimen of the usual caprice and uncertainty attending the motions of militia, was given.
One of the party, whose voice had been loud and resolute while on the Kentucky shore, all at once managed to discover that the enterprise was rash, ill advised, and if prosecuted, would certainly prove disastrous. A keen debate ensued, in which young Spencer Calvin, then a lad of eighteen, openly accused the gentle- man alluded to of cowardice, and even threatened to take the measure of his shoulders with a ramrod, on the spot. By the prompt interference of Kenton and the elder Calvin, the young man's wrath was appeased for the time, and all those who preferred safety to honor, were invited instantly to return. The permission was promptly accepted, and no less than fifteen men, headed by the recreant al-

ready mentioned, turned their horses' heads and re-crossed the river. The remainder, consisting chiefly of experienced warriors, continued the pursuit.

The trail led them down on the Miami, and about noon on the second day, they heard a bell in front, apparently from a horse grazing. Cautiously approaching it, they beheld a solitary Indian, mounted on horseback, and leisurely advancing towards them. A few of their best marksmen fired upon him and brought him to the ground. After a short consultation, it was then determined to follow his back trail, and ascertain whether there were more in the neighborhood. A small, active, resolute woodsman, named McIntyre, accompanied by three others, was pushed on in advance, in order to give them early notice of the enemy's appearance, while the main body followed at a more leisurely pace. Within an hour, McIntyre returned, and reported that they were then within a short distance of a large party of Indians, supposed to be greatly superior to their own. That they were encamped in a bottom upon the borders of a creek, and were amusing themselves, apparently awaiting the arrival of the Indian whom they had just killed, as they would occasionally halloo loudly, and then laugh immoderately, supposing, probably, that their comrade had lost his way.

This intelligence fell like a shower bath upon the spirits of the party, who, thinking it more prudent to put a greater interval between themselves and the enemy, set spurs to their horses, and galloped back in the direction from which they had come. Such was the panic, that one of the footmen, a huge hulking fellow, six feet high, in his zeal for his own safety, sprung up behind Capt. Calvin, (who was then mounted upon Capt. Ward's horse, the captain having dismounted in order to accommodate him), and nothing short of a threat to blow his brains out, could induce him to dismount. In this orderly manner they scampered through the woods for several miles, when, in obedience to the orders of Kenton and Calvin, they halted, and prepared for resistance in case (as was probable) the enemy had discovered them, and were engaged in the pursuit. Kenton and Calvin were engaged apart in earnest consultation. It was proposed that a number of saplings should be cut down and a temporary breastwork erected, and while the propriety of these measures was under discussion, the men were left to themselves.

Finding themselves not pursued by the enemy, as they had expected, it was determined that they should remain in their present position until night, when a rapid attack was to be made, in two divisions, upon the Indian camp, under the impression that the darkness of the night, and the surprise of the enemy, might give them an advantage, which they could scarcely hope for in daylight. Accordingly, every thing remaining quiet at dusk, they again mounted and advanced rapidly, but in profound silence, upon the Indian camp. It was ascertained that the horses which the enemy had stolen were grazing in a rich bottom below their camp. As they were advancing to the attack, therefore, Calvin detached his son with several halters, which he had borrowed from the men, to regain their own horses, and be prepared to carry them off in case the enemy should overpower them. The attack was then made in two divisions.

Calvin conducted the upper and Kenton the lower party. The wood was thick, but the moon shone out clearly, and enabled them to distinguish objects with sufficient precision. Calvin's party came first in contact with the enemy. They had advanced within thirty yards of a large fire in front of a number of tents, without having seen a single Indian, when a dog, which had been watching them for several minutes, sprung forward to meet them, baying loudly. Presently an Indian appeared approaching cautiously towards them, and occasionally speaking to the dog in the Indian tongue. This sight was too tempting to be borne, and Calvin heard the tick of a dozen rifles in rapid succession, as his party cocked them in order to fire. The Indian was too close to permit him to speak, but turning to his men he earnestly waved his hand as a warning to be quiet. Then cautiously raising his own rifle, he fired with a steady aim, just as the Indian had reached the fire, and stood fairly exposed to its light.

The report of the rifle instantly broke the stillness of the night, and their ears were soon deafened by the yells of the enemy. The Indian at whom Calvin had fired, fell forward into the burning pile of faggots, and, by his struggles to extricate himself, scattered the brands so much, as almost to extinguish the light. Several dusky forms glanced rapidly before them for a moment, which drew a volley from his men, but with what effect could not be ascertained. Calvin, having discharged his piece, turned so rapidly as to strike the end of his ramrod against a tree behind him, and drive it into its sheath with such violence, that he was unable to extricate it for several minutes, and finally fractured two of his teeth in the effort.

A heavy fire now commenced from the Indian camp, which was returned with equal spirit by the whites, but without much effect on either side. Trees were barked very plentifully, dogs bayed, the Indians yelled, the whites shouted, the squaws screamed, and a prodigious uproar was maintained for about fifteen minutes, when it was reported to Calvin that Kenton's party had been overpowered, and was in full retreat. It was not necessary to give orders for a similar movement. No sooner had the intelligence been received, than the Kentuckians of the upper division broke their ranks, and every man attempted to save himself as he best could. They soon overtook the lower division, and a hot scramble took place for horses. One called upon another to wait for him until he could catch his horse, which had broken his bridle, but no attention was paid to the request. Some fled upon their own horses, others mounted those of their friends. " First come, first served," seemed to be the order of the night, and a sad confusion of property took place, in consequence of which, to their great terror, a few were compelled to return on foot. The flight was originally caused by the panic of an individual. As the lower division moved up to the attack, most of the men appeared to advance with alacrity. The action quickly commenced, and at the first fire from the Indians, Barre, a young Kentuckian, was shot by ——'s side. This circumstance completely overthrew the courage of this one of the party, who had been the most boisterous and blustering when the chase commenced, but whose courage had visibly declined since the first encounter of the morning : and, elevating his voice to its shrillest notes, he shouted, " boys ! it won't do for us to be here ; Barre is killed, and the Indians are crossing the creek !" Bonaparte has said, that there is a critical period in every battle, when the bravest men will eagerly seize an excuse to run away. The remark is doubly true with regard to militia.

No sooner had this speech been uttered by one who had never yet been charged with cowardice, than the rout instantly took place, and all order was disregarded. Fortunately, the enemy were equally frightened, and probably would have fled themselves, had the whites given them time. No pursuit took place for several hours, nor did they then pursue the trail of the main body of fugitives. McIntyre, however, who had turned off from the main route, was pursued by the Indians, overtaken, tomahawked and scalped.

It is somewhat remarkable, that a brother of Capt. Ward's was in the Indian camp at the moment when it was attacked. He had been taken by the Indians in 1758, being at that time only three years old, had been adopted as a member of the Shawanee tribe, and had married an Indian woman by whom he had several children, all of whom, together with their mother, were then in camp. Capt. Ward has informed the writer of this narrative, that, a few seconds before the firing began, while he stood within rifle shot of the encampment, an Indian girl, apparently fifteen years of age, attracted his attention. She stood for an instant in an attitude of alarm, in front of one of the tents, and gazed intently upon the spot where he then stood. Not immediately perceiving that it was a female, he raised his gun, and was upon the point of firing, when her open bosom announced her sex, and her peculiarly light complexion caused him to doubt for a moment whether she could be an Indian by birth. He afterwards ascertained that she was his brother's child.

The celebrated Tecumseh commanded the Indians. His cautious yet fearless intrepidity made him a host wherever he went. In military tactics night attacks are not allowable, except in cases like this, when the assailing party are far inferior in numbers. Sometimes, in such attacks, panics and confusion are created in the attacked party, which may render them a prey to inferior numbers. Kenton trusted to this on the present occasion, but Tecumseh's presence and influence over the minds of his followers infused such confidence that superior numbers only could prevail over them.

Some time in the spring of 1793, Tecumseh and a few of his followers, while hunting in the Scioto valley, on the waters of Paint creek, were unexpectedly attacked by a party of white men from Mason county, Kentucky. The circumstances which led to this skirmish were the following : Early that spring, an express reached the settlement in Mason, that some stations had been attacked and captured on Slate creek, in Bath county, Kentucky, and that the Indians were returning with their prisoners to Ohio. A party of thirty-three men was immediately raised to cut off their retreat. They were divided into three companies of ten men each; Simon Kenton commanding one, ———— Baker another, and Captain James Ward the third. The whole party crossed the Ohio at Limestone, and aimed to strike the Scioto above Paint creek. After crossing this creek near where the great road from Maysville to Chillicothe now crosses it, evening came on, and they halted for the night. In a short time they heard a noise, and a little examination disclosed to them that they were in the immediate vicinity of an Indian encampment. Their horses were promptly taken back some distance and tied, to prevent an alarm. A council was held, and Captain Baker offered to go and reconnoitre, which being agreed to, he took one of his company and made the examination. He found the Indians encamped on the bank of the creek, their horses being between them and the camp of the whites. After Baker's report was made, the party determined to remain where they were until near daylight the next morning. Captain Baker and his men were to march round and take a position on the bank of the stream in front of the Indian camp; Captain Ward was to occupy the ground in the rear; and Captain Kenton one side, while the river presented a barrier on the fourth, thus guarding against a retreat of the Indians. It was further agreed that the attack was not to commence until there was light enough to shoot with accuracy. Before Kenton and Ward had reached the positions they were respectively to occupy, the bark of a dog in the Indian camp was heard, and then the report of a gun. Upon this alarm, Baker's men instantly fired, and Captains Kenton and Ward, with their companies, raising the battle cry, rushed towards the camp. To their surprise, they found Baker and his men in the rear, instead of the front of the Indians, thus deranging the plan of attack, whether from design or accident is unknown. The Indians sent back the battle cry, retreated a few paces and treed. It was still too dark to fire with precision, but random shots were made, and a terrible shouting kept up by the Indians. While the parties were thus at bay, Tecumseh had the address to send a part of his men to the rear of the Kentuckians for their horses; and when they had been taken to the front, which was accomplished without discovery, the Indians mounted and effected their escape, carrying with them John Ward, the brother of Captain James Ward, the only one of their party who was shot. He died of his wound a few days after the engagement. One Kentuckian only, Jacob Jones, was killed, a member of Baker's detachment. No pursuit of the Indians was made, nor did they prove to be the same party who had attacked the Slate creek station.

After the fatal disaster which befel our troops at the river Raisin, during the late war, Captain Isaac Baker, a son of the late Colonel Baker, of Mason county, attempted to make good his retreat with the remnant of his company, some fifteen or twenty in number. They were pursued by a much larger party of Indians on horseback. When they came in sight, Captain Baker told his men that as they were on foot there was no possibility of escape, and that it only remained for them as brave men to sell their lives as dearly as possible. He ordered every man to *tree* and await the approach of the enemy. The order was promptly obeyed. The Indians approached within good rifle distance and then dismounted. As they did so, Captain Baker's little Spartan band poured in simultaneously a destructive fire, which brought the Indian force nearly to an equality with his own party. The Indians immediately *treed*, and the action continued in the true Indian manner of fighting, neither party firing except when there was a fair prospect of its taking effect. Unfortunately Captain Baker's men, at the commencement of the action, had but five rounds each. The fight was continued until the last load of ammunition was expended. Captain Baker then hoisted his handkerchief as the signal of surrender. The Indians approached, received the arms of the prisoners, counted the loss sustained on each side, and finding that theirs was the greater, began to make preparations to sacrifice as many as would bring the loss on each side to an equality. The first selected as a victim was the son of George Shinglebower, of Lexington, who was a red haired man, and as such an object of peculiar aversion to the Indians. A warrior approached him, tomahawk in hand, and took off his hat, the better to execute his dire purpose. Shinglebower, being a stout man, at the very moment the Indian was removing his hat, seized his tomahawk and sunk it into his head. The Indians, aroused to the utmost pitch of rage by this daring deed, now rushed upon the prisoners with their tomahawks, determined to massacre the whole party. At this moment, an aged chief stepped forward and took two of the prisoners, one in each hand, and led them aside, claiming them as his, and protecting them from the enraged savages. These two men were Captain Baker, since deceased, and Captain McCarty, now a citizen of Pendleton county. They were purchased from the Indian chief at the restoration of peace; the residue of Captain Baker's brave little band were all tomahawked on the spot where they surrendered.

Gen. HENRY LEE, a native of Virginia, was one of the earliest pioneers who settled in the county of Mason. He was a man of considerable intelligence and remarkably strong natural powers of mind. He was a member of the Virginia legislature from the district of Kentucky, and also of the convention which adopted the federal constitution. He served in the convention at Danville which met in 1787, and was one of the commissioners who located the seat of government at Frankfort. He was county lieutenant for all the territory north of Licking river, and was appointed judge of the quarter sessions court, and associate judge of the circuit court for Mason county, and was president of the Washington Branch of the old Bank of Kentucky. He came to Kentucky originally as a surveyor, and acted in that capacity for many years. He was a very sagacious man, of fine business habits, and by his position and great application, amassed a very large fortune. He was tall and powerfully made, very erect, and a man of remarkably fine and imposing personal appearance. He died in the spring of 1846, in the eighty-ninth year of his age.

Judge WILLIAM McCLUNG settled in Mason at an early period, and was a very prominent and influential citizen, and took an active part in advancing the interests of the new settlements. He was judge for many years of the district and circuit courts of the county, and was distinguished for his high attainments as a lawyer, but most eminently for his great unswerving and unapproachable integrity as a judge. He died while filling that office, leaving his venerable widow, the sister of Chief Justice Marshall, who is still living with her son, John A. McClung, Esq., of this county. Colonel Alexander K. McClung, of Mississippi, is also a son of Judge McClung.

ALEXANDER K. MARSHALL, Esq. a son of Colonel Thomas Marshall, and brother of the chief justice, was a pioneer lawyer of Mason county, and one of the very ablest of his day. In 1818 he was appointed reporter to the court of appeals, and during the period he held the office, published three volumes of reports.

Captain THOMAS MARSHALL, another son of Colonel Thomas Marshall, was the first clerk of the Mason county court. He was remarkable for his strong sense, benevolence and kind feelings, and was very generally beloved. He was a member of the convention that formed the present constitution of Kentucky.

Colonel ALEXANDER D. ORR, came to Kentucky from Virginia at an early period and settled in Mason on the farm lately occupied by John A. McClung, Esq. on the Ohio river, and built the first brick house ever erected in the county. He was elected to Congress in 1792 (after having been elected the same year to the state legislature), upon the admission of Kentucky into the Union, and took his seat at the session of 1792–3, in conjunction with his colleagues John Brown and John Edwards. He continued a member of Congress until 1797. He was a man of commanding personal appearance, and a polished gentleman of the old school. He died in Paris a few years since at an advanced age.

Doctor BASIL DUKE was born in Calvert county, Maryland. He obtained a classical education in the school of a Scotchman of eminent scholarship. He studied medicine in the city of Baltimore. After practicing his profession a short time in his native county, he emigrated to Kentucky, and settled in Lexington in the year 1791, then about twenty-five years of age. During his residence at Lexington, his professional ability secured him a large practice. In '94 he married Charlotte, the daughter of Colonel Thomas Marshall, then of Woodford, and in 1798 removed to Mason county. At the head of his profession in that part of

Kentucky, his practice for the greater part of his life was large and laborious, extending over Mason and the adjoining counties. His kind and benevolent character endeared him to the people, to whom his medical services rendered him greatly useful. He died in the town of Washington in 1828.

Colonel DEVALL PAYNE was born on the 1st of January, 1764, in the county of Fairfax, Virginia, within seven miles of the city of Alexandria. He was the son of William Payne, whose paternal ancestor accompanied Lord Fairfax from England when he came over to colonize his grant in Virginia. At the time Gen. Washington was stationed in Alexandria as a colonel of a British regiment, before the war of the revolution, an altercation took place in the court-house yard, between him and William Payne, in which Payne knocked Washington down. Great excitement prevailed, as Payne was known to be firm, and stood high, and Washington was beloved by all. A night's reflection, however, satisfied Washington that he was the aggressor and in the wrong, and in the morning he, like a true and magnanimous hero, sought an interview with Payne, which resulted in an apology from Washington, and a warm and lasting friendship between the two, founded on mutual esteem. During the revolutionary war, whilst Washington was on a visit to his family, Mr. Payne, with his son Devall, went to pay his respects to the great American chief. Washington met him some distance from the house, took him by the hand, and led him into the presence of Mrs. Washington, to whom he introduced Mr. Payne as follows: "My dear, here is the little man, whom you have so frequently heard me speak of, who once had the courage to knock me down in the court-house yard in Alexandria, *big as I am.*"

Devall Payne was married to Hannah, youngest daughter of Major Hugh Brent, of Loudon county, Virginia, December 1st, 1785. In 1789 he removed to Kentucky and settled near Lexington. Shortly afterwards he joined Captain Kenneth M'Coy's troop of cavalry, and served under Governor Charles Scott in his campaign against the Weaw Indians on the Wabash. He was with Captain M'Coy when he was wounded, and assisted him from the battle field. During the engagement, as his horse leaped a log in the charge, he encountered an Indian chief who was laying beside it. Payne instantly dismounted and grappled with the Indian, determined, if possible, to take him prisoner. The Indian was armed with gun, tomahawk and butcher knife, and resisted furiously. Payne pressed him so closely, and was so active and athletic, that the Indian could not use his weapons. The contest was very severe, and lasted for several minutes, exciting the interest and admiration of half a dozen soldiers, who had collected around to witness the struggle. Payne finally conquered, having thrown the Indian down three times before he would surrender.

In 1792, he removed to Mason county, and settled on his farm, on Mill creek, where he resided till his death. He was twice shot at by the Indians, near his own house, and had his horses stolen out of his stable. He was an active and resolute woodsman, and was one of almost every party in pursuit of the enemy. He was a scientific and practical surveyor, and for many years a member of the bench of magistrates for the county. His tastes, however, were decidedly military; and, as an officer of the militia, he took great pride in their drill and discipline. In 1813, when Col. R. M. Johnson raised his regiment of mounted riflemen, for service in the north-west, he received the appointment of major commanding the first battalion; and, on the 10th of October of that year, at the battle of the Thames, he, at the head of his battalion, charged through the British line, and, after the surrender, by special order from the general-in-chief, led in pursuit of Proctor. Mounted on a splendid charger, with Capt. (now Colonel) Todd, Maj. Wood, and John Chambers, Esq., one of Gen. Harrison's volunteer aids, close behind him, he dashed off with the battalion at his heels,—which, however, was soon left far in their rear,—and did not rein up till they had gone ten miles beyond the battle-field. The pursuit was so hot, that Gen. Proctor was forced to abandon his carriage and take refuge in the swamp, leaving all his baggage and his papers, public and private, which fell into the hands of the victors. In the report of this battle, it is stated that "Maj. Devall Payne, of the first battalion, inspired confidence wherever he appeared."

JOHN CHAMBERS, Esq., one of those who followed Maj. Payne in this daring pursuit, was, for many years afterwards, a leading lawyer of the Mason bar; frequently a member of the legislature and of congress; and, lately, distinguished as the able and efficient governor of Iowa.

After this campaign, Col. Payne retired to private life. He was extremely popular in his county—was, for a long series of years, a member of the lower house, and, for eight years, in the senate, of the Kentucky legislature, where he was distinguished for his strong common sense and practical view of legislation; and was always elected, when he would consent to serve. He was a member of every electoral college from the time of Jefferson till his death, except the one which cast its vote for Jackson. A democrat of the Jeffersonian school, he was associated with Hughes, George Nicholas, John Breckenridge, Judge Coburn, Gen. Bodley, and other leading men of the olden time in Kentucky; and, in his political course, was firm and inflexible in his own principles, yet tolerant of the opinions of those opposed to him.

Affectionate, tender and assiduous as a husband and father, he was benevolent and gentle in all his social relations. He was bold, resolute, and perfectly honorable in his purposes; fearless and ready in the discharge of all his duties. Tall and erect, with fine symmetry of form, a lofty brow, dark and piercing eyes, and a Roman contour of face, his personal appearance was very commanding.

He died on the 25th of June, 1830, having been a member of the Baptist church for about two years before his death.

Judge JOHN COBURN was a native of Philadelphia, where he received an excellent education, and was bred to the bar. In 1784, under the advice of the distinguished Luther Martin, Esq., of Baltimore, who cherished a deep interest for him, young Coburn emigrated to Kentucky. Abandoning the profession to which he had been reared, however, he located himself in Lexington, and commenced the mercantile business, which was at that time very lucrative. In August, 1786, he married Miss Mary Moss, of Fayette county. He seems to have been successful in mercantile operations, and remained in Lexington till about the year 1794, when he removed to Mason county; and, in partnership with Dr. Basil Duke, continued his mercantile pursuits. Shortly afterwards, he was appointed judge of the district court of Mason, and, upon the reorganization of the courts, became a judge of the circuit court, which office he held till the year 1805.

He was appointed, by Mr. Jefferson, judge of the territory of Michigan, which office he declined, and was subsequently appointed to the judgeship of the territory of Orleans, and held his courts in St. Louis. This office he resigned in 1809, and was afterwards appointed, by Mr. Madison, during the late war, collector of the revenue for the fourth district of Kentucky. This office, which he held for several years, was his last public employment.

Judge Coburn was a man of most decided political principles, and stood high in the confidence of the democratic party. As early as 1785,—a few months after his arrival in the State,—he was elected a member of the convention, called at Danville in that year, to take preliminary steps to procure the admission of Kentucky into the Union, and for other purposes. In 1796, he was appointed a commissioner, in conjunction with Robert Johnson, to run and settle the boundary line between Virginia and Kentucky, upon which subject he made a very able report. Upon its being intimated to the citizens of St. Louis that Judge Coburn intended to resign his office as judge of the Orleans territory, they addressed him a petition complimentary of his "talents, industry, and conciliating manners," and urging him to relinquish the idea of resigning his office.

In 1813, Governor Shelby wrote him an urgent invitation to accompany him and become a member of his military family, which was accepted by the judge, although he held that post for only a short period.

To the able and indefatigable efforts of Judge Coburn is to be attributed, in a great degree, the act of Congress appropriating one thousand acres of land to Col. Daniel Boone. The judge was an ardent friend of the old pioneer, and addressed to Congress some powerful appeals in his behalf.

Judge Coburn never practised law, although he took out license in 1788. He was one of the most indefatigable, efficient and accomplished political writers of his day, and was in close correspondence and intimate relationship with the leading democratic statesmen of Kentucky. So high an estimate was placed upon his ability, that, as early as 1800, he was spoken of in connection with the exalted station of senator in the congress of the United States; but he declined his pretensions to that office in favor of his friend, the distinguished John Breckinridge, who was elected to the senate at the succeeding session of the legislature. Judge Coburn died in February, 1823, aged about sixty years.

AARON H. CORWINE, a portrait painter of much character, was born on the 31st day of August, 1802, at his father's farm, on what is called Jersey Ridge, in Mason county, Kentucky. His father, Amos Corwine, emigrated to Kentucky from Huntington county, New Jersey, at a very early day, and settled in Mason county, where he resided until the period of his death. About the same time, the father of Thomas Corwin, late governor of Ohio, and now a member of the United States' senate from that State, removed with his family from the same State, and settled in Mason county, near Mayslick. Preferring, however, to go further into the interior of Kentucky, he moved with his family to Bourbon county, where Thomas Corwin was born. Aaron H. Corwine was the youngest son, and early evinced a genius in drawing and sketching. It is said that in his tenth year, so fond was he of drawing, he marked and scored his father's board fences and barn with grotesque figures of men, beasts and fowls. So faithful and striking were some of these figures as likenesses, they attracted his father's attention, and induced him to inquire which one of his boys had drawn them. Before then, young Aaron was a ploughboy, for which he never showed much taste, and had scarcely been off of the farm. His father determined to give him an opportunity to pursue the inclination of his mind; and, after bestowing upon him as good an education as could be acquired, at that early day, in Kentucky, in a country school, he placed him with a portrait painter then located in Maysville, whose name was Turner. But he did not remain with him long. He soon mastered all that Mr. Turner knew, and, by the advice of that good man, he was induced to seek other sources of instruction, and a wider field in which to pursue his profession. Cincinnati was then the largest town in the west, and even at that early day was famed for the fostering care her wealthier citizens extended to young artists. Whilst he was yet in his *teens,* young Corwine sought a home in the Queen City. Like the majority of the children of genius, he had but a scanty proportion of this world's goods, when he reached his new home; no knowledge, whatever, of men; and no friends whose wealth and influence could bring him business, or make him known to those who would encourage him by giving employment to his yet immature pencil. Nothing daunted at this gloomy prospect, young Corwine applied himself assiduously to such business as was thrown in his way, until his glowing and life-like pictures attracted the attention and won the admiration of those citizens of Cincinnati who were able and willing to contribute their means, and loan their influence, to lift the young artist into notoriety and business. Amongst these was Nathan Guilford, Esq., who was the first friend of the young artist in that city. These early friends never deserted him; and as he rose, step by step, in his profession, they stood by him—cheering him with their smiles, and strengthening him with their counsel, in the devious and slippery pathway to fame. By their advice, he sought the instruction of that master in his profession, Thomas Sully, then residing in Philadelphia. After a few years spent in the studio of Mr. Sully, young Corwine returned to Cincinnati, where he continued to apply himself to his profession until the year 1828. About this time it was found that his close application to his easel for many years, had seriously impaired his health. For the twofold purpose of improving his health and studying the masters in the old country, he departed for Europe. When he reached London, he deposited all his means with a banker of reputed wealth, who soon after failed, leaving Corwine in a strange city, without means and wholly destitute of friends, to struggle for the necessaries of life. His courage and his genius rose with the occasion. He visited all the galleries in London, that were accessible to one so poor and friendless. He caught the spirit of the mighty masters, and soon his own canvass was made to glow with the genius and taste of Italy and England's mighty dead. The high-born and the noble of England sought his rooms, and the faithful likenesses, the accurate delineations, and the animated and life-like coloring of the young American, were appreciated, and he was rewarded by numerous orders for the most costly pictures. But the close application consequent upon this state of the affairs of Mr. Corwine, was too much for his already enfeebled constitution, and his friends were pained to see him gradually wasting away under the influence of disease. He turned his face towards his native land, to die amongst his friends and in the arms of his kindred. But, alas! this last and dearest hope he was destined never to realize. When he reached Philadelphia, he was borne from the vessel to his lodgings, and, after a few days' struggling, died in that city, on the 4th day of July, 1830, in the twenty-eighth year of his age.

Many of the early productions of Mr. Corwine adorn the parlors of his Cincinnati patrons. Had he lived a few years longer, Mr. Corwine would have stood at the head of his profession.

McCRACKEN COUNTY.

McCRACKEN county was formed in 1824, and named in honor of Captain VIRGIL McCRACKEN. It is situated in the extreme western part of the state, and lies on the Ohio and Tennessee rivers— bounded on the north by the Ohio river; east by Marshall; south by Graves, and west by Ballard. Tobacco is the staple of the county, but grain is generally cultivated, and hogs are exported in considerable quantities.

Number of acres of land in McCracken county, 147,918; average value of land per acre, $2.28; total valuation of taxable property in 1846, $902,653; number of white males over twenty-one years of age, 652; number of children between five and sixteen years old, 861. Population in 1840, 4,745.

PADUCAH, the seat of justice and only town of any size in McCracken, is situated at the mouth of Tennessee river, two hundred and seventy-nine miles by land from Frankfort. It contains four churches, three schools, eight lawyers, six physicians, ten stores, six groceries, three taverns, and a large number of mechanics' shops. In 1830, the population was 105—in 1845, 1500 —in 1847, supposed to be nearly 2000. It was laid out in 1827, by General Clark, of St. Louis, and named after the celebrated Indian chief *Paducah*.

There is a prevailing opinion that there is silver ore in McCracken county, and considerable time and money have been expended in searching for it; hitherto, however, with but very partial success. Lead ore, it is believed, abounds in the county.

Captain VIRGIL McCRACKEN, in honor of whom this county received its name, was a native of Woodford county. His father, Cyrus McCracken, was one of the first adventurers to Kentucky. In conjunction with Hancock Lee, he raised cabins one mile below where Frankfort stands, and named it Leestown. Captain McCracken was an intelligent, patriotic and fearless young man; and when, in 1812, war was declared by the United States against Great Britain, and a call made upon Kentucky for volunteers, he raised a company of riflemen, and joined the regiment of the lamented Colonel John Allen. In the battle of the river Raisin, on the 22d of January, 1813, he fell at the head of his company, while bravely maintaining the honor of his native state on that fatal field.

MEADE COUNTY.

MEADE county was formed in 1823, and called for Capt. JAMES MEADE. It is situated in the north-west middle part of the State, and lies on the Ohio river—bounded on the north by the Ohio river; east by Bullitt; south by Hardin and Breckinridge, and west by Breckinridge and the Ohio river. The Ohio river opposite Meade makes a great bend, and skirts the county on the north, north-west and west about sixty miles, while the Rolling fork of Salt river forms its eastern boundary. The face of the country, with the exception of the river bottoms, is rolling; about two-thirds of the county is what is commonly termed "barrens," interspersed with a few groves of fine timber, the remainder wood land. The soil is based upon clay, with a limestone foundation, and is generally rich and fertile. The principal productions of the county are hemp, tobacco, pork, beef, wheat, corn and oats.

Number of acres of land in Meade county, 152,719; average value per acre, $4.39; total valuation of taxable property in the county in 1846, $1,307,740; number of white males over twenty-one years of age, 1,034; number of children between five and sixteen years of age, 1,360. Population in 1840, 5,780.

There are six towns in the county, viz:—Brandenburg, Big Spring, Concordia, Grahampton, Garnetsville and Rock Haven. BRANDENBURG, the seat of justice, is situated on the Ohio river, forty miles below Louisville and ninety miles from Frankfort. It contains a court-house, two churches (Baptist and Methodist), ten lawyers, seven doctors, ten stores, one drug-store, three groceries, three taverns, one steam and one water flouring mill, four warehouses, one tobacco inspection and eighteen mechanics' shops. Population 600. Incorporated in 1825, and named after Colonel Solomon Brandenburg, the proprietor.

Big Spring is situated at the extreme southern border of the county—and contains a Methodist church, five stores, three taverns and a number of mechanics' shops—the population embracing about twenty families. The town derives its name from a large spring which bursts from the earth near the centre, and flows off two or three hundred yards in a stream of sufficient size to turn a mill, when it sinks beneath the surface, and altogether disappears. At this spring, three counties have their corner, viz: Hardin, Breckinridge and Meade—and this neat little village not only enjoys the luxury of an abundant supply of cold and delicious water, but possesses the rare felicity of incorporating within its bounds, a portion of the territory of three counties.

Concordia is a small village, situated immediately on the bank of the Ohio river, two miles above Flint Island—and contains one store, one doctor, and six or seven families. *Grahampton* is situated at the falls of Otter creek, five miles from the Ohio—contains one tavern, two stores, one Methodist church, one common school, one grist mill, a large cotton and woolen factory, with twelve power looms in constant operation, and three or four mechanics' shops. *Garnetsville* is three miles from the Ohio, on Otter creek, and contains one Methodist church, (and there are two Baptist churches in the vicinity,) two doctors, two stores, one tavern, one water grist and saw mill, and five mechanics' shops. *Rock-Haven* is situated at the Narrows, on the Ohio river, and contains two stores and groceries, and several mechanical trades.

There are several caves in Meade county, but they have not been explored to any extent. In some of these human bones have been discovered of an extraordinary size. A skull bone, sufficiently large to encase the head of a living man of ordinary size, was found in a cave on the lands of Captain Nathan D. Anderson, near Brandenburg.

There are several "Knobs" and "Groves" in Meade county, which are places of considerable notoriety, viz :—The Indian Hill, on Otter creek ; Jennie's Knob ; Bee Knob ; Buck Grove; Jackey's Grove; Hill Grove ; Indian Grove, and Hogback Grove. These places lie very nearly in a range a few miles back or south of the Ohio, and stretch from the mouth of Salt river to the mouth of Sinking creek, a distance of forty miles by land and about eighty miles by the river. These knobs and groves being well known to many individuals before the settlement of the county, especially to the spies, they became points of observation, with the view of detecting the approach of Indians, and giving the alarm to the settlements in Hardin county.* The spies sent out from these settlements, were directed to traverse the country lying between Salt river and Sinking creek, these "knobs" and "groves" serving as places of observation, and giving direction to their course ; and thereby they were enabled to discover the trails of the Indians as soon as they crossed the Ohio river, on their route to attack the settlements. In this way, the Indians were generally discovered and routed, and the settlements protected from their incursions.

The Indians that harassed these settlements were in the habit, uniformly, of crossing the Ohio river between the points before named. On one occasion, they were discovered after they had got some miles into the country, and pursued back to the river at the point where Brandenburg is now situated. They had secreted their bark canoes at the mouth of a small creek, and when the pursuing whites reached the river, the Indians were just landing on the opposite shore. One Indian was seen standing erect in a skiff, having on a *red coat*, when some one of the party exclaimed, "down with the red coat." Joe Logston, a noted Indian fighter at that time, instantly elevated his rifle, and fired at the *red* Indian. He fell forward into the river, causing quite a splashing of the water around him, and as he was not seen to rise again, the inference was irresistible that Joe's bullet had proved fatal.†

This county received its name in honor of Captain JAMES MEADE, a native of Woodford county, Kentucky. Captain Meade, when quite a youth, volunteered his services under the lamented Colonel Joseph H. Daviess, in the Wabash expedition, and fought side by side with that gallant officer in the battle of Tippecanoe. For his bravery on this occasion, combined with his intelligence and military qualifications, he was promoted to the rank of captain in the regular service. In 1813, at the battle of the river Raisin, where so many of the gallant young men of Kentucky found a bloody grave, the company of Captain Meade composed a part of the regular force. He occupied a very exposed position, and fell at the head of his company, while gallantly leading them on, early in the action.

*These settlements comprised several stations and many highly respectable families—among them, the Hynes, the Helms. the Rawlings, the Millers, the Ventrees, the Vanmatres, the Harts, the Fairleighs, the Larues, the Hodgens, &c., &c., and extended into what is now Larue county.
† This individual was no doubt Big Joe Logston. See an account of his rencounter with two Indians under the head of Greene county.

VIEW OF HARRODSBURG SPRINGS, KY.

MERCER COUNTY.

MERCER county is one of the nine counties formed by Virginia in 1786, and received its name in honor of General HUGH MERCER. It is situated near the centre of the State, on the waters of the Kentucky river—bounded on the north by Anderson, on the east by Woodford, Jessamine and Garrard, on the south by Boyle, and on the west by Washington. The surface is undulating, and the land generally of a good quality—some portions very rich, and the whole finely watered. Mercer is a heavy grain growing and stock raising county, and before Boyle county was stricken from it, produced a much larger quantity of corn than any other county in the State. In 1840, Mercer gathered 3,397,406 bushels of corn, while Harrison, the next highest on the list, gathered 1,716,484 bushels. This county, being settled at the very earliest period of the history of Kentucky, has been finely improved; and the population, consisting principally of the descendants of pioneer families, are generally in independent circumstances, well educated and intelligent.

Number of acres of land reported in Mercer, 153,923; average value of land per acre, $14.32; valuation of taxable property in 1846, $4,026,469; number of white males over twenty-one years of age, 2,027; number of children between the ages of five and sixteen years, 2,037. Population in 1840, 12,353.

The towns of Mercer consist of Harrodsburg, the seat of justice, Pleasant Hill, Salvisa, Lucto, Cornishville, and Oregon.

HARRODSBURG is situated on a commanding eminence, thirty miles from Frankfort, eight miles from the Kentucky river, one mile from Salt river, and near the geographical centre of the State.* Contains a court-house, five churches, (Methodist, Presbyterian, Baptist, Christian, and African), one college, two female academies, one male seminary, ten lawyers, ten physicians, five taverns, eighteen dry goods stores and groceries, two book and drug stores, one printing office, two hemp factories, two wool carding establishments, and forty-five mechanics' shops, embracing all the industrial trades—population 1,700. Named after the Harrod family.

The HARRODSBURG SPRINGS, one of the most fashionable watering places in the State, have become deservedly celebrated for the medicinal virtue of the water,† and as a delightful summer resort, both to the votaries of health and pleasure. Dr. Christopher Graham, the amiable, enterprising and intelligent proprietor, has spared no pains or expense in the preparation of accommodations for visitors, the improvements having already cost about $300,000. The main hotel is one of the

---

* The history of its settlement will be found in the succeeding pages, for which we are indebted to General R. B. McAfee.

† Dr. Drake, in the Western Journal of Medical and Physical Sciences, gives the following analysis of the water in one of the springs: 1. Sulphate of magnesia, in large quantities; 2. Carbonate of magnesia, in small quantities; 3. Sulphate of soda, do.; 4. Sulphate of lime, do.; 5. Carbonate of lime, in minute do.; 6. Iron, do; 7. A minute quantity of sulphuretted hydrogen. There are seven or eight springs at Harrodsburg, which vary somewhat in the character of their waters. The Epsom closely resembles that of the celebrated Seidlitz Springs, of Bohemia.

29

finest and most commodious buildings in the west, and the surrounding cottages are admirably arranged, alike to promote the comfort and convenience of the occupants. The grounds are elevated and extensive; adorned with every variety of shrubbery grown in America, interspersed with some of the most beautiful and rare exotics from Europe and Asia, and traversed by wide gravel walks, intersecting and crossing each other in every direction. A small and beautiful lake, three hundred yards long, one hundred yards in width, and fifteen feet deep, lately excavated, is well stored with fish of the finest flavor, and its glassy surface enlivened by the presence of many wild and tame water-fowls.

BACON COLLEGE, HARRODSBURGH, KY.

BACON COLLEGE,* located in Harrodsburg, under the care of the Christian body, is a flourishing institution, with some eighty or one hundred students. It was founded in 1836. The Rev. JAMES SHANNON is president, assisted by four professors. The library contains fifteen hundred volumes. Commencement on the last Friday in September.

There are also in Harrodsburg, two flourishing FEMALE SEMINARIES—one under the management of Mr. Mullens, of the Christian church, containing sixty or seventy scholars; and the other under the care of the Rev. John Montgomery, of the Presbyterian church, with from one hundred to one hundred and twenty students.

---

* For a more full account of Bacon College, see article headed "Christian Church."

MAIN HOUSE AT SHAKER VILLAGE, KY.

Pleasant Hill, or *Union Village*, is a small village of rare beauty and neatness, situated on a commanding eminence, about one mile from the Kentucky river, and seven miles from Harrodsburg. It belongs exclusively to that orderly and industrious society called *Shakers*, and contains between three and four hundred inhabitants, divided into families of from sixty to eighty each. Their main edifice is a large, handsome and costly structure, built of Kentucky marble; the others, generally, are built of brick, and all admirably arranged for comfort and convenience. The internal and external arrangement and neatness of their dwellings—the beauty and luxuriance of their gardens and fields—the method and economy displayed in their manufacturing and mechanical establishments—their orderly and flourishing schools—their sleek and well fed stock, are all characteristic of this singular people, and evidence a high degree of comfort and prosperity. Every important family arrangement is governed by the *clock*, and moves on with the harmony and regularity of *clock-work*, in BEAUTIFUL ORDER.

Salvisa is a handsome village on the turnpike road from Frankfort to Harrodsburg, eleven miles from the latter place—contains four churches,* (Presbyterian, Christian, Baptist and Methodist), an excellent school, three physicians, four stores, one tavern, one woolen factory, and eight or ten mechanics' shops—population, 130. Laid out by general McAfee in 1816. *Lucto* and *Cornishville* are small places on Salt river, and *Chapline* has a post-office, mill and two stores. *Oregon* is a new village on the Kentucky river, at the head of slack water navigation, and promises to be a place of considerable trade. Seven or eight thousand hogs were slaughtered there in 1846.

The scenery on the Kentucky and Dick's rivers, is among the grandest and most picturesque in the United States. Next to the highlands of the Hudson, it is probably unequalled for its imposing effect. Those towering cliffs, rising in perpendicular walls for many hundred feet above the beach, variegated by marble strata of every conceivable thickness and color, overpower the beholder with a sense of Nature's majesty. They look like the battlements of a world, standing there so stern and erect in their massive proportions, and as we gaze upon their bald fronts, against which the storms of ages have beaten, we can almost realize the fable of the Titans, and suppose they have been thrown up in some long-forgotten battle of the gods.

An incident occurred at Shaker ferry in 1845, nearly opposite the most elevated of these cliffs, which shows that men sometimes bear a charmed life. A stranger from Connecticut, believed to be an artist, was seen in the neighborhood for several days—his object unknown. A short time before the hour of dinner, in the month of June or July, while the occupant of a little cabin on the left bank of the river was engaged in his corn field on the bottom immediately opposite the ferry, his attention was attracted by a rattling noise above him, and looking up, he saw a man falling down the fearful precipice—now touching and grasping at a twig, now at a root, without being able to arrest his descent. He finally lodged in the top of a small buckeye tree, about fifty feet above the general level of the bottom. The total distance of the fall was one hundred and seventy feet; and from the last point at which he touched the rock to the top of the tree, was forty-five feet. The next day he was walking about, apparently but little injured.

---

* There are but few towns in the United States, it is believed, with so small a population, which contains so many places of religious worship.

ANCIENT TOWNS AND FORTIFICATIONS.—There are two of these in Mercer county both on Salt river, one about four miles above Harrodsburg, containing ditches and a mound some ten or twelve feet high, filled with human bones and broken pieces of crockery ware. On one side of the mound a hickory tree about two feet in diameter grew, and was blown up by its roots, making a hole some three or four feet deep. Its lower roots drew up a large piece of crockery ware, which had been on some fire coals—the handle was attached to it, and human hair lay by the coals. This was probably a place of human sacrifice. The other ruins are about a mile and a half above, both being on the west side of the river. There is no mound near this, but only the remains of earth dug out of the ditches. Each place is of quadrangular form.

There are also remains of ancient Indian villages on and near Salt river, and close by petrified muscle shells, conglomerated into large lumps of rocks, exist; and generally some two feet of soil covers them, showing many years of abandonment. One of these is on General R. B. McAfee's plantation, four miles northwest of Harrodsburg, near a large cave spring.

Colonel DANIEL BOONE spent the winter of 1769–70, in a cave, on the waters of *Shawanee*, in Mercer county. A tree marked with his name, is yet standing near the head of the cave.

The settlements in Mercer county commenced in March, 1775, and gradually increased till 1779, when the commissioners to grant land titles met in Harrodsburg. A flood of emigrants succeeded, and the number was more than doubled the succeeding three years. Among the emigrants previous to the year 1786, are found the names of Harrod, Ray, McAfee, McGary, Denton, Hogan, Thompson, Adams, Curry, Wood, Haggin, McBride, Mosby, Smith, Armstrong, Buchanan, Cowan, Field, Jordan, McCoun, Moore, Prather, Wilson, Irvine, Caldwell, Rice and Harbison. The first county court met in Harrodsburg on Tuesday, August —, 1786, and appointed Thomas Allin, who had served in the staff of General Greene in his southern campaigns during the latter years of the revolutionary war, its first clerk. Justices of the peace present: John Cowan, Hugh McGary, Gabriel Madison, Alexander Robertson, Samuel Scott, Samuel McAfee, John Irvine and Samuel McDowell, Senior.

Harrodsburg has the honor of being the first settled place in the state of Kentucky.[*] In July, 1773, the McAfee company, from Bottetourt county, Virginia, visited this region, and surveyed lands on Salt river, from the mouth of Hammond's creek to a point two miles above the mouth of the town branch. Captain James Harrod, with forty-one men, descended the Ohio river from the Monongahela country in May, 1774, and penetrating the intervening forest, made his principal camp about one hundred yards below the town spring, (which is a very ·fine one,) under the branches of a spreading elm tree, which is now standing in full vigor. Here he held his nightly councils, and explored the surrounding country, during which time Captain Alexander Chapline, one of his men, discovered Chapline's fork of this river, which yet bears his name. About the middle of June, Captain Harrod and his company agreed to lay off a town, including their camp, and extending down and south of the town branch; and proceeded to erect a number of cabins on their respective lots of one half acre, and a five acre out-lot. The town thus laid off received the name of *Harrodstown*; subsequently it was called *Oldtown*—and, finally, its present name of *Harrodsburg*. The first corn raised in Kentucky was in 1775, by John Harman, in a field at the east end of Harrodsburg. Here Colonel Boone found them on his way to the falls of Ohio, being sent out by Governor Dunmore to warn the surveyors in that region that the northern Indians had become hostile, which eventuated in General Lewis' battle at the mouth of the Kenawha, October 10th, 1774. Harrod and his company remained at his town until about the 20th of July, when three or four of his men having discovered a large spring about three miles below their town, which was called *Fontainbleau*, stopped to rest about noon. The Indians fired on them, and killed James Cowan, who was engaged at the time drying his papers in the sun, which had got wet from a heavy rain in the morn-

---

[*] So says General R. B. McAfee, in a letter to the author, and he is not disposed to controvert the statement, although it has been questioned by others.

ing. The others dispersed. Two of them, Jacob Sandusky and another, taking the trail to the falls of Ohio, descended that river and the Mississippi in a bark canoe, and went round to Philadelphia by sea. The other got back to Harrod's camp and gave the alarm. Captain Harrod raised a company of his men and went down and buried Cowan, and secured his papers, which they found very much scattered; when they returned to their camp.

On the 11th of March of the succeeding year, 1775, the McAfee company returned to Salt river to renew their improvements—cleared two acres of ground, and planted peach stones and apple seeds at what was afterwards known as McAfee's station on Salt river, about one-fourth of a mile above what is now known as Providence church. Four days after their arrival, Captain Harrod and a greater part of the men who had been with him the year before, passed them on their way to Harrodsburg, then called Harrodstown, and reached there on the same day, March 15, 1775. The McAfee company started home the 11th of April, and left two of their men, John Higgins and Swein Poulson, with Captain Harrod, to notify other companies not to intrude on their lands. Harrodsburg was always occupied afterwards. On the 8th day of September following, Captain Hugh McGary, Thomas Denton and —— Hogan with their wives, arrived at Harrodsburg, having traveled as far as the Hazle patch with Colonel Daniel Boone and his family, on his way to Boonsborough. We have been thus particular, as some dispute has grown out of this matter between Harrodsburg and Boonsborough. When the whole State was known as Kentucky county, the first court ever held in the State, convened in Harrodsburg on the second day of September, 1777, at which time its population, taken by Captain John Cowan, was 198, as follows:

Men in service, ... 81
Do. not in service,....................................... 4
Women,.. 24
Children over ten years,.. 12
Children under ten years,... 58
Slaves above ten years,.. 12
Do. under ten years,... 7

Total,......................... 198

In the years 1771–2, the sons of James McAfee, sen., fired by the glowing description of the beauty and fertility of Kentucky, and particularly of this region, as given by Dr. Walker and others, determined to visit it in search of a new home. Accordingly, after holding a family council, it was resolved that James, George, and Robert McAfee, James McCoun, jr., (the brother-in-law of Robert McAfee), and Samuel Adams, a youth of eighteen years, and a cousin of James McCoun, should constitute the company. They departed from their homes, in Bottetourt county, Virginia, on the 10th of May, 1773, and, proceeding across the mountains, struck the Kanawha river about four miles above the mouth of Elk river, and from this point sent back their horses by two boys, (John McCoun and James Pawling), who had accompanied them for the purpose. Here they constructed two canoes, and, on the 28th of May, descended the Kanawha—meeting, in their descent, by previous arrangement, Hancock Taylor and his company of surveyors, and finding at the mouth of the river, which they reached on the 1st of June, Capt. Bullitt and his company.* The three parties proceeded from the mouth of the Kanawha, down the Ohio, in company, and, on the 22d of June, arrived at the mouth of Limestone creek, where Maysville now stands. On the 24th, the boats were shoved off, and the party continued to descend the river, while Robert McAfee made an excursion through the contiguous country. Passing up Limestone creek to its source, he struck across the dividing ridge, to the

---

* Capt. Bullitt left his companions at this place, and went alone, through the woods, to the Indian town at Old Chillicothe. He arrived in the midst of the town undiscovered by the Indians, until seen waving his white handkerchief as a token of peace. The Indians were, very naturally, startled—but the intrepidity, courage, and fine address of Bullitt, disarmed their hostility. He held a friendly conversation with them—attended a council—assured them of the friendly disposition of the whites, who were solicitous, in return, of the good will of the Indians—spoke of the lands he was about to settle—promised them presents—and, leaving them in good humor, rejoined his company at the mouth of the Scioto.

waters of the north fork of Licking, and proceeded down that stream some twenty or twenty-five miles, and then directed his course over the hills of the present county of Bracken, to the Ohio river. When he reached the river, he ascertained that his company had passed down. Determined to follow as speedily as possible, he instantly went to work, and, with the use of his tomahawk and knife, cut down and skinned a tree, and constructed a bark canoe, which he completed about sundown on the same day of his arrival. Committing himself to this frail craft, he floated down the river, and on the succeeding day—the 27th of June—overtook his company at the mouth of Licking.

The 4th and 5th of July the company spent at Big Bone Lick, in the present county of Boone,—making seats and tent poles, while there, of the enormous backbones and ribs of the mastodon, which were found in large quantities at that time. At the mouth of the Kentucky, the companies separated—Capt. Bullitt's proceeding to the falls of the Ohio, and Hancock Taylor and the McAfee company directing their course up the Kentucky river. They ascended the Kentucky to the mouth of Drennon's Lick creek, where they found the river nearly closed by a rocky bar. Here, on the 9th of July, they left their canoes, and went out to the lick, where they discovered immense numbers of buffalo, elk, deer, wolves, bears, &c. They continued either at or in the neighborhood of the lick, until the 15th of July. While there, quite a ludicrous and yet dangerous scene occurred. A large herd of buffalo being in the lick, Samuel Adams was tempted to fire his gun at one of them, when the whole herd, in terrible alarm, ran directly towards the spot where Adams and James McAfee stood. Adams instantly sprang up a leaning tree, but James McAfee, being less active, was compelled to take shelter behind a tree barely large enough to cover his body. In this condition the whole herd passed them—the horns of the buffalo scraping off the bark on both sides of the tree behind which McAfee was standing, drawn up to his smallest dimensions. After all had passed, Adams crawled down, and McAfee mildly said: "My good boy, you must not venture that again."

On the 15th of July, the company left Drennon's lick, and, on the succeeding day, crossed the Kentucky river below where Frankfort now stands, where Robert McAfee had two surveys made, embracing six hundred acres, and including Frankfort bottom. On the 17th, they left their encampment, and, proceeding up the Kentucky river, on the 18th reached the Cave Springs.* Tarrying here two days, they continued their march, in a westerly direction, to Salt river, which they called Crooked creek, and made their surveys of four hundred acres each, from the mouth of Hammond's creek, up Salt river, to about two miles above where Harrodsburg now stands.

The further history of the McAfee company we quote, in a condensed form, from a small work by the Rev. Dr. Davidson:

"On the 31st of July, they (the McAfee company), turned their faces homeward. They proceeded under showers of rain, and suffering various hardships. When they reached the foot of the mountains, their stock of provisions failed, and game was difficult to procure. To cross the mountains proved likewise a very laborious undertaking, covered as they were with laurel, underbrush, and pine.

"The 12th of August was a gloomy day to this little band. They had gained the highest point of the craggy range dividing the head waters of the Kentucky and Clinch rivers; a region that seemed the abode of desolation. Nothing but barren rocks frowned on every side, and silence and solitude reigned uninterrupted. Not a living animal was to be seen, nor a bird to cheer them with its wild notes. They were exposed to a broiling sun; their feet were blistered; and their legs were torn and raw from the effect of the briers; add to which, they were literally starving, not having had a mouthful to eat for two days. Such a combination of misfortunes was enough to appal the stoutest heart.

"The day was drawing to a close; the sun was sinking in the west, and gilding the mountain's top with his last setting beams; they had not as yet seen a solitary animal that could serve for food ; and the herbage was not only scanty but unfit for sustenance. To complete their distress, they found the head-springs of the water-courses dried up by the excessive heat, and not affording a drop to

---

* This is a remarkable spring, situated under a rock, on the road between Frankfort and Harrodsburg,—at that time called Cave Spring, but now known as Lillard's Spring.

allay their thirst. Exhausted by fatigue, hunger and despair, George McAfee and young Adams threw themselves on the ground, declaring themselves unable to proceed any farther. As a last desperate effort, Robert McAfee then determined to compass the ridge in quest of game, leaving James with the two others to rally their spirits. He had not proceeded a quarter of a mile, when a young buck crossed his path ; and although agitated by intensely anxious feelings, he was so good a marksman as to bring him down at the first shot. On hearing the report of his gun, the rest of the company, forgetting their fatigue, sprang up, and ran to the spot whence the sound proceeded. The meal, thus opportunely furnished, they devoured with keen appetites, and slaked their thirst from a branch which they discovered adjacent ; while their hearts overflowed with gratitude to that Providence, which, by so timely an interposition, had rescued them from the jaws of death. Recruited in strength, they resumed their journey, and soon reached their homes ; where, in spite of the hardships and hazards attending the exploit, the accounts they published inspired a general enthusiasm to imitate their example.

"Indian wars and the battle of Kenhawa, detained them in Virginia during the succeeding year ; but the year 1775 found them among the cane-brakes. Robert, Samuel, and William McAfee, allowed themselves to be persuaded by Colonel Henderson, to unite their fortunes with his, against the wholesome advice of their elder brother James, who assured them that Henderson's claim could not be valid, because without the sanction of government. They went to Boonsborough, entered land and raised corn, but, as was predicted, the scheme proved abortive. In the fall, we find the company reunited, consisting of William, George, and Robert McAfee, George McGee, David Adams, John McCoun, and some others, and under the protection of the newly erected Harrod's station, they cleared fifteen acres of ground below the mouth of Armstrong's Branch, in Mercer county, and planted it in corn. A part of the company wintered here, while the rest went back to Virginia, leaving forty head of cattle to fatten on the luxuriant cane and herbage. These last mentioned persons took measures to return in the spring following, calculating that the corn and cattle would, by this time, be in a condition to support them.

"Accordingly, in May, 1776, they packed up their household property and farming utensils, with a quantity of seeds of various kinds, barrels of corn and flour, and stores of coffee, sugar, and spices, not omitting a few bottles of whisky and spirits, (*by way of medicine, no doubt,*) which they placed, for security, in the middle of the flour and corn barrels, and attempted to convey them in canoes down the Gauley and Kenhawa rivers ; but finding this impracticable, they resolved to go back for pack horses. Having built a strong log cabin, resembling the *caches* described by Washington Irving in his Astoria, as used by the fur-traders, they deposited in it all their property, and covering it with bark, left it in this situation in the wilderness. The rumor of hostilities, and the war of the Revolution caused a delay of several months; and when they returned in September, they found the *cache*, to their dismay, broken open, the roof torn off, and rugs, blankets, barrels, and stores, strewed in confusion around, and totally ruined. On making some search, they found evidences of some one having taken out the bedding to sleep on, under an adjacent cliff, and that the same person had rummaged their kegs and barrels, in order to get at the liquor.

"No Indian *sign*, as the traces of the savages were called, was visible; but upon searching by parties of two, they found, within half a mile of the spot, a diminutive red-haired man, on whose person they discovered some of the missing articles. Vexed at the wanton destruction of so many valuable stores of coffee, sugar, spices, and the like articles, which they had been for years collecting, at a time too, when they were so much needed, and could not be replaced where they were going; and provoked beyond endurance by the wretch's denial, although proofs were on his person, one of the party felled him to the ground with his tomahawk, and was on the point of dispatching him with his knife, when his brother seized his arm and prevented the rash act.

"The fellow's name was Edward Sommers. He was a convict servant, who had ran off from his master in the interior of Virginia, and was making the best of his way to the Indians. As soon as he recovered from the stunning effect of the blow he had received, he was led to the cabin, where a council was held upon the case. He was adjudged to have forfeited his life according to the laws of the land, but as none of the company was willing to execute the hangman's office, the miserable wretch escaped with his life. He was compelled, however, to accompany them back to Virginia, where he was delivered up into the hands of his master, and very probably received such a scourging as made him more desirous to run away than ever.

"The war with Great Britain, in which the members of this company and all their connexions heartily united, hindered the resumption of their darling project for the next two years, during which time the cattle they had left ran wild, in the woods, or fell the prey of Indian marauders, and were irrecoverably lost.

"The year 1779 saw these enterprising adventurers settled with their families on their new territory, having passed the Cumberland Gap with pack-horses. Their first care was to fortify themselves in a quadrangular enclosure of cabins and stockades, to which was given the name of *McAfee's station*. A winter of unexampled severity ensued; and from the middle of November to the middle of February, snow and ice continued on the ground without a thaw. Many of the cattle perished; and numbers of bears, buffalo, deer, wolves, beavers, otters, and wild turkeys were found frozen to death. Sometimes the famished wild animals would come up in the yard of the stations along with the tame cattle. Such was the scarcity of food, that a single jonny-cake would be divided into a dozen parts, and distributed around to the inmates to serve for two meals. Even this resource failed, and for weeks they had nothing to live on but wild game. Early in the spring, some of the men went to the Falls of the Ohio, now Louisville, where they gave sixty dollars (continental money) for a bushel of corn; which was considered an enormous price, even making allowance for its depreciated value; but the only alternative was starvation.

"A delightful spring, and the rapid growth of vegetation, promised to repay them for the hardships they had undergone. The peach-trees they had planted five years before, were loaded with fruit, and the apple-trees were also in a thriving condition. Plenty and happiness smiled upon the settlement, when, by one of those unexpected reverses, which seem designed by Providence to admonish us of what we are too apt to forget, the uncertain tenure of our earthly prosperity, and the small reliance to be placed upon present appearances, their flattering prospects were all at once damped by a melancholy event that filled every heart with gloom.

"Joseph McCoun, a promising lad, the youngest and the darling son of his father, and the favourite of the whole family, was surprised and carried off by a party of Shawanee Indians, while looking after some cattle in an adjoining glade. His companion escaped, and immediately gave the alarm; but pursuit was vain. The savages carried their unhappy victim to a little town on the head waters of Mad river, about six miles above the spot now occupied by the town of Springfield, Ohio, where they tied him to a stake and burned him with excruciating tortures. After this heart-rending event, which took place in March, 1781, the families, seven in number, abandoned the farms they had been cultivating, and took refuge in the station. This step was rendered absolutely necessary, for the Indians were prowling in every direction, stealing horses, attacking the armed companies that passed from one station to another, and killing and scalping every unfortunate straggler that fell into their hands. The expedition under General George Rogers Clark, in which the men of the Salt river settlement, burning for vengeance, participated, daunted them for a time, and restored quiet."

The insecurity of the settlers, and the hazards to which they were exposed about this period, appear to have been very great. There was no communication between the stations, of which there were now several, except by armed companies. The inhabitants, not daring to spend the night out of the forts, cultivated their corn during the day, with the hoe in one hand and a gun in the other. A large party went one morning to a neighboring plantation to assist in pulling flax, a friendly office always cheerfully tendered, but were unconsciously waylaid by eight or nine Indians. The wily savages, afraid to make an open attack, cut down bushes, and constructed a screen in a fit situation for an ambuscade, so that no one would be able to discover them till within a few yards. Behind this leafy screen they lay, watching for the return of their unsuspecting victims, and anticipating with savage eagerness the pleasure of scalping the whole party. But

Providence ordered otherwise. One of the young men (John McCoun, Jr.) proposed to his companions, on their way homeward, to deviate a little for the sake of gathering plums, a quantity of which grew at no great distance. As the sun was not yet down, they consented ; and in consequence of this happy suggestion, they reached home by a more circuitous but safer route. We may imagine the mingled amazement and delight with which they discovered next day what an escape they had made from imminent danger. The deserted blind, and the spot where the Indians lay, till their impatience and chagrin became insupportable, were objects of curiosity for several years. Surprise, however, was not the only emotion excited on this occasion ; it is gratifying to be able to add, that a deep and salutary impression was made on the whole party, of the obligations under which they were placed to Providence for so signal a deliverance.

And it may be here mentioned to the credit of the McAfees and McCouns, that when a few years after they erected a rural church in their settlement, (the same over which the venerable Dr. Cleland now presides), mindful of the frequent interpositions of benignant Heaven in their favor, from the relief on the Alleghany mountains, through the entire progress of their history, they gave it the appropriate name of *Providence* church. Who can doubt, that from this humble structure built of logs, this church in the woods, the hymn and the prayer went up, as acceptable to the ear of the Almighty, as though it had been one of those stately and elegant temples which have been reared in later years, attesting, if not the increased devotion, at least the increased wealth of the west.

The incursions of the savages gradually diminished from this period, as the country was more and more occupied by numerous emigrants, or *Long Knives*, as the Indians termed the whites. The McAfee station, like all the others, became a prominent centre of population, and was looked up to as one of the main props of the country. Grist-mills began now to be erected ; improvements of all kinds were projected ; and uninterrupted prosperity finally crowned the enterprising pioneers. Having mentioned grist-mills, it may not be amiss to relate, out of the MSS., how their grain had been ground hitherto. Hand-mills were in use, of a primitive and almost oriental character, consisting of a pair of slabs of limestone, about two feet in diameter, which were placed in a hollow tree, generally sycamore or gum ; and every morning each family would grind as much as would supply them through the day.

General George Rogers Clark first came to Kentucky in 1775, and penetrated to Harrodsburg, which had been re-occupied by Colonel Harrod. In this visit, from his well known and commanding talents, he was voluntarily placed in command of the irregular troops then in Kentucky. In the fall, he returned to Virginia, and came back again to Kentucky in 1776. Mr. Butler relates the following anecdote, received from the lips of General Ray, as having occurred with General Clark upon his second visit : "I had come down," said General Ray, " to where I now live, (about four miles north of Harrodsburg,) to turn some horses in the range. I had killed a small blue-wing duck, that was feeding in my spring, and had roasted it nicely on the brow of the hill, about twenty steps east of my house. After having taken it off to cool, I was much surprised on being suddenly arrested by a fine, soldierly looking man, who exclaimed, 'How do you do, my little fellow ? What is your name ? A'nt you afraid of being in the woods by yourself ?' On satisfying the inquiries, I invited the traveler to partake of my duck, which he did without leaving me a bone to pick, his appetite was so keen, though he should have been welcome to all the game I could have killed, when I afterwards became acquainted with his noble and gallant soul." After satisfying his questions, he inquired of the stranger his own name and business in this remote region. "My name is Clark," he answered, " and I have come out to see what you brave fellows are doing in Kentucky, and to lend you a helping hand if necessary." General Ray, then a boy of sixteen, conducted Clark to Harrodsburg, where he spent his time in observations on the condition and prospects of the country, natural to his comprehensive mind, and assisting at every opportunity in its defence.

At a general meeting of the settlers at Harrodstown, on the 6th of June, 1775, General George Rogers Clark, and Gabriel John Jones were chosen to represent them in the assembly of Virginia.* For the manner in which they discharged the trust committed to them, see sketch of General Clark.

In March, 1777, while James Ray, his brother, and another man were engaged in clearing some land about four miles from Harrodstown, (the same place which afterwards continued to be the residence of the venerable pioneer, General James Ray, until his death,) they were attacked by a party of forty-seven hostile Indians, under the command of the celebrated chief, Blackfish. The Indians were attracted to the place by the noise of the axes, and rushing upon the choppers, killed the younger Ray, and took the third prisoner. The elder Ray, (distinguished afterwards as General James Ray) being uninjured by the discharge of rifles, fled in the direction of the fort. Several of the swiftest Indians followed him in full chase, but such was his fleetness and activity, that he distanced them all, and reached the fort in safety. The remarkable swiftness of Ray elicited the admiration of the Indians, and Blackfish himself remarked to Boone after his capture at the Blue Licks the succeeding year, that some boy at Harrodstown had outrun all his warriors.

The speed of Ray was a fortunate circumstance for the fort at Harrodstown, as his information enabled the garrison to prepare for the expected attack. The militia was organised, ammunition prepared, water and provision secured, and the fort put in the best possible state of defence. On the morning of the 7th of March, 1777, several days after the escape of Ray, the Indians approached the vicinity of the fort, and preliminary to an attack, fired an out cabin on the east side of the town. The garrison, unconscious of the proximity of the enemy, and supposing the fire to be the result of accident, rushed out of the fort with a view to extinguish the flames. The Indians, doubtless intending to decoy the garrison, instantly attempted to intercept their return to the fort. The whites retreated, keeping up a random fire, until they reached a piece of woods on the hill, (now occupied by the court house in Harrodsburg,) where each man took a tree, and soon caused the Indians, in turn, to give back, when they succeeded in regaining the fort. The Indians soon afterwards withdrew. In this conflict, one Indian was killed, and four of the whites wounded, one of whom subsequently died.

In the "Sketches of the Early Catholic Missions of Kentucky," by the Rev. Dr. Spalding, of the Catholic church, recently published, a different version is given of the attack on the wood-choppers, than that published by Mr. Butler. "The *third man*," Dr. Spalding says, "was William Coomes; but there was yet a *fourth* man, named Thomas Shores," who, and not William Coomes, "was taken prisoner by the Indians, at the Shawanee Springs." The statement of Mr. Coomes, as furnished Dr. Spalding by his son, is as follows:

"The party of choppers alluded to, consisted of the two Rays, Wm. Coomes, and Thomas Shores, who were engaged in clearing land, at the Shawanee Springs, for Hugh McGary, the father-in-law of the two Rays. On the 6th of March, 1777, the two Rays, and Shores, visited a neighboring sugar-camp, to slake their thirst, leaving Mr. Coomes alone at the clearing. William Coomes, alarmed at their protracted absence, had suspended his work, and was about to start in search of them, when he suddenly spied a body of Indians—fifteen in number—coming directly towards him, from the direction of the sugar-camp. He instantly concealed himself behind the trunk of the tree which he had just felled, at the same time seizing and cocking his rifle. Fortunately, the Indians had not observed him, owing to the thick cane-brake and undergrowth: they passed by him, in Indian file, to a temporary log cabin, which the woodmen had erected for their accommodation.

"So soon as they were out of sight, Coomes escaped towards the sugar-camp, to find out what had become of his companions. Discovering no trace of them, he concealed himself amidst the boughs of a fallen hickory tree, the yellow leaves of which were of nearly the same color as his garments. From his hiding-place he had a full view of the sugar-camp; and, after a short time, he observed a party of forty Indians halt there, where they were soon rejoined by the fifteen whom he had previously seen. They tarried there for a long time, drinking the syrup, singing their war-songs, and dancing their war-dance. Coomes was a breathless spectator of this scene of revelry, from the distance of only fifty or sixty yards.

---

* They hailed as representatives from "the western part of Fincastle county, on the Kentucky river."

Other straggling parties of savages also came in, and the whole number amounted to about seventy, instead of forty-seven, as stated by Butler and Marshall.

" Meantime, James Ray had escaped, and communicated the alarm to the people of Harrodstown. Great was the terror and confusion which ensued there. The hot-headed McGary openly charged James Harrod with having been wanting in the precautions and courage necessary for the defence of the fort. These two men, who had a personal enmity against each other, quarreled, and leveled their fatal rifles at each other's bosoms. In this conjuncture, the wife of McGary rushed in and turned aside the rifle of her husband, when Harrod immediately withdrew his, and the difficulty was temporarily adjusted.

" McGary insisted that a party of thirty should be immediately dispatched with him, in search of Coomes, Shores, and his son-in-law, William Ray. Harrod, the commandant of the station, and Col. George Rogers Clark, thought this measure rash and imprudent, as all the men were necessary for the defence of the place, which might be attacked by the Indians at any moment. At length, however, the request of McGary was granted, and thirty mounted men were placed under his command, for the expedition.

" The detachment moved with great rapidity, and soon reached the neighborhood of the sugar-camp, which the Indians had already abandoned. Near it they discovered the mangled remains of William Ray, at the sight of which, McGary turned pale, and was near falling from his horse, in a fainting fit. As soon as the body was discovered, one of the men shouted out: ' See there ! they have killed poor Coomes !' Coomes, who had hitherto lurked in his hiding-place, now sallied forth, and ran towards the men, exclaiming : ' No, they haven't killed me, by Job ! I'm safe !'

" The party, having buried Ray and rescued Coomes, returned in safety to Harrodstown, which they reached about sunset."

During the year 1777, the Indians collected in great numbers around Harrodstown, in order, it is supposed, to prevent any corn from being raised for the support of the settlers. In this period of distress and peril, Ray, at that time but seventeen years old, rendered himself an object of general favor, by his intrepidity, courage and enterprise. He often rose before day, and left the fort, on an old horse,—the only one left by the Indians, of forty brought to the country by Maj. McGary,—in order to procure food for the garrison. Proceeding cautiously to Salt river, (generally riding in the water, or in the bed of some small stream, in order to conceal his route), when sufficiently out of hearing, he would kill his load of game, and bring it in to the suffering inhabitants after night-fall. Older and more experienced hunters, in similar hazardous enterprises, were killed by the Indians.[*]

During the same year, while Ray and a man named M'Connell were shooting at a mark near the fort, the latter was suddenly shot down by the Indians. Ray instantly glanced his eye in the direction of the shot, and perceiving the enemy, raised his rifle to avenge the death of his friend, when he was suddenly attacked by a large body of Indians, who had crept near him unseen. His powers as a runner were again called into requisition, and Ray bounded towards the fort, distant a hundred and fifty yards, with the speed of an antelope, amidst showers of bullets from the savages. But when he approached the gates of the fort, he found them closed, and the garrison too much under the influence of their fears to open them for his admission. In this critical situation, pursued by the savages, and refused shelter by his friends, Ray threw himself flat upon the ground, behind a stump just large enough to protect his body. Here, within seven steps of the fort wall, in sight of his mother, he lay for four hours, while the Indians kept up an incessant fire, the balls often striking and tearing up the ground on either side of him. At last, becoming somewhat impatient, he called out to the garrison, " for God's sake dig a hole under the cabin wall, and take me in." Strange as may have appeared the suggestion, it was immediately carried out, and the noble young hunter was speedily within the shelter of the fort and in the arms of his friends !

During the fall of this year, (1777),[†] in order to make up the deficiency arising from having raised no corn, the people of the fort determined to make a tur-

---

nip patch, about two hundred yards north-west of the station. While clearing the ground, an Indian was shot at by the guard, and the men retired. The next day the cattle were perceived to be disturbed, and snuffing the air about a small field in the furthest corner, that had been allowed to grow up in very high weeds. The presence of concealed Indians was instantly suspected, so sure were the cattle to betray their vicinity, either from the sight of the Indians themselves, or from the smell of the paint upon their persons. This indication prompted Major George Rogers Clark to turn the ambuscade upon the enemy. For this purpose, some men were still kept at work in the turnip patch nearest the fort, and, in order to prevent suspicion by the Indians of any movement from within, they occasionally hallooed to their companions to come out to their work, while Clark, with a party of the garrison, sallied out of the fort with great secrecy, and making a circuit, came up on the rear of the Indians as they lay concealed in the weeds. A volley was discharged at the concealed foe, and four of their number killed—one by Clark and another by Ray. The Indians instantly retreated, and were pursued by the whites about four hundred yards down the creek, where they came upon the remains of a deserted Indian encampment, of sufficient extent for the accommodation of five or six hundred warriors. From this camp the enemy had issued during the preceding summer to assail the stations, which they had kept in a state of constant alarm, and had destroyed the greater portion of their horses and cattle. The Indians had now abandoned their position, and the party which had just been pursued was supposed to be the remnant of the Indian force which had occupied the encampment. Major Clark complimented James Ray (subsequently General James Ray) with the gun of the Indian which he had shot, and which was the first he had ever killed. The property found in the Indian camp, consisting, principally, of cooking utensils, was, as usual, divided by lottery among the captors.

In Dr. Spalding's "Sketches," we find a record of the following adventure, in which William Coomes was an actor:

"In the spring of 1778, he [Mr. Coomes] was one of a party of thirty men sent out under Colonel Bowman, for the purpose of shelling corn at a plantation about seven miles distant from Harrodstown. The men were divided into pairs, each of which had a large sack, which was to be filled and brought back to the fort. While engaged in filling the sacks, they were fired on by a party of about forty Indians, who had lain concealed in a neighboring cane-brake. At the first fire, seven of the white men were shot down, and among them Mr. H. Berry, the person standing by the side of William Coomes, whose face was bespattered with the blood from the wounds of his fallen comrade. Eight others of the white men fled for shelter to the cane-brake; but the rest of them, rallied by the loud cries of Colonel Bowman, seized their rifles, and sheltering themselves in an adjoining cabin, or behind the trees, prepared to defend themselves to the last. One of the men, observing the face of Coomes reddened with blood, mistook him for an Indian, and was leveling his rifle at him, when the latter, fortunately remarking his movement, cried out, and thus saved his life.

" Meantime, Colonel Bowman dispatched a courier on horseback to Harrodstown, to carry the alarm and to obtain a re-inforcement. The messenger sped his way unharmed to the fort, though many a rifle was aimed at him, and though another strong party of savages were lying in ambush on the way he had to travel. In a few hours, the expected reinforcement arrived; when the Indians, baffled in their object, betook themselves to flight. The white men, after burying their dead, returned to Harrodstown in the evening, with their replenished sacks of corn."

During the year 1779, an expedition was set on foot, from Harrodsburg against the Indian town at old Chillicothe, under the command of Colonel Bowman. The number of men who rendezvoused at Harrodsburg, is stated by Mr. Butler at three hundred, and by Mr. McClung at one hundred and sixty. Captains Benjamin Logan, John Holder, James Harrod and John Bulger, accompanied the expedition, of which Captain (afterwards general) Logan was second in command—and Major George M. Bedinger, of Nicholas county, lately deceased, was adjutant. The expedition, owing to bad management on the part of Colonel Bowman, proved a failure. The particulars will be found in the biographical sketch of General Logan, under the head of Logan county.

From McClung's Sketches, we copy the following account of an attack on McAfee's station, in the year 1781 :

" Early in May, 1781, McAfee's station, in the neighborhood of Harrodsburg, was alarmed. On the morning of the 9th, Samuel McAfee, accompanied by another man, left the fort, in order to visit a small plantation in the neighborhood, and at the distance of three hundred yards from the gate, they were fired upon by a party of Indians in ambush. The man who accompanied him instantly fell, and McAfee attempted to regain the fort. While running rapidly for that purpose, he found himself suddenly intercepted by an Indian, who, springing out of the cane-brake, placed himself directly in his path. There was no time for compliments, each glared upon the other for an instant in silence, and both raising their guns at the same moment, pulled the triggers together. The Indian's rifle snapped, while McAfee's ball passed directly through his brain. Having no time to reload his gun, he sprung over the body of his antagonist, and continued his flight to the fort.

" When within one hundred yards of the gate, he was met by his two brothers, Robert and James, who, at the report of the guns, had hurried out to the assistance of their brother. Samuel hastily informed them of their danger, and exhorted them instantly to return. James readily complied, but Robert, deaf to all remonstrances, declared that he must have a view of the dead Indian. He ran on, for that purpose, and having regaled himself with that spectacle, was hastily returning by the same path, when he saw five or six Indians between him and the fort, evidently bent upon taking him alive. All his activity and presence of mind was now put in requisition. He ran rapidly from tree to tree, endeavoring to turn their flank, and reach one of the gates, and after a variety of turns and doublings in the thick wood, he found himself pressed by only one Indian. McAfee hastily throwing himself behind a fence, turned upon his pursuer and compelled him to take shelter behind a tree.

" Both stood still for a moment, McAfee having his gun cocked, and the sight fixed upon the tree, at the spot where he supposed the Indian would thrust out his head in order to have a view of his antagonist. After waiting a few seconds he was gratified. The Indian slowly and cautiously exposed a part of his head, and began to elevate his rifle. As soon as a sufficient mark presented itself, McAfee fired, and the Indian fell. While turning, in order to continue his flight, he was fired on by a party of six, which compelled him again to tree. But scarcely had he done so, when, from the opposite quarter he received the fire of three more enemies, which made the bark fly around him, and knocked up the dust about his feet. Thinking his post rather too hot for safety, he neglected all shelter, and ran directly for the fort, which, in defiance of all opposition, he reached in safety, to the inexpressible joy of his brothers, who had despaired of his return.

" The Indians now opened a heavy fire upon the fort, in their usual manner; but finding every effort useless, they hastily decamped, without any loss beyond the two who had fallen by the hands of the brothers, and without having inflicted any upon the garrison. Within half an hour, Major McGary brought up a party from Harrodsburg at full gallop, and uniting with the garrison, pursued the enemy with all possible activity. They soon overtook them, and a sharp action ensued. The Indians were routed in a few minutes, with the loss of six warriors left dead upon the ground, and many others wounded, who as usual were borne off. The pursuit was continued for several miles, but from the thickness of the woods, and the extreme activity and address of the enemy, was not very effectual. McGary lost one man dead upon the spot, and another mortally wounded."

ROBERT McAFEE, the father of General Robert B. McAfee, moved to and built a cabin on the place where General McAfee now lives, in November, 1779, and remained during that winter, generally known as the "hard winter." Often, during the winter, and while the weather was intensely cold, he shot buffalo, deer and turkeys, while standing in his own door. The death of Joseph McCoun, noticed in the preceding pages, induced Mr. McAfee, with six other families, to move to James McAfee's station, where they remained till the spring of 1783, before they ventured to remove to their own farms. During the same year, a small party of Indians passed through the neighborhood and stole the greater portion of their horses. In the spring of 1795, Robert McAfee took a boat load of flour and bacon to New Orleans, where, before day light on the morning of the 10th of May, he was killed by a Spaniard, in his boat, receiving the stroke of an axe in his temple, the object of the miscreant being to rob him. His eldest son, Samuel, experienced great difficulty with the Spanish government in his efforts to save the money and other property of his father. His remains were interred near the hospital, and after steamboat navigation was commenced on the river, his son, Robert B. McAfee, attempted to recover his bones, with a view to their interment at the homestead in Kentucky, but they were found in a state of decomposition.

WILLIAM McAFEE commanded a company, under Gen. Clark, in 1780, in an expedition against the Shawanee Indians, on the Big Miami. In a skirmish, near Piqua, he was shot through the body, and mortally wounded; but, through the aid of his brothers, he was enabled to return to the Ohio river, descend that river to the Falls, and then travel as far as Floyd's station, (where his wife met him), before he died. He left two infant daughters, and another daughter was born to him a few months after, who afterwards became the wife of Major Willis A. Lee, for many years clerk of the senate of Kentucky. The eldest married Capt. Elijah Craig, who was killed at the battle of the Thames, in October, 1813. These two sisters now live in the town of Salvisa, near their relatives, in humble, but comfortable circumstances, upon the remains of an extensive landed estate left them by their father.

GEORGE McAFEE, sen., died on his farm, near Salvisa, on Salt river, on the 14th of April, 1803, and was the first person buried at New Providence church.

SAMUEL McAFEE died in 1801, and was buried in the family grave-yard; but, after the death of his wife, in 1817, his remains were removed to Providence, and interred with her.

JAMES McAFEE, the eldest brother, died on his farm, in 1817, and was buried in the family burying-ground, near New Providence.

JANE McAFEE, sen., the mother of the above sons, came to Kentucky in 1779, with her children, and died in 1788. She was buried on a beautiful eminence, on the east side of Salt river, west of Wilson's station, on the land now owned by Archibald Adams.

JAMES HARROD was emphatically the *leader* of the first settlers at Harrodsburg. Emigrating to the country in the year 1774, he has been rendered conspicuous, as the builder of the "first log cabin" in Kentucky. Possessing qualities of a high and generous nature—tall, erect, and commanding in his personal appearance—bold, resolute, active and energetic—inured to the life of a backwoodsman, and familiar with its dangers and capable of supporting its hardships—he was singularly adapted to the position that he was to occupy.* His open, manly countenance—his mild and conciliating manners—his integrity, kindness and generosity—all conspired to render him the idol of his associates. Expert in the use of the rifle, he was a successful hunter, and a skillful and dangerous antagonist of the Indian. If he was an unlettered, he was not an ignorant man. The defects of his education were supplied by the masculine energy of his natural endowments; and, at a period when the cultivation of the intellect was not only impracticable, but was deemed subordinate to the discipline of the body, his claim of rank, as a leader of the pioneers, was universally allowed. His attention to the safety and wants of his companions was as unremitted, as his magnanimity was proverbial. If he received information that a party of hunters had been surprised by the savages, "let us go and beat the red rascals," was his instantaneous order; and the command and its execution were synonymous with him. If a plow horse were missing—having strayed from the station,—and the owner, unaccustomed to the range, or unwilling to encounter the risk of making search for him,

*Morehead's Address. Marshall's History.

was idle in consequence, Harrod would disappear, and it would not be long before the horse would be driven to the owner's premises. Of a restless and active temperament, the dull routine of life in a station was unsuited to him. He loved, like Boone, the free and unrestrained occupation of a hunter. While others were standing still for want of employment, disdaining repose, he would range through the forest, hunt the wild game, or attach himself to expeditions into the Indian country or exploring parties on the frontier. Having built his cabin on the site of the beautiful village of Harrodsburg in the spring or summer of 1774, we find him on the 10th of October with Col. Lewis, at the Point, giving, by a decisive victory over the north-western tribes of savages, a death-blow to their supremacy. On the return of spring he is again at his chosen station in the wilderness, fortifying himself against their inroads, and, as we shall presently see, representing his little settlement in the Transylvania Assembly. Thenceforward Harrodsburg became a prominent place of refuge and resort : and she has never ceased to insist upon the validity of her claims to precedence, as the honored spot of the first settlement of Kentucky.

Harrod survived the stormy scenes of his manhood. But age could not tranquilize the restless elements of his character. In after times, when peace and quiet had ensued, and the range of the buffalo was filled up with a civilized and enterprizing population, and he had become the father of an interesting family, the veteran pioneer would turn away from the scenes of domestic and social life, and plunge again into the solitudes of the wilderness, to indulge himself in the cherished enjoyments of his earlier years. From one of those excursions, into a distant part of the country, he never returned.

Such are some of the outlines of the character of James Harrod, one of the pioneers of Kentucky.*

Among the early settlers of Harrodsburg, distinguished for their bravery, activity and enterprise, were Major Hugh McGary, Harlan, McBride, and Chaplain. The former was ardent, impetuous and rash, but withal a man of daring courage, indomitable energy, and untiring perseverance.

Colonel GABRIEL SLAUGHTER, governor of Kentucky, was a native of Virginia, but emigrated in his youth to Kentucky, and settled in Mercer county, some few miles from Harrodsburg. His residence was widely known under the attractive name of "Traveler's Rest."

Early in life he became a member of the Baptist denomination of Christians, and was extensively known as a prominent and useful member of that numerous and respectable society. He was frequently employed as messenger to its associated churches, and generally presided as moderator of their assemblies.

He rendered gallant and distinguished service in the battle of New Orleans on the 8th of January, 1815, as a colonel of a regiment of Kentucky troops. On one occasion, while acting as president of a court-martial—whose decision was not in accordance with the views of General Jackson—the court were ordered to reverse their proceedings ; but Colonel Slaughter declined to comply, saying, " He knew his duty, and had performed it." General Jackson entertained the highest respect for his character as a soldier and patriot.

Colonel Slaughter was elected in 1816 to the office of lieutenant governor, and upon the death of George Madison, succeeded him in the executive chair, and administered the government as acting governor of Kentucky for the four years of Madison's term. He appointed John Pope, Esq., secretary of state, who, at that time, was somewhat unpopular in Kentucky, on account of his opposition to the war with England while senator of the United States. In consequence, it is thought, of this unexpected appointment, the new election question was fiercely agitated during the first session of the legislature after Governor Slaughter's inauguration, and at the succeeding session also. The new election movement failed, and the construction or exposition then given to the constitution, in regard to the succession of the lieutenant governor to the office of governor, upon the " death, resignation, or refusal to qualify," of the governor elect, has been acquiesced in ever since, and regarded as a settled precedent.

Governor Slaughter, during this exciting controversy, displayed great indepen-

* Morehead's Address.

dence of opinion, and much firmness and decision of character. After one or two legislative sessions had passed, in unavailing and violent discussions of the question of new election, Mr. Pope, regarding himself as the principal cause of the continued and turbulent agitation of the question, resigned the office of secretary of state. The governor was advised by timid and panic-stricken friends to yield to the arrogant and disorganizing demands of the legislature. The firm and pugnacious old patriot declared his fixed resolution to administer the government alone and without a secretary, (for he had offered the vacant secretaryship to Martin D. Hardin, who declined it), rather than submit to a violation of his rights in the overthrow of the constitution. A common sense and literal interpretation of the organic law, resumed its sway over the public mind, while partisan purpose and sophisticated opinion yielded the contest. Successive vacancies by death in the office of governor have since occurred, in the instances of Governor Breathitt, Clarke, &c., without a renewal of the long mooted question.

At the end of his gubernatorial term, Governor Slaughter retired to his farm in Mercer, where he died in 1830, at the age of sixty-three years. The legislature, by joint resolution, some years since, ordered a marble monument to be erected to his memory on the spot where he was buried.

Captain SAMUEL DAVEISS, a well known citizen of Mercer, is a brother of the celebrated Colonel Joseph H. Daveiss, and is a fine specimen of the old Kentucky gentleman. He is a lawyer of considerable eminence, and has frequently represented his county in the legislature of the State, of which body he was a very useful member. Having emigrated to Kentucky at an early day, he is extensively acquainted with the facts connected with the first settlement of the country, which renders his conversation exceedingly interesting and instructive.

Gen. ROBERT B. MCAFEE was born in the district of Kentucky, at his present residence, on Salt river, in February, 1784. His ancestors came to Kentucky, and settled at this place, in the fall of 1779. Robert McAfee, the father of Gen. McAfee, had to cultivate his farm gun in hand, for four or five years after he settled in Kentucky; and the subject of this sketch was born and reared amid the confusion and perils of continued Indian alarms. He was placed at school while yet very young, and continued at various institutions of instruction until he had obtained a good education. He lost his father when he was eleven years of age; and being thus left an orphan, (his mother having died the year previous), he was placed under the charge of the Hon. John Breckinridge and James McCoun, who had been appointed his guardians. In the year 1796, he entered Transylvania Seminary, (the germ of the present university of that name), then under the control of the Rev. James Moore, a gentleman of learning and estimable character. He also attended, for a brief period, a private school, in Mercer county. When he had completed his classical education, he commenced the study of the law under the Hon. John Breckinridge, in whose office he continued three years. When he had completed his studies, he returned to Mercer county and commenced the practice of the law. In October, 1807, he was united in marriage to Miss Mary Cardwell, a niece of Col. Anthony Crockett, a revolutionary officer, who was with Gen. George Rogers Clark in the expedition against Kaskakias and Vincennes. In the year 1800 he was elected to represent Mercer county in the legislature; and, with the exception of two or three years, has been in public life ever since. Upon the breaking out of the late war, he volunteered as a private, in a company of mounted riflemen, and was among the first Kentuckians who joined the north-western army. In this company he was appointed sergeant, and was, subsequently, elected ensign, and, afterwards, second lieutenant. He was also made quarter-master of Col. R. M. Johnson's regiment. This regiment aided in relieving fort Wayne, at a very critical period, when surrounded by hostile Indians. A detachment having been sent, under Col. Wells, against the Indian town of Five Medals, sixty miles north-west of fort Wayne, McAfee accompanied the expedition. In 1813, he received from Governor Shelby a captain's commission in Col. Johnson's regiment of mounted riflemen, having, previously, raised a company of eighty men, by whom he had been elected captain. Col. Johnson's regiment marched on the 25th of May, 1813, and was employed in active service on the frontiers. Capt. McAfee's company, having been increased to one hundred and fifty men, were in the battle of the Thames, on the 5th of

October, 1813, and did good service. At the close of the war, Capt. McAfee returned to his farm, in Mercer county, and spent two or three years in private life. In 1819, he was elected to the legislature; and, in 1821, was chosen a member of the State senate. In 1824, he resigned his seat in the senate, and was elected lieutenant governor, in which capacity he served four years. He presided over the deliberations of the senate during those bitter and exciting contests, which are known in history as the new and old court questions. In 1829, he became a candidate for Congress, but declined before the election came on. In 1830, he was again elected to the legislature; and again in 1831-2. He was a member of the convention which assembled at Baltimore in 1832, and nominated Gen. Jackson as candidate for president, and Martin Van Buren for vice-president. In 1833, he was appointed charge d'affaires to the republic of Colombia, in South America, and proceeded to the city of Bogota, where he remained, engaged in the discharge of his duties, until 1837, when he returned to the United States. In this mission he was accompanied by his son James, as private secretary. In 1841, he was again elected to the senate of Kentucky; and, in 1842, was appointed one of the visitors to West Point, and elected president of the board. In 1845, he retired from public life, and has since resided on his farm, in Mercer county. He is now in the sixty-third year of his age. It should not be omitted, that Gen. McAfee is a member of the Royal Antiquarian Society of Denmark, and an honorary member of the Kentucky Historical Society.

Gen. HUGH MERCER, of Virginia, from whom this county received its name, was a native of Scotland, and graduated at an early age in the science of medicine. At the memorable battle of Culloden, he acted as assistant surgeon, and with many of the vanquished sought a refuge in America. In the Indian war of 1755, he served as a captain, under Washington. For his gallantry and military skill in this war, the corporation of Philadelphia presented him with an appropriate medal. In 1775, he was in command of three regiments of minute-men; and in 1776, he was made colonel in the army of Virginia. Having joined the continental army, he was promoted to the rank of brigadier general, and served in that capacity with efficiency and distinction, until the period of his death, which occurred in the battle of Princeton, where he fell mortally wounded, while leading the vanguard of the American forces. He survived nine days, and then died of his wounds.

During the last war with Great Britain a very remarkable circumstance occurred in connection with the invasion of Canada by the Kentucky troops, which from its singularity merits preservation. A company of volunteers destined for Shelby's army, rendezvoused at Harrodsburg, Mercer county, and formed a nucleus around which the military recruits of the country gathered, obtaining fresh accessions of strength with their progress towards the Ohio. When they marched from Harrodsburg, about a mile or two out, they saw two pigs fighting, and delayed their march to see it out. When the march was recommenced, it was observed that the victorious pig was following in the route, and at night, when they encamped, the animal also busied itself a shelter, and halted for the night. The following day, the pig accompanied the troops as before, and thus night and morning, in their progress to the river, the animal halted, rested, and started onwards when they resumed their journey. When they came opposite Cincinnati, at which place they crossed in a ferry boat, the pig on getting to the water's edge, promptly plunged in, waiting on the other side until the whole *cortege* crossed over, and resumed its post as customary in the flank of the moving column. In this way the animal kept on with the troops, until they got to the lake. On the whole journey, as the men grew more familiar with their comrade, it became a pet, receiving a full share of the rations issued to the soldiers, and destitute as the troops found themselves at times of sustenance, no one thought of putting the knife to the throat of their fellow *soldier*. What they had was still shared, and if the pig fared at times as scantily as the rest, it grunted on, and manifested as much patriotism in its own line, as the bipeds it accompanied in theirs. At the margin of the lake she embarked with the troops and went as far as Bass Island. She was there offered a passage into Canada, but obstinately refused to embark a second time. Some of the men attributed her conduct to *constitutional scruples*, and observed that she knew it was contrary to the constitu-

30

tion to force a *militia pig* over the line. In consequence of this remark they gave her leave to remain. After the campaign had closed, the troops recrossed the lake, having left their horses on the American side. As soon as the line was formed, to the great surprise of many, and inspiring a deep interest in all, there was the pig on the right of the line, ready to resume her march with the rest. By this time the winter frosts had set in, and the animal suffered greatly on its homeward march. It made out, however, to reach Maysville, at which point the troops recrossed the Ohio river. There it gave out, and was placed in trusty hands by Governor Shelby; and finally taken to the Governor's home, where the animal passed the rest of its days in ease and indolence. The facts contained in this narrative are strictly true, and can be attested by many living witnesses.[*]

The following account of some singular natural formations among the cliffs of the Kentucky river, should have appeared under the head of Jessamine county, but was not prepared until the description of that county had gone to press. They are situated immediately opposite the county of Mercer, which is the reason of its insertion in this place.

The most picturesque of these natural objects is called the Devil's Pulpit. We are indebted for the following account of a visit to this remarkable curiosity, to the pen of a well known citizen of Kentucky, Dr. Graham, the enterprising and intelligent proprietor of the Harrodsburg Springs. He says :

"After much vexation and annoyance occasioned by the difficulties of the road, we arrived near the object of our visit, and quitting our horses, proceeded on foot. Upon approaching the break of the precipice, under the direction of our guide, we suddenly found ourselves standing on the verge of a yawning chasm, and immediately beyond, bottomed in darkness, the Devil's Pulpit was seen rearing its black, gigantic form, from amid the obscurity of the deep and silent valley. The back ground to this gloomy object presented a scene of unrelieved desolation. Cliff rose on cliff and crag surmounted crag, sweeping off on either hand in huge semicircles, until the wearied eye became unable to follow the countless and billowy-like mazes of that strange and awful scene. The prevailing character of the whole was that of savage grandeur and gloom. A profound silence broods over the place, broken only by the muffled rushing of the stream far down in its narrow passage, cleaving its way to its home in the ocean. Descending by a zigzag path to the shore of the river, while our companions were making preparations to cross, I strayed through the valley. The air was cool, refreshing and fragrant, and vocal with the voices of many birds. The bending trees, the winding stream with its clear and crystal waters, the flowering shrubs, and clustering vines walled in by these adamantine ramparts—which seem to tower to the skies—make this a place of rare and picturesque beauty. The dew drops still hung glittering on the leaves, the whispering winds played with soft music through the rustling foliage, and. the sunbeams struggling through the overhanging forest kissed the opening flowers, and all combined made up a scene of rural loveliness and romance, which excited emotions of unmingled delight. The boat having arrived, the river was crossed without difficulty, and we commenced the ascent, and after measuring up two hundred and seventy feet, arrived at the base of the "Pulpit." Fifty paces from this point, and parallel with it, in the solid ledge of the cliff, is a cave of considerable extent. At its termination, there passes out like the neck of a funnel, an opening, not larger than a hogshead. Upon pitching rocks into this cave, a rumbling was heard at an immense distance below the earth. Some are of opinion that this cave contains a bottomless pit. We now ascended the cliffs some fifty feet further, clambering up through a fissure in the rocks, having the Pulpit on our right, and a range of cliffs on our left. To look up here makes the head dizzy. Huge and dark masses roll up above you, upon whose giddy heights vast crags jut out and overhang the valley, threatening destruction to all below. The floating clouds give these crags the appearance of swimming in mid air. The ascent up these rocks, though somewhat laborious, is perfectly safe, being protected by natural walls on either side, and forming a perfect stairway with steps from eight to ten feet thick. At the head of this passage, there is a hole through the river side of the wall, large enough to admit the body, and through which one may crawl, and look down

* Vide Cist's Cincinnati Miscellany for 1845–6, and McAfee's History of the Late War.

upon the rushing stream below. At the foot of the stairway stands the Pulpit, rising from the very brink of the main ledge, at more than two hundred feet of an elevation above the river, but separated from the portion which towers up to the extreme heights. The space is twelve feet at bottom, and as the cliff retreats slightly at this point, the gap is perhaps thirty feet at the top. The best idea that can be formed of this rock is to suppose it to be a single column, standing in front of the continuous wall of some vast building or ruin, the shaft standing as colonnades are frequently built upon an elevated platform. From the platform to the capital of the shaft is not less than one hundred feet, making the whole elevation of the "Devil's Pulpit" three hundred feet. It is called by some the inverted candlestick, to which it has a striking resemblance. There are two swells, which form the base moulding and occupy about forty feet of the shaft. It then narrows to an oblong of about three feet by six, at which point there are fifteen distinct projections. This narrow neck continues with some irregularity for eight or ten feet, winding off at an angle of more than one degree from the line of gravity. Then commences the increased swell, and craggy offsets, first overhanging one side, and then the other, till they reach the top or cap rock, which is not so wide as the one below it, but is still fifteen feet across.

~~~~~~~~~~

MONROE COUNTY.

MONROE county was formed in 1820, and named in honor of President JAMES MONROE. It is situated on the southern border of the State, and lies on the head waters of Big Barren river, the Cumberland passing through its south-west corner : bounded on the north by Barren, east by Cumberland, south by the State of Tennessee, and west by Allen county. The face of the county is diversified—level, undulating and hilly—the principal growth walnut, hickory, beech, and white, black and chesnut oak, &c. Wheat, oats and corn are the principal products, and hogs are exported in considerable numbers.

Number of acres of land in Monroe, 155,571 ; average value of land per acre, $2.29 ; valuation of taxable property in 1846, $755,397 ; number of white males over twenty-one years of age, 1,118 ; number of children between five and sixteen years old, 1,650. Population in 1840, 6,526.

TOMPKINSVILLE, the seat of justice of Monroe county, is one hundred and forty miles from Frankfort. Contains a court-house and jail, Presbyterian and Methodist churches, one school, four lawyers, four doctors, one tavern, five stores, and five mechanics' shops—population 150. Incorporated in 1819, and named after Daniel D. Tompkins, vice-president of the United States *Centre Point* is a small village on the Cumberland river.

This county received its name in honor of JAMES MONROE, the fifth president of the United States. He was a native of Virginia, and was born in Westmoreland county, on the 28th day of April, 1758. He was educated at William and Mary college, and graduated in 1776. Upon leaving college, he entered as a cadet in a corps then organizing under General Mercer. He was soon after appointed a lieutenant, and joined the army at York. He was in the engagement at Harlaem heights, and at White Plains, and accompanied the army in its retreat through the Jerseys. He was with Washington when he crossed the Delaware, and made the successful attack on the Hessians at Trenton. Here he was wounded in the shoulder. On recovering, he served as aid to Lord Sterling, and was with him in the battles of Brandywine, Germantown, and Monmouth. Retiring from the army, he entered the office of Mr. Jefferson, as a student of law. In 1780 he was sent by Mr. Jefferson, then governor of Virginia, as a commissioner to the southern army, then under De Kalb, to ascertain its effective force, its wants and ulterior prospects. In 1782 he was elected a member of the legislature of Virginia, and the next year was sent to the continental Congress, when only twenty-four years of age. He continued in Congress three years. Upon retiring from Congress, he was again sent to the legislature of his native State. In 1788 he was a member of the Virginia convention which adopted the constitution of the United States, but voted against the adoption of that instrument. From 1790 to 1794, he was a member of the Senate of the United States, and was taken from that body to be envoy extraordinary and minister plenipotentiary to France. In 1796 he was recalled. Upon his return, he was elected governor of Virginia, and served in that capacity three years. In 1803 he was again sent by Mr. Jefferson to France, to act with Mr. Livingston, the resident minister there. From France he was transferred to London, as successor to Mr. King. From England he was ordered to Spain, from whence he returned to England on the death of Mr. Pitt. Upon his return to the United States, he spent several years in retirement upon his farm in Virginia, but in 1810 was sent to the legislature of Virginia. A few months after he was elected governor of the commonwealth, and remained in that office until he was appointed secretary of state under Mr. Madison. In 1817 he was elected president of the United States, and continued in that office eight years. After he retired from office, he continued to reside on his farm in Virginia till the 4th of July, 1831, when he expired, in the seventy-third year of his age.

MONTGOMERY COUNTY.

MONTGOMERY county was formed in 1796, and named in honor of Gen. RICHARD MONTGOMERY, of the revolutionary army. It lies on the waters of Hinkston and Red rivers : bounded on the north by Bath ; east, by Bath and Morgan ; south, by Estill and Owsley ; and west, by Clark and Bourbon,—and, originally, included Bath, part of Morgan, Floyd, Letcher, Perry, Breathitt, Owsley and Estill. The south-eastern half of the county is very thinly settled, being very mountainous, and does not embrace one hundred voters. Most of the residue of the county is first rate, rich, limestone land,—more broken and rolling than Bourbon, Clark, or Fayette, but the soil is considered as rich and productive as it is in those counties. Hemp is raised, to some extent, in the county ; but the principal exports are fat cattle, mules, horses and hogs. There are nineteen schools in the county, two of which are in Mount-Sterling.

MOUNT-STERLING, the county seat, is situated on Hinkston creek, near its head, about five miles east of the Clark county line, and seven miles west of the Bath county line,—being sixty miles from Frankfort. It has improved rapidly for a few years past, and now contains 1,000 inhabitants. The public buildings are, a very large, commodious, and well arranged brick court house, clerks' offices, three churches, (Presbyterian, Methodist, and Reformed), a male academy—a large, fine, new brick building, built under a charter from the legislature, and in which is kept the Highland Institute, one of the most flourishing literary institutions in the State, having four teachers, and from one hundred to one hundred and eighty pupils each session. There are sixteen lawyers and seven physicians in the town, sixteen dry goods stores, one hardware store, one drug store, three groceries, one book store, printing office, two taverns, one shoe store, and a large number of mechanics' shops. *Jeffersonville* is a small village, eight miles east of Mount-Sterling, on the State road to Prestonsburg, with one tavern, a store, and a blacksmith shop.

Number of acres of land in Montgomery, 176,276; average value of land per acre, $13.14; number of white males over twenty-one years of age, 1,360; number of children between five and sixteen years old, 1,778. Total valuation of taxable property in 1846, $4,039,948. Population in 1840, 9,332.

No county in Kentucky has suffered more from land litigation than Montgomery. The laws of Virginia for the appropriation of lands, were the greatest curse that ever befell Kentucky. Sometimes as many as five or six patents covered the same piece of land; and the occupant, besides the title under which he entered, frequently had to buy two or three times more, or lose his home and his labor. The difficulties in the land titles belong to the State at large, and need not be specially pointed out here.

The MOUND which gave name to *Mount-Sterling*, was cut down during the year 1846. Many curious things were found, interspersed with human bones—among which were, a copper and two white queensware breastplates, about the size of a man's hand; a great number of large beads, some of copper and others of ivory; bracelets of copper, &c. Thirty years ago, there were trees on this mound as large as those in the neighboring forest.

About five miles west of Mount-Sterling, on the farm belonging to the heirs of Mr. Jacob Johnson, is another mound, near to what was once an entrenchment. The latter was square, and when cleared, the timber which was growing in the trenches and on the banks was of the largest and richest growth,—just such as that which surrounded it in the forest. On the eastern side of the square, was, evidently, a gate, some twenty feet wide, which was on the brow of the hill; thence down to a spring, some thirty yards off, for the width of the gate, there were no trees of any kind, when the country was first settled by the whites.

Montgomery county was not settled as early as those west of it. The first corn raised in it, was by Capt. JOHN A. CRAWFORD, in the year 1790. He was employed, in that year, to clear the land and cultivate a few acres of corn, for which he was to receive one hundred acres of choice land. In conjunction with a negro man, he cleared four acres and cultivated the same, for which he received his hundred acres, and which lies adjoining Mount-Sterling, and upon which he has resided ever since, and raised a large and respectable family. He is now a vigorous, sprightly old man, about eighty-two years old. He was under Gen. Wayne in the north-west, and, also, commanded a volunteer company during the last war with Great Britain.

In 1782 Montgomery county was the scene of a rencontre between the whites and the Indians, which was marked by a display of cool intrepidity, on both sides, worthy of veteran troops. This event is known in history as Estill's defeat, and is perhaps more honorable to the Indian character than any other battle fought during those times.

In the month of May, a party of about twenty-five Wyandots invested Estill's station, on the south of the Kentucky river. They killed a white man, took a negro prisoner, and after destroying the cattle, retreated. Soon after the Indians had disappeared, Captain Estill raised a company of twenty-five men, and with these pursued the enemy with the design of inflicting summary vengeance for these outrages. He came up with them at the Hinkston fork of Licking river. They had just crossed the creek, which is here very narrow, and were leisurely ascending a hill of moderate elevation which arose on the opposite side. Estill's men immediately opened a fire on the retreating Indians, who at first manifested a disposition to run, but their chief, being severely wounded, ordered them in a loud voice to stand and fight. Upon this the Indians promptly prepared for battle, each man taking a tree, in which position they returned the fire of the whites.

Estill and his men had also, in the mean time, formed a line of battle, and protecting themselves as well as they could by the trees and bushes in the vicinity, kept up a rapid discharge of rifles. The opposing foemen were formed on opposite sides of the creek, and maintained the fight for some time with great deliberation and coolness.

The numbers were equal on each side, and the battle was more like a single combat, than an engagement between organized forces. Each rifleman singled out his man, and fired only when he saw his mark. The firing was deliberate, although life itself was often the forfeit. And thus both sides firmly stood, or bravely fell, for more than one hour. Upwards of one-fourth of the combatants on both sides had fallen. Never was the native bravery of men put to a more severe test. In the clangour and uproar of a general battle, death is forgotten, and even cowards die like brave men; but in the cool and lingering expectation of death, none but the man of true courage can stand: and such was the situation of these combatants. Captain Estill clearly perceived that no advantage had been gained over the Indians up to this period of the contest, and that while the action was continued in the manner in which it had been commenced, no decided change could be produced in the relative fortunes of the fight. Victory itself, could it have been purchased with the loss of his last man, would be but a mournful triumph; but even of victory, without some successful manœuvre, he could not assure himself. His situation was critical; the promptest action was required. He cast his eyes over the field, and saw that the creek before him opposed a charge in front; but on the other hand he observed a valley running from the creek towards the rear of the enemy's line, and prompted by the urgency of his situation, he determined to detach six of his men by this valley, to gain the flank or rear of the enemy; while himself, with the residue, maintained their position in front.

The detachment accordingly moved off under the command of Lieutenant Miller; but either mistaking his way, or not comprehending the orders of his superior, this officer did not proceed with the requisite dispatch, and the movement was not executed in time. The Indian leader, in the meantime, discovering from the slackening of the fire in front, that the line had been weakening, made a rapid charge across the creek with his whole force, drove the whites from their coverts, and compelled them to retreat with great slaughter. In the charge, Captain Estill and eight of his men were killed. Four others were badly wounded, who made their escape. In this affair the Indians lost more than half of their number; the loss of the whites was much greater. The action lasted two hours, and there was nothing wanting in its circumstances, but numbers and the pomp and tactics of modern war, to make it memorable.

The last incursion by the Indians on the interior of the State, was made on Easter Monday, being the 1st day of April, 1793, on which occasion they took Morgan's station, on Slate creek, about seven miles east of Mount-Sterling, and carried away nineteen prisoners, all of whom were women and children. The men, not anticipating danger, were engaged in the neighborhood preparing to raise their crops. One old man and one woman were killed near the station, and pursuit having been made by the whites, the savages killed several of the prisoners, and the remainder were taken to the north-west and sold. After the treaty of Greenville, in 1795, they were all restored to their families and friends.

General RICHARD MONTGOMERY, in memory of whom this county received its name, was a major general in the American revolutionary army, and a native of Ireland—born in 1737. He embraced the profession of arms at an early period, and was with Wolfe at the capture of Quebec, in 1759. On his return to England, he resigned his commission and removed to America, purchased an estate in New York, and married a daughter of Judge Livingston. On the commencement of the revolutionary struggle, his feelings in favor of the colonies being well known, he was entrusted with the command of the continental forces in the northern department, in conjunction with General Schuyler. The indisposition of the latter devolved the chief command upon Montgomery, who, after various successes, (the reduction of fort Chamblee, the capture of St. John's, and of Montreal), proceeded to the siege of Quebec. Having formed a junction with Colonel Arnold, a combined attack was made on the place on the 1st of December, 1775; but for the want of artillery of sufficient calibre, although the attack was well planned, the assailants were defeated. General Montgomery and his two aids were killed by the only gun fired from the battery of the enemy. He was buried in Quebec, without the honors due his rank, but his remains, by order of Congress, were removed to New York in 1816, and placed in front of St. Paul's church, where a monument was erected to his memory. He had received an excellent education, and was gifted with fine abilities. His military talents especially were of a high order, and the sorrow for his loss was heightened by the esteem which his amiable character had gained him. At the period of his death he was only thirty-eight years of age.

MORGAN COUNTY.

MORGAN county was formed in 1822, and named for General DANIEL MORGAN. It is situated in the eastern part of the State— Licking river flowing in a north-western direction through the centre : Bounded on the north by Carter ; east by Lawrence and Johnson ; south by Breathitt and Owsley ; west by Montgomery and Bath, and north-west by Fleming. The face of the country is hilly, interspersed with fertile valleys. The soil is based on free stone, with red clay foundation. Iron ore, coal, alum and copperas, with mineral and oil springs, abound in the county. Principal productions are, Indian corn, oats, potatoes and flax— the exports, pork, beef and horses. Besides Licking river, which flows through this county, the head waters of Little Sandy and Red river have their rise here—the former flowing into the Ohio river in Greenup county, and the latter into the Kentucky river in Clark county.

Number of acres of land in Morgan,* 515,962 ; average value of lands per acre, 96 cents ; valuation of taxable property in 1846, $602,494 ; number of white males over twenty-one years of age, 1,068 ; number of children between five and sixteen years old, 1,547 : Population in 1840, 4,603.

---

* The territory of this county is full six times as large as that of some other counties of the State.

The towns of the county are—West Liberty and Hazle-Green. WEST-LIBERTY, the seat of justice, is one hundred and seven miles from Frankfort—contains a court-house, a Methodist church, a Christian church, two lawyers, one physician, two taverns, three stores, and eight mechanics' shops : Population 100—established in 1825. *Hazle-Green* is a pleasant little village, with a population of about 40 souls.

General DANIEL MORGAN, from whom this county received its name, was a distinguished officer of the war of the revolution, and was born in New Jersey in 1736. His first employment was that of a wagoner. In this capacity he was with the army at Braddock's defeat. On the return of the army he received a commission as ensign in the English service. From this period until 1774 nothing distinct is known of the history of General Morgan. In this year he commanded a company in Dunmore's expedition against the Indians. He commanded a detachment consisting of three rifle companies under Arnold at Quebec, and led the forlorn hope in the assault. Here he was taken prisoner. On his exchange he received the appointment of colonel in the continental army. He was at the head of Lis riflemen in the decisive and victorious battle of Saratoga. For his gallantry in this action, the legislature of Virginia passed a resolution presenting him with a horse, pistols, and a sword.

MUHLENBURG COUNTY.

MUHLENBURG county was formed in 1798, and named in honor of Gen. PETER MUHLENBURG, of the revolutionary army. It is situated in the south-western middle part of the State, and lies on the waters of Greene river : Bounded on the north and north-east by Greene river, which separates it from Daviess and Ohio ; east by Butler ; south by Todd and Logan ; and west by Hopkins. In the southern portion of the county the surface is broken, and the lands comparatively poor ; while the middle and northern divisions are undulating, and the soil productive. Corn, pork, and tobacco, are the staples. The county abounds in coal and iron ore. The " Henry Clay Iron Works," four miles from Greeneville is supplied with ore of a superior quality from the contiguous high grounds, which, as the quantity is inexhaustible, has obtained the name of the " *Iron Mountain*." There are several mineral springs in Muhlenburg ; and salt, in small quantities, was at one time manufactured in the county.

Number of acres of land in Muhlenburg, 274,809 ; average value of lands per acre, $1.93 ; valuation of taxable property in 1846, $1,298,019 ; number of white males over twenty-one years old, 1,366 ; number of children between five and sixteen years old, 1,744 ; population in 1840, 6,964.

There are five towns in the county, viz : Greeneville, Lewisburg, Rumsey, South Carrollton, and Skilesville. GREENEVILLE, the seat of justice, is one hundred and twenty miles from Frankfort. It contains, besides the usual public buildings, one Presbyterian and one Methodist church, six lawyers, three physicians, one seminary, six stores, one grocery, two taverns, one wool carding factory, two tobacco factories, and eight mechanics' shops. Population, 400. Established in 1812, and named after the distinguished revolutionary general, Greene. *Lewisburg* is a small village, situated on Greene river, nine miles from Greeneville, containing two stores, one warehouse, and about 50 souls. *Rumsey* lies on Greene river, at lock and dam No. 2, about twenty-five miles north of Greeneville—contains one Union church, one lawyer, two physicians, two taverns, five stores, two groceries, one school, two saw-mills, two grist-mills, one carding factory, and six mechanics' shops. Population, 300. Named after James Rumsey, for whom the honor is claimed of having built the first steamboat in the United States. *South Carrollton*, situated on Greene river, two miles below Lewisburg—has two stores, three warehouses, one Cumberland Presbyterian church, one physician, one tavern, and four mechanics' shops. Population, 75. *Skilesville* is situated on Greene river, at lock and dam No. 3, fourteen miles east of Greeneville, and contains one physician, two stores, and about 15 souls. Named after James R. Skiles, who introduced the first steamboat upon Greene river, and who spent a fortune in promoting the navigation of the river.

Gen. PETER MUHLENBURG was a native of Pennsylvania, and by profession a clergyman of the Lutheran church. At the breaking out of the revolution, he was a young man of about thirty years of age, and pastor of a Lutheran church at Woodstock. In 1776, he received the commission of colonel, and was requested to raise his regiment among the Germans of the valley. Having in his pulpit inculcated the principles of liberty, he found no difficulty in enlisting a regiment. He entered the pulpit with his sword and cockade, preached his farewell sermon, and the next day marched at the head of his regiment to join the army. His regiment was the eighth Virginia, or, as it was commonly called, the German regiment. This corps behaved with honor throughout the war. They were at Brandywine, Monmouth, and Germantown, and in the southern campaigns. In 1777, Mr. Muhlenburg was promoted to the rank of brigadier general. After the war, he returned to Pennsylvania—was for many years treasurer of that State, and served three terms in Congress, after the adoption of the constitution. In person, Gen. Muhlenburg was tall and well-proportioned, and, in his address, remarkably courteous. He was a fine disciplinarian, an excellent officer, and esteemed and beloved by both officers and soldiers.

NELSON COUNTY.

NELSON county was formed in 1781, and named for Governor THOMAS NELSON, of Virginia. It is situated in the middle part of the state, and lies on the waters of Salt river : Bounded on the north by Spencer ; east by Washington and Marion ; south by Larue ; west by Hardin ; and north-west by Bullitt. The surface of the county is undulating The soil in the northern portion is of an excellent quality, and well adapted to the growth of hemp ; while that of the southern portion is rather thin, though there are detached parcels of good land, particularly in the bottoms of the Beech and Rolling forks, and Pottinger creeks. This county grows almost every variety of grain and grasses. The exports are, principally, hemp, flour, hay, corn, apples, hogs, cattle, horses, mules, and whisky.

Number of acres of land in Nelson, 252,597 ; average value of lands per acre, $9.00 ; total valuation of taxable property in 1846, $4,967,176 ; number of white males over twenty-one years of age, 1,987; number of children between five and sixteen years old, 1,754. Population in 1840, 13,637.

CATHOLIC COLLEGE, BARDSTOWN, KY.

The towns of Nelson are, Bardstown, Bloomfield, Fairfield, Chaplin and New-Haven. BARDSTOWN, the principal town and county seat, is situated on an elevated plain, three-fourths of a mile north of the Beech fork of Salt river, about fifty miles from Frankfort, and forty miles south-west from Louisville. It contains a fine brick court-house, four churches, (Baptist, Methodist, Presbyterian and Roman Catholic,) fourteen lawyers, nine physicians, ten dry goods stores, one drug store, several grocery stores, one bagging factory, one wool factory, one steam cotton factory, and twenty-five mechanics' shops. Population about 2,000. *St. Joseph's College*, located in this town, was founded in

1819, and is under the control of the Roman Catholic denomination. Rev. Edward McMahon is president, assisted by four professors. Numbers about one hundred and fifty students, with five thousand volumes in the library. Commencement in August. The college edifice is a very commodious and imposing structure. There is a Roman Catholic *Female Institution* two and a half miles north-west of Bardstown—and Presbyterian and Methodist *Female Academies* in Bardstown—all extensively patronised and in a flourishing condition. Bardstown is one of the handsomest towns of the west, and contains an enterprising, intelligent and remarkably moral population.

There is a natural tunnel under Bardstown, of circular form and several feet in diameter, commencing at the eastern and terminating at the western declivity of the eminence on which the town is built. We have not learned to what extent this subterranean passage has been penetrated.

Bloomfield is a handsome town, containing one Baptist church, two physicians, five stores, two taverns, and sixteen mechanics' shops, with a population of 400. *New Haven* has a Roman Catholic church, one Methodist Episcopal church, one tavern, four physicians, four stores, and ten mechanics' shops : Population 300. *Fairfield* contains one Catholic church, three physicians, one tavern, four stores and six mechanics' shops—with a population of 150. *Chaplin* has three physicians, three stores, one tavern, and seven mechanics' shops—population 150.

FEMALE COURAGE.—The following record of the indomitable courage and amazing physical strength of one of the pioneer females of Kentucky, we copy from the interesting work of Mr. McClung, the Sketches of Western Adventure :

" During the summer of 1787, the house of Mr. John Merril, of Nelson county, Ky., was attacked by the Indians, and defended with singular address and good fortune. Merril was alarmed by the barking of a dog about midnight, and upon opening the door in order to ascertain the cause of the disturbance, he received the fire of six or seven Indians, by which his arm and thigh were both broken. He instantly sunk upon the floor and called upon his wife to close the door. This had scarcely been done when it was violently assailed by the tomahawks of the enemy, and a large breach soon effected. Mrs. Merril, however, being a perfect Amazon, both in strength and courage, guarded it with an axe, and successively killed or badly wounded four of the enemy as they attempted to force their way into the cabin.

" The Indians then ascended the roof, and attempted to enter by way of the chimney ; but here again they were met by the same determined enemy. Mrs. Merril seized the only feather bed which the cabin afforded, and hastily ripping it open, poured its contents upon the fire. A furious blaze and stifling smoke instantly ascended the chimney, and brought down two of the enemy, who lay for a few moments at the mercy of the lady. Seizing the axe, she quickly dispatched them, and was instantly afterwards summoned to the door, where the only remaining savage now appeared, endeavoring to effect an entrance, while Mrs. Merril was engaged at the chimney. He soon received a gash in the cheek, which compelled him, with a loud yell, to relinquish his purpose, and return hastily to Chillicothe, where, from the report of a prisoner, he gave an exaggerated account of the fierceness, strength, and courage of the " long knife squaw !"

In August, 1792, information was communicated to Major Brown, of Nelson county, that a party of Indians were committing depredations on the Rolling fork of Salt river. He immediately raised a company of volunteers, and commenced

a vigilant search for the marauders. Falling on their trail, he pursued and overtook them, when a brisk skirmish ensued between his men and the rear of the
Indian force, consisting of twelve warriors. In this spirited conflict, four of the
Indians were left dead upon the field, and the remainder were dispersed. The
loss of the whites was one man killed, and two wounded.

The Hon. CHARLES A. WICKLIFFE, who has filled a considerable space in the
political history of his State and country, is a native of Kentucky. His father,
C. Wickliffe, removed from Virginia to Kentucky in 1784, when the few and
feeble settlements in the western forests were still exposed to the horrors of savage warfare. His mother was a sister of Col. John Hardin, so celebrated in the
traditions of the west, for his heroism and tragical fate. The subject of our
sketch is the youngest of nine children. His father, with small means and a
large family, was unable, partly from the condition of the country at that early
period, to bestow an education upon any of his sons, beyond the rudiments of the
English language. The whole family, however, were brought up in habits of
industry and economy.

The oldest brother, Robert Wickliffe, after he had attained the age of twenty-
one, commenced the study of the law under the celebrated George Nicholas, and,
by his vigorous talents, and industry, has raised himself to well known eminence
at the bar and in the councils of his country. The other two brothers, one of
whom is dead, engaged in mercantile pursuits, and attained great respectability
and high standing in the society in which they moved. Charles A. Wickliffe remained at home until his seventeenth year, when, manifesting a desire to obtain
an education, he was sent to a grammar school in Bardstown, under the care of
the Rev. Dr. Wilson, where he remained about one year. He afterwards enjoyed
the benefit of Dr. Blythe's instructions, at Lexington, for about nine months.

Expressing a desire to study law, he was placed under the tuition of his relative, Gen. Martin D. Hardin. He was forced to enter upon the practice of his
profession, after a shorter term of preparation than was usual at that day,—for his
father's property was little more than adequate to the support of his family ; and
young Wickliffe found himself almost wholly dependent upon his own exertions
for the means of subsistence. His appearance at the bar was greeted by many
warm friends of his youth, to whose kindness he was much indebted for his subsequent success, and for whom he has ever expressed the most grateful regard.
Yet he had to struggle against a tremendous competition.

The bar of Bardstown, when he commenced his professional career, was the
ablest west of the Alleghany mountains. It comprised such men as Rowan,
who, as an advocate, was excelled by few, if any, of his day : afterwards a judge
of the highest court of the commonwealth, and senator in the Congress of the
United States ; Pope, who has been pronounced, by good judges, one of the
ablest debaters that this country has ever produced ; Hardin, who is well known
as a skillful and learned jurist; and, at a subsequent period, that prodigy, John
Hays, whose marvellous eloquence is never spoken of without enthusiasm, by
those who had the good fortune to hear him. In this battle of giants, Mr. Wickliffe, by fair and honorable exertion, forced his way to that high place in public
estimation which he has ever since maintained.

When the popular mind began to be deeply moved in reference to the vindication of our national rights and honor against the maritime tyranny of England,
Mr. Wickliffe took an active part, by public addresses, in preparing the people
of that part of Kentucky in which he was then known, to support a declaration
of war, and to take a share in the struggle worthy of her renown for courage and
patriotism. After war had been declared in 1812, he entered the service as a volunteer, but was soon after appointed aid to Gen. Winlock. He had been chosen
to represent Nelson county in the legislature, which met in December, 1812. This
was an important session. Kentucky had responded, with her usual alacrity, to
the call of the country. During the preceding summer, great numbers of volunteers had left their homes for the hardships and perils of the north-western campaign. The general government having failed, in a great measure, to provide for
the wants, the legislature threw open the treasury of the State ; and, at the same
time hat they devoted her revenues to the public service, pledged the lives of her
sons to the cause of the nation.

While this legislature was in session, came the news of that dreadful disaster at the Raisin, which covered the State with mourning. The two houses requested the venerable Gov. Shelby, then in the executive chair, to take command of the Kentuckians, and lead them to victory and vengeance. Of all these measures for the vigorous prosecution of the war, Mr. Wickliffe was the zealous and efficient advocate. His re-election, in 1813, was the best proof that his constituents approved his legislative conduct.

In this year, he was married to Miss Margaret Cripps, a lady who is justly admired for her colloquial powers and social accomplishments, and esteemed by her intimate friends for other less brilliant, but still more valuable qualities. Her father, some months before her birth, had fallen in a dreadful conflict with the Indians, near Bullitt's Lick, after a display of courage and generosity unsurpassed in the annals of western adventure.

When Gov. Shelby issued his proclamation, inviting his fellow-citizens to meet him at Newport, Mr. Wickliffe again volunteered, and was appointed aid to Gen. Caldwell, of the Kentucky troops, in which capacity he was present, and rendered valuable service, at the battle of the Thames. After that battle, he returned to Kentucky, and served in the ensuing session of the legislature. He then withdrew from public life, being under the necessity of providing for a family, by undivided attention to his professional business.

In 1820, he was again elected to the legislature. In the session of that year the commonwealth bank was chartered. Mr. Wickliffe made an able speech against that measure, basing his opposition to it not only upon constitutional ground, but also upon the evils and dangers of the paper system. He continued a member of the legislature until his election to Congress in 1822. In 1825, when the choice of a president devolved upon the house of representatives, Mr. Wickliffe, in opposition to most of his colleagues, voted for General Jackson, in accordance with the wishes of a large majority of the people whom he represented. He preferred General Jackson to Mr. Adams, from his personal knowledge of their characters, as well as of their views in relation to the fundamental principles of the federal government. His re-election to Congress, by the unusually large majority of two thousand votes, was a decisive proof of the approbation of his constituents. He continued to represent the same district in Congress until 1833, when the pressure of domestic cares and professional business compelled him once more to retire from public life.

During his ten years' service in the councils of the nation, his reputation steadily rose as a debater and a man of business. He was for several years chairman of the important committee of public lands, and was chosen by the house one of the managers of the impeachment of Judge Peck, in which capacity he appeared before the senate, and made one of the ablest speeches reported in the proceedings of that celebrated trial.

Mr. Wickliffe was not long permitted to remain in retirement. The same year in which he left Congress, he was called upon by the people of Nelson county to represent them in the legislature. In the session of 1834, he was chosen speaker of the house of representatives. At a subsequent session Mr. Wickliffe drafted, supported and carried through the legislature, in the face of violent opposition, the bill establishing the present jury system of Kentucky. Every one acquainted with the defects of the former system, must admit that we are indebted to Mr. Wickliffe for a valuable reform in the administration of justice—perhaps the most important of all the objects for which governments are instituted.

Scarcely had he left the legislature, when, in 1836, he was chosen lieutenant governor of Kentucky, by which he became president of the senate. His commanding person, dignified manners, and prompt decision, well qualify him to preside over a deliberative body. In 1839, by the death of Governor Clarke, he became the acting governor of the commonwealth, and discharged the duties of that high office with ability, integrity, and to the general satisfaction of the public. He found the finances of the commonwealth in such a condition, owing to the excesses of the internal improvement system, as threatened to impair the credit of the State. He saw that this state of things required a prompt remedy, and in his annual message, he called upon the legislature to prevent the further issue and sale of bonds, without an adequate provision for paying the interest on the vast liabilities already incurred.

In 1841, he was called by Mr. Tyler to a seat in his cabinet, as post master general of the United States. All who know him will acknowledge that he was well qualified for that responsible office, by methodical habits of business, sagacity, combined with scrupulous attention to details, and unswerving determination to do his duty according to law, regardless of the clamors of interested men. The close of his official career was signalized by a transaction, perhaps the most memorable of his public life. It was his fortune to take a considerable share in bringing to its final consummation the annexation of Texas; a measure which may be regarded as a link in a chain of events that will girdle the North American continent with a wide belt of illumination: which has given an impulse to the extension of anglo American institutions, that cannot be arrested until the circuit of empire shall have been completed on the shores of the Pacific.

In conclusion, we may remark that, though, like all men who have been prominently connected with public transactions, Mr. Wickliffe has given offence to many, his conduct in all the domestic relations, as a citizen, as a man of business, and as a christian gentleman, secures the respect and confidence even of his bitterest political enemies.

The Hon. BENJAMIN HARDIN is one of the ablest men in the State. He has frequently been a member of the legislature, and elector for president and vice-president. He was a member of Congress from 1815 to 1817, from 1819 to 1823, and from 1833 to 1837. While in Congress, few occupied higher rank as a debater than Mr. Hardin. His style is peculiar, pungent, sarcastic, pointed and energetic; making him an antagonist to be feared. The late eccentric John Randolph, of Roanoke, in allusion to Hardin's peculiar style of oratory, used to call him " the kitchen knife," rough and homely, but keen and trenchant. As an advocate at the bar, he has few if any superiors in the State. In 1844, when William Owsley became governor of the State, he appointed Hardin his secretary of state, which office he held until February, 1847, when he resigned. His person is tall and commanding, his eye remarkably keen and penetrating, and his countenance exhibits striking indications of decided talent. In his politics he is a whig.

THOMAS NELSON, one of the signers of the declaration of independence, from whom this county received its name, was a native of Virginia. He was educated in England; and entered the Virginia house of burgesses, in 1774. In the military organization of Virginia, at the breaking out of the war, he was appointed to the command of a regiment. In 1775, he was sent to the general Congress, at Philadelphia, and was a member of that body at the time of the declaration of independence. About this time he was appointed, by the State of Virginia, a brigadier general, and invested with the chief command of the military of the State. In 1779, he was again, for a short time, a member of Congress, but was forced by ill health to resign his seat. In 1781, he succeeded Mr. Jefferson as governor of Virginia; and continued to unite in himself the two offices of governor and commander of the military forces, until the surrender of Lord Cornwallis. He died in 1789, aged fifty years.

The following incidents, from an esteemed and valuable contributor, were designed to appear under the head of Bullitt, but were not received until after the description of that county had passed through the hands of the stereotyper. They are too interesting to be lost, and we therefore transfer them to Nelson:

" If I could have taken the time, I might have given you many other interesting particulars of the early times about Bullitt's Lick—when the fires of an hundred salt furnaces gleamed through the forest, and the Wyandot sat on Caha's knob and looked down on five hundred men on the plain below. I have sat in the fork of the chesnut-oak to which Caha was bound by the Indians, while they procured his funeral pile out of the dead limbs of the pitch-pine that grows on the mountain's side—(they intended to burn him in sight of Bullitt's Lick). Some oxen had been turned out to graze, and were straggling up the hill side. The Indians heard the cracking of the brush, and supposing it to be their enemies (the whites) coming in search of their lost companion, darted into the thicket on the opposite side of the hill. Caha improved their temporary absence—slipped his bands, and escaped in the darkness, and in a half hour arrived safe at the licks. A company was immediately raised, and made pursuit. They followed the trail of about twenty Indians to the bank of the Ohio river, and saw the Indians crossing on dead timber they had rolled into the river. Some shots were exchanged, but no damage was known to be done on either side.

"I have sat under the shade of the elm, about three miles north of Shepherdsville, where Col. Floyd fell; and have a thousand times walked the path that May and his companions pursued, as they returned from making surveys in the new county of Washington, when they were waylaid by some twelve Indians, about a mile and a half above Shepherdsville, on the south side of Salt river. The surveyors, including the elder May, were all killed but one—his name was Hardin. He fled to the river bank, pursued by the Indians. There was a small station on the opposite side, (called Brashear's station, I think), about a quarter of a mile above the site of the present beautiful watering place called Paroquette Springs. The men in the station, about twenty-five in number, sallied out. Hardin ran under the river bank and took shelter. The whites, on the opposite side, kept the Indians off of him with their rifles, until a part of their company ran down and crossed at the ford, (Shepherdsville), came up on the side Hardin was on, and drove the Indians from their prey. May's field-notes of his surveys were preserved, and subsequently sustained by the supreme court of the commonwealth."

In 1778, JOHN FITCH, for whom the honor has been claimed of having invented the steamboat, came to Kentucky, located a tract of land in Nelson county, and appears to have resided there for some time. He was a native of Connecticut— a man of robust person and vigorous intellect—inclined to mechanics in his studies and habits, but not educated as a practical mechanic. The idea of applying steam as a propelling power in navigation, first suggested itself to his mind while sitting on the bank of the Ohio river, and thinking of the vastness and fertility of the great valley watered by that and the Mississippi river. After repeated trials, and much annoyance from unsuccessful applications for assistance, he finally succeeded in carrying his project into execution, and made a boat which was propelled by steam. He visited Europe, in the course of his labors, and availed himself of the knowledge to be obtained from an examination of Watts' improvement in the steam engine. He endeavored to procure a patent for his invention, but failed. The remainder of his life was spent in harassing efforts to make his invention productive, but without avail. His disappointments preyed upon his spirit. He resorted to the bottle, and died in extreme poverty. He was interred in the public burial ground at Bardstown.

NICHOLAS COUNTY.

NICHOLAS county was formed in 1799, and named in honor of Colonel GEORGE NICHOLAS. It is situated in the north-east middle part of the State, and lies on both sides of the Licking river, which flows through the county in a north-western direction. The other more important streams of the county are, Flat, Somerset and Cassady's creeks. That portion of the county which borders upon Bourbon and Bath, is generally level or gently undulating, and is quite rich and productive: the remainder of the county, with the exception of the vallies of Licking and its tributaries, is broken oak lands. The soil is based on limestone, with red clay foundation. The staple articles of trade and commerce are, corn, hemp, cattle and hogs. Carlisle is the present seat of justice, 58 miles from Frankfort. It is a singular fact that the county seat has been located at every prominent point in the county. First at the Blue Licks; next at Bedinger's mill, two miles above; then at Ellisville, on the road from Maysville to Lexington; and finally it found a permanent location at Carlisle in 1816.

Number of acres of land in Nicholas, 142,305; average value of land per acre, $11.55; total valuation of taxable property in 1846, $2,456,145; number of white males over twenty-one years old, 1,623; number of children between five and sixteen years old, 2,121. Population in 1840, 8,745.

CARLISLE, the seat of justice for Nicholas county, is situated two miles east of the Maysville and Lexington road, thirty-four miles from Maysville, fifty-eight miles from Frankfort, and five hundred and ten miles from Washington city : contains a new brick court-house, two churches, six lawyers, three physicians, two taverns, five dry goods stores, one drug and hat store, two tanneries and fifteen mechanics' shops. Population about 300. Incorporated in 1817. *Moorefield* is a small village, six miles east of Carlisle —containing one church, two physicians, four mechanics' shops, and about 40 inhabitants.

The BLUE LICK SPRINGS have, from various causes, become the most celebrated watering place in the west. It was here that the bloody battle was fought with the Indians, which shrouded Kentucky in mourning; and next to Braddock's defeat, has become famous in the annals of savage warfare. At an early day, the Licks became a point of great importance to the settlers, as it was chiefly here that they procured, with great labor, and at much expense, their supply of salt. In modern times, it has become a favorite and fashionable resort, where hundreds of the elite of the land annually assemble in the pursuit of health or pleasure. The largest and most valuable spring, whose supply of water appears to be inexhaustible, is situated on the northern bank of the Licking river, about two hundred yards from that stream. The water has been analyzed by experienced chemists, and contains the following ingredients :—Sulphurated hydrogen, carbonic acid, muriate of soda, muriate of magnesia, muriate of lime, sulphate of lime, sulphate of soda, sulphate of magnesia, and carbonate of lime. In its action on the system, it is purgative, diaphoretic and alterative.

Since this watering place has passed into the possession of the Messrs. Holliday, the buildings have been greatly extended, the accommodations increased, and the grounds improved and beautifully adorned. The main hotel is six hundred and seventy feet in length, three stories high, and surrounded by large and airy galleries, eighteen hundred feet in extent. It has a large and commodious dining room, ball room, and three elegantly furnished parlors. The large cedar grove which occupies the site of the battle ground, has been enclosed and set in blue grass, and affords a delightful retreat to visitors in the hot months of July and August. The Blue Lick water has become an important article of commerce, several thousand barrels being annually exported.

On the 25th of September, 1776, Colonel John Todd, with a party of ten men, left Hinkston's station, for the purpose of removing the military stores secreted by General George Rogers Clark on Limestone creek,* (near Maysville,) to Harrodsburg. When near the Blue Licks, they met a small body of Indians, which was following the trail of Clark and his companions, who had made their way a few days previous to Harrodsburg. The savages made a sudden and vigorous onset upon the whites, killing Jones and one or two others, making two or three prisoners, and putting the remainder to flight.

In January, 1778, accompanied by thirty men, Boone went to the Blue Licks to make salt for the different stations ; and on the seventh of February following, while out hunting, he fell in with one hundred and two Indian warriors, on their march to attack Boonsborough. He instantly fled, but, being upwards of fifty

---

* See sketch of General George Rogers Clark.

VIEW OF THE BLUE LICK SPRINGS, K.Y.

years old, was unable to contend with the fleet young men who pursued him, and was a second time taken prisoner. As usual he was treated with kindness until his final fate was determined, and was led back to the Licks, where his men were still encamped. Here his whole party, to the number of twenty-seven, surrendered themselves, upon promise of life and good treatment, both of which conditions were faithfully observed.*

In 1782, the Indians having committed some depredations at Hoy's station, and taken two boys prisoners, Captain Holder raised a party of seventeen men and pursued them. Near the Upper Blue Licks, he came in sight of the enemy, and a spirited conflict ensued; but Captain Holder finding his force greatly inferior in number to the Indians, very prudently gave orders to retreat, which was effected with the loss of four men killed and wounded. The loss on the part of the Indians was never ascertained.

On the 19th of August, 1782, the fatal battle to which we have previously referred, took place, on the old State road, about half a mile north of the Lower Blue Licks. The Kentuckians who fought this battle left Bryant's station on the afternoon of the 18th, and was composed of one hundred and eighty-two men, according to General G. R. Clark, and of one hundred and sixty-six, according to Mr. Marshall. The subjoined account of the troops, pursuit, and battle, we copy from McClung's Sketches :

" Colonel Daniel Boone, accompanied by his youngest son, headed a strong party from Boonsborough; Trigg brought up the force from the neighborhood of Harrodsburg, and Todd commanded the militia around Lexington. Nearly a third of the whole number assembled was composed of commissioned officers, who hurried from a distance to the scene of hostilities, and for the time took their station in the ranks. Of those under the rank of colonel, the most conspicuous were Majors Harland, McBride, McGary, and Levi Todd, and Captains Bulger and Gordon. Of the six last named officers, all fell in the subsequent battle, except Todd and McGary. Todd and Trigg, as senior colonels, took the command, although their authority seems to have been in a great measure nominal. That, however, was of less consequence, as a sense of common danger is often more binding than the strictest discipline.

" A tumultuous consultation, in which every one seems to have had a voice, terminated in an unanimous resolution to pursue the enemy without delay. It was well known that General Logan had collected a strong force in Lincoln, and would join them at farthest in twenty-four hours. It was distinctly understood that the enemy was at least double, and, according to Girty's account, more than treble their own numbers. It was seen that their trail was broad and obvious, and that even some indications of a tardiness and willingness to be pursued, had been observed by their scouts, who had been sent out to reconnoitre, and from which it might reasonably be inferred that they would halt on the way, at least march so leisurely, as to permit them to wait for the aid of Logan! Yet so keen was the ardor of officer and soldier, that all these obvious reasons were overlooked, and in the afternoon of the 18th of August, the line of march was taken up, and the pursuit urged with that precipitate courage which has so often been fatal to Kentuckians. Most of the officers and many of the privates were mounted.

" The Indians had followed the buffalo trace, and as if to render their trail still more evident, they had chopped many of the trees on each side of the road with their hatchets. These strong indications of tardiness, made some impression upon the cool and calculating mind of Boone; but it was too late to advise retreat. They encamped that night in the woods, and on the following day reached the fatal boundary of their pursuit. At the Lower Blue Licks, for the first time since the pursuit commenced, they came within view of an enemy. As the miscellaneous crowd of horse and foot reached the southern bank of Licking, they saw a number of Indians ascending the rocky ridge on the other side.

" They halted upon the appearance of the Kentuckians, gazed at them for a few moments in silence, and then leisurely disappeared over the top of the hill. A halt immediately ensued. A dozen or twenty officers met in front of the ranks,

---

* Life of Boone.

31

and entered into consultation. The wild and lonely aspect of the country around them, their distance from any point of support, with the certainty of their being in the presence of a superior enemy, seems to have inspired a portion of serious-ness, bordering upon awe. All eyes were now turned upon Boone, and Colonel Todd asked his opinion as to what should be done. The veteran woodsman, with his usual unmoved gravity, replied:

"That their situation was critical and delicate; that the force opposed to them was un-doubtedly numerous and ready for battle, as might readily be seen from the leisurely retreat of the few Indians who had appeared upon the crest of the hill; that he was well acquain-ted with the ground in the neighborhood of the Lick, and was apprehensive that an ambus-cade was formed at the distance of a mile in advance, where two ravines, one upon each side of the ridge, ran in such a manner that a concealed enemy might assail them at once both in front and flank, before they were apprised of the danger.

"It would be proper, therefore, to do one of two things. Either to await the arrival of Logan, who was now undoubtedly on his march to join them, or if it was determined to at-tack without delay, that one half of their number should march up the river, which there bends in an elliptical form, cross at the rapids and fall upon the rear of the enemy, while the other division attacked in front. At any rate, he strongly urged the necessity of recon-noitering the ground carefully before the main body crossed the river."

" Such was the counsel of Boone. And although no measure could have been much more disastrous than that which was adopted, yet it may be doubted if any thing short of an immediate retreat upon Logan, could have saved this gallant body of men from the fate which they encountered. If they divided their force, the enemy, as in Estill's case, might have overwhelmed them in detail ; if they remained where they were, without advancing, the enemy would certainly have attacked them, probably in the night, and with a certainty of success. They had committed a great error at first, in not waiting for Logan, and nothing short of a retreat, which would have been considered disgraceful, could now repair it.

" Boone was heard in silence and with deep attention. Some wished to adopt the first plan ; others preferred the second ; and the discussion threatened to be drawn out to some length, when the boiling ardor of McGary, who could never endure the presence of an enemy without instant battle, stimulated him to an act, which had nearly proved destructive to his country. He suddenly interrupted the consultation with a loud whoop, resembling the war-cry of the Indians, spur-red his horse into the stream, waved his hat over his head, and shouted aloud :— " Let all who are not cowards, follow me ! " The words and the action together, produced an electrical effect. The mounted men dashed tumultuously into the river, each striving to be foremost. The footmen were mingled with them in one rolling and irregular mass.

" No order was given, and none observed. They struggled through a deep ford as well as they could, McGary still leading the van, closely followed by Majors Harland and McBride. With the same rapidity they ascended the ridge, which, by the tramping of buffalo foragers, had been stripped bare of all vegetation, with the exception of a few dwarfish cedars, and which was rendered still more desolate in appearance, by the multitude of rocks, blackened by the sun, which were spread over its surface. Upon reaching the top of the ridge, they followed the buffalo trace with the same precipitate ardor ; Todd and Trigg in the rear ; McGary, Harland, McBride, and Boone in front. No scouts were sent in ad-vance ; none explored either flank ; officers and soldiers seemed alike demented by the contagious example of a single man, and all struggled forward, horse and foot, as if to outstrip each other in the advance.

" Suddenly, the van halted. They had reached the spot mentioned by Boone, where the two ravines head, on each side of the ridge. Here a body of Indians presented themselves, and attacked the van. McGary's party instantly returned the fire, but under great disadvantage. They were upon a bare and open ridge ; the Indians in a bushy ravine. The center and rear, ignorant of the ground, hur-ried up to the assistance of the van, but were soon stopped by a terrible fire from the ravine which flanked them. They found themselves enclosed as if in the wings of a net, destitute of proper shelter, while the enemy were in a great mea-sure covered from their fire. Still, however, they maintained their ground. The action became warm and bloody. The parties gradually closed, the Indians emerged from the ravines, and the fire became mutually destructive. The officers suffered dreadfully.   Todd and Trigg in the rear; Harland, McBride, and young Boone, in front, were already killed.

"The Indians gradually extended their line, to turn the right of the Kentuckians, and cut off their retreat. This was quickly perceived by the weight of the fire from that quarter, and the rear instantly fell back in disorder, and attempted to rush through their only opening to the river. The motion quickly communicated itself to the van, and a hurried retreat became general. The Indians instantly sprang forward in pursuit, and falling upon them with their tomahawks, made a cruel slaughter. From the battle ground to the river, the spectacle was terrible. The horsemen generally escaped, but the foot, particularly the van, which had advanced farthest within the wings of the net, were almost totally destroyed. Colonel Boone, after witnessing the death of his son and many of his dearest friends, found himself almost entirely surrounded at the very commencement of the retreat.

Several hundred Indians were between him and the ford, to which the great mass of the fugitives were bending their flight, and to which the attention of the savages was principally directed. Being intimately acquainted with the ground, he, together with a few friends, dashed into the ravine which the Indians had occupied, but which most of them had now left to join in the pursuit. After sustaining one or two heavy fires, and baffling one or two small parties, who pursued him for a short distance, he crossed the river below the ford, by swimming, and entering the wood at a point where there was no pursuit, returned by a circuitous route to Bryant's station. In the mean time, the great mass of the victors and vanquished crowded the bank of the ford.

"The slaughter was great in the river. The ford was crowded with horsemen and foot and Indians, all mingled together. Some were compelled to seek a passage above by swimming ; some, who could not swim, were overtaken and killed at the edge of the water. A man by the name of Netherland, who had formerly been strongly suspected of cowardice, here displayed a coolness and presence of mind, equally noble and unexpected. Being finely mounted, he had outstripped the great mass of the fugitives, and crossed the river in safety. A dozen or twenty horsemen accompanied him, and having placed the river between them and the enemy, showed a disposition to continue their flight, without regard to the safety of their friends who were on foot, and still struggling with the current.

"Netherland instantly checked his horse, and in a loud voice, called upon his companions to halt, fire upon the Indians, and save those who were still in the stream. The party instantly obeyed ; and facing about, poured a close and fatal discharge of rifles upon the foremost of the pursuers. The enemy instantly fell back from the opposite bank, and gave time for the harassed and miserable footmen to cross in safety. The check, however, was but momentary. Indians were seen crossing in great numbers above and below, and the flight again became general. Most of the foot left the great buffalo track, and plunging into the thickets, escaped by a circuitous route to Bryant's station.

"But little loss was sustained after crossing the river, although the pursuit was urged keenly for twenty miles. From the battle ground to the ford, the loss was very heavy ; and at that stage of the retreat, there occurred a rare and striking instance of magnanimity, which it would be criminal to omit."

The foregoing account of the battle of the Blue Licks, we copy from McClung's Sketches, who, we suppose, derived his facts from Marshall. A letter to the author, from a distinguished citizen of Kentucky, far advanced in years, makes the following statement in reference to the battle, which differs, in some important particulars, from Mr. McClung. The writer says :

"Will you include the battle of the Blue Licks in your notes upon Nicholas county ? If so, and you are not in possession of the true account of that battle, I believe I can supply you, and on information derived from Gen. Clark and Simon Kenton ; and, also, Capt. Samuel Johnson and Judge Twyman, both of whom were in the battle. It substantially varies from Marshall, &c., who have, most erroneously, blamed the conduct of the officers. Johnson was a captain, and Judge Twyman a man of high intelligence and perfect veracity. I went over the ground with him, many years since, and was not only shown the spot where the battle began, and where Trigg was killed, but the position of Trigg's, Todd's and Boone's lines. These statements agreed with Kenton's and Gen. Clark's—

the latter receiving his information from his friends in the action, and the Indian chief who fought it. Indeed, Boone's short letter, when correctly understood, corroborates my information, and proves Marshall and others to be in error.

"The whole force assembled in the open Lick ground, and formed three lines —Todd commanding the centre, Trigg the right, and Boone the left lines ; while Capt. Harlan, with twenty-five picked men, formed an advance guard. The whole road from the Lick to the forks was examined by two *spies*, who reported that they could find no Indians between the two points—the latter, as was soon ascertained, having fallen behind the river hills on either side of the horse-shoe, leaving a few of their number concealed in the grass, in the right hand hollow. As the troops moved on, Trigg's battalion came upon the small number last mentioned, who fired upon his command, and killed him and two or three of his men. This threw Trigg's line into confusion, and, being attacked by the Indians from the right hill side of the river, before order could be restored, the whole battalion broke. This exposed Todd to a fire in flank, while Harlan and his twenty-five men were attacked in front, and the whole, with three exceptions, cut down. Todd's line, in consequence, became exposed to the Indian fire in front as well as on his flank, when a large portion of his men gave ground, leaving the left and front ranks exposed to the galling fire of the enemy. A general and tumultuous retreat soon followed, &c.

' "Equally untrue is the statement, that Todd hurried the pursuit, without waiting the arrival of Logan, for fear of being superseded in the command. The fact is, that Todd was then both a militia colonel and a colonel in the State line, and Logan was but a captain.* Logan did not reach Bryant's station until the day after the action, so that, if the battle had been delayed, the Indians would have crossed the Ohio before he reached Lexington."

There are few objects of more interest than the struggle of a great mind with all the disadvantages of poverty and obscurity ; nor is there any sight more grand and imposing—more eminently worthy of contemplation—than the ultimate triumph of such a mind. Of such struggles and such triumphs, our country affords many bright examples ; though there are few, if any, more illustrious than the subject of this brief memoir.

THOMAS METCALFE was born on the 20th of March, 1780, in the county of Fauquier and State of Virginia. His parents were poor and humble, aspiring to no distinction saving that of a good name and spotless reputation. At an early day they emigrated to Kentucky, and settled in the county of Fayette.

The necessity growing out of the poverty and misfortunes of his father and family, contributed, in no small degree, to stamp the character of the boy with the elements of greatness, which his natural industry and enterprize subsequently so fully developed. In his early youth he was sent to school only long enough to attain to moderate perfection in the then recognized rudiments of an English education—sufficient, however, to inspire an ardent love for knowledge. At the age of *sixteen*, he was apprenticed to an elder brother, to learn the trade of a stone mason. Here it was that the character he had displayed in boyhood, shone out in its fullness. The hours which other boys devoted to idleness and unprofitable amusements, were by him assiduously devoted to study and to books. What to other boys was labor, was to him relaxation and repose. At the age of nineteen, his father died, leaving his mother and several children extremely poor, and dependent, partially, upon him for sustenance and support. To enable him more effectually to render them the aid their circumstances required, his brother cancelled his indentures, and he was declared *free*. With his accustomed energy, he set about providing for his widowed mother and her orphan children ; and he most faithfully performed his duty towards them,—rearing and educating the children—protecting and sustaining all of them.

In 1809, he made his first public speech. A requisition had been made upon the State, to vindicate the honor of the nation in the contemplated difficulties with

* The writer of this letter evidently labors under a mistake in relation to the rank of Gen. Logan at this period. In the year 1780, according to Mr. Butler, (History of Kentucky, pp. 114 and 115), Benjamin Logan was comm'ssioned colonel, and Stephen Trigg lieutenant colonel, of Lincoln; and John Todd colonel, and Daniel Boone lieutenant colonel, of Fayette. Marshall, McClung, and Morehead, agree with Butler, as to the rank of Logan.

GOV. METCALFE'S RESIDENCE, FOREST RETREAT, KY.

old Spain. In the language of one who witnessed this effort of the young soldier, "the fire of his language spread through the ranks of the regiment, and imparted to the men the same noble ardor that animated his own bosom. Nothing could withstand the eloquence of his call ; and volunteers flocked to the standard of this Norval of the Grampian hills, until an overflowing complement proved the success of his undertaking."

His expectations were disappointed,—as indeed they had been on two former occasions, on which he had raised volunteers for the contemplated war. He quietly again doffed his title, and betook himself to the labor of his trade. In 1812, he was elected a member of the lower branch of the general assembly of Kentucky. Here his worth was as manifest as in the station of a private citizen. In the spring of 1813, he raised a company of volunteers ; and, at the memorable battle of fort Meigs, he commanded one of the companies under Boswell, on the left flank of the line on this side of the river, which defeated more than double its number of Indians. He displayed an intrepidity and gallantry which secured him the favorable notice of his commander-in-chief, the lamented Harrison. While absent on the campaign of 1813, he was again elected to the legislature, receiving the suffrage of every voter in the county but *thirteen*. He served in this body several years ; and, in 1818, was elected a member of Congress, under circumstances most gratifying to his friends. He remained in Congress until 1827, when he received the nomination of the national republican party as their candidate for governor of Kentucky. He resigned his seat in Congress, returned to Kentucky, and accepted the nomination. He entered at once, fearlessly, and with his accustomed energy, upon the duties of the canvass ; and though the majority was understood to be in favor of the party of his distinguished competitor, Major Barry, he overcame every obstacle, and bore his banner proudly and victoriously through the contest.

After the expiration of his term of service as governor, he retired to his farm, in Nicholas county ; but he was not permitted to leave the field of active service —he was soon recalled to public life. In 1834, he was returned a member of the senate, from the district of Nicholas and Bracken. In 1840, he was appointed president of the board of internal improvements,.which office he has ever since filled,—the arduous and responsible duties of which, he has most faithfully and honorably performed. The venerable man is now, as ever, the honored and beloved of all who know him—a true and worthy specimen of a "fine old Kentucky gentleman."

Major GEORGE M. BEDINGER was a pioneer of Kentucky, and an early settler in Nicholas county. In 1779, he acted as adjutant in the unfortunate expedition of Col. Bowman against the Indian town of old Chillicothe ; and, in 1782, he was a major at the fatal battle of the Blue Licks. In both the expedition and battle he bore himself gallantly, as a brave and efficient officer. In 1792, he was elected a member of the house of representatives of the first legislature of Kentucky, from Bourbon county—the territory of Nicholas then constituting a part of that county. In 1802, he was elected a member of Congress, and served two terms in that body,—retiring to private life in 1807. He lived to an advanced age, and died a few years since, on his farm, near the lower Blue Licks.

Colonel GEORGE NICHOLAS, in honor of whom Nicholas county was named, was an eminent lawyer of Virginia, who served for some years as colonel during the revolutionary war. He came to Kentucky just before it became a State. He was a prominent and influential member of the Virginia convention, and a zealous advocate in favor of the adoption of the Federal Constitution. He was a prominent, if not the most influential member of the convention which framed the first constitution of Kentucky. He enjoyed in an eminent degree the confidence of the people of Kentucky, and contributed largely, by speaking and writing, to influence the course they took in the great political contest of '98. He died when between fifty and sixty years of age, in 1799. As indicating the tone of Colonel Nicholas' moral sentiments, it may be stated that in theory and practice he was opposed to dueling. The following extract from a letter written by him to A. S. Bullitt, in 1792, is honorable alike to his head and his heart. "You ask ' if I expect any further satisfaction from you, on this subject.' I make no scruple to declare, that I have long been of opinion that fighting does no real service to the reputation; that I think it wrong to hazard life in that way contrary both to the laws of God and man; and that for these reasons I shall never call any person to the field. But I hold myself at full liberty to resent any aspersion that may be cast on me; and to defend myself against any personal attack that may be made on me.

"Your obedient servant,

" G. NICHOLAS."

OHIO COUNTY.

Oнιο county was formed in 1798, and named from the Ohio river. It is situated in the west middle portion of the State, lying on the waters of Greene river, which forms its southern and a part of its south-western boundary—Rough creek, quite a considerable stream, flowing, in a meandering course, through its northern territory : bounded on the north by Hancock ; east by Grayson ; south-east by Butler ; south-west by Muhlenburg ; and north-west by Daveiss. The soil of this county is considered equal to that of the Greene river lands generally, producing excellent crops of corn, tobacco, oats, potatoes, clover and other grasses, but supposed not to contain sufficient lime for the profitable growing of wheat. The timber is heavy and of a superior quality. Iron ore abounds in the county, and the beds of excellent coal are inexhaustible. The morus multicaulis flourishes here, and the culture of silk might be carried on to any extent. Some specimens of the manufactured article have been pronounced equal to the best Italian.

Valuation of taxable property in Ohio county, in 1846, $1,280,-237 ; number of acres of land in the county, 309,630 ; average value of lands per acre, $2.08 ; number of white males over twenty one years of age, 1,407 ; number of children between five and seventeen years old, 2,032. Population in 1840, 6,592—but supposed to be one-third greater in 1847.

HARTFORD, the seat of justice, is situated on the bank of Rough creek, about twenty-eight miles by water from its junction with Greene river, and one hundred and sixty miles from Frankfort. Its location is pleasant and agreeable, remarkable for its fine water, and the general health of the population, which numbers about 400. It contains a brick court-house and other county buildings, two churches (Methodist and Free,) six lawyers, six physicians, two taverns, fifteen stores and groceries and ten mechanics' shops. Established in 1808.

Ohio was the first county formed below Hardin, and once included all of the present counties of Ohio, Daveiss and Hancock, with portions of Breckinridge, Grayson and Butler. The immediate vicinity of Hartford was settled at a very early period, and was often the scene of bloody strife and acts of noble daring. Hartford and Barnett's stations were about two miles apart, and although never regularly besieged, were frequently harassed by straggling parties of Indians, and a number of persons, who imprudently ventured out of sight of the stations,

killed or captured. The following facts we have derived from Mr. Stephen Stateler, a pioneer and venerable and esteemed citizen of Ohio county:

In April, 1790, the Indians waylaid Barnett's station, and killed two of the
children of John Anderson. One of the party assaulted Mrs. Anderson with a
sword, inflicted several severe wounds upon her person, and while in the act of
taking off her scalp, John Miller ran up within about twenty steps, and snapped
his rifle at him. The Indian fled, leaving his sword, but succeeded in carrying
off the scalp of Mrs. Anderson. She however recovered and lived some ten or
twelve years afterwards. The same party captured and carried off Hannah Barnett, a daughter of Colonel Joseph Barnett, then a girl of about ten years of age.
They retained her as a captive until October of the same year, when through the
instrumentality of her brother-in-law, Robert Baird, she was recovered and restored to her friends.

In August, of the same year, three men were attacked by a party of Indians,
near the mouth of Greene river. John McIlmurray, one of the whites, was killed,
a man named Faith was wounded, and Martin Vannada was made a prisoner.
The Indians immediately crossed the Ohio river, and, after traveling for some
days in the direction of their towns, struck, as they supposed, the trail of some
white men. In order to pursue them with the utmost celerity and without impediment, they tied Vannada to a tree. With the view of rendering his escape
hopeless, during their absence, they spread a blanket at the root of a tree, and
caused him to sit upon it, with his back against the tree. His hands were then
pinioned behind him, and fastened to the tree with one rope, while they tied another rope around his neck, and fastened it to the tree above. In this painful position they left him, and commenced the pursuit of their supposed enemies. But
no sooner had they departed, than he commenced the work of extricating himself.
With much difficulty he succeeded in releasing his hands, but his task appeared
then only to have begun. He ascertained that he could not reach round the tree
so as to get to the knot; and it was so twisted or tied between his neck and the
tree, that it was impossible for him to slip it one way or the other. Without a
knife, he made powerful efforts to get the rope between his teeth, that he might
gnaw it in two. Failing in this, he almost regretted having made any effort to
effect his escape, as, upon the return of the Indians, the forfeit of his life would,
in all probability, be the consequence. At this moment he recollected that there
were some metal buttons on his waistcoat. Instantly tearing one off, he placed
it between his teeth, and, by great efforts, broke it into two pieces. With the
rough edge of one of these, he succeeded in fretting rather than cutting the cord
in two which bound his neck to the tree, and was once more free. But in what
a condition! In a wilderness and an enemy's country, with no clothing save a
shirt, waistcoat, breeches and moccasins!—no provisions, no gun, no ammunition,
no knife, not even a flint to strike fire with! He did not, however, hesitate or
falter, but instantly struck into the trackless forest, in the direction of home,—
and, under the direction of a kind Providence, reached Hartford the ninth day
after his escape, having subsisted upon such small animals and insects as he could
catch and eat raw. He was nearly famished, and greatly emaciated; but having
fallen into good hands, he was soon recruited, and returned to his family in fine
health.

In the year 1786 or 1787, an incident occurred at a fort on Greene river, which
displays the dangers which beset the emigrants of that period, and illustrates the
magnanimity of the female character.

About twenty young persons—male and female—of the fort, had united in a
flax pulling, in one of the most distant fields. In the course of the forenoon two
of their mothers made them a visit, and the younger took along her child, about
eighteen months old. When the whole party were near the woods, one of the
young women, who had climbed over the fence, was fired upon by several Indians
concealed in the bushes, who at the same time raised the usual war-whoop. She
was wounded, but retreated, as did the whole party,—some running with her
down the lane, which happened to open near that point, and others across the
field. They were hotly pursued by the enemy, who continued to yell and fire
upon them. The older of the two mothers who had gone out, recollecting in her
flight that the younger, a small and feeble woman, was burthened with her child,
turned back in the face of the enemy, they firing and yelling hideously, took the

child from its almost exhausted mother, and ran with it to the fort, a distance of three hundred yards. During the chase, she was twice shot at with rifles, when the enemy were so near that the powder burned her, and one arrow passed through her sleeve; but she escaped uninjured. The young woman who was wounded almost reached the place of safety, when she sunk, and her pursuer, who had the hardihood to attempt to scalp her, was killed by a bullet from the fort.

OLDHAM COUNTY.

OLDHAM county was formed in 1823, and named in honor of Colonel WILLIAM OLDHAM. It is situated in the north middle part of the State, and lies on the Ohio river : bounded on the north by Trimble, east by Henry, south by Jefferson and Shelby, and west and north-west by the Ohio river, and contains a surface of about one hundred and seventy square miles. The face of the country along the Ohio river and Eighteen Mile creek, and in the upper part of the county, adjoining Trimble, is hilly and broken. The remainder of the county is gently undulating, and generally good, arable land—based on limestone. The principal products and exports consist of wheat, hemp, tobacco, hogs and cattle. The principal streams of the county are Harrod's creek and Curry's fork of Floyd's fork, both having their source in Henry county.

The taxable property of Oldham in 1846 was assessed at $2,-517,505 ; number of acres of land in the county, 102,423 ; average value of land per acre, $13.13 ; number of white males over twenty-one years of age, 1,066 ; number of children between five and sixteen years of age, 1,169. Population in 1840, 7,380.

LaGRANGE, the county seat, contains a court-house and other county buildings, one church, six lawyers, three physicians, five stores and groceries, twelve or fifteen mechanics' shops, and about 300 inhabitants. *Masonic College*, under the supervision and sustained by the funds of the grand lodge of Kentucky—located in LaGrange—is quite a flourishing institution. LaGrange took its name from General Lafayette's residence in France. *Ballardsville* is a small village four miles south-east of Lagrange, and contains one church, one physician, two stores, and several mechanics' shops. *West-Port*, formerly the county seat, is a small town on the Ohio river, containing two physicians, two merchants, with several mechanics. *Brownsborough*, a small village, has two physicians and two merchants—and *Floydsburg* has one physician and three merchants. LaGrange, the seat of justice, is about forty miles from Frankfort.

Oldham county was named in compliment to Colonel WILLIAM OLDHAM, who was killed by the Indians at *St. Clair's defeat*, on the 4th of November, 1791. Colonel Oldham was a brave and experienced officer, and commanded a regiment of Kentucky militia in that memorable battle.

He was a native of Berkely county, Virginia, and entered the revolutionary army in 1775, as an ensign, and continued in active service until the spring of

1779, when he resigned, (being then a captain), and came to the Falls of the Ohio, where he remained until his death in 1791.

Col. Oldham was a chivalrous and enterprising man, and was very efficient in defending the country against the incursions of the Indians : and in other respects contributed much to advance its settlement.

The following incident we find in Cist's "Cincinnati Miscellany" for 1846. It is from the "Recollections of the Last Sixty Years," by J. Johnston, Esq., of Piqua, Ohio. The writer, in speaking of the celebrated Indian chief, Little Turtle, says :

"The Little Turtle used to entertain us with many of his war adventures, and would laugh immoderately at the recital of the following :—A white man, a prisoner for many years in the tribe, had often solicited permission to go on a war party to Kentucky, and had been refused. It never was the practice with the Indians to ask or encourage white prisoners among them to go to war against their countrymen. This man, however, had so far acquired the confidence of the Indians, and being very importunate to go to war, the Turtle at length consented, and took him on an expedition into Kentucky. As was their practice, they had reconnoitered during the day, and had fixed on a house recently built and occupied, as the object to be attacked next morning a little before the dawn of day. The house was surrounded by a clearing, there being much brush and fallen timber on the ground. At the appointed time, the Indians, with the white man, began to move to the attack. At all such times no talking or noise is to be made. They crawl along the ground on their hands and feet ; all is done by signs from the leader. The white man all the time was striving to be foremost, the Indians beckoning him to keep back. In spite of all their efforts, he would keep foremost ; and having at length got within running distance of the house, he jumped to his feet and went with all his speed, shouting at the top of his voice, "Indians ! Indians ! " The Turtle and his party had to make a precipitate retreat, losing forever their white companion, and disappointed in their fancied conquest of the unsuspecting victims of the log cabin. From that day forth, this chief would never trust a white man to accompany him again to war."

OWEN COUNTY.

Owen county was formed in 1819, and named in honor of Colonel Abraham Owen. It is situated in the north middle part of the State, and lies on the Kentucky river, which borders it on the west: bounded on the north by Carroll and Gallatin ; east by Grant and Pendleton ; south by Scott and Franklin ; and west by Henry. The face of the country is undulating and the soil good —producing fine tobacco, corn, oats, buckwheat, &c. Sheep are raised in large numbers, and do well. The county is watered by the Kentucky river and Big Eagle creek, with many smaller streams. Big Eagle rises in Scott, and flows through the southern part of Owen into Grant in a northern direction ; then, making a sudden bend, takes a direction somewhat south of west, and running parallel with the Ohio river, flows into the Kentucky in Carroll, skirting the northern boundary of Owen in its progress. Many valuable mineral springs are found in the county, the medicinal virtues of some of which are supposed to be equal to any in the State.

Valuation of taxable property in Owen in 1846, $2,014,066;

number of acres of land in the county, 185,462 ; average value of lands per acre $6.28 ; number of white males over twenty-one years old, 1,602 ; number of children between the ages of five and sixteen years, 1,963. Population in 1830, 5,792—in 1840, 8,232.

The towns of the county are—Owenton, the seat of justice, Marion, New-Liberty and Williamsburg. OWENTON is about thirty miles from Frankfort—and contains a court-house and the usual county buildings, three churches, three lawyers, five physicians, five stores and groceries, two taverns and nine mechanics' shops. Established in 1828—population 200. *Marion* is a small village, with but few houses. *New-Liberty* has four lawyers, four physicians, seven or eight merchants, fourteen mechanics' shops, two taverns, with a population of 400. Incorporated in 1827. *Williamsburg* is a small village with one tavern, one store, one physician, and about fifty inhabitants. The whole county contains fourteen Baptist, six Methodist, and five Christian churches, and one Presbyterian church.

There are several remarkable places in Owen, which merit a description. The " Jump Off," on the Kentucky river, is a perpendicular precipice, at least one hundred feet high, with a hollow passing through its centre about wide enough for a wagon road. The " Point of Rocks," on Cedar creek, just above its mouth, and near Williamsburg, is a beautiful and highly romantic spot, where an immense rock, about seventy-five feet high, overhangs a place in the creek called the " Deep Hole," to which no bottom has ever been found, and which abounds with fish of a fine quality. " Pond Branch" is a stream of water which flows from a large pond in a rich, alluvial valley, which, from its general appearance, is supposed to have been at one time the bed of the Kentucky river. It is about a mile and a half distant from Lock and Dam number 3. The water flows from the pond and empties into the river, by two outlets, and thus forms a complete mountain island, two and a half miles long and a mile and a half wide in its broadest part.

Colonel ABRAHAM OWEN, in honor of whom this county received its name, was born in Prince Edward county, Virginia, in the year 1769, and emigrated to Shelby county, Kentucky, in 1785. The particulars of his early life are not known, and his first appearance on the public theatre and in the service of the country, was upon Wilkinson's campaign, in the summer of 1791, on the White and Wabash rivers. He was a lieutenant in Captain Lemon's company in St. Clair's defeat, November 4th, 1791, and received two wounds in that engagement —one on the chin, and the other in the arm. He was in the expedition led by Colonel Hardin to White river, and participated in the action which routed the Indians in their hunting camps. His brother John, James Ballard and others of Shelby county, were his associates on this occasion. It is not known that he was in Wayne's campaign ; but in 1796, he was surveyor of Shelby county, and afterwards a magistrate. He commanded the first militia company raised in the county, and the present venerable Singleton Wilson, of Shelbyville, brother of the late Dr. Wilson of Cincinnati, was the lieutenant. They had been associates in Wilkinson's campaign, and the humane efforts of Colonel Owen to provide for the wants and promote the comforts of his companion, were illustrative of his general good character. Owen was soon promoted to be a major, and then colonel of the regiment. Lieutenant Wilson was promoted to the rank of captain, having served with distinction as a spy in the campaign led by General Wayne.

Col. Owen was, soon after, elected to the legislature, by the largest vote ever before polled in the county ; and, in 1799, was chosen a member of the convention which framed our present constitution. Shortly before his death, he was a member of the senate of Kentucky. No man in the county had a stronger hold on the affections of the people, whom he was always ready to serve in peace or in war. In 1811, he was the first to join Gov. Harrison at Vincennes, for the purpose of aiding in the effort to resist the hostile movements of the Indian bands collected by the energy and influence of Tecumseh and his brother, the Prophet. He was chosen by Gen. Harrison to be one of his aids-de-camp; and, at the memorable battle of Tippecanoe, fell at the side of his heroic chief, bravely fighting for his country, deeply regretted by the whole army and by his numerous friends in Kentucky. In battle he was fearless—as a citizen, mild and gentlemanly. He was esteemed an excellent officer on parade, and possessed a high order of military talent.

In the following December, the legislature of Kentucky went into mourning for the loss of colonels Daveiss and Owen, and others who had fallen at Tippecanoe; and, in 1819–20, the memory of Col. Owen was perpetuated by a county bearing his name. McAfee, in his history of the late war, says: "His character was that of a good citizen and a brave soldier;" which Butler, in his history of Kentucky, speaking of him, pronounces to be "no little praise in a republic and in a warlike State."

He left a large family to unite with his country in deploring his premature fall. His daughters intermarried with the most respectable citizens of Henry county, and his son Clark is a distinguished citizen of Texas, having won a high rank in her civil and military annals. His brothers, Robert and William, survive him, and are highly respectable citizens of Shelby county. His father was an early settler, of high standing and marked character. His fort, near Shelbyville, was the resort of intrepid families of that day, and may be said to have been the foundation of the capital of the flourishing county of Shelby. The chivalric patriotism of Col. Owen, in leaving a position of ease and civil distinction at home, to volunteer his services against the north-western savages, is truly illustrative of the Kentucky character; and after ages will look back upon the deeds of heroism at Tippecanoe, with the same veneration with which the present generation regards the memory of those who fought and fell at Thermopylæ.

OWSLEY COUNTY.

Owsley county was formed in 1842, and named after Gov. William Owsley. It is situated in the eastern part of the State, on each side of the Kentucky river,—the three forks of that river— the north fork, the middle fork, and the south-east fork,—forming a junction within the territory of the county : bounded on the north by Montgomery and Morgan ; east by Breathitt; south by Clay; and west by Estill. The soil along the river valleys is rich and remarkably productive ; but the face of the country is generally broken, and the soil not sufficiently strong for profitable cultivation. Corn is the staple production—but rye, wheat and oats, are also raised. At the confluence and on the banks of each fork of the Kentucky, there are inexhaustible supplies of bituminous coal, in strata of from three to six feet thick. The cannel or English coal, of a very superior quality, is also found in great abundance along the banks of these rivers.

In 1846, the valuation of taxable property in Owsley county amounted to $238,396; number of acres of land in the county, 153,141; average value of land per acre, $1.22 ; number of white males over twenty-one years old, 512 ; number of children between five and sixteen years of age, 669.

The county seat bears the name of OWSLEY COURT-HOUSE. It contains one Methodist church, four stores, two physicians, two lawyers, one tavern, school, &c. Population, 75. *Proctor* is a very small village, containing about 20 inhabitants.

WILLIAM OWSLEY, the present governor of Kentucky, was born in the State of Virginia, in the year 1782. In 1783, his father, (William Owsley), left that State and moved to the then "county of Kentucky," and settled on the waters of Drake's creek, near where the town of Crab Orchard, in Lincoln county, now stands. It was but fourteen years previous that Daniel Boone had first penetrated this western wilderness, so that William Owsley can date his citizenship in the State over which he presides, with the very first settlement made in her borders.

The father of William Owsley was one of eleven children, and the family being in very moderate circumstances in life, his share of fortune and education was meagre enough. But being of an adventurous disposition, he struck out boldly, resolved to find a home and fortune in this wild land. With his young family he sat down in the woods where the tomahawk and scalping knife of the stealthy savage still frequently gleamed and bathed itself in the white man's blood. In the midst of such perils, common to all the early settlers of Kentucky, our emigrant lived, labored and throve ; and, in worthy imitation of paternal example, he had in due time surrounded himself with ten or twelve children, a majority of whom were daughters.

William and Joel, two of the sons, by their devotion to study, succeeded in getting a better education than was common for boys at that day. Joel studied medicine, and he is now living, a highly esteemed physician, in Cumberland county, in this State.

William Owsley taught for a while a country school, and, while thus engaged, improved his education and learned plain surveying. He shortly after became deputy surveyor, and afterwards deputy sheriff, his father being high sheriff of the county.

It may be proper to add, just here, that among the pupils of William Owsley, the young school master, was a young Miss of near seventeen, whose name was Elizabeth Gill. It so fell out that the lessons taught and learned between this pupil and teacher soon pertained to other matters than books. In a short time William Owsley, being about twenty-one years of age, married his young and blooming scholar: and this connexion, thus early and happily commenced, has, by a kind Providence, been full forty-four years continued—the wife as much distinguished for all the virtues and devotion of a Kentucky housewife, as the man for the plain, unostentatious manners of the olden time.

It was whilst William Owsley was engaged in his early official pursuits as deputy sheriff, &c., that he attracted the attention of John Boyle, afterwards chief justice of Kentucky. Judge Boyle, perceiving the promise that was in young Owsley, offered him the use of his library, and the advantage of his instructions in the study of law. The offer was accepted, and by perseverance and close application, Owsley soon obtained license and commenced the practice of law in Garrard county. His success was immediate. He ranked high at the bar, and became the intimate and firm friend of Judge Boyle. He afterwards represented Garrard county several years in the legislature, and became so favorably known to the public as a legislator and lawyer, that, in 1812, when he was only thirty-one years of age, and had been but few years at the bar, Governor Scott appointed him to the supreme bench of the State, as the colleague of Judge Boyle, who had been honored by a seat on the appellate bench three years previously. Judge Owsley resigned this office in a short time, in consequence of the passage of a law reducing the number of judges of the court to three. But a vacancy occurring in 1813, he was immediately re-appointed by Governor Shelby.

During the service of Boyle, Owsley and Mills, on the supreme bench, that ever memorable controversy between the old and new court parties was waged. The annals of Kentucky's history will attest the momentous character of that struggle, and duly commemorate the virtues of the men that were then made conspicuous. Never before did the fires of discord burn more fiercely in any civil community. Never before was a State so near anarchy, revolution and ruin.

Firmness, wisdom and coolness alone could save the country in that time of dread and peril. All these qualities were pre-eminent in the judges who then sat upon the bench. They were equal to the crisis. They withstood the storm of popular tumult, careless of the rage of disappointed partisans, flushed with temporary triumph, but crossed in the enjoyment of victory. It seems Providential that such men were on the bench to save the State in that stormy trial.

Having seen the constitution of his country safe through the dangers that beset it, Judge Owsley remained at his high and honorable post till the year 1828, when, after having served upon the bench longer than any man in the State, except Judge Boyle, he resigned his office, and retired to private life on his farm in Garrard county, which he had held and cultivated as a successful practical farmer, for about twenty-five years. Sometime after this, he again represented his old county, Garrard, in the legislature. But finding it inconvenient to attend to his circuit court practice and his growing practice in the court of appeals, he gave up the former, and having parcelled out his farm among his children, (of whom he has five,) he removed to Frankfort. Here he resided until 1843, when, out of the gains of his practice, he purchased himself a splendid farm in Boyle county, to which he removed, giving up his practice altogether. In 1844, after one of the most exciting and hard fought contests ever witnessed in the State, William Owsley was elected governor of Kentucky over Colonel William O. Butler, by far the most popular and formidable candidate the democratic party has ever run in the State. The vote received by Governor Owsley was 59,680, which is larger by 1,191 than the great vote received by General Harrison in 1840.

Governor Owsley's administration is not yet ended, and therefore can not now have the verdict of history. But his friends confidently look to the future for as full justification of all his present and recent acts as the present has already awarded to his past acts. As governor of the State, he is distinguished for his devotion to the duties of his office—his laborious and faithful examination into the affairs of the State, particularly its public debt—and his clear and concise statements thereof in his annual messages ; and for his unshaken determination to bring every officer up to his duty, and as far as in him lies, to have the laws "faithfully executed" in every department of the government.

But his friends claim, as the chief glory of his administration, that the public debt has been checked in its fearful and rapid increase, and for the first time since the debt was created, has been from year to year, during his administration, sensibly diminished. Already has Governor Owsley paid off upwards of *one hundred thousand dollars* of the public debt, and he has all the means in constant operation for the continued payment and reduction of the State debt.

In person, Governor Owsley is very tall, being about six feet two inches high, and is slender for such height. His disposition is reserved, and he talks very little. His deportment is ever calm and quiet, and in times of greatest excitement, when he might be supposed to be intensely anxious, there is no perceptible change in his spirits or demeanor. He is proverbial for honesty, firmness and impartiality, and making the principle of *right* the ground of every action. He seems wholly indifferent to falsely raised popular clamor or the present judgment of men, and relies with unshaken confidence on the calm afterthought of the people. His manners are very plain, simple and purely republican, and he has ever been the sturdy foe of all new fangled fashions in social intercourse, and new notions in law and politics.

PENDLETON COUNTY.

PENDLETON county was formed in 1798, and named for the Honorable EDMUND PENDLETON, of Virginia. It is situated in the northern section of the State, nearly square in shape, and embraces about three hundred square miles. Bounded on the north by

Kenton and Campbell; on the east by Bracken; south by Harrison; and west by Grant and Owen. Pendleton is drained by Main and South Licking rivers, which flow into the county on the south-eastern and southern borders, form a junction near its centre, and passing out near the middle of its northern border—having, as their tributaries, Fork Lick, Kincade, Flour and Grassy creeks. Along the rivers and smaller streams, there are many thousand acres of fine bottom lands, which produce rich and luxuriant crops of corn and grasses. Receding from the streams, the surface is undulating and hilly, but the soil, based upon limestone, is comparatively good, and yields excellent crops of tobacco, wheat, oats, rye, &c. A large portion of the lands, although within from twenty to thirty miles of the fine markets of Cincinnati, Covington and Newport, are yet in a state of nature. In the hands of enterprising men, these lands might be converted into beautiful and profitable stock farms, being well adapted for grasses of all kinds, and particularly the *blue* grass, the favorite of stock raisers—Licking river affording a safe downward navigation through the year, except at very low water. The timber along the water courses in some of the up-lands, is remarkably luxuriant, and well adapted for all the purposes of civilized life—embracing the oak, the walnut, the poplar, the ash, &c.

Valuation of taxable property, in Pendleton county, for 1846, $927,469; number of acres of land in the county, 180,760; average value of lands per acre,$3.95; number of white males over twenty-one years old, 1,128; number of children between the ages of five and sixteen years,1,156. Population in 1830,3,886—in 1840,4,455.

FALMOUTH is the seat of justice, and only town of Pendleton county. It is situated on an elevated and very beautiful and extensive bottom, at the confluence of main Licking and the south branch of Licking river, about sixty miles from Frankfort: contains a court-house and other county buildings, four churches, (Baptist, Presbyterian, Methodist and Christian,) two lawyers, two physicians, male and female school, four stores, two taverns, one wool factory, and ten mechanics' shops. Population, 300. Established in 1793; and being settled by Virginians, was named after Falmouth, Virginia.

There are several salt and sulphur springs in Pendleton; iron ore abounds, and some coal has been discovered.

Within a few hundred yards of the boundaries of Falmouth, the remains of an ancient fortification are yet distinctly visible. It is situated upon elevated and commanding ground, near midway between the two rivers, and commanding the junction, and some distance up both streams. In form, it is a regular circle, with four apertures or openings, opposite to each other, and corresponding very nearly to the four cardinal points of the compass. Twenty years ago,* trees, from two and a half to three feet in diameter, were standing upon the circular embankment of earth which formed the fortification; while the enclosure, covering probably upwards of a quarter of an acre of ground, was grown up in trees, bearing the same

---

* More than thirty-five years since, when the author was a very small boy, he recollects to have examined these ancient remains. The circular embankment, at that time, he thinks, was upwards of three feet high.

marks as to age, size, &c. The timber of the surrounding forest was about the same size of that growing within and upon the embankment, and must have grown up many years after this fortification had been abandoned by its ancient builders. This fortification, combined with the fact, that every height and hill surrounding the junction of the two rivers and overlooking the fort, as well as for miles around, are crowned with one or more Indian graves, or small mounds, present strong and abiding evidence that a warfare, of a bloody and desolating character, once prevailed here, between a people possessing and occupying the ground, and an invading and aggressive enemy.

Pendleton is not the scene of any Indian battle or bloody rencounter, within the recollection of its "oldest inhabitant." But her territory has been desecrated by the feet of hostile Britons, as well as of the blood-thirsty savages. In June, 1779, Col. Byrd, with his Canadian and Indian force of six hundred men, in his route to attack Ruddell's station, ascended the Licking river to its junction with the south branch, where Falmouth now stands. Here he landed his cannon, concentrated his forces, and took up his line of march for that station. The track he pursued was distinctly marked by blazing the forest trees, and may still be traced where the trees are left standing. After capturing Ruddell's and Martin's stations, he returned by the same route, took water at Falmouth, and descended the Licking to its mouth. The traces of his march, south of Falmouth, served to give notoriety, in the surveyors' books, to the entries of land subsequently made.

EDMUND PENDLETON, in honor of whom this county was named, was born in Caroline county, Virginia, in 1741, and died in Richmond in 1803. He was president of the Virginia court of appeals, and of the Virginia convention of 1775—was twice elected a member of Congress—in 1778, was chosen president of the Virginia convention which met to consider the federal constitution, and when the federal government was organized, he was selected by Congress to be district Judge of Virginia, but declined the appointment. Wirt says, " he had in a great measure overcome the disadvantages of an extremely defective education, and by the force of good company, and the study of correct anthors, had attained a great accuracy and perspicuity of style. His manners were elevated, graceful, and insinuating. His person was spare, but well proportioned, and his countenance one of the finest in the world ; serene, contemplative, benignant ; with that expression of unclouded intelligence and extensive reach, which seemed to denote him capable of any thing that could be effected by the power of the human mind. His mind itself was of a very fine order. It was clear, comprehensive, sagacious and correct; with a most acute and subtle faculty of discrimination ; a fertility of expedient which never could be exhausted ; a dexterity of address which never lost an advantage and never gave one, and a capacity for a continued and unremitting application which was perfectly invincible. As a lawyer and a statesman, he had few equals and no superiors. For parliamentary management, he was without a rival. With all these advantages of person, manners, address, and intellect, he was also a speaker of distinguished eminence. He had that silver voice of which Cicero makes such frequent and honorable mention; an articulation uncommonly distinct ; a perennial stream of transparent, cool and sweet elocution, and the power of presenting his arguments with great simplicity and striking effect. He was always graceful, argumentative, persuasive; never vehement, rapid or abrupt. He could instruct and delight; but he had no pretensions to those high powers which are calculated to " shake the human soul."

PERRY COUNTY.

PERRY county was formed in 1820, and named in honor of Commodore OLIVER HAZARD PERRY, of the United States' navy. It is situated in the south-eastern section of the State, and lies on the head waters of the Kentucky river: bounded on the north by

Breathitt; east by Floyd and Letcher; south by Harlan, and west by Clay. This county is drained by the north and middle forks of Kentucky river, with their tributaries, which are navigable, for descending boats, the greater portion of the year. The surface is hilly and mountainous, and a large portion is unsuitable for cultivation, but well adapted for wool growing. The valleys are fertile and productive, with a sandstone foundation. The principal articles of export are—horses, cattle, hogs, salt, coal, ginseng and wool.

Valuation of taxable property in Perry in 1846, $202,068; number of acres of land in the county, 109,863; average value of lands per acre, $1.64; number of white males over twenty-one years old, 338; number of children between the ages of five and sixteen, 678. Population in 1840, 3,089.

HAZARD, the county seat, is a small village, situated on the north fork of the Kentucky river, about one hundred miles from Frankfort.

Early in the summer of 1794, a party of Indians passed through the scattered settlements of Russell or Lee county, Virginia, to the residence of the Livingstons, in Washington county, of the same State. The two Livingstons had gone out into the field, unarmed and unsuspicious of danger, when the Indians broke into the house, and killed their mother (an old woman) and a negro child, and took the two Mrs. Livingstons, all the children, a negro fellow and a negro boy, prisoners; and, taking such other property as they fancied, commenced a retreat. As the children were running along the path, in advance of their mother, she made signs to them to take a path which turned off to a neighbor's house, and the Indians permitted them to run on, only retaining the two women and negroes. Knowing that the Indians must pass either through Russell or Lee to gain the wilderness, expresses were instantly sent to both these counties. The court was in session when the express reached the court-house, and it immediately adjourned, and a party was organized upon the spot, under the command of Capt. Vincent Hobbs, to waylay a gap in Cumberland mountain, called the Stone gap, through which, it was supposed, the Indians would most probably pass. On his arrival at the gap, Hobbs discovered that Indians had just passed through before him; he, therefore, pursued with eagerness, and soon discovered two Indians kindling a fire. These they instantly dispatched; and, finding some plunder with them which they knew must have been taken out of Livingston's house, they at once came to the conclusion, that these two had been sent forward to hunt for provisions, and that the others were yet behind, with the prisoners.

The object of Hobbs was now to make a quick retreat, to cover his own sign, if possible, at the gap, before the Indians should discover it, and perhaps kill the prisoners and escape. Having gained this point, he chose a place of ambuscade: but not exactly liking his position, he left his men there, and taking one with him, by the name of Van Bibber, he went some little distance in the advance, in order, if possible, to find a position better suited to his purpose. As they stood looking round for such a place, they discovered the Indians advancing, with the prisoners. They cautiously concealed themselves, and each singled out his man. Benje, (a noted Indian), having charge of the younger Mrs. Livingston, led the van, and the others followed in succession; but the Indian who had charge of the elder Mrs. Livingston was considerably behind, she not being able to march with the same light, elastic step of her sister. When the front came directly opposite to Hobbs and Van Bibber, they both fired, Hobbs killing Benje, and Van Bibber the next behind him. At the crack of the guns the other men rushed forward, but the Indians had escaped into a laurel thicket, taking with them the negro fellow. The Indian who had charge of the elder Mrs. Livingston tried his best to kill her, but he was so hurried that he missed his aim. Her arms were badly cut by defending her head from the blows of his tomahawk.

The prisoners had scarcely time to recover from their surprise, before the two Livingstons, who heard the guns and who were now in close pursuit with a party of men from Washington, came rushing up, and received their wives at the hands of Hobbs with a gust of joy.   Four Indians were killed, and five had escaped; and it appears they were separated into parties of three and two.   The first had the negro fellow with them, and, by his account, they lodged that night in a cave, where he escaped from them and got home.

In the meantime, a party of the hardy mountaineers of Russell collected and proceeded in haste to waylay a noted Indian crossing-place high up on the Kentucky river, (in the present county of Perry.)   When they got there, they found some Indians had just passed.   These they pursued, and soon overtook two, whom they killed.   They immediately drew the same conclusion that Hobbs had done, and hastened back to the river for fear those behind should discover their sign.   Shortly after they had stationed themselves, the other three made their appearance; the men fired upon them, two fell and the other fled, but left a trail of blood behind him, which readily conducted his pursuers to where he had taken refuge in a thick cane-brake.   It was thought imprudent to follow him any farther, as he might be concealed and kill some of them before they could discover him.   Thus eight of the party were killed, and the other perhaps mortally wounded.*

Commodore OLIVER HAZARD PERRY, in honor of whom this county received its name, was a distinguished officer in the United States' navy, and was born at Newport, Rhode Island, in August, 1785.   He was entered as a midshipman on the sloop of war General Greene, in 1798.   He served in the Tripolitan war, and secured the affection and respect of all the officers and men in the squadron.   In 1810 he was a lieutenant commandant in the schooner Revenge.   In this vessel, in the spring of 1811, he was wrecked in a fog near Stonington.   He demanded a court of inquiry, which acquitted him of all blame in the affair.   In 1812 he was promoted to the rank of master and commander, and appointed to the command of the gun boats in the harbor of New York.   Disliking his situation here, he solicited to be transferred to the lakes, and the greater portion of his men went with him.   On his arrival at Sackett's Harbor, he was ordered by Commodore Chauncey to Lake Erie, to superintend the building of vessels in order to meet the British force on those waters.   On the 4th of August, he got his squadron over the bar, and on the 10th of September met the British squadron under Commodore Barclay.   This fight resulted in a complete victory to the Americans, and Perry was promoted to the rank of Captain.   In the battle of the Thames, on the 5th of October, he served as aid to General Harrison, and rendered important assistance.   At the conclusion of the war, he was appointed to the command of the Java, a frigate of the first class.   In this frigate he attended Commodore Decatur, to chastise the Dey of Algiers, who had committed depredations on our commerce.   In 1819 he was sent to the West India station, where he died of the yellow fever on the 23d of August, 1820.

PIKE COUNTY.

PIKE county was formed in 1821, and named in honor of General ZEBULON M. PIKE.   It is situated in the extreme eastern part of the State, and is drained by the West and Tug forks of Big Sandy river : bounded on the north by Johnson and Floyd; northeast, east, and south-east and south by Virginia ; west by Letcher ; and north-west by Floyd.   The surface of the county presents quite a variegated appearance.   Along the water courses, the lands are of a superior quality and very productive : but the up-

---

* Benjamin Sharp, in the Western Pioneer, Vol. I, pp. 466-7-8.

lands are broken and mountainous, and the soil generally comparatively poor. Stone coal, of a fine quality, abounds—some
banks have been opened, where the seam is from five to eight feet
thick. Iron ore is found in small bodies, but has not been worked.
There are a number of salt wells in the county, at two of which
salt has been manufactured. Corn is the staple product, but
oats, wheat, rye, buck-wheat and potatoes are also cultivated.

Value of taxable property in Pike in 1846, $450,984; number of
acres of land in the county, 104,100; average value of lands per
acre, $2.82: number of white males over twenty-one years old,
698; number of children between five and sixteen years old, 1,112.
Population in 1840, 3,567.

PIKEVILLE, the seat of justice, is situated on the West fork of
Big Sandy river, near the centre of the county, and about one
hundred miles from Frankfort—being at the head of navigation
on the river named; it contains a court-house and other county
buildings, three lawyers, three physicians, nine stores and groceries, and eight or ten mechanics' shops. Established in 1824.

This county was named in honor of General ZEBULON M. PIKE, who was born
at Lamberton, in the State of New Jersey, January 5th, 1779. His father was a
respectable officer in the army of the United States. He entered the army while
yet a boy, and served for some time as a cadet in his father's company, which
was then stationed on the western frontiers of the United States. At an early
age he obtained a commission as ensign, and some time after that of lieutenant.
In 1805 he was sent by the government of the United States to explore the Mississippi river to its sources. After his return from this expedition, he was sent
by General Wilkinson on an excursion into the interior of Louisiana, with a
view of fixing the boundary line between New Mexico and the United States.
This expedition proved a partial failure, and after a variety of adventures, he
returned with his little band to the United States, July 1, 1807. Upon his return
he was appointed a captain, subsequently a major, and in 1810 a colonel of
infantry. In 1812 he was stationed with his regiment on the northern frontier,
and at the beginning of the campaign of 1813 appointed a brigadier general. He
was selected to command the land forces in an expedition against York, the capital of Upper Canada, and April 25th sailed from Sackett's Harbor in the squadron commanded by Commodore Chauncey. On the 27th he arrived at York with
seventeen hundred chosen men. A landing having been effected under a heavy
fire from the enemy, General Pike assaulted the works, and in the course of the
attack, the British magazine exploded, throwing large stones in every direction,
one of which struck Pike on the breast, inflicting a mortal wound, of which he
died in a few hours.

PULASKI COUNTY.

PULASKI county was formed in 1798, and named for Count
PULASKI. It is situated in the south middle part of the State, and
is drained by the Cumberland river, which skirts it on the south
and east: bounded by Lincoln on the north; Casey and Laurel
on the east; Wayne on the south; and Russell and Casey on the
west. The northern part of the county is gently undulating—
the remainder hilly or mountainous. There are extensive coal

mines in the county, principally bordering on the Cumberland river, from which large quantities are shipped annually to the city of Nashville and other points on the river. Salt is manufactured in considerable quantities at Fishing creek salt works, about five miles from Somerset. The Cumberland river is navigable for steamboats of the smaller class as high up as Stegall's ferry and Waitsborough, and within six miles of Somerset. The staple products of the county are—corn, wheat, rye, oats and tobacco.

Valuation of taxable property in Pulaski in 1846, $1,264,975 ; number of acres of land in the county, 288,509 ; average value of lands per acre, $2.16 ; number of white males over twenty-one years of age, 2,097 ; number of children between the ages of five and sixteen years, 3,197. Population in 1840, 9,620.

SOMERSET, the seat of justice, is about eighty miles nearly south from Frankfort. It contains three churches, (Baptist, Methodist and Christian,) one school, six lawyers, five physicians, thirteen stores and groceries, four taverns, one iron foundry, one tannery, ten mechanical trades, with a population of about three hundred. Incorporated in 1812. *Waitsborough* is a small village, laid out in 1845, and situated on the Cumberland—containing a warehouse and a few residences.

In the month of December, 1786, a body of Indians defeated a small party of whites, at the mouth of Buck creek, under the command of Captain Hargrove. The Indians made their attack in the night, killed one man, and severely wounded Hargrove. An Indian, who had probably fired his rifle, made an onset on Captain Hargrove with his tomahawk, and a fierce encounter ensued. Each party exerted himself to the utmost. Hargrove finally succeeded in wresting the tomahawk from the hand of the Indian, and bore it off.

In May, 1788, a party of southern Indians stole some horses near the Crab Orchard. Nathan McClure, lieutenant to Captain Whitley, with a portion of his company, pursued the trail to the ridge between Rockcastle and Buck creek. Here he incidentally fell in with another party, and a fierce skirmish ensued. After several discharges of their guns, both parties precipitately retreated—but not until after Lieutenant McClure was mortally, and several of his men, slightly wounded. The loss on the part of the Indians was not ascertained. McClure died the succeeding night in a cave, where, at his own instance, he had been left—and on the next day, when a party came for him, his remains were found shockingly mangled and torn by wild beasts. He was an active officer, and his loss was deeply deplored.

This county was named in honor of Count JOSEPH PULASKI, a distinguished Pole, who after in vain attempting to restore the independence of his own country, entered the American service. Pulaski had followed the profession of the law, and in 1768 was at the head of the patriots who formed the confederation of Bar. Eight noblemen only constituted the first assembly of that confederation; and of these, three were the sons and one the nephew of Pulaski. In 1771, at the head of a few accomplices, he seized the person of the king, but the latter having procured his liberation, Pulaski was condemned to death, and obliged to save himself by flight. He soon after came to America, and offered his services to the United States against the mother country. Being appointed brigadier general in the American service, he served both in the northern and in the southern army. October 9, 1779, he was mortally wounded in the attack on Savannah, and died two days afterwards.

ROCKCASTLE COUNTY.

ROCKCASTLE county was formed in 1810, and named after Rockcastle river, which forms its south-eastern border. It is situated in the south-east middle section of the State: bounded on the north by Madison and Garrard; north-east by Madison; south-east by Laurel; south-west by Pulaski; and west by Lincoln. The north-eastern and south-eastern parts of the county are broken and hilly, but interspersed with numerous creeks and branches, along which there are some fine, rich bottom lands. In the western part of the county, the surface is level, or gently undulating, and the soil quite productive. The timber consists, principally, of hickory, poplar, white, chesnut, black and spotted oak; lynn, walnut, and dogwood; and, on the watercourses, large and lofty sycamore. In some locations there are fine sugar orchards, which yield a large quantity of sugar for domestic consumption. The staple products are corn, wheat and oats.

Valuation of taxable property in Rockcastle in 1846, $518,876; number of acres of land in the county, 124,214; average value of lands per acre, $2.19; number of white males in the county over twenty-one years of age, 812; number of children between the ages of five and sixteen years, 1,176. Population in 1840, 4,238.

MOUNT VERNON, the seat of justice, is situated on the main road from Crab Orchard to the Cumberland Gap,—thirteen miles from the former, seventy-eight miles from the latter, and about seventy miles from Frankfort. It contains a court-house and other county buildings; one Presbyterian, one Methodist, one Baptist, and one Christian church, (with four others in the county); one school in town, (and various schools in the county on the free school system); eight lawyers, two physicians, two taverns, six stores, five tanneries, and a number of mechanics' shops. Established in 1818, and contains about 200 inhabitants.

Rockcastle river, from its source to the mouth, is about seventy-five miles. It is lined by numerous banks of bituminous coal; but, for the want of navigation, they have not been opened to any extent. The river is about eighty yards wide, but the navigation is obstructed, near its mouth, by what are called "the narrows." By some freak of nature, or powerful concussion of the earth, the rocks have broken loose from the adjoining cliffs and tumbled into the bed of the river, forming an impenetrable barrier to water crafts for about three-fourths of a mile. The whole bed is so closely obstructed, that the largest size fish in Cumberland river do not pass. The expenditure of forty thousand dollars, according to the report of the state engineer, would render the river navigable, and open a market to one of the finest coal regions in the State.

Among the hills of Rockcastle there are numerous saltpetre caves, at which large quantities of saltpetre were manufactured during the late war. One of these, called the " Big Cave," eight miles north-east of the county seat, extends through a spur of the mountain, usually termed the " Big Hill," about six hundred yards. It was discovered by John Baker, who, in company with his wife, commenced exploring it with a torchlight. At the distance of about three hundred yards, their light went out, and they were forced to crawl about, in perfect darkness, for forty hours, before they found the place at which they entered. The arch is from ten to twenty feet high. Large rooms branch off several hundred yards long, and the end of one has not been reached. Some of the rooms cover an area of several acres. The saltpetre manufactured here, before and during the late war, gave employment to some sixty or seventy laborers. There is a fine, bold running stream of water in the cave, and works were constructed inside, for the manufacture of saltpetre by torchlight. Carts and wagons passed through, from one side of the mountain to the other, without difficulty. The way is so level and straight, that oxen were soon taught to pass through in perfect darkness, without a driver.

There are several mineral springs in the county, but their waters have never been analyzed.

Boone's old trace, and Skegg's trace, pass through this county,—the former leading to Boonsborough, and the latter to the Crab Orchard. On Skegg's trace, there were two defeats among the emigrants, in the early settlement of Kentucky. McClure's family and company were defeated near the head of the east fork of Skegg's creek, and Capt. Baughman and company on Negro creek.

The following incident appears in Cist's " Cincinnati Miscellany," for 1846. It is characteristic of the female character, in times of emergency:

" About the year 1790, several families emigrating together into the interior of Kentucky, encamped at the distance of a mile from a new settlement of five cabins. Before they had laid down, and were still sitting around the blazing brush, a party of Indians approached behind the trees, and fired upon them. One man was killed on the spot, and another fled to the village, leaving *behind* him a young wife and infant child! As no danger had been apprehended, the men had not their ammunition at hand, and were so confused by the fire of the savages, that it was left for one of the mothers of the party to ascend into the wagon where it was deposited, break open the box with an axe, hand it out, and direct the men to return the fire of the enemy. This was done, and they dispersed."

<hr>

RUSSELL COUNTY.

Russell county was formed in 1825, and named for Col. William Russell. It is situated in the south middle section of the State, and lies on both sides of Cumberland river: bounded on the north by Casey; east by Pulaski and Wayne; south by Clinton; and west and north-west by Cumberland and Adair. The beautiful level bottom lands on the Cumberland are very fertile; but the surface of the county, generally, is hilly and broken, and the soil not well adapted for profitable agriculture. The water power of the county is remarkably fine—one cotton and two woollen factories have been already erected, and many others might be profitably established.

Russell is a small county, embracing 118,544 acres of land, the average value of which, in 1846, was $2.01; total valuation of taxable property, same year, $523,967; number of white males over twenty-one years old, 825; number of children between five and sixteen years of age, 1,307. Population in 1840, 4,238.

JAMESTOWN, the seat of justice, contains four lawyers, five physicians, six stores, three taverns, eight or ten mechanics' shops,
the usual public buildings, and about 150 inhabitants. *Creelsburg*
is a small village, situated on the Cumberland river, and contains
about 50 inhabitants.

Colonel WILLIAM RUSSELL, in honor of whom this county was named, was
born in the year 1758, in the county of Culpepper, in the then province of Virginia. Whilst yet a boy, his father, a man of an enterprising and adventurous
disposition, and who afterwards attained considerable distinction in the struggles of the revolution, removed into the extreme south-western portion of the
province—then an exposed frontier settlement. Here the youthful days of William Russell were spent in acquiring such information as the means of a new
settlement afforded him, or in the hardy and robust exercises incident to a frontier residence.

It is not our purpose, in this sketch, to detail minutely the various transactions
of his useful life. The limits to which we are necessarily prescribed, will permit us only to glance at some of the most prominent events of his military and
political career. In the year 1774, young Russell, at the early age of fifteen,
was engaged with a party under the command of the illustrious Daniel Boone,
in repelling the aggressions made upon the settlement by a tribe of southern
Indians. During his expedition, his comrades, from his tender age, were compelled to relieve the weight of his rifle, by carrying his portion of baggage and
provisions. From this period, until the year 1779, both before and after the
epoch of Independence, he was engaged in frequent excursions against the savages, who waged a continued warfare with the white settlers. In the spring of
1780 he visited Kentucky, and thence proceeded to West Tennessee, where a
settlement had just been effected on what now forms the site of the flourishing
city of Nashville. Here he spent the summer, generously aiding the settlers in
defending their infant home against the repeated assaults of the neighboring Indians. He returned to Virginia the ensuing fall. During his absence the war
of the Revolution which hitherto had raged at a distance, had now, besides
assuming a much more appalling aspect, approached the vicinity of his own
abode. That courage and intrepidity so often evinced in his previous engagements with the Indians, combined with a natural love of liberty, soon nerved his
still youthful arm for the patriotic struggle. The memorable battle of " King's
Mountain," which may be considered the most decisive of the revolution, burst
like a meteor light upon the drooping spirits of the American army. The immediate results of this victory proved an epoch in the struggle, and has conferred
the boon of immortality upon the principal actors. In this glorious contest, young
Russell bore a valiant and distinguished part. He was a lieutenant in the mounted regiment from Virginia. and owing to the indisposition of his captain, led his
company in the action. He was, it is believed, the first man in the advance, to
reach the summit of the mountain, and among the first to receive a sword from
the vanquished enemy. In the course of the same season, Captain Russell joined
an expedition against the Cherokee Indians, which led in its results to a treaty
of peace. The succeeding spring he joined a company of volunteers under the
command of Colonel William Campbell, and in the capacity of his lieutenant,
marched to the assistance of the southern army. During the service that ensued,
he fought in the battle of Whitsell's mills, and subsequently was engaged in the
memorable action of Guilford court-house. Soon after the conclusion of the war,
Captain Russell migrated to Kentucky, and settled himself in Fayette county,
then the constant scene of Indian depredations. Hence the event of peace, far
from terminating his military operations, served only to enlarge their field and
add to his exposures. The promptitude and alacrity which he ever displayed in
leaving his home and fireside, and marching to repel the slightest encroachment
of the savage upon the defenceless inhabitants, endeared him to the early settlers,
and rendered him distinguished for all the noble traits of the western pioneer.
In almost every general expedition in the western country, he bore an active participation. In each of the expeditions which were conducted in the course of
the same season respectively by the late Governor Scott and General Wilkinson

against the Indian towns in the North-western Territory, he volunteered as a private. His patriotic services, however, had been too conspicuous to permit his merit to escape the attention of his commanders. In the first he was invested under General Hardin, by the intrepid Scott, with the command of the advance of the army. In the second, he was selected by General Wilkinson and assigned to the chief command of the same post of danger and of honor.

In the celebrated expedition under Wayne, Colonel Russell commanded one of the regiments of Kentucky volunteers, and when in the second campaign of that distinguished officer, these regiments were reduced to battalions, he again appeared in the field at the head of a battalion. At the close of this campaign, which led in its results to the restoration of peace to all of our savage frontier, Colonel Russell returned to the pursuits of agriculture. But the patriotism, zeal and fidelity which he had so often exhibited in a military capacity, soon pointed him out to his fellow citizens as eminently qualified to do service in another department. Accordingly, in 1789, he was elected a delegate to the Virginia legislature which passed the act separating the district of Kentucky from the parent State. Immediately after the organization of the State government, he was annually returned a member of the legislature from Fayette, except one or two years, until 1808. During the whole of this period, he was the intimate associate of Nicholas and Breckinridge. In 1808, Colonel Russell was again called to resume his original profession ; Mr. Madison, in anticipation of the rupture with Great Britain, having appointed him to the command of a regiment in the regular army. In 1811, after the battle of Tippecanoe, where as much gallantry and intrepidity was evinced as on any subsequent occasion during the war, General Harrison by a combination of circumstances was transferred to the command of the north-western army, and it became important that he should be succeeded by an officer of judgment and experience. The whole frontier of Indiana, Illinois and Missouri was nakedly exposed to the depredations of the Indians, and Colonel Russell was assigned to this important command by General Harrison. Taking into consideration the almost boundless frontier which he had to protect from the merciless attacks of the savage, and the comparatively small force under his command, consisting only of one regiment of rangers, scattered in forts at great distances apart, we must admire, even at this day, when much of the character of the Indian warfare is forgotten, the activity, sagacity and courage of the man who could thus avert the ruthless butchery of so many innocent women and children.

After Hopkins' campaign, Col. Russell, in conjunction with Gov. Edwards, of Illinois, planned the expedition against the *Peoria Indians.* The secrecy and celerity attending the movements of this expedition, together with the complete success that crowned the enterprise, exhibit the strongest evidences of the skill of the commander. When peace was restored, Col. Russell retired again to his farm, in Fayette county, where, surrounded by a large family and numerous connexions, he devoted his time and attention to the cultivation of the soil. In 1823, during the prevalence of great political excitement in the State, the attention of his fellow-citizens was, with one accord, directed to Col. Russell ; and he was induced, reluctantly, to leave the quiet and retirement of his farm, and to become a candidate for the legislature. The contending parties seemed to forget their feuds, and all rallied around the "*old soldier.*" Subsequently, he was urgently solicited to offer as a candidate for the chief magistracy of the State. The modesty of his nature shrunk from the solicitation as the result of the partiality of friendship. He was urged to it by some of the most distinguished men of the State. In fact, he seemed to be the only individual of his party who offered any promise of success. He was presented as a candidate, and when both parties seemed, in consideration of his public services, about to forget the difference of sentiment that divided them, and unite in his unanimous choice, some strange infatuation seized the minds of his own party, and he was suddenly discarded in favor of another candidate, and the State thus deprived of his ripe experience and valuable services. In the spring of 1825, he was called from his sick room to preside over a public meeting ; and, from the exposure of the occasion, contracted an illness which resulted, in a few weeks, in his death.

Possessing an amiable disposition, a kind heart, and a high moral character, few men were more useful in society. From the age of sixteen to that of sixty-seven, in the field or in the cabinet, he may literally be said to have been employed in the service of his country. In both stations, many have served their country with a greater glare of personal renown—some more successfully ; but no man ever served his country with a more steady and persevering zeal, or with a more fervent and devoted patriotism.   J. H. T.

SCOTT COUNTY.

Scott county was formed in 1792, and named in honor of Governor Charles Scott. It is situated in the north middle part of the State, and watered by North Elkhorn and Eagle creeks—both of which flow into the Kentucky river : bounded on the north by Owen ; east by Harrison and Bourbon ; south by Fayette and Woodford ; and west by Franklin. The surface of the county presents quite a variegated appearance—level, undulating, and hilly. The southern and south-eastern portion, bordering on Woodford, Fayette and Bourbon, is embraced in that beautiful region known as the " Garden of Kentucky ;" with a level or very gently undulating surface, and a deep, rich, black soil, based on limestone, and unsurpassed in fertility. In the northern and north-western parts of the county, which are drained by Big Eagle and Elkhorn, the surface is hilly and broken, and the soil less rich and productive. The exports consist, principally, of horses, mules, cattle and hogs. Hemp and corn are the staple products, and wheat is cultivated to some extent.

Valuation of taxable property in Scott in 1846, $5,945,662 ; number of acres of land in the county, 167,179 ; average value of land per acre, $20.73 ; number of white males over twenty-one years old, 1,917 ; number of children between the ages of five and sixteen years, 1,697. Population in 1840, 13,668.

There are five towns in Scott, viz : Georgetown, Great Crossings, Marion, Newtown, and Stamping Ground.

Georgetown, the seat of justice, occupies an elevated site, seventeen miles east of Frankfort, sixteen miles west of Paris, twelve miles north of Lexington, and seventy miles south of Covington and Cincinnati. Contains six churches,—Regular Baptist, Particular Baptist, Presbyterian, Methodist, Christian, and African, under the Regular Baptists,—one college, two female schools, four primary schools, (including a common school), ten lawyers, ten physicians, ten dry goods stores, two drug and book stores, thirteen grocery stores, one shoe store, five taverns, two woollen manufactories, two carding factories, two bagging and rope factories, one printing office, (Georgetown Herald), one tannery, and forty-five mechanics' shops. Population, 1,800. Incorporated by the legislature of Virginia in 1790, and named in honor of George Washington. One of the finest springs in the State,—called at an early period the " Royal Spring "—and affording an ample supply of water for the entire population,—bursts from a high bluff of limestone rock, and flows through the west end of the town, and empties into Elkhorn five-eighths of a mile from its source. The stream from this spring affords sufficient water power for a woollen factory and grist mill, which are located upon it. The late Nathaniel Hart, of Woodford county, advanced the opinion, that the first settlement in Kentucky was made at this spring.

GEORGETOWN COLLEGE GEORGETOWN, KY

GEORGETOWN COLLEGE occupies a fine swell, on the south-eastern border of the town, and affords a handsome view of the surrounding country. The buildings consist, 1, of a *President's House,** with fifty acres of land. 2. The *Main Edifice*, one hundred feet long by sixty wide, two stories high, and a basement. It contains a handsome chapel, sixty by forty feet—spacious halls for library, philosophical rooms, cabinets, museum, laboratory, &c. 3. *Paulding Hall*, appropriated to the use of candidates for the ministry. It contains, besides chapel and dining-room, apartments for a steward's family and thirty-two students. 4. *Rittenhouse Academy,*

---

*This building does not appear in the engraving.

FEMALE COLLEGIATE INSTITUTE, GEORGETOWN, KY.

WESTERN MILITARY INSTITUTE, GEORGETOWN, KY.

forty-five feet square, two stories high, with a cupola. The lower story accommodates the preparatory department, and the upper furnishes two good halls for the voluntary societies connected with the college. The lawn embraces about sixteen acres, beautifully elevated, and laid out with trees and shrubbery.

The library contains about four thousand volumes, many of them rare and valuable; besides a large collection of ancient and modern maps, charts, &c. The philosophical apparatus is of the most recent construction, and has been procured at great expense. It includes a standing telescope, for astronomical observations, Chamlain's great air-pump, fine magnetic and galvanic implements, and abundant means of illustrating mechanical powers. Chemical experiments are given; and the cabinets of minerals, fossils, shells, and natural productions, furnish many facilities in the natural sciences.

The institution began its chartered existence in 1829, but the faculty was never full till 1840, and the usual classes were not all formed till 1842. The commencement of the enterprise was a legacy of $20,000 from Issachar Paulding, a native of New Jersey, long settled in Kentucky: but most of the endowment was obtained in 1839, by the Rev. Rockwell Giddings, from New England, who had settled in Shelbyville, over the Baptist church in that place. He was elected President of the college, and obtained, in less than a year, about $70,000 in subscriptions, but died before he had completed his great work. In 1840, Rev. HOWARD MALCOM, D. D., was chosen president, and is still in office— (1847).

Besides the usual four years' course, there is a shorter or scientific course, which may be completed in two or three years, according to the proficiency of the student at the time of entering. It embraces the regular course, except the Latin and Greek languages, and on completing it, the student is entitled to a diploma certifying the fact. Persons whose circumstances do not permit them to complete either course, may study particular branches and receive certificates of their actual attainments. Chemistry is now taught in the institution with special reference to agriculture and the improvement of soils.

The college is not in debt, and possesses revenues, aside from tuition, sufficient to maintain the faculty even with the present average of students, which is about 130. The Institution is deservedly enjoying great prosperity; and from the high qualifications of the faculty, combined with its salubrious location, the intelligence, refinement and elevated morality of the inhabitants of the beautiful and thriving town, it must continue to grow in popular favor.

Two flourishing Female Institutions, of high grade, are located at Georgetown.

The *Female Collegiate Institute*, T. F. JOHNSON, Esq., principal, was organized in March, 1838, and has continued steadily to advance in public estimation. The number of students at present (1847) in attendance is about 100. The Institute is provided with splendid philosophical and chemical apparatus, and has a select library containing five hundred volumes. The pupils have free use of these without charge. The assistants, who are experienced teachers from the best female schools in the United States, reside at the Institute, and are constant in their attentions to the pupils. The pupils are permitted to attend any place of worship they may prefer, but are not allowed to visit or receive visits, or to attend night meetings or parties of pleasure. The collegiate year is divided into two sessions ; the first commencing on the first Monday in March, and closing on the third Friday in July ; the second opens on the first Monday in August, and closes at Christmas.

The advantages possessed by this school, together with the high character of the estimable gentleman at the head, makes it one of the most eligible institutions of the kind in the United States ; and it bids fair to have a career of extensive usefulness and prosperity.

The *Western Military Institute*, also under the superintendence of Professor JOHNSON, was recently established with a view to unite civil education with military discipline. It has been incorporated by an act of the legislature, with all the powers, privileges and rights in conferring literary degrees and honors, and granting diplomas, which are exercised by any college in the State. The professors are men of science, and have had a large experience in the instruction of youth. The principal, together with several of the professors, were educated at the National Military Academy at West Point. The design of the Institution is to afford to youth a course of instruction as varied and more *practical* than can be obtained at most seminaries of learning. In the scientific and mathematical departments, are taught chemistry, mineralogy, civil engineering, architecture, navigation, surveying, drawing, &c. In the languages, Greek, Latin, French German and Spanish. In the department of law, is taught the elements of constitutional, international and common law. In the *military department*, special attention is paid to field fortifications, infantry, rifle and artillery drills ; and, where circumstances justify, to the sword exercise, cavalry drill, &c. The institute, already, has a large number of students, and is in a most flourishing condition.

Great Crossings is a small but neat village, containing one Baptist church, one school, one physician, two stores, one grocery, one tavern, one paper and flouring mill, six mechanics' shops, and a population of 130. Took its name from the fact that the great buffalo trace from the southern part of Kentucky to the Ohio river, *crossed* North Elkhorn at that point. *Marion* is a small village, having a population of about fifty souls—with one Methodist and one Christian church, one school, one physician, and five mechanical trades. *Newtown* contains Methodist and Presbyterian churches, one school, store, grocery, post office, and several mechanics' shops—population 100. *Stamping Ground* has a Baptist and a Christian church, two schools, three physicians, two taverns, four stores and groceries, one tannery, ten mechanics' shops, with a population of 150. Incorporated in 1834. Derived its name from the fact that the herds of buffalo which resorted here for salt water, *tramped* down the undergrowth as well as the soil for a great distance around—hence the name of " *Stamping Ground.*"

During the summer of 1776, several families, collected from the mouth of Kentucky river, from Kingston's settlement, and from Drennon's Lick, built a fort at Royal Spring, where Georgetown now stands, which received the name of McClellan's fort or station. On the 29th of December, of the same year, a large body of Indians made an attack on this fort, and killed McClellan and two others. The terror inspired by this event, caused the occupants to abandon the fort and retire to Harrodsburg. Col. Patterson* assisted in building the fort, and was one of its defenders until the beginning of October, 1776. The supply of powder being nearly exhausted, he and six others started to Pittsburgh to procure ammunition and other necessaries. On their way they spent several days at the Blue Licks, curing buffalo jerk and tallow for their journey up the river. At Limestone (now Maysville) they procured a canoe, commenced their journey, and arrived at Point Pleasant, at the mouth of the Great Kanawha, without encountering any Indians. From the Point they proceeded on their journey, traveling very cautiously,—starting before daybreak and going on until after dark, and sleeping without fire.

Late in the evening of the 12th of October, they landed a few miles below the mouth of Hockhocking, in the present State of Ohio, and, contrary to their usual practice, made a fire,—having become less cautious in consequence of their near approach to the settlements. They laid upon their arms around the fire, and in the night were attacked by a party of eleven Indians, who gave them a volley, and then fell upon them with their tomahawks. Col. Patterson received two balls in his right arm, by which it was broken; and a tomahawk was struck into his side, between two of his ribs, penetrating into the cavity of the body. He sprang out into the darkness and got clear, supposing all his companions were killed. He made for the river, in hopes of getting into the canoe and floating down to Point Pleasant; but as he approached it, he discovered that there was an Indian in it. In a short time the whole party of Indians went on board, and floated down the river. Col. Patterson then made an attempt to get to the fire, in which he succeeded. He found a companion, named Templeton, wounded in a manner very similar to his own case; another, named Wernock, wounded dangerously; and another, named Perry, slightly. Of the other three, one was killed, one was missing, and the other, named Mitchell, was unhurt. They had saved one gun and some ammunition. They remained on the ground until morning, when they attempted to proceed up the river on foot; but Wernock was unable to move, and they were forced to leave him. They, however, found themselves unable to proceed farther than a quarter of a mile from the camp, and it was then agreed that Perry should endeavor to reach Grave creek, and bring them aid, while Mitchell was to remain and take care of the others. Wernock, who was left behind, died in the evening; and Mitchell, who had gone back to assist him, lost his way in returning to Patterson and Templeton, and did not find them until next morning. They then moved a couple of hundred yards further from the river, and the next day got under a cliff, which sheltered them from the rain, where they remained until Perry returned from Grave creek with assistance. They were removed to that place, after lying eight days in their suffering condition. Patterson laid twelve months under the surgeon's care.†

In the latter part of May, 1778, a party of Indians stole twenty horses, near

---

* See the interesting incident in the battle of the Blue Licks. Col. Patterson was a brave and meritorious officer and valuable citizen. He removed from Lexington in 1804, to the vicinity of Dayton, Ohio, where he resided on a farm till his death, in August, 1827, in the seventy-fifth year of his age.
† American Pioneer, vol. 2, pp. 344–5.

Col. Johnson's mill. They were pursued by Capt. Herndon with a small body of whites, but escaped. On this occasion, a most singular manœuvre was executed by one of the Indians, probably the leader. The party, after traveling about twenty miles, halted in a brushy copse of wood, and were overtaken by the pursuers, who came upon them before they were discovered or saw their adversary. The whites, on discovering the marauders, made instant preparation to fire; and, at the same moment, the Indians gave a loud yell, sprang to their feet, and, with one exception, ran in various directions. One, who remained in view of the whites, continued to yell and scream and jump—now flying to one tree, then to another—now dodging, then springing aloft, as one perfectly frantic. This strange exhibition attracted and so engrossed the attention of the whites, that they did not even fire—thus, without doubt, effecting the very object intended by this dexterous and wily savage. In the mean time, the other Indians had secured their guns and blankets, and made their escape, as did also the partisan hero, in an instant after his followers were safe—leaving an enemy, superior in numbers, to express their wonder at the enchantment which had thus deluded them.*

About the 20th of June, 1788, three Indians made an incursion into Scott county, and stole three horses from the farm of Jacob Stucker, on North Elkhorn. On the succeeding day, a lad was killed near Col. Johnson's mill. The neighborhood was roused, and Capt Henderson, immediately assembling a company, gave pursuit. He struck the horse trail, and, pursuing it with great vigor, soon overhauled the Indians. At the first fire, two of the Indians fell dead, and the third, though wounded, effected his escape. The horses were recovered, and the whites returned to their homes without having received the slightest injury.

The first paper mill in Kentucky was erected by Messrs. Craig and Parkers, near Georgetown, in the year 1795.

Captain WILLIAM HUBBELL.—The subject of this brief notice was a native of Vermont, and served five and a half years in the revolutionary army, in the various stations of private, sergeant, ensign, and second and first lieutenant. He participated in the capture of St. John's and Montreal, and was engaged in many skirmishes during the war. Some years after the close of the revolutionary war, Captain Hubbell removed to Kentucky, and settled in Scott county, where he resided until his death at a very advanced age—enjoying throughout life, in an eminent degree, the confidence and esteem of the community among whom his lot was cast. In the year 1791, while the Indians were yet troublesome, especially on the banks of the Ohio, Captain Hubbell, who had been compelled to go to the eastward on business, was returning to his home in Kentucky. On one of the tributary streams of the river Monongahela, he procured a flat bottomed boat, and embarked in company with Mr. Daniel Light, and Mr. William Plascut and his family, consisting of a wife and eight children, destined for Limestone, Kentucky. On their progress down the river Ohio, and soon after passing Pittsburgh, they saw evident traces of Indians along the banks, and there is every reason to believe that a boat which they overtook, and which, through carelessness, was suffered to run aground on an island, became a prey to the merciless savages. Though Captain Hubbell and his party stopped some time for it in a lower part of the river, it did not arrive, and has never to their knowledge been heard of since. Before they reached the mouth of the Great Kenhawa, they had, by several successive additions, increased their number to twenty, consisting of nine men, three women, and eight children. The men, besides those mentioned above, were one John Stoner, an Irishman, and a Dutchman, whose names are not recollected, Messrs. Ray and Tucker, and a Mr. Kilpatrick, whose two daughters also were of the party. Information received at Gallipolis confirmed the expectation which appearances previously raised, of a serious conflict with a large body of Indians; and as Captain Hubbell had been regularly appointed commander of the boat, every possible preparation was made for a formidable and successful resistance of the anticipated attack.

The nine men were divided into three watches for the night, who were alternately to continue awake and be on the look-out for two hours at a time. The arms on board, which consisted principally of old muskets much out of order, were collected, loaded, and put in the best possible condition for service. At about sunset on that day, the 23d of March, 1791, our party overtook a fleet of six boats descending the river in company, and intended to have continued with them; but as their passengers seemed more disposed to dancing than fighting, and as, soon after dark, notwithstanding the remonstrances of Captain Hubbell, they commenced fiddling and dancing instead of preparing their arms and taking the necessary rest preparatory to battle, it was wisely considered more hazardous to be in such company than to be alone.

It was therefore determined to proceed rapidly forward by aid of the oars, and to leave those thoughtless fellow-travelers behind. One of the boats, however, belonging to the fleet, commanded by a Captain Greathouse,* adopted the same plan, and for a while kept up with Captain Hubbell, but all its crew at length falling asleep, that boat also ceased to be propelled by the oars, and Captain Hubbell and his party proceeded steadily forward *alone*. Early in the night a canoe was dimly seen floating down the river, in which were probably Indians reconnoitering, and other evident indications were observed of the neighborhood and hostile intentions of a formidable party of savages.

It was now agreed, that should the attack, as was probable, be deferred till morning, every man should be up before the dawn, in order to make as great a show as possible of numbers and of strength; and that, whenever the action should take place, the women and children should lie down on the cabin floor and be protected as well as they could by the trunks and other baggage, which might be placed around them. In this perilous situation they continued during the night, and the captain, who had not slept more than one hour since he left Pittsburgh, was too deeply impressed with the imminent danger which surrounded him to obtain any rest at that time.

Just as daylight began to appear in the east, and before the men were up and at their posts agreeably to arrangement, a voice at some distance below them in a plaintive tone repeatedly solicited them to come on shore, as there were some white persons who wished to obtain a passage in their boat. This the captain very naturally and correctly concluded to be an Indian artifice, and its only effect was to rouse the men and place every one on his guard. The voice of entreaty was soon changed into the language of indignation and insult, and the sound of distant paddles announced the approach of the savage foe. At length three Indian canoes were seen through the mist of the morning rapidly advancing. With the utmost coolness the captain and his companions prepared to receive them. The chairs, tables, and other incumbrances were thrown into the river, in order to clear the deck for action.

Every man took his position, and was ordered not to fire till the savages had approached so near, that (to use the words of Captain Hubbell,) " the flash from the guns might singe their eyebrows; " and a special caution was given that the men should fire successively, so that there might be no interval. On the arrival of the canoes, they were found to contain about twenty-five or thirty Indians each. As soon as they approached within the reach of musket shot, a general fire was given from one of them, which wounded Mr. Tucker through the hip so severely that his leg hung only by the flesh, and shot Mr. Light just below the ribs. The three canoes placed themselves at the bow, stern, and on the right side of the boat, so that they had an opportunity of raking in every direction. The fire now commenced from the boat, and had a powerful effect in checking the confidence and fury of the Indians.

The captain, after firing his own gun, took up that of one of the wounded men, raised it to his shoulder, and was about to discharge it, when a ball came and took away the lock; he coolly turned round, seized a brand of fire from the kettle which served for a caboose, and applying it to the pan, discharged the piece with effect. A very regular and constant fire was now kept up on both sides. The captain was just in the act of raising his gun a third time, when a ball passed through his right arm, and for a moment disabled him. Scarcely had he recovered from the shock and re-acquired the use of his hand, which had been suddenly *drawn up* by the wound, when he observed the Indians in one of the canoes just about to board the boat in its bow, where the horses were placed

* Captain Greathouse was on shore hunting, and shot in the river while swimming to his boat.

belonging to the party. So near had they approached, that some of them had actually seized with their hands the side of the boat.

Severely wounded as he was, he caught up a pair of horseman's pistols, and rushed forward to repel the attempt at boarding. On his approach the Indians fell back, and he discharged a pistol with effect at the foremost man. After firing the second pistol, he found himself without arms, and was compelled to retreat; but stepping back upon a pile of small wood which had been prepared for burning in the kettle, the thought struck him, that it might be made use of in repelling the foe, and he continued for some time to strike them with it so forcibly and actively that they were unable to enter the boat, and at length he wounded one of them so severely that with a yell they suddenly gave way. All the canoes instantly discontinued the contest and directed their course to Captain Greathouse's boat, which was then in sight. Here a striking contrast was exhibited to the firmness and intrepidity which had been displayed.

Instead of resisting the attack, the people on board of this boat retired to the cabin in dismay. The Indians entered it without opposition, and rowed it to the shore, where they instantly killed the captain and a lad of about fourteen years of age. The women they placed in the centre of their canoes, and manning them with fresh hands, again pursued Captain Hubbell and party. A melancholy alternative now presented itself to these brave but almost desponding men, either to fall a prey to the savages themselves, or to run the risk of shooting the women, who had been placed in the canoes in the hope of deriving protection from their presence. But "self preservation is the first law of nature," and the captain very justly remarked, there would not be much humanity in preserving their lives at such a sacrifice, merely that they might become victims of savage cruelty at some subsequent period.

There were now but four men left on board of Captain Hubbell's boat, capable of defending it, and the captain himself was severely wounded in two places. The second attack, however, was resisted with almost incredible firmness and vigor. Whenever the Indians would rise to fire, their opponents would commonly give them the first shot, which in almost every instance would prove fatal. Notwithstanding the disparity of numbers, and the exhausted condition of the defenders of the boat, the Indians at length appeared to despair of success, and the canoes successively retired to the shore. Just as the last one was departing, Captain Hubbell called to the Indian, who was standing in the stern, and on his turning round, discharged his piece at him. When the smoke, which for a moment obstructed the vision, was dissipated, he was seen lying on his back, and appeared to be severely, perhaps mortally wounded.

Unfortunately the boat now drifted near to the shore where the Indians were collected, and a large concourse, probably between four and five hundred, were seen rushing down on the bank. Ray and Plascut, the only men remaining unhurt, were placed at the oars, and as the boat was not more than twenty yards from shore, it was deemed prudent for all to lie down in as safe a position as possible and attempt to push forward with the utmost practicable rapidity. While they continued in this situation, nine balls were shot into one oar, and ten into the other, without wounding the rowers, who were hidden from view and protected by the side of the boat and the blankets in its stern. During this dreadful exposure to the fire of the savages, which continued about twenty minutes, Mr. Kilpatrick observed a particular Indian, whom he thought a favorable mark for his rifle, and, notwithstanding the solemn warning of Captain Hubbell, rose to shoot him. He immediately received a ball in his mouth, which passed out at the back part of his head, and was almost at the same moment shot through the heart. He fell among the horses that about the same time were killed, and presented to his afflicted daughters and fellow travelers, who were witnesses of the awful occurrence, a spectacle of horror which we need not further attempt to describe.

The boat was now providentially and suddenly carried out into the middle of the stream, and taken by the current beyond the reach of the enemy's balls. Our little band, reduced as they were in numbers, wounded, afflicted, and almost exhausted by fatigue, were still unsubdued in spirit, and being assembled in all their strength, men, women and children, with an appearance of triumph gave three hearty cheers, calling to the Indians to come on again if they were fond of the sport.

Thus ended this awful conflict, in which, out of nine men, two only escaped unhurt. Tucker and Kilpatrick were killed on the spot, Stoner was mortally wounded, and died on his arrival at Limestone, and all the rest, excepting Ray and Plascut, were severely wounded. The women and children were all uninjured, excepting a little son of Mr. Plascut, who, after the battle was over, came to the captain, and, with great coolness, requested him to take a ball out of his head. On examination, it appeared that a bullet, which had passed through the side of the boat, had penetrated the forehead of this little hero, and remained under the skin. The captain took it out, and the youth, observing, "*that is not all*," raised his arm, and exhibited a piece of bone at the point of his elbow, which had been shot off, and hung only by the skin. His mother exclaimed, "why did you not tell me of this?" "Because," he coolly replied, "the captain directed us to be silent during the action, and I thought you would be likely to make a noise if I told you."

The boat made the best of its way down the river, and the object was to reach Limestone that night. The captain's arm had bled profusely, and he was compelled to close the sleeve of his coat in order to retain the blood and stop its effusion. In this situation, tormented by excruciating pain and faint through loss of blood, he was under the necessity of steering the boat with his left arm, till about ten o'clock that night, when he was relieved by Mr. William Brooks, who resided on the bank of the river, and who was induced, by the calls of the suffering party, to come out to their assistance. By his aid, and that of some other persons, who were in the same manner brought to their relief, they were enabled to reach Limestone about twelve o'clock that night.

Immediately on the arrival of Mr. Brooks, Capt. Hubbell, relieved from labor and responsibility, sunk under the weight of pain and fatigue, and became for a while totally insensible. When the boat reached Limestone, he found himself unable to walk, and was obliged to be carried up to the tavern. Here he had his wound dressed, and continued several days, until he acquired sufficient strength to proceed homewards.

On the arrival of our party at Limestone, they found a considerable force of armed men, about to march against the same Indians, from whose attacks they had so severely suffered. They now learned, that on the Sunday preceding, the same party of savages had cut off a detachment of men ascending the Ohio from Fort Washington, at the mouth of Licking river, and had killed with their tomahawks, without firing a gun, twenty-one out of twenty-two men, of which the detachment consisted.

Crowds of people, as might be expected, came to witness the boat which had been the scene of so much heroism, and such horrid carnage, and to visit the resolute little band by whom it had been so gallantly and perseveringly defended. On examination, it was found that the sides of the boat were literally filled with bullets and with bullet holes. There was scarcely a space of two feet square, in the part above water, which had not either a ball remaining in it, or a hole through which a ball had passed. Some persons who had the curiosity to count the number of holes in the blankets which were hung up as curtains in the stern of the boat, affirmed that in the space of five feet square there were one hundred and twenty-two. Four horses out of five were killed, and the escape of the fifth, amidst such a shower of balls, appears almost miraculous.

The day after the arrival of Capt. Hubbell and his companions, the five remaining boats, which they had passed on the night preceding the battle, reached Limestone. Those on board remarked, that during the action they distinctly saw the flashes, but could not hear the reports of the guns. The Indians, it appears, had met with too formidable a resistance from a single boat to attack a fleet, and suffered them to pass unmolested ; and since that time, it is believed that no boat has been assailed by Indians on the Ohio.

The force which marched out to disperse this formidable body of savages, discovered several Indians dead on the shore, near the scene of action. They also found the bodies of Capt. Greathouse and several others,—men, women and children,—who had been on board of his boat. Most of them appeared to have been *whipped to death*, as they were found stripped, tied to trees, and marked with the appearance of lashes ; and large rods, which seemed to have been worn with use, were observed lying near them.

33

In the year 1788, a party of hunters,—five in number,—from the station near Georgetown, Kentucky, landed at the mouth of Deer creek, in Cincinnati, in two canoes.* After hiding the canoes among the willows and weeds, that grew thick and rank upon that little stream, they proceeded to ascend the creek along the left bank. At the distance of about one hundred and fifty yards from the mouth, in the shade of a branching elm, they halted for refreshment, and sat down to partake of the rude repast of the wilderness. The month was September, the day clear and warm, and the hour that within which the sun would "sink to rest." After having partaken of their coarse evening meal, the party, at the suggestion of a man named Hall,—one of their number,—proposed, as a matter of safety and comfort, that they should go among the northern hills, and there encamp until the morning's dawn, as the musquitoes and the frogs, amongst the creek's marshes, dinned the night with most annoying cherivari. The proposition of Hall was acceded to, and the party packed up for their journey.

Emerging from a thicket of iron weed, through which a deer-path was open, and into which the party walked single file, they entered, one after another, upon a grassy, weedless knob, which being elevated some distance above the tops of the blossomed iron weeds around, had the appearance of a green island in the midst of a purple sea. The deer-path crossed the knob, and entered the weed thicket again on the northern side. The hunters did not pause for a moment, but entered the narrow avenue, one after another.

As the last man was about to enter the path, he fell simultaneously with the crack of a rifle, discharged from amongst the weeds on the western slope. The whole party dashed into the thicket on either side, and "squatted," with rifles cocked, ready for any emergency. Quietly in this position they waited until nightfall; but every thing around being still, and no further hostile demonstrations being made, one after another they again ventured out into the path and started towards the opening—observing, however, the utmost caution.

Hall, a bold fellow, and connected by ties of kindred with the man who had been shot, whose name was Baxter, crawled quietly upon his hands and knees to the spot where his comrade had fallen, and found him dead, lying with his face downward, a bullet having entered his skull forward of the left temple. Baxter had fallen some ten feet from the thicket's entrance, and Hall, after getting out of the thicket, *rolled* slowly to the side of the dead man, lest he should be observed by the skulking enemy—as, in an upright position, notwithstanding the gloom of nightfall, he would have been. He lay for several minutes by the side of the corpse, analyzing, as it were, the sounds of the night, as if to detect in them the decoying tricks so common with the Indian. There was nothing, however, that, even to his practiced ear, indicated the presence of an enemy; and he ventured, at length, to stand erect. With rifle ready, and eye-ball strained to penetrate the gloom that hung like a marsh-mist upon the purple fields around, he stood for several seconds, and then gave a signal for the approach of his companions. The party cautiously approached the spot where Hall stood, and after a moment's consultation in whispers, agreed to bury the unfortunate man, and then pursue their journey. Poor Baxter was carried to the bank of the river, and silently interred under a beech, a few feet from the bluff, the grave being dug by the knives and tomahawks of his late companions. Yet in the warmth of recent life, the body was laid in its rude resting-place, and the sod which was to shut it out from the glow of star or planet—the light of sun or moon—was moistened with many a tear from many an eye that danger never blenched.

Having performed the last sad duties to the departed, the party prepared to leave, and had advanced, silently, a step or two, when they were startled by a sound upon the water. "A canoe!" whispered Hall. A suspicion flashed upon his mind, and he crawled to the spot where the canoes had been hidden, and found one of them gone.

Quick to decide, and fired with a spirit of vengeance, he proposed to his comrades that immediate pursuit be made. The proposition was agreed to, and in less than five minutes three of the hunters, armed and determined for a deadly mission, were darting silently through the quiet waters, in the direction of the sound which they had recently heard. About one hundred yards below the mouth of Licking, on the Kentucky side, they came within rifle-shot of the canoe, fired at the person who was paddling it, scarcely visible in the dim starlight, and a short exclamation of agony evidenced the certainty of the shot.

Paddling up along side, the canoe was found to contain but a single person, and that an old Indian, writhing in death's agony, the blood gushing from his shaven brow. In the bottom of the canoe lay a rifle, and near it a pouch of parched corn, and a gourd about half filled with *whisky*. It was this Indian, evidently, who shot Baxter, and it seemed equally evident that he was alone upon the war-path. The savage was scalped, and his body thrown into the river.

Hall and his party returned to the mouth of the creek—again hid the canoes—encamped near Baxter's grave for the night, and with the morning's dawn started upon their journey to the north.

Col. Robert Johnson (the father of colonels Richard M., James, and Major John T. Johnson,) was a native of Virginia, and emigrated to Kentucky, then a county of that State, during the stormy period of the revolution. He was distinguished for that high-toned integrity and courage which marked the age and country in which he lived ; and took an active and prominent part in the sanguinary conflicts which raged between the settlers and natives, in the early settlement of Kentucky. So great was the confidence reposed in his skill and courage, by the adventurers of that age, by whom he was surrounded, that he was called to take a conspicuous position in almost every hazardous enterprise. The sentiments of patrio ism and integrity which marked the history of his active life, he did not fail to inculcate upon the minds of his children ; and the character of those children, as developed, shows that they were not without their proper effect. Of Col. Richard M. Johnson, the eldest son, a sketch will be found under the head of Johnson county. Col. James Johnson was the lieutenant-colonel of the mounted regiment of Col. R. M. Johnson, during the late war, and distinguished himself at the battle of the Thames, as well as on several occasions while in the service. He subsequently served several sessions in the Congress of the United States, with general acceptance. At the time of his death, which occurred many years since, he was in communion with the Baptist church, and was esteemed a zealous and devoted christian. Major John T. Johnson was, for a short time, a member of the appellate court of Kentucky ; subsequently, for several sessions, a member of Congress ; and is now, (1847), and has been for some eight or ten years, a distinguished minister of the Christian church.

Gen. Joseph Desha was a descendant of the Huguenots of France, his paternal grandfather being one of that persecuted sect, who in the middle of the seventeenth century fled to America, to avoid the fury of intolerance, and enjoy, unmolested, the religion of their choice. The subject of this notice was born on the 9th day of December, 1768, in the western part of the then colony of Pennsylvania. In July, 1781, his father emigrated to Kentucky, and in the following year removed to that part of the present State of Tennessee which was then known as the Cumberland District. In the month of December, 1789, Joseph Desha was united in marriage with the daughter of Col. Bledsoe ; and in the year 1792, settled permanently in Mason county, Kentucky.

As early as the year 1794, he volunteered under General Wayne, and served in his campaigns against the Indians, with distinction. Indeed, at the early age of fifteen, and between that age and twenty-two, he took an active part in various skirmishes with the foe, who at that period in the early history of the west, proved so fatal an annoyance to the settlers. In one of these skirmishes he had the misfortune to lose two of his brothers, who were shot down by his side ; an event which no doubt stimulated his courage and greatly excited his vengeance against the perfidious enemy. His gallant bearing as a soldier, and amiable qualities as a man, rendered him justly popular with the people, and for several years previous to 1806, he represented the county of Mason in the State legislature. In 1816 he was elected to Congress, and by successive re-elections was continued in that body until the year 1819.

While in Congress he acted with the republican party, and was devotedly zealous in the prosecution of all such measures as were calculated in his judgment to advance the interest and glory of the nation. He was a warm supporter of the war of 1812, and in 1813 accepted a commission as major general of volunteers, and was present with his division, in the battle of the Thames.

In 1824 he was elected governor of Kentucky, and served the usual term of four years. His administration of the State government was efficient and vigorous. At the expiration of his term he retired from public life, and continued engaged in his private affairs upon his farm, in Harrison county, until his death, which occurred, at Georgetown, Scott county, on the 11th of October, 1842.

General CHARLES SCOTT, from whom this county received its name, a distinguished officer of the revolution, was born in Cumberland county, Virginia. He served as a corporal in a volunteer company of militia in the memorable campaign of 1755, which terminated in Braddock's defeat. Upon the breaking out of the revolutionary war, he raised the first company of volunteers south of James river that entered into actual service, and so distinguished himself that when the county of Powhatan was formed in 1777, the county of Scott was named in honor of him. Having been appointed by General Washington to the command of a regiment in the continental line, he was with General Wayne at the storming of Stony Point. He was in Charleston when it surrendered to Sir Henry Clinton. When marching out of the gate a British officer spoke to him very abruptly ; ordered him to march faster to give room for others. Scott turned upon him, ripped out a tremendous oath, (one of his characteristics,) and shamed the officer for having let so few men stand out so long against so large an army. The officer molested him no further. After the war terminated he removed to Kentucky, and in 1785 settled in Woodford county. He was with General St. Clair in his defeat on the 4th of November, 1791, when there were about six hundred men killed in one hour. In 1763, he and General Wilkinson conducted a corps of horsemen against the Indian towns on the Wabash, killed some of the warriors and took a number of prisoners. In 1794 he commanded a portion of Wayne's army at the battle of the Fallen Timber, where the Indians were defeated and driven under the walls of the British fort. In 1808 he was elected to the office of Governor of Kentucky, and discharged its duties faithfully.

General Scott was a man of strong natural powers, but somewhat illiterate, and rough in his manners. He was very eccentric, and many amusing anecdotes are related of him. The following anecdote we believe is literally authentic :

While Scott, as governor of Kentucky, was reposing on his military renown, a puny whipster, himself just about as brave a man as any of the descendants of Ezekiel Polk, took it into his head to distinguish his own prowess, and as a mark for its exhibition, pretending some offence, singled out General Scott, to whom he sent a challenge to a duel. The old veteran very properly returned no answer to the summons. Meantime the braggart had been ostentatiously speculating on the occurrence in advance, not anticipating the turn it took. Being committed by the knowledge of the public, he was in a desperate predicament. After waiting in vain for an acceptance, and not even receiving an answer, he went personally to demand an explanation.

" General Scott, you received a challenge from me ? "

" Your challenge was delivered, sir."

" But I have received neither an acknowledgment nor an acceptance of it."

" I presume not sir, as I have sent neither."

" But of course you intend to accept ? "

" Of course I do not."

" What ! Not accept my challenge ? Is it possible that you, General Scott, brought up in the army, decline a combat ? "

" I do with you, sir," coolly answered the hero.

" Then I have no means of satisfaction left, but to post you a coward."

" Post *me* a coward ? Ha, ha, ha ! Post and be ———— ; but if you do, you will only post yourself a ———— liar, and every body else will say so."

And that was the end of it.

General Scott was a faithful and constant friend, but a bitter and implacable enemy. He died about the year 1820, at a very advanced age.

SHELBY COUNTY.

SHELBY county was formed in 1792, and named in honor of Gov. ISAAC SHELBY. It is drained by the waters of Kentucky and Salt rivers: bounded on the north by Oldham and Henry; east by Franklin; south by Spencer; and west by Jefferson. The streams of the county are—Clear, Beech, Brashear's, Bullskin, Fox, Jeffrey's and Fitch's creeks, which flow into the Kentucky, and Six Mile creek, which enters into Salt river. The general surface is gently undulating, and the lands finely timbered, and in a high state of cultivation. The soil is based upon limestone, with red clay foundation, and is black, friable, and remarkably fertile. The grasses succeed well; but hemp, corn and wheat, form the staple products; horses, mules, cattle, hogs, bagging and bale rope, the principal articles of export. The exports of Shelby, in 1846, amounted to the sum of $630,750—the imports to $350,000,— leaving an excess, in favor of the exports, of $280,750.

Valuation of the lands of Shelby, $4,852,725; total valuation of taxable property in 1846, $8,331,400; number of acres of land in the county, 241,523; average value of land per acre, $19.94; number of white males over twenty-one years of age, 2,348; number of children between five and sixteen years old, 2714. Population in 1840, 17,768.

The towns of Shelby consist of Shelbyville, the seat of justice, Christiansburg, Hardinsville, Simpsonville, Clay village, and Harrisonville.

SHELBYVILLE is situated on the waters of Clear creek, thirty miles from Louisville, and twenty-one miles from Frankfort, immediately on the turnpike road from the former to the latter place. It has a population of about 1,600; seven churches, with four denominations, viz: Baptists, Methodists, Presbyterians and Christians; ten lawyers, nine physicians, fourteen merchants, thirty-one mechanics' shops, and nine manufacturing establishments. It contains, also, one college, and two male and two female schools. The court-house is a large three story new brick building, ninety feet in length and seventy-five feet in width, including court room, and the various offices of the clerks, sheriff, &c.

Trustees to lay off a town at Shelby court-house, were appointed by an act of the general assembly of Kentucky, passed in 1792; and on the 15th day of January, 1793, the said trustees met, and laid off fifty-one acres of land, "around and adjacent to the place whereon the public buildings are to be erected, into suitable lots and streets." The "gentlemen trustees," as they styled themselves in the record, among their first acts, passed the following resolution, indicating, very clearly, the plainness and simplicity of the style of building of our ancestors: "Ordered, that every purchaser or purchasers of lotts in the town of Shelbyville, shall build thereon a hued log house, with a brick or stone chimney, not less than one story and a half high, otherwise the lot or lots shall be forfeited for the use of the town." These trustees were David Standiford, Joseph Winlock, and Abraham Owen—the last of whom was the Col. Owen who fell at the battle of Tippecanoe.

SHELBY COLLEGE, which is located here, was organized in 1836,

and transferred to the Episcopal church in 1841. Its presidency
is now (1847) temporarily vacant. The college edifice is a handsome brick building, forty-two feet by seventy, with a president's
house on the grounds, which include about eighteen acres. The
FEMALE SEMINARIES are very popular institutions, and embrace a
large number of pupils. The one under the superintendence of
W. F. Hill, has a beautiful edifice, lately constructed. The location of Shelbyville is very favorable to health ; and the zeal and
liberality displayed by the citizens in the cause of education,—
resulting in the organization of an unusual number of flourishing schools,—is a guaranty of its permanent prosperity. The
population of the town and county, generally, is intelligent, refined, and remarkably moral.

Christiansburg is a small village, situated on the New-Castle
road, eight miles east of Shelbyville ; and contains two churches,
(Baptist and Methodist), two physicians, two taverns, four stores
and groceries, a steam saw-mill, woollen factory, and three or
four mechanics' shops. *Hardinsville* is situated at the east corner
of the county, at the junction of the Louisville, Frankfort, and
Harrodsburg turnpike roads, fifteen miles from Shelbyville, and
nine miles from Frankfort : contains one tavern, two stores, post-
office, and several mechanics' shops. Population, 60. *Simpsonville* is situated on the turnpike from Louisville to Shelbyville,
eight miles west of the latter ; was laid out in 1816, and named
after Capt. John Simpson, who was killed at the battle of the
river Raisin, during the late war with Great Britain. It has
a population of 200 ; three churches, (Baptist, Methodist and
Presbyterian,) three physicans, three merchants, four mechanics'
shops, one steam saw-mill, and a school for males and females.
Clay Village lies on the road from Louisville to Frankfort, six miles
east of Shelbyville ; was established in the year 1820, and named
after Henry Clay, the great statesman of Kentucky : has a population of about 100 souls ; two physicians, five merchants, fourteen mechanics' shops, two manufacturing establishments, and
one Universalist church. *Harrisonville* is situated in the south-
east corner of the county, about sixteen miles from Shelbyville ;
was established about the year 1825, and originally known by
the name of Connersville, after the proprietor, but is now called
for Gen. William H. Harrison. It is a small village.

In the month of September, 1781, a station settled by Squire Boone, (a brother
of the great hunter,) near where Shelbyville is built, became alarmed at the appearance of Indians in the neighborhood, and determined to remove to the stronger
settlements on Beargrass. In effecting this object, the party—necessarily encumbered with women, children and household goods—was attacked by a large body
of Indians near Long run, defeated and dispersed with considerable loss. Colonel Floyd, on hearing of the disaster, immediately collected a party of twenty-five
men, and repaired with honorable promptitude to relieve the whites and chastise
the Indians. He advanced with his usual caution, dividing his men into two
parties ; and yet, in spite of his prudence, he fell into an ambuscade of two hundred Indians. He was defeated with the loss of half his men, and nine or ten of
the Indians were killed. While Colonel Floyd was retreating on foot, nearly
exhausted and closely pursued by the Indians, Captain Samuel Wells, who

retained his horse, dismounted and gave it to Floyd, and ran by his side to support him. The magnanimity of the action, is enhanced by the previous hostility between these officers, which was, however, cancelled forever—" they lived and died friends."

WILLIAM LOGAN was the eldest son of General Benjamin Logan, and was born at Harrodsburg on the 8th of December, 1776. He was, probably, the first white child born in Kentucky. In 1799 he was a member of the convention which formed the present constitution of the state, being then only twenty-three years of age. His selection to this responsible office, so early in life, evinced the high opinion entertained of his character and talents, by his fellow-citizens. About the same time he commenced the practice of the law, and soon attained considerable eminence in his profession. He was frequently elected to represent his county in the legislature, and on several occasions was made speaker of the house of representatives. He was twice appointed a judge of the court of appeals, in which station he was noted for the propriety with which he discharged its various duties. In 1820, he was elected a Senator in the Congress of the United States. He resigned his seat in this body in 1820, for the purpose of becoming a candidate for governor of the State, but was not elected.

He died at his residence in Shelby county, on the 8th of August, 1822, in the 46th year of his age. At the time of his decease he was generally looked to by the people of the State, as the candidate for Governor in 1824, and had he lived would no doubt have succeeded General Adair in that office.

When he was not prevented from mingling in politics by his duties as a judge, he was an active and influential member of the republican party, and was warmly engaged in the controversy which arose on the question of a new election upon the death of Governor Madison. On this occasion he took the ground which was finally settled as the true construction of the constitution, that upon the death of the governor, the lieutenant-governor should succeed to his place, and serve out the term. He was also an active partizan on the new and old court questions, having espoused the cause of the old court. In his private and social relations he was a gentleman of great moral worth, courteous in his manners, and of inflexible integrity. His early death was a loss to the State, and was very generally deplored.

The Rev. ARCHIBALD CAMERON, a distinguished minister of the Presbyterian church, was a native of Scotland, but was brought to America by his parents when very young. He was of good parentage, his father, John Cameron, of the "clan Cameron," being a man of sound understanding, correct principles and decided integrity of character. His mother, whose maiden name was Janet McDonald, of the "McDonald clan," was a lady of superior capacity, and distinguished for extensive and general information, sterling integrity, exemplary piety, and great force of character. She was a "Scotch Presbyterian" of the genuine stamp.

Archibald, the youngest of six children, was born in the Highlands, in the vicinity of Fort William, about the year 1770 or 1771. The family soon after his birth removed to America, and settled on the Monongahela river; where they resided till April, 1781, when they removed to Kentucky, and settled on a farm at the foot of " Cameron's Knob," about six miles from Bardstown.

Little is known of Mr. Cameron's early history; but as his father was a farmer, and in moderate circumstances, he was probably employed in agricultural pursuits. His education, however, was not neglected; and he commenced the study of the Latin and Greek languages with his eldest brother, Angus Cameron, who had received a thorough education before he left Scotland. At about the age of fifteen, he was sent to a school then kept in Bardstown by Dr. Priestly. His companions at this school were John Rowan, Felix Grundy, John Pope, Col. John Allen, John Simpson, and others, all of whom became distinguished in after life. Mr. Cameron took a high stand, and was considered the best scholar in the school. Upon leaving this school, he spent about one year at the "Transylvania Seminary," then under the charge of Mr. James Moore. At the age of nineteen he professed religion, and connected himself with the Presbyterian church at Bardstown. His religious experience, written about this time, and preserved among his papers, agrees most strikingly with those evangelical doctrines for which his preaching was afterwards distinguished. He studied theology unde. the Rev. David Rice, and was licensed by Transylvania Presbytery, February 14, 1795.

He preached at many points in the counties of Nelson, Shelby and Jefferson where he laid the foundations of Presbyterianism, and at most of which he afterwards organized churches. Having received a call from Simpson's creek church, in Nelson county, and from Ackron and Fox run, new churches in Shelby county, he was ordained and installed over them, June 2, 1796. The first administration of the Lord's supper in Shelby county, was in the fall of 1796, when the number of members had increased to thirty-five, mostly received on examination. His labors were spread over a wide region, now occupied by the congregations of Shelbyville, Mulberry, Six Mile, Shiloh, Olivet, and Big Spring, and embracing a circuit of from thirty to forty miles.

All these churches were planted and built up by him; but the field being too extensive, in 1803 he relinquished Simpson's creek, and devoted his whole time to the churches in Shelby county. In these he labored with great self-denial and success, till 1818, when the churches now called Shiloh and Olivet secured the services of Rev. Dr. Crow. In this extended field his labors were much blessed, constant accessions being received to his churches; but these accessions did not increase their members in proportion, which were constantly reduced by removals. He spent a long, eventful, a happy and useful life, among the people of these counties—having been their pastor for more than forty years; and long will his name be borne in memory by them.

In intellect Mr. Cameron had few equals. His mind was cast in the finest mould, and cultivated to a high degree. The distinctive characteristics of his mind were strength, originality and discrimination. He was a man of great shrewdness, and gifted with keen powers of satire. His discourses were always systematic, instructive and practical. As a doctrinal and experimental preacher, he was excelled by none; and his appeals were often most eloquent and impressive. As a pastor, he was highly esteemed and much beloved by the people of his charge; as a friend, he was frank, generous, and confiding; as a divine, he ranked in the very first class, and was regarded by all who knew him as the ablest man in the synod. He was the author of many published writings of high repute, and extensively known. Among these may be mentioned—

1. The Faithful Steward: against baptizing adults who do not give evidence of faith and repentance, or the children of such adults. 1806—pp. 53.

2. The Monitor: on Religious Liberty, Church Government, Discipline, &c. 1806—pp. 109.

3. An Appeal to the Scriptures, on the Design, Extent, and Effect of the Propitiation made by Christ. 1811—pp. 79.

4. A Discourse between the Confession of Faith of the Presbyterian Church, and a Preacher in that Society who holds the Doctrine of Indefinite, Universal Atonement. 1814—pp. 24.

5. A Defence of the Doctrines of Grace: A Series of Letters in Reply to Judge Davidge's publication addressed to the "Advocates of a Partial Gospel." 1816—pp. 49.

6. A Reply to some Arminian Questions on Divine Predestination, and to a doggerel poem, "The Trial of Cain." 1822—pp. 36.

7. An Anonymous Letter on Fore-ordination; pp. 22.

8. Two pamphlets, addressed to the Rev. George Light, a Methodist preacher.

9. A Sketch of the Transylvania Presbytery, for the General Assembly's committee appointed to write a History of the Presbyterian Church.

During his last illness, which was protracted, his mind was sustained by the spirit of that gospel which, with so much faithfulness and success, he had preached to his fellow men. The exercises of his mind were in unison with the general tenor of his religious sentiments. The prevailing feeling of his heart was submission to God, and reliance on Christ. His brethren of the Presbytery can never forget, that at their meeting the spring before his death, when he was supposed, by himself and others, to be on the very borders of the grave, he sent them a message full of tenderness, saying, that the nearer he approached to the eternal world, the more precious did the doctrines of the Bible, as held in our standards, become; and from the very waters of Jordan did he look back, and bid them all tc hold fast those truths so precious while we live—so unspeakably precious when we come to die.   He died on the 4th of December, 1836.

Colonel CHARLES S. TODD, late minister to Russia, so favorably known as a soldier and a diplomatist, is a son of the late Thomas Todd, who for many years filled the high office of judge of the supreme court of the United States.   He was born near Danville, Kentucky, on the 22d January, 1791—and having entered at an early age on a classical course of education in the best schools of Kentucky, in 1807, entered the ancient university of William and Mary, in Virginia, as a junior, and graduated with high reputation in 1809.   His thesis at the time of his graduation was the subject of encomium by the faculty.   He returned to Kentucky in 1809, and commenced the study of law with his father, and in 1810 he proceeded to Litchfield, Connecticut, to attend a course of lectures by the celebrated Judges Reeves and Gould.

In 1811–12 Colonel Todd established a law office in Lexington, but having cherished an ardent military spirit during his residence at college, where he was elected ensign in a volunteer company raised on account of the attack on the Chesapeake, he volunteered his services in June, 1812, and was elected ensign in one of the companies from Lexington, though before the march of the troops in August, he was appointed to a situation in the quarter master general's department, which made him the acting quarter master of the advance of the left wing of the north-western army.   In December he was appointed into General Harrison's staff as division judge advocate of the Kentucky troops.   In this capacity he was the bearer, one hundred miles across the wilderness, on snow and ice, of the confidential instructions from the commander-in-chief to General Winchester, previous to the disastrous affair of the river Raisin.   At the close of the campaign Ensign Todd returned to Kentucky, with a letter from General Harrison recommending him for a captaincy in the regular army, adding the beautiful compliment that " he appeared to combine the ardor of youth with the maturity of age."   McAfee's History of the War, Butler's History of Kentucky, and Judge Hall's Life of Harrison, all speak of incidents in this campaign in which Ensign Todd's enterprise and intrepidity were commended.   He was, on *personal application at the war office of Secretary Monroe,* appointed to a vacancy of captain in the 17th regiment of infantry.   Captain Todd, after commanding the recruiting rendezvous of the regiment, at Newport, was transferred to an original vacancy in the 28th infantry, attached to the brigade of General Cass, and was appointed aid to General Harrison.   Captain Todd's conduct on the campaign, and particularly in the battle of the Thames, is thus noticed in General Harrison's official report : " My aids-de-camp, Lieutenant O'Fallon and Captain Todd, of the line, and my volunteer aids, John Speed Smith and John Chambers, Esqs., have rendered me the most important services from the opening of the campaign."   " Major Wood, of the engineers, already distinguished by his conduct at Fort Meigs, attended the army with two six pounders.   Having no use for them in the action, he joined in the pursuit of the enemy, and with Major Payne of the mounted regiment, two of my aids-de-camp, Todd and Chambers, and three privates, continued it for several miles after the rest of the troops had halted, and made many prisoners."   After the capture of the British troops, he was sent with an order to Governor Shelby, to bring up Simrall's regiment to reinforce the crotchet, and participated in the operations on the left against the Indians.   He was then dispatched with Major Payne's battalion to pursue General Proctor, whose *sword, papers, &c.* were the joint prize of Major Wood, and Captain Todd.   He accompanied General Harrison down the lakes to the Niagara frontier, and Sackett's Harbor, and thence, via New York and Washington, to Cincinnati, having succeeded Major Hukill as deputy inspector general of the 8th military district.   During the summer of 1814, Major Todd acted also as adjutant general of the district, and is thus handsomely noticed in General McArthur's report of the expedition into Canada during that fall : " I have the support of the troops in assuring you, sir, that to the military talents, activity and intelligence of Major Todd, who acted as my adjutant general, much of the fortunate progress and issue of this expedition is attributable, and I cheerfully embrace this occasion to acknowledge the important services which he has at all times rendered me whilst in command of the district.   His various merits, justly entitle him to the notice of government."

In march following, he was promoted to the situation of inspector general, with the brevet rank and pay of colonel of cavalry. Subsequently to the war, General Harrison, in a letter to a member of the cabinet at Washington, expressed the opinion " that Colonel Todd was equal in bravery, and superior in intelligence to any officer of his rank in the army."

At the peace in 1815, and upon the disbandment of the army in 1815, he returned to his original profession at Frankfort, Kentucky, and in 1816 married the youngest daughter of Governor Shelby. He was soon after appointed secretary of state by the new Governor Madison. Upon the death of Governor Madison, Colonel Todd resigned his office, and the year following was returned to the legislature from Franklin county, and again in 1818, highest over Judges Bibb and Marshall and General Hardin. His conduct in the legislature was so acceptable to his fellow citizens that he could have been re-elected at any time, but unexpectedly he was invited by President Monroe to proceed to the government of Colombia, in South America, upon a confidential mission, with the pay and duties of a charge d'affaires. He was deputed to complete negotiations which had been in part effected by the lamented Perry, and to look into the actual condition of affairs in that country. He returned to the United States in 1821, and resumed his position at the capital of Colombia in 1822, bearing the recognition of the independence of that government. In these two trips to South America, Colonel Todd passed through seas infested with pirates, encountering hurricanes and malignant diseases, and passed one thousand miles over the Andes on mules at a time when the country was involved in a sanguinary civil war. In the summer of 1821, he received a letter from the department of state, announcing that his conduct on the mission had been approved by the president. In June, 1823, Mr. Adams, in his dispatch, said, " I have been directed by the president to assure you of his undiminished confidence in your talents, zeal and usefulness."

Colonel Todd, after declining an acceptance of several important offices, established himself as a cultivator of the soil, in Shelby county. For a number of years whilst engaged in improving his beautiful farm, his pen was devoted to the great subjects of religion, agriculture and politics. In 1837 and '39 he served as a commissioner in the Presbyterian General Assembly, in Philadelphia, by which the separation was effected, he sustaining the old school party. For several years he was vice president of the State agricultural society, and in 1839 delivered the annual address in the legislative hall. He had always sustained the claims of that distinguished orator and statesman, Mr. Clay, with whom from his youth up, he had maintained relations of the most intimate friendship; but as Mr. Clay had been withdrawn from the canvass in 1835, he advocated the claims of General Harrison to the presidency. In the spring of 1840, he was invited by the committees of Ohio and Kentucky, in connection with the late Benjamin Drake, of Cincinnati, to prepare sketches of the civil and military history of that distinguished patriot. These were received with great favor. He then moved to Cincinnati, and assumed the editorial charge of the Cincinnati Republican, devoted to the support of General Harrison's claims to the presidency. His efficiency was acknowledged by both parties. In February, '41 he accompanied General Harrison to Washington, and at the hour of that death which covered his country as with a pall, he was near the pillow of that illustrious patriot, whose confidence he enjoyed in an eminent degree, and who designed to engage his services for the country, in the mission to Vienna, as envoy extraordinary and minister plenipotentiary: but in the subsequent arrangements of President Tyler, it was thought best to send Colonel Todd to Russia, a decision which, so far as the country was concerned, was most eminently judicious.

He reached St. Petersburg early in November, 1841. As the intimate friend and companion-in-arms of the lamented Harrison, he was at once commended to the respect of the Russian government; and being invited by the emperor to attend his military parades, thus had access to many sources of information and influence, which a mere politician could not have enjoyed. He traveled into the interior of Russia, having visited Moscow and the annual fair at Nishnii Novogorod, on the Volga, where he encountered two hundred thousand people, speaking twenty different languages. He afterwards visited Sweden, and had the good fortune of being presented to the celebrated Bernadotte, the only marshal of Napoleon who retained his crown. As an evidence of the estimation in which Col.

Todd was held in the capital of Russia, he was elected a member of the Imperial Agricultural Society—the only instance in which a foreigner was admitted. A vote of thanks was entered on the journal; and upon his leaving the capital, he was presented with a gold medal. The merchants in the American trade tendered him a letter, with assurances of high regard and esteem, and of their great regret at his departure. A touching compliment, which any minister might be proud to receive, was extended to Col. Todd a few days before he left St. Petersburg, by Gen. Kaveline, the governor-general of the city, who drank the health of the American minister in the following language :

" Though our respective countries be situated on two different parts of the world, and consequently very distant from each other, yet I hope that you will acknowledge with me, that there is no distance for friendship. I then dare say, Hon. Mr. Todd, that when on the distant shores of the New World, you will sometimes remember the friends you leave here, whose hearts you have won by your eminently good qualities, and in whose bosom and memory your remembrance will remain engraved forever."

An extract from a dispatch from Mr. Webster, will show the estimation in which Col. Todd was held by both governments :

" The president directs me to express to you his approbation of the manner in which you have discharged your duties, as the representative of your country at the imperial court of Russia. While he is satisfied that you have sedulously sought, on all occasions, to promote the interests of the United States, it gives him much pleasure to understand that your public conduct and personal deportment have been quite satisfactory to the government to which you have been accredited."

President Polk thought proper to terminate Col. Todd's mission to Russia, in the fall of 1845; the secretary of state having communicated, in a private letter, that this act had not proceeded from any unfriendly feeling, but was the result of a change in the administration, and the application of what he was pleased to term the four years rule or practice, as to the continuance in office of our ministers.

In the course of a long public career, in war and in peace, at home and abroad, there are many interesting incidents connected with the subject of this memoir, a recital of which would gratify the public taste, but for want of space they are omitted. It will be seen that Col. Todd was reared in the military school of Harrison, and was a pupil in the diplomatic school of Monroe. Having returned to his country, in all the vigor of life, after a long and distant service, attended with great sacrifices, and maintaining a high moral standard, with a ripe experience in public affairs, and high mental accomplishments united to courteous and graceful manners, he has shown himself worthy to have been associated with such eminent patriots and illustrious statesmen as Madison, Monroe, Adams, Harrison, Clay and Webster.

Isaac Shelby, the subject of this memoir, was born on the 11th day of December, 1750, near to the North Mountain, a few miles from Hagerstown, in Maryland, where his father and grandfather settled after their arrival in America from Wales. In that early settlement of the country, which was annoyed during the period of his youth by Indian wars, he obtained only the elements of a plain English education; but like his father, General Evan Shelby, born with a strong constitution, capable of bearing great privation and fatigue, he was brought up to the use of arms and the pursuit of game.

At the age of twenty-one, he took up his residence in Western Virginia, beyond the Alleghany mountains, having previously acquired a knowledge of surveying and of the duties of sheriff at Fredericktown. He was engaged, in his new residence, in the business of feeding and attending to herds of cattle in the extensive range which distinguished that section of country. He was a lieutenant in the company of his father, the late General Evan Shelby, in the memorable battle fought 10th of October, 1774, at the mouth of the Kenhawa, at the close of which his father was the commanding officer, Colonels Lewis, Fleming and Field being killed or disabled. The result of this battle gave peace to the frontier, at the critical period of the colonies venturing into the eventful contest of the revolution, and deterred the Indians from uniting with the British until 1776. This was, probably, the most severely contested conflict ever maintained with the north-western Indians; the action continued from sunrise to sunset, and the ground for half a mile along the bank of the Ohio, was alternately occupied by each of the parties in the course of the day. So sanguinary was the contest, that blood was found on each of the trees behind which the parties were posted. The Indians, under the celebrated chief Cornstalk, abandoned the ground under cover of the night. Their loss, according to the official report, exceeded that of the Americans, the latter amounting to sixty-three killed and eighty wounded. This report was drawn up by Captain Russell, reputed to be the best scholar in camp, and the father of the late Colonel William Russell, of Kentucky. The fortune of the day, as stated in Doddridge's Notes of Border War, was decided by a bold movement, to the rear of the left wing of the Indians, led by Captain Evan Shelby, in which the subject of this memoir bore a conspicuous part.

The garrison at Kenhawa was commanded by Captain Russell, and Lieutenant Shelby continued in it until the troops were disbanded, in July, 1775, by order of Governor Dunmore, who was apprehensive that the post might be held for the benefit of the rebel authorities. He proceeded immediately to Kentucky, and was employed as a surveyor under Henderson & Co.; who styled themselves proprietors of the country, and who had established a regular land office under their purchase from the Cherokees. He resided in the then wilderness of Kentucky, for nearly twelve months, and being without bread or salt, his health was impaired, and he returned home.

In July, 1776, during his absence from home, he was appointed captain of a minute company by the committee of safety of Virginia. In the year 1777, he was appointed, by Governor Henry, a commissary of supplies for an extensive body of militia, posted at different garrisons to guard the frontier settlements, and for a treaty to be held at the Long Island of Holston river, with the Cherokee tribe of Indians. These supplies could not have been obtained nearer than Staunton, Va., a distance of three hundred miles; but by the most indefatigable perseverance, (one of the most conspicuous traits of his character,) he accomplished it to the satisfaction of his country.

In 1778, he was engaged in the commissary department, providing supplies for the continental army, and for an expedition, by the way of Pittsburg, against the north-western Indians. In the early part of 1779, he was appointed by Governor Henry to furnish supplies for the campaign against the Chicamauga Indians, which he effected upon *his own individual credit.* In the spring of that year, he was elected a member of the Virginia legislature from Washington county, and in the fall of that year was commissioned a major, by Governor Jefferson, in the escort of guards to the commissioners for extending the boundary line between that State and the State of North Carolina. By the extension of that line, his residence was found to be within the limits of the latter State, and shortly afterwards, he was appointed by Governor Caswell a colonel of the new county of Sullivan, established in consequence of the additional territory acquired by the running of that line.

In the summer of 1780, Colonel Shelby was in Kentucky, locating and securing those lands, which he had five years previously marked out and improved for himself, when the intelligence of the surrender of Charleston, and the loss of the army, reached that country. He returned home in July of that year, determined to enter the service of his country and remain in it until her independence should be secured. He could not continue to be a cool spectator of a contest in which the dearest rights and interests of his country were involved. On his arrival in Sullivan, he found a requisition from General Charles McDowell, requesting him to furnish all the aid in his power to check the enemy, who had overrun the two southern States, and were on the borders of North Carolina. Colonel Shelby assembled the militia of his county, called upon them to volunteer their services for a short time on that interesting occasion, and marched, in a few days, with three hundred mounted riflemen, across the Alleghany mountains.

In a short time after his arrival at McDowell's camp, near the Cherokee ford of Broad river, Col. Shelby, and Lieutenant-colonels Sevier and Clarke,—the latter a refugee officer from Georgia,—were detached with six hundred men, to surprise a post of the enemy in front, on the waters of Pacolet river. It was a strong fort, surrounded by abbatis, built in the Cherokee war, and commanded by that distinguished loyalist, Capt. Patrick Moore; who surrendered the garrison, with one British sergeant-major, ninety-three loyalists, and two hundred and fifty stand of arms. Major Ferguson, of the British army, though a brigadier general in the royal militia, and the most distinguished partisan officer in the British army, made many ineffectual efforts to surprise Col. Shelby. His advance, about six or seven hundred strong, came up with the American commander, at Cedar Spring, and before Ferguson approached with his whole force, the Americans took two officers and fifty men prisoners, and safely effected their retreat. It was in the severest part of this action, that Col. Shelby's attention was arrested by the heroic conduct of Col. Clarke. He often mentioned the circumstance of his ceasing in the midst of the battle, to look with astonishment and admiration at Clarke fighting.

The next important event was the battle fought at Musgrove's mill, on the south side of the Enoree river, distant forty miles, with seven hundred men, led by Cols. Shelby, Clarke, and Williams, of South Carolina. This affair took place on the 19th of August, and is more particularly described in the sketch of Col. Shelby, inserted in the first volume of the "National Portrait Gallery," published in 1834, under the direction of the American Academy of Fine Arts. It has been introduced into the historical romance called "Horse-Shoe Robinson," and noticed, also, in McCall's History of Georgia, where the British loss is stated to be sixty-three killed, and one hundred and sixty wounded and taken; the American loss, four killed and nine wounded: amongst the former, Capt. Inman; and amongst the latter, Col. Clarke and Capt. Clarke. Col. Innes, the British commander of the "Queen's American Regiment," from New York, was wounded; and all the British officers, except a subaltern, were killed or wounded; and Capt. Hawsey, a noted leader among the tories, was killed.

The Americans intended to be that evening before Ninety-Six—but at that moment an express from Gen. McDowell came up, in great haste, with a short note from Gov. Caswell, dated on the battle-ground, apprising McDowell of the defeat of the American grand army under Gen. Gates, on the 16th, near Camden. Fortunately, Col. Shelby knew Caswell's handwriting, and by distributing the prisoners among the companies, so as to make one to every three men, who carried them, alternately, on horseback, the detachment moved directly towards the mountains. The Americans were saved by a long and rapid march that day and night, and until the evening of the next day, without halting to refresh. Col. Shelby, after seeing the party and prisoners out of danger, retreated to the western waters, and left the prisoners in the charge of Clarke and Williams, to convey them to a place of safety in Virginia; for at that moment there was no corps of Americans south of that State. The brilliancy of this affair was obscured, as indeed were all the minor events of the previous war, by the deep gloom which overspread the public mind after the disastrous defeat of Gen. Gates.

Ferguson was so solicitous to recapture the prisoners, and to check these daring adventures of the mountaineers, that he made a strenuous effort, with his main body, to intercept them; but failing of his object, he took post at a place called Gilbert-town, from whence he sent the most threatening messages, by paroled prisoners, to the officers west of the mountains, proclaiming devastation to their country, if they did not cease their opposition to the British government.

This was the most disastrous and critical period of the revolutionary war, to the south. No one could see whence a force could be raised to check the enemy in their progress to subjugate this portion of the continent.

Cornwallis, with the main army, was posted at Charlotte-town, in North Carolina, and Ferguson, with three thousand, at Gilbert-town; while many of the best friends of the American government, despairing of the freedom and independence of America, took protection under the British standard. At this gloomy moment, Col. Shelby proposed to Cols. Sevier and Campbell to raise a force from their several counties, march hastily through the mountains, and attack and surprise Ferguson in the night. Accordingly, they collected with their followers, about one thousand strong, on Doe run, in the spurs of the Alleghany, on the 25th of September, 1780, and the next day commenced their march, when it was discovered that three of Col. Sevier's men had deserted to the enemy. This disconcerted their first design, and induced them to turn to the left, gain his front, and act as events might suggest. They traveled through mountains almost inaccessible to horsemen. As soon as they entered the level country, they met with Col.

Cleveland with three hundred men, and with Cols. Williams and Lacy, and other refugee officers, who had heard of Cleveland's advance, by which three hundred more were added to the force of the mountaineers. They now considered themselves to be sufficiently strong to encounter Ferguson; but being rather a confused mass, without any head, it was proposed by Col. Shelby, in a council of officers, and agreed to, that Col. Campbell, of the Virginia regiment,—an officer of enterprise, patriotism, and good sense,—should be appointed to the command. And having determined to pursue Ferguson with all practicable dispatch, two nights before the action they selected the best horses and rifles, and at the dawn of day commenced their march with nine hundred and ten expert marksmen. As Ferguson was their object, they would not be diverted from the main point by any collection of tories in the vicinity of their route. They pursued him for the last thirty-six hours without alighting from their horses to refresh but once, at the Cowpens, for an hour, although the day of the action was so extremely wet, that the men could only keep their guns dry by wrapping their bags, blankets, and hunting shirts around the locks, which exposed their bodies to a heavy and incessant rain during the pursuit.

By the order of march and of battle, Col. Campbell's regiment formed the right, and Col. Shelby's regiment the left column, in the centre : the right wing was composed of Sevier's regiment, and Maj. Winston's and McDowell's battalions, commanded by Sevier himself; the left wing was composed of Col. Cleveland's regiment, the followers of Cols. Williams, Lacy, Hawthorn, and Hill, headed by Col. Cleveland in person. In this order the mountaineers pursued, until they found Ferguson, securely encamped on King's Mountain, which was about half a mile long, and from which, he declared the evening before, that "God Almighty could not drive him." On approaching the mountain, the two centre columns deployed to the right and left, formed a front, and attacked the enemy, while the right and left wings were marching to surround him. In a few minutes the action became general and severe—continuing furiously for three-fourths of an hour ; when the enemy, being driven from the east to the west end of the mountain, surrendered at discretion. Ferguson was killed, with three hundred and seventy-five of his officers and men, and seven hundred and thirty captured. The Americans had sixty killed and wounded ; of the former, Col. Williams.

This glorious achievement occurred at the most gloomy period of the revolution, and was the first link in the great chain of events to the south, which established the independence of the United States. History has, heretofore, though improperly. ascribed this merit to the battle of the Cowpens, in January, 1781 ; but it belongs, justly, to the victory on King's Mountain, which turned the tide of war to the south, as the victory of Trenton, under Washington, and of Bennington, under Stark, did to the north. It was achieved by raw, undisciplined riflemen, without any authority from the government under which they lived,— without pay, rations, ammunition, or even the expectance of reward, other than that which results from the noble ambition of advancing the liberty and welfare of their beloved country. It completely dispirited the tories, and so alarmed Cornwallis, who then lay only thirty miles north of King's Mountain with the main British army, that, on receiving information of Ferguson's total defeat and overthrow by the riflemen from the west, under Cols. Campbell, Shelby, Cleveland and Sevier, and that they were bearing down upon him, he ordered an immediate retreat—marched all night, in the utmost confusion—and retrograded as far back as Winnsborough, sixty or eighty miles, whence he did not attempt to advance until reinforced, three months after, by Gen. Leslie, with two thousand men from the Chesapeake. In the meantime, the militia of North Carolina assembled in considerable force at New Providence, on the border of South Carolina, under Gen. Davidson ; and Gen. Smallwood, with Morgan's light corps, and the Maryland line, advanced to the same point. Gen. Gates, with the shattered remains of his army, collected at Hillsborough, also came up, as well as the new levies from Virginia, of one thousand men, under Gen. Stevens. This force enabled Gen. Greene, who assumed the command early in December, to hold Cornwallis in check.

The legislature of North Carolina passed a vote of thanks to Colonel Shelby and several other officers, and directed each to be presented with an elegant sword, for their patriotic conduct in the attack and defeat of the enemy on King's mountain, on the memorable 7th of October, 1780. This resolution was carried into effect as to Colonel Shelby, in the summer of 1813, just at the moment when, in the language of Secretary Monroe, " disclaiming all metaphysical distinctions tending to enfeeble the government," he was about to lead his troops far beyond the limits of the State of which he was governor. The presentation at that particular time, afforded a presage of the new glory he was to acquire for himself and country in that eventful campaign.

If any were entitled to special commendation in this band of heroic spirits on King's mountain, the claim of Colonel Shelby would be well founded. He originated the expedition, and his valor and unshaken resolution, contributed to rally the right of the front line, when driven down the mountain by a tremendous charge from the enemy, at the onset of the battle. Nor have the histories of the war at the south done justice to the sagacity and judgment of Colonel Shelby upon another interesting occasion, just following the affair on King's mountain. As soon as he had placed the prisoners beyond the reach of the enemy, he repaired to the head quarters of General Gates, and suggested to him the plan of detaching General Morgan towards the mountains. The details of this arrangement were submitted by him, and approved by Gates, and Greene had the good sense to adopt them, after he assumed the command. The result of his advice was exhibited in the splendid affair at the Cowpens, which added fresh laurels to the veteran brows of *Morgan, Howard* and *Washington.*

In the campaign of the fall of 1781, Colonel Shelby served under General Marion, a distinguished partizan officer, of the boldest enterprise. He was called down by General Greene to that lower country, with five hundred mounted riflemen from the western waters, in September, 1781, to aid the general in intercepting Cornwallis, at that time blockaded by the French fleet in the Chesapeake, and who, it was suspected, would endeavor to make good his retreat through North Carolina to Charleston; but, upon his lordship's surrender in Virginia, Colonel Shelby was attached to General Marion's command below, on the Santee, and was second in command of a strong detachment of dragoons, under Colonel Mayhem, ordered to carry a British post at Fairlawn, near Monk's Corner, eight or ten miles below the enemy's main army, under General Stuart. Information had been received by General Marion that five hundred Hessians at that post were in a state of mutiny, and would surrender to any considerable force that might appear before it. But the officer commanding the post having some apprehensions of their fidelity, had marched them off to Charleston, the day before Colonel Mayhem appeared before it. The post, however, was surrendered, with one hundred and fifty British prisoners. The British general at Ferguson's Swamp, nine miles in the rear, made great, though unavailing efforts to intercept Mayhem's party on their return with the prisoners to General Marion's encampment. Immediately after this excursion, the British commander retreated with his whole force to Charleston.

As the period for which the mounted volunteers had engaged to serve was about to expire, and no further active operations being contemplated, after the retreat of the enemy towards Charleston, Colonel Shelby obtained leave of absence from General Marion, to attend the assembly of North Carolina, of which he was a member, which would sit two hundred miles distant, about the first of December. Marion addressed a letter on the subject to General Greene, which Colonel Shelby was permitted to see, speaking in high terms of the conduct of the mountaineers, and assigning particular credit to Colonel Shelby for his conduct in the capture of the British post, as it surrendered to him after an ineffectual attempt by an officer of the dragoons.

In 1782, Colonel Shelby was elected a member of the North Carolina assembly, and was appointed one of the commissioners to settle the pre-emption claims upon the Cumberland river, and to lay off the lands allotted to the officers and soldiers of the North Carolina line, south of where Nashville now stands. He performed this service in the winter of 1782–3, and returned to Boonsborough, Kentucky, in April following, where he married Susanna, second daughter of Captain Nathaniel Hart, one of the first settlers of Kentucky, and one of the proprietors styled Henderson & Co., by their purchase of the country from the Cherokees. He established himself on the first settlement and pre-emption granted in Kentucky, for the purpose of pursuing his favorite occupation, the cultivation of the soil; and it is a remarkable fact, pregnant with many curious reflections, that at the period of his death, forty-three years after, he was the only individual in the State residing upon his own settlement and pre-emption.

He was a member of the early conventions held at Danville for the purpose of obtaining a separation from the State of Virginia; and was a member of that convention which formed the first constitution of Kentucky, in April, 1792. In May following, he was elected the first chief magistrate, and discharged its arduous duties with signal advantage to the State. The history of his administration of an infant republic in the remote wilderness, would fill a volume with deeply interesting incidents, exhibiting him advantageously in the character of a soldier, of a lawgiver, and a diplomatist; but the limits prescribed to this sketch will not permit a detail of them.

After completing the organization of the government under the provisions of the constitution, by filling the various offices created by it, the earnest attention of the governor was directed to the defence of the State against the Indian incursions, and the border war to which the people were exposed by their remote and unprotected position in the wilderness. Gen. Washington's paternal regard to the same high object was manifested in the cautious and extensive arrangements which were made under the direction of Gen. Wayne for a strong expedition against the north-western Indians, who were stimulated and aided by the British and provincial forces occupying posts within our boundary. The confidence of Washington, as well as of the people of Kentucky, was reposed in the energy and patriotism of Gov. Shelby. This was evinced in his almost unanimous elevation to the chief magistracy, as well as in the answer of the first legislature to his message, and in a letter from Gen. Knox, secretary of war, of July 12, 1792.

In the subsequent letter from the war department, the defensive operations for the protection of Kentucky were committed exclusively to his judgment and discretion, and whenever there was a prospect of acting offensively against the Indians of the north-west, the president made an appeal to his patriotism and that of the State, in furnishing mounted volunteers in aid of the regular force. His energy and the gallantry of Kentucky was signally displayed in the valuable succour rendered to Gen. Wayne on the memorable 20th of August, 1794. His enlightened forecast, and the valor of Kentucky, presented on this occasion, as on the equally glorious 5th of October, 1813, the means of victory both in men and transportation, at a critical moment to the scene of action—to victories the most decisive in their results to any heretofore known in Indian warfare.

Whilst the people of Kentucky were interrupted in their business and prosperity by the attention necessary to the progress of the Indian war, they were annoyed by continued apprehensions of losing the navigation of the Mississippi, on which their commercial existence depended. In the midst of these difficulties, a new and unexpected occasion presented itself for the display of Gov. Shelby's diplomatic sagacity. The complaints and remonstrances of the Spanish minister induced the general government to open a correspondence with Gov. Shelby, for the purpose of suppressing an expedition, which was represented to be in contemplation, by La Chaise and other French agents, against the possessions of Spain on the Mississippi. Gov. Shelby had no apprehensions that they would succeed in organizing the necessary force, and under this impression his reply to the department of state, October 5th, 1793, was forwarded, without considering that he had not authority under existing laws to interfere in preventing it. But the granting of commissions to Gen. Clark and other influential individuals, and the actual attempt to carry the plans of French emissaries into effect, induced the governor to examine the subject more thoroughly, and conceiving that he had no legal authority to interfere, he addressed a letter, January 13th, 1794, to the secretary of state, expressing these doubts, and assuming an attitude, which, though professing the most devoted regard to the Union, had the effect of drawing from the general government a full development of the measures which had been pursued for securing the navigation of the Mississippi. These explanations by the department of state, and by the special commissioner, the eloquent Col. James Innes, attorney general of Virginia, who was deputed by Gen. Washington to proceed to Kentucky to communicate with the governor and legislature, removed all ground of uneasiness, and created a tranquillity in the public mind which had not existed since the first settlement of the State.

The whole subject was communicated by Gov. Shelby to the legislature on the 15th of November, 1794, and the part he took in it was approved by that body. The act of Congress on the subject, passed after the receipt of Gov. Shelby's letter, shows conclusively that the legislature of the United States did not conceive that previously he had authority to interfere in the mode recommended by the department of state. This measure on the part of Gov. Shelby, though it might seem to conflict with the opinions and policy of Gen. Washington, did not produce in the mind of the father of his country any diminution of the respect and confidence he had theretofore reposed in him; for in May following, Gen. Knox, secretary of war, in a letter detailing the plans of the general government, in relation to Wayne's proposed campaign, takes occasion to say, that "the president, confiding in the patriotism and good disposition of your excellency, requests that you will afford all the facilities, countenance and aid in your power, to the proposed expedition, from which, if successful, the State of Kentucky will reap the most abundant advantages." In the next paragraph, he is appointed president of the board for selecting the field and company officers, and concludes with the assurance that "Gen. Wayne has been written to, not to interfere in the defensive protection of Kentucky, which is hereby, in the name of the president of the United States, confided to your excellency, under the following general paragraph," etc.

At the close of his gubernatorial term, he returned to his farm in Lincoln, with renewed relish for the cares and enjoyments which its management necessarily created. He was as distinguished for the method and judgment and industry, which he displayed in agricultural pursuits, as he had exemplified in the more conspicuous duties of the general and the statesman. He was the model of an elevated citizen, whether at the plow, in the field, or in the cabinet.

He was repeatedly chosen an elector of president, and voted for Mr. Jefferson and Mr. Madison. He could not yield to the repeated solicitations of influential individuals in different parts of the State, requesting him to consent to be a candidate for the chief magistracy, until the exigencies of our national affairs had brought about a crisis which demanded the services of every patriot. In this contingency, he was elected, upon terms very gratifying to his feelings, a second time to the chief magistracy, at the commencement of the war, in 1812, with Great Britain.

Of his career at that eventful period, it would be impracticable, in the limits of this sketch, to present even an outline. His energy, associated with a recollection of his revolutionary fame, aroused the patriotism of the State. In every direction he developed her resources, and aided in sending men and supplies to the support of the north-western army under Gen. Harrison. The legislature of Kentucky, in the winter of 1812–13, contemplating the necessity of some vigorous effort, in the course of that year, to regain the ground lost by the disasters at Detroit and at the river Raisin, passed a resolution authorising and requesting the governor to assume the personal direction of the troops of the State, whenever, in his judgment, such a step would be necessary. Under this authority, and at the solicitation of Gen. Harrison, he invited his countrymen to meet him at Newport, and to accompany him to the scene of active, and, as he predicted, of decisive operations. Upon his own responsibility he authorized the troops to meet him with their horses. Four thousand men rallied to his standard in less than thirty days; and this volunteer force reached the shore of Lake Erie just in time to enable the commander-in-chief to profit by the splendid victory, achieved by the genius and heroism of Perry and his associates. It was a most interesting incident, which augured favorably of the issue of the campaign, that Gov. Shelby should arrive at the camp of Gen. Harrison precisely at the moment when Commodore Perry was disembarking his prisoners. The feelings of congratulation which were exchanged by the three heroes, at the tent of the general on the shore of Lake Erie, may be more readily conceived than described. The writer of this article had been previously dispatched by Gen. Harrison to Commodore Perry, to ascertain the result of the naval battle, and, returning with Perry, was present at this interview.

In the organization which Governor Shelby made of his forces, he availed himself of the character and respectability of the materials at his command Generals Henry and Desha were assigned to the command of the two divisions

34

and General Calmes, Caldwell, King, Chiles and Calloway to the brigades. His confidential staff was composed, among other respectable citizens, of the names of Adair, Crittenden and Barry, so well known in the history of the State and of the nation. As governor of Kentucky, his authority ceased as soon as he passed the limits of the State; but the confidence of General Harrison and of all the troops, in his judgment and patriotism was so exalted, that he was regarded as the Mentor of the campaign, and recognized as the senior major-general of the Kentucky troops. In the general order of march and of battle, the post assigned to him was the most important, and the subsequent battle evinced that the arrangement was as creditable to the sagacity of General Harrison as it was complimentary to the valor of Governor Shelby.

In all the movements of the campaign, whether in council or execution, monuments of his valor and of his energetic character were erected by the gratitude of the commander-in-chief, of all his troops, and of the president of the nation, who spoke officially of his services with the veneration which belongs only to public benefactors. The legislature of Kentucky and the Congress of the United States expressed their sense of his gallant conduct in resolutions which will transmit his name to posterity, 'as a patriot without reproach and a soldier without ambition.'

The vote of Congress assigning to him and to General Harrison each a gold medal, commemorative of the decisive victory on the Thames, was delayed one session in consequence of some prejudice prevailing in the public mind in relation to General Harrison. As soon as Governor Shelby was advised of this fact, he solicited his friends in Congress, through Mr. Clay, *to permit no expression of thanks to him, unless associated with the name of General Harrison.* This magnanimous conduct and the unqualified commendation which he gave of the career of General Harrison on that campaign, connected with a favorable report of a committee at the next session of Congress, instituted at the request of the general, of which Colonel R. M. Johnson was chairman, led to the immediate adoption of the original resolution.

Governor Shelby was unremitting in the aid which he extended to the operations of the general government during the war. He furnished troops to defend the country around Detroit, and dispatched an important reinforcement to General Jackson for the defence of New Orleans. His sagacity led him to send General Adair as adjutant-general, with the rank of brigadier-general, to meet the precise contingency, which actually occurred, of General Thomas being sick or disabled. The result of this measure was exhibited in the critical succor afforded by General Adair on the memorable 8th of January.

In the civil administration of the State, Governor Shelby's policy continued to establish and confirm the sound principles of his predecessors. Integrity, fidelity to the constitution, and capacity, were the qualifications which he required in public officers: and his recommendations to the legislature enforced a strict regard to public economy and to the claims of public faith. In the fall of 1816, his term expired, and he retired again to the sweets of domestic life, in the prosecution of his favorite pursuit.

In March, 1817, he was selected by President Monroe to fill the department of war; but his advanced age, the details of the office, and his desire, in a period of peace, to remain in private life, induced him to decline an acceptance of it. In 1818, he was commissioned by the president to act in conjunction with General Jackson in holding a treaty with the Chickasaw tribe of Indians, for the purchase of their lands west of the Tennessee river within the limits of Kentucky and Tennessee, and they obtained a cession of the territory to the United States, which unites the western population, and adds greatly to the defence of the country, in the event of future wars with the savages, or with any European power. This was his last public act.

In February, 1820, he was attacked with a paralytic affection, which disabled his right arm, and which was the occasion of his walking lame on the right leg. His mind continued unimpaired until his death, by apoplexy, on the 18th July, 1826, in the seventy-sixth year of his age. It was a consolation to his afflicted family to cherish the hope that he was prepared for this event. In the vigor of life he professed it to be his duty to dedicate himself to God, and to seek an interest in the merits of the Redeemer. He had been for many years a member of the Presbyterian church, and in his latter days, he was the chief instrument in erecting a house of worship upon his own land.

The vigor of his constitution fitted him to endure active and severe bodily exercise, and the energetic symmetry of his person, united with a peculiar suavity of manner, rendered his deportment impressively dignified; his strong natural sense was aided by close observation on men and things; and the valuable qualities of method and perseverance, imparted success to all his efforts.

SIMPSON COUNTY.

SIMPSON county was formed in 1819, and named in honor of Capt. JOHN SIMPSON. It is situated in the southern part of the State, and is drained by Big Barren river and its tributaries: bounded on the north by Warren; east by Allen; south by the State of Tennessee; and west by Logan. The surface is generally level, or very slightly undulating; the soil, based upon limestone, with red clay foundation, is rich and very productive. The staple products are Indian corn, wheat, and tobacco.

Valuation of the taxable property of Simpson in 1846, $1,368,-842; number of acres of land in the county, 115,948; average value of lands per acre, $4.49; number of white males over twenty-one years of age, 955; number of children between five and sixteen years old, 1,197. Population in 1840, 6,537.

FRANKLIN, the seat of justice and only town of Simpson, is situated near the centre of the county, about one hundred and fifty miles from Frankfort. It contains the court-house and other county buildings, two churches, (Union and Christian,) five lawyers, eight physicians, two schools, two taverns, ten stores and groceries, and eighteen mechanical trades—population, 300. Established in 1820, and named after Dr. Franklin.

The Hon. JOHN SIMPSON (for whom this county was named) came to Lincoln county at an early day, having migrated with his father from Virginia. The date and place of his birth is not recollected—but he arrived in Kentucky at a period when she was subject to the predatory incursions of the savage foe. He, when quite a lad, accompanied the intrepid Wayne on several expeditions, and contributed his part in the eventful scenes of the border war which afflicted the first republic in the wilderness.

The decisive victory of Wayne having established a general peace, young Simpson availed himself of the kind counsel of the late lamented and illustrious jurist, Col. John Allen, to remove to Shelby county, and to enter upon the study of the law,—a pursuit which, after arms, exercised the strongest influence upon the ambitious youth of the country. Young Simpson soon established himself in his profession, as well by the accuracy and soundness of his judgment, as by the amenity of his manners. He rose, at an early day, to distinction, professionally and politically, having been repeatedly elected to the legislature. In 1811–12, he was elected speaker of the house of representatives; and in August, 1812, was chosen to a seat in the Congress of the United States.

In the meantime, however, the aggressions of Great Britain upon the rights and interests of the United States, led to a declaration of war, and Kentucky was called upon to furnish 5,500 men, her quota of the 100,000 authorised to be received into service by Congress. Mr. Simpson raised a company of volunteer riflemen, and was attached to the regiment commanded by his old friend, Col.

Allen. This regiment formed part of the brigade of Gen. Payne, and marched with the first troops from Kentucky, to reinforce Gen. Hull at Detroit.

The events of the campaign are given in McAfee's history of the war in the western country. The regiment of Allen performed its part in the timely relief afforded by Gen. Harrison to the important post of fort Wayne; and the company of Capt. Simpson participated in the gallant though disastrous events at the river Raisin, brought on by the unauthorised movement under Gen. Winchester. Allen and Simpson sealed their devotion to their country by their blood, on that memorable occasion; and the patriots who were united in life by so many ties, were not divided in their deaths. Simpson was distinguished by his uncommon height, as well as that of his first sergeant, the present venerable Col. S. Harbison, of Shelbyville. His bones yet rest where they fell, with no monument to mark the spot; but the State which he served and honored in his life and in his death, has perpetuated his memory in the name of one of her counties. He left no family, but the rich legacy of his fame descends to his country.

SPENCER COUNTY.

SPENCER county was formed in 1824, and named in honor of Captain SPEAR SPENCER. It is situated in the middle portion of the State, and watered by Salt river, which flows through the county from east to west: bounded on the north by Jefferson and Shelby; east by Anderson; south by Nelson; and west by Bullitt. The tributaries of Salt river are, Brashear's, Big Beech, Ash's, Simpson's, Plumb and Elk creeks. Along the river and creeks, there are numerous fertile valleys; but the surface of the county is generally undulating or hilly, with a rich soil, based on limestone. The principal products are—corn, wheat, rye, oats, hemp, tobacco and grass. The articles of export are, horses, mules, cattle, hogs, hemp, whisky and tobacco.

Valuation of taxable property in Spencer in 1846, $2,115,577; number of acres of land in the county, 111,313; average value of land per acre, $10.73; number of white males over twenty-one years old, 979; number of children between five and sixteen years of age, 1,103. Population in 1840, 6,585.

TAYLORSVILLE, the seat of justice of Spencer county, is situated on Salt river, thirty-one miles east from Louisville, and about thirty-two miles from Frankfort: contains a brick court-house and other county buildings; Baptist, Presbyterian, Methodist and Roman Catholic churches—the two latter large and handsomely finished edifices; a very neat and substantial Seminary building, with eighty pupils connected with the seminary, in which the Latin and Greek languages are taught in connection with the higher branches of English; a female school with twenty-four scholars; four lawyers, two physicians, seven merchants, two taverns, and thirty mechanics' shops: population 500. Incorporated in 1829—named after Richard Taylor, the proprietor of the land. *Mount Eden* is a small village about twelve miles from Taylorsville—containing a post office, two physicians, three stores, two taverns and five mechanical trades. Population 150.

Taylorsville is located in a beautiful valley, comprising about one hundred and sixty acres of land, lying immediately in the forks of Salt river and Brashear's creek. The creek runs parallel with the river for several hundred yards, and then making an abrupt turn, flows into it at right angles : this, with the elevation in the rear, leaves the bottom or valley in an oblong square, the longest sides extending up and down the river and creek. In this bottom, about equi-distant from the river and creek, and nearer the upper than the lower end, is a *hill* or *mound*, rising to an elevation of from seventy to eighty feet above the general level, and containing an area of six acres. The shape of this mound is oval, resembling an egg, ranging from north to south ; the south end of easy ascent, while the north is steep and more abrupt. Within the recollection of aged persons still living, the timber upon this mound was observed to be of the same size and character of that upon the bottom land, and the whole was remarkably heavy. The mound has the appearance of being a natural, rather than an artificial embankment. A Catholic church has been recently built on one side of it.

In August, 1782, shortly after the battle of the Blue Licks, some western bands of Indians, believed to have been engaged in that conflict, infested the settlements along Salt river. Intelligence was promptly communicated to Colonel Floyd, who instantly ordered out a party of militia to scour the country where the savages were suspected to be lurking. Some of the party were from Kincheloe's station on Simpson's creek, which consisted of six or seven families. On the first of September the militia, unable to discover any Indians, dispersed and returned to their homes. There had been no alarm at Kincheloe's station during the absence of the men, and upon reaching home late in the evening, greatly fatigued and without apprehension of danger, they retired to rest. At the dead hour of the night, when the inmates of the station were wrapt in the most profound sleep, the Indians made a simultaneous attack upon the cabins of the station, and, breaking open the doors, commenced an indiscriminate massacre of men, women and children. The unconscious sleepers were awakened but to be cut down, or to behold their friends fall by their side. A few only, availing themselves of the darkness of the night, escaped the tomahawk or captivity. Among those who effected their escape, was Mrs. Davis, whose husband was killed, and another woman whose name is not given. They fled to the woods, where they were fortunately joined by a lad, by the name of Ash, who conducted them to Cox's station.

William Harrison, after placing his wife and a young woman of the family, under the floor of the cabin, made his escape under cover of the darkness. He remained secreted in the neighborhood until he was satisfied the Indians had retired, when he returned to the cabin and liberated his wife and her companion from their painful situation.

Thomas Randolph occupied one of the small cabins, with his wife and two children, one an infant. The Indians succeeded in breaking into his house, and although they outnumbered him four or five to one, he stood by his wife and children with heroic firmness. He had succeeded in killing several Indians, when his wife, and the infant in her arms, were both murdered by his side. He instantly placed his remaining child in the loft, then mounting himself, made his escape through the roof. As he alighted on the ground from the roof of the cabin, he was assailed by two of the savages whom he had just forced out of the house. With his knife he inflicted a severe wound upon one, and gave the other a stunning blow with the empty gun, when they both retreated. Freed from his foes, he snatched up his child, plunged into the surrounding forest, and was soon beyond the reach of danger.

Several women and children were cruelly put to death after they were made prisoners, on the route to the Indian towns. On the second day of her captivity, Mrs. Bland, one of the prisoners, made her escape in the bushes. Totally unacquainted with the surrounding country, and destitute of a guide, for eighteen successive days she rambled through the woods, without seeing a human face, without clothes, and subsisting upon sour grapes and green walnuts, until she became a walking skeleton. On the eighteenth day she was accidentally discovered and taken to Lynn's station, where, from kind attention and careful nursing, her health and strength were soon restored.

The situation of Mrs. Polk, another prisoner, with four children, was almost as pitiable as that of Mrs. Bland. She was far advanced in a state of pregnancy, and compelled to walk until she became almost incapable of motion. She was then threatened with death, and the tomahawk brandished over her head by one Indian, when another, who saw it, begged her life—took her under his care—mounted her on a horse with two of the children, and conducted her safely to Detroit. Here she was purchased by a British trader, well treated, and enabled to write to her husband, who, though a resident of the station, was absent at the time of her capture. On the receipt of her letter, the husband immediately repaired to Detroit, obtained his wife and five children, and returned with them safely to Kentucky. After the peace of the succeeding year, the remainder of the prisoners were also liberated and returned home.

This county was named in honor of Captain SPEAR SPENCER, a young man of ardent patriotism and undaunted courage, who fell at the head of his company in the battle of Tippecanoe. He commanded a fine rifle company in that severe engagement, and occupied a most exposed position. In the midst of the action, he was wounded on the head, but continued at his post, and exhorted his men to fight on. Shortly after, he received a second ball, which passed through both thighs, and he fell—but still resolute and unyielding, he refused to be carried from the field, and urged his men to stand to their duty. By the assistance of one of his men he was raised to a sitting posture, when he received a third ball through his body, which instantly killed him. Both of his lieutenants, Messrs. McMahan and Berry, were also killed. Captain Spencer was a warm friend and bosom companion of the gifted and gallant Daviess, who perished with him in that battle.

TODD COUNTY.

TODD county was formed in 1819, and named in honor of Col. JOHN TODD. It is situated in the southern part of the State, on the Tennessee line : bounded on the north by Muhlenburg ; east by Logan ; south by the Tennessee line ; and west by Christian. The county is watered by Elk, west and east forks of Pond river, Whippoorwill, and Big, Little, and West Clifty creeks. But for a small portion in the north-western end of the county, the territory would form an oblong square, comprising about three hundred and fifty square miles. The southern, and a portion of the northern part of the county, is level or gently undulating—the soil based upon limestone, and very productive,—the remainder rolling and hilly, the soil of an inferior quality, but producing fine grass. Stone coal abounds ; and the tall cliffs on Big Clifty creek, rising in some places to the height of three hundred feet, afford some as grand and magnificent scenery as any in the State. The greatest natural curiosity in the county is the " *Pilot Rock*," situated on the dividing line between Christian and Todd.* The principal products of the county are corn, wheat, oats and tobacco ; exports—horses, mules, cattle, sheep and hogs.

Valuation of taxable property of Todd in 1846, $3,034,658, number of acres of land in the county, 192,694 ; average value of land per acre, $5.79 ; number of white males over twenty-one

---

* See Christian county.

years of age, 1,388; number of children between five and sixteen years old, 1763. Population in 1840, 9,991.

The towns of the county consist of Elkton, Haydensville, Trenton, Allensville, and Fairview. ELKTON, the seat of justice, is a beautiful town, situated near the centre of the county, on the bank of Elk creek, and about one hundred and eighty miles from Frankfort: contains the usual public buildings, three churches, (Baptist, Methodist, and Cumberland Presbyterian,) one male and one female academy, ten lawyers, six physicians, two taverns, six stores, one grocery, and twenty-five mechanics' shops. Population, 750. Established in 1820. *Haydensville* is a small village, containing a tavern, post-office, school, store, four mechanics' shops, with a population of sixty souls. *Trenton* contains one free church, post-office, school, tavern, five physicians, (including vicinity), four stores, and ten mechanics' shops. Population, 200. *Allensville* contains one Baptist and one Christian church, school, post-office, tavern, two physicians, two stores, and three or four mechanics' shops. Population, 60. *Fairview* is a small village, containing but a few families.

Col. JOHN TODD, for whom this county was named, was the eldest of three brothers, and a native of Pennsylvania. He was educated in Virginia, at his uncle's —the Rev. John Todd,—and, at maturity, entered upon the study of the law, and finally obtained a license to practice. He left his uncle's residence, and settled in the town of Fincastle, in Virginia, where he practiced law for several years; but Daniel Boone and others having discovered Kentucky, Col. Todd, lured with the descriptions given him of the fertility of the country, about the year 1775, came first to Kentucky, where he found Col. Henderson and others at Boonsborough. He joined Henderson's party, obtained a pre-emption right, and located sundry tracts of land in the now county of Madison, in Col. Henderson's land office. He afterwards returned to Virginia; and, in the year 1786, again set out from Virginia with his friend, John May, and one or two others, for Kentucky. They proceeded some distance together on the journey, when, for some cause, Mr. May left his servant with Col. Todd, to proceed on to Kentucky, and returned to Richmond, Virginia. Col. Todd proceeded on to the place where Lexington now stands, and, in its immediate vicinity, improved two places,—the one in his own name, and the other in that of his friend, John May,—for both of which he obtained certificates for settlement and pre-emption, of fourteen hundred acres. These pre-emptions adjoin, and lie in the immediate vicinity of the now city of Lexington. It appears from depositions, taken since his death, that he accompanied Col. Clark, since Gen. Clark, in his expedition against Kaskaskia and Vincennes, and was at the capture of those places. After the surrender of those places, it is supposed that he returned to Kentucky; of this there is no record or living evidence; but it appears from a letter written by Gen. Clark, that Col. Todd was appointed to succeed him in the command at Kaskaskia. Under an act of the Virginia legislature, passed in 1777, by which that part of Virginia conquered by Clark, and all other of her territory north-west of the Ohio river, was erected into the county of Illinois, of which John Todd was appointed colonel commandant and county lieutenant, with all the civil powers of governor. He was further authorised, by enlistment or volunteers, to raise a regiment for the defence of the frontier. His commission and many papers, all show that he immediately entered upon the duties of his office, and was seldom absent from his government, up to the time of his death. The regiment was only raised for one year, but was continued in service until about 1779, when the State of Virginia raised four additional regiments—two for the eastern, and two for the western part of Virginia. It is supposed that Col. Joseph Crockett was promoted to the command of one of these regiments, and Col. Todd was appointed to the other. No commission has been found, appointing him a colonel in the regular service ; but depositions on file in Richmond, and old papers, show that he was acting as a regular colonel, from about the time the regiments were expected to be raised.

In the spring of 1780, Col. Todd was sent a delegate to the legislature of Virginia, from the county of Kentucky. While attending on the legislature, he married Miss Hawkins, and returned again to Kentucky, and settled his wife in the fort at Lexington ; but again visited the county of Illinois, and was engaged continually in the administration of its government, and in other military affairs, so that he was seldom with his family, until the summer of 1782, when, in the month of August, the Indians besieged Bryant's station in great force.

Col. Todd fell at the battle of the Blue Licks, in the midst of his usefulness, and in the prime of life, leaving a wife, an only child, (and that a daughter,) about twelve months old. That daughter was born in Lexington, and is supposed to be now the eldest female ever born in that place. She is the wife of R. Wickliffe, Esq., who has still in his family the colonel's body servant—George ; who, at the advanced age of eighty-odd years, retains his health, hearing, and intelligence, perfectly. George has passed through many trying scenes, with his master and others, and often speaks with great accuracy. He assisted, he says, to build the forts at Harrodsburg, Wilson's station, and Lexington, and several times narrowly escaped with his life, when the parties he was with were attacked by the savages.

Col. Todd was a man of fine personal appearance and talents, and an accomplished gentleman ; was universally beloved, and died without a stain upon his character, and it is believed without even one enemy upon earth. From the year 1778, he might be considered as residing in Illinois, (himself,) until he married, in the year 1780. When he married, settling his family in Lexington, he was, up to the time of his death, enabled to stay but little with them. It is believed, that besides aiding in the councils held by Clark, and accompanying him in one or more of his expeditions, he passed the dangerous regions from Lexington to Kaskaskia twice (and often four times) in every year.

An anecdote, illustrative of the benevolence of his heart, was told by his widow, after his death, to his child : That, during the winter succeeding their marriage, the provisions of the fort at Lexington became exhausted to such an extent, that, on her husband's return home with George one night, almost famished with hunger, she had been able to save for him a small piece of bread, about two inches square, and about a gill of milk, which she presented to him ; on which he asked, if there was nothing for George ? She answered, not a mouthful. He called George, and handed him the bread and the milk, without taking any of it himself.

George was tendered his liberty by the daughter, on her arriving at age, and often since, but he has wisely preferred to remain with the child of his benefactor, in the state in which he left him.

TRIGG COUNTY.

TRIGG county was formed in 1820, and named in honor of Colonel STEPHEN TRIGG. It is situated in the south-west part of the State, triangular in form, and drained by the Cumberland and Tennessee rivers : bounded on the north-west and north by Caldwell ; east by Christian ; south by the State of Tennessee ; and west by Caldwell, the Tennessee river forming the division line. The Cumberland river flows through the south-west part of the county, in a direction north thirty degrees west, eight and a half miles distant from the Tennessee, and about the same general direction. Between the rivers, and on the east side of the Cumberland, for about seven miles, the surface of the country is generally broken, but not mountainous. Receding from the river and creek bottoms, the country becomes hilly or undulating. The eastern half of the county is called *barrens*, which is generally level or undulating. The soil is based on limestone, with red clay foundation. Little river is the principal tributary of the Cumberland, which flows through the county—entering on the eastern border, and taking a north-west direction, disembogues its waters in the Cumberland at the north-western extremity of the county. The bottom lands on the rivers and creeks are generally fine for farming, and the hills abound with iron ore, and timber of the best quality for charcoal—while there are fine seams of stone coal near the north-east corner of the county. Lead has been discovered. Tobacco, corn, wheat and oats are the staple products—exports, hogs, cattle, mules and horses.

Valuation of taxable property in Trigg county in 1846, $1,750,-538; number of acres of land in the county, 199,048; average value of lands per acre, $3.59; number of white males over twenty-one years of age, 1,346; number of children between five and sixteen years old, 1,777. Population in 1840, 12,353.

There are five towns in Trigg county, viz: Cadiz, Canton, Ferry Corner, Rockcastle and Wallonia.

Cadiz, the seat of justice, is situated on Little river, about two hundred and thirty miles south-west of Frankfort—and contains a court house and other county buildings, three churches, (Methodist, Baptist and Christian,) two academies, five lawyers, four physicians, nine stores, three groceries, two taverns, twelve mechanical trades, and 500 inhabitants. *Canton* is a small village, containing a Republican church, one school, two physicians, four stores, one grocery, two taverns, five or six mechanics' shops, and 200 inhabitants. *Ferry Corner* has one physician, one store, with several mechanics, and 50 inhabitants. *Rockcastle* contains a tavern, grocery, post-office and several mechanics—population 50. Derived its name from a large cave in the vicinity, somewhat resembling a castle. *Wallonia* has a physician, store, grocery, post-office, several mechanics, with a population of 75. Named after Mr. Wall, who owned the lands on which it is built.

Colonel Stephen Trigg, for whom this county received its name, was a native of Virginia. He came to Kentucky in the fall of 1779, as a member of the court of land commissioners; and in the spring of 1780, after the dissolution of that body, he determined to make the new country his permanent home. He accordingly, in the same year, settled a station at the mouth of Dick's river, and soon became noted for his activity against the Indians. He fell, two years afterwards, in the fatal and bloody battle of the Blue Licks, while bravely leading his men to the charge. Though he had been but a few years in the country, his amiable qualities had endeared him to the hearts of the people of Kentucky, and his memory is still cherished with fond veneration as one of the noblest of the early pioneers. He fell in the prime and flower of his years, and in the midst of his usefulness, mourned and regretted by the whole community. If he had lived, he would have taken rank among the most distinguished men of his time.

TRIMBLE COUNTY.

TRIMBLE county was formed in 1836, and named after the Honorable ROBERT TRIMBLE. It is situated in the northern part of the state, immediately on the Ohio river : bounded on the west and north by the Ohio river; north-east by Carroll; and south by Oldham and Henry. The territory of Trimble is small, comprising about one hundred and forty square miles. The vallies on the Ohio are unsurpassed in fertility; and the up-lands, though hilly and broken, are quite productive. Tobacco and corn are cultivated in large quantities, and wheat and oats succeed well.

Valuation of the taxable property of Trimble in 1846, $1,078,-675 ; number of acres of land in the county, 85,384 ; average value of lands per acre, $8.01 ; number of white males over twenty-one years of age, 944 ; number of children between the ages of five and sixteen years, 1,255. Population in 1840, 4,480.

The towns of Trimble county are Bedford, Milton and Palmyra. BEDFORD, the seat of justice, is situated near the centre of the county, about fifty miles from Frankfort : contains a court house and the usual public buildings ; three churches, viz: Methodist, Baptist and Christian; two schools, three lawyers, four physicians, six stores and groceries, three taverns and eight mechanics' shops : population 300. *Milton* is a small village, situated on the Ohio river, and containing two stores and groceries, post-office, &c. *Palmyra* is also a small village, with one store, post-office, &c.

The Hon. ROBERT TRIMBLE, in honor of whom this county received its name, was born in Berkeley county, Virginia, and when three years old, his father emigrated to Kentucky. His parents were not affluent, but occupied a respectable position in the agricultural population of the country. He received but the imperfect rudiments of an education,—such only as could be had in a new settlement, so distant from the seats of learning in the older States. He, however, improved himself, by teaching for a few years, and reading carefully the scanty libraries afforded by his neighborhood. After so imperfect a probation, he commenced the study of the law, under George Nicholas. That eminent man dying before he had completed his studies, he continued them under James Brown; and, in 1803, was licensed by the court of appeals to practice his profession. He commenced his career in Paris, and in the same year was elected a member of the legislature from the county of Bourbon. But the stormy life of a politician not being congenial to his disposition or taste, he ever afterwards refused to be a candidate for political office—even to be nominated, on two occasions, for the United States' senate, when his assent only was necessary to secure his election. He devoted himself exclusively to his profession, and rapidly rose to the first class of jurists. In 1808, he was commissioned second judge of the court of appeals. He retained this place but a short time, but long enough to greatly distinguish himself in it by his rectitude, learning and ability. He was appointed chief justice of Kentucky in 1810, but, in consequence of his limited circumstances, declined the first judicial station in the commonwealth. After retiring from the bench, he resumed, with great assiduity, the practice of his profession ; and, in 1813, was appointed a district attorney for the State. He continued at the bar, with eminent and profitable success, until 1816, when he was appointed by President Madison judge of the Kentucky district. He filled this office until 1826, when he was promoted by John Quincy Adams to the supreme court of the United States. He died the 25th day of August, 1828, in the fifty-second year of his age, and in the full vigor of his powers.

It is not often that the august tribunal to which he belonged, has sustained a greater loss. His mind was characterized by deliberation, clearness, expansion and force. As a forensic debater, he combined flowing eloquence and powerful argumentation. He studied law upon principle, and comprehended it as a science. Such was his ripe though early proficiency, that, in the year 1818, the sole professorship of law for Transylvania University was tendered to him by the board of trustees, and his acceptance earnestly urged upon him by Mr. Clay. A necessary change of residence induced him to decline a place so honorable and responsible.

As a judge of the highest State court, he had no superior in diligence, learning, ability and uprightness; and on being transferred to the supreme tribunal of the nation, both Chief Justice Marshall and Judge Story pronounced him to be not only a lawyer of the first order, but also one of the most improvable men they had ever known. Had Providence spared his life to ordinary old age, he would have fully vindicated his title to rank with those great jurists. But his private virtues, and his simple, noble nature, shed a lustre upon his name above all that which was derived from great intellect, ripe attainments, and high station. It was these which made all who knew him friends through his life, and mourners upon his death.

UNION COUNTY.

Union county was organized in 1811, and so called in consequence of being formed from other counties, all agreeing, with perfect unanimity, upon the boundary lines of the new county. It is situated on the Ohio river, which forms its western, and a part of its northern boundary; Henderson forming the north-eastern, Hopkins the south-eastern, and Christian the south-western boundary. Besides the Ohio, this county is drained by Tradewater and Highland creeks, and their tributaries—the first forming the south-western, and the latter the north-eastern border. The face of the country, like most of the river counties, is diversified: level, undulating, and hilly. The soil is good. Corn is the staple product of the county—but oats, rye, wheat, tobacco, hemp, hay and clover, are cultivated, and sweet potatoes grow finely. Horses, mules, cattle, sheep and hogs, are exported.

Valuation of taxable property in Union in 1846, $1,467,091; number of acres of land in the county, 205,442; average value of lands per acre, $3.53; number of white males over twenty-one years of age, 1,189; number of children between five and sixteen years old, 1,339. Population in 1840, 6,673.

The towns of Union county consist of Morganfield, Caseyville, Raleigh and Uniontown. Morganfield is the seat of justice, situated near the centre of the county, and about two hundred and five miles from Frankfort: contains two churches, (Methodist and Presbyterian,) two academies, one common school, seven lawyers, seven physicians, six stores, one grocery, two taverns, and sixteen mechanics' shops. Population about 400. Incorporated in 1812, and named after Gen. Morgan, of the revolutionary army. Caseyville is a small town, situated on the Ohio river, fifteen miles from Morganfield, containing one lawyer, two physicians, three stores, one grocery, one tavern, one school, and six mechanics' shops. This town has an abundant supply of stone coal in its immediate vicinity. *Raleigh* is a very small village, also situated on the Ohio river, nine miles west of Morganfield; has one store and tavern. *Uniontown* lies on the Ohio river, seven miles northwest of Morganfield, and contains three physicians, four stores, one grocery, one tavern, and six mechanics' shops. Derived its name from the *union* of two small villages.

The county of Union abounds in mineral springs. One of these,—a fine white sulphur spring,—five miles from Morganfield, has been handsomely improved, and has become quite a popular and fashionable watering place. The other springs which possess any notoriety, contain chalybeate water of fine quality.

About eight miles from Morganfield, there is a large, flat *rock*, with a number of deeply indented and perfectly distinct impressions of the naked foot of human beings, of all sizes, together with very plain footprints of the dog. About three miles from Caseyville, there is a rock, called the "*Anvil Rock*," which closely resembles a blacksmith's anvil. It is about fifty feet high, twenty feet in width, and two feet thick, with a projection or spur like the horn of an anvil. This rock stands upon level bottom land, entirely isolated; and by what process it was placed there, in an erect position, must forever remain a mystery. There is also a *hill*, in the centre of an extended river bottom or plain, which is about three-fourths of a mile long, half a mile wide, and from eighty to one hundred feet in height. There is, likewise, a *cave* in the county, which is believed to be of great extent, but heretofore very partially explored. In this cave a number of human bones have been found. A few miles from Uniontown, on Highland creek, there is a *tar* or *American oil spring*, from which tar or oil constantly flows, in considerable quantities.

WARREN COUNTY.

Warren county was formed in 1796, and named in memory of General Joseph Warren, who fell at Bunker Hill. It embraces about five hundred and sixty square miles; and is bounded on the north by Butler and Edmonson; east by Barren; south by Allen and Simpson; and west by Logan and Butler. Big Barren river, which heads near the Cumberland, runs through this county. Its tributaries, in the county, are, Bay's fork, Drake's and Jennings' creeks, and Gasper river. Several mineral springs in the county —one, three miles from Bowling-Green, (Mr. Jackson's,) in character of its water, much like the Blue Lick. Face of the country gently undulating. Soil fertile and productive, based mostly on red clay and limestone foundation. Principal articles of export, tobacco, wheat, corn and pork.

Valuation of taxable property in Warren in 1846, $3,918,312; number of acres of land in the county, 292,588; average value of land per acre, $5.39; number of white males over twenty-one years of age, 2,083; number of children between five and sixteen years old, 2,831. Population in 1840, 15,446.

Bowling-Green, the county seat of Warren, is a neat and thriving town, situated at the head of slack water navigation on Big Barren river, one hundred and forty-five miles from Frankfort, and six hundred and eighty-five miles from Washington city. Several steamboats make their weekly arrivals here from Louisville and elsewhere; the turnpike from Louisville to Nashville passes through it; and the Bowling-Green portage rail road from the river, terminates here. Besides the ordinary county buildings, there are four church edifices, Presbyterian, Baptist, Methodist, and Episcopalian. The court-house, on the public square, is handsomely enclosed with a neat stone wall, ornamented by iron railing. It contains also, a branch of the Bank of Kentucky, two newspapers, (the *Bowling-Green Press* and the *Bowling-Green Argus,*) fifteen lawyers, eight physicians, five schools, twenty-four stores, two wholesale groceries and commission warehouses, one drug store, one foundry, one candle factory, one wool factory, two steam saw mills, three taverns, and thirty or forty mechanics' shops. Population 1700. Established by the legislature in 1808.

Ancient Marks on Trees.—On the north side of Barren river, about three miles from Bowling-Green, and about a quarter of a mile above Vanmeter's ferry, there are some beech trees which indicate the camping ground of a party, perhaps the " Long Hunters," as they were called, in June, 1775. The most conspicuous tree has engraven on its bark, on the north side, the names of thirteen persons. The letters were handsomely cut with some instrument adapted to the purpose. The highest name is about nine feet from the ground, the lowest four feet. They stand in the following order, beginning with the uppermost and descending to the lowest, to wit: J. Newell or Neaville,* E. Bulger. I. Hite, V. Harman, J. Jackman, W. Buchannon, A. Bowman, J. Drake, N. Nall, H. Skaggs, J. Bowman, Tho. Slaughter, J. Todd. The date is thus given: "1775, June Th 13." The apparent age of the marks corresponds with the date. About five steps south of the above named tree, and near the verge of the river bank, stands a beech, marked on the north side with the name of "Wm. Buchanan," and dated "June 14th, 1775." On the south side of the same tree, there is the name of "J. Todd," dated "June 17, 1775." About twenty steps north of the first tree, there stands a third beech, with the names of I. Drake, and Isaac Hite engraved, and each with the date "15 June, 1775." Above the names the date "June 23, 1775." The names and dates on this tree seem to be as old as any, but made with a different instrument from that which cut the names on the first tree, and they are not so well executed. These dates from the 13th to the 23d, prove that the party encamped at that place ten days. About fifty yards up the river from the first named tree, there stands a beech with a name now illegible, cut in the bark over the date 1779. On the same tree, the name of H. Lynch is carved over the date 1796.

Where are now those pioneers? They have ceased to follow the deer, the elk, the bear, the buffalo and beaver, which were then abundant in this region; and their children are hunters no more. The animals which their fathers pursued, have become extinct. The wilderness they traversed, now blooms with the arts and refinements of civilized life.

Caves are very numerous in this county. Some of them would be regarded as considerable curiosities, if there were no mammoth cave. About six miles northeast of Bowling-Green, there is a cave with a perpendicular descent from the north of about thirty or forty feet. At the bottom are vast quantities of human bones. How and when they were put there, can of course only be conjectured. About three miles south of Bowling-Green, and on the turnpike to Nashville, is the Cave Mill, in level barrens. A creek breaks up from the ground, runs about two hundred yards, then disappears in the cave; and, after a course under ground of a mile and a half, again appears, and runs into Barren river. Immediately under the roof of the cave, Mr. Shanks has a water grist mill and wool-carding ma-

---

* Judge Graham supposed it to be Neaville.

chine, with no covering but the rocky arch above. Directly over the mill, and within a few feet of the precipice, runs the turnpike over which thousands pass, many of them unconscious of the deep chasm beneath.

MOUNDS.—There are very many in this county, mostly near watercourses—some of them quite large. They all contain human bones. In one of them was found a smooth, circular, well polished flint, near two inches broad, three-fourths of an inch thick, and weighing one-fourth of a pound, apparently made as a four-ounce weight. On the north bank of the river, near Bowling-Green, are a great many ancient graves,—some of them with a row of stones set on edge around them. These graves, with a large mound on which large trees are growing, are included within the remains of an old fort, built of earth. Some ancient relics were found here in 1838, and are now in the possession of Lloyd Berry, Esq. One of these is in the shape of a bowl, hollow, and composed of earth and pounded shells; and seems to have been burnt or dried in the sun. Its color is dark. The other two are composed of the same materials, but of lighter color, and in the shape of flat-bottomed candlesticks, the stem being shorter and solid; the upper surface of the bottom slightly concave; the under surface convex, and about half an inch in thickness.

On the south bank of Greene river, about twelve miles from Bowling-Green, is an old fort, situated on a hill or bluff, inaccessible save on the south-west corner. The remainder of the hill is level on top, with perpendicular, or, rather, overhanging cliff or bluff, about thirty feet high. Near the centre, lengthwise, of this hill, is an old fort, which seems to have been erected with stone and earth. The walls are now about one foot high.

The annexed is a rough sketch of the hill and fort. One of the projections

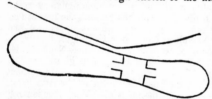

from the fort is twenty feet, the other thirty feet in length—each fifteen feet wide. The area of the fort seven acres. There is nothing to indicate who were its tenants, nor when it was erected. From it, to the distance of more than a mile, there is a line of mounds, diminishing in size as they recede from the fort, perhaps showing a running fight, and the most bloody contest nearest the fort. There are other ancient works in the county, which have not been examined.

Eight miles east of Bowling-Green, there is in the level open barrens, a large deep sink, about fifty yards wide, and a hundred yards in length. On the south side, the descent is near twenty feet; on the north, it is one hundred and fifty feet deep. Large river trees are growing in it. Shortly after the first settlement here, a blind horse fell in this sink. A hungry wolf had the folly to jump in after its prey, and being unable to get out, was found and shot. Since that time it has been known by the name of the "*Wolf Sink*."

Four miles above Bowling-Green, on the river, is McFadin's old station. Some anecdotes are connected with it, one of which we relate: A dashing young Virginian came to the station, and began his brag that he could outrun any man "in all Kaintuck." McFadin, who was a quizzical old genius, inquired whether he would run barefooted or shod, and was promptly answered "barefoot." Let me fix time and place, said McFadin, and I will risk a gallon of whisky I find a man to beat you. The bet was made and the day fixed. The old hunter Raymer was sent for. The parties repaired to the track selected by McFadin. It was probably the most flinty bed in all the country. At the word the racers started. They had gone but a few yards when the Virginian was compelled to hold up. But as Raymer's feet were hard as a buffalo's, he kept ahead like a quarter horse, to the great amusement of old McFadin and his friends. That ground has since been called "*Raymer's Race Track*."

JOSEPH ROGERS UNDERWOOD was born in Goochland county, Virginia, on the 24th of October, 1791. He was the eldest child of John Underwood, who for many years represented that county in the legislature, during those periods in the history of that State when political honors were rarely bestowed but as the reward of personal merit. His mother, Frances Rogers, was a daughter of George Rogers, of Caroline county, Va., a gentleman eminently distinguished for the purity of his life and the integrity of his character.

The parents of young Underwood being in humble circumstances, and having a large family of other children to provide for, were induced to commit him to his maternal uncle, Mr. Edward Rogers, a soldier of the revolution, who had emigrated to Kentucky as early as 1783. He brought his youthful charge to Barren county in the spring of 1803, and nobly did he fulfil the promises made to the parents of the little boy, " to be unto him as a father."

The Greene river country was then a wilderness, and contained but few schools, and those not of the best class. Joseph was placed at school with the Rev. John Howe, near Glasgow. About a year thereafter he was placed under the tuition of the Rev. Samuel Findley at Danville, and afterwards at Lancaster, and after that with McMurrel, who taught a French and Latin school at Glasgow. Having under these several teachers acquired the rudiments of his education, he was sent by his parental uncle to the Transylvania University, at which, in 1811, he finished it.

On leaving the university he commenced the study of the law in Lexington, with Robert Wickliffe, Esq., and under the instructions of this learned and accomplished lawyer, he completed his course of elementary reading.

About this time Kentucky was thrown into great excitement by the war with Great Britain, then raging with violence on the Canada border. The melancholy affair of the river Raisin had deprived the state of some of its best citizens, and plunged the commonwealth in mourning. The impulse to arms was universal, and pervaded all classes. In March, 1813, a company of volunteers being about to be raised in Lexington, to be commanded by Captain John C. Morrison, and attached to the regiment of Colonel William Dudley, young Underwood was the first to volunteer on that occasion, and seizing the colors, marched alone with the musicians down the ranks of the assembled citizens. This little incident caused him to be elected lieutenant. He proceeded with the regiment to which he belonged to join the northern army, commanded by General Harrison. He was in Dudley's defeat on the 5th of May, 1813, when the captain of his company being killed, the command devolved on Lieutenant Underwood. The remnant of Dudley's regiment were compelled to surrender as prisoners of war. Lieutenant Underwood after being badly wounded, and the ball still remaining in the wound, was stripped of his clothing and compelled to run the gauntlet. He and his comrades were thrown into the old fort built by General Wayne on the left bank of the river, and forced to sit down in the mud and water, and whilst thus confined, the infuriated savages stalked round upon the embankment that overlooked them, and singled out and shot down their victims. In the meantime, an angry controversy arose among the Indians themselves, whether they should make one general slaughter of all the prisoners or not. It was a moment of intense and terrible interest to the poor soldiers who were within hearing of it, helplessly awaiting the issue. Mercy, however, prevailed, and their lives were spared. Lieutenant Underwood was finally released on his parol, and returned home to his uncle in the summer of 1813.

In the fall of 1813, Mr. Underwood obtained license to practice law, and settled in Glasgow. He rose rapidly, and soon stood in the first rank of his profession.

In 1816 he was elected to represent Barren county in the legislature; and continued to represent that county in the same body, for four successive years. In March, 1817, he married Miss Eliza M. Trotter, daughter of Mr. John Trotter, of Glasgow; and grand-daughter, on her mother's side, of the Rev. David Rice. This lady died in July, 1835.

Mr. Underwood having removed, in the year 1823, to Bowling-Green, was elected, in 1825, to represent the county of Warren in the legislature. He served two years in that body with great distinction and eminent usefulness, and then retired to private life and the practice of his profession. In 1828 he was a candidate for lieutenant-governor, but the vote resulted in the election of Mr. Breathitt. In the same year he was commissioned as a judge of the court of appeals; which office he held until February, 1835, when he resigned, and was elected to Congress. He continued, with high reputation, to serve as a member of Congress until 1843, when he again retired to private life. In August, 1845, he was elected, by a very large majority, to represent the county of Warren in the legislature, and was made speaker of the house of representatives. At the session of the legislature of 1846–7, he was elected by that body to succeed the Hon. James T. Morehead as senator in the Congress of the United States from Kentucky.

In his politics, Mr. Underwood has always been a firm and consistent whig. In 1824, and again in 1844, he was one of the presidential electors of the State, and both times cast his vote for Henry Clay. As a lawyer, Judge Underwood has few superiors in the State; his decisions, while on the bench of the court of appeals, being distinguished for their soundness and general equity. On the whole, it may be said that he stands deservedly conspicuous among the distinguished men of Kentucky. Learned as a jurist, experienced as a statesman, an ardent patriot, he is qualified to adorn any station to which the partiality of his countrymen may elevate him.

Gen. JOSEPH WARREN, in memory of whom this county was named, was a distinguished patriot, and was one of the earliest of those who sealed with their blood the charter of their country's liberties. He was born at Roxbury, near Boston, in 1741. His father was a respectable farmer. Joseph entered Harvard University in 1755, being then fourteen years of age, and there established a character for talents, address, a generous, bold, and independent spirit, which his subsequent life only confirmed and rendered more striking. On leaving college, he studied medicine under the instruction of Dr. Loyd, an eminent physician of that day; and, upon the completion of his studies, commenced the practice. His affable manners, handsome person, and thorough skill in his profession, soon rendered him a general favorite; and his success was rapid and complete. Possessing fine talents as an orator and writer, he soon became prominent as a politician and public speaker; and, on two occasions, was appointed to deliver orations on the 5th of March—the anniversary of the Boston massacre. In that brilliant constellation of talent which then gave the New England States an enviable intellectual prominence in the colonies, Dr. Warren was a star of the first magnitude. An ardent patriot, he was foremost among those who took measures to arouse the country to resistance, against the aggressions of the mother country. On the 18th of April, 1775, discovering the design of the British commander to seize our public stores at Concord, he instantly dispatched faithful messengers, who removed everything except three old cannon, a few gun-carriages, and sixty barrels of flour: these the British soldiery destroyed. He participated in the battle of Lexington, where, while pressing on the enemy with daring impetuosity, he had a lock of hair, close to his ear, shot away by a musket ball. He was the president of the provincial congress of Massachusetts, of 1775; and, on the 14th day of June, was appointed, by that body, major-general of the military force of the province. When congress adjourned, he rode to the camp; and, mingling familiarly with the soldiers, infused into them his own undaunted spirit. In the memorable battle of the 17th of June, on Bunker Hill, when their ammunition was expended, the Americans, after having thrice repulsed the charge of the British regulars, were compelled to retire. Gen. Warren was one of the last to leave the entrenchments, and had proceeded from the works but a few steps, when he was struck by a random shot, and instantly expired. Congress passed a resolution to erect a monument to his memory, which long occupied the site of the present Bunker Hill monument.

WASHINGTON COUNTY.

WASHINGTON county was formed in 1792, and named in honor of the father of his country, Gen. GEORGE WASHINGTON. It is situated near the centre of the State, and is drained by Salt river:

bounded on the north by Anderson ; east by Mercer ; south by Marion : west and north-west by Nelson. The face of the country is undulating—the soil rich and fertile. Staple products, hemp, wheat and corn ; exports, beef, pork, hemp and whisky.

Valuation of taxable property in Washington in 1846, $2,832,-853 ; number of acres of land in the county, 188,367 ; average value of land per acre, $7.55 ; number of white males over twenty-one years of age, 1,653 ; number of children between the ages of five and sixteen years, 2,261. Population in 1840, 10,596.

The towns of Washington county are Springfield, Maxville, and Fredericktown. SPRINGFIELD, the seat of justice, is about forty miles from Frankfort. It contains a large brick court-house and other county buildings, three churches, (Methodist, Presbyterian and Catholic,) twelve lawyers, six physicians, ten stores, three groceries, and twelve mechanics' shops. Population, 700. Incorporated in 1793, and took its name from a spring in the bounds of the town. *Maxville* has two physicians, four stores, six mechanics' shops, post-office, and 320 inhabitants. *Fredericktown* is eight miles from Springfield, on the Beech fork of Salt river, and contains a physician, tavern, carding machine, manufacturing mill, several mechanics' shops, with a population of 60. Established in 1818.

In the year 1776, James Sodowsky, or Sandusky, removed from Virginia to Washington county, and built Sandusky's station, on Pleasant run. On the breaking up of Harrod's settlement, in 1774, Jacob Sandusky, a brother of James, and connected with Harrod's settlement, traveled to Cumberland river ; there procured a canoe, descended the Cumberland, Ohio and Mississippi rivers, to New Orleans ; from thence he took shipping, and went round to Virginia, via Baltimore. He is believed to have been the first white man that ever descended those rivers, except French or Spanish. Shortly after, he returned to Kentucky, and settled with James, at Sandusky's station. From this station the brothers removed, in 1785, to Jessamine county. Jacob died in Jessamine, and James in Bourbon county. The nephews of Jacob state that he kept very full notes of the settlement of the country, and often pronounced the published histories to be incorrect in many particulars.

The following account of the adventures of John Lancaster, in 1788, we copy from " Early Sketches of Catholic Missions in Kentucky," by the Rev. M. J. Spalding, D. D. :

" John Lancaster was descending the Ohio river in a flat boat, bound from Maysville to Louisville. His companions on the boat were Col. Joseph Mitchell and son, and Alexander Brown. When they had reached the mouth of the Miami river, on the 8th of May, 1788, the boatmen discovered a large party of Indians lying in wait for them. They did not make this fearful discovery until they were very near the party ; and unfortunately the current bore the boat directly towards them. Escape was hopeless. The savages displayed a white flag, in token of friendship : but at the same time leveled their muskets at the man who was at the oar, and would have shot him down, had not the chief interposed. This man was called Captain Jim, or *Shawnese* Jim, and he spoke a little broken English, which he had probably learned at some of the British military posts in the north-west. He assured the white men that his people meant them no harm, and that they merely wished to trade with them.

" Meantime, a skiff, manned by four Indians, was seen to put off from the shore, and was rowed rapidly towards the boat, which it struck with so much violence as to upset the skiff, and to precipitate three of the Indians into the river. John Lancaster here showed great presence of mind, by leaping promptly into the river, and aiding the struggling Indians in their efforts to escape from a watery grave. He succeeded, and had reason to hope that he had done much to conciliate their good will—a hope which the event did not, however, justify. On entering the boat, the Indians seized on the white men, and made them prisoners, two of them struggling violently for the possession of Mr. Lancaster. Some time after they had reached the shore, these same two savages came to blows, and had a desperate fight on the same ground of quarrel, when Captain Jim interposed, and decided in favor of the first who had seized the person of the captive.

"The boat was soon rowed to the shore and robbed of all its effects. The Indians then decamped with the booty, and the four prisoners whom they had taken. The first night was devoted to revelry and drunkenness; the savages having carried with them the whisky with which the boat was partly laden. The prisoners were bound down on their backs to the earth, with cords which were passed around their limbs and bodies, and tied closely to stakes driven in the ground. During the whole night, the rain poured down in torrents, on their faces and bodies; while their only covering was a blanket, their Indian captors having already stripped them of their clothing and money. They passed a sleepless night, witnessing the wild revelry of the Indians, and musing sorrowfully on the dreadful fate which probably awaited them on the morrow.

"On the next morning they were released from their confinement, and were hurried on towards the Indian village in the interior, which Mr. Lancaster estimates was about sixty-five miles from the mouth of the Miami, and twenty-five miles lower down the Ohio river. After they had reached their encampment, which was probably one of the Shawnese towns, they were made to witness new scenes of stirring interest. While the captives were gloomily meditating on their probable doom to the stake, the Indian master of John Lancaster suddenly came up to him, and embraced him, shedding tears, and exclaiming, amidst sobs and lamentations that 'he was his brother, who should take the place of one who had been slain during the previous year!' Immediately the Indian ceremony of adoption took place. Mr. Lancaster was stripped of his blanket, and had his body greased with bear's oil, and painted of a vermilion color. He was then taught some scraps of Indian song, and was made to join in the savage festival which ensued. This consisted of songs and the war-dance, one Indian beating time with a stick, the head of which was curiously wrought and trimmed with the hoofs of deer. After the performance of this singular ceremony, he was viewed as having been regularly adopted into the Indian tribe.

"Mr. Lancaster continued a captive in the Indian camp for eight days, during which he made great proficiency in the knowledge of Indian manners and customs. He was called *Kiohba*, or the *Running Buck*, from his remarkable activity and fleetness of foot. He was placed on an equal footing with the Indians, and his new brother treated him with great kindness. After some days, however, this foster brother was sent off from the camp, and then he experienced rougher treatment. Captain Jim, under whose charge he was now left, became sullen and vindictive. He quarreled with his wife, who, fearing his vengeance, fled from the camp. Jim immediately pursued her, threatening vengeance, and was soon perceived returning to the camp, after having, in all probability, been her murderer. As he was returning, his daughter, who was well acquainted with her father's moods, and who had entertained a partiality for *Kiohba*, said to the latter: *puck-e-te—run!* He took her advice, and instantly darted from the camp.

"On casting a glance backward, from a neighboring eminence, he perceived Captain Jim beating the elder Mitchell with a tent pole. After his final escape from the Indians, he learned that, soon after his departure, young Mitchell was painted black and burned at the stake; but that his father and Alexander Brown, after suffering almost incredible hardships and privations, were finally ransomed by their friends, and returned to Pittsburgh.

"John Lancaster was soon out of sight of the Indian encampment. He took the direction of the Ohio river, but ran in different directions, and crossed repeatedly the various Indian trails, in order the more easily to elude pursuit. He was particularly fearful of about fifty Indian dogs, who had been trained to following the footsteps of man. He was, however, fortunate enough to escape all these multiplied dangers; and after running for six days, during which his only subsistence was four turkey eggs, which he had found in the hollow of a fallen tree, he safely reached the Ohio river. Exhausted as he was, he immediately tied himself with bark to the trunk of a box-elder tree, and after four hours' unremitting toil, succeeded in crossing to the Kentucky side. While crossing he had swallowed much water; and he now perceived that his strength had almost entirely failed.

"After resting a short time, he determined to float down the river, to the station at the Falls, which he estimated was between twenty and thirty miles distant. Accordingly, he made a small raft, by tying two trees together with bark, on which he placed himself, with a pole for an oar. When a little above Eighteen Mile Island, he heard the sharp report of a rifle, when, thinking that his pursuers had overtaken him, he crouched down on his little raft, and concealed himself as best he could. Hearing no other noise, however, he concluded that his alarm was without foundation. But shortly after, a dreadful storm broke upon the river; night had already closed in, and he sank exhausted and almost lifeless on his treacherous raft, drenched with the rain, benumbed with cold, and with the terrible apprehension on his mind, that he might be precipitated over the Falls during the night.

"At break of day, he was aroused from his death-like lethargy, by one of the most cheering sounds that ever fell on the ears of a forlorn and lost wanderer— the crowing of a cock,—which announced the immediate vicinity of a white settlement. The sound revived him; he collected all his energies for one last effort, and sat upright on his little raft. Soon, in the gray light of the morning, he discovered the cabins of his countrymen, and was enabled to effect a landing at the mouth of Beargrass—the site of the present city of Louisville. He immediately rejoined his friends, and their warm welcome soon made him forget all his past sufferings. He lived for many years to recount his adventures; and died a few years ago of a good old age, surrounded by his children and his children's children."

JOHN POPE, a distinguished politician and statesman, was for many years a resident of this county, where he died in 1842. He was a native of Prince William county, Virginia, where he was born about the year 1770, but emigrated to Kentucky while quite a boy. In early life he had the misfortune to lose his arm, from a severe wound received while attending a cornstalk mill. Owing to this accident, he was induced to turn his attention to the profession of the law, and being a man of great native vigor of intellect, soon attained eminence. He first settled in Shelby county, but afterwards removed to Lexington. He was frequently a member of the legislature, in which body his great talents rendered him eminently conspicuous and influential. In 1807, he was elected to the senate of the United States, and was for many years a distinguished member of the house of representatives. In 1829 he was appointed governor of the territory of Arkansas, which office he held for six years. He died at his residence in Washington county, in the year 1842. In early life, Mr. Pope belonged to the federal party; but in after years attached himself to that party which has assumed to itself the name of democratic, and of which General Jackson was the founder.

The late Honorable FELIX GRUNDY, of Tennessee, was also for some years a citizen of this county, to which he was brought by his parents from Virginia, in his early boyhood. He was a native of Berkely county, Va., where he was born in September, 1777. Mr. Grundy was for many years a distinguished member of the Kentucky legislature, and while he remained a citizen of the State, was appointed chief justice of the court of appeals. In 1808 he removed to Tennessee, and was subsequently a member of Congress from that State. He represented the State of Tennessee in the Senate of the United States for many years, and during the administration of Mr. Van Buren, was appointed attorney general of the United States.

Mr. Grundy was one of the most distinguished lawyers and statesmen of the western country. When in the councils of the nation he had but few superiors. His politics were democratic, of which party he was always a most zealous and efficient supporter.

Another distinguished citizen of Washington county was General MARTIN D. HARDIN, the son of Colonel John Hardin. He was a lawyer of great eminence, and practiced his profession in Frankfort with distinguished success. He was a man of marked talent and very decided character, as were indeed all the members of this family. He was secretary of state under Governor Shelby, and in 1817 was appointed by Governor Slaughter to the senate of the United States, in which body he served one session. He was a major in the rifle regiment of Colonel John Allen, in the campaign on the northern border during the last war with Great Britain, in which situation he approved himself a brave, vigilant and efficient officer. General Hardin died at Frankfort in the fall of 1823. He was the father of the late Colonel John J. Hardin, of Illinois, who fell in the battle of Buena Vista in Mexico.

Washington county derived its name from General GEORGE WASHINGTON, commander-in-chief of the American armies during the war of the revolution, and first president of the United States under the federal constitution. Any narrative of his life is almost superfluous; for what citizen of the republic has it not engraven upon his heart? A patriot without blemish, a statesman without guile, a leader of armies without ambition, a magistrate without severity, yet inflexible in uprightness, a citizen exemplary in the discharge of every duty, a man in whose character weakness and faults appeared but as specks on the brightness of the sun—who had religion without austerity, dignity without pride, modesty without diffidence, courage without rashness, politeness without affectation, affability without familiarity:—such was the man whose memory the great and the good of all nations have delighted to honor.

WAYNE COUNTY.

WAYNE county was formed in the year 1800, and named after General ANTHONY WAYNE. It is watered by the Cumberland river and its tributaries, the south fork passing entirely through the county from the south in a direction a little west of north: bounded on the north by the Cumberland river, which separates it from Pulaski county; east by Whitley; south by the State of Tennessee; and west by Clinton and Russell. The surface of the county is somewhat broken with hills, but the valley lands are fertile and productive—the soil very generally based upon limestone. The county abounds with stone coal; and on the Big South fork of the Cumberland, there is a continuous strata or seam of coal upwards of thirty miles in length. There is, also, an abundance of iron ore and salt water of a rich quality. Numerous small caves are found, in which there are large quantities of alum and salt petre, and some marine petrifactions have been discovered. The principal exports of the county are, horses, mules, cattle and hogs.

Valuation of the taxable property of Wayne in 1846, $1,214,-579; number of acres of land in the county, 198,853; average value of lands per acre, $3.02; number of white males over twenty-one years of age, 1,335; number of children between the ages of five and sixteen years, 2,406. Population in 1840, 15,446.

MONTICELLO, the seat of justice and only town of Wayne county, is ninety miles south of Frankfort. It contains a brick court house and other county buildings; two churches, Methodist and Christian; five lawyers, four physicians, six stores, three groceries, two tanyards and ten mechanics' shops. Population 300. Established in 1810, and named after President Jefferson's residence.

General ANTHONY WAYNE, in honor of whom this county was named, was a distinguished officer in the United States' service, and was born in Chester county, Pennsylvania, January 1st, 1745. He received a good education, and after leaving school at the age of eighteen, took up the business of surveying, in which he acquired great reputation and success. He was one of the provincial deputies who early in 1774 were chosen by the different counties of Pennsylvania to take into consideration the state of affairs with Great Britain; and a member of the convention which shortly after assembled at Philadelphia. In the same year he was elected to the legislature, and in 1775 appointed a member of the committee of safety. In September of this year he raised a company of volunteers, and in the ensuing January, was appointed by Congress, colonel of one of the Pennsylvania regiments, and at the opening of the campaign received orders to join the army under General Lee at New York. In 1777 he was promoted to the rank of brigadier general. In the battle of Brandywine he commanded a division stationed at Chad's ford, to resist the passage of Knyphausen. He maintained the contest until near sunset, when he was compelled to retreat. He was in the battle of Germantown, where he evinced his wonted valor; he was also present at the battle of Monmouth. In July, 1779, he stormed the strong fortress of Stony Point by a night assault. He was present at Yorktown, and witnessed the surrender of Lord Cornwallis. He was subsequently sent to the south, where he remained until the conclusion of peace. In 1789 he was a member of the Pennsylvania convention and an advocate of the constitution of the United States. In 1792, he was appointed by Washington, successor to General St. Clair in the command of the army engaged against the Indians on the western frontier. It was at first supposed that his ardor would render him an unfit opponent of a foe remarkable for caution. He soon, however, proved the incorrectness of this idea. He established admirable discipline among his troops, and by his wise and prudent measures in preparing for an engagement, and the skill and bravery with which he fought and gained the battle of August 20th, 1794, near the river Miami of the lakes, he brought the war to a completely successful termination. In 1795, he concluded a definite treaty of peace with the Indians. He died in December, 1796.

WHITLEY COUNTY.

WHITLEY county was formed in 1818, and named in honor of Col. WILLIAM WHITLEY. It is situated in the south-east section of the State, and is drained by the Cumberland river and its tributaries. This river penetrates the county on the north-eastern border, and meanders in a general western course to within a few miles of its western border, when it makes a bend, and runs directly north, to near the northern border; here it again makes a sudden bend, and flows out of the county on the north-western border: bounded on the north by Laurel; on the east by Knox; on the south by the State of Tennessee; and on the west by Wayne. The face of the country, except the river valleys, is hilly and broken, two spurs of the Cumberland mountain penetrating the south-eastern corner to within a short distance of Williamsburg, on the Cumberland river. Corn is the staple product, and hogs the principal export of the county.

The falls of the Cumberland river, in Whitley county, about fourteen miles below Williamsburg, are among the most remarkable objects in the State. The river here is precipitated over a sheer fall of sixty-three feet, perpendicular. On a clear morning, the roar of the waters may be heard for a distance of ten or twelve miles above and below the falls. Immediately behind the falling sheet of water, there is a considerable cave in the surface of the rock; and a person can go almost across the river by this passage, through an arch formed on one side by the rock, and on the other by the flashing waters. Just below the falls, large fish are to be caught in great numbers. The country, for six or eight miles above and below the falls, is very irregular, and presents to the eye of the traveler a succession of scenery as romantic and picturesque as any to be found in the State. The hills and mountains rise upon each other, like clouds upon the horizon.

Valuation of the taxable property of Whitley in 1846, $388,-332; number of acres of land in the county, 167,967; average value of land per acre, $1.42; number of white males over twenty-one years of age, 877; number of children between five and sixteen years old, 1,435. Population in 1840, 6,673.

WILLIAMSBURG, the seat of justice of Whitley county, is situated on the right bank of the Cumberland river, about one hundred miles from Frankfort, and contains a Methodist church, two lawyers, four stores and groceries, one tavern, and several mechanics' shops. Population, 75. *Boston* is a very small village, containing a Baptist church, a store, post-office, &c. Population, 30.

In October, 1786, a large number of families, traveling by land to Kentucky, known by the name of McKnitt's company, were surprised in their camp at night, between the Big and Little Laurel rivers, by a party of Indians, and totally defeated, with the loss of twenty-one persons killed, and the rest dispersed or made prisoners.

Shortly before settlements were formed in what is now Whitley county, John Tye, his son, and some two or three other men, having encamped on the head of Big Poplar creek, were attacked after night by a party of Cherokee Indians. Tye's son was killed, and the old man wounded. The other men fled after the first fire of the Indians, and made their escape. The Indians rushed upon the camp, and two of them entered it, but were immediately met by two large cur dogs, which defended the wounded sire and the dead son with a fearlessness and bravery which would have done credit to animals of a higher order. In this conflict, one of the Indians was very severely wounded; and, as soon as he extricated himself from the jaws of the enraged dogs, the party precipitately fled, leaving their moccasins and leggings on the opposite side of the creek, where they had left them in order to ford the stream.

In the early settlement of the county, Joseph Johnson was killed by three Cherokees, on Lynn camp. They entered his house in the dusk of the evening, when there was no men about it but himself, and killed him with their tomahawks and knives. His wife was out milking the cows at the time, and was ignorant of what was passing within until she reached the door of the cabin, when she beheld her prostrate and bleeding husband in the agonies of death, and the Indians standing over and around him, inflicting additional wounds upon the now unconscious body. The savages discovered her almost at the instant she reached the door, and one of them sprang at her with his tomahawk. She dropped her milk pail, and precipitately fled in the direction of the house of the elder Johnson, about a hundred and fifty yards off, the Indian in full chase. Mrs. Johnson was a remarkably stout, active young woman, and the race was one for life. Getting a few yards the start of the savage, she maintained the relative distance between them, until she reached the yard fence of the old gentleman; and as with one bound she cleared the obstruction, the savage made an unsuccessful thrust at her head, gave a yell of disappointment, and instantly retreated.

WILLIAM WHITLEY, from whom this county received its name, was one of the most distinguished of those early pioneers, whose adventurous exploits have shed a coloring of romance over the early history of Kentucky. He was born on the 14th of August, 1749, in that part of Virginia then called Augusta, and which afterwards furnished territory for Rockbridge county. Unknown to early fame, he grew to manhood in the laborious occupation of tilling his native soil, in which his corporeal powers were fully developed, with but little mental cultivation. He possessed, however, the spirit of enterprise, and the love of independence. In 1775, having married Esther Fuller, and commenced house-keeping in a small way, with health and labor to season his bread, he said to his wife, he heard a fine report of Kentucky, and he thought they could get their living there with less hard work. "Then, Billy, if I was you I would go and see," was the reply. In two days he was on his way, with axe and plow, and gun and kettle. And she is the woman who afterwards collected his warriors to pursue the Indians.

Whitley set out for Kentucky, accompanied by his brother-in-law, George Clark; in the wilderness they met with seven others, who joined them.

We are not in possession of materials for a detailed narrative of Whitley's adventures after his arrival in Kentucky, and shall have to give only such desultory facts as we have been enabled to collect.

In the year 1785, the camp of an emigrant by the name of McClure, was assaulted in the night by Indians, near the head of Skagg's creek, in Lincoln county, and six whites killed and scalped.

Mrs. McClure ran into the woods with her four children, and could have made her escape with three, if she had abandoned the fourth; this, an infant in her arms, cried aloud, and thereby gave the savages notice where they were. She heard them coming: the night, the grass, and the bushes, offered her concealment without the infant, but she was a mother, and determined to die with it; the like feeling prevented her from telling her three eldest to fly and hide. She *feared* they would be lost if they left her side; she *hoped* they would not be killed if they remained. In the meantime the Indians arrived, and extinguished both fears and hopes in the blood of three of the children. The youngest, and the mother they made captives. She was taken back to the camp, where there was plenty of provisions, and compelled to cook for her captors. In the morning they compelled her to mount an unbroken horse, and accompany them on their return home.

Intelligence of this sad catastrophe being conveyed to Whitley's station, he was not at home. A messenger, however, was dispatched after him by Mrs. Whitley, who at the same time sent others to warn and collect his company. On his return he found twenty-one men collected to receive his orders. With these he directed his course to the war path, intending to intercept the Indians returning home. Fortunately, they had stopped to divide their plunder; and Whitley succeeded in gaining the path in advance of them. He immediately saw that they had not passed, and prepared for their arrival. His men being concealed in a favorable position, had not waited long before the enemy appeared, dressed in their spoils. As they approached, they were met by a deadly fire from the concealed whites, which killed two, wounded two others and dispersed the rest. Mrs. McClure, her child, and a negro woman, were rescued, and the six scalps taken by the Indians at the camp, recovered.

Ten days after this event, a Mr. Moore, and his party, also emigrants, were defeated two or three miles from Rackoon creek, on the same road. In this attack, the Indians killed nine persons, and scattered the rest. Upon the receipt of the news, Captain Whitley raised thirty men, and under a similar impression as before, that they would return home, marched to intercept them. On the sixth day, in a cane-brake, he met the enemy, with whom he found himself face to face, before he received any intimation of their proximity. He instantly ordered ten of his men to the right, as many to the left, and the others to dismount on the spot with him. The Indians, twenty in number, were mounted on good horses, and well dressed in the plundered clothes. Being in the usual Indian file, and still pressing from the rear when the front made a halt, they were brought into full view ; but they no sooner discovered the whites than they sprang from their horses and took to their heels. In the pursuit, three Indians were killed ; eight scalps retaken ; and twenty-eight horses, fifty pounds in cash, and a quantity of clothes and household furniture captured. Captain Whitley accompanied Bowman and Clark in their respective expeditions against the Indians.

In the years 1792, '93 and '94, the southern Indians gave great annoyance to the inhabitants of the southern and south-eastern portions of the State. Their hostile incursions were principally directed against the frontiers of Lincoln county, where they made frequent inroads upon what were called the outside settlements, in the neighborhood of Crab Orchard, and Logan's and McKinney's stations. Their depredations became, at length, so frequent, that Col. Whitley determined to take vengeance, and deprive them of the means of future annoyance ; and, with this view, conceived the project of conducting an expedition against their towns on the south side of the Tennessee river.

In the summer of 1794 he wrote to Major Orr, of Tennessee, informing him of his design, and inviting the major to join him with as large a force as he could raise. Major Orr promptly complied ; and the two corps, which rendezvoused at Nashville, numbered between five and seven hundred men. The expedition is known in history as the Nickajack expedition, that being the name of the principal town against which its operations were directed. The march was conducted with such secrecy and dispatch, that the enemy were taken completely by surprise. In the battle which ensued, they were defeated with great slaughter, their towns burned, and crops destroyed. This was the last hostile expedition in which Whitley was engaged during the war.

Very soon after the general peace, he went to some of the southern Indian towns to reclaim some negroes, that had been taken in the contest ; when he was put under more apprehension than he had been at any time during the war. A half-breed, by the name of Jack Taylor, who spoke English, and acted as interpreter, if he did not intend to procure Whitley's death, at least determined to intimidate him. The Indians being assembled, as soon as Whitley had declared the purpose of his visit, Taylor told him he could not get the negroes ; and taking a bell that was at hand, tied it to his waist, then seizing and rattling a drum, raised the war-whoop. Whitley afterwards said, when telling the story, "I thought the times were squally ; I looked at Otter Lifter : he had told me I should not be killed :—his countenance remained unchanged. I thought him a man of honor, and kept my own." At this time the Indians gathered about him armed, but fired their guns in the air, to his great relief. Whitley finally succeeded in regaining his negroes, and returned home.

Sometime after the affair of the negroes, he again visited the Cherokees, and was everywhere received in the most friendly manner.

In the year 1813, being then in the sixty-fifth year of his age, he volunteered with the Kentucky militia, under Gov. Shelby, and fell in the decisive and victorious battle of the Thames, on the 5th of October.

Col. Whitley was a man above the ordinary size, of great muscular power, and capable of enduring great fatigue and privation. His courage as a soldier was unquestionable, having been foremost in seventeen battles with the Indians, and one with a more civilized foe. In the battle of the Thames, he fell at the first fire. His memory is cherished throughout Kentucky with profound respect, as that of one uniting the characters of patriot and hero.

WOODFORD COUNTY.

Woodford county was formed in 1788, and named after Gen. William Woodford. It was the last of the nine counties organized by Virginia previous to the separation of Kentucky, and her admission into the Union. It is situated in the heart of the State, and drained by Kentucky river and its tributary streams: bounded on the north by Franklin and Scott; east and south-east by Fayette and Jessamine; and south-west by Mercer and Anderson, the Kentucky river forming the dividing line. The county is triangular in shape, and comprises between one hundred and eighty and one hundred and ninety square miles. The face of the country is level, or very gently undulating—the soil equal to any in the State in fertility, being based on limestone, and deep, rich and friable. The timber is luxuriant, and of the finest quality—embracing the black walnut, blue and black ash, hickory, black locust, sugar-tree, &c. Woodford has been appropriately termed the "asparagus bed" of Kentucky. The farms are large, generally under fence, and in a high state of cultivation; the population intelligent, refined and independent. Hemp, corn, oats and wheat, are the staple products; horses, mules, cattle, hogs, bagging and bale rope, the principal exports.

Valuation of taxable property in Woodford in 1846, $6,607,-906; number of acres of land in the county, 116,693; average value of land per acre, $32.58; number of white males over twenty-one years of age, 1,367; number of children between five and sixteen years old, 1,038. Population in 1840, 11,740.

VERSAILLES, the seat of justice of Woodford, is situated near the centre of the county, directly on the turnpike road from Lexington to Frankfort, twelve miles from the former and fourteen from the latter place—and is a beautiful, thriving town, with a population of about 1400 hundred souls. It contains a handsome brick court-house, and other county buildings; four churches, Baptist, Presbyterian, Methodist and Christian; three female schools, one seminary, averaging nearly two hundred scholars; twelve lawyers, fourteen physicians, two taverns, eight stores, four groceries, eight bagging factories, one wool factory, masonic hall, and twenty mechanics' shops. Established in 1792, and named after the city of Versailles in France. On the southern border of the town, about one hundred yards from the court-house, a large cave spring, of clear, crystal water, issues from an abrupt break on gradually descending ground, and flows off in a stream of sufficient size to afford water power for a small grist mill or manufacturing establishment; and a wool carding factory, which has been burnt down, was formerly located upon it. This cave or natural conduit runs under the town in a general direction from north to south. Immediately over it, in front of the court-house, a public well has been dug, which affords at all seasons, an ample and inexhaustible supply of water for the town.

Midway is a handsome village, situated on the Lexington rail road, and contains four hundred inhabitants. It has three churches, five physicians, two taverns, three stores, two groceries, three hemp factories, two schools, and a number of mechanics' shops. Took its name from its central position on the rail road between

Lexington and Frankfort. *Mortonsville* is also a neat village, situated four miles south of Versailles, and two miles from the Kentucky river—contains a Christian church, three physicians, one female school, four stores and groceries, one bagging factory and eight mechanics' shops, with a population of 350. Named after Mr. Morton, the proprietor.

From the RECOLLECTIONS of Major HERMAN BOWMAR, senior, a venerable pioneer of Woodford, now nearly eighty years of age, active, sprightly, and intelligent, we glean the following facts, concerning the settlement of that county, sketches of character, incidents, &c. The father of Major Bowmar removed to Kentucky in 1779, and settled at Colonel Bowman's station in Mercer, and in 1789, removed to Woodford. In 1791, Major Herman Bowmar, then twenty-two years of age, was qualified as a deputy sheriff of Woodford—the county then embracing portions of the present counties of Franklin and Scott, being divided into two sheriff's districts. His acquaintance, consequently, became extensive, and his *recollections*, kindly furnished for this work, show a remarkable tenacity of memory.

As late as the year 1782, there were no settlements within the bounds of the present county of Woodford. In the winter of 1782–3, Captain Elijah Craig, who commanded the fort at Bryant's station, in 1782, removed to Woodford, and settled a station about five miles from Versailles, and ten miles from Lexington—the county of Woodford then composing a part of the territory of Fayette. The close of the revolutionary war caused an immense emigration to Kentucky, and during the years 1783–4–5–6–7 and 8, the increase of population in Woodford was so great, as to give the county, at the close of the year last mentioned, as many voters as there are at present (1847) in her reduced territory. That portion of the original territory of Woodford, lying on the lower Elkhorn and the lower Mercer, on the north side of the Kentucky river, was an exposed and guarded frontier from 1783 to 1793.

On the opposite side of the river, in Mercer county, there was no man of his day who excelled Capt. James Ray, (the late Gen. James Ray,) in his activity, bravery and efficiency, as a pioneer commander and Indian fighter. But lower down, as the frontier extended, the most active and efficient was the late Capt. John Arnold, who settled a station on the waters of Little Benson creek in 1783, about seven or eight miles above the site of Frankfort. Several other stations were settled higher up than that of Arnold, his being the extreme frontier; but not having sufficient men to guard them with safety, against the apprehended incursions of the savages, they were abandoned in about a year, and the occupants returned to the older settlements, in Mercer. These settlements were re-occupied in the year 1786. Capt. John Arnold was the commandant of a company of spies for several years, and, with Samuel Hutton and others as his associates, ranged the country as far as Drennon's lick.

In 1792, Jacob Coffman, who owned and resided on the land on which Lawrenceburg, the county seat of Anderson, is now located, was killed and scalped. Maj. Bowmar was of the party raised to pursue the savages and avenge his death; but the pursuit was unsuccessful. During the same year, Capt. Todd, residing then in Woodford, but now embraced in the territory of Scott, was riding alone down the river hill where South Frankfort is situated, when he was fired at by several Indians, who waylaid his path, and killed and scalped. The men in Frankfort heard the report of the guns and the scalp halloo, but were unable to cross the river in time to render him any assistance. Todd was an estimable man, and his death was greatly lamented.

The Saturday before the first Monday in May, 1792, (the first election day under the government of Kentucky,) twenty-five Indians crossed the Lexington road about two miles above Frankfort, and fired at William Chinn, who was riding down the road. Chinn escaped unhurt, and gave the alarm. About a mile further in their progress, they took John Dimint prisoner. They then proceeded about five miles further up into Woodford, and encamped in a rocky cliff of Main Glenn's creek, eight or nine miles from Versailles. Here they remained during the night and succeeding day (Sunday). The alarm being spread through the surrounding country, several hundred men were out during Sunday, scouring the neighborhood; twenty-five of whom lodged at Lewis Easterday's, about three miles above Frankfort, on Sunday night. The Indians, on the same night, were induced by Dimint to go to Easterday's still-house, where they were unsuccessful in obtaining whisky, but managed to steal the horses of the twenty-five whites, and by a rapid movement soon crossed Main Elkhorn. A party under Col. John Grant, and another under captains Nathaniel Sanders and Anthony Bartlett,—the former from the neighborhood of Georgetown, and the latter from the south side of Elkhorn,—having been united, got upon the trail of the Indians, and commenced a rapid pursuit. As they approached the Eagle hills, the Indians were overtaken by the whites, several shots exchanged, and one of their number killed.* The Indians abandoned their horses, and fled precipitately to the hills with their prisoner. Dimint effected his escape while the Indians were engaged in crossing the Ohio, and returned in safety to his family, bringing home the evidence of his captivity—the " buffalo tug " with which his arms had been confined.

Among the most active and reliable men in the defence of the North Elkhorn frontier, the settlement at the main forks of Elkhorn, and those at Frankfort and its immediate neighborhood, were Col. John K. Grant and Capt. Samuel Grant, with their brothers; Maj. Thomas Herndon and Jacob Tucker; the late Col. James Johnson and Capt. Lucket, as they grew up; Capt. Nathaniel Sanders, Capt. A. Bartlett, Capt. Pemberton, (the late Gen. Bennet Pemberton,) and William Haydon and sons. On the Elkhorn, below the forks, old Mr. Church and sons, Jeremiah Craig, and others, distinguished themselves by their bravery and zeal.

Woodford was principally settled by emigrants from eastern and western Virginia; but there were many families from the states of North Carolina, Maryland, Pennsylvania and New Jersey, and quite a respectable number from Ireland and Germany.

The Honorable GEORGE M. BIBB,† is a native of Virginia—emigrated to Kentucky when young—studied law, and soon distinguished himself at the bar for his legal acquirements, solid judgment and cogent reasoning. He rose rapidly in his profession, and it was not long before he was numbered among the ablest and soundest lawyers in the country. He became well known in a short time—was in politics a republican—acquired the esteem and confidence of his countrymen, to which his honest, consistent and undeviating advocacy of the rights of the occupying claimants contributed not a little. He was appointed by the legislature of Kentucky to defend the occupying claimant laws before the supreme court of the United States and against the State of Virginia—a trust which he discharged with great ability and in a very satisfactory manner to his countrymen.

Judge Bibb has been three times chief justice of the State of Kentucky—the second time upon the reorganization of the court of appeals at the session of 1824-5—consequently belonged to the *new court* side of the *old* and *new court* question, by which the State was so long and so fearfully agitated about that time, and of course believed in the competency of the legislature to enact what were called *relief* laws—including laws for the stay of execution, replevin laws, and laws for the valuation of property taken in execution—without which power, the legislative branch of the government would seem to be imperfect.

Judge Bibb has been twice elected to the senate of the United States—the last time when General Jackson was first elected president of the United States —to whom he gave his cordial support, both when the general was first a candidate in 1824, and when he was elected in 1828—which support was in a short time withdrawn, however. What cause of dissatisfaction he had with that illustrious patriot, is but imperfectly known to the writer of this sketch.

Upon the Judge's retirement from the Senate, he was appointed chancellor of the chancery court of the city of Louisville, in which tribunal he fully sustained his high character as an able and impartial administrator of justice. And in that office he continued until invited in 1844, by President Tyler, to take charge of the treasury department of the United States. From this he retired in 1845, upon

---

* The respective friends of Col. Grant and Capt. Sanders, claimed for their commander the honor of shooting this Indian.

† The sketch of Judge Bibb properly belongs to Franklin or Jefferson, but was not received until after the descriptions of those counties were stereotyped.

the inauguration of President Polk ; and since then he has resided at Washington city, practicing law in the supreme court of the United States, and in the courts of the district of Columbia ; and has the rare good fortune of enjoying in the evening of his life, much of the activity, with all the mental vigor and vivacity of his younger days.

The Honorable John J. Crittenden, of the United States' senate ; the Honorable John J. Marshall, late judge of the Louisville circuit court ; and the Honorable Thomas A. Marshall, chief justice of the State of Kentucky, were all natives of Woodford county.

General William Woodford, in honor of whom this county received its name, a revolutionary officer of high merit, was born in Caroline county, Virginia. He early distinguished himself in the French and Indian war. Upon the assembling of the Virginia troops in Williamsburg, in 1775, consequent upon the hostile attitude of Lord Dunmore, he was appointed colonel of the second regiment. In the military operations immediately subsequent, in that section of the State, his name is honorably mentioned in history, particularly at the battle of Great Bridge, fought December 9th, upon which occasion he had the chief command, and gained a signal victory over the enemy. He was finally promoted to the command of the first brigade, in which station he served through the war. He was in various actions, in one of which, the battle of Brandywine, he was wounded. He was made prisoner by the British in 1780, during the siege of Charleston, and taken to New York, where he died on the 13th of November, of that year, in the 46th year of his age.

APPENDIX.

The following account of the last excursion of the Indians into Kentucky, is copied from M'Donald's Sketches. It should have appeared under the head of Mason County, but was accidentally omitted :

"In the course of this summer (1793), the spies who had been down the Ohio, below Limestone, discovered where a party of about twenty Indians had crossed the Ohio, and sunk their canoes in the mouth of Holt's creek. The sinking of their canoes, and concealing them, was evidence of the intention of the Indians to re-cross the Ohio at the same place. When Kenton received this intelligence, he dispatched a messenger to Bourbon county, to apprise them that the Indians had crossed the Ohio, and had taken that direction ; whilst he forthwith collected a small party of choice spirits, whom he could depend upon in cases of emergency. Among them was Cornelius Washburn, who had the cunning of a fox, for ambuscading, and the daring of a lion for encountering. With this party, Kenton crossed the Ohio, at Limestone, and proceeded down to opposite the mouth of Holt's creek, where the Indian canoes lay concealed. Here his party lay concealed four days, before they saw or heard anything of the Indians. On the fourth day of their ambuscade, they observed three Indians come down the bank, and drive six horses into the river. The horses swam over. The Indians then raised one of their canoes they had sunk, and crossed over. When the Indians came near the shore, Kenton discovered, that of the three men in the canoe, one was a white man. As he thought the white man was probably a prisoner, he ordered his men to fire alone at the Indians, and save the white man. His men fired ; the two Indians fell. The headway which the canoe had, ran it upon the shore ; the white man in the canoe picked up his gun, and as Kenton ran down to the water's edge, to receive the man, he snapped his gun at the whites. Kenton then ordered his men to kill him. He was immediately shot. About three or four hours afterwards, on the same day, two more Indians, and another white man, came to the river, and drove in five horses. The horses swam over ; and the Indians raised another of their sunk canoes, and followed the horses across the Ohio. As soon as the canoe touched the shore with the Indians, Kenton's party fired upon them, and killed them all. The white man, who was with this party of Indians, had his ears cut, his nose bored, and all the marks which distinguish the Indians. Kenton and his men still kept up the ambuscade, knowing there were still more Indians, and one canoe behind. Some time in the night, the main body of the Indians came to the place where their canoes were sunk, and hooted like owls ; but not receiving any answer, they began to think all was not right. The Indians were as vigilant as weasels. The two parties who had been killed, the main body expected to find encamped on the other side of the Ohio ; and as no answer was given to their hooting, which was doubtless agreed upon as a countersign, one of the Indians must have swum the river to reconnoitre, and discover what had become of their friends. The Indian who swam the river, must have discovered the ambuscade. He went upon a high hill, or knob, which was immediately in Kenton's rear, and gave three long and loud yells ; after which he informed his friends that they must immediately make their escape, as there was a party of whites waylaying them. Kenton had several men who understood the Indian language. Not many minutes after the Indian on the hill had warned his companions of their danger, the Bourbon militia came up. It being dark, the Indians broke and run, leaving about thirty horses, which they had stolen from about Bourbon. The next morning, some attempts were made to pursue the Indians; but they had scattered and straggled off in such small parties, that the pursuit was abandoned, and Kenton and his party returned home, without the affair making any more noise or eclat than would have taken place on the return of a party from a common hunting tour. Although Kenton and his party did not succeed as well as they could wish, or their friends expected, yet the Indians were completely foiled and defeated in their object; six of them were killed, and all the horses they had stolen were retaken, and the remainder of the Indians scattered, to return home in small squads. This was the last inroad the Indians made in Kentucky; from henceforward they lived free from all alarms."

SCIENCE AND LITERATURE, IN KENTUCKY.

BY A KENTUCKIAN.

THE following contribution to the literary history of the West, is but a fragment; yet, it is hoped, that it may serve as a stimulus to those who have opportunity and ability to do full justice to western talent. In presenting the casual sketches which follow, we aim merely to call attention to the subject. We are by no means indifferent to the merits of many other distinguished and gifted sons of Kentucky; and would gladly, were it in our power, at present, enlarge this sketch to a full outline of the science and literature of our native state.

In literature, science. and the arts, the condition of the Western States has not been favorable to progress. The talent, and force of character, which Kentuckians have so often manifested in a brilliant manner, have found their field in business, in personal adventures, enterprise, war and emigration, or in forensic and political strife. The calm pursuit of letters was not the natural vocation of the brave pioneers, or of their immediate descendants. Yet even under these adverse circumstances, Kentucky has had not only orators, soldiers, and statesmen of the first rank, but artists, scholars, and literary men of whom she may be justly proud. The bar of Kentucky, some thirty or forty years since, was probably unsurpassed in any other State. Her Allen, Rowan, Clay, Daviess, Hays, and others, were truly intellectual giants. Her artists have won high distinction. The productions of Jouett display the hand of a master, and compare favorably with European standards. Among her male and female poetical writers, we might name several who have an American reputation. Her men of science and invention have produced works of ability, and inventions of the highest importance. We do not propose even to enumerate these, but we cannot abstain from alluding to one of Kentucky's brave and hardy pioneers, JOHN FITCH, who while engaged in exploring the wilderness and rivers of the west, and wielding his rifle in expeditions against the hostile savages, conceived the great invention of the STEAMBOAT at a time when he was not even aware of the existence of a steam engine. Having demonstrated the practicability of his invention long before the more successful Fulton introduced the steamboat into general use, he is undoubtedly entitled to the highest rank among American inventors. No invention has contributed more to the wealth and power of the West than the *Steamboat*. To John Fitch belongs the honor of demonstrating more than sixty years ago, that the rivers of the West would be navigated, and the Atlantic ocean crossed by steam; and although he was not sustained by public or private co-operation in carrying out his whole scheme—he was enabled to build a steamboat which in 1786 at Philadelphia made a speed of eight miles an hour. Fitch was truly one of our greatest national benefactors. The comparative neglect of his high claims upon the gratitude of his countrymen inspires us with a lively sympathy in his behalf. He enjoys however that honor which Cato preferred—for we may well ask why his countrymen have *not* erected a monument to his memory.

In medical science, Kentucky has not been backward. Her two medical colleges are the most prosperous in the West, and some fifteen or twenty of her talented sons have been called to occupy professorships in the medical colleges of other states. We do not propose to enumerate her distinguished medical men, but offer the following sketches—the materials for which happened to be within our reach, as specimens of Kentucky talent.

DR. BENJAMIN WILKINS DUDLEY has long been conspicuous as an eminent surgeon. Dr. D. was born in Spottsylvania Co., Virginia, April 12, 1785. Some months after his birth, his father emigrated to Kentucky. Dr. D. was educated in Transylvania University. In his professional studies he attended the courses of lectures at Philadelphia, and graduated in 1806. After thus receiving the instructions of Rush, Barton, Physic, Shippen, Woodhouse and Wistar, he practised his profession at Lexington until 1810,—then visited London and Paris, and spent four years in those cities, profiting by the instructions of Cooper, Dupuytren, Larrey, Boyer, Dubois, Abernethey, Cline, Cuvier, &c. After a pupilage of two years in the hospitals of London. he was honored with a degree, which constituted him a member of the Royal College of Surgeons. Not only were his pecuniary means exhausted by this long residence abroad, but his books and instruments, and a cabinet of rare minerals, were destroyed by the burning of the custom house at London.

He returned to Lexington, and soon stood in the front rank of the profession. His fame filled the southwest, and in 1818 he was appointed to fill the anatomical and surgical chair of the Medical Department of Transylvania University. His appointment was co-eval with the successful establishment of the Medical College at Lexington, of which he has been ever since, the principal support. For about thirty years past Dr. D. has enjoyed an amount of reputation and influence which few professional men have ever attained. Standing for many years at the head of Western surgery, his lectures were highly prized by students, and the clear impressive manner in which he imparted his instruction made an indelible impression upon their minds.

As a surgeon he has not been a mere mechanical operator, but has strictly attended to constitutional treatment. Hence his success in the use of the knife. As a lithotomist he is probably unsurpassed. He has operated upon 192 cases of stone in the bladder. His operations upon the eye have been very numerous. Among other important operations, he has perforated the cranium in some twelve or more cases for the relief of epilepsy. In the treatment of chronic affections of the urethra and bladder. his views are quite original. The most remarkable peculiarities of his practice, however, are based upon his views of the utility of his favorite instrument—the bandage. Its efficiency in the treatment of aneurism, fractures, ulcers &c., has been amply illustrated in his hands.

The merits of Dr. Dudley are strictly professional. In general literature and science he has no pretensions. In his profession, his reputation is based upon his practice and his lectures; having done nothing by his pen for the benefit of the science, notwithstanding his ample fund of professional experience. With no intellectual reputation at the commencement of his career, he has achieved by his energy, skill and address, an enviable distinction; and will long be remembered as the distinguished surgeon of Kentucky. As the prominent man of the Transylvania school, the fact of his occupying for many years the two chairs of Anatomy and Surgery, illustrates the importance attached to his services. The aggregate numbers of the classes to which he has lectured. amount to near six thousand;—1660 is the number of graduates under his teachings. His personal appearance and manner as a lecturer, are striking and impressive. His stature is moderate, his voice strong, though not sonorous or loud; his face marked by the lines which indicate a strong character; and his head such as would indicate to the phrenologist an influential and original mind.

DR. DANIEL DRAKE, for about thirty years, has been distinguished as a medical professor in the medical colleges of Lexington, Philadelphia, Cincinnati and Louisville. In the latter city he holds at present the chair of Theory and Practice of Medicine, in the most flourishing institution of the Western country. No medical name is more extensively known in the Western and Southwestern states, than that of Dr. Drake.

Dr. D. was born in New Jersey, about sixty two years since. In his second year the family removed to Kentucky . In his professional career he has been identified with the West. Unlike Dr. Dudley, the talents of Dr. Drake have been as showy in other departments as in his own profession. In general literature and science, and in the various social, moral and literary enterprises of the times, Dr. D. has been actively engaged. Having an extensive fund of information, an easy and fluent delivery; with a fund of humour, and even eloquence; he has often been conspicuous as a public speaker on popular and professional subjects. The professional distinction of Dr. Drake has not been of that solid practical character which commands the highest reverence of the members of the profession. Though familiar with medical literature, and capable of lecturing or writing in a pleasing style upon the current topics of interest; his productions have not been of that extent or elaborateness necessary to a very lasting reputation. Nor has his practical professional skill been conceded by all. In the course of a long and restless career, he has sometimes been engaged in strife with his professional brethren, and has therefore, decided enemies or opponents as well as friends; between whom there is some difference in their estimate of his professional worth. An impartial spectator, however, cannot but concede to Dr. D. the possession of decided talent, varied acquirements and versatile powers; with remarkable excellence as a public lecturer and miscellaneous professional writer. It has been said that Dr. D. contemplates the publication of an elaborate medical work, upon which he has been engaged some years. Such a publication would give his reputation a more permanent basis.

DR. CHARLES CALDWELL, one of the most distinguished medical Professors and most voluminous writers of America, is at present Professor of the Institutes of Medicine in the Louisville Medical Institute. As a cotemporary of Rush and Physic, he may be said to belong to a past generation; but he still retains in an extraordinary degree his inexhaustible vigor of mind and body.

Dr. Caldwell was born in Caswell Co., N. C., about the year 1772. At nine years of age•he was sent to school, and after two years in the log cabin schools of Caswell and Cabarrus counties, was considered master of all their teachers could impart. Having surpassed all his schoolfellows, he was permitted by his father to attend a Latin school. on condition that he allowed no fellow pupil to surpass him in his studies. The condition was fulfilled, and by the age of fourteen he had mastered the Latin, Greek and all the other studies of the classical schools. His father wished him to study Divinity, but he declined; and taking an independent course, opened a grammar school in Iredell county, which was attended by several pupils much older than himself. One year spent in this, and two in another grammar school in that county, completed his seventeenth year. He then commenced the study of medicine with Dr. Harris, of Salisbury, N. C. After a year and a half of private study, he removed to Philadelphia. and graduated in the medical school of that city, in which Rush, Wistar and Shippen were professors. In 1795 he commenced his career of authorship by the translation of Blumenbach's Elements of Physiology. This period of his life was one of extraordinary mental activity, being often engaged from eighteen to twenty hours of the twenty-four, in active mental labour, and taking but four hours sleep! In this respect Dr. C. was been throughout his life an admirable model for the ambitious student; and even at the present time there are few young men who can rival his mental activity and scholastic assiduity. Knowing his habits, one need not be surprised at the extent of his literary labors. Dr. C. has written and published in the course of his life, a vast number of productions—his essays, translations, pamphlets and books on various subjects have been estimated to amount in the aggregate to more than ten thousand pages, and perhaps eleven thousand would be nearer the truth. In reviewing the voluminous collection, we are struck with the great diversity of his writings—Medicine, History, Biography, Poetry and Fiction, Jurisprudence, Phrenology, Education, Penal Law, Hygiene, Mesmerism, Philosophy, the Languages, Morals, the Physical Sciences, and the Ancient Classics have each been the subject of essays or volumes. He has made in the aggregate two hundred and eleven distinct publications. Four-fifths of this number do not exceed fifty pages in length—twenty-one are above 100 pages—thirteen above 200, and six of three hundred and upwards. Notwithstanding the extent of his literary, and scientific labors, Dr. C. has not achieved the solid and commanding reputation to which his abilities, energy and perseverance were justly entitled. This may be attributed partly to the lack of concentration. Writing upon all subjects with graceful facility, he has produced no imposing original work upon which his fame might rest. At the same time delighting in philosophy and argumentative discussion, rather than in practical details. he has acquired the character of a speculative, rather than practical writer; and having a higher degree of mental liberality than his cotemporaries, he has generally been too much in advance of the age, to be fully appreciated. His position has always been in the van. In Medical Jurisprudence he was in conjunction with Dr. Stringham, the first in the United States to deliver a course of lectures. The first course of clinical lectures in the Philadelphia Almshouse (now Blockley Hospital) was delivered by Dr. C. He was the first prominent champion of Phrenology in the United States, and may be regarded as the father of the science in this country. In Mesmerism too, he was one of the few distinguished men who openly and manfully espoused the cause of scientific truth, in the face of public ridicule and opposition.

The principal professional labors of Dr. C. have been in the teaching of philosophical medicine, in which he has been engaged nearly thirty years, as Professor of the Institutes at Lexington and Louisville. In the former city he was the most distinguished member of the Faculty, by whom the medical department was successfully established; and in the latter he may be regarded as the founder of the Medical Institute, having been the most prominent actor in its establishment.

Prof. Caldwell has received many honors in the course of his life, and enjoys a European, as well as American reputation. He has a remarkably venerable and distinguished personal appearance; a dignified bearing; a great flow of conversation, and inexhaustible energy. As a writer, he is always clear and instructive. Though somewhat diffuse in style, he has no idle verbiage—no absurdities in thought—no violations of good taste. In conversation, writing, or lecturing, he has ever the same strong, steady current of thought. Never inventive, but always independent in his views, never brilliant, but always polished; never sublime, but generally elevated; never enthusiastic, but always earnest; never very practical, yet always rational, instructive and useful; never rash in his intellectual progress, yet always in advance of most of his cotemporaries. It may be said, upon the whole, that few have done so much, and done so well; and although not adapted to general popularity, he has gained a wide-spread reputation among liberal minds.

DR. JOHN MILTON HARNEY, a distinguished poet, was the son of Major Thos. Harney, of Delaware, who emigrated to Tennessee, and settled near Nashville, in 1791. The birth of Dr. Harney occurred in Sussex Co., Delaware, March 9th, 1789. Major Harney was a gallant and accomplished gentleman, and his traits of character have been inherited by his descendants. His youngest son, Col. W. S. Harney, has been distinguished as a brave and efficient officer in the Florida campaigns, and in the present war with Mexico. His eldest son, Dr. Benj. F. Harney, is the oldest surgeon in the U. S. Army. His second son, Dr. Jno. M. Harney, the subject of our sketch, manifested not only a vigorous and brilliant intellect, but an exalted sense of honor, purity of life and dignity of character.

We have but few details of the life of Dr. H. It is known that he settled at Bardstown, Ky., in the practice of his profession, where he was much esteemed and admired. He married a daughter of Judge Rowan, in 1814, by whom he had a daughter (now living.) Mrs. H. did not long survive the birth of her daughter. After her death, Dr. H. went to New York, visited England, Ireland, France and Spain; and spent some time as surgeon in the naval service of Buenos Ayres. Subsequently he settled at Savannah, where he edited with ability a political newspaper. Being out of health at the time that a fire broke out in Savannah, his exposure while laboring to extinguish the flames, produced an impression upon his constitution from which he never recovered. He returned to Kentucky, and died at Bardstown, Jan. 15, 1825, in his 36th year. In his latter years, Dr. H. became deeply impressed with the truth of Christianity, and after full investigation, adopted the Roman Catholic faith.

Dr. Harney possessed a highly poetical temperament. Ardent and firm, yet keenly, almost morbidly sensitive; generous, affectionate, grave and pensive, full of romance and chivalry, his personal character was just what we should look for in the true epic poet. As a poet, although most of his productions have been lost, there is sufficient evidence that he was entitled to a high rank. Critics and poets who have been familiar with his writings, affirm that his genius was truly of a high order. In reading, after his, the works of Milton, Thompson, Pope and Cowper, we feel that Harney's was a kindred spirit, and that he might have won a place in the brightest constellations of either hemisphere.

The principal evidences of his powers are now unfortunately lost, in consequence of the sudden deaths of individuals who had his manuscripts in charge; but in his Crystallina, Fever Dream, and some other of his productions, there is the evident impress of genius; and on the memories of those who knew him, the impression of his mental superiority was firmly stamped. Owing to his extreme sensitiveness, he suppressed nearly the whole of the edition of his Crystallina, when he experienced the annoyance of unfriendly criticism. Subsequently for some years he occupied his leisure in the preparation of an epic poem of some length, which is believed to have been worthy of his abilities. This, and many other productions of his pen, are probably irrecoverably lost; but in the memory of those who knew and honored him, there was a consciousness of his powers, independent of any written manifestation, and among those who enjoyed the perusal of his manuscript, there was an ardent admiration of his genius. The classical scholar, the critic and the poet alike honored the name of Harney.

DR. JOSEPH BUCHANAN, a philosopher, mathematician and mechanical inventor, was born in Washington Co. Va., Aug. 24, 1785, removed to Tennessee in 1795, visited Kentucky for the completion of his education in 1804, and spent the remainder of his life chiefly in that state, in scientific and literary occupations.

His boyhood in Tennessee (on the Cumberland) was spent amid the usual hardships of a frontier life and poverty, with but trifling opportunities of education. In 1802 he repaired to a grammar school near Nashville; where he spent five months, and by his remarkable proficiency astonished his class-mates and "obtained the reputation of a great genius." Having made as he conceived an important invention for mills, he wished to devote his attention to the execution of his invention, but upon a critical review of his plan, discovered a defect, and gave it up. In 1803 he returned to the Academy, and in the course of nine months mastered the Latin language, and distinguished himself by original composition. "He was so fond of originality in all his essays, that he would not even condescend to write on any subject on which he had ever read anything."

In 1804 he was sent by his guardian Major Edmonson, to Transylvania University at Lexington, Ky. Rustic and diffident—enfeebled by intense study and a pulmonary fever, he passed for a simpleton, until his proficiency in mathematical studies again made him conspicuous. In studying Ferguson's Optics, he detected an error of the author in regard to the focal distances of lenses. His professor sustained the author and put him down by authority. When the weekly theses were handed in, Buchanan gave in as his, the disputed proposition concerning the lenses, and proposed to render it sufficiently long by a demonstration on the black board. The professor, however, would not permit him to use the board and gain a mathematical triumph. During the vacation he published a mathematical pamphlet of 20 pages, demonstrating the sufficiency of gravitation for the celestial motions, and the incorrectness of "the projectile velocity assigned by Newton." In this, as usual, he relied upon his own genius, with but little assistance from authors.

In 1805 he commenced the study of medicine with Dr S. Brown; invented a new musical instrument, producing its music from glasses of different chemical composition; and originated the grand conception of the MUSIC OF LIGHT, to be executed by means of harmonific colors luminously displayed. The invention has never been put into operation, but there can be no doubt that it would produce one of the grandest and most imposing spectacles ever witnessed by the human eye. To perfect his invention it was necessary to study music, colors, and the laws of vision; in doing which he discovered that Father Castel and the Darwins had anticipated the fundamental principles of his discovery, and this precluded his hopes of immortality. Nevertheless he read before the medical society, an essay of 80 pages upon his discovery, strongly characterised by critical acumen, and ingenious originality.

To procure the means of finishing his education at Philadelphia, he removed to settle and practice for a short time at Port Gibson, Mississippi Territory. In 1807 he resolved to that place, where he spent eight months, suffered from the climate, practised his profession, and wrote a volume of 175 pages on the subject of Fever, with which he removed to Philadelphia. Professors Barton and Rush spoke highly of the style, ability, and ingenuity of his essay, and offered their friendly services. But being now destitute of resources. he could neither publish his work, nor remain in attendance upon the lectures; and in 1808 he walked out in 27 days to Lexington, Ky., and settled at that place, empty in purse, but improved in health. The degree of A. B. was soon after conferred upon him, by the University, at the instance of President Blythe.

He now directed his attention to the medical department of Transylvania, which had only a nomi nal existence, there being but one professor, who gave no lectures. The Trustees co-operating with him, a regular Faculty was organized, and he received (in 1809) the appointment of Professor of the INSTITUTES OF MEDICINE, being then in his 24th year—five years from his arrival as a rustic student from the wilds of Tennessee.

The fall of 1811 was fixed upon as the time for the opening of the medical session; prior to which he was engaged in preparing his lectures. Dr. B. had, unfortunately, but little faith in the success of the enterprise—not expecting an efficient support from any of his colleagues but Dr. Overton; in whom he had the highest confidence. Nevertheless he prepared his lectures, and being wholly engrossed in writing and inventions, made no effort to obtain practice. When he abandoned the attempt to establish a school, he published his philosophical views (in 1812) in a volume of 336 pages, under the title of "THE PHILOSOPHY OF HUMAN NATURE," of which a thousand copies were issued. This established his reputation as a profound thinker. It is a work of rare merit, and notwithstanding the subsequent progress of physiological and phrenological science, (with the latter of which he was unacquainted,) it is still a valuable and interesting book.

Not long after this publication he determined with the advice of his friends to abandon the medical profession, and give his attention to introducing into Kentucky the Pestalozzian system of education. He visited Philadelphia, to study the new system, as introduced by Mr. Neef, and spent some years in Pestalozzian teaching in Kentucky. But his indomitable mental activity withdrew him from this field, and in his 32d year he entered the profession of law, and delivered a course of law lectures to a private class; being meanwhile engaged in editing the Reporter, and writing on other subjects; or as he expressed it "wearing out my days in hard study without deriving much profit from it." The principles of materialism inculcated in his "Philosophy" he reviewed in a masterly manner—showing that without destroying the force of his former arguments, one might by a deeper analysis arrive at a system of universal spiritualism.

Subsequently he took an active interest in politics, as a Jeffersonian democrat, a friend of Mr. Clay and a supporter of the old-court party. He edited the Palladium, at Frankfort; the Western Spy and Literary Cadet, at Cincinnati; and the Focus, at Louisville. The latter, which he projected in 1826, he edited until he died in 1829, leaving a wife and son, (Dr. J. R. Buchanan, Prof. Institutes of Medicine &c., Cincinnati). He left behind valuable manuscripts and sketches of important mechanical inventions. In 1821-2 he constructed an extremely economical steam engine, which he successfully applied to the propulsion of the machinery of a factory, and to steam navigation on the Ohio. The invention was of some importance, from its economy of fuel; but it was found that the spiral tubes which he substituted for boilers, became encrusted by the impurities of the river water; and hence were adapted only to the use of the pure fluid. From the superior lightness and efficiency of his engine, he supposed at first that it would be applicable to ærial navigation. An experiment however, demonstrated that certain scientific facts upon which he had relied, had been erroneously stated by English authors. In 1824 or 5 he applied his engine upon land, to demonstrate its applicability to land carriage. The engine and wagon ran through the streets of Louisville in the presence of an astonished throng of spectators.

His discovery of a new motive power derived from combustion without the aid of water or steam, has a high degree of scientific plausibility, and it is to be regretted that he never attempted its execution.

Dr. B. was theoretically and practically devoted to education. He published at Louisville a grammar, very valuable for its simplicity; designed to facilitate the study of grammar by youth. His views of education were profound and enlarged—his methods admirable, and incalculably superior to those generally in vogue. His sanguine predictions were fully realized, in the education of his own son, who was so rapidly advanced, that by the age of twelve, he was placed at the study of Blackstone's Commentaries; having previously mastered a course of studies embracing grammar, geography, history, arithmetic. algebra, geometry, surveying, astronomy, natural philosophy, chemistry, mental philosophy, political economy, and constitutional law. Similar methods of education, adopted since his death by the Rev. B. O. Peers, of the Eclectic Institute of Lexington, produced similar results. In competing for an educational prize, the pupils of Mr. Peers—little boys, such as we find in common schools engaged with their primer and first lessons—were seen gravely lecturing before the Kentucky legislature, in the statehouse, upon chemistry and natural philosophy, with illustrative experiments!

The life of Dr. Buchanan affords an instructive moral. Simple in his manners and tastes, amiable in private life, elevated in his aims—full of philosophy and philanthropy—original and ingenious—ardent and enthusiastic, yet subjecting everything to the searching analysis of critical reason, he might have attained the highest rank in any pursuit upon which his energies had been concentrated; but cultivating his intellect to the neglect of other powers, he scorned the pursuit of wealth; abstracted himself from society, lived in continual pecuniary embarrassment—abandoned the road to wealth whenever it ceased to present intellectual attraction and novelty—wasted his powers in desultory labors, lived and died comparatively indifferent to fame—and as soon as the depths of human knowledge had been sounded, and its novelties exhausted, became indifferent to all the other incentives of ambition.

THE END.

The First American Frontier

AN ARNO PRESS/NEW YORK TIMES COLLECTION

Agnew, Daniel.
A History of the Region of Pennsylvania North of the Allegheny River. 1887.

Alden, George H.
New Government West of the Alleghenies Before 1780. 1897.

Barrett, Jay Amos.
Evolution of the Ordinance of 1787. 1891.

Billon, Frederick.
Annals of St. Louis in its Early Days Under the French and Spanish Dominations. 1886.

Billon, Frederick.
Annals of St. Louis in its Territorial Days, 1804-1821. 1888.

Littel, William.
Political Transactions in and Concerning Kentucky. 1926.

Bowles, William Augustus.
Authentic Memoirs of William Augustus Bowles. 1916.

Bradley, A. G.
The Fight with France for North America. 1900.

Brannan, John, ed.
Official Letters of the Military and Naval Officers of the War, 1812-1815. 1823.

Brown, John P.
Old Frontiers. 1938.

Brown, Samuel R.
The Western Gazetteer. 1817.

Cist, Charles.
Cincinnati Miscellany of Antiquities of the West and Pioneer History. (2 volumes in one). 1845-6.

Claiborne, Nathaniel Herbert.
Notes on the War in the South with Biographical Sketches of the Lives of Montgomery, Jackson, Sevier, and Others. 1819.

Clark, Daniel.
Proofs of the Corruption of Gen. James Wilkinson. 1809.

Clark, George Rogers.
Colonel George Rogers Clark's Sketch of His Campaign in the Illinois in 1778-9. 1869.

Collins, Lewis.
Historical Sketches of Kentucky. 1847.

Cruikshank, Ernest, ed,
Documents Relating to Invasion of Canada and the Surrender of Detroit. 1912.

Cruikshank, Ernest, ed,
The Documentary History of the Campaign on the Niagara Frontier, 1812-1814. (4 volumes). 1896-1909.

Cutler, Jervis.
A Topographical Description of the State of Ohio, Indian Territory, and Louisiana. 1812.

Cutler, Julia P.
The Life and Times of Ephraim Cutler. 1890.

Darlington, Mary C.
History of Col. Henry Bouquet and the Western Frontiers of Pennsylvania. 1920.

Darlington, Mary C.
Fort Pitt and Letters From the Frontier. 1892.

De Schweinitz, Edmund.
The Life and Times of David Zeisberger. 1870.

Dillon, John B.
History of Indiana. 1859.

Eaton, John Henry.
Life of Andrew Jackson. 1824.

English, William Hayden.
Conquest of the Country Northwest of the Ohio. (2 volumes in one). 1896.

Flint, Timothy.
Indian Wars of the West. 1833.

Forbes, John.
Writings of General John Forbes Relating to His Service in North America. 1938.

Forman, Samuel S.
Narrative of a Journey Down the Ohio and Mississippi in 1789-90. 1888.

Haywood, John.
Civil and Political History of the State of Tennessee to 1796. 1823.

Heckewelder, John.
History, Manners and Customs of the Indian Nations. 1876.

Heckewelder, John.
Narrative of the Mission of the United Brethren. 1820.

Hildreth, Samuel P.
Pioneer History. 1848.

Houck, Louis.
The Boundaries of the Louisiana Purchase: A Historical Study. 1901.

Houck, Louis.
History of Missouri. (3 volumes in one). 1908.

Houck, Louis.
The Spanish Regime in Missouri. (2 volumes in one). 1909.

Jacob, John J.
A Biographical Sketch of the Life of the Late Capt. Michael Cresap. 1826.

Jones, David.
A Journal of Two Visits Made to Some Nations of Indians on the West Side of the River Ohio, in the Years 1772 and 1773. 1774.

Kenton, Edna.
Simon Kenton. 1930.

Loudon, Archibald.
Selection of Some of the Most Interesting Narratives of Outrages. (2 volumes in one). 1808-1811.

Monette, J. W.
History, Discovery and Settlement of the Mississippi Valley. (2 volumes in one). 1846.

Morse, Jedediah.
American Gazetteer. 1797.

Pickett, Albert James.
History of Alabama. (2 volumes in one). 1851.

Pope, John.
A Tour Through the Southern and Western Territories. 1792.

Putnam, Albigence Waldo.
History of Middle Tennessee. 1859.

Ramsey, James G. M.
Annals of Tennessee. 1853.

Ranck, George W.
Boonesborough. 1901.

Robertson, James Rood, ed.
Petitions of the Early Inhabitants of Kentucky to the Gen. Assembly of Virginia. 1914.

Royce, Charles.
Indian Land Cessions. 1899.

Rupp, I. Daniel.
History of Northampton, Lehigh, Monroe, Carbon and Schuykill Counties. 1845.

Safford, William H.
The Blennerhasset Papers. 1864.

St. Clair, Arthur.
A Narrative of the Manner in which the Campaign Against the Indians, in the Year 1791 was Conducted. 1812.

Sargent, Winthrop, ed.
A History of an Expedition Against Fort DuQuesne in 1755. 1855.

Severance, Frank H.
An Old Frontier of France. (2 volumes in one). 1917.

Sipe, C. Hale.
Fort Ligonier and Its Times. 1932.

Stevens, Henry N.
Lewis Evans: His Map of the Middle British Colonies in America. 1920.

Timberlake, Henry.
The Memoirs of Lieut. Henry Timberlake. 1927.

Tome, Philip.
Pioneer Life: Or Thirty Years a Hunter. 1854.

Trent, William.
Journal of Captain William Trent From Logstown to Pickawillany. 1871.

Walton, Joseph S.
Conrad Weiser and the Indian Policy of Colonial Pennsylvania. 1900.

Withers, Alexander Scott.
Chronicles of Border Warfare. 1895.